BUSINESS RESEARCH METHODS

FOURTH EDITION

ALAN **BRYMAN** & EMMA **BELL**

OXFORD

UNIVERSITY PRESS

OXFORD

UNIVERSITY PRESS

Great Clarendon Street, Oxford OX2 6DP
United Kingdom

Oxford University Press is a department of the University of Oxford.
It furthers the University's objective of excellence in research, scholarship,
and education by publishing worldwide. Oxford is a registered trade mark of
Oxford University Press in the UK and in certain other countries

First edition 2003
Second edition 2007
Third edition 2011

Impression: 1

Published in the United States of America by Oxford University Press
198 Madison Avenue, New York, NY 10016, United States of America

British Library Cataloguing in Publication Data

Data available

Library of Congress Control Number: 2014952418

ISBN 978–0–19–966864–9

Printed in Italy by L.E.G.O. S.p.A.

Brief contents

Detailed contents

Abbreviations

ABTA	Association of British Travel Agents
ALS	average leadership style
AoIR	Association of Internet Researchers
AoM	Academy of Management
ASA	American Sociological Association
ASHE	Annual Survey of Hours and Earnings
BHPS	British Household Panel Study
BRES	Business Register and Employment Survey
BSA	British Social Attitudes
BSA	British Sociological Association
CA	conversation analysis
CAPI	computer-assisted personal interviewing
CAQDAS	computer-assisted qualitative data analysis software
CATI	computer-assisted telephone interviewing
CDA	critical discourse analysis
CEO	chief executive officer
CMD	common mental disorder
CSR	corporate social responsibility
CV	curriculum vitae
CWP	Changing Workforce Programme
DA	discourse analysis
ECA	ethnographic content analysis
ESRC	Economic and Social Research Council
EWCS	European Working Conditions Survey
FTSE	Financial Times (London) Stock Exchange
GICS	Global Industry Classifications Standard
GM	General Motors
GMID	General Market Information Database
GSS	General Social Survey
HISS	hospital information support system
HP	Hewlett Packard
HR	human resources
HRM	human resource management
HRT	hormone replacement therapy
ICI	Imperial Chemical Industries
IiP	Investors in People
ISIC	International Standard Industrial Classification
ISO	International Organization for Standardization
ISP	Internet service provider
ISSP	International Social Survey Programme
IT	information technology

JDS	Job Diagnostic Survey
LFS	Labour Force Survey
LGI	Looking Glass Inc.
LPC	least-preferred co-worker
MBA	Master of Business Administration
MORI	Market & Opinion Research International
MPS	Motivating Potential Score
MRS	Market Research Society
NACE	*Nomenclature statistique des Activités économiques dans la Communauté Européenne*
NAICS	North American Industrial Classification System
NASA	National Air and Space Administration
NHS	National Health Service
NOS	National Organisations Survey
NUD*IST	Non-numerical Unstructured Data Indexing Searching and Theorizing
OCB	organizational citizenship behaviour
OCS	Organizational Culture Scale
OD	organizational development
OECD	Organization for Economic Cooperation and Development
ONS	Office for National Statistics
ORACLE	Observational Research and Classroom Learning Evaluation
R&D	research and development
REPONSE	Relations Professionnelles et Négociations d'Enterprise
RTW	return to work
SIC	Standard Industrial Classification
SME	small or medium-sized enterprise
SOGI	society, organization, group, and individual
SSCI	Social Sciences Citation Index
SRA	Social Research Association
TDM	Total Design Method
TGI	Target Group Index
TQM	Total Quality Management
UKDA	UK Data Archive
VDL	vertical dyadic linkage
WERS	Workplace Employment Relations Survey (previously Workplace Employee Relations Survey)
WOMM	word-of-mouth marketing
WoS	Web of Science

About the authors

Alan Bryman was appointed Professor of Organizational and Social Research at the University of Leicester in August 2005. Prior to this he was Professor of Social Research at Loughborough University for thirty-one years.

His main research interests are in leadership, especially in higher education, research methods (particularly mixed methods research), and the 'Disneyization' and 'McDonaldization' of modern society. In 2003–4 he completed a project on the issue of how quantitative and qualitative research are combined in the social sciences, as part of the Economic and Social Research Council's Research Methods Programme.

He has published widely in the field of Social Research, including: *Quantitative Data Analysis with SPSS 17, 18 and 19: A Guide for Social Scientists* (Routledge, 2011) with Duncan Cramer; *Social Research Methods* (Oxford University Press, 2008); *The SAGE Encyclopedia of Social Science Research Methods* (Sage, 2004) with Michael Lewis-Beck and Tim Futing Liao; *The Disneyization of Society* (Sage, 2004); *Handbook of Data Analysis* (Sage, 2004) with Melissa Hardy; *Understanding Research for Social Policy and Practice* (Policy Press, 2004) with Saul Becker; and the *SAGE Handbook of Organizational Research Methods* with David Buchanan (Sage, 2009), as well as editing the *Understanding Social Research* series for the Open University Press.

He has contributed articles to a range of academic journals, including *Journal of Management Studies*; *Human Relations*; *International Journal of Social Research Methodology*; *Leadership Quarterly*; and *American Behavioral Scientist*. He is also on the editorial board of *Leadership* and *Qualitative Research in Organizations and Management: An International Journal*. He was a member of the ESRC's Research Grants Board and has recently completed research into effective leadership in higher education, a project funded by the Leadership Foundation for Higher Education.

Emma Bell is Professor of Management and Organization Studies and Head of the Centre for Economics and Management at Keele Management School, Keele University. She graduated with a Ph.D. from Manchester Metropolitan University in 2000 which was based on an ethnographic study of payment systems and organizational time in the chemical industry.

Her research approach involves qualitative analysis of organizational culture and change and adopts a critical perspective. She has focused on topics including organizational badging and learning initiatives, spirituality and belief in organizations, and loss and organizational death; this work has been published in various journals, including the *British Journal of Management*; the *British Journal of Industrial Relations*; *Human Relations*; *Organization*; the *Journal of Management Studies*; *Management Learning*; and *Time & Society*.

Emma also has an enduring interest in methods and methodologies of management research and the ways in which management knowledge is created. She has published on a number of issues related to this subject, including *A Very Short, Fairly Interesting and Reasonably Cheap Book about Management Research* (Sage, 2013) with Richard Thorpe. She is a founding member of *in*Visio (International Network of Visual Studies in Organizations), and has worked on an ESRC Researcher Development Initiative to promote the development of visual analysis in management research. She is the author of *Reading Management and Organization in Film* (Palgrave, 2008) and co-editor of the *Routledge Companion to Visual Organisation* (Routledge, 2013), with Samantha Warren and Jonathan Schroeder.

About the students and supervisors

Six undergraduate and two postgraduate students have provided valuable input that has informed our writing of the **Telling it like it is** feature of the book. We are extremely grateful to them for being willing to share their experiences of doing a research project and we hope that sharing what they have learned from this process with the readers of this book will enable others to benefit from their experience. Video-taped interviews with the students are available to view on the Online Resource Centre that accompanies this book.

Angharad Jones

Angharad did her undergraduate degree in Commerce at the University of Birmingham and completed her final year of study in 2005. Her dissertation project was a qualitative interview study exploring why women are under-represented in senior management. Although it was not a requirement of the dissertation to do a research project, Angharad felt that this was something that would help to give her dissertation a focus. She carried out her research in a department of a county council organization where women constitute over 60 per cent of the workforce.

Chris Phillips

Chris did an undergraduate degree in Commerce at Birmingham Business School and graduated in June 2004. His third year involved a final-year dissertation based on a small research project. Chris gained access to study women in management in a global banking organization as a result of his internship during the summer of his second year. He focused on the role of women employed by the bank, asking questions about why they progress, why they don't progress, and what affects their career progression. He was interested in the literature on the 'glass ceiling' and its effects on women's careers and wanted to find out whether or not it existed within the bank. His research design was qualitative and involved semi-structured interviews with women in the organization.

Karen Moore

In 2005 Karen was in her last year of study at Lancaster University on a four-year degree programme for the award of a Bachelor's in Business Administration in Management. Her final year research project came about as the result of her third-year placement in a company based in Leeds, where she worked in the Human Resources department. Karen became interested in the concept of person–organizational culture fit, having done courses in human resource management at university. She carried out an audit of the organizational culture in her placement company and explored the way that the recruitment and selection process operated to ensure person–organization fit. Her research design involved a questionnaire and semi-structured interviewing.

Lisa Mellors

Lisa studied at Lancaster University Management School for a Bachelor's Degree in Business Administration in Management. Her four-year course included a one-year work placement in industry. In 2004/5 she undertook a dissertation that formed a compulsory part of her final year of study. She based her research on the organization where she undertook her work placement and carried out an action research project involving a team that she was managing. She explained: 'on my work placement I was given a team to manage that were in trouble. The management had found problems in the team in terms of errors, and the morale was very low. There was a high turnover in the team as well, and they asked me if I could solve the problems and go in and kind of find out what was wrong. So I thought it was kind of a useful, real life project to do.' The action research project ran for a period of three months and involved Lisa in making changes to the team and then monitoring the effects of these changes. For more on action research see Chapter 17 or turn to the Glossary.

Lucie Banham

At the time we interviewed her, Lucie had just completed an MA in Organization Studies at Warwick Business School. She had also studied psychology as an undergraduate at the University of Warwick. Her dissertation project was about how governments employ action at a distance to encourage people towards identities that are supportive of their policies. Her specific focus was on how governments seek to foster the development of enterprising behaviour amongst students and young people. Her fieldwork was concentrated on the activities of one of the government-funded institutes that is responsible for promoting enterprise. She explained: 'I researched an . . . institute . . . that runs these kind of programmes [including] big events and competitions and courses that students can attend, so they. . . can learn about how to be an entrepreneur or how to be an enterprising subject.' Lucie's research design combined participant observation, unstructured and semi-structured interviews, and documentary data collection.

Nirwanthi De Vaz

Nirwanthi was an undergraduate on a three-year course studying for a BA in Management Studies at the University of Leicester. She finished her studies in 2005. In her third year she was required to do a dissertation, and she was encouraged to undertake some primary research as part of the dissertation project. Her research interest was in the role of informal organization, including personal relationships and friendships, in affecting how things get done efficiently in organizations outside the formal structure. The company she studied is based in Sri Lanka, and its business involves exporting fresh fish, so the nature of the product meant that efficiency was particularly important to the company. Her research strategy was qualitative and involved semi-structured interviews with managers in the company.

Tom Easterling

When he spoke to us, Tom had recently finished studying for an M.Sc. in occupational psychology at Birkbeck College, University of London, where he had been studying part-time over two years, combining this with his full-time job as an NHS manager in London. His dissertation research project focused on the development of wellbeing in the workplace, focusing on telephone call centres as the research context in which he explored this subject. Having done a project based on quantitative research methods several years previously when he was an undergraduate, this time Tom was keen to develop a research design that was more qualitative in nature. His research was based on a single case study of a public-sector call centre, where he interviewed people at different levels of the organization.

Tore Opsahl

Tore was in his final year at Queen Mary, University of London, studying for a B.Sc. in Business Management when he spoke to us about his experiences of doing a dissertation project. His project emerged from a business plan competition in which he got involved during an exchange visit in his second year at the University of California. For the competition Tore had set up a website for students to enable them to meet and socialize with each other. Upon returning to London in his third year he realized that the website had also generated a large amount of quantitative data, which he could usefully analyse for his research project. Guided by his interest in social network theory, he was able to analyse this existing dataset for his dissertation research project.

Seven supervisors also provided helpful feedback to inform the **Telling it like it is** feature of the book. They kindly agreed to share their experiences of supervising students doing research projects, and we hope that this will add an interesting new perspective for readers of the book. While they provided their feedback anonymously, we would like to acknowledge their affiliations, which were Coventry University, Uppsala University, the University of Portsmouth, the University of Hull, Southampton Solent University, Edinburgh Napier University, and Queen Mary University of London.

Guided tour of textbook features

Research in focus boxes

It is often said that the three most important features to look for when buying a house are location, location, location. A parallel for the teaching of research methods is examples, examples, examples! Research in focus boxes are designed to provide a sense of place for the theories and concepts being discussed in the chapter text, by providing real examples of published research.

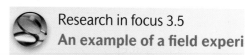

Research in focus 3.5
An example of a field experi

Frayne and Geringer (2000) examined the possibility that, if indi
they do usually, their performance in their jobs will be positively
the literature on 'self-management', as well as on relevant psych
Their primary hypothesis was expressed as follows: 'This study's
management is a causal or independent variable that affects em

Chapter outline

The goal of this chapter is to provide advice to students on t
have to prepare a dissertation based upon a research projec
students are required to produce such a dissertation as part
addition to needing help with the conduct of research, whic
aim to provide, the student may find it useful to have more s

Chapter outline

Each chapter opens with a chapter outline that provides a route map through the chapter material and summarizes the goals of each chapter, so that you know what you can expect to learn as you move through the text.

Key concept boxes

The world of research methods has its own language. To help you build your research vocabulary, key terms and ideas have been defined in Key concept boxes that are designed to advance your understanding of the field and help you to apply your new learning to new research situations.

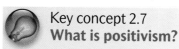

Key concept 2.7
What is positivism?

Positivism is an epistemological position that advocates the appl
the study of social reality. Although the term stretches beyond th
between authors, positivism is widely understood to rely on the

1. Only phenomena and hence knowledge confirmed by the se
   (the principle of phenomenalism).

Telling it like it is
Researching your own workplace

Chris, Karen, and Lisa all gained access to their research sites as the result of internship or opportunitie:
organized by their universities as part of their degree course.

Chris used the contacts he had established during his internship to make contact with individuals within
who could facilitate his access and provide him with important information. 'I ended up ringing the fourt
most senior person in the bank saying 'I'm doing this. Can I chat to you?' and she was absolutely great at
Then I spoke to somebody beneath her, who agreed to put me in contact with other women in the bank
good chat with her. She gave me lots of information regarding percentage of women at different levels of
management, progression over the years, information on competitors and things like that, so by the time
my internship I'd organized three interviewees and I could go back to university with my idea.'

Telling it like it is boxes

We have called these boxes 'Telling it like it is' because they provide you with insights based on personal experience rather than abstract knowledge. Many of these insights are based on interviews with real research students and business school supervisors and lecturers from business schools around the UK. In this way we hope to represent both sides of the supervision relationship, including the problems faced by students and how they are helped to overcome them and the advice that supervisors can provide. These boxes will help you to anticipate and resolve research challenges as you move through your dissertation or project.

Tips and skills boxes

Tips and skills boxes provide guidance and advice on key aspects of the research process. They will help you to avoid common research mistakes and equip you with the necessary skills to become a successful business researcher in your life beyond your degree.

Tips and skills
Reasons for writing a literat

The following is a list of reasons for writing a literature review:

1. You need to know what is already known in connection witl be accused of reinventing the wheel.

2. You can learn from other researchers' mistakes and avoid m

3. You can learn about different theoretical and methodologic

Thinking deeply 6.5
The assumption of anonymit

Grinyer (2002) argues that, although protecting the anonymity of integral feature of ethical research, there may be certain circumst remain anonymous because making their identity explicit is an ir stories. In the UK, the legal requirements of the Data Protection protect anonymity, since the Act states that anonymization shoul the security of data processing. These guidelines are based on the

Thinking deeply boxes

Business research methods can sometimes be complex: to raise your awareness of these complexities, Thinking deeply boxes feature further explanation of discussions and debates that have taken place between researchers. These boxes are designed to take you beyond the introductory level and think in greater depth about current research issues.

Checklists

Many chapters include checklists of issues to be considered when undertaking specific research activities (such as writing a literature review or conducting a focus group), to remind you of key questions and concerns and to help you progress your research project.

Checklist
Planning a research project

○ Do you know what the requirements for your dissertatior department?

○ Have you made contact with your supervisor?

Key points

- Follow the dissertation guidelines provided by your instit
- Thinking about your research subject can be time-consur the dissertation process.
- Use your supervisor to the fullest extent allowed and foll

Key points

At the end of each chapter there is a short bulleted summary of crucial themes and arguments explored by that chapter. These are intended to alert you to issues that are especially important and to reinforce the areas that you have covered to date.

Questions for review

Review questions have been included at the end of every chapter to test your grasp of the key concepts and ideas being developed in the text and to help you to reflect on your learning in preparation for coursework and assessment.

Questions for review

Managing time and resources

- What are the main advantages and disadvantages associated wit research?

Formulating suitable research questions

- What are the main sources of research questions?

Guided tour of the Online Resource Centre

What is involved in a small-scale research project or dissertation?

Chapter 3

- Get to know what is expected of you by your institution
- Start thinking about your research early
- Asking research questions
- Use your supervisor
- Manage your past resources
- Search and read the existing literature to produce a critical review
- Prepare for your research
- Collect your data
- Analyse your results
- Write up your research

For students
Research guide

This interactive research guide takes you step by step through each of the key research phases, ensuring that you do not overlook any research step and providing guidance and advice on every aspect of business research. The guide features checklists, web links, research activities, case studies, examples, and templates and is conveniently cross-referenced back to the book.

Interviews with students

Six undergraduate and two postgraduate students have provided valuable input that has informed our writing of the **Student experience** feature of *Business Research Methods*. We are extremely grateful to them for being willing to share their experiences. OUP would also like to express their gratitude to Emma Bell for conducting and filming the interviews with these students.

Video clips showing the students talking about their research projects are provided on this site. These clips are linked in to the 'student experience' boxes throughout the text.

Angharad Jones

Karen Moore

Interviews with research students

Learn from the real research experiences of students who have recently completed their own research projects! Download video-taped interviews with undergradute and postgraduate students from business schools around the UK and hear them describe the research processes they went through and the problems they resolved as they moved through each research phase.

Multiple-choice questions

The best way to reinforce your understanding of research methods is through frequent and cumulative revision. To support you in this, a bank of self-marking multiple-choice questions is provided for each chapter of the text, and they include instant feedback on your answers to help strengthen your knowledge of key research concepts.

Instructions

Choose your answer by clicking the radio button next to your choice and then press 'Submit' to get your score.

Question 1

What is distinctive about "Mode 2" knowledge production?

- a) It proceeds in a linear fashion building on existing knowledge.
- b) It is driven primarily by an academic agenda.
- c) It involves academics, policy makers and practitioners in problem solving.

Dataset

The dataset that relates to the gym survey in Chapters 15 and 16 of the text is available in both Excel and SPSS formats for use in course-work and independent study.

	C	D	E	F	G	H	I	J	K	L
1	2	1	1	3	1	2	0	33	17	5
2	1	3	1	4	3	1	2	10	23	10
3	3	1	2	2	1	1	1	27	18	12
4	3	2	1	2	1	2	0	30	17	3
5	2	1	3	2	3	1	4	22	0	15
6	3	1	1	3	1	1	3	34	17	0
7	5	2	1	5	1	1	5	17	48	10
8	3	1	2	2	2	1	1	25	18	7
9	2	1	1	3	1	2	0	34	15	0
10	2	2	2	4	3	2	0	16	18	11
11	5	2	1	3	1	1	1	0	42	16
12	2	1	2	3	1	2	0	34	22	12
13	5	1	1	2	1	2	0	22	31	7
14	2	1	3	4	2	1	3	37	14	12
15	3	1	1	5	2	2	0	26	9	4
16	3	1	2	2	3	1	4	22	7	10

Web links

A series of annotated web links organized by chapter are provided to point you in the direction of important articles, reviews, models, and research guides. These links will help keep you informed of the latest issues and developments in business research.

The Association of Business Schools
http://www.the-abs.org.uk

This is a link to the homepage for The Association of Business Schools (ABS) who are a representative body for the UK's leading higher education business institutions. There is a really useful Academic Journal Quality Guide, a system which ranks the quality of published journals based on the frequency that they are cited by other researchers. The ABS also contains a handy directory of schools and courses associated with business and management in the UK.

Paradigms and research methods
http://division.aomonline.org/rm/1999_RMD_Forum_Paradigms_and_Research_Methods.htm

Guide to using Excel in data analysis

This interactive workbook takes you through step-by-step from the very first stages of using Excel to more advanced topics such as charting, regression, and inference, giving guidance and practical examples.

Using Excel in data analysis

This resource has been authored by David Whigham, Senior Lecturer in Economics at Glasgow Caledonian University.

The workbooks contain instructions and practical examples to help you make the most of using Excel in data analysis.

Click on the links below to download the workbooks.

Excel 1: Basic Excel Techniques

For registered adopters of the text
Lecturer's guide

A comprehensive lecturer's guide is included to assist both new and experienced instructors in their teaching. The guide includes reading guides, discussion points, and some pointers to assist with problem-solving for each chapter.

Lecturer's Guide:
Chapter 1 – Business Research Strategies

Reading guide

The chief aim of this chapter is to show that a variety of considerations enter into the process of doing management and business research. The distinction that is commonly drawn between *quantitative research* and *qualitative research* is explored in relation to these considerations. This chapter explores:

- the nature of the relationship between theory and research, in

The nature of business research

Business research does not 'exist in a bubble' in a world from the social sciences -it is integrated with them;

The variety and diversity of business and management studies makes it hard to find agreement on how busin research claims should be evaluated;

PowerPoint slides

A suite of customizable PowerPoint slides is included for use in lecture presentations. Arranged by chapter theme the slides may also be used as hand-outs in class.

Figures and plates from the text

All figures and plates from the text have been provided in high-resolution format for downloading into presentation software or for use in assignments and exam material.

About the book

The focus of the book

This is a book that will be of use to all students in business schools who have an interest in understanding research methods as they are applied in management and organizational contexts. *Business Research Methods* gives students essential guidance on how to carry out their own research projects and introduces readers to the core concepts, methods, and values involved in doing research. The book provides a valuable learning resource through its comprehensive coverage of methods that are used by experienced researchers investigating the world of business as well as introducing some of the philosophical issues and ethical controversies that these researchers face. So, if you want to learn about business research methods, from how to formulate research questions to the process of writing up your research, *Business Research Methods* will provide a clear, easy to follow, and comprehensive introduction.

The book is based on the first-named author's *Social Research Methods*, which was written for students of the social sciences. The success of this book and the interest that it attracted in business schools led to this book, which has entailed an extensive adaptation for students of business and management studies. This has meant completely changing the examples that are used in the book; removing the discussion of issues that are not central to the concerns of students of business and management; and including completely new sections on areas that are important to business school students. The book has also been comprehensively updated to reflect the growing use of the Internet as a medium for conducting research and also as a source of data, so that there is now a chapter that deals with these newly emerging research opportunities (Chapter 28). Chapters 4, 5, and 29 take the reader through the process of doing a research project. In writing the fourth edition of the book we have created two new chapters in response to the many helpful comments we have received from colleagues and students in relation to previous editions. Chapter 1 is an entirely new chapter which we wrote in order to set the scene of the book and to indicate what is to come in subsequent chapters. Several people told us that they found the start of the book quite hard going, particularly the chapter about business research strategies (now Chapter 2), which deals with epistemological issues that many students find difficult. The revised structure hopefully provides a gentler introduction. Chapter 18 is also a brand new chapter which focuses on sampling in qualitative research. Feedback from our readers suggested that there was a rationale for including a separate chapter on this (as there is for sampling in quantitative research: see Chapter 7), rather than having it dispersed throughout the book in different chapters. This enables specific consideration of the quite different way in which qualitative researchers address the issue of sampling.

Because this book is written for a business school audience, it is intended to reflect a diverse range of subject areas, including organizational behaviour, marketing, strategy, organization studies, and HRM. In using the term 'business research methods', we have in mind the kinds of research methods that are employed in these fields, and so we have focused primarily on methods that are used in areas of business and management that have been influenced by the social sciences. Consequently, we do not claim to cover the full gamut of business research methods. Certain areas of business and management research, such as economic research and financial and accounting research, are not included within our purview. Our reason for not including such disciplines is that they are very much self-contained fields with their own traditions and approaches that do not mesh well with the kinds of methods that we deal with in this book.

This book has been written with two groups of readers in mind. The first comprises undergraduates and postgraduates in business and management schools and departments who invariably take at least one module or course in the area of research methods. This book covers a wide range of research methods, approaches to research, and ways of carrying out data analysis, so it is likely to meet the needs of the vast majority of students in this position. Research methods are not tied to a particular nation; many, if not most, of the principles transcend national boundaries.

The second group, which in most cases overlaps with the first, comprises undergraduates and postgraduates who do a research project as part of the requirement for their degree programmes. This can take many forms, but one of the most common is that a research project is carried out and a dissertation based on the investigation is presented. In addition, students are often expected to carry out mini-projects in relation to certain modules. The chapters in Part One of the book have been written specifically for students who are doing research projects, especially Chapters 3 and 4, which include a discussion of formulating research questions and reviewing the literature, reinforcing topics that we see as key to the whole process of doing research. In Parts Two and Three the accent is on the practice of business research and the methods that may be used. These chapters will be extremely useful in helping students make informed decisions about doing their research. In addition, when each research method is examined, its uses and limitations are explored in order to help students to make these decisions. Chapter 29 in Part Four provides advice on writing up business research.

In addition to providing students with practical advice on doing research, the book also explores the nature of business and management research. This relates to fundamental concerns about what doing business and management research involves. For example:

- What is the aim or function of business research?

- Is it conducted primarily in order to find ways of improving organizational performance through increasing effectiveness and efficiency?

- Or is it mainly about increasing our understanding of how organizations work, and their impact on individuals and on society?

- Who are the audiences of business research?

- Is business research conducted primarily for managers and, if not, for whom else in organizations is it conducted?

- Is the purpose of business research to further the academic development of the field?

- What is the politics of management research and how does this frame the use of different methods and the kinds of research findings that are regarded as legitimate and acceptable?

- To what extent do researchers' personal values impact upon the research process?

- Should we worry about the feelings of people outside the research community concerning what we do to people during our investigations?

These questions are the subject of considerable ongoing debate. Being aware of them is important in understanding what influences a student's choice of research topic and how he or she addresses it. This also enables understanding of the practices of business researchers. There are four points that can be made in relation to this.

1. In order to evaluate the quality of management and business research it is necessary to know as much as possible about researchers' *own* role in this process—including how they collected and analysed the data and the theoretical perspective that informed their interpretation of it. This understanding relies on examination of methods used by business researchers, which is why, throughout this book, we have used real examples of published research to illustrate how researchers deal with and justify these methodological choices.

2. This leads to a second point in relation to the use of examples. Business research methods tend on the whole to be more eclectic and explained in less detail than in some other social sciences such as sociology. Perhaps this is due to the emergent nature of the field or because it draws from such a diverse range of disciplines. In practice, it means that novice researchers can sometimes find it difficult to identify examples of existing research to inform their own practice. One of the reasons we use so many examples in this book is to draw attention to the range of methods that business researchers use in a way that can be understood by those who are new to this field of study.

3. The third point relates to the kinds of methods used in business research. In some instances, it is hard to identify examples of particular research methods, while in others, such as the **case study** method, there are numerous studies to choose from. We believe, however, that this creates opportunities for new researchers to make use of less popular or less commonly used methods to gain insight into a research problem. In other words, we hope that through reading this book students will possibly be encouraged to use research methods that are less common, as well as those that are well established in the field.

4. Finally, despite the sometimes limited availability of examples that illustrate the use of various research methods, we have tried to confine our choice of examples to business and management. This is because by getting to know how other researchers in the field have approached its study we can build up an understanding of how research methods might be improved and developed.

These and many other issues impinge on research in a variety of ways and will be confronted at different stages throughout the book.

Why use this book?

There are likely to be two main circumstances in which this book is in your hands at the moment. One is that you have to study one or more modules in research methods for a degree in business and management or there are methodological components to one of your taught modules (for example, a course in organizational behaviour). The other is that you have to do some research, perhaps for a dissertation or project report, and you need some guidelines about how to approach your study. You may find yourself reading this book for either or both of these reasons during the course of doing your degree. It may be that you are wondering why you need to study research methods and why such people as the authors of this book do business research at all. In the rest of this section, we will try briefly to address these issues and concerns, but before that, what do we mean by 'business research'?

What do we mean by 'business research'?

The term 'business research', as it is used in this book, refers to *academic* research on topics relating to questions that are relevant to the field of business and management and have a social science orientation. We include in this category research in areas such as organizational behaviour, marketing, accounting, HRM, and strategy, which draw on the social sciences for conceptual and theoretical inspiration.

In the previous paragraph, the word 'academic' is emphasized, and there is an important reason for this in setting out this book's approach. Academics carry out research to investigate research questions that arise out of the existing literature on topics (such as 'What are the implications of low levels of job satisfaction in a workforce?'), or that may be influenced by developments in business and management generally (such as 'What is the impact of the introduction of Total Quality Management in companies?'). We discuss in some detail in Chapter 4 what research questions are and how they arise in the research process, but for the time being the purpose of this discussion is to make it clear that, when we use the term 'business research', we are referring to research conducted for the illumination of issues that arise in the context of academic thinking in the area of business and management. The term 'business research' in this book

does not include research conducted by organizations for the investigation of issues of concern to them. For example, commercial organizations conduct market research to explore how their products or services are received or when they want to launch a new product or service. This is not the kind of research that we focus on in this book. This is not because we view such research as unimportant or irrelevant or because we view it as inferior in some way. Rather, it is because the rationales for doing such research and the ways in which it is done are different from academic research. Consequently, it would be difficult to incorporate both approaches to business and management research within the covers of a manageable volume. This is the reason why almost all of our examples in this book are based on academic research. To include commercial business research would make the book unmanageable and potentially confusing.

We do not wish to drive a wedge between academic research and that originating from business and management practitioners. Indeed, there is a great deal of soul-searching among academics in the business and management field concerning this issue (see, in particular, the June 2006 special issue of the *Journal of Occupational and Organizational Psychology*), and in Chapter 1 we address further some of these issues in the context of a discussion of what are known as Mode 1 and Mode 2 forms of knowledge (the first is more or less synonymous with traditional academic research in this area; the second is research conducted by academics *and* practitioners to address applied organizational issues and problems). The point of this discussion is to highlight our point of departure and our rationale for emphasizing academic research in this field. It is also worth pointing out that there is often considerable cross-fertilization between academic and practitioner-based research in the field. Practitioners often draw on methodological developments in academic fields, such as sampling, to refine their techniques, while a research method such as focus groups was largely developed in the applied context of market research before making its way into academic research. Further, the skills from one domain are invariably transferable to the other.

Why do business research?

The rationale for doing business research has been outlined in the previous subsection to a certain extent. Academics conduct such research because, in the course of reading the literature on a topic or when reflecting on what is going on in modern organizations, questions occur to them. They may notice a gap in the literature or an inconsistency between a number of studies or an unresolved issue in the literature. These provide common circumstances that act as springboards for business research in academic circles. Another is when there is a development in organizations that provides an interesting point of departure for the investigation of a research question. For example, noting the widespread use of email in organizations, a researcher might be interested in studying its introduction in an organization and whether this is accompanied by changes in the nature and quality of interaction. In exploring this issue, the researcher is likely to draw upon the literature on technology and organizational change to provide insights into how to approach the issue. As we say in Chapter 1, there is no single reason why people do business research of the kind emphasized in this book, but at its core, it is done because there is an aspect of understanding of what goes on in organizations that is to some extent unresolved.

Why is it important to study methods?

For some students, there does not seem a great deal of point to studying research methods. They might take the view that, if they have to conduct an investigation, why not adopt a 'need to know' approach? In other words, why not just look into how to do your research when you are on the verge of carrying out your investigation? Quite aside from the fact that this is an extremely risky approach to take, it neglects the opportunities that training in research methods offers. In particular, you need to bear in mind the following:

- Training in research methods sensitizes you to the *choices* that are available to business and management researchers. In other words, it makes you aware of the range of research methods that can be employed to collect data and the variety of approaches to the analysis of data. Such awareness will help you to make the most appropriate choices for your project, since you need to be aware of when it is appropriate or inappropriate to employ particular techniques of data collection and analysis.

- Training in research methods provides you with an awareness of the 'dos' and 'don'ts' when employing a particular approach to collecting or analysing data. Thus, once you have made your choice of research method (for example, a questionnaire), you need to be aware of the practices you need to follow in order to implement that method properly. You also need to be aware of the many pitfalls to be avoided.

- Training in research methods provides you with insights into the overall research process. It provides a general vantage point for understanding how research is done. As such, it illuminates the various stages of research, so that you can plan your research and think about such issues as how your research methods will connect with your research questions.

- Training in research methods provides you with an awareness of what constitutes good and poor research. It therefore provides a platform for developing a critical awareness of the limits and limitations of research that you read. This can be helpful in enabling you to evaluate critically the research that you read about for modules in fields such as organizational behaviour and HRM.

- The skills that training in research methods imparts are transferable ones. How to sample, how to design a questionnaire, how to conduct semi-structured interviewing or focus groups, and so on are skills that are relevant to research in other spheres (such as firms, public-sector organizations, etc.).

Thus, we feel that training in research methods has much to offer and that readers of this book will recognize the opportunities and advantages that it provides.

The structure of the book

Business and management research has many different traditions, one of the most fundamental of which is the distinction between quantitative and qualitative research. This distinction lies behind the structure of the book and the way in which issues and methods are approached.

The book is divided into four parts.

- **Part One** deals with basic ideas about the nature of business and management research and with the considerations in planning and starting a student research project.

  - Chapter 1 outlines the main stages involved in doing most kinds of business research. It also explores how business research is understood in a wider context, including discussion of the political and wider societal issues that affect its current practice. This provides the basic foundations from which you will be able to explore these issues in more detail and depth.

  - Chapter 2 examines such issues as the nature of the relationship between theory and research and the degree to which a natural science approach is appropriate for the study of business and management. It is here that the distinction between quantitative and qualitative research is first encountered. They are presented as different **research strategies** with different ways of conceptualizing how business and management should be studied. It is also shown that there is more to the distinction between them than whether or not an investigation includes the collection of quantitative data.

- In Chapter 3, the idea of a **research design** is introduced. This chapter allows an introduction to the basic frameworks within which social research is carried out, such as social survey research, case study research, and experimental research. Chapters 2 and 3 provide the basic building blocks for the rest of the book.

- Chapter 4 takes you through the main steps that are involved in planning and designing a research project and offers advice on how to manage this process. It also includes a discussion of **research questions**—what they are, why they are important, and how they come to be formulated.

- Chapter 5 is designed to help you to get started on your research project by introducing the main steps in conducting a critical review of the literature.

- Chapter 6 considers the ways in which ethical and political issues impinge on researchers and the kinds of principles that are involved in addressing them.

○ **Part Two** contains ten chapters concerned with quantitative research.

- Chapter 7 explores the nature of quantitative research and provides a context for the later chapters. The next four chapters are largely concerned with aspects of social survey research.

- Chapter 8 deals with sampling issues: how to select a sample and the considerations that are involved in assessing what can be inferred from different kinds of sample.

- Chapter 9 is concerned with the kind of interviewing that takes place in survey research—that is, structured interviewing.

- Chapter 10 covers the design of questionnaires. This involves a discussion of how to devise self-completion questionnaires such as postal questionnaires.

- Chapter 11 examines the issue of how to ask questions for questionnaires and structured interviews.

- Chapter 12 covers structured observation, which is a method that has been developed for the systematic observation of behaviour. It has been especially influential in the areas of business and management research.

- Chapter 13 presents content analysis, a method that provides a rigorous framework for the analysis of a wide range of documents.

- Chapter 14 deals with the analysis of data collected by other researchers and by official bodies. The emphasis then switches to the ways in which we can analyse quantitative data.

- Chapter 15 presents a range of basic tools for the analysis of quantitative data. The approach taken is non-technical. The emphasis is upon how to choose a method of analysis and how to interpret the findings. No formulae are presented.

- Chapter 16 shows you how to use computer software—in the form of SPSS, the most widely used software for analysing quantitative data—in order to implement the techniques you learned in Chapter 15.

○ **Part Three** contains nine chapters on aspects of qualitative research.

- Chapter 17 has the same role in relation to Part Three as Chapter 7 has in relation to Part Two. It provides an overview of the nature of qualitative research and as such supplies the context for the other chapters in this part.

- Chapter 18 examines the main sampling strategies used in qualitative research. Just like quantitative researchers, qualitative researchers often have to sample research participants, documents, or organizations as units of analysis. As this chapter shows, the sampling principles used are quite different from those usually employed by quantitative researchers.

- Chapter 19 is concerned with ethnography and participant observation, which are the source of some of the best-known studies in business and management research. The two terms are often used interchangeably and refer to the immersion of the researcher in a social setting.

- Chapter 20 deals with the kinds of interview used by qualitative researchers, typically semi-structured interviewing or unstructured interviewing.

- Chapter 21 explores the focus group method, whereby groups of individuals are interviewed on a specific topic.

- Chapter 22 examines two ways in which qualitative researchers analyse language: conversation analysis and discourse analysis.

- Chapter 23 deals with the examination of documents in qualitative research, including historical documents. The emphasis then shifts to the interpretation of documents.

- Chapter 24 explores some approaches to the analysis of qualitative data.

- Chapter 25 shows you how to use computer software to assist with your analysis of quantitative data.

It is striking that certain issues recur across Parts Two and Three: interviewing, observation, documents, and data analysis. However, as you will see, quantitative and qualitative research constitute contrasting approaches to these activities.

○ **Part Four** contains chapters that go beyond the quantitative/qualitative research contrast.

- Chapter 26 deals with some of the ways in which the distinction between quantitative and qualitative research is less fixed than is sometimes supposed.

- Chapter 27 presents some ways in which quantitative and qualitative research can be combined to produce what is referred to as mixed methods research.

- Chapter 28 is concerned with e-research, including the use of the Internet as a context or platform for conducting research.

- Chapter 29 has been included to help with writing up research, an often neglected area of the research process.

How to use the book

The book can be used in a number of different ways. However, we would encourage all readers at least to look at the chapter guide at the beginning of each chapter to decide whether or not they need the material covered there and also to gain a sense of the range of issues that are addressed.

- *Setting the scene*. Chapter 1 is a scene-setting chapter which outlines the main stages involved in doing most kinds of business research. Most of the topics introduced in this chapter are covered in much greater depth and detail later in the book. The aim of this chapter, then, is to give an overview of some of the main issues that will be considered as the book progresses.

- *Wider philosophical and methodological issues*. If you do not need to gain an appreciation of the wider philosophical context of enquiry in business and management research, Chapter 2 can largely be ignored. If an emphasis on such issues *is* something you are interested in, Chapter 2 along with Chapter 26 should be a particular focus of attention.

- *Survey research*. Chapters 7 to 16 deal with the kinds of topics that need to be addressed in survey research. In addition, Chapter 15 examines ways of analysing the kinds of data that are generated by survey researchers. Also, sections in Chapter 28 explore issues to do with the conduct of surveys via email or the Internet.

- *Practical issues concerned with doing quantitative research*. This is the province of the whole of Part Two. In addition, you would be advised to read Chapter 3, which maps out the main research designs employed, such as experimental and cross-sectional designs, which are frequently used by quantitative researchers.

- *Practical issues concerned with doing qualitative research*. This is the province of the whole of Part Three. In addition, you would be advised to read Chapter 3, which maps out the main research designs employed, such as the case study, which is frequently employed in qualitative research.

- *Analysing data*. Chapters 15 and 24 explore the analysis of quantitative and qualitative research data, respectively, while Chapters 16 and 25 introduce readers to the use of computer software in this connection. It may be that your module on research methods does not get into issues to do with analysis, in which case these chapters may be omitted.

- *Formulating research questions*. As we have already said in this Guide, we see the asking of research questions as fundamental to the research process. Advice on what research questions are, how they are formulated, where they come from, and so on is provided in Chapter 4.

- *Doing your own research project*. We hope that the whole of this book will be relevant to students doing their own research projects or mini-projects, but Chapters 4 and 5 are the ones where much of the specific advice relating to this issue is located. In addition, we would alert you to the Tips and skills and Telling it like it is features that have been devised and to the checklists of points to remember.

- *Writing*. This issue is very much connected with the last point. It is easy to forget that your research has to be *written up*. This is as much a part of the research process as the collection of data. Chapter 29 discusses a variety of issues to do with writing up business research, including writing up your research as a dissertation or similar product.

- **_Wider responsibilities of researchers_**. It is important to bear in mind that as researchers we bear responsibilities to the people and organizations that are the recipients of our research activities. Ethical issues are raised at a number of points in this book and Chapter 6 is devoted to a discussion of them. The fact that we have an entire chapter focused on a discussion of ethics is a measure of the importance of these issues and the need for all researchers to be aware of them. There is also a discussion of the ethical issues involved in Internet research in Chapter 28.

- **_The quantitative/qualitative research contrast_**. We use the distinction between quantitative and qualitative research in two ways: as a means of organizing the research methods and methods of analysis available to you; and as a way of introducing some wider philosophical issues about business and management research. Chapter 2 outlines the chief areas of difference between quantitative and qualitative research.

These are followed up in Chapter 26. We also draw attention to some of the limitations of adhering to an excessively strict demarcation between the two research strategies in Chapter 26, while Chapter 27 explores ways of integrating them. If you do not find it a helpful distinction, these chapters can be avoided or skimmed.

- **_The Internet_**. The Internet plays an increasingly important role in the research process. At various junctures we provide important websites where key information can be gleaned. We also discuss in Chapter 5 the use of the Internet as a route for finding references for your literature review, itself another important phase of the research process. You will find that many of the references that you obtain from an online search will then themselves be accessible to you in electronic form. Finally, Chapter 28 discusses the use of the Internet as a source of material that can be analysed and as a platform for doing research in the form of such research methods as Web surveys, electronic focus groups, and email surveys.

Acknowledgements

This book has benefited from the large number of students who have shared their ideas about, experiences of, and problems encountered in business and management and social science research. These individuals, many of them unwittingly, have made a significant contribution to the development of the text.

Alan Bryman's teaching of research methods at Loughborough University and the University of Leicester and Emma Bell's experience of teaching in business and management schools have provided major sources of inspiration in this respect, and we would therefore like to express our appreciation for the support provided by all these institutions, as well as by our current institutions, which are respectively the University of Leicester and Keele University.

As this is the fourth edition of this book, the number of colleagues who have provided advice and suggestions grows ever longer. We would particularly like to acknowledge colleagues Alan Beardsworth, Michael Billig, Dave Buchanan, and Cliff Oswick for their constructive comments on various parts of the book, as well as Dave McHugh, Steve Carter, and Nick Wylie for their imaginative contribution to the Online Research Guide that accompanies this text. In addition, our thanks go to the referees for their detailed and helpful comments on this and previous editions of the book; their criticisms and advice, informed by substantial experience of teaching research methods to business and management students, have proved invaluable. We would also like to say a big thank you to Albert Mills and Tony Yue for generously allowing us to use some of their valuable insights into historical research, which they developed in the Canadian adaptation of this book, in the section in Chapter 23 on historical analysis (Bryman, Bell, Mills, and Yue © Oxford University Press Canada 2011. Reprinted by permission of the publisher). We are also grateful to Samantha Warren and Jonathan Schroeder for their advice on visual methods, to Jane Davison and Samantha Warren for kindly agreeing to let us use photographs from their research, and to Karam Ram and Jaguar Heritage for permission to reproduce images from the Jaguar Archive. We would also like to thank Roland Miller for his technical support in relation to the student interviews, and the students themselves who agreed to be interviewed about their research experiences. In addition, we are grateful to the business and management librarians at Queen Mary, Bath, Exeter, and Birmingham for their invaluable advice and suggestions concerning Chapter 5 of the book. We would also like to thank the business school lecturers who shared their experiences of supervising students through the dissertation research process and agreed for us to share their expertise in the 'Telling it like it is' feature of this book.

We also wish to thank several people at or connected with Oxford University Press: Patrick Brindle and Angela Adams, both formerly of OUP, Antony Hey and the whole editorial team, for their support and enthusiasm, their firm handling of the book's production, and their astute and careful copy-editing of the typescript, on this and previous editions.

However, we have reserved our most important acknowledgements until last. Alan would like to thank Sue and Sarah as usual for their support in putting up with him without a murmur. Alan would also like to thank Sue for her wonderful work on the proofs for this book. Finally, we take full responsibility for the final text, including its inevitable deficiencies, from which everyone except us must, of course, be absolved.

Part One
The research process

Part One of this book provides the groundwork for more specialized chapters in Parts Two, Three, and Four. In Chapter 1, the purpose and process of business research are outlined. Chapters 2 and 3 present two ideas that recur throughout the book—**research strategy** and **research design**. Chapter 2 outlines a variety of considerations that impinge on the practice of business research and relates these to research strategy. Two research strategies are identified: **quantitative** and **qualitative research**. Chapter 3 identifies different kinds of research design employed in business research. Chapters 4 and 5 provide advice on issues to consider if you have to prepare a dissertation based on a student research project. Chapter 4 deals with planning and formulating **research questions**, including principles and considerations to be taken into account in designing a student research project, while Chapter 5 is about how to get started with a review of the literature. Chapter 6 deals with ethics and politics in business research.

1

The nature and process of business research

Chapter guide

This chapter introduces some fundamental considerations in conducting business research. It begins by outlining what we mean by business research and the reasons why we conduct it. The bulk of the chapter considers three areas:

- *Business research methods in context.* This deals with issues such as the role of theory, the role of values and ethical considerations, debates about relevance versus rigour, and how political considerations affect business research.

- *The elements of the research process.* The whole book is dedicated to the elements of business research, but here the essential stages are given a preliminary treatment. The elements are: a literature review; formulating concepts and theories; devising research questions; sampling; data collection; data analysis; and writing up.

- *The messiness of business research.* This section acknowledges that business research often does not conform to a neat, linear process and that researchers may find themselves facing unexpected contingencies and difficulties. At the same time, it is suggested that a familiarity with the nature of the research process and its principles is crucial to navigating through the unexpected.

All of the issues presented here are treated in greater detail in later chapters, but they are introduced at this stage to provide you with an early opportunity to think about them.

Introduction

This book is concerned with the ways that business researchers go about their craft. We take this to mean the approaches employed by business researchers to go about the research process in all its phases—formulating research objectives; choosing research methods; securing research participants; collecting, analysing, and interpreting data; and disseminating findings. An understanding of business research methods is important for several reasons, but three stand out. First, it will help you to avoid the many pitfalls that are common when relatively inexperienced people try to do business research, such as failing to match research questions to research methods, asking ambiguous questions in **questionnaires**, or engaging in practices that are ethically dubious. If you are expected to conduct a research project, an education in research methods is important, not just for ensuring that the correct procedures are followed but also for gaining an appreciation of the choices that are available to you. Second, an understanding of business research methods is important from the point of view of a consumer of published research. When people take degrees in business subjects, they read a lot of published research in the substantive areas they study. A good grounding in the research process and a knowledge of the potential pitfalls provides an invaluable critical edge when reading the research of others. Finally, an understanding of research methods will enable you to satisfy your curiosity about topics that interest you by undertaking your own research project, either for a dissertation or perhaps in a work-related context. Such a project may generate insight into important business issues and thus allow you, in a small and incremental way, to contribute to business knowledge.

What is meant by 'business research'?

The term 'business research' as used here denotes academic research on topics relating to questions relevant to business and management. Business research includes studies that draw on the social sciences, such as sociology, psychology, anthropology, and economics, for conceptual and theoretical inspiration. Business research may be motivated by developments and changes in organizations and societies, such as concerns about rising levels of executive pay or a desire to improve the environmental sustainability of businesses, but social scientific ideas are used to illuminate those changes. The social sciences also provide ideas about how to formulate research topics and how to interpret and draw implications from research findings. In other words, what distinguishes business research as discussed in this book is that it is deeply rooted in the ideas and intellectual traditions of the social sciences.

Why do business research?

Academics conduct research because in the course of reading the literature on a topic or reflecting on what is going on in organizations, questions occur to them. They may notice a gap in the literature or an inconsistency between a number of studies or an unresolved issue in the literature. Another rationale is a societal development that provides a point of departure for the development of a research question. For example, observing the behaviours of consumers who prefer a particular brand of technology such as Apple, a researcher might decide to study how consumer groups develop and express strong loyalty to a particular brand. In exploring this issue, the researcher is likely to draw upon the literature on identity and culture to generate insights. As we note in Chapter 2, there is no single reason why people do business research, but, at its core, it is done when there is an aspect of business and management that is believed to be inadequately understood.

Business research methods in context

Business research and its associated methods do not exist in a vacuum. The following factors form part of the context within which business research takes place:

- The *theories* that social scientists develop to understand the social world influence what is researched and how research findings are interpreted. The topics of business research are profoundly influenced by available theoretical positions. Drawing on our earlier example, if a researcher were interested in understanding the behaviours of brand-loyal consumers, it is quite likely that he or she would take into account theories concerning the collective cultural processes whereby groups of people develop a shared identity. This illustrates how current research is informed and influenced by existing theory. Research also contributes to theory because new research feeds into the stock of knowledge to which the theory relates.

- Existing knowledge about an area also forms an important part of the background in which business research takes place. This means that someone planning to conduct research must be familiar with the *literature* on the area of interest. You have to be familiar with what is already known so that you can build on it and avoid covering the same ground as others. Reviewing literature is the main focus of Chapter 5 and is also discussed in other chapters, such as Chapter 29.

The researcher's views about the nature of the *relationship between theory and research* are also important. For some researchers, theory should be addressed at the beginning of a research project. The researcher engages in theoretical reflections from which a **hypothesis** or hypotheses are formulated and then tested. This was the approach taken in the study discussed in Research in focus 1.3 by Elsesser and Lever (2011: 1559), who proposed nine hypotheses based on their review of relevant theory. An alternative position is to view theory as an outcome of the research process—that is, as something that is arrived at after the research has been carried out. The first approach implies that a set of theoretical ideas drive data collection and analysis, whereas the second suggests a more open-ended strategy in which theoretical ideas emerge out of data. Of course, the choice is rarely as stark as this, but there are contrasting views about the role of theory in research. This issue will be a major focus of Chapter 2.

- Assumptions and views about how research should be conducted influence the research process. It is often assumed that a 'scientific' approach should be followed, in which a hypothesis is formulated and then tested using precise measurement techniques. Such research exists, but the view that this is how business research should be done is not universally accepted. These are **epistemological** considerations. They focus on how the social world should be studied. Some researchers argue that people and their social institutions are very different from the subject matter of the scientist and require an approach that is more sensitive to the special qualities of people and social life. This issue will be a major focus of Chapter 2.

- Assumptions about the nature of social phenomena influence the research process too. It is sometimes suggested that the social world is external to social actors and that they have no control over it. It is simply there, acting upon and influencing their behaviour, beliefs, and values. The culture of an organization, for example, can be seen as a set of values and behavioural expectations that exert a powerful influence over people who work in it, and into which new recruits have to be socialized. But we could also view culture as something that is constantly being reformulated and reassessed, as members of the organization modify it through practices and through small innovations. Considerations of this kind are **ontological**. They focus on the nature of social phenomena—are they relatively inert and beyond our influence or are they a product of social interaction? This issue will be a major focus of Chapter 2.

- The *quality criteria* used to evaluate research are a further important influence on the research process. How do you do good research and how do you know it when you read it? The assessment of quality relates to all phases of the research process. As we will see, quality has become a prominent issue among business researchers and policy-makers with an interest in academic research. There are several reasons for this, but the key point here is that debates have arisen about whether there can be quality criteria that apply to all forms of research. As we will see, especially in Chapter 17, some methodologists argue that a 'horses for courses' approach is required whereby quality criteria need to take into account the kind of investigation to which they are being applied.

- The *values* of the research community have significant implications for research. *Ethical issues* have always been a point of discussion and controversy in research, but in recent times they have become even more prominent. It is now almost impossible to do certain kinds of research without risking the opprobrium of the research community and censure from the funder or university. There is an elaborate framework of bodies that scrutinize research proposals for ethical integrity, so that transgression of ethical principles is less likely. Ethical values and the institutional arrangements that researchers must respond to have implications for what and who can be researched and for how research can be conducted, to the point that some research methods are no longer used. Ethical issues are addressed in Chapter 6 and touched on in several other chapters.

- So far, we have stressed the academic nature and role of business research. However, many researchers feel that what they do should have a practical purpose and make a difference to the world around us. This means that studies should focus on issues that will have *implications for practice*. For Alvesson (2013), this involves researchers going beyond the narrow confines of their academic field, and asking 'whether one has something to say that makes a difference to our understanding of the phenomena targeted; something that would lead the intellectually-minded practitioner to think and act differently and thus somehow be supportive in improving the functioning of organizations and/or people's working life' (Alvesson, 2013: 80). This can involve critique of the business function, as long as this is framed in a way which is understandable and helpful. Some business research, such as **action research**, discussed in Chapter 17, involves those being researched (such as managers, employees, and consumers, as well as policy-makers) participating in the research process, perhaps by helping to formulate research questions. While opinions differ about the need for business research to be directly relevant to practice, this is an issue that researchers are expected to reflect upon.

- Business research operates within a wider *political context*. This complex feature is explored in Chapter 6. For example, much business research is funded by government bodies, and these often reflect the orientation of politicians in power. This will mean that certain research issues are somewhat more likely to receive financial support than others. Research supported by the Economic and Social Research Council (ESRC), a major funding body for UK business research, requires applicants to demonstrate how users of the research will be involved or engaged. There is also a growing expectation that people will be able to access published research, requiring researchers to publish findings in a form that is public and freely available, such as on a research project website or in an 'open-access' journal (see Key concept 5.1). A further political issue relates to the status of the journal in which research is published, as this is used to inform rankings of business schools, which in turn affects the decisions of fee-paying students concerning which university they apply to. Highly ranked journals tend to favour particular kinds of research, and some fear that this may result in a narrowing of the type of research that is done in business schools.

- The *training and personal values* of the researcher form part of the context of business research in that they may influence the research area, the research questions, and the methods chosen. The influence of personal experience can be seen clearly in the study by Clarke et al. (2012) of business school academics in UK universities, discussed later in this chapter. They explain: 'prior to the research we (as academics employed by a UK business school), held ideas about the concerns with identity amongst our academic colleagues in business and management schools … we cannot claim the interview schedule we used was independent of these ideas' (Clarke et al. 2012: 17). Issues relating to the management of individual performance and how this affects identities were of personal interest to them, but they also used the data to engage with issues of managerialism, audit, and performativity which have been of interest to business researchers for well over a decade. Researchers, as a result of their training and sometimes from personal preference, frequently develop attachments to, or at least preferences for, certain methods and approaches. One of the reasons we try to cover a wide range of research methods in this book is because we are convinced that it is important for practising and prospective researchers to be familiar with a diversity of methods and how to implement them. The development of methodological preferences carries the risk of becoming blinkered and restricted, but such preferences often do emerge and have implications for the conduct of research.

 # Relevance to practice

The diverse nature of business research means there is considerable debate about how it should be evaluated. Some have suggested that management research can be understood solely as an applied field because it is concerned with understanding the nature of organizations and solving problems of managerial practice. Gummesson (2000) sees academic researchers and management consultants as groups of knowledge workers who place a different emphasis on theory and practice. He writes: 'Backed by bits and pieces of theory, the consultant contributes to practice, whereas the scholar contributes to theory supported by fragments of practice' (2000: 9), but fundamentally he views their roles as closely related. Gummesson sees researchers and consultants as both involved in addressing problems that concern management, so that the value of both groups is determined by their ability to convince the business community that their findings are relevant and useful. Tranfield and Starkey (1998) argue that much management research has lost touch with the concerns and interests of practitioners and that researchers must learn to be responsive to them in order for research to retain value and purpose. In recent years, there has been much debate around the concept of evidence-based management (Key concept 1.1). A leading advocate of evidence-based management, Rousseau, argues that managers need to move their 'professional decisions away from personal preference and unsystematic experience toward those based on the best available scientific evidence' (Rousseau 2006: 256). However, others have been more cautious, arguing that the changing and pluralistic nature of organizations makes it difficult to identify generally applicable best practices. Reay et al. (2009) carried out a review of articles that used evidence-based analysis and found that none of them demonstrated a link between the adoption of evidence-based management and improved organizational performance. They conclude that managers should

Key concept 1.1
What is evidence-based management?

Evidence-based management is 'the systematic use of the best available evidence to improve management practice' (Reay et al. 2009). The concept has been developed since the 1990s in medical and health research to try to reduce variation in clinical practice and to ensure that diagnostic and therapeutic procedures are based on the best research evidence. It later expanded into other fields such as education (Sebba 2004; Petticrew and Roberts 2006). There are four sources of information that contribute to evidence-based management:

1. practitioner expertise and judgement;

2. evidence from the local context;

3. critical evaluation of the best available research evidence;

4. perspectives of those who may be affected by a particular decision (Briner et al. 2009: 19).

Point 3 is based on the practice of systematic review of the literature (see Chapter 5), which is a cornerstone of evidence-based management practice. The success of evidence-based management depends in part on the transfer and translation of research findings into practice, through 'knowledge translation'. While responsibility for knowledge translation rests partly on management researchers, who need to make sure they highlight the practical implications of their research findings, it also depends on managers being engaged with research. Reay et al. (2009: 16) argue that 'it is crucial to teach students how to evaluate research evidence so that when they become practicing managers they will be able to understand and appropriately apply new research evidence in practice'.

not adopt evidence-based management 'in advance of evidence demonstrating its impact on organizational performance' (Reay et al. 2009: 13). Other commentators are concerned that evidence-based management privileges certain kinds of research evidence, in particular positivistic, quantitative studies. Learmonth (2008) argues that evidence-based management constitutes a backlash against methodological pluralism by limiting what counts as legitimate research. He suggests that evidence-based management obscures the fact that management research is not a neutral science, but rather is constructed in line with the interests of those who hold and seek to maintain power. In other words, '"evidence" is never just there, waiting for the researcher to find. Rather it is always necessary to construct it in some way—a process that is inherently ideological and always contestable—not merely a technical, "scientific" task' (Learmonth 2009: 95). Finally, he argues that because management research operates from within conflicting paradigms (see Key concept 2.14), it is not possible to develop a consensus-based notion of evidence that transcends these fundamental differences.

Other writers suggest that management and business research is too concerned with lengthy 'fact-finding' exercises and is insufficiently guided by theoretical concerns. They argue that application is not a primary purpose to which management research should be directed (Burrell 1997). For these scholars, making research

relevant to managerial practice is not the main aim of academic study (Clegg 2002; Hinings and Greenwood 2002). They believe that research should not be dictated by non-academic interests, such as professional associations and government agencies, who may seek to influence its focus and guide its development in a way that is 'useful' to current practice but susceptible to the whim of current management fads and fashions.

A further debate that influences understandings of the role of management and business research stems from the thesis developed by Gibbons et al. (1994). These writers suggest that the process of knowledge production in contemporary society falls into two contrasting categories or types, which they describe as 'mode 1' and 'mode 2':

- *Mode 1.* Within this traditional, university-based model, knowledge production is driven primarily by an academic agenda. Discoveries tend to build upon existing knowledge in a linear fashion. The model makes a distinction between theoretically pure knowledge and applied knowledge, the latter being where theoretical insights are translated into practice. Only limited emphasis is placed on the dissemination of knowledge, because the academic community is the most important audience or consumer of knowledge.

- *Mode 2.* This model draws attention to the role of *transdisciplinarity* in research, which refers to a process that causes the boundaries of single contributing disciplines to be exceeded. Findings are closely related to context and may not easily be replicated, so knowledge production is less of a linear process. Moreover, the production of knowledge is not confined to academic institutions. Instead, it involves academics, policy-makers, and practitioners, who apply a broad set of skills and experiences in order to tackle a shared problem. Knowledge is disseminated more rapidly and findings are more readily exploited in order to achieve practical advantage.

Although mode 2 research is intended to exist alongside mode 1, rather than to replace it, some have suggested that management and business research is more suited to mode 2 knowledge production (Tranfield and Starkey 1998).

The process of business research

In this section and the rest of this chapter, we will introduce what we think are the main elements of most research projects. It is common for writers of textbooks on business research methods to compile flow charts of the research process, and we are not immune to this temptation—as you will see from, for example, Figures 2.1, 8.1, and 17.1! At this point, however, we are not going to sequence the stages or elements of the research process, as the sequencing varies according to different research strategies and approaches. All we want to do is introduce the main elements—in other words, elements that are common to all or most varieties of business research. Some have already been touched on, and all will be addressed in more detail in later chapters.

Literature review

Existing literature represents an important element in all research. When we have a topic or issue that interests us, we must read further to determine:

- what is already known about the topic;
- what concepts and theories have been applied to it;
- what research methods have been applied in studying it;
- what controversies exist about the topic and about how it is studied;
- what clashes of evidence (if any) exist;
- who the key contributors to research on the topic are.

Many topics have a rich tradition of research, so it is unlikely that many people will be able to conduct an exhaustive review of the literature. What is crucial is that you identify and read key books and articles by some of the main figures who have written in the field. As we suggest in Chapter 5, you must know what is known, so that you cannot be accused of naively going over old ground. Linking your research questions, findings, and discussion to existing literature is an important and useful way of demonstrating the credibility of your research and the contribution it is making. However, as will become clear in Chapter 5, a literature review is not simply a summary: it is expected to be critical. This does not necessarily mean that you must be highly critical of existing work, but it does mean that you should assess its significance and how each item fits into the narrative that you construct about the literature.

Concepts and theories

Concepts are the way that we make sense of the social world. They are labels that we give to aspects of the social world that seem to have significant common features. As outlined in Chapter 7, the social sciences have a strong tradition of concepts, many of which have become part of the language of everyday life. Concepts such as bureaucracy, power, social control, status, charisma, labour process, McDonaldization, and alienation are all part of the body of theory that generations of social scientists have constructed. Concepts are a key ingredient of theories. Indeed, it is almost impossible to imagine a theory that did not have at least one concept embedded in it.

Concepts serve several purposes in business research. They are important to how we organize and signal our research interests. They help us to think and be more disciplined about what we want to find out about, and help with the organization of our research findings. The relationship between theory and research is often depicted as involving a choice between theories driving the research process in all its phases, or theories as a product of the research process. This is invariably depicted as a choice between **deductive** and **inductive** approaches and will be expanded upon in Chapter 2. Unsurprisingly, this choice has implications for concepts. Concepts may be something we start out with that represent key areas around which data are collected in an investigation. In other words, we might collect data in order to shed light on a concept (or more likely several concepts and how they are connected). This is the approach taken in the investigation reported in Research in focus 1.3. The alternative view is that concepts are outcomes of research. According to this second view, concepts help us to reflect on and organize the data that we collect.

One of the reasons why familiarity with existing literature is so important is that it alerts us to the main concepts already in use in an area of research and enables us to assess how useful or limited those concepts have been in helping to unravel the main issues. Research in focus 1.3 provides an example of this. Even when we are reading the literature solely as consumers of research—for example, when writing an essay—it is crucial that we know what the main concepts are, who is responsible for them, and what controversies (if any) surround them.

Research questions

Research questions are extremely important in the research process, because they force you to consider that most basic of issues—what is it that you want to know? Most people begin research with a general idea of what they are interested in. Research questions require you to consider much more precisely what you want to find out about, as discussed in Key concept 1.2.

Having no research questions or poorly formulated research questions will lead to poor research. If you do not specify clear research questions, there is a great risk that your research will be unfocused and that you will be unsure about what it is about or why you are collecting data. It does not matter how well you design a questionnaire or how skilled an interviewer you are; you must be clear about your research questions. Equally, it does not matter whether your research is for a project with a research grant of £300,000, a doctoral thesis, or a student project—research questions are crucial because they will

- guide your literature search;
- guide your decisions about the kind of research design to employ;
- guide your decisions about what data to collect and from whom;
- guide your analysis of data;
- guide your writing-up of data;
- stop you going off in unnecessary directions; and
- provide your readers with a clear sense of what your research is about.

Key concept 1.2
What are research questions?

A research question provides an explicit statement of what it is the researcher wants to know about. A research purpose can be presented as a statement (for example, 'I want to find out whether [or why] . . .'), but a question forces the researcher to be more explicit about what is to be investigated. A research question must have a question mark at the end of it or else it is not a question. It must be interrogatory. A hypothesis is in a sense a form of research question, but it is not stated as a question and provides an anticipation of what will be found out.

Denscombe (2010) provides a list of types of research question:

1. Predicting an outcome (does y happen under circumstances a and b?).
2. Explaining causes and consequences of a phenomenon (is y affected by x or is y a consequence of x?).
3. Evaluating a phenomenon (does y exhibit the benefits that it is claimed to have?).
4. Describing a phenomenon (what is y like or what forms does y assume?).
5. Developing good practice (how can we improve y?).
6. Empowerment (how can we enhance the lives of those we research?).

White (2009) is uneasy about Denscombe's last category, arguing that an emphasis on political motives of this kind can impede the conduct of high-quality research. To some extent, this difference of opinion can be attributed to differences in viewpoint about the purposes of research. White proposes an alternative:

7. Comparison (do a and b differ in respect of x?).

There are many ways that research questions can be categorized, but these seven types provide a rough indication of the possibilities as well as drawing attention to a controversy about the wider goals of research.

Research in focus 1.3
A research question about gender bias in attitudes towards leaders

The research question posed in the title of the article by Elsesser and Lever (2011) is 'Does gender bias against female leaders persist?' They begin by reviewing the literature which suggests that negative attitudes towards female leaders still persist. However, they question whether prior research can be generalised to 'real world scenarios' because much of it is based on 'student samples surveyed on vignettes of hypothetical leaders, attitudes about ideal leaders, or ratings of task leaders in laboratory settings' (Elsesser and Lever 2011: 1556). The aim of their study was therefore to examine whether biases exist towards actual female leaders and, if so, the conditions and management styles that cause such biases to emerge. At one level, this research addresses a practical issue by identifying factors which prevent or discourage women from assuming leadership positions. As noted earlier, it is generally viewed as a good thing that researchers address relevant problems with the potential to improve practice. But the authors also draw on theory, in this case role congruity theory, to help explain the processes whereby gender bias against female leaders persists. This theory states that individuals who behave in ways that are incongruent with stereotypically defined sex roles are likely to be viewed negatively. Based on their literature review, the authors present nine hypotheses which they aim to test through data collection and statistical analysis, including:

> *Hypothesis 3a:* When stating their preference for managers in general, respondents will show a preference for male over female managers.
>
> *Hypothesis 3b:* The general preference for male management will be strongest for those in male-dominated environments, by those with no previous experience with a female boss, and by those who currently report to a male boss.
>
> (Elsesser and Lever 2011: 1559).

Their method of data collection was a US-based national survey, titled 'Rate Your Boss', which was posted on the popular news website msnbc.com in 2007 for 10 days. 60,470 people responded to the survey. The majority (68%) had a male boss but most (89% of women and 78% of men) had experience of both male and female management. Measures included 'relationship quality', 'competence', 'competitiveness', 'sensitivity and directness' and 'preference for a male or female boss'. Preliminary findings were reported in *Elle* magazine before being written up academically. In addition to statistical analysis, the researchers identified a random stratified subsample from 12,440 responses to an optional open-ended follow-up question which asked participants who had expressed a preference for the gender of their boss to explain why. The researchers identified common themes that emerged from these narratives using a grounded theory approach (see Key concept 24.3), providing quotes supportive of the themes.

The researchers found a cross-sex bias in how respondents rated their bosses: men judged female bosses more favourably, and women judged male bosses more favourably. A further finding from the qualitative results of the study was that while respondents who said they preferred female bosses cited such things as their compassion or understanding, those who said they preferred male bosses justfied this by referring to the negative attributes of female leaders, describing them as too 'emotional', 'moody', 'gossipy', and 'bitchy'. The authors conclude that the answer to their research question is 'yes' and 'no', as participants were less likely to show gender bias when evaluating their own boss, indicating minimal 'bias against women for violating their sex role by adopting a leadership position', but a high level of descriptive bias—'where women are seen as having less potential for management' (Elsesser and Lever 2011: 1571).

It is possible that reading the literature may prompt you to revise your research questions and may even suggest some new ones. Therefore, at an early stage of a research study, research questions and the literature relating to them are likely to be intertwined. At the beginning of a research project the initial contact with the literature may generate one or two research questions; further reading guided by the initial research questions may lead to revision of them and possibly generate new ones. In Chapter 4, there will be more discussion of research questions and how they can be developed.

Sampling

As will be seen in later chapters, there are a number of different principles behind the idea of sampling. Many people associate sampling with surveys and the quest for **representative samples**. Such sampling is usually based on constructing a sample that can represent (and therefore act as a microcosm of) a wider **population**. The principles that lie behind the quest for the representative sample will be explained in Chapter 8. These principles often apply to questionnaire **survey research** of the kind described in Research in focus 1.3. In that research, Elsesser and Lever (2011) point out that their sample was unusually large and broadly representative in terms of gender (51% men and 49% women). Respondents covered a wide range in terms of their educational experience and the sector of employment they worked in. However, the sample 'was not nationally representative, and the survey did not include information on race or ethnicity' (Elsesser and Lever, 2011: 1574). The sample may have been affected by the fact that participation relied on Internet access, although in the US, Internet samples are relatively diverse with respect to gender, age, and socio-economic status. A final limitation relates to the self-selecting nature of the sample, which means that it may be skewed in ways that do not reflect overall patterns of employment. For example, 94% of respondents were employed full-time and 36% of female and 51% of male participants described themselves as managers; these proportions are not representative of the overall population.

As this example illustrates, even business research which is traditionally seen as prioritizing representative samples involves convenience, i.e. making use of the data collection opportunities that are available. In Part Three we encounter sampling principles based not on the idea of representativeness but on the notion that samples should be selected on the basis of their appropriateness to the purposes of the investigation. This is common in **case study** research, where there may be just one or two units of analysis. Here, the goal is to understand the selected case or cases in depth. Sampling issues are still relevant to such research because cases have to be chosen according to criteria relevant to the research, and individuals who are members of the case study context have to be sampled according to criteria too. The key issue is that sampling is an inevitable feature of most

kinds of business research and therefore constitutes an important stage of any investigation.

It is also important to remember that business research is not always carried out on people. For example, we may want to examine mass-media content and employ a technique such as **content analysis**, covered in Chapter 13. In such a situation, we are collecting our data from newspapers or television programmes rather than from people. Because of this, it is common for writers on business research methods to use the term 'case' to cover the wide variety of objects on whom or from whom data will be collected. Much if not most of the time, 'cases' will be people. In business research we are rarely in a position in which we can interview, observe, or send questionnaires to all possible individuals who are appropriate to our research; equally, we are unlikely to be able to read and analyse the content of all articles in all newspapers relating to an area of media content that interests us. Time and cost issues will always constrain the number of cases we can include in our research, so we almost always have to sample.

Data collection

Data collection is the key point of any research project, and therefore this book gives more space to this stage in the research process than to any other. Some methods of data collection, such as interviewing and questionnaires, are likely to be more familiar to readers than others. Some methods require a structured approach—that is, the researcher establishes in advance the broad contours of what he or she needs to find out about and designs research instruments accordingly. The questionnaire is an example of a structured instrument; the researcher designs questions that will allow data to be collected to answer specific research questions. Similarly, a **structured interview**—the kind of interview used in survey investigations—includes questions designed for exactly the same purpose. It is unfortunate that we use the same word—question—for both research questions and the kinds of questions posed in questionnaires and interviews. They are very different: a research question is a question designed to indicate what the purpose of an investigation is; a questionnaire question is one of many questions that are posed in a questionnaire that will help to shed light on and answer one or more research questions.

There are many methods of data collection that are less structured than this. In Part Three we concentrate on research methods that emphasize an open-ended view of the research process, so that there is less restriction on the topics and issues being studied. Research methods such as **participant observation** and **semi-structured interviewing** allow the researcher to keep an open mind about what he or she needs to know about, so that concepts and theories can emerge out of the data. This is the inductive approach to theorizing and conceptualization that was referred to above. Such research is usually still geared to answering research questions, but these are expressed less explicitly than in more structured research. This can be seen by comparing the specificity of the hypotheses developed by Elsesser and Lever (2011, Research in focus 1.3) to address their overarching research question with the question that guided the study of academics in business schools in UK universities by Clarke et al. (2012):

> Our objective is to understand how the historical, cultural, economic, political and institutional relations in higher education (and in our case specifically UK business schools) shape or reshape the conditions of identity work and how academic subjectivities are sustained or transformed. In particular, we examine how the cultural, institutional and managerial changes of the last decade or so have affected academic identities.
>
> (Clarke et al. 2012: 6)

This research question, which the authors describe as an 'objective', is derived from and illuminated by concepts of managerialism, audit, and performativity. To explore the research question, semi-structured interviews were conducted with 48 academics in business schools in UK universities. The interviews were '"conversations with a purpose" (Burman 1994)—that of elucidating the impact of new public management on academic identities' (Clarke et al. 2012: 8). This is a noticeably less structured approach to data collection, which reflects the open-ended nature of the research question. Data collection, then, can entail different approaches in terms of how structured or open-ended the methods are.

Data analysis

Data analysis is a stage that incorporates several elements. At the most obvious level, this might mean the application of statistical techniques to data. However, even when data is amenable to quantitative data analysis, there are other things going on when it is analysed. For a start, the raw data has to be *managed*. This means the researcher has to check the data to establish whether there are any obvious flaws. For example, in the research by Clarke et al. (2012), the interviews were audio-recorded and transcribed.

Transcription enables the researcher to upload the transcripts into a computer software program of the kind discussed in Chapter 25. In the research by Clarke et al., once the transcripts had been uploaded into the software, the authors began by **coding** each transcript. This is a process whereby the data are broken down into component parts which are then given labels. The analyst searches for recurrences of sequences of coded text within and across cases and for links between different **codes**. Clarke et al. began by identifying a number of 'descriptive first order' categories such as 'emotion' and 'changes in the higher education system' (2012: 8), which they later expanded or collapsed as the analysis progressed, refining them into more analytic categories such as 'professionalism', eventually arriving at core themes which they concentrated on. This approach is referred to as **thematic analysis**. There is a lot going on here: data are being made more manageable than they would be if the researcher just kept listening and relistening to the recordings; the researcher is making sense of data through coding; and data are being interpreted—that is, the researcher is linking the process of making sense of the data with the research question, as well as with the literature and theoretical concepts.

The data analysis stage is fundamentally about *data reduction*—that is, reducing the large corpus of information gathered in order to make sense of it. Unless the researcher reduces the data collected—for example, in the case of quantitative data by producing tables or averages and in the case of qualitative data by grouping textual material into categories such as themes—it is more or less impossible to interpret the material.

Data analysis can also refer to interpretation of secondary data. Primary data analysis means that the researcher who collected the data conducts the analysis, as was the case with Elsesser and Lever (2011) and with Clarke et al. (2012). Secondary data analysis occurs when someone else analyses such data. Researchers in universities are encouraged to deposit their data in archives, which allows others to analyse it. Given the time and money involved in business research, this is a sensible thing to do: it increases the value of an investigation, and a researcher conducting secondary analysis can explore the research questions in which he or she is interested without having to go through the time-consuming and lengthy process of collecting primary data. **Secondary analysis** is discussed in Chapters 14 and 24.

Writing up

The finest piece of research is useless if it is not disseminated so that others can benefit from it. We do research so that others can read about what we have done and our findings. Writing up is often neglected, so we devote the final chapter of this book to this issue.

There are different ways to write up research. More structured research, like that presented in Research in focus 1.3, is sometimes written up differently from more open-ended research of the sort represented by Clarke et al. (2012). However, there are core ingredients that dissertations, theses, research articles, and books will include.

- *Introduction*. The research area and its significance are outlined. The research questions will also probably be introduced.
- *Literature review*. What is already known about the research area is examined critically. This section often relates to theoretical concepts that are the focus of the research, as shown in Table 1.1.
- *Research methods*. The research methods (sampling, methods of data collection, methods of data analysis) are presented and justified.
- *Results*. The findings are presented.
- *Discussion*. The findings are discussed in relation to the literature and the research questions.
- *Conclusion*. The significance of the research is reinforced.

These elements are discussed in detail in Chapter 29. They are not an exhaustive list, because writing conventions differ, but they are recurring elements of the completed research. Table 1.1 summarizes the seven elements of the research process.

Table 1.1

Stages in the research process in relation to two studies

Stage	Description of stage	Example: Elsesser and Lever 2011 *	Example: Clarke et al. 2012
Literature review	Critical examination of existing research relating to the phenomena of interest and relevant theoretical ideas.	Literature concerning gender bias in organizational leadership, focusing on role congruity theory.	Literature concerning identity and new public management (including managerialism, audit, and performativity), related to business school academics.
Concepts and theories	Ideas that drive the research process and shed light on interpretation of resulting findings.	Stereotypes; role congruity; female managers; female bosses.	Audit and performative culture; new public management; identity; managerialism.
Research questions	Question that provides an explicit statement of what the researcher wants to know about.	'Does gender bias against female leaders persist?' (Elsesser and Lever 2011: 1555)—followed by nine hypotheses (see Research in focus 1.3)	'Our objective is to understand how the historical, cultural, economic, political and institutional relations in higher education (and in our case specifically UK business schools) shape or reshape the conditions of identity work and how academic subjectivities are sustained or transformed.' (Clarke et al. 2012: 6).
Sampling	Selection of sample relevant to the research questions.	60,470 men and women who responded to a US-based national survey, 'Rate Your Boss', posted on the msnbc.com website for 10 days in 2007. Subsample of 1000 narratives from 12,440 responses to an open-ended follow-up question asking respondents to explain their gender preferences for a boss.	Sample of 48 lecturers, senior lecturers, readers, and professors working in 8 different UK business schools in the field of organization studies who were interviewed in 2009/10. The sampling approach was both purposeful (i.e. participants worked in a range of different universities) and self-selecting 'because the onus was on participants to respond to a detailed invitation to take part in this study' (Clarke et al. 2012: 8).
Data collection	Gathering data from sample so that research questions can be answered.	Large-scale web survey involving a questionnaire which was accessed online (see Chapter 28).	Semi-structured interviews between 45 and 70 minutes in length.
Data analysis	Management, analysis, and interpretation of data.	Statistical analysis of the questionnaire data.	Thematic analysis of interview transcripts.

(continued)

Table 1.1

Continued			
Stage	Description of stage	Example: Elsesser and Lever 2011 *	Example: Clarke et al. 2012
Writing up	Dissemination of research and findings.	Initial descriptive findings published in *Elle* magazine and in msnbc.com's financial section in 2007, before being written up as an academic article. Main sections in Elsesser and Lever (2011): • Introduction • Role congruity theory • Goals of the present study • Method • Results • Discussion	Research written up as an article in Clarke et al. (2012) and also in Clarke and Knights (2014). Main sections: • Introduction • Loving to labour: Identity in business schools • Methodology • Research findings • Discussion • Summary and conclusion

* Clarke and Knights (2014) consulted for further information.

The messiness of business research

There is one final point we want to make before you read on. Business research is often a lot less smooth than accounts of the process you read in books such as this. Our purpose is to provide an overview of the research process and to give advice on how it should ideally be done. In reality, research is full of false starts, blind alleys, mistakes, and enforced changes. We know that research is messy from the confessional accounts that have been written over the years (e.g. Hammond 1964; Bell and Newby 1977; Bryman 1988*b*; Townsend and Burgess 2009*a*; Streiner and Sidani 2010). It is therefore important for business researchers to remain flexible and to modify and adapt their research plans in response to opportunities and problems that arise. Of course, research often does go relatively smoothly and, in spite of minor difficulties, may proceed roughly according to plan. However, what we read in reports of research are often quite sanitized accounts of how the research was carried out, without a sense of the difficult problems the researcher faced. This is not to say that business researchers seek to deceive us, but rather that research when written up tends to follow an implicit template that emphasizes some aspects of the research but not others. Most accounts emphasize how specific findings were arrived at and use standard methodological terminology to describe the underlying process. Research reports typically display the various

elements discussed in the previous section—relevant literature is reviewed, key concepts and theories are discussed, research questions are presented, sampling procedures and methods of data collection are explained and justified, findings are presented and discussed, and conclusions are drawn. The vicissitudes of research tend not to feature within this template. This tendency is not unique to *business* research: in Chapter 26 a study of how natural scientists present and discuss their work shows that here too certain core aspects of the production of 'findings' tend to be omitted from the written account (Gilbert and Mulkay 1984).

It is also the case that, regardless of the various ways in which research happens, this book can deal only with generalities. It is quite possible that when doing your research you will find that these generalities do not fit perfectly. It is important to be aware of that possibility; you need not interpret departures that you make from the advice provided in this book as a problem with your skills and understanding. This uncertainty and messiness leads some to argue that a book on research methods, outlining how research is and should be conducted, is of little value. Needless to say, we disagree with this. However, we do urge a degree of caution in the way that you read this book. Like a cookery book, it provides written instruction and guidance. A great deal of success in cooking is derived not only from the ability to read a recipe but also from the cook's skill and confidence in understanding, interpreting, and adapting the recipe to suit the circumstances. Bell and Thorpe (2013) have written about the importance of research communities, including the relationship between research student and supervisor, in passing on these skills: for example by telling stories about their research experience and by doing research in groups. As Chapter 4 explains, developing a good working relationship with your supervisor is crucial in undertaking a successful research project, for example for a dissertation, because he or she will be able to support you in dealing with unexpected events.

A second comparison can be made to the construction of buildings. Many years ago, Alan Bryman was involved in several studies of construction projects. A recurring theme in the findings was the different ways that projects could be knocked off course: unpredictable weather, sudden shortages of key supplies, illness, accidents,

previously reliable subcontractors letting the project manager down, clients changing their minds or being unavailable at key points, sudden changes in health and safety regulation, poor-quality supplies, poor-quality work, early excavation revealing unanticipated problems—any of these could produce significant interruptions to even the best-planned construction project. But it was never suggested that the principles of construction and of construction management should be abandoned. Much the same is true of research projects. There are plenty of things that can go wrong. As Townsend and Burgess (2009b) write in the introduction to their collection of 'research stories you won't read in textbooks', two of the recurring themes from the accounts they collected are the need for flexibility and the need for perseverance. However, it is also crucial to have an appreciation of the methodological principles and the debates and controversies that surround them, and these are outlined in the next 28 chapters. These principles provide a road map for the journey ahead.

 ## Key points

- Business research and business research methods are embedded in wider contextual factors. They are not practised in a vacuum.

- Business research practice comprises elements that are common to all or at least most forms of business research. These include: conducting a literature review; concepts and theories; research questions; sampling of cases; data collection; data analysis; and a writing-up of the research finding.

- Attention to these steps is what distinguishes academic business research from other kinds of business research, such as market research done by private companies.

- Although we can attempt to formulate general principles for conducting business research, we have to recognize that things do not always go entirely to plan.

 ## Questions for review

What is meant by 'business research'?

- What is distinctive about academic business research?

Why do business research?

- If you were about to embark on a research project now or in the near future, what would be the focus of it and why?

Business research methods in context

- What contextual factors affect the practice of business research and researchers' choice of methods?

Relevance to practice

- What are the differences between mode 1 and mode 2 forms of knowledge production and why is this distinction important?

Elements of the process of business research

- Why is a literature review important when conducting business research?

- What role do concepts and theories play in the process of business research?

- Why are researchers encouraged to specify their research questions? What kinds of research question are there?

- Why do researchers need to sample? Why is it important for them to outline the principles that underpin their sampling choices?

- Outline one or two factors that might affect a researcher's choice of data-collection instrument.

- What are the main differences between the kinds of data analysed by Elsesser and Lever (2011) and by Clarke et al. (2012)?

- How might you structure a report of the findings of a research project that you conducted?

The messiness of business research

- If research does not always go according to plan, why should we bother with methodological principles at all?

....

Online Resource Centre

www.oxfordtextbooks.co.uk/orc/brymanbrm4e/

Visit the Online Resource Centre that accompanies this book to enrich your understanding of business research strategies. Consult web links, test yourself using multiple choice questions, and gain further guidance and inspiration from the Interactive Research Guide.

....

2

Business research strategies

Chapter outline

This chapter shows that a variety of considerations enter into the process of doing business research. The distinction that is commonly drawn among writers on and practitioners of business research between **quantitative research** and **qualitative research** is explored in relation to these considerations. This chapter explores:

- the nature of the relationship between theory and research, in particular whether theory guides research (a **deductive** approach) or whether theory is an outcome of research (an **inductive** approach);

- *epistemological issues*—that is, what is regarded as appropriate knowledge about the social world, and whether a natural science model of research is suitable for studying the social world;

- *ontological issues*—that is, whether the social world is regarded as something external to social actors or as something that people are in the process of constructing;

- how these issues relate to the widely used types of **research strategy**, quantitative and qualitative research; there is also a preliminary discussion, followed up in Chapter 26, which shows that while quantitative and qualitative research represent different approaches, we should be wary of driving a wedge between them;

- the ways in which *values* and *practical issues* are also central to business research.

Introduction: the nature of business research

Business research is situated in the context of the social science disciplines, such as sociology, psychology, anthropology, and economics, which inform the study of business and its specific fields, which include marketing, HRM, strategy, organizational behaviour, accounting and finance, industrial relations, and operational research. It would be much easier to 'cut to the chase', explore the nature of methods in business research, and provide the reader with advice on how best to choose between and implement them. After all, many people might expect a book with this title to be concerned mainly with the ways in which the different methods in the business researcher's arsenal can be employed.

But the practice of business research does not exist in a bubble, hermetically sealed off from the social sciences. Two points are particularly relevant here. First, the methods of management and business research are closely tied to different visions of how organizational reality should be studied. Methods are not simply neutral tools: they are linked to how social scientists envisage social reality and how it should be examined. However, while methods

are not neutral, they are not entirely dependent on intellectual inclinations either. Second, there is the question of how business research methods and practice connect with the wider social scientific enterprise. Research data are invariably collected in relation to something. The 'something' may be a pressing organizational problem, such as the effect of a merger on corporate culture or the impact of new technology on employee motivation. Research is also done when a specific opportunity arises. For example, the NASA space shuttle *Challenger* disaster in 1986 stimulated business and management research into the decision-making processes and group dynamics that had led to the decision to launch the shuttle despite indications that there were significant safety problems (Shrivasta et al. 1988; Vaughan 1990). Yet another stimulus for research comes from personal experiences. Lofland and Lofland (1995) note that many research projects emerge out of the researcher's personal biography. Certainly, Bryman traces his interest in Disney theme parks back to a visit to Disney World in Florida in 1991 (Bryman 1995, 1999), while his interest in the representation of social science research in the mass media (Fenton, Bryman, and Deacon 1998) can be attributed to a difficult experience with the press (reported in Haslam and Bryman 1994). Similarly, the experience of being involved in the implementation of a quality management initiative in a UK National Health Service hospital trust prompted Bell to explore the meaning of

badging in an organizational context (Bell, Taylor, and Thorpe 2002).

Whatever the stimulus, research data become significant and contribute to knowledge when they are viewed in relation to theoretical concerns. This means that the nature of the relationship between theory and research is crucial.

Theory and research

Understanding the nature of the link between theory and research is complex. There are several important issues, but two stand out. First, the link depends on what form of theory is being referred to. Secondly, there is the question of whether data are collected to test or to build theories.

What type of theory?

The term 'theory' is used in a variety of ways, but its most common meaning is as a way of explaining observed regularities: for example, why women and ethnic minorities are under-represented in higher-paid managerial positions, or why alienation associated with the introduction of new technology varies according to methods of production. However, theories do not in themselves constitute a theoretical *perspective*, which is characterized by a higher level of abstraction in relation to research findings. Examples of this kind of theory include structural functionalism, **symbolic**

interactionism, critical theory, poststructuralism, or structuration theory. This is a distinction between theories of the former type, or *theories of the middle range* (Merton 1967), and *grand theories*, which operate at a more abstract and general level.

According to Merton, grand theories do not help researchers to think about how they collect empirical evidence. So, if someone wanted to test a theory or to draw an inference from it that could be tested, the level of abstraction is so great that the researcher would find it difficult to make the necessary links with the real world. However, as the example in Research in focus 2.1 shows, an abstract theory such as structuration theory (Giddens 1984) can be very helpful. Middle-range theories are 'intermediate to general theories of social systems which are too remote from particular classes of social behavior, organization and change to account for what is observed and to those detailed orderly descriptions of particulars that are not generalized at all' (Merton 1967: 39).

Research in focus 2.1
Grand theory and researching project-based organizations

Giddens's (1984) structuration theory is an attempt to bridge the gulf between notions of structure and agency in social life. It is interpreted as a way of overcoming the dichotomy between 'structural' perspectives such as traditional theories of bureaucracy and 'interactional' perspectives that emphasize informal processes of talk and action (Ranson, Hinings, and Greenwood 1980). Structuration theory has informed a number of empirical studies of managerial control, agency, and strategy, including Pettigrew's (1985) study of strategic change at ICI, which shows how organizational forms both enable and constrain human action. Combining a focus on the role of executive leadership and managerial action with a sensitivity to the contexts in which managers work, Pettigrew suggests that managerial actions are framed by the business and economic environment encountered by the organization.

Bresnen, Goussevskaia, and Swan (2004) use structuration theory in their analysis of project-based organization, applying it to a longitudinal case study of a construction firm implementing a new managerial initiative. They use this to understand how the **relationship** between structural form and individual agency influences the diffusion

(continued)

and enactment of managerial knowledge. They argue that 'project management practices can be seen as the outcome of a complex, recursive relationship between structural attributes and individual agency, in which actors (in this case project managers and project team members) draw upon, enact, and hence reproduce (and, under certain circumstances modify) the structural properties of the system in which they are embedded' (2004: 1540). Their analysis highlights the influence of structural conditions, such as decentralization, that created circumstances in which individual actors could act upon the new managerial initiative by drawing on shared local perspectives. They conclude that 'the rules of signification and legitimization . . . gave project managers considerable latitude in being able to choose how to respond to the introduction of the new practices . . . project managers were able to transform the initiative and the implementation process with responses like "playing the scoring game"' (2004: 1549). Their analysis suggests that the diffusion of new managerial knowledge in project-based organizations is shaped by a complex interplay between structural conditions and actors' social practices.

Empirical enquiry

To summarize, then, it is not grand theory that typically guides management and business research. Middle-range theories are much more likely to frame empirical enquiry. Merton formulated the idea as a means of bridging a widening gulf between grand theory and empirical findings. Although there were middle-range theories before he wrote, what Merton did was to clarify what social scientists mean by 'theory' when writing about the relationship between theory and research.

Middle-range theories, unlike grand ones, operate in a limited domain. Whether it is research on strategic choice or the labour process (see Research in focus 2.2), they vary in the purpose of their application. In other words, they sit between grand theories and empirical findings. They represent attempts to understand and explain a limited aspect of social life. For example, contingency theory has been used widely in management and business research to explain interrelationships among subsystems, as well as the relationship between an organization and its environment. It relies on a number of assumptions: first, there is no one best way to organize; second, one way of organizing is not equally effective under all conditions; and, third, to be most effective, organizational structures should be appropriate to the type of work and environmental conditions (Schoonhoven 1981). However, contingency theory has been applied in different ways and for different purposes. Some researchers, such as Lawrence and Lorsch (1967), used it descriptively to show the factors in the environment that should be taken into account. Others applied the theory in a normative sense, adopting a solution-seeking focus to develop a guide to managerial action based on 'best fit' in a particular situation (e.g. Fiedler 1967). A normative stance suggests that, although factors within the environment should be taken into account, it is up to managers to make decisions about how they respond to these in order to achieve the impact on organizational performance that they want.

The grand/middle-range distinction is useful but it does not entirely clarify the issues involved in asking the

Research in focus 2.2
Labour process theory: an example of a contested middle-range theory

In the sociology of work, labour process theory can be regarded as a middle-range theory. The publication of *Labor and Monopoly Capital* (Braverman 1974) inaugurated a stream of thinking and research around the idea of the labour process, especially the degree to which there is an inexorable trend towards greater and greater control over the manual worker and deskilling of manual labour. P. Thompson (1989) described the theory as having four elements: the principle that the labour process entails extraction of surplus value; the need for capitalist businesses constantly to transform production processes; the quest for control over labour; and the essential conflict between capital and labour. Labour process theory has generated considerable research, including recently in India (e.g. Taylor et al. 2013).

deceptively simple question of 'What is theory?' This is because the term 'theory' is frequently used to refer to the background literature in an area of social enquiry. Contingency theory is a good example of this: Schoonhoven (1981) suggests that it is not a theory at all, in the sense of being a well-developed set of interrelated propositions. Willmott (1990) suggests contingency theory is based on empirical evidence without any acknowledgement of the social theories that affect the political realities of organizations, and so it is unable to deal with complex organizational problems.

In many cases, the relevant background literature on a topic defines the focus of research and thereby acts as the equivalent of a theory. In Ghobadian and Gallear's (1997) article on Total Quality Management (TQM) and the competitive position of small or medium-sized enterprises (SMEs), there are no, or virtually no, allusions to theory. Instead, the literature informs the generation of research questions about what the authors argue is a neglected topic, as the majority of TQM research focuses on large companies. Other ways in which background literature influences the focus of research include: an aspect of a topic having been neglected; certain ideas not having been tested; and existing approaches used to study a topic being deficient.

Social scientists are sometimes dismissive of research that has no obvious connections with theory—in either the grand or middle-range senses of the term. Such research is often dismissed as naïve **empiricism** (see Key concept 2.3). It would be harsh and inaccurate to brand the numerous studies in which the publications-as-theory strategy is employed as naïve empiricism simply because their authors have not been preoccupied with theory. Such research is conditioned by and directed towards research questions that arise out of critical reading of the literature. Data collection and analysis are subsequently geared to illumination or resolution of the research issue or problem identified. The literature acts as a proxy for theory; theory is latent or implicit.

Research that has the characteristics of a 'fact-finding exercise' should not be prematurely dismissed as naïve empiricism either. For example, research in industrial relations that focuses on the detail of current employment practices in a variety of sectors or cultural contexts has sometimes been criticized for its empiricism and lack of theoretical development (Marsden 1982; Godard 1994). The problem with this, according to Marsden (1982: 234), is that 'empiricists tend to assume that theory will somehow arise from the facts "like steam from a kettle". But facts are never given, they are selected or produced by theory'. To explore the accuracy of such claims, Frege (2005) examined patterns of publication in leading American, German, and British journals between 1970 and 1973 and between 1994 and 2000. She found that empirical publications were much more common in the USA (72 per cent in the 1970s and 91 per cent in the 1990s) than in Germany (41 per cent over both time periods), with Britain in between (72 per cent over both periods). However, Frege detects a shift away from empirical-descriptive articles towards empirical-deductive and empirical-inductive papers in US journals. She concludes 'the notion of what is empirical research shifted over time away from purely descriptive towards more sophisticated analytical work' (Frege 2005: 194).

As Figure 2.1 implies, research is guided by theoretical ideas and the aim of research is to make a contribution to theory. However, researchers frequently come to an investigation with particular intellectual preferences. Orlitzky (2011) provides a fascinating insight into this tendency in a quantitative analysis of the literature on the relationship between corporate social performance and corporate financial performance. He used a technique called meta-analysis (see Key concept 14.9) to do this. Meta-analysis summarizes quantitatively the findings of areas of literature. He notes that in the field of organization studies, articles about the relationship between corporate social performance and corporate

Key concept 2.3
What is empiricism?

The term 'empiricism' is used in a number of ways, but two stand out. First, it is used to refer to an approach to the study of reality that suggests that only knowledge gained through experience and the senses is acceptable. In other words, ideas must be subjected to the rigours of testing before they can be considered knowledge. The second meaning of the term is related to this and refers to a belief that the accumulation of 'facts' is a legitimate goal in its own right. It is this second meaning that is sometimes referred to as 'naïve empiricism'.

Figure 2.1

The process of deduction

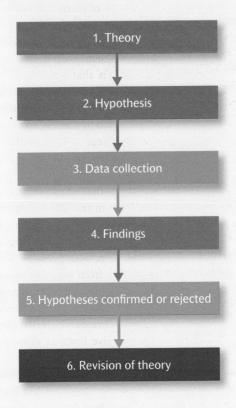

1. Theory

2. Hypothesis

3. Data collection

4. Findings

5. Hypotheses confirmed or rejected

6. Revision of theory

theory guides and influences the collection and analysis of data. In other words, research is done in order to answer questions posed by theoretical puzzles. But an alternative position is to view theory as something that develops after collection and analysis of data. There is a second factor in considering the relationship between theory and research—whether we are referring to deductive or inductive theory.

Deductive and inductive theory

Deductive theory is the most common view of the relationship between theory and research. The researcher, on the basis of what is known about a domain and the theoretical considerations within it, deduces a **hypothesis** (or hypotheses) that must be subjected to empirical scrutiny. Embedded within the hypothesis will be concepts that need to be translated into researchable entities. The social scientist must skilfully deduce a hypothesis and then translate it into operational terms. This means there is a need to specify how data can be collected in relation to the concepts that make up the hypothesis.

This view of the role of theory is very much what Merton had in mind with middle-range theory, which 'is principally used in sociology to guide empirical inquiry' (Merton 1967: 39). Theory and the hypotheses deduced come first and drive the process of gathering data (see Research in focus 2.4 for an example of this). The sequence can be depicted as a series of steps, as outlined in Figure 2.1.

The last step involves a movement that is in the opposite direction from deduction—it involves *induction*, as the researcher infers the implications of his or her findings for the theory that prompted the whole exercise. In other words, the findings are fed back into the stock of theory. This can be seen in Whittington's (1989) case study research on strategic choice in the domestic appliance and office furniture industries. Whittington's approach is primarily deductive, since it is based on the contention that a critical realist approach to strategic choice enables recognition of plural and contradictory social structures for human agency. However, as he points out towards the end of his book, 'after the empirical interlude of the last four chapters, it is time now to return to the theoretical fray' (1989: 244) to assess how well realist approaches to strategic choice account for the behaviour within the eight case study firms. At this stage he claims that, although dominant actors within the firms 'began from their structural positions within the capitalist enterprise, this starting point was neither unambiguous or exhaustive' (1989: 282). This finding thus confirms his central

financial performance have been published in three types of journal: accounting, economics, and finance journals; journals in areas such as business ethics and social issues in management; and general management journals. Orlitzky shows that articles published in accounting journals typically found the relationship between the two variables to be smaller than did articles published in business ethics journals. Articles published in general management journals tended to be closer to those articles published in business ethics journals in terms of the strength of the relationship between the two variables. As Orlitzky notes, such findings cast doubt on the notion of objective, value free knowledge, but also show that research is profoundly affected by the different intellectual traditions in which researchers are trained and to which they orientate themselves.

This brings us to our next question: in so far as any piece of research is linked to theory, what was the role of that theory? Up to now, we have written as though

Research in focus 2.4
A deductive study

Parboteeah, Hoegl, and Cullen (2009) tested the influence of religious values on individuals' work obligation norms. They argue that 'given the prominent role of religion in societies, it is imperative that international management research acknowledges its potential influences on how organizations and people within them operate' (2009: 121). Based on a review of the literature on how major religions around the world describe work, the researchers suggest that 'all major religions prescribe work as an individual's obligation' (2009: 123). This leads them to propose that 'if an individual is raised and educated in a country with a stronger religious environment, that individual is more likely to get exposed to values consistent with stronger work obligation than a similar individual residing in a country with a weaker religious environment. Individuals in stronger religious environments are thus more likely to see work as an obligation' (2009: 124). The researchers use the 'country institutional profile', a theoretical model developed by Kostova (1999) to explain how a country's government policies, shared knowledge, and values affect domestic business activity. This enabled them to specify the contextual determinants of work obligation in different countries and to propose the following five hypotheses:

- *Hypothesis 1*. There is a **positive relationship** between the cognitive aspect of religious institutions and work obligation.

- *Hypothesis 2*. There is a positive relationship between the normative aspect of religious institutions and work obligation.

- *Hypothesis 3*. There is a **negative relationship** between the regulative aspect of religion and work obligation.

- *Hypothesis 4*. Religious pluralism moderates the relationship between the cognitive aspect of religion and work obligations, such that the effect of the cognitive component decreases with more religious pluralism.

- *Hypothesis 5*. Religious pluralism moderates the relationship between the normative aspect of religion and work obligations, such that the effect of the cognitive component decreases with more religious pluralism.

The researchers used data from the World Values Survey conducted in 2000, in which a consortium of universities from around the world work together to conduct political and social research. The **sample** comprised 62,218 individuals in 45 different countries. The researchers designed a **questionnaire** that was translated into different languages and permitted **secondary analysis** of the dataset. The results revealed that hypotheses 1, 2, and 3 were supported. However, the effects of religious pluralism were found to be mixed, and hypothesis 4 was not supported. The researchers conclude that religious institutions do have a significant influence on the work-related attitudes of individuals, regardless of the individual's personal religiosity. They note that this finding is consistent with Max Weber's (1930) thesis on the importance of religious values in shaping the development of modern capitalism.

proposition that organizational structures could be converted into 'the effective instruments of private agency'.

The deductive process appears very linear—one step follows the other in a clear, logical sequence. However, this is not always the case. A researcher's view of theory or literature may change as a result of analysis of collected data for several reasons:

- new theoretical ideas or findings may be published before the researcher has generated his or her findings;

- the relevance of a dataset for theory may become apparent only *after* data have been collected;

- data may not fit with the original hypotheses.

The Hawthorne studies (see Research in focus 3.8), undertaken at the Western Electric Company's Hawthorne plant between 1927 and 1932, illustrate how deductive research can produce unexpected findings. This research explored the human effects of work and working conditions (Roethlisberger and Dickson 1939); the aim was to examine the relationship between conditions of work and fatigue and monotony among employees. To test this relationship, a series of experiments were undertaken to establish the effects of variables such as lighting, temperature, humidity, and hours of sleep that could be isolated and measured separately. These first experiments involved adjusting the level of artificial illumination at stated intervals to see if this had any effect on efficiency. However, researchers were not able to make sense of changes in productivity, which increased and remained high despite manipulation of a **range** of variables. This led them to move away from the 'test room method' and adopt a more qualitative strategy based on interview and observation. By moving to a more inductive position, researchers made sense of the data through an alternative hypothesis that focused on informal social relationships. Eventually, this led to an alternative method for the study of the informal work group. In the Bank Wiring Observation Room investigators spent a total of six months observing informal social relationships within a group of male operators. The Hawthorne research thus made an important methodological contribution to the study of work organizations by showing that research questions and methods could change over the course of an investigation (Schwartzman 1993).

Similarly, the study of the impact of Total Quality Management (TQM) on the competitive position of small and medium-sized enterprises (SMEs) by Ghobadian and Gallear (1997) explored the relationship between organizational size and the implementation of TQM in SMEs and large organizations. A number of research questions were developed through analysis of the TQM literature. Although Ghobadian and Gallear describe their research as deductive, they also point out that hypotheses were not easily formulated, because variables and issues identified were mainly contextual and therefore did not translate into simple **constructs**. They therefore shift towards a more inductive approach in the later stage of the study, using four case studies to explore the research questions and develop a ten-step framework for the implementation of TQM in SMEs.

This may seem rather surprising and confusing. There is a certain logic to the idea of developing theories and then testing them. In everyday contexts, we think of theories as things that are quite illuminating but that need to be tested before they can be considered valid or useful. However, while the process of deduction in Figure 2.1 does undoubtedly occur, it is better considered as a general orientation to the link between theory and research. Its broad contours may frequently be discernible in business research, but it is also the case that we often find departures from it.

However, in some research *no* attempt is made to follow the sequence outlined in Figure 2.1. Some researchers prefer an approach to the relationship between theory and research that is primarily *inductive*. With an inductive stance, theory is the *outcome* of research. In other words, the process of induction involves drawing generalizable inferences out of observations. To put it crudely, whereas deduction entails a process in which:

theory → observations/findings,

with induction the connection is reversed:

observations/findings → theory.

However, just as deduction often entails an element of induction, the inductive process is likely to involve some deduction. Once theoretical reflection on data has been carried out, the researcher may want to collect further data to establish the conditions in which a theory will or will not hold. This strategy is often called *iterative*: it involves weaving back and forth between data and theory. It is particularly evident in **grounded theory**, examined in Chapter 24, but in the meantime the basic point is that induction represents an alternative strategy for linking theory and research.

However, as with the deductive approach, we have to be cautious about the use of the term 'theory' in the context of the inductive strategy too. Some researchers undoubtedly develop theories, but it is important to be aware that many researchers end up with little more than empirical generalizations of the kind Merton (1967) wrote about. Inductive researchers often use a grounded theory approach to data analysis and theory generation. This approach was first outlined by Glaser and Strauss (1967) and is regarded as useful in generating theories out of data. This contrasts with many supposedly inductive studies, which generate interesting and illuminating findings but whose theoretical significance is not entirely clear. Secondly, in much the same way that the deductive strategy is associated with a quantitative research approach, an inductive strategy of linking data and theory is typically associated with a qualitative research approach. Research in focus 2.5 describes research that is inductive in the sense that it uses a grounded analysis of **focus groups**, interview data, and participants' drawings to develop a theoretical understanding of the metaphors that workers use to describe their emotional experience of bullying. However, as will be shown below, the inductive strategy is not always associated with qualitative research: not only does much qualitative research *not* generate theory, but also theory is often used as a background to qualitative investigations.

It is useful to think of the relationship between theory and research in terms of deductive and inductive strategies. However, as we have emphasised, the issues are not as clear-cut as sometimes presented. Deductive and inductive strategies are better thought of as tendencies rather than as a hard-and-fast distinction. In recent years

Research in focus 2.5
An inductive study

Tracy, Lutgen-Sandvik, and Alberts (2006) wanted to understand what bullying feels like to those who are the target of it. They suggest that workplace bullying encompasses a range of persistent abusive workplace behaviours including harassment and mobbing (when a group of co-workers gang up on an employee). However, they argue that previous research has overlooked the emotional experience of bullied workers. Using focus groups, in-depth interviews, and creative drawing, they asked participants to tell stories about workplace bullying. As they explain, through early interpretation of the data 'we found that participants often spoke metaphorically' (2006: 157). This led them to focus on the metaphors that bullied workers used to articulate and explore the emotional pain associated with these experiences. This in turn led them to revise their research question to: 'What types of metaphorical language do participants use to describe the emotional experience of bullying?' The authors suggest the complexity and diversity of workplace bullying meant that 'an inductive approach is especially worthwhile for making sense of messy interactive processes, such as bullying, that have no definite "face"' (2006: 174). They identified a series of metaphorical themes in the data that reflected bullied workers' experiences, including the bullying process as noxious substance, the bully as demon, and the target of bullying as a slave or animal. Importantly, the researchers did not commence their study with a view that metaphors were the key to understanding their chosen topic, but came to this conclusion through the collection and analysis of the data. By focusing on metaphorical images of bullying, they shift the focus 'from how researchers label workplace abuse to how those targeted perceive and make sense of abuse and its impacts' (2006: 173).

it has become popular, especially among qualitative researchers, to approach their research as an **abductive** rather than either a deductive or an inductive process (Key concept 2.6). Mantere and Ketokivi (2013) distinguish between three types of reasoning in organizational research:

- *Theory-testing research:* this involves developing hypotheses from *a priori* theoretical considerations, enabling them to be confirmed or disconfirmed through statistical inference. This is closely associated with the deductive approach described above.
- *Inductive case research:* this involves theory being developed in a 'data-driven manner' using qualitative data, often taking a grounded theory approach. As in theory-testing research, theory is understood as 'a set of propositional statements linking the key concepts in the theory to one another' (Mantere and Ketokivi 2013: 75). The idea is that, once developed, theories can be tested. Both theory-testing and inductive case

researchers tend to adopt a realist ontology: see Key concept 2.8 for more on this.

- *Interpretive research:* while this also involves qualitative data, theory is developed in quite a different way involving a dialogical process between theory and the empirical phenomenon; this results in the production of 'reflexive narratives, not explanatory models or theoretical propositions' (Mantere and Ketokivi 2013: 75). Interpretive research is founded on an interpretive epistemology (Key concept 2.9) and is sometimes associated with abductive reasoning (Key concept 2.6). It is also associated with analogical reasoning, which involves interpretation of one entity in terms of its similarity to another, as in metaphorical analysis.

As these distinctions highlight, the way in which business researchers build theory reveals much about their epistemological and ontological positions, which are the focus of the next two sections.

Epistemological considerations

An epistemological issue concerns the question of what is (or should be) regarded as acceptable knowledge in a discipline. A particularly central issue in this context is

the question of whether or not the social world can and should be studied according to the same principles, procedures, and ethos as the natural sciences. The position that

Key concept 2.6
What is abductive reasoning?

Abduction is a mode of reasoning which has grown in popularity in business research, as well as in other social scientific research disciplines. Like inductive and deductive approaches, abduction is used to make logical inferences and build theories about the world. However, abduction is proposed as a way of overcoming the limitations associated with deductive and inductive positions. The weakness associated with deductive reasoning is its reliance on a strict logic of theory-testing and falsifying hypotheses, but a problem arises because it is not clear how to select the theory to be tested. The difficulty with inductive reasoning arises from the criticism that no amount of empirical data will necessarily enable theory-building. Abductive logic is proposed as a third way which overcomes these limitations. It is based on the pragmatist perspective (in particular the work of philosopher Charles Pierce). Abduction starts with a puzzle or surprise and then seeks to explain it. Puzzles may arise when researchers encounter empirical phenomena which existing theory cannot account for. Abductive reasoning involves seeking to identify the conditions that would make the phenomenon less puzzling, turning surprising facts into a matter of course (Mantere and Ketokivi 2013). This involves back-and-forth engagement with the social world as an empirical source for theoretical ideas, and with the literature, in a process of 'dialectical shuttling' (Atkinson, Coffey, and Delamont, 2003; Schwartz-Shea and Yanow, 2012).

Abduction involves the researcher selecting the 'best' explanation from competing explanations or interpretations of the data (Mantere and Ketokivi 2013). It highlights the limited ability of researchers to think rationally, in terms of computational reasoning, and acknowledges the importance of cognitive reasoning in theory building. This is related to the philosophical idea of the 'hermeneutic circle', through which understanding is seen as a continuous dialogue between the data and the researcher's preunderstandings. Researchers such as Alvesson and Kärreman (2007) see this as crucial in enabling the researcher to remain open to the possibility of being surprised by the data, rather than using it to confirm their preunderstandings.

affirms the importance of imitating the natural sciences is invariably associated with an epistemological position known as **positivism** (see Key concept 2.7).

A natural science epistemology: positivism

The doctrine of **positivism** is extremely difficult to pin down and outline precisely, because it is used in a number of ways by researchers. For some writers, it is a descriptive category—one that describes a philosophical position that can be discerned in research; for others, it is a pejorative term used to describe crude and often superficial data collection.

The five principles in Key concept 2.7 link the points that have already been raised about the relationship between theory and research. For example, positivism contains elements of both a deductive approach (2) and an inductive strategy (3). Also, a sharp distinction is drawn between theory and research. The role of research is to test theories and to provide material for the development of laws. An example of positivism can be seen from the Aston studies, the objective of which to was to make

generalizations about the relationship between organizational size, technology, and structure through systematic comparison across a wide range of organizations. One of the Aston researchers, Pugh (1983), describes the research task as entailing the collection of data upon which to base generalizable propositions that can be tested. The researchers were guided by the belief that organizations exist as concrete entities about which data can be collected. This 'appeal to data' is underpinned by a distinction between facts and values, the former being the goal towards which data collection is directed, leading to the development of a 'conceptual framework' made up of 'analytical constructs' that can be used to analyse the regularities of the data. Conclusions could then be drawn about the 'structure and functioning of organizations' and the 'behaviour of groups and individuals within them' (Pugh 1983: 48). The researchers were committed to the generation of generalizable propositions, from which it would be possible to discover 'how to organize better' (see also Research in focus 3.6).

These connections between theory and research imply that it is possible to collect observations in a way that is not influenced by pre-existing theories. Moreover,

Key concept 2.7
What is positivism?

Positivism is an epistemological position that advocates the application of the methods of the natural sciences to the study of social reality. Although the term stretches beyond this principle and constituent elements vary between authors, positivism is widely understood to rely on the following principles:

1. Only phenomena and hence knowledge confirmed by the senses can genuinely be warranted as knowledge (the principle of phenomenalism).

2. The purpose of theory is to generate hypotheses that can be tested and that will allow explanations of laws to be assessed (the principle of deductivism).

3. Knowledge is arrived at by gathering facts that provide the basis for laws (the principle of inductivism).

4. Science must (and can) be conducted in a way that is value free (that is, objective).

5. There is a clear distinction between scientific statements and normative statements and the former are the true domain of the scientist.

This last principle is implied by the first because the truth of normative statements cannot be confirmed by the senses.

theoretical terms that are not directly amenable to observation are not considered genuinely scientific; they must be susceptible to the rigours of observation. This implies that greater epistemological status is given to observation than to theory.

Even so, it would be a mistake to treat positivism as synonymous with science and the scientific. Philosophers of the natural and social sciences differ over how best to characterize scientific practice, and, since the early 1960s, there has been a drift away from viewing it in positivist terms. When writers complain about the limitations of positivism, it is not entirely clear whether they mean the philosophical term or a scientific approach more generally. **Realism** (in particular **critical realism**) is another philosophical position that provides an account of the nature of scientific practice (see Key concept 2.8).

The central issue is the rejection of the application of natural scientific principles to the study of social reality. It is not easy to disentangle the natural science model from positivism. This means it may be unclear whether writers are objecting to the application of a general natural scientific approach or of positivism. The controversy outlined here about the appropriateness of a natural science model for the study of society has largely taken the form of a controversy about positivism. This is because the description of the natural science model has mainly been one that been highly influenced by positivism rather than other accounts of scientific practice (such as critical realism—see Key concept 2.8).

Interpretivism

Interpretivism is a contrasting **epistemology** to positivism (see Key concept 2.9). The term comes from writers who have been critical of the application of the scientific model to the study of the social world. They share a view that the subject matter of the social sciences—people and their institutions—is fundamentally different from that of the natural sciences. The study of the social world therefore requires a different logic of research that reflects the distinctiveness of humans as against the natural order. Wright (1971) depicts the epistemological clash as being between positivism and **hermeneutics** (a term drawn from theology that has been imported into the social sciences; it refers to the theory and method of interpretation of human action). This arises from a difference of emphasis between the *explanation* of human behaviour (as in the positivist approach to the social sciences) and the *understanding* of human behaviour. Interpretivism is concerned with the empathic understanding of human action rather than with the forces that act on it. This contrast reflects long-standing debates that precede the emergence of the modern social sciences. They are expressed through notions such as a *Verstehen* approach advocated by Max Weber (1864 – 1920). Weber described sociology as a 'science which attempts the interpretive understanding of social action in order to arrive at a causal explanation of its course and effects' (1947: 88). Weber's definition seems to embrace both explanation *and* understanding, but the task of 'causal explanation' must refer to

Key concept 2.8
What is realism?

Realism shares two features with positivism: a belief that the natural and the social sciences can and should apply the same approach to data collection and explanation, and a commitment to the view that there is an external reality to which scientists direct their attention (in other words, there is a reality that is separate from our descriptions of it). There are two major forms of realism:

- *Empirical realism* simply asserts that, through the use of appropriate methods, reality can be understood. As such, it 'fails to recognise that there are enduring structures and generative mechanisms underlying and producing observable phenomena and events' and is therefore 'superficial' (Bhaskar 1989: 2). This is perhaps the most common meaning of the term. When writers employ the term 'realism' in a general way, it is invariably this meaning they refer to.

- *Critical realism* is a specific form of realism which recognizes the reality of the natural order and the events and discourses of the social world. Critical realists argue that 'we will only be able to understand—and so change—the social world if we identify the structures at work that generate those events and discourses . . . These structures are not spontaneously apparent in the observable pattern of events; they can only be identified through the practical and theoretical work of the social sciences' (Bhaskar 1989: 2).

Critical realism implies two things. First, whereas positivists take the view that the scientist's conceptualization of reality actually directly reflects that reality, realists argue that the scientist's conceptualization is simply a way of knowing that reality. As Bhaskar (1975: 250) puts it: 'Science, then, is the systematic attempt to express in thought the structures and ways of acting of things that exist and act independently of thought.' Critical realists acknowledge and accept that the categories they use to understand reality are likely to be provisional. Thus, unlike naïve realists, critical realists see a distinction between the objects that are the focus of their enquiries and the terms they use to describe, account for, and understand them. Secondly, critical realists, unlike positivists, are content to include theoretical terms that are not directly amenable to observation. As a result, hypothetical entities to account for regularities in the natural or social orders (the 'generative mechanisms' to which Bhaskar refers) are perfectly admissible for realists, but not for positivists. This emphasis on causal mechanisms can be attractive to researchers who are dissatisfied with the emphasis in many areas of research on uncovering relationships between variables. Referring to strategic management, Miller and Tsang (2011) bemoan the fact that emphasis on correlations between variables means that researchers rarely explore the causal mechanisms that are implied by the field's theories. They propose some strategies for studying mechanisms directly as a means of providing more satisfactory explanations. What makes critical realism *critical* is the identification of generative mechanisms, which offers the prospect of change that can transform the status quo.

the 'interpretive understanding of social action' rather than to external forces that have no meaning for those involved in social action. An example of an interpretative understanding of leadership is given in Research in focus 2.10. Grint (2000) argues that the concept of leadership can be understood through researching the meaning of the concept for those involved in it. His approach to this subject is thus broadly interpretive.

One of the main intellectual traditions responsible for the anti-positivist position has been **phenomenology**, a

Key concept 2.9
What is interpretivism?

Interpretivism is an alternative to the positivist orthodoxy that held sway for many years in business research. It is based on the view that a strategy is required that respects the differences between people and the objects of the natural sciences and therefore requires the social scientist to grasp the subjective meaning of social action. Its intellectual heritage includes Weber's notion of *Verstehen*; the hermeneutic–phenomenological tradition; and symbolic interactionism.

Research in focus 2.10
Interpretivism in practice

Leitch, Hill, and Harrison (2010) discuss research conducted on women business owners that was interpretivist in terms of the approach to both data collection and analysis. They were interested in how women perceived their experiences of obtaining external finance for their businesses at the initial start-up stage and later in nurturing the growth of the businesses. The interpretivist stance was apparent in the researchers' commitment to giving "'voice' to women's experiences in their own right' (Leitch et al. 2010: 77). Semi-structured interviews were carried out with a purposive sample of ten women business owners (Hill, Leitch, and Harrison 2006). One strand of the interview included the use of the critical incident technique (see Research in focus 20.5) when interviewees were asked to reflect on specific experiences in raising venture finance. The researchers elicited the women's 'personal perspectives and in their own words' and the analysis was undertaken to reflect 'the issues and topics identified by research participants as being important in understanding the phenomenon of interest' (Leitch et al. 2010: 77, 79). This focus on the perspectives of research participants during data collection and analysis stages is the motif of the interpretivist approach. For example, the researchers found that their interviewees had predominantly negative perceptions of banks as routes to financial support. One commented: 'The company is not interested in bank finance because the banks are risk averse and don't understand the needs of small businesses' (quoted in Hill et al. 2006: 171). What we see in an interpretivist stance is a preference for research methods that elicit participants' world views in relation to the topic of interest, and for analyses that ground concepts and connections between them in the words and elicited perspectives of participants.

philosophy concerned with how individuals make sense of the world around them and how, in particular, the philosopher should bracket out preconceptions in his or her own engagement with that world. The initial application of phenomenological ideas to the social sciences is attributed to Alfred Schutz (1899–1959), whose work did not come to the notice of English-speaking social scientists until its translation from German in the 1960s. His work was profoundly influenced by Weber's concept of *Verstehen*, as well as by phenomenological philosophers such as Husserl. Schutz's position is well captured in the following often-quoted passage:

> The world of nature as explored by the natural scientist does not 'mean' anything to molecules, atoms, and electrons. But the observational field of the social scientist—social reality—has a specific meaning and relevance structure for the beings living, acting, and thinking within it. By a series of common-sense constructs they have pre-selected and pre-interpreted this world which they experience as the reality of their daily lives. It is these thought objects of theirs which determine their behaviour by motivating it. The thought objects constructed by the social scientist, in order to grasp this social reality, have to be founded upon the thought objects constructed by the common-sense thinking of men [and women!], living their daily life within the social world.
>
> (Schutz 1962: 59)

Two points are worth noting in this quotation. First, Schutz asserts that there is a fundamental difference between the subject matter of the natural sciences and that of the social sciences and that an epistemology is required to reflect and capitalize upon that difference. The fundamental difference is in the fact that social reality has a meaning for human beings and therefore human action is meaningful—that is, it has meaning for human beings and they act on the basis of the meanings that they attribute to their acts and to the acts of others. This leads to the second point—that it is the job of the social scientist to gain access to people's 'common-sense thinking' and hence to interpret their actions and their social world from their point of view. It is this feature that social scientists claiming allegiance to phenomenology typically emphasize. As the authors of a research methods text whose approach is phenomenological state: 'The phenomenologist views human behavior . . . as a product of how people interpret the world . . . . In order to grasp the meanings of a person's behavior, *the phenomenologist attempts to see things from that person's point of view*' (Bogdan and Taylor 1975: 13–14, emphasis in original).

This explanation skates over some complex issues. In particular, Weber's examination of *Verstehen* is more complex than the above suggests, because the empathetic understanding that seems to be implied above was not how he applied it (Bauman 1978), while the question of what is and is not a genuinely phenomenological approach to the social sciences is disputed (Heap and Roth 1973). However, the writings of the hermeneutic–phenomenological tradition and the *Verstehen* approach, with their emphasis on social action as meaningful to actors and therefore needing to be interpreted from their point of view, coupled with the rejection of positivism, contributed to a stream of thought often referred to as interpretivism (e.g. Hughes 1990).

Verstehen and the hermeneutic–phenomenological tradition do not exhaust the intellectual influences on interpretivism. The theoretical tradition in sociology known as *symbolic interactionism* is also regarded as an influence. The implications of the ideas of the founders of symbolic interactionism, in particular George Herbert Mead (1863–1931), who discusses the way in which our notion of self emerges through an appreciation of how others see us, have been hotly debated. The school of research known as the Iowa school has drawn heavily on Mead's concepts and ideas but has proceeded in a direction that most people would prefer to depict as largely positivist (Meltzer, Petras, and Reynolds 1975). Some writers have argued that Mead's approach is far more consistent with a natural science approach than has typically been recognized (McPhail and Rexroat 1979). However, symbolic interactionism is generally viewed as occupying similar intellectual space to the hermeneutic–phenomenological tradition and so broadly interpretative in approach. This is largely the result of writings of Herbert Blumer, a student of Mead's who acted as his mentor's spokesman and interpreter, and his followers (Hammersley 1989; R. Collins 1994). Not only did Blumer coin the term 'symbolic interaction'; he also provided a gloss on Mead's writings that has interpretative overtones. Symbolic interactionists argue that interaction takes place in such a way that the individual is continually interpreting the symbolic meaning of his or her environment (which includes the actions of others) and acts on the basis of this imputed meaning. According to Blumer (1962: 188), 'the position of symbolic interaction requires the student to catch the process of interpretation through which [actors] construct their actions', a statement that brings out clearly his views of the research implications of symbolic interactionism and of Mead's thought.

Although the connection between symbolic interactionism and the hermeneutic–phenomenological tradition should not be exaggerated, the two are united in their antipathy for positivism and have in common an interpretative stance. However, symbolic interactionism is usually understood as a type of social theory that has distinctive epistemological implications; the hermeneutic–phenomenological tradition, by contrast, is best thought of as a general epistemological approach in its own right. There are other intellectual currents that have affinities with the interpretative stance, such as the working-through of the ramifications of the works of the philosopher Ludwig Wittgenstein (Winch 1958), but the hermeneutic–phenomenological, *Verstehen*, and symbolic interactionist traditions are the major influences.

Taking an interpretative stance can mean that the researcher comes up with surprising findings, or at least findings that appear surprising if a largely external stance is taken—that is, a position from outside the particular social context being studied. The Hawthorne studies, referred to earlier (see also Research in focus 3.8), provide an interesting example of this: it was the failure of the investigation to come up with answers to the original research questions that stimulated the researchers to change their approach and methods and adopt a more interpretative epistemological position. Of course, when the social scientist adopts an interpretative stance, he or she is not simply exposing how members of a social group interpret the world around them. The social scientist will almost certainly be aiming to place the interpretations that have been elicited into a theoretical frame. As Research in focus 2.10 illustrates, there is a double interpretation here, where the researcher is providing an interpretation of others' interpretations of effective leadership. Indeed, there is a third level of interpretation going on, because the researcher's interpretations have to be further interpreted in terms of the concepts, theories, and literature of a discipline.

This section has outlined how epistemological considerations—especially the question of whether a natural science, and in particular a positivist approach, can supply legitimate knowledge of the social world—are related to research practice. This links to the earlier discussion in this chapter about the relationship between theory and research, in that a deductive approach is typically associated with a positivist position. Key concept 2.7 does try to suggest that inductivism is also a feature of positivism (third principle), but, in the working-through of its implementation in the practice of research, it is the deductive element (second principle) that is emphasized. Similarly, the third level of interpretation that a researcher engaged in interpretative research must bring into operation is part of the inductive strategy described in the previous section. However, while such interconnections between epistemological issues and research practice exist, it is important not to overstate them, since they represent tendencies rather than definitive points of correspondence. Epistemological principles and research practices do not necessarily go hand in hand in a neat, unambiguous manner. For example, Hofstede's (1984) study of cultural differences between members of a large multinational business organization, referred to as the HERMES Corporation, shows that inductive researchers do not always rely on qualitative methods. Survey data were collected between 1967 and 1973, from employees in over forty different countries where HERMES had subsidiaries, producing a total of 116,000 self-completion questionnaires. Statistical analysis based on **factor analysis** formed the basis for Hofstede's development of a theoretical framework consisting of four main **dimensions** on which country cultures differ, labelled 'power distance', 'uncertainty avoidance', 'individualism', and 'masculinity'. The dimensions were not developed deductively as hypotheses prior to data collection; instead they emerged inductively through the process of analysis. We will return to this point on several occasions and will focus on it in Chapter 26.

Ontological considerations

Social **ontology** is concerned with the nature of social entities. The central question here is whether social entities can and should be considered objective entities that have a reality external to social actors, or whether they can and should be considered as social constructions built up from the perceptions and actions of social actors. These positions are frequently referred to respectively as **objectivism** and **constructionism**. Their differences can be illustrated by reference to two of the most common terms in social science—organization and culture.

Objectivism

Objectivism is an ontological position that implies that social phenomena confront us as external facts beyond our reach or influence (see Key concept 2.11). We can discuss organization or *an* organization as a tangible object. It has rules and regulations. It adopts standardized procedures for getting things done. People are appointed to different jobs as part of the division of labour. There is a hierarchy. It has a mission statement. And so on. The degree to which these features exist from organization to organization is variable, but in thinking in these terms we take the view that an organization has a reality that is external to the individuals who inhabit it. Moreover, the organization represents a social order in that it exerts pressure on individuals to conform to certain requirements. People learn and apply the rules and regulations. They follow the standardized procedures. They do the jobs to which they are appointed. People tell them what to do and they tell others what to do. They learn and apply the values in the mission statement. If they do not do these things, they may be reprimanded or even fired. The organization is therefore a constraining force that acts on and inhibits its members.

The same can be said of culture. Cultures and subcultures can be viewed as repositories of widely shared values and customs into which people are socialized so that they can function as good citizens or full participants. Cultures and subcultures constrain us because we internalize their beliefs and values. In the case of both organization and culture, the social entity in question comes across as something external to the actor with an almost tangible reality of its own. It has the characteristics of an object and hence of having an objective reality.

Constructionism

However, we can consider an alternative ontological position—*constructionism* (see Key concept 2.12). This position challenges the suggestion that categories such as organization and culture are pre-given and therefore confront social actors as external realities that they have no role in fashioning.

Let us take organization first. Strauss et al. (1973), drawing on insights from symbolic interactionism, carried out

Key concept 2.11
What is objectivism?

Objectivism is an ontological position that asserts that social phenomena and their meanings have an existence that is independent of social actors. It implies that social phenomena and the categories that we use in everyday life have an existence that is independent or separate from actors.

Key concept 2.12
What is constructionism?

Constructionism is an ontological position (often also referred to as constructivism) which asserts that social phenomena and their meanings are continually being accomplished by social actors. It implies that social phenomena and categories are not only produced through social interaction but are also in a constant state of revision.

In recent years, the term has also been used to show researchers' own accounts of the social world as constructions. In other words, the researcher always presents a specific version of social reality, rather than one that can be regarded as definitive. Knowledge is viewed as indeterminate. This is related to the concept of **postmodernism** (Key concept 17.2). This sense of constructionism is usually allied to the ontological version of the term. In other words, these are linked meanings. Both meanings are antithetical to *objectivism* (see Key concept 2.11), but the second meaning is also antithetical to *realism* (see Key concept 2.8). The first meaning might be thought of usefully as constructionism in relation to the social world, the second as constructionism in relation to the nature of knowledge of the social (and indeed the natural) world.

Increasingly, constructionism is being discussed in relation to the nature of knowledge, but in this book we use the term in relation to the first meaning, as an ontological position in relating to social objects and categories—that is, one that views them as socially constructed.

research in a psychiatric hospital and proposed that it was best conceptualized as a 'negotiated order'. Instead of taking the view that order in organizations is a pre-existing characteristic, they argue that it is worked at. Rules were far less extensive and less rigorously imposed than might be supposed from classic accounts of organization. Strauss et al. refer to them as 'much less like commands, and much more like general understandings' (1973: 308). Because relatively little of the spheres of action of doctors, nurses, and other personnel was prescribed, the social order of the hospital was an outcome of agreed-upon patterns of action that were themselves the products of negotiations between the people involved. The social order is in a constant state of change because the hospital is 'a place where numerous agreements are continually being terminated or forgotten, but also as continually being established, renewed, reviewed, revoked, revised . . . . In any pragmatic sense, this is the hospital at the moment: this is its social order' (Strauss et al. 1973: 316–17). The authors argue that preoccupation with the formal properties of organizations (rules, organizational charts, regulations, roles) neglects the degree to which order in organizations is accomplished in everyday interaction. This is not to say that the formal properties have *no* element of constraint on individual action, but it is not the primary reality.

The same point can be made about culture. Instead of culture being seen as an external reality that acts on and constrains people, it can be taken to be an emergent reality in a continuous state of construction and reconstruction. Becker (1982: 521) has suggested that 'people create culture continuously . . . . No set of cultural understandings . . . provides a perfectly applicable solution to any problem people have to solve in the course of their day, and they therefore must remake those solutions, adapt their understandings to the new situation in the light of what is different about it.' Like Strauss et al., Becker recognizes that the constructionist position cannot be pushed to the extreme: it is necessary to appreciate that culture has a reality that 'persists and antedates the participation of particular people' and shapes their perspectives, but it is not an inert objective reality that possesses only a sense of constraint: it acts as a point of reference but is always in the process of being formed.

Neither the work of Strauss et al. nor that of Becker pushes the constructionist argument to the extreme. Each accepts the pre-existence of their objects of interest (organization and culture, respectively). However, they both have an intellectual preference for stressing the active role of individuals in the social construction of social reality. Not all writers adopting a constructionist position are similarly prepared to acknowledge the existence or importance of an objective reality. Walsh, for example, has written that 'we cannot take for granted, as the natural scientist does, the availability of a preconstituted world of phenomena for investigation' and that we must instead 'examine the processes by which the social world is constructed' (1972: 19). It is this apparent split between viewing the social world as an objective reality and as a subjective reality in a continuous state of

Research in focus 2.13
Constructionism in action

Much research has been devoted to considering the impact of delayering and downsizing on middle management. Some studies draw attention to increased job insecurity and rising levels of stress experienced by those who remain in employment. Others strike a more optimistic tone, suggesting that managerial work can be transformed through delayering into a more strategic, intrinsically motivating form. These pessimistic and optimistic predictions for the future of middle management form the basis for empirical testing and debate.

Adopting a social constructionist framework, Thomas and Linstead (2002) suggest an alternative way of thinking about the 'reality' of middle management based on the assumption that the term itself is a social construct. This leads them to a focus on how middle managers' identity is continually created and contested through prevailing discourses. In other words, they are interested in understanding how managers make sense of the language and practice associated with their changing work roles.

Through the analysis of individual managers' subjective accounts of their work, Thomas and Linstead analyse how they construct identity and deal with feelings of insecurity, ambiguity, and confusion that cause them to 'feel that they are losing the plot in their organizations' (2002: 88). Constant changes in terms of roles and status make it difficult for middle managers to retain a sense of identity. The authors conclude: 'What is apparent . . . is that these middle managers, for a range of reasons, are searching for stability and sense in their reflections on their lives' (2002: 88).

In sum, the social constructionist perspective enables the question of 'What has become of middle management?' to be recast. Instead it asks: 'How are middle managers becoming?'

---

flux that Giddens sought to resolve through his theory of structuration (see Research in focus 2.1).

Constructionism also suggests that the categories people use to understand the natural and social world are in fact social products. The categories do not have built-in essences; instead, their meaning is constructed in and through interaction. Thus, a category such as 'masculinity' can be treated as a social construction. This notion implies that, rather than being treated as a distinct inert entity, masculinity is construed as something whose meaning is built up during interaction. That meaning is likely to be ephemeral, in that it will vary according to

both time and place. This stance displays a concern with the language used to present categories. It suggests that the social world and its categories are not external to us but are built up and constituted in and through interaction. This tendency can be seen in **discourse analysis**, examined in Chapter 22. As Potter (1996: 98) observes: 'The world . . . is *constituted* in one way or another as people talk it, write it and argue it.' This sense of constructionism is antithetical to realism (see Key concept 2.8). Constructionism frequently results in an interest in the representation of social phenomena, as Research in focus 2.13 shows.

Epistemology and ontology in business research

Questions of social ontology cannot be divorced from the conduct of business research. Ontological assumptions and commitments feed into the formulation of research questions and the way research is carried out. If a research question is formulated in a way that suggests that organizations and cultures are objective social entities

that act on individuals, the researcher is likely to emphasize the formal properties of organizations or the beliefs and values of members of the culture. Alternatively, if the researcher formulates a research problem so that the tenuousness of organization and culture as objective categories is stressed, an emphasis will be placed on the active involvement of people in reality construction. In each case, different approaches to the design of research and the collection of data will be required.

Competing paradigms

A key influence on understanding the epistemological and ontological foundations of business research is Burrell and Morgan's (1979) four paradigms, which reflect the assumptions researchers make about the nature of organizations and how we find out about them. Their use of the notion of **paradigm** draws on the work of Kuhn (1970; see Key concept 2.14). Burrell and Morgan suggest that each paradigm contains assumptions that are either:

- *objectivist*—there is an external viewpoint from which it is possible to view the organization, which is comprised of consistently real processes and structures; or
- *subjectivist*—an organization is a socially constructed product, a label used by individuals to make sense of their experience.

Each paradigm makes assumptions about the function and purpose of research in investigating the world of business as either:

- *regulatory*—the purpose of business research is to describe what goes on in organizations, possibly to suggest minor changes to improve them, but not make any judgement; or
- *radical*—the point of management and business research is to make judgements about the way that

organizations ought to be and to make suggestions about how this could be achieved.

Plotting the assumptions of researchers along these two axes provides a framework for four paradigmatic positions in the study of organizations:

- *functionalist*—the dominant framework for the study of organizations, based on a problem-solving orientation which leads to rational explanation;
- *interpretative*—focuses on the conceptions of social actors and implies that understanding must be based on the experience of those who work in organizations;
- *radical humanist*—proposes that organizations are social arrangements from which individuals need to be emancipated and that research should be guided by the need for change;
- *radical structuralist*—views an organization as a product of structural power relationships, which result in conflict.

Each paradigm results in the generation of a quite different type of organizational analysis to address specific organizational 'problems' in different ways. Research in focus 2.15 illustrates the different organizational insights produced by each paradigm.

One of the most significant controversies generated by this model relates to the commensurability or otherwise of the four paradigms. Burrell and Morgan were quite specific in arguing that 'a synthesis between paradigms cannot be achieved' (Jackson and Carter 1991: 110) because

Key concept 2.14
What is a paradigm?

Kuhn's (1970) highly influential use of the term 'paradigm' derives from his analysis of revolutions in science. A paradigm is 'a cluster of beliefs and dictates which for scientists in a particular discipline influence what should be studied, how research should be done, [and] how results should be interpreted' (Bryman 1988*a*: 4). Kuhn depicted the natural sciences as going through periods of revolution, whereby normal science (science carried out in terms of the prevailing paradigm) is increasingly challenged by anomalies that are inconsistent with the assumptions and established findings in the discipline. The growth in anomalies eventually gives way to a crisis in the discipline, which in turn occasions a revolution. The period of revolution is resolved when a new paradigm emerges as ascendant and a new period of normal science sets in. An important feature of paradigms is that they are *incommensurable*—that is, they are inconsistent with each other because of divergent assumptions and methods. Disciplines in which no paradigm has emerged as pre-eminent, such as the social sciences, are deemed pre-paradigmatic, in that they feature competing paradigms. One of the problems with the term is that it is not very specific: Masterman (1970) was able to discern twenty-one different uses of it by Kuhn. Nonetheless, its use is widespread in the social sciences (e.g. Ritzer 1975; Guba 1985).

Research in focus 2.15
An illustration of multiple paradigms

Hassard (1991) uses the multiple paradigm model, developed by Burrell and Morgan (1979), to conduct an empirical analysis of work behaviour in the British Fire Service. He shows how different insights into organization can be gained through using each paradigm as a distinct frame of reference. Because each paradigm community defines its research problems differently, the study was adapted in order to focus on issues of work organization that each paradigm community would consider legitimate. The four main subjects were:

- job motivation (functionalist paradigm);
- work routines (interpretative paradigm);
- management training (radical humanist paradigm);
- employment relations (radical structuralist paradigm).

Although there is no necessary connection between, for example, the study of job motivation and the functionalist paradigm, Hassard states that it was logically and practically difficult to focus on a single issue examined from each of the four perspectives, because each paradigm considers specific research problems as important.

For the functionalist investigation, the aim was to assess how full-time firemen evaluate the motivating potential of their jobs using the Job Diagnostic Survey developed by Hackman and Oldham (1980; see Research in focus 7.4). Questionnaires were distributed to a stratified sample of 110 firemen, differentiated by age and length of service, and an 85 per cent response rate was achieved. Analysis of the results using statistical tests showed that, although the fireman's job possesses modest levels of motivation potential, 'this is not in fact a problem for employees whose needs for psychological growth at work are also modest' (Hassard 1991: 285).

For the interpretative part of the study, firemen were asked to describe and explain their daily tasks in order to enable an ethnomethodological study of Fire Service work routines and activities (see Key concept 17.1 on **ethnomethodology**). Analysis of conversational data collected over a three-month period highlighted how routine events in the Fire Service are accomplished in a context of uncertainty, which stems from the constant threat of emergency calls. The research suggests that the Fire Service organization 'is a cultural phenomenon which is subject to a continuous process of enactment' (Hassard 1991: 288).

The radical humanist investigation was conducted in the style of critical theory; it describes how management training in the Fire Service contributes towards the reproduction of an ideology that supports and reinforces capitalist values. Data were collected on training practices used to prepare firemen for promotion to first-line supervision. Analysis of audio recordings of formal classroom sessions and discussions between participants showed how the in-house training programmes allow the organization to retain tight control over the messages delivered, selectively using theories that reinforced the existing authority structure.

Finally, the radical structuralist paradigm was represented through the application of labour process theory, focusing on the development of employment relations and conflicts over working time. Historical analysis of contractual negotiations and strike action showed how, as firemen's working hours were reduced to a level comparable with other manual occupations, 'measures have been taken which at once enhance management's control over the work process whilst yielding greater productivity from the working period' (Hassard 1991: 294).

Hassard thus challenges the notion of paradigm incommensurability, suggesting instead that multiple paradigm research can enable greater variety in organizational research, to challenge the kind of absolutist analysis typical within such journals as *Administrative Science Quarterly*. Yet, according to Johnson and Duberley (2000), the diversity in subject focus between the four investigations merely confirms the fundamental differences between the paradigms and hence their incommensurability. Rather than showing how paradigms can be combined, Hassard's study demonstrates how they can be displayed side by side, as competing versions of reality.

paradigms are founded upon a commitment to fundamentally opposing beliefs; in other words they are incompatible with one another. Each paradigm must therefore develop independently of the others. Jackson and Carter argue that paradigm incommensurability is important because it protects the diversity of scientific thought and resists the hegemony of functionalist approaches, which have tended to dominate business research, particularly in North American-based journals. Reed (1985), on the other hand, suggests that the boundaries between paradigms are not as clear as Burrell and Morgan suggest and that overstatement of differences leads to isolationism and reduces 'the potential for creative theoretical development' (1985: 205). Willmott (1993) takes a different tack. He suggests that, although the four-paradigm model challenges the intellectual hegemony of functionalism and opens up possibilities for alternative forms of analysis, its central thesis is distinctly double-edged. For Willmott, the division between subjectivist and objectivist forms of analysis leads to a polarization of methodological approaches. Instead he suggests that paradigms arise through critical reflection upon the limitations of competing approaches. For example, labour process theory has sought to incorporate an appreciation of the subjective dimension of work while at the same time retaining a commitment to structural analysis of the dynamics involved in

capitalist production. Willmott argues that this example draws attention to the 'practical indivisibility' of subjective and objective dimensions in research. Writers such as Willmott have therefore called for a 'bracketing' of paradigms, building awareness of practices and principles that researchers from different paradigmatic traditions hold in common. In a recent review, Shepherd and Challenger (2013) argue that the paradigms debate continues to be influential within business research, including in subfields such as marketing, accounting, and operations research, as well as in organization studies where it was originally applied. However, the ways in which the concept is used varies considerably, encompassing notions such as 'perspective', 'theory', 'discipline', 'school', and 'method'.

Whatever view is held in relation to the relative commensurability of the four paradigms, it is clear that this model has significantly influenced business researchers by encouraging exploration of the assumptions that they make about the nature of the social world and how it can be studied. The paradigm debate thereby draws attention to the relationship between epistemology and ontology in business and management research. The choice of which paradigm to adopt also has implications for the design of the research and the data collection approach that will be taken; it is to this question that we turn in the following section.

Research strategy: quantitative and qualitative

Many writers on methodological issues find it helpful to distinguish between quantitative and qualitative research. The status of the distinction is ambiguous, because it is regarded by some writers as a fundamental contrast and by others as no longer useful or even simply as 'false' (Layder 1993: 110). However, there are no signs that the use of the distinction is decreasing and there is considerable evidence of its continued, even growing, currency. The quantitative/qualitative distinction will be used frequently in this book, because it represents a useful means of classifying different methods of business research and because it is a helpful umbrella for a range of issues concerned with its practice.

On the face of it, there seems little to the quantitative/qualitative distinction other than the fact that quantitative researchers employ measurement and qualitative researchers do not. It is certainly true that there is a predisposition along these lines, but many writers have suggested that the differences are deeper than the superficial issue of the

presence or absence of quantification. Many writers see quantitative and qualitative research as having different epistemological foundations. If we take the areas that have been the focus of the last three sections—the connection between theory and research, epistemological considerations, and ontological considerations—quantitative and qualitative research can be understood as two distinctive clusters of *research strategy*. By a research strategy, we simply mean a general orientation to the conduct of business research. Table 2.1 outlines the differences between quantitative and qualitative research in terms of the three areas.

Thus, quantitative research is a research strategy that emphasizes quantification in the collection and analysis of data and that:

• entails a deductive approach to the relationship between theory and research, in which the emphasis is on the testing of theories;

- has incorporated the practices and norms of the natural scientific model and of positivism in particular; and
- takes a view of social reality as an external, objective reality.

By contrast, qualitative research is a research strategy that usually emphasizes words rather than quantification in the collection and analysis of data and that:

- predominantly emphasizes an inductive approach to the relationship between theory and research, in which the emphasis is placed on the generation of theories;
- has rejected the practices and norms of the natural scientific model and of positivism in particular in preference for an emphasis on the ways in which individuals interpret their social world; and
- takes a view of social reality as a constantly shifting emergent property of individuals' creation.

There is, in fact, considerably more to the quantitative/qualitative distinction than this contrast. In Chapters 7 and 17 the natures of quantitative and then qualitative research are outlined in much greater detail, while in Chapters 26 and 27 the contrasting features will be further explored. In particular, a number of distinguishing features flow from the commitment of the quantitative research strategy to a positivist epistemology and from the rejection of that epistemology by practitioners of the qualitative research strategy. In other words, the three contrasts in Table 2.1 are basic, though fundamental.

However, the interconnections between different features of quantitative and qualitative research are not as straightforward as Table 2.1 and the previous paragraph imply. While it is useful to contrast the two research strategies, it is necessary to be careful about hammering a wedge between them too deeply.

For example, it is common to describe qualitative research as concerned with the generation rather than the testing of theories. However, there are examples of studies in which qualitative research has been employed to test rather than to generate theories. For example, Hochschild's (1983) theory of emotion work (see Research in focus 17.4) emerged from a questionnaire study of university students. The theory was subsequently tested to establish its wider significance in employment using two occupational groups, where a wider range of qualitative methods, including interviews and **participant observation**, were used. This enabled development of the theory to incorporate the idea of emotional labour, which is emotion work that forms part of paid employment. This study shows that although qualitative research is typically associated with generating theories, it can also be used to test them. Moreover, it is striking that, although Hochschild's study is broadly interpretivist in epistemological orientation, with its emphasis on how flight attendants view their work role identity, the findings have objectivist, rather than constructionist, overtones. When Hochschild describes the marketing and advertising strategies used by Delta Airlines, she explains how, by creating a discrepancy between promise and fact, flight attendants are forced to cope with the disappointed expectations of customers through their emotional labour. She relates the demand for emotional labour to the structural conditions of the airline industry market, thus suggesting a social world that is 'out there' and as having a formal, objective quality. It is an example of qualitative research in the sense that there is no quantification or very little of it, but it does not have *all* the other features outlined in Table 2.1. As such, it has interpretivist overtones despite the use of quantitative research methods.

The point is that quantitative and qualitative research represent different research strategies and that each carries with it striking differences in terms of the role of theory, epistemological issues, and ontological concerns. However, the distinction is not a hard-and-fast one: studies that have the broad characteristics of one research

Table 2.1

Fundamental differences between quantitative and qualitative research strategies		
	Quantitative	Qualitative
Principal orientation to the role of theory in relation to research	Deductive; testing of theory	Inductive; generation of theory
Epistemological orientation	Natural science model, in particular positivism	Interpretivism
Ontological orientation	Objectivism	Constructionism

Research in focus 2.16
Mixed methods research—an example

Holmberg et al. (2008) conducted an investigation of the role of leadership in the implementation of evidence-based treatment practices for drug abuse and criminal behaviour in Sweden. The chief method of data collection—a **self-completion questionnaire** administered by mail to treatment personnel involved in the implementation of treatment programmes—resulted in largely quantitative data that allowed the researchers to examine hypotheses relating to the factors that are likely to enhance or inhibit the implementation of evidence-based programmes. These quantitative data showed that the leadership behaviour of those charged with leading such programmes was related to the job satisfaction, work output, and perceptions of the organization by those members of staff who had to implement the programmes on a day-to-day basis. The questionnaire data therefore allowed the authors to demonstrate the ways in which leadership behaviour had implications for the everyday work lives of staff working on the implementation of the programmes. The success or failure of the programmes could depend critically on the organizational setting that leaders created for the process of implementation. Qualitative data were drawn from in-depth interviews, which were conducted with sixty-five individuals who worked for organizations associated with the programmes. Over half were treatment staff and the rest were managers and others. Further qualitative data were obtained from observation of meetings where the programmes were discussed and from participation in training workshops. The interviews revealed the importance of managers taking an active interest in what staff were doing to implement the programmes and being available for support. Where staff had difficulties with implementation, a key factor was that managers were uninterested and failed to provide support and resources that were important to success. The authors write in the discussion of their findings: 'Methods that focus on subordinates' perceptions and reports about leader behaviour through questionnaires may be insufficient for capturing the dynamics of managers' impact on processes of implementation and a combination of methods will probably give a more balanced understanding of leadership . . . . In this study we conducted interviews and observations in order to be able to make a more context-sensitive interpretation of the implantation process. This study can be seen as a step towards more elaborated studies that capture a little bit more of the complexities involved in implementing new practices in human service organisations' (Holmberg et al. 2008: 168). The point that the authors are making is that the use of a mixed methods approach that combined quantitative and qualitative research enabled a more rounded and complete picture to be drawn. At the same time, the study draws out the complexity of the notion of evidence-based management (see Key concept 1.1), as it points to the significance and the complexity of the implementation of evidence-based practices.

strategy may have a characteristic of the other. Many writers argue that the two can be combined within an overall research project, and Chapter 27 examines precisely this possibility. In Chapter 27 we will explore the ways in which management researchers combine these two strategies.

Research in focus 2.16 is an example of a mixed methods study. It is presented here partly to provide an early insight into the possibility of doing **mixed methods research**, but also to show how a wedge need not and should not be driven between quantitative and qualitative research. By contrasting the two approaches, it is easy to see them as incompatible. As the example in Research in focus 2.16 shows, they can be fruitfully combined within a single project. This point will be amplified further throughout Chapter 27.

Influences and politics on the conduct of business research

We are beginning to get a picture now that business research is influenced by a variety of factors. Figure 2.2 summarizes the influences that have been examined so far, but adds two more—the impact of *personal values* and *practical considerations*.

Figure 2.2

Influences on business research

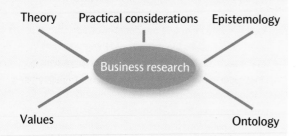

Values

Values reflect either the personal beliefs or the feelings of a researcher. On the face of it, we would expect that social scientists should be value free and objective in their research. After all, one might argue that research that simply reflected the personal biases of its practitioners could not be considered valid and scientific because it was bound up with the subjectivities of its practitioners. This view is held with less and less frequency among social scientists nowadays. Émile Durkheim (1858 – 1917) wrote that one of the corollaries of his injunction to treat social facts as things was that all 'preconceptions must be eradicated' (1938: 31). Since values are a form of preconception, his exhortation was at least implicitly to do with suppressing them when conducting research. His position is unlikely to be regarded as credible nowadays, because there is a growing recognition that it is not feasible to keep the values that a researcher holds totally in check. These can intrude at any or all of a number of points in the process of business research:

- choice of research area;
- formulation of research question;
- choice of method;
- formulation of **research design** and data collection techniques;
- implementation of data collection;
- analysis of data;
- interpretation of data;
- conclusions.

There are numerous points at which bias and the intrusion of values can occur (see Thinking deeply 2.17). Values can materialize at any point during the course of research. The researcher may develop an affection or

sympathy, which was not necessarily present at the outset of an investigation, for the people being studied. It is quite common, for example, for researchers working within a qualitative research strategy, and in particular when they use participant observation or very intensive interviewing, to develop a close affinity with the people whom they study to the extent that they find it difficult to disentangle their stance as social scientists from their subjects' perspective. This possibility may be exacerbated by the tendency of some researchers to be very sympathetic to underdog groups. For example, following publication of his classic study of the Ford factory in Dagenham, Beynon (1975) was criticized by the press for having become too emotionally involved in the lives of workers. Equally, researchers may feel unsympathetic towards the people they study. Having sympathy for the people or organizations studied is a particular issue for business researchers, many of whom are part-time students who choose to study issues or problems in their employing organization. Hence they are already immersed in the organization as complete participants and have an understanding of it that is based on this. This is particularly pronounced in an action research project (see Chapter 17), where the aim is to intervene in situations and study them at the same time. According to Coghlan (2001), researchers in such situations face three interrelated sets of issues:

- *their preunderstanding of the setting*—this refers to the knowledge, insight, and experience that researchers have about the lived experience of their own organization; for example, they already know the history, key events, and jargon used within the organization and who to turn to for information;
- *their role duality*—sets them apart from other organizational members and can affect the data that are generated, particularly when they are engaged in research that may threaten existing organizational norms;
- *organizational politics*—this relates to the potential role of action research in destabilizing organizational norms and questioning established ways of doing things, requiring a high level of political skill. Although this particularly salient in action research, the ability to deal with organizational politics is common to much business research (see Thinking deeply 2.17).

Another perspective in relation to values and bias suggests that research cannot be value free. Researchers can therefore only ever try to be self-reflective and so exhibit *reflexivity* about the part played by such factors. This view is born of the assumption that the researcher's prior knowledge, experience, and attitudes will influence not

Thinking deeply 2.17
Factors that influence methods choice in organizational research

Buchanan and Bryman (2007) identify six types of factor that influence researchers' choice of methods in organizational research:

- *Organizational*: this includes factors such as organizational size and pace of change. For example, Buchanan describes a situation where the question 'What is your job title?' produced a bemused response from managers whose roles were shifting every few weeks.

- *Historical*: this relates to previous studies of the topic.

- *Political*: this type of influence includes negotiating research objectives, obtaining permission to access respondents, aligning with groups of stakeholders, and the way that different methods are perceived by journals, which affects researchers' ability to publish their findings.

- *Ethical*: this relates to the increased ethical scrutiny that is faced by researchers and the role of ethical review in regulating their conduct (see Chapter 6).

- *Evidential*: this relates to the different expectations that academic and managerial audiences have of business research; the former expect knowledge and insight and the latter want practical recommendations. The rise of evidence-based management, which will be discussed in Chapter 4 (see also Key concept 1.1), has only amplified these tensions and debates.

- *Personal*: researchers are also influenced in their choice of methods by such factors as the extent to which they enjoy face-to-face contact, some researchers opting for methods that rely heavily on interpersonal interaction and others choosing methods that confine them to the computer screen.

Buchanan and Bryman (2007) argue that these unavoidable issues that should be treated not as unwelcome distractions but as a central aspect of the research process. They conclude that, as a result, it is difficult to sustain a view of the researcher as a neutral observer. Methods choice is not a single rational process of selecting the most effective tool to address a particular question but rather a highly complex and continually evolving process.

only how the researcher sees things but also *what* he or she sees. The example in Research in focus 2.18 considers some of these issues in relation to organization research.

Another approach is to argue for consciously value-laden research. This is a position taken by some feminist writers, who argue that only research on women that is intended *for* women will be consistent with the wider political needs of women. Mies (1993: 68) has argued that in feminist research the 'postulate of *value free research*, of neutrality and indifference towards the research objects, has to be replaced by *conscious partiality*, which is achieved through partial identification with the research objects' (emphases in original).

The significance of feminism in relation to values goes further than this. Several feminist researchers proposed in the early 1980s that the principles and practices associated with quantitative research were incompatible with feminist research on women. For writers such as

Oakley (1981), quantitative research was informed by masculine values of control that can be seen in the general orientation of the research strategy—control of the research subject/respondent and control of the research context and situation. Moreover, the research process was seen as one-way, in that researchers extract information from the people being studied and give little or more usually nothing in return. For many feminists, such a strategy bordered on exploitation and was incompatible with feminism's values of emancipation and non-hierarchical relationships. The antipathy towards quantitative research resulted in a preference for qualitative research among feminists. Not only was qualitative research seen as more consistent with the values of feminism; it was seen as more adaptable to those values. Thus, feminist qualitative research came to be associated with an approach in which the investigator rejects the possibility of a value-neutral approach and engages

Research in focus 2.18
Influence of an author's biography on research values

Brewis (2005) explains that her research on sexual harassment and the sex industry impacts on her being-in-the-world more generally. She considers the reasons why she chose to research sex and organization, even though 'links between my life story and my research, whilst they indubitably exist, are not causal or easily drawn' (2005: 540). For Brewis, readers act as biographers, 'shaping and constructing authors as particular types of individual' (2005: 494). In her own case this has involved them making 'certain assumptions' about her personal life based on her research interests. She explains: 'whether others meet me in settings such as conferences, listen to my presentations, read or hear about my work, their constructions of who I am and what I do derive in no small part from the ways in which they attribute a gender and a sexuality to me . . . Certain deeply embedded paradigms seem to have constructed me as the kind of author who has intimate relationships with her collaborators. Because I am gendered-as-female, and because I tend to collaborate with others who are gendered-as-male, these signs have apparently been read—through the heterosexual matrix—to imply that my relationships with these individuals go further than straightforward "professional" contact' (2005: 498). This biographic construction of professional identity serves to confirm the sexist belief that women can progress in organizations only if they trade on their sexuality. Brewis's analysis suggests a cyclical dynamic to the role of values on the choice of research subject. Not only does biography influence the choice of research subject, but the chosen research subject can also affect how readers construct the researcher's biography.

with the people being studied as people and not simply as respondents to research instruments. The stance of feminism in relation to both quantitative and qualitative approaches demonstrates the ways in which values have implications for the process of social investigation. In more recent years, there has been a softening of the attitudes of feminists towards quantitative research. Several writers have acknowledged a viable and acceptable role for quantitative research, particularly when it is employed in conjunction with qualitative research (Jayaratne and Stewart 1991; Oakley 1998). This issue will be picked up in Chapters 17, 26, and 27.

There are, then, different positions that can be taken up in relation to values and value freedom. Far fewer researchers than in the past overtly subscribe to the position that the principle of objectivity can be put into practice. Quantitative researchers sometimes seem to be writing in a way that suggests an aura of objectivity (Mies 1993), but we simply do not know how far they subscribe to such a position. There is a greater awareness today of the limits to objectivity, so that some of the highly confident, not to say naïve, pronouncements on the subject, such as Durkheim's, have fallen into disfavour. A further way in which values are relevant to the conduct of business research is through the following of ethical principles or standards (see Chapter 6).

Practical considerations

Finally, we must not neglect the importance and significance of *practical issues* in decisions about how business research should be carried out. There are a number of dimensions to this. Choices of research strategy, design, or method have to be dovetailed with the specific research question being investigated. If we are interested in teasing out the relative importance of a number of causes of a social phenomenon, it is quite likely that a quantitative strategy will fit our needs, because, as will be shown in Chapter 7, the assessment of cause is one of its keynotes. Alternatively, if we are interested in the world views of members of a certain social group, a qualitative research strategy that is sensitive to how participants interpret their social world may be the direction to choose. If a researcher is interested in a topic on which very little research has been done, the quantitative strategy may be difficult to employ, because there is little prior literature from which to draw leads. A more exploratory stance may be preferable and, in this connection, qualitative research may serve the researcher's needs better, since it is typically associated with the generation of, rather than the testing of, theory (see Table 2.1) and with a relatively unstructured approach to the research process (see Chapter 17). Another dimension may have to do with the nature of the topic and of the people being investigated. For example, if the researcher needs to engage with individuals or groups involved in illicit activities, such as industrial sabotage (Sprouse 1992) or theft (Ditton 1977), it is unlikely that a social survey would gain the confidence of the subjects involved or achieve the necessary rapport. It is not surprising, therefore, that researchers in these areas have tended to use a qualitative strategy.

While practical considerations may seem rather mundane and uninteresting compared with the lofty realm of philosophical debates surrounding discussions about epistemology and ontology, they are important. All business research is a coming together of the ideal and the feasible. There will be many circumstances in which the nature of the topic or of the subjects of an investigation and the constraints on a researcher loom large in decisions about how best to proceed. Consequently, in certain circumstances, business researchers exercise a degree of opportunism in their choice of research setting and focus on a particular subject. Alvesson (2003) draws a distinction within qualitative research between a '*planned-systematic*' approach to data collection and an '*emergent-spontaneous*' one. The researcher who takes a planned-systematic approach has a reasonably clear idea of his subject of study and plans the process of data collection with the aim of producing a pile of notes and interview transcripts to analyse at the end of it. For example, to study organizational identity, notes made during fieldwork and questions asked in interviews reflect this subject focus. The results of this data collection process then form the basis for writing up findings.

An emergent-spontaneous study, on the other hand, is carried out when something revealing happens. 'In such a study the researcher waits for something interesting/generative to pop up' (Alvesson 2003: 181). Although there are disadvantages associated with this—namely, it might appear somewhat arbitrary and unscientific—Alvesson suggests there are some advantages: 'the most significant one is that it increases the likelihood of coming up with interesting material. The researcher does not find the empirical material, it finds him or her' (2003: 181). By developing sensitivity to rich empirical data and willingness to respond to situations where such data may emerge, the researcher takes a more opportunistic approach to the task. The experience of Bell (2012) in researching the closure of the Jaguar car manufacturing plant in the UK city of Coventry, which was near where she lived, illustrates how such an emergent-spontaneous study might arise. In this case it was the result of existing local contacts she already had with members of the local community that enabled her to trace events relating to the closure as they unfolded. However, Alvesson recommends care in presenting studies based on emergent-spontaneous research, as the conventions that guide some researchers might cause them to respond unfavourably to this more unsystematic method of research topic selection, even if the research strategy and research design are well informed. It is also potentially a risky strategy, in that it presumes that something important or significant will materialize while the researcher is around. It also requires a high level of vigilance on the part of the researcher—blink and you might miss it!

Telling it like it is
The influence of personal values on student research

Many students are influenced in their choice of research subject by their own personal values and life experiences. This can be positive, because it helps to ensure that they remain interested in their chosen subject throughout the project.

For example, Chris's interest in women in management stemmed from seeing how this had formed the basis for his mother's career: 'My mum runs residential courses on women in management for various large, global organizations, so there had always been books around the house about this and we'd sit and talk about it. So it's always been something that's kind of been in my mind and at the front of what's going on in my life. I had access to an organization that had a large number of women who were doing reasonably well in their careers and I felt it was something that would be really, really interesting to explore. So before I did the internship which allowed me access to the organization I had already decided that I wanted to look at this issue. I don't really know exactly why,

(continued)

looking back on it, but I just thought it was something that not a lot of men would necessarily research. I think a few people were a bit surprised when I chose to do it. I suppose also I wanted to put the argument forward that men aren't necessarily part of the old boy network and doing all the bad stuff. Maybe it's also a positive defence mechanism—I don't know.'

What is also interesting from Chris's account is that he is very aware of the importance of his own gender as potentially affecting how others perceive his interest in this subject.

The extent to which personal values influence the research project will obviously vary. Angharad's decision to study the under-representation of women in senior management was driven by academic interest and personal values. 'It was something that I'd wanted to look at for my dissertation all along but I was also concerned about my own future career as a woman manager and I was worried that I might one day find myself stuck in the wrong job.'

The experience of these students highlights the importance of researcher reflexivity, an issue we will cover in more depth in Chapter 27 (see also **reflexivity** in the Glossary).

Telling it like it is
Researching your own workplace

Chris, Karen, and Lisa all gained access to their research sites as the result of internship or opportunities organized by their universities as part of their degree course.

Chris used the contacts he had established during his internship to make contact with individuals within the bank who could facilitate his access and provide him with important information. 'I ended up ringing the fourth or fifth most senior person in the bank saying 'I'm doing this. Can I chat to you?' and she was absolutely great about it. Then I spoke to somebody beneath her, who agreed to put me in contact with other women in the bank. I had a good chat with her. She gave me lots of information regarding percentage of women at different levels of management, progression over the years, information on competitors and things like that, so by the time I finished my internship I'd organized three interviewees and I could go back to university with my idea.'

Karen also found that gaining the agreement of her line manager to carry out the research was relatively straightforward. 'Once I had decided that this was a topic I was interested in doing, I had a discussion with my manager and discovered that it was something that she was quite interested in as well and other people in the department who did recruitment were all quite interested in it. So access wasn't really a problem. Obviously it was difficult to get time with people but the management wasn't opposed to me doing it.'

However, gaining access through her placement meant that Karen was constrained by the need to combine her full-time employment with a research role. 'Obviously when you're involved in the organization it's quite good because you can get access to people that you know. If I asked them for a favour, they helped me because I'd helped them with something else, so that was quite good. But then, on the other hand, because I was so involved in the organization, I was concerned that I had brought my own opinions into the analysis. I think to some extent I probably did do this, although I tried as much as possible to keep my university head on and remain distanced from it a little bit.'

However, in some situations it may be impractical to research your own workplace, as Tom found. 'When I started the course I was doing a job which was on a fixed-term basis and I knew I was going to be moving on, so I wasn't in a settled work environment and I knew that it might be tricky to get access and keep it going in the organization where I was working. Also, it wasn't like I'd been working in one organization for a long time and had things that I could explore in that environment.'

Of course, opportunities to do research in an organization where you are an intern are not available to all students, so in setting up a student research project it can be important to make use of personal contacts. Researching your own workplace also introduces particular ethical and analytical considerations that stem from having to maintain the dual roles of being a colleague and a researcher. These issues will be discussed further in Chapters 6 and 19.

Key points

- Business research is subject to considerable debate concerning its relevance to practitioners and its fundamental purpose.

- Quantitative and qualitative research constitute different approaches to social investigation and carry with them important epistemological and ontological considerations.

- Theory can be depicted as something that precedes research (as in quantitative research) or as something that emerges out of it (as in qualitative research).

- Epistemological considerations loom large in considerations of research strategy. To a large extent, these revolve around the desirability of employing a natural science model (and in particular positivism) versus interpretivism.

- Ontological considerations, concerning objectivism versus constructionism, also constitute important dimensions of the quantitative/qualitative contrast.

- These considerations have informed the four-paradigm model, which has been an important influence on business research.

- Values may impinge on the research process at different times.

- Practical considerations in decisions about research methods are also important.

- Feminist researchers have tended to prefer a qualitative approach, though there is some evidence of a change of viewpoint in this regard.

Questions for review

Theory and research

- If you had to conduct some business research now, what would the topic be and what factors would influence your choice? How important was theory in your consideration?

- Outline, using examples of your own, the difference between grand and middle-range theory.

- What are the differences between inductive and deductive theory and why is the distinction important?

Epistemological considerations

- What is meant by each of the following terms: positivism; realism; and interpretivism? Why is it important to understand each of them?

- What are the implications of epistemological considerations for research practice?

Ontological considerations

- What are the main differences between epistemological and ontological considerations?

- What is meant by objectivism and constructionism?

- Which theoretical ideas have been particularly instrumental in the growth of interest in qualitative research?

- What are the main arguments for and against paradigm commensurability within management and business research?

Relationship of epistemology and ontology to business research

- What are the four main paradigms in business research and how do they influence the insights that are gained?

Research strategy: quantitative and qualitative research

- Outline the main differences between quantitative and qualitative research in terms of: the relationship between theory and data; epistemological considerations; and ontological considerations.

- To what extent is quantitative research solely concerned with testing theories and qualitative research with generating theories?

Influences on the conduct of business research

- How might your own personal values influence your choice of research topic?

- List the three most important practical considerations that need to be taken into consideration in your research project.

....

 Online Resource Centre

www.oxfordtextbooks.co.uk/orc/brymanbrm4e/

Visit the Interactive Research Guide that accompanies this book to complete an exercise in Business Research Strategies.

....

3

Research designs

Chapter outline

In focusing on the different kinds of research design, we are paying attention to the different frameworks for the collection and analysis of data. A research design relates to the criteria that are employed when evaluating business research. It is, therefore, a framework for the generation of evidence that is suited both to a certain set of criteria and to the research question in which the investigator is interested. This chapter is structured as follows:

- **Reliability, replication, and validity** are presented as criteria for assessing the quality of business research. The latter entails an assessment in terms of several criteria covered in the chapter: **measurement validity**; **internal validity**; **external validity**; and **ecological validity**.

- The suggestion that such criteria are mainly relevant to quantitative research is examined, along with the proposition that an alternative set of criteria should be employed in relation to qualitative research. This alternative set of criteria, which is concerned with the issue of **trustworthiness**, is outlined briefly.

- Five prominent research designs are then outlined:
  - experimental and related designs (such as the quasi-experiment);
  - cross-sectional design, the most common form of which is social survey research;
  - longitudinal design and its various forms, such as the panel study and the cohort study;
  - case study design;
  - comparative design.

- Each research design is considered in terms of the criteria for evaluating research findings.

Introduction

In Chapter 2, the idea of research strategy was introduced as a broad orientation to business research. The specific context for its introduction was the distinction between quantitative and qualitative research as different research strategies. However, the decision to adopt one or the other strategy will not get you far along the road of doing a piece of research. Two other key decisions will have to be made (along with a host of tactical decisions about the way in which the research will be carried out and the data analysed). These decisions concern choices about research design and research method. On the face of it, these two terms would seem to mean the same thing, but it is crucial to draw a distinction between them (see Key concepts 3.1 and 3.2).

Research methods can be and are associated with different kinds of research design. The latter represents a structure that guides the execution of a research method and the analysis of the subsequent data. The two terms are often confused. For example, one of the research designs to be covered in this chapter—the case study—is very often referred to as a method. As we will see, a case study entails the detailed exploration of a specific case, which could be a community, organization, or person. But, once a case has been selected, a research method or research methods are needed to collect data. Simply selecting an organization and deciding to study it intensively are not going to provide data. Do you observe? Do you conduct interviews? Do you examine documents? Do you administer questionnaires? You may in fact use any or all of these research methods, but the crucial point is that deciding to choose a case study approach will not in its own right provide you with data. This choice is further complicated by the fact that what counts as data is not an entirely straightforward matter. Bartunek, Bobko, and Venkatraman (1993) acknowledge the diversity in the way that management researchers define the concept

Key concept 3.1
What is a research design?

A research design provides a framework for the collection and analysis of data. A choice of research design reflects decisions about the priority being given to a range of dimensions of the research process. These include the importance attached to:

- expressing causal connections between variables;
- generalizing to larger groups of individuals than those actually forming part of the investigation;
- understanding behaviour and the meaning of that behaviour in its specific social context;
- having a temporal (i.e. over time) appreciation of social phenomena and their interconnections.

Key concept 3.2
What is a research method?

A research method is simply a technique for collecting data. It can involve a specific instrument, such as a self-completion questionnaire or a **structured interview** schedule, or participant observation whereby the researcher listens to and watches others.

of data to include responses to questionnaire items, transcripts of public inquiry hearings, case studies, and advertisements.

In this chapter, five different research designs will be examined: experimental design and its variants, including quasi-experiments; cross-sectional or social survey design; longitudinal design; case study design; and comparative design. However, before embarking on the nature of and differences between these designs, it is useful to consider some recurring issues in business research that cut across some or all of these designs.

Quality criteria in business research

Three of the most prominent criteria for the evaluation of business and management research are reliability, replication, and validity. All of these terms will be treated in much greater detail in later chapters, but in the meantime a fairly basic treatment of them can be helpful.

Reliability

Reliability is concerned with the question of whether the results of a study are repeatable. The term is commonly used in relation to the question of whether or not the measures that are devised for concepts in business and management (such as teamworking, employee motivation, organizational effectiveness) are consistent. In Chapter 7, we will be looking at the idea of reliability in greater detail, in particular the different ways in which it can be conceptualized. Reliability is particularly at issue in connection with quantitative research. The quantitative researcher is likely to be concerned with the question of whether a measure is stable or not. After all, if we found that scores on IQ tests, which were designed as measures of intelligence, were found to fluctuate, so that people's IQ scores were often wildly different when administered on two or more occasions, we would be concerned about the IQ test as a measure. We would consider it an unreliable measure—we could not have faith in its consistency.

Replication

The idea of reliability is very close to another criterion of research—replication and more especially replicability. It sometimes happens that researchers choose to replicate the findings of others. There may be a host of different reasons for doing so, such as a feeling that the original results do not match other evidence that is relevant to the domain in question. In order for replication to take place, a study must be capable of replication—it must be replicable. This is a very obvious point: if a researcher does not spell out his or her procedures in great detail, replication is impossible. Similarly, in order for us to assess the reliability of a measure of a concept, the procedures that constitute that measure must be replicable by someone else. Ironically, replication in business research is not common. In fact, it is probably truer to say that it is quite rare. When Burawoy (1979) found that by accident he was conducting case study research in a US factory that had been studied three decades earlier by another researcher (Donald Roy), he thought about treating his own investigation as a replication. However, the low status of replication in academic research persuaded him to resist this option. He writes: 'I knew that to replicate Roy's study would not earn me a dissertation let alone a job . . . [In] academia the real reward comes not from replication but from originality!' (Burawoy 2003: 650). Nonetheless, an investigation's capacity to be replicated—replicability—is highly valued by many business researchers working within a quantitative research tradition. See Research in focus 7.11 for an example of a replication study.

Validity

A further and in many ways the most important criterion of research is validity. Validity is concerned with the integrity of the conclusions that are generated from a piece of research. Like reliability, we will be examining the idea of validity in greater detail in later chapters, but in the meantime it is important to be aware of the main facets of validity that are typically distinguished.

- *Measurement validity*. This criterion applies primarily to quantitative research and to the search for measures of social scientific concepts. Measurement validity is also often referred to as *construct validity*. Essentially, it is to do with the question of whether or not a measure that is devised of a concept really does reflect the concept that it is supposed to be denoting. Does the IQ test really measure variations in intelligence? If we take the study reported in Research in focus 3.5, there

are two issue-related concepts that need to be measured in order to test the hypotheses: 'magnitude of consequences' and 'issue framing'; there are also two context-related concepts that also need to be measured: 'perceived social consensus' and 'competitive context'. The question then is: do the measures really represent the concepts they are supposed to be tapping? If they do not, the study's findings will be questionable. It should be appreciated that measurement validity is related to reliability: if a measure of a concept is unstable in that it fluctuates and hence is unreliable, it simply cannot be providing a valid measure of the concept in question. In other words, the assessment of measurement validity presupposes that a measure is reliable.

- *Internal validity*. This form of validity relates mainly to the issue of **causality**, which will be dealt with in greater detail in Chapter 7. Internal validity is concerned with the question of whether a conclusion that incorporates a causal relationship between two or more variables holds water. If we suggest that x causes y, can we be sure that it is x that is responsible for variation in y and not something else that is producing an apparent causal relationship? In the study examined in Research in focus 3.5, Frayne and Geringer (2000) conclude that moral awareness is more likely when an individual perceives the issue to have significant harmful consequences, such as putting a competitor out of business ('magnitude of consequences'), and when the individual perceives a social consensus within the organization that the activity in question is ethically problematic ('perceived social consensus'). Internal validity raises the question: can we be sure that 'magnitude of consequences' and 'perceived social consensus' really do cause variation in moral awareness and that this apparent causal relationship is genuine and not produced by something else? In discussing issues of causality, it is common to refer to the factor that has a causal impact as the **independent variable** and the effect as the **dependent variable** (see Key concept 3.3). In the case of the research of Parboteeah, Hoegl, and Cullen (2009) in Research in focus 2.4, 'religious belief' was an independent variable and 'work obligation' the dependent variable. Thus, internal validity raises the question: how confident can we be that the independent variable really is at least in part responsible for the variation that has been identified in the dependent variable?

- *External validity*. This issue is concerned with the question of whether the results of a study can be generalized beyond the specific research context. It is in this context that the issue of how people or organizations are selected to participate in research becomes crucial. This is why Scase and Goffee (1989) go to such great lengths to detail the process whereby their sample of UK managers was generated (see Research in focus 3.15). External validity is one of the main reasons why quantitative researchers are so keen to generate representative samples (see Chapter 8).

- *Ecological validity.* This criterion is concerned with the question of whether or not social scientific findings are applicable to people's everyday, natural social settings. As Cicourel (1982: 15) has put it: 'Do our instruments capture the daily life conditions, opinions, values, attitudes, and knowledge base of those we study as expressed in their natural habitat?' This criterion is concerned with the question of whether business research sometimes produces findings that may be technically valid but have little to do with what happens in people's everyday lives. If research findings are not ecologically valid, they are in a sense artefacts of the social scientist's arsenal of data collection and analytic tools. The more the social scientist intervenes in natural settings or creates unnatural ones, such as a laboratory or even a special room to carry out interviews, the more likely it is that findings will be ecologically invalid. This was an important finding to have emerged from the Hawthorne studies (see Research in focus 3.8). Furthermore, the conclusions deriving from a study using questionnaires may have measurement validity and a reasonable level of internal validity, and they may be externally valid, in the sense that the findings can be generalized to other samples confronted by the same questionnaire, but the unnaturalness of the fact of having to answer a questionnaire may mean that the findings have limited ecological validity.

One feature that is striking about most of the discussion so far is that it seems to be geared mainly to quantitative rather than to qualitative research. Both reliability and measurement validity are essentially concerned with the adequacy of measures, which are most obviously a concern in quantitative research. Internal validity is concerned with the soundness of findings that specify a causal connection, an issue that is most commonly of concern to quantitative researchers. External validity may be relevant to qualitative research, but the whole question of representativeness of research subjects with which the issue is concerned has a more obvious application to the realm of quantitative research, with its preoccupation with sampling procedures that maximize the opportunity for generating a **representative sample**. The issue of ecological validity relates to the naturalness of the research approach and seems to have considerable relevance to both qualitative and quantitative research.

Some writers have sought to apply the concepts of reliability and validity to the practice of qualitative research (e.g. LeCompte and Goetz 1982; Kirk and Miller 1986; Peräkylä 1997), but others argue that the grounding of these ideas in quantitative research renders them inapplicable to or inappropriate for qualitative research. Writers such as Kirk and Miller (1986) have applied concepts of validity and reliability to qualitative research but have changed very slightly the sense in which the terms are used. Qualitative researchers sometimes propose that the studies they produce should be judged or evaluated according to different criteria from those used in relation to quantitative research. Lincoln and Guba (1985) propose that alternative terms and ways of assessing qualitative research are required. For example, they propose trustworthiness as a criterion of how good a qualitative study is. Each aspect of trustworthiness has a parallel with the previous quantitative research criteria.

Key concept 3.3
What is a variable?

A variable is simply an attribute on which cases vary. 'Cases' can obviously be organizations, but they can also include things such as people, offices and shops, production plants, cities, or nations. If an attribute does not vary, it is a **constant**. If all manufacturing organizations had the same ratio of male to female managers, this attribute of such organizations would be a constant and not a variable. Constants are rarely of interest to business researchers. It is common to distinguish between different types of variable. The most basic distinction is between independent variables and dependent variables. The former are deemed to have a causal influence on the latter.

- *Credibility*, which parallels internal validity—i.e. how believable are the findings?

- *Transferability*, which parallels external validity—i.e. do the findings apply to other contexts?

- *Dependability*, which parallels reliability—i.e. are the findings likely to apply at other times?

- *Confirmability*, which parallels objectivity—i.e. has the investigator allowed his or her values to intrude to a high degree?

These criteria will be returned to in Chapter 17.

Hammersley (1992a) occupies a kind of middle position here in that, while he proposes validity as an important criterion (in the sense that an empirical account must be plausible and credible and should take into account the amount and kind of evidence used in relation to an account), he also proposes relevance as a criterion. Relevance is taken to be assessed from the vantage point of the importance of a topic within its substantive field or the contribution it makes to the literature on that field. The issues in these different views have to do with

the different objectives that many qualitative researchers argue are distinctive about their craft. The distinctive features of qualitative research will be examined in later chapters.

However, it should also be borne in mind that one of the criteria previously cited—ecological validity—may have been formulated largely in the context of quantitative research, but is in fact a feature in relation to which qualitative research fares rather well. Qualitative research often involves a naturalistic stance (see Key concept 3.4). This means that the researcher seeks to collect data in naturally occurring situations and environments, as opposed to fabricated, artificial ones. This characteristic probably applies particularly well to ethnographic research, in which participant observation is a prominent element of data collection, but it is sometimes suggested that it applies also to the sort of interview approach typically used by qualitative researchers, which is less directive than the kind used in quantitative research. We might expect that much qualitative research is stronger than quantitative investigations in terms of ecological validity.

Key concept 3.4
What is naturalism?

Naturalism is an interesting example of a—mercifully relatively rare—term that not only has different meanings, but also has meanings that can actually be contradictory! It is possible to identify three different meanings.

1. *Naturalism means viewing all objects of study—whether natural or social ones—as belonging to the same realm and a consequent commitment to the principles of natural scientific method.* This meaning, which has clear affinities with positivism, implies that all entities belong to the same order of things, so that there is no essential difference between the objects of the natural sciences and those of the social sciences (M. Williams 2000). For many naturalists, this principle implies that there should be no difference between the natural and the social sciences in the ways they study phenomena. This version of naturalism essentially proposes a unity between the objects of the natural and social sciences and, because of this, there is no reason for social scientists not to employ the approaches of the natural scientist.

2. *Naturalism means being true to the nature of the phenomenon being investigated.* According to Matza, naturalism is 'the philosophical view that strives to remain true to the nature of the phenomenon under study' (1969: 5) and 'claims fidelity to the natural world' (1969: 8). This meaning of the term represents a fusion of elements of an interpretivist epistemology and a constructionist ontology, which were examined in Chapter 2. Naturalism is taken to recognize that people attribute meaning to behaviour and are authors of their social world rather than passive objects.

3. *Naturalism is a style of research that seeks to minimize the intrusion of artificial methods of data collection.* This meaning implies that the social world should be as undisturbed as possible when it is being studied (Hammersley and Atkinson 1995: 6).

The second and third meanings overlap considerably, in that it could easily be imagined that, in order to conduct a naturalistic enquiry in the second sense, a research approach that adopted naturalistic principles in the third sense would be required. Both the second and third meanings are incompatible with, and indeed opposed to, the first meaning. Naturalism, in the first sense, is invariably viewed by writers drawing on an interpretivist epistemology as not 'true' to the social world, precisely because it posits that there are no differences between humans and the objects of the natural sciences; it therefore ignores the capacity of humans to interpret the social world and to be active agents; and, in its preference for the application of natural science methods, it employs artificial methods of data collection. When writers are described as *anti-naturalists,* it is invariably the first of the three meanings that they are deemed to be railing against.

By and large, these issues in business research have been presented because some of them will emerge in the context of the discussion of research designs (below), but in a number of ways they also represent background considerations for some of the issues to be examined. They will be returned to later in the book.

 # Research designs

In this discussion of research designs, five different types will be examined: experimental design; cross-sectional or social survey design; longitudinal design; case study design; and comparative design. Variations on these designs will be examined in their relevant subsections.

Experimental design

True field experiments are rare in business and management research, mainly because of the problems of achieving the requisite level of control when dealing with organizational behaviour. Why, then, bother to introduce experimental designs at all in the context of a book written for business and management researchers? The chief reason, quite aside from the fact that they are sometimes employed, is that a true **experiment** is often used as a yardstick against which non-experimental research is assessed. Experimental research is frequently held up as a touchstone because it engenders considerable confidence in the robustness and trustworthiness of causal findings. In other words, true experiments tend to be very strong in terms of internal validity.

Manipulation

If experiments are so strong in this respect, why then do business researchers not make far greater use of them? The reason is simple: in order to conduct a true experiment, it is necessary to manipulate the independent variable in order to determine whether it does in fact have an influence on the dependent variable. Experimental subjects are likely to be allocated to one of two or more experimental groups, each of which represents different types or levels of the independent variable. It is then possible to establish how far differences between the groups are responsible for variations in the level of the dependent variable. Manipulation, then, entails intervening in a situation to determine which of two or more things happens to subjects. However, the vast majority of independent variables with which business researchers are concerned cannot be manipulated. If we are interested in the effects of gender on work experiences, we cannot manipulate gender so that some people are made male and others female. If we are interested in the effects of variations in the economic environment on organizational performance, we cannot alter share prices or interest rates. As with the huge majority of such variables, the levels of social engineering that would be required are beyond serious contemplation.

Before moving on to a more complete discussion of experimental design, it is important to introduce a basic distinction between the *laboratory experiment* and the *field experiment.* As its name implies, the laboratory experiment takes place in a laboratory or in a contrived setting, whereas field experiments occur in real-life settings, such as in workplaces or retail spaces, as the example in Research in focus 3.5 illustrates. It is experiments of the latter type that are most likely to touch on areas of interest to business and management researchers. However, in business and management research it is more common to find field experiments in which a scenario is employed as a substitute for a real-life setting. Furthermore, and somewhat confusingly, researchers will sometimes refer to their research as a field study. This simply means that the research was conducted in a real-life setting; it need not imply that a field experiment was involved.

Classic experimental design

In what is known as the classical experimental design, two groups are established and this forms the basis for experimental manipulation of the independent variable. The *experimental group*, or *treatment group*, receives the treatment, and it is compared against the *control group*, which does not. The dependent variable is measured before and after the experimental manipulation, so that a before-and-after analysis can be conducted. Moreover, the subjects are assigned randomly to their respective groups. This enables the researcher(s) to feel confident that any difference between the two groups is attributable to manipulation of the independent variable.

In order to capture the essence of this design, the following simple notation is employed:

Obs An **obs**ervation made in relation to the dependent variable; there may well be two or more observations, before (the pre-test) and after (the post-test) the experimental manipulation.

Exp The **exp**erimental treatment (manipulation of the independent variable). **No Exp** refers to the absence of an experimental treatment and represents the experience of the control group.

T The **t**iming of the observations made in relation to the dependent variable.

Thus, the classical experimental design comprises the following elements: random assignment to the experimental and control groups; pre-testing (Obs) of both groups at T_1; manipulation of the experimental treatment so that

the experimental group receives it (Exp) but the control group does not (No Exp); and post-testing (Obs) of the two groups at T_2. The difference between each group's pre- and post-test scores is then computed to establish whether or not Exp has made a difference. See Figure 3.1 for an outline of these elements.

Classic experimental design and validity

The purpose of the control group in a true experiment is to control (in other words, eliminate) the possible effects of rival explanations of a causal finding. We might then be in a position to take the view that the study is internally valid. The presence of a control group and the random assignment of subjects to the experimental and control groups enable us to eliminate rival explanations and eliminate threats to internal validity. These threats include the following:

- *Testing*. This threat refers to the possibility that subjects may become sensitized to the aims of the experiment (see Research in focus 3.8). The presence of a control group, which presumably also experiences the same 'experimenter effect', allows us to discount this possibility if there is no difference between the experimental and control groups.

- *History*. This threat refers to the possibility that events in the experimental environment that are unrelated to manipulation of the independent variable may have caused the changes. If there is no control group, we would be less sure that changes to the independent variable are producing the change. If there is a control group, differences between the control and experimental groups can be more confidently attributed to manipulation of the independent variable.

- *Maturation*. Quite simply, people change, and the ways in which they change may have implications for the dependent variable. Since maturation should affect the control group subjects as well, the control group allows us to discount the possibility that changes would have occurred anyway, with or without manipulation of the independent variable.

- *Selection*. If there are differences between the two groups, which would arise if they had been selected by a non-random process, variations between the experimental and control groups could be attributed to pre-existing differences in their membership. However, if a random process of assignment to the experimental and control groups is employed, this possibility can be discounted.

Figure 3.1

Classical experimental design

T_1		T_2
Obs_1	Exp	Obs_2
Obs_3	No Exp	Obs_4

Research in focus 3.5
An example of a field experiment

Frayne and Geringer (2000) examined the possibility that, if individuals are able to manage themselves more than they do usually, their performance in their jobs will be positively affected. Their reasoning was based on some of the literature on 'self-management', as well as on relevant psychological theory such as social cognitive theory. Their primary hypothesis was expressed as follows: 'This study's primary hypothesis was that skill in self-management is a causal or independent variable that affects employee job performance positively' (2000: 363).

Experimental participants were salespeople working for a large North American insurance company. Those salespeople who had not achieved the company's performance targets were sent a memo inviting them to participate in the study. Staff were informed 'only persons who could commit themselves to four weekly training sessions, each of 2 hours' length and offered during normal work hours, should volunteer for the training program' (2000: 364). Sixty individuals volunteered and were assigned randomly to experimental and control groups. Members of the experimental group received training in self-management over several weeks. Members of the control group did not receive the training but were informed that they would receive it in the future. In fact, a year after the experimental group had begun its training, the control group was then trained. The effectiveness of the training in self-management was assessed using 'reaction, learning, cognitive, and behavioral criteria' (2000: 364). Effectiveness was assessed at 3, 6, 9, and 12 months for both groups. The hypothesis was confirmed in that the experimental group performed much better than the control group at each point on the various effectiveness criteria employed. Further, when the control group was trained after the 12 months had elapsed, it exhibited an increase in its effectiveness comparable to that of the experimental group.

This field experiment is fairly unusual in that it is often difficult for researchers to assign participants randomly to experimental and control groups. Often, field experiments are 'quasi-experiments' (see below)—that is, studies that have some if not many of the features of a real experiment but are lacking in one or possibly more ways. This arises because organizations are unable to surrender sufficient control to researchers to allow **random assignment** because of the ongoing work that has to be attended to. However, field experiments are not without their problems, even when they exhibit the features of a true experiment. As Frayne and Geringer note, it is possible that the members of the experimental and control groups communicated with one another about their experiences, which, if it occurred, might have contaminated the findings.

- *Ambiguity about the direction of causal influence.* The very notion of an independent variable and dependent variable presupposes a direction of causality. However, there may be occasions when the temporal sequence is unclear, so that it is not possible to establish which variable affects the other. The existence of a control group can help to make this clear.

These threats are taken from Campbell (1957) and Cook and Campbell (1979), but not all the threats to internal validity they refer to are included here. The presence of a control group coupled with random assignment allows us to eliminate these threats. As a result, our confidence in the causal finding is greatly enhanced.

Simply because research is deemed to be internally valid does not mean that it is beyond reproach or that questions cannot be raised about it. When a quantitative research strategy has been employed, other criteria can be applied to evaluate a study. In the case of the study by Nielsen et al. (2010), for example (see Research in focus 3.9), there is a potential question of measurement validity. Even though measures of intrinsic job motivation and intrinsic job satisfaction may appear to exhibit a correspondence with manager training—that is, to possess **face validity**—in the sense that they appear to exhibit a correspondence with what they are measuring, we might feel somewhat uneasy about how far increases in job motivation and satisfaction can be regarded as indicative of improvements in training. Does it really measure what it is supposed to measure? The second question relating to measurement validity is whether or not the experimental manipulation really worked. In other words, did the training programme create the conditions for improvements in employee involvement and work satisfaction to be examined?

Secondly, is the research externally valid? Campbell (1957) and Cook and Campbell (1979) identify five major threats to the external validity and hence **generalizability** of an investigation. These can be summarized as follows:

- *Interaction of selection and treatment*. This threat raises the question: to what social and psychological groups can a finding be generalized? Can it be generalized to a wide variety of individuals who might be differentiated by gender, ethnicity, social class, and personality? For instance, many influential studies of leadership, conducted on samples comprising a majority of men, rarely treat gender as a significant variable (Wilson 1995). It is possible that the findings of these studies simply reflect the characteristics of the predominantly male samples and therefore cannot provide a theory of effective leadership that is generalizable across both men and women.

- *Interaction of setting and treatment*. This threat relates to the issue of how confident we can be that the results of a study can be applied to other settings. For example, in the example in Research in focus 3.5, Frayne and Geringer (2000) had a particularly large amount of influence over the experimental arrangements, given that this research took place in a company rather than in a laboratory. The reason for this control over the arrangements may have been that the company had a significant number of salespersons who were not meeting its performance criteria and was therefore keen to find a way to redress the situation. Also, the sales staff themselves may have been keen to redress a situation in which they were perceived to be under-performing. As a result, the setting may have been unusual, and this may have had an influence on the experimental participants' receptivity to the training programme.

- *Interaction of history and treatment*. This raises the question of whether or not the findings can be generalized to the past and to the future. The original Aston studies, for example, were conducted in the early 1960s (see Research in focus 3.6). How confident can we be that these findings would apply today?

- *Interaction effects of pre-testing*. As a result of being pre-tested, subjects in an experiment may become sensitized to the experimental treatment. Consequently, the findings may not be generalizable to groups that have *not* been pre-tested and, of course, in the real world people are rarely tested in this way. The findings may, therefore, be partly determined by the experimental treatment as such and partly by how pre-test sensitization has influenced the way in which subjects respond to the treatment. This may have occurred in Nielsen et al.'s research (see Research in focus 3.9).

- *Reactive effects of experimental arrangements*. People are frequently, if not invariably, aware that they are participating in an experiment. Their awareness may influence how they respond to the experimental treatment and therefore affect the generalizability of the findings. This was a major finding of the Hawthorne studies (see Research in focus 3.8).

Thirdly, are the findings ecologically valid? The fact that the research is a field experiment rather than a laboratory experiment seems to enhance this aspect of the Nielsen et al. (2010) research. The fact that Nielsen et al. did not randomly assign their subjects to the control and treatment groups and that the memberships of the two groups are therefore of unknown equivalence might be considered a source of concerns about ecological validity, though this is an area in which much quantitative research is likely to be implicated.

A fourth issue that we might want to raise relates to the question of replicability. For example, Pugh et al. (1968) lay out very clearly the procedures and measures that were employed in the Aston studies, and these have been used by several other researchers seeking to carry out replication of this research, both in business and non-business organizations, including trade unions, churches, schools, and public bureaucracies. Consequently, the research is replicable. However, analysis of the same data by Aldrich (1972) and Hilton (1972) using a different statistical technique showed other possible patterns of relationships between the variables in the Aston studies (see Research in focus 3.6). This failure to replicate casts doubt on the external validity of the original research and suggests that the first three threats referred to above may have played an important part in the differences between the two sets of results.

The laboratory experiment

Many experiments in such fields as social psychology are laboratory experiments rather than field experiments. Some of the most well known of these, such as Milgram's (1963) electric-shock experiments or Zimbardo's prison experiments (see Research in focus 6.3), have informed our understanding of how individuals and groups behave within modern work organizations. One of the main advantages of laboratory experiments is that the researcher has far greater influence over the experimental arrangements. For example, it is easier to randomly assign subjects to different experimental conditions in the laboratory than to do the same in an ongoing, real-life organization. The researcher therefore has a higher level of control, and this is likely to enhance the internal validity of the study. It is also likely that laboratory experiments will be more straightforward to replicate, because they are less bound up with a certain milieu that is difficult to reproduce.

However, laboratory experiments such as the one described in Research in focus 3.7 suffer from a number of limitations. First, the external validity is likely to be difficult to establish. There is the interaction of setting and treatment, since the setting of the laboratory is likely to be unrelated to real-world experiences and contexts. Also, there is likely to be an interaction of selection and treatment. In the case of the experiment by Krause et al. (2014; see Research in focus 3.7), there are a number of difficulties. The subjects were students, who are unlikely to be representative of the general population, so that their responses to the experimental treatment may be distinctive. Also, they were volunteers, and it is known that volunteers differ from non-volunteers (Rosnow and Rosenthal 1997: Chapter 5). There will have been no problem of interaction effects of pre-testing, because, as in many experiments, there was no pre-testing. However, it is quite possible that reactive effects may have been set in motion by the experimental arrangements. As Research in focus 3.8 illustrates, reactive effects associated with an experiment can have a profound effect on the outcomes of the research. Secondly, the ecological validity of the study may be poor because we do not know how well the findings are applicable to the real world and everyday life. However, while the study may lack what is often called mundane realism, it may nonetheless enjoy experimental realism (Aronson and Carlsmith 1968). The latter means that the subjects are very involved in the experiment and take it very seriously.

Quasi-experiments

A number of writers have drawn attention to the possibilities offered by quasi-experiments—that is, studies that have certain characteristics of experimental designs but that do not fulfil all the internal validity requirements.

Research in focus 3.6
Establishing the direction of causality

The Aston studies (Pugh et al. 1968) consisted of a highly influential programme of research that derived from an initial survey study of the correlates of organizational structure carried out in forty-six West Midlands organizations during the early 1960s. While the study was guided by the hypothesis that characteristics of an organization's structure would be related to characteristics of its context, there was little in the way of detailed hypothesis formulation on exactly how these characteristics were related. The view taken by the researchers was that, although there was a considerable amount of case study research describing the functioning of organizations, very little in the way of systematic comparison had been attempted. Moreover, generalization was made difficult because it was not possible to assess the representativeness of a particular case study. The strategy developed by the Aston researchers was therefore 'to carry out comparative surveys across organizations to establish meaningful stable relationships which would enable the particular idiosyncracies of case studies to be placed into perspective' (Pugh 1998: p. xv). One of the key assumptions on which the research was based was that 'the nature, structure and functioning of an organization will be influenced by its objectives, context and environment, all of which must be taken into account' (1998: p. xv). The researchers concluded that organizational size and production technology were important potential correlates of organization structure, though their findings implied that size, rather than technology, was the more critical factor. This finding contradicted other studies conducted at the time, such as Woodward (1965), which suggested that technology was a more important causal factor. However, in later analysis of the same data using a different statistical technique, Aldrich (1972) and Hilton (1972) were able to show other possible patterns of relationships between the three variables, which suggested that technology was an important cause of organizational structure, which in turn affected size. From this example we can see some of the difficulties in identifying the causal relationship between variables using survey data.

Research in focus 3.7
A laboratory experiment on voting on CEO pay

Krause, Whitler, and Semadeni (2014) were interested in the factors that influence the way shareholders vote on the pay of their chief executive officers (CEOs). In particular, they were interested in the relative impacts of CEOs' current levels of pay and of firm performance on shareholders' propensity to vote in favour of an increase. They formulated hypotheses concerning the impacts of these variables on voting. MBA students were randomly assigned to one of four scenarios which simulated notices to shareholders about the opportunity to vote on CEO pay. The scenarios were identical but varied in terms of information supplied about the two variables of interest— CEOs' current levels of pay and firm performance. Firm performance was described as either strong or weak. For scenarios in which firm performance was strong, the CEO's pay was either described as currently high or as low. Thus, there were four groups to which students had been randomly assigned. The students were told to imagine that they were shareholders of a Fortune 500 company and were being given the opportunity to vote on pay. CEO pay was found to have no impact on propensity to vote for an increase, whereas poor performance by the firm was found to have an adverse effect on 'shareholders'' inclination to vote for an increase. However, Krause et al. also showed that whether an increase in a CEO's pay is approved is highly affected by firm performance.

Research in focus 3.8
The Hawthorne effect

The effect of the experimenter, or the fact of being studied, on the subject is commonly referred to as the 'Hawthorne effect'. This phrase was coined as a result of the series of interlinked investigations carried out during the late 1920s and early 1930s at the Hawthorne works of the Western Electric Company in the USA (Roethlisberger and Dickson 1939).

One phase of the investigations entailed a group of women carrying out manual tasks being taken away from their department and working in a separate room. The aim of the study was to discover how changes in the number and duration of rest pauses, in length of the working day, in heating and lighting, and so on affected productivity, as this quotation from the study illustrates:

> First, the amount of light was increased regularly day by day, and the girls were asked each day how they liked the change. As the light was increased, the girls told the investigator that they liked the brighter lights. Then for a day or two the investigator allowed the girls to see the electrician come and change the light bulbs. In reality, the electrician merely took out bulbs of a given size and inserted bulbs of the same size, without in any way changing the amount of light. The girls, thinking that the light was still being 'stepped up' day by day, commented favourably about the increase of light. After a few days of this, the experimenter started to decrease the intensity of light, keeping the girls informed of the change and soliciting their reaction. After a period of this day-by-day decrease in illumination, he again allowed the girls to see the electrician change the bulbs without really changing the intensity of illumination. Again the girls gave answers that were to be expected, in that they said the 'lesser' light was not so pleasant to work under as the brighter light. Their production did not change at any stage of the experiment.
>
> (Roethlisberger and Dickson 1939: 17)

However, as the study went on, it was found that productivity *did* increase, irrespective of the changes that were being introduced. Eventually it was recognized that the women were responding to the positive attention and special treatment they were receiving. The researchers concluded that increases in worker productivity were due not to any changes in the conditions of the working environment, but instead to the favourable circumstances that the experimental arrangements had produced. While this finding did much to stimulate the 'human-relations' approach to the study of work, by pointing to the potential advantages of providing people with psycho-social support in the workplace, it also neatly demonstrates that experimental arrangements may induce an effect—a '**reactive effect**'—over and above the intentions of the investigator. This has been referred to, more generally, as the 'experimenter effect', where the researcher creates a bias in the data through participation in the research situation or by inadvertently communicating his or her preferred research outcome.

The Hawthorne effect also draws attention to the way in which researchers themselves represent 'an audience to the actors being studied', and it is therefore likely that the researcher's activities will have an influence on the research setting. This draws attention to the fact that, 'while the researcher attends to the study of other persons and their other activities, these other persons attend to the study of the researcher and his activities' (Van Maanen and Kolb 1985: 6). The results of fieldwork thus depend in part upon the outcomes of the unofficial study that the observed make of the physical nature and psychological character of the observer, as well as the other way around.

Research in focus 3.9
A quasi-experiment

Nielsen, Randall, and Christensen (2010) were interested in whether providing managers with training during the change process when a team working intervention is being introduced might enhance the impact of the intervention. To this end, the researchers employed a quasi-experiment in the course of which they employed a mixed methods approach whereby they collected qualitative as well as quantitative data. The research was driven by hypotheses, such as:

> *Hypothesis 1*: Implementing teams will bring about improvements in employees' perceptions of task design (increased team interdependence and autonomy) and team processes (increased motivation and improved social climate). Because of the change in the role of the manager brought about by the change we predict that employees will also rate their manager as exerting more transformational leadership behaviours. In addition, organizational and individual outcome measures will improve (for example, perceptions of increased team effectiveness, employee involvement and job satisfaction).
>
> (Nielsen et al. 2010: 1721).

The experiment was conducted at two elderly care centres in Denmark. The centres are described by the authors as 'almost identical'. In both centres employees experienced a teamwork intervention, but in one of them managers were trained in the course of the change and were therefore treated as the intervention group; in the other they were not trained and that group was therefore treated as a comparison or control group. The two groups were compared in terms of how far they changed over time (18 months) for a wide range of dependent variables that would allow the researchers' hypotheses to be tested. Nielsen et al. found that the effects of the introduction of teamwork on most of the dependent variables was limited when it was not accompanied by manager training. Overall, they found that teamwork accompanied by training made a difference for several variables, notably employee involvement and job satisfaction. Contrary to expectations, the control group fared better than the intervention group in respect of one variable (interdependency).

This study uses a quasi-experimental design, in which a control group is compared to a treatment group. It bears some of the hallmarks of a classic experimental design, but there is no random assignment; participants were assigned to the groups according to their work location. Subjects were not randomly assigned to the two groups because of practical constraints. While the two centres are viewed as nearly identical, the memberships of the two groups are of unknown equivalence, so that we cannot be certain that the findings associated with the comparison of the groups are not due to differences between them. On the other hand, the fact that this is a real-world study makes it of considerable interest, especially in view of the known difficulty of conducting experiments with random assignment in the field. Further, the study collected qualitative data which allowed the researchers to gather a wide range of additional information; this allowed them to make inferences about such issues as the mechanisms that lay behind the changes that teamwork and the training intervention engendered.

A large number of types of quasi-experiment have been identified (Cook and Campbell 1979), and it is not proposed to cover them here. A particularly interesting form of quasi-experiment occurs in the case of 'natural experiments'. These are 'experiments' in the sense of entailing manipulation of a social setting, but as part of a naturally occurring attempt to alter social arrangements. In such circumstances, random assignment to experimental and control groups is invariably not possible. An example is provided in Research in focus 3.9.

The absence of random assignment in the quasi-experiment described in Research in focus 3.9 casts a certain amount of doubt on the study's internal validity, since the groups may not have been equivalent. However, the results of such studies are still compelling, because they are not artificial interventions in social life and because their ecological validity is therefore very strong. Hofstede's study of cultural differences (discussed in Chapter 2) falls into this category, because the research design enabled some degree of control to be maintained over variables—all employees belonged to the same multinational organization, even though the research took place in a natural setting. This meant that corporate culture constituted the dependent variable and differences in national cultures and mentalities of employees constituted independent variables, where Hofstede anticipated the main differences would be seen. In addition, some requirements of internal validity were fulfilled through replication of the questionnaire survey on two separate occasions, once in 1967–9 and again in 1971–3.

Most writers on quasi-experimentation discount experiments in which there is no control group or basis for comparison (Cook and Campbell 1979). However, some experiments do involve manipulation of the independent variable within experimental groups without a control group as the basis for comparison. For example, in an experimental study of electronic brainstorming, Gallupe et al. (1992) wanted to test the effect of group size on performance. The researchers wanted to find out if electronic brainstorming could more effectively support the generation of ideas within large groups (six and twelve persons), as well as in small groups (two, four, and six persons)—unlike the traditional, verbal brainstorming technique. In this study, both the large and the small groups received the experimental treatment—that is, electronic brainstorming—and both received the control treatment—that is, verbal brainstorming. It was anticipated that large and small groups would show similar levels of productivity in the verbal brainstorming experiment, but that large groups would outperform small groups in the electronic brainstorming experiment. Because there was no control

group, where no manipulation of the independent variable occurs, this study cannot be seen as a classic experimental design. However, the internal validity of the findings was reinforced by the fact that both the experiments were also carried out on small groups, where it was found that electronic brainstorming made no difference to group performance. Comparison between large and small experimental groups helped to reduce threats to the internal validity of the findings. The study thus exhibits some of the characteristics of an experimental design, even though no control group was used.

Finally, experimental designs, and more especially quasi-experimental designs, have been particularly prominent in **evaluation research** studies (see Key concept 3.10 and Research in focus 3.11).

Possibly because of the various difficulties with quasi-experiments that have been noted in this section, Grant and Wall (2009) have noted that they are used relatively infrequently in organizational research. However, they also note that there may be ways of addressing some of the concerns regarding internal validity that beset quasi-experiments. For example, they suggest that it may be possible to strengthen causal inferences when it is not possible to assign experimental and control group participants randomly and the researcher has limited or no control over the experimental manipulation. This might be done by seeking out further information that will help to discount some of the rival interpretations of a causal link that arise from the lack of a true experimental design. However, it is unlikely that such a view will find favour among writers who adopt a purist view about the need for experimental designs in order to generate robust causal inferences.

Significance of experimental design

As was stated at the outset, the chief reason for introducing the experiment as a research design is because it is frequently considered to be a yardstick against which quantitative research is judged. This occurs largely because of the fact that a true experiment will allow doubts about internal validity to be allayed and reflects the considerable emphasis placed on the determination of causality in quantitative research. As we will see in the next section, cross-sectional designs of the kind associated with social survey research are frequently regarded as limited, because of the problems of unambiguously imputing causality when using such designs.

Logic of comparison

However, before exploring such issues, it is important to draw attention to an important general lesson that an

Key concept 3.10
What is evaluation research?

Evaluation research, as its name implies, is concerned with the evaluation of such occurrences as organizational programmes or interventions. The essential question that is typically asked by such studies is: has the intervention (for example, a new policy initiative or an organizational change) achieved its anticipated goals? A typical design may have one group that is exposed to the treatment—that is, the new initiative—and a control group that is not. Since it is often not feasible or ethical to randomly assign research participants to the two groups, such studies are usually quasi-experimental. The use of the principles of experimental design is fairly entrenched in evaluation research, but other approaches have emerged in recent years. Approaches to evaluation based on qualitative research have also been developed. While there are differences of opinion about how qualitative evaluation should be carried out, the different views typically coalesce around a recognition of the importance of an in-depth understanding of the context in which an intervention occurs and the diverse viewpoints of the stakeholders (Greene 1994, 2000). Pawson and Tilley (1997) advocate an approach that draws on the principles of critical realism (see Key concept 2.8) and that sees the outcome of an intervention as the result of generative mechanisms and the contexts of those mechanisms. A focus of the former element entails examining the causal factors that inhibit or promote change when an intervention occurs. Pawson and Tilley's approach is supportive of the use of both quantitative and qualitative research methods.

examination of experiments teaches us. A central feature of any experiment is the fact that it entails a *comparison*: at the very least it entails a comparison of results obtained by an experimental group with those engendered by a control group. In the case of the experiment in Research in focus 3.7, there is no control group: the research entails a comparison of the effects of CEO pay and firm performance. The advantage of carrying out any kind of comparison like this is that we understand the phenomenon that we are interested in better when we compare it with something else that is similar to it. The case for arguing that charismatic leadership is an effective, performance-enhancing form of leadership is much more persuasive when we view it in relation to other forms of leadership. Thus, while the specific considerations concerning experimental design are typically associated with quantitative research, the potential of comparison in business research represents a more general lesson that transcends matters of both research strategy and research design. In other words, while the experimental design is typically associated with a quantitative research strategy, the specific logic of comparison provides lessons of broad applicability and relevance. This issue is given more specific attention below in the section on comparative design.

Cross-sectional design

The **cross-sectional design** is often called a social survey design, but the idea of the social survey is so closely connected in most people's minds with questionnaires

and structured interviewing that the more generic-sounding term *cross-sectional design* is preferable. While the research methods associated with social surveys are certainly frequently employed within the context of cross-sectional research, so too are many other research methods, including **structured observation, content analysis,** official statistics, and diaries. All these research methods will be covered in later chapters, but in the meantime the basic structure of the cross-sectional design will be outlined.

The cross-sectional design is defined in Key concept 3.12. A number of elements of this definition have been emphasized.

- *More than one case*. Researchers employing a cross-sectional design are interested in variation. That variation can be in respect of people, organizations, nation states, or whatever. Variation can be established only when more than one case is being examined. Usually, researchers employing this design will select a lot more than two cases for a variety of reasons: they are more likely to encounter variation in all the variables in which they are interested; they can make finer distinctions between cases; and the requirements of sampling procedure are likely to necessitate larger numbers (see Chapter 8).

- *At a single point in time*. In cross-sectional research design, data on the variables of interest are collected more or less simultaneously. When an individual completes a questionnaire, which may contain fifty or more

Research in focus 3.11
An evaluation study of role redesign

The purpose of research conducted by Hyde et al. (2006) was to examine the introduction of role redesign in the NHS (the UK's National Health Service) under the Changing Workforce Programme (CWP), to highlight implications for employment relations, and to identify characteristics of successful CWP initiatives. This was a qualitative, rather than an experimental, evaluation that was based on secondary data analysis, semi-structured interviews, and observations. The two-phase study was carried out by the research team in 2003 and funded by the Department of Health. The first phase of the evaluation focused on the thirteen pilot sites where the CWP had been introduced and 'involved documentary review of reports relating to this initiative. In addition, individual interviews were conducted with participants from each of the pilot sites' (2006: 700); in total thirty interviews were conducted across the thirteen sites. The second phase involved a case study design 'to study the process of role redesign and identify examples of good practice' (2006: 700). Four of the thirteen pilot sites were selected as case studies 'to illustrate varying degrees of progress in relation to individual roles; variation in type of redesign attempted; different types of partnership arrangement; differing means of involving those receiving the service; and relevance to the wider NHS and other care sectors' (2006: 700). The fifth case study involved the CWP team itself, to gain an overview of the development of the programme. A further sixty-four interviews were carried out in the five case study sites. In addition, the research team attended meetings and conducted role observations. This approach to evaluation enabled the researchers to 'take account of the heterogeneity and complexity of CWP interventions' (2006: 703) in different health service contexts.

Key concept 3.12
What is a cross-sectional research design?

A cross-sectional design entails the collection of data on more than one case (usually quite a lot more than one) and at a single point in time in order to collect a body of quantitative or quantifiable data in connection with two or more variables (usually many more than two), which are then examined to detect patterns of association.

variables, the answers are supplied at essentially the same time. This contrasts with an experimental design. Thus, in the classical experimental design, someone in the experimental group is pre-tested, then exposed to the experimental treatment, and then post-tested. Days, weeks, months, or even years may separate the different phases.

- *Quantitative or quantifiable data.* In order to establish variation between cases (and then to examine associations between variables—see next point), it is necessary to have a systematic and standardized method for gauging variation. One of the most important advantages of quantification is that it provides the researcher with a consistent benchmark. The advantages of quantification and of measurement will be addressed in greater detail in Chapter 7.

- *Patterns of association.* With a cross-sectional design it is possible to examine only relationships between variables. There is no time ordering to the variables, because the data on them are collected more or less simultaneously, and the researcher does not (invariably because he or she cannot) manipulate any of the variables. This creates the problem referred to in Research in focus 3.6 in establishing the direction of causal influence. If the researcher discovers a relationship between two variables, he or she cannot be certain whether this denotes a causal relationship, because the features of an experimental design are not present. All that can be said is that the variables are related. This is not to say that it is not possible to draw causal inferences from research based on a cross-sectional design. As will be shown in Chapter 15, there are a number of ways in which the researcher is able to draw certain inferences about causality, but these inferences rarely have the credibility of causal findings deriving from an experimental design. As a result, cross-sectional research invariably lacks the internal validity that one finds in most experimental research.

In this book, the term 'survey' will be reserved for research that employs a cross-sectional research design and in which data are collected by questionnaire or by structured interview (see Key concept 3.13). This will allow us to retain the conventional understanding of what a survey is while recognizing that the cross-sectional research design has a wider relevance—that is, one that is not necessarily associated with the collection of data by questionnaire or by structured interview. An example of a survey that is widely used and cited in the study of UK human resource management and industrial relations is given in Research in focus 3.14.

Key concept 3.13
What is survey research? *cosssʃop*

Survey research comprises a cross-sectional design in relation to which data are collected predominantly by questionnaire or by structured interview on more than one case (usually quite a lot more than one) and at a single point in time in order to collect a body of quantitative or quantifiable data in connection with two or more variables (usually many more than two), which are then examined to detect patterns of association.

Research in focus 3.14
An example of survey research: the Workplace Employment Relations Survey

The 2011 Workplace Employment Relations Survey (WERS) was the sixth in a series started in 1980 looking at changing employment relations policies and practices in Britain. The survey population is all workplaces in Britain that have five or more employees. The main objectives of the survey are to:

- map British employment relations over time;
- inform policy and practice and stimulate debate;
- provide a comprehensive and statistically reliable dataset on British workplace employment relations for public use.

2011 WERS contains data from a representative sample of 2680 British workplaces collected from:

- 2680 workplace managers responsible for employment relations and personnel;
- 1002 worker representatives;
- 2981 employees.

The main unit of analysis in WERS is the 'workplace', which is defined as comprising 'the activities of a single employer at a single set of premises' (van Wanrooy et al. 2013: 5). This definition means that a local branch of a bank is classed as a workplace and the head office of the bank as another, even though they legally form part of the same organization. The cross-section survey contains the following elements:

- *Employee profile questionnaire*—self-completion questionnaire given to the manager respondent prior to the interview;

(continued)

- *Management questionnaire*—face-to-face structured interview with the most senior manager responsible for staff and employment relations at the workplace;
- *Financial performance questionnaire*—self-completion questionnaire distributed after the management interview;
- *Worker representative questionnaire* –structured interview conducted either face-to-face or by telephone with the most senior representative of the largest recognized (or if none present, non-recognized) trade-union and most senior non-union representative at the workplace;
- *Survey of employees questionnaire*—self-completion questionnaire distributed to up to 25 randomly selected employees in the workplace.

The overall workplace response rates to WERS 2011 (see Table 10.1) were lower than in the 2004 study; the researchers attribute this to the difficult economic climate and the long-term decline in response to business surveys in recent years.

These data enable researchers to build up a picture of employee relations that links the view of employees with those of managers and workers in the same workplace. A key strength of the survey is thus derived from its representation of multiple interests in the workplace, rather than just relying on the account given by a senior manager. One of the primary interests of the researchers has been to track changes over time. The 2011 workplace sample therefore comprised:

a) a cross-section of workplaces randomly selected from the UK's Inter-Departmental Business Register, which contains details of all private and publicly owned 'going concerns' operating in the UK. This sample is stratified by employment size and by industrial activity;

b) a panel of workplaces that had been surveyed in 2004 and met the criteria to be surveyed again in 2011.

The panel survey data for 989 workplaces means that responses from 2011 can be directly compared with responses 'collected from the same workplace in 2004 in order to assess the extent to which practices, behaviours and experiences have changed' (van Wanrooy et al. 2013: 7). In the 2011 survey, the cross-sectional sample and the panel sample were integrated, enabling them to be analysed together and making the overall cross-sectional sample larger.

Most of the survey data is made available in an anonymous form to researchers via the UK Data Service (see Chapter 14 for information on how to access this resource).

Reliability, replicability, and validity

How does cross-sectional research measure up in terms of the previously outlined criteria for evaluating quantitative research: reliability, replicability, and validity?

- The issues of *reliability* and *measurement validity* are primarily matters relating to the quality of the measures that are employed to tap the concepts in which the researcher is interested, rather than matters to do with a research design. In order to address questions of the quality of measures, some of the issues outlined in Chapter 7 would have to be considered.

- *Replicability* is likely to be present in most cross-sectional research to the degree that the researcher spells out procedures for selecting respondents; designing measures of concepts; administration of research instruments (such as structured interview or self-completion questionnaire); and the analysis of data. Most quantitative research based on cross-sectional research designs specifies such procedures to a large degree.

- *Internal validity* is typically weak. As has just been suggested above, it is difficult to establish causal direction from the resulting data. Cross-sectional research designs produce associations rather than findings from which causal inferences can be unambiguously made. However, procedures for making causal inferences from cross-sectional data will be referred to in Chapter 15, though most researchers feel that the resulting causal findings rarely have the internal validity of those deriving from experimental designs.

- *External validity* is strong when, as in the case of the Workplace Employee Relations Survey (see Research in focus 3.14), the sample from which data are collected has been randomly selected. When non-random methods of sampling are employed, external validity becomes questionable. Sampling issues will be specifically addressed in Chapter 8.

- Since much cross-sectional research makes a great deal of use of research instruments, such as self-completion questionnaires and structured observation schedules, *ecological validity* may be jeopardized because these very instruments disrupt the 'natural habitat', as Cicourel (1982) put it.

Non-manipulable variables

As was noted at the beginning of the section on experimental design, in much, if not most, business research it is not possible to manipulate the variables in which we are interested. This is why most quantitative business research employs a cross-sectional research design rather than an experimental one. Moreover, some of the variables in which social scientists are interested, and which are often viewed as potentially significant independent variables, simply cannot be manipulated, other than by extreme measures. At the individual level of analysis, age, ethnicity, gender, and social background are 'givens' that are not really amenable to the kind of manipulation that is necessary for a true experimental design. To a lesser extent this also applies at the organizational level of analysis to variables such as size, structure, technology, and culture. On the other hand, the very fact that we can regard certain variables as givens provides us with a clue as to how we can make causal inferences in cross-sectional

research. Many of the variables in which we are interested can be *assumed* to be temporally prior to other variables. For example, we can assume that, if we find a relationship between gender and entrepreneurial behaviour, then the former is more likely to be the independent variable, because it is likely to be temporally prior to entrepreneurial behaviour. In other words, while we may not be able to manipulate the gender variable, we can draw some causal inferences from cross-sectional data.

Structure of the cross-sectional design

The cross-sectional research design is not easy to depict in terms of the notation previously introduced, but Figure 3.2 captures its main features, except that in this case Obs simply represents an observation made in relation to a variable.

Figure 3.2 implies that a cross-sectional design comprises the collection of data on a series of variables (Obs_1 Obs_2 Obs_3 Obs_4 Obs_5 . . . Obs_n) at a single point in time, T_1. The effect is to create what Marsh (1982) referred to as a 'rectangle' of data that comprises variables Obs_1 to Obs_n and cases $Case_1$ to $Case_n$, as in Figure 3.3. For each case (which may be a person, household, city, nation, etc.) data are available for each of the variables, Obs_1 to Obs_n, all of which will have been collected at T_1. Each **cell** in the matrix will have data in it.

Cross-sectional design and research strategy

This discussion of the cross-sectional design has placed it firmly in the context of quantitative research. Also, the evaluation of the design has drawn on criteria associated

Figure 3.2

A cross-sectional design

T_1
Obs_1
Obs_2
Obs_3
Obs_4
Obs_5
. . .
Obs_n

Figure 3.3

The data rectangle in cross-sectional research

	Obs_1	Obs_2	Obs_3	Obs_4	. . .	Obs_n
$Case_1$						
$Case_2$						
$Case_3$						
$Case_4$						
$Case_5$						
. . .						
$Case_n$						

with the quantitative research strategy. It should be noted, however, that qualitative research often entails a form of cross-sectional design. A fairly typical form of such research is when the researcher employs unstructured interviewing or semi-structured interviewing with a number of people. Research in focus 3.14 provides an illustration of such a study.

While not typical of the qualitative research tradition, the study described in Research in focus 3.15 bears some research design similarities to cross-sectional studies within a predominantly quantitative research tradition, such as the WERS (see Research in focus 3.14), while retaining some research design features more typical of qualitative studies. The research was not directly preoccupied with such criteria of quantitative research as internal and external validity, replicability, measurement validity, and so on, but it is clear that the researchers took considerable care to ensure the representativeness of their sample of managers in relation to the overall **population**. In fact, it could be argued that the use of interviews in conjunction with self-completion questionnaires makes the study more ecologically valid than research that just uses more formal instruments of data collection. It is common within business and management research to see such a *triangulated* approach, where attempts are made to cancel out the limitations of one method by the use of another in order to cross-check the findings. Hence, cross-sectional studies in business and management tend not to be so clearly divided into those that use either quantitative or qualitative methods.

Longitudinal design(s)

The longitudinal design represents a distinct form of research design that is typically used to map change in business and management research. Pettigrew (1990) has emphasized the importance of longitudinal study in understanding organizations as a way of providing data on the mechanisms and processes through which changes are created. Such a 'contextualist' research design involves drawing on 'phenomena at vertical and horizontal levels of analysis and the interconnections between those levels through time' (1990: 269). However, partly because of the time and cost involved, longitudinal design is relatively little used in business and management research. In the form in which it is typically found, it is usually an extension of social survey research based on self-completion questionnaire or structured interview research within a cross-sectional

design. Consequently, in terms of reliability, replication, and validity, the longitudinal design is little different from cross-sectional research. However, a longitudinal design can allow some insight into the time order of variables and therefore may be more able to allow causal inferences to be made. This was one of the aims of the WERS series (see Research in focus 3.14).

With a longitudinal design, a sample is surveyed and is then surveyed again on at least one further occasion. It is common to distinguish two types of longitudinal design: the *panel study* and the *cohort study*. With the former type, a sample, often a randomly selected national one, is the focus of data collection on at least two (and often more) occasions. Data may be collected from different types of case within a panel study framework: individuals, organizations, and so on. An illustration of this kind of study is that incorporated into the 2011 WERS (see Research in focus 3.14).

The cohort study selects either an entire cohort of people or a randomly selected sample of them as the focus of data collection. The cohort is made up of people who share a certain characteristic, such as all being born in the same week, or having a certain experience, such as being unemployed or getting married on a certain day or in the same week. However, this design is rarely used in business and management research.

Panel and cohort studies share similar features. They have a similar design structure: Figure 3.4 portrays this structure and implies that data are collected in at least two waves on the same variables on the same people or organizations. Both panel and cohort studies are concerned with illuminating social change and improving

Figure 3.4

The longitudinal design

T_1	$\cdots$	T_n
Obs_1		Obs_1
Obs_2		Obs_2
Obs_3		Obs_3
Obs_4		Obs_4
Obs_5		Obs_5
$\cdots$		$\cdots$
Obs_n		Obs_n

Research in focus 3.15
A representative sample?

Scase and Goffee (1989) conducted a survey of 374 managers employed in six large organizations—four of which were privately owned and two of which were in the public sector. A number of issues were taken into account in order to ensure that the sample was representative of a wider population.

1. The sample of 323 men and 51 women chosen for the questionnaire survey was designed to reflect gender proportions within the wider UK management population.
2. The researchers attempted to achieve a broad spread of ages within their sample, to reflect the relative proportions of male and female managers in each group.
3. They also sought to reflect labour market patterns and functional groupings—for example, by including more women in the sample who were engaged in personnel management, training, and industrial relations.
4. They included more men in senior and middle-level management positions to reflect the fact that women are under-represented in these positions.
5. Finally, the sample was selected to reflect patterns of employment, levels of education, salary levels, and marital status broadly representative of patterns in the wider population.

From the questionnaire survey, a smaller representative group of 80 men and women was selected for in-depth interviews. However, Scase and Goffee make no claim for the statistical representativeness of their sample. Instead they suggest that their findings can be 'regarded as indicative of broader trends . . . affecting the work, careers and personal experiences of men and women managers during the closing decades of the twentieth century' (1989: 197).

the understanding of causal influences over time. The latter means that longitudinal designs are somewhat better able to deal with the problem of ambiguity about the direction of causal influence that plagues cross-sectional designs. Because certain potentially independent variables can be identified at T_1, the researcher is in a better position to infer that purported effects that are identified at T_2 or later have occurred *after* the independent variables. This does not deal with the entire problem about the ambiguity of causal influence, but it at least addresses the problem of knowing which variable came first. In all other respects, the points made above about cross-sectional designs are the same as those for longitudinal designs.

Panel and cohort studies share similar problems. First, there is the problem of sample attrition through employee job changes, companies going out of business, and so on, and through subjects choosing to withdraw at later stages of the research. The first problem with attrition is largely that those who leave the study may differ in some important respects from those who remain, so that the latter do not form a representative group. Secondly, there are few guidelines as to when is the best juncture to conduct further waves of data collection. Thirdly, it is often suggested that many longitudinal studies are poorly thought out and that they result in

the collection of large amounts of data with little apparent planning. Fourthly, there is evidence that a *panel conditioning* effect can occur whereby continued participation in a longitudinal study affects how respondents behave.

Case study design

The basic case study entails the detailed and intensive analysis of a single case. As Stake (1995) observes, case study research is concerned with the complexity and particular nature of the case in question. The case study approach is a very popular and widely used research design in business research (Eisenhardt and Graebner 2007), and some of the best-known studies in business and management research are based on this design. A case can be:

- *a single organization*, such as Pettigrew's (1985; see Research in focus 3.16) research at Imperial Chemical Industries (ICI), Joanne Martin's (1992) study of organizational culture at 'OzCo', a high-technology industry company based in California, or Born's (2004) study of managerialism in the BBC;

- *a single location*, such as a factory, production site, or office building—for example, Pollert's (1981; see Research in focus 19.12) research in a tobacco factory,

Linstead's (1985) study of humour in a bakery, or Milk-man's (1997) investigation of an automobile assembly plant (see Chapter 20);

- *a person*, as in Marshall's (1995; see Key concept 17.5) study of women managers, where each woman constitutes a separate case—such studies are characterized as using the life history or biographical approach; or

- *a single event*, such as the NASA space shuttle *Challenger* disaster in 1986 (Vaughan 1990; see Chapter 23) or the events surrounding a pipeline accident in Canada (Gephart 1993; see Research in focus 23.4).

What is a case?

The most common use of the term associates the case study with a geographical location, such as a workplace or organization. What distinguishes a case study from other research designs is the focus on a bounded situation or system, an entity with a purpose and functioning parts. The emphasis tends to be upon intensive examination of the setting. There is a tendency to associate case studies with qualitative research, but such an identification is not appropriate. It is certainly true that exponents of the case study design often favour qualitative methods, such as participant observation and unstructured interviewing, because these methods are viewed as particularly helpful in the generation of an intensive, detailed examination of a case. Knights and McCabe (1997) suggest that the case study provides a vehicle through which several qualitative methods can be combined, thereby avoiding too great a reliance on one single approach. In their study of quality management in a UK retail bank, they were able to combine participant observation with semi-structured interviewing and documentary data collection of company reports, Total Quality Management (TQM) guides, and newsletters. They suggest that the findings from the case study can be used to identify insights into why so many quality management programmes have failed. However, case studies are frequently sites for the employment of both quantitative and qualitative research, an approach that will receive attention in Chapter 27. Indeed, within business research the dominance of positivism has meant that the way that case studies are conducted has been heavily influenced by this epistemological tradition. For example, Lee (1999) reports that qualitative research that is published in American journals tends to cite the work of Yin (1984), who adopts a relatively narrow view of case study research (Lee, Collier, and

Cullen 2007) (see Thinking deeply 3.17). In some instances, when an investigation is based exclusively upon quantitative research, it can be difficult to determine whether it is better described as a case study or as a cross-sectional research design. The same point can often be made about case studies based upon qualitative research.

With a case study, the case is an object of interest in its own right, and the researcher aims to provide an in-depth elucidation of it. Unless a distinction of this or some other kind is drawn, it becomes impossible to distinguish the case study as a special research design, because almost any kind of research can be construed as a case study. However, it also needs to be appreciated that when specific research illustrations are examined they can exhibit features of more than one research design. However, for some case study research, cases are selected in order to represent a population, and in such instances more formal sampling is required. What distinguishes a case study is that the researcher is usually concerned to elucidate the unique features of the case. This is known as an *idiographic* approach. Research designs such as the cross-sectional design are known as *nomothetic* in that they are concerned with generating statements that apply regardless of time and place.

Stake (1995) suggests that the selection of cases should be based first and foremost on the anticipation of the opportunity to learn. Researchers should, therefore, choose cases where they expect learning will be greatest. He distinguishes between three different types of case study. Intrinsic case studies are undertaken primarily to gain insight into the particularities of a situation, rather than to gain insight into other cases or generic issues. Instrumental case studies are those that focus on using the case as a means of understanding a broader issue or allowing generalizations to be challenged. Finally, there is the category of multiple or collective case studies that are undertaken jointly to explore a general phenomenon. Stake (2005) notes, however, that the boundaries between these three types of case study are often blurred.

With experimental and cross-sectional designs, the typical orientation to the relationship between theory and research is a deductive one. The research design and the collection of data are guided by specific research questions that derive from theoretical concerns. However, when a qualitative research strategy is employed within a cross-sectional design, the approach tends to be inductive. In other words, whether a cross-sectional design is inductive or deductive tends to be affected by

Research in focus 3.16
A longitudinal case study of ICI

Pettigrew (1985) conducted research into the use of organizational development (OD) expertise at Imperial Chemical Industries (ICI). The fieldwork was conducted between 1975 and 1983. He carried out 'long semi-structured interviews' in 1975–7 and again in 1980–2. Some individuals were interviewed more than once, and care was taken to ensure that interviews included people from all hierarchical levels in the company and from the different functional and business areas within the firm. The total number of interviews conducted during this period amounted to 175. During the period of the fieldwork Pettigrew also had fairly regular contact with members of the organization through his involvement with the company as a consultant, and he had access to archival materials that explained how internal OD consultants were recruited and how external OD consultants were used. He writes: 'The continuous real-time data collection was enriched by retrospective interviewing and archival analysis . . .' (1985: 40). The study thus covered ten years of 'real-time' analysis, complemented by over twenty years of retrospective data. This longitudinal case study thus spans more than thirty years, although Pettigrew (1990) acknowledges that this is rarely feasible in organizational research.

whether a quantitative or a qualitative research strategy is employed. The same point can be made of case study research. When the predominant research strategy is qualitative, a case study tends to take an inductive approach to the relationship between theory and research; if a predominantly quantitative strategy is taken, it tends to be deductive. Thinking deeply 3.17 illustrates how the strategy adopted affects the type of case study approach that is taken.

Reliability, replicability, and validity

The question of how well the case study fares in the context of the research design criteria cited early on in this chapter—measurement validity, internal validity, external validity, ecological validity, reliability, and replicability—depends in large part on how far the researcher feels that these are appropriate for the evaluation of case study research. Some writers on case study research, such as Yin (1984), consider that they are appropriate criteria and suggest ways in which case study research can be developed to enhance its ability to meet the criteria; for others, like Stake (1995), they are barely mentioned, if at all. Writers on case study research whose point of orientation lies primarily with a qualitative research strategy tend to play down or ignore the salience of these factors, whereas those writers who have been strongly influenced by the quantitative research strategy tend to depict them as more significant.

However, one question on which a great deal of discussion has centred concerns the *external validity* or *generalizability* of case study research. How can a single case possibly be representative so that it might yield findings

that can be applied more generally to other cases? For example, how could the findings from Pettigrew's (1985) research into ICI (see Research in focus 3.16) be generalizable to all large multinational pharmaceutical corporations? The answer, of course, is that they cannot. It is important to appreciate that case study researchers do not delude themselves that it is possible to identify typical cases that can be used to represent a certain class of objects, whether it is factories, managers, or critical events. In other words, they do not think that a case study is a sample of one.

However, although many researchers emphasize that they are interested in the detail of a single case, they do sometimes claim a degree of theoretical generalizability on the basis of it. For example, in her study of Indsco Supply Corporation, Kanter (1977) explains that the case enabled her to generate concepts and give meaning to abstract propositions, which she then sought to test in three other large corporations. It is, therefore, clear that she is seeking to achieve a degree of theoretical generalizability from this case. Lee, Collier, and Cullen (2007) suggest that particularization rather than generalization constitutes the main strength of case studies. The goal of case study analysis should, therefore, be to concentrate on the uniqueness of the case and to develop a deep understanding of its complexity.

Types of case

Following on from the issue of external validity, it is useful to consider a distinction between different types of case that is sometimes made by writers. Yin (2003) distinguishes five types.

Thinking deeply 3.17
The case study in business research

Piekkari, Welsh, and Paavilainen (2009) suggest that the way that researchers in the area of international business use case study designs is different from how they are used in other social science disciplines. To find out how the case study research design is used, the authors argue that it is necessary to look at how researchers use it, rather than at how methods textbooks say it can be used. Based on a review of 135 case study articles in international business journals, Piekkari, Welsh, and Paavilainen argue that the way that case studies are conducted is relatively narrow and is dominated by the positivist tradition as developed by Yin (1984) and Eisenhardt (1989), at the expense of alternative, interpretative approaches. They distinguish between:

- *positivistic approaches*, such as propounded by Eisenhardt (1989), where the goal is to extract variables from their context in order to generate generalizable propositions and build theory, often through conducting multiple case studies and using a variety of data collection methods to triangulate and improve the validity of the study;

- *alternative approaches*, where the aim is to produce rich, holistic, and particularized explanations that are located in situational context through using multiple methods of data collection to uncover conflicting meanings and interpretations.

They argue that these conventions 'affect judgments about the proper role of case studies in research, how case studies should be conducted, and the criteria for evaluating the quality of case research' (Piekkari, Welsh, and Paavilainen 2009: 570). The authors express the concern that variable-oriented approaches can be constraining for international business researchers by limiting the extent to which they are flexible in their research. They conclude that researchers need to be more aware of the type of case study approach they are adopting and to justify their choice more explicitly.

- *The critical case*. Here the researcher has a clearly specified hypothesis, and a case is chosen on the grounds that it will allow a better understanding of the circumstances in which the hypothesis will and will not hold.

- *The unique case*. The unique or extreme case is, as Yin observes, a common focus in clinical studies.

- *The revelatory case*. The basis for the revelatory case exists 'when an investigator has an opportunity to observe and analyse a phenomenon previously inaccessible to scientific investigation' (Yin 1984: 44). While the idea of the revelatory case is interesting, it seems unnecessary to restrict it solely to situations in which something has not previously been studied. Much qualitative case study research that is carried out with a predominantly inductive approach to theory treats single case studies as broadly 'revelatory'.

- *The representative* or *typical case*. This type seeks to explore a case that exemplifies an everyday situation or form of organization.

- *The longitudinal case*. This type of case is concerned with how a situation changes over time.

Any particular study can involve a combination of these elements, which can be viewed as rationales for choosing particular cases. However, Lee, Collier, and Cullen (2007) argue that Yin's categorization of cases is still rather narrow and defers to the positivist tradition.

> Unfortunately, the majority of these uses are best understood as poor relations to positivistic, quantitative research. Exploratory case studies tend to be conducted as preliminary research in advance of wide-scale surveys to map out the themes for the subsequent research. Descriptive case studies are often used to expand on trends and themes already discovered by survey research. It is only the explanatory case that seeks to derive a detailed understanding of a particular phenomenon where the case is not seen as ancillary to more quantitative methods. (Lee, Collier, and Cullen 2007: 170)

Exponents of case study research counter suggestions that the evidence they present is limited because it has restricted external validity by arguing that it is not the purpose of this research design to generalize to other cases or to populations beyond the case. This position is very different from that taken by practitioners of survey research. Survey researchers are invariably concerned to be able to generalize their findings to larger populations and frequently use random sampling to enhance the representativeness of the samples on which they conduct their investigations and therefore the external validity of their findings. Case study researchers argue strenuously that this is not the purpose of their craft.

However, the notion of the case study is by no means straightforward. Tight (2010) has reviewed a range of methodological writings on the case study, including a book that was written by Bryman (2004a) for students of social research methods. He notes that the term is used in a wide variety of ways and that there is a sense in which many different kinds of study can end up being described as case studies. Indeed, he proposes that 'we simply use case study as a convenient label for our research—when we can't think of anything "better"—in an attempt to give it some added respectability' (Tight 2010: 337). He goes on to propose 'why don't we just call this kind of research what it is—small-sample, in-depth study, or something like that?' (Tight 2010: 338). While this is one solution to the problem of the term 'case study' being employed in different ways, it is not one that we advocate. It ought to be possible for an agreed-upon definition to be arrived at and for researchers who describe their work as based on a case study to justify why the label is warranted.

Case study as intensive analysis

Instead, case study researchers tend to argue that they aim to generate an intensive examination of a single case, in relation to which they then engage in a theoretical analysis. The central issue of concern is the quality of the theoretical reasoning in which the case study researcher engages. How well do the data support the theoretical arguments that are generated? Is the theoretical analysis incisive? For example, does it demonstrate connections between different conceptual ideas that are developed out of the data? The crucial question is not whether or not the findings can be generalized to a wider universe, but how well the researcher generates theory out of the findings (Mitchell 1983; Yin 1984). Such a view places case study research firmly in the inductive tradition of the relationship between theory and research. However, a case study design is not necessarily associated with an inductive approach, as can be seen in the research by Whittington (1989) referred to in Chapter 2. Thus, case studies can be associated with both theory generation and

theory testing. However, within this, case study researchers vary in their approach to theory generation and testing. Eisenhardt's (1989) article on case studies has been highly influential in promoting a view of case-based theory-building that relies on strategic sampling of cases from which generalizations can be made. She further recommends that researchers avoid getting too involved in the particularities of individual cases, because this will lead them to develop overly complex theory. Other researchers see case studies as a means of refining or refuting existing theories, rather than building entirely new explanatory frameworks (Jack and Kholief 2007).

It may be that it is only at a late stage in the research process that the nature and significance of the case becomes apparent. An example of this phenomenon is provided by Buchanan's (2012) account of his work with a team of researchers on the implementation of strategic change in six hospitals and five primary care organizations within the UK's NHS. This was a multiple-case study design (see next section and the discussion of comparative design below). Each case focused upon an area of activity which exhibited change. Buchanan himself was mainly involved in research on one of the hospitals (referred to as Grange) which had significantly improved its prostate cancer services. He found that responsibility for the changes had been widely distributed and varied over the change process itself. When compared to other hospitals that were included in the research, Grange and its cancer care specialty in particular emerged as a case study of 'distributed leadership' as it is referred to in the literature (e.g. Gronn 2011), though they use the term 'distributed change leadership'. However, Buchanan and his co-researchers had not set out to conduct a case study of distributed change leadership at this hospital. That it was a case study of distributed change leadership only emerged once the data had been collected and analysed.

More than one case

Case study research is not confined to the study of a single case. Multiple-case study designs have become increasingly common in business and management research. They are extensions of the case study design. The multiple-case study design is considered in the section on comparative design because multiple-case studies are largely undertaken for the purpose of comparing the cases that are included. As such, they allow the researcher to compare and contrast the findings deriving from each of the cases. This in turn encourages researchers to consider what is unique and what is common across cases, and frequently promotes theoretical reflection on the findings.

It might be asked what the difference is between a multiple-case study involving several cases and a cross-sectional design. After all, if an investigation involved, say, eight cases, it could be viewed as either a multiple-case study involving several cases or as a cross-sectional design. A simple rule of thumb is to ask: what is the focus? If the focus is on the cases and their unique contexts, it is a multiple-case study and as such is an extension of the case study approach; if the emphasis is on producing general findings, with little regard for the unique contexts of each of the eight cases, it is better viewed as a cross-sectional design. In other words, with a multiple-case study design, the emphasis is on the individual case; with a cross-sectional design, it is on the sample of cases.

Longitudinal research and the case study

Case study research frequently includes a longitudinal element. The researcher is often a participant of an organization for many months or years. Alternatively, he or she may conduct interviews with individuals over a lengthy period. Moreover, the researcher may be able to inject an additional longitudinal element by analysing archival information and by retrospective interviewing. Research in focus 3.16 provides an illustration of longitudinal case study research.

Another way in which a longitudinal element occurs is when a case that has been studied is returned to at a later stage. An interesting instance of this is Burawoy's (1979) study of a factory in Chicago, which he claims was the same one as was originally studied by Roy in the 1950s. This is a somewhat loose connection, however, as the theoretical focus adopted by the two researchers was markedly different, although their research methods, based on participant observation, were quite similar. A further example of **longitudinal research** carried out by different researchers is given in Research in focus 3.18. This study is interesting because it relies on social survey methods in addition to preliminary interviews with managers, union officials, and employees. Generally speaking, however, it is difficult for the researcher to establish how far change over the two time periods is the result of real differences or of other factors, such as different people in the organization, different ownership of the company between the two time periods, and the possible influence of the initial study itself.

Comparative design

It is worth distinguishing one further kind of design: **comparative design**. Put simply, this design entails the study using more or less identical methods on two or more contrasting cases. It embodies the logic of comparison, in that it implies that we can understand social phenomena better when they are compared in relation to two or more meaningfully contrasting cases or situations. The comparative design may be realized in the context of either quantitative or qualitative research. Within the former, the data collection strategy will take the form outlined in Figure 3.5. This figure implies that there are at least two cases (which may be organizations, nations, people, etc.) and that data are collected from each, usually within a cross-sectional design format.

One of the more obvious forms of such research is in cross-cultural or cross-national research (see Key concept 3.19). In a useful definition, Hantrais (1996) has suggested that such research occurs when individuals or teams set out to examine particular issues or phenomena in two or more countries with the express intention of comparing their manifestations in different sociocultural settings (institutions, customs, traditions, value systems, lifestyles, language, thought patterns), using the same research instruments either to carry out secondary analysis of national data or to conduct new empirical work. The aim may be to seek explanations for similarities and differences or to gain a greater awareness and a deeper understanding of social reality in different national contexts.

Figure 3.5

A comparative design

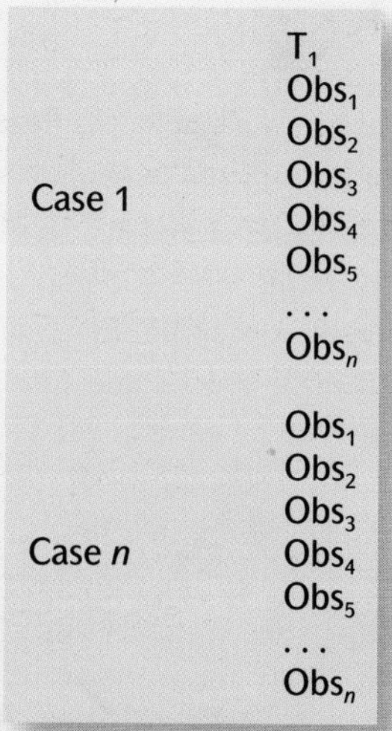

$$
\begin{array}{ll}
& T_1 \\
& Obs_1 \\
& Obs_2 \\
& Obs_3 \\
\text{Case 1} & Obs_4 \\
& Obs_5 \\
& \ldots \\
& Obs_n \\
\\
& Obs_1 \\
& Obs_2 \\
& Obs_3 \\
\text{Case } n & Obs_4 \\
& Obs_5 \\
& \ldots \\
& Obs_n \\
\end{array}
$$

Research in focus 3.18
A study of a steelworks spanning fifty years

One way of overcoming some of the difficulties associated with longitudinal study is by revisiting case study organizations that have previously been studied by other researchers in order to explore how they have changed over time. This was the approach taken by Bacon and Blyton (2001) in their case study of a North Wales steelworks. These researchers sought to replicate and extend survey research carried out in the 1950s (Scott et al. 1956), which looked at the social systems of industrial organizations to explain the positive orientation of steelworkers to technical change. Even though the steelworks was not actually named in the original study, information about its size, location, history, and activities meant that it was relatively easy for Blyton and his colleagues to identify it as the Shotton plant.

In 1991, Blyton, Bacon, and Morris (1996) conducted an employee attitude survey at the plant in order to explore the impact of teamworking on employee attitudes and behaviour, focusing on a variety of aspects of job satisfaction, change, attitudes to management, and industrial relations issues. This survey formed part of a broader study of the role of industrial relations and workplace change in the UK and German steel industries. They found that, despite the massive changes that had affected the plant between the 1950s and the 1990s, the social system of the works continued to influence steelworkers' attitudes to work, contributing towards their positive attitude to workplace change. However, at the end of the 1990s, when they returned to the plant to conduct a similar survey, they found that employee attitudes had changed. In particular, the steelworkers, who had been deeply affected by competitive pressures leading to increased job insecurity, were no longer as positively oriented towards change. As the authors note, the 'almost fifty year time span between the first and last surveys provides a unique research setting upon which to base some broader reflections on organisational change, management practices and employee attitudes' (Bacon and Blyton 2001: 224).

Cross-cultural research in business and management tends to presuppose that culture is a major explanatory variable that exerts profound influence on organizational behaviour. In business and management research, there has been a tendency to question the adaptability of many management theories and practices to other, particularly non-Western, cultural contexts. There has also been mounting criticism of the universalist vision that business and management research has promoted, based predominantly on unacknowledged Anglo-Saxon values. These pressures have led to greater interest in cross-cultural research. Within this overall category, however, there are some important distinctions. International management research concerns itself with how and why companies internationalize; it may focus on a specific country, or make cross-cultural comparisons between several countries. Usunier (1998) distinguishes between:

- *cross-cultural approaches*—which compare national management systems and local business customs in various countries; and
- *intercultural approaches*—which focus on the study of interaction between people and organizations with different national/cultural backgrounds.

Comparative research should not be treated as solely concerned with comparisons between nations. The logic of comparison can be applied to a variety of situations to inform a number of levels of analysis. For example, Hofstede's (1984) research on cultural differences has informed a generation of studies that have explored cultural differences in organizations other than IBM, and the framework has also been applied to understanding specific organizational behaviours, such as ethical decision-making.

Cross-cultural research is not without problems: for example, managing and gaining the funding for such research (see Key concept 3.19); ensuring, when existing data, such as official statistics or survey evidence, are submitted to a secondary analysis, that the data are comparable in terms of categories and data collection methods; and ensuring, when new data are being collected, that the need to translate data collection instruments (for example, interview schedules) does not undermine genuine comparability. This raises the further difficulty that even when translation is carried out competently, there is still the potential problem of an insensitivity to specific national and cultural contexts. On the other hand, cross-cultural research helps to reduce the risk of failing to appreciate that social science findings are often, if not invariably, culturally specific. Cross-cultural research also creates particular issues in achieving equivalence—between the samples, variables, and methods that are used (McDonald 2000). For example, in many cases nationality is used as a surrogate for culture; differences may thus be attributed to culture even if they could be more readily attributed to national situation. Equally, people inhabiting a country under the same government may belong to quite different cultures that reflect historical or religious affiliations. Further issues are raised by language differences, which can cause translation problems. Adler (1983) claims that many comparative cross-cultural studies in business and management do not adequately acknowledge these distinctions.

In terms of issues of reliability, validity, replicability, and generalizability, the comparative study is no different from the cross-sectional design. The comparative design is essentially two or more cross-sectional studies carried out at more or less the same point in time.

The comparative design can also be applied in relation to a qualitative research strategy. When this occurs, it takes the form of a multiple-case study (see Research in focus 3.20). Essentially, a multiple-case (or multi-case) study occurs whenever the number of cases examined exceeds one. In business research this is a popular research design that usually takes two or more organizations as cases for comparison, but occasionally a number of people are used as cases. For example, Marshall (1984) adopts a multiple-case study approach in her study of women managers; she retains a focus on intensive examination of each case, but there is qualitative comparison of each woman manager's situation with the others. The main argument in favour of the multiple-case study is that it improves theory-building. By comparing two or more cases, the researcher is in a better position to establish the circumstances in which a theory will or will not hold (Yin 1984; Eisenhardt 1989). Moreover, the comparison may itself suggest concepts that are relevant to an emerging theory.

Research in focus 3.20 describes one approach to selecting cases for a multiple-case study that involved researchers in each country selecting two workplaces from retail and financial service sectors. Another example is found in the study of TQM by Edwards, Collinson,

Key concept 3.19
What is cross-cultural and international research?

As its name implies, cross-cultural research entails the collection and/or analysis of data from two or more nations. Possible models for the conduct of cross-cultural research are as follows:

1. A researcher, perhaps in conjunction with a research team, collects data in a number of countries. Hofstede's (1984) research on the cultural differences between IBM workers in different countries (discussed in Chapter 2) is an illustration of this model, in that he took comparable samples of IBM employees from all hierarchical levels, allowing for a similar representation of gender and age, in sixty-six national subsidiaries of the company. More than forty countries were eventually compared using this method.

2. A central organization coordinates a portion of the research work of national organizations or groups. An example is the Global Disney Audiences Project (Wasko, Phillips, and Meehan 2001), whereby a research group in the USA recruited researchers in a variety of countries who were interested in the ways Disney products are viewed, and then coordinated the ways questions were asked in the research. Each nation's research groups were responsible for sampling and other aspects of the interview process.

3. Secondary analysis is carried out using data that are comparable, but where the coordination of their collection is limited or non-existent. This kind of cross-cultural analysis might occur if researchers seek to ask survey questions in their own country that have been asked in another country. The ensuing data may then be analysed cross-culturally. A further form of this model is through the secondary analysis of officially collected data, such as unemployment statistics. However, this kind of cross-cultural research makes it particularly important to be sure about the accuracy of data, which will probably have been produced by several different agencies, in providing a suitable basis for cross-cultural comparison. For example, Roy, Walters, and Luk (2001) suggest that business researchers have tended to avoid relying on secondary data about China because of concerns about the reliability and representativeness of government sources. Research units associated with local authorities may overstate certain factors to give the impression that the economy is doing better than it

really is, statistical approaches and classification schemes may differ from one province to another, and data may have been censored at certain points in time or even lost. Business researchers must therefore be cautious in their use of secondary data for the purpose of cross-cultural analysis.

4. Teams of researchers in participating nations are recruited by a person or body that coordinates the programme. Each researcher or group of researchers has the responsibility of conducting the investigation in his, her, or their own country. The work is coordinated in order to ensure comparability of research questions, survey questions, and procedures for administering the research instruments. This model differs from (2) above in that it usually entails a specific focus on certain research questions. The article by Terence Jackson (2001) provides an example of this model: Jackson relied on academic associates to collect data in their respective countries using the questionnaire instrument he had designed for this purpose (see Research in focus 9.14).

and Rees (1998), where the researchers selected two case studies from each of the three main sectors of the UK economy: private services, public sector, and manufacturing. Their selection of two cases in each sector, rather than just one, was intended to allow for variation; the limitation to two cases, rather than three, was due to time and resource constraints. To identify their cases the researchers searched press reports and listings of leading quality institutes such as the National Society for Quality through Teamwork. However, they were also keen to avoid companies that had a high profile as 'success stories', instead choosing cases that 'had made significant moves' in quality management but 'were not among the leading edge examples' (1998: 454). From this they identified twenty-five potential cases, and, on the basis of interviews with quality or human resources managers in each one, narrowed their sample down to just six. With a case selection approach such as this, the findings that are common to the firms can be just as interesting and important as those that differentiate them.

However, not all writers are convinced about the merits of multiple-case study research. Dyer and Wilkins (1991), for example, argue that a multiple-case study approach tends to mean that the researcher pays less attention to the specific context and more to the ways in which the cases can be contrasted. Moreover, the need to forge comparisons tends to mean that the researcher has to develop an explicit focus at the outset, whereas it may be advantageous to adopt a more open-ended approach in many instances. These concerns about retaining contextual insight and a rather more unstructured research approach are very much associated with the goals of the qualitative research strategy (see Chapter 17).

The key to the comparative design is its ability to allow the distinguishing characteristics of two or more cases to act as a springboard for theoretical reflections about contrasting findings. It is something of a hybrid, in that

in quantitative research it is frequently an extension of a cross-sectional design and in qualitative research it is frequently an extension of a case study design. It even exhibits certain features that are similar to experiments and quasi-experiments, which also rely on the capacity to forge a comparison.

Level of analysis

A further consideration for business researchers that applies to the research designs covered in this chapter relates to the concept of level; in other words, what is the primary unit of measurement and analysis? Hence, research might focus on:

- *individuals*: this would include studies that focus on specific kinds of individuals such as managers or shop-floor employees;

- *groups*: this would include research that considered certain types of groupings—for example, human resources departments or boards of directors;

- *organizations*: in addition to studies that focused on companies, this would include surveys, such as WERS (see Research in focus 3.14), that treat the workplace as the principal unit of analysis;

- *societies*: the main focus of this kind of analysis would be on the national, political, social, environmental, and economic contexts in which business organizations are located.

Differences in level of analysis are commonly referred to in terms of the SOGI model (societies, organizations, groups, and individuals). However, some research designs draw on samples that combine different levels of analysis—for example, organizations and departments. This begs the question as to whether it is possible to combine data from different levels to produce a meaningful analysis. The complexity of organizational

Research in focus 3.20
A comparative analysis and a panel study of female employment

Collins and Wickham (2004) used data from 'Servemploi', which is a study of women's employment and career prospects in the information society. The project had eight European Union partners, comprising members of universities or research institutes in Ireland, Denmark, Germany, Italy, Spain, Sweden, and Belgium. The main objective of the study was 'to examine the implications for women workers of technical and organizational changes in the retail and financial services sectors' (2004: 36). Each national team studied four workplaces, two in each sector, and each case involved workplace observation and interviews with managers and employees.

However, as well as being comparative, the study was also longitudinal, as it involved a two-year panel study of women based on semi-structured interviews. As the researchers explain: 'using a variety of sources, in particular, contacts in the trade unions, we located four women working in each sector (but not in the case study companies) who would be prepared to participate in the study' (2004: 36). The reason for keeping the sample for the panel study separate from the comparative cases was because they wanted to follow the women as they moved between workplaces, so it made sense to focus on individuals rather than on workplaces, as WERS has done (see Research in focus 3.14). This generated a total of 500 interviews.

types can make the issue of level particularly difficult to determine. Rousseau (1985) suggests it is important to make explicit the problems of using data derived from one level to represent something at another level in order to avoid misinterpretation. For example, processes of individual and organizational learning may be constructed quite differently at different levels. If researchers make inferences about organizational learning on the basis of data about individuals, they are at risk of making a cross-level misattribution. Since the phenomenon of learning is an essentially human characteristic, as organizations do not behave but people do, this leads to the attribution of human characteristics to a higher-level system. Misattribution can also occur when metaphors are used to interpret organizational behaviour. It is, therefore, good practice to identify and

make clear in your research design the level of analysis that is being used and then to switch to another level only after having made this clear (Rousseau 1985).

Another illustration of mixed-level research cited by Rousseau (1985) is found in the area of leadership studies. The average leadership style (ALS) approach assumes that leaders display the same behavioural style toward all subordinates. Research therefore relies on eliciting subordinate perceptions of the leader, which are averaged and treated as group-level characteristics. In contrast, the vertical dyadic linkage (VDL) model assumes that a leader's style may be different with each subordinate, thereby treating leadership as an individual-level phenomenon rather than as a group one. Each model thus conceptualizes leadership at a different level.

Bringing research strategy and research design together

Finally, we can bring together the two research strategies covered in Chapter 2 with the research designs outlined in this chapter. Table 3.1 shows the typical form associated with each combination of research strategy and

research design and a number of examples that either have been encountered so far or will be covered in later chapters. Table 3.1 refers also to research methods that will be encountered in later chapters but that have not been referred to so far. The Glossary at the end of this book will give you a quick reference to terms used that are not yet familiar to you.

The distinctions are not always perfect. In particular, in some qualitative and quantitative research it is not obvious whether a study is an example of a longitudinal design or a case study design. Life history studies, research that concentrates on a specific issue over time, and **ethnography**, in which the researcher charts change in a single case, are examples of studies that cross the two types. Such studies are perhaps better conceptualized as longitudinal case studies rather than as belonging to one category of research design or another. A further point to note is that there is no typical form in the qualitative research strategy/experimental research design cell. Qualitative research

in the context of true experiments is very unusual. However, as noted in the table, the Hawthorne studies (Roethlisberger and Dickson 1939) provide an interesting example of the way that a quasi-experimental research design can change over time. What you will also notice as you encounter many of the examples in this book is that business research designs often use a combination of quantitative and qualitative methods, so the distinction between quantitative and qualitative research strategies that is suggested in Table 3.1 is rarely as clear as this table suggests. In Chapters 26 and 27 of the book we will consider the implications of this and discuss research that combines quantitative and qualitative methods. Increasingly, research that combines quantitative and qualitative approaches is referred to as mixed methods research.

Table 3.1

Research strategy and research design

Research design	Research strategy Quantitative	Qualitative
Experimental	*Typical form.* Most researchers using an experimental design employ quantitative comparisons between experimental and control groups with regard to the dependent variable. See, for example, the study of CEO pay by Krause et al. (2014) (Research in focus 3.7).	*No typical form*; however, the Hawthorne experiments (Chapter 2 and Research in focus 3.8) provide an example of experimental research design that gradually moved away from the 'test room method' towards use of qualitative methods.
Cross-sectional	*Typical form.* Social survey research or structured observation on a sample at a single point in time. See, for example, the Aston studies of organizational size, technology, and structure (Chapter 2 and Research in focus 3.6); Parboteeah, Hoegl, and Cullen's (2009) study of the influence of religious values on work obligation norms (Research in focus 2.4); and Berg and Frost's (2005) telephone survey of low-skill, low-wage workers (Research in focus 9.3). This can also include content analysis on a sample of documents such as in Kabanoff, Waldersee, and Cohen's (1995) study of organizational values (Chapter 13).	*Typical form.* Qualitative interviews or focus groups at a single point in time. See, for example, Scase and Goffee's (1989) research into managers in large UK organizations (Research in focus 3.15); or Blackburn and Stokes's (2000) study of small business owner-managers (Research in focus 21.4). Can also be based upon **qualitative content analysis** of a set of documents relating to a single event or a specific period in time such as in Gephart's (1993) study of an organizational disaster (Research in focus 23.4).
Longitudinal	*Typical form.* Social survey research on a sample on more than one occasion, as in the five Workplace Employment Relations Surveys (Research in focus 3.14) or the 1997 and 2001 Skills Survey (Research in focus 8.3); or may involve content analysis of documents relating to different time periods, as in Boyce and Lepper's (2002) study of information in a joint venture involving two shipping firms between 1904 and 1975 (Research in focus 13.8).	*Typical form.* Ethnographic research over a long period, qualitative interviewing on more than one occasion, or qualitative content analysis of documents relating to different time periods. Such research warrants being dubbed longitudinal when there is an effort to map change, as in Pettigrew's (1985) study of ICI (Research in focus 3.16) or in the Work Foundation's study of what happened to workers following the closure of the MG Rover plant in Longbridge (Research in focus 20.10).

Table 3.1

Continued

Research design	Research strategy Quantitative	Qualitative
Case study	*Typical form.* Social survey research on a single case with a view to revealing important features about its nature. Examples include Hofstede's study of cultural differences based on a survey study of a large multinational business organization (discussed in Chapter 2); and Sørensen's (2004) study of the racial composition of workplaces based on a large multidivisional financial services institution (Research in focus 14.2).	*Typical form.* The intensive study by ethnography or qualitative interviewing of a single case, which may be an organization—such as Tracy, Lutgen-Sandvik, and Alberts's (2006) study of organizational bullying (Research in focus 2.5); a group of employees within an organization—as in Perlow's (1997) study of software engineers in a high-tech organization (Key concept 19.1); or an individual—as in Marshall's (1995) study of women managers (Key concept 17.5).
Comparative	*Typical form.* Social survey research in which there is a direct comparison between two or more cases, including cross-cultural research. An example is Brengman et al.'s (2005) study of Internet shoppers in the United States and Belgium (Research in focus 8.4).	*Typical form.* Ethnographic or qualitative interview research on two or more cases where some comparison is sought between them, as in Hyde et al.'s (2006) evaluation study of role redesign in the NHS (Research in focus 3.11); and Collins and Wickham's (2004) panel study of patterns of female employment across Europe (Research in focus 3.20).

Key points

- There is an important distinction between a research method and a research design.

- It is necessary to become thoroughly familiar with the meaning of the technical terms used as criteria for evaluating research: reliability; validity and the types of validity (measurement, internal, external, ecological); and replicability.

- It is also necessary to be familiar with the differences between the five major research designs covered (experimental, cross-sectional, longitudinal, case study, and comparative) and to consider the level of analysis (individual, group, organization, and society) that research may focus on. In this context, it is important to realize that the term 'experiment', which is often used somewhat loosely in everyday speech, has a specific technical meaning.

- There are various potential threats to validity in non-experimental research.

- Although the case study is often thought to be a single type of research design, it in fact has several forms. It is also important to be aware of the key issues concerned with the nature of case study evidence in relation to issues such as external validity (generalizability).

Questions for review

- In terms of the definitions used in this book, what are the chief differences between each of the following: a research method; a research strategy; and a research design?

Quality criteria in business research

- What are the differences between reliability and validity and why are these important criteria for the evaluation of business research?

- Outline the meaning of each of the following: measurement validity; internal validity; external validity; and ecological validity.
- Why have some qualitative researchers sought to devise alternative criteria besides reliability and validity when assessing the quality of investigations?
- What is the 'experimenter effect' and how might it contribute towards bias?
- What is social desirability bias and how might its effects be reduced?

Research designs

- What are the main research designs that have been outlined in this chapter?
- Why is level of analysis a particular consideration in business and management research?

Experimental design

- 'The main importance of the experimental design for the business researcher is that it represents a model of how to infer causal connections between variables.' Discuss.
- Following on from the last question, if experimental design is so useful and important, why is it not used more?
- What is a quasi-experiment?

Cross-sectional design

- What is meant by a cross-sectional research design?
- In what ways does the social survey exemplify the cross-sectional research design?
- Assess the degree to which the survey researcher can achieve internally valid findings.
- To what extent is the survey design exclusive to quantitative research?

Longitudinal design(s)

- Why might a longitudinal research design be superior to a cross-sectional one?
- What are the main differences between panel and cohort designs in longitudinal research?

Case study design

- What is a case study?
- Is case study research exclusive to qualitative research?
- What are some of the principles by which cases might be selected?

Comparative design

- What are the chief strengths of a comparative research design?
- Why might comparative research yield important insights?

....

 Online Resource Centre

www.oxfordtextbooks.co.uk/orc/brymanbrm4e/

Visit the Interactive Research Guide that accompanies this book to complete an exercise in Research Designs.

....

4

Planning a research project and formulating research questions

Chapter outline

The goal of this chapter is to provide advice to students on the issues that they need to consider if they have to prepare a dissertation based upon a research project. Increasingly, business and management students are required to produce such a dissertation as part of the requirements for their degrees. In addition to needing help with the conduct of research, which the chapters that come later in this book will aim to provide, the student may find it useful to have more specific advice on tactics in doing and writing up research for a dissertation. It is against this background that this chapter has been written. The chapter explores a wide variety of issues such as:

- advice on timing;
- advice on generating research questions;
- advice on writing to help you produce compelling findings;
- advice on understanding the requirements of a dissertation project;
- advice on what makes a good dissertation.

Chapter 5 will then focus on how to get started with your research project by conducting a literature review.

Introduction

This chapter provides some advice for readers who might be carrying out a research project of their own. The chapters that follow in Parts Two, Three, and Four of this book will then provide more detailed information about the choices available to you and how to implement them. But, beyond this, how might you go about conducting a small project of your own? We have in mind here the kind of situation that is increasingly common among business and management degree programmes—the requirement to write a dissertation of between 7000 and 15,000 words. In particular we have in mind the needs of undergraduate students, while students on postgraduate degree programmes will also find some of the observations we make helpful. The advice is really aimed at students conducting projects with a component of empirical research in which they collect new data or perhaps conduct a secondary analysis of existing data.

Getting to know what is expected of you by your institution

Your institution or department will have specific requirements concerning a wide variety of different features that your dissertation should comprise and a range of other matters relating to it. These may include such things as the form of binding; how the dissertation is to be presented; whether or not an abstract is required; how big the page margins should be; the format for referencing; the number of words; the structure of the dissertation; how much advice you can get from your supervisor; whether or not a proposal is required; plagiarism; deadlines; how much (if any) financial assistance you can expect; and so on.

The advice here is simple: *follow the requirements, instructions, and information you are given*. If anything in this book conflicts with your institution's guidelines and requirements, ignore this book! We very much hope this is not something that will occur very much, but if it does, keep to the guidelines your institution gives you.

Thinking about your research area

The chances are that you will be asked to start thinking about what you want to do research on well before you are due to start work on your dissertation. It is worth giving yourself a good deal of time for this. As you are doing your various modules, begin to think about whether there are any topics that might interest you and that might provide you with a researchable area. This may at times feel like a rather unproductive process in which a number of false starts or changes of direction are made. However, taking the time to explore different avenues at the point of problem identification can prevent difficulties at a much later stage.

Telling it like it is
The importance of starting early

For Lisa, one of the main lessons she learned from her experience of doing a research project was the importance of starting early. 'Time management is definitely a big thing with your dissertation. Starting it early, starting the reading early as well, because the paper trail can take for ages to trace back authors and what they've written in the past. It's really important to start early, I think.' Karen expressed a similar view: 'I started my dissertation very early on. A lot of people didn't start it until they got back to University in September/October time, whereas I'd already started mine in January. I actually finished it a bit early because it was due in at the beginning of May and I finished it for the beginning of April.'

Angharad also said that this was something that she had learned from the experience of doing a research project. 'I'm quite organized so it wasn't too big a deal for me, but I know people have left it to the last minute and they're having a big panic. So getting organized is probably the main thing.'

Tom also felt that one of the main lessons he had learned from doing a research project was the importance of starting early, even though the demands of other taught courses might discourage this. 'It's very tempting when you've got taught modules of the course as well to do to put the project back and back, but you've kind of got to force yourself to get on with it even when it feels difficult and it's good to have some milestones . . . some things to aim for rather than just the end of the project.'

These views were also confirmed by the supervisors we surveyed.

Telling it like it is
Why do a research project?

For some students, doing a research project is an optional part of their degree programme or dissertation requirement. In this case, the decision whether or not to do research becomes more personal. For Chris, doing a research project was an opportunity 'to find things out from the horse's mouth' by investigating how things worked in the 'real world' after three years of studying theories of business and management. 'I thought it would be interesting to actually find out what people really think about a subject. When you read these textbooks you read theories, you know, papers, and you get told things in lectures or newspapers or whatever and you think "Right, great. That's interesting and I'm sure that must be right." I mean sometimes I used to question. "Well, I don't agree with that." And I thought "Well, now I've got this really good opportunity to find out things" in an organization.'

(continued)

For Tom, a research-based dissertation stood apart from dissertations that did not include research. 'Some of my friends for their dissertations took a load of information commented on it and came up with a conclusion and essentially, you know, that's an essay like any other that we've been doing throughout the three years at university, just a bit longer. For me, it was worth putting the extra effort in because it was an entire module. And it was fun. It was enjoyable and I got exposure to people that I wouldn't otherwise have had which has helped me recently in my graduate scheme. And maybe it's just me, but it's nice to question theories that you don't necessarily believe and it's very easy to say "Oh well, I don't believe it, but there we go." The way I [saw] it was: "Well, I don't believe it, so [let's] see if I can find out anything to back that up."'

Karen explained that doing her research on something that she was genuinely interested in was crucial in maintaining her enthusiasm for the project. 'My manager said "Just make sure that it's something you're interested in, because, if it isn't, then you're not going to get through it and you're going to get disheartened." If it is something you're interested in, you can really enjoy doing the research and it becomes really good for you. You feel like you're really getting something out of it.'

Tom found that doing a research project helped him to feel that he had become a specialist in a particular subject area. 'I did like getting really into a topic and feeling like, you know, "I'm a bit of an expert on this now." You know, I know a lot about this and I've read more than 99 per cent of the population about this now and actually I feel kind of, you know, if anyone's going to have anything sensible to say about call centres it might be me.' Lucie felt that the experience of doing a research project had equipped her with skills that had the potential to be useful in other contexts. As she explained, 'In every job there's some element of research. A lot of my friends have gone into consultancy; you have to do research there. And a lot of my friends have gone into banking and there's a lot of research there as well. So you can apply the skills that you gain from research to everyday life and everyday jobs.'

These views were confirmed by one of the supervisors we questioned, who said: 'A piece of research can be a talking point for a job interview, as it is something the student has done!' Another commented: 'By the end of the research project, students have an awareness of the need for flexible thinking and the ability to adapt in order to make progress.'

 # Using your supervisor

Most institutions that require a dissertation or similar component allocate students to supervisors. Institutions vary quite a lot in what can be expected of supervisors; in other words, they vary in terms of what kinds of and how much assistance supervisors will give to students allocated to them. Equally, students vary a great deal in how frequently they see their supervisors and in their use of them. Our advice here is simple: use your supervisor to the fullest extent that you are allowed and follow the pointers you are given by him or her. Your supervisor will almost certainly be someone who is well versed in the research process and who will be able to provide you with help and feedback at all stages of your research, subject to your institution's strictures in this regard. If your supervisor is critical of your research questions, your **interview schedule**, drafts of your dissertation, or whatever, try to respond positively. Follow the suggestions that he or she provides, since the criticisms will invariably be accompanied by reasons for the criticisms and suggestions for revision. It is not a personal attack. Supervisors regularly have to go through the same process themselves when they submit an article to a peer-refereed journal, apply for a research grant, or give a conference paper. So respond to criticisms and suggestions positively and be glad that you are being given the opportunity to address deficiencies in your work before it is formally examined.

A further point is that students who get stuck at the start of their dissertations or who get behind with their work sometimes respond to the situation by avoiding their supervisors. They then get caught up in a vicious circle that results in their work being neglected and perhaps rushed at the end. Try to avoid this situation by confronting the fact that you are experiencing difficulties in getting going or are getting behind and seek out your supervisor for advice.

Telling it like it is
Maintaining a good relationship with your supervisor

The expectations concerning the frequency and format of meetings between students and supervisors vary considerably from one university course to another. Of the supervisors we contacted, the majority met students individually, but some held meetings with a group of dissertation students so that common issues could be shared. Face-to-face meetings were also complemented by email communication, telephone calls, and online discussion groups. The students whom we spoke to had different experiences of their relationship with supervisors. Angharad valued the expertise of her supervisor and his knowledge of the subject. She advised: 'Make sure you use your supervisor, because they know the subject area and they're marking your dissertation, so you might as well draw on their expertise as much as possible.' From her own experience and that of other students, Karen observed differences in the expectations that students had of their supervisors. 'All supervisors are different anyway, but I think that students have different needs as well. My supervisor was really good for me, because he wasn't very prescriptive about what to do and what not to do. He was really good in that sense for me, but he wasn't, I don't think, the right type of tutor for everybody, because he didn't tell me anything, I don't think. He never said that that's wrong or that's right. He just used to ask questions and guide me and that type of thing. He read the plan and he gave that a good mark and then that was it; he didn't actually read any of my dissertation during the supervision process. I think it's really good, because hopefully now when he looks at it, it'll be really fresh for him as well. I was really excited about him reading it, because I thought "I'm really looking forward to seeing what he thinks!" ' Karen enjoyed the independence afforded to her by her supervisor but felt this would not have suited all students equally. 'I think that, if a supervisor thinks you are a bit lost, that's when they come in and they say, "Right, well let me have a look at it," or something like that, because they think you need guidance. But the good thing about him was that he recognized I had my own ideas. I think that when they start to read it and give you feedback, it becomes more their work than your work. Whereas the reason I feel so good about my dissertation is because it is all my work and my supervisor hasn't put anything into it.'

Tom, a postgraduate student, saw his relationship with his supervisor as quite different from when he had been an undergraduate. 'When I did my undergraduate dissertation I was such a poor student I actively avoided my supervisor in case he asked me any questions and I hadn't done any reading or anything. This time I was determined I was going to make active use of my supervisor and so I did programme in to meet him at various points. At Birkbeck they're very keen that, when you go and see your supervisor, you don't just go and have a chat. Instead you go with some questions to ask and specific issues to talk about. So having those dates in the diary kind of really forced me to say, "Right, I'll go and see my supervisor and I need to have done A, B, and C before I go." You know, "I need to have done the interviews and done some preliminary data analysis before I go and see him." So that was quite helpful in terms of planning—you know, in spurring me on.' These views were confirmed by several of the supervisors we surveyed who echoed the importance of preparation beforehand by both parties in making supervision meetings successful. One stated: 'I adopt a fairly demanding regime for the production of draft material and require plans for activity between meetings.'

Lucie emphasized she was expected to be proactive in seeking support from her supervisor rather than expecting him to be constantly checking her progress. 'It wasn't like he would chase me up or anything. It was purely up to me. He was there as much as I wanted to use him. So he wouldn't chase me up and say "Have you written your dissertation yet?" or "Have you written your literature review yet?" It was purely up to me to go to him.' Another supervisor in our survey talked about the importance of a mature relationship between supervisor and student. 'Doing research and writing a thesis are things that you very much learn by doing. Supervision at higher levels therefore becomes much more guiding and discussing ideas (like working *with* the student) than teaching or suggesting how to do something (working *for* the student).' We feel that this is a really helpful distinction for students to make. Students can find these expectations disconcerting at first, but in the long run they tend to pay off.

When asked what makes for a successful supervision meeting, one supervisor replied: 'the moment when you know the student sparks off a new insight for you . . . or vice versa'. This comment highlights the reciprocal nature of the learning involved in supervision relationships that rely on the commitment of both parties to be successful.

Managing time and resources

All research is constrained by time and resources. There is no point in working on research questions and plans that cannot be seen through because of time pressure or because of the costs involved. Two points are relevant here.

1. Work out a timetable—preferably in conjunction with your supervisor—detailing the different stages of your research (including the review of the literature and writing up). This is particularly important if you are a part-time student combining your studies with full-time work. The timetable should specify the different stages and the calendar points at which you should start and finish them. Some stages of the research are likely to be ongoing—for example, searching the literature for new references—but that should not prove an obstacle to developing a timetable.

2. Find out what, if any, resources can be put at your disposal for carrying out your research. For example, will you receive help from your institution with such things as travel costs, photocopying, secretarial assistance, postage, stationery, and so on? Will the institution be able to loan you hardware such as audio recorders and **transcription** machines if you need to record and transcribe your interviews? Has it got the software you need, such as **SPSS** or a qualitative data analysis package such as **NVivo**? This kind of information will help you to establish how far your research design and methods are financially feasible and practical. The imaginary gym survey used in Chapter 15 is an example of an investigation that would be feasible within the kind of time frame usually allocated to undergraduate and postgraduate dissertations. However, it would require the availability of a quantitative data analysis package such as SPSS; it would also require such facilities as typing up and formatting the questionnaire, which nowadays students can usually do for themselves with the help of word-processing programs; photocopying covering letters and questionnaires; postage for sending the questionnaires out and for any follow-up letters to non-respondents; and return postage for the questionnaires. Alternatively, participants could be contacted by email and either attach the questionnaire to the email or provide a URL where a web-based questionnaire can be found and answered; see Chapter 28 for more on e-research.

Telling it like it is
Finding time to do a research project

For part-time MBA, undergraduate, and postgraduate students, doing a research project sometimes has to be combined with the intense demands of work and family, which in themselves may constitute more than a full-time job. From our experience of supervising such students, we have observed that they develop many different and creative ways of managing the time pressures associated with doing a dissertation project, but this can often involve an element of personal sacrifice for them. Female MBA students from Warwick Business School interviewed by Bell (2004) described some of the effects of these time pressures—for example, causing them temporarily to give up social activities or family time in order to work on their dissertation at weekends or during holidays. Students also highlighted the importance of partners and other family members in helping to enable them to find time and giving them emotional and practical support in doing their research project. Students who don't fully take these time pressures into account can sometimes find that they are unable to meet the deadlines for submitting the dissertation and have repeatedly to postpone this final stage of their degree study. One female MBA student working full-time with two young children interviewed by Bell (2004: 69–70) summarized the pressures associated with these conflicting demands. 'My son is growing up really quickly and, yes, people can take him off so I can work on my MBA dissertation, but I'm at work all week and I actually quite like seeing him at the weekend. I'm just conscious that, as the gap between the MBA course and the project gets longer, the project gets harder because you can't remember anything that you've done.'

Tom, a part-time student at Birkbeck, took a different approach, cutting down on his work time to create time for his research project. 'This isn't going to be any help to people that are working full time, but I reduced my hours to

(continued)

work four days a week for the second half of the course so I had a day a week to do my studies; that was a big help . . . A lot of people did extend their studies over a third year because it was just really difficult to fit it all in.' Even so, Tom found the pressures of doing a research project daunting at times. 'It's very easy to feel like it's this huge mountain that you'll never get to the top of and just feel like you can never do. You can never sit down and watch telly or relax because this thing's always there; living with it can be annoying at times; and there are times when you get stuck and it doesn't feel great.'

Tips and skills
Constructing a Gantt chart for your research project

One way of keeping track of your research project is through the use of a Gantt chart. This is a horizontal bar chart that was originally developed as a production control tool in 1917 by Henry L. Gantt, an American engineer and social scientist. Although Gantt charts are more commonly used in project management, they can also help you to plan, coordinate, and track specific tasks in your research project by providing a graphical illustration of your timetable and the key tasks involved in it. Simple Gantt charts may be designed on graph paper or as a table in Microsoft Word. More complex automated versions can be created using project management applications such as Microsoft Project or Excel. The horizontal axis of the chart represents the total time span of the project divided into units such as weeks or months. The vertical axis represents the tasks involved in the project. An example of a Gantt chart for a student research project is provided in Figure 4.1. As Figure 4.1 shows, you shade the squares on

Figure 4.1

An example of a Gantt chart for a student research project

	Sept.	Oct.	Nov.	Dec.	Jan.	Feb.	Mar.	Apr.
Identify research area	▓							
Formulate research questions		▓						
Formulate research strategy, research design, and select methods		▓	▓					
Write research proposal			15th					
Negotiate access			▓					
Literature review				▓				
Data collection				▓				
Data analysis					▓			
Write first draft						▓		
Write second draft							▓	
Write final draft								▓
Dissertation due								21st

(continued)

the graph to represent the amount of time you expect to spend on each task. The filled-in squares may overlap, to reflect the fact, for example, that you may continue to review the literature in the same time span as starting to collect your data. As the research project progresses, the chart may be amended to indicate the portions of tasks that have been completed. However, one of the limitations of Gantt charts is that they do not indicate task dependencies, so you cannot tell, for example, how falling behind with your literature review will affect the timing of other tasks in your research project. This is a particular problem for student research projects, where you will almost certainly be working to a fixed and immovable deadline for completion of the dissertation, so falling behind in your timetable will necessarily reduce the amount of time that you have to devote to other stages of the project. A further difficulty with Gantt charts is that, even though they allow for overlaps between different tasks, they do encourage you to see the research process as a linear, sequential activity. This may be inappropriate, particularly for qualitative research projects where many of the tasks are iterative. Such a project might produce a Gantt chart where tasks overlap to such an extent that the graph becomes impossible to follow.

Telling it like it is
When doing a research project doesn't turn out to be a linear process

Tom found that his experience of doing a research project contradicted some of what he had been told to expect. 'People talk about the research process being this linear thing. You review the literature, find your question and identify your methods and, you know, it kind of neatly follows on. I didn't really experience it like that to be perfectly honest.' Our experience in supervising research projects suggests Tom is by no means unusual in this and there is not necessarily anything to feel concerned about—particularly in a qualitative research project such as Tom's. Tom also found himself revisiting his research questions throughout the research project. As he explained, 'I found identifying a question that I was able to investigate and that was meaningful was the most difficult bit of my whole project. I kept coming back to that throughout the year I was doing the project refining it, changing it.' The main thing in planning your research project is to be conscious of the deadlines imposed by your university and to be active in setting achievable milestones along the way, so you are less likely to get discouraged and more likely to feel you are making progress.

Formulating suitable research questions

Many students want to conduct research into areas that are of personal interest to them. This is not a bad thing at all and, as we noted in Chapter 2, many business researchers start from this point as well (see also Lofland and Lofland 1995: 11–14). However, you must move on to develop research questions. This recommendation applies to qualitative research as well as to quantitative research. As we will go on to explain in Chapter 17, qualitative research is more open-ended than quantitative research, and in Chapter 19 we will mention some notable studies that appear not to have been driven by specific

research questions. However, very open-ended research is risky and can lead to the collection of too much data and, when it comes to writing up, to confusion about your focus. So, unless your supervisor advises you to the contrary, we would definitely advise you to formulate some research questions, even if they turn out to be somewhat less specific than the kinds we often find in quantitative research. In other words, what is it about your area of interest that you want to know?

Research questions are, therefore, important. Not having research questions or having poorly formulated research questions will lead to poor research. If you do not specify clear research questions, there is a great risk that your research will be unfocused and that you will be unsure about what your research is about and what you are collecting data for. It does not matter how well you design a questionnaire or how skilled an interviewer you are; you must be clear about your research questions. Equally, it does not matter whether your research is for a research contract or a dissertation project. Research questions are crucial because they will:

- guide your literature search;
- guide your decisions about the kind of research design to employ;
- guide your decisions about what data to collect and from whom;
- guide your analysis of your data;
- guide your writing-up of your data;
- stop you from going off in unnecessary directions.

Marx (1997) has suggested a wide range of sources of research questions (see Thinking deeply 4.1) and outlines some of the features that your research questions should exhibit. Figure 4.2 brings out the main steps in developing research questions. Research questions in quantitative research are sometimes more specific than in qualitative research. Indeed, some qualitative researchers advocate a very open approach with no research questions. This is a very risky approach and can be a recipe for collecting masses of data without a clear sense of what to observe or what to ask your interviewees. There is a growing tendency for qualitative researchers to advocate a somewhat more focused approach to their craft (e.g. Hammersley and Atkinson 1995: 24–9).

Thinking deeply 4.1
Marx's sources of research questions

Marx (1997) suggests the following as possible sources of research questions:

- Intellectual puzzles and contradictions.
- The existing literature.
- Replication.
- Structures and functions. For example, if you point to a structure such as a type of organization, you can ask questions about the reasons why there are different types and the implications of the differences.
- Opposition. Marx identifies the sensation of feeling that a certain theoretical perspective or notable piece of work is misguided and exploring the reasons for your opposition.
- A social problem. But remember that this is just a source of a research question; you still have to identify business and management research issues in relation to a social problem: 'Gaps between official versions of reality and the facts on the ground' (Marx 1997: 113). An example here is something like Delbridge's (1998) fascinating ethnographic account of company **rhetoric** about Japanized work practices and how they operate in practice.
- The counter-intuitive. For example, when common sense seems to fly in the face of social scientific truths.
- Empirical examples that 'trigger amazement' (Marx 1997: 114). Marx gives, as examples, deviant cases and atypical events.
- New methods and theories. How might they be applied in new settings?
- New social and technical developments and social trends (Marx 1997: 114).
- Personal experience.
- Sponsors and teachers. But do not expect your teachers to provide you with detailed research questions.

We usually start out with a general research area that interests us. It may derive from any of several sources:

- *Personal interest/experience*. As we pointed out in Chapter 2, Bryman's interests in theme parks can be traced back to a visit to Disney World in Orlando in 1991, while Bell's interest in 'Investors in People' stems from her involvement in managing the implementation of this quality standard in a UK National Health Service trust hospital.

- *Theory*. Someone might be interested in testing aspects of labour process theory or the contingency perspective on organization structure.

- *The research literature*. Studies relating to a research area such as the Japanization of work in British industry could be an example of a literature that might stimulate an interest in the nature of shopfloor work in such a context. Sandberg and Alvesson (2011) note that spotting gaps in the literature is a good way of identifying research questions. The chief strategies for doing this are spotting overlooked or under-researched areas and identifying areas of research that have not been previously examined using a particular theory or perspective. Alvesson and Sandberg (2011) recommend greater development of research questions through what they call 'problematization', which entails challenging the assumptions that are embedded in the literature. Such assumptions might be located within a root metaphor (Morgan 1997) or paradigm (Burrell and Morgan 1979). Challenging them can result in the formulation of alternative assumptions that can be used as a springboard for generating innovative research questions. However, as Alvesson and Sandberg recognize, 'gap spotting' is itself a creative process because gaps in the literature are frequently identified by arranging or positioning the literature in certain ways. However, because such a process rarely involves challenges to assumptions, research questions are rarely innovative and rarely likely to engender significant theoretical departures.

- *Puzzles*. For example, how are team and individual empowerment, both of which have been themes in research on quality initiatives, compatible?

- *New developments in organizations*. Examples might include the rise of the Internet or the diffusion of new models of organization—for example, Total Quality Management (TQM), customer service programmes, call centres.

- *Organizational problems*. An example might be how staff in call centres should handle consumer rage when consumers are interrupted by unwanted telephone calls.

As these types of source suggest, in research we often start out with a general research area or research objective that has to be narrowed down so that we can develop a tighter focus out of which research questions can be developed. We can depict the process of generating research questions as a series of steps, as suggested in Figure 4.2. The series of stages is meant to suggest that, when developing research questions, the researcher is involved in a process of progressive focusing down, so that we move from a general research area down to specific research questions. In making this movement, we have to recognize the following restrictions:

- Remember that a research question should end with a question mark. If there is no question mark, it is not a research question.

- We cannot answer all the research questions that occur to us. This is not just to do with issues of time and the cost of doing research. It is very much to do with the fact that we must keep a clear focus: our research questions must relate to each other to form a coherent set of issues.

- We therefore have to select from the possible research questions that we arrive at.

- In making our selection, we should be guided by the principle that the research questions we choose should be related to one another. If they are not, our research will probably lack focus and we may not make as clear a contribution to understanding as would be the case if research questions were connected. Thus, in the example in Figure 4.2, the selected research questions relating to TQM are closely connected.

The section below on 'Criteria for evaluating research questions' provides some suggestions about the kinds of considerations that should be taken into account when developing your own research questions.

Research in focus 4.2 describes some considerations that went into Watson's (1994*a*, *b*) exploration of management at ZTC Ryland, a UK-based telecommunications firm.

Watson (1994*a*, *b*) has also provided a useful account of the process of 'crafting research', as he puts it. Before embarking on the task of research design and choice of research methods, it is a good idea to ask yourself a series of questions about your research and the findings that you hope to produce. Crafting a research design relies on addressing a series of what, why, and how questions

Figure 4.2

Steps in selecting research questions

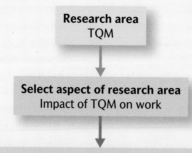

Research area
TQM

Select aspect of research area
Impact of TQM on work

Research questions
Does TQM have a positive or negative impact on job satisfaction?
Does the effect of TQM on job satisfaction vary by level in the organization?
Does TQM disrupt traditional methods of working in firms?
Do workers try to resist TQM and if so how far are they successful?
Does TQM lead to empowerment or disempowerment?
Does the way that TQM is introduced have an influence on the nature of
its impact on job satisfaction?

Select research questions
Does TQM have a positive or negative impact on job satisfaction?
Does the way that TQM is introduced have an influence on the nature of
its impact on job satisfaction?
Does the effect of TQM on job satisfaction vary by level in the organization?

Telling it like it is
Finding a research area

Lucie's choice of research subject reflected her personal experience of having been exposed to entrepreneurial discourses while she was a student at university. 'As a student I was being exposed to kind of these enterprise courses. I was bombarded with messages like "Join this course", and I was quite interested in enterprise, so I attended one of these courses as an undergraduate and that's how I became interested in it. Also, a lot of my friends are really interested in enterprise, and a lot of them kind of have started to try and run businesses while at university. So I was interested in what was provoking students to do this.' Lucie's choice of research area illustrates how practical considerations (see Chapter 2) can impact upon choice of research area, since Lucie already had social contact with the kinds of people who might become the focus of her research, in this case university students, and had already had contact with the research setting on which she was intending to base her study. Lucie was thus studying a social group of which she was a member—university students. This is interesting, because it raises particular considerations about the nature of the relationship between the researcher and research subjects, an issue that we will return to in Chapter 17.

(continued)

Tom's research interest was driven initially by his curiosity about the rise of telephone call centres as a new type of workplace environment. 'I guess that I started by probably not thinking about testing a theory so much—like "How does goal-setting theory affect behaviour in the workplace?" or something. I was more interested in looking at a type of workplace. There had been a lot of stuff in the media about call centres and there were quite a lot of references to call centres in the literature that I'd read in my first term and so that's how my interest evolved.' A further advantage to Tom's choice of research subject stems from its clearly defined parameters. He was attracted to the subject of call centres because it constituted a relatively clearly defined literature that did not go back very far in time. This helped to make it suitable for a student research project. As he explained 'If you type in "call centre" to a database you get a compact set of references and it's quite attractive because call centres have only been in existence for sort of ten years or something, so actually the literature is not that extensive, which makes kind of getting into it a lot easier.'

Telling it like it is
Using your supervisor to help develop your research questions

Tom found it was common for students on his course to be too ambitious in forming their research questions. 'We all came up with really big questions like "How does leadership impact on the NHS?" Some huge question like that—you know, not the sort of thing that's very easy to test in a student research project. We were encouraged to knock these ideas around. Most of them were pretty impractical, because they were sort of like five-year research projects needing thousands and thousands of hours to be operationalized, whereas we only had very limited time. So we were encouraged to kind of focus down.'

Karen had a similar experience: 'I used to send my supervisor drafts of my proposal and get his feedback, to check that I was on the right lines. But to be honest, I don't think he ever actually told me anything. He just used to ask me questions, which I think was the best thing for me, because that just sort of got me thinking about it and that was really what I needed at that time. He kind of narrowed me down when I was trying to take on too much, when I was saying: "Well, I think I might do this and I might do that as well." Then he would just sort of ask me questions and get me to narrow it down.'

This experience was echoed by the supervisors we spoke to, who said that it was common for students to be too broad in designing their research questions. One said: 'Undergraduate students tend to be unrealistic about what can be achieved and to assume that doing research is easy and not very time consuming. Many choose something which is "fashionable" or "current", often without much apparent initial investigation, only to find later that the topic has limited foundations in the existing literature. Apart from the usual problem of students having a broad question, underpinned by multiple more focused research questions, each of which might be the basis for a more effective proposal, it is striking that many students will not narrow the focus, despite numerous signals that it is necessary. I also notice that very few revisit and refine the research question as they proceed. Another substantial minority of students feel that they have to have both a qualitative and a quantitative aspect to the project, irrespective of the context or the specific research question. The outcome is that the project typically falls "between both stools" and lacks conviction.' While this supervisor's comments might sound a little harsh, they are based on substantial experience of trying to help students to avoid these common pitfalls.

Research in focus 4.2
Developing research questions

Watson (1994*b*) gives a very frank account of the process by which he developed his research questions for his participant observation study of ZTC Ryland, 'a plant of three thousand or so employees engaged in developing, making and selling telecommunications products' (Watson 1994*a*: 4). The fact that the company was involved in several change initiatives at the time made it particularly interesting to Watson. His initial aim, therefore, was to improve understanding of how people doing managerial work 'shape' their own lives and identities in the context of organized work efforts (1994*b*). He writes that he 'sharpened' this general area of interest somewhat by reflecting on the impact on managers of the emergence of what were then fairly new developments, such as the rise of cultural change programmes and of HRM (human resource management) principles. In developing this set of interests into research questions, Watson was influenced by writers and researchers on managerial work who had been critical of existing knowledge in this area. In particular he notes that these critics recommended greater attention to the terms managers use to reflect on their work; a greater emphasis on explaining why managers engage in the forms of behaviour that have been uncovered; and a greater appreciation of the way in which managerial behaviour is embedded in organizational arrangements. These reflections on the literature on managerial work gave rise to Watson's research questions and led to an emphasis on the linguistic categories and rhetorical processes involved in managers' constructions of their work and jobs; explaining patterns of behaviour observed; and exploring the ways in which organizational arrangements have implications for managerial behaviour and indeed are influenced by it.

(see Figure 4.3), which eventually result in the production of a set of 'findings' or conclusions. Watson (1994*b*) sees management research as an intellectual craft that relies on the acquisition of a set of skills, which, when combined imaginatively, result in the production of an artefact.

Watson's figure illustrates how central research questions are to the overall research process and the way in which they are embedded in the many decisions that have to be made during it. In the case of his own research, Watson found that his research questions were pushing him in the direction of needing to appreciate 'issues of language and meaning'. He goes on to say:

> This implies investigative techniques which take one close to individuals, which allow close attention to the way people use language and which enable the researcher to relate closely the individual to the context in which they work. The basic research design shaped to meet these criteria was one of participant observation within the management team of a single organization combined with detailed interviews with a cross-section of that group of managers.
>
> (Watson 1994*b*: S82)

In other words, the way in which Watson's research questions were framed profoundly influenced both his research design (a case study) and his research methods (participant observation and semi-structured interviewing). Decisions about research questions are therefore crucial to how research is designed and how data are collected. You are advised not to begin thinking about your research methods until you have established what your research questions are. Some people do prefer to use particular methods and frame their research questions in terms of those preferences (Bryman 2007*b*); that is not regarded as a good practice (P. White 2009).

One final point to make is that a research question is not the same as a hypothesis. A hypothesis is a specific type of research question. It is an informed speculation, which is set up to be tested, about the possible relationship between two or more variables. Hypotheses are not as common in quantitative research as is sometimes supposed and in qualitative research they are typically avoided, other than as speculations that arise in the course of fieldwork.

If you are still stuck about how to formulate research questions (or indeed about other phases of your research), it is always a good idea to look at journal articles or research monographs to see how other researchers have formulated them. Look at past dissertations for ideas as well.

Figure 4.3

A 'what, why, and how' framework for crafting research questions

What?	Why?
What puzzles/intrigues me? What do I want to know more about/understand better? What are my key research questions?	Why will this be of enough interest to others to be published as a thesis, book, paper, guide to practitioners or policy-makers? Can the research be justified as a 'contribution to knowledge'?
How—conceptually?	**How—practically?**
What models, concepts, and theories can I draw on/develop to answer my research questions? How can these be brought together into a basic conceptual framework to guide my investigation?	What investigative styles and techniques shall I use to apply my conceptual framework (both to gather material and analyse it)? How shall I gain and maintain access to information sources?

Source: Watson (1994b: S80). Reprinted with permission of Wiley Publishing.

Criteria for evaluating research questions

Research questions for a dissertation or project should meet the following criteria:

- *Questions should be clear.* They must be understandable to you and to others.

- *Questions should be researchable.* They should be capable of development into a research design, so that data may be collected in relation to them. This means that extremely abstract terms are unlikely to be suitable.

- *Questions should connect with established theory and research.* This means that there should be a literature on which you can draw to help illuminate how your research questions should be approached. Even if you find a topic that has been scarcely addressed by social scientists, it is unlikely that there will be no relevant literature (for example, on related or parallel topics). Making connections with theory and research will also allow you to show how your research has made a contribution to knowledge and understanding.

- *Questions should be linked to each other.* Unrelated research questions are unlikely to be acceptable, since you should be developing an argument in your dissertation. You will not very readily be able to construct a single argument in connection with unrelated research questions.

- *Questions should have potential for making a contribution to knowledge.* They should at the very least hold out the prospect of being able to make a contribution—however small—to the topic.

- *Questions should be neither too broad nor too narrow.* The research questions should be neither too large (so that you would need a massive grant to study them) nor too small (so that you cannot make a reasonably significant contribution to your area of study).

Writing your research proposal

You may be required as part of your dissertation to write a short proposal or plan outlining what your research project will be about and how you intend to go about it. This is a useful way of preparing for your research, and it will encourage you to think about many of the issues that are covered in the next section. In addition to outlining the research design and methods that you intend to use, the topic area in which your study is going to be located, and the research questions that you intend to address, the proposal will ask you to demonstrate some knowledge of the literature in your chosen field—for example, by identifying several key authors or important research studies. This information may be used as the basis for allocating a supervisor who is knowledgeable in your area of research interest. The proposal is also a useful basis for discussion of your research project with your supervisor, and if it includes a timetable for the project this can provide a basis for planning regular meetings with your supervisor to review your progress. Developing a timetable can be very important in making you think about aspects of the overall research process, such as the different stages of your research and their timing, and in giving you a series of ongoing goals to aim for. Even if you are not required to produce a research proposal, it is worthwhile constructing a timetable for your research and asking your supervisor to look at it, so that you can assess how (un)realistic your goals are and whether you are allowing enough time for each of the components of the research process.

When writing a research proposal, there are a number of issues that you will probably need to cover:

- What is your research topic or, alternatively, what are your research objectives?
- Why is your research topic (or why are those research objectives) important?
- What is your research question or what are your research questions?

- What does the literature have to say about your research topic/objectives and research question(s)?
- How are you going to go about collecting data relevant to your research question(s)? In other words, what research methods are you intending to use?
- Why are the research methods/sources you have selected the appropriate ones for your research question?
- Who will your research participants be and how will they be selected (or if the research will employ documents, what kinds of documents will be the focus of your attention and how will they be selected)?
- If your research requires you to secure access to organizations, have you done so, and if not, what obstacles do you anticipate?
- What resources will you need to conduct your research (for example, postage, travel costs, recording and transcription equipment, photocopying, software) and how will those resources be funded?
- What is your timetable for the different stages of the project?
- What problems do you anticipate in doing the research (for example, access to organizations)?
- What are the possible ethical problems associated with your research?
- How will you analyse your data?

Writing a proposal is, therefore, useful in getting you started on your research project and encouraging you to set realistic objectives for your research project. An important thing to remember about the research proposal is that it is a working document and the ideas that you set out in it can be refined and developed as your research progresses. But it is also important to bear in mind that, if you keep changing your mind about your area of research interest and research design, you will be using up valuable time needed to complete the dissertation within the deadline.

Preparing for your research

Do not begin your data collection until you have identified your research questions reasonably clearly and conducted your literature review. Decide on your data collection methods with these research questions at the forefront of your thinking. If you do not do this, there is the risk that your results will not allow you to illuminate

Telling it like it is
The importance of planning

Karen found one of the things she had learned from the experience of doing a research project was the importance of planning. 'For our dissertation we actually had to do a proposal and submit it and get that approved by our dissertation tutor before we started the actual writing. I think that's really important for them to check that you're on the right lines and just to clarify for you because I think when you first start you think "Oh, it's such a lot of pages or a lot of words" and you have the desire to do so much, but then once you start writing you realize that it's much better to be a lot more focused and then you can go a lot deeper into things. So I think having that plan right at the beginning is really important.'

the research questions. If at all possible, conduct a small pilot study to determine how well your research methods work.

You will also need to think about access and sampling issues. If your research requires you to gain access to or the cooperation of one or more closed settings such as an organization, you need to confirm at the earliest opportunity that you have the necessary permission to conduct your work. You also need to consider how you will go about gaining access to people. These issues lead you into sampling considerations, such as the following:

- Who do you need to study in order to investigate your research questions?

- How easily can you gain access to a **sampling frame**?

- What kind of sampling strategy will you employ (for example, **probability sampling**, **quota sampling**, **theoretical sampling**, **convenience sampling**)?

- Can you justify your choice of sampling method?

Also, at this stage, if you are using a case study design, you will almost certainly need to find out more about the organization that you intend to investigate. What is its financial position? Has it been in the news recently? Where are its premises? What market conditions does it face? There are a wide variety of sources available on the Web that can provide this kind of background information to inform your research. Company accounts are available through Companies House; some free company information is available from *www.companieshouse.gov.uk* (accessed 15 October 2014).

In addition, the largest multinational corporations often make their annual reports and accounts available through their homepages. Although this is for them primarily a marketing exercise, you can often obtain the full text, as it appears in hard copy, free of charge. The best way to find these pages is by entering the full company name as a phrase in your search engine.

Newspapers such as the *Financial Times* are also accessible on the Web, although there are some limitations on the amount of information that you can obtain free of charge. Newslink is a collection of links to countries and then to newspapers all over the world. It can be found at *www.newslink.org* (accessed 15 October 2014).

Also, while preparing for your data collection, you should consider whether there are any possible ethical problems associated with your research methods or your approach to contacting people (see Chapter 6).

Doing your research and analysing your results

Since this is what the bulk of this book will be about, it is not necessary at this point to go into detail, but here are some useful reminders of practicalities.

- Keep good records of what you do. A research **diary** can be helpful, but there are several other things to bear in mind. For example, if you are doing a survey by postal questionnaire, keep good records of who has replied, so that you know who should be sent reminders. If participant observation is a component of your research, remember to keep good **field notes** and not to rely on your memory.

- Make sure that you are thoroughly familiar with any hardware you are using in collecting your data, such as audio recorders for interviewing, and check that it is in good working order (for example, that the batteries are not low or exhausted).

- Do not wait until all your data have been collected to begin coding. This recommendation applies to both quantitative and qualitative research. If you are conducting a questionnaire survey, begin coding your data and entering them into SPSS or whatever package you are using after you have put together a reasonably sized batch of completed questionnaires. In the case of qualitative data, such as interview transcripts, the same point applies, and, indeed, it is a specific recommendation of the proponents of grounded theory that data collection and analysis should be intertwined.

- Remember that the transcription of recorded interviews takes a long time. Allow at least six hours' transcription for every one hour of recorded interview talk, at least in the early stages of transcription.

- Become familiar with any data analysis packages as soon as possible. This familiarity will help you to establish whether or not you definitely need them and will ensure that you do not need to learn everything about them at the very time you need to use them for your analysis.

- Do not at any time take risks with your personal safety (see Tips and skills 'Safety in research').

Tips and skills
Safety in research

You must bear in mind that, even though the majority of business research carries a low risk of personal harm to the researcher, there are occasions when doing research places you in potentially dangerous situations. You should avoid taking personal risks at all costs and you should resist any attempts to place yourself in situations where personal harm is a possibility. Just as you should ensure that no harm comes to research participants (as prescribed in the discussion of ethical principles in Chapter 6), individuals involved in directing others' research should not place students and researchers in situations in which they might come to harm. Equally, lone researchers should avoid such situations. There are also situations in which there is no obvious reason to think that a situation may be dangerous, but the researcher is faced with a sudden outburst of abuse or threatening behaviour. This can arise when people react relatively unpredictably to an interview question or to being observed. If there are signs that such behaviour is imminent (for example, through body language), begin a withdrawal from the research situation. R. M. Lee (2004) draws an important distinction between two kinds of danger in fieldwork: ambient and situational. The former refers to situations that are avoidable and in which danger is an ingredient of the context. Situational danger occurs 'when the researcher's presence or activities evoke aggression, hostility or violence from those in the setting' (R. M. Lee 2004: 1285). While problems surrounding safety may be easier to anticipate in the case of ambient danger, they are less easy to foresee in connection with situational danger.

Telling it like it is
Listen to the advice of your supervisor, but make your own choices

We asked the supervisors we surveyed to tell us what the most important advice they gave to students at the start of their research project was. Here's what they told us!

- Choose a topic that interests *you*.

- Ask yourself whether you can answer the research question.

- Read a lot; read thoroughly and appropriately (this includes articles in refereed journals).

- Identify your strengths, weaknesses, interests, and personal development opportunities and take them into account in designing the project.

- Don't pre-commit to one idea, approach, research design, data source, and so on, to the exclusion of other possibilities.

- Use opportunities to talk to others in your own field and other fields about your proposed research and assess its importance, characteristics, and possible relationship to what others are doing.

- Research something that is likely to be interesting to others: either practitioners or researchers (or both).

- Start writing early. Build in a cushion round the deadline; analysis takes much longer than you think. This is where 'added value' can be gained.

- Remember that this is not your life work or a bid for a Nobel Prize.

- Listen to my advice, but make your own choices.

Checklist
Planning a research project

- ○ Do you know what the requirements for your dissertation are, as set out by your university or department?

- ○ Have you made contact with your supervisor?

- ○ Have you left enough time for planning your research, collecting and analysing data, and writing up your research project?

- ○ Do you have a clear timetable for your research project with clearly identifiable milestones for the achievement of specific tasks?

- ○ Have you got sufficient financial and practical resources (for example, money to enable travel to research site, audio recorder) to enable you to carry out your research project?

- ○ Have you formulated some research questions and discussed these with your supervisor?

- ○ Are the research questions you have identified capable of being answered through your research project?

- ○ Do you have the access that you require in order to carry out your research?

○ Do you know which research participants or what sources (e.g. documents) are needed to answer your research questions and how to locate and sample them?

○ Have you established which research method(s) you are planning to use and why?

○ Are you familiar with the data analysis software that you will be using to analyse your data?

Key points

- Follow the dissertation guidelines provided by your institution.

- Thinking about your research subject can be time-consuming, so allow plenty of time for this aspect of the dissertation process.

- Use your supervisor to the fullest extent allowed and follow the advice offered by him or her.

- Plan your time carefully and be realistic about what you can achieve in the time available.

- Formulate some research questions to express what it is about your area of interest that you want to know.

- Writing a research proposal is a good way of getting started on your research project and encouraging you to set realistic objectives.

- Consider access and sampling issues at an early stage and consider testing your research methods by conducting a pilot study.

- Keep good records of what you do in your research as you go along and don't wait until all of your data have been collected before you start coding.

Questions for review

Managing time and resources

- What are the main advantages and disadvantages associated with using a Gantt chart to plan your research?

Formulating suitable research questions

- What are the main sources of research questions?

- What are the main steps involved in developing research questions?

  What criteria can be used to evaluate research questions?

Writing your research proposal

- What is the purpose of the research proposal and how can it be useful?

Online Resource Centre

www.oxfordtextbooks.co.uk/orc/brymanbrm4e/

Visit the Interactive Research Guide that accompanies this book to complete an exercise in Planning a Research Project and Formulating Research Questions.

5

Getting started: reviewing the literature

Chapter outline

The goal of this chapter is to provide guidance for students on how to get started on their research project. Once you have identified your research questions (see Chapter 4), the next step in any research project is to search the existing literature and write a literature review. The principal task at this early stage involves reviewing the main ideas and research relating to your chosen area of interest. This provides the basis for the writing of a literature review, which forms an important part of the dissertation.

The chapter explores:

- how to go about searching the literature and engaging critically with the ideas of other writers;
- what is expected in a literature review and the criteria that are used to evaluate it;
- how to assess the quality of existing research in your subject area;
- the role of the bibliography and the importance of referencing the work of others;
- the importance of understanding what constitutes plagiarism and the penalties that are associated with it.

Introduction

This chapter is intended to help you to get started on one of the most important tasks in carrying out a research project of your own—reviewing the literature in your chosen subject area. The literature review is a crucial part of an undergraduate or postgraduate dissertation, often constituting a separate chapter or substantial section that is usually positioned towards the beginning of the finished document. It provides the basis on which you justify your research questions and build your research design. The literature review also informs how you collect your data and enables you to analyse your data in an informed way. However, doing a literature review can initially feel quite daunting, either because so many other researchers have written so many books and articles about your chosen subject often based on much larger-scale studies than your own, or because your subject area does not seem to have a clearly defined boundary, hence there are various literatures that you could review and you are not sure how to choose between or combine them. The process of reviewing the literature therefore involves making judgements about what to include and exclude from your literature review and then reading what other researchers have written about your subject and writing about it in a way that demonstrates your understanding. The advice we give in this chapter is designed to assist in this process. A substantial proportion of this literature will have been published in academic journals (see Key concept 5.1).

Reviewing the existing literature and engaging with what others have written

Why do you need to review the existing literature? The most obvious reason is that you want to know what is already known about your area of interest so that you do not simply 'reinvent the wheel'. Your literature review is where you demonstrate that you are able to engage in scholarly review based on your reading and understanding of the work of others in the same field as you. Beyond this, using the existing literature on a topic is a means of developing an argument about the significance of your research and where it leads. The simile of a *story* is also sometimes used in this context (see Thinking deeply 5.2). Whatever different understandings of the literature review process you adopt, it is perhaps easier to be clear about the goal that the process is directed towards achieving. A competent review of the literature is at least in part a means of affirming your credibility as someone who is knowledgeable in your chosen area. This is not simply a matter of reproducing the theories and opinions of other scholars, but also of being able to interpret what they have written, possibly by using their ideas to support a particular viewpoint or argument. The purpose of exploring the existing literature should be to identify the following issues:

- What is already known about this area?
- What concepts and theories are relevant to this area?

- What research methods and research strategies have been employed in studying this area?
- Are there any significant controversies?
- Are there any inconsistencies in findings relating to this area?
- Are there any unanswered research questions in this area?

This last issue points to the possibility that you will be able to revise and refine your research questions in the process of reviewing the literature.

Key concept 5.1
What is an academic journal?

An academic journal, also referred to as a scholarly, peer-reviewed, or refereed journal, is one where the research papers submitted for consideration must go through a process of, usually 'blind' (i.e. anonymous), review by between two and four experts in the specialist subject, and a decision is made by the editor based on these reviews. Usually, the editor will require certain revisions of the author (or authors) on the basis of the referees' comments, and the editor will then decide whether or not to accept the revised paper, often after sending it back out to the referees for further comment, a process that may result in the author having to revise the draft for a second or third time. If the editor is still not satisfied with the changes the authors have made to the paper, this process may still result in rejection. In prestigious academic journals in the business and management field, it is common for more than 90 per cent of articles to be rejected, and it is very unusual for an article to be accepted on its first submission. This process is referred to as 'peer review'. Consequently, the articles that are eventually published are not just the culmination of a research process but are also the outcome of an often lengthy feedback and review process than can take in excess of two years. Many of the examples used in the Research in focus boxes in this book have been published in academic journals, which means that they have gone through a review process similar to the one just described. This enables the reader to have confidence in the quality of the research because it has been reviewed and approved for publication by other experts in the field.

Most academic journals are published by a commercial publisher such as Sage Publishing or John Wiley & Sons, sometimes in association with a professional association, such as the British Academy of Management or the Academy of Management. In recent years, commercial publishers have come under increasing critical scrutiny as a consequence of their journal publishing practices, which are extremely lucrative and generate substantial profits (Lilley et al., 2012). The rapidly rising costs of subscription to academic journals is born by university libraries, at a time when universities are facing greater budgetary constraints and students, in the UK at least, are being asked to pay increasingly large fees for their university education. This has led to calls for more 'open-access' journal publishing, where research can be read, free of charge, online for an unlimited time. An example is the independent journal of organization studies, *Ephemera*, which was founded in 2001 and provides its content free of charge. The research published in the journal goes through peer review, and several articles published have become well cited in their fields. Many universities also now have institutional repositories, where a pre-publication version of the accepted journal article can be posted by the author online. This is an entirely respectable way of accessing an academic article if you do not have institutional access to the published version, since it should contain exactly the same text as the published version; the only difference is that it is not typeset, so citing specific page numbers for direct quotes can be a problem.

(continued)

Open-access publishing has the potential to enable the majority of the world's population to access research even if they cannot afford access to academic journals via expensive institutional or individual subscription. On the other hand, the rise in open-access journal publishing has also led to some more unscrupulous practices. The website Scholarly Open Access, commonly referred to as Beall's List, is the work of Jeffrey Beall, a US-based university librarian. Beall has taken issue with the sudden proliferation of open-access journals and the unscrupulous publishers behind them, who use a variety of tricks to try to fool people into thinking that their journals are legitimate scholarly publications. Some publishers have objected to Beall's classifications, so they should be treated with caution. Examples from Beall's List in the field of business include a Taiwan-based organization which hosts the bogus Global Business and International Management Conference and publishes papers in its conference proceedings and in three open-access journals, including the *Journal of Global Business Management*. This relies on each author paying a publication fee of between $500 and $700. Beall's List may be seen at **http://scholarlyoa.com/** (accessed 17 October 2014).

Tips and skills
Ways of conceptualizing a literature review

Bruce's (1994) study of research students' early experiences of the dissertation literature review identified six qualitatively different ways in which the review process was experienced or understood by postgraduates. The six conceptions included:

1. *List*. The literature review is understood as a list comprising pertinent items representing the literature of the subject.

2. *Search*. The review is a process of identifying relevant information and the focus is on finding or looking, which may involve going through sources (for example, article, database) to identify information.

3. *Survey*. Students also see the literature review as an investigation of past and present writing or research on a subject. This investigation may be active (critical/analytical) or passive (descriptive).

4. *Vehicle*. The review is also seen as having an impact on the researcher because it is seen as a vehicle for learning that leads to an increase in their knowledge and understanding. Within this conception the review acts as a sounding board through which the student can check ideas or test personal perceptions.

5. *Facilitator*. The literature review can be understood as directly related to the research that is about to be or is being undertaken, the process helping them to identify a topic, support a methodology, provide a context, or change research direction. The review thus helps to shape the course of the student's research.

6. *Report*. The review is understood as a written discussion of the literature drawing on previously conducted investigations. The focus is on 'framing a written discourse about the literature which may be established as a component part of a thesis or other research report' (1994: 223).

These six conceptions reflect the varying relationship between the student and the literature, the earlier ones being more indirect—the student works with items that represent the primary literature such as bibliographic citations, and the latter conceptions being more direct—the student works with source material rather than, for example, a representative abstract. The conceptions can also be seen as cumulative, since a student who adopts the facilitator conception may also continue to hold the conception of the literature review as a survey. Bruce therefore recommends that students be encouraged to adopt the higher level conceptions (4–6) because through this the other ways of experiencing the literature review (1–3) become more meaningful.

Telling it like it is
Using the literature to develop your research questions

One of the most common ways that students develop their research questions is by reviewing the literature. Angharad explained: 'I started off reading through my literature review I think and I just pulled out questions from that, things that had cropped up in research. There were things that had come up that I wanted answering, but a lot of it was things that I wanted to test out from the literature and then I went to see my supervisor and said, "This is the area I want to look at," and he said, "Well, that's a big area. You need to think of a question. Have you got something you want to know?" And I said, "Yeah, I want to know why women aren't senior managers and specifically whether they're choosing not to go that way or whether something is holding them back." And that was my question.'

Sometimes the experience of searching the literature for a research project can be more difficult than for taught courses, in which you would probably be given extensive reading lists and would have recommended textbooks. In doing a research project you are focusing on a specialized subject of your own choosing. It is, therefore, unlikely that there will be a textbook that precisely matches your subject focus, so you may have to be persistent in your search for existing literature, as Karen's experience illustrates: 'I became quite interested in the relationship between person and organization culture fit and so I started doing a little bit more reading and then I stumbled upon this one article in a human resources journal but then I sort of hit a wall after this first article where I thought, "Great! There's something about it!" I hit a wall where there was just nothing else that I could find and I went to all you know, all sorts of mainstream human resources textbooks and recruitment textbooks and they were just talking all the time about evaluating job criteria and nothing about culture fit. And so then I started to look a bit more broadly and then it was just all of a sudden I just hit on this one article and it just led to loads of things. I just looked in the bibliography and it was just one thing really that opened up the whole sphere to me and said like "There is some stuff written about this." Because at that point I was thinking "Argh! There's nothing and I'm not going to be able to do it because there's nothing else written about it."'

Of course, you may find that there really is nothing written about your chosen subject, although you would probably already have been advised against taking on such a research project in the first place. If you do become worried that there is not enough literature on which to base your research project, you should discuss this with your supervisor.

To find out more about Karen's research experiences, go to the Online Resource Centre that accompanies this book: **www.oxfordtextbooks.co.uk/orc/brymanbrm4e/**

Getting the most from your reading

Since a great deal of time during the early stages of your research project will be taken up with reading the existing literature in order to write your review, it is important to make sure that the process of reading is also preparing you for this. Getting the most from your reading involves developing your skills in being able to read actively and critically. When you are reading the existing literature, try to do the following:

- Take good notes, including publication details of the material you read. It is infuriating to find that you forgot to record the volume number of an article you read and that needs to be included in your bibliography.

This may necessitate a trip to the library on occasions when you are already hard pressed for time.

- Develop critical reading skills. In reviewing the literature you should do more than simply summarize what you have read; you should, whenever appropriate, be critical in your approach. It is worth developing these skills and recording relevant critical points in the course of taking notes. Developing a critical approach is not necessarily one of simply criticizing the work of others. It entails moving beyond mere description and asking questions about the significance of the work. It entails attending to such issues as: how does the item relate to others you have read? Are there any apparent strengths and deficiencies—perhaps in terms of methodology or in terms of the credibility of the conclusions drawn? What theoretical ideas have influenced the item?

- Use your review of the literature as a means of showing why your research questions are important. For example, if one of your arguments in arriving at your research questions is that, although a lot of research has been done on X (a general topic or area, such as the psychological contract, female entrepreneurship, or employee absenteeism), little or no research has been done on X_1 (an aspect of X), the literature review is the point where you can justify this assertion. Alternatively, it might be that there are two competing positions with regard to X_1 and you are going to investigate which one provides a better understanding. In the literature review, you should outline the nature of the differences between the competing positions. The literature review, then, allows you to locate your own research within a tradition of research in an area. Indeed, reading the literature is itself often an important source of research questions.

- Bear in mind that you will want to return to much of the literature that you examine in the discussion of your findings and conclusion.

- Do not try to get everything you read into a literature review. Trying to force everything you have read into your review (because of all the hard work involved in uncovering and reading the material) is not going to help you. The literature review must assist you in developing an argument, and bringing in material of dubious relevance may undermine your ability to get your argument across.

- Bear in mind that reading the literature is not something that you should stop doing once you begin designing your research. You should continue your search for and reading of relevant literature more or less throughout your research. This means that, if you have written a literature review before beginning your data collection, you will need to regard it as provisional. Indeed, you may want to make quite substantial revisions of your review towards the end of writing up your work.

- Further useful thoughts about how to develop your use of the literature can be found in Thinking deeply 5.2. The different ways of construing the literature that are presented in this box are derived from a review of qualitative studies of organizations, but the approaches identified have a much broader applicability, including to quantitative research.

Systematic review

In recent years, considerable thought has been devoted to the notion of **systematic review** (see Key concept 5.3). This is an approach to reviewing the literature that adopts explicit procedures. An example of systematic review is given in Research in focus 5.4.

Systematic review has emerged as a focus of interest for two main reasons. First, it is sometimes suggested that many reviews of the literature tend to 'lack thoroughness' and to reflect the biases of the researcher (e.g. Tranfield, Denyer, and Smart 2003). Proponents of systematic review suggest that adopting explicit procedures makes such biases less likely to arise. Second, as discussed in Chapter 1, in fields such as medicine and latterly business there has been a growing movement towards evidence-based solutions. Systematic reviews of the literature are seen as a cornerstone of evidence-based approaches. Their purpose is to provide advice for practitioners based on all the available evidence. Such reviews are deemed to be valuable for decision-makers, particularly in areas where there is conflicting evidence concerning the best way of doing things (as in the case of business).

Thinking deeply 5.2
Presenting literature in articles based on qualitative research on organizations

Further useful advice on relating your own work to the literature can be gleaned from an examination of the ways in which articles based on qualitative research on organizations are composed. In their examination of such articles, Golden-Biddle and Locke (1993, 1997) argue that good articles in this area develop a

(continued)

story—that is, a clear and compelling framework around which the writing is structured. This idea is very much in tune with Wolcott's (1990: 18) recommendation to 'determine the basic story you are going to tell'. Golden-Biddle and Locke's research suggests that the way the author's position in relation to the literature is presented is an important component of storytelling. They distinguish two processes in the ways that the literature is conveyed.

- Constructing intertextual coherence—refers to the way in which existing knowledge is represented and organized; the author shows how contributions to the literature relate to each other and the research reported. The techniques used are:
  - *Synthesized coherence*—puts together work that is generally considered unrelated; theory and research previously regarded as unconnected are pieced together. There are two prominent forms:
    1. the organization of very incompatible references (bits and pieces);
    2. connections forged between established theories or research programmes.
  - *Progressive coherence*—portrays the building-up of an area of knowledge around which there is considerable consensus.
  - *Non-coherence*—recognition that there have been many contributions to a certain research programme, but there is considerable disagreement among practitioners. Each of these strategies is designed to leave room for a contribution to be made.
- Problematizing the situation—the literature is then subverted by locating a problem. The following techniques were identified:

  Incomplete—the existing literature is not fully complete; there is a gap.

  Inadequate—the existing literature on the phenomenon of interest has overlooked ways of looking at it that can greatly improve our understanding of it; alternative perspectives or frameworks can then be introduced.

  Incommensurate—argues for an alternative perspective that is superior to the literature as it stands; differs from 'inadequate' because it portrays the existing literature as 'wrong, misguided, or incorrect' (Golden-Biddle and Locke 1997: 43).

The key point about Golden-Biddle and Locke's account of the way the literature is construed in this field is that it is used by writers to achieve a number of things:

- They can demonstrate their competence by referring to prominent writings in the field (Gilbert 1977).
- They develop their version of the literature in such a way as to show and to lead up to the contribution they will be making in the article.
- The gap or problem in the literature that is identified corresponds to the research questions.

The idea of writing up one's research as storytelling acts as a useful reminder that reviewing the literature, which is part of the story, should link seamlessly with the rest of the article and not be considered a separate element.

However, Tranfield, Denyer, and Smart (2003) acknowledge that, unlike medical science, business research is a relatively young field that stems from the social, rather than the biological, sciences and is characterized by low consensus concerning key research questions. Also, medical science is often concerned with research questions to do with whether or not particular interventions (such as a medicine or a therapy) are effective. Such issues are well suited to systematic review, but are not often encountered in business and management research. So, can a review process developed in a discipline that is largely based on a quantitative research strategy inform the development of a more systematic literature review process in business research?

Telling it like it is
Getting help from your supervisor
at the literature review stage

Nirwanthi found that her supervisor was influential in helping her to identify an area of existing literature that helped her to better understand her research data. She explained: 'I got a lot of help from my supervisor. He actually found an important article for me that was very close to what I was studying. What was useful was that he had a whole list of references that I started reading. I picked a few—like ten to fifteen that I thought would be useful and started reading and then it just started to materialise, you know. It became specific.'

Angharad also found that she turned to her supervisor to advise her at the literature review stage. 'I had absolutely no idea where to start. It was all up in the air. Basically I was encouraged and I did do some reading around the subject, so I knew what the issues were. My supervisor recommended three or four books and told me, "These are central to what you're doing." He was very good. He just said, "If you want to do this topic, start with this and see what you think." So I read those and I could see what the issues were and what I was looking for.'

Angharad also went a step further than this by contacting the author of one of the studies that was key to her research project to ask for her advice. 'Just by chance I came across her email address on a search on Google and I emailed her and said, "I'm doing interviews tomorrow and I've read your book and it really helped me." Her book really helped me in getting an idea of how you go about doing research into these kinds of things. So I emailed her and told her what I was doing and she wrote back and said, "Ask what you want to know." So I did! [*laughs*].'

Although we do not recommend that you should rely on authors responding to emails of this nature from students doing a research project, or that you start sending emails left, right, and centre to management academics across the world, Angharad's experience does show that the process of doing a research project can bring you closer to the community of researchers who have contributed to the literature on which you seek to build.

Key concept 5.3
What is a systematic review?

Systematic review has been defined as 'a replicable, scientific and transparent process, in other words a detailed technology, that aims to minimize bias through exhaustive literature searches of published and unpublished studies and by providing an audit trail of the reviewer's decisions, procedures and conclusions' (Tranfield, Denyer, and Smart 2003: 209). Such a review is often contrasted with traditional narrative review, which is the focus of the next section. Proponents of systematic review argue that it is more likely than the traditional review to generate unbiased and comprehensive accounts of the literature, especially in relation to fields where the aim is to understand whether a particular intervention has benefits. A systematic review that includes only quantitative studies and which seeks to summarize those studies quantitatively is a **meta-analysis** (see Key concept 14.9). Very recently, the development of systematic review procedures for qualitative studies has attracted a great deal of attention, especially in the social sciences. **Meta-ethnography** (see Key concept 24.10) is one such approach to the synthesis of qualitative findings, but currently there are several methods, none of which is in widespread use (Mays, Pope, and Popay 2005).

Research in focus 5.4
A systematic review of networking and innovation

Pittaway et al. (2004) carried out a review on the impact of business networking on the innovative capacity of firms. The objectives of the review were:

1. to establish the nature of the relationship between networking and innovation;

2. to compare the degree and impact of networking behaviour in the UK with that in other competing countries;

3. to explore the literature on failure of business-to-business networks;

4. to generate insights that could inform policies aimed at fostering business-to-business networking;

5. to identify areas for future research.

The review team comprising the five authors of the paper started by identifying subject keywords based on their prior experience, which were then constructed into search strings such as

> Network* AND Innovat*

An initial search on the bibliographic database ABI/INFORM via Proquest was analysed in Procite, and this was used to generate further keywords and extend the search using six other search engines. The citations generated were reviewed according to inclusion and exclusion criteria defined by the team. An example of the inclusion criteria used is 'Working papers'—to ensure coverage of the most current research. An example of the exclusion criteria is 'Pre-1980'—because few contributions to networking theory were published before this date. The articles were then separated into three lists:

A articles of particular relevance with interesting empirical approaches;

B articles where there 'may have been some question' (2004: 139) over the value of the empirical work;

C articles of little relevance or predominantly conceptual.

Then the AIM Fellows (a group of academics who are appointed to the Advanced Institute of Management) were invited to comment on the A-list and add to it, and this list was then reviewed according to pre-established quality criteria. Abstracts of the A-list articles were imported into NVivo and coded according to their content. Finally, the sections of the review were written to reflect the eleven subject themes identified.

One of the challenges faced by the researchers was related to the keywords used, since networking and innovation are inherently ambiguous terms that are used in a variety of subject disciplines from economic geography to sociology. A further challenge related to the sheer volume of papers that were identified as relevant—623 in total. The authors claim it was therefore very important to rank the papers according to relevance, so that an A-list of 179 papers could then be used as the primary basis for the review.

The main steps of the systematic review process are:

- *Specifying the question and planning the review*. This involves specifying the research question, which must be clearly answerable. Denyer and Tranfield (2009) suggest that this involves looking at the relationship between variables and why, and in what circumstances, the relationship occurs. There are four elements to this: *Context* (what individuals/relationships/ institutional settings/systems are being studied); *Intervention* (what effects, relating to events, actions, or activities, are being studied); *Mechanisms* (what mechanisms explain the relationship between interventions and outcomes), and *Outcomes* (the intended and unintended effects of the intervention and how they will be measured). Denyer and Tranfield (2009: 682) give an example of a suitable question to illustrate: 'Under what conditions (C) does leadership style (I) influence the performance of project teams (O), and what mechanisms operate in the influence of leadership style (I) on project team performance?' Next, a group of stakeholders, including practitioners and researchers, meets at regular intervals, first to define and clarify the boundaries of the review and later to monitor its progress. This includes setting the criteria for inclusion and exclusion of studies from the review. 'This helps ensure that reviews are impartial and balanced, preventing reviewers from including only those studies supporting their particular argument' (Briner, Denyer, and Rousseau 2009: 26).

- *Conducting the review*. This involves carrying out 'a comprehensive, unbiased search' (Tranfield, Denyer, and Smart 2003: 215) based on keywords and search terms. The search strategy must be described in terms that allow it to be replicated and searches should include unpublished (for example, working or conference papers) as well as published articles. The information search leads to the production of a list of all the articles and books on which the review will be based. These articles and books are examined and sifted on the basis of two types of consideration. First, all studies that fail to relate to the review's research question have to be excluded. Second, those studies that are relevant are examined for study quality. Sometimes, systematic reviewers will exclude studies that fail to meet minimum criteria, although that can sometimes mean that the review is then conducted on an extremely small sample of remaining studies. More often, reviewers will categorize studies in terms of the extent to which they meet the quality criteria that are specified. Checklists for assessing quality are available, but it is necessary to use those that are appropriate for the kinds of research being examined. The issue of quality criteria in relation to quantitative and qualitative research is covered in Chapters 7 and 17. Once the items to be included in the review have been identified, the analysis begins. The aim of this is to achieve a cumulative understanding of what is known about the subject through applying techniques of research synthesis. Often, systematic reviewers seek to arrive at a 'narrative synthesis' of the research: this uses text to summarize key findings relating to the research question, often accompanied by simple statistical summaries such as the percentage of studies that examined a certain issue or that adopted a particular perspective. One advantage of a narrative synthesis is that it can be used as a platform for reviewing and summarizing both quantitative and qualitative studies.

- *Reporting and dissemination*. This involves reporting in a way that provides a descriptive map of the research on the subject, including who the contributors are, where they are based, and when the main temporal periods of research activity on the subject occurred. A further criterion for reporting is accessibility and readability. The review process should make it easier for the practitioner to understand the research, so that it is more likely that it will be translated into practice.

Tranfield, Denyer, and Smart (2003) suggest that the systematic review process provides a more reliable foundation on which to design research, because it is based on a more comprehensive understanding of what we know about a subject. Research that involves systematic literature review is argued to be more strongly evidence-based because it is concerned with seeking to understand the effects of a particular variable or intervention that has been found in previous studies. This is useful in subjecting widely held assumptions about a subject to empirical scrutiny. For example, it is widely assumed that workplace stress produces ill-health effects in employees. Systematic review provides a way for the researcher who is interested in this subject to find out whether or not previous studies have found this to be the case. This can be helpful in encouraging researchers to think critically about their subject. Proponents of systematic review also commend the approach for its transparency; in other words, the grounds on which studies were selected and how they were analysed are clearly articulated and are potentially replicable.

Tips and skills
Using systematic review in a student research project

The systematic review approach does contain some elements that cannot easily be applied in a student research project because of limitations of time and resources. For example, you are unlikely to be able to assemble a panel of experts in methodology and theory to meet regularly with you and discuss the boundaries of the review.

(continued)

However, there are some aspects of the approach that can be applied to students' research. For example, meeting regularly with your supervisor during the planning stage of your literature review to define the boundaries of the subject and to come up with likely search terms is extremely useful. Your supervisor's knowledge of the subject can be invaluable at this stage, as some of the students we interviewed indicated. Also, a systematic review approach to the literature requires a transparent way of searching for and examining the literature as well as keeping records of what you have done. These practices are feasible for a student research project. However, the experience of one student who was intending to conduct a systematic review for a Ph.D. in the field of political science suggests that students can become engulfed by the sheer volume of literature that has to be screened and analysed (Daigneault et al. 2012). The student in question had intended the systematic review to be the core of his thesis and not a literature review that would act as a precursor to data collection, but he had to give up due to the sheer volume of material he was having to consider as well as other reasons. Clearly, the decision to include a systematic review should not be taken lightly and may be difficult for students doing undergraduate or postgraduate dissertations to implement. In Daigneault's case, he underestimated the amount of time required to screen articles for relevance, and the difficulty of doing so, in the face of large numbers of article titles and abstracts that were not as informative as he would have liked.

On the other hand, there has been growing interest in **rapid reviews**, which conform to many of the principles of systematic reviews but are deliberately limited in scope in one or more respects so that the review can be completed in a much shorter time frame than would normally apply with a full systematic review, for example by restricting the scope of the review to a particular year or years or by economizing on effort in areas such as number of databases used. Gannan et al. (2010) examined a substantial number of such reviews in medicine and uncovered some that took as little as a month, but as they note, the shorter the time frame the greater the risk that the principles and strengths of a systematic review will be compromised. Harker and Kleijnen (2012) uncovered 46 rapid reviews in the Health Technology Assessment field and found that there was a wide variety of departures from the typical systematic review. For example, 47 per cent of studies were found to have no research question(s), which in itself is a big departure from a fully-fledged systematic review. The mean length of time taken from start to finish was 9.7 months when one 'outlier' that took an inordinately long time was excluded. While the prospect of doing a rapid review may appear attractive to many students lacking the time to conduct a full systematic review, the lack of agreement about what a rapid review is and the uncertainty about the value of the approach (Harker and Kleijnen 2012) suggest that it should only be considered with a great deal of caution.

However, a limitation of systematic review stems from situations where research questions are not capable of being defined in terms of the effect of a particular variable, or when the subject boundaries are more fluid and open or subject to change. Since, as we discussed in Chapter 1, business is an applied field of study that borrows theory from a range of social science and other disciplines, this is more common than it might first seem. Another criticism of the approach is that it can lead to a bureaucratization of the process of reviewing the literature because it is more concerned with the technical aspects of how it is done than with the analytical interpretations generated by it. A third potential limitation of the approach relates to its application to qualitative research studies and in particular the methodological judgements that inform decisions about quality that determine the inclusion or exclusion of an article from a literature review. These stem from differences between qualitative and quantitative research in relation to the criteria used to assess their methodological quality (see Chapters 7 and 17). The systematic review approach assumes that an objective judgement about the quality of an article can be made. Such judgements have the potential to be controversial for all research, but are likely to be especially so for ones based on qualitative research. Among quantitative researchers there is somewhat more agreement about the criteria that might be applied than among qualitative researchers, who have not achieved even a near consensus (see Chapter 17). The growth of interest in systematic review and of the inclusion of qualitative studies within such reviews has almost certainly added an increased focus on quality criteria among qualitative and mixed methods researchers (Bryman, Becker, and Sempik 2008).

Some researchers would say that they measure the quality of published research in terms of what they find interesting. This may or may not include empirical study, but this view is not compatible with the systematic approach, which requires articles to be evaluated in terms of methodological criteria. In addition, researchers in the medical sciences have found the process of identifying relevant qualitative studies is quite time-consuming and cannot be done on the basis of the abstract or summary in the way that quantitative research studies can (M. L. Jones 2004). Finally, whether or not the systematic review approach makes sense to you depends somewhat on your epistemological position (see Chapter 2). As Noblit and Hare (1988: 15) state: 'Positivists have had more interest in knowledge synthesis than interpretivists. For them, knowledge accumulates. The problem has been how best to accomplish that accumulation.' For these reasons, researchers who adopt an interpretative approach to understanding the social sciences and use qualitative methods may find the systematic review approach more problematic.

Narrative review

Rather than reviewing the literature to find out what their research project can add to existing knowledge about a subject, interpretative researchers (see Chapter 2 for an explanation of interpretivism) can have quite different reasons for reviewing the literature on a particular subject, since their purpose is to enrich human discourse (Geertz 1973) by generating understanding rather than by accumulating knowledge. The literature review is for them a means of gaining an initial impression of the topic area that they intend to understand through their research. Narrative reviews therefore tend to be less focused and more wide-ranging in scope than systematic reviews. They are also less explicit about the criteria for exclusion or inclusion of studies. An example of this type of review is given in Research in focus 5.5.

If your approach to the relationship between theory and research is inductive rather than deductive (see Chapter 2), setting out all the main theoretical and conceptual terms that define your area of study prior to data collection is extremely problematic, because theory is the outcome of the study, rather than the basis for it. Hence, in the process of researching a topic, researchers may discover issues that they did not previously anticipate as likely to be important to their area of study. As a result, they become aware of the limitations of the topic

area that they originally intended to inform, and this can lead them towards an unanticipated understanding of it (Noblit and Hare 1988). Interpretative researchers are thus more likely than deductive researchers to change their view of the theory or literature as a result of the analysis of collected data, and so they require greater flexibility to modify the boundaries of their subject of study as they go along. This means that narrative review may be more suitable for qualitative researchers, whose research strategy is based on an interpretative epistemology, and systematic review should not be automatically accepted as a better way of dealing with the literature.

Most reviews are of the narrative kind, regardless of whether they are meant to be springboards for the reviewer's own investigation (for example, when the literature is reviewed as a means of specifying what is already known in connection with a research topic, so that research questions can be identified that the reviewer will then examine) or are ends in their own right (as a means of summarizing what is known in an area). When we examine some examples of writing up research in Chapter 29, we will see that the literature relevant to the researcher's area of interest is always reviewed as a means of establishing why the researcher conducted the research and what its contribution is likely to be. Such reviews are still mainly narrative reviews.

However, the gap between systematic and narrative reviews is beginning to narrow, as sometimes some of the procedures associated with systematic reviews are incorporated into a narrative review. As a result, there is a growing tendency for researchers to spell out in some detail such things as the procedures they used for conducting a literature search and the quality criteria that guided inclusion and exclusion (e.g. Bryman 2007a). For example, Purkayastha et al. (2012) conducted a narrative review of the literature on the relationship between firm diversification and performance in developed and emerging markets. They were very explicit about the two questions they employed in selecting articles for inclusion. For the research on diversification in emerging economies, the researchers used two online databases—ABI-Inform and EBSCO—using such keywords as 'diversification', 'firm performance', and 'emerging economy/ies'. Each of the articles found in this way was examined to establish how well it dovetailed with the review's research questions. In the end, 37 relevant articles concerned with diversification and firm performance in emerging economies were employed.

Research in focus 5.5
A narrative review of narrative research

Rhodes and Brown (2005) conducted a review of the management literature on **narrative analysis** (see Chapter 22 for an explanation of narrative analysis). Their use of narrative review is consistent with the focus of their review, which was on a qualitative research method. They identify five principal research areas that narrative analysis has explored, assessing the theoretical value each has added:

1. *Sensemaking*—focuses on the role of stories as a device through which people make sense of organizational events.

2. *Communication*—explores how narratives are used to create and maintain organizational culture and power structure.

3. *Learning/change*—analyses how stories help people to learn and subjectively to make sense of change.

4. *Politics and power*—considers the role of shared narratives in the control of organizational meaning.

5. *Identity and identification*—focuses on the role of stories in creating and maintaining organizational identity.

While they do not make explicit their criteria for inclusion or exclusion of certain studies, the authors assess the main contributions, implications, and limitations of narrative analysis. They also cite a number of their own publications in this subject area. This helps to convince the reader of the credibility of the authors' evaluations of other people's research on the subject from the 1970s to 2004.

Tips and skills
Reasons for writing a literature review

The following is a list of reasons for writing a literature review:

1. You need to know what is already known in connection with your research area because you do not want to be accused of reinventing the wheel.

2. You can learn from other researchers' mistakes and avoid making the same ones.

3. You can learn about different theoretical and methodological approaches to your research area.

4. It may help you to develop an analytic framework.

5. It may lead you to consider the inclusion of variables in your research that you might not otherwise have thought about.

6. It may suggest further research questions for you.

7. It will help with the interpretation of your findings.

8. It gives you some pegs on which to hang your findings.

9. It is expected!

Searching the existing literature and looking for business information

Usually, students will have in mind a few initial references when they begin work on a project. These will probably come from recommended reading in course modules, or from textbooks. The bibliographies provided at the end of textbook chapters or articles will usually provide you with a raft of further relevant references that can also be followed up. A literature search relies on careful reading of books, academic journals, and reports in the first instance. Once you have identified a few keywords that help to define the boundaries of your chosen area of research (see below), electronic databases of published literature can be searched for previously published work in the field.

Electronic databases

Online bibliographical databases are an invaluable source of academic journal references. An increasing number of these will also provide access to the full text of an article in electronic format—these are usually referred to as e-journals. You will need to check what electronic resources are available at your institution. A good place to start is on your university library's homepage or you can ask a member of library staff. Here are three resources that we would recommend:

1. ABI/INFORM provides business information from a wide range of periodicals and reports, coverage is international, and it is possible to search by keyword or to browse by topic to search for relevant articles by subject. The database can be accessed at: *proquest. com* (accessed 17 October 2014).

2. EBSCO Business Source Premier/Complete is an increasingly widely used business periodical database that now rivals ABI/INFORM in scope and coverage. Its popularity is in part due to the provision of extremely comprehensive full text access to certain key business and management journals, including titles such as *Harvard Business Review* and *Academy of Management Review*, although older issues of journals are not all included. In addition, it provides indexing and abstracts for over 3000 business journals as well as access to some company and market reports. It can be accessed via EBSCO Publishing at: *ebscohost.com* (accessed 17 October 2014).

3. We also recommend use of the Social Sciences Citation Index (SSCI), which fully indexes over 1700 major social science journals covering all social science disciplines dating back to 1970. The Citation indexes collectively are also known as Web of Science. The SSCI can be accessed from the ISI Web of Knowledge at: *wokinfo.com* (accessed 17 October 2014).

Tips and skills
Using email alerts

One way of expanding your literature search is through email alerts. These supply you with an email when an issue of a journal that you are interested in is published. You can also be sent email alerts when articles with certain keywords or written by certain authors are published. One of the main ways of setting up email alerts is by signing up for this service with the main journal publishers. Publishers such as Sage and Elsevier allow you to do this; you can customize your search results according to areas of interest and receive alerts when relevant articles are cited.

The SSCI database is a little less easy to use than the others, but it provides references and abstracts. Some libraries add full-text links for articles from some of the most important business journals published worldwide. The database also covers related fields such as accountancy and finance, economics, and public administration. It is, therefore, very useful as an initial source in your literature search because, if you search the database effectively, you can be relatively confident that you have covered the majority of recent academic journals that may have published articles on your topic of interest. Here are some introductory guidelines for searching SSCI which is accessed via Web of Science:

- Click on GO beside Web of Science;

- Click on 'More Settings' and leave only 'Social Science Citation Index' checked.

- Use the 'Basic Search' box. Note that the default is to search 1900 to date. You can change this by using the pull-down menus;

- You can then search by a number of fields including TOPIC or AUTHOR.
- You can also use the CITED REF SEARCH to search for articles that cite an article you know about already. This can help you find other related research and also see what other authors thought of your original article. This is particularly useful if your article is a few years old.

In the mid-2000s some academic publishers began to make full text of their journals available through their own websites; Cambridge University Press (Cambridge Journals Online) and Sage (HighWire) are the two most prominent examples. Again, you will need to check with your librarian to find out which of these resources you can use and how to access them. The INGENTA website offers full text from various publishers, but you will be able to access full text only to titles to which your library subscribes. In addition to scholarly books and journals, newspaper archives can provide a valuable supplementary resource through which to review the emergence of new topics in business and management. Most newspapers require subscriptions to be able to search their online databases (e.g. *Financial Times*, *Daily* and *Sunday Telegraph*, *Wall Street Journal*, *The Economist*). However, most academic libraries will have a subscription to some individual newspapers or to a service such as Proquest or Nexis UK, which allow you to search several newspapers at once; you may need a password to access them. Newspapers and periodicals can be a rich source of information about certain topics that make good stories for journalists, such as financial scandals, discrimination, or trade union disputes. The level of analysis can also be high; however, for an academic dissertation newspapers should always be seen as secondary to published literature in books and journals. On the other hand, it should be remembered that it takes some time for academic articles to be published, so for recent events newspapers may be the only source of information.

Telling it like it is
Using newspapers and the Internet to get information on a current management topic

In addition to using academic books and journal sources, Chris found that newspaper databases provided a valuable source of information on the subject of diversity and in the debate about women in management and the 'glass ceiling' effect. The Equal Opportunities Commission website was also a useful source. He observed: 'I picked a relatively hot topic in the management field. It was interesting to learn that it isn't just the most obvious places that you do research. It's typing something into Google and looking in the newspaper daily. The *Independent* regularly had articles on this subject and so did the *Guardian*, so it wasn't just, you know, academic views that I was using.'

However, it is important not to regard these sources of information as a substitute for academic research, which should provide the basis of your literature review. It is also important to remember that fashionable topics in management research will almost certainly have connections with former managerial practices. Therefore, an established theory can provide an invaluable means of understanding what is currently happening in the managerial context.

Another valuable resource to supplement your literature searching is provided by the various non-academic institutions that publish policy-oriented research on issues related to business and management, such as the Equal Opportunities Commission, Work Foundation, World Bank, Institute for Public Policy Research, the Chartered Institute of Personnel and Development, and Demos. Reports are often published via the Web in PDF form and they can usually be downloaded free, thereby providing a faster route to publication than more academic routes. This is particularly useful when researching a currently emerging topic in management and business, or a government-led initiative such as Investors in People or Public Private Partnerships.

A word of warning about using Google and other search engines for research. Internet search engines are very useful for researching all sorts of things. However, they merely find sites, they do not evaluate them, so be prepared to look critically at what you've found. Remember that anyone can put information on the Web, so when looking at websites you need to evaluate whether the information you have found is useful. The following points are worth considering:

- Who is the author of the site and what is his or her motive for publishing?
- Where is the site located? The URL can help you here. Is it an academic site (often .ac or .edu) or a government site (.gov), a non-commercial organization (.org) or a commercial one (.com or.co)?

- How recently was the site updated? Many sites will give you a 'last updated' date, but you can get clues as to whether a page is being well maintained by whether or not the links are up-to-date and by its general appearance.

Try to confine your literature search to reliable websites such as those mentioned in this chapter.

The catalogue of your own institution is an obvious route to finding books, but so too are the catalogues of other universities. COPAC contains the holdings of twenty-seven of the largest university research libraries in the UK and Ireland, plus the British Library. It can be found at: *copac.ac.uk* (accessed 17 October 2014).

Telling it like it is
Different approaches to finding information

From our experience as supervisors, it is clear that students have different approaches to finding business and management information. Some prefer to organize articles and books according to specific themes or topics, while others choose to focus on understanding the paradigm (see Chapter 2) adopted by the authors. The following accounts of Nirwanthi, Tore, and Angharad illustrate the diverse nature of these approaches. Many students also feel that by the time they reach this stage of their degree studies they are confident of their ability to look for information, precisely because this is what a great deal of their learning has required them to do.

Nirwanthi: 'First of all I just wanted to know what past authors had written about this subject so that I had something to compare and contrast my own data with. Then I just read through the references and I selected about 15 to 20 of the topics that I thought would be relevant. I started grouping the journal articles and the textbook bits that I had under headings, making it more concise, I guess, and focusing on whichever I thought was relevant to my own data. To start off with I didn't think I was going to find so much literature on this particular research topic that I was studying, but there was so much! There was some that I didn't agree with and some that I did agree with, so I had a lot to work on.'

Tore: 'My supervisor gave me a stack of articles, so that was kind of the beginning. Then I went about cross-referencing the articles that he gave me. Then when an article mentioned something that I found was interesting, I would look up that reference and find the article. Because most of the research in this field is published in articles, they were easy to find online. So it was very easy to get a broad literature review.'

Angharad: 'You've been to the library so you know where to get everything. A lot of it was just going to the library and I found the section and just pulled out books and had a look what was in them really. I tended to look to textbooks and things for the main arguments, ideas in the field, and then draw upon articles and journals to perhaps back that up and support what I'd already got.'

Catalogues from 10,000 libraries worldwide are brought together by the Online Computer Library Center and may be found at: *worldcat.org* (accessed 17 October 2014)

You may also need to find out background information about the markets or companies in which you are interested. There are numerous database sources that can provide you with this kind of company and market research data, including the General Market Information Database (GMID), which contains marketing profiles, consumer market sizing for 52 countries, consumer lifestyle reports, data for over 200 countries, market forecasts, and information about 100,000 brands and 12,000 companies. Mintel provides comprehensive market research reports on the UK retail and leisure sectors and conducts its own market research, and Reuters Business Insight provides access to hundreds of market research reports focused

on energy, consumer goods, finance, health care, and technology. Depending on the library you belong to, you might also be able to access Datastream, Amadeus, or Investext, all of which contain company-specific information. Others such as Creative Club are more subject-specific; it provides an archive of advertisements in all UK media from 1997 on.

Again, you will need to check with your library to find out which of these is available to you.

Finally, the UK National Statistics website offers a wide range of statistics about the UK, including Social Trends, Regional Trends, Consumer Trends, and the results of the General Household Survey: *www.statistics.gov.uk/ hub/index.html* (accessed 17 October 2014)

European statistics relating to specific countries, industries, and sectors can be found on Europa, the portal to the European Union website: *europa.eu* (accessed 17 October 2014)

Tips and skills
Using information on the Web

The Internet provides freely available information about business and management that can be quickly and easily obtained without the need for university agreements to access it. However, there is a difficulty in this, because the strength of the Internet in providing access to huge amounts of information is also its weakness in that it can be very difficult to differentiate what is useful and reliable from that which is too simplistic, too commercially oriented, too highly opinionated, or just not sufficiently academic. The worst thing that can happen is that you end up quoting from sources from the Web that are quite simply misleading and incorrect. Therefore, it is important to be selective in your use of information on the Internet and to build up a list of favourite websites that you can check regularly.

'Google Scholar' can be accessed from the Google homepage. This product provides a simple way to broadly search for academic literature. It searches only on sites which contain scholarly works, but it is not clear how this is defined. This includes published academic papers, theses, books, and items in open-access repositories, as well as universities and other scholarly organizations. Searching is done using keywords, including via the Advanced Search option, which is accessed with the down arrow at the end of the main search box. However, Google Scholar should not be the only search tool you use because it is not clear what the coverage is (in terms of dates, sources, and frequency of update), and it is not comprehensive in terms of disciplines (business and management, for example, is less well covered than science and medicine). Also, owing to the algorithms involved to rank the relevance of results, Google Scholar is better at finding commonly used rather than unusual or specialist material, even though the latter can be very important to researchers.

scholar.google.com (accessed 17 October 2014)

Also worth exploring, especially for information about current research, are sites that support the development of management research, such as the Academy of Management, British Academy of Management, and Advanced Institute of Management: *www.aomonline.org* (accessed 17 October 2014) *www.bam.ac.uk* (accessed 17 October 2014)

www.aimresearch.org (accessed 17 October 2014)

However, there are numerous sites that contain material which is not suitable for academic study, either because the theories are too simplistically presented or because the information is incorrect. Examples include:

humanresources.about.com (accessed 17 October 2014)

www.wisegeek.com (accessed 17 October 2014)

www.businessballs.com (accessed 17 October 2014)

Keywords and defining search parameters

For all of these online databases, you will need to work out some suitable keywords that can be entered into the search engines and that will allow you to identify suitable references. There are a number of business dictionaries that can help you to define your area of research and to identify changes in the language used to describe the subject. For example, the term 'personnel management' has now been largely superseded by 'HRM', and 'payment systems' are now more widely referred to under the umbrella of 'reward management'. You will also need to think of synonyms and try to match your language to that of the source you are searching. For example, performance management may be more usually referred to in practitioner publications as 'employee evaluation' or 'appraisal'. Sometimes opposites are useful—for example, employment/unemployment. You also need to think about alternative spellings—for example, organization/ organisation, labor/labour. Be prepared to experiment and to amend your keywords as your research progresses—you may find that, as you search the literature, there are other ways of describing your subject.

In most databases, typing in the title of your project, or a sentence or long phrase, as your search term is not advisable: unless someone has written something with the same title, you are unlikely to find very much. You need to think in terms of keywords. For example, if you are interested in 'the role of women in the management of banks' your keywords would be WOMEN and MANAG* and BANK*. This would mean that you captured articles containing the words mana*ger*, mana*gers*, mana*ging*, and manag*ement*, as well as bank*ing*, bank*s*, and bank*ers*, because the asterisk acts as a wild card that searches for all words that begin in this way.

Use the HELP provided in the databases themselves to find out how to use your keywords to best effect.

Telling it like it is
The importance of identifying suitable keywords

Karen's experience of literature searching highlights the importance of identifying the most accurate term to describe the subject in which you are interested. 'I went to Leeds University Library then and asked them, but it was just such a small area that not many people knew anything about it and so it was just a case really of going onto databases and searching on different words and seeing if that brought anything up. I was searching on "cultural fit" and that didn't work. There was nothing. Nobody had written anything on the term "cultural fit," but then I tried "organisational fit" and that was when it opened up and there were lots of things; and then once I had one, I had lots of other references and that was how it sort of snowballed.'

Karen's metaphor of the snowball is striking here. Literature reviews frequently begin in this way—namely, by beginning with a small number of references, following up citations within those, and continuing the process until a sizeable number of items has been accumulated.

In some areas of research, there are very many references. Try to identify the major ones and work outwards from there. Move on to the next stage of your research at the point that you identified in your timetable (see Chapter 4), so that you can dig yourself out of the library. This is not to say that your search for the literature will cease, but that you need to force yourself to move on. Seek out your supervisor's advice on whether or not you need to search the literature much more. Figure 5.1 outlines one way of searching the literature. The most important thing to remember, as the note at the end says, is to keep a record of the process so that you can keep track of what you have done.

Figure 5.1

One way of searching the literature

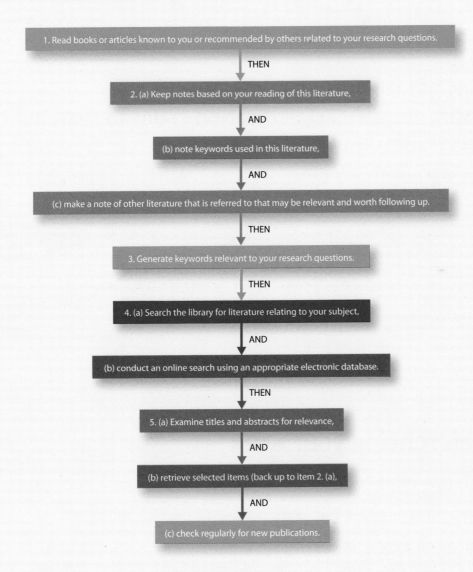

1. Read books or articles known to you or recommended by others related to your research questions.

THEN

2. (a) Keep notes based on your reading of this literature,

AND

(b) note keywords used in this literature,

AND

(c) make a note of other literature that is referred to that may be relevant and worth following up.

THEN

3. Generate keywords relevant to your research questions.

THEN

4. (a) Search the library for literature relating to your subject,

AND

(b) conduct an online search using an appropriate electronic database.

THEN

5. (a) Examine titles and abstracts for relevance,

AND

(b) retrieve selected items (back up to item 2. (a),

AND

(c) check regularly for new publications.

Note: At each stage, keep a record of what you have done and your reasons for certain decisions. This will be useful to you for remembering how you proceeded and for writing up a description and justification of your literature search strategy, which can form part of your methods section. When making notes on literature that you read, make notes on content and method, as well as relevance, and keep thinking about how each item will contribute to your critical review of the literature.

Telling it like it is
Learning from others

Lisa found that other students on her degree course provided a valuable source of support in addition to the feedback she gained from her supervisor. Her advice to others was to communicate 'with other people on your degree that are doing dissertations, find out how they're doing it, what their stance is, perhaps people that are doing similar subjects to you'. Lisa discussed her ideas with another student who was also doing a research project in the field of human resource management that related to the same subject as her project, looking at performance management. By talking about what literature they had read, they were able to point each other towards articles and books they had each found interesting or useful, and in this way to make the process of reviewing the literature easier.

Tips and skills
Using industrial classification codes to search an electronic database

When you are searching for literature related to a particular service or industry, it can be useful to refine your search strategy by using the appropriate code for the sector from an industrial classification system such as SIC or NAICS (see Tips and skills 'A guide to industry classification systems' in Chapter 8)). Ojala (2005: 43) claims that few business people know how to do this. Instead they just tend to 'put the words that describe their industry into a Web search engine and that's it. If they're researching the shoe industry, they don't think to add in the word footwear, let alone the particular type of shoe they want to know about, such as sandals, baby, or boots. It would not occur to them to look up the industry code for shoes (314).' This is particularly useful when using search engines such as Business Source Premier run by the EBSCO host, which indexes journal content using the NAICS and SIC systems. By typing the relevant code into your search string, you can obtain articles that relate to the particular service or sector that you are interested in.

Referencing your work

Referencing the work of others is an important academic convention because it emphasizes that you are aware of the historical development of your subject, particularly if you use the Harvard method of referencing, and shows that you recognize that your own research builds on the work of others. Referencing in your literature review is thus a way of emphasizing your understanding and knowledge of the subject. In other parts of your dissertation referencing will serve somewhat different purposes. For example, it will show your understanding of methodological considerations or help to reinforce your argument. A reference is also sometimes described as a citation and the act of referencing as citing.

As we mentioned earlier on in this chapter, a key skill in writing your literature review is to keep a record of what you have read, including all the bibliographic details about the articles or books that will go into your bibliography or references. For larger research projects it can be useful to use note cards or software packages that are designed specifically for this purpose, such as Procite or Endnote. However, for a student research project it will probably be sufficient to keep an electronic record of all the items that you have read in a Word document, although you should bear in mind that you may not include all of these in your final bibliography. The main thing to make sure of is that you keep your bibliographic records up to date and do not leave this until the very end of the writing-up process, when you will probably be under significant time pressure.

Your institution will probably have its own guidelines as to which style of referencing you should use in your dissertation, and if it does you should definitely follow them. However, the two main methods used are:

- *Harvard*. The essence of this system is that whenever you paraphrase the argument or ideas of an author or authors in your writing, you add in parentheses immediately afterwards the surname of the author(s) and the year of publication. If you are quoting the author(s), you put quotation marks around the quotation and after the year of publication you include the page number where the quotation is from. All books, articles, and other sources that you have cited in the text are then provided in full in a reference list at the end of the dissertation in alphabetical order by author surname. This is by far the most common referencing system in business and management research and the one that

we follow in this book. It is, therefore, the style that we would encourage you to use if your university does not require you to follow its own guidelines.

- *Note or numeric*. This approach involves the use of superscript numbers in the text that refer to a note at the foot of the page or the end of the text, where the reference is given in full, together with the page number if it is a direct quotation. If a source is cited more than once, an abbreviated version of the reference is given in any subsequent citation (which is why this is often called the short-title system). As well as being used to refer to sources, notes are often used to provide additional detail, including comments from the writer about the source being cited. This is a particular feature of historical writing. One of the advantages of the numeric or note method is that it can be less distracting to the reader in terms of the flow of the text than the Harvard method, where sometimes particularly long strings of references can make a sentence or a paragraph difficult for the reader to follow. Furthermore, software packages such as Word make the insertion of notes relatively simple, and many students find that this is a convenient way of referencing their work. However, when students use this method, they often use it incorrectly—it is quite difficult to use it well—and are sometimes unsure whether or not also to include a separate bibliography. For books and dissertations a bibliography is always recommended, and indeed this can be important in the assessment of students' work (see the section on avoiding plagiarism at the end of this chapter).

Tips and skills
The Harvard and note approaches to referencing

The examples below show some fictitious examples of referencing in published work. Note that in published articles there is usually a list of references at the end; books using the Harvard system usually have a list of references, whereas a bibliography is used with the short-title system of notes. The punctuation of references—such as where to place a comma, whether to capitalize a title in full or just the first word—varies considerably from source to source. For example, with Harvard referencing, in some books and journals the surname of the author is separated from the date in the text with a comma—for example (Name, 1999)—but in others, like this book, there is no comma. However, the main thing is to be consistent. Select a format for punctuating your references, such as the one adopted by a leading journal in your subject area, and then stick to it.

An example of a Harvard reference to a book

In the text:

As Name and Other (1999) argue, motivation is a broad concept that comprises a variety of intrinsic and extrinsic factors . . .

. . . and in the list of references:

Name, A., and Other, S. (1999). *Title of Book in Italics: Throughout*. Place of Publication: Publisher.

An example of a Harvard reference with a direct quotation from a book

In the text:

However, the importance of intrinsic factors often tends to be overlooked since 'studies of motivation have tended predominantly to focus on the influence of extrinsic factors' (Name and Other 1999: 123).

. . . and in the list of references:

Name, A., and Other, S. (1999). *Title of Book in Italics: Throughout*. Place of Publication: Publisher.

An example of a Harvard reference to a journal article

In the text:

Research by Name (2003) has drawn attention to the importance of intrinsic factors in determining employee motivation.

. . . and in the list of references:

Refers to volume (issue) number

Name, A. (2003). 'Title of Journal Article', *Journal Title*, 28(4): 109–38.

An example of a Harvard reference to a chapter in an edited book

In the text:

As Name (2001) suggests, individual motivation to work is affected by a range of intrinsic and extrinsic factors . . .

. . . and in the list of references:

Name, A. (2001). 'Title of Book Chapter', in S. Other (ed.), *Title of Book in Italics*. Place of Publication: Publisher, pp. 124–56.

Abbreviation for 'Editor'

An example of a secondary reference using the Harvard Method

In the text:

Individual motivation to work is affected by a range of intrinsic and extrinsic factors (Name 1993, cited in Other 2004).

. . . and in the list of references:

Name, A. (1993). *Title of Book in Italics*. Place of Publication: Publisher, cited in S. Other (2004). *Title of Textbook in Italics*. Place of Publication: Publisher.

An example of a Harvard reference to an Internet site

In the text:

'we use a comprehensive product life cycle analysis that measures the carbon footprint throughout the entire life of our products' (Apple 2014).

. . . and in the list of references:

Apple (2014). 'Climate Change', **www.apple.com/uk/environment/climate-change**/ (accessed 17 October 2014).

Note: it is very important to give the date accessed, as some websites change frequently (or even disappear!).

An example of a note reference to a book

In the text:

On the other hand, research by Name[3] has drawn attention to the influence of intrinsic factors on employee motivation . . .

. . . and the corresponding note should read:

[3] A. Name, *Title of Book in Italics: Throughout*, Place of Publication, Publisher, 2000, 170–7.

An example of a note reference to an Internet site

In the text:

'we use a comprehensive product life cycle analysis that measures the carbon footprint throughout the entire life of our products'.[39]

. . . and the corresponding note should read:

[39] Apple, 'Climate Change', **www.apple.com/uk/environment/climate-change**/ (accessed 17 October 2014).

Tips and skills
Using bibliographic software

EndNote and Reference Manager are Windows-based software tools used for publishing and managing bibliographies. Your university may have a site licence for one of these packages. They are used by academic researchers, information specialists, and students to create bibliographic records equivalent to the manual form of index cards, which allow you to compile your own personal reference database. These records can then be automatically formatted to suit different requirements—for example, to comply with the referencing requirements of a particular scholarly journal. A further advantage to the software is that it can enable you to export references directly from databases such as the Social Sciences Citation Index (SSCI). The software also has search options that help you to locate a particular reference, although the extent of these features varies from one package to another.

In the long run, this can save you time and effort, and reduce the possibility of errors. However, for a student research project it may not be worthwhile for you to take the time to learn how to use this software if it is only to be used for the dissertation. On the other hand, if knowledge of the software may be useful to you in the longer term, for example if you are thinking of going on to pursue an academic career by doing a Ph.D. or if you are intending to work in a field where research skills are valued, then it may be worth learning how to use the software. More details about these products can be found on the following websites, and a short guide to using Endnote is provided in the following section:

thomsonreuters.com/endnote (accessed 17 October 2014)

www.refman.com (accessed 17 October 2014)

However, if you do not have access to one of these packages, similar software is often freely available and can be downloaded from the Internet. A basic version of EndNote Web is available free and allows up to 50,000 references to be stored.

http://endnote.com (accessed 17 October 2014)

Research in focus 5.6
A direct quotation that has been referenced for more than fifteen years

The importance of referencing and the role it plays in communicating ideas between a group of scholars is aptly illustrated by an example concerning the debate between academics in US and UK business schools about the role of management education. The now infamous quotation is from an article written by Harold Leavitt of Stanford University in the USA and published in a 1989 issue of the *California Management Review*, where he stated:

> While we teach many of the right things in our MBA programs, we don't teach some critical things we ought to teach. The major reason we don't is because if we teach those untaught things it will become more difficult to teach and to justify what we already teach. So, we have built a weird, almost unimaginable design for MBA-level education. We then lay it upon well-proportioned young men and women, distorting them (when we are unlucky enough to succeed) into critters with lopsided brains, icy hearts, and shrunken souls.
>
> (Leavitt 1989: 39)

The highly emotive and evocative tone of Leavitt's pronouncement meant that it has often been quoted, and sometimes misquoted, by other authors over the years. Moreover, progressive summarizing of the quotation means that the original context setting involved in Leavitt's argument is sometimes lost and only the pithy phrase remains. For example, in his 1996 book *The Collapse of the American Management Mystique*, R. Locke references a 1991 issue of *The Economist* as the source for his direct quotation about 'critters with lopsided brains, icy hearts, and shrunken souls' (p. 53). However, he makes no reference to the original author to whom the quotation is attributed, so this is an example of rather sloppy secondary referencing. In the article in *The Economist*, an abbreviated version of the quotation is attributed to Leavitt, who it is said was 'writing over a decade ago'. No original source is cited (although we would not really expect it to be, since *The Economist* is more journalistic than academic and so is less rigorous about referencing).

In 2002, an abbreviated version of the quotation pops up again, this time in an influential article in *Academy of Management Learning and Education* by Pfeffer and Fong, who cite Leavitt's (1989) article as the original source. After this, use of Leavitt's quotation mushrooms. A Google search on 'icy hearts and shrunken souls' produces 39 hits, all related to this particular use of the phrase, from sources as diverse as the Portland State University Magazine, Warwick Business School, The European Foundation for Management Development, and The UK Council for Excellence in Management and Leadership. In an article prompted by Pfeffer and Fong's (2002) piece, Tinker (2004) cites a version of Leavitt's quotation (although the page number for it is wrong), and so do Starkey, Hatchuel, and Tempest (2004) in an article in *Journal of Management Studies*.

The use of Leavitt's words over a time span of over fifteen years is interesting, because it illustrates how referencing allows the words of one author to continue to be invoked, appropriated, and interpreted long after their original usage. However, it is also interesting that Leavitt's phrase has come to be associated with the writers who quoted it—i.e. Pfeffer and Fong (2002)—as well as the original author. Moreover, the example illustrates how the reputation of authors who use a powerful phrase is in part derived from the reputation of the scholar whom they reference. This is because one of the ways that academics evaluate each other's work is through judgements they make about the quality of the work that the author is citing. Perhaps the 'icy hearts and shrunken souls' quotation would not have been so widely used over the years and broadly accepted had it not been written by a well-known Stanford professor.

The role of the bibliography

What makes a good bibliography? You might initially think that length is a good measure, since a longer bibliography containing more references might imply that the author has been comprehensive in his or her search of the existing literature. This is undoubtedly true, but only up to a point, since it is also important for the bibliography to be selectively focused—that is, not to try to include everything that has ever been written about a subject but instead to reflect the author's informed judgement of the importance and suitability of sources. This incorporates some of the judgements about quality that were discussed earlier in this chapter. One common proxy for quality is the reputation of the journal in which an article is published. However, although this is a useful indicator, we recommend that it is not one you should rely on exclusively; there might be articles in lesser-status journals, for instance those targeted at practitioners, that have relevance to your subject. It is important to be aware of these judgements of quality and to seek the advice of your supervisor when making them.

Another important feature of a good bibliography relates to secondary referencing. This is when you refer to an article or book that has been cited in another source such as a textbook and you do not, or cannot, access the original article or book from which it was taken. However, relying heavily on secondary references can be problematic because you are dependent upon the interpretation of the original text that is offered by the authors of the secondary text. This may be adequate for some parts of your literature review, but there is always the potential for different interpretations of the original text; this increases the further removed you are from the original source. So it is a good idea to be cautious in the use of secondary references and to go back to the original source if you can, particularly if the reference is an important one for your subject. Research in focus 5.6 gives an example of how an author's work can be referenced in ways that involve reinterpretation and misquotation long after the date of publication.

A further feature of a good reference list stems from the relationship between the entries and the way they are used in the main body of the text. It should go without saying that it is not very helpful to include references in the bibliography that are not even mentioned in the text. If references are integrated into the text in a way that shows that you have read them in detail and understood the theoretical perspective from which they are written, this is much more impressive than if a reference is inserted into the text in a way that does not closely relate to what is being said in the text. Finally, Barnett (1994) argues that a good bibliography gives no indication of the quality of a piece of work, pointing out that some of the most influential academic books ever written do not even include one. Drawing on the ideas of Bourdieu (1984), he suggests that the main purpose of the bibliography is to enable you to understand the habitus that the author is claiming to reside in, this being about understanding the beliefs and dispositions of the author combined with the constraints associated with his or her situation.

Tips and skills
Helping your supervisor to understand your literature review

If you are planning to give a first draft of your literature review to your supervisor for him or her to comment on, make sure that you include your list of references in this version. Otherwise your supervisor will not know what literature you have used to compile the review, and this will make it harder for him or her to comment meaningfully on the quality of your work.

Avoiding plagiarism

An issue to bear in mind when writing up your literature review is the need to avoid plagiarizing the work that you are reading. Plagiarism is a notoriously slippery concept. It is defined in *The Oxford Dictionary of English* (2nd edn, 2003: 1344) as 'the practice of taking someone else's work or ideas and passing them off as one's own'. In the Wikipedia entry on 'Academic dishonesty', plagiarism is defined as 'The adoption or reproduction of original creations of another author (person, collective, organization, community or other type of author, including anonymous authors) without due acknowledgment' (accessed 27 February 2013). Plagiarism does not just relate to the literature you read in the course of preparing an essay or report. Taking material in a wholesale and unattributed way from sources such as essays written by others or from websites is also plagiarism. Further, it is possible to self-plagiarize (something that is not apparent in the Wikipedia definition above), as when a person lifts material that he or she has previously written and passes it off as new and original work. Plagiarism is commonly regarded as a form of academic cheating and as such differs little if at all in the minds of many academics from other academic misdemeanours such as fabricating research findings.

There is a widespread view that plagiarism among students is increasing in incidence, though whether this is in fact the case is difficult to establish unambiguously. Indeed, it is difficult to establish how widespread plagiarism is, and there are quite substantial variations in estimates of its prevalence. In a study of two assignments for a business course at a New Zealand university, Walker (2010) found that just over one-quarter of the two assignments together exhibited some level of plagiarism. He also found that the level of plagiarism declined between the two assignments, suggesting that students were less inclined to plagiarise for the second assignment when they had been notified of the marker's comments on the first assignment. It is widely viewed that the Internet is a prominent—if not the main—driver behind the perceived increase in the prevalence of plagiarism. The ease with which text can be copied from websites, e-journal articles, e-books, online essays sold commercially, and numerous other sources and then pasted into essays is often viewed as one of the main factors behind the alleged rise in plagiarism cases among students in UK universities and elsewhere.

There are several difficulties with plagiarism as an issue in higher education. One is that universities vary in their definitions of what plagiarism is (Stefani and Carroll 2001). Further, they vary in their response to it when it is uncovered. They also vary in both the type and the severity of punishment. Further, within any university, academic and other staff differ in their views of the sinfulness of plagiarism and how it should be handled (Flint, Clegg, and Macdonald 2006). There is also evidence that students are less convinced than academic staff that plagiarism is wrong and that it should be punished.

In view of all these uncertainties of both the definition of plagiarism and the appropriate response to it, students may wonder whether they should take issues of plagiarism seriously. Our answer is that they most definitely should take it seriously. Academic research places a high value on the originality of the work that is presented in any kind of output. To pass someone else's ideas and/or writings off as your own is widely regarded as morally dubious at best. Thus, while there are several grey areas with regard to plagiarism, as outlined in the previous paragraph, it is important not to overstate their significance. There *is* widespread condemnation of plagiarism in academic circles and it *is* nearly always punished when found in the work of students (and indeed that of others). You should, therefore, avoid plagiarizing the work of others at all costs. So concerned are universities about the growth in the number of plagiarism cases that come before examination boards, and the likely role of the Internet in facilitating plagiarism, that they are making more and more use of plagiarism detection software, which trawls the Internet for such things as strings of words. Thus, as several writers (for example, McKeever 2006) have observed, the very technological development that is widely perceived as promoting the incidence of plagiarism—the Internet—is increasingly the springboard for its detection. Even well-known and ubiquitous search engines such as Google are sometimes employed to detect student plagiarism through the search for unique strings of words.

The most important issue from the student's point of view is that he or she should avoid plagiarism at all costs, as the penalties may be severe, regardless of the student's own views on the matter. First, do not 'lift' large sections of text without making it clear that they are in fact quotations. This makes it clear that the text in question is not your own work but that you are making a point by quoting someone. It is easy to get this wrong. In June 2006,

it was reported that a plagiarism expert at the London School of Economics had been accused of plagiarism in a paper he published on plagiarism! A paragraph was found that copied verbatim a published source by someone else and that had not been acknowledged properly as from another source. The accused person defended himself by saying that this was due to a formatting error. It is common practice in academic publications to indent a large section of material that is being quoted, thus:

> The most important issue from the student's point of view is that he or she should avoid plagiarism at all costs, as the penalties may be severe, regardless of the student's own views on the matter. First, do not 'lift' large sections of text without making it clear that they are in fact quotations. This makes it clear that the text in question is not your own work but that you are making a point by quoting someone. It is easy to get this wrong. In June 2006, it was reported that a plagiarism expert at the London School of Economics had been accused of plagiarism in a paper he published on plagiarism! A paragraph was found that copied verbatim a published source by someone else and that had not been acknowledged properly as from another source. The accused person defended himself by saying that this was due to a formatting error. It is common practice in academic publications to indent a large section of material that is being quoted.
>
> (Bryman and Bell 2015: 124)

The lack of indentation meant that the paragraph in question looked as though it was his own work. While it may be that this is a case of 'unintentional plagiarism' (Park 2003), distinguishing the intentional from the unintentional is by no means easy. Either way, the credibility and possibly the integrity of the author may be undermined. It is also important to realize that, for many if not most institutions, simply copying large portions of text and changing a few words will also be regarded as plagiarism.

Secondly, do not pass other people's ideas off as your own. This means that you should acknowledge the source of any ideas that you present that are not your own.

Academics are on their guard against plagiarism by their peers too. Colquitt (2012) notes that when authors submit articles via the Academy of Management's online portal for submitting articles for consideration, they encounter an automatic message that warns the author that all articles are screened for plagiarism. Honig and Bedi (2012) examined 279 papers that were presented at a conference associated with one of the divisions of the Academy of Management in 2009. They found evidence of some plagiarism in 25 per cent of the papers and, even more alarming, 'significant plagiarism' (where 5 per cent or more of the paper is found to be plagiarised) in 13 per cent of the papers. As Honig and Bedi note, the fact that papers undergo peer review when they are submitted clearly does not act as a deterrent and does not serve to identify cases of plagiarism.

One of the most important messages of this section is that you should guard against plagiarism at all costs. The fact that there is evidence that academics themselves are sometimes guilty of plagiarism should not be taken as a justification for student plagiarism. In the words of the old saying, 'two wrongs don't make a right'. But it should also be clear that you should find out what your university and possibly departmental guidelines on the matter are. Quite aside from the rights and wrongs of plagiarism, it is not likely to impress your tutor if it is clear from reading the text that large chunks of your essay or report have been lifted from another source with just your own words interspersing the plagiarized text. In fact, that is often in our experience a giveaway—the contrast in styles is frequently very apparent and prompts the tutor to explore the possibility that some or much of the assignment you submit has in fact been plagiarized. Nor is it likely to impress most tutors if much of the text has been lifted but a few words changed here and there, along with a few sprinkled words written by you. However, equally it has to be said that frequent quoting with linking sentences by you is not likely to impress either. When we have been presented with essays of that kind, we have frequently said to the student concerned that it

is difficult to establish what his or her own thoughts on the issue are.

Try, therefore, to express your ideas in your own words and acknowledge properly those ideas that are not your own. Plagiarism is something you may get away with once or twice, but it is so imprinted on the consciousness of many of us working in universities nowadays that you are unlikely to get away with it regularly. It is also extremely irritating to find that your own work has been plagiarized. Bryman was asked to act as an external examiner of a doctoral thesis and found that large sections of one of his books had been taken and presented as the student's own work. He found this extremely annoying. A colleague he mentioned the incident to remarked that the only thing worse than plagiarism is incompetent plagiarism—incompetent because the student had plagiarized the work of someone he or she knew would be the external examiner. However, on reflection, we see that the colleague was mistaken. Plagiarism is wrong—regardless of whether it is competently implemented or not.

One final point to note is that plagiarism is like a moving target. What it is, how it should be defined, how it can be detected, how it should be penalized: all of these issues and others are in a state of flux as we write this chapter. It is very much a shifting situation precisely because of the perception that it is increasing in frequency. The penalties can be severe, and, as we have witnessed when students have been presented with evidence of their plagiarism, it can be profoundly embarrassing and distressing for them. The message is simple: do not do it, and make sure that you know exactly what it is and how it is defined at your institution so that you do not inadvertently commit the sin of plagiarism.

Checklist

Questions to ask yourself when reviewing the literature

○ Is your list of references up to date in your current areas of interest? Are there new areas of interest that you need to search for?

○ What literature searching have you done recently?

○ What have you read recently? Have you found time to read?

○ What have you learned from the literature? Has this changed your understanding of the subject in which you are working in any way?

○ Is your search for the literature and the review you are writing being guided by your research questions? Has your reading of the literature made you think about revising your research questions?

○ Is what you have read going to influence your research design in any way? Has it given you ideas about what you need to consider and incorporate?

○ Have you addressed any key controversies in the literature and any different ways of conceptualizing your subject matter?

○ Have you been writing notes on what you have read? Do you need to reconsider how what you have read fits into your research?

○ Have you adopted a critical approach to presenting your literature review?

○ What story are you going to tell about the literature? In other words, have you worked out what is going to be the message about the literature that you want to tell your readers?

○ Has someone read a draft of your review to check on your writing style and the strength of your arguments about the literature?

Adapted from Bruce (1994); Holbrook et al. (2007); Reuber (2010).

Key points

- Writing a literature review is a means of reviewing the main ideas and research relating to your chosen area of interest.
- A competent literature review confirms you as someone who is competent in the subject area.
- A great deal of the work of writing a literature review is based upon reading the work of other researchers in your subject area; key skills can be acquired to help you get the most from your reading.
- Systematic review is a method that is gaining in popularity in business research as a way of enhancing the reliability of literature searching and review.
- Narrative review is a more traditional approach that has the advantage of flexibility, which can make it more appropriate for inductive research and qualitative research designs.

Questions for review

Reviewing the existing literature

- What are the main reasons for writing a literature review?
- How can you ensure that you get the most from your reading?
- What are the main advantages and disadvantages associated with systematic review?
- What type of research question is systematic review most suited to addressing?
- What are the main reasons for conducting a narrative literature review?
- In what type of research is narrative review most appropriate?

Searching the existing literature

- What are the main ways of finding existing literature on your subject?

- What is a keyword and how is it useful in searching the literature?

Referencing your work

- Why is it important to reference your work?

- What are the two main referencing styles used in academic work and which of these is preferred by your institution?

- What is the role of the bibliography and what makes a good one?

Avoiding plagiarism

- What is plagiarism?

- Why is it taken so seriously by researchers?

....

Online Resource Centre

www.oxfordtextbooks.co.uk/orc/brymanbrm4e/

Visit the Interactive Research Guide that accompanies this book to complete an exercise in Getting Started: Reviewing the Literature.

....

6

Ethics and politics in business research

Chapter outline

Ethical issues arise at a variety of stages in business and management research. This chapter is concerned with the concerns about ethics that might arise in the course of conducting research. The professional bodies concerned with the social sciences have been keen to spell out the ethical issues that can arise, and some of their statements will be reviewed in this chapter. Ethical issues cannot be ignored, in that they relate directly to the integrity of a piece of research and of the disciplines that are involved. This chapter explores:

- some famous, even infamous, cases in which transgressions of ethical principles have occurred, though it is important not to take the view that ethical concerns arise only in relation to these extreme cases;
- different stances that can be and have been taken on ethics in business research;
- the significance and operation of four areas in which ethical concerns particularly arise: whether or not harm comes to participants; **informed consent**; invasion of privacy; and deception;
- some of the difficulties associated with ethical decision-making;
- the political context of business research and the ethical concerns this raises.

Introduction

Discussions about the ethics of business research bring into focus the role of values in the research process. Ethical issues revolve around such concerns as the following:

- How should we treat the people on whom we conduct research?
- Are there activities in which we should or should not engage in our relations with them?

Questions about ethics in business and management research also bring in the role of professional associations, such as the American Academy of Management (AoM) and the Market Research Society (MRS), which have formulated codes of ethics on behalf of their members. Statements of professional principles are frequently accessible from the Internet. Some useful codes of ethics for business and management researchers can be found at the URLs below.

Association of Business Schools (ABS), *Ethics Guide* (2012):
www.associationofbusinessschools.org/sites/default/files/abs_ethics_guide_-_2012.pdf

Academy of Management (AoM), *Code of Ethical Conduct* (2005):
www.aomonline.org/governanceandethics/aomrevisedcodeofethics.pdf

Market Research Society (MRS), *Code of Conduct* (2010):
www.mrs.org.uk/pdf/Code%20of%20Conduct%20(2012%20rebrand).pdf

(also includes specific guidelines on qualitative and quantitative research, Internet research, and employee research).

However, it is also useful to look at the way that researchers within the social sciences more generally have dealt with ethical research issues—for example, the Social Research Association (SRA), the British Sociological Association (BSA), and the American Psychological Association (APA). In this chapter, the codes of ethics of these professional associations will also be referred to on several occasions.

Social Research Association (SRA) [UK], *Ethical Guidelines* (2003):
the-sra.org.uk/wp-content/uploads/ethics03.pdf

British Sociological Association (BSA), *Statement of Ethical Practice* (2002):
www.britsoc.co.uk/media/27107/StatementofEthicalPractice.pdf

American Sociological Association (ASA), *Code of Ethics* (1999):
www.asanet.org/images/asa/docs/pdf/CodeofEthics.pdf

American Psychological Association (APA), *Ethical Principles and Code of Conduct* (2002):
www.apa.org/ethics/code/principles.pdf

Economic and Social Research Council (ESRC) [UK], *Framework for Research Ethics* (2012) (see Tips and skills 'ESRC recommendations for ethical review of student research projects'):

www.esrc.ac.uk/_images/framework-for-research-ethics-09-12_tcm8-4586.pdf

[All statements and codes accessed 18 October 2014]

Writings about ethics in business and other social science research are frequently frustrating for four reasons.

1. Writers often differ quite widely from each other over ethical issues and questions. In other words, they differ over what is and is not ethically acceptable.

2. The main elements in the debates do not seem to move forward a great deal. The same kinds of points that were made in the 1960s were being rehashed in the late 1990s and at the start of the present century.

3. Debates about ethics have often accompanied well-known cases of alleged ethical transgression. Some of them, such as Dalton's (1959) covert ethnography of unofficial managerial activity, will also be encountered later on in this book (see Chapter 19). One of the central issues that Dalton addresses in his study is the unofficial use of company resources, including pilfering or corporate theft (see Research in focus 6.1). There is considerable debate as to whether it was ethical to obtain such data through the method of covert observation (see Key concept 6.2). There are also several well-known psychological studies (e.g. Milgram 1963; Haney, Banks, and Zimbardo 1973) that continue to be widely cited in the field of organizational behaviour, despite the fact that they were based on research designs that would now be widely considered extremely unethical (see Research in focus 6.3). However, the problem with this emphasis on notoriety is that it can be taken to imply that ethical concerns reside only in such extreme cases, when in fact the potential for ethical transgression is much more general than this.

4. Related to this last point is that these extreme and notorious cases of ethical violation tend to be associated with particular research methods—notably disguised observation and the use of deception in experiments. Again, the problem with this association of ethics with certain studies (and methods) is that it implies that ethical concerns reside only or even primarily in some methods but not others. As a result, the impression can be gleaned that other methods, such as questionnaires or overt ethnography, are immune from ethical problems. Moreover, as the recent popularization of television experiments suggests, disguised observation is as popular today as it was when researchers such as Milgram and Zimbardo carried out their classic studies.

Research in focus 6.1
A covert study of unofficial rewards

One of Dalton's (1959) central themes in his study of American managers and unofficial action revolves around the use of company materials and services as supplementary rewards for the variable contributions of individuals. He presents several cases, including the Milo carpenter, Ted Berger, who was rewarded for his loyalty by not being required to operate machines, instead making such things as baby beds, tables, and rocking horses—custom-built objects for various managers—in exchange for which he was given 'gifts'. Another case concerns staff who routinely filled their car fuel tank from the company garage and with this obtained free washing and waxing. Similarly, there is the case of Jim Speier, a factory foreman, who made use of machinery and materials to have constructed a rose arch, storm windows, and a set of wooden lawn sprinklers cut in the form of dancing girls and brightly painted!

Dalton's main strategy for preventing harm to his participants is to protect their anonymity, but the reader is left in no doubt as to the seriousness of consequences for the individuals concerned if their identities were to have been discovered. As Dalton explains, these individuals 'gave information and aid that, if generally known, would have jeopardized their careers' (1959: 275). One of the key ethical issues in this study concerns the lack of informed consent: participants were in no position to be able to judge whether or not to become involved in the research, as they were only vaguely aware of the nature of Dalton's interest. Furthermore, they were almost certainly unaware of the risk of harm that could result from the study in relation to their employment prospects. In his defence, Dalton adopts a situational stance (see Key concept 6.2), arguing that it is impossible to study unofficial action other than by using covert methods that enable the researcher to get sufficiently close to the subject. As there has been very little study of this subject, it is difficult to see how we could compare Dalton's findings with those produced using overt methods, and therefore we have little choice but to take his word for this.

Key concept 6.2
Stances on ethics

Authors on social research ethics can be characterized in terms of the stances they take on the issue. The following stances can be distinguished:

- *Universalism.* A universalist stance takes the view that ethical precepts should never be broken. Infractions of ethical principles are wrong in a moral sense and are damaging to social research. This kind of stance can be seen in the writings of Erikson (1967), Dingwall (1980), and Bulmer (1982). Bulmer does, however, point to some forms of what appears to be disguised observation that may be acceptable. One is retrospective covert observation, which occurs when a researcher writes up his or her experiences in social settings in which he or she participated but not as a researcher. An example would be Van Maanen (1991*b*), who wrote up his experiences as a ride operator in Disneyland many years after he had been employed there in vacation jobs. Even a universalist like Erikson (1967: 372) recognizes that it 'would be absurd . . . to insist as a point of ethics that sociologists should always introduce themselves as investigators everywhere they go and should inform every person who figures in their thinking exactly what their research is all about'.

- *Situation ethics.* Goode (1996) has argued for deception to be considered on a case-by-case basis. In other words, he argues for what J. Fletcher (1966: 31) has called a 'situation ethics', or more specifically 'principled relativism', which can be contrasted with the universalist ethics of some writers. This argument has two ways of being represented:

  1. *The end justifies the means.* Some writers argue that, unless there is some breaking of ethical rules, we would never know about certain social phenomena. Dalton (1959) essentially argues for this position in relation to his study of managers and the differences between official and unofficial action. Without some kind of disguised observation, this important aspect of organizational life would not have been studied. This is usually linked to the second form of a situationist argument in relation to social research ethics.

  2. *No choice.* It is often suggested that we have no choice but to engage in dissimulation on occasions if we want to investigate the issues in which we are interested.

- *Ethical transgression is pervasive.* It is often observed that virtually all research involves elements that are at least ethically questionable. This occurs whenever participants are not given absolutely all the details on a piece of research, or when there is variation in the amount of knowledge about the research. Punch (1994: 91), for example, observes that 'some dissimulation is intrinsic to social life and, therefore, to fieldwork'. He quotes Gans (1962: 44) in support of this point: 'If the researcher is completely honest with people about his activities, they will try to hide actions and attitudes they consider undesirable, and so will be dishonest. Consequently, the researcher must be dishonest to get honest data.'

- *Anything goes (more or less).* The writers associated with arguments relating to situation ethics and a recognition of the pervasiveness of ethical transgressions are not arguing for an 'anything-goes' mentality, but for a certain amount of flexibility in ethical decision-making. However, Douglas (1976) has argued that the kinds of deception in which social researchers engage are trivial compared to those perpetrated by powerful institutions in modern society (such as the mass media, the police, and industry). His book is an inventory of tactics for deceiving people so that their trust is gained and they reveal themselves to the researcher. Very few researchers subscribe to this stance. Denzin (1968) comes close to an anything-goes stance when he suggests that social researchers are entitled to study anyone in any setting provided the work has a 'scientific' purpose, does not harm participants, and does not deliberately damage the discipline. The harm-to-participants criterion can also be seen in the cases reported in Research in focus 6.3.

Research in focus 6.3
Two infamous studies of obedience to authority

Milgram's (1963) electric-shock experiments and Haney, Banks, and Zimbardo's (1973) prison studies have come to be seen as infamous because of the ethical issues they raise. Both studies were concerned to measure the effects of group norms on the behaviour of the individual, and they have been widely applied in the field of organizational behaviour. Milgram was concerned with the processes whereby a person can be induced to cause extreme harm to another by virtue of being ordered to do so. To investigate this issue further, he devised a laboratory experiment. Volunteers were recruited to act out the role of teachers who punished learners (who were accomplices of the experimenter) by submitting them to electric shocks when they gave incorrect answers to questions.

The shocks were not, of course, real, but the teachers/volunteers were not aware of this. The level of electric shock was gradually increased with successive incorrect answers until the teacher/volunteer refused to administer more shocks. Learners had been trained to respond to the rising level of electric shock with simulated but appropriate howls of pain. In the room was a further accomplice of Milgram's, who cajoled the teacher/volunteer to continue to administer shocks, suggesting that it was part of the study's requirements to continue and that they were not causing permanent harm, in spite of the increasingly shrill cries of pain. However, in a later adaptation of the experiment, the teacher/volunteer was accompanied by a colleague who acted out the part of someone who refused to administer the shocks beyond a certain level. In this situation, the real subject continued to administer the shocks for a shorter period and then declined as the first teacher/volunteer had done. Milgram's study demonstrates the extent to which individuals display obedience to authority even if this involves causing considerable pain to others. It also shows how peer rebellion can be a powerful means of resisting the experimenter's authority.

Experiments conducted by Zimbardo and his graduate students from the Department of Psychology at Stanford University, California, involved creating a mock prison, in order to examine the roles played by prisoners and guards. Twenty-one male participants were selected from a group of seventy-five who responded to an advertisement in a local newspaper. Individuals were selected on the basis that they were mature, emotionally stable, middle class, well educated, and had no criminal record. Each was paid $15 per day to participate in the study. A coin was flipped in order to decide if the participant was to play the role of prisoner or guard. There were ten prisoners and eleven guards. However, only a few days into the planned fourteen-day study, the experiment took an unexpected turn. The relationship between prisoners and guards deteriorated to such an extent that guards began to subject prisoners to psychological cruelty. Within the first few days several of the prisoners had been released, suffering from severe depression and mental breakdown. Only six days into the study the experiment was abandoned owing to the extreme symptoms experienced by the prisoners. Haney, Banks, and Zimbardo's study shows that individual behaviour is determined by social and environmental conditions to a far greater extent than is commonly assumed.

Both studies raise complex ethical issues, particularly in relation to the potential harm incurred by participants as a result of the experiments. It is worth noting that both studies were conducted over forty years ago, and it is extremely unlikely that either would be considered acceptable to a university human subjects committee or indeed to most social researchers today. However, in 2006 Burger (2009) conducted what he refers to as a 'partial replication' of the Milgram experiment. Burger hypothesized that there would be little or no difference between Milgram's findings and his own some forty-five years later. The replication is 'partial' for several reasons such as: participants did not proceed beyond the lowest simulated voltage level that Milgram used (150 volts; 79 per cent of Milgram's teachers went beyond this point); participants were intensively screened for emotional and psychological problems and excluded if there was evidence of such problems; people who had studied some psychology were excluded (because the Milgram studies are so well known); and participants of all adult ages were included, rather than up to the age of 50, as in the original studies. Burger also reckons that his sample was more ethnically diverse than Milgram's would have been. The replication had to be partial because, as Burger puts it, 'current standards for the ethical treatment of participants clearly place Milgram's studies out of bounds' (Burger 2009: 2). Burger found that the propensity for obedience was only slightly lower than forty-five years previously, though, as Miller (2009) observes, the adjustments Burger had to make probably render comparisons with Milgram's findings questionable.

Researchers' ethical qualms do not extend to television, however. In March 2010, newspapers reported a French documentary based on a supposed game show called Game of Death and broadcast on prime-time television. Eighty contestants signed contracts agreeing to inflict electric shocks on other participants. Shocks were administered when the other contestant failed to answer a question correctly. The shocks continued up to the highest voltage with the contestants being egged on by an audience and a presenter. Only sixteen contestants stopped before administering the highest shock level, which would have been fatal. As in the Milgram experiment, the participants receiving the shocks were actors who simulated howls of agony and the shocks themselves were, of course, also fake. An account of this programme, which refers to Milgram, can be found at:

news.bbc.co.uk/1/hi/world/europe/8573755.stm (accessed 18 October 2014).

Tips and skills
Ethics committees

In addition to needing to be familiar with the codes of practice produced by professional associations such as the Academy of Management, the Market Research Society, and the Social Research Association, you should be acquainted with the ethical guidelines of your university or college. Most higher education institutions have ethics committees that issue guidelines about ethical practice to researchers employed by the university and students. Ethical guidelines and ethics committees are there to protect research participants, but they are also involved in protecting researchers and institutions from the possibility of adverse publicity or legal action being taken against them. These guidelines are often based on or influenced by the codes developed by professional associations. Universities' and colleges' guidelines will provide indications of what practices are considered ethically unacceptable. Sometimes, you will need to submit your proposed research to an ethics committee of your university or college for approval. As part of this you may need to complete a form to show that you have considered potential ethical issues that might arise from your study (see Tips and skills 'A sample university ethics form'). You may also be advised to submit a study information sheet which you propose to distribute to research participants, together with a consent form which participants will be asked to complete (see Tips and skills 'A sample study information sheet' and 'A sample study consent form'). If your university requires you to apply for ethical approval as part of your research project, be aware that this process can be time-consuming, so it is important to leave sufficient time for this. It is also essential that you do not start the research until approval has been granted.

In this chapter, we will introduce the main issues and debates about ethics. We are not going to try to resolve them, because they are not readily capable of resolution. This is why the ethical debate has scarcely moved on since the 1960s. What *is* crucial is to be aware of the ethical principles involved and of the nature of the concerns about ethics in business research. It is only if researchers are aware of the issues involved that they can make informed decisions about the implications of certain choices. If nothing else, you should be aware of the possible opprobrium that will be coming your way if you make certain kinds of choice. Our chief concern lies with the ethical issues that arise in relations between researchers and research participants in the course of an investigation. This focus by no means exhausts the range of ethical issues and dilemmas that arise, such as those that might arise in relation to the funding of business research or how findings are used by non-researchers. However, the

Tips and skills
A sample university ethics form

This form is intended to help researchers consider the ethical implications of research activity. Researchers are responsible for deciding, guided by university guidelines and professional disciplinary standards, whether a more extensive review is necessary.

Title of study:

Names of investigators:

Yes No (please tick)

1. Is the study funded (if yes, name the source)? ☐ ☐

2. Is the research compromised by the source of funding? ☐ ☐

3. Are there potential conflicts of interest in the financial or organizational arrangements? ☐ ☐

4. Will confidentiality be maintained appropriately at all stages of enquiry: at collection, storage, analysis, and reporting? ☐ ☐

5. Will human rights and dignities be actively respected? ☐ ☐

6. Will highly personal, intimate, or other private or confidential information be sought? ☐ ☐

7. Will there be any harm, discomfort, physical, or psychological risks? ☐ ☐

8. Will participants be involved whose ability to give informed voluntary consent may be limited? ☐ ☐

9. Will the study involve obtaining or processing personal data relating to living individuals (e.g. recording interviews with subjects even if the findings will subsequently be made anonymous)? (*Note: if the answer to this question is 'yes' you will need to ensure that the provisions of the Data Protection Act (1988) are complied with. In particular you will need to ensure that subjects provide sufficient consent and that personal data will be properly stored for an appropriate period of time.*) ☐ ☐

10. Please provide a paragraph explaining any additional ethical issues that are relevant to the study. If none, explain why.

I confirm that the ethical issues pertaining to this study have been fully considered.

Signed (lead investigator): _____ Date:

On behalf of University Research Ethics Committee: _____ Date:

ethical issues that arise in the course of doing research are the ones that are most likely to impinge on students. Writers on research ethics adopt different stances concerning the ethical issues that arise in connection with relationships between researchers and research participants. Key concept 6.2 outlines some of these stances.

Ethical principles

Discussions about ethical principles in business research, and perhaps more specifically transgressions of them, tend to revolve around certain issues that recur in different guises. They have been usefully broken down by Diener and Crandall (1978) into four main areas:

- whether there is *harm to participants*;
- whether there is a *lack of informed consent*;
- whether there is an *invasion of privacy*;
- whether *deception* is involved.

We will look at each of these in turn, but it should be appreciated that these four issues overlap somewhat. For example, it is difficult to imagine how the principle of informed consent could be built into an investigation in which research participants were deceived. However, there is no doubt that these four areas form a useful classification of ethical issues in and for business research.

Harm to participants

Research that is likely to harm participants is regarded by most people as unacceptable. But what is harm? Harm can entail a number of facets: physical harm; harm to participants' development or self-esteem; stress; harm to career prospects or future employment; and 'inducing subjects to perform reprehensible acts', as Diener and Crandall (1978: 19) put it. In several studies that we have encountered in this book, there has been real or potential harm to participants.

- In Dalton's (1959) study, his 'counselling' relationship with the female secretary in exchange for access to valuable personnel files (see Research in focus 19.4) was potentially harmful to her, both in terms of the personal relationship and in jeopardizing the security of her employment.

- In Haney, Banks, and Zimbardo's (1973) prison experiments (see Research in focus 6.3), several participants experienced severe emotional reactions, including mental breakdown.

- Many of the participants in the Milgram experiment (1963) on obedience to authority (see Research in focus 6.3) experienced high levels of stress and anxiety as a consequence of being incited to administer electric shocks. It could also be argued that Milgram's observers were 'inducing subjects to perform reprehensible acts'. Indeed, yet another series of studies in which Milgram was involved placed participants in positions where they were being influenced to steal (Milgram and Shotland 1973).

The AoM *Code of Ethical Conduct* states that it is the responsibility of the researcher to assess carefully the possibility of harm to research participants, and, to the extent that it can be, the possibility of harm should be minimized. Similar views are expressed by the MRS's *Code of Conduct*, which advocates that 'the researcher must take all reasonable precautions to ensure that respondents are in no way directly harmed or adversely affected as a result of their participation in a marketing research project'. However, some commentators cast the scope of ethical consideration far wider, suggesting that it is also necessary to consider non-participants in evaluating the risk of harm (see Thinking deeply 6.4). This is consistent with recent changes in social research guidelines that extend the definition of what constitutes an ethical issue (see the section below on 'Ethics and legal considerations' for more discussion of these changes).

A further area of ethical consideration relates to the possibility of harm to the researcher, an issue that was introduced in Tips and skills 'Safety in research' (Chapter 4). In addition to the possibility of physical or emotional harm through exposure to a fieldwork setting, certain research methods, such as auto-ethnography (see Key concept 19.20), may carry a greater risk of emotional or professional harm to the researcher because the researcher's own personal self-disclosures constitute the basis for the analysis (Doloriert and Sambrook 2009). If this analysis is made public, a great deal of sensitive, personal information pertaining to the researcher is placed in the public domain. The anonymity of the researcher thus cannot be maintained. Doloriert and Sambrook (2009) argue that this is a particular concern for student researchers whose work will be examined by more experienced and more powerful senior researchers.

The issue of harm to participants is further addressed in ethical codes by advocating care over maintaining the

Thinking deeply 6.4
Harm to non-participants?

Gorard (2002) argues that, although much ethical guidance focuses on the responsibilities of the researcher in relation to research participants, there is also a need to consider the interests of non-participants in the research who constitute the majority, especially when research has practical implications in determining social policies such as those relating to health, housing, transport, and education. He argues that 'most discussions of ethical considerations in research focus on possible harm to the research participants, to the exclusion of the possible harm done to future users of the evidence which research generates. They almost never consider the wasted resources, and worse, used in implementing treatments and policies that do not work' (2002: 3).

confidentiality of records and anonymity of accounts. This means that the identities and records of individuals and organizations should be maintained as confidential. For example, the AoM *Code of Ethical Conduct* recommends that issues relating to confidentiality and anonymity should be negotiated and agreed with potential research participants, and, 'if confidentiality or anonymity is requested, this must be honored'. This injunction also means that care needs to be taken when findings are being published to ensure that individuals and organizations are not identified or identifiable, unless permission has been given for data to be passed on in a form that allows them to be identified. The MRS *Code of Conduct* states that researchers 'should be particularly careful if sample sizes are very small (such as in business and employee research) that they do not inadvertently identify organisations or departments and therefore individuals'.

In quantitative research, it is often easier to anonymize records and to report findings in a way that does not allow individuals to be identified. However, even in quantitative studies there are sometimes instances where it is virtually impossible to make a company anonymous. The use of pseudonyms is a common recourse, but it may not eliminate entirely the possibility of identification. For example, in the case of Hofstede's (1984) research, although a company pseudonym was used

throughout the published study, it was virtually impossible to conceal the company's identity without completely distorting the original data, partly because IBM is such a large and well-known organization. Similarly, although W. Scott et al. (1956) did not actually name their case study organization, the details they provided in their analysis about the firm's size, location, history, and activities made it clear to Bacon and Blyton (2001; see Research in focus 3.18), and to other researchers, exactly which large steelworks in North Wales they had studied. Issues of anonymity are particularly complex in relation to visual data. Sometimes researchers who use visual data have to go to quite extreme lengths in order to protect the anonymity of their research participants (see Research in focus 6.6).

The issues of confidentiality and anonymity raise particular difficulties for many forms of qualitative research, where great care has to be taken with regard to the possible identification of persons, organizations, and places. Moreover, as Thinking deeply 6.5 illustrates, in some qualitative research projects research participants may not wish to remain anonymous. The consequences of failing to protect individual anonymity are illustrated by M. Parker (2000: 238; see Chapter 19), who describes how a quotation in his report about the managing director was traced to an 'insufficiently anonymized source' whose reputation was damaged as a result of the incident.

Tips and skills
Confidentiality agreements

As part of the process of negotiating access, it is becoming increasingly common for companies where research is to be carried out to ask their legal departments to prepare a confidentiality agreement, which you may be asked to sign on your own behalf, or someone from your university may be asked to sign on behalf of the institution. The main purpose of this is to define what type of information you can have access to and to establish what information you are and are not able to disclose about the company. This usually involves agreeing that you will not pass on information to a third party, particularly that which pertains to commercially sensitive or valuable issues such as new product development. In addition, there may be a clause that specifies that the company must have sight of the research once it has been written up, so that it can comment on the findings, particularly if they are going to be published. This legally binding agreement can thus grant a considerable amount of power to the company, and it has the potential to cause considerable difficulties if your research throws up issues that the company would rather were kept out of the public domain. If you are asked to sign a confidentiality agreement, before signing it, take it to your supervisor to ask for advice and get it checked by someone who deals with legal issues on behalf of the university. It may be that there is some room for negotiation in relation to the exact wording of the agreement, and the company may be reassured if there is an undertaking that the research will guarantee its anonymity.

Thinking deeply 6.5
The assumption of anonymity

Grinyer (2002) argues that, although protecting the anonymity of research participants is assumed to be an integral feature of ethical research, there may be certain circumstances where research participants do not wish to remain anonymous because making their identity explicit is an important way of retaining ownership of their stories. In the UK, the legal requirements of the Data Protection Act mean there is also a legal requirement to protect anonymity, since the Act states that anonymization should be maintained wherever possible to increase the security of data processing. These guidelines are based on the assumption that research participants 'not only deserve the protection of anonymity, but that they actively desire it' (Grinyer 2002: 2). Grinyer argues that the allocation of pseudonyms to protect anonymity can cause unanticipated stress, since research participants sometimes feel that keeping their real names is an important recognition of their involvement in the research project. This, according to Grinyer, makes clear 'how problematic it is to make judgments on behalf of others, however well intentioned' (2002: 3). Grinyer recommends that this issue is dealt with on a case-by-case basis, through consultation with research participants throughout the research and publication process, so that individuals have the freedom to make a more informed choice and are less likely to feel that they have lost ownership of their stories.

Telling it like it is
Ethical considerations in a student research project

Tom was encouraged by his university to consider the ethical implications of his study of well-being among call-centre workers. His main focus was on protecting the anonymity of interviewees so that managers could not trace back comments to specific individuals. 'Birkbeck are very concerned with encouraging an ethical approach to research and considering the implications of it. Given what I was doing, I didn't think there were huge ethical implications. I suppose my main concern was to make sure that I wasn't in any way harming the well-being of the people I was talking to and I suppose there was a vague possibility that, you know, we might have talked about very traumatic stuff in the interview, which might make them very stressed and so on, but I didn't think that was very likely. What was more likely was that they'd somehow feel that I'd kind of betrayed their confidentiality by feeding back to management what they were saying, even if it was in some sort of anonymized format. Because I only had a small sample size, you know, the boss could have said "Right, who said this? I want to see all of you in my office." So I wanted to set out as clearly as I could how I was going to use their data. What I did was when I transcribed my tapes I called them Interviewee A, Interviewee B, or whatever, and then I destroyed the tapes, so all I had was an anonymized interview. I did use quotes from interviews in my dissertation, but these were attributed to Interviewee A or Call handler B or whatever, but that report was confidential to Birkbeck. It didn't go to the organization that I did my research in.' In the report that went back to the organization Tom 'made sure that there was nothing in there that could be linked back to any individual. So it didn't say "A middle aged, Asian call handler said" because that could have been attributable back to individuals.'

However, Tom also became aware that employees could be pursuing their own political agendas through the research process. 'Although I made it clear that I wasn't there to check up on call handlers on behalf of the management and that it was all confidential and I wasn't going to make recommendations which would be traceable back to any individual, there'd still be a question about to what extent people thought that it was safe to talk to me or that all sorts of stuff was going on. People were asking themselves: "Was it safe to talk to me?" Actually, I was possibly a mouthpiece for them to make comments back to management and they could say things that hopefully might get relayed on to management about working conditions or whatever.'

The issues of confidentiality and anonymity involve legal as well as ethical considerations. For example, in Cavendish's (1982) study of women factory workers on an assembly line, great care was taken by the researcher to invent names for all the women so that they could not be identified, to protect them from possible victimization by the company. However, Cavendish deliberately left the name of the firm unchanged in order to preserve the realism of the study and to provide 'concrete facts about the factory' (1982: vi). However, as Cavendish explains, this proved very naive: 'if the firm was named, there was a risk both to me and to the publisher that the firm might bring a libel action against us' (1982: vi). For this reason, after consultation with lawyers, she decided to rewrite the account prior to publication in order to make the firm unidentifiable. This involved changing not only the name of the firm, but also its location, the details of the components manufactured, and the name of the trade union representing the women. In contrast, there are other instances where organizations do consent to be named in publications, for example in Pettigrew's (1985) study of changing culture at Imperial Chemical Industries.

The issues of confidentiality and anonymity also raise particular problems with regard to the secondary analysis of qualitative data (see Chapter 24), since it is very difficult, though by no means impossible, to present field notes and interview transcripts in a way that will prevent people and places from being identified. As Alderson (1998) has suggested, the difficulty is one of being able to ensure that the same safeguards concerning confidentiality can be guaranteed when secondary analysts examine such records as those provided by the original primary researcher.

One of the problems with the harm-to-participants issue is that it is not possible to identify in all circumstances whether or not harm is likely, though that fact should not be taken to mean that there is no point in seeking to protect participants. For example, in the prison experiments conducted by Haney, Banks, and Zimbardo (see Research in focus 6.3) the extreme reactions of participants surprised the researchers. Arguably they did not anticipate this level of harm to be incurred when they planned the study. This is partly why the ESRC *Framework for Research Ethics* makes it a requirement of funding that research involving human participants and sensitive personal data is reviewed by a research ethics committee, usually within the university where the researcher works or studies.

Telling it like it is
Maintaining anonymity in a student research project

Karen devised an innovative way of keeping her research participants anonymous that still enabled her to reveal important details about a participant's position within the organization. She said, 'I didn't put any names in the dissertation. It was very difficult to actually work out what I was going to do. With the questionnaire it was just a tick-box so it was a lot easier, but with the actual interviews I wanted to use quotes and that type of thing. So it was a lot more difficult so in the appendix I had a table which was a profile of all the people that I questioned, but with no names on it. So it just had the department that they were from and their level in the organization—not the job title—and then some other information like the length of the time they'd been there in the organization because I used that in the analysis. I could cross-reference that with the quotes that I used and say "This person from the HR department or from another department said this." So it maintained their anonymity.'

Chris agreed to protect the anonymity of the bank where he did his research and he sought informed consent from each of the interviewees who agreed to take part in the study. He gave the company and each of the people interviewed a pseudonym. 'The individuals knew from the beginning what I was doing and why I was doing it. I asked them would they want me to keep their names anonymous or not. One person said she did want to be kept anonymous, two said they weren't really bothered. So I thought if I'm going to do it with one, I'd best do it with the other two as well, which I did. I also had to get permission from the organization because I had information about the percentage of women at different levels of management within the organization, which I was freely given, but obviously I sought permission about actually putting that in my dissertation. They said they were fine about it as long as it's sort of not going to be published.'

After having completed his degree, Chris was offered a job with the bank as a graduate management trainee. Since then he has become involved in diversity management within the company. Chris's experience shows how the need to act ethically in a research project cannot be separated from one's other roles, as his colleagues' impressions of him now will have undoubtedly been influenced by the way in which he conducted the research project. More generally, the importance of ethics in building trust through the research relationship is something that Chris feels strongly about, as he explains: 'It's who you know and not what you know—and if you can get organizations to trust you and let you in, then you never know what that might lead to in the end.'

Lack of informed consent

The issue of informed consent is in many respects the area within business research ethics that is most hotly debated. The bulk of the discussion tends to focus on what is variously called disguised or covert observation. Such observation can involve covert participant observation (see Key concept 19.5), or simple or contrived observation (see, for example, Thinking deeply 12.9 and Research in focus 12.10), in which the researcher's true identity is unknown. The principle of informed consent means that prospective research participants should be given as much information as might be needed to make an informed decision about whether or not they wish to participate in a study. Covert observation transgresses that principle, because participants are not given the opportunity to refuse to cooperate. They are involved whether they like it or not.

Lack of informed consent is a feature of Research in focus 6.1 and Research in focus 6.3. For example, in Dalton's research, informed consent is almost entirely absent. Dalton went to great lengths in order to keep the purpose of his research from participants, presumably to maximize his chances of obtaining specific information about such things as unofficial use of resources or pilfering. Even those who became key informants, or 'intimates', knew only of Dalton's general interest in 'personnel problems', and Dalton took great care not to arouse suspicion. Dalton describes his undercover role as similar in indirect actions to that of an espionage agent or spy, although he stresses that his interest was in scientific rather than criminal evidence. It is striking that some of the most notorious violations of the principle of informed consent are in the relatively distant past (especially those discussed in Research in focus 6.3). However, an experiment on Facebook users by Kramer, Guillory, and Hancock (2014) suggests that such incidents should not be regarded as indicative of problems rooted in the past. A massive sample of 689,003 Facebook users was randomly selected in order to investigate whether exposure to positive or negative emotional expressions caused a change in users' own affective expressions as expressed in their own posts. Two experiments were created: one in which an experimental group was exposed for a one-week period to a reduction in positive emotions in friends' news feeds compared to a control group and one in which the experimental group was exposed to a reduction in negative emotions. However, participants were not offered the opportunity to give explicit informed consent. Instead, the researchers claim that their investigation 'was consistent with Facebook's Data Use Policy, to which all users agree prior to creating an account on Facebook, constituting informed consent for this research' (Kramer et al. 2014: 8789). In other words, the researchers were relying on an implicit informed consent. The research engendered a storm of protest in the mass media in both the UK (e.g. **www.theguardian.com/ technology/2014/jun/29/facebook-users-emotions-news-feeds**, accessed 18 October 2014) and the USA (e.g. **www.nytimes.com/2014/06/30/technology/ facebook-tinkers-with-users-emotions-in-news-feed-experiment-stirring-outcry.html?_r=0**, accessed 18 October 2014). It is the lack of explicit informed consent that lies at the heart of this outcry.

The principle of informed consent also entails the implication that, even when people know they are being asked to participate in research, they should be fully informed about the research process. The ABS *Ethics Guide* recommends that researchers

Ensure that participants in research and scholarship, from within or outside the University, understand enough about the process to be able to make an informed decision about taking part, including what their participation entails, why their participation is necessary, how data will be used, and how and to whom findings will be reported.

The MRS *Code of Conduct* also states that informed consent means that respondents should be told, normally at the beginning of the interview, if observation techniques or recording equipment are to be used. Thus, while Milgram's and Haney, Banks, and Zimbardo's experimental subjects (see Research in focus 6.3) were volunteers and therefore knew they were going to participate in research, there was a lack of informed consent because they were not given full information about the nature of the research and its possible implications for them.

However, as Homan (1991: 73) has observed, implementing the principle of informed consent 'is easier said than done'. At least two major points stand out here.

- It is extremely difficult to present prospective participants with absolutely all the information that might be required to make an informed decision about their involvement. In fact, relatively minor transgressions probably pervade most business research, such as deliberately underestimating the amount of time that an interview is likely to take so that people are not put off being interviewed, and not giving absolutely all the details about one's research for fear of contaminating people's answers to questions.

- In ethnographic research, the researcher is likely to come into contact with a wide spectrum of people, and ensuring that absolutely everyone has the opportunity for informed consent is not practicable because it would be extremely disruptive in everyday contexts. Also, even when all research participants in a certain setting are aware that the ethnographer is a researcher, it is doubtful whether they are all similarly (let alone identically) informed about the nature of the research. For example, in C. K. Lee's (1998) study of women factory workers in Hong Kong and China, she found it difficult to convey her 'version' of what she was doing to her co-workers. This was partly because the academic term 'thesis' did not make sense to them, so the women developed an alternative explanation, which involved the idea that Lee was writing a novel based on her experiences as a worker 'toiling side by side with "real" workers'. Lee explains: 'I had to settle for that definition too' (1998: 173). This example aptly illustrates how it is not always possible for the researcher fully to explain the purposes and nature of the research, and so sometimes a compromise understanding is reached.

- The difficulties of obtaining informed consent are further complicated when data is collected in a public place, or using publicly available information about people or organizations. In such cases, it may not be practical to seek informed consent from all those present. This also applies to some research involving the Internet, where the boundaries between public and private spaces are often unclear (see Chapter 28 for more on this). The ASA *Code of Ethics* states that researchers 'may conduct research in public places or use publicly-available information about individuals (e.g., naturalistic observations in public places, analysis of public records, or archival research) without obtaining consent. If, under such circumstances, sociologists have any doubt whatsoever about the need for informed consent, they consult with institutional review boards or, in the absence of such boards, with another authoritative body with expertise on the ethics of research before proceeding with such research.'

In spite of the widespread condemnation of violations of informed consent and the view that covert observation is especially vulnerable to accusations of unethical practice in this regard, studies such as Dalton's (1959) are still regarded as important in providing insight into subversive or illegitimate organizational behaviour. The defence is usually of the 'end-justifies-the-means' kind, which is further discussed below. What is interesting in the context of this discussion is that some ethical codes essentially leave the door ajar for covert observation. The BSA *Statement of Ethical Practice* does suggest that researchers should 'as far as possible' seek to achieve informed consent, but it then goes even further in relation to **covert research**:

> There are serious ethical and legal issues in the use of covert research but the use of covert methods may be justified in certain circumstances. For example, difficulties arise when research participants change their behaviour because they know they are being studied. Researchers may also face problems when access to spheres of social life is closed to social scientists by powerful or secretive interests.
>
> (BSA, Statement of Ethical Practice 2002: 4)

While this statement hardly condones the absence of informed consent associated with covert research, it is not unequivocally censorious either. The statement recognizes that covert research may avoid certain problems and refers, without using the term, to the possibility of **reactivity** associated with overt observational methods. It also recognizes that covert methods can help to get over the difficulty of gaining access to certain kinds of setting. The passage entails an acknowledgement that covert research jeopardizes informed consent, along with the privacy principle (see below), but the BSA *Statement of Ethical Practice* goes on to say that covert research can be used 'where it is impossible to use other methods to obtain essential data'. The difficulty here clearly is how a researcher is to decide whether or not it is in fact impossible to obtain data other than by covert work. We suspect that, by and large, covert observers typically make their judgements in this connection on the basis of the *anticipated* difficulty of gaining access to a setting or of encountering reactivity problems, rather than as a response to difficulties they have actually experienced. For example, Dalton (1959) has written that it is impossible to get sufficiently close to unofficial managerial activities to access the meanings assigned to them by participants, other than through covert observation. The issue of the circumstances in which violations of ethical principles such as informed consent are deemed acceptable will reappear in the discussion below.

The principle of informed consent is also bound up to some extent with the issue of harm to participants. Erikson (1967) has suggested that, if a researcher fails to seek informed consent and if participants are harmed as a result of the research, the investigator is more culpable than if there was no informed consent. For example, he writes: 'If we happen to harm people who have agreed to act as subjects, we can at least argue that they knew something of the risks involved' (1967: 369). While this might seem like a recipe for seeking a salve for the researcher's conscience, it does point to an important issue—namely, that the business researcher is more likely to be vilified if participants are adversely affected

when they were not willing accomplices than when they were. However, it is debatable whether that means that the researcher is any less culpable for that harm. Erikson implies that researchers are less culpable, but this is a potential area for disagreement. In the Facebook experiment referred to above (Kramer et al. 2014), there is a very real possibility that some of the participants may have been adversely affected by a sudden change to their exposure to positive and/or negative emotions.

The need to take precautions to ensure that respondents are in no way harmed as a result of their participation in research is of particular concern in situations involving vulnerable persons who may not be in a position to give their fully informed consent. An example of this might be marketing research that explores the effect of advertising on children. For example, Lawlor and Prothero (2007) conducted focus groups and individual interviews involving fifty-two children aged between 7 and 9 to explore their understanding of television advertisements. They carried out their data collection in two Irish primary schools during school hours. Consent to participate in the study was requested from the parents of the children, who expressed a preference that the interviews be conducted in the neutral setting of the school, rather than in the children's homes. Permission was also requested for the interviews to be tape-recorded. In cases such as this one, extreme diligence must be exercised over the gaining of informed consent because of the greater vulnerability of children as research participants and the difficulties in ensuring that they fully understand the implications of their agreement to participate in research.

Tips and skills
A sample study information sheet

Study Information

[Study Title]

You are being invited to consider taking part in the research study [insert title]. This study is being undertaken by [researcher name]. Before you decide whether or not you wish to take part, it is important for you to understand why this research is being done and what it will involve. Please take time to read this information carefully. Please ask if there is anything that is unclear or if you would like more information.

You have been invited to participate because [reason for participant selection]. The study will involve [brief details of methods in language the reader will be able to understand]. You are free to decide whether you wish to take part or not. If you do decide to take part you will be asked to sign two consent forms; one is for you to keep and the other is for my records. You are free to withdraw from this study at any time and without giving reasons. Should you decide to withdraw from the study, your data will not be used and will be destroyed. The

(continued)

study is [details of how the research is being funded or, if it is part of a student project, explain: e.g. 'the study forms part of my MSc qualification at {name of university}'].

If you agree to take part, [explain what will happen from participant's perspective, e.g. 'you will be interviewed by the researcher involved in the study; the interview will last approximately one hour and will be audio-recorded for research purposes. The data will be anonymized and will not be used in a way which would enable identification of your individual responses. Data will be stored securely on a password-protected computer, and in hard copy in a locked filing cabinet, by the research investigators for a period not exceeding five years after which point it will be disposed of securely. The data will not be shared with any third parties.'].

If you have any questions about the study, please feel free to contact me at [researcher details: use university contact information rather than private phone number or personal email address]. Alternatively, if you are concerned about any aspect of this study you may contact [named contact within the university to whom issues should be addressed].

Tips and skills
A sample study consent form

Consent Form

[Title of Research Project]

[Contact details of researcher: include university postal address, university telephone number and university email address]

Request for informed consent:

- I have read the Study Information sheet provided and been given adequate time to consider it.
- I have been given the opportunity to ask questions about the Study and any questions have been answered to my satisfaction.
- I understand that my participation in the Study is voluntary.
- I understand that taking part in the Study will involve me being interviewed and I agree to this interview being audio-recorded.
- I understand that my personal details such as name and employer address will not be revealed to people outside the project.
- I understand that my words may be quoted in publications, reports, web pages, and other research outputs, but data collected about me during the Study will be anonymized before it is submitted for publication.
- I understand that I can withdraw from the Study at any time and I will not be asked any questions about why I no longer want to take part.
- I understand that if I withdraw from the Study my data will not be used.

Name of Participant: _____ Signature: _____ Date: _____

Name of Researcher: _____ Signature: _____ Date: _____

[Based on examples from UK Data Archive (2009) and several UK universities]

It is increasingly common for researchers to be advised by their universities, via their research ethics committees, to gain written, rather than verbal, consent from research participants by asking them to fill out and sign a form, particularly if the research involves the collection of personal data (see the section in this chapter on 'Data management'). This is typically accompanied by a study information sheet, which explains what the research is about and how the researchers plan to use the data. If data are collected using audio or video recording equipment, informed consent can also be formally recorded in this way, by asking the participant for their informed consent at the start of the process, rather than by completing a form. However, some researchers have expressed concerns about what they see as a 'tick-box approach' to informed consent, saying that it encourages ethical issues to be seen as a one-time consideration, rather than as something that needs to be considered throughout the research process (Sin 2005). The form-filling method of gaining informed consent is particularly problematic in certain qualitative research designs, where data collection can extend over a period of time and involve methods such as participant observation (see Chapter 19) for which it would be inappropriate to ask research participants to sign a form. Also, the direction of qualitative studies can be somewhat less predictable than with quantitative ones, so it is difficult to be specific within forms about some issues.

Invasion of privacy

This third area of ethical concern relates to the issue of the degree to which invasions of privacy can be condoned. The right to privacy is a tenet that many of us hold dear, and transgressions of that right in the name of research are not regarded as acceptable. Under the heading 'Avoiding undue intrusion', the SRA guidance on this issue cites Cassell (1982) and states:

> People can feel wronged without being harmed by research: they may feel they have been treated as objects of measurement without respect for their individual values and sense of privacy. In many of the social enquiries that have caused controversy, the issue has had more to do with intrusion into subjects' private and personal domains, or by overburdening subjects by collecting 'too much' information, rather than with whether or not subjects have been harmed. In some cases a researcher's attitudes, demeanour or even their latent theoretical or methodological perspective can be interpreted as doing an injustice to subjects. Examples include an offhand manner on the part of a survey interviewer or studies which depend upon some form of social disruption. By exposing subjects to a sense of being wronged, perhaps by such attitudes, by such approaches, by the methods of selection or by causing them to acquire self knowledge that they did not seek or want, social researchers are vulnerable to criticism. Participants' resistance to future social enquiries in general may also increase as a consequence of such 'inconsiderateness'.
>
> (SRA, *Ethical Guidelines* 2003: 27)

Privacy is very much linked to the notion of informed consent, because, to the degree that informed consent is given on the basis of a detailed understanding of what the research participant's involvement is likely to entail, he or she in a sense acknowledges that the right to privacy has been surrendered for that limited domain. Of course, the research participant does not entirely abrogate the right to privacy by providing informed consent. When people agree to be interviewed, they may refuse to answer certain questions on whatever grounds they feel are justified. Often, these refusals will be based on a feeling that certain questions delve into private realms or cover topic areas that they find sensitive and they do not wish to make these public, regardless of the fact that the interview is conducted in private. However, the SRA statement highlights the potentially very broad and varied nature of the issues that can be interpreted as intrusive. Although there are some topics that can be judged sensitive to everyone, because of the nature of the subject, it is impossible for the researcher to know beforehand which topics may be sensitive to a particular individual. It therefore recommends that the researcher 'treat each case sensitively and individually, giving respondents a genuine opportunity to withdraw'.

Covert methods are usually deemed to be violations of the privacy principle on the grounds that participants are not being given the opportunity to refuse invasions of their privacy. Such methods also mean that they might reveal confidences or information that they would not have revealed if they had known about the status of the confidant as researcher. The issue of privacy is invariably linked to issues of anonymity and confidentiality in the research process, an area that has already been touched on in the context of the question of whether or not harm comes to participants. The BSA *Statement* forges this kind of connection: 'The anonymity and privacy of those who participate in the research process should be respected. Personal

Research in focus 6.6
Invasion of privacy in visual research

As S. Warren (2002: 240) notes, 'the very act of holding a camera up to one's eye and pointing it at someone is an obvious and potentially intrusive activity which cannot be "disguised" in the same way as making field-notes in a journal or even tape-recording an interview'. Ethical issues of anonymity and confidentiality are potentially more problematic because of the instant recognizability of photographic images. Legal issues can also be more complex, especially those pertaining to copyright ownership (Pink 2001). As a precaution, in her study of organizational aesthetics (see Research in focus 17.11), Warren did not use any photographs that revealed distinguishing organizational features, such as logos. She also used digital image manipulation software to obscure the faces of the few people in the photographs in order to protect their anonymity.

Another example of the consequences of the ethical sensitivity of using photographs in research is found in Bolton, Pole, and Mizen's (2001) research into child employment, where the researchers gave the young people involved in the study a disposable camera for them to take photographs of their place of work. Several of the young people chose to opt out of the photographic part of the study because they were worried that taking photographs might jeopardize their employment, while others, who had wanted to participate in the photographic study, found that when they took the camera into work they were able to take only one or two shots before being asked by their employer not to take photographs. The researchers conclude: 'in these situations it is the absence of photographs that begins to tell us something about the work experiences of the children by providing an insight into the power relations that govern their employment' (2001: 512).

information concerning research participants should be kept confidential. In some cases it may be necessary to decide whether it is proper or appropriate to record certain kinds of sensitive information.' Invasion of privacy can also be a particular issue when dealing with certain kinds of data, such as photographs (see Research in focus 6.6).

Issues about ensuring anonymity and confidentiality in relation to the recording of information and the maintenance of records relate to all methods of business research. In other words, while covert research may pose certain kinds of problem regarding the invasion of privacy, other methods of business research are implicated in possible difficulties in connection with anonymity and confidentiality.

Deception

Deception occurs when researchers represent their research as something other than what it is. Deception in various degrees is probably quite widespread in much research, because researchers often want to limit participants' understanding of what the research is about so that they respond more naturally to experimental treatment. The obedience-to-authority study by Milgram referred to in Research in focus 6.3 involved deception, because participants were led to believe they were administering

real electric shocks. A less extreme example is provided by Holliday (1995) in her ethnographic study of small firms (see Research in focus 6.7). In pretending to be a student interested in small firms in order to get information about a competitor's product, Holliday was clearly engaged in an element of deception.

The ethical objection to deception seems to turn on two points. First, it is not a nice thing to do. While the SRA *Guidelines* recognizes that deception is widespread in social interaction, it is hardly desirable. Secondly, there is the question of professional self-interest. If business researchers became known as snoopers who deceived people as a matter of professional course, the image of our work would be adversely affected and we might experience difficulty in gaining financial support and the cooperation of future prospective research participants. As the SRA *Guidelines* puts it:

It remains the duty of social researchers and their collaborators, however, not to pursue methods of inquiry that are likely to infringe human values and sensibilities. To do so, whatever the methodological advantages, would be to endanger the reputation of social research and the mutual trust between social researchers and society which is a prerequisite for much research.

Research in focus 6.7
An example of an ethical fieldwork dilemma

Holliday (1995: 17–18) describes an ethical dilemma that she faced during her fieldwork.

> I arranged to visit a small electronics company owned by a friend of a colleague. The night before I was due to visit the company my temperature soared to 103 degrees and I went down with 'flu. However, I felt that I could not break the arrangement at such short notice, so I decided to go to the factory anyway . . . I got to the factory at 10 am. Eventually Raj, the owner-manager, arrived. We had spent 10 minutes touring the factory when he asked me if I could drive. I said that I could, so he asked me if I would drive him to another factory about fifteen miles south . . . Business and lunch over we walked back to the car (to my great relief—at last I could go home) . . . As we pulled out of the car park, Raj turned to me and said, 'I'd just like to pop down to an exhibition in Birmingham—is that okay?' My heart sank, but I didn't have the strength to protest, so off to Birmingham we went.
>
> During the journey down, Raj told me about a crisis which had occurred very recently within his company. Another small firm had ordered a very substantial piece of equipment from him, which had required a huge amount of development work. Once the item was supplied the company which placed the order promptly declared itself bankrupt and refused to pay . . . By the time we reached Birmingham my sense of injustice was well and truly inflamed . . . 'So', Raj continued, 'this company has a display of *our product* here today and I want to get their brochure on it. The trouble is they'll know me, so you'll have to get it. We'll split up at the door and I'll meet you in an hour. Tell them you're a customer or something . . .' I couldn't believe it. I was being asked to commit industrial espionage in my first few hours of fieldwork . . .
>
> I got the brochure pretending to be a student—from Southampton, interested in researching small firms. I even got an invitation to the factory to come and research them. Then I passed the intelligence to Raj and began the long drive back. I arrived home at 8.30 pm exhausted and feverish, and with a very guilty conscience.

One of the chief problems with the discussion of this aspect of ethics is that deception is, as some writers observe, widespread in business research (see the stance 'Ethical transgression is pervasive' in Key concept 6.2). As the example from C. K. Lee's (1998) research illustrates, it is rarely feasible or desirable to provide participants with a totally complete account of what your research is about. Bulmer (1982), whose stance is predominantly that of a universalist in ethics terms (see Key concept 6.2), none-theless recognizes that there are bound to be instances such as this and deems them justifiable. However, it is very difficult to know where the line should be drawn here.

Ethics and legal considerations

In addition to the four main ethical issues identified by Diener and Crandall (1978), there are other ethical considerations that need to be taken into account in planning a research project that have been made more prominent as the result of recent changes within the social science research community. These relate to work carried out by research funding bodies such as the ESRC and the European Union, which have been active in recent years in developing ethical frameworks that apply to all social science researchers, including those in the field of business and management. The ESRC *Framework for Research Ethics,* mentioned at the start of this chapter, is the result of discussion and consultation with the social science community and other key stakeholders. Although the guidelines apply specifically to research projects funded by these organizations, which will have to show that they have met the requirements set out in the framework in order to receive funding, they are a useful point of reference for all university social science researchers. The *Respect Code of Practice for Socio-Economic Research* (2004), covering research in Europe, can be found at: *www.respectproject. org/code/respect_code.pdf* (accessed 18 October 2014).

Another example of the heightened awareness of ethical issues in university-based research is the *Missenden Code of Practice for Ethics and Accountability* (2002), which aims to address the challenges posed by the increased commercialization of research and shifts in the source of research funding. This code is available at: *www.missendencentre. co.uk/Ethics_report.pdf* (accessed 18 October 2014).

Rather than being intended as a replacement for the ethics codes developed by professional associations such as those described earlier in this chapter, these frameworks are intended to supplement existing codes and to encourage their further development. Because of this, it is worthwhile reviewing here the main areas that they cover in addition to the four main ethical issues that we have already discussed. These relate to:

- the impact of data protection legislation;
- the role of reciprocity in determining the relationship between the researcher and research participants;
- the need to declare sources of funding and support that may affect the affiliations of the researcher, causing conflicts of interest.

In the UK, a further issue that you may encounter if you intend to conduct research in a National Health Service (NHS) organization, such as a hospital, or a local authority social care organization is that it will come within the terms of reference of the *Research Governance Framework for Health and Social Care* issued by the Department of Health in 2005. This document can be found at: *www. dh.gov.uk/en/Publicationsandstatistics/Publications/ PublicationsPolicyAndGuidance/DH_4108962* (accessed 18 October 2014).

This document includes recommendations about ethics and ethics-related issues. In the views of many commentators, this *Framework* considerably expands the range of issues covered by ethical considerations. For example, in paragraph 2.3.1, it is suggested that: 'Research which duplicates other work unnecessarily or which is not of sufficient quality to contribute something useful to existing knowledge is in itself unethical.' Such a position enlarges the scope of ethical considerations well beyond the kinds of issues addressed by Diener and Crandall (1978). Further information on the ethics of research in the NHS can also be found at the *National Research Ethics Service* of the NHS: *www.nres.nhs.uk/* (accessed 18 October 2014).

Data management

The routine collection and storing of digital data and the practices of data sharing raise new concerns about confidentiality and other ethical issues. They raise questions about the extent to which information can legitimately be used for research purposes that may be different from the original reason for collecting the data. This issue focuses on who owns the data and under what circumstances people are entitled to use it. In obtaining informed consent from research participants, any long-term preservation and sharing plans should be made explicit, so these decisions need to be made at the outset of a project. A good source of advice on the management and sharing of data is the UK Data Archive (2009), which states:

> The ease with which digital data can be stored, disseminated and made accessible to secondary users via the internet means that many institutions embrace the sharing of research data to increase the impact and visibility of their research.
>
> (UK Data Archive 2009: 3)

As this statement highlights, it is increasingly common for researchers to be encouraged to make their data available to the wider scientific community so that maximum potential benefit may be gained from it. This raises issues relating to data security: the extent to which data need to be protected from unauthorized access or usage, particularly if they contain personal information relating to individuals, such as their names, addresses, occupations, or photographs. The specific piece of legislation that determines the extent to which personal data may be used for research purposes in the UK is the 1998 Data Protection Act. Common techniques for enhancing security include separating personal identifiers from expressions of opinion and storing them separately. The physical as well as technical security of data should be attended to—for example, by keeping filing cabinets and offices containing data locked and having password-protected databases.

There is a further category in the Data Protection Act that relates to sensitive personal data, such as information about a data subject's political or religious beliefs, ethnic origin, or whether he or she belongs to a trade union. This type of data is more rigorously protected, and there is greater onus on the researcher to obtain explicit, usually written, consent from data subjects for the processing of this type of personal data. However, the Act does provide for certain exemptions in the case of personal data that are collected for research purposes—namely, that where personal data are processed for research that is not likely to cause damage or distress to any of the data subjects concerned, they may be kept and further processed at a later stage for other purposes. Additionally, as long as the results of the research are not published in any form that identifies any particular data subject, respondents do not have right of access to the data.

Because the legislation surrounding data protection varies from country to country, the Respect project set out to identify some common principles for European researchers to bear in mind when dealing with data-protection issues. This involved a group of legal specialists who reviewed the existing EU legislation and came up with a common set of guidelines for researchers to follow in dealing with this issue. These guidelines, which are extremely detailed and run for over eighty pages, can be viewed in full at: *www.respectproject.org/data/415data.pdf* (accessed 18 October 2014)

The length and detail of this report highlights the complexity of this issue, for which researchers may be advised to take legal advice. However, it is worth highlighting three of the recommendations that the authors of the report make. These are:

- Researchers should draft an outline of the processing operations (this is not limited to electronic processing) involved in their use of the data *before* they start to process it, so they can assess the legality of their usage in advance, rather than perform the operations and then find out afterwards whether or not they are permitted to use the data in this way. This point highlights the potential seriousness of using data unlawfully, for which criminal or administrative sanctions may be applied.

- Researchers should decide who is the controller of the data and thus responsible for its usage, and on the basis of this determine which national legislation applies to their study. This is a particular issue in situations involving a group of researchers working together on a research project but based in different countries. This decision also depends on where the data processing will be carried out.

- Prior to the data processing, the researcher should define who will be the data subjects and take precautions to respect their rights in relation to the data.

Copyright

A further issue affected by legal considerations is copyright. Copyright is an intellectual property right that protects the owner of copyright from unauthorized copying. Most research publications, reports, and books, as well as raw data such as spreadsheets and interview transcripts, are protected by copyright. For employed researchers, the first owner of copyright is usually the employer. However, many universities waive this right in relation to research data and publications and give it to the researcher. Some researchers use Creative Commons licences, which allow the creators of works to waive some of their rights in order to allow their work to be used more freely. The UK Data Archive provides a very helpful explanation of the situation regarding copyright:

> In the case of interviews, the interviewee holds the copyright in the spoken word. If a transcription is a substantial reproduction of the words spoken, the speaker will own copyright in the words and the transcriber will have separate copyright of the transcription.
>
> (UK Data Archive 2009: 23)

The important thing to remember is that, if you want to share your data with other researchers, you will need to get copyright clearance from the interviewee for this at the time of the interview. There are also particular copyright issues pertaining to the use of visual data. For example, in order to reproduce a photograph in publication, consent may be required from the subject in the photograph as well as from the person who took it, who is usually the first owner of copyright; in such cases copyright is jointly shared.

Reciprocity and trust

We have argued elsewhere (Bell and Bryman 2007, Bell and Wray Bliss 2007) that ethics codes increasingly emphasize the importance of openness and honesty in communicating information about the research to all interested parties. Although this issue is related to the ethical principles of informed consent and avoiding deception discussed above, it goes further than these existing principles in placing the responsibility on researchers for taking action that helps to overcome the power inequalities between themselves and research participants, and for ensuring that the research has benefits for them both. For example, the ESRC *Framework for Research Ethics* makes frequent mention of the need to communicate benefits to research participants. At its most advanced, this incorporates the concept of reciprocity, the idea that the research should be of mutual benefit to researcher and participants and that some form of collaboration or active participation should be built into the research project from the outset.

This encourages a view of the research relationship as a mutually beneficial exchange between researcher and participants who see each other as moral beings and enforce on each other adherence to a set of agreed-upon moral norms (Wax 1982). It also resonates with developments in qualitative research that have sought to reconceptualize researcher–subject relationships (see Chapter 17).

Telling it like it is
Seeking to establish reciprocity by sharing research findings

One of the ways in which students can establish a degree of reciprocity within a student research project is through agreeing to share their findings with research participants by sending them a report based on the dissertation project or a copy of the dissertation. As Karen explained: 'There were a lot of people while I was doing the research who said, "Oh, I'd love to see what your findings are and what your conclusions are" and that sort of thing. 'Cos it brings up a lot of issues sort of even more broadly than just recruitment as to, you know, "Well, is it a good idea that we're doing this sort of thing?" and "What is it doing to the whole organizational culture?" So there were lots of people who were very interested in it. So I sent them a copy [of the dissertation once I had] finished it. I don't know what they'll do with it! [*chuckles*] Whether anybody'll actually sit down and read all fifty pages of it I don't know.'

In Tom's study of call centres he agreed to produce a report for the organization as a condition of his access arrangements. However, it was not entirely clear from the start whether or not this report was principally for management or call-centre employees. 'There [was] an interesting question about who was I working for. Was I reporting back to the management or to the work force or to both? I kind of fudged it and said I was reporting back to both of them and I came back and I tried to produce an even-handed report which would say, "Here are some things that you could think about doing which might be useful." My job was made a lot easier because I got the sense that relationships between the management and the work force were pretty good. If I'd gone in and found a lot more antagonism or a much more difficult relationship, it would have been much more difficult to think how I was going to pitch that. I could easily have fallen into a trap on that and I didn't think about it very carefully beforehand. As it was, it turned out okay, and the circumstances meant that it wasn't a contentious issue.'

The decision to share findings with research participants also raises particular ethical issues relating to the protection of anonymity, since it is especially important that individuals cannot be identified if decisions might be made by the organization based on the information collected through your research (see Chapter 17 for some examples of this). If you have agreed to provide feedback findings from your research to people within the organization, especially if these are people with decision-making authority, you need to be very clear in explaining this when seeking the fully informed consent of individuals involved in the study.

On the other hand, sharing your findings with research participants can also help to make the research process a more open exchange, because it helps to take account of the power relations between the researcher and the people being studied (see the section on researcher–subject relationships in Chapter 17 for further discussion of this). This is particularly so if you share your findings during the research rather than at the end of it, so that research participants have the opportunity to question and add to your interpretations of the data. The views of research participants in response to your initial findings can then be written into the dissertation project. This helps to overcome the tendency towards interpretative omnipotence—a common feature of academic writing (see Chapter 29). However, these practices are more common in qualitative than quantitative research, because the former is less concerned with the possibility that this might introduce bias into the study.

Affiliation and conflicts of interest

In all areas of scientific study, it is recognized that affiliations, particularly those related to funding, have the potential to influence the way that research issues are defined and findings presented. The Missenden Code aims to address the challenges posed by the increased commercialization in universities and shifts in the sources of research funding. The code, which was set up following a number of high-profile ethical controversies (see Thinking deeply 6.8), recommends that universities set up ethics committees to monitor the sources of sponsorship and funding, and to ensure that the source of funding is acknowledged in any publication. The code claims that ethical implications arise when research is financially underwritten by a source that has a vested interest in the results.

However, this does not mean that it is automatically biased but rather that it may be perceived to be biased, for example by the media, and therefore able to be discredited. Moreover, no research is truly independent. Even if it is not in receipt of funding from commercial sources, it is clear that the money must come from somewhere, such as a government source, which will also have interests in funding certain kinds of research and coming up with particular findings. Similarly, in many postgraduate MBA student research projects, the study forms part of a dissertation for a degree that is at least partly funded by the student's employer. Therefore, the main thing for researchers to be conscious of is the possibility that questions about funding have the potential to affect the credibility of the research; in any publication, researchers should be explicit and open about the resources that enabled their research.

Thinking deeply 6.8
A funding controversy in a university business school

In December 2000, Nottingham University accepted £3.8 million from British American Tobacco to set up the International Centre for Corporate Social Responsibility within Nottingham University Business School. This prompted the professor leading one of Nottingham's top research teams working in the field of cancer research to leave, taking fifteen of his staff with him. Cancer Research UK, which was funding medical research at the university, subsequently withdrew its £1.5 million grant and launched a new code of conduct that recommended research support not be provided to any university faculty that is in receipt of tobacco industry funding. However, Nottingham University insisted that it had been following these guidelines, because the money that funded the International Centre for Corporate Social Responsibility was kept completely separate from any area of research funded by Cancer Research UK. The case prompted a heated exchange among academics, one letter angrily commenting that it must only be a matter of time before someone founded a Pinochet Centre for the study of human rights. Because the tobacco industry has a history of subverting scientific research that does not support its commercial interests, as portrayed in the feature film *The Insider*, it was seen as unacceptable by some that Nottingham University should accept financial support from this source.

(C. Clark, 'Letter: Stub out BAT Cash', *Times Higher Education Supplement*, 8 December 2000; T. Tysome, 'Tobacco Link Causes Cancer Team to Leave', *Times Higher Education Supplement*, 23 March 2001.)

Tips and skills
ESRC recommendations for ethical review of student research projects

In line with Kent et al.'s (2002) prediction that developments within the social sciences would mean that ethical oversight regimes would become less 'light touch' in orientation than previous structures, the ESRC *Framework for Research Ethics* has a section entitled 'Student research and ethics approval', which deals specifically with undergraduate and postgraduate students. It states:

(continued)

> ... research organizations should establish procedures specifically for reviewing research projects undertaken by undergraduate students and students on taught postgraduate courses. ... Student research poses particular challenges in relation to ethical review because of the large numbers, short timescales and limited scope of the projects involved.
>
> Nevertheless, the same high ethical standards should be expected in student research. ... Student projects involving more than minimal risk ... may need careful consideration and possibly a full ethics review. However, in many cases student research may be managed at school/department level and overseen by a light touch Departmental Ethics Committee using an initial checklist. ... It should be made clear to potential research participants that the study is a student project. Research organisations also need to ensure that students are not exposed to undue risk in conducting their research.
>
> (ESCR, *Framework for Research Ethics* 2010: Section 1.14)

A case could be made for considering student research through a particular form of expedited review. Undergraduate and taught postgraduate research might be reviewed by multidisciplinary committees with a proportion of the members from outside the school or faculty but within the university. As student projects are not externally funded individually, there is less risk of a conflict of interests within the university.

 # The difficulties of ethical decision-making

The difficulty of drawing the line between ethical and unethical practices can be revealed in several ways. The issue of some members of social settings being aware of the researcher's status and the nature of his or her investigation has been mentioned on several occasions. Manuals about interviewing are full of advice about how to entice interviewees to open up about themselves. Researchers using Likert scales reword items to identify 'yeasayers' and 'naysayers'. Interviewers frequently err on the low side when asked how long an interview will take. Women may use their identity as women to influence female interviewees in in-depth interviews to probe into their lives and reveal inner thoughts and feelings, albeit with a commitment to feminist research (Oakley 1981; Finch 1984; Freeman 2000). Qualitative research is frequently very open-ended, and, as a result, research questions are either loose or not specified, so that it is doubtful whether or not ethnographers in particular are able to inform others accurately about the nature of their research. Perhaps, too, some interviewees find the questions we ask unsettling or find the cut and thrust of a focus group discussion stressful, especially if they inadvertently reveal more than they might have intended.

There are, in other words, many ways in which there is the potential for deception and, relatedly, lack of informed consent in business research. These instances are, of course, a far cry from the deceptions perpetrated in the research summarized in Research in focus 6.1 and Research in focus 6.3, but they point to the difficulty of arriving at ethically informed decisions. Ethical codes give advice on patently inappropriate practices—though sometimes leaving some room for manoeuvre, as we have seen—but provide less guidance on marginal areas of ethical decision-making. Indeed, guidelines may even be used by research participants against the researcher when they seek to limit the boundaries of a fieldworker's investigation (Punch 1994). Finally, computer technology, and in particular the use of the Internet as a data collection method, has introduced new ethical challenges for researchers that will be discussed in Chapter 28.

This might lead business researchers to regard ethical issues as a series of obstacles that need to be overcome so that they can get on with their study. There is no doubt that the level of ethical scrutiny business researchers face in relation to their activities has increased in recent years, and the burden of responsibility for demonstrating that ethical issues have been satisfactorily addressed has been placed firmly on the shoulders of researchers. Some universities require even undergraduate and post-graduate student research projects to go through an ethical approval process, and the prospect of having one's research scrutinized by an ethics committee can seem daunting for a new researcher. Moreover, these requirements can encourage a bureaucratic compliance-based approach whereby, once ethical approval has been obtained, the researcher tends to assume that ethical considerations can be set to one side as having been dealt with. However, nothing could be farther from the truth; we believe it is vitally important for qualitative and quantitative researchers continually to revisit ethical issues throughout their study and to see them as an integral part of the research process.

The politics of business research

It is relatively rare for management and business researchers to talk openly about the tacit rules that determine the conduct of research, but it is important to understand how this process works in order to appreciate how it shapes the field. One of the most common dissemination outlets for management research is through publishing research findings in academic journals (see Key concept 5.1, 'What is an academic journal?'). In recent years there has been increasing debate about the pressure that the requirement to publish in certain high-profile academic journals can place on researchers concerning their choice of methods. The pressure to publish business research in a few highly regarded journals in the field has increased because staff publishing in such journals contribute indirectly towards business school performance, affecting their school's position in the global rankings. Publishing in these journals is therefore an important determinant of career success for individual researchers. Ranking systems, such as the EAJG International Guide to Journal Quality (**www.bizschooljournals.com**, accessed 18 October 2014), have been developed as a means of assessing the quality of journals in business and management by drawing on a range of quantitative measures, such as the journal 'impact factor', which is based on the frequency with which the articles published in the journal are cited by other researchers. Macdonald and Kam (2007) argue that this 'publish or perish' culture has resulted in business researchers employing gamesmanship to maximize their likelihood of success within the system. These political strategies include self-citation and citation of articles in other high-ranking management journals, especially if they are in the same journal as the one to which the author is submitting an article. They also suggest that this encourages authors to write articles that reviewers are likely to see as uncontroversial and to use methods that are broadly accepted within the field, rather than to experiment with pioneering new research approaches or to challenge existing theory.

A further impact of the politics of publishing business research arises from how this affects researchers' choice of methods. It has been widely suggested that the journal

publishing hierarchy tends to favour quantitative more than qualitative research. Many of the highest-ranking business journals are North American and are dominated by the positivist tradition (Singh, Haddad, and Chow 2007; Grey 2010). As Grey (2010: 682) notes, in addition to macro-political context which locates North American authors and journals as at the centre of knowledge production and European authors and journals as peripheral knowledge producers, international rankings of business schools and journals generate 'micro-political issues' that impact on management research, including 'the status of journals; the social and institutional norms that police who publishes what, where and with what impact; the capacity of dominant elites and research traditions to marginalize alternative voices and intellectual dissent'.

Qualitative researchers also tend to face greater difficulty than researchers who use quantitative methods in convincing key gatekeepers, including journal editors, reviewers, and funding bodies, of the credibility and quality of their research (Easterby-Smith, Golden-Biddle, and Locke 2008; Symon et al. 2008). Qualitative researchers can also encounter difficulties as a consequence of journals working to contribution-to-length ratios, as quantitative findings can often be presented more tersely and authors who use these methods encounter less pressure to justify and explain in detail their choice of methods (Pratt 2008). The challenges encountered by qualitative researchers have the potential to affect the methods choices that business researchers make (see also Bell and Thorpe 2013). We have already noted the importance of real examples of published research for students who are learning how to use business research methods. If the politics of business research results in a marginalization of certain methods in the highest-status journals, this could mean that future researchers have a less diverse resource on which to draw in making methods choices. Journal editors often feel compelled to defend their journals and their publishing practices against the charge of bias towards quantitative investigations (see, for example, the defence of the *Academy of Management Journal* by Rynes et al. 2005).

This political context also has implications for the ethics of business research. Bell and Clarke's (2014) study of undergraduate student perceptions of management researchers in UK business schools found that the dominant image of the management researcher is as untouchable, solitary, aggressive, competitive, and careerist. Inspired by Gummeson's (2000) pictorial representation of management researchers and consultants, Bell and Clarke asked students: 'if a management researcher were an animal, what kind of animal would they be?' A free drawing method was used to focus on symbolic and mythological meaning, and to encourage students to express their feelings as well as thoughts. The students then participated in a follow-up focus group interview where they discussed the images, a selection of which are shown in Plates 6.1 and 6.2. A key finding to emerge from this study was that undergraduate students hold an impression of management researchers as a community 'engaged in instrumental, game-playing and primarily self-serving activities' that is based on 'personal possession of intellectual knowledge and the domination of other researchers and research participants' (Bell and Clarke, 2014: 14). This is of obvious concern as it suggests that management researchers are giving students the impression that they are not interested in ethical and reciprocal (Bell and Bryman, 2007) engagement with practice.

Since writing the first edition of this book, we have noticed a shift in emphasis in codes of ethics for business and management researchers such as the Academy of Management (AoM) *Code of Ethical Conduct*. In recent years much greater emphasis has been placed on the ethics of publishing; this has been accompanied by a reduction in emphasis on the process of doing research (e.g. collecting data and forming relationships with research participants). This includes issues such as 'honorary authorship' (Greenland and Fontanarosa, 2012), which

Plate 6.1

The 'great wild beast' metaphor of a management researcher

Plate 6.2

The 'exotic creature' metaphor of a management researcher

is where someone is listed as an author when they have not made a substantive intellectual contribution to the work. As Greenland and Fontanarosa state, there can be several reasons for this, including 'coercive authorship', which is where 'a senior person informs a junior colleague that the senior person must be listed as an author even though she/he did not contribute substantially—or at all—to the work. In other cases, the principal investigator may add the name of a prominent scientist in the field as a guest author in an attempt to boost the paper's chance of publication. Both types of behaviour have fraudulent aspects, distorting the ethical culture that is central to a healthy academic environment' (2012: 1019). To guard against this, the AoM code states that its members should take 'authorship credit, only for work they have actually performed or to which they have contributed'. The code further states that its members should 'usually list a student as principal author on

multiple-authored publications that substantially derive from the student's dissertation or thesis'.

Other ethical concerns relate to plagiarism, discussed in Chapter 5, and self-plagiarism, where researchers re-use material which they have already published elsewhere. The AoM code states that members should 'explicitly cite others' work and ideas, including their own, even if the work or ideas are not quoted verbatim or paraphrased. This standard applies whether the previous work is published, unpublished, or electronically available'. Basbøll's (2010) analysis of plagiarism in the work of the influential organization theorist Weick identifies a number of instances where the author's attribution of literary and other sources is unclear, and expresses concern that while students are warned not to engage in these practices, academics sometimes seem to get away with them. In relation to self-plagiarism, when researchers 'publish data or findings that overlap with work they have previously published elsewhere', the AoM code states that researchers should 'cite these publications' in their work to ensure that appropriate checks can be made. A recent example involved the author of an article that, somewhat ironically, was about publishing ethics. The piece was written by an individual who had been chair of the Ethics Education Committee of the Academy of Management for three years (2008–2011). It was retracted from *Management and Organization Review* (Schminke and Ambrose 2011) following identification of unattributed overlap with work that the author had previously published in *Academy of Management Review* (Schminke 2009). The online retraction statement provides detailed insight into how this situation arose and how it was dealt with; in his account of this process Schminke states 'as scientists, we make our living by being careful, conscientious, and precise. Failure to cite prior work properly, even when it's yours, does not meet those expectations. Don't let it happen to you' (Schminke, 2014).

A final ethical issue related to publishing involves 'coercive citation', which can arise when journal editors, in an attempt to enhance the impact factor of their journal, put pressure on authors to add citations to their journal when no intellectual rationale for doing so exists (Wilhite and Fong, 2012). Analysing 6672 responses to a survey sent to researchers across the social science disciplines, and data from 832 journals in those disciplines, Wilhite and Fong (2012: 542) conclude that 'coercion is uncomfortably uncommon and appears to be practiced opportunistically', particularly in the business disciplines. They also found that senior researchers were more likely than junior researchers to resist coercive demands put upon them by journal editors. With the growth in prevalence of metric-based systems for literature searching and measuring the academic impact of researchers, such as Google Scholar, the potential for this kind of ethical transgression, and the need for measures to be taken to guard against it, is only likely to increase.

Checklist
Ethical issues to consider

○ Have you read and incorporated into your research the principles associated with at least one of the major professional associations mentioned in this book?

○ Have you read and incorporated your institution's requirements for doing ethical research?

○ Have you found out whether or not all proposed research needs to be submitted to the body in your institution that is responsible for the oversight of ethical issues?

○ If only certain types of research need to be submitted, have you checked to see whether or not your proposed research is likely to require clearance?

○ Have you checked to ensure that there is no prospect of any harm coming to participants?

○ Does your research conform to the principle of informed consent, so that research participants understand:

    ○ what the research is about?

    ○ the purposes of the research?

    ○ who is sponsoring it?

    ○ the nature of their involvement in the research?

    ○ how long their participation is going to take?

    ○ that their participation is voluntary?

    ○ that they can withdraw from participation in the research at any time?

    ○ what is going to happen to the data (e.g. how are the data going to be kept)?

○ Are you confident that the privacy of the people involved in your research will not be violated?

○ Do you appreciate that you should not divulge information or views to your research participants that other research participants have given you?

○ Have you taken steps to ensure that your research participants will not be deceived about the research and its purposes?

○ Have you taken steps to ensure that the confidentiality of data relating to your research participants will be maintained?

○ Once the data have been collected, have you taken steps to ensure that the names of your research participants and the location of your research (such as the name of the organization(s) in which it took place) are not identifiable?

○ Does your strategy for keeping your data in electronic form comply with data-protection legislation?

○ Once your research has been completed, have you met obligations that were a requirement of doing the research (for example, submitting a report to an organization that allowed you access)?

Key points

- This chapter has been concerned with a limited range of issues concerning ethics in business research, in that it has concentrated on ethical concerns that might arise in the context of collecting and analysing data. Our concern has mainly been with relations between researchers and research participants. Other ethical issues can arise in the course of business research.

- While the codes and guidelines of professional associations provide some guidance, their potency is ambiguous, and they often leave the door open for some autonomy with regard to ethical issues.

- The main areas of ethical concern relate to: harm to participants; lack of informed consent; invasion of privacy; and deception.

- Covert observation and certain notorious studies have been particular focuses of concern.

- The boundaries between ethical and unethical practices are not clear cut; writers on social research ethics have adopted several different stances in relation to the issue.

- While the rights of research participants are the chief focus of ethical principles, concerns about professional self-interest arising from the politics of publishing are also of concern.

Questions for review

- Why are ethical issues important in relation to the conduct of business research?
- Outline the different stances on ethics in social research.

Ethical principles

- Does 'harm to participants' refer to physical harm alone?
- What are some difficulties with following the ethical principle of avoiding harm to subjects?
- Why is the issue of informed consent so hotly debated?
- What are some of the difficulties with following the ethical principle of informed consent?

- Why is the privacy principle important?
- What principles concerning the use of personal data are expressed in the 1998 Data Protection Act?
- Why does deception matter?
- How helpful are studies such as Milgram's, Zimbardo's, and Dalton's in terms of understanding the operation of ethical principles in business research?

The difficulties of ethical decision-making

- How easy is it to conduct ethical research?
- Read one of the ethical guidelines referred to in this chapter. How effective is it in guarding against ethical transgressions?
- Were the actions taken by Holliday (1995) and described in Research in focus 6.7 ethical? (Explain your viewpoint using the framework provided in this chapter.) Would you have behaved differently in these circumstances? If so, how?

The politics of business research

- What political issues might affect your choice of research project and the methods you use?
- Should we be concerned about the ethics of publishing in business research?

....

Online Resource Centre

www.oxfordtextbooks.co.uk/orc/brymanbrm4e/

Visit the Interactive Research Guide that accompanies this book to complete an exercise in Ethics in Business Research.

....

Part Two
Quantitative research

Part Two of this book is concerned with quantitative research. Chapter 7 explores the main features of this research strategy. Chapter 8 discusses how we sample people on whom we carry out research. Chapter 9 focuses on the structured interview, which is one of the main methods of data collection in quantitative research, and survey research in particular. Chapter 10 is concerned with another important method of gathering data through survey research—questionnaires that people complete themselves. Chapter 11 provides guidelines on how to ask questions for structured interviews and questionnaires. Chapter 12 discusses structured observation, a method that provides a systematic approach to the observation of people. Chapter 13 addresses content analysis, which is a distinctive and systematic approach to the analysis of a wide variety of documents. Chapter 14 discusses the possibility of using, in your own research, data collected by other researchers or official statistics. Chapter 15 presents some of the main tools you will need to conduct quantitative data analysis. Chapter 16 shows you how to use computer software in the form of SPSS—a widely used package of programs—to implement the techniques learned in Chapter 15.

These chapters will provide you with the essential tools for doing quantitative research. They will take you from the very general issues to do with the generic features of quantitative research to the very practical issues of conducting surveys and analysing your own data.

7

The nature of quantitative research

Chapter outline

This chapter is concerned with the characteristics of quantitative research. This approach has been the dominant strategy for conducting business research, although its influence has waned slightly since the mid-1980s, when qualitative research became more influential. However, quantitative research continues to exert a powerful influence in many quarters. The emphasis in this chapter is very much on what quantitative research typically entails, although at a later point in the chapter the ways in which there are frequent departures from this ideal type are outlined. This chapter explores:

- the main steps of quantitative research, which are presented as a linear succession of stages;

- the importance of concepts in quantitative research and the ways in which measures may be devised for concepts; this discussion includes a discussion of the important idea of an *indicator*, which is devised as a way of measuring a concept for which there is no direct measure;

- the procedures for checking the reliability and validity of the measurement process;

- the main preoccupations of quantitative research, which are described in terms of four features: measurement; causality; generalization; and replication;

- some criticisms that are frequently levelled at quantitative research.

Introduction

In Chapter 2, quantitative research was outlined as a distinctive research strategy. In very broad terms, it was described as entailing the collection of numerical data and as exhibiting a view of the relationship between theory and research as deductive, a predilection for a natural science approach (and for positivism in particular), and an objectivist conception of social reality. A number of other features of quantitative research were outlined, but in this chapter we will be examining the strategy in much more detail.

It should be abundantly clear by now that the description of this research strategy as 'quantitative research' should not be taken to mean that quantification of aspects of social life is all that distinguishes it from a qualitative research strategy. The very fact that it has a distinctive epistemological and ontological position suggests that there is a good deal more to it than the mere presence of numbers. In this chapter, the main steps in quantitative research are outlined. We also examine some of the principal preoccupations of the strategy and how certain issues of concern among practitioners are addressed, such as questions about measurement validity.

The main steps in quantitative research

Figure 7.1 outlines the main steps in quantitative research. This is very much an ideal-typical account of the process: it is probably never or rarely found in this pure form, but this outline represents a useful starting point for getting to grips with the main ingredients of the approach and the links between them. Research is rarely as linear and as straightforward as the figure implies, but its aim is to do no more than capture the main steps and provide a rough indication of their interconnections.

Some of the chief steps have been covered in the first two chapters of this book. The fact that we start off with theory signifies that a broadly deductive approach to the relationship between theory and research is taken. It is common for outlines of the main steps of quantitative research to suggest that a hypothesis is deduced from the theory and is tested. This notion has been incorporated into Figure 7.1. However, a great deal of quantitative research does not entail the specification of a hypothesis, and instead theory acts loosely as a set of concerns in relation to which the business researcher collects data. The specification of hypotheses to be tested is particularly likely to be found in experimental research. Although other research designs sometimes entail the testing of

Figure 7.1

The process of quantitative research

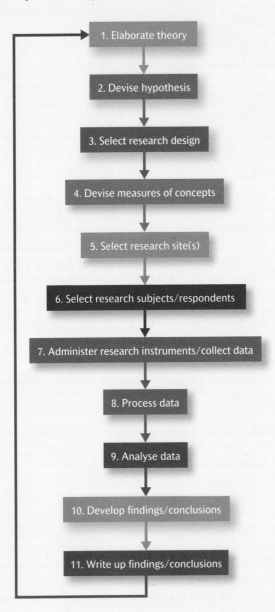

1. Elaborate theory
2. Devise hypothesis
3. Select research design
4. Devise measures of concepts
5. Select research site(s)
6. Select research subjects/respondents
7. Administer research instruments/collect data
8. Process data
9. Analyse data
10. Develop findings/conclusions
11. Write up findings/conclusions

hypotheses, as a general rule, we tend to find that Step 2 is more likely to be found in experimental research.

The next step entails the selection of a research design, a topic that was explored in Chapter 3. As we have seen, the selection of research design has implications for a variety of issues, such as the external validity of findings and researchers' ability to impute causality to their findings. Step 4 entails devising measures of the concepts in which the researcher is interested. This process is often referred to as *operationalization*, a term that originally derives from physics to refer to the operations by which a concept (such as temperature or velocity) is measured (Bridgman 1927). Aspects of this issue will be explored later on in this chapter.

The next two steps entail the selection of a research site or sites and then the selection of subjects/respondents. (Experimental researchers tend to call the people on whom they conduct research 'subjects', whereas social survey researchers typically call them 'respondents'.) Thus, in social survey research an investigator must first be concerned to establish an appropriate setting for his or her research. A number of decisions may be involved. The *Affluent Worker* research undertaken by Goldthorpe et al. (1968: 2–5) involved two decisions about a research site or setting. First, the researchers needed a community that would be appropriate for the testing of the 'embourgeoisement' thesis (the idea that affluent workers were becoming more middle-class in their attitudes and lifestyles). As a result of this consideration, Luton was selected. Secondly, in order to come up with a sample of 'affluent workers' (Step 6), it was decided that people working for three of Luton's leading employers should be interviewed. Moreover, the researchers wanted the firms selected to cover a range of production technologies, because of evidence at that time that technologies had implications for workers' attitudes and behaviour. As a result of these considerations, the three firms were selected. Industrial workers were then sampled, also in terms of selected criteria that were to do with the researchers' interests in embourgeoisement and in the implications of technology for work attitudes and behaviour. Research in focus 7.1 provides a much more recent example of research that involved similar deliberations about selecting research sites and sampling respondents. In experimental research, these two steps are likely to include the assignment of subjects into control and treatment groups.

Step 7 involves the administration of the research instruments. In experimental research, this is likely to entail pre-testing subjects, manipulating the independent variable for the experimental group, and

Research in focus 7.1
Selecting research sites and sampling respondents: the Quality of Work and Life in Changing Europe project

The 'Quality of Work and Life in Changing Europe' is a European Commission funded research project (Abendroth and Den Dulk, 2011; Lippe et al. 2009) that analyses international comparative data on the social wellbeing of citizens and social quality in European workplaces in eight partner countries: UK, Finland, Sweden, Germany, the Netherlands, Portugal, Hungary, and Bulgaria. The focus of the study was to understand the quality of working life among European workers, including how public and organizational policies in different countries affect these issues. The overall survey sample of 7867 service sector workers varied in size by country, ranging from 676 respondents in Sweden to 1373 respondents in Portugal. Service sector workers were chosen as the focus of the study because this is a growing sector of the economy that comprises both professional and lower-skilled workers. In each of the eight countries, a national team of researchers surveyed employees from:

1. a bank/insurance company: included because these organizations are often at the forefront of supportive work–life policies and are highly visible, therefore susceptible to institutional pressures to provide work–life balance support (total of 1918 respondents)

2. a retail company: chains of shops were included because of the higher proportion of lower-skilled jobs and female workers employed there (total of 1670 respondents)

3. an IT/telecom company: included because of the high proportion of professional workers and the highly competitive nature of careers in these organizations (total of 2628 respondents)

4. a public hospital: large hospitals in major cities were included as representative of public sector organizations (total of 1651 respondents)

Because this was a non-random quota sample to represent various categories of organization (see Chapter 78), in each country attempts were made to select similar service sector organizations in order to increase comparability. These sector comparisons acted as a control variable on the sample. A questionnaire survey was developed by the researchers and translated into the language of each country, before being back-translated for comparability. Employees in the selected organizations received a letter in which they were asked to fill in the questionnaire, either on paper or in a web-based form (see Chapter 28 for more on web surveys). The response rates in different countries were variable, ranging from 17 per cent (Hungary and the UK both being low) to 89 per cent (Bulgaria, Finland, and Sweden being relatively high). These findings enabled the researchers to trace differences between countries in terms of the level of support available (from the state, the workplace, and the family) for the development of work–life balance.

post-testing subjects. In cross-sectional research using social survey research instruments, it will involve interviewing the sample members by structured interview schedule or distributing a self-completion questionnaire. In research using structured observation, this step will mean an observer (or possibly more than one) watching the setting and the behaviour of people and then assigning categories to each element of behaviour.

Step 8 simply refers to the fact that, once information has been collected, it must be transformed into 'data'. In the context of quantitative research, this is likely to mean that it must be prepared so that it can be quantified.

With some information this can be done in a relatively straightforward way—for example, for information relating to such things as people's ages, incomes, number of years spent at school, and so on. For other variables, quantification will entail *coding* the information—that is, transforming it into numbers to facilitate the quantitative analysis of the data, particularly if the analysis is going to be carried out by computer. Codes act as tags that are placed on data about people to allow the information to be processed by the computer. This consideration leads into Step 9—the analysis of the data. In this step, the researcher is concerned to use a number of techniques of quantitative data analysis to reduce the amount of data collected, to test for relationships between variables, to develop ways of presenting the results of the analysis to others, and so on.

On the basis of the analysis of the data, the researcher must interpret the results of the analysis. It is at this stage that the 'findings' will emerge (Step 10). The researcher will consider the connections between the findings that emerge out of Step 9 and the various preoccupations that acted as the impetus of the research. If there is a hypothesis, is it supported? What are the implications of the findings for the theoretical ideas that formed the background to the research?

Then the research must be written up (Step 11). It cannot take on significance beyond satisfying the researcher's personal curiosity until it enters the public domain in some way by being written up as a paper to be read at a conference, or as a report to the agency that funded the research, or as a book or journal article for academic business researchers. In writing up the findings and conclusions, the researcher is doing more than simply relaying to others what has been found: readers must be convinced that the research conclusions are important and that the findings are robust. Thus, a significant part of the research process entails convincing others of the significance and validity of one's findings.

Once the findings have been published, they become part of the stock of knowledge (or 'theory' in the loose sense of the word) in their domain. Thus, there is a feedback loop from Step 11 back up to Step 1. The presence of both an element of deductivism (Step 2) and inductivism (the feedback loop) is indicative of the positivist foundations of quantitative research. Similarly, the emphasis on the translation of concepts into measures (Step 4) is symptomatic of the principle of phenomenalism (see Key concept 2.7), which is also a feature of positivism. It is to this important phase of translating concepts into measures that we now turn. As we will see, certain considerations follow on from the stress placed on measurement in quantitative research. By and large, these considerations are to do with the validity and reliability of the measures devised by social scientists. These considerations will figure prominently in the following discussion.

As we noted before presenting the model in Figure 7.1, this sequence of stages is a kind of ideal-typical account that is probably rarely found in this pure form. At the end of this chapter, the section 'Is it always like this?' deals with three ways in which the model may not be found in practice.

Concepts and their measurement

What is a concept?

Concepts are the building blocks of theory and represent the points around which business research is conducted. Think of the numerous concepts that are mentioned in relation to just some of the research examples cited in this book:

> structure, agency, deskilling, organizational size, technology, charismatic leadership, followers, TQM, functional subcultures, knowledge, managerial identity, motivation to work, moral awareness, productivity, stress management, employment relations, organizational development, competitive success.

Each represents a label that we give to elements of the social world that seem to have common features and that strike us as significant. As Bulmer succinctly puts it, concepts 'are categories for the organization of ideas and observations' (1984: 43). One item mentioned in Chapter 3 but omitted from the list of concepts above is IQ. It has been omitted because it is not a concept! It is a *measure* of a concept—namely, intelligence. This is a rare case of a social scientific measure that has become so well known that the measure and the concept are almost as synonymous as temperature and the centigrade or Fahrenheit scales, or as length and the metric scale. The concept of intelligence has arisen as a result of noticing that some people are very clever, some are quite clever, and still others are not at all bright. These variations in what we have come to call the concept of 'intelligence' seem important, because we might try to construct theories to explain these variations. We may try to incorporate the concept of intelligence into theories to explain variations in such things as job competence or entrepreneurial success. Similarly, with indicators of organizational performance such as productivity or return on investment, we notice that some organizations improve their relative performance, others remain static, and others decline in economic value. Out of such considerations, the concept of organizational performance is reached.

If a concept is to be employed in quantitative research, it will have to be measured. Once they are measured, concepts can be in the form of independent or dependent variables. In other words, concepts may provide an explanation of a certain aspect of the social world, or they may stand for things we want to explain. A concept such as organizational performance may be used in either capacity: for example, as a possible explanation of culture (are there differences between highly commercially successful organizations and others, in terms of the cultural values, norms, and beliefs held by organizational members?) or as something to be explained (what are the causes of variation in organizational performance?). Equally, we might be interested in evidence of changes in organizational performance over time or in variations between comparable nations in levels of organizational performance. As we start to investigate such issues, we are likely to formulate theories to help us understand why, for example, rates of organizational performance vary between countries or over time. This will, in turn, generate new concepts, as we try to tackle the explanation of variation in rates.

Why measure?

There are three main reasons for the preoccupation with measurement in quantitative research.

- Measurement allows us to delineate *fine differences* between people in terms of the characteristic in question. This is very useful, since, although we can often distinguish between people in terms of extreme categories, finer distinctions are much more difficult to recognize. We can detect clear variations in levels of job satisfaction—people who love their jobs and people who hate their jobs—but small differences are much more difficult to detect.

- Measurement gives us a *consistent device* or yardstick for making such distinctions. A measurement device provides a consistent instrument for gauging differences. This consistency relates to two things: our ability to be consistent over time and our ability to be consistent with other researchers. In other words, a measure should be something that is influenced neither by the timing of its administration nor by the person who administers it. Obviously, saying that the measure is not influenced by timing is not meant to indicate that measurement readings do not change: they are bound to be influenced by the process of social change. What it means is that the measure should generate consistent results, other than those that occur as

a result of natural changes. Whether a measure actually possesses this quality has to do with the issue of *reliability*, which was introduced in Chapter 3 and which will be examined again below.

- Measurement provides the basis for *more precise estimates of the degree of relationship between concepts* (for example, through **correlation** analysis, which will be examined in Chapter 15). Thus, if we measure both job satisfaction and the things with which it might be related, such as stress-related illness, we will be able to produce more precise estimates of how closely they are related than if we had not proceeded in this way.

Indicators

In order to provide a measure of a concept (often referred to as an **operational definition**, a term deriving from the idea of operationalization), it is necessary to have an **indicator** or indicators that will stand for the concept (see Key concept 7.2). There are a number of ways in which indicators can be devised:

- through a question (or series of questions) that is part of a structured interview schedule or self-completion questionnaire; the question(s) could be concerned with the respondents' report of an attitude (for example, job satisfaction) or their employment status (for example, job title) or a report of their behaviour (for example, job tasks and responsibilities);

- through the recording of individuals' behaviour using a structured **observation schedule** (for example, managerial activity);

- through official statistics, such as the use of Workplace Employment Relations Survey (WERS) data (see Research in focus 3.14) to measure UK employment policies and practices;

- through an examination of mass media content through content analysis—for example, to determine changes in the salience of an issue, such as courage in managerial decision-making (Harris 2001).

Indicators, then, can be derived from a wide variety of sources and methods. Very often the researcher has to consider whether one indicator of a concept will be sufficient. This consideration is frequently a focus for social survey researchers. Rather than have just a single indicator of a concept, the researcher may feel that it may be preferable to ask a number of questions in the course of a structured interview or a self-completion questionnaire that tap that concept (see Research in focus 7.3 and Research in focus 7.4).

Key concept 7.2
What is an indicator?

It is worth making two distinctions here. First, there is a distinction between an *indicator* and a *measure*. The latter can be taken to refer to things that can be relatively unambiguously counted. At an individual level, measures might include personal salary, age, or years of service, whereas at an organizational level they might include annual turnover or number of employees. Measures, in other words, are quantities. If we are interested, for example, in some of the correlates of variation in the age of employees in part-time employment, age can be quantified in a reasonably direct way. We use indicators to tap concepts that are less directly quantifiable. If we are interested in the causes of variation in job satisfaction, we will need indicators that will stand for the concept. These indicators will allow job satisfaction to be measured and we can treat the resulting quantitative information as if it were a measure. An indicator, then, is something that is devised or already exists and that is employed *as though it were a measure of a concept*. It is viewed as an indirect measure of a concept, like job satisfaction. An IQ test is a further example, in that it is a battery of indicators of the concept intelligence. We see here a second distinction between *direct* and *indirect* indicators of concepts. Indicators may be direct or indirect in their relationship to the concepts for which they stand. Thus, an indicator of marital status has a much more direct relationship to its concept than an indicator (or set of indicators) relating to job satisfaction. Sets of attitudes always need to be measured by batteries of indirect indicators. So too do many forms of behaviour. When indicators are used that are not true quantities, they will need to be coded to be turned into quantities. Directness and indirectness are not qualities inherent to an indicator: data from a survey question on amount earned per month may be a direct measure of personal income, but, if we treat it as an indicator of social class, it becomes an indirect measure. The issue of indirectness raises the question of where an indirect measure comes from—that is, how does a researcher devise an indicator of something like job satisfaction? Usually, it is based on common-sense understandings of the forms the concept takes or on anecdotal or qualitative evidence relating to that concept.

Research in focus 7.3
A multiple-indicator measure of a concept

The research on cultural values and management ethics by T. Jackson (2001) involved a questionnaire survey of part-time MBA and post-experience students in Australia, China, Britain, France, Germany, Hong Kong, Spain, India, Switzerland, and the USA. This contained twelve phrases, each describing a specific action, and respondents were asked to judge the extent to which they *personally* believed the action was ethical on a five-point **scale**, 1 = unethical; 5 = ethical. There was a middle point on the scale that allowed for a neutral response. This approach to investigating a cluster of attitudes is known as a **Likert scale**, though in some cases researchers use a seven-point scale rather than a five-point scale for responses. The twelve phrases were as follows:

- accepting gifts/favours in exchange for preferential treatment;
- passing blame for errors to an innocent co-worker;
- divulging confidential information;
- calling in sick to take a day off;
- pilfering organization's materials and supplies;
- giving gifts/favours in exchange for preferential treatment;
- claiming credit for someone else's work;
- doing personal business on organization's time;
- concealing one's errors;

(*continued*)

- taking extra personal time (breaks, etc.);
- using organizational services for personal use;
- not reporting others' violations of organizational policies.

Respondents were also asked to judge the extent to which they thought their *peers* believed the action was ethical, using the same scale. Finally, using the same Likert scale, they were asked to evaluate the frequency with which they and their peers act in the way implied by the statement: 1 = infrequently; 5 = frequently. 'Hence, respondents make a judgement as to the extent to which they believe (or they think their colleagues believe) an action is ethical: the higher the score, the higher the belief that the action is ethical' (2001: 1283). The study found that, across all national groups, managers saw their colleagues as less ethical than themselves. The findings also supported the view that ethical attitudes vary according to cultural context.

Research in focus 7.4
Specifying dimensions of a concept: the case of job characteristics

A key question posed by Hackman and Oldham (1980) was: 'How can work be structured so that employees are internally motivated?' Their answer to this question relied on development of a model identifying five job dimensions that influence employee motivation. At the heart of the model is the suggestion that particular job characteristics ('core job dimensions') affect employees' experience of work ('critical psychological states'), which in turn have a number of outcomes for both the individual and the organization. The three critical psychological states are:

- *experienced meaningfulness*: individual perceives work to be worthwhile in terms of a broader system of values;
- *experienced responsibility*: individual believes him or herself to be personally accountable for the outcome of his or her efforts;
- *knowledge of results*: individual is able to determine on a regular basis whether or not the outcomes of his or her work are satisfactory.

In addition, a particular employee's response to favourable job characteristics is affected by his or her 'growth need strength'—that is, his or her need for personal growth and development. It is expected that favourable work outcomes will occur when workers experience jobs with positive core characteristics; this in turn will stimulate critical psychological states.

In order to measure these factors, Hackman and Oldham devised the Job Diagnostic Survey (JDS), a lengthy questionnaire that can be used to determine the Motivating Potential Score (MPS) of a particular job—that is, the extent to which it possesses characteristics that are necessary to influence motivation. Below are the five dimensions; in each case an example is given of an item that can be used to measure it.

1. *Skill variety*: 'The job requires me to use a number of complex or high-level skills.'
2. *Task identity*: 'The job provides me with the chance completely to finish the pieces of work I begin.'
3. *Task significance*: 'This job is one where a lot of other people can be affected by how well the work gets done.'
4. *Autonomy*: 'The job gives me considerable opportunity for independence and freedom in how I do the work.'
5. *Feedback*: 'The job itself provides plenty of clues about whether or not I am performing well.'

Respondents are asked to indicate how far they think each statement is accurate, from 1 = very inaccurate, to 7 = very accurate. In Hackman and Oldham's initial study, the JDS was administered to 658 individuals working in

62 different jobs across 7 organizations. Interpreting an individual's MPS score involves comparison with norms for specific job 'families', which were generated on the basis of this original sample. For example, professional/technical jobs have an average MPS of 154, whereas clerical jobs normally have a score of 106. Understanding the motivational potential of job content thus relies on interpretation of the MPS relative to that of other jobs and in the context of specific job families. Workers who exhibit adequate knowledge, high growth need strength, and skill, and who are satisfied with their job context, are expected to respond best to jobs with a high MPS.

Using multiple-indicator measures

What are the advantages of using a multiple-indicator measure of a concept? The main reason for its use is a recognition that there are potential problems with a reliance on just a single indicator:

- It is possible that a single indicator will incorrectly classify many individuals. This may be due to the wording of the question or it may be a product of misunderstanding. If there are a number of indicators, however, then even if people are misclassified through a particular question it will be possible to offset its effects.

- One indicator may capture only a portion of the underlying concept or be too general. A single question may need to be of an excessively high level of generality and so may not reflect the true state of affairs for the people replying to it. Alternatively, a question may cover only one aspect of the concept in question. For example, if you were interested in job satisfaction, would it be sufficient to ask people how satisfied they were with their pay? Almost certainly not, because most people would argue that there is more to job satisfaction than just satisfaction with pay. A single indicator such as this would be missing out on such things as satisfaction with conditions, with the work itself, and with other aspects of the work environment. By asking a number of questions, the researcher can get access to a wider range of aspects of the concept.

- You can make much finer distinctions. Taking the Terence Jackson (2001) measure as an example (see Research in focus 7.3), if we just took one of the indicators as a measure, we would be able to array people only on a scale of 1 to 5, assuming that answers indicating that a manager believed an item was unethical were assigned 1 and answers indicating a manager believed an item was ethical were assigned 5, with the three other points being scored 2, 3, and 4. However, with a multiple-indicator measure of twelve indicators the range is 12 (12×1) to 60 (12×5).

However, the use of single indicators of concepts is widespread. Boyd et al. (2012) have expressed concern about the fact that comparing articles published in *Strategic Management Journal* in 1998–2000 with those published in 2010, there has been an increase in the proportion of articles using single indicators. Moreover, this increase was from an already high level. The increase in the use of single indicators was particularly prominent for measures of dependent variables, with an increase from 57.7 per cent of articles in the earlier period to 76.5 per cent in 2010. It is striking that Boyd et al. view the high levels of reliance on single indicators as a cause for concern.

Dimensions of concepts

One elaboration of the general approach to measurement is to consider the possibility that the concept in which you are interested comprises different dimensions. This view is associated particularly with Lazarsfeld (1958). The idea behind this approach is that, when the researcher is seeking to develop a measure of a concept, the different aspects or components of that concept should be considered. This specification of the dimensions of a concept would be undertaken with reference to theory and research associated with that concept. For his research on corporate social responsibility among Indian IT companies, Dhanesh (2014) needed to distinguish between the different dimensions of corporate social responsibility (CSR) because one of his research questions was: 'What dimensions of CSR are most significantly related to the employees' relationships with their employing organizations?'. Following a review of theory and research on the subject, he proposed four dimensions of CSR, each of which was measured through a multiple-item scale comprising several statements requiring respondents to reply in terms of level of agreement or disagreement. The four dimensions are presented here, each with a representative item:

- *Discretionary CSR*. Example item: 'This organization has a program in place to reduce the amount of energy and materials wasted in its business.'

- *Ethical CSR*. Example item: 'In this organization, fairness toward co-workers and/or business partners is an integral part of the employee evaluation process.'

- *Legal CSR*. Example item: 'The managers of this organization try to comply with the law'.
- *Economic CSR*. Example item: 'This organization has been successful at maximizing its profits'. (Dhanesh 2014: 144–5).

Dhanesh found that CSR was indeed associated with better relationships between employees and their organizations but that legal CSR was particularly important in this regard. He attributes this to India's recent economic past, in which it has emerged from a period of 'crippling crony capitalism' as he calls it (Dhanesh 2014: 141).

However, in much if not most quantitative research, there is a tendency to rely on a single indicator of concepts. For many purposes this is quite adequate. It would be a mistake to believe that investigations that use a single indicator of core concepts are somehow deficient. In any case, some studies employ both single- and multiple-indicator measures of concepts. What *is* crucial is whether or not measures are reliable and whether or not they are valid representations of the concepts they are supposed to be tapping. It is to this issue that we now turn.

Reliability

Although the terms 'reliability' and 'validity' seem to be almost like synonyms, they have quite different meanings in relation to the evaluation of measures of concepts, as was seen in Chapter 3. We deal with reliability in this section of the chapter and with validity in the next. As Key concept 7.5 suggests, reliability is fundamentally concerned with issues of consistency of measures. There are at least three different meanings of the term 'reliability'. These are outlined in Key concept 7.5 and elaborated upon below.

Stability

The most obvious way of testing for the stability of a measure is the *test–retest* method. This involves administering a test or measure on one occasion and then readministering it to the same sample on another occasion, i.e.

$$T_1 \qquad\qquad T_2$$
$$Obs_1 \qquad\qquad Obs_2$$

We should expect to find a high correlation between Obs_1 and Obs_2. Correlation is a measure of the strength of the relationship between two variables. This topic will be covered in Chapter 15 in the context of a discussion about quantitative data analysis. Let us imagine that we develop a multiple-indicator measure that is supposed to tap a concept that we might call 'designerism' (a preference for buying goods, and especially clothing, with 'designer' labels). We would administer the measure to a sample of respondents and readminister it some time later. If the correlation is low, the measure would appear to be unstable, implying that respondents' answers cannot be relied upon.

However, there are a number of problems with this approach to evaluating reliability. First, respondents' answers at T_1 may influence how they reply at T_2. This may result in greater consistency between Obs_1 and Obs_2 than is in fact the case. Secondly, events may intervene between T_1 and T_2 that influence the degree of consistency. For example, if a long span of time is involved, changes in the economy or in respondents' personal financial circumstances could influence their views about and predilection for designer goods. There are no obvious solutions to these problems, other than by introducing a complex research design and so turning the investigation of reliability into a major project in its own right. Perhaps for these reasons, many if not most reports of research findings do not appear to carry out tests of stability. Indeed, longitudinal research is often undertaken precisely in order to identify social change and its correlates.

Internal reliability

This meaning of reliability applies to multiple-indicator measures such as those examined in Research in focus 7.3 and Research in focus 7.4. When you have a multiple-item measure in which each respondent's answers to each question are aggregated to form an overall score, the possibility is raised that the indicators do not relate to the same thing; in other words, they lack coherence. We need to be sure that all our designerism indicators are related to each other. If they are not, some of the items may actually be unrelated to designerism and therefore indicative of something else. An example of a study that assessed internal reliability is given in Research in focus 7.9.

One way of testing internal reliability is the *split-half* method. We can take the management ethics measure developed by Terence Jackson (2001) as an example (see

Key concept 7.5
What is reliability?

Reliability refers to the consistency of a measure of a concept. The following are three prominent factors involved when considering whether a measure is reliable.

- *Stability*. This consideration entails asking whether or not a measure is stable over time, so that we can be confident that the results relating to that measure for a sample of respondents do not fluctuate. This means that, if we administer a measure to a group and then readminister it, there will be little variation over time in the results obtained.

- **Internal reliability**. The key issue is whether or not the indicators that make up the scale or index are consistent—in other words, whether or not respondents' scores on any one indicator tend to be related to their scores on the other indicators.

- *Inter-rater reliability*. When a great deal of subjective judgement is involved in such activities as the recording of observations or the translation of data into categories and where more than one rater is involved in such activities, there is the possibility that there is a lack of consistency in their decisions. This can arise in a number of contexts, for example: in content analysis where decisions have to be made about how to categorize media items; when answers to open-ended questions have to be categorized; or in structured observation when observers have to decide how to classify subjects' behaviour.

Key concept 7.6
What is Cronbach's alpha?

To a large extent we are leaping ahead too much here, but it is important to appreciate the basic features of what this widely used test means. Cronbach's alpha is a commonly used test of internal reliability. It essentially calculates the average of all possible split-half reliability coefficients. A computed alpha coefficient will vary between 1 (denoting perfect internal reliability) and 0 (denoting no internal reliability). The Figure 0.8 is typically employed as a rule of thumb to denote an acceptable level of internal reliability, though many writers accept a slightly lower figure. For example, in the case of the burnout scale replicated by Schutte et al. (2000; see Research in focus 7.11), alpha was 0.7, which they suggest 'as a rule of thumb' is 'considered to be efficient' (2000: 56).

Research in focus 7.3). The twelve indicators would be divided into two halves, with six in each group. The indicators would be allocated on a random or an odd–even basis. The degree of correlation between scores on the two halves would then be calculated. In other words, the aim would be to establish whether respondents scoring high on one of the two groups also scored high on the other group of indicators. The calculation of the correlation will yield a figure, known as a coefficient, that varies between 0 (no correlation and therefore no internal consistency) and 1 (perfect correlation and therefore complete internal consistency). It is usually accepted that

a result of 0.8 and above implies an acceptable level of internal reliability, although for many purposes 0.7 and above is accepted. Do not worry if these figures appear somewhat opaque. The meaning of correlation will be explored in much greater detail later on. The chief point to carry away with you at this stage is that the correlation establishes how closely respondents' scores on the two groups of indicators are related.

Nowadays, most researchers use a test of internal reliability known as *Cronbach's alpha* (see Key concept 7.6). Its use has grown as a result of its incorporation into computer software for quantitative data analysis.

Inter-rater reliability

The idea of inter-rater reliability is briefly outlined in Key concept 7.5. The issues involved are rather too advanced to be dealt with at this stage and will be briefly touched on in later chapters. Cramer (1998: Chapter 14) provides a very detailed treatment of the issues and appropriate techniques.

Validity

As noted in Chapter 3, the issue of measurement validity has to do with whether or not a measure of a concept really measures that concept (see Key concept 7.7). When people argue about whether or not a person's IQ score really measures or reflects that person's level of intelligence, they are raising questions about the measurement validity of the IQ test in relation to the concept of intelligence. Similarly, one often hears people say that they do not believe that the UK's Retail Price Index really reflects inflation and the rise in the cost of living. Again, a query is being raised in such comments about measurement validity. And whenever students or lecturers debate whether or not formal examinations provide an accurate measure of academic ability, they too are raising questions about measurement validity.

Writers distinguish between a number of ways of testing measurement validity, which really reflect different ways of gauging the validity of a measure of a concept. These different ways of testing validity will now be outlined.

Face validity

At the very minimum, a researcher who develops a new measure should establish that it has *face validity*—that is, that the measure apparently reflects the content of the concept in question. Face validity might be established by asking other people whether or not the measure seems to be getting at the concept that is the focus of attention. In other words, people, possibly those with experience or expertise in a field, might be asked to act as judges to determine whether or not on the face of it the measure seems to reflect the concept concerned. Face validity is, therefore, an essentially intuitive process. See Research in focus 14.8 for a discussion that uses the face validity test in order to establish the quality of some measures in the field of strategic management.

Concurrent validity

The researcher might seek also to gauge the *concurrent validity* of the measure. Here the researcher employs a *criterion* on which cases (for example, people) are known to differ and that is relevant to the concept in question. A new measure of job satisfaction can serve as an example. A criterion might be absenteeism, because some people are more often absent from work (other than through illness) than others. In order to establish the concurrent validity of a measure of job satisfaction, we might see if people who are satisfied with their jobs are less likely than those who are not satisfied to be absent from work. If a lack of correspondence was found, such as there being no difference in levels of job satisfaction among frequent absentees, doubt might be cast on whether or not our measure is really addressing job satisfaction. An example of a study that measured concurrent validity is given in Research in focus 7.9.

Key concept 7.7
What is validity?

Validity refers to the issue of whether or not an indicator (or set of indicators) that is devised to gauge a concept really measures that concept. Several ways of establishing validity are explored in the text: **face validity**; **concurrent validity**; **predictive validity**; **construct validity**; and **convergent validity**. Here the term 'validity' is being used as a shorthand for what was referred to as **measurement validity** in Chapter 3. Measurement validity should therefore be distinguished from the other terms introduced in Chapter 3: internal validity; external validity; and ecological validity.

Predictive validity

Another possible test for the validity of a new measure is *predictive validity*, whereby the researcher uses a *future* criterion measure, rather than a contemporary one, as in the case of concurrent validity. With predictive validity, the researcher would take future levels of absenteeism as the criterion against which the validity of a new measure of job satisfaction would be examined. The difference from concurrent validity is that a future rather than a simultaneous criterion measure is employed. Research in focus 7.9 provides an example of research that administered the criterion measure at a point in the future. Sometimes, predictive validity is assessed by asking respondents whether they are likely to engage in a certain activity in the future. For example, Sonenshein et al. (2014) were interested in how people's self-evaluations influence their support for environmental issues. They developed a scale of 'self-assets' which asked respondents their level of agreement or disagreement with statements such as 'I stay up to date on environmental issues' and 'I am well practiced at making positive environmental change'. As a test of the predictive validity of the scale, the authors also asked respondents about such issues as the likelihood of them engaging in environmental issue-supportive behaviour and found a clear relationship between the two.

Construct validity

Some writers advocate that the researcher should also estimate the *construct validity* of a measure. Here, the researcher is encouraged to deduce hypotheses from a theory that is relevant to the concept. For example, drawing upon ideas about the impact of technology on the experience of work, the researcher might anticipate that people who are satisfied with their jobs are less likely to work on routine jobs; those who are not satisfied are more likely to work on routine jobs. Accordingly, we could investigate this theoretical deduction by examining the relationship between job satisfaction and job routine. However, some caution is required in interpreting the absence of a relationship between job satisfaction and job routine in this example. First, either the theory or the deduction that is made from it might be misguided. Secondly, the measure of job routine could be an invalid measure of that concept.

Convergent validity

In the view of some methodologists, the validity of a measure ought to be gauged by comparing it to measures of the same concept developed through other methods. For example, if we develop a questionnaire measure of how much time managers spend on various activities (such as attending meetings, touring their organization, informal discussions, and so on), we might examine its validity by tracking a number of managers and using a structured observation schedule to record how much time is spent in various activities and their frequency. An example of convergent *in*validity is described in Research in focus 7.8.

Research in focus 7.8
The study of strategic HRM: a case of convergent invalidity?

Researchers in the field of human resource management (HRM) have sought to develop and test basic hypotheses concerning the impact of strategic HRM on firm performance. They have set out to measure the extent to which 'high performance work practices' (including comprehensive recruitment and selection procedures, incentive compensation and performance management systems, employee involvement, and training) are related to organizational performance.

In one of the earliest empirical studies of this topic, published in the *Academy of Management Journal*, Arthur (1994) focused on a sample of US steel minimills (relatively small steel-producing facilities) and drew on his previous research in which two types of human resource systems were identified—labelled 'control' and

(continued)

'commitment'. He explains his approach as follows: 'I developed and tested propositions regarding the utility of this human resource system taxonomy for predicting both manufacturing performance, measured as labor efficiency and scrap rate, and the level of employee turnover' (1994: 671). Based on questionnaire responses from human resource managers at 30 minimills, Arthur's conclusions are that commitment systems were more effective than control systems of HRM, being associated with lower scrap rates and higher labour efficiency than with control. In the following year, Huselid (1995) published a paper in the same journal claiming that high-performance work practices associated with a commitment model of HRM have an economically and statistically significant impact on employee outcomes such as turnover and productivity and on measures of corporate financial performance. Results were based on a sample of nearly 1000 US firms drawn from a range of industries, and data were collected using a postal questionnaire, which was addressed to the senior human resources professional in each firm.

However, this strong tradition of questionnaire-based research is not without its critics. One assumption they tend to make is that HRM effectiveness affects firm performance, but it may be that human resource managers who work in a firm that is performing well tend to think the firm's HRM system must be effective. Moreover, the reliance of these researchers on questionnaire data implies a lack of convergent validity, and their tendency to focus on HRM managers as the main or only respondents implies a potential managerial bias. This has been the focus of more recent critiques (Pfeffer 1997) and has led to more qualitative empirical study (e.g. Truss 2001; see Chapter 27) in order to overcome the limitations of earlier work. Some of this research calls into question the validity of the proposed relationship between high-performance human resources practices and firm performance identified in earlier studies.

Discriminant validity

Discriminant validity entails ensuring that when a measure is used for one construct (Construct A) it is different in terms of its content from a measure used to measure another construct (Construct B). For example, Little et al. (2012) developed a scale comprising 20 items in order to measure 'interpersonal emotion management'. They sought to ensure that the scale did not overlap substantially (i.e. had discriminant validity from) measures of related constructs such as self-reported emotional intelligence. As the authors put it, the tests of discriminant validity 'provided support for its distinctiveness' (Little et al. 2012: 417). Testing for discriminant validity is important in terms of ensuring that there is not excessive overlap between measures of constructs that are related.

 # Reflections on reliability and validity

There are, then, a number of ways of investigating the merit of measures that are devised to represent social scientific concepts. However, the discussion of reliability and validity is potentially misleading, because it would be wrong to think that all new measures of concepts are submitted to the rigours described above. In fact, most typically, measurement is undertaken within a stance that Cicourel (1964) described as 'measurement by fiat'. By the term 'fiat', Cicourel was referring not to a well-known Italian car manufacturer but to the notion of 'decree'. He meant that most measures are simply asserted. Fairly straightforward but minimal steps may be taken to ensure that a measure is reliable and/or valid, such as testing for internal reliability when a **multiple-indicator measure**

has been devised and examining face validity. But in many, if not the majority, of cases in which a concept is measured, no further testing takes place. This point will be further elaborated below.

It should also be borne in mind that, although reliability and validity are analytically distinguishable, they are related because validity presumes reliability. This means that if your measure is not reliable, it cannot be valid. This point can be made with respect to each of the three criteria of reliability that have been discussed. If the measure is not stable over time, it simply cannot be providing a valid measure. The measure could not be tapping the concept it is supposed to be related to if the measure fluctuated. If the measure fluctuates, it may be measuring

Research in focus 7.9
Assessing the internal reliability and the concurrent and predictive validity of a measure of organizational climate

Patterson et al. (2005) describe the way they went about validating a measure they developed of organizational climate. This is a rather loose concept that was first developed in the 1960s and 1970s to refer to the perceptions of an organization by its members. Four main dimensions of climate were developed, based around the following notions:

1. *human relations model*: feelings of belonging and trust in the organization and the degree to which there is training, good communication, and supervisory support;

2. *internal process model*: the degree of emphasis on formal rules and on traditional ways of doing things;

3. *open systems model*: the extent to which flexibility and innovativeness are valued;

4. *rational goal model*: the degree to which clearly defined objectives and the norms and values associated with efficiency, quality, and high performance are emphasized.

An Organizational Climate Measure, comprising 95 items in a 4-point Likert format (definitely false, mostly false, mostly true, definitely true) was developed and administered to employees in 55 organizations, with 6869 completing a questionnaire—a response rate of 57 per cent. A factor analysis (see Key concept 7.12) was conducted to explore the extent to which there were distinct groupings of items that tended to go together. This procedure yielded seventeen scales, such as autonomy, involvement, innovation and flexibility, and clarity of organizational goals.

The *internal reliability* of the scales was assessed using Cronbach's alpha, showing that all scales were at a level of 0.73 or above. This suggests that the measure's constituent scales were internally reliable.

Concurrent validity was assessed following semi-structured interviews with each company's managers in connection with their organization's practices. The interview data were coded to provide criteria against which the validity of the scales could be gauged. In most cases, the scales were found to be concurrently valid. For example, the researchers examined the correlation between a scale designed to measure the emphasis on tradition and the degree to which practices associated with the 'new manufacturing paradigm' (Patterson et al. 2005: 397) were adopted, as revealed by the interview data. The correlation was –0.42, implying that those firms that were perceived as rooted in tradition tended to be less likely to adopt new manufacturing practices. Here the adoption of new manufacturing practices was treated as a criterion to assess the extent to which the scale measuring perceptions of tradition really was addressing tradition. If the correlation had been small or positive, the concurrent validity of the scale would have been in doubt.

To assess *predictive validity*, the researchers asked a senior **key informant** at each company to complete a questionnaire one year after the main survey had been conducted. The questionnaire was meant to address two of the measure's constituent scales, one of which was the innovation and flexibility scale. It asked the informants to assess their companies in terms of their innovativeness in a number of areas. For example, the correlation between the innovation and flexibility scale and informants' assessment of their companies in terms of innovativeness with respect to products achieved a correlation of 0.53. This implies that there was indeed a correlation between perceptions of innovativeness and flexibility and a subsequent indicator of innovativeness.

different things on different occasions. If a measure lacks internal reliability, it means that a multiple-indicator measure is actually measuring two or more different things; therefore, the measure cannot be valid. Finally, if there is a lack of inter-observer consistency, it means that observers cannot agree on the meaning of what they are observing, which in turn means that a valid measure cannot be in operation.

The main preoccupations of quantitative researchers

Both quantitative and qualitative research can be viewed as exhibiting a set of distinctive but contrasting preoccupations. These preoccupations reflect epistemologically grounded beliefs about what constitutes acceptable knowledge. In this section, four distinctive preoccupations that can be discerned in quantitative research will be outlined and examined: measurement, causality, generalization, and replication.

Measurement

The most obvious preoccupation is with measurement, a feature that is scarcely surprising in the light of much of the discussion in the present chapter so far. From the position of quantitative research, measurement carries a number of advantages that were previously outlined. It is not surprising, therefore, that issues of reliability and validity are a concern for quantitative researchers, though this is not always manifested in research practice.

Causality

There is a very strong concern with explanation in most quantitative research. Quantitative researchers are rarely concerned merely to describe how things are, but are keen to say why things are the way they are. This emphasis is also often taken to be a feature of the ways in which the natural sciences proceed. Thus, researchers are often not only interested in a phenomenon such as motivation to work as something to be described, for example, in terms of how motivated a certain group of employees are, or what proportion of employees in a sample are highly motivated and what proportion are largely lacking in motivation. Rather, they are likely to want to explain it, which means examining its causes. The researcher may seek to explain motivation to work in terms of personal characteristics (such as 'growth need strength', which refers to an individual's need for personal growth and development—see Research in focus 7.4) or in terms of the characteristics of a particular job (such as task interest or degree of supervision). In reports of research you will often come across the idea of 'independent' and 'dependent' variables, which reflect the tendency to think in terms of causes and effects. Motivation to work might be regarded as the dependent variable, which is to be explained, and

'growth need strength' as an independent variable, which therefore has a causal influence upon motivation.

When an experimental design is being employed, the independent variable is the variable that is manipulated. There is little ambiguity about the direction of causal influence. However, with cross-sectional designs of the kind used in most social survey research, there is ambiguity about the direction of causal influence in that data concerning variables are simultaneously collected. Therefore, we cannot say that an independent variable precedes the dependent one. To refer to independent and dependent variables in the context of cross-sectional designs, we must *infer* that one causes the other, as in the example concerning 'growth need strength' and motivation to work in the previous paragraph. We must draw on common sense or theoretical ideas to infer the likely temporal precedence of variables. However, there is always the risk that the inference will be wrong (see Research in focus 27.9 for an example of this possibility).

The concern about causality is reflected in the preoccupation with internal validity that was referred to in Chapter 3. There it was noted that a criterion of good quantitative research is frequently the extent to which there is confidence in the researcher's causal inferences. Research that exhibits the characteristics of an experimental design is often more highly valued than cross-sectional research, because of the greater confidence that can be enjoyed in the causal findings associated with the former. For their part, quantitative researchers who employ cross-sectional designs are invariably concerned to develop techniques that will allow causal inferences to be made. Moreover, the emergence of longitudinal research such as WERS (see Research in focus 3.14) almost certainly reflects a desire on the part of quantitative researchers to improve their ability to generate findings that permit a causal interpretation.

Generalization

In quantitative research the researcher is usually concerned to be able to say that his or her findings can be generalized beyond the confines of the particular context in which the research was conducted. Thus, if a study of motivation to work is carried out using a questionnaire with a number of people answering the questions, we often want to say that the results can apply to individuals other than those who responded in the study. This concern reveals itself in survey research in the attention that is often given to the question of how one can create a representative sample. Given that it is rarely feasible to send questionnaires to or interview whole populations (such as all members of a town, or the whole population of a country, or all members of an organization), we have to sample. However, we will want the sample to be as representative as possible in order to be able to say that the results are not unique to the particular group upon whom

the research was conducted; in other words, we want to be able to generalize the findings beyond the cases (for example, the people) that make up the sample. The preoccupation with generalization means some researchers become focused on developing law-like principles about human behaviour that can be used to predict what people will do in certain situations. To complicate matters further, this research is sometimes based on studies of animal rather than human behaviour, thus raising the question of whether or not behaviour can be generalized from one species to another (see Research in focus 7.10).

Research in focus 7.10
Generalizability and behaviour: Maslow's (1943) hierarchy of needs

The study of animals has formed an important part of the research design used in several psychological studies of human behaviour (e.g. Skinner 1953). The logic behind this strategy relies on the assumption that non-human behaviour can provide insight into the essential aspects of human nature that have ensured our survival as a species. This has made non-human study particularly attractive in areas such as motivational research, where early studies conducted on mice, rats, pigeons, monkeys, and apes have been used to inform understanding of human behaviour and in particular the relationship between motivation and performance (see Vroom 1964 for a review). However, some writers have cast doubt on the potential generalizability of such findings. In other words, do results from these studies apply equally to humans or should the findings be treated as unique to the particular species on which the study was conducted?

An interesting illustration of this debate is to be found in Maslow's (1943) hierarchy of needs, which remains one of the most well-known theories of motivation within business and management, even though much subsequent research has cast doubt on the validity of Maslow's theory. One of these critics has been Cullen (1997), who has drawn attention to the empirical research on which the theory is based. Cullen argues that Maslow developed the needs hierarchy using his observations of primate behaviour, which revealed differences between individuals in terms of dominant behaviour. Maslow used these observations as a basis for arguing that people vary in the extent to which they are inclined to progress through the needs hierarchy.

However, as Cullen points out, the fundamental problem with motivation theory's use of Maslow's hierarchy is not necessarily the fact that the theory is based on data generated through the study of primates, since several other management theories rely on insights drawn from animal studies. The problem instead relates to the nature of the animal data on which Maslow based his understanding of dominance. In particular, his conclusion that the confidence of some monkeys allowed them to dominate others was based on the study of caged animals that were largely kept isolated from each other: 'If we rely on a theory based on animal data that was collected more than 60 years ago, we are obligated to consider the accuracy and validity of that data' (1997: 368). Cullen suggests that recent studies of free-living primates in their natural habitats have called into question previous understandings of dominance and aggression but 'the experimental methods Maslow used did not permit him to see the social skills involved in establishing and maintaining dominance in non-human primate societies' (1997: 369). This alternative interpretation of dominance 'would seem to have more relevance for complex social settings such as organizations than does Maslow's individualistic interpretation' (1997: 369). Her main argument is that, if we intend to apply insights from the study of primates in order to understand the behaviour of humans in organizations, we cannot afford to ignore current debates and changes in understanding that occur in other research fields.

Probability sampling, which will be explored in Chapter 8, is the main way in which researchers seek to generate a representative sample. This procedure largely eliminates bias from the selection of a sample by using a process of random selection. The use of a random selection process does not guarantee a representative sample, because, as will be seen in Chapter 8, there are factors that operate over and above the selection system used that can jeopardize the representativeness of a sample. A related consideration here is this: even if we did have a representative sample, what would it be representative *of*? The simple answer is that it will be representative of the population from which it was selected. This is certainly the answer that sampling theory gives us. Strictly speaking, we cannot generalize beyond that population. This means that, if the members of the population from which a sample is taken are all inhabitants of a town, city, or region, or are all members of an organization, we can generalize only to the inhabitants or members of the town, city, region, or organization. But it is very tempting to see the findings as having a more pervasive applicability, so that, even if the sample was selected from a single large organization such as IBM, the findings are relevant to all similar organizations. We should not make inferences beyond the population from which the sample was selected, but researchers frequently do so. The wish to be able to generalize is often so deeply ingrained that the limits to the generalizability of findings are frequently forgotten or sidestepped.

The concern with generalizability or external validity is particularly strong among quantitative researchers using cross-sectional and longitudinal designs. There is a concern about generalizability among experimental research, as the discussion of external validity in Chapter 3 suggested, but users of this research design usually give greater attention to internal validity issues.

Replication

The natural sciences are often depicted as wishing to reduce to a bare minimum the contaminating influence of the scientist's biases and values. The results of a piece of research should be unaffected by the researcher's special characteristics or expectations. If biases and lack of objectivity were pervasive, the claims of the natural sciences to provide a definitive picture of the world would be seriously undermined. As a check upon the influence of these potentially damaging problems, scientists may seek to replicate—that is, to reproduce—each other's experiments. If there was a failure to replicate, so that a scientist's findings repeatedly could not be reproduced, serious questions would be raised about the validity of his or her findings. Consequently, scientists often attempt to be highly explicit about their procedures so that an experiment is capable of replication. Likewise, quantitative researchers in the social sciences often regard replication, or more precisely the ability to replicate, as an important ingredient of their activity. It is easy to see why: the possibility of a lack of objectivity and of the intrusion of the researcher's values would appear to be much greater when examining the social world than when the natural scientist investigates the natural order. Consequently, it is often regarded as important that the researcher spells out clearly his or her procedures so that they can be replicated by others, even if the research does not end up being replicated. The study by Schutte et al. (2000) described in Research in focus 7.11 relies on replication of the Maslach Burnout Inventory—General Survey,

Research in focus 7.11
Testing validity through replication: the case of burnout

The Maslach Burnout Inventory relies on the use of a questionnaire to measure burnout, which is characterized by emotional exhaustion, depersonalization, and reduced personal accomplishment. This syndrome is particularly associated with individuals who do 'people work of some kind'. Findings from the original North American study (Maslach and Jackson 1981) led the authors to conclude that burnout has certain debilitating effects, resulting ultimately in a loss of professional efficacy.

A study by Schutte et al. (2000) attempted to replicate these findings across a number of occupational groups (managers, clerks, foremen, technicians, blue-collar workers) in three different nations—Finland, Sweden, and Holland. However, subsequent tests of the Maslach Burnout Inventory scale suggested a need for revisions that would enable its use as a measure of burnout in occupational groups other than the human services, such as nurses, teachers, and social workers, for whom the original scale was intended. Using this revised, General Survey version, the researchers sought to investigate its *factorial validity*, or the extent to which the dimensions of burnout could be measured using the same questionnaire items in relation to different occupational and cultural groupings than the original study (see Key concept 7.12 for an explanation of *factor analysis*).

Following Hofstede (1984; see Chapter 2), employees were drawn from the same multinational corporation in different countries, in order to minimize the possibility that findings would reflect 'idiosyncrasies' associated with one company or another. The final sample size of 9055 reflected a response rate to the questionnaire of 63 percent.

The inventory comprises three subscales, each measured in terms of a series of items. An example of each is given below:

- *Exhaustion (Ex)*: 'I feel used up at the end of the workday.'
- *Cynicism (Cy)*: 'I have become less enthusiastic about my work.'
- *Professional Efficacy (PE)*: 'In my opinion I am good at my job.'

The individual responds according to a seven-point scale, from 0 = never, to 6 = daily. High scores on Ex and Cy and low scores on PE are indicative of burnout. A number of statistical analyses were carried out; for example, the reliability of the subscales was assessed using Cronbach's alpha as an indicator of internal consistency, meeting the criterion of 0.70 in virtually all the (sub)samples.

Schutte et al. conclude that their study:

- confirms that burnout is a three-dimensional concept;
- clearly demonstrates the factorial validity of the scale across occupational groups;
- reveals that the three subscales are sufficiently internally consistent.

Furthermore, significant differences were found in the pattern of burnout among white- and blue-collar workers, the former scoring higher on PE and lower on Cy. In interpreting these findings they argue that the higher white-collar PE scores may have arisen because 'working conditions are more favourable for managers than for workers, offering more autonomy, higher job complexity, meaningful work, and more respect for co-workers' (2000: 64).

Conversely: 'The relatively high scores on Cy for blue-collar workers reflect indifference and a more distant attitude towards their jobs. This might be explained by the culture on the shopfloor where distrust, resentment, and scepticism towards management and the organization traditionally prevail' (2000: 64).

Finally, Schutte et al. note that there were significant differences across national samples, the Dutch employees having scores that were consistently lower than those of their Swedish or Finnish colleagues. The authors conclude that the Maslach Burnout Inventory—General Survey is a suitable instrument for measuring burnout in occupational groups other than human services and in nations apart from those that are North American. Although alternative measurement scales exist, the majority of quantitative studies of burnout continue to rely on the Maslach Burnout Inventory—General Survey and the number of studies carried out is expanding rapidly. A recent meta-analysis (Key concept 14.9) of quantitative research on burnout identified 86 primary studies conducted since 2000, 48 of which had been published since 2006. This demonstrates the ongoing popularity of the measurement tool, especially in European and English-speaking countries (Reichl, Leiter, and Spinath, 2014).

a psychological measure that has been used by the authors to test for emotional exhaustion, depersonalization, and reduced personal accomplishment across a range of occupational groups and nations.

It has been relatively straightforward and therefore quite common for researchers to replicate the Job Characteristic Model, developed by Hackman and Oldham (1980, see Research in focus 7.4), in order to enhance confidence in the theory and its findings. Several of these have attempted to improve the generalizability of the model through its replication in different occupational settings—for example, on teachers, university staff, nursery school teachers, and physical education and sport administrators. However, some criticism has been levelled at the original research for failing to make explicit how the respondent sample was selected, beyond the fact that it involved a diverse variety of manual and non-manual occupations in both manufacturing and service sectors, thus undermining the potential generalizability of the investigation (Bryman 1989*a*). A further criticism relates to the emphasis that the model places on particular characteristics of a job, such as feedback from supervisors, which may be less of a feature in today's working context than they were in the late 1970s. A final criticism made of subsequent replications of the initial study is that they fail to test the total model, focusing on the core job characteristics rather than incorporating the effects of the mediating psychological states, which Hackman and Oldham suggest are the 'causal core of the model' (1976: 255).

A study by Johns, Xie, and Fang (1992) attempts to address this last criticism by specifically focusing on the mediating and moderating effects of psychological states on the relationship between job characteristics and outcomes. Basing their research on a random sample of 605 first- and second-level managers in a large utility company (response rate approximately 50 percent), the authors used a slightly modified version of the JDS questionnaire to determine the relationship between job characteristics, psychological states, and outcome variables. Their results provide some support for the mediating role of psychological states in determining outcomes based on core job characteristics—however, not always in the way that is specified by the model. In particular, some personal characteristics, such as educational level, were found to affect psychological states in a reverse manner to that which was expected—those with less education responded more favourably to elevated psychological states.

Another significant interest in replication stems from the original Aston studies (see Research in focus 3.6), which stimulated a plethora of replications over a period of more than thirty years following publication of the first generation of research in the early 1960s. Most clearly associated with replication were the 'fourth-generation' Aston researchers, who undertook studies that

- used a more homogenous sample drawn from a single industry, such as electrical engineering companies, 'to further substantiate the predictive power of the Aston findings' (Grinyer and Yasai-Ardekani 1980: 405); or

- extended the original findings to other forms of organization, such as churches (e.g. Hinings, Ranson, and Bryman 1976) or educational colleges (Holdaway et al. 1975).

Later proponents of the 'Aston approach' made international comparisons of firms in different countries in order to test the hypothesis that the relationship between the context and the structure of an organization was dependent on the culture of the country in which it operates. Studies conducted in China, Egypt, France, Germany, India, and Japan (e.g. Shenoy 1981) sought to test the proposition that some of the characteristic differences in organizational structure originally identified by the Aston researchers remained constant across these diverse national contexts.

However, replication is not a high-status activity in the natural or the social sciences, partly because it is often regarded as a pedestrian and uninspiring pursuit. Moreover, standard replications do not form the basis for attractive articles, so far as many academic journal editors are concerned. Consequently, replications of research appear in print far less frequently than might be supposed. A further reason for the low incidence of published replications is that it is difficult to ensure in business research that the conditions in a replication are precisely the same as those that pertained in an original study. So long as there is some ambiguity about the degree to which the conditions relating to a replication are the same as those in the initial study, any differences in findings may be attributable to the design of the replication rather than to some deficiency in the original study.

Nonetheless, it is often regarded as crucial that the methods taken in generating a set of findings are made explicit, so that it is *possible* to replicate a piece of research. Thus, it is *replicability* that is often regarded as an important quality of quantitative research.

The critique of quantitative research

Over the years, quantitative research, along with its epistemological and ontological foundations, has been the focus of a great deal of criticism, particularly from exponents and spokespersons of qualitative research. To a very large extent, it is difficult to distinguish between different

kinds of criticism when reflecting on the different critical points that have been proffered. These include: criticisms of quantitative research in general as a research strategy; criticisms of the epistemological and ontological foundations of quantitative research; and criticisms of specific methods and research designs with which quantitative research is associated.

Criticisms of quantitative research

To give a flavour of the critique of quantitative research, four criticisms will be covered briefly.

- *Quantitative researchers fail to distinguish people and social institutions from 'the world of nature'.* The phrase 'the world of nature' is from the writings of Schutz (the passage from which it has been taken is quoted in Chapter 2 of this volume). Schutz and other phenomenologists charge social scientists who employ a natural science model with treating the social world as if it were no different from the natural order. In so doing, they draw attention to one of positivism's central tenets—namely, that the principles of the scientific method can and should be applied to all phenomena that are the focus of investigation. As Schutz argues, this tactic essentially means turning a blind eye to the differences between the social and natural world. More particularly, as was observed in Chapter 2, it therefore means ignoring and riding roughshod over the fact that people interpret the world around them, whereas this capacity for self-reflection cannot be found among the objects of the natural sciences ('molecules, atoms, and electrons', as Schutz put it).

- *The measurement process possesses an artificial and spurious sense of precision and accuracy.* There are a number of aspects to this criticism. For one thing, it has been argued that the connection between the measures developed by social scientists and the concepts they are supposed to be revealing is assumed rather than real; hence, Cicourel's (1964) notion of 'measurement by fiat'. Testing for validity in the manner described in the previous section cannot really address this problem, because the very tests themselves entail measurement by fiat. A further way in which the measurement process is regarded by writers like Cicourel as flawed is that it presumes that when, for example, members of a sample respond to a question on a questionnaire (which is itself taken to be an indicator of a concept), they interpret the key terms in the question similarly. For many writers, respondents simply do not interpret such terms similarly. An often-used reaction to this problem is to use questions with fixed-choice answers, but this approach merely provides 'a solution to the problem of meaning by simply ignoring it' (Cicourel 1964: 108).

- *The reliance on instruments and procedures hinders the connection between research and everyday life.* This issue relates to the question of ecological validity that was raised in Chapter 3. Many methods of quantitative research rely heavily on administering research instruments to subjects (such as structured interviews and self-completion questionnaires) or on controlling situations to determine their effects (such as in experiments). However, as Cicourel (1982) asks, how do we know if survey respondents have the requisite knowledge to answer a question or if they are similar in their sense of the topic being important to them in their everyday lives? Thus, if respondents answer a set of questions designed to measure motivation to work, can we be sure that they are equally aware of what it is and its manifestations, and can we be sure that it is of equal concern to them in the ways in which it connects with their everyday working life? One can go even further and ask how well their answers relate to their everyday lives. People may answer a question designed to measure their motivation to work, but respondents' actual behaviour may be at variance with their answers (LaPiere 1934).

- *The analysis of relationships between variables creates a static view of social life that is independent of people's lives.* Blumer argued that studies that aim to bring out the relationships between variables omit 'the process of interpretation or definition that goes on in human groups' (1956: 685). This means that we do not know how what appears to be a relationship between two or more variables has been produced by the people to whom it applies. This criticism incorporates the first and third criticisms that have been referred to—that the meaning of events to individuals is ignored and that we do not know how such findings connect to everyday contexts—but adds a further element—namely, that it creates a sense of a static social world that is separate from the individuals who make up that world. In other words, quantitative research is seen as carrying an objectivist ontology that reifies the social world.

We can see in these criticisms the application of a set of concerns associated with a qualitative research strategy that reveals the combination of an interpretivist epistemological orientation (an emphasis on meaning from the individual's point of view) and a constructionist ontology (an emphasis on viewing the social world as the product of individuals rather than as something beyond them). The criticisms may appear very damning, but, as we will see in Chapter 17, quantitative researchers have a powerful battery of criticisms of qualitative research in their arsenal as well!

Is it always like this?

One of the problems with characterizing any research strategy, research design, or research method is that to a certain extent one is always outlining an ideal-typical approach. In other words, one tends to create something that represents that strategy, design, or method, but that may not be reflected in its entirety in research practice. This gap between the ideal type and actual practice can arise as a result of at least two major considerations. First, it arises because those of us who write about and teach research methods cannot cover every eventuality that can arise in the process of business research, so that we tend to provide accounts of the research process that draw upon common features. Thus a model of the process of quantitative research, such as that provided in Figure 7.1, should be thought of as a general *tendency* rather than as a definitive description of all quantitative research. A second reason why the gap can arise is that, to a very large extent, when writing about and teaching research methods we are essentially providing an account of *good practice*. The fact of the matter is that these practices are often not followed in the published research that students are likely to encounter in the substantive courses that they will be taking. This failure to follow the procedures associated with good practice is not necessarily due to incompetence on the part of business researchers (though in some cases it can be!), but is much more likely to be associated with matters of time, cost, and feasibility—in other words, the pragmatic concerns that cannot be avoided when one does business research.

Reverse operationism

As an example of the first source of the gap between the ideal type and actual research practice we can take the case of something that Bryman has referred to as 'reverse operationism' (1988a: 28). The model of the process of quantitative research in Figure 7.1 implies that concepts are specified and measures are then provided for them. As we have noted, this means that indicators must be devised. This is the basis of the idea of 'operationism' or 'operationalism', a term that derives from physics (Bridgman 1927) and that implies a deductive view of how research should proceed. However, this view of research neglects the fact that measurement can entail much more of an inductive element than Figure 7.1 implies. Sometimes, measures are developed that in turn lead to conceptualization. One way in which this can occur is when a statistical technique known as *factor analysis* is employed (see Key concept 7.12). In order to measure the concept of 'charismatic leadership', a term that owes a great deal to Weber's (1947) notion of charismatic authority, Conger and Kanungo (1998) generated twenty-five items to provide a multiple-item measure of the concept. These items derived from their reading of existing theory and research on the subject, particularly in connection with charismatic leadership in organizations. When the items were administered to a sample of respondents and the results were factor analysed, it was found that the items bunched around six factors, each of which to all intents

Key concept 7.12
What is factor analysis?

Factor analysis is employed in relation to multiple-indicator measures to determine whether groups of indicators tend to bunch together to form distinct clusters, referred to as factors. Its main goal is to reduce the number of variables with which the researcher needs to deal. It is used in relation to multiple-item measures, such as Likert scales, to see how far there is an inherent structure to the large number of items that often make up such measures. Researchers sometimes use factor analysis to establish whether the dimensions of a measure that they expect to exist can be confirmed. The clusters of items that are revealed by a factor analysis need to be given names (for example, 'innovation and flexibility' or 'autonomy' in the example in Research in focus 7.9). It is a complex technique that is beyond the level at which this book is pitched (see Bryman and Cramer 2008: Chapter 13), but it has considerable significance for the development of measures in many social scientific fields.

and purposes represents a dimension of the concept of charismatic leadership:

- strategic vision and articulation behaviour;
- sensitivity to the environment;
- unconventional behaviour;
- personal risk;
- sensitivity to organizational members' needs;
- action orientation away from the maintenance of the status quo.

The point to note is that these six dimensions were not specified at the outset: the link between conceptualization and measurement was an inductive one. Nor is this an unusual situation so far as research is concerned (Bryman 1988a: 26–8).

Reliability and validity testing

The second reason why the gap between the ideal type and actual research practice can arise is because researchers do not follow some of the recommended practices. A classic case of this tendency is that, while, as in the present chapter, much time and effort are expended on the articulation of the ways in which the reliability and validity of measures should be determined, a great deal of the time these procedures are not followed. There is evidence from analyses of published quantitative research in organization studies (Podsakoff and Dalton 1987) that writers rarely report tests of the stability of their measures and even more rarely report evidence of validity (only 3 per cent of articles provided information about measurement validity). A large proportion of articles used Cronbach's alpha, but, since this device is relevant only to multiple-item measures because it gauges internal consistency, the stability and validity of many measures that are employed are unknown. Boyd et al. (2013) found that for articles published in *Strategic Management Journal* 1998–2000, 49.8 per cent of all possible reliability estimates were reported for measures of independent variables and 41 per cent for dependent variables; in 2010, these percentages had increased considerably to 87.5 and 64.7 per cent respectively. This is not to say that research that fails to report reliability estimates

is necessarily *un*stable and *in*valid, but that we simply do not know. The reasons why the procedures for determining stability and validity are rarely used are almost certainly the cost and time that are likely to be involved. Researchers tend to be concerned with substantive issues and are less than enthusiastic about engaging in the kind of development work that would be required for a thoroughgoing determination of measurement quality. However, what this means is that Cicourel's (1964) previously cited remark about much measurement in sociology being 'measurement by fiat' has considerable weight.

The remarks on the lack of assessment of the quality of measurement should not be taken as a justification for readers to neglect this phase in their work. Our aim is merely to draw attention to some of the ways in which practices described in this book are not always followed and to suggest some reasons why they are not followed.

Sampling

A similar point can be made in relation to sampling, which will be covered in Chapter 8. As we will see, good practice is strongly associated with the use of random samples or **probability samples**. However, quite a lot of research is based on **non-probability samples**—that is, samples that have not been selected in terms of the principles of probability sampling to be discussed in Chapter 8. Sometimes the use of non-probability samples will be due to the impossibility or extreme difficulty of obtaining probability samples. Yet another reason is that the time and cost involved in securing a probability sample are too great relative to the level of resources available. And a third reason is that sometimes the opportunity to study a certain group presents itself and represents too good an opportunity to miss. Again, such considerations should not be viewed as a justification and hence a set of reasons for ignoring the principles of sampling to be examined in the next chapter, not least because not following the principles of probability sampling carries implications for the kind of statistical analysis that can be employed (see Chapter 15). Instead, our purpose, as before, is to draw attention to the ways in which gaps between recommendations about good practice and actual research practice can arise.

 ## *Key points*

....

- Quantitative research can be characterized as a linear series of steps moving from theory to conclusions, but the process described in Figure 7.1 is an ideal type from which there are many departures.

- The measurement process in quantitative research entails the search for indicators.

- Establishing the reliability and validity of measures is important for assessing their quality.

- Quantitative research can be characterized as exhibiting certain preoccupations, the most central of which are: measurement; causality; generalization; and replication.

- Quantitative research has been subjected to many criticisms by qualitative researchers. These criticisms tend to revolve around the view that a natural science model is inappropriate for studying the social world.

Questions for review

The main steps in quantitative research

- What are the main steps in quantitative research?

- To what extent do the main steps follow a strict sequence?

- Do the steps suggest a deductive or inductive approach to the relationship between theory and research?

Concepts and their measurement

- Why is measurement important for the quantitative researcher?

- What is the difference between a measure and an indicator?

- Why might multiple-indicator approaches to the measurement of concepts be preferable to those that rely on a single indicator?

Reliability and validity

- What are the main ways of thinking about the reliability of the measurement process? Is one form of reliability the most important?

- 'Whereas validity presupposes reliability, reliability does not presuppose validity.' Discuss.

- What are the main criteria for evaluating measurement validity?

The main preoccupations of quantitative researchers

- Outline the main preoccupations of quantitative researchers. What reasons can you give for their prominence?

- Why might replication be an important preoccupation among quantitative researchers, in spite of the tendency for replications in business research to be fairly rare?

The critique of quantitative research

- 'The crucial problem with quantitative research is the failure of its practitioners to address adequately the issue of meaning.' Discuss.

- How central is the adoption by quantitative researchers of a natural science model of conducting research to the critique by qualitative researchers of quantitative research?

Online Resource Centre
www.oxfordtextbooks.co.uk/orc/brymanbrm4e/

Visit the Interactive Research Guide that accompanies this book to complete an exercise in The Nature of Quantitative Research.

8

Sampling in quantitative research

Chapter outline

This chapter and the three that follow it are very much concerned with principles and practices associated with social survey research. Sampling principles are not exclusively concerned with survey research; for example, they are relevant to the selection of documents for content analysis (see Chapter 13). However, in this chapter the emphasis will be on sampling in connection with the selection of people who would be asked questions by interview or questionnaire. The chapter explores:

- the related ideas of generalization (also known as external validity) and of a representative sample; the latter allows the researcher to generalize findings from a sample to a population;

- the idea of a *probability sample*—that is, one in which a random selection process has been employed;

- the main types of probability sample: the **simple random sample**; the **systematic sample**; the **stratified random sample**; and the multi-stage **cluster sample**;

- the main issues involved in deciding on sample size;

- different types of **non-probability sample**, including quota sampling, which is widely used in market research and opinion polls;

- potential sources of error in survey research.

Introduction

This chapter is concerned with some important aspects of conducting a survey, but it presents only a partial picture, because there are many other steps. In this chapter we are concerned with the issues involved in selecting individuals for survey research, although the principles involved apply equally to other approaches to **quantitative research**, such as content analysis. Chapters 9, 10, and 11 deal with the data collection aspects of conducting a survey, while Chapter 15 deals with the analysis of data.

Figure 8.1 aims to outline the main steps involved in planning survey research. Initially, the survey will begin with general research issues that need to be investigated. These are gradually narrowed down so that they become research questions, which may take the form of hypotheses, though this is not necessarily the case. The movement from research issues to research questions is likely to be the result of reading the literature relating to the issues, such as relevant theories and evidence.

Once the research questions have been formulated, the planning of the fieldwork can begin. In practice, decisions relating to sampling and the research instrument will overlap, but they are presented in Figure 8.1 as part of a sequence. The figure is meant to illustrate the main phases of a survey, and these different steps (other than those to do with sampling, which will be covered in this chapter) will be followed through in the next three chapters and in Chapters 15 and 16. The survey researcher needs to decide what kind of population is suited to the investigation of the topic and also needs to formulate a research instrument and how it should be administered. By 'research instrument' is meant simply something like a **structured interview** schedule or a **self-completion questionnaire**. Moreover, there are several different ways of administering such instruments. Figure 8.2 outlines the main types that are likely to be encountered. Types 1 to 4 are covered in Chapter 9. Types 5 and 6 are covered in Chapter 10. Types 7 to 9 are covered in Chapter 28 in the context of the use of the Internet generally.

Figure 8.1

Steps in planning a social survey

Figure 8.2

Main modes of administration of a survey

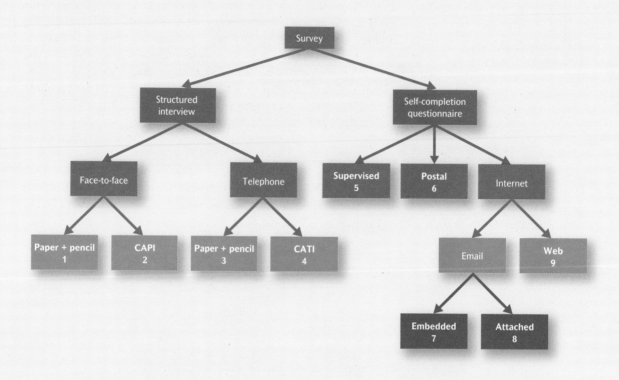

 # Introduction to sampling

Many of the readers of this book will be university or college students. At some point in your stay at your university (we will use this term from now on to include colleges) you may have wondered about the attitudes of your fellow students to various matters, or about their behaviour in certain contexts, or something about their backgrounds. If you were to decide to examine any or all of these three areas, you might consider conducting structured interviews or sending out questionnaires in order to find out about their behaviour, attitudes, and backgrounds. You would, of course, have to consider how best to design your interviews or questionnaires, and the issues that are involved in the decisions that need to be made about designing these research instruments and administering them will be the focus of Chapters 9–11.

However, before getting to that point, you are likely to be confronted with a problem. Let us say that your university is quite large and has around 9000 students. It is extremely unlikely that you will have the time and resources to conduct a survey of all these students. It is unlikely that you would be able to send questionnaires to all 9000 and even more unlikely that you would be able to interview all of them, since conducting survey research by interview is considerably more expensive and time-consuming, all things being equal, than by postal questionnaire (see Chapter 10). It is almost certain that you will need to *sample* students from the total population of students in your university.

The need to sample is one that is almost invariably encountered in quantitative research. In this chapter, we will be almost entirely concerned with matters relating to sampling in relation to social survey research involving data collection by structured interview or questionnaire. In social survey research, sampling constitutes a key step in the research process, as illustrated in Figure 8.1. However, other methods of quantitative research also involve sampling considerations, as will be seen in Chapters 12 and 13, when we will examine structured observation and content analysis, respectively. The principles of sampling involved are more or less identical in connection with these other methods, but frequently other considerations come to the fore as well.

But will any old sample suffice? Would it be sufficient to locate yourself in a central position on your campus (if your university has one) and then interview the students who come past you and whom you are in a position to interview? Alternatively, would it be sufficient to

go around your student union asking people to be interviewed? Or again to send questionnaires to everyone on your course?

The answer, of course, depends on whether or not you want to be able to *generalize* your findings to the entire student body in your university. If you do, it is unlikely that any of the three sampling strategies proposed in the previous paragraph would provide you with a *representative sample* of all students in your university. In order to be able to generalize your findings from your sample to the population from which it was selected, the sample must be representative. See Key concept 8.1 for an explanation of key terms concerning sampling.

Why might the strategies for sampling students previously outlined be unlikely to produce a representative sample? There are various reasons, of which the following stand out.

Key concept 8.1
Basic terms and concepts in sampling

- **Population**: basically, the universe of units from which the sample is to be selected. The term 'units' is employed because it is not necessarily people who are being sampled—the researcher may want to sample from a universe of nations, cities, regions, firms, etc. Thus, 'population' has a much broader meaning than the everyday use of the term, whereby it tends to be associated with the total number of people in a nation or town.

- **Sample**: the segment of the population that is selected for investigation. It is a subset of the population. The method of selection may be based on a probability or a non-probability approach (see below).

- **Sampling frame**: the listing of all units in the population from which the sample will be selected.

- **Representative sample**: a sample that reflects the population accurately so that it is a microcosm of the population.

- **Sampling bias**: a distortion in the representativeness of the sample that arises when some members of the population (or more precisely the sampling frame) stand little or no chance of being selected for inclusion in the sample.

- **Probability sample**: a sample that has been selected using random selection so that each unit in the population has a known chance of being selected. It is generally assumed that a *representative sample* is more likely to be the outcome when this method of selection from the population is employed. The aim of probability sampling is to keep sampling error (see below) to a minimum.

- **Non-probability sample**: a sample that has not been selected using a random selection method. Essentially, this implies that some units in the population are more likely to be selected than others.

- **Sampling error**: the difference between a sample and the population from which it is selected, even though a probability sample has been selected.

(continued)

- **Non-sampling error**: differences between the population and the sample that arise either from deficiencies in the sampling approach, such as an inadequate sampling frame or non-response (see below), or from such problems as poor question wording, poor interviewing, or flawed processing of data.

- **Non-response**: a source of non-sampling error that is particularly likely to happen when individuals are being sampled. It occurs whenever some members of the sample refuse to cooperate, cannot be contacted, or for some reason cannot supply the required data (for example, because of mental incapacity).

- **Census**: the enumeration of an entire population. Thus, if data are collected in relation to all units in a population, rather than in relation to a sample of units of that population, the data are treated as census data. The phrase '*the* census' typically refers to the complete enumeration of all members of the population of a nation state—that is, a national census. This form of enumeration occurs once every ten years in the UK. However, in a statistical context, like the term *population*, the idea of a census has a broader meaning than this.

- The first two approaches depend heavily upon the availability of students during the time or times that you search them out. Not all students are likely to be equally available at that time, so the sample will not reflect those students who are not available.

- The first two approaches also depend on the students going to the locations. Not all students will necessarily pass the point where you locate yourself or go to the student union, or they may vary hugely in the frequency with which they do so. Their movements are likely to reflect such things as where their halls of residence or accommodation are situated, or where their departments are located, or their social habits. Again, to rely on these locations would mean missing out on students who do not frequent them.

- It is possible, not to say likely, that your decisions about which people to approach will be influenced by your judgements about how friendly or cooperative the people concerned are likely to be or by how comfortable you feel about interviewing students of the same (or opposite) gender to yourself, as well as by many other factors.

- The problem with the third strategy is that students on your course by definition take the same subject as each other and therefore will not be representative of all students in the university.

In other words, in the case of all of the three sampling approaches, your decisions about whom to sample are influenced too much by personal judgements, by prospective respondents' availability, or by your implicit criteria for inclusion. Such limitations mean that, in the language of survey sampling, your sample will be *biased*. A biased sample is one that does not represent the population from which the sample was selected. As far as possible, bias should be removed from the selection of your sample. In fact, it is incredibly difficult to remove bias

altogether and to derive a truly representative sample. What needs to be done is to ensure that steps are taken to keep bias to an absolute minimum.

Three sources of bias can be identified (see Key concept 8.1 for an explanation of terms).

- *If a non-probability or non-random sampling method is used.* If the method used to select the sample is not random, there is a possibility that human judgement will affect the selection process, making some members of the population more likely to be selected than others. This source of bias can be eliminated through the use of probability or random sampling, the procedure for which is described below.

- *If the sampling frame is inadequate.* If the sampling frame is not comprehensive or is inaccurate or suffers from some other kind of similar deficiency, the sample that is derived cannot represent the population, even if a random or probability sampling method is employed.

- *If some sample members refuse to participate or cannot be contacted—in other words, if there is non-response.* The problem with non-response is that those who agree to participate may differ in various ways from those who do not agree to participate. Some of the differences may be significant to the research question or questions. If the data are available, it may be possible to check how far, when there is non-response, the resulting sample differs from the population. It is often possible to do this in terms of characteristics such as gender or age, or, in the case of something like a sample of university students, whether the sample's characteristics reflect the entire population in terms of the students' areas of study. However, it is usually impossible to determine whether differences exist between the population and the sample after non-response in terms of 'deeper' factors, such as attitudes or patterns of behaviour.

Sampling error

In order to appreciate the significance of sampling error for achieving a representative sample, consider Figures 8.3–8.7. Imagine we have a population of 200 employees and we want a sample of 50. Imagine as well that one of the variables of concern to us is whether or not employees receive regular performance appraisals from their immediate supervisor and that the population is equally divided between those who do and those who do not. This split is represented by the vertical line that divides the population into two halves (see Figure 8.3). If the sample is representative, we would expect our sample of 50 to be equally split in terms of this variable (see Figure 8.4). If there is a small amount of sampling error, so that we have one employee too many who is not appraised and one too few who is, it will look like Figure 8.5. In Figure 8.6 we see a rather more serious degree of over-representation of employees who do not receive appraisals. This time there are three too many who are not appraised and three too

Figure 8.3

Having performance appraisals in a population of 200

| Have performance appraisal | Do not have performance appraisal |

Figure 8.4

A sample with no sampling error

| Have performance appraisal | Do not have performance appraisal |

Figure 8.5

A sample with very little sampling error

| Have performance appraisal | Do not have performance appraisal |

Figure 8.6

A sample with some sampling error

| Have performance appraisal | Do not have performance appraisal |

few who are. In Figure 8.7 we have a very serious over-representation of employees who do not receive performance appraisals, because there are 35 employees in the sample who are not appraised, which is much larger than the 25 who should be in the sample.

It is important to appreciate that, as suggested above, probability sampling does not and cannot eliminate sampling error. Even with a well-crafted probability sample, a degree of sampling error is likely to creep in. However, probability sampling stands a better chance than non-probability sampling of keeping sampling error in check so that it does not end up looking like the outcome featured in Figure 8.7. Moreover, probability sampling allows the researcher to employ tests of statistical significance that permit inferences to be made about the sample from which the sample was selected. These will be addressed in Chapter 15.

Figure 8.7

A sample with a lot of sampling error

Have performance appraisal	Do not have performance appraisal

Types of probability sample

Imagine that we are interested in levels of training, skill development, and learning among employees and the variables that relate to variation in levels of training they have undertaken. We might decide to conduct our research in a single nearby company. This means that our population will all be employees in that company, which in turn will mean that we will be able to generalize our findings only to employees of that company. We simply cannot assume that levels of training and their correlates will be the same in other companies. We might decide that we want our research to be conducted only on full-time employees, so that part-time and subcontracted workers are omitted. Imagine too that there are 9000 full-time employees in the company.

Simple random sample

The simple random sample is the most basic form of probability sample. With random sampling, each unit of the population has an equal probability of inclusion in the sample. Imagine that we decide that we have enough money to interview 450 employees at the company. This means that the probability of inclusion in the sample is

$$\frac{450}{9000} \text{ i.e. 1 in 20.}$$

This is known as the *sampling fraction* and is expressed as

$$\frac{n}{N}$$

where n is the sample size and N is the population size.

The key steps in devising our simple random sample can be represented as follows:

1. Define the population. We have decided that this will be all full-time employees at the company. This is our N and in this case is 9000.

2. Select or devise a comprehensive sampling frame. It is likely that the company's personnel department will keep records of all employees and that this will enable us to exclude those who do not meet our criteria for inclusion—i.e. part-time employees and those who work on the premises but are not employees of the company.

3. Decide your sample size (n). We have decided that this will be 450.

4. List all the employees in the population and assign them consecutive numbers from 1 to N. In our case, this will be 1 to 9000.

5. Using a table of random numbers, or a computer program that can generate random numbers, select n (450) different random numbers that lie between 1 and N (9000).

6. The employees to which the n (450) random numbers refer constitute the sample.

Two points are striking about this process. First, there is almost no opportunity for human bias to manifest itself. Employees would not be selected on such subjective criteria as whether they looked friendly and approachable. The selection of whom to interview is entirely mechanical. Secondly, the process is not dependent on the employees' availability. They do not have to be working in the interviewer's proximity to be included in the sample. The process of selection is done without their knowledge. It is not until they are contacted by an interviewer that they know that they are part of a social survey.

Step 5 mentions the possible use of a table of random numbers. These can be found in the appendices of many statistics books. The tables are made up of columns of five-digit numbers, such as:

09188
90045
73189
75768
54016
08358
28306
53840
91757
89415

The first thing to notice is that, since these are five-digit numbers and the maximum number that we can sample from is 9000, which is a four-digit number, none of the random numbers is usable for our purposes except for 09188 and 08358, although the former is larger than the largest possible number. The answer is that we should take just four digits in each number. Let us take the last four digits. This would yield the following:

9188
0045
3189
5768
4016
8358
8306
3840
1757
9415

However, two of the resulting numbers—9188 and 9415—exceed 9000. We cannot have an employee with either of these numbers assigned to him or her. The solution is simple: we ignore these numbers. This means that the employee who has been assigned the number 45 will be the first to be included in the sample; the employee who has been assigned the number 3189 will be next; the employee who has been assigned the number 5768 will be next; and so on.

An alternative but very similar strategy to the one that has been described is to write (or get someone to write for you) a simple computer program that will select n random numbers (in our case 450) that lie between 1 and N (in our case 9000). As with using a table of random numbers, you may be faced with the possibility of some random numbers turning up more than once. Since you will want to interview the person to whom those recurring random numbers refer on only one occasion, you will want to ignore any random number that recurs. This procedure results in a sample known as a simple random sample *without replacement*. More or less all simple random samples will be of this kind in the context of business research and so the qualifier 'without replacement' is invariably omitted.

Systematic sample

A variation on the simple random sample is the **systematic sample**. With this kind of sample, you select units directly from the sampling frame—that is, without resorting to a table of random numbers.

We know that we are to select 1 employee in 20. With a systematic sample, we would make a random start between 1 and 20 inclusive, possibly by using the last two digits in a table of random numbers. If we did this with the ten random numbers above, the first relevant one would be 54016, since it is the first one where the last two digits yield a number of 20 or below, in this case 16. This means that the sixteenth employee on our sampling frame is the first to be in our sample. Thereafter, we take every twentieth employee on the list. So the sequence will go:

16, 36, 56, 76, 96, 116, etc.

This approach obviates the need to assign numbers to employees' names and then to look up names of the employees whose numbers have been drawn by the random selection process. It is important to ensure, however, that there is no inherent ordering of the sampling frame, since this may bias the resulting sample. If there is some ordering to the list, the best solution is to rearrange it.

Stratified random sampling

In our imaginary study of company employees, one of the features that we might want our sample to exhibit is a proportional representation of the different departments in which employees work. It might be that the kind of department an employee works in is viewed as relevant to a wide range of attitudinal features that are in turn relevant to the study of skill development and training. Generating a simple random sample or a systematic sample *might* yield such a representation, so that the proportion of employees from the sales and marketing department in the sample is the same as that in the employee population and so on. Thus, if there are 1800 employees in the sales and marketing department, using our sampling fraction of 1 in 20, we would expect to have 90 employees in our sample from this department of the company. However, because of sampling error, it is unlikely that this will occur and more likely that there will be a difference, so that there may be, say, 85 or 93 from this department.

Because it is very likely that the company will include in its records the department in which employees are based, or indeed may have separate sampling frames for each department, it will be possible to ensure that employees are accurately represented in terms of their departmental membership. In the language of sampling, this means stratifying the population by a criterion (in this case, departmental membership) and selecting either a simple random sample or a systematic sample from each of the resulting strata. In the present example, if there are five departments we would have five strata, with the numbers in each stratum being one-twentieth of the total for each department. Table 8.1 reflects this and also shows a hypothetical outcome of using a simple random sample, which results in a distribution of employees across departments that does not mirror the population all that well.

The advantage of stratified sampling in a case like this is clear: it ensures that the resulting sample will be distributed in the same way as the population in terms of the stratifying criterion. If you use a simple random or systematic sampling approach, you *may* end up with a distribution like that of the stratified sample, but it is unlikely. Two points are relevant here. First, you can conduct stratified sampling sensibly only when it is relatively easy to identify and allocate units to strata. If it is not possible or it would be very difficult to do so, stratified sampling will not be feasible. Secondly, you can use more than one stratifying criterion. Thus, it may be that you would want to stratify by department, by gender, and by whether or not employees are above or below a certain salary level or occupational grade. If it is feasible to identify employees in terms of these stratifying criteria, it is possible to use pairs of criteria or several criteria (such as departmental membership plus gender plus occupational grade).

Stratified sampling is really feasible only when the relevant information is available. In other words, when data are available that allow the ready identification of members of the population in terms of the stratifying criterion (or criteria), it is sensible to employ this sampling method. But it is unlikely to be economical if the identification of population members for stratification purposes entails a great deal of work because there is no available listing in terms of strata.

Multi-stage cluster sampling

In the example we have been dealing with, employees to be interviewed are located in a single company. Interviewers will have to arrange their interviews with the sampled employees, but, because they are all working on the same premises, they will not be involved in a lot of travel. However, imagine that we wanted a *national* sample of employees. It is likely that interviewers would have to travel the length and breadth of the UK to interview

Table 8.1

The advantages of stratified sampling			
Department	Population	Stratified sample	Possible simple random or systematic sample
Sales and marketing	1800	90	85
Finance and accounts	1200	60	70
Human resource management and training	1000	50	60
Technical, research, and new-product development	1800	90	84
Production	3200	160	151
TOTAL	9000	450	450

the sampled individuals. This would add a great deal to the time and cost of doing the research. This kind of problem occurs whenever the aim is to interview a sample that is to be drawn from a widely dispersed population, such as a national population, or a large region, or even a large city.

One way in which it is possible to deal with this potential problem is to employ *cluster sampling*. With cluster sampling, the primary sampling unit (the first stage of the sampling procedure) is not the units of the population to be sampled but groupings of those units. It is the latter groupings or aggregations of population units that are known as *clusters*. Imagine that we want a nationally representative sample of 5000 employees who are working for the 100 largest companies in the UK (this

information is publicly available and generated through the FTSE [Financial Times Stock Exchange] index; company size is measured in terms of market capitalization). Using simple random or systematic sampling would yield a widely dispersed sample, which would result in a great deal of travel for interviewers. One solution might be to sample companies and then employees from each of the sampled companies. A probability sampling method would need to be employed at each stage. Thus, we might randomly sample ten companies from the entire population of the 100 largest companies in the UK, thus yielding ten clusters, and we would then interview 500 randomly selected employees at each of the ten companies. Research in focus 8.2 gives an example of a study that used cluster sampling.

Research in focus 8.2
A cluster sample survey of small ventures in the tourism industry

In a study aimed at identifying the performance measures of small ventures in the Israeli tourism industry, Haber and Reichel (2005) designed a cluster sample as the basis for their questionnaire survey. The first stage of their sampling strategy involved the use of information held by the twelve regional tourism associations run by the Ministry of Tourism in Israel. These then formed the basis for the second stage of their sample design, which involved selecting approximately 25 per cent of the total population of the country's small tourism ventures, which were sampled across each of the twelve regional areas, thus ensuring the sample was representative of the national population. The 305 ventures that participated in the survey represented a very high response rate of 94 per cent. This was achieved by preliminary telephone calls followed up by face-to-face interviews to conduct the questionnaire survey.

Tips and skills
A guide to industry classification systems

Industry classification systems are used to divide firms and other organizations into groups based on the type of business they are in or the kind of products they make. The oldest of these systems is the Standard Industrial Classification (SIC) scheme, which was developed by the US government in 1939 to delineate industrial activities. Over the years there have been several revisions to this system to reflect the emergence of new industries and product markets. The SIC system forms the basis for the ISIC (International SIC) developed by the United Nations and also for the UK version of the system, the most recent of which is UK SIC 2007. Under the system, economic activities are divided into seventeen sections, each denoted by a letter; these are in turn divided into sixteen subsections, denoted by a second letter, which are then divided into divisions (60), groups (222), classes (503), and subclasses (253). The seventeen main sections are:

A. Agriculture, hunting, and forestry

B. Fishing

(continued)

C. Mining and quarrying

D. Manufacturing

E. Electricity, gas, and water supply

F. Construction

G. Wholesale and retail trade and repair

H. Hotels and restaurants

I. Transport, storage, and communication

J. Financial intermediation (including banking)

K. Real estate, renting, and business activities

L. Public administration and defence; compulsory social security

M. Education

N. Health and social work

O. Community, social, and personal service activities

P. Private households with employees

Q. Extra-territorial organizations and bodies

More information about UK SIC 2007 is available from the Office for National Statistics website: **www.ons.gov.uk/ons/guide-method/classifications/current-standard-classifications/standard-industrial-classification/index.html** (accessed 21 October 2014).

This includes information about the major revision of the UK SIC that took place in 2007, timed to coincide with the revision of the European Union's industrial classification system—Nomenclature statistique des Activités économiques dans la Communauté Européenne (known as NACE)—which aims to establish a common statistical classification of economic activities between European Community countries. More information about NACE is available via the Eurostat website at: **epp.eurostat.ec.europa.eu** (accessed 21 October 2014)

However, in 1997 in response to changes in world economies, the SIC codes were supplanted in North America by a more comprehensive system, called the North American Industrial Classification System (NAICS), which is starting to replace the SIC scheme. NAICS classifies establishments based on production processes—in other words, on what they do rather than what they make. NAICS also focuses more on emerging industries and services—of the 358 five-digit industry codes, 250 deliver services (Krishnan and Press 2003). A full list of the codes, which were revised in 2007, can be found at the US Census Bureau website, which explains the NAICS coding system and gives information on new industries and sectors: **www.census.gov/eos/www/naics/** (accessed 22 October 2014).

Eventually NAICS is intended to replace SIC in relation to all North American reporting of statistics, but it is only gradually becoming accepted worldwide and most databases continue to use both the SIC and NAICS systems. However, SIC codes are by far the most commonly used scheme among business researchers (Jacobs and O'Neill 2003; Ojala 2005). Bhojraj, Lee, and Oler (2003) suggest this is because, although researchers acknowledge the limitations of the SIC scheme in terms of its inability to provide homogenous categories, there isn't a system that is significantly better, so researchers have tended to stick with it.

There are also other industry classification schemes, including the Global Industry Classifications Standard (GICS) system, which was developed by two leading investment banks with the needs of the financial community in mind. Unlike SIC and NAICS codes, which focus primarily on identifying the type of product or service as the basis for categorization, GICS classifies companies according to their principal business activity. GICS also provides guidelines for classifying companies that don't fit neatly into a particular business activity—for example, because a company has diversified across several sectors that contribute equally to revenues (Bhojraj, Lee, and Oler 2003). This is a particularly important challenge for industry classification systems in dealing with the rise of multinational businesses whose activities may span several sectors of activity.

Research in focus 8.3
An example of a multi-stage cluster sample

The UK Skills and Employment Survey (SES) is a national study of people aged 20–65 who are in paid work. It focuses upon the work that people do and how working life has changed over time. The 2012 survey (SES2012) is the sixth in a series which began in 1986. A total of 3200 working adults took part in the 2012 survey. At the first stage, the researchers sampled from postcode sectors in order to ensure coverage of Britain and a reflection of its socio-economic composition. Then, from each of the sampled postcode sectors, addresses were selected using a systematic sampling approach based on a random starting point. The sample was weighted to take into account differential probabilities of sample selection, oversampling of certain areas and small response rate variations between groups (defined by sex, age, and occupation). One respondent per address was selected for interview and 49 per cent completed the survey. Findings have been published in a series of themed mini-reports on topics including fear at work, work intensification, well-being, skills, and training:
www.cardiff.ac.uk/socsi/ses2012/ (accessed 21 October 2014).

This is fine, but there is no guarantee that these ten companies reflect the diverse range of industrial activities that are engaged in by the population as a whole. One solution to this problem would be to group the 100 largest UK companies by Standard Industrial Classification (SIC) codes (see Tips and skills 'A guide to industry classification systems') and then randomly sample companies from each of the major SIC groups. We might follow the example of the Workplace Employment Relations Survey (WERS) researchers (see Research in focus 3.14) and exclude the less common SIC groups (agriculture, hunting, and forestry; fishing; mining and quarrying—A to C, and private households—P). One company might then be sampled from each of the twelve remaining major SIC code categories (D to O) and then approximately 400 employees from each of the twelve companies would be interviewed. Thus, there are three separate stages:

- group 100 largest UK companies by market capitalization;

- sample one company from each of the twelve major SIC categories;

- sample 400 employees from each of the twelve companies.

In a sense, cluster sampling is always a multi-stage approach, because one always samples clusters first and then something else—either further clusters or population units—is sampled.

Many examples of multi-stage cluster sampling entail stratification. We might, for example, want further to stratify the companies according to whether their headquarters are located in the UK or abroad. To do this we would group companies according to whether their headquarters were based in the UK or elsewhere and then select one or two companies per major SIC code from each of the two strata.

Research in focus 8.3 provides an example of a multi-stage cluster sample. It entailed three stages: the sampling of sub-regions within the UK, the sampling of socio-economic groups, and the sampling of individuals. In a way, there are four stages, because addresses are randomly sampled (using the Postcode Address File) and then, if there was more than one eligible individual at the same address, one person was randomly selected.

The advantage of multi-stage cluster sampling should be clear by now: it allows interviews to be far more concentrated geographically than would be the case if a simple random or stratified sample was selected. The advantages of stratification can be capitalized upon because the clusters can be stratified. However, even when a rigorous sampling strategy is employed, sampling error cannot be avoided, as the example in Research in focus 8.9 clearly shows.

The qualities of a probability sample

The reason why probability sampling is such an important procedure in social survey research is that it is possible to make inferences from information about a random sample to the population from which it was selected. In other words, we can generalize findings derived from a sample to the population. This is different

Tips and skills
Generalizing from a random sample to the population

Using our imaginary study of training and skill development in a single nearby company, let us say that the sample mean is 6.7 days of training per employee (the average amount of training received in the previous twelve months in the sample). A crucial consideration here is: how confident can we be that the mean number of 6.7 training days is likely to be found in the population, even when probability sampling has been employed? If we take an infinite number of samples from a population, the sample estimates of the mean of the variable under consideration will vary in relation to the population mean. This variation will take the form of a bell-shaped curve known as a *normal distribution* (see Figure 8.8). The shape of the distribution implies that there is a clustering of sample means at or around the population mean. Half the sample means will be at or below the population mean; the other half will be at or above the population mean. As we move to the left (at or lower than the population mean) or the right (at or higher than the population mean), the curve tails off, implying fewer and fewer samples generating means that depart considerably from the population mean. The variation of sample means around the population mean is the *sampling error* and is measured using a statistic known as the **standard error of the mean**. This is an estimate of the amount that a sample mean is likely to differ from the population mean.

This consideration is important, because sampling theory tells us that 68 per cent of all sample means will lie between plus or minus 1.00 standard error from the population mean and that 95 per cent of all sample means will lie between plus or minus 1.96 standard errors from the population mean. It is this second calculation that is crucial, because it is at least implicitly employed by survey researchers when they report their statistical findings. They typically employ 1.96 standard errors as the crucial criterion in how confident they can be in their findings. Essentially, the criterion implies that you can be 95 per cent certain that the population mean lies within plus or minus 1.96 sampling errors from the sample mean.

If a sample has been selected according to probability sampling principles, we know that we can be 95 per cent certain that the population mean will lie between the sample mean plus or minus 1.96 multiplied by the standard error of the mean. This is known as the *confidence interval*. If the mean number of training days in the previous twelve months in our sample of 450 employees is 6.7 and the standard error of the mean is 1.3, we can be 95 per cent certain that the population mean will lie between

$$6.7 + (1.96 \times 1.3)$$

and

$$6.7 - (1.96 \times 1.3),$$

i.e. between 9.248 and 4.152.

If the standard error was smaller, the range of possible values of the population mean would be narrower; if the standard error was larger, the range of possible values of the population mean would be wider.

If a stratified sample is selected, the standard error of the mean will be smaller; this is because the variation between strata is essentially eliminated, because the population will be accurately represented in the sample in terms of the stratification criterion or criteria employed. This consideration demonstrates the way in which stratification injects an extra increment of precision into the probability sampling process, since a possible source of sampling error is eliminated.

By contrast, a cluster sample without stratification exhibits a larger standard error of the mean than a

Figure 8.8

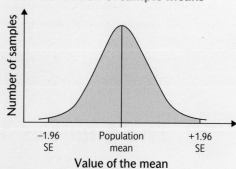

The distribution of sample means

Note: 95 per cent of sample means will lie within the shaded area. SE = standard error of the mean.

comparable simple random sample. This occurs because a possible source of variability between employees (that is, membership of one department rather than another, which may affect levels of training undertaken) is disregarded. If, for example, some departments have a culture of learning in which a large number of employees were involved, and if these departments were not selected because of the procedure for selecting clusters, an important source of variability would have been omitted. It also implies that the sample mean would be on the low side, but that is another matter.

Research in focus 8.4
Ensuring sampling equivalence in a cross-cultural validation study

The main purpose of research carried out by Brengman et al. (2005) was to validate cross-culturally a previously designed measurement instrument called the 'Internet shopper lifestyle' scale by conducting an online email survey of Internet shoppers in the United States and Belgium. The researchers claim that, although lifestyle studies are considered to be an interesting aspect of cross-cultural research, the cross-cultural validity of instruments 'remains to be demonstrated'. By replicating the study, they intended 'to test for cross-cultural differences in the basic meaning and structure of the Internet shopper lifestyle scale' (2005: 79).

The main focus of the sample design was therefore not to obtain a sample with the same cross-national socio-demographic characteristics, or to draw a sample that was representative of the population as a whole. Instead, their aim was to generate a sample that was representative of the relevant target population, which in this case was heads of household with home Internet and email connection. Therefore, in each country the sample was drawn in a very similar way. The American sample was obtained by email requests to participate in the survey sent to 20,000 representative users. In Belgium an invitation email requesting that recipients visit the site where the questionnaire was posted was sent to 11,500 Internet users; response rates were 11 per cent and 19 per cent, respectively. The authors explain, 'since the purpose of the current study is not to provide a cross-cultural segmentation but rather to validate a scale and to compare which segments can be detected in the United States and Belgium, the sample sizes in the United States and Belgium need not be proportionate to the respective population sizes' (2005: 81).

from equivalence sampling, which aims to ensure findings are equivalent between samples rather than representative of the population (see Research in focus 8.4). This is not to say that we treat the population data and the sample data as the same. If we take the example of the level of skill development in our sample of 450 employees, which we will treat as the number of training days completed in the previous twelve months, we will know that the mean number of training days undertaken by the sample (X) can be used to estimate the population mean (m) but with known margins of error. The mean, or more properly the **arithmetic mean**, is the simple average.

In order to address this point it is necessary to use some basic statistical ideas. These are presented in Tips and skills 'Generalizing from a random sample to the population' and can be skipped if just a broad idea of sampling procedures is required.

Sample size

One question about research methods that we are asked by students almost more than any other relates to the size of the sample: 'How large should my sample be?' or 'Is my sample large enough?' The decision about sample size is not a straightforward one: it depends on a number of considerations, and there is no one definitive answer. This is frequently a source of great disappointment to those who pose such questions. Moreover, most of the time decisions about sample size are affected by considerations of time and cost. Therefore, invariably decisions about sample size represent a compromise between the constraints of time and cost, the need for precision, and a variety of further considerations that will now be addressed.

Absolute and relative sample size

One of the most basic considerations, and one that is possibly the most surprising, is that, contrary to what you might have expected, it is the *absolute* size of a sample that is important, not its *relative* size. This means that a national probability sample of 1000 individuals in the UK has as much validity as a national probability sample of 1000 individuals in the USA, even though the latter has a much larger population. It also means that increasing the size of a sample increases the precision of a sample. This means that the 95 per cent confidence interval referred to in Tips and skills 'Generalizing from a random sample to the population' narrows. However, a large sample cannot *guarantee* precision, so that it is probably better to say that increasing the size of a sample increases the *likely* precision of a sample. This means that, as sample size increases, sampling error decreases. Therefore, an important component of any decision about sample size should be how much sampling error one is prepared to tolerate. The less sampling error one is prepared to tolerate, the larger a sample will need to be. Fowler (1993) warns against a simple acceptance of this criterion. He argues that in practice researchers do not base their decisions about sample size on a single estimate of a variable. Most survey research is concerned to generate a host of estimates—that is, of the variables that make up the research instrument that is administered. He also observes that it is not normal for survey researchers to be in a position to specify in advance 'a desired level of precision' (1993: 34). Moreover, since sampling error will be only one component of any error entailed in an estimate, the notion of using a desired level of precision as a factor in a decision about sample size is not realistic. Instead, to the extent that this notion does enter into decisions about sample size, it usually does so in a general rather than a calculated way.

Time and cost

Time and cost considerations become very relevant in this context. In the previous paragraph it is clearly being suggested that the larger the sample size, the greater the precision (because the amount of sampling error will be less). However, by and large up to a sample size of around 1000, the gains in precision are noticeable as the sample size climbs from low figures of 50, 100, 150, and so on upwards. After a certain point, often in the region of 1000,

Tips and skills
Sample size and probability sampling

As we have said in the text, the issue of sample size is the matter that most often concerns students and others. Basically, this is an area where size really does matter—the bigger the sample, the more representative it is likely to be (provided the sample is randomly selected), regardless of the size of the population from which it is drawn. However, when doing projects, students clearly need to do their research with very limited resources. You should try to find out from your department or business school if there are any guidelines about whether or not samples of a minimum size are expected. If there are no such guidelines, you will need to conduct your mini-survey in such a way as to maximize the number of interviews you can manage or the number of postal questionnaires you can send out, given the amount of time and resources available to you. Also, in many if not most cases, a truly random approach to sample selection may not be open to you. The crucial point is to be clear about and to justify what you have done. Explain the difficulties that you would have encountered in generating a random sample. Explain why you really could not include any more in your sample of respondents. But, above all, do not make claims about your sample that are not sustainable. Do not claim that it is representative or that you have a random sample when it is clearly not the case that either of these is true. In other words, be frank about what you have done. People will be much more inclined to accept an awareness of the limits of your sample design than claims about a sample that are patently false. Also, it may be that there are lots of good features about your sample—the range of people included, the good response rate, the high level of cooperation you received from the firm. Make sure you play up these positive features at the same time as being honest about its limitations.

the sharp increases in precision become less pronounced, and, although it does not plateau, there is a slowing-down in the extent to which precision increases (and hence the extent to which the sample error of the mean declines). Considerations of sampling size are likely to be profoundly affected by matters of time and cost at such a juncture, since striving for smaller and smaller increments of precision becomes an increasingly uneconomic proposition.

Non-response

However, considerations about sampling error do not end here. The problem of *non-response* should be borne in mind. Most sample surveys attract a certain amount of non-response. Thus, it is likely that only some of our sample will agree to participate in the research. If it is our aim to ensure as far as possible that 450 employees are interviewed and if we think that there may be a 20 per cent rate of non-response, it may be advisable to sample 540–550 individuals, on the grounds that approximately 90 will be non-respondents. For example, of the 143 survey questionnaires posted to companies in T. C. Powell's (1995) study of Total Quality Management, only 40 were returned and of these only 36 were usable, making a response rate of 25 per cent. This raises the question of whether or not this sample is significant enough to represent companies in the geographical area

of the north-eastern USA that the study claims to represent (see Chapter 10 for a further discussion of acceptable response rates). The issue of non-response, and in particular of refusal to participate, is of particular significance, because it has been suggested by some researchers that response rates (see Key concept 8.5) to surveys are declining in many countries. This implies that there is a growing tendency towards people refusing to participate in survey research. In 1973, an article in the American magazine *Business Week* carried an article ominously entitled 'The Public Clams up on Survey Takers'. The magazine asked survey companies about their experiences and found considerable concern about declining response rates. Similarly, in Britain, a report from a working party on the Market Research Society's Research and Development Committee in 1975 pointed to similar concerns among market research companies. However, an analysis of this issue by T. W. Smith (1995) suggests that, contrary to popular belief, there is no consistent evidence of such a decline. Moreover, Smith shows that it is difficult to disentangle general trends in response rates from such variables as the subject matter of the research, the type of respondent, and the level of effort expended on improving the number of respondents to individual surveys. The strategies that can improve responses to survey instruments such as structured interviews and postal questionnaires will be examined in Chapter 10.

Key concept 8.5
What is a response rate?

The notion of a response rate is a common one in social survey research. When a social survey is conducted, whether by structured interview or by self-completion questionnaire, it is invariably the case that some people who are in the sample refuse to participate. The response rate is, therefore, the percentage of a sample that does, in fact, agree to participate. However, the calculation of a response rate is a little more complicated than this. First, not everyone who replies will be included: if a large number of questions are not answered by a respondent, or if there are clear indications that he or she has not taken the interview or questionnaire seriously, it is better to employ only the number of *usable* interviews or questionnaires as the numerator. Similarly, it also tends to occur that not everyone in a sample turns out to be a suitable or appropriate respondent or can be contacted. Thus the response rate is calculated as follows:

$$\frac{\text{number of usable questionnaires}}{\text{total sample} - \text{unsuitable or uncontactable members of the sample}} \times 100$$

Heterogeneity of the population

Yet another consideration is the homogeneity and heterogeneity of the population from which the sample is to be taken. When a sample is very heterogeneous, such as a sample of a whole country or city, the population is likely to be highly varied. When it is relatively homogeneous, such as members of a company or of an occupation, the amount of variation is less. The implication of this is that, the greater the heterogeneity of a population, the larger a sample will need to be.

Kind of analysis

Finally, researchers should bear in mind the *kind of analysis* they intend to undertake. A case in point here is the **contingency table**. A contingency table shows the relationship between two variables in tabular form. It shows how variation in one variable relates to variation in another variable. To understand this point, consider our example of employee skill development and learning in the 100 largest UK companies. A contingency table would show how far the 5000 employees that comprise the sample vary in terms of skill and learning, measured in terms of training received during the previous twelve months. In addition, the table would need to reflect differences between companies that represent the seventeen main SIC code sections. However, it is unlikely that the initial criterion of selecting the 100 largest companies would enable all the SIC sections, such as education, community activities, or fishing, to be represented; therefore, some of the cells of the table would remain empty. In order to overcome this problem, the sample would have to be designed to reflect a much wider range of public and private organizational activity, perhaps by removing the criterion of size of company from the study. This would have a bearing on the number of employees who would be sampled from each company.

Types of non-probability sampling

The term *non-probability sampling* is essentially an umbrella term to capture all forms of sampling that are not conducted according to the canons of probability sampling outlined above. It is not surprising, therefore, that the term covers a wide range of types of sampling strategy, at least one of which—the **quota sample**—is claimed by some practitioners to be almost as good as a probability sample. Also covered under non-probability sampling is the practice of surveying one individual per organization, often a human resources manager or senior manager, in order to find out about the organization (see Thinking deeply 8.6). In this section we will also cover two main types of non-probability sample: the **convenience sample** and the quota sample.

Convenience sampling

A convenience sample is one that is simply available to the researcher by virtue of its accessibility. Imagine that a researcher who teaches at a university business school

Thinking deeply 8.6
Using a single respondent to represent an organization

It is fairly common practice in business and management survey research for one respondent, often a senior manager, to be asked to complete a questionnaire or to be interviewed about issues that are related to their organization or workplace. One of the advantages of gathering data from a single executive respondent is that it enables a larger number of organizations to be surveyed with a lower investment of time and resources than if multiple respondents were surveyed within each organization. However, it can also be argued that it is unwise to rely on a single respondent to know everything about the organization. In addition, if the respondent is a senior manager, he or she may also be inclined to represent organizational practices in a way that portrays his or her own role and responsibilities more favourably than other respondents in the organization would. It is therefore important to acknowledge the potential limitations associated with such a sampling strategy.

is interested in the way that managers deal with ethical issues when making business decisions. The researcher might administer a questionnaire to several classes of students, all of whom are managers taking a part-time MBA degree. The chances are that the researcher will receive all or almost all the questionnaires back, so that there will be a good response rate. The findings may prove quite interesting, but the problem with such a sampling strategy is that it is impossible to generalize the findings, because we do not know of what population this sample is representative. They are simply a group of managers who are available to the researcher. They are almost certainly not representative of managers as a whole—the very fact they are taking this degree programme marks them out as different from managers in general.

This is not to suggest that convenience samples should never be used. Let us say that our lecturer/researcher is developing a battery of questions that are designed to measure the ethical decision-making processes used by managers. It is highly desirable to pilot such a research instrument before using it in an investigation, and administering it to a group who are not a part of the main study may be a legitimate way of carrying out

some preliminary analysis of such issues as whether or not respondents tend to answer in identical ways to a question, or whether or not one question is often omitted when managers respond to it. In other words, for this kind of purpose, a convenience sample may be acceptable, though not ideal. A second kind of context in which it may be at least fairly acceptable to use a convenience sample is when the chance presents itself to gather data from a convenience sample and it represents too good an opportunity to miss. The data will not allow definitive findings to be generated, because of the problem of generalization, but they could provide a springboard for further research or allow links to be forged with existing findings in an area.

It also perhaps ought to be recognized that convenience sampling probably plays a more prominent role than is sometimes supposed. Certainly, in the field of business and management, convenience samples are very common and indeed are more prominent than are samples based on probability sampling (Bryman 1989*a*: 113–14), and in some areas such as consumer behaviour research they have become the norm. Research in focus 8.7 provides two examples of the use of

Research in focus 8.7
Convenience samples involving university students

It is relatively common for business researchers to make use of the opportunities they have to draw a sample from their own organization, usually a university, when carrying out research. The use of convenience samples reflects this, as the following two examples illustrate.

Hall, Workman, and Marchioro (1998) were interested in whether or not leadership perceptions are dependent on an individual's sex and behavioural flexibility, as well as the sex type of the group task. Their convenience sample comprised undergraduate and graduate students at the University of Akron, Oklahoma, where all three of the researchers were employed. More than 200 potential participants were pre-screened, and a sample of 112 was selected on the basis of their responses to a questionnaire that was designed to measure behavioural flexibility—that is, the extent to which individuals are able and willing to adapt their responses to fit their social context. This stratified sample of socially adaptable and socially inflexible participants was then subdivided into experimental groups of sixteen people made up of four four-person groups. Each four-person group consisted of two males and two females, one pair being adaptable and the other inflexible. High attendance at the experimental session was ensured by the fact that the students received course credit for their participation. The laboratory experiment involved two group tasks, each lasting around 20 minutes. The first was a manufacturing game, which the authors expected would be congruent with a masculine sex role; the second was a brainstorming task related to children's health, which the authors expected would be more gender-neutral. After completing the task, the participants rated the other group members according to their leadership impressions, on such questions as 'To what degree did this person fit your image of a leader?' Response options ranged from 5 = very much, to 1 = not at all, on a five-point Likert scale. The researchers claim that their use of student subjects instead of working

(continued)

adults was driven by their experimental research design, which 'would have been difficult, if not impossible to implement in an organizational setting' (1998: 27). That said, because their sample involved persons who had not worked together before, may not have known each other, and were not in paid employment, the ability of the research to detect the cumulative effects of disparity between the sexes on leader perceptions in an organizational setting is limited.

Lucas (1997) describes a study of university students that was undertaken to find out about the extent and kinds of part-time employment among students. Data were collected from students in five of the seven faculties at the university where she was a lecturer. Self-completion questionnaires were given out to students in the first, final, and either second or third years of their degrees (depending on whether the course lasted three or four years). The choice of subjects was designed to maximize the amount of variety in the type of degree programme and to provide similar numbers of males and females (since one gender frequently predominates in particular degree programmes). The questionnaire 'was issued, completed, and collected at the end of class contact time by one of the researchers, or by a member of teaching staff' (1997: 6001). These procedures represent a very good attempt to generate a varied sample. It is a convenience sample, because the choice of degree programmes was selected purposively rather than randomly and because absentees from classes were unable to complete the questionnaires. On the other hand, this meant there was a high rate of response among those students to whom the questionnaires were administered. An interesting question is whether or not absence from classes might be connected in some way to part-time working; in other words, might absence be due to students working at the time of the class or to students perhaps being too tired to go to the class because of their part-time work?

There is also an important difference between these two convenience samples that should be noticed. The first involves a convenience sample where the principal shared characteristic of the group—that is, that they are all university students—is in no way directly related to the subject of study, which is leadership perceptions. In other words, the convenience sample could as easily have been drawn from employees of a large corporation or members of a professional association if the researchers had found it convenient to draw their sample from this population. However, in the second, Lucas was studying the incidence of part-time employment among university students; therefore, her choice of convenience sample is directly related to her subject of study. This raises the issue of whether or not convenience samples can be used as the basis for generalization to a population that is wider than that to which the group belongs. In the case of the study of leadership, we cannot assume that the leadership perceptions of university students are representative of employees working in an organization. This is a limitation of convenience sampling.

convenience samples involving university students. The growing tendency across the social sciences to use university undergraduate students as a convenience sample, particularly in experimental research, has been criticised by Hooghe et al. (2010) who argue that this can endanger the validity and generalizability of findings because undergraduate students are likely to act differently from the general population. For instance, people from lower socio-economic groups are underrepresented in undergraduate student populations; students have more socio-economic resources; and students may be inclined to exert more cognitive effort in order to give the 'right' answer. Hooghe et al. therefore encourage researchers to systematically include non-student samples in laboratory experiments, even if this causes problems such as lower response rates.

Quota sampling

Quota sampling is used intensively in commercial research, such as market research and political opinion polling (see Thinking deeply 8.8). The aim of quota sampling is to produce a sample that reflects a population in terms of the relative proportions of people in different categories, such as gender, ethnicity, age groups, socio-economic groups, and region of residence, and in combinations of these categories. However, unlike a stratified sample, the sampling of individuals is not carried out randomly, since the final selection of people is left up to the interviewer. Information about the stratification of the UK population or about certain regions can be obtained from sources such as the census and from surveys based on probability samples such as the WERS (see Research in focus 3.14) or the UK Skills and Employment Survey (see Research in focus 8.3).

Once the categories and the number of people to be interviewed within each category (known as *quotas*) have been decided upon, it is then the job of interviewers to select people who fit these categories. The quotas will typically be interrelated. In a manner similar to stratified sampling, the population may be divided into strata in terms of, for example, gender, social class, age, and ethnicity. Census data might be used to identify the number of people who should be in each subgroup. The numbers to be interviewed in each subgroup will reflect the population. Each interviewer will probably seek out individuals who fit several subgroup quotas. Accordingly, an interviewer may know that among the various subgroups of people, he or she must find and interview five Asian, 25-to-34-year-old, lower-middle-class females in the area in which the interviewer has been asked to work (say, the Wirral). The interviewer usually asks people who are available to him or her about their characteristics (though gender will presumably be self-evident) in order to determine their suitability for a particular subgroup. Once a subgroup quota (or a combination of subgroup quotas) has been achieved, the interviewer will no longer be concerned to locate individuals for that subgroup.

The choice of respondents is left to the interviewer, subject to the requirement of all quotas being filled, usually within a certain time period. Those of you who have ever been approached on the street by a person toting a clipboard and interview schedule and have been asked about your age, occupation, and so on, before being asked a series of questions about a product or whatever, have almost certainly encountered an interviewer with a quota sample to fill. Sometimes, he or she will decide not to interview you because you do not meet the criteria required to fill a quota. This may be due to a quota already having been filled or to the criteria for exclusion meaning that a person with a certain characteristic that you possess is not required.

A number of criticisms are frequently levelled at quota samples.

- Because the choice of respondent is left to the interviewer, the proponents of probability sampling argue that a quota sample cannot be representative. It may accurately reflect the population in terms of superficial characteristics, as defined by the quotas. However, in their choice of people to approach, interviewers may be unduly influenced by their perceptions of how friendly people are or by whether the people make eye contact with the interviewer (unlike most of us, who look at the

ground and shuffle past as quickly as possible because we do not want to be bothered in our leisure time).

- People who are in an interviewer's vicinity at the times he or she conducts interviews, and are therefore available to be approached, may not be typical. There is a risk, for example, that people in full-time paid work may be under-represented and that those who are included in the sample are not typical.

- The interviewer is likely to make judgements about certain characteristics in deciding whether or not to approach a person, in particular, judgements about age. Those judgements will sometimes be incorrect—for example, when someone who is eligible to be interviewed, because a quota that he or she fits is unfilled, is not approached because the interviewer makes an incorrect judgement (perhaps that the person is older than he or she looks). In such a case, a possible element of bias is being introduced.

- It has also been argued that the widespread use of social class as a quota control can introduce difficulties, because of the problem of ensuring that interviewees are properly assigned to class groupings (Moser and Kalton 1971).

- It is not permissible to calculate a standard error of the mean from a quota sample, because the non-random method of selection makes it impossible to calculate the range of possible values of a population.

All of this makes the quota sample look a poor bet, and there is no doubt that it is not favoured by academic researchers. It does have some arguments in its favour, however.

- It is undoubtedly cheaper and quicker than an interview survey on a comparable probability sample. For example, interviewers do not have to spend a lot of time travelling between interviews.

- Interviewers do not have to keep calling back on people who were not available at the time they were first approached.

- Because calling back is not required, a quota sample is easier to manage. It is not necessary to keep track of people who need to be recontacted or to keep track of refusals. Refusals occur, of course, but it is not necessary (and indeed it is not possible) to keep a record of which respondents declined to participate.

- When speed is of the essence, a quota sample is invaluable when compared to the more cumbersome probability sample. Newspapers frequently need to know how a national sample of voters feel about a certain

Thinking deeply 8.8
Using quota sampling in telephone market research

H. Taylor (1997) conducted a questionnaire survey of the methods used by eighty-three leading marketing research firms in seventeen countries, which revealed great variation in the way that they understood the notion of sampling within public opinion surveys using telephone interviewing (see Chapter 9). Firms are divided according to whether they are committed to probability or quota sampling; 40 per cent of firms described their methods as quota sampling. 'In many so-called quota samples, telephone numbers are selected on some kind of random basis, and individual respondents at those numbers are interviewed if they fit in the quotas' (1997: 424). However, the distinction between probability and quota sampling is unclear within many firms, virtually all of which use some form of quota sampling, by region, sex, gender, or age, and in telephone surveys almost all firms use some form of quota to accept or reject some individual respondents. Taylor concludes that concepts of probability and quota sampling 'seem to be loosely defined in the minds of many researchers; this suggests the need for a better and common research language for use worldwide, with unambiguous definitions' (1997: 432).

topic or how they intend to vote at that time. Alternatively, if there is a sudden major news event, such as the terrorist attacks on the World Trade Center in New York, the news media may seek a more or less instant picture of the nation's views or responses. Again, a quota sample will be much faster.

- As with convenience sampling, it is useful for conducting development work on new measures or on research instruments. It can also be usefully employed in relation to exploratory work from which new theoretical ideas might be generated.

- Although the standard error of the mean should not be computed for a quota sample, it frequently is. As Moser and Kalton (1971) observe, some writers argue that the use of a non-random method in quota sampling should not act as a barrier to such a computation because its significance as a source of error is small when compared to other errors that may arise in surveys (see Figure 8.9). However, they go on to argue that at least with random sampling the researcher can calculate the amount of sampling error and does not have to be concerned about its potential impact.

Figure 8.9

Four sources of error in social survey research

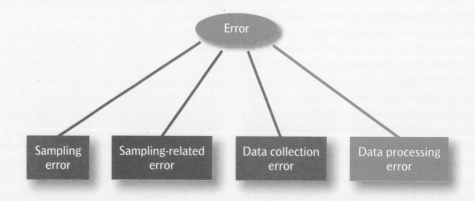

There is some evidence to suggest that, when compared to random samples, quota samples often result in biases. They under-represent people in lower social strata, people who work in the private sector and manufacturing, and people at the extremes of income, and they over-represent women in households with children and people from larger households (Marsh and Scarbrough 1990; Butcher 1994). On the other hand, it has to be acknowledged that probability samples are often biased too.

Limits to generalization

One point that is often not fully appreciated is that even when a sample has been selected using probability sampling, any findings can be generalized only to the population from which that sample was taken. This is an obvious point, but it is easy to think that findings from a study have some kind of broader applicability. If we take our imaginary study of training and skill development among employees of a company, any findings could be generalized only to that company. In other words, you should be very cautious about generalizing to employees at other companies. There are many factors that may imply that the level of training and skill development is higher (or lower) than among company employees as a whole. There may be a higher (or lower) level of skill required in order to do the jobs that the company requires its employees to do, there may be more (or less) money in the company's training budget, there may be more (or less) of a culture of learning at this company, or the company may recruit a higher (or lower) proportion of employees who are already skilled. There may be many other factors too.

Similarly, we should be cautious of overgeneralizing in terms of locality. Hence a frequent criticism made in relation to research on employee motivation relates to the extent to which it can be assumed to be generalizable beyond the confines of the national culture on which the study is based. For example, Herzberg, Mausner, and Snyderman (1959) conducted semi-structured interviews with 203 accountants and engineers in the Pittsburgh area in the USA. Most of the companies that constituted sites for the study were involved in heavy industry, such as steel making or shipbuilding. The population from which the sample was selected consisted of all accountants and engineers who worked for these companies. Respondents were chosen randomly according to certain criteria for stratification, including age, job title, level in the company, and length of service. It is interesting that there is no mention of gender in the study, although we can fairly safely assume that, given that this was a study of accountants and engineers in the late 1950s, there is likely to be a male bias to the study. The maximum number of individuals selected for interview in each company was approximately 50. As the authors acknowledge, 'the fact that this work was done within a thirty-mile radius around Pittsburgh will inevitably raise questions about the degree to which the findings are applicable in other areas of the country' (1959: 31). The findings may also reflect the values of high individualism, self-interest, and high masculinity that have been identified as characteristic of American culture (Hofstede 1984). This is part of the reason there have been so many attempts to replicate the study on other occupational groups and in other localities, including different cultures and nationalities.

However, there could even be a further limit to generalization that is implied by the Herzberg et al. sample. The main study was conducted in the late 1950s. One issue that is rarely discussed in this context, and that is almost impossible to assess, is whether or not there is a time limit on the findings that are generated. Quite aside from the fact that we need to appreciate that the findings cannot (or at least should not) be generalized beyond the Pittsburgh area, is there a point at which we have to say, 'Well, those findings applied to the Pittsburgh area then but things have changed and we can no longer assume that they apply to that or any other locality?' We are, after all, used to thinking that things have changed when there has been some kind of prominent change. To take a simple example: no one would be prepared to assume that the findings of a study in 1980 of UK university students' budgeting and personal finance habits would apply to students in the early twenty-first century. Quite aside from changes that might have occurred naturally, the erosion and virtual dismantling of the student grant system in the UK has changed the ways students finance their education, including perhaps a greater reliance on part-time work (Lucas 1997), a greater reliance on parents, and use of loans. But, even when there is no definable or recognizable source of relevant change of this kind, there is nonetheless the possibility (or even likelihood) that findings are temporally specific. Such an issue is impossible to resolve without further research (Bryman 1989b).

Error in survey research

We can think of 'error', a term that has been employed on a number of occasions, as being made up of four main factors (see Figure 8.9).

- *Sampling error*. See Key concept 8.1 for a definition. This kind of error arises because it is extremely unlikely that one will end up with a truly representative sample, even when probability sampling is employed.

- We can distinguish what might be thought of as *sampling-related error*. This is error that is subsumed under the category *non-sampling error* (see Key concept 8.1) but that arises from activities or events that are related to the sampling process and are connected with the issue of generalizability or external validity of findings. Examples are an inaccurate sampling frame and non-response.

- There is also error that is connected with the implementation of the research process. We might call this

data collection error. This source of error includes such factors as: poor question wording in self-completion questionnaires or structured interviews; poor interviewing techniques; and flaws in the administration of research instruments.

- Finally, there is *data processing error*. This arises from faulty management of data, in particular errors in the *coding* of answers.

The third and fourth sources of error relate to factors that are not associated with sampling and instead relate much more closely to concerns about the validity of measurement, which was addressed in Chapter 7. An example of the way that non-response can impact upon the external validity and generalizability of findings is shown in Research in focus 8.9. The kinds of steps that need to be taken to keep these sources of error to a minimum in the context of social survey research will be addressed in the next three chapters.

Research in focus 8.9
Sources of sampling and non-sampling error in a survey of the effects of privatization

In a study of the effects of privatization on corporate culture and employee well-being, Cunha and Cooper (2002) describe, first, the difficulties they experienced in obtaining access to companies in Portugal that were going through privatization and, secondly, the impact of a high non-response rate on their research design. Commenting on the first issue, the authors explain, 'we faced a very strong resistance on the part of top management of the companies we contacted, which is understandable considering the "sensitive" [*sic*] political and human resource decisions that were being taken' (2002: 27). In relation to the second point, samples were selected by the human resource managers, forming the basis for the questionnaire survey, which was sent directly by the researchers to the employees' home address. The three companies are listed below, with the associated samples and non-response rates.

- The first was a cement company. It had approximately 2500 employees and a stratified sample of 750 employees was chosen, in managerial, technical/professional, clerical, and manual jobs; 133 valid responses were obtained (18 per cent response rate).

- The second was a smaller cement company. From a population of 500 a stratified sample of 125 employees was chosen, but no manual workers were included in the sample owing to the low literacy levels among workers. Thirty-five valid responses were received (28 per cent response rate). By occupational level this sample consisted of 22 managers, 11 technical/professional, and 2 clerical employees.

- The third was a paper pulp company with 2800 employees. A stratified sample of 1244 employees was chosen. In this case a longitudinal element was built into the survey—questionnaires were sent in 1994 (before partial privatization) and again in 1996 (after partial privatization). However, the number of employees who responded to both these surveys was quite small ($n = 545$), so the researchers had to select different kinds of sample that focused on subgroups that were involved in privatization.

This study raises a number of questions in relation to possible sources of sampling error. The fact that samples were chosen by the human resources manager in the company means that they were non-random and thus may have reflected a bias on the part of the individual who was making these choices. The researchers' original aim—to conduct a longitudinal analysis based on surveying employees before and after privatization—had to be modified owing to insufficient access. This meant that the researchers were limited in the extent to which they were able to suggest that changes in corporate culture were caused by privatization.

A further possible source of bias associated with the sampling frame related to the exclusion of manual workers from the survey in the second company, owing to their low levels of literacy. However, it is worth noting that this problem could potentially have been overcome through the use of a **structured interview** approach instead of a **self-completion questionnaire**. In addition, we can see from the profile of responses in this company (22 managers, 11 technical/professional, and 2 clerical employees) that this sample consists of significantly more managers than other kinds of employees. It is, therefore, extremely likely that the sample does not reflect the actual population. Finally, the high non-response rate in the third company introduced a further source of sample bias (this forced the researchers to find other ways of breaking down the sample in ways that were more statistically meaningful).

The example shows how various sources of sampling and non-sampling error are sometimes closely interrelated. In particular, it illustrates how non-response rates and sampling frames can be affected by the sensitivity of the issue that is being investigated and the consequent willingness or reluctance of companies and employees to participate in the research.

Key points

- Probability sampling is a mechanism for reducing bias in the selection of samples.
- Ensure you become familiar with key technical terms in the literature on sampling such as: representative sample; random sample; non-response; population; sampling error; etc.
- Randomly selected samples are important because they permit generalizations to the population and because they have certain known qualities.
- Sampling error decreases as sample size increases.
- Quota samples can provide reasonable alternatives to random samples, but they suffer from some deficiencies.
- Convenience samples may provide interesting data, but it is crucial to be aware of their limitations in terms of generalizability.
- Sampling and sampling-related error are just two sources of error in social survey research.

Questions for review

- What does each of the following terms mean: population; probability sampling; non-probability sampling; sampling frame; representative sample; and sampling and non-sampling error?
- What are the goals of sampling?
- What are the main areas of potential bias in sampling?

Sampling error

- What is the significance of sampling error for achieving a representative sample?

Types of probability sample

- What is probability sampling and why is it important?

- What are the main types of probability sample?

- How far does a stratified random sample offer greater precision than a simple random or systematic sample?

- If you were conducting an interview survey of around 500 people in Manchester, what type of probability sample would you choose and why?

- A researcher positions herself on a street corner and asks one person in five who walks by to be interviewed: she continues doing this until she has a sample of 250. How likely is she to achieve a representative sample?

The qualities of a probability sample

- A researcher is interested in levels of job satisfaction among manual workers in a firm that is undergoing change. The firm has 1200 manual workers. The researcher selects a simple random sample of 10 per cent of the population. He measures job satisfaction on a Likert scale comprising ten items. A high level of satisfaction is scored 5 and a low level is scored 1. The mean job satisfaction score is 34.3. The standard error of the mean is 8.57. What is the 95 per cent confidence interval?

Sample size

- What factors would you take into account in deciding how large your sample should be when devising a probability sample?

- What is non-response and why is it important to the question of whether or not you will end up with a representative sample?

Types of non-probability sampling

- Are non-probability samples useless?

- 'Quota samples are not true random samples, but in terms of generating a representative sample there is little difference between them, and this accounts for their widespread use in market research and opinion polling.' Discuss.

Limits to generalization

- 'The problem of generalization to a population is not just to do with the matter of getting a representative sample.' Discuss.

Error in survey research

- 'Non-sampling error, as its name implies, is concerned with sources of error that are not part of the sampling process.' Discuss.

Online Resource Centre

www.oxfordtextbooks.co.uk/orc/brymanbrm4e/

Visit the Interactive Research Guide that accompanies this book to complete an exercise in Sampling.

9

Structured interviewing

Chapter outline

Once sampling issues have been taken into consideration, the next stage of the survey research process (see Figure 8.1) involves considering whether to administer the questionnaire face to face or to rely on self-completion. This chapter deals with the first option, the structured interview, while Chapter 10 addresses issues relating to self-completion. A further option to consider is whether to administer the questionnaire by email or by using the Web; this possibility will be covered in Chapter 28.

The structured interview is one of a variety of forms of research interview, but it is the one that is most commonly employed in survey research. The goal of the structured interview is for the interviewing of respondents to be standardized so that differences between interviews in any research project are minimized. As a result, there are many guidelines about how structured interviewing should be carried out so that variation in the conduct of interviews is small. This chapter explores:

- the reasons why the structured interview is a prominent research method in survey research; this issue entails a consideration of the importance of standardization to the process of measurement;

- the different contexts of interviewing, such as the use of more than one interviewer and whether the administration of the interview is in person or by telephone;

- various prerequisites of structured interviewing, including establishing rapport with the interviewee; asking questions as they appear on the interview schedule; recording exactly what is said by interviewees; ensuring there are clear instructions on the interview schedule concerning question sequencing and the recording of answers; and keeping to the question order as it appears on the schedule;

- problems with structured interviewing, including the influence of the interviewer on respondents and the possibility of systematic bias in answers (known as *response sets*). The feminist critique of the structured interview, which raises a distinctive cluster of problems with the method, is also examined.

Introduction

The interview is a common occurrence in social life, because there are many different forms of interview. There are job interviews, media interviews, social work interviews, police interviews, appraisal interviews. And then there are research interviews, which represent the kind of interview that will be covered in this and other chapters (such as Chapters 20 and 21). These different kinds of interview share some common features, such as the eliciting of information by the interviewer from the interviewee and the operation of rules of varying degrees of formality or explicitness concerning the conduct of the interview.

In the business research interview, the aim is for the interviewer to elicit from the interviewee or *respondent*, as he or she is frequently called in survey research, all manner of information: interviewees' own behaviour or that of others, attitudes, norms, beliefs, and values. There are many different types or styles of research interview, but the kind that is primarily employed in survey research is the structured interview, which is the focus of this chapter. Other kinds of interview will be briefly mentioned in this chapter but will be discussed in greater detail in later chapters.

The structured interview

The research interview is a prominent data collection strategy in both quantitative and qualitative research. The social survey is probably the chief context within which business researchers employ the structured interview (see Key concept 9.1) in connection with quantitative research, and it is this form of the interview that will be emphasized in this chapter. The reason why survey researchers typically prefer this kind of interview is that it promotes standardization of *both* the asking of questions *and* the recording of answers. This feature has two closely related virtues from the perspective of quantitative research.

Reducing error due to interviewer variability

The standardization of both the asking of questions and the recording of answers means that, if the interview is properly executed, variation in people's replies will be due to 'true' or 'real' variation and not due to the interview context. To take a simple illustration, when we ask a question that is supposed to be an indicator of a concept, we want to keep error to a minimum, an issue that was touched on at the end of Chapter 8. We can think of the answers to a question as constituting the values that a variable takes. These values, of course, exhibit variation. This could be the question on skill development and training among employees that was a focus of Chapter 8 at certain points. Employees will vary in the number of training days they receive (see Figure 9.1). However, some respondents may be inaccurately classified in terms of the variable. There are a number of possible reasons for this.

Most variables will contain an element of error, so that it is helpful to think of variation as made up of two components: true variation and error. In other words:

$$\text{variation} = \text{true variation} + \text{variation due to error}.$$

The aim is to keep the error component to a minimum (see Figure 9.2), since error has an adverse effect on the validity of a measure. If the error component is quite high (see Figure 9.3), validity will be jeopardized. The significance for error of standardization in the structured interview is that two sources of variation due to error—the second and fifth in Tips and skills 'Common sources of error in survey research'—are likely to be less pronounced, since the opportunity for variation in interviewer behaviour in these two areas (asking questions and recording answers) is reduced.

The significance of standardization and of thereby reducing interviewer variability is this: assuming that there is no problem with an interview question owing to such things as confusing terms or ambiguity (an issue that will be examined in Chapter 11), we want to be able to say as far as possible that the variation that we find is

Figure 9.1

A variable

Variation

Key concept 9.1
What is a structured interview?

A structured interview, sometimes called a *standardized interview*, entails the administration of an interview schedule by an interviewer. The aim is for all interviewees to be given exactly the same context of questioning. This means that each respondent receives exactly the same interview stimulus as any other. The goal of this style of interviewing is to ensure that interviewees' replies can be aggregated, and this can be achieved reliably only if those replies are in response to identical cues. Interviewers are supposed to read out questions exactly and in the same order as they are printed on the schedule. Questions are usually very specific and very often offer the interviewee a fixed range of answers (this type of question is often called *closed, closed ended, pre-coded,* or *fixed choice*). The structured interview is the typical form of interview in social survey research.

Figure 9.2

A variable with little error

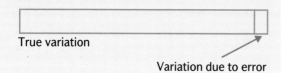

Figure 9.3

A variable with considerable error

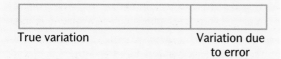

connected with true variation between interviewees and not to variation in the way a question was asked or the answers recorded in the course of the administration of a survey by structured interview. Variability can occur in either of two ways: first, *intra-interviewer variability*, whereby an interviewer is not consistent in the way he or she asks questions and/or records answers; secondly, when there is more than one interviewer, there may be *inter-interviewer variability*, whereby interviewers are not consistent with each other in the ways they ask questions and/or record answers. Needless to say, these two sources of variability are not mutually exclusive; they can coexist, compounding the problem even further. In view of the significance of standardization, it is hardly

surprising that some writers prefer to call the structured interview a *standardized interview* (e.g. Oppenheim 1992) or *standardized survey interview* (e.g. Fowler and Mangione 1990).

Accuracy and ease of data processing

Like self-completion questionnaires, most structured interviews contain mainly questions that are variously referred to as *closed*, *closed ended*, *pre-coded*, or *fixed choice*. This issue will be covered in detail in Chapter 11. However, this type of question has considerable relevance to the current discussion. With the **closed question**, the respondent is given a limited choice of possible answers. In other words, the interviewer provides respondents with two or more possible answers and asks them to select which one or ones apply. Ideally, this procedure will simply entail the interviewer placing a tick in a box by the answer(s) selected by a respondent or circling the selected answer or using a similar procedure. The advantage of this practice is that the potential for interviewer variability is reduced: there is no problem of whether the interviewer writes down everything that the respondent says or of misinterpretation of the reply given. If an *open* or *open-ended* question is asked, the interviewer may not write down everything said, may embellish what is said, or may misinterpret what is said.

However, the advantages of the closed question in the context of survey research go further than this, as we will see in Chapter 11. One advantage that is particularly significant in the context of the present discussion is that closed questions greatly facilitate the processing of data. When an **open question** is asked, the answers need to be sifted and *coded* in order for the data to be analysed quantitatively. Not only is this a laborious procedure, particularly if there is a large number of open questions

Tips and skills
Common sources of error in survey research

There are many sources of error in survey research, in addition to those associated with sampling. This is a list of the principal sources of error:

1. a poorly worded question;
2. the way the question is asked by the interviewer;
3. misunderstanding on the part of the interviewee;
4. memory problems on the part of the interviewee;
5. the way the information is recorded by the interviewer;
6. the way the information is processed, either when answers are coded or when data are entered into the computer.

and/or of respondents; it also introduces the potential for another source of error, which is the sixth in Tips and skills 'Common sources of error in survey research': it is quite likely that error will be introduced as a result of variability in the coding of answers. When open questions are asked, the interviewer is supposed to write down as much of what is said as possible. Answers can, therefore, be in the form of several sentences. These answers have to be examined and then categorized, so that each person's answer can be aggregated with other respondents' answers to a certain question. A number will then be allocated to each category of answer so that the answers can then be entered into a computer database and analysed quantitatively. This general process is known as coding, and will be examined in greater detail in Chapter 11.

Coding introduces yet another source of error. First, if the rules for assigning answers to categories, collectively known as the **coding frame**, are flawed, the variation that is observed will not reflect the true variation in interviewees' replies. Secondly, there may be variability in the ways in which answers are categorized. As with interviewing, there can be two sources: *intra-coder variability*, whereby the coder varies over time in the way in which the rules for assigning answers to categories are implemented; and *inter-coder variability*, whereby coders differ from each other in the way in which the rules for assigning answers to categories are implemented. If either (or both) source(s) of variability occur, at least part of the variation in interviewees' replies will not reflect true variation and instead will be caused by error.

The closed question sidesteps this problem neatly, because respondents allocate *themselves* to categories. The coding process is then a simple matter of attaching a different number to each category of answer and of entering the numbers into a computer database. It is not surprising, therefore, that this type of question is often referred to as pre-coded, because decisions about the coding of answers are typically undertaken as part of the design of the schedule—that is, before any respondents

have actually been asked questions. There is very little opportunity for interviewers or coders to vary in the recording or the coding of answers. Of course, if some respondents misunderstand any terms in the alternative answers with which they are presented, or if the answers do not adequately cover the appropriate range of possibilities, the question will not provide a valid measure. However, that is a separate issue and one to which we will return in Chapter 11. The chief point to register about closed questions for the moment is that, when compared to open questions, they reduce one potential source of error *and* are much easier to process for quantitative data analysis.

Other types of interview

The structured interview is by no means the only type of interview, but it is certainly the main type that is likely to be encountered in survey research and in quantitative research generally. Unfortunately, a host of different terms have been employed by writers on research methodology to distinguish the diverse forms of research interview. Key concept 9.2 represents an attempt to capture some of the major terms and types.

All of the forms of interview outlined in Key concept 9.2, with the exception of the *structured interview* and the *standardized interview*, are primarily used in connection with qualitative research, and it is in that context that they will be encountered again later in this book. They are rarely used in connection with quantitative research, and survey research in particular, because the absence of standardization in the asking of questions and recording of answers makes respondents' replies difficult to aggregate and to process. This is not to say that they have no role at all. For example, as we will see in Chapter 11, the **unstructured interview** can have a useful role in relation to developing the fixed-choice alternatives with which respondents are provided in the kind of closed question that is typical of the structured interview.

Key concept 9.2
Major types of interview

- *Structured interview*; see Key concept 9.1.

- *Standardized interview*; see Key concept 9.1.

- **Semi-structured interview**. This is a term that covers a wide range of instances. It typically refers to a context in which the interviewer has a series of questions that are in the general form of an interview schedule but is able to vary the sequence of questions. The questions are frequently somewhat more general in their frame of reference than that typically found in a structured interview schedule. Also, the interviewer usually has some latitude to ask further questions in response to what are seen as significant replies.

(continued)

- *Unstructured interview*. The interviewer typically has only a list of topics or issues, often called an **interview guide** or *aide-mémoire*, that are covered. The style of questioning is usually informal. The phrasing and sequencing of questions will vary from interview to interview.

- *Intensive interview*. This term is employed by Lofland and Lofland (1995) as an alternative term to the *unstructured interview*. Spradley (1979) uses the term *ethnographic interview* to describe a form of interview that is also more or less synonymous with the *unstructured interview*.

- *Qualitative interview*. For some writers, this term seems to denote an *unstructured interview* (e.g. Mason 1996), but more frequently it is a general term that embraces interviews of both the semi-structured and unstructured kind (e.g. Rubin and Rubin 1995).

- *In-depth interview*. Like the term *qualitative interview*, this one sometimes refers to an *unstructured interview* but more often refers to both semi-structured and unstructured interviewing.

- *Focused interview*. This is a term devised by Merton, Fiske, and Kendall (1956) to refer to an interview using predominantly open questions to ask interviewees questions about a specific situation or event that is relevant to them and of interest to the researcher.

- *Focus group*. This is the same as the *focused interview*, but interviewees discuss the specific issue in groups. See Key concept 21.1 for a more detailed definition.

- *Group interview*. Some writers see this term as synonymous with the *focus group*, but a distinction may be made between the latter and a situation in which members of a group discuss a variety of matters that may be only partially related.

- **Oral history interview**. This is an *unstructured* or *semi-structured interview* in which the respondent is asked to recall events from his or her past and to reflect on them (see also Key concept 22.4). There is usually a cluster of fairly specific research concerns to do with a particular epoch or event, so there is some resemblance to a focused interview.

- **Life history interview**. This is similar to the *oral history interview*, but the aim of this type of *unstructured interview* is to glean information on the entire biography of each respondent (see also Key concept 22.4).

Interview contexts

In an archetypal interview, an interviewer stands or sits in front of the respondent, asking the latter a series of questions and writing down the answers. However, there are several possible departures from it, although this archetype is the most usual context for an interview.

More than one interviewee

In the case of group interviews or focus groups, there is more than one, and usually quite a few more than one, respondent or interviewee. Nor is this the only context in which more than one person is interviewed. Bell, Taylor, and Thorpe (2001) carried out interviews with two managers in the same company, both of whom had been involved in the implementation of the people-management initiative Investors in People. The managers, who had often had different roles in relation to the initiative or been involved with it at different stages of its development, were together able to build a chronological understanding of its implementation. Similarly, in Bryman's research on visitors to Disney theme parks, not just couples but often their children took part in the interview as well (Bryman 1999). However, it is very unusual for structured interviews to be used in connection with this kind of questioning. In survey research, it is almost always a specific individual who is the object of questioning. Indeed, in survey interviews it is very advisable to discourage as far as possible the presence and intrusion of others during the course of the interview. Investigations in which more than one person is being interviewed tend to be exercises in qualitative research, though this is not always the case.

More than one interviewer

This is a relatively unusual situation in business research, because of the considerable cost that is involved in dispatching two (or indeed more than two) people to interview someone. Bechhofer, Elliott, and McCrone (1984) (see Chapter 20) describe research in which two people interviewed individuals in a wide range of occupations. However, while their approach achieved a number of benefits for them, their interviewing style was of the unstructured kind that is typically employed in qualitative research, and they argue that the presence of a second interviewer is unlikely to achieve any added value in the context of structured interviewing.

In person or by telephone?

A third way in which the archetype may not be realized is that interviews may be conducted by telephone rather than face to face. While telephone interviewing is quite common in such fields as market research, it is less common in business research. In market research opinion has shifted in recent years away from the perception that face-to-face surveys are more representative than telephone surveys, towards thinking that telephone surveys are either more or at least as representative as face-to-face surveys. This is noteworthy, since, as H. Taylor (1997: 429) notes, 'it is not very long since telephone surveys were regarded as a cheap and dirty substitute for face-to-face interviewing by many survey firms'. See Research in focus 9.3 for an example of the use of telephone interviewing.

There are several advantages of telephone over personal interviews.

- On a like-for-like basis, they are far cheaper and also quicker to administer. This arises because, for personal interviews, interviewers have to spend a great deal of time and money travelling between respondents. This factor will be even more pronounced when a sample is geographically dispersed, a problem that is only partially mitigated for in personal interview surveys by strategies such as cluster sampling. Of course, telephone interviews take time, and hired interviewers have to be paid, but the cost of conducting a telephone interview will still be lower than a comparable personal one.

- The telephone interview is easier to supervise than the personal interview. This is a particular advantage when there are several interviewers, since it becomes easier to check on interviewers' transgressions in the asking of questions, such as rephrasing questions or the inappropriate use of probes by the interviewer. Probes are stimuli introduced by the interviewer to elicit further information from the interviewee when the latter's response is inadequate either because it fails to answer the question or because it answers the question but there is insufficient detail.

- Telephone interviewing has a further advantage that is to do with evidence (which is not as clear-cut as one might want) that suggests that, in personal interviews, respondents' replies are sometimes affected by characteristics of the interviewer (for example, class or ethnicity) and indeed by his or her mere presence (implying that the interviewees may reply in ways they feel will be deemed desirable by interviewers). The remoteness of the interviewer in telephone interviewing removes this potential source of bias to a significant extent. The interviewer's personal characteristics cannot be seen and the fact that he or she is not physically present may offset the likelihood of respondents' answers being affected by the interviewer.

Research in focus 9.3
A telephone survey of dignity at work

Berg and Frost (2005) used results from a telephone survey of over 500 low-skill, low-wage workers in hospitals in the USA in order to explore the features that affect workers' perceptions of dignity at work. They also wanted to find out if union representation and/or changes in worker representation influenced workers' perceptions of dignity at work. The researchers identified three main dimensions to the concept of dignity at work: fair treatment, intrinsically satisfying work, and economic security. The kinds of jobs that their sample were engaged in included food service, housekeepers, and nursing assistants doing tasks that the authors describe as 'dead end jobs with

(continued)

little or no chance of upward mobility' (2005: 663). They observe that workers who do these jobs typically earn only the minimum wage and there tends to be a high level of annual turnover, between 50 and 100 per cent.

The data came from a sample of fifteen community hospitals from across the United States, focusing on the most representative group, hospitals with between 200 and 400 beds. The researchers chose telephone interviewing because of the 'inherent instability in the lives of this sector of the workforce' (2005: 669). This method was seen as being one way of reliably reaching the workers. The researchers carried out telephone interviews with 589 workers, asking them about all aspects of their jobs and careers. Telephone numbers were obtained from employers. However, there were a number of difficulties associated with the telephone interview method that stemmed from the nature of the population in which the research was interested. 'Many of the phone numbers we secured from employers were simply no good: the phone service had been disconnected; the person no longer lived at that phone number; or the respondent would not answer the telephone' (2005: 669). One of the reasons why the phone call was not answered was because respondents had call display. If they did not recognize the number, they would not pick up the phone, because they were trying to avoid debt collection agents. These difficulties adversely affected the response rate, which ended up at 45 per cent. The researchers conclude that the people they were able to survey probably represent the most stable part of this population, so the results are likely to overstate the positive aspects associated with these jobs: 'those whose work lives keep them living in a precarious fashion are likely those not responding to our telephone survey' (2005: 669).

Telephone interviewing suffers from certain limitations when compared to the personal interview.

- People who do not own or who are not contactable by telephone obviously cannot be interviewed by telephone. In business research, this characteristic is most likely to be a feature of lower-status employees and, therefore, the potential for sampling bias exists. Lower-income households are more likely not to own a telephone; also, many people choose to be ex-directory—that is, they have taken action for their telephone numbers not to appear in a telephone directory. Again, these people cannot be interviewed by telephone. One possible solution to this last difficulty is *random digit dialling*. With this technique, the computer randomly selects telephone numbers within a predefined geographical area. Not only is this a random process that conforms to the rules about probability sampling examined in Chapter 8; it also stands a chance of getting at ex-directory households, though it cannot, of course, gain access to those without a telephone at all.

- The length of a telephone interview is unlikely to be sustainable beyond 20–25 minutes, whereas personal interviews can be much longer than this (Frey 2004).

- The question of whether response rates (see Key concept 8.5) are lower with surveys by telephone interview than with surveys by personal interview is unclear, in that there is little consistent evidence on this question. However, there is a general belief that telephone interviews achieve slightly lower rates than personal interviews (Frey and Oishi 1995; Shuy 2002; Frey 2004) (see Table 28.1).

- There is some evidence to suggest that telephone interviews fare less well for the asking of questions about sensitive issues, such as workplace bullying or drug and alcohol use. However, the evidence is not entirely consistent on this point, though it is probably sufficient to suggest that, when many questions of this kind are to be used, a personal interview may be superior (Shuy 2002).

- Developments in telephone communications, such as answerphones, other forms of call screening, and mobile phones, have almost certainly had an adverse effect on telephone surveys in terms of response rates and the general difficulty of getting access to respondents through conventional landlines. Households that rely exclusively on mobile phones represent a particular difficulty.

- Telephone interviewers cannot engage in observation. This means that they are not in a position to respond to signs of puzzlement or unease on the faces of respondents when they are asked a question. In a personal interview, the interviewer may respond to such signs by restating the question or attempting to clarify the meaning of the question, though this has to be handled in a standardized way as far as possible. A further issue relating to the inability of the interviewer to observe is that, sometimes, interviewers may be asked to collect subsidiary information in connection with their visits (for example, whether or not health and safety procedures are made evident at a business premises). Such information cannot be collected when telephone interviews are employed.

- It is frequently the case that specific individuals in households or firms are the targets of an interview. In other words, simply anybody will not do. This requirement is likely to arise from the specifications of the population to be sampled, which means that people in a certain role or position or with particular characteristics are to be interviewed. It is probably more difficult to ascertain by telephone interview whether or not the correct person is replying.

- The telephone interviewer cannot readily employ visual aids such as show cards (see Tips and skills 'A show card' and Tips and skills 'Another show card') from which respondents might be asked to select their replies, or use diagrams or photographs.

- There is some evidence to suggest that the quality of data derived from telephone interviews is inferior to that of comparable face-to-face interviews. A series of experiments reported by Holbrook, Green, and Krosnick (2003) on the mode of survey administration in the USA using long questionnaires found that respondents interviewed by telephone were more likely to express no opinion or 'don't know' (see Chapter 11 for more on this issue); to answer in the same way to a series of linked questions; to express socially desirable answers; to be apprehensive about the interview; and to be more likely to be dissatisfied with the time taken by the interview (even though interviews were invariably shorter than in the face-to-face mode). Also, telephone interviewees tended to be less engaged with the interview process. While these results should be viewed with caution, since studies like these are bound to be affected by such factors as the use of a large questionnaire on a national sample, they do provide interesting food for thought.

Computer-assisted interviewing

In recent years, increasing use has been made of computers in the interviewing process, especially in commercial survey research of the kind conducted by market research and opinion polling organizations. There are two main formats for computer-assisted interviewing: computer-assisted personal interviewing (CAPI) and computer-assisted telephone interviewing (CATI). A very large percentage of telephone interviews are conducted with the aid of computers. Among commercial survey organizations, almost all telephone interviewing

is of the CATI kind, and this kind of interview has become one of the most popular formats for such firms. The main reasons for the growing use of CAPI has been that the increased portability and affordability of laptop computers, and the growth in the number and quality of software packages that provide a platform for devising interview schedules, provide greater opportunity for them to be used in connection with face-to-face interviews.

With computer-assisted interviewing, the questions that comprise an interview schedule appear on the screen. As interviewers ask each question, they input the appropriate reply and proceed to the next question. This process has the great advantage that, when *filter questions* are asked, so that certain answers may be skipped as a result of a person's reply, the computer 'jumps' to the next relevant question. This removes the possibility of interviewers inadvertently asking inappropriate questions or failing to ask ones that should be asked. In these ways, computer-assisted interviewing enhances the degree of control over the interview process and can therefore improve standardization of the asking and recording of questions. However, there is very little evidence to suggest that the quality of data deriving from computer-assisted interviews is demonstrably superior to comparable paper-and-pencil interviews (Couper and Hansen 2002). If the interviewer is out in an organization all day, he or she may take a removable storage device with the saved data to the research office or transfer the data electronically. It is possible that technophobic respondents may be a bit alarmed by their use, but, by and large, the use of computer-assisted interviewing seems destined to grow. One of us has had personal experience of this technique as a respondent in a market research survey: in this instance the laptop started to beep part of the way through the interview because the battery was about to expire and needed to be replaced with a back-up. An incident such as this could be disruptive to the flow of an interview and be alarming for technophobic respondents.

There is evidence that professional interviewers generally like computer-assisted interviewing, often feeling that it improves the image of their occupation, though there are many who are concerned about the problems that might arise from technical difficulties and the inconvenience of correcting errors with a computer as opposed to a pen. One issue that sometimes disconcerts interviewers is the fact that they can see only part of the schedule at any one time (Couper and Hansen 2002).

CAPI and CATI have not infiltrated academic survey research to anything like the same degree that they have in commercial survey research, although that picture is likely to change considerably because of the many advantages they possess. In any case, many of the large datasets that are used for secondary analysis (see Chapter 14 for examples) derive from computer-assisted interviewing studies undertaken by commercial or large social research organizations. One further point to register in connection with computer-assisted interviewing is that so far we have avoided discussion of Internet surveys. The reason for this is that such surveys are self-completion questionnaires rather than interviews. We cover them in Chapter 28.

Conducting interviews

Issues concerning the conduct of interviews are examined here in a very general way. In addition to the matters considered here, there is clearly the important issue of how to word the interview questions themselves. This area will be explored in Chapter 11, since many of the rules of question-asking relate to self-completion questionnaire techniques such as postal or online questionnaires as well as to structured interviews. One further general point to make here is that the advice concerning the conduct of interviews provided in this chapter relates to structured interviews. The framework for conducting the kinds of interviewing used in qualitative research (such as unstructured and semi-structured interviewing and focus groups) will be handled in later chapters.

Know the schedule

Before interviewing anybody, an interviewer should be fully conversant with the schedule. Even if you are the only person conducting interviews, make sure you know it inside out. Interviewing can be stressful for interviewers, and it is possible that under duress standard interview procedures such as filter questions (see Tips and skills 'Instructions for interviewers in the use of a filter question') can cause interviewers to get flustered and miss questions out or ask the wrong questions. If two or more interviewers are involved, they need to be fully trained to know what is required of them and to know their way around the schedule. Training is especially important in order to reduce the likelihood of interviewer variability in the asking of questions, which is a source of error.

Introducing the research

Prospective respondents have to be provided with a credible rationale for the research in which they are being asked to participate and for giving up their valuable time. This aspect of conducting interview research is of particular significance at a time when response rates to social survey research appear to be declining, though, as noted in Chapter 8, the evidence on this issue is the focus of some disagreement. The introductory rationale may be either spoken by the interviewer or written down. In many cases, respondents may be presented with both modes. It comes in spoken form in such situations as when interviewers make contact with respondents on the street or when they 'cold call' respondents in their homes or at their place of work, whether in person or by telephone. A written rationale will be required to alert respondents that someone will be contacting them in person or on the telephone to request an interview. Respondents will frequently encounter both forms—for example, when they are sent a letter and then ask the interviewer who turns up to interview them what the research is all about. It is important for the rationale given by telephone to be consistent with the one given by letter, as if respondents pick up inconsistencies they may well be less likely to participate in the survey.

Introductions to research should typically contain the bits of information outlined in Tips and skills 'Topics and issues to include in an introductory statement'. Since interviewers represent the interface between the research and the respondent, they have an important role in maximizing the response rate for the survey. In addition, the following points should be borne in mind:

- Interviewers should be prepared to keep calling back if interviewees are out or unavailable. This will require taking into account people's likely work and leisure habits—for example, there is no point in calling at home on people who work during the day. In addition, first thing in the morning may not be the best time to contact a busy manager who is likely to be briefing colleagues and responding to queries.

- Be self-assured; you may get a better response if you presume that people will agree to be interviewed rather than that they will refuse.

- Reassure people that you are not a salesperson. Because of the tactics of certain organizations whose representatives say they are doing market or business research, many people have become very suspicious of people saying they would just like to ask you a few questions.
- Dress in a way that will be acceptable to a wide spectrum of people.
- Make it clear that you will be happy to find a time to suit the respondent.

Rapport

It is frequently suggested that it is important for the interviewer to achieve *rapport* with the respondent. This means that very quickly a relationship must be established that encourages the respondent to want (or at least be prepared) to participate in and persist with the interview. Unless an element of rapport can be established, some respondents may initially agree to be interviewed but then decide to terminate their participation because of the length of time the interview is taking or perhaps because of the nature of the questions being asked.

While this injunction essentially invites the interviewer to be friendly with respondents and to put them at ease, it is important that this quality is not stretched too far. Too much rapport may result in the interview going on too long and the respondent suddenly deciding that too much time is being spent on the activity. Also, the mood of friendliness may result in the respondent answering questions in a way that is designed to please the interviewer. The achievement of rapport between interviewer and respondent is therefore a delicate balancing act. Moreover, it is probably somewhat easier to achieve in the context of the face-to-face interview rather than the telephone interview, since in the latter the interviewer is unable to offer obvious visual cues of friendliness like smiling or maintaining good eye contact, which is also frequently regarded as conducive to gaining and maintaining rapport (see Thinking deeply 9.4 for a more detailed discussion of rapport in telephone interviewing).

Asking questions

It was suggested above that one of the aims of the structured interview is to ensure that each respondent is asked exactly the same questions. It was also pointed

Tips and skills
Topics and issues to include in an introductory statement

There are several issues to include in an introductory statement to a prospective interviewee. The following list comprises the principal considerations:

- Make clear the identity of the person who is contacting the respondent.
- Identify the auspices under which the research is being conducted—for example, a university, a market research agency.
- Mention any research funder, or, if you are a student doing an undergraduate or postgraduate dissertation or doing research for a thesis, make this clear.
- Indicate what the research is about in broad terms and why it is important, and give an indication of the kind of information to be collected.
- Indicate why the respondent has been selected—for example, selected by a random process.
- Provide reassurance about the confidentiality of any information provided.
- Make it clear that participation is voluntary.
- Reassure the respondent that he or she will not be identified or be identifiable in any way. This can usually be achieved by pointing out that data are anonymized when they are entered into the computer and that analysis will be conducted at an aggregate level.
- Provide the respondent with the opportunity to ask any questions—for example, provide a contact telephone number if the introduction is in the form of a written statement, or, if in person, simply ask if the respondent has any questions.

These suggestions are also relevant to the covering letter that accompanies mail questionnaires, except that researchers using this method need to remember to include a stamped addressed envelope!

Thinking deeply 9.4
The problem of laughter in telephone survey interviews

Lavin and Maynard (2001) explore the tension within telephone interviews between the desire for standardization that leads some survey research centres to prohibit interviewers from laughing during a telephone interview, and the need to develop an affiliative social relationship, or rapport, with the interviewee, which even in structured interviewing is important in ensuring completion of the interview and accuracy of the data that are collected. Using data from recorded telephone interviews from a survey research centre, they focus on the occurrence of 'reciprocated laughter', which is defined as when 'an interviewer responds positively to the laughter initiated by a respondent during the course of a telephone survey interview' (2001: 455), taking laughter to be an indication of rapport. The interviews were related to two different surveys, one about television viewing habits and the other about respondents' opinions concerning their local neighbourhoods. Although the survey centre formally and informally prohibits interviewers from engaging in emotional displays including laughter, the researchers found an average of three laughter incidences per interview. They also collected data from a survey centre that did not have a policy of prohibiting laughter, instructing interviewers to be 'natural' and to speak in a conversational manner, where they found an average of eight laughter incidences per interview. They conclude that interviewers sometimes deal with respondent laughter by adhering to the structure of the interview, asking questions, talking seriously, or typing audibly into the computer. However, they also engage in pseudo-laughter, whereby they respond in a cheery way to ensure that the interview relationship is maintained but any supervisor listening in on the call would not actually be able to hear any laughter, for which they might be penalized. They conclude that this reveals the considerable taken-for-granted conversational skill involved in survey interviewing. It also reveals the conventions of survey research centres as sites where practitioners seek to generate objective, scientific knowledge.

out that variation in the ways a question is asked is a potential source of error in survey research. The structured interview is meant to reduce the likelihood of this occurring, but it cannot guarantee that this will not occur, because there is always the possibility that interviewers will embellish or otherwise change a question when it is asked. There is considerable evidence that this occurs, even among centres of social research that have a solid reputation for being rigorous in following correct methodological protocol (Bradburn and Sudman 1979). The problem with such variation in the asking of questions was outlined above: it is likely to engender variation in replies that does not reflect 'true' variation—in other words, error. Consequently, it is important for interviewers to appreciate the importance of keeping exactly to the wording of the questions they are charged with asking.

You might say: 'Does it really matter?' In other words, surely small variations to wording cannot make a significant difference to people's replies? While the impact of variation in wording obviously differs from context to context and is in any case difficult to quantify exactly, experiments in question wording suggest that even small variations in wording can exert an impact on replies (Schuman and Presser 1981). Three experiments in England conducted by Social and Community Planning

Research concluded that a considerable number of interview questions are affected by interviewer variability. The researchers estimated that, for about two-thirds of the questions that were considered, interviewers contributed to less than 2 per cent of the total variation in each question (M. Collins 1997). On the face of it, this is a small amount of error, but the researchers regarded it as a cause for concern.

The key point to emerge, then, is the importance of getting across to interviewers the importance of asking questions as they are written. There are many reasons why interviewers may vary question wording, such as reluctance to ask certain questions, perhaps because of embarrassment (M. Collins 1997), but the general admonition to keep to the wording of the question needs to be constantly reinforced when interviewers are being trained. It also needs to be borne in mind for your own research.

Recording answers

An identical warning for identical reasons can be registered in connection with the recording of answers by interviewers, who should write down respondents' replies as exactly as possible. Not to do so can result in interviewers distorting respondents' answers and hence introducing error. Such errors are less likely to occur when the interviewer has merely to allocate respondents' replies to a category, as in a closed question. This process can require a certain amount of interpretation on the part of the interviewer, but the error that is introduced is far less than when answers to open questions are being written down (Fowler and Mangione 1990).

Clear instructions

In addition to instructions about the asking of questions and the recording of answers, interviewers need instructions about their progress through an interview schedule. An example of the kind of context in which this is likely to occur is in relation to *filter questions*. Filter questions require the interviewer to ask questions of some respondents but not others. For example, the question

> How many days of on-the-job training have you received in the past twelve months?

presumes that the respondent is in employment. This option can be reflected in the fixed-choice answers that are provided, so that one of these is a 'not-in-employment' alternative. However, a better solution is not to presume anything about respondents' work behaviour but to ask them if they are currently in employment and then to filter out those respondents who are not. A further consideration in relation to this filter question is how many hours or days they are employed for. For example, in the Skills and Employment Survey (see Research in focus 8.3) the researchers were interested in anyone who was employed for one hour per week or more. In this case, there was no point in asking those who were not in paid work about the training opportunities they had received as part of their employment. Tips and skills 'Instructions for interviewers in the use of a filter question' provides a simple example in connection with an imaginary study of feedback and job performance. The chief point to register about this example is that it requires clear instructions for the interviewer. If such instructions are not provided, there is the risk either that respondents will be asked inappropriate questions (which can be irritating for them) or that the interviewer will inadvertently fail to ask a question (which results in missing information).

Question order

In addition to warning interviewers about the importance of not varying the asking of questions and the recording of answers, they should be alerted to the importance of keeping to the order of asking questions. For one thing,

varying the question order can result in certain questions being accidentally omitted, because the interviewer may forget to ask those that have been leapfrogged during the interview. Also, variation in question order may have an impact on replies: if some respondents have been previously asked a question that they should have been asked whereas others have not, a source of variability in the asking of questions will have been introduced and therefore a potential source of error.

Quite a lot of research has been carried out on the general issue of question order, but few if any consistent effects on people's responses that derive from asking questions at different points in a questionnaire or interview schedule have been unveiled. Different effects have been demonstrated on various occasions. A study in the USA found that people were less likely to say that their taxes were too high when they had been previously asked whether or not government spending ought to be increased in a number of areas (Schuman and Presser 1981: 32). Apparently, some people perceived an inconsistency between wanting more spending and lower taxes, and adjusted their answers accordingly. However, it is difficult to draw general lessons from such research, at least in part because experiments in question order do not always reveal clear-cut effects of varying the order in which questions are asked, even in cases where effects might legitimately have been expected. There are two general lessons.

- Within a survey, question order should not be varied (unless, of course, question order is the subject of the study!).

- Researchers should be sensitive to the possible implications of the effect of early questions on answers to subsequent questions.

The following rules about question order are sometimes proposed:

- Early questions should be directly related to the topic of the research, about which the respondent has been informed. This removes the possibility that the respondent will be wondering at an early stage in the interview why he or she is being asked apparently irrelevant questions. This injunction means that personal questions about age, social background, and so on should *not* be asked at the beginning of an interview.

- As far as possible, questions that are more likely to be salient to respondents should be asked early in the interview schedule, so that their interest and attention are more likely to be secured. This suggestion

Tips and skills
Instructions for interviewers in the use of a filter question

1. Have you received any feedback concerning your job performance during the last twelve months?

   Yes _____

   No _____

   (if No proceed to question 4)

2. (*To be asked if interviewee replied* Yes *to question 1*)

   Who provided you with this feedback?

   (Ask respondent to choose the category that represents the person who most often gives them feedback and to choose one category only.)

   Line manager _____

   Personnel manager _____

   Other _____ (specify) _____

3. How frequently do you receive feedback concerning your job performance?

   (Ask interviewee to choose the category that comes closest to his or her current experience.)

   Once or twice a week _____

   Once or twice a month _____

   A few times a year _____

   Once or twice a year _____

4. (*To be asked if interviewee replied* No *to question 1*)

   Have you received feedback concerning your job performance at any time during your employment by this organization?

   Yes _____

   No _____

may conflict with the previous one, in that questions specifically on the research topic may not be obviously salient to respondents, but it implies that as far as possible questions relating to the research topic that are more likely to grab their attention should be asked at or close to the start of the interview.

- Potentially embarrassing questions or ones that may be a source of anxiety should be left till later. In fact, research should be designed to ensure that as far as possible respondents are not discomfited, but it has to be acknowledged that with certain topics this effect may be unavoidable.

- With a long schedule or questionnaire, questions should be grouped into sections, since this allows a better flow than skipping from one topic to another.

- Within each group of questions, general questions should precede specific ones. Research in focus 9.5 provides an illustration of such a sequence.

- A further aspect of the rule that general questions should precede specific ones is that it has been argued that, when a specific question comes before a general one, the aspect of the general question that is covered by the specific one is discounted in the minds of respondents because they feel they have already covered it. Thus, if a question about how people feel about the amount they are paid precedes a general question about job satisfaction, there are grounds for thinking that respondents will discount the issue of pay when responding about job satisfaction.

- It is sometimes recommended that questions dealing with opinions and attitudes should precede questions to do with behaviour and knowledge. This is because it is felt that behaviour and knowledge questions are less affected by question order than questions that tap opinions and attitudes.

Research in focus 9.5
A question sequence

The question sequence given below follows the recommendations of Gallup (1947, cited in Foddy 1993: 61–2). The example demonstrates how this approach might operate in connection with building society demutualization, the process whereby several British mutual building societies turned themselves into banks and hence into public companies quoted on the Stock Exchange. The question order sequence is designed with a number of features in mind. It is designed to establish people's levels of knowledge of demutualization before asking questions about it and to distinguish those who feel strongly about it from those who do not. According to Foddy (1993), the second question is always open-ended, so respondents' frames of reference can be established with respect to the topic at hand. However, it seems likely that, if sufficient pilot research has been carried out, a closed question could be envisaged, a point that applies equally to question 4.

1. Have you heard of demutualization?

   Yes _____ No _____

2. What are your views about demutualization?

3. Do you favour or not favour demutualization?

   Favour _____ Not favour _____

4. Why do you favour (not favour) demutualization?

5. How strongly do you feel about this?

   Very strongly _____

   Fairly strongly _____

   Not at all strongly _____

• During the course of an interview, it sometimes happens that a respondent provides an answer to a question that is to be asked later in the interview. Because of the possibility of a question order effect, when the interviewer arrives at the question that appears already to have been answered, it should be repeated.

However, question order effects remain one of the more frustrating areas of structured interview and questionnaire design, because of the inconsistent evidence that is found and because it is difficult to formulate generalizations or rules from the evidence that does point to their operation.

Probing

Probing is a highly problematic area for researchers employing a structured interview method. It frequently happens in interviews that respondents need help with their answers. One obvious case is where it is evident that they do not understand the question—they may either ask for further information or it is clear from what they say that they are struggling to understand the question or to provide an adequate answer. The second kind

of situation the interviewer faces is when the respondent does not provide a sufficiently complete answer and has to be probed for more information. The problem in either situation is obvious: the interviewer's intervention may influence the respondent and the nature of interviewers' interventions may differ. A potential source of variability in respondents' replies that does not reflect 'true' variation is introduced—that is, error.

Some general tactics with regard to probes are as follows:

• If further information is required, usually in the context of an open-ended question, standardized probes can be employed, such as 'Could you say a little more about that?' or 'Are there any other reasons why you think that?' or simply 'Mmmm . . . ?' Probes have to be handled carefully. If they are not introduced in a consistent way or if they suggest a particular kind of answer to the interviewee, error will increase.

• If the problem is that when presented with a closed question the respondent replies in a way that does not allow the interviewee to select one of the pre-designed answers, the interviewer should repeat the fixed-choice alternatives and make it apparent that the answer needs to be chosen from the ones that have been provided.

- If the interviewer needs to know about something that requires quantification, such as the number of visits to building societies in the last four weeks or the number of building societies in which the respondent has accounts, but the respondent resists this by answering in general terms ('quite often' or 'I usually go to the building society every week'), the interviewer needs to persist with securing a number from the respondent. This will usually entail repeating the question. The interviewer should not try to second guess a figure on the basis of the respondent's reply and then suggest that figure to him or her, since the latter may be unwilling to demur from the interviewer's suggested figure.

Prompting

Prompting occurs when the interviewer suggests a possible answer to a question to the respondent. The key prerequisite here is that all respondents receive the same prompts. All closed questions entail standardized prompting, because the respondent is provided with a list of possible answers from which to choose. An unacceptable approach to prompting would be to ask an open question and to suggest possible answers only to some respondents, such as those who appear to be struggling to think of an appropriate reply.

During the course of a face-to-face interview, there are several circumstances in which it will be better for the interviewer to use 'show cards' rather than rely on reading out a series of fixed-choice alternatives. Show cards (sometimes called 'flash cards') display all the answers from which the respondent is to choose and are handed to the respondent at different points of the interview. Three kinds of context in which it might be preferable to employ show cards rather than to read out the entire set of possible answers are as follows:

- There may be a very long list of possible answers. For example, respondents may be asked which daily newspaper they each read most frequently. To read out a list of newspapers would be tedious and it is probably better to hand the respondent a list of newspapers from which to choose.

- Sometimes, during the course of interviews, respondents are presented with a group of questions to which the same possible answers are attached. An example of this approach is Likert scaling, which is an approach to attitude measurement. A typical strategy entails providing respondents with a series of statements and asking them how far they agree or disagree with the statements (see Chapter 7). These are often referred to as *items* rather than as *questions*, since, strictly speaking, the respondent is not being asked a question. An example was provided in Research in focus 7.3. It would be excruciatingly dull to read out all five possible answers twelve times. Also, it may be expecting too much of respondents if the interviewer reads out the answers once and then requires respondents to keep the possible answers in their heads for the entire batch of questions to which they apply. A show card that can be used for the entire batch and to which respondents can constantly refer is an obvious solution. As was mentioned in Research in focus 7.3, most Likert scales of this kind comprise five levels of agreement/disagreement and it is this more conventional approach that is illustrated in Tips and skills 'A show card'.

- Some people are not keen to divulge personal details such as their age or their income. One way of neutralizing the impact of such questioning is to present respondents with age or income bands with a letter or number attached to each band. They can then be asked to say which letter applies to them (see Tips and skills 'Another show card'). This procedure will obviously not be appropriate if the research requires *exact* ages or incomes.

Tips and skills
A show card

Card 6

Strongly agree

Agree

Undecided

Disagree

Strongly disagree

Tips and skills
Another show card

Card 11

(*a*) Below 20

(*b*) 20–29

(*c*) 30–39

(*d*) 40–49

(*e*) 50–59

(*f*) 60–69

(*g*) 70 and over

Leaving the interview

Do not forget common courtesies such as thanking respondents for giving up their time. However, the period immediately after the interview is one in which some care is necessary, in that sometimes respondents try to engage the interviewer in a discussion about the purpose of the interview. Interviewers should resist elaboration beyond their standard statement, because respondents may communicate what they are told to others, which may bias the findings.

Training and supervision

On several occasions, reference has been made to the need for interviewers to be trained. The standard texts on survey research and on interviewing practice tend to be replete with advice on how best to train interviewers. Such advice is typically directed at contexts in which a researcher hires an interviewer to conduct a large number of or even all the interviews. It also has considerable importance in research in which several interviewers (who may be either collaborators or hired interviewers) are involved in a study, since the risk of interviewer variability in the asking of questions needs to be avoided.

For many readers of this book who are planning to do research, such situations are unlikely to be relevant, because they will be 'lone' researchers. You may be doing an undergraduate dissertation, or an exercise for a research methods course, or you may be a postgraduate conducting research for a Master's dissertation or for a Ph.D. thesis. Most people in such a situation will not have the luxury of being able to hire a researcher to do any interviewing (though you may be able to find someone to help you a little). When interviewing on your own, you must train yourself to follow the procedures and advice provided above. This is a very different situation from a large research institute or market research agency, which relies on an army of hired interviewers who carry out the interviews. Whenever people other than the lead researcher are involved in interviewing, they will need training and supervision in the following areas:

- contacting prospective respondents and providing an introduction to the study;
- reading out questions as written and following instructions in the interview schedule (for example, in connection with filter questions);
- using appropriate styles of probing;
- recording exactly what is said;
- maintaining an interview style that does not bias respondents' answers.

Fowler (1993) cites evidence that suggests that training of less than one full day rarely creates good interviewers.

Supervision of interviewers in relation to these issues can be achieved by:

- checking individual interviewers' response rates;
- making audio recordings of at least a sample of interviews;
- examining completed schedules to determine whether any questions are being left out or if they are being completed properly;
- call-backs on a sample of respondents (usually around 10 per cent) to determine whether or not they were interviewed and to ask about interviewers' conduct.

Other approaches to structured interviewing

A number of other methods or techniques are used in business and management research as part of either the structured or the semi-structured interview. Four main types will be discussed in this section:

- critical incident method;
- projective methods, pictorial and photo-elicitation;
- verbal protocol approach;
- repertory grid technique.

We have grouped these four methods together here because they can form part of a structured interview. However, they can also form part of a semi-structured interview (see Chapter 20) in a qualitative investigation and so to an extent they cut across the quantitative/qualitative divide (see Chapter 26). They are sometimes used as one part of an interview, in combination with other questions that form part of a more conventional interview schedule, or in other research designs they form the basis for the entire interview. A further use of these methods is to check findings from more conventional quantitative approaches such as structured interviews or questionnaire surveys.

Critical incident method

The **critical incident method** involves asking respondents to describe *critical incidents*, which are defined very broadly by Flanagan (1954) as any observable human activity where the consequences are sufficiently clear as to leave the observer with a definite idea as to their likely effects. The term is derived from the analysis of near-disaster situations, where a version of the technique can be used to build up a picture of the events that contribute to a potential disaster and to develop a plan of action for dealing with them. The most common use of the critical incident method involves interviewing respondents about particular types of event or behaviour in order to develop an understanding of their sequence and their significance to the individual.

One of the earliest and most well-known illustrations of this method in business research is the study by Herzberg, Mausner, and Snyderman (1959), which was mentioned in Chapter 8. The authors explain: 'We decided to ask people to tell us stories about times when they felt exceptionally good or bad about their jobs. We decided that from these stories we could discover the kinds of situations leading to negative or positive attitudes toward the job and the effects of these attitudes' (1959: 17). Their initial interview strategy was followed up by a series of probe questions that filled in missing information in the spontaneously told accounts. Content analysis (see Chapter 13) was then used to focus on exploring the essential features of the critical incident in order to reveal the values that they reflected. A more recent example of the use of the critical incident method is found in the study of self-managing work teams described in Research in focus 9.7.

Finally, although we have introduced the critical incident method in Part Two of the book, which deals with

Telling it like it is
Using critical incident method in a student research project

Tom followed the advice of his supervisor and used the critical incident technique when he was interviewing call centre workers about wellbeing and the experience of working in a call centre. He explained, 'I did use critical incident technique in the interview to try and get people to give an example of a time when things have gone particularly well at work or particularly badly. It was quite a useful tool to get people to talk in an interesting way really about their work experience. And sometimes it wasn't really necessary because they would give lots of examples anyway, but it was quite a useful prompt to get people to be more specific and give examples of the sort of stuff that their work life was like.'

Research in focus 9.7
An example of the critical incident method

Urch Druskat and Wheeler (2003) used the critical incident technique in interviews with self-managing work team leaders and team members as part of a mixed-method case study. Their research site was a Fortune 500 durable consumer goods manufacturing plant in the mid-western United States with 3500 employees that had introduced self-managing work teams five years previously. The critical incident interview technique involved 'asking interviewees to alternate between describing incidents on the job in which they felt effective and incidents in which they felt ineffective' (2003: 440). The role of the interviewer in this context is to 'obtain detailed descriptions of events while remaining as unobtrusive as possible in order to avoid leading interviewees' (2003: 440). The questions consisted of the following:

- What led up to the event?
- Who did and said what to whom?
- What happened next?
- What were you thinking and feeling at that moment?
- What was the outcome?

To enhance the validity and reliability of the critical incident interviews, events were limited to those that had happened within approximately the last year. The kinds of events that respondents recalled included specific team meetings, production or equipment changes, and times when production goals were met or times when they were not met due to adverse conditions.

quantitative research, we should point out that this method is often used as part of a qualitative research investigation. An example of this is the study of small business owner-managers by Blackburn and Stokes (2000) (see Research in focus 21.2). In this instance, respondents were asked to recall a situation that had arisen in the previous two years in which they had lost a major customer and to explain what had happened and how they had coped with it. Blackburn and Stokes's analysis of the data was primarily qualitative, relying on the use of themes illustrated by the inclusion of direct quotes from respondents.

Projective methods, pictorial and photo-elicitation

Projective methods classically involve the presentation of ambiguous stimuli to individuals, and responses are interpreted by the researcher to reveal underlying characteristics of the individual concerned. A common example is the Rorschach inkblot test, where respondents are asked to describe random inkblots. Analysis relies on expert psychological interpretation of the way that respondents have described the inkblots, and this is suggested to be indicative of their dominant channels of thinking.

Another form of projective analysis involves the 'sentence completion test', where the individual is asked to complete a number of unfinished sentences; this technique has been used in the context of recruitment and selection, often as an assessment centre exercise.

One of the best-known examples of the use of **projective techniques** in management research involves the study by McClelland (1961) of leadership and the need for individual achievement. Informed by experimental psychology and the psychoanalytic insights of Freud, McClelland's study first involved stimulating the achievement motive in a group of subjects. He then sought to elicit their 'spontaneous thoughts' and fantasies in order to determine the effect of achievement motivation. The subjects were male college students who were told that they were going to be tested to determine their intelligence and leadership ability; it was assumed that this would arouse a desire in the subjects to do well. After the 'tests' had been completed, subjects were asked to write short 5-minute stories suggested by pictures that flashed onto a screen for a few seconds. 'The pictures represented a variety of life situations centering particularly around work' (1961: 40). The stories were compared with those that had been written by a control group under normal conditions. The experimental group was found to refer more often in their stories to ideas related to achievement. From this, McClelland concluded that, if someone 'in writing his stories consistently uses achievement-related ideas of the same kind as those elicited in everyone under achievement "pressure," then he would appear to be someone with a "bias," a "concern," or a "need" for achievement' (1961: 43). This led him to develop a score for the need for achievement, defined as the number of achievement-related ideas in stories written by an individual under normal conditions.

A more recent example of projective methods can also be found in advertising research (see Research in focus 9.8). Using a range of methods including collage, storytelling, sentence completion, and word associations, the authors of this study sought to investigate the nature of consumer desire among students in three countries. However, the use of projective methods is relatively uncommon in business research. They have largely been superseded by the use of visual techniques to stimulate creative thinking and problem solving, and to explore feelings, emotions, and values. For example, Stiles (2004) asked members of UK and North American business schools to express how they saw their organization's identity by drawing pictures (see Research in focus 9.9). The use of **photo-elicitation** can also be seen as an adaptation of projective methods (see Key concept 9.10 for an explanation and Research in focus 9.11 for an example).

Verbal protocol approach

The **verbal protocol approach** builds on the work of Newell and Simon (1972) in the area of human problem solving and has since been used in relation to a number of topics that are relevant to business and management

Research in focus 9.8
Using projective methods in consumer research

In a cross-cultural study of consumer desire, Belk, Ger, and Askegaard (1997) wanted to explore the cultural differences in consumer desire among students in the USA ($n = 38$), Turkey ($n = 29$), and Denmark ($n = 17$).

Desire is defined by the authors as belief-based passions that involve longing or wishing for something. Hence, 'we may speak of hungering for, lusting after, or craving certain consumer goods as if they were delicious foods, alluring sexual mates, or addictive drugs' (1997: 24). Research informants were graduate and undergraduate students at the three universities where each of the three authors was employed. The projective methods used included:

- *collage*: using popular magazines, informants were asked to create a collage to express their understanding of desire;

- *associations*: informants were asked to imagine swimming in a sea of things (objects, experiences, people) that bring them pleasure and to describe them;

- *sketches*: they were told to imagine themselves as artists commissioned to create artworks called 'desire' and 'not desire';

- *synonyms*: they were asked to name an object, experience, or person (X) that they desired and to list as many words or phrases that might be used in the sentence, 'I____X';

- *synonym examples and feelings*: informants were asked to name things a person might strongly desire and to describe the feelings a person might have (1) before he or she gets it, (2) at the moment he or she gets it, and (3) after he or she has got it.

Perhaps unsurprisingly, the study found that men and women tended to focus on different objects of desire: objects that emerged with greater frequency for men included luxury cars; for women they included food, and especially chocolates. Although both sexes focused on people as objects of desire, women were more likely to specify relationships as the interpersonal objects of their desire whereas men were more likely to desire women as objects. American and Turkish women were more likely than Danish women to see desire as sinful. The authors conclude that desire is a positive emotional state that is at the same time interpersonal, whether in a competitive sense of wanting more or better things than others, or in the sense of wanting approval and love from others.

researchers. The approach involves asking respondents to 'think aloud' while they are performing a task. The idea is to elicit the respondent's thought processes while he or she is making a decision or judgement or solving a problem. The subject's account of what he or she is doing and why is usually audio-recorded and transcribed and then content analysed using a coding scheme to discern different categories of thinking. An interesting example of the use of verbal protocol analysis can be found in a study by Cable and Graham (2000), who wanted to explore the factors that job-seekers consider when evaluating employers' reputations (see Research in focus 9.12).

Repertory grid technique

Repertory grid technique is based on G. A. Kelly's (1955) personal construct theory, and it is used to identify the interpretative processes whereby an individual constructs meaning in relation to his or her social context. The theory portrays the individual as a scientist, striving to make sense of his or her environment in order to predict and cope with future events. Kelly claimed that sense-making occurs through an individual's personal construct system, which provides an order for dealing with incoming information. This system is composed of a series of interlinked and hierarchically related constructs, which are the bipolar sorting mechanisms that distinguish between similarity and dissimilarity for a given event. In order to make sense of an event, the individual must

assign information to either one pole of the construct or the other. The researcher's task therefore involves identifying the *constructs* that people use to make sense of their world and seeking to understand the way in which a person's thought processes are conditioned by events that he or she anticipates.

The first stage in developing a repertory grid involves the researcher, sometimes together with the participant, identifying a number of (usually between six and twelve) *elements*, which are terms or categories that are deemed relevant to the subject of study—they may be persons, events, or objects. These elements are then written on cards and presented to the respondent, typically in groups of three. The researcher then asks questions that encourage respondents to express how they see the relationship between these elements, such as: 'In what way are two similar?' or 'How does one differ?' The process is then repeated with another three cards, until eventually a picture is built up about how the person construes his or her particular context. This procedure, which is known as the *sequential triadic method*, enables the elements to be sorted. These data can then be entered into the grid, which relates elements to the constructs that underlie the individual's rationale for sorting decisions, and the respondent is asked to rank each element in relation to each construct, using a five- or seven-point scale, as shown in Figure 9.4.

Repertory grids have been used in the study of strategic management and decision-making, and in studies of

Research in focus 9.9
Using pictorial exercises in a study of business school identity

Stiles (2004) used pictorial methods in a study of strategy in UK and North American business schools. The first stage of the research involved asking individual interviewees to imagine their organization as having a personality and then asking them to draw a picture of what that personality looks like. The second stage of the research involved showing these drawings to members of a focus group (see Chapter 21), who are invited to reach a consensus in choosing five pictures, ranging from an unfavourable depiction of the organization, to neutral, through to a favourable one. 'The group then produces a composite *free-drawn personality image* of its own' (2004: 130). The focus group discussion was video-recorded and transcribed. The importance of the pictures stems from the discussion that respondents had around their selection decisions, which revealed insights into the way academics perceived the management styles associated with their organizations and leaders. Stiles notes that, although this study was conducted in a business school setting, it could equally be applied in relation to a variety of other organizational settings. Stiles concludes that the pictorial exercises revealed constructs that were not identified using verbal research instruments, thus introducing the possibility that images are useful in revealing more latent perceptions.

Key concept 9.10
What is photo-elicitation?

This method involves integrating photographs into the interview by asking the respondent questions about photographs that the researcher has taken of the research setting. Respondents are asked to reflect, explain, and comment on the meaning of the objects in the photograph, the events that are taking place, or the emotions they associate with them. Photographs can provide a point of reference for the discussion and can help to move the interview from 'the concrete (a cataloguing of the objects in the photograph) to the socially abstract (what the objects in the photograph mean to the individual being interviewed)' (Harper 1986: 25). Harper suggests that the most useful photographs tend to be those that are visually arresting, because they are more likely to get the respondent's attention and provoke a response.

Research in focus 9.11
Using photo-elicitation to study the patient trail

Buchanan's (1998) single case study of business process re-engineering was intended to assess the impact of a project introduced by the management of a UK hospital to improve the 'patient trail'—the process whereby patients are transferred from one part of the hospital to another. Part of Buchanan's research design involved the use of photo-elicitation. This involved him documenting the steps in the patient trail photographically on approximately 150 35mm colour transparencies. These were made into a slide presentation that was shown to five groups of hospital staff of mixed job levels in open groups. Hospital staff were then invited to comment on the photographic representation of the patient trail, and these comments were incorporated into the written research account of the patient trail process. (For more about this research see Chapter 17.) Although Buchanan's use of photo-elicitation involved a type of focus group interviewing (see Chapter 21), this method could equally apply in interviewing individuals.

Research in focus 9.12
The use of the verbal protocol method to enable experimental testing

Cable and Graham (2000) were interested in the factors affecting graduate job-seekers' assessment of employers' reputations. Their sample consisted of fourteen undergraduate students at two large state universities in the USA. Half of the students were on engineering degree programmes and the other half were doing management degrees. The subjects were given a task that involved evaluating the reputations of three employers. They were given a management trainee job description, which was the same for all three organizations, and recruitment brochures from the three companies—General Electric, Wal-Mart, and Broadview Associates. In making their decision, the subjects were told that they should speak all their thoughts aloud. The 'thinking-aloud' process was audio-recorded, and content analysis was conducted on the transcripts using categories that were drawn from the recruitment and job search literatures. Frequently mentioned categories included 'opportunities for growth' and 'organizational culture'. Typical of the former was the comment: 'They have a vast array of opportunities no matter what you do your major in or what you want to do'; a comment typical of the latter was: 'It talks about integrity which is high on my list. I don't want to work for a company that doesn't value integrity and morals.'

The second stage of the research was designed to improve confidence in the findings generated from the first part of the study. It relied on an experimental design involving sixty-six undergraduate job-seekers, who were asked to read a series of scenarios that described an organization. After reading the scenarios, they reported their perceptions of each company's reputation.

The third stage of the research involved the use of an experimental design to examine the effects of some of the attributes of organizational reputation that had been identified through the verbal protocol analysis. The field experiment involved 126 undergraduate and postgraduate job-seekers, who were asked to complete a questionnaire survey about six organizations with diverse reputations that recruited at the two universities they attended. The survey was repeated three weeks later, in order to limit potential survey biases such as mood effects.

Using these three methods—verbal protocol analysis, an experiment based on scenarios, and a questionnaire survey—the theory of organizational reputation that was developed inductively from the first part of the study using verbal protocol method can then be subjected to further empirical testing using other methods.

Figure 9.4

An example of a repertory grid designed to elicit an applicant's perceptions of preferred job tasks

Construct—emergent pole (1)	Present job	Disliked past job	Elements Liked past job	Neutral past job	Ideal job	Construct—contrast pole (5)
1. Career opportunities*	4	5	2	3	1	No career opportunities
2. Close supervision	4	2	4	3	5	Discretionary*
3. Changeable*	2	5	2	4	1	Fixed
4. Challenging*	1	5	2	4	1	Not challenging
5. Innovative*	2	4	2	3	2	Repetitive
6. Deskbound	5	1	5	4	5	Mobile*
7. No leadership responsibility	4	5	4	2	4	Leadership responsibilities*
8. Administrative work	4	1	4	3	5	Planning work*
9. Enjoyed variety*	2	5	1	3	1	Monotonous/repetitive
10. 'Standing still'	2	2	5	3	5	Career development*

*Denotes preferred pole.
Source: adapted from N. Anderson (1990).

recruitment, personnel management, and other areas of organizational behaviour. For example, a study conducted by Neil Anderson (1990) explored how the technique could be used in employee selection to assess the task reactions of applicants in a recruitment situation. In this study, it was used to focus on the job–person match for a marketing manager vacancy. An example of a completed grid for a marketing manager applicant, which has been adapted and simplified for our purposes of illustration, is provided in Figure 9.4. The grid illustrates ten elicited constructs relating to five elements, which in this case are 'present job', 'disliked past job', 'liked past job', 'neutral past job', and 'ideal job'. The participant was presented with these elements in triads and asked to identify two that were alike and to explain what differentiated them from the third element. This process resulted in the generation of a series of constructs, such as 'career opportunities', which the participant used to relate one kind of job to another. The participant was then asked to indicate the preferred pole for each of the constructs he or she had identified, so 'career opportunities' was identified as preferred to 'no career opportunities'. Finally, the applicant was asked to assess each element against each construct using a five-point scale, with 1 = 'emergent pole' and 5 = 'contrast pole'. As Figure 9.4 illustrates, this managerial applicant has ranked the elements 'ideal job' and 'disliked past job' at opposite ends of these poles, as might be expected. Once the grid is completed, analysis can be either interpretative or statistical in nature. Anderson's use of the technique involved feedback of the results of the analysis to each participant as a basis for counselling and discussion. However, as you will probably by now have gathered, one of the difficulties with using repertory grids is that the technique is quite complex, both for the researcher to use and for the respondent to complete. Some researchers therefore suggest that the primary

value of repertory grid technique derives from its use as a tool for enabling in-depth discussion and thinking about a topic.

A qualitative application of the repertory grid technique can be found in the study of recruiters' perceptions of job applicants conducted by Kristof-Brown (2000; see Research in focus 9.13). In this study, semi-structured interviews were used to determine what the recruiters thought about each applicant, but the data generated were analysed quantitatively in order to gain an impression of the relative importance of each characteristic. This study illustrates a further important aspect of the technique, which is that it requires that participants base their responses on a common set of stimuli. The use of video-recorded interviews in this study of recruiters' selection of job applicants meant that all participants were basing their responses on exactly the same set of interviews.

Research in focus 9.13
An example of the use of repertory grid technique

Kristof-Brown (2000) carried out a study using repertory grid technique to assess whether recruiters form perceptions of an applicant based on:

- the match between the person and the requirements of a specific job; or
- the match between the applicant and the broader organizational attributes.

In the first part of the study, thirty-one recruiters from four consulting organizations participated in the study. The repertory grid method was chosen because it allowed recruiters to articulate their own criteria for evaluating applicants. The recruiters watched a video recording showing a series of short mock interviews with job applicants, who were also MBA students, and then they reviewed the applicants' work history and qualifications. This allowed recruiters to view applicants' verbal and non-verbal behaviour, appearance, and interpersonal skills in a realistic setting. After the recruiters had watched the video, individual interviews were carried out with each recruiter. Each person was presented with the details of three randomly selected applicants, and questions were asked about the degree to which each one matched (a) the job, and (b) the organization. For example, the researcher might ask: 'Comparing applicants four, five, and two, which of these people is the best fit with your company?'

After having identified the best-fitting applicant in terms of the person and the job, recruiters were then asked to describe the characteristics of the applicant that had led them to make this choice. The process of presenting three applicants at a time to recruiters was repeated until all applicants had been evaluated and this information could be represented in the form of a repertory grid.

The researchers then coded the data from the interviews to generate a list of 119 characteristics of applicants, which were judged by five independent raters for similarity, resulting in the eventual generation of 62 applicant characteristics. The coders then analysed the responses from each interview to generate frequency data, including the number and type of characteristics that were reported by each recruiter. The study thus combined qualitative data collection with quantitative analysis of data that were generated using the repertory grid technique.

In sum, the repertory grid technique has been used as a supplement and as an alternative to structured interviewing, both as a basis for qualitative exploration and analysis and as a device for generating data that can be statistically analysed using quantitative methods. For an illustration of some of the potential applications of the repertory grid interview in management research you might want to consult the following website: *www.enquirewithin.co.nz* (accessed 23 October 2014)

Problems with structured interviewing

While the structured interview is a commonly used method of business research, certain problems associated with it have been identified over the years. These problems are not necessarily unique to the structured interview, in that they can sometimes be attributed to kindred methods, such as the self-completion questionnaire in survey research or even semi-structured interviewing in qualitative research. However, it is common for the structured interview to be seen as a focus for the identification of certain limitations that are briefly examined below.

Characteristics of interviewers

There is evidence that interviewers' attributes can have an impact on respondents' replies, but, unfortunately, the literature on this issue does not lend itself to definitive generalizations. In large part, this ambiguity in the broader implications of experiments relating to the effects of interviewer characteristics is due to several problems, such as: the problem of disentangling the effects of interviewers' different attributes from each other ('race', gender, socio-economic status); the interaction between the characteristics of interviewers and the characteristics of respondents; and the interaction between any effects observed and the topic of the interview. Nonetheless, there is undoubtedly some evidence that effects due to characteristics of interviewers can be discerned.

The ethnicity of interviewers is one area that has attracted some attention. Schuman and Presser (1981) cite a study that asked respondents to nominate two or three of their favourite actors or entertainers. Respondents were much more likely to mention black actors or entertainers when interviewed by black interviewers than when interviewed by white ones. Schuman and Converse (1971) interviewed 619 black Detroiters shortly after Martin Luther King's assassination in 1968. The researchers found significant response differences between black and white interviewers in around one-quarter of the questions asked.

Although this proportion is quite disturbing, the fact that the majority of questions appear to have been largely unaffected does not give rise to a great deal of confidence that a consistent biasing factor is being uncovered. Similarly inconclusive findings tend to occur in relation to experiments with other sets of characteristics of interviewers. These remarks are not meant to play down the potential significance of interviewers' characteristics for measurement error, but to draw attention to the limitations of drawing conclusive inferences about the evidence. All that needs to be registered at this juncture is that almost certainly the characteristics of interviewers do have an impact on respondents' replies but that the extent and nature of the impact are not clear and are likely to vary from context to context.

Response sets

Some writers have suggested that the structured interview is particularly prone to the operation among respondents of what Webb et al. (1966) call 'response sets', which they define as 'irrelevant but lawful sources of variance' (1966: 19). This form of response bias is especially relevant to multiple-indicator measures (see Chapter 7), where respondents reply to a battery of related questions or items, of the kind found in a Likert scale (see Research in focus 7.3). The idea of a **response set** implies that people respond to the series of questions in a consistent way but one that is irrelevant to the concept being measured. Two of the most prominent types of response set are known as the 'acquiescence' (also known as the 'yeasaying' and 'naysaying') effect and the 'social desirability' effect.

Acquiescence

Acquiescence refers to a tendency for some people consistently to agree or disagree with a set of questions or items. Imagine respondents who replied to all the items in Research in focus 7.3 stating that they believed they were all unethical (scale = 5) and judging that they and their peers infrequently acted in the way implied by the statement (scale = 1). The problem with this multiple-item measure is that none of the item measure statements is written in a way that implies an opposite stance. In other words, there are no items that are ethical or likely to be engaged in frequently by many ethically responsible people. This could be seen as a potential source of bias in this multiple-item measure. A wording that would imply an opposite stance might be 'being prepared to take responsibility for errors' or 'refusing to accept gifts/favours in exchange for preferential treatment'. This would help to weed out those respondents who were replying within the framework of an acquiescence response set.

Social desirability bias

The social desirability effect refers to evidence that some respondents' answers to questions are related to their perception of the social desirability of those answers. An answer that is perceived to be socially desirable is more likely to be endorsed than one that is not. This phenomenon has been demonstrated in studies of ethical behaviour and managerial decision-making (see Research in focus 9.14). In order to try to prevent **social desirability bias**, Terence Jackson (2001) framed the questions in a way that was intended to enable the respondents to distance themselves from their responses, by imagining what a peer might do rather than having to state what they would do. It was expected that this would reduce the likelihood that individuals would respond in a way that they anticipated would be more acceptable. However, Steenkamp, de Jong, and Baumgartner (2010) have proposed that it is crucial to distinguish between social desirability bias that is conscious and that which is unconscious. The underlying motives and psychological processes associated with each are likely to differ, so that it is not obvious whether a procedure like that employed in Research in focus 9.14 applies to both or just one of the two forms.

In so far as these forms of response error go undetected, they represent sources of error in the measurement of concepts. However, while some writers have proposed outright condemnation of social research on the basis of evidence of response sets (e.g. Phillips 1973), it is important not to get carried away with such findings. We cannot be sure how prevalent these effects are, and to some extent awareness of them has led to measures to limit their impact on data (for example, by weeding out cases obviously affected by them) or by instructing interviewers to limit the possible impact of the social desirability effect by not becoming overly friendly with respondents and by not being judgemental about their replies.

Research in focus 9.14
Reducing social desirability bias

Terence Jackson (2001) wanted to understand the effect of underlying cultural values on ethical attitudes towards management decision-making. He proposed that national differences could be attributed to differences in underlying cultural values. His research design therefore relied upon exploration of Hofstede's (1984) cultural dimensions of 'individualism' and 'uncertainty avoidance' (see Chapter 2), which Jackson took to be important in determining ethical attitudes.

Jackson's study involved 425 managers across ten nations and four continents who were chosen to reflect diverse positions along the two cultural dimensions. In each country a postal questionnaire survey was carried out using samples drawn from university business schools, of part-time MBA participants, most of whom were middle-ranking managers. Although the study was based on postal questionnaires (which will be covered in Chapter 10), it raises issues concerning the management of bias that are also very relevant to the conduct of structured interviewing. In an attempt to reduce social desirability response bias, managers were asked to respond to each questionnaire item according to:

1. 'what I believe; what I would do', i.e. as a 'participant';
2. 'what my peers believe; what my peers would do', i.e. as an 'observer'.

However, an almost universal finding to emerge from the study was that managers appeared to see others as less ethical than themselves. In this case, did the former represent a biased response and the latter a 'true' response, as other researchers had suggested? This would be to imply that the 'observer' response was actually a projection of the respondents' own attitudes, rather than a reflection of how they perceived the attitudes of others. However, the finding may indicate that managers really do judge their colleagues to be less ethical than they are in an absolute sense. The conclusions drawn thus depend ultimately on how one interprets these data.

The problem of meaning

A critique of survey interview data and findings gleaned from similar techniques was developed by social scientists influenced by phenomenological and other interpretivist ideas of the kinds touched on in Chapter 2 (Cicourel 1964, 1982; Filmer et al. 1972; Briggs 1986; Mishler 1986). This critique revolves around what is often referred to in a shorthand way as the 'problem of meaning'. The kernel of the argument is that when humans communicate they do so in a way that not only draws on commonly held meanings but also simultaneously creates meanings. 'Meaning' in this sense is something that is worked at and achieved—it is not simply pre-given. Allusions to the problem of meaning in structured interviewing draw attention to the notion that survey researchers presume that interviewer and respondent share the same meanings of terms employed in the interview questions and answers. In fact, the problem of meaning implies that the possibility that interviewer and respondent may not be sharing the same meaning systems and may hence imply different things in their use of words is simply sidestepped in structured interview research. The problem of meaning is resolved by ignoring it.

The feminist critique

The feminist critique of structured interviewing is difficult to disentangle from the critique launched against quantitative research in general, which was briefly outlined in Chapter 2. However, for many feminist social researchers the structured interview symbolizes more readily than other methods the limitations of quantitative research, partly because of its prevalence but also partly because of its nature. By 'its nature' is meant the fact that the structured interview epitomizes the asymmetrical relationship between researcher and subject that is seen as an ingredient of quantitative research: the researcher extracts information from the research subject and gives nothing in return. For example, standard textbook advice of the kind provided in this chapter implies that *rapport* is useful to the interviewer but that he or she should guard against becoming too familiar. This means that questions asked by respondents (for example, about the research or about the topic of the research) should be politely but firmly rebuffed on the grounds that too much familiarity should be avoided and because the respondents' subsequent answers may be biased.

This is perfectly valid and appropriate advice from the vantage point of the canons of structured interviewing with its quest for standardization and for valid and reliable data. However, from the perspective of feminism, when women interview women, a wedge is hammered between them that, in conjunction with the implication of a hierarchical relationship between the interviewer and respondent, is incompatible with feminist values. An impression of exploitation is created, but exploitation of women is precisely what feminist social science seeks to fight against. Hence Cotterill (1992) claims the methods that feminists adopt are crucially important in developing an understanding of women that relies on breaking down the artificial split between researcher and researched. According to Oakley (1981), this entails the interviewer investing her own personal identity in the research relationship, by answering questions, giving support, and sharing knowledge and experience in a way that can lead to long-term friendships with interviewees. Oakley's point is that to act according to the canons of textbook practice would be impossible for a feminist in such a situation. It was this kind of critique of structured interviewing and indeed of quantitative research in general that ushered in a period in which a great many feminist social researchers found qualitative research more compatible with their goals and norms. In terms of interviewing, this trend resulted in a preference for forms of interviewing such as unstructured and semi-structured interviewing and focus groups. These will be discussed in later chapters. However, as noted in Chapter 2, there has been some softening of attitudes towards the role of quantitative research among feminist researchers, although there is still a tendency for qualitative research to remain the preferred research strategy.

 Key points

....

- The structured interview is a research instrument that is used to standardize the asking of questions and often the recording of answers in order to keep interviewer-related error to a minimum.

- The structured interview can be administered in person or over the telephone.

- It is important to keep to the wording and order of questions when conducting social survey research by structured interview.

- While there is some evidence that interviewers' characteristics can influence respondents' replies, the findings of experiments on this issue are somewhat equivocal.

- Response sets can be damaging to data derived from structured interviews and steps need to be taken to identify respondents exhibiting them.

- The structured interview symbolizes the characteristics of quantitative research that feminist researchers find distasteful—in particular, the lack of reciprocity and the taint of exploitation.

Questions for review

The structured interview

- Why is it important in interviewing for survey research to keep interviewer variability to a minimum?

- How successful is the structured interview in reducing interviewer variability?

- Why might a survey researcher prefer to use a structured rather than an unstructured interview approach for gathering data?

- Why do structured interview schedules typically include mainly closed questions?

Interview contexts

- Are there any circumstances in which it might be preferable to conduct structured interviews with more than one interviewer?

- 'Given the lower cost of telephone interviews as against personal interviews, the former are generally preferable.' Discuss.

Conducting interviews

- Prepare an opening statement for a study of manual workers in a firm, in which access has already been achieved.

- To what extent is rapport an important ingredient of structured interviewing?

- How strong is the evidence that question order can significantly affect answers?

- How strong is the evidence that interviewers' characteristics can significantly affect answers?

- What is the difference between probing and prompting? How important are they and what dangers are lurking with their use?

Other approaches to structured interviewing

- What is the critical incident method and how has it been applied in business and management research?

- Make a list of the projective methods that could be used in a study of organizational culture and consider how they might be applied.

- How might repertory grids be used in qualitative analysis?

Problems with structured interviewing

- What are response sets and why are they potentially important?
- What are the main issues that lie behind the critique of structured interviewing by feminist researchers?

Online Resource Centre

www.oxfordtextbooks.co.uk/orc/brymanbrm4e/

Visit the Interactive Research Guide that accompanies this book to complete an exercise in Structured Interviewing.

10

Self-completion questionnaires

Chapter outline

Questionnaires that are completed by respondents themselves are one of the main instruments for gathering data using a social survey design, along with the structured interview that was covered in Chapter 9. Probably the most common form is the mail or postal questionnaire. The term *self-completion questionnaire* is often preferred because it is somewhat more inclusive than *postal questionnaire*, as not all questionnaires are sent through the post. This chapter explores:

- the advantages and disadvantages of the questionnaire in comparison to the structured interview;
- how to address the potential problem of poor response rates, which is often a feature of the postal questionnaire;
- how questionnaires should be designed in order to make answering easier for respondents and less prone to error;
- the use of diaries as a form of self-completion questionnaire.

Introduction

In a very real sense, the bulk of the previous chapter was about questionnaires. The structured interview is in many, if not most, respects a questionnaire that is administered by an interviewer. However, there is a tendency, which borders on a convention, to reserve the term 'questionnaire' for contexts in which a battery of usually closed questions is completed by respondents themselves.

Self-completion questionnaire or postal questionnaire?

The *self-completion questionnaire* is sometimes referred to as a *self-administered questionnaire*. The former term will be followed in this book. With a self-completion questionnaire, respondents answer questions by completing the questionnaire themselves. As a method, the self-completion questionnaire can come in several forms. Probably the most prominent of these forms is the **mail** or **postal questionnaire**, whereby, as its name implies, a questionnaire is sent through the post to the respondent. The latter, following completion of the questionnaire, is usually asked to return it by post; an alternative form of return is when respondents are requested to deposit their completed questionnaires in a certain location, such as a box in a supervisor's office in a firm or on the top of a cashier's desk in a restaurant or shop. The self-completion questionnaire also covers forms of administration, such as when a researcher hands out questionnaires to all students in a class and collects them back after they have been completed. A variant of this is the 'drop-off and collect' approach that was used in a study of cardholders' satisfaction with loyalty programmes in Malaysia. Omar et al. (2011) delivered questionnaires to employees in several organizations. Each respondent was requested to select a loyalty programme of which he or she was a member and to answer questions about that programme. The questionnaires were then collected from the respondents. A high response rate of 87 per cent was achieved. 'Self-completion questionnaire' is, therefore, a more inclusive term than 'postal questionnaire', though it is probably true to say that the latter is the most prominent form of the self-completion questionnaire.

In the discussion that follows, when points apply to more or less all forms of self-completion questionnaire, this term will be employed. When points apply specifically or exclusively to questionnaires sent through the post, the term 'postal questionnaire' will be used.

Evaluating the self-completion questionnaire in relation to the structured interview

In many ways, the self-completion questionnaire and the structured interview are very similar methods of business research. The obvious difference between them is that, with the self-completion questionnaire, there is no interviewer to ask the questions; instead, respondents must read each question themselves and answer the questions themselves. Beyond this obvious, but central, difference, they are remarkably similar. However, because there is no interviewer in the administration of the self-completion questionnaire, the research instrument has to be especially easy to follow and its questions have to be particularly easy to answer. After all, respondents cannot be trained in the way interviewers can be; nor do they know their way around a research instrument in the way a 'lone researcher' might.

As a result, self-completion questionnaires, as compared to structured interviews, tend to:

- have fewer open questions, since closed ones tend to be easier to answer;

- have easy-to-follow designs to minimize the risk that the respondent will fail to follow filter questions or will inadvertently omit a question;

- be shorter, to reduce the risk of 'respondent fatigue', since it is manifestly easier for a respondent who becomes tired of answering questions in a long questionnaire to consign it to a waste paper bin than it is for a subject being interviewed to terminate the interview.

Advantages of the self-completion questionnaire over the structured interview

Cheaper to administer

Interviewing can be expensive. The cheapness of the self-completion questionnaire is especially advantageous if you have a sample that is geographically widely dispersed. When this is the case, a postal questionnaire will be much cheaper, because of the time and cost of travel for interviewers. This advantage is obviously less pronounced in connection with telephone interviews, because of the lower costs of telephone charges relative to travel and time spent travelling. But, even in comparison to telephone interviewing, the postal questionnaire enjoys cost advantages.

Quicker to administer

Self-completion questionnaires can be sent out by post or otherwise distributed in very large quantities at the same time. A thousand questionnaires can be sent out by post in one batch, but, even with a team of interviewers, it would take a long time to conduct personal interviews with a sample of that size. However, it is important to bear in mind that the questionnaires do not all come back immediately and that they may take several weeks to be returned. Also, there is invariably a need to send out follow-up letters and/or questionnaires to those who fail to return them initially, an issue that will be returned to below.

Absence of interviewer effects

It was noted in Chapter 9 that various studies have demonstrated that characteristics of interviewers (and respondents) may affect the answers that people give. While the findings from this research are somewhat equivocal in their implications, it has been suggested that such characteristics as ethnicity, gender, and the social background of interviewers may combine to bias the answers that respondents provide. Obviously, since there is no interviewer present when a self-completion questionnaire is being completed, interviewer effects are eliminated. However, this advantage probably has to be regarded fairly cautiously, since few consistent patterns have emerged over the years from research to suggest what kinds of interviewer characteristics bias answers.

Probably of greater importance to the presence of an interviewer is the tendency for people to be more likely to exhibit social desirability bias when an interviewer is present. Research by Sudman and Bradburn (1982) suggests that postal questionnaires work better than personal interviews when a question carries the possibility of such bias. There is also evidence to suggest that respondents are less likely to under-report activities that induce anxiety or about which they feel sensitive in self-completion questionnaires than in structured interviews (Tourangeau and Smith 1996).

No interviewer variability

Self-completion questionnaires do not suffer from the problem of interviewers asking questions in a different order or in different ways.

Convenience for respondents

Self-completion questionnaires are more convenient for respondents, because they can complete a questionnaire when they want and at the speed that they want to go.

Disadvantages of the self-completion questionnaire in comparison to the structured interview

Cannot prompt

There is no one present to help respondents if they are having difficulty answering a question. It is always important to ensure that the questions that are asked are clear and unambiguous, but this is especially so with the self-completion questionnaire, since there is no interviewer to help respondents with questions they find difficult to understand and hence to answer. Also, great attention must be paid to ensure that the questionnaire is easy to complete; otherwise questions will be inadvertently omitted if instructions are unclear.

Cannot probe

There is no opportunity to probe respondents to elaborate an answer. Probing can be very important when open-ended questions are being asked. Interviewers are often trained to get more from respondents. However, this problem largely applies to open questions, which are not used a great deal in self-completion questionnaire research.

Cannot ask many questions that are not salient to respondents

Respondents are more likely than in interviews to become tired of answering questions that are not very salient to them, and that they are likely to perceive as boring. Because of the risk of a questionnaire being consigned to a waste paper bin, it is important to avoid including many non-salient questions in a self-completion questionnaire. However, this point suggests that, when a research issue *is* salient to the respondent, a high response rate is feasible (Altschuld and Lower 1984). This means that, when questions are salient, the self-completion questionnaire may be a good choice for researchers, especially when the much lower cost is borne in mind.

Difficulty of asking other kinds of question

In addition to the problem of asking many questions that are not salient to respondents, as previously suggested, it is also important to avoid asking more than a very small number of open questions (because respondents frequently do not want to write a lot). Questions with complex structures, such as filters, should be avoided as far as possible (because respondents often find them difficult to follow).

Questionnaire can be read as a whole

Respondents are able to read the whole questionnaire before answering the first question. When this occurs, none of the questions asked is truly independent of the others. It also means that you cannot be sure that questions have been answered in the correct order. It also means that the problems of question order effects, of the kind discussed in Chapter 9, may occur.

Do not know who answers

With postal questionnaires, you can never be sure that the right person has answered the questionnaire. If a questionnaire is sent to a certain person in a household, it may be that someone else in that household completes the questionnaire. It is also impossible to have any control over the intrusion of non-respondents (such as other members of a household) in the answering of questions. Similarly, if a questionnaire is sent to a manager in a firm, the task may simply be delegated to someone else. This advantage of the structured interview over the postal questionnaire does not apply when the former is administered by telephone, since the same problem applies. There is a feeling among some commentators that when a self-completion questionnaire is administered over the Internet (see Chapter 28 for more on this), the problem of not knowing who is replying is exacerbated because of the propensity of some Web users to assume online identities (Couper 2004).

Cannot collect additional data

With an interview, interviewers might be asked to collect snippets of information about the workplace, firm, manager, or whatever. This is not going to be possible in connection with a postal questionnaire, but, if self-completion questionnaires are handed out in an organization, it is more feasible to collect such additional data.

Difficult to ask a lot of questions

As signalled above, because of the possibility of 'respondent fatigue', long questionnaires are rarely feasible. They may even result in a greater tendency for questionnaires not to be answered in the first place, since they can be daunting.

Not appropriate for some kinds of respondent

Respondents whose literacy is limited or whose facility with English is restricted will not be able to answer the questionnaire, as illustrated by the example in Research in focus 8.9 of the exclusion of manual workers in a cement factory from a questionnaire survey owing to low levels of literacy. The second of these difficulties cannot be entirely overcome when interviews are being employed, but the difficulties are likely to be greater with postal questionnaires.

Greater risk of missing data

Partially answered questionnaires are more likely, because of a lack of prompting or supervision, than in interviews. It is also easier for respondents actively to decide not to answer a question when on their own than when being asked by an interviewer. For example, questions that appear boring or irrelevant to the respondent may be especially likely to be skipped. If questions are not answered, this creates a problem of missing data for the variables that are created.

Lower response rates

One of the most damaging limitations is that surveys by postal questionnaire typically result in lower response rates (see Key concept 8.5) than comparable interview-based studies. The significance of a response rate is that, unless it can be proven that those who do not participate do not differ from those who do, there is likely to be the risk of bias. In other words, if, as is likely, there are differences between participants and refusals, it is probable that the findings relating to the sample will be affected. If a response rate is low, it seems likely that the risk of bias in the findings will be greater.

The problem of low response rates seems to apply particularly to postal questionnaires. This explains why some researchers who use postal questionnaires as a data collection method tend to employ a mixed methods research design (see Chapter 27 for a discussion of this kind of research). This is because they anticipate the likelihood of a low response rate to the questionnaire survey and therefore seek to increase the validity of their research through triangulation (see Key concept 17.6) with other methods. However, there are strategies that can be employed by researchers to improve self-completion questionnaire response rates. These can sometimes include the provision of a small financial incentive. Alternatively, researchers may choose to administer self-completion questionnaires to samples drawn from a population that is more within their control—for example, by sampling from a group of practising managers who are part-time students at the university where the researcher also works. Lucas's (1997) research involved a survey by self-completion questionnaire that was answered by all students to whom it was administered; the only non-respondents were those who were absent from the lecture (see Research in focus 8.7). When a self-completion questionnaire is employed in this kind of context, it seems less vulnerable to the problem of a low response rate.

Mangione (1995: 60–1) has provided the following classification of bands of response rate to postal questionnaires:

over 85 per cent	excellent
70–85 per cent very	good
60–70 per cent	acceptable
50–60 per cent	barely acceptable
below 50 per cent	not acceptable.

Steps to improve response rates to postal questionnaires

Because of the tendency for postal questionnaire surveys to generate lower response rates than comparable structured interview surveys (and the implications this has for the validity of findings), a great deal of thought and research has gone into ways of improving survey response. The following steps are frequently suggested:

- Write a good covering letter explaining the reasons for the research, why it is important, and why the recipient has been selected; mention sponsorship if any, and provide guarantees of confidentiality. The advice provided in Tips and skills 'Topics and issues to include in an introductory statement' (Chapter 9) in connection with the kind of letter that might go out in advance of a respondent being asked to be interviewed can also be followed to good effect in connection with a postal questionnaire.

- Postal questionnaires should always be accompanied by a stamped addressed envelope or, at the very least, return postage.

- Follow up individuals who do not reply at first, possibly with two or three further mailings. The importance of reminders cannot be overstated—they do work. Our preferred and recommended approach is to send out a reminder letter to non-respondents two weeks after the initial mailing, reasserting the nature and aims of the survey and suggesting that the person should contact either the researcher or someone else in the research team to obtain a replacement copy of the questionnaire if the initial mailing has been mislaid or lost. Then, two weeks after that, all further non-respondents should be sent another letter along with a further copy of the questionnaire. These reminders have a demonstrable effect on the response rate. Some writers argue for further mailings of reminder letters to non-respondents. If a response rate is worryingly low, such further mailings would certainly be desirable. Some of the tactics used by Fey and Denison (2003; see Research in focus 10.1) can also be used.

- Unsurprisingly, shorter questionnaires tend to achieve better response rates than longer ones. However, this is not a clear-cut principle, because it is difficult to specify when a questionnaire becomes 'too long'. Also, the evidence suggests that the effect of the length of questionnaires on response rates cannot be separated very easily from the salience of the topic(s) of the research for respondents and from the nature of the sample. Respondents may be highly tolerant of questionnaires that contain many questions on topics that interest them.

- Clear instructions and an attractive layout improve postal questionnaire response rates. Dillman (1983), as part of what he calls the Total Design Method (TDM) for postal questionnaire research, recommends lower case for questions and upper case for closed-ended answers. However, with the growing use of electronic communication and the associated rise of 'netiquette', upper case is increasingly associated with shouting, so that this recommendation may become less desirable.

- Do not allow the questionnaire to appear unnecessarily bulky. Dillman (1983) recommends a booklet format for the questionnaire and using the photocopier to reduce the size of the questionnaire to fit the booklet

format. This also gives the impression of a more professional approach.

- As with structured interviewing (see Chapter 9), begin with questions that are more likely to be of interest to the respondent. This advice is linked to the issue of salience (see above) but has particular significance in the context of research that may have limited salience for the respondent.

- There is some controversy about how significant for response rates it is to personalize covering letters by including the respondent's name and address (Baumgartner and Heberlein 1984). However, one of the features of the TDM approach advocated by Dillman (1983) is that these details are supplied on covering letters and each is individually signed.

- We are inclined to the view that, in general, postal questionnaires should comprise as few open questions as possible, since people are often deterred by the prospect of having to write a lot. In fact, many writers on the subject recommend that open questions are used as little as possible in self-completion questionnaires.

- Providing monetary incentives can be an effective way of increasing the response rate, although it is very unlikely to be an option for most students undertaking project work or research for their dissertation. Incentives are more effective if the money comes with the questionnaire rather than if it is promised once the questionnaire has been returned. Apparently, respondents typically do not cynically take the money and discard the questionnaire! The evidence also suggests that quite small amounts of money have a positive impact on the response rate, but that larger amounts do not necessarily improve the response rate any further.

Some advantages and disadvantages of the self-completion questionnaire, as compared to the structured interview, are illustrated by the example provided in Research in focus 10.2. The Workplace Employment Relations (WERS) study employed a research design that combined face-to-face and telephone structured interviewing and postal/online questionnaires in order to overcome some of the limitations of each and to represent the perspectives of managers, worker representatives, and employees on a range of employment relations issues. Table 10.1 illustrates their combined use of these methods and provides details of the response rates obtained in each case. However, despite these measures, response rates in the WERS 2011 survey (shown in Table 10.1) are lower than in the 2004 survey, falling close to levels that

Research in focus 10.1
Following up on a questionnaire survey

In a survey of foreign firms operating in Russia, Fey and Denison (2003) describe how they personally delivered a copy of the questionnaire to each firm for a senior manager to complete. 'Wherever possible, the researcher described the project and had the manager complete the questionnaire at that time. However, sometimes the manager opted to complete the questionnaire later and return it by fax' (2003: 690). They then go on to explain how they followed up on individuals who did not initially respond: 'If questionnaires were not received within one week, we began a follow-up procedure including three telephone calls, faxing another questionnaire, and a fourth telephone call as a final reminder. Companies whose questionnaires had not been returned by the end of this procedure were considered nonrespondents' (2003: 690–1). However, even with all of this effort on the part of the researchers, it is worth noting that they obtained only 179 usable questionnaires, representing a 37 per cent response rate.

could be seen as a problem. This decline is not unique to WERS and has been attributed to 'a reduced sense of obligation to participate in government-sponsored research, greater reluctance to provide potentially sensitive data and research saturation' (van Wanrooy et al., 2013: 209). This last point draws attention to the fatigue that can arise when potential respondents are inundated with requests to participate in research studies.

In a sense, the choice between structured interviews or self-administered questionnaires as a method of data collection is an issue that is primarily about mode of administration. The advantages and disadvantages of postal questionnaires versus other modes of questionnaire administration, including telephone interviewing, email, and web-based surveys, are summarized in Table 28.1.

Table 10.1

Outcomes from the WERS 2011 cross-section survey sample			
	Total responses (number)	Response rate (%)	Average duration (minutes)
Survey of managers	2680	46	87
Survey of worker representatives	1002	64	30
Survey of employees	21,981	54	–

Source: adapted from van Wanrooy et al. (2013)

Tips and skills
Response rates

As we have explained, response rates are important because, the lower a response rate, the more questions are likely to be raised about the representativeness of the achieved sample. This is likely, however, to be an issue only with randomly selected samples. With samples that are not selected on the basis of a probability sampling method, it could be argued that the response rate is less of an issue, because the sample would not be representative of a population, even if everyone participated! Postal questionnaire surveys in particular are often associated with low response rates and, as Mangione's classification illustrates, according to some authorities a response rate of below 50 per cent is not acceptable. On the other hand, many published articles report the results of studies that are well below this level. In an examination of published studies in the field of organizational research in the years 1979–83, Terence Mitchell(1985) found a range of response rates of 30–94 per cent. Bryman (1989*a*: 44) points to two articles in the early 1980s that achieved response rates of 21 and 25 per cent. Moreover, these articles were published in two of the most highly regarded journals in the field: *Academy of Management Journal* and *Strategic Management Journal*. One of the surveys reported by Cunha and Cooper (2002;) (see Research in focus 8.9) achieved a sample of just 18 per cent. The point we are making is that, if you achieve a low response rate, do not despair. Although such writers as Mangione(1995) may regard response rates of 18, 21, and 25 per cent as unacceptable (and he may be right about this judgement), a great deal of published research also achieves low response rates. The key point is to recognize and acknowledge the implications of the possible limitations of a low response rate. On the other hand, if your research is based on a convenience sample, ironically it could be argued that a low response rate is less significant. Many students find postal and other forms of self-completion questionnaire attractive because of their low cost and quick administration. The point of this discussion is that you should not be put off using such techniques because of the prospect of a low response rate.

Research in focus 10.2
Combining the use of structured interviews with self-completion questionnaires

Structured interviews can be used in conjunction with self-completion questionnaires to gain understanding of the perspectives of different groups of participants. The 2011 Workplace Employment Relations Survey (WERS 2011) (see also Research in focus 3.14) is an example of a project that has been concerned to use different research methods to reach different categories of respondent. The structured interviews with managers involved a Central Contacting Team of 120 experienced telephone interviewers, who contacted the workplaces to arrange face-to-face or telephone interviews with the senior managers who were responsible for workplace relations and with worker representatives. They also administered questionnaires to staff members at each workplace.

The WERS survey is designed to combine the views of different groups of participants in order to overcome the limitations and partiality of any one group of respondents. The combined use of structured interviews and self-completion questionnaires together enables this aim to be achieved, despite the vast scale of the project.

Designing the self-completion questionnaire

Do not cramp the presentation

Because of the well-known problem of low response rates to the postal questionnaire in particular, it is sometimes considered preferable to make the instrument appear as short as possible in order for it to be less likely to deter prospective respondents from answering. However, this is almost always a mistake. As Dillman(1983) observes, an attractive layout is likely to enhance response rates, whereas the kinds of tactics that are sometimes employed to make a questionnaire appear shorter than it really is—such as reducing margins and the space between questions—make it look cramped and thereby unattractive. Also, if questions are too close together, there is a risk that they will be inadvertently omitted.

This is not to say that you should be ridiculously liberal in your use of space, as this does not necessarily provide for an attractive format either and may run the risk of making the questionnaire look bulky. As with so many other issues in business research, a steady course needs to be steered between possible extremes.

Clear presentation

Far more important than making a self-completion questionnaire appear shorter than is the case is to make sure that it has a layout that is easy on the eye, as Dillman emphasizes, and that it facilitates the answering of all questions that are relevant to the respondent. Dillman's recommendation of lower case for questions and upper case for closed answers is an example of one consideration, but at the very least a variety of print styles (for example, different fonts, print sizes, bold, italics, and capitals) can enhance the appearance *but must be used in a consistent manner*. This last point means that you should ensure that you use one style for general instructions, one for headings, perhaps one for specific instructions (e.g., 'Go to question 7'), one for questions, and one for closed-ended answers. Mixing print styles, so that one style is sometimes used for both general instructions and questions, can be very confusing for respondents.

Vertical or horizontal closed answers?

Bearing in mind that most questions in a self-completion questionnaire are likely to be of the closed kind, one consideration is whether to arrange the fixed answers vertically or horizontally. Very often, the nature of the answers will dictate a vertical arrangement because of their sheer length. Many writers prefer a vertical format whenever possible, because, in some cases where either arrangement is feasible, confusion can arise when a horizontal one is employed (Sudman and Bradburn 1982). Consider the following:

What do you think of the CEO's performance in his job since he took over the running of this company? (*Please tick the appropriate response*)

Very ____ Good ____ Fair ____ Poor ____ Very ____
good   poor

There is a risk that, if the questionnaire is being answered in haste, the required tick will be placed in the wrong space—for example, indicating Good when Fair was the intended response. Also, a vertical format more clearly distinguishes questions from answers. To some extent, these potential problems can be obviated through the judicious use of spacing and print variation, but they represent significant considerations. A further reason why vertical alignments can be superior is that they are probably easier to code, especially when **pre-codes** appear on the questionnaire. Very often, self-completion questionnaires are arranged so that to the right of each question are two columns: one for the column in which data relating to the question will appear in a data matrix; the other for all the pre-codes. The latter allows the appropriate code to be assigned to a respondent's answer by circling it for later entry into the computer. Thus, the choice would be between the formats presented in Tips and skills 'Closed question with a horizontal format' and Tips and skills 'Closed question with a vertical format'. In the second case, not only is there less ambiguity about where a tick is to be placed; the task of coding is easier. However, when there is to be a battery of questions with identical answer formats, as in a Likert scale, a vertical format will take up too much space. One way of dealing with this kind of questioning is to use abbreviations with an accompanying explanation. An example can be found in Tips and skills 'Formatting a Likert scale'. The four items presented there are taken from an eighteen-item Likert scale designed to measure job satisfaction (Brayfield and Rothe 1951).

Identifying response sets in a Likert scale

One of the advantages of using closed questions is that they can be pre-coded, thus turning the processing of data for computer analysis into a fairly simple task (see Chapter 11 for more on this). However, some thought has to go into

Tips and skills
Closed question with a horizontal format

What do you think of the CEO's performance in his job since he took over the running of this company?

(*Please tick the appropriate response*)

Very good ____ Good ____ Fair ____ Poor ____ Very poor ____   5 4 3 2 1

Tips and skills
Closed question with a vertical format

What do you think of the CEO's performance in his job since he took over the running of this company?
(Please tick the appropriate response)

Very good	____	5
Good	____	4
Fair	____	3
Poor	____	2
Very poor	____	1

Tips and skills
Formatting a Likert scale

In the next set of questions, you are presented with a statement. You are being asked to indicate your level of agreement or disagreement with each statement by indicating whether you: Strongly Agree (SA), Agree (A), are Undecided (U), Disagree (D), or Strongly Disagree (SD).

Please indicate your level of agreement by circling the appropriate response.

23. My job is like a hobby to me.

    SA   A   U   D   SD

24. My job is usually interesting enough to keep me from getting bored.

    SA   A   U   D   SD

25. It seems that my friends are more interested in their jobs.

    SA   A   U   D   SD

26. I enjoy my work more than my leisure time.

    SA   A   U   D   SD

the scoring of the items of the kind presented in Tips and skills 'Formatting a Likert scale'. We might for example score question 23 as follows:

Strongly agree = 5

Agree = 4

Undecided = 3

Disagree = 2

Strongly disagree = 1

Accordingly, a high score for the item (5 or 4) indicates satisfaction with the job and a low score (1 or 2) indicates low job satisfaction. The same applies to question 24. However, when we come to question 25, the picture is different. Here, agreement indicates a *lack* of job satisfaction. It is disagreement that is indicative of job satisfaction. We would have to reverse the coding of this item, so that:

Strongly agree = 1

Agree = 2

Undecided = 3

Disagree = 4

Strongly disagree = 5

The point of including such items is to identify people who exhibit response sets, such as acquiescence (see Chapter 9). If someone were to agree with all eighteen items, when some of them indicated *lack* of job satisfaction, it is likely that the respondent was affected by a response set and the answers are unlikely to provide a valid assessment of job satisfaction for that person.

Clear instructions about how to respond

Always be clear about how you want respondents to indicate their replies when answering closed questions. Are they supposed to place a tick by or circle or underline the appropriate answer, or are they supposed to delete inappropriate answers? Also, in many cases it is feasible for the respondent to choose more than one answer—is this acceptable to you? If it is not, you should indicate this in your instructions, for example:

(Please choose the one answer that best represents your views by placing a tick in the appropriate box.)

If you do not make this clear and if some respondents choose more than one answer, you will have to treat their replies as if they had not answered. This possibility increases the risk of missing data from some respondents.

If it is acceptable to you for more than one category to be chosen, you need to make this clear, for example:

(Please choose all answers that represent your views by placing a tick in the appropriate boxes).

It is a common error for such instructions to be omitted and for respondents either to be unsure about how to reply or to make inappropriate selections.

Keep question and answers together

This is a simple and obvious, though often transgressed, requirement—namely, that you should never split up a question so that it appears on two separate pages. A common error is to have some space left at the bottom of a page into which the question can be slotted but for the closed answers to appear on the next page. Doing so carries the risk of the respondent forgetting to answer the question or providing an answer in the wrong group of closed answers (a problem that is especially likely when a series of questions with a common answer format is being used, as with a Likert scale).

Diaries as a form of self-completion questionnaire

When the researcher is specifically interested in precise estimates of different kinds of behaviour, the diary warrants serious consideration, though it is still a relatively underused method. Unfortunately, the term 'diary' has somewhat different meanings in business research (see Key concept 10.3). It is the first of the three meanings— what Elliott (1997) calls the *researcher-driven diary*—that is the focus of attention here, especially in the context of its use in relation to quantitative research. When employed in this way, the researcher-driven diary functions in a similar way to the self-completion questionnaire.

Equally, it could be said that the researcher-driven diary is an alternative method of data collection to observation in the sense that the research participants observe and record their own behaviour. As such it can be thought of as the equivalent of structured observation (see Chapter 12) in the context of research questions that are framed in terms of quantitative research, or of ethnography (see Chapter 19) in the context of research questions framed in terms of qualitative research.

Corti(1993) distinguishes between 'structured diaries' and 'free text diaries'. Either may be employed by

Key concept 10.3
What is a research diary?

There are three major ways in which the term 'diary' has been employed in the context of business research.

The diary as a method of data collection. Here the researcher devises a structure for the diary and then asks a sample of diarists to complete the instruments so that they record what they do more or less contemporaneously with their activities. Elliott (1997) refers to this kind of use of the diary as *researcher-driven diaries*. Such diaries can be employed for the collection of data within the context of both quantitative and qualitative research. Sometimes, the collection of data in this manner is supplemented by a personal interview in which the diarist is asked questions about such things as what he or she meant by certain remarks. This *diary-interview*, as it is often referred to (Zimmerman and Wieder 1977), is usually employed when diarists record their behaviour in prose form rather than simply indicating the amount of time spent on different kinds of activity.

The diary as a document. The diary in this context is written spontaneously by the diarist and not at the behest of a researcher. Diaries in this sense are often used by historians but have some potential for business researchers working on issues that are of social scientific significance. As John Scott (1990) observes, the diary in this sense often shades into autobiography. Diaries as documents will be further addressed in Chapter 23.

The diary as a log of the researcher's activities. Researchers sometimes keep a record of what they do at different stages as an *aide-mémoire*. For example, the famous social anthropologist Malinowski (1967) kept an infamous log of his activities ('infamous' because it revealed his distaste for the people he studied and his inappropriate involvement with females). This kind of diary often shades into the writing of field notes by ethnographers, about which more is written in Chapter 19.

Research in focus 10.4
A diary study of managers and their jobs

R. Stewart's (1967) now classic study of managerial time use focused on:

* the amount of time managers spent on particular activities;
* the frequency with which they undertook particular tasks.

'The diary method was chosen instead of observation because the research aimed to study more than 100 managers in a large number of companies. This aim could not be achieved by observation without a large team of observers' (1967: 7). In addition to recording the nature of the task that was being undertaken (such as paperwork, telephone calls, discussions, and so on), managers were asked to record in their diary:

1. the duration of the incident (hours and minutes);
2. where the work was done (own office, travelling, etc.);
3. who else was involved (boss, secretary, colleagues, etc.).

The diary entry took the form of a grid, which was filled in by ticking the appropriate boxes, which were subsequently coded. A distinction was made between episodes of work lasting 5 minutes or more, and 'fleeting contacts' of less than 5 minutes. The latter were recorded separately from the main section of the diary so managers could record as many of these short incidents as possible. Each day, the managers completed in addition to the main diary entry a form asking them to describe the three activities that had taken up the most work time. Each week, the managers filled in a form designed to check how well they had kept the diary, asking for example, 'How often did you fill in the diary?' 160 managers kept diaries for a period of four weeks, a time period that Stewart considered was long enough to gain an impression of variations in the job but not so long that managers would lose interest in the exercise.

Research in focus 10.5
A diary study of responses to psychological contract breach

Conway and Briner (2002) suggest that one of the limitations of existing studies of psychological contract breach—when an organization breaks a promise made to the employee—stems from the methods that are used for study—that is, questionnaire surveys. In particular, 'breaches of an employee's psychological contract are *events* that happen at work or in relation to work. For accurate measurement they therefore need to be assessed soon after they occur' (2002: 288).

(*continued*)

This led the researchers to conduct a daily diary study in order to develop a better understanding of the psychological contract. The sample comprised:

- 21 managers who worked for a UK bank; and
- a convenience sample of 24 participants who were part-time M.Sc. students at Birkbeck College, where both of the researchers were employed.

All 45 participants were in employment, mostly in professional occupations. The researchers anticipated that exceeded promises would be construed positively, whereas broken promises would be construed negatively.

The diary was completed over ten consecutive working days. Participants were posted their diary booklets and asked to complete their daily diary schedules immediately at the end of each working day. The first three pages of the daily diary booklet provided instructions on how to complete the diary (2002: 291).

On each occasion, participants were first asked how they had felt at work on that particular day; items were assessed on a six-point scale denoting the frequency with which certain emotions were felt by workers on that day. The scale categories were: 'not at all'; 'occasionally'; 'some of the time'; 'much of the time'; 'most of the time'; and 'all of the time'. For example, workers were asked to indicate how frequently they felt depressed rather than enthusiastic on the day in question. They were then asked (a) if the organization had broken any promises to them on that day, and (b) if the organization had exceeded any promises during that day. If a promise had been either broken or exceeded, they were asked to provide written details of the event and to complete emotion checklists by responding to a list of words that represented possible reactions, such as 'resentment' (reaction to broken promise) and 'excitement' (reaction to exceeded promise).

The research suggests a far greater incidence of psychological contract breach than previous survey studies had suggested. This, suggest the authors, may be in part attributable to the method used, in particular the sensitivity of the diary method in picking up events as they occur on a day-to-day basis.

quantitative researchers. The research on managers and their jobs by R. Stewart (1967) is an illustration of the structured kind of diary (see Research in focus 10.4). The diary has the general appearance of a questionnaire with largely closed questions. The kind of diary employed in this research is often referred to as a 'time-use' diary, in that it is designed so that diarists can record more or less contemporaneously the amount of time engaged in certain activities, such as time spent travelling, doing paperwork, in committee meetings, and so on. Estimates of the amount of time spent in different activities are often regarded as more accurate, because the events are less subject to memory problems or to the tendency to round up or down. Structured diaries are also regarded as more accurate in tracking events as they occur, as the example in Research in focus 10.4 illustrates. However, the diary method is more intrusive than answering a questionnaire, and it could be argued that it causes changes in behaviour or behavioural awareness of an issue. For example, in their study of psychological contract breach, Conway and Briner (2002) (see Research in focus 10.5) note that their research design may have encouraged respondents to report very minor breaches of the psychological contract that they perhaps otherwise would not

have regarded as significant. They thus conclude that 'it is a matter of debate as to what can be considered as lying inside or outside a psychological contract' (2002: 299).

An example of a free-text diary is provided by Huxley et al.'s (2005) study of stress and pressures among mental health social workers. In this study, a diary relating to the previous working week was sent to each of the 237 respondents, along with a postal questionnaire. The issues that diarists were invited to cover were based on findings from two focus groups the researchers ran prior to the diary study involving mental health social workers. The diary invited open-ended responses, which were entered into the qualitative software analysis package NVivo and were analysed thematically. One of the advantages of the diary in conjunction with a self-completion questionnaire in this study was that it provided contextual information about factors that had an impact on employee stress, such as the burden of paperwork and bureaucratic procedures, staff shortages and excessive workloads, and constant change and restructuring. This kind of information would probably have been much more difficult to glean from the questionnaires alone.

Using free-text recording of behaviour carries the same kinds of problems as those associated with coding answers to structured interview open questions—namely, the time-consuming nature of the exercise and the increased risks associated with the coding of answers. However, the free-text approach is less likely to be problematic when, as in Huxley et al. (2005), diarists can be instructed on what kind of information to write about, such as that relating to pressures of work, their affective commitment, and job satisfaction. It would be much more difficult to code free-text entries relating to more general questions such as in R. Stewart's (1967) study of how managers use their time.

Corti (1993) recommends that the person preparing the diary should:

- provide explicit instructions for diarists;
- be clear about the time periods within which behaviour is to be recorded—for example, day, twenty-four hours, week;
- provide a model of a completed section of a diary;
- provide checklists of 'items, events, or behaviour' that can jog people's memory—but the list should not become too daunting in length or complexity;
- include fixed blocks of time or columns showing when the designated activities start and finish (for example, diaries of the kind used by R. Stewart (1967), which show how managers spend their time).

Advantages and disadvantages of the diary as a method of data collection

The two studies that have been used to illustrate the use of diaries also suggest its potential advantages.

- When fairly precise estimates of the frequency and/or amount of time spent in different forms of behaviour are required, the diary may provide more valid and reliable data than questionnaire data (see Research in focus 10.6).
- When information about the sequencing of different types of behaviour is required, the diary is likely to perform better than questionnaires or interviews.
- The first two advantages could be used to suggest that structured observation would be just as feasible, but structured observation is probably less appropriate for producing data on behaviour that is personally sensitive, such as work-related gossip (see Research in focus 10.7). Moreover, although data on such behaviour can be collected by structured interview, it is likely that respondents will be less willing to divulge personal details. If such information were collected by

questionnaire, there is a greater risk of recall and rounding problems (see the first point in this list).

On the other hand, diaries may suffer from the following problems:

- They tend to be more expensive than personal interviews (because of the costs associated with recruiting diarists and of checking that diaries are being properly completed).
- Diaries can suffer from a process of attrition, as people decide they have had enough of the task of completing a diary.
- This last point raises the possibility that diarists become less diligent over time about their record keeping.
- There is sometimes failure to record details sufficiently quickly, so that memory recall problems set in.

However, diary researchers argue that the resulting data are more accurate than the equivalent data based on interviews or questionnaires.

Experience and event sampling

Scherbaum and Meade (2013) have called for greater use in management research of various methods that would reduce the reliance on questionnaires and other traditional techniques. Among these is **experience sampling** or *event sampling*, which capture participants' 'transient affective states'. With this method, participants are prompted to reply to questions about their behaviour and/or their affective states at particular points in time (or within a narrow timeframe). The method allows something approximating to real-time data about the occurrence and possibly intensity of the issue being asked about. The authors write:

> Individuals are typically prompted at specific points in time (e.g. every hour, once a day, during work breaks) or after specific events (e.g. after an interaction with a customer) to respond about their current states.
>
> (Scherbaum and Meade 2013: 140)

In addition, the participant might be prompted to complete the research instrument when a device that he or she carries around emits a sound. Experience/event sampling operates in a similar way to a diary in that participants record their feelings or impressions in terms of a predetermined format at the appropriate juncture.

Research in focus 10.6
A diary study of text messaging

Faulkner and Culwin (2005) used a questionnaire and a diary study to explore the uses of text messaging among UK university students. The diary study involved twenty-four mobile phone users who had also used text messaging. The researchers used a convenience sample made up of students in their mid-20s on a computer studies course at a UK university and the study formed part of their course work. The group was asked to keep diaries of sent and received text messages for a two-week period. 'The study started at midnight on February 15th to avoid the sample being affected by Valentine's Day greetings' (2005: 176). The following information was recorded in a structured format:

Book number

Message number

Date

Time

Send or receive

The original message

A translation if it was not in English

Sender's details

Relationship of sender to receiver.

Although structured observation could have been used in this study, it would have entailed researchers following users around and waiting for participants to text someone, so a diary study is in this case a more directed method of focusing on one particular type of activity. This study focused on text messages that were predominantly of a personal nature, but text messaging is also a method of communication within business, where similar research methods could be applied.

Research in focus 10.7
Using diaries to study a sensitive topic:
work-related gossip

K. Waddington (2005) argues that diary methods offer a solution to the problems of researching the often private, unheard, and unseen world of gossip in organizations. However, she also argues that diary methods alone are insufficient. Her mixed-method research design of nursing and health care organizations thus involved three phases. The first was aimed at exploring the characteristics of gossip and individual differences in relation to gender and organizational position; repertory grid technique (see Chapter 9) was used to ascertain categories related to these distinctions. Phase two of the research addressed the role of gossip in sensemaking and socialization and as an aspect of the expression and management of emotion in relation to workplace stress; in-depth interviews with nurses were used as the main method of data collection. The third phase of the study is where diary methods were used, along with a critical incident method (see Chapter 9) and telephone interviewing. The aim of this stage of the study was to add to the findings of the first two phases. Twenty health care workers were asked to keep an event-contingent structured diary record. When an incident of gossip occurred, they were asked to record it on the incident sheet (see Figure 10.1) as soon as possible after it had occurred and at least once a day. The respondents were also asked to reflect upon an episode of work-related gossip in the form of a critical incident account detailing: (1) reasons for choosing the incident; (2) how they felt at the time it took place; (3) where and when it occurred and who was involved; (4) the content of the gossip; and (5) organizational factors contributing to the occurrence of the incident. Within four weeks of completion and return of the diaries and critical incident accounts, follow-up telephone interviews were carried out to clarify details relating to the critical incident accounts and to discuss the perceived accuracy and practicality of the diary records.

Figure 10.1

A sample diary record sheet

Record Sheet

Date......... Time.........am/pm   Length of time incident approx............... minutes

Number of people involved........ Females/.........Males

Where the incident took place:

Nature of *your* interpersonal relationship with the person(s) involved (please circle):
Work relationship only/friends at work/friends outside of work/partner/family member/other—please specify

I disclosed	Very little	1 2 3 4 5 6 7	A great deal
Others disclosed	Very little	1 2 3 4 5 6 7	A great deal
Social integration	I didn't feel part of the group	1 2 3 4 5 6 7	I felt part of the group
Quality	Unpleasant	1 2 3 4 5 6 7	Very unpleasant
Initiation	I initiated	1 2 3 4 5 6 7	Others initiated

What did you gossip about?
How did you feel at the time the above took place?

Source: K. Waddington (2005).

An experience sampling study of 78 bus drivers in the USA was conducted by Wagner et al. (2013). The authors were interested in how far having to enact emotional labour has implications for people's home lives. The researchers arranged for a computer terminal to be set up close to the bus drivers' lounge. Over a two-week period, prior to beginning their shifts, each bus driver logged into the computer and completed a questionnaire regarding how well they had slept the previous night. Following each shift, drivers logged on again and completed a questionnaire about how far they had engaged in emotional labour that day and their level of anxiety at that moment. Then, each evening drivers completed a paper-and-pencil questionnaire which assessed the level of emotional exhaustion and whether the driver had experienced 'work-to-family conflict' during the evening. The researchers were able to show that enacting emotional labour on a daily basis did indeed have adverse implications for drivers' home lives.

The chief advantages of the method over the traditional way of administering a self-completion questionnaire is that the ensuing data tend to be more immediate (since particpants reply *in situ*), less general (replies are not about feelings over a period of time), and less prone to memory distortions, though they share most of the limitations associated with the diary method (see above). Experience sampling may become popular as people's familiarity with and use of smartphones increases, since they provide a very useful platform for prompting research participants to complete a research instrument and for completing and submitting answers. Hofmans et al. (2013) used smartphones to gather experience sampling data from 50 employees in a study of task characteristics and work effort. The employees were prompted via a beep five times a day for five working days to complete questions about their task at that time and their feelings about it. Beeps were not always responded to, so that there is an element of non-response, but the immediacy of the data that were received provides a significant alternative to conventional questionnaire answers. Uy et al. (2010) distinguish between three types of experience sampling approach:

a) *interval contingent*—where responses are provided at predetermined intervals, e.g. every hour, or at the same time each day, such as in Wagner et al.'s (2013) study of emotional labour and bus drivers;

b) *event contingent*—participants respond when the event takes place, such as when they experience certain moods;

c) *signal contingent*—participants are prompted to respond by a signalling device, such as an alarm, at randomly selected points in the day, as in Hofmans' (2013) study mentioned above.

Uy et al. suggest that experience sampling may offer benefits in terms of being able to capture dynamic processes as they unfold over time and offer greater **ecological validity** through the fact that reactions to events are recorded in naturalistic contexts where they occur (Uy et al., 2010). Chapter 12 returns to the issue of time sampling in relation to structured observation, where the observer records the observed behaviour of respondents at regularly timed intervals.

Key points

- Many of the recommendations relating to the self-completion questionnaire apply equally or almost equally to the structured interview, as has been mentioned on several occasions.

- Closed questions tend to be used in survey research rather than open ones. Coding is a particular problem when dealing with answers to open questions.

- Structured interviews and self-completion questionnaires both have their respective advantages and disadvantages, but a particular problem with questionnaires sent by post is that they frequently produce a low response rate. However, steps can be taken to boost response rates for postal questionnaires.

- Presentation of closed questions and the general layout constitute important considerations in the design of the self-completion questionnaire.

- The researcher-driven diary was also introduced as a possible alternative to using questionnaires and interviews when the research questions are very specifically concerned with aspects of people's behaviour.

Questions for review

Self-completion questionnaire or postal questionnaire?

- Are the self-completion questionnaire and the postal questionnaire the same thing?

Evaluating the self-completion questionnaire in relation to the structured interview

- 'The low response rates frequently achieved in research with postal questionnaires mean that the structured interview is invariably a more suitable choice.' Discuss.

- What steps can be taken to boost postal questionnaire response rates?

Designing the self-completion questionnaire

- Why are self-completion questionnaires usually made up mainly of closed questions?

- Why might a vertical format for presenting closed questions be preferable to a horizontal format?

Diaries as a form of self-completion questionnaire

● What are the main kinds of diary used in the collection of business research data?

● Are there any circumstances when the diary approach might be preferable to the use of a self-completion questionnaire?

Online Resource Centre

www.oxfordtextbooks.co.uk/orc/brymanbrm4e/

Visit the Interactive Research Guide that accompanies this book to complete an exercise in Self-Completion Questionnaires.

11

Asking questions

Chapter outline

This chapter is concerned with the considerations that are involved in asking questions that are used in structured interviews and questionnaires of the kinds discussed in Chapters 9 and 10. As such, it continues the focus upon survey research that began in Chapter 7 and moves on to the next stage in the process that we outlined in Figure 8.1. The chapter explores:

- the issues involved in deciding whether or when to use open or closed questions;
- the different kinds of question that can be asked in structured interviews and questionnaires;
- rules to bear in mind when designing questions;
- vignette questions in which respondents are presented with a scenario and are asked to reflect on the scenario;
- the importance of piloting questions;
- the possibility of using questions that have been used in previous survey research.

Introduction

To many people, how to ask questions represents the crux of considerations surrounding the use of survey instruments such as the structured interview or the self-completion questionnaire. As the previous two chapters have sought to suggest, there is much more to the design and administration of such research instruments than how best to phrase questions. However, there is no doubt that the issue of how questions should be asked is a crucial concern for the survey researcher and it is not surprising that this aspect of designing survey instruments has been a major focus of attention over the years and preoccupies many practising researchers.

Open or closed questions?

One of the most significant considerations for many researchers is whether to ask a question in an open or closed format. This distinction was first introduced in Chapter 9. The issue of whether to ask a question in an open or closed format is relevant to the design of both structured interview and self-administered questionnaire research.

With an open question, respondents are asked a question and can reply however they wish. With a closed question, they are presented with a set of fixed alternatives from which they have to choose an appropriate answer. All of the questions in Tips and skills 'Instructions for interviewers in the use of a filter question' (Chapter 9) are of the closed kind. So too are the Likert-scale items in Research in focus 7.3 and Research in

focus 7.4, as well as Tips and skills 'Closed question with a horizontal format', and Tips and skills 'Closed question with a vertical format' (Chapter 10); these form a particular kind of closed question. What, then, are some of the advantages and limitations of these two types of question format?

Open questions

Open questions present both advantages and disadvantages to the survey researcher, though, as the following discussion suggests, the problems associated with the processing of answers to open questions tend to mean that closed questions are more likely to be used.

Advantages

Although survey researchers typically prefer to use closed questions, open questions do have certain advantages over closed ones, as outlined in the list below.

- Respondents can answer in their own terms. They are not forced to answer in the same terms as those foisted on them by the closed answers.

- They allow unusual responses to be derived. Replies that the survey researcher may not have contemplated (and that would therefore not form the basis for fixed-choice alternatives) are possible.

- The questions do not suggest certain kinds of answer to respondents. Therefore, respondents' levels of knowledge and understanding of issues can be tapped. The salience of issues for respondents can also be explored.

- They are useful for exploring new areas or ones in which the researcher has limited knowledge.

- They are useful for generating fixed-choice format answers. This is a point that will be returned to below.

Disadvantages

However, open questions present problems for the survey researcher, as the following list reveals:

- They are time-consuming for interviewers to administer. Interviewees are likely to talk for longer than is usually the case with a comparable closed question.

- Answers have to be 'coded'. This is very time-consuming. For each open question, it entails reading through answers, deriving themes that can be employed to form the basis for codes, and then going through the answers again so that the answers can be coded for entry into a computer spreadsheet. The process is essentially identical to that involved in *content analysis* and is sometimes called *post-coding* to distinguish it from *pre-coding*, whereby the researcher designs a coding frame in advance of administering a survey instrument and often includes the pre-codes in the questionnaire (as in Tips and skills 'Processing a closed question'). However, in addition to being time-consuming, post-coding can be an unreliable process, because it can introduce the possibility of variability in the coding of answers and therefore of measurement error (and hence lack of validity). This is a form of data processing error (see Figure 8.8). Research in focus 11.1 deals with aspects of the coding of open questions.

- They require greater effort from respondents. Respondents are likely to talk for longer than would be the case for a comparable closed question, or, in the case of a self-completion questionnaire, would need to write for much longer. Therefore, it is often suggested that open questions have limited utility in the context of self-completion questionnaires. Because of the greater effort involved, many prospective respondents are likely to be put off by the prospect of having to write

Research in focus 11.1
Coding a very open question

Coding an open question usually entails reading and rereading transcripts of respondents' replies and formulating distinct themes in their replies. A **coding frame** then needs to be designed that identifies the types of answer associated with each question and their respective codes (i.e. numbers). A **coding schedule** may also be necessary to keep a record of rules to be followed in the identification of certain kinds of answer in terms of a theme. The numbers allocated to each answer can then be used in the computer processing of the data.

Foddy (1993) reports the results of an exercise in which he asked a small sample of his students, 'Your father's occupation is (was) . . . ?' and requested three details: nature of business; size of business; and whether owner or employee. In answer to the size of business issue, the replies were particularly variable in kind, including: 'big', 'small', 'very large', '3000 acres', 'family', 'multinational', '200 people', and 'Philips'. The problem here is obvious: you simply cannot compare and therefore aggregate people's replies. In a sense, the problem is only partly to do with the difficulty of coding an open question. It is also due to a lack of specificity in the question. If, instead, Foddy had asked, 'How many employees are (were) there in your father's organization?', a more comparable set of answers should have been forthcoming. Whether his students would have known this information is, of course, yet another issue. However, the exercise does illustrate the potential problems of asking an open question, particularly one such as this that lacks a clear reference point for gauging size.

Tips and skills
Processing a closed question

What do you think of the CEO's performance in his job since he took over the running of this company?

(Please tick the appropriate response)

Very good	____	5
Good	✓	④
Fair	____	3
Poor	____	2
Very poor	____	1

extensively, which may exacerbate the problem of low response rates with postal questionnaires in particular (see Chapter 10).

- There is the possibility in research based on structured interviews of variability between interviewers in the recording of answers. This possibility is likely to arise as a result of the difficulty of writing down verbatim what respondents say to interviewers. The obvious solution is to use an audio recorder; however, this may not be practicable, for example, in a noisy environment. Also, the transcription of answers to audio-recorded open questions is immensely time-consuming and adds additional costs to a survey. The problem of transcription is one continually faced by qualitative researchers using semi-structured and unstructured interviews (see Chapter 20).

Closed questions

The advantages and disadvantages of closed questions are in many respects implied in some of the considerations relating to open questions.

Advantages

Closed questions offer the following advantages to researchers:

- It is easy to process answers. For example, the respondent in a self-completion questionnaire or the interviewer using a structured interview schedule will place a tick or circle an answer for the appropriate response. The appropriate code can then be almost mechanically derived from the selected answer, since the pre-codes are placed to the side of the fixed-choice answers. See Tips and skills 'Processing a closed question' for an

example based on Tips and skills 'Closed question with a vertical format' (Chapter 10).

- Closed questions enhance the comparability of answers, making it easier to show the relationship between variables and to make comparisons between respondents or types of respondents. For example, in the research described in Research in focus 11.2, Guest and Dewe (1991) were able to generate a contingency table on the basis of their pre-coding of respondents' answers. Although contingency tables can also be generated by post-coding respondents' answers to open questions, with post-coding there is always a problem of knowing how far respondents' answers that receive a certain code are genuinely comparable. As previously noted, the assignment of codes to people's answers may be unreliable (see the sixth point in Tips and skills 'Common sources of error in survey research' in Chapter 9). Checks are necessary to ensure that there is a good deal of agreement between coders and that coders do not change their coding conventions over time. Closed questions essentially circumvent this problem.

- Closed questions may clarify the meaning of a question for respondents. Sometimes respondents may not be clear about what a question is getting at, and the availability of answers may help to clarify the situation for them.

- Closed questions are easy for interviewers and/or respondents to complete. Precisely because interviewers and respondents are not expected to write extensively and instead have to place ticks or circle answers, closed questions are easier and quicker to complete.

- In interviews, closed questions reduce the possibility of variability in the recording of answers in structured interviewing. As noted in Chapter 9, if interviewers do

Research in focus 11.2
Coding closed questions to create a contingency table

In order to establish whether employees were more strongly committed to their company or their union, Guest and Dewe (1991) selected a sample of 716 workers at random from three electronics plants in the south-east of England as the basis for a self-completion questionnaire survey. Just under half of the sample belonged to a trade union. The questions were developed and piloted specifically for the survey and covered a broad range of issues, including:

- *management role*: 'How well do the decisions of local management on this site reflect your opinions?' Responses were on a five-point scale from 'very well' to 'I do not expect anything from the management';

- *union role*: 'How far are the unions successful in properly representing the interests of employees at plant *X*?' Responses were on a five-point scale from 1 = very successful to 5 = unsuccessful.

The results were used to construct a *contingency table* (see Table 11.1). This included, on the one hand, employees who perceived both management and unions to represent their interests very well or fairly well (dual identity), and, at the other extreme, employees who perceived that neither management nor unions represented their interests at all (alienated). This showed that the majority of employees did not identify either with the union or with the company.

Table 11.1

A contingency table to show employee identity			
Identity	Union members (%)	Non-unionists (%)	Total sample (%)
Dual identity	16.9	2.5	9.7
Union identity	27.1	1.2	14.2
Management identity	11.1	35.7	23.4
No identity	44.9	60.6	52.8
Of which: Alienated	8.0	22.1	15.1

Source: adapted from Guest and Dewe (1991).

not write down exactly what respondents say to them when answering questions, a source of bias and hence of invalidity is in prospect. Closed questions reduce this possibility, though there is still the potential problem that interviewers may have to *interpret* what is said to them in order to assign answers to a category.

Disadvantages

However, closed questions exhibit certain disadvantages.

- There is a loss of spontaneity in respondents' answers. There is always the possibility that they might come up with interesting replies that are not covered by the fixed answers that are provided. One solution to this possible problem is to ensure that an open question is used to generate the categories (see Research in focus 11.3). Also, there may be a good case for including a possible response category of 'Other' and allowing respondents to indicate what they mean by this category.

- It can be difficult to make forced-choice answers mutually exclusive. The fixed answers with which respondents are provided should not overlap. If they do overlap, respondents will not know which one to choose and so will arbitrarily select one or the other or

Research in focus 11.3
A comparison of results for a closed and an open question

Schuman and Presser (1981) conducted an experiment to determine how far responses to closed questions can be improved by asking the questions first as open questions and then developing categories of reply from respondents' answers. They asked a question about what people look for in work in both open and closed format. Different samples were used. They found considerable disparities between the two sets of answers (40 per cent of the open-format categories were not capable of being subsumed by the closed-format answers). They then revised the closed categories to reflect the answers they had received from people's open-ended answers. They readministered the open question and the revised closed question to two large samples of Americans. The question and the answers they received are as follows:

This next question is on the subject of work. People look for different things in a job. Which one of the following five things do you most prefer in a job? [closed question]. What would you most prefer in a job? [open question]

Closed format		Open format	
Answer	%	Answer	%
Work that pays well	13.2	Pay	16.7
Work that gives a feeling of accomplishment	31.0	Feeling of accomplishment	14.5
Work where there is not too much supervision and you make most decisions yourself	11.7	Control of work	4.6
Work that is pleasant and where the people are nice to work with	19.8	Pleasant work	14.5
Work that is steady + little chance of being laid off	20.3	Security	7.6
	96% of sample		57.9% of sample
		Opportunity for promotion	1.0
		Short hours/lots of free time	1.6
		Working conditions	3.1
		Benefits	2.3
		Satisfaction/liking a job	15.6
Other/DK/NA	4.0	Other responses	18.3

With the revised form for the closed question, Schuman and Presser were able to find a much higher proportion of the sample whose answers to the open question corresponded to the closed one. They argue that the new closed question was superior to its predecessor and is also superior to the open question. However, it is still disconcerting that only 58 per cent of respondents answering the open question could be subsumed under the same categories as those answering the closed one. Also, the distributions are somewhat different: for example, twice as many respondents answer in terms of a feeling of accomplishment with the closed format than with the open one. Nonetheless, the experiment demonstrates the desirability of generating forced-choice answers from open questions.

alternatively may tick both answers. If a respondent were to tick two or more answers when one is required, it would mean that you would have to treat the respondent's answer as missing data, since you would not know which of the ticked answers represented the true one. One of the most frequently encountered forms of this problem can be seen in the following age bands:

18–30

30–40

40–50

50–60

60 and over.

In which band would a 40-year-old position him or herself?

- It is difficult to make forced-choice answers exhaustive. All possible answers should really be catered for, although in practice this may be difficult to achieve, since this rule may result in excessively long lists of possible answers. Again, a category of 'Other' may be desirable to provide a wide range of answers.

- There may be variation among respondents in the interpretation of forced-choice answers. There is always a problem when asking a question that certain terms may be interpreted differently by respondents. If this is the case, then validity will be jeopardized. The presence of forced-choice answers can exacerbate this possible problem, because there may be variation in the understanding of key terms in the answers.

- Closed questions may be irritating to respondents when they are not able to find a category that they feel applies to them.

- In interviews, a large number of closed questions may make it difficult to establish rapport, because the respondent and interviewer are less likely to engage with each other in a conversation. The interview is more likely to have an impersonal feel to it. However, because it is difficult to determine the extent to which rapport is a desirable attribute of structured interviewing (see Chapter 9), this is not necessarily too much of a problem.

Types of question

It is worth bearing in mind that, when you are employing a structured interview or self-completion questionnaire, you will probably be asking several different types of question. There are various ways of classifying these, but here are some prominent types of question.

- *Personal factual questions*. These are questions that ask the respondent to provide *personal information*, such as age, gender, education, employment status, income, and so on. This kind of question also includes questions about *behaviour*. Such factual questions may have to rely on the respondents' memories, as when they are asked about such things as frequency of individual performance appraisal meetings, how often they visit certain shops, or when they last had any time off work. For example, in the study by Deery, Iverson, and Walsch (2002) (see Research in focus 11.5), in addition to being asked to provide demographic details, telephone call centre workers were asked about the number of calls they took on an average day and the average length of calls taken.

- *Factual questions about others*. Like the previous type of question, this one asks for personal information about others, sometimes in combination with the respondent. An example of such a question would be one about team performance, which would require respondents to consider their own productivity (measured in terms of such things as daily work rate, frequency of lateness for work, and so on) in conjunction with the productivity of fellow team members. However, a criticism of such research is precisely that it relies on the possibly distorted views of respondents concerning their own and others' behaviour. Like personal factual questions, an element of reliance on memory recall is likely to be present.

- *Informant factual questions*. Sometimes, we place people who are interviewed or who complete a questionnaire in the position of informants rather than as respondents answering questions about themselves. This kind of question can also be found when people are asked about such things as the size of the firm for which they work, who owns it, whether it employs certain technologies, and whether it has certain specialist functions. Such questions are essentially about characteristics of an entity of which they have knowledge, in this case, a firm. However, informant factual questions may also be concerned with behaviour; for example, in the study by Deery, Iverson, and Walsch (2002; see Research in focus 11.5), telephone call centre employees were asked about the demands placed upon them by customers and priorities of the call centre management.

- *Questions about attitudes.* Questions about attitudes are very common in both structured interview and self-completion questionnaire research. The Likert scale is one of the most frequently encountered formats for measuring attitudes. Tips and skills 'Response formats for scales' provides a number of ways of presenting response formats.

- *Questions about beliefs.* Respondents are frequently asked about their beliefs. Another form of asking questions about beliefs is when respondents are asked whether they believe that certain matters are true or false—for example, a question asking whether or not the respondent believes the UK is better off as a result of being a member of the European Union. Or a survey about workplace stress might ask respondents to indicate whether or not they believe that the incidence of stress-related absence from work is increasing.

- *Questions about normative standards and values.* Respondents may be asked to indicate what principles of behaviour influence them or they hold dear. The elicitation of such norms of behaviour is likely to have considerable overlap with questions about attitudes and beliefs, since norms and values can be construed as having elements of both.

- *Questions about knowledge.* Questions can sometimes be employed to 'test' respondents' knowledge in an area. For example, a study of health and safety in the workplace might ask questions about the legal requirements that companies must comply with, in order to test respondents' awareness of these issues.

Most structured interview schedules and self-completion questionnaires will comprise more than one, and often several, of these types of question. It is important to bear in mind the distinction between different types of question. There are a number of reasons for this.

- It is useful to keep the distinctions in mind because they force you to clarify in your own mind what you are asking about, albeit in rather general terms.

- It will help to guard against asking questions in an inappropriate format. For example, a Likert scale is entirely unsuitable for asking factual questions about behaviour.

- When building scales like a Likert scale, it is best not to mix different types of question. For example, attitudes and beliefs sound similar and you may be tempted to use the same format for mixing questions about them. However, it is best not to do this and instead to have separate scales for attitudes and beliefs. If you mix them, the questions cannot really be measuring the same thing, so that measurement validity is threatened.

Tips and skills
Response formats for scales

There are several ways of presenting the response formats for the individual items that make up a scale like a Likert scale. The kind used in Tips and skills 'Formatting a Likert scale' (Chapter 10) is an example of a verbal format (see below).

Binary response format
My job is usually interesting enough to keep me from getting bored
Agree _____   Disagree _____
(This format is sometimes elaborated to include a 'don't know' response.)

(*continued*)

Numerical response format

My job is usually interesting enough to keep me from getting bored

5   4   3   2   1

(where 5 means Strongly agree and 1 means Strongly disagree)

Verbal format

My job is usually interesting enough to keep me from getting bored

Strongly agree _____   Agree _____   Undecided _____   Disagree _____   Strongly disagree _____

Bipolar numerical response format

I love my job   7   6   5   4   3   2   1   I hate my job

Frequency format

My job is usually interesting enough to keep me from getting bored

All of the time _____   Often _____   Fairly often _____   Occasionally _____   None of the time _____

The bipolar numerical response format is used in connection with semantic differential scales. With such scales, the respondent is given lists of pairs of adjectives. Each pair represents adjectival opposites (for example, masculine/feminine). A well-known example is the Fiedler (1967) least-preferred co-worker (LPC) scale. With this scale, each leader in a sample of leaders is given a set of between sixteen and twenty-five pairs of adjectives and is asked to describe with whom he or she has least preferred co-working. Examples of the pairs are:

Pleasant   8   7   6   5   4   3   2   1   Unpleasant
Friendly   8   7   6   5   4   3   2   1   Unfriendly
Rejecting   1   2   3   4   5   6   7   8   Accepting
Distant   1   2   3   4   5   6   7   8   Close

Each leader's score on each pair is aggregated to give a total score for that leader. Fiedler argued that leaders who describe their least-preferred co-workers in largely positive terms (pleasant, friendly, accepting, close) were predominantly relationship-oriented; those who described their least-preferred co-workers in largely negative terms (unpleasant, unfriendly, rejecting, distant) were predominantly task-oriented.

Rules for designing questions

Over the years, numerous rules (and rules of thumb) have been devised in connection with the dos and don'ts of asking questions. In spite of this, it is one of the easiest areas for making mistakes. There are three simple rules of thumb as a starting point; beyond that the rules specified below act as a means of avoiding further pitfalls.

General rules of thumb

Always bear in mind your research questions

The questions that you will ask in your self-completion questionnaire or structured interview should always be geared to answering your research questions. This first rule of thumb has at least two implications. First, it means that you should make sure that you ask questions that relate to your research questions. Ensure, in other words, that the questionnaire questions you ask will allow your research questions to be addressed. You will definitely not want to find out at a late stage that you forgot to include some crucial questions. Secondly, it means that there is little point in asking questions that do not relate to your research questions. It is also not fair to waste your respondents' time answering questions that are of little value.

What do you want to know?

Rule of thumb number two is to decide exactly what it is you want to know. Consider the seemingly harmless question:

Do you have a car?

What is it that the question is seeking to tap? Is it car ownership? If it is car ownership, the question is inadequate, largely because of the ambiguity of the word 'have'. The question can be interpreted as: personally owning a car; having access to a car in a household; and 'having' a company car or a car for business use. Thus, an answer of 'yes' may or may not be indicative of car ownership. If you want to know whether your respondent owns a car, ask him or her directly about this matter. Similarly, there is nothing wrong with the question:

How many people does your company employ?

However, this question does not clarify whether you are interested in the workplace, the company, or in the business as a whole—which may include a number of subsidiary companies. In addition, it does not distinguish between full- and part-time workers, or temporary and permanent employees. Hence, if you are interested in knowing how many full-time or full-time equivalent employees there are, then you need to specify this. Similarly, if you are interested only in people who are employed directly by the firm (rather than temporary or contract staff who work on the premises), you need to make this clear in your question.

How would *you* answer it?

Rule of thumb number three is to put yourself in the position of the respondent. Ask yourself the question and try to work out how you would reply. If you do this, there is at least the possibility that the ambiguity that is inherent in the 'Do you have a car?' question will manifest itself and its inability to tap car ownership would become apparent. Let us say as well that there is a follow-up question to the previous one:

Have you driven the car this week?

Again, this looks harmless, but, if you put yourself in the role of a respondent, it will be apparent that the phrase 'this week' is vague. Does it mean the last seven days or does it mean the week in which the questioning takes place, which will, of course, be affected by such things as whether the question is being asked on a Monday or a Friday? In part, this issue arises because the question designer has not decided what the question is about. Equally, however, a moment's reflection in which

you put yourself in the position of the respondent might reveal the difficulty of answering this question.

Taking account of these rules of thumb and the following rules about asking questions may help you to avoid the more obvious pitfalls.

Specific rules when designing questions

Avoid ambiguous terms in questions

Avoid terms such as 'often' and 'regularly' as measures of frequency. They are very ambiguous, because respondents will operate with different frames of reference when employing them. Sometimes their use is unavoidable, but, when there is an alternative that allows actual frequency to be measured, this will nearly always be preferable. So, a question like

How often do you usually visit the cinema?

Very often	____
Quite often	____
Not very often	____
Not at all	____

suffers from the problem that, with the exception of 'not at all', the terms in the response categories are ambiguous. Instead, try to ask about actual frequency, such as:

How frequently do you usually visit the cinema?
(*Please tick whichever category comes closest to the number of times you visit the cinema.*)

More than once a week	____
Once a week	____
Two or three times a month	____
Once a month	____
A few times a year	____
Once a year	____
Less than once a year	____

Alternatively, you might simply ask respondents about the number of times they have visited the cinema in the previous four weeks.

Words like 'colleagues' or 'management' are also ambiguous, because people will have different notions of who their colleagues are or who makes up the management. As previously noted, words like 'have' can also be sources of ambiguity.

It is also important to bear in mind that certain common words, such as 'quality' and 'customer', mean different things to different people. For some, quality is dependent on the purpose of the product, whereas for others it is an absolute measure of the standard of the product. Similarly, some people refer to colleagues from different departments as customers, whereas others take the word to mean those external to the organization who consume the products or services that the firm provides. In such cases, it will be necessary to define what you mean by such terms.

Avoid long questions

It is commonly believed that long questions are undesirable. In a structured interview the interviewee can lose the thread of the question, and in a self-completion questionnaire the respondent may be tempted to omit such questions or to skim them and therefore not give them sufficient attention. However, Sudman and Bradburn (1982) have suggested that this advice applies better to attitude questions than to ones that ask about behaviour. They argue that, when the focus is on behaviour, longer questions have certain positive features in interviews—for example, they are more likely to provide memory cues and they facilitate recall because of the time taken to complete the question. However, by and large, the general advice to keep questions short is the main piece of advice to be followed.

Avoid double-barrelled questions

Double-barrelled questions are ones that in fact ask about two things. The problem with this kind of question is that it leaves respondents unsure about how best to respond. Take the question:

> How satisfied are you with pay and conditions in your job?

The problem here is obvious: the respondent may be satisfied with one but not the other. Not only will the respondent be unclear about how to reply, but any answer that is given is unlikely to be a good reflection of the level of satisfaction with pay *and* conditions. Similarly,

> How frequently does your boss give you information concerning your daily work schedule and new developments within the company?

suffers from the same problem. A boss may provide extensive information about the daily work schedule but be totally uninformative about what is going on in the company more generally, so any stipulation of frequency of information is going to be ambiguous and will create uncertainty for respondents.

The same rule applies to fixed-choice answers. In Research in focus 11.3, one of Schuman and Presser's (1981) answers is:

> Work that is pleasant and where the people are nice to work with.

While there is likely to be a symmetry between the two ideas in this answer—pleasant work and nice people—there is no necessary correspondence between them. Pleasant work may be important for someone, but he or she may be relatively indifferent to the issue of how pleasant their co-workers are. Further instances of double-barrelled questions are provided in Tips and skills 'Matching question and answers in closed questions'.

Tips and skills
Matching question and answers in closed questions

You can sometimes find examples of badly designed questions in situations that you encounter in your everyday life. A recent example we have come across is of a feedback questionnaire produced by a publisher and inserted into the pages of a novel that one of us was reading. At one point in the questionnaire there was a series of Likert-style items regarding the book's quality. In each case, the respondent is asked to indicate whether the attribute being asked about is poor; acceptable; average; good; or excellent. However, in each case, the items are presented as questions, for example:

> Was the writing elegant, seamless, imaginative?

The problem here is that an answer to this question is 'yes' or 'no'. At most, we might have gradations of yes and no, such as: definitely; to a large extent; to some extent; not at all. However, 'poor' or 'excellent' cannot be answers to this question. The problem is that the questions should have been presented as statements, such as:

Please indicate the quality of the book in terms of each of the following criteria:

The elegance of the writing:

Poor ____ Acceptable ____ Average ____ Good ____ Excellent ____

Of course, we have changed the sense slightly here, because, as it was stated, a further problem with the question is that it is a double-barrelled question. In fact, it is 'treble-barrelled', because it actually asks about three attributes of the writing in one. The reader's views about the three qualities may vary. A similar question asked:

Did the plot offer conflict, twists, and a resolution?

Again, not only does the question imply a 'yes' or 'no', it actually asks about three attributes. How would you answer if you had different views about each of the three criteria?

It might be argued that the issue is a nit-picking one: someone reading the question obviously knows that he or she is being asked to rate the quality of the book in terms of each attribute. The problem is that we simply do not know what the impact might be of a disjunction between question and answer, so you may as well get the connection between question and answers right (and do not ask double- or treble-barrelled questions either!).

Avoid very general questions

It is easy to ask a very general question when in fact what is wanted is a response to a specific issue. The problem with questions that are very general is that they lack a frame of reference. Thus,

How satisfied are you with your job?

seems harmless, but it lacks specificity. Does it refer to pay, conditions, the nature of the work, or all of these? If there is the possibility of such diverse interpretations, respondents are likely to vary in their interpretations too, and this will be a source of error. One of our favourite general questions comes from Karl Marx's *Enquête Ouvrière*, a questionnaire that was sent to 25,000 French socialists and others (though there is apparently no record of any being returned). The final (one-hundredth) question reads:

> What is the general, physical, intellectual, and moral condition of men and women employed in your trade?
>
> (Bottomore and Rubel 1963: 218)

Avoid leading questions

Leading or loaded questions are ones that appear to lead the respondent in a particular direction. Questions of the kind 'Do you agree with the view that . . . ?' fall into this class of question. The obvious problem with such a question is that it is suggesting a particular reply to respondents, although invariably they do have the ability to rebut any implied answer. However, it is the fact that they might feel pushed in a certain direction that they do not naturally incline towards that is the problem. Such a question as

Do you think that UK corporate directors receive excessive financial compensation?

is likely to make it difficult for some people to answer in a way that indicates they do not believe that UK corporate directors are overpaid for what they do. But once again, Marx is the source of a favourite leading question:

> If you are paid piece rates, is the quality of the article made a pretext for fraudulent deductions from wages?
>
> (Bottomore and Rubel 1963: 215)

Avoid questions that are actually asking two questions

The double-barrelled question is a clear instance of the transgression of this rule, but in addition there is the case of a question like:

When did you last discuss your training needs with your supervisor/line manager?

What if the respondent has never discussed his or her training needs with the line manager? It is better to ask two separate questions:

Have you ever discussed your training needs with your supervisor/line manager?

Yes ____

No ____

If yes, when did your most recent discussion take place?

Another way in which more than one question can be asked is with a question like:

How effective have your different job search strategies been?

Very effective	____
Fairly effective	____
Not very effective	____
Not at all effective	____

The obvious difficulty is that, if the respondent has used more than one job search strategy, his or her estimation of effectiveness will vary for each strategy. A mechanism is needed for assessing the success of each strategy, rather than forcing respondents to average out their sense of how successful the various strategies were.

Avoid questions that include negatives

The problem with questions with 'not' or similar formulations in them is that it is easy for the respondent to miss the word out when completing a self-completion questionnaire or to miss it when being interviewed. If this occurs, a respondent is likely to answer in the opposite way from the one intended. There are occasions when it is impossible to avoid negatives, but a question like the following should be avoided as far as possible:

Do you agree with the view that students should not have to take out loans to finance higher education?

Instead, the question should be asked in a positive format. Questions with double negatives should be totally avoided, because it is difficult to know how to respond to them. Oppenheim (1966) gives the following as an example of this kind of question:

Would you rather not use a non-medicated shampoo?

It is quite difficult to establish what an answer of 'yes' or 'no' would actually mean in response to this question.

One context in which it is difficult to avoid using questions with negatives is when designing Likert scale items. Since you are likely to want to identify respondents who exhibit response sets and will therefore want to reverse the direction of your question asking (see Chapter 10), the use of negatives will be difficult to avoid.

Tips and skills
Common mistakes when asking questions

Over the years, we have read many projects and dissertations based on structured interviews and self-completion questionnaires. We have noticed that a small number of mistakes recur. Here is a list of some of them.

1. An excessive use of open questions. Students sometimes include too many open questions. While a resistance to closed questions may be understandable, although not something we would agree with, open questions are likely to reduce your response rate and will cause you analysis problems. Keep the number to an absolute minimum.

2. An excessive use of yes/no questions. Sometimes students include lots of questions that provide just a yes/no form of response. This is usually the result of lazy thinking and preparation. The world rarely fits into this kind of response. Take a question like:

   Are you satisfied with opportunities for promotion in the firm?

   Yes ____ No ____

   This does not provide for the possibility that respondents will vary in their satisfaction. So why not rephrase it as:

   How satisfied are you with opportunities for promotion in the firm?

Very satisfied	____
Satisfied	____
Neither satisfied nor dissatisfied	____
Dissatisfied	____
Very dissatisfied	____

3. Students often fail to give clear instructions on self-completion questionnaires about how the questions should be answered. Make clear whether you want a tick, something to be circled or deleted, or whatever. If only one response is required, make sure you say so—for example, 'Tick the answer that comes closest to your view'.

4. Be careful about letting respondents choose more than one answer. Sometimes it is unavoidable, but questions that allow more than one reply are often a pain to analyse.

5. In spite of the fact that we always warn about the problems of overlapping categories, students still formulate closed answers that are not mutually exclusive. In addition, some categories may be omitted. For example:

How many times per week do you consult with your line manager?

1–3 times _____   3–6 times _____   6–9 times _____   More than 10 times _____

Not only does the respondent not know where to answer if his or her answer might be 3 or 6; there is no answer for someone who would want to answer 10.

6. Students sometimes do not ensure the answers correspond to the question. For example:

Do you regularly meet with your appraiser for an appraisal interview?

Never	_____
Once a year	_____
Twice a year	_____
More than twice a year	_____

The problem here is that the answer to the question is logically either 'yes' or 'no'. However, the student quite sensibly wants to gain some idea of frequency (something that we would agree with in the light of our second point in this list!). The problem is that the question and the response categories are out of kilter. The question should be:

How frequently do you meet with your appraiser in any year (January to December)?

Never	_____
Once a year	_____
Twice a year	_____
More than twice a year	_____

If you never committed any of these 'sins', you would be well on the way to producing a questionnaire that would stand out from the rest, provided you took into account the other advice we give in this chapter as well!

Avoid technical terms

Use simple, plain language and avoid jargon. Do not ask a question like

Do you sometimes feel alienated from work?

The problem here is that many respondents will not know what is meant by 'alienated', and furthermore they are likely to have different views of what it means, even if it is a remotely meaningful term to them.

Consider the following question:

The influence of the TUC on management–worker relations has declined in recent years.

Strongly__Agree__Undecided__Disagree__Strongly__
agree   disagree

The use of acronyms like TUC can be a problem, because some people may be unfamiliar with what they stand for.

Does the respondent have the requisite knowledge?

There is little point in asking respondents lots of questions about matters of which they have no knowledge. It is very doubtful whether or not meaningful data about computer use could be extracted from respondents who have never used or come into direct contact with a computer.

Make sure that there is a symmetry between a closed question and its answers

A common mistake is for a question and its answers to be out of phase with each other. Tips and skills 'Matching question and answers in closed questions' describes such an instance.

Make sure that the answers provided for a closed question are balanced

A fairly common error when asking closed questions is for the answers that are provided to be unbalanced. For example, imagine that a respondent is given a series of options such as:

Excellent   ____

Good   ____

Acceptable   ____

Poor   ____

In this case, the response choices are balanced towards a favourable response. Excellent and Good are both positive; Acceptable is a neutral or middle position; and Poor is a negative response. In other words, the answers are loaded in favour of a positive rather than a negative reply, so that a further negative response choice (perhaps Very Poor) is required.

Memory problems

Do not rely too much on stretching people's memories to the extent that the answers for many of them are likely to be inaccurate. It would be nice to have accurate replies to a question about the number of times respondents have visited the cinema in the previous twelve months, but it is highly unlikely that most will in fact recall events accurately over such a long space of time (other perhaps than those who have not gone at all or only once or twice in the preceding twelve months). It was for this reason that, in the question on cinema visiting above, the time frame was predominantly just one month.

Don't know

One area of controversy when asking closed questions is whether to offer a 'don't know' or 'no opinion' option. The issue chiefly relates to questions concerning attitudes. The

chief argument for including the 'don't know' option is that *not* to include one risks forcing people to express views that they do not really hold. Converse and Presser (1986: 35–6) strongly advocate that survey respondents should be offered a 'don't know' option but argue that it should be implemented by a filter question to filter out those who do not hold an opinion on a topic. This means that the interviewer needs to ask two questions, with the second question just relating to those respondents who do not hold an opinion.

The alternative argument in connection with 'don't know' is that presenting it as an option allows respondents to select it when they cannot be bothered to think about the issue. In other words, presenting the option may prevent some respondents from thinking about the issue. A series of experiments conducted in the USA suggests that many respondents who express a lack of opinion on a topic do in fact hold an opinion (Krosnick et al. 2002). It was found that respondents with lower levels of education were especially prone to selecting the 'don't know' option and that questions that are later on in a questionnaire are more likely to suffer from a tendency for 'don't know' to be selected. The latter finding implies a kind of question order effect, a topic that was addressed in Chapter 9. It implies that respondents become increasingly tired or bored as the questioning proceeds and therefore become prone to laziness in their answers. The researchers conclude that data quality is not enhanced by the inclusion of a 'don't know' option and that it may even be the case that some respondents become inhibited from expressing an opinion that they probably hold. Consequently, these researchers err on the side of *not* offering a 'don't know' option unless it is felt to be absolutely necessary.

Vignette questions

A form of asking mainly closed questions that has been used in connection with the examination of people's normative standards is the vignette technique. The technique essentially comprises presenting respondents with one or more scenarios and then asking them how they would respond when confronted with the circumstances of that scenario. Research in focus 11.4 describes a vignette that was employed in the context of a longitudinal study of the ethical behaviour of managers.

Sixteen different vignettes were used in this study to tease out respondents' responses to questionable ethical practices of different kinds. The scenarios presented in Research in focus 11.4 were concerned with a wide variety of business situations and were designed to address different functional areas of business. Each one dealt with a different questionable ethical practice, including some that were illegal. For example, scenario A concerns the issue of corporate theft; scenario B, law breaking,

Research in focus 11.4
Using vignette questions in a tracking study of ethical behaviour

The following vignettes were used by Longenecker et al. (2006: 177) in a study of ethical perceptions of managers of large corporations and owner/managers of smaller companies over 17 years. Using a postal questionnaire which contained 16 vignettes of business decisions with ethical overtones, a random sample of 10,000 respondents was surveyed at three points in time, in 1985, 1993 and 2001. The nationwide sample of US business professionals was generated from a mailing list used by publishers of major business periodicals. While some of the situations described in the vignettes were illegal, others involved debatable ethical characteristics. Respondents were asked to what extent they found the action compatible with their own ethical views using a seven-point scale ranging from (1) never acceptable to (7) always acceptable. Three of the 16 vignettes are presented below.

A) An executive earning $50,000 a year padded his expense account by about $1500 a year.

B) In order to increase profits, a general manager used a production process which exceeded legal limits for environmental pollution.

C) Because of pressure from his brokerage firm, a stockbroker recommended a type of bond which he did not consider a good investment.

This longitudinal study enabled the researchers to track whether the ethical decision-making of managers was changing over time. However, unlike in a panel or a cohort study (see Chapter 3), the samples surveyed in each case were not the same, which limits the comparability of the data over time. Also, the nature of these questions makes it clear that they are all involve ethical transgression of some sort, so respondents may be tempted to indicate the unacceptability of the actions because of **social desirability bias** (see Chapter 9), even if they might take a different view in practice.

and scenario C, professional malpractice. Many aspects of the issues being tapped by the vignette questions could be accessed through attitude items, such as:

> If a senior marketing professional has private business interests that are also related to the business of the firm, he has a duty to declare these interests to other senior executives immediately they arise.
>
> Strongly agree__ Agree __ Undecided __ Disagree __ Strongly disagree__

The advantage of the vignette over such an attitude question is that it anchors the choice in a situation and as such reduces the possibility of an unreflective reply. In addition, when the subject matter is a sensitive area (in this case, dealing with ethical behaviour), there is the possibility that the questions may be seen as threatening by respondents. Respondents may feel that they are being judged by their replies. If the questions are about other people (and imaginary ones at that), this permits a certain amount of distance between the questioning and the respondent and results in a less threatening

context. However, it is hard to believe that respondents will not feel that their replies will at least in part be seen as reflecting on them, even if the questions are not about them as such.

One obvious requirement of the vignette technique is that the scenarios must be believable, so that considerable effort needs to go into the construction of credible situations. Finch (1987) points out two further considerations in relation to this style of questioning. First, it is more or less impossible to establish how far assumptions are being made about the characters in the scenario (such as their ethnicity) and what the significance of those assumptions might be for the validity and comparability of people's replies. Secondly, it is also difficult to establish how far people's answers reflect their own normative views or indeed how they themselves would act when confronted with the kinds of choices revealed in the scenarios. However, in spite of these reservations, the vignette technique warrants serious consideration when the research focus is concerned with an area that lends itself to this style of questioning.

Piloting and pre-testing questions

It is always desirable, if at all possible, to conduct a pilot study before administering a self-completion questionnaire or structured interview schedule to your sample. In fact, the desirability of piloting such instruments is not solely to do with trying to ensure that survey questions operate well; piloting also has a role in ensuring that the research instrument as a whole functions well. Pilot studies may be particularly crucial in relation to research based on the self-completion questionnaire, since there will not be an interviewer present to clear up any confusion. Also, with interviews, persistent problems may emerge after a few interviews have been carried out, and these can then be addressed. However, with self-completion questionnaires, since they are sent or handed out in large numbers, considerable wastage may occur prior to any problems becoming apparent.

Here are some uses of pilot studies in survey research.

- If the main study is going to employ mainly closed questions, open questions can be asked in the pilot to generate the fixed-choice answers. Glock (1988), for example, extols the virtues of conducting qualitative interviews in preparation for a survey for precisely this kind of reason.

- Piloting an interview schedule can provide interviewers with some experience of using it and can infuse them with a greater sense of confidence.

- If everyone (or virtually everyone) who answers a question replies in the same way, the resulting data are unlikely to be of interest because they do not form a variable. A pilot study allows such a question to be identified.

- In interview surveys, it may be possible to identify questions that make respondents feel uncomfortable and to detect any tendency for respondents' interest to be lost at certain junctures.

- Questions that seem not to be understood (more likely to be realized in an interview than in a self-completion questionnaire context) or questions that are often not answered should become apparent. The latter problem of questions being skipped may be due to confusing or threatening phrasing, poorly worded instructions, or confusing positioning in the interview schedule or questionnaire. Whatever the cause might be, such missing data are undesirable, and a pilot study may be instrumental in identifying the problem.

- Pilot studies allow the researcher to determine the adequacy of instructions to interviewers, or to respondents completing a self-completion questionnaire.

- It may be possible to consider how well the questions flow and whether it is necessary to move some of them around to improve this feature.

The pilot should not be carried out on people who might have been members of the sample that would be employed in the full study. One reason for this is that, if you are seeking to employ probability sampling, the selecting-out of a number of members of the population or sample may affect the representativeness of any subsequent sample. If possible, it is best to find a small set of respondents who are comparable to members of the population from which the sample for the full study will be taken.

Using existing questions

One final observation regarding the asking of questions is that you should also consider using questions that have been employed by other researchers for at least part of your questionnaire or interview schedule. This may seem like stealing and you would be advised to contact the researchers concerned regarding the use of questions they have devised. However, employing existing questions allows you to use questions that have in a sense been piloted for you. If any reliability and validity testing has taken place, you will know about the measurement qualities of the existing questions you use. A further advantage of using existing questions is that they allow you to draw comparisons with other research. This might allow you to indicate whether change has occurred or whether place makes a difference to findings. For example, if you are researching job satisfaction, using one of the standard job satisfaction scales would allow you to compare your findings with another researcher's. Alternatively, using the same questions as another researcher may allow you to explore whether the location of your sample appears to make a difference to the findings. While you need to be cautious about inferring too much from such comparisons between your own and other researchers' data, the findings can none the less be illuminating. At the very least, examining questions used by others might give you some ideas about how best to approach your own questions, even if you decide not to make use of them as they stand. An example of how questions developed by other researchers were used in a study of telephone call centre operators is given in Research in focus 11.5.

The process of finding questions has been made a great deal easier by the creation of 'question banks', which act as repositories of questions employed in surveys and elsewhere. The UK Data Archive (UKDA), which aims to improve standards in UK survey research, has a very good question bank providing access to questionnaires from major surveys (including the Census) and associated commentary to assist survey design. It is freely available and can be found at the following site: *discover. ukdataservice.ac.uk/variables* (accessed 24 October 2014)

Research in focus 11.5
Using scales developed by other researchers in a survey of call centre operators

In a study of call centre operators working in the telecommunications industry in Australia, Deery, Iverson, and Walsch (2002) were interested in the possible negative effects of this form of work on the psychological well-being of employees. Specifically, they sought:

1. to identify the factors leading to feelings of emotional exhaustion among operators; and

2. to analyse the effects of emotional exhaustion on employee absence.

Emotional exhaustion was defined as the extent to which individuals feel emotionally drained from their work. It was predicted that emotional exhaustion would be higher among employees who felt they had a high workload and among those who felt they lacked the skills needed to do the job.

In designing the questionnaire used to test these relationships, Deery, Iverson, and Walsch used scales that had been devised by other researchers in earlier studies. These included:

* a five-item scale taken from Wharton (1993) used to measure emotional exhaustion; item statements included: 'I feel emotionally drained from my work';

* emotional expressivity measured by four items adapted from Kring, Smith, and Neale (1994), including, 'I can't hide the way I'm feeling when talking to customers';

* workload and role overload measured by items taken from Caplan et al. (1975), including, 'My job requires me to work very fast';

* team leader and team member support measured using items adapted from House (1981), such as, 'My team members are willing to listen to my job-related problems'.

Deery, Iverson, and Walsch supplemented these scales with items they developed themselves to measure other variables in the study, such as:

* *customer interactions*—with the statement, 'I now have more abusive customer calls than I used to have'; and

* *management focus on quality*—using item statements such as, 'I believe senior management are more concerned about the quantity rather than the quality of work'.

The study illustrates how item scales developed by other researchers can be combined with those developed by those conducting the present study to create a questionnaire instrument that is sensitive to the context and relevant to the questions that the research is seeking to address.

Telling it like it is
Using a questionnaire designed by another researcher

Karen used a questionnaire designed by an author that she had identified during her literature review to measure the cultural profile of the company where she was doing her research. For each of the fifty-four characteristics of the culture, each respondent had to 'identify whether it was highly characteristic, moderately characteristic or not characteristic at all of the culture'. This quantitative element of her research project was combined with qualitative semi-structured interviews involving a sample of fifteen managers within the business from different departments and different levels of the organization. Each research participant completed the questionnaire and was also interviewed. In explaining her research design, she said: 'I chose [a sample of] fifteen because I only had a limited amount of time and I thought, "If I go for more than that, then I'm going to end up with like an overwhelming amount of data and information to sift through." I thought, "I'd rather get more valuable information and sort of have longer interviews and get more sort of time to explore things, than to just cut them short and only have a few."' For a detailed discussion of the issues involved in combining quantitative and qualitative research see Chapter 27.

To hear more about Karen's research experiences, go to the Online Resource Centre that accompanies this book at: www.oxfordtextbooks.co.uk/orc/brymanbrm4e/

Tips and skills
Getting help in designing questions

When designing questions, as we suggested earlier, try to put yourself in the position of someone who has been asked to answer the questions. This can be difficult, because some (if not all) of the questions may not apply to you—for example, if you are a student doing a survey of managers. However, try to think about how you would reply. This means concentrating not just on the questions themselves but also on the links between the questions. For example, do filter questions work in the way you expect them to? Then try the questions out on some people you know, as in a pilot study. Ask them to be critical and to consider how well the questions connect to each other. Also, do look at the questionnaires and structured interview schedules that experienced researchers have devised. They may not have asked questions on your topic, but the way they have asked the questions and the flow of the questions should give you an idea of what to do and what to avoid when designing such instruments.

Checklist
Issues to consider for your structured interview schedule or self-completion questionnaire

○ Have you devised a clear and comprehensive way of introducing the research to interviewees or questionnaire respondents?

○ Have you considered whether or not there are any existing questions used by other researchers to investigate this topic that could meet your needs?

○ Do the questions allow you to answer all your research questions?

○ Could any questions that are not strictly relevant to your research questions be dropped?

○ Have you tried to put yourself in the position of answering as many of the questions as possible?

○ Have you piloted the questionnaire with some appropriate respondents?

○ If it is a structured interview schedule, have you made sure that the instructions to yourself and to anyone else involved in interviewing are clear (for example, which questions should be answered next with filter questions)?

○ If it is a self-completion questionnaire, have you made sure that the instructions to the respondent are clear (for example, which questions should be answered next with filter questions)?

○ Are instructions about how to record responses clear (for example, whether to tick or circle; whether or not more than one response is allowable)?

○ Have you included as few open questions as possible?

○ Have you allowed respondents to indicate levels of intensity in their replies, so that they are not forced into 'yes' or 'no' answers where intensity of feeling may be more appropriate?

○ Have you ensured that questions and their answers do not span more than one page?

○ Have socio-demographic questions been left until the end of the questionnaire?

○ Are questions relating to the research topic at or very close to the beginning?

○ Have you taken steps to ensure that the questions you are asking really do supply you with the information you need?

○ Have you taken steps to ensure that there are no:

   ○ ambiguous terms in questions or closed answers?

   ○ long questions?

   ○ double-barrelled questions?

   ○ very general questions?

   ○ leading questions?

   ○ questions that are asking about two or more things?

   ○ questions that include negatives?

   ○ questions using technical terms?

○ Have you made sure that your respondents will have the requisite knowledge to answer your questions?

○ Is there an appropriate match between your questions and your closed answers?

○ Do any of your questions rely too much on your respondents' memory?

○ If you are using a Likert scale approach:

   ○ Have you included some items that can be reverse scored in order to minimize response sets?

   ○ Have you made sure that the items really do relate to the same underlying cluster of attitudes so that they can be aggregated?

○ Have you ensured that your closed answers are exhaustive?

○ Have you ensured that your closed answers do not overlap?

○ Have you ensured that there is a category of 'other' (or similar category such as 'unsure' or 'neither agree nor disagree') so that respondents are not forced to answer in a way that is not indicative of what they think or do?

Key points

- While open questions undoubtedly have certain advantages, closed questions are typically preferable for a survey, because of the ease of asking questions and recording and processing answers.

- This point applies particularly to the self-completion questionnaire.

- Open questions of the kind used in qualitative interviewing have a useful role in relation to the formulation of fixed-choice answers and piloting.

- It is crucial to learn the rules of question asking to avoid some of the more obvious pitfalls.

- Remember always to put yourself in the position of the respondent when asking questions and to make sure you will generate data appropriate to your research questions.

- Piloting or pre-testing may clear up problems in question formulation.

Questions for review

Open or closed questions?

- What difficulties do open questions present in survey research?

- Why are closed questions frequently preferred to open questions in survey research?

- What are the limitations of closed questions?

- How can closed questions be improved?

Types of question

- What are the main types of question that are likely to be used in a structured interview or self-administered questionnaire?

Rules for designing questions

- What is wrong with each of the following questions?

    What is your annual salary?

    Below £10,000

    £10,000–15,000

    £15,000–20,000

    £20,000–25,000

    £25,000–30,000

    £30,000–35,000

    £35,000 and over.

Do you ever feel alienated from your work?

> All the time
>
> Often
>
> Occasionally
>
> Never.

How satisfied are you with the customer services and products provided by this company?

> Very satisfied
>
> Fairly satisfied
>
> Neither satisfied nor dissatisfied
>
> Fairly dissatisfied
>
> Very dissatisfied.

Vignette questions

● In what circumstances are vignette questions appropriate?

Piloting and pre-testing questions

● Why is it important to pilot questions?

Using existing questions

● Why might it be useful to use questions devised by others?

 Online Resource Centre

www.oxfordtextbooks.co.uk/orc/brymanbrm4e/

Visit the Interactive Research Guide that accompanies this book to complete an exercise in Asking Questions.

12

Structured observation

Chapter outline

Structured observation attracted a good deal of attention in business and management research during the 1970s and early 1980s. However, in more recent years it has been less commonly employed as a research method. It entails the direct observation of behaviour and the recording of that behaviour in terms of categories that have been devised prior to the start of data collection. This chapter explores:

- the limitations of survey research for the study of behaviour;
- the different forms of observation in business research;
- the potential of structured observation for the study of behaviour;
- how to devise an observation schedule;
- different strategies for observing behaviour in structured observation;
- sampling issues in structured observation research; with this method, the issue of sampling is to do not just with people but also with the sampling of time and contexts;
- issues of reliability and validity in structured observation;
- field stimulations, whereby the researcher actively intervenes in social life and records what happens as a consequence of the intervention, as a form of structured observation;
- some criticisms of structured observation.

Introduction

Structured observation is a method for systematically observing the behaviour of individuals in terms of a schedule of categories. It is a technique in which the researcher employs explicitly formulated rules for the observation and recording of behaviour. One of its main advantages is that it allows behaviour to be observed directly, unlike in survey research, which only allows behaviour to be inferred. In survey research, respondents frequently report their behaviour, but there are good reasons for thinking that such reports may not be entirely accurate. Structured observation constitutes a possible solution in that it entails the direct observation of behaviour. Interest in structured observation within business and management stemmed initially from the fact that it was seen as having the potential to provide researchers with far greater insight into the issue of what managers actually do. In this respect it was seen by many as providing an alternative to the diary study method (see Chapter 10) used by R. Stewart (1967).

Problems with survey research on behaviour

Chapters 8–11 have dealt with several different aspects of survey research. In the course of outlining procedures associated with the social survey, certain problems with the techniques with which it is typically associated have been identified. For example, in the field of leadership research, which relies a great deal on questionnaire measures, researchers have relied heavily on the responses of subordinates and what they say leaders do, rather than what leaders actually do (the two are often used interchangeably). To some extent the deficiencies associated with the survey are recognized by researchers, who have developed ways of dealing with them, or at least of offsetting their impact to some degree. When survey techniques such as the structured interview

Tips and skills
Problems with using social survey research to investigate behaviour

- *Problem of meaning*. People may vary in their interpretations of key terms in a question.
- *Problem of omission*. When answering the question, respondents may inadvertently omit key terms in the question.
- *Problem of memory*. They may misremember aspects of the occurrence of certain forms of behaviour.
- *Social desirability effect*. They may exhibit a tendency towards replying in ways that are meant to be consistent with their perceptions of the desirability of certain kinds of answer.
- *Question threat*. Some questions may appear threatening and result in a failure to provide an honest reply.
- *Interviewer characteristics*. Aspects of the interviewer may influence the answers provided.
- *Gap between stated and actual behaviour*. How people say they are likely to behave and how they actually behave may be inconsistent.

or the self-completion questionnaire are employed in connection with the study of respondents' *behaviour*, certain characteristic difficulties are encountered, some of which have been touched on in earlier chapters. Tips and skills 'Problems with using social survey research to investigate behaviour' identifies some of these difficulties. The list is by no means exhaustive but it does capture some of the main elements.

So why not observe behaviour?

An obvious solution to the problems identified is to observe people's behaviour directly rather than to rely on research instruments such as questionnaires to elicit such information. In this chapter, we are going to outline a method called **structured observation** (see Key concept 12.1), also often called systematic observation.

Key concept 12.1
What is structured observation?

Structured observation, often also called *systematic observation*, is a technique in which the researcher employs explicitly formulated rules for the observation and recording of behaviour. The rules inform observers about what they should look for and how they should record behaviour. Each person who is part of the research (we will call these people 'participants') is observed for a predetermined period of time using the same rules. These rules are articulated in what is usually referred to as an *observation schedule*, which bears many similarities to a structured interview schedule with closed questions. The aim of the observation schedule is to ensure that each participant's behaviour is systematically recorded so that it is possible to aggregate the behaviour of all those in the sample in respect of each type of behaviour being recorded. The rules that constitute the observation schedule are as specific as possible in order to direct observers to exactly what aspects of behaviour they are supposed to be looking for. The resulting data resemble questionnaire data considerably, in that the procedure generates information on different aspects of behaviour that can be treated as variables. Moreover, structured observation research is typically underpinned by a cross-sectional research design (see Key concept 3.12 and Figures 3.2 and 3.3).

Key concept 12.2
Major types of observation research

- *Structured observation*, also called *systematic observation*. See Key concept 12.1.

- *Participant observation*. This is one of the best-known methods of data collection in business and management research. It is primarily associated with qualitative research and entails the relatively prolonged immersion of the observer in a social setting in which he or she seeks to observe the behaviour of members of that setting (group, organization, community, etc.) and to elicit the meanings they attribute to their environment and behaviour. Participant observers vary considerably in how much they participate in the social settings in which they locate themselves. See Key concept 19.1 and Chapter 19 generally for a more detailed treatment.

- *Non-participant observation*. This is a term that is used to describe a situation in which the observer observes but does not participate in what is going on in the social setting. Structured observers are usually non-participants in that they are in the social setting being observed but rarely participate in what is happening. The term can also be used in connection with unstructured observation.

- *Unstructured observation*. As its name implies, unstructured observation does not entail the use of an observation schedule for the recording of behaviour. Instead, the aim is to record in as much detail as possible the behaviour of participants, with the aim of developing a narrative account of that behaviour. In a sense, most participant observation is unstructured, but the term unstructured observation is usually employed in conjunction with non-participant observation.

- **Simple observation** and *contrived observation*. Webb et al. (1966) write about forms of observation in which the observer is unobtrusive and is not observed by those being observed. With simple observation, the observer has no influence over the situation being observed; in the case of contrived observation, the observer actively alters the situation to observe the effects of an intervention. These two types of observation are invariably forms of non-participant observation and can entail either structured or unstructured observation.

Much like the interview (see Key concept 9.2), there are many different forms of the observation approach in business research. Key concept 12.2 outlines some major ways of conducting observation studies in business research.

It has been implied that structured observation can be viewed as an alternative to survey methods of research. After all, in view of the various problems identified in Tips and skills 'Problems with using social survey research to investigate behaviour', it would seem an obvious solution to observe people instead. However, structured observation has not attracted a large following and instead tends to be in use in certain specific research areas, such as in educational research, where it is used to study the behaviour of school teachers and pupils and the interaction between them.

Central to any structured observation study will be the *observation schedule* or *coding scheme*. This specifies the categories of behaviour that are to be observed and how behaviour should be allocated to those categories. It is best to illustrate what this involves by looking at examples. One of the best-known studies to have used structured observation is Mintzberg's (1973) study of managerial work. Mintzberg studied five chief executives, each for one week, as they went about their normal business day, took phone calls, attended scheduled and unscheduled meetings, scanned mail, received visitors, and walked around buildings. The detailed nature of his investigation restricted the amount of quantitative data that could be generated but it also enabled more detailed analysis of the kind of work that managers do. The activity categories used in the study were: scheduled meetings, unscheduled meetings, desk work, telephone calls, and tours (see Research in focus 12.3).

Structured data were collected using three records:

- *chronology record*: described activity patterns, noting the time, nature, and duration of the activity;

Research in focus 12.3
Mintzberg's categories of basic activities involved in managerial work

Mintzberg (1973) identified five categories into which the activities of managerial work could be placed. They are listed below.

- *Scheduled meeting*. A prearranged face-to-face meeting involving the manager and one or more other participants is defined as scheduled.
- *Unscheduled meeting*. A meeting is defined as unscheduled if it is arranged hastily, as when someone just 'drops in'.
- *Desk work*. This refers to the time the manager spends at his or her desk, processing mail, scheduling activities, writing letters, or communicating with the secretary.
- *Call*. This category refers to telephone calls.
- *Tour*. This refers to a chance meeting in the hall, or to the 'promenades' taken by the manager to observe activity and to deliver information.

- *mail record*: described each piece of incoming/outgoing mail and the action that was taken in order to respond to it;
- *contact record*: described each verbal contact, noting the participants and where it took place.

In Mintzberg's coding scheme, time and activities were coded separately, so that the distribution of clock time might overlap an activity or vice versa. For example, 'tours' of the work site and 'desk work' included time spent talking. Almost 40 per cent of activities were meetings; this accounted for 70 per cent of the managers' work time. From such data a number of features could be derived. Mintzberg's main conclusions were that managerial work is highly fragmented, varied, and brief, and that managers have a need for instant communication, on which to base further verbal contact and action. These findings ran contrary to the traditional view that was dominant at the time, which suggested that managerial activity was planned and rational. Research in focus 12.4

Research in focus 12.4
Structured observation of managerial work

Mintzberg's (1973) research was highly influential and generated several other studies that replicated and extended his study of what managers do in their day-to-day work. In part, these later studies are an attempt to redress two of the criticisms that have been made of Mintzberg's study: not actually reflecting the variation between different kinds of managerial work and not relating managerial work to managerial and organizational efficiency and effectiveness.

The first example described here by Martinko and Gardner (1990) extends the research question that informs Mintzberg's study from 'How do senior managers spend their work time?' to 'How does senior managers' use of work time affect their performance?' Their sample consisted of forty-one school principals. This group of managers was selected because they have a relatively high level of autonomy in their work (and therefore an ability to influence organizational performance). Also, because they are a relatively homogenous group, their performance levels can be more easily compared. The observations were conducted mainly by doctoral students who attended a two-day training session in which they were taught the principles of structured observation. Minute-by-minute observation led to the production of written protocols that recorded managerial events, the time they started and ended, and their purpose. The mean number of observations was 6.7 days per principal. The sample was stratified into high- and moderate-performing managers, based on the assumption that the performance of the principal would be reflected by the performance of the school. Although the research confirmed Mintzberg's earlier finding that managerial work is brief, varied, fragmented, and interpersonal, there was no evidence to suggest that managerial behaviour was related to performance level. In other words, there was no significant difference in the behaviours of highly effective and less effective managers in terms of how they organized their daily activities. It is interesting to note that the researchers deliberately excluded low-performing managers from their sample because they had anticipated difficulties in securing the cooperation of individuals who had been labelled as low performers. However, it may have been that a comparison of high- and low-performing managers would have revealed greater differences between principals in terms of the time spent on events and the number of events that were associated with certain activities.

O'Gorman, Bourke, and Murray (2005) also used Mintzberg's (1973) observational study of managerial work as the basis for their investigation into managerial work in small growth-oriented businesses. A purposive sample of ten owner-managers of small high-growth manufacturing companies was selected based on their participation in growth seminars at the Department of Business Studies at Trinity College in Dublin. The chief executive officers (CEOs) were all male and their businesses represented the printing, construction, chemicals, pharmaceuticals, and agri-food sectors. The researchers describe their observational method as follows: 'two days were spent with the CEO, during the Spring and Summer of 1992 . . . . Using a chronological record, based on the data-recording format used by Mintzberg, the daily activities of each CEO were recorded' (O'Gorman, Bourke, and Murray 2005: 9). In addition, two other types of activity were recorded: the first recorded CEOs' attendance at social functions related to the business, and the second classified the type of functional duty being performed in each activity (production, research and development, sales and marketing, market research, finance, engineering, legal affairs, distribution, personnel, and general management). They found that managerial work in these organizations was even more fragmented than for the managers in Mintzberg's study.

gives two examples of studies that involve a replication of Mintzberg's methods.

It is interesting to think about how a scheme like this might be employed in connection with higher-education teaching and in particular in tutorials and seminars. In the following imaginary scheme, the focus is on the tutor. The categories might be:

Tutor

1. asking question addressed to group;
2. asking question addressed to individual;
3. responding to question asked by member of group;
4. responding to comment by member of group;
5. discussing topic;
6. making arrangements;
7. silence.

Student(s)

8. asking question;

9. responding to question from tutor;
10. responding to comment from tutor;
11. responding to question from another student;
12. responding to comment from another student;
13. talking about arrangements.

We might want to code what is happening every 5 seconds. The coding sheet for a 5-minute period in the tutorial might look like Figure 12.1. In this grid, each cell represents a 5-second interval so that a row constitutes twelve 5-second intervals—that is, a minute. The numbers in each cell are the codes used to represent the classification of behaviour. Thus, the top left-hand cell has a 3 in it, which refers to a tutor 'responding to question asked by member of group'. We might try to relate the amount of time that the tutor is engaged in particular activities to such things as: number of students in the group; layout of the room; subject discipline; gender of tutor; age of tutor; and so on.

Figure 12.1

Coding sheet for imaginary study of university tutors

3	3	3	3	10	10	10	10	10	10	10	10
10	10	10	10	10	10	7	7	7	8	8	8
8	8	8	8	8	8	8	8	11	11	11	11
11	11	11	11	11	11	11	11	11	11	11	11
7	7	7	7	7	4	4	4	4	4	4	1

Note: Each cell represents a 5-second interval and each row is 1 minute. The number in each cell refers to the code used to represent a category of behaviour that has been observed.

The observation schedule

Devising a schedule for the recording of observations is clearly a crucial step in the structured observation project. The considerations that go into this phase are very similar to those involved in producing a structured interview schedule. The following considerations are worth taking into account.

- A clear focus is necessary. There are two aspects to this point. First, it should be clear to the observer exactly who or what (and possibly both) is to be observed. For example, if people are the focus of attention, the observer needs to know precisely who is to be observed. Also, the observer needs to know which if any aspects of the setting are to be observed and hence recorded. The second sense in which a clear focus is necessary is that the research problem needs to be clearly stated so that the observer knows which of the many things going on in any setting are to be recorded.

- As with the production of a closed question for a structured interview schedule or self-completion questionnaire, the forms taken by any category of behaviour must be both mutually exclusive (that is, not overlap) and inclusive. Taking the earlier example of coding behaviour in a university tutorial, we might

conceivably run into a problem of the twelve categories not being exhaustive if a student knocks on the tutor's door and quickly asks him or her a question (perhaps about the tutorial topic, if the student is from another of the tutor's groups). An observer unfamiliar with the ways of university life might well be unsure about whether this behaviour needs to be coded in terms of the twelve categories and whether the coding should be temporarily suspended. Perhaps the best approach would be to have another category of behaviour to be coded as what we might term 'interruption'. It is often desirable for a certain amount of unstructured observation to take place prior to the construction of the observation schedule and for there to be some piloting of it so that possible problems associated with a lack of inclusiveness can be anticipated.

- The recording system must be easy to operate. Complex systems with large numbers of types of behaviour will be undesirable. In a similar way to interviewers using a structured interview schedule, observers need to be trained, but even so it is easy for an observer to become flustered or confused if faced with too many options.

Research in focus 12.5
Observing jobs

Jenkins et al. (1975) report the results of an exploratory study employed to measure the nature of jobs. The research focused on several types of job in a number of types of organization. An observation schedule was devised to assess the nature of twenty aspects (dimensions) of the jobs in question. Most of the dimensions were measured through more than one indicator, each of which took the form of a question that observers had to answer on a six- or seven-point scale. These were then aggregated for each dimension. While the research has a predominantly psychological slant, many of the twenty dimensions relate to issues that have been raised in the sociology of work by labour process theorists and others (e.g. Braverman 1974). One dimension relates to 'Worker pace control' and comprises three observational indicators such as:

> How much control does the employee have in setting the pace of his/her work?

Another dimension was 'Autonomy', which comprised four indicators, such as:

> The job allows the individual to make a lot of decisions on his/her own.

Most of the observers were university students. The procedure for conducting the observations was as follows: 'Each respondent was observed twice for an hour. The observations were scheduled so that the two different observations were separated by at least 2 days, were usually made at different times of the day, and were always made by two different observers' (Jenkins et al. 1975: 173).

- One possible problem with some observation schedules is that they sometimes require a certain amount of interpretation on the part of the observer. For example, it might be difficult to distinguish in any meaningful sense between an unscheduled meeting and a discussion with two or three colleagues that takes place in a corridor, apart from the fact that in the first instance the participants are more likely to be seated!

To the extent that it may be difficult to distinguish between the two, a certain amount of interpretation on the part of the observer may be needed. If such interpretation is required, there would need to be clear guidelines for the observer and considerable experience would be required (see Research in focus 12.5 for an illustration of a study in which a good deal of interpretation seems to have been necessary).

Strategies for observing behaviour

There are different ways of conceptualizing how behaviour should be recorded.

- We can record in terms of *incidents*. This means waiting for something to happen and then recording what follows from it. Essentially, this is what Mintzberg (1973) did, as the following account of his method illustrates: 'The researcher observes the manager as he performs his work. Each observed event (a verbal contact or a piece of incoming or outgoing mail) is categorized by the researcher in a number of ways (for example, duration, participants, purpose)' (1973: 231). In this study, the categories, or activity codes, are developed either during the observation or shortly after it takes place,

rather than beforehand. Only after the observation had taken place did Mintzberg begin to draw connections between the activities in order to develop his final activity codes. Similarly, a newspaper story several years ago reported that someone placed a ladder over a pavement and then observed whether people preferred to go under the ladder or to risk life and limb in the face of oncoming traffic. A considerable number preferred the latter option, confirming the persistence of superstitious beliefs in an apparently secular society. Once again, an incident (someone approaching the ladder) triggered the observation. Webb et al. (1966) would regard this as an example of *contrived observation*, because the researchers fabricated the situation. The discussion later in this chapter of *field stimulations* provides further illustrations of this kind of research.

- We can observe and record in terms of *short periods* of time, observing one individual for a couple of minutes but returning at structured intervals to conduct further observations. This can help to ensure the generalizability of what goes on in the setting. For example, if a manager holds regular meetings each day at 4 p.m., three observations, each lasting 20 minutes, conducted in the morning, at lunchtime, and in the afternoon, will ensure a more representative sample of activities than would an observation lasting an hour at 4–5 p.m.

- We can observe and record observations for quite *long periods* of time. The observer watches and records more or less continuously. Consider, for example, the study of job characteristics by Jenkins et al. (1975), which entailed the observation of each worker on two occasions but for an hour on each occasion (see Research in focus 12.5): 'The observation hour was structured so that the observer spent 10 min becoming oriented to the job, 30 min observing specific job

actions, and 20 min rating the job in situ. The observers then typically spent an additional 15 min away from the job completing the observation instrument' (Jenkins et al. 1975: 174). This last study is an example of what Martin and Bateson (1986) refer to as '**continuous recording**', whereby the observer observes for extended periods, thus allowing the frequency and duration of forms of behaviour to be measured. They contrast this approach with **time sampling**.

- *Time sampling* is a further approach to the observation of behaviour. An example here would be a study of schools known as the ORACLE (Observational Research and Classroom Learning Evaluation) project (Galton, Simon, and Croll 1980). In this research, eight children (four of each gender) in each class in which observation took place were observed for around 4 minutes but on ten separate occasions. A mechanical device made a noise every twenty-five seconds and on each occasion this occurred the observer made a note of what the teacher or pupils were doing in terms of the observation schedule. The sampling of time periods was random.

Sampling

Just like survey research, structured observation necessitates decisions about sampling. Mintzberg's study was somewhat unusual in that it relied on a very small sample of only five individuals—a decision that he explains was forced partly by practical constraints, as the research was done for his doctoral dissertation. This meant that 'the time of only one researcher was available, and that for only 12 months or so' (Mintzberg 1973: 237). However, with structured observation it is more usual not only to sample a larger number of people, but also to incorporate several other sampling issues as well.

Sampling people

When people are being sampled, considerations very similar to those encountered in Chapter 8 in respect of probability sampling come to the fore. This means that the observer will ideally want to sample on a random basis. In the study of job characteristics (see Research in focus 12.5), the individuals who were observed at work were randomly selected (Jenkins et al. 1975). However, structured observation

can also be based on non-probability sampling, such as in the example in Research in focus 12.6.

Sampling in terms of time

As implied by the idea of time sampling (see above), it is often necessary to ensure that, if certain individuals are sampled on more than one occasion, they are not always observed at the same time of the day. This means that, if particular individuals are selected randomly for observation on several different occasions for short periods, it is desirable for the observation periods to be randomly selected. For example, it would not be desirable for a certain manager working in his office always to be observed at the end of the day. He or she might be tired and this would give a false impression of that manager's behaviour. Experience and event sampling, discussed in Chapter 10, offers a means of structuring the selection of time intervals through the use of technologies such as smartphones—techniques that could also be applied in sampling for structured observation.

Research in focus 12.6
Structured observation with a sample of one

Louhiala-Salminen (2002) observed a Finnish business manager who works in a multinational corporation for one day to identify the features that characterize the discourse in a multinational corporation. The aim of the study 'was to describe the discourse activities of a professional who is a non-native speaker of English and uses English "as a business lingua franca"' (2002: 215). Most of the day was recorded using audio tapes, and an observation protocol was used to make notes about the nature of the activity, including type of communication and language used. Louhiala-Salminen undertook the observation between 09.00 and 16.00 and followed the manager all day except for one 20-minute meeting that entailed confidential information. The manager stayed at work for a further 90 minutes after the observation ended 'catching up with some planning and writing which he was not able to do in the day' (2002: 217). On the day following the observation, the manager, his superior, and subordinates were interviewed to seek clarification of events the previous day and to gain background information about the manager's education, experience, and attitudes towards language, communication, and culture.

One of the issues this study had to deal with is the impact of technology on managerial time use, specifically the use of email as a communication medium as opposed to writing letters or making telephone calls. The researcher explains: 'The written documents that the manager read or wrote during the day were e-mail messages. Because of the large number of the messages (about 150 altogether) it would have been impossible to have copies of all without seriously disturbing the normal flow of work. Therefore about one third of the email messages were printed as examples' (2002: 214). Louhiala-Salminen notes the crucial role of email in structuring the events of the working day. The manager spent the first two hours of his day working through the ninety-five emails that had arrived for him during the previous two days when he had been out of the office, and the majority of subsequent interactions were initiated by email messages. The study also highlights the blurred boundaries between different kinds of activity: 'throughout the day spoken and written communication were totally intertwined, there was hardly any activity in either mode where the other would not be present as well; many of the phone calls were to confirm an issue in an e-mail message, e-mail messages referred to phone calls, and they were constantly discussed in face-to-face communication with colleagues' (2002: 217).

This study is also interesting in terms of reactive effects (see Key concept 12.8). When discussing the nature of the observation and in particular the low number of direct spoken encounters, which Louhiala-Salminen found puzzling given the open-plan nature of the office, the manager suggested that more people would have stopped to talk to him had the researcher not been sitting near his desk. Finally, although this study involved the structured observation of just one manager for one day, it was intended to form part of a bigger international comparative study across four different countries once the research design and data collection methods had been tested. One of the things that Louhiala-Salminen discovered from the study was that, because of the hectic pace of work involving different communication media, the observation protocol was too detailed to be completed during the observation. She suggests that a video recording would make analysis of simultaneous and interconnected activities easier.

Further sampling considerations

The sampling procedures mentioned so far conform to probability sampling principles, because it is feasible to construct a sampling frame for individuals. However, this is not always possible for different kinds of reason. Studies in public areas, like the research on superstition mentioned above, do not permit random sampling, because we cannot very easily construct a sampling frame of people walking along a street. Similarly, it is not feasible to construct a sampling frame of interactions—for

example, of meetings between managers and their subordinates. The problem with doing structured observation research on such a topic is that it does not lend itself to the specification of a sampling frame, and therefore the researcher's ability to generate a probability sample is curtailed.

As suggested in Chapter 8, considerations relating to probability sampling derive largely from concerns surrounding the external validity of findings. Such concerns are not necessarily totally addressed by resorting to probability sampling, however. For example, if a structured observation study is conducted over a relatively short span of time, issues of the representativeness of findings are likely to arise. If the research was conducted in estate agents' offices, observations conducted over the summer, when most people are on holiday and the housing market is quite quiet, may be affected by these factors compared to observations at a different point in the year. Consequently, consideration has to be given to the question of the timing of observation. Furthermore, how are the sites in which structured observation is to take place selected? Can we presume that they are themselves representative? Clearly, a random sampling procedure for the selection of organizations may assuage any worries in this connection. However, in view of the difficulty of securing access to settings such as schools and business organizations, it is likely that the organizations to which access is secured may not be representative of the population of appropriate ones.

A further set of distinctions between types of sampling in structured observation have been drawn by Martin and Bateson (1986):

- 'ad libitum sampling', whereby the observer records whatever is happening at the time;

- 'focal sampling', in which a specific individual is observed for a set period of time; the observer records all examples of whatever forms of behaviour are of interest in terms of a schedule;

- 'scan sampling', whereby an entire group of individuals is scanned at regular intervals and the behaviour of all of them is recorded at that time; this sampling strategy allows only one or two types of behaviour to be observed and recorded; and

- 'behaviour sampling', whereby an entire group is watched and the observer records who was involved in a particular kind of behaviour.

Most structured observation research seems to employ focal sampling, such as Mintzberg's (1973) study, the research by Martinko and Gardner (1990) and O'Gorman, Bourke, and Murray (2005) (see Research in focus 12.4), and Jenkins et al. (1975) (see Research in focus 12.5).

 # Issues of reliability and validity

One writer has concluded that, when compared to interviews and questionnaires, structured observation 'provides (a) more reliable information about events; (b) greater precision regarding their timing, duration, and frequency; (c) greater accuracy in the time ordering of variables; and (d) more accurate and economical reconstructions of large-scale social episodes' (McCall 1984: 277). This is a very strong endorsement for structured observation, but, as McCall notes, there are several issues of reliability and validity that confront practitioners of the method. Some of these issues are similar to those faced by researchers when seeking to develop measures in business research in general (see Chapter 7) and by those using survey research in particular. However, certain concerns are specific to structured observation.

Reliability

Practitioners of structured observation have been concerned with the degree of inter-observer consistency. Essentially, this issue entails considering the degree to which two or more observers of the same behaviour agree in terms of their coding of that behaviour on the observation schedule—that is, *inter-observer consistency*. The chief mechanism for assessing this component of reliability is a statistic called *kappa* (see Key concept 12.7; *this can be ignored if you feel unsure about addressing more complex statistical issues at this stage*).

A second consideration in relation to reliability is the degree of consistency of the application of the observation schedule over time—that is, *intra-observer consistency*. This is clearly a difficult notion, because of the capacity for and often necessity for people to behave in different ways on different occasions and in different contexts. Assessing the consistency of observation ratings across all possibilities is clearly a difficult undertaking. The procedures for assessing this aspect of reliability are broadly similar to those applied to the issue of inter-observer consistency. The Jenkins et al. (1975) research addressed the issue of inter-observer consistency over time and found that the measures fared even worse in this respect.

It is clearly not an easy matter to achieve reliability in structured observation. This is a point of some significance in view of the fact that validity presupposes reliability (see Chapter 7). Reliability may be difficult

Key concept 12.7
What is Cohen's kappa?

Cohen's kappa is a measure of the degree of agreement over the coding of items by two people. As such, it could be applied to the coding of any textual information, as in the content analysis of newspaper articles or of answers to open interview questions, as well as to the coding of observation. Much like Cronbach's alpha (see Key concept 7.6), you will end up with a coefficient that will vary between 0 and 1. The closer the coefficient is to 1, the higher the agreement and the better the inter-observer consistency. A coefficient of 0.75 or above is considered very good; between 0.6 and 0.75, it is considered good; and between 0.4 and 0.6, it is regarded as fair. The meaning of kappa is that it measures the degree of agreement between observers beyond that which would occur by chance. Croll (1986) refers to a very similar statistic, the Scott coefficient of agreement, which can be interpreted in an identical way.

The values of kappa in the study of job characteristics referred to in Research in focus 12.5 were mainly in the 'fair' category. The two indicators referred to in Research in focus 12.5 achieved kappa values of 0.43 and 0.54, respectively (Jenkins et al. 1975). These are not very encouraging and suggest that the coding of job characteristics was not very reliable.

to achieve on occasions, because of the effects of such factors as observer fatigue and lapses in attention. However, this point should not be exaggerated, because some studies have been able to achieve high levels of reliability for many of their measures, and indeed two critics of structured observation have written that 'there is no doubt that observers can be trained to use complex coding schedules with considerable reliability' (Delamont and Hamilton 1984: 32).

Validity

Measurement validity relates to the question of whether or not a measure is measuring what it is supposed to measure. The validity of any measure will be affected by:

- whether or not the measure reflects the concept it has been designed to measure (see Chapter 7); and

- error that arises from the implementation of the measure in the research process (see Chapter 9).

The first of these issues simply means that in structured observation it is necessary to attend to the same kinds of issues concerning the checking of validity (assessing face validity, concurrent validity, and so on) that are encountered in research-based interviews and questionnaires. The second aspect of validity—error in implementation—relates to two matters in particular.

- Is the observation instrument administered as it is supposed to be? This is the equivalent of ensuring that interviewers using a structured interview schedule follow the research instrument and its instructions exactly as they are supposed to. If there is variability between observers or over time, the measure will be unreliable and therefore cannot be valid. Ensuring that observers have as complete an understanding as possible of how the observation schedule should be implemented is therefore crucial.

- Do people change their behaviour because they know they are being observed? This is an instance of what is known as the 'reactive effect' (see Key concept 12.8)—after all, if people adjust the way they behave because they know they are being observed (perhaps because they want to be viewed in a favourable way by the observer), their behaviour would have to be considered atypical. As a result, we could hardly regard the results of structured observation research as indicative of what happens in reality. As McCall (1984) notes, there is evidence that a reactive effect occurs in structured observation, but that by and large research participants become accustomed to being observed, so that the researcher essentially becomes less intrusive the longer he or she is present. Moreover, it should be borne in mind that frequently people's awareness of the observer's presence is offset by other factors. For example, managers have many tasks to accomplish that reflect the demands of the organization, so that the observer's ability to make a big impact on behaviour may be curtailed by the requirements of the situation.

Key concept 12.8
What is the reactive effect?

Webb et al. (1966) wrote about the 'reactive measurement effect', by which they meant that 'the research subject's knowledge that he is participating in a scholarly search may confound the investigator's data' (1966: 13). They distinguished four components of this effect.

- *The guinea pig effect—awareness of being tested.* Examples of the kind of concern that Webb et al. were writing about are such effects as the research participant wanting to create a good impression or feeling prompted to behave in ways (or express attitudes) that would not normally be exhibited.

- *Role selection.* Webb et al. argue that participants are often tempted to adopt a particular kind of role in research. An example is that there is a well-known effect in experimental research (but which may have a broader applicability) whereby some individuals seek out cues about the aims of the research and adjust what they say and do in line with their perceptions (which may, of course, be false) of those aims (this is also known as the Hawthorne effect—see Research in focus 3.8).

- *Measurement as a change agent.* The very fact of a researcher being in a context in which no researcher is normally present may itself cause things to be different. For example, the fact that there is an observer sitting in on a management meeting means that there is space and a chair being used that otherwise would be unoccupied. This very fact may influence behaviour.

- *Response sets.* This is an issue that primarily relates to questionnaire and interview research and occurs when the respondent replies to a set of questions in a consistent but clearly inappropriate manner. Examples of this kind of effect are measurement problems such as the social desirability effect and yeasaying and naysaying (consistently answering yes or no to questions or consistently agreeing or disagreeing with items regardless of the meaning of the question or item).

Reactive effects are likely to occur in any research in which participants know they are the focus of investigation. Webb et al. called for greater use of what they call *unobtrusive measures* or *non-reactive methods*, which do not entail participants' knowledge of their involvement in research (see Key concept 14.12 for a more complete explanation). The Hawthorne effect, mentioned in Chapter 3, is a form of reactive effect, but Webb et al.'s categories provide a more inclusive summary of this term.

Other forms of structured observation

Field stimulation

Salancik (1979) has used the term '**field stimulation**' to describe a form of observation research that shares many of structured observation's characteristics. Although he classifies field stimulations as a qualitative method, they are in fact better thought of as operating with a quantitative research strategy, since the researcher typically seeks to quantify the outcomes of his or her interventions. In terms of the classification offered in Key concept 12.2, it is in fact 'contrived observation'. A field stimulation is a study in which the researcher directly intervenes in and/ or manipulates a natural setting in order to observe what

happens as a consequence of that intervention. However, unlike most structured observation, in a field stimulation participants do not know they are being studied, which makes it a form of unobtrusive measure as defined by Webb et al. (1966) (see Key concept 14.12). In business and management, consumer researchers use field stimulations to study the behaviour of retail front-line staff using the 'mystery shopper' technique (see Thinking deeply 12.9). An example of the use of this technique in the study of travel agents' recommendations is given in Research in focus 12.10.

While such research provides some quite striking findings and gets around the problem of reactivity by not

Thinking deeply 12.9
Field stimulation and the mystery shopper

A popular technique used in consumer research to evaluate the effectiveness of retail staff is the 'mystery shopper' technique. This typically involves sending people into a shop to buy products. After the interaction, the shoppers typically fill out a rating sheet detailing the nature of the interaction and service they received. This information is then fed back via the consumer research organization to the firm concerned so that it can make any necessary improvements to front-line service. More recent developments have included supplying mystery shoppers with wireless hidden cameras that can be concealed in their cap, button, or cellphone in order to record the transactions and interaction between the customer and the assistant.

The mystery shopper technique is a type of field stimulation, because it involves the researcher entering the shop (a natural setting) and intervening in order to see what happens. In addition, the retail staff are not aware that they are being studied. However, because this involves observing people without their informed consent, the mystery shopper technique raises numerous ethical issues (see Chapter 6), including those related to the lack of informed consent, and misrepresentation and deceit, since an inherent feature of mystery shopping is to pretend to be a customer (Ng Kwet Shing and Spence, 2002). These issues are particularly pronounced if the encounter is recorded in some way, as this has even greater potential to violate their privacy, also thereby potentially raising legal considerations. Ng Kwet Shing and Spence (2002) investigated the ethics of mystery shopping in the UK mobile phone industry from the perspective of those affected by it. In particular, they highlight the practice of using students on an industrial placement as part of their degree to collect competitor information. Their research suggests students on placements felt they had little choice over whether or not to participate in mystery shopping, and they conclude that those most suited to it seem to be individuals 'who lie easily, find face-to-face deceit unproblematic, and are not stressed by misrepresentation' (Ng Kwet Shing and Spence, 2002: 349), hardly desirable ethical characteristics in an employee. They also raise concern that companies are condoning and encouraging young people to pursue unethical practices by becoming mystery shoppers.

Research in focus 12.10
A mystery shopper investigation into the selling behaviour of travel agents

In a study designed to assess the influence of travel agency recommendations on UK consumers who were choosing a holiday, Hudson et al. (2001) conducted research that combined focus groups, semi-structured interviews, and 'mystery shoppers'.

Travel agents have come under scrutiny for directional selling, placing pressure on consumers to purchase package holidays that are linked to their parent companies. The researchers wanted to investigate the extent to which this bias influenced consumer choice. They wanted to gain an insight into the interaction that occurs between travel agent and customer when the latter books a holiday. The focus groups and interviews provided the researchers with an insight into the process whereby consumers choose a holiday, and this formed the basis for the construction of scenarios that were used in the second stage of data collection, which relied on the mystery shopper technique.

Fifty-two agencies from the three largest UK travel agency chains, Lunn Poly (owned by Thomson), Going Places (owned by Airtours, later renamed MyTravel), and Thomas Cook/Carlson (owned by Thomas Cook), were selected using a quota sampling technique. A list of travel agents obtained from the Association of British Travel Agents (ABTA) constituted the sampling frame from which the travel agencies were selected.

A total of 36 visits and 120 telephone calls were made by the mystery shoppers to travel agents in the London area. The 'shoppers' were trained, using role plays, to ensure that they adopted a neutral rather than an aggressive

(continued)

or defensive approach in the encounter with agents. None of the respondents was aware that he or she was being studied. The mystery shoppers were given one of four different scenarios.

- *Scenario 1.* The customer has a specific holiday from one brochure/operator in mind. (It was hypothesized that, in this situation, the agent would not attempt to influence the customer but would book the holiday as requested.)

- *Scenario 2.* The customer has a number of alternatives chosen from different brochures. (In this situation it was suggested that the agent would try to influence the customer's choice, attempting to sell the holiday of the parent company.)

- *Scenario 3.* The customer has a certain amount of money in mind (£2000), as well as a destination (Spain). (Here it was speculated that the travel agent would strongly influence the customer's choice, recommending the holiday of the parent company.)

- *Scenario 4.* The customer is looking for a last-minute holiday and calls the agent to see what is available. (In this circumstance it was predicted that the travel agent would exert strong influence over the customer's eventual decision.)

Each face-to-face interview lasted on average 30 minutes, while telephone encounters lasted an average of 15 minutes. Following the interaction, 'shoppers' completed a report form, detailing, for example, how forcibly the agent used directional selling tactics (that is, did the agent try to guide the shopper towards purchasing a holiday offered by his or her parent company?) using a five-point scale.

Findings from the study showed that in the first scenario none of the agents made an attempt to guide the customer towards an alternative holiday, but in the third scenario all the agencies employed directional selling tactics. The study also found that the agencies owned by Airtours and Thomas Cook gave more biased advice than those owned by Thomson. Of Going Places agencies, 90 per cent pushed the Airtours brand, while 75 per cent of agencies owned by Thomas Cook tried to sell their own brands, the largest being JMC holidays.

The use of the mystery shopper technique produced findings that appear to confirm the view of smaller agents and operators—that directional selling tactics are much more widespread than the larger operators or the Monopolies and Mergers Commission would like to admit. Moreover, given the publicity and interest in this issue, it is unlikely that the agents would have used directional selling tactics to such an extent if they had known that they were being studied.

alerting research participants to the fact that they are being observed, ethical concerns are sometimes raised, such as the use of deception. Moreover, the extent to which an observation schedule can be employed is inevitably limited (unless the researcher is carrying a hidden camera, as some 'mystery shoppers' have done), because excessive use will blow the observer's cover. All that can usually be done is to engage in limited coding at the time of the interaction, paying particular attention to the nature of the effect of the intervention, or to document the interaction immediately after the observation has taken place, as the Hudson et al. (2001) research in Research in focus 12.10 did.

Organizational simulation

An alternative method for observing behaviour in which participants are made aware of the fact that they are being studied involves the organizational simulation. A simulation involves representing a situation by creating an artificial setting in which individual or group behaviour can be observed. An example of an organizational simulation is provided in Research in focus 12.11. In a sense, a simulation is similar to a laboratory experiment (see Chapter 3), except that it does not seek to control participants' activities as much as in an experimental research design. Simulations can thus give participants much greater freedom to act according to their judgement and to make decisions, and their actions become the focus of observation. Hough and White (2003) used a version of the Looking Glass Inc. (LGI) organizational simulation to explore the effects of 'environmental dynamism' on strategic decision-making and firm performance. Their 216 participants were members of a technology company which 'sent senior managers and executives to one of 18 executive development programs, which included participation in the LGI study'

Research in focus 12.11
Looking Glass Inc.: an organizational simulation

Looking Glass Inc. is a simulation developed by the Centre for Creative Leadership (see McCall and Lombardo 1982), which requires participants to act as managers in a hypothetical glass-manufacturing organization. Unlike many other simulations, which tend to be developed for training, Looking Glass was based on research, involving interviews with executives, site visits, and the collection of data from business publications. The simulation lasts approximately six hours. Twenty participants are assigned to twenty top management roles ranging from President to Plant Manager and spanning three divisions. Their task is to run the company for a day in any way they want.

The simulation begins the evening before, with events that are designed to familiarize participants with the company, including a slide show explaining the structure of the company. Participants are assigned roles and spend some time in their offices; job descriptions and annual reports are distributed. The following morning, the simulation of a business day commences. 'Each participant spends the first 45 minutes at his or her desk reviewing an in-basket containing today's mail . . . After 45 minutes the telephone system is turned on and the managers are free to call meetings, send memos, place phone calls, etc. Using memo or phone, participants can contact anyone inside or outside the company' (1982: 535).

The simulation includes a wide range of management problems and issues that participants must deal with (or ignore if they see fit). These cover a range of functional areas and include:

- an opportunity to acquire a new plant;
- a lawsuit with a major customer;
- technological innovation and obsolescence.

The three divisions within the company face different external environments:

- *Advanced Products*: makes products for electronics and communications industries and exists in a highly uncertain and rapidly changing business environment;
- *Commercial Glass*: makes light bulb casings and flat glass, and faces a relatively predictable, stable market;
- *Industrial Glass*: faces a mixed environment because of the wide variety of products it makes, from auto glass (stable) to spacecraft windows (unstable).

The simulation enables a variety of data collection methods to be used, including the possibility of structured observation. Observers can be assigned to observe specific roles or to time sample all the roles on a scheduled basis. Memos sent by participants and telephone calls made provide a further unobtrusive source of data. However, McCall and Lombardo claim that, 'in many respects, studying Looking Glass presents the same challenges as studying a real organization' (1982: 540), because it is impossible to control the variables involved.

(Hough and White, 2003: 483). Participants were given reports and memos relating to their self-selected fictitious job role and asked to prepare the previous evening, before participating in a day-long staff meeting. The authors argue that this methodology enabled them to focus on the multi-level nature of decision-making and to tease out the effect of complex variables, including those related to the environment in which decision-making takes place.

Simulations create large amounts of data in a relatively short period of time, thereby overcoming some of the difficulties of cost and access that are often associated with business and management research. They also enable access to issues that may not be amenable to observation in real life, such as problem-solving or decision-making. Moreover, simulation enables the researcher to create and alter the situation in order to examine the effect of an intervention; if the effects of such interventions are studied in 'real' organizations, research is likely to take a considerable length of time. Developments in computing technology are suggested to have opened up greater opportunities for development of simulation models based on 'agent' interactions, where 'agents' represent 'real social actors' (Fioretti, 2012: 228) who interact in an artificial environment, not unlike in a videogame. However, simulations are subject to the charge of artificiality. For example, there is no guarantee that the participants attending an executive development programme, as in the study by Hough and White (2003), will respond in the same way in the simulation as they would if they were making decisions in their real workplace.

Criticisms of structured observation

Although it is not very extensively used in business and management research, structured observation has, in the past, been quite controversial. Certain criticisms have been implied in some of the previous discussion of reliability and validity issues, as well as in connection with the issue of generalizability. However, certain other areas of criticism warrant further discussion.

- There is a risk of imposing a potentially inappropriate or irrelevant framework on the setting being observed. This point is similar to the problem of the closed question in questionnaires. This risk is especially great if the setting is one about which little is known. One solution is for the structured observation to be preceded by a period of unstructured observation, so that appropriate variables and categories can be specified.

- Because it concentrates upon directly observable behaviour, structured observation is rarely able to get at intentions behind behaviour. Sometimes, when intentions are of concern, they are imputed by observers. Thus, in Mintzberg's basic activity categories of managerial behaviour, it is not entirely clear what the difference is between an 'unscheduled meeting' and a 'tour' that involves a chance meeting. Essentially, the problem is that structured observation does not readily allow the observer to get a grasp of the meaning of behaviour.

- There is a tendency for structured observation to generate lots of bits of data. The problem here can be one of trying to piece them together to produce an overall picture, or one of trying to find general themes that link the fragments of data together. It becomes difficult, in other words, to see a bigger picture that lies behind the segments of behaviour that structured observation typically uncovers. It has been suggested, for example, that the tendency for structured observation studies of managers at work to find little evidence of planning in their everyday work (e.g. Mintzberg 1973) is due to the tendency for the method to fragment a manager's activities into discrete parts. As a result, something like planning, which may be an element in many managerial activities, becomes obscured from view (Snyder and Glueck 1980).

- It is often suggested that structured observation neglects the context within which behaviour takes place. For example, Martinko and Gardner (1990) found that some of Mintzberg's categories of basic activity were represented differently among school principals, rather than general managers, and, in particular, the amount of time spent on unscheduled meetings was much greater. Of course, were data collected about the context in which behaviour takes place, this criticism would have little weight, but the tendency of structured observation researchers to concentrate on overt behaviour tends to engender this kind of criticism.

On the other hand . . .

It is clear from the previous section that there are undeniable limitations to structured observation. However, it also has to be remembered that, when overt behaviour is the focus of analysis and perhaps issues of meaning are less salient, structured observation is almost certainly more accurate and effective than getting people to report on their behaviour through questionnaires. It may also be that structured observation is a method that works best when accompanied by other methods. Since it can rarely provide reasons for observed patterns of behaviour, if it is accompanied by another method that can probe reasons, it is of greater utility.

In laboratory experiments in such fields as social psychology and medical research, observation with varying degrees of structure is quite commonplace, but in business and management research, with the exception of Mintzberg's classic study, structured observation has not been used very frequently. Perhaps one major reason is that, although interviews and questionnaires are limited in terms of their capacity to tap behaviour accurately, as noted above, they do offer the opportunity to reveal information about both behaviour *and* attitudes and social backgrounds. In other words, they are more flexible and offer the prospect of being able to uncover a variety of correlates of behaviour (albeit reported behaviour), such as social background factors. They can also ask questions about attitudes and investigate explanations that people proffer for their behaviour. As a result, researchers using questionnaires are able to gain information about some factors that may lie behind the patterns of behaviour they uncover. Also, not all forms of behaviour are liable to be accessible to structured observation, and it is likely that survey research or researcher-driven diaries (see Key concept 10.3) are the only means of gaining access to them. However, greater use of structured observation may result in greater facility with the method, so that reliable measures might emerge.

Checklist

Structured observation research

○ Have you clearly defined your research questions?

○ Is the sample to be observed relevant to your research questions?

○ Can you justify your sampling approach?

○ Does your observation schedule indicate precisely which kinds of behaviour are to be observed?

○ Have your observation categories been designed so that there is no need for the observer to interpret what is going on?

○ Have you made sure that the categories of behaviour do not overlap?

○ Do all the different categories of behaviour allow you to answer your research questions?

○ Have you piloted your observation schedule?

○ Are the coding instructions clear?

○ Are the categories of behaviour inclusive?

○ Is it easy to log the behaviour as it is happening?

Key points

- Structured observation is an approach to the study of behaviour that is an alternative to survey-based measures.

- It comprises explicit rules for the recording of behaviour.

- Structured observation has tended to be used in relation to a rather narrow range of forms of behaviour, such as that of managers.

- It shares with survey research many common problems concerning reliability, validity, and generalizability.

- Reactive effects have to be taken into account but should not be exaggerated.

- Field stimulations represent a form of structured observation but suffer from difficulties concerning ethics.

- Problems with structured observation revolve around the difficulty of imputing meaning and ensuring that a relevant framework for recording behaviour is being employed.

Questions for review

Problems with survey research on behaviour

● What are the chief limitations of survey research with regard to the study of behaviour?

So why not observe behaviour?

● What are the chief characteristics of structured observation?

● To what extent does it provide a superior approach to the study of behaviour than questionnaires or structured interviews?

The observation schedule

● What is an observation schedule?

● 'An observation schedule is much like a self-completion questionnaire or structured interview except that it does not entail asking questions.' Discuss.

● Devise an observation schedule of your own for observing an area of social interaction in which you are regularly involved. Ask people with whom you normally interact in those situations how well they think it fits what goes on. Have you missed anything out?

Strategies for observing behaviour

● What are the main ways in which behaviour can be recorded in structured observation?

Sampling

● Identify some of the main sampling strategies in structured observation.

Issues of reliability and validity

● How far do considerations of reliability and validity in structured observation mirror those encountered in relation to the asking of questions in structured interviews and self-completion questionnaires?

● What is the reactive effect and why might it be important in relation to structured observation research?

Other forms of structured observation

● What are field stimulations and what ethical concerns are posed by them?

● What are the advantages and disadvantages of simulation as a form of structured observation?

Criticisms of structured observation

● 'The chief problem with structured observation is that it does not allow us access to the intentions that lie behind behaviour.' Discuss.

● How far do you agree with the view that structured observation works best when used in conjunction with other research methods?

Online Resource Centre
www.oxfordtextbooks.co.uk/orc/brymanbrm4e/

Visit the Interactive Research Guide that accompanies this book to complete an exercise in Structured Observation.

13

Content analysis

Chapter outline

Content analysis is an approach to the analysis of documents and texts (which may be printed or visual) that seeks to quantify content in terms of predetermined categories and in a systematic and replicable manner. It is a very flexible method that can be applied to a variety of media. In a sense, it is not a research method, in that it is an approach to the analysis of documents and texts rather than a means of generating data. However, it is usually treated as a research method because of its distinctive approach to analysis. This chapter explores:

- the kinds of research question to which content analysis is suited;
- how to approach the sampling of documents to be analysed;
- what kinds of features of documents or texts are counted;
- how to go about *coding*, which is probably the central and most distinctive stage of doing a content analysis;
- the advantages and disadvantages of content analysis.

Introduction

Imagine that you are interested in the amount and nature of the interest shown by the mass media, such as newspapers, in a business news item such as the collapse of Enron and WorldCom and the impact this has had on corporate accountability and ethical behaviour. You might ask such questions as:

- When did news items on this topic first begin to appear?
- Which newspapers were fastest in generating an interest in the topic?
- Which newspapers have shown the greatest interest in the topic?
- At what point did media interest begin to wane?
- Have journalists' stances on the topic changed, for example, in terms of their support for business accountants and consultants, such as Arthur Andersen, or in calling for increased government regulation of corporate behaviour?

If you want to know the answers to research questions such as these, you are likely to need to use content analysis to answer them.

Probably the best-known definition of content analysis is as follows:

> Content analysis is a research technique for the objective, systematic and quantitative description of the manifest content of communication.
>
> (Berelson 1952: 18)

Another well-known and apparently similar definition is:

> Content analysis is any technique for making inferences by objectively and systematically identifying specified characteristics of messages.
>
> (Holsti 1969: 14)

It is striking that both of these definitions contain a reference to two qualities: objectivity and being systematic. The former quality means that, as with something like an observation schedule (see Chapter 12), rules are clearly specified in advance for the assignment of the raw material (such as newspaper stories) to categories. Objectivity in this sense resides in the fact that there is transparency in the procedures for

Tips and skills
Avoiding rater bias in a coding scheme

R. Weber (1990) recommends eight steps for creating, testing, and implementing a coding scheme in order to avoid rater bias. These steps are widely applied and are sometimes referred to as the Weber Protocol.

1. definition of the recording units (for example, word, phrase, sentence, paragraph);
2. definition of the coding categories;
3. test of coding on a sample of text;
4. assessment of the accuracy and reliability of the sample coding;
5. revision of the coding rules;
6. return to Step 3 until sufficient reliability is achieved;
7. coding of all the text;
8. assessment of the achieved reliability or accuracy.

assigning the raw material to categories so that the analyst's personal biases intrude as little as possible in the process. The content analyst is simply applying the rules in question. The quality of being systematic means that the application of the rules is done in a consistent manner so that bias is again suppressed. As a result of these two qualities, anyone could employ the rules and (hopefully) come up with the same results. The process of analysis is one that means that the results are not an extension of the analyst and his or her personal biases. The rules in question may, of course, reflect the researcher's interests and concerns and therefore these might be a product of subjective bias, but the key point is that, once formulated, the rules can be (or should be capable of being) applied without the intrusion of bias.

Berelson's definition also makes reference to 'quantitative description'. Content analysis is firmly rooted in the quantitative research strategy, in that the aim is to produce quantitative accounts of the raw material in terms of the categories specified by the rules. The feature of quantification adds to the general sense of the systematic and objective application of neutral rules, so that it becomes possible to say with some certainty and in a systematic way that, for example, broadsheet newspapers carried far more coverage of a particular issue than tabloid newspapers.

Two other elements in Berelson's definition are striking, especially when juxtaposed against Holsti's. First, Berelson refers to 'manifest content'. This means that content analysis is concerned with uncovering the apparent

content of the item in question: what it is clearly about. Holsti makes no such reference, alluding only to 'specified characteristics'. The latter essentially opens the door to conducting an analysis in terms of what we might term 'latent content'—that is, of meanings that lie beneath the superficial indicators of content. Uncovering such latent content means interpreting meanings that lie beneath the surface, such as whether the impression is given that the author construes the Enron scandal as an issue solely of concern to US shareholders and accountancy practices, or as having a broader set of implications for business practice and corporate accountability across the globe. A related distinction is sometimes made between an emphasis on the linguistic structure of the text (in particular, counting certain words) and an emphasis on themes within the text, which entails searching for certain ideas within the text (Beardsworth 1980).

A second element in Berelson's definition not found in Holsti's is the reference to 'communication'. Berelson's (1952) book was concerned with communication research, a field that has been especially concerned with newspapers, television, and other mass media. Holsti refers somewhat more generally to 'messages', which raises the prospect of quite a wide applicability of content analysis beyond the specific boundaries of the mass media and mass communications. Content analysis becomes applicable to many different forms of unstructured information, such as transcripts of semi- and unstructured interviews (e.g. Bryman, Stephens, and A Campo 1996) and even qualitative case studies of organizations (e.g. Hodson 1996). Nor is it necessary for the medium being analysed to be in a written form. Research has been conducted on:

- the visual images (as well as the text) of company annual reports to explore how these reflect organizational beliefs about customers (Dougherty and Kunda 1990);

- motivational videos featuring management guru Frederick Herzberg giving a live lecture to managers (Jackson and Carter 1998);

- the pictures drawn by managers to express their views about organizational change (Broussine and Vince 1996).

However, the main use of content analysis has been to examine mass media items, as well as texts and documents that are either produced by the organization, such as annual reports, or written about it, such as articles in the business press. For example, Bettman and Weitz (1983) examined letters to stockholders from the annual reports of 181 companies in 4 industries. A good year (1972) and a bad year (1974) were compared, based on GNP and stock market performance. In this regard, content analysis is one of a number of approaches to the examination of texts that have been developed over the years (see Key concept 13.1). Insch, Moore, and

Murphy (1997) suggest that one of the reasons for the limited popularity of content analysis in business and management is because researchers are unsure how to use it. They advocate a step-by-step process whereby the researcher reviews the literature to develop understanding of the construct of interest and then identifies texts that are likely to capture it. It is the intention of this chapter to provide a framework through which systematic content analysis can be conducted. However, Duriau, Reger, and Pfarrer (2007) claim that the use of content analysis in organizational research has grown since the 1990s, not least because it is a relatively low-cost method that can be applied to student research projects. The advent of computer programs that facilitate the analysis of textual data and the increase in the number of searchable electronic databases available have also enabled some of the tediousness associated with the method to be removed, have enhanced reliability and speed, and have further lowered costs, and this may have further contributed to the increase in popularity of content analysis. Duriau, Reger, and Pfarrer (2007) also suggest that the potential of this method has yet to be fully exploited, particularly in relation to the vast amount of text and graphic content, as well as audio and video data, contained on organizational websites.

Key concept 13.1
What is content analysis?

- *Content analysis*. An approach to the analysis of documents and texts that seeks to quantify content in terms of predetermined categories and in a systematic and replicable manner.

Content analysis can usefully be contrasted with two other approaches to the analysis of the content of communication:

- **Semiotics**. The study/science of signs. An approach to the analysis of documents and other phenomena that emphasizes the importance of seeking out the deeper meaning of those phenomena. A semiotic approach is concerned to uncover the processes of meaning production and how signs are designed to have an effect upon actual and prospective consumers of those signs. This approach will be explored in Chapter 23.

- *Ethnographic content analysis*. A term employed by Altheide (1996) to refer to an approach to documents that emphasizes the role of the investigator in the construction of the meaning of and in texts. It is sometimes also referred to as qualitative content analysis. As with most approaches that are described as ethnographic, there is an emphasis on allowing categories to emerge out of data and on recognizing the significance for understanding meaning in the context in which an item being analysed (and the categories derived from it) appeared. This approach will be explored in Chapter 23.

When the term 'content analysis' is employed in this chapter, it will be referring to quantitative content analysis—that is, the first of the three forms of analysis referred to in the list above, which is the kind of analysis to which Berelson (1952) and Holsti (1969) refer.

What are the research questions?

As with most quantitative research, it is necessary to specify the research questions precisely, as these will guide both the selection of the media to be content analysed and the coding schedule. If the research questions are not clearly articulated, there is a risk that inappropriate media will be analysed or that the coding schedule will miss out key dimensions. Most content analysis is likely to entail several research questions. For example, the aim of Harris's (2001) study was to investigate the way the word 'courage' was used in the business community. In itself this is not very specific and hardly directs you to a clear specification of the media to be examined or the development of a coding schedule. However, to achieve this aim Harris sought to content analyse stories in broadsheet newspapers that were about courage in order to compare a definition of courage derived from the literature with the way the word 'courage' is used in the community (especially in business, commerce, and government). This gave rise to other, more specific research questions, including:

- Is it possible to categorize the types of courage event described in the newspaper stories?

- What tools, if any, are said to have helped people show courage?

- Are obstacles identified in accounts of courage, and, if so, what are they?

- Are aspects of the accounts linked to specific professions or sectors of activity?

- Is courage used to describe dispositions, actions, or a virtue?

Such questions seem to revolve around the questions of: *who* (gets reported); *what* (gets reported); *where* (does the issue get reported); *location* (of coverage within the items analysed); *how much* (gets reported); and *why* (does the issue get reported).

As with much content analysis, the researchers were just as interested in omissions in coverage as in what *does* get reported. For example, details about the profession, qualifications, and beliefs of the courageous person were frequently omitted. Such omissions are in themselves potentially interesting, as they may reveal what is and is not important to reporters and their editors.

Another kind of issue that is frequently encountered in content analysis is:

> How far does the amount of coverage of the issue change over time?

This kind of research question or problem is particularly asked by researchers who are keen to note trends in coverage to demonstrate ebbs and flows in interest. An example of this kind of research is a study by Barley, Meyer, and Gash (1988), which used content analysis to assess whether or not members of two distinct subcultures, business and management academics and practitioners, have influenced each other's interpretations. Content analysis focused on 192 articles published on the subject of organizational culture between 1975 and 1984. This time span was chosen to reflect changes in discussion of organizational culture at a time when understanding of this topic in the business and management field was still emerging. Content analysis focused on changes in the language used by the two groups to frame this particular issue. The research showed that, although in the mid-1970s academics and practitioners conceptualized organizational culture quite differently, by the mid-1980s academics had moved towards greater appreciation of the practitioners' point of view while practitioners' interpretations were little influenced by academics.

Selecting a sample

There are several phases in the selection of a sample for content analysis. Because it is a method that can be applied to many kinds of document, the case of applying it to the mass media will be explored here. However, the basic principles have a broader relevance to a wide range of applications of content analysis.

Sampling media

Many studies of the mass media entail the specification of a research problem in the form of 'the representation of X in the mass media'. The X may be trade unions, HRM, or women and leadership. But which mass media might one choose to focus upon? Will it be newspapers or television or radio or magazines, or whatever? And, if newspapers, will it be all newspapers or tabloids or broadsheets? And, if both tabloids and broadsheets, will it be all of them and will it include Sunday papers? If it will be a sample of newspapers, including Sunday ones, will these be national or local or both? And will it include free newspapers? And if newspapers, will all news items be candidates for analysis—for example, would feature articles and letters to the editor be included? And if newspapers, will newspapers from more than one country be included?

Typically, researchers will opt for one or possibly two of the mass media and may sample within that type or types. In the research described in Research in focus 13.2, Harris (2001) chose to focus on just four broadsheet newspapers over one year, 1996, which is just as well, since the author was able to locate a large number of appropriate items (news items containing one or more of the words 'courage', 'courageous', or 'courageously')—610 in total. However, the study also incorporated a cross-cultural element by sampling one newspaper each from Australia, the UK, the USA, and China. Other media that typically have a smaller, more carefully selected audience can also form the focus for content analysis. For example, Barley, Meyer, and Gash (1988) conducted content analysis on items from business and management journals. Although

these periodicals cannot be classified as mass media in the conventional sense, as the average peer-reviewed journal article is read by only a handful of people, these journals do represent a highly influential medium for the subcultural groups that Barley and his colleagues were concerned to investigate.

Sampling dates

Sometimes, the decision about dates is more or less dictated by the occurrence of a phenomenon. For example, the timing of representation of the Enron scandal will have been more or less dictated by the speed of the US government investigation into the company's downfall and its accounting practices. One could hardly examine the issue fully prior to this investigation, though there may be an important consideration in deciding at what point the content analysis should cease, since discussions about Enron and what it means for other businesses could continue for some time after the cessation of the investigation and may entail a reappraisal as a result of subsequent events, such as the demise of Andersen Consulting.

With a research question that entails an ongoing general phenomenon, such as the representation of courage in managerial decision-making or the cultural values of companies, the matter of dates is more open. The principles of

Research in focus 13.2
A content analysis of courage and managerial decision making

The aim of Harris's (2001) study was to investigate the way the word 'courage' was used in the business community and to compare this with a theoretical definition of the construct defined prior to data collection—based on a selective review of the literature. The content analysis procedure that followed relied on searching through the 1996 editions of four daily newspapers—the *Australian Financial Review*, the *Guardian* (UK), the *Los Angeles Times*, and the *South China Morning Post*. These newspapers were selected because they all had substantial coverage of business and commerce, they covered a wide geographical spread, and they could provide information about the way that courage was perceived in the business community.

Using a searchable database, Harris included items where the word 'courage', or derivatives such as 'courageous', appeared in the text. This gave him a total population of 610 items. Each of the items was coded by the researcher using a specially designed form that allowed for inclusion of information about the nature of the article, the characteristics of the individual who was described as courageous, and the features of the courage that was being described. A coding 'dictionary' was devised that showed the coding rules, so that more than one coder could be involved in the classification and thereby increase validity. Findings showed that the newspaper stories about courage confirmed the theoretical definition of the construct that had been developed during the first stage of the study.

probability sampling outlined in Chapter 8 can readily be adapted for sampling dates—for example, generating a systematic sample of dates by randomly selecting one day of the week and then selecting every *n*th day thereafter. Alternatively, Monday newspapers could provide the first set of newspapers for inclusion, followed by Tuesday the following week, Wednesday the week after, and so on.

One important factor is whether the focus will be on an issue that entails keeping track of representation as it happens, in which case the researcher may begin at any time and the key decision becomes when to stop, or whether or not it is necessary to go backwards in time to select media from one or more time periods in the past. For example, because the topic of organizational culture had attracted 'only sporadic interest before the late 1970s', Barley, Meyer, and Gash (1988: 32) stipulated that content analysis should be carried out only on articles, written in English, that appeared in periodicals or collections of readings published after January 1975. The researchers' own informed judgement of interest in this topic thus determined their decision as to how far back to go in their sampling of the journals. Moreover, content analysis of texts was seen by the authors to be a more favourable method for studying the way that concepts of organizational culture have changed over time because journal articles are preserved at the point in time when they were written. This makes them less prone to retrospective construction than other, observational methods that could have been used to capture the author's point of view.

What is to be counted?

Obviously, decisions about what should be counted in the course of a content analysis are bound to be profoundly affected by the nature of the research questions under consideration. Content analysis offers the prospect of different kinds of 'units of analysis' being considered. The following kinds of units of analysis are frequently encountered and can be used as guides to the kinds of objects that might be the focus of attention. However, what you would actually *want* or *need* to count will be significantly dictated by your research question.

Significant actors

Particularly in the context of mass media news reporting, the main figures in any news item and their characteristics are often important items to code. These considerations are likely to result in the following questions being asked in the course of a content analysis:

- What kind of person has produced the item (for example, general or specialist news reporter)?
- Who is or are the main focus of the item (for example, senior executive of an organization, manager, politician, or employee representative)?
- Who provides alternative voices (for example, consumer representative, official from a professional association, or employee)?
- What was the context for the item (for example, publication of financial results, major organizational event, or disaster)?

In the case of the content analysis of managerial courage (see Research in focus 13.2), the significant actors and their characteristics included:

- the courage event or events described in the newspaper story;
- the type of newspaper item (for example, long or short general article, biography or obituary, book review, etc.) in which the courage event was reported;
- the details of the actor associated with the courageous act or action in the item (for example, personal details, status, and the kinds of obstacles he or she faced and the tools he or she used to help him or her to take courageous action).

The chief objective in recording such details is to map the main protagonists in news reporting in an area and to begin to reveal some of the mechanics involved in the production of information for public consumption.

Words

While it may seem a dull and time-consuming activity, counting the frequency with which certain words occur is sometimes undertaken in content analysis. Deciding what the unit of analysis will be, whether word, phrase, or sentence, is an important consideration in content analysis research. It would be difficult to contemplate using manual analysis for such a large sample, and so researchers tend to use computer-aided content analysis (see Research in focus 13.3). Gephart (1993; see Research in

Research in focus 13.3
A computer-aided content analysis of microlending to entrepreneurs

Allison, McKenny, and Short (2013) were interested in the factors that might be associated with the propensity of investors to lend through microlending to entrepreneurs in developing countries. They anticipated that one set of factors involved in the decision to invest was how entrepreneurs represent themselves in entrepreneurial investment profiles. These provide narratives about the entrepreneurs, their businesses, and rationale for investing in them. One of their hypotheses was: 'There is a negative correlation between use of accomplishment rhetoric and the speed with which individual investors fund microloans' (Allison et al. 2014: 695). Narratives were acquired through a microlending organization (Kiva.org). In order to examine the narratives, the researchers employed DICTION 6.0, a program that compares texts to dictionaries comprising groups of words that are thematically organized. Thus, the word 'accomplishment' is described as associated with a series of words associated with task-completion. For this dictionary, the authors supply the following example with the relevant words that trigger an attribution of accomplishment in bold:

> When she **started** her business she actually had no car but now due to her **success** and **increased** working capital she has bought a car to **expand** her territory.
>
> (Allison et al. 2014: 699)

The number of narratives analysed varied greatly across the 39 countries in the dataset, with a range of four in Haiti to 1804 in Philippines. The length of the narratives also varied greatly with a range of 27 to 1379 words and a mean of 163 words. In line with the hypothesis quoted above, it was found that an accomplishment rhetoric reduced the speed with which investors were prepared to fund ventures. Information about DICTION can be found at **http://www.dictionsoftware.com/** (accessed 25 October 2014).

focus 23.4) also used data analysis software to assist his qualitative study of accounts of a pipeline disaster, taking the phrase, rather than the word, to be the unit of analysis. In Bettman and Weitz's (1983) study of corporate annual reports, the unit of analysis was defined as a phrase or sentence in which there is some sort of causal reasoning about a performance outcome. The use of some words rather than others can often be of some significance because they have the potential to reveal the interpretative frameworks used by different subcultural groupings. For example, Barley, Meyer, and Gash (1988) proposed that practitioner-oriented papers on organizational culture would use words associated with rational organizing strategies. In order to test their proposition, they calculated the percentage of a paper's paragraphs that contained words associated with bureaucracy, such as 'hierarchy', and words associated with structural differentiation, such as 'departments' or 'divisions'. Similarly, they suggested practitioner-oriented papers would make more references to external forces and environmental uncertainty that posed a threat to corporate performance. Words associated with this discourse included 'changing

technology', 'foreign competition', 'fluctuating interests', and 'Japanese management'.

Subjects and themes

Frequently in a content analysis the researcher will want to code text in terms of certain subjects and themes. Essentially, what is being sought is a categorization of the phenomenon or phenomena of interest. In the study by Barley, Meyer, and Gash (1988), the researchers further posited that academically orientated articles would exhibit a number of key themes. In addition, words associated with the causal framework employed in the papers that were written for a practitioner audience would be 'conspicuously absent'. While categorizations of specific words are often relatively straightforward, when the process of coding is thematic a more interpretative approach needs to be taken. At this point, the analyst is searching not just for manifest content but for latent content as well. It becomes necessary to probe beneath the surface in order to ask deeper questions about what is happening. One theme that cut across all the papers was the

Tips and skills
Counting words in electronic news reports

The growing availability of the printed media in electronic form greatly facilitates the search for and counting of keywords in this kind of context. Most of the main UK newspapers and many others are available in electronic format, either through their own websites or through a website such as British Media Online:

www.wrx.zen.co.uk/britnews.htm (accessed 25 October 2014)

—which acts as a launch pad for a host of different electronic newspapers. An alternative source is Nexis UK, which allows you to search a number of newspapers at once. The newspapers can then usually be searched for keywords and phrases.

www.provalisresearch.com/wordstat/Wordstat.html (accessed 25 October 2014)

justification of organizational culture as an alternative paradigm for understanding organizational phenomena. Hence the researchers found that, 'although the precise nature of the alternative varied from article to article, the perception that culture offered a radical departure from traditional organizational theory was nearly invariant' (1988: 44). Like the practitioner-orientated articles, academic articles also viewed organizational culture as a source of social integration, but, unlike the articles aimed at practitioners, they did not seek to portray culture as a force for social control. The researchers therefore sought to classify academically orientated articles according to the percentage of paragraphs that contained sentences that expressed gain or loss of control through culture. They speculated that articles written for an academic audience from a functionalist perspective would see culture as a means of gaining control, but that very few of the articles would see culture as leading to loss of control because this would not fit with the academics' anthropologically informed paradigm. To test the model, the

Tips and skills
Making content analysis more efficient

The main disadvantages associated with content analysis arise from the fact that it can be very labour-intensive. Franzosi (1995) therefore suggests several strategies for making it more efficient. The first involves identifying the different parts or the schemata that are associated with the genre of text that is being analysed. For example, newspaper articles have a schema that comprises a summary and a story, containing 'background' (history and context) and 'episode' (main events and consequences). Franzosi suggests that the time and cost of content analysis can be reduced by excluding parts of the article that contain summary and background information. 'The longer an event lasts, the more likely that the "background" section of the articles dealing with an event become increasingly repetitive. The percentage of new material in each article is thus likely to decrease with the temporal position of the article in the sequence of articles that report an event' (1995: 159). Franzosi also suggests that a Taylorist approach to coding can help to make it more efficient. In this, several coders read the same article, with each of them coding a specific type of information, such as keywords, within a limited set of coding categories. However, he acknowledges that such a Taylorist approach would not be suitable for more complex thematic analyses. His final strategy for increasing the efficiency of content analysis entails a focus on sampling, not just of the time period of interest and the data sources (for example, newspapers) to be used, but also of the articles that are going to be coded and the kinds of information coded within each article.

three researchers therefore coded all 192 of the articles according to these indicators and arrived at a final score that comprised a percentage average of the three individual ratings. Their analysis showed that, although practitioners and academics initially saw culture quite differently, over time academics changed their understanding of organizational culture to incorporate the practitioner's point of view, even though practitioners' understanding of culture was little influenced by the academic viewpoint.

Dispositions

A further level of interpretation is likely to be entailed when the researcher seeks to demonstrate a disposition in the texts being analysed. For example, it may be that the researcher wants to establish whether the journalists, in the reporting of an issue in the news media, are favourably inclined or hostile towards an aspect of it, such as their stances on the practice of paying chief executives large financial bonuses. Alternatively, the researcher may be interested in the views of a news article reader, rather than the writer. For example, in the case of the study by Chen and Meindl (1991), the authors wanted to discern the image formed by news article readers about the owner of the airline People Express, entrepreneur Donald Burr. Each item was coded in terms of whether the reader had interpreted the editorial commentary on the leader's image in a way that was positive or negative. In many cases, it was necessary to infer whether the editorial commentary was implicitly positive or negative on the basis of image themes. For example, positive image themes were defined by the authors to include 'motivation'—that is, Burr as an individual who is motivated, ambitious, and energetic—whereas the theme 'overdone' was interpreted by the authors as a negative image, characterized by descriptions of the leader as overzealous, idealistic, and lacking in realism. Such an analysis entails establishing whether a judgemental stance can be discerned in the items being coded and, if so, what the nature of the judgement is.

Images

A further alternative focus for content analysis involves counting the frequency and type of images contained within a text. For example, Hunter (2008), a researcher in the field of tourism studies, analysed photographic representations appearing in tourist brochures and guidebooks relating to twenty-one destinations. In fact such methods are relatively common in tourism research and have been applied in the analysis of a wide range of documents such as postcards. Hunter (2008) analysed a sample of 10 per cent or 375 of the photographic images contained in the selected brochures and guidebooks. Images were categorized in terms of space, defined as 'the kind of physical tourism environment that is represented by means of the photograph' (Hunter 2008: 359); categories included 'natural landscapes', 'cultivated landscapes', 'heritage and material culture', and 'tourism products' such as cuisine. They were also categorized by 'subject', defined as the kinds of people found in the photograph; categories include 'no people', 'host only', 'guest only', and 'host and guest'. He could thereby analyse the frequency with which each category appeared, using this as the basis for critical analysis of the social effects of tourism on places and peoples.

A further example is provided by Prichard (2001), who uses content analysis to explore the representation of images of men and women in tourism marketing. Prichard used a content analysis technique called the 'consciousness scale' to classify more than 12,000 images contained in a random, stratified sample of UK tour operators' brochures along a four-point continuum from sexist to non-sexist portrayals of male and female roles and relationships as follows:

- *Level 1* includes images that depict men and women in very limited, essentially sexual and decorative roles;
- *Level 2* contains traditional images that show women and men engaged in highly traditional gender roles;
- *Level 3* is used to classify images that portray women and men in non-traditional gender roles—for example, men caring for children or women playing team sports;
- *Level 4* refers to images where women and men are represented as equal individuals.

Account was also taken of the size of the images as they appeared in the brochures, larger images being interpreted as more influential than smaller ones. This content analysis technique enabled Prichard to quantify the extent of gendered representations in UK tour operators' brochures, which were found to be extremely stereotypical, women being portrayed in sexual and 'decorative' poses with men playing more active roles. The content analysis of images has significant application in other areas of business research such as marketing, where the visual plays an influential role.

Coding

As much of the foregoing discussion has implied, coding is a crucial stage in the process of doing a content analysis. There are two main elements to a content analysis coding scheme: designing a **coding schedule** and designing a **coding manual**. To illustrate their use, imagine a student who is interested in newspaper reports of employment tribunal hearings dealing with sex, race, or disability discrimination in the workplace and reported in a national daily newspaper over a three-month period. The student chooses to focus on the reporting of the employment tribunal hearing and the outcomes of the hearing. To simplify the issue, the following variables might be among those considered:

1. nature of the claim (for example, denial of promotion);
2. gender of the complainant;
3. ethnicity of the complainant;
4. occupation of the complainant;
5. age of the complainant;
6. marital status of the complainant;
7. nature of the employer's business;
8. number of employees;
9. outcome of tribunal (case sustained/not sustained; nature of award);
10. position of the news item;
11. number of words in the item.

Analysis would enable the student to record information about the kinds of sex, race, or disability discrimination issues that employment tribunals deal with and also to look for patterns in the characteristics of complainants and employers. The content analysis could thereby provide valuable insight—for example, into the way that gendered managerial structures, cultures, and organizational practices are reproduced. Content analysts would normally be interested in a much larger number of variables than this, but a simple illustration like this can be helpful to show the kinds of variables that might be considered.

Coding schedule

The coding schedule is a form into which all the data relating to an item being coded will be entered. Figure 13.1 provides

Figure 13.1

Coding schedule

No.	Information about the actor	Code	No.	Features of courage displayed, sought, or observed	Code
i	Gender of actor		viii	Word used to describe courage	
ii	Age of actor		ix	Tools mentioned	
iii	Qualifications		x	Obstacles mentioned	
iv	Profession		xi	Involves choice between personal values and corporate values	
v	Place		xii	Involves defence of corporate/ organizational values or vision	
vi	Rank		xiii	Involves choice between personal advantage and corporate/community good	
vii	Evidence of being a risk-taker		xiv	Courage refers to the action or to disposition of actor or to a virtue	

Source: adapted from Harris (2001).

an example of a coding schedule based on the study of managerial courage and decision-making described in Research in focus 13.2. The schedule is very much a simplification in order to facilitate the discussion of the principles of coding in content analysis and of the construction of a coding schedule in particular.

Each of the roman numerals in Figure 13.1 relates to a specific dimension that is being coded—for example, 'iii' relates to the dimension 'qualifications' of the actor. The blank cells on the coding form are the places where codes are written. A new coding schedule form would be used for each media item coded. The codes can then be transferred to a computer data file for analysis with a software package such as IBM SPSS (see Chapter 16).

Coding manual

On the face of it, the coding schedule in Figure 13.1 seems very bare and does not appear to provide much information about what is to be done or where. This is where the coding manual comes in. The coding manual, sometimes referred to as the content analysis dictionary, is a statement of instructions to coders that specifies the categories that will be used to classify the text based on a set of written rules that define how the text will be classified. It provides: a list of all the dimensions; the different categories subsumed under each dimension; the letters or numbers (that is, *codes*) that correspond to each category; and guidance on what each dimension is concerned with, the definitions or rules to be used in assigning words to categories, and any factors that should be taken into account in deciding how to allocate any particular code to each dimension. The coding manual enables the message content to be coded in a consistent manner. The coding categories for each dimension need to be mutually exclusive and exhaustive so that there is no sense of overlap. There are a number of off-the-shelf content analysis dictionaries (for example, Harvard VI Psychosocial Dictionaries) that are often used as a starting point from which the researcher him or herself constructs a coding manual that relates to the particular research project.

For example, in his study of managerial courage and managerial decision-making, Harris (2001) constructed a coding manual to define the features of courage that he was looking for in the newspaper stories. Figure 13.2 provides a simplified version of the coding manual that corresponds to the coding schedule developed by Harris in this study (see Figure 13.1 and Research in focus 13.4). The coding manual includes all the dimensions that would be employed in the coding process, indications of guidance for coders, and the lists of categories

that were created for each dimension. The coding manual includes instructions for classification of information about the actor in addition to categories for various features of the courage referred to in the newspaper article, how it was displayed, sought, or observed. The coding schedule and manual permit only one obstacle or tool to be recorded in relation to a particular phrase or sentence in a newspaper article. However, if a phrase contains two or more obstacles or tools, the coder may break down the phrase and code a single word or a few words at a time.

The coding manual is crucial, because it provides coders with complete listings of all categories for each dimension they are coding and guidance about how to interpret the dimensions. At this stage, decisions must be made regarding the treatment of words that have more than one meaning. For example, Harris (2001) had to filter out items that were referring to 'Courage' as a brand of beer or its brewer from those that were dealing with courage as a quality or personal trait. It is on the basis of these lists and guidance that a coding schedule of the kind presented in Figure 13.1 will be completed. Even if you are a lone researcher, such as a student conducting a content analysis for a dissertation or thesis, it is important to spend a lot of time providing yourself with instructions about how to code. While you may not face the problem of **inter-rater reliability**, the issue of **intra-rater reliability** is still significant for you and you will probably need to use the coding manual to keep reminding yourself of your rules for coding the data.

Figure 13.3 illustrates how a fictitious example of a news item that presents an act of courage might be coded according to Harris's coding manual. The news story, published in the UK newspaper the *Guardian*, focuses on a 35-year-old female entrepreneur and small business-owner who is described as having acted courageously in taking the decision to turn down a contract with a major distributor and retailer because of concerns, which were subsequently proved correct, about the tactics being used to undermine the competition. The coding of the incident would then appear as in Figure 13.3 and the data would be entered into a computer program like SPSS as follows:

2 35 1 6 14 4 2 1 4 4 3 1 2 1

Each newspaper item that mentions the word 'courage' would create a row of data with an identical structure.

Potential pitfalls in devising coding schemes

There are several potential dangers in devising a content analysis coding scheme, and they are very similar to the kinds of consideration that are involved in the

Figure 13.2

Coding manual

Information about the actor	Features of courage displayed, sought, or observed
i. Gender of actor Male (1); Female (2); Unknown (3)	**viii. Word used to describe courage** Courage/ous/ly (1); Moral courage (2); Brave/ry (3); Dare/ing (4); Moral fibre (5); Strong will (6); Persevere/nce (7)
ii. Age of actor (at the time the event occurred) Record age in years (0 if unknown)	**ix. Tools mentioned (activities, circumstances, or events that facilitated the courage)** Bind (1) = made a public statement so as to make it harder to avoid the intended action Devil's advocate (2) = a person specifically designated to put contrary views Example (3) = e.g. 'seeing what A did gave me courage' Horror (4) = can't allow it to continue, sheer enormity (to the actor) of what is proposed/happening meant that major obstacles had to be overcome Others (5) = support expressed by others who may not necessarily be being courageous themselves Vision (6) = clear focus Faith (7) = inspiration or belief in a higher force
iii. Qualifications (only include if unambiguous) Degree/professional (1); Trade (2); Unknown (3)	**x. Obstacles mentioned (something faced or overcome, a difficulty, concern, temptation, or hurdle)** Easy path (1) = temptation to avoid the hard work Name calling (2) = personal abuse directed at the actor Physical threat (3) = violence or threat of violence to actor, family, etc. Commercial risk (4) = includes potential financial consequences Unpopular (5) = what is planned is unpleasant or trenchantly opposed
iv. Profession (only include if unambigious) Law (1); Medicine (2); Engineering (3); Accounting (4); Journalism (5); Other (6); Not clear or combined (7)	**xi. Involves choice between personal values and corporate values** Yes, personal values chosen (1); Yes, corporate and community values chosen (2); Unknown (3)
v. Place in which the event occurred Use 2-letter ISO country code (see Research in focus 12.5 for some examples); if many, code as World (–1)	**xii. Involves defence of corporate/organizational values or vision** Yes (1); No (2)
vi. Rank (only include if unambiguous) Minister and ranking opposition, US senator (1); Member of Parliament (2); Manager (3); Company owner (4); Board member (5); Self-employed (6); Corporate professional, e.g. engineer or lawyer (7); other (8)	**xiii. Involves choice between personal advantage and corporate/community good** Yes, personal advantage chosen (1); Yes, corporate and community good chosen (2); Unknown (3)
vii. Evidence of being a risk-taker (evidence in the item apart from courage event of the actor being a risk-taker) Yes (1); No (2)	**xiv. Courage refers to the action or to disposition of actor or to a virtue** The word 'courage' is used to describe an act or action, or some other outcome—*a courageous act, acted courageously, acted with courage* (1); Courage is attributed to the actor in relation to the act(s)—*to show courage, to be courageous* (2); Courage is mentioned without attribution to either act or person— *e.g. reference to a disembodied virtue* (3)

Source: adapted from Harris (2001).

design of structured interview and structured observation schedules.

- *Discrete dimensions*. Make sure that your dimensions are entirely separate; in other words, there should be no conceptual or empirical overlap between

them. For example, coding manual rules may be needed to distinguish between 'management' positions (such as the administrators of a firm) and 'management' actions (like the management of innovation).

Figure 13.3

Completed coding schedule

No.	Information about the actor	Code	No.	Features of courage displayed, sought, or observed	Code
i	Gender of actor	2	viii	Word used to describe courage	1
ii	Age of actor	35	ix	Tools mentioned	4
iii	Qualifications	1	x	Obstacles mentioned	4
iv	Profession	6	xi	Involves choice between personal values and corporate values	3
v	Place	14	xii	Involves defence of corporate/ organizational values or vision	1
vi	Rank	4	xiii	Involves choice between personal advantage and corporate/community good	2
vii	Evidence of being a risk-taker	2	xiv	Courage refers to the action or to disposition of actor or to a virtue	1

Source: adapted from Harris (2001).

Research in focus 13.4
Some of the ISO country codes used in Harris's (2001) study

The International Organization for Standardization (ISO) produces codes for the representation of names of countries and their subdivisions, some of which are listed below. Each one is also allocated a number to facilitate SPSS data entry.

AR   Argentina (1)

AU   Australia (2)

BR   Brazil (3)

CH   Switzerland (4)

CN   China (5)

DK   Denmark (6)

FI   Finland (7)

JP   Japan (8)

LK   Sri Lanka (9)

MZ   Mozambique (10)

PT   Portugal (11)

RU   Russian Federation (12)

TW   Taiwan (13)

UK   United Kingdom (14)

ZA   South Africa (15)

This forms part of the organization's broader mission to produce documentary agreements, such as the ISO 9000 series, which are designed to enable international trade through establishing criteria that can be used consistently as rules, guidelines, or definitions. What this means in terms of coding is that their work could provide a basis for the development and definition of categories, as Harris (2001) has done (see Figure 13.2).

- *Mutually exclusive categories*. Make sure that there is no overlap in the categories supplied for each dimension. If the categories are not mutually exclusive, coders will be unsure about how to code each item.

- *Exhaustive*. For each dimension, all possible categories should be available to coders.

- *Clear instructions*. Coders should be clear about how to interpret what each dimension is about and what factors to take into account when assigning codes to each category. Sometimes, these will have to be very elaborate. Coders should have little or no discretion in how to allocate codes to units of analysis.

- *Be clear about the unit of analysis*. For example, in Harris's (2001) study of courage and managerial decision-making, more than one courage event per media item can be recorded. The coding schedule needs to be clear in distinguishing between the

media item (for example, a newspaper article) and the event being coded. In practice, a researcher is interested in both but needs to keep the distinction in mind.

In order to be able to enhance the quality of a coding scheme, it is highly advisable to pilot early versions of the scheme, as Todd, McKeen, and Gallupe (1995) did (see Research in focus 13.5). Piloting will help to identify difficulties in applying the coding scheme, such as uncertainty about which category to employ when considering a certain dimension or discovering that no code was available to cover a particular case. Piloting will also help to identify any evidence that one category of a dimension tends to subsume an extremely large percentage of items. If this occurs, it may be necessary to consider breaking that category down so that it allows greater discrimination between the items being analysed.

Research in focus 13.5
A content analysis of job advertisements

Todd, McKeen, and Gallupe (1995) carried out a content analysis of job advertisements in four major newspapers for information systems positions to determine changes in the knowledge and skill requirements for these posts over a twenty-year period from 1970 to 1990. One of the advantages of this methodology stems from the use of secondary data (see Chapter 14), which enables a bigger sample than is usually possible in interview or survey research and therefore enables assessment of a wider range of jobs. Three types of jobs were examined: program managers, systems analysts, and information systems managers. Data were collected from two US newspapers: the *Wall Street Journal* and the *New York Times*; and from two Canadian newspapers: the *Globe and Mail* and the *Toronto Star*, at five-year intervals—1970, 1975, 1980, 1985, 1990. The researchers explain that 'the choice of five-year intervals was made to have a window that was broad enough to allow for a reasonable chance to observe differences . . . Ads were chosen from each month of the year to avoid the possibility of seasonal or cyclical effects in the data . . . Selection from a given newspaper, for a given month, continued until between five and ten ads were extracted' (1995: 26–7). A total of 1634 information systems job advertisements were collected: 581 were for programmers, 348 for systems analysts, and 305 for information systems managers. The remaining 400 advertisements were for a variety of other jobs that were excluded from the analysis. A coding scheme was developed based on the literature on skills needed by information systems workers. Phrases relating to skill mentioned in each advertisement were coded into one of three basic knowledge/skill categories: technical (subdivided into hardware and software knowledge), business (comprising functional or industry expertise, general management skills, and social/ interpersonal skills), and systems (consisting of problem-solving and development methodology knowledge/ skills). These seven skill categories formed the basis for the analysis. Prior to the main study a pilot sample of 200 advertisements was analysed by research assistants who attempted to classify each word or phrase into the seven categories. 'From this, an index was built that included the specific phrases used in the ads and the coding categories to which they belonged' (1995: 26). They found that skill requirements specified in advertisements had grown during the time period under investigation, especially those relating to technical knowledge.

Research in focus 13.6
Issues of inter-coder reliability in a study of text messaging

The results of the diary study of patterns of text messaging carried out by Faulkner and Culwin (2005) described in Research in focus 10.6 were analysed according to the content of text messages by the participants in the study. The categories identified were:

1. advertisements;
2. questions;
3. rendezvous immediate and ongoing;
4. rendezvous near future;
5. events;
6. instructions;
7. reminders;
8. jokes;
9. signon;
10. signoff;
11. gossip;
12. dates;
13. information—personal;
14. information—commercial;
15. information—operational.

The results of the coding exercise were entered onto a web-based database. To check for inter-coder reliability, the participants were then shown a random selection of text messages from the entire pool and asked to code them; a consensus was drawn up based on the number of times a text message was assigned to a particular category. However, the degree of consensus between coders was not high. Total consensus was achieved for approximately 16 per cent of the items and 50 per cent consensus was achieved for 75 per cent of the items. Faulkner and Culwin explain this in terms of the specificity of text messaging, which is a method of communication between one sender and receiver, unlike newspapers, which are a medium of mass communication. They conclude: 'these classifications were applied by people who had not necessarily received nor sent the individual text message. To a large extent the interpretation of content depends on the receiver of that content' (2005: 180).

The reliability of coding is a further potential area of concern. Coding must be done in a consistent manner. As with structured observation, coding must be consistent between coders (**inter-rater reliability**) and each coder must be consistent over time (**intra-rater reliability**). An important part of piloting the coding scheme will be testing for consistency between coders and, if time permits,

intra-coder reliability. However, coding may not be consistent, and the extent of inter-coder reliability may vary depending on the type of content that is being analysed (see Research in focus 13.6 for an example). The process of gauging reliability is more or less identical to that briefly covered in the context of structured observation in Key concept 12.6.

Advantages of content analysis

Kabanoff, Waldersee, and Cohen (1995) suggest that content analysis offers an important method for the cultural study of organizations because it enables researchers to

analyse organizational values, traces of which can be observed in organizational documents. Moreover, by measuring the frequency with which values occur, researchers are able to discern their importance. Content analysis has several further advantages, which are outlined below.

- Content analysis is a very transparent research method. The coding scheme and the sampling procedures can be clearly set out so that replications and follow-up studies are feasible. It is this transparency that often causes content analysis to be referred to as an objective method of analysis.

- It can allow a certain amount of longitudinal analysis with relative ease. Several of the studies referred to above allow the researcher to track changes in frequency over time (Barley, Meyer, and Gash 1988; Chen and Meindl 1991; Kabanoff, Waldersee, and Cohen 1995; Todd, McKeen, and Gallupe 1995). For example, Kabanoff et al.'s (1995) research entailed an analysis of organizational values over a four-year time period, Todd et al. (1995) examined information systems job advertisements over a twenty-year period (see Research in focus 13.5), while Research in focus 13.7 gives an example of a content analysis that spanned an even longer time period. Similarly, in the example of employment tribunal hearings concerning sex, race, or disability discrimination, a temporal analysis could be introduced through comparison of employment tribunal reporting in newspapers during two different time periods, such as the 1960s and the 1990s. Changes in emphasis could thus be examined.

- Content analysis is often referred to favourably as an *unobtrusive method*, a term devised by Webb et al. (1966) to refer to a method that does not entail participants in a study having to take the researcher into account (see Key concept 14.12). It is therefore a *non-reactive method* (see Key concept 12.8). However, this point has to be treated with a little caution. It is

certainly the case that, when the focus of a content analysis is upon things such as newspaper articles or television programmes, there is no reactive effect. Newspaper articles are obviously not written in the knowledge that a content analysis may one day be carried out on them. Hence Harris (2001) suggests that the content analysis of secondary data such as newspaper articles is particularly useful when researching sensitive issues such as the ethical behaviour of managers, because the method overcomes the problematic tendency of individuals to deny socially undesirable traits and only to admit to socially desirable ones (see Chapter 9 on social desirability as a source of error). On the other hand, if the content analysis is being conducted on documents, such as interview transcripts or ethnographies (e.g. Hodson 1996; see Research in focus 13.8), while the process of content analysis does not itself introduce a reactive effect, the documents may have been at least partly influenced by such an effect.

- It is a highly flexible method. It can be applied to a wide variety of kinds of unstructured information. While content analysis in the social sciences is primarily associated with the analysis of mass-media outputs, in business and management research it has a much broader applicability than this, including content analysis of websites. Research in focus 13.8 presents an illustration of a rather unusual application of content analysis.

- Content analysis can allow information to be generated about social groups that are difficult to gain access to. For example, most of our knowledge of the social backgrounds of elite groups, such as company directors, derives from content analyses of such publications as *Who's Who* and *Burke's Peerage* (Bryman 1974).

Research in focus 13.7
A content analysis spanning thirty-six years

Boyce and Lepper (2002) examined the company records relating to a successful joint venture that existed for seventy-five years between the Union Steam Ship Company in New Zealand and William Holyman and Sons to assess the importance of information quality in its success. The study is based on data collected from the company archives relating to the dates 1904, 1919, 1920, 1924, and 1935. The authors explain that these years were chosen for pragmatic reasons—namely, there were more data in the archives for these years and they 'appeared to be the most interesting' (2002: 118). Data from the files relating to the joint venture were then entered onto a spreadsheet, which recorded 'the number of words in each document, the source of each exchange and recipient,

(continued)

the nature of each exchange, and a subjective assessment as to the level of trust implicit in each exchange' (2002: 89). Words and phrases classified as indicating high trust included 'I am glad to say', 'we are willing to do so', 'trusting to the future'; words and phrases indicating low trust included 'unfortunately', 'we do not feel inclined', 'our hands cannot be tied too tightly'. The results of the content analysis indicate that information exchanges between the joint venture partners involved a high level of trust. However, the authors acknowledge some of the limitations of content analysis for an archival study of this nature. Namely, deciding on whether an item indicates high or low trust involves the coder in making a judgement as to what constitutes high or low trust. The authors suggest that the content analysis relied on their background knowledge and understanding of the material contained in the archive, and thus involved an element of subjective judgement.

Research in focus 13.8
A content analysis of qualitative research on the workplace

Hodson (1996) reports the results of a content analysis of 'book-length ethnographic studies based on sustained periods of direct observation' (1996: 724). There is an excellent website in connection with the Workplace Ethnography Project, which can be found at:

www.sociology.ohio-state.edu/rdh/Workplace-Ethnography-Project.html (accessed 25 October 2014)

As a method, ethnography (see Chapter 19) entails a long period of participant observation in order to understand the culture of a social group. Hodson's content analysis concentrated on ethnographic studies of workplaces that had been published in book form (published articles were excluded because they rarely included sufficient detail). Thousands of case studies were assessed for possible inclusion in the sample. The sample was made up of studies from different countries and included some well-known British ones (Beynon 1975; Nichols and Beynon 1977; Pollert 1981; Cavendish 1982). According to the Workplace Ethnography Project website: 'The study generated 204 ethnographic cases. These cases were derived from 156 separate books since the observations reported in some books allowed the coding of multiple cases.'

Hodson (1996) states that each case was coded in terms of one of five types of workplace organization (craft, direct supervision, assembly line, bureaucratic, and worker participation). This was the independent variable. Various dependent variables and 'control' variables (variables deemed to have an impact on the relationships between independent and dependent variables) were also coded. Here are two of the variables and their codes:

Job satisfaction

1 = very low; 2 = moderately low; 3 = average; 4 = high; 5 = very high

Autonomy

1 = none (the workers' tasks are completely determined by others, by machinery, or by organizational rules); 2 = little (workers occasionally have the chance to select among procedures or priorities); 3 = average (regular opportunities to select procedures or set priorities within definite limits); 4 = high (significant latitude in determining procedures and setting priorities); 5 = very high (significant interpretation is needed to reach broadly specified goals).

(Hodson 1996: 728)

Hodson's findings suggest that some pessimistic accounts of worker participation schemes (for example, that they do not genuinely permit participation and do not necessarily have a beneficial impact on the worker) are incomplete. A more detailed treatment of this research can be found in Hodson (1999). Since the early 1996 publication, many others have been published in major journals. Not only does the website provide a list of publications deriving from the project (including downloadable PDF files of most of the articles), it also includes the coding information, and you can download the data into SPSS (see Chapter 16 for more information on SPSS).

Research in focus 13.9
A content analysis of Swedish job advertisements 1960–2010

Rosén (2014) used content analysis to evaluate changes in the description and requirements of professional communicators in Swedish job advertisements from 1960 to 2010. A total of 196 job advertisements were collected at ten-year intervals over the period from the largest morning newspapers in Sweden—*Dagens Nyheter*, *Svenska Dagbladet*, and *Sydsvenska Dagbladet*. In each case, the sample was taken from thirty-one days in August, which is a busy recruitment month in Sweden. Advertisements relating to information, marketing, communication, and consultancy were selected. A coding scheme covering seventeen major recruitment aspects was developed, including job title, function/role, education, and qualifications. This enabled understanding of the process whereby strategic communication roles have become increasingly professionalized, requiring college-level qualifications and specialist expertise. As might be expected, the analysis also indicated a shift over time in job titles, away from those that used the term 'man', e.g. 'advertising man' in the 1960s, towards more gender-neutral labels by 2010.

Disadvantages of content analysis

Like all research techniques, content analysis suffers from certain limitations, which are described below.

- A content analysis can only be as good as the documents on which the practitioner works. John Scott (1990) recommends assessing documents in terms of such criteria as: authenticity (that the document is what it purports to be); credibility (whether there are grounds for thinking that the contents of the document have been or are distorted in some way); and representativeness (whether or not the documents examined are representative of all possible relevant documents, as, if certain kinds of document are unavailable or no longer exist, generalizability will be jeopardized). These kinds of consideration will be especially important to bear in mind when a content analysis is being conducted on documents such as company reports or internal memoranda. These issues will be explored in further detail in Chapter 23.

- It is almost impossible to devise coding manuals that do not entail some interpretation on the part of coders. Coders must draw upon their everyday knowledge as participants in a common culture in order to be able to code the material with which they are confronted (Cicourel 1964; Garfinkel 1967). To the extent that this occurs, it is questionable whether or not it is justifiable to assume a correspondence of interpretation between

the persons responsible for producing the documents being analysed and the coders (Beardsworth 1980).

- Particular problems are likely to arise when the aim is to impute latent rather than manifest content. In searching for traditional markers of organizational leadership, as in Chen and Meindl's study (1991), the potential for invalid inference being made is magnified.

- It is difficult to ascertain the answers to 'Why?' questions through content analysis. For example, Barley, Meyer, and Gash (1988) found that over the course of nearly a decade academically oriented papers on the subject of organizational culture gradually adopted or accommodated practitioners' concerns. Why? Although the authors provide a number of speculative answers to these questions, content analysis alone cannot provide the answers. As they claim, 'the convergence may have resulted because academics were subtly influenced to adopt a more managerial agenda in order to secure valued resources and a larger audience for their work, but given the nature of the data, other explanations are equally plausible' (1988: 55). Hence, the authors claim that to establish the motives for the convergence would require interviewing the paper authors 'and studying networks of citations to determine who influenced whom' (1988: 55). Similarly, although Rosén (2014) was able to trace the increasing level of professionalization in job advertisements for strategic communication experts in Sweden, she was unable to explain in any detail why this had occurred (see Research in focus 13.9).

- Content analytic studies are sometimes accused of being atheoretical. It is easy to see why an atheoretical approach might arise. The emphasis in content analysis on measurement can easily and unwittingly result in an accent being placed on what is measurable rather than on what is theoretically significant or important. However, content analysis is not necessarily atheoretical. For example, Barley et al. (1988) place their findings about academic and practitioner subcultures in the context of a political perspective of knowledge creation and diffusion, suggesting that the research interests of academics are ultimately defined by the interests of practitioners who influence the research process, through exercising constraints on funds, sites, and objectives. Similarly, Hodson's (1996) content analysis of workplace ethnographies was underpinned by theoretical ideas deriving from the work of influential writers such as Blauner (1964) and R. Edwards (1979) concerning developments in modes of workplace organization and their impacts on workers' experiences.

Checklist

Doing content analysis

- ○ Have you clearly defined your research questions?
- ○ Is the population of documents to be content analysed relevant to your research questions?
- ○ Can you justify your sampling approach?
- ○ Have you made sure that your dimensions do not overlap?
- ○ Have you made sure that the categories used for each of your dimensions do not overlap?
- ○ Do all the dimensions allow you to answer your research questions?
- ○ Have you piloted your coding schedule?
- ○ Are the coding instructions clear?
- ○ If your research is based on the mass media, can you justify the time span of your coverage?
- ○ Are you clear about the unit of analysis?

Key points

- Content analysis is very much located within the quantitative research tradition of emphasizing measurement and the specification of clear rules that exhibit reliability.
- While traditionally associated with the analysis of mass-media content, content analysis is in fact a very flexible method that can be applied to a wide range of phenomena.
- It is crucial to be clear about your research questions in order to be certain about your units of analysis and what exactly is to be analysed.
- You also need to be clear about what is to be counted.
- The coding schedule and coding manual are crucial stages in the preparation for a content analysis.
- Content analysis becomes particularly controversial when it is used to seek out latent meaning and themes.

Questions for review

- To what kinds of documents and media can content analysis be applied?
- What is the difference between manifest and latent content? What are the implications of the distinction for content analysis?

What are the research questions?

- Why are precise research questions especially crucial in content analysis?
- With what general kinds of research questions is content analysis concerned?

Selecting a sample

- What special sampling issues does content analysis pose?

What is to be counted?

- What kinds of things might be counted in the course of doing a content analysis?
- To what extent do you need to infer latent content when you go beyond counting words?

Coding

- Why is coding so crucial in content analysis?
- What is the difference between a coding schedule and a coding manual?
- What potential pitfalls need to be guarded against when devising coding schedules and manuals?

Advantages of content analysis

- 'One of the most significant virtues of content analysis is its immense flexibility in that it can be applied to a wide variety of documents.' Discuss.

Disadvantages of content analysis

- To what extent does the need for coders to interpret meaning undermine content analysis?
- How far are content analysis studies atheoretical?

Online Resource Centre
www.oxfordtextbooks.co.uk/orc/brymanbrm4e/

Visit the Interactive Research Guide that accompanies this book to complete an exercise in Content Analysis.

14

Secondary analysis and official statistics

Chapter outline

This chapter explores the possibilities associated with the analysis of data that have been collected by others. There are two main types discussed in this chapter:

- the secondary analysis of data collected, either for commercial or research purposes, by other people;
- the secondary analysis of **official statistics**—that is, statistics collected by government departments in the course of their work or specifically for statistical purposes.

This chapter explores:

- the advantages and disadvantages of carrying out secondary analysis of data collected by other researchers, particularly in view of many datasets being based on large, high-quality investigations that are invariably beyond the means of students;
- how to obtain such datasets;
- the potential of official statistics in terms of their reliability and validity;
- the growing recognition of the potential of official statistics after a period of neglect as a result of criticisms levelled at them;
- the notion that official statistics are a form of *unobtrusive method*—that is, a method that is not prone to a reaction on the part of those being studied to the fact that they are research participants.

Introduction

Many of the techniques we have covered so far—survey research by questionnaire or structured interview, structured observation, and content analysis—can be extremely time-consuming and expensive to conduct. Students in particular may have neither the time nor the financial resources to conduct very extensive research. Yet we know that large amounts of quantitative data about business and management are collected by social scientists, market intelligence firms, professional associations, and others. Some of this information, such as that produced by market research organizations, can be expensive. However, many organizations, most notably government departments and their various representatives, collect data that are presented in statistical form and that may be usable without charge by students and university researchers. Would it not be a good idea to analyse such data rather than collect new data? It would have the additional advantage for managers and employees that they would not be bothered by interviewers and by questionnaires popping through their letter boxes.

This is where *secondary analysis* comes in. Secondary analysis offers this kind of opportunity. Key concept 14.1

contains a brief definition of secondary analysis and raises one or two basic points about what it involves. As the opening paragraph suggests, in this chapter we will be concerned with two kinds of issue:

- the secondary analysis of data that have been collected by other researchers;
- the secondary analysis of data that have been collected by other organizations in the course of their business.

In business and management, secondary analysis is of increasing interest to researchers. Traditionally, it has been the province of economists to analyse secondary data and draw conclusions about how it relates to the world of business. However, since the 1960s, more researchers, particularly those from an industrial relations background, have begun to take greater interest in the analysis of large-scale workplace survey data. Part of the reason for this relates to the success of the UK's Workplace Employment Relations Survey (WERS; see Research in focus 3.14), which considerably opened up the potential for secondary analysis of work-related issues, largely because of its breadth and scope. The success of

Key concept 14.1
What is secondary analysis?

Secondary analysis is the analysis of data by researchers who will probably not have been involved in the collection of those data, for purposes that in all likelihood were not envisaged by those responsible for the data collection. Secondary analysis may entail the analysis of either quantitative data (Dale, Arber, and Proctor 1988) or qualitative data (Corti, Foster, and Thompson 1995), but it is with the former that we will be concerned in this chapter. To some extent, it is difficult to know where primary and secondary analysis start and finish. If a researcher is involved in the collection of survey interview data and analyses some of the data, resulting in some publications, but then some time later decides to rework the data, it is not entirely clear how far the latter is primary or secondary analysis. Typically, secondary analysis entails the analysis of data that others have collected, but, as this simple scenario suggests, this need not necessarily be the case.

the WERS has encouraged these researchers to explore other secondary datasets, such as the Labour Force Survey (LFS), and to engage in greater cross-national, comparative analysis. Moreover, their experience of designing survey research has informed the way that these data were collected and used, by bringing insights from a tradition based more on a qualitative case study to bear on the design and development of large-scale surveys and by ensuring that the right kinds of question continue to be asked (Marginson 1998).

Other researchers' data

There are several reasons why secondary analysis should be considered a serious alternative to collecting new data. These advantages of secondary analysis have been covered by Dale, Arber, and Proctor (1988), from whom we have borrowed most of the following observations. In considering the various advantages of secondary analysis, we have in mind the particular needs of the lone student conducting a small research project as an undergraduate or a more substantial piece of work as a postgraduate. However, this emphasis should definitely not be taken to imply that secondary analysis is really appropriate or relevant only to students. Quite the contrary: secondary analysis should be considered by all business researchers, and, indeed, the Economic and Social Research Council (ESRC) requires applicants for research grants who are proposing to collect new data to demonstrate that relevant data are not already available in the UK Data Archive (see the section on 'Accessing the UK Data Archive' below). However, secondary data need not necessarily be collected by other researchers; instead, they may be collected by a company or another type of organization for its own purposes (see Research in focus 14.2). It is also possible for secondary analysis to be used in combination with the collection of primary data, as the example in Research in focus 14.3 illustrates. This can enable a comparative element to be incorporated into the research design. However, we have one other reason for emphasizing the prospects of secondary analysis for students that is simply based on our personal experience that students tend to assume that any research they carry out has to entail the collection of primary data. Provided secondary analysis does not conflict with the guidelines students are given regarding projects they are asked to complete, we feel there is a strong case for students considering the use of secondary analysis, as it frees them up to spend more time on searching the literature, designing their research questions, and analysing and interpreting their data.

Advantages of secondary analysis

Secondary analysis offers numerous benefits to students carrying out a research project. These are outlined below.

- *Cost and time.* As noted at the outset, secondary analysis offers the prospect of having access to good-quality data, such as that available from the UK Data

Research in focus 14.2
Secondary analysis of data collected by a business

Sørensen's (2004) study of the racial composition of workplaces was based on secondary data that he obtained from a large multidivisional financial services organization. Access to the personnel records was provided on the condition that no identifying information about the firm would be revealed (see discussion of anonymity in Chapter 6). Analysis focused on groups of newly hired staff in retail branches of the company, where interaction between employees was considered to be more likely. 'These data selection rules resulted in a dataset covering 1,673 employees from 263 district branches' (Sørensen 2004: 643). Sørensen explains that 'a distinct advantage of this dataset is that it contains the demographic characteristics not only of the focal employees who are tracked from the time of hire, but also of all other employees at the branch, regardless of the date of hire. I can therefore continuously measure the demographic composition of the branches from the time a sampled employee is hired into the branch until the time of exit or censoring' (Sørensen 2004: 643). The use of a quantitative case study design enabled a longitudinal element to be designed into the study (see Chapter 3), as the dataset contained information about the exact point at which employees joined and left the company over the time period under investigation, 1 January 1996 to 31 May 1999. This enabled Sørensen to explore changes in turnover rates over time. The results of this analysis revealed that employees were more likely to leave the organization if the number of employees of the same racial grouping as themselves declined during the time that they worked there.

Research in focus 14.3
Combining primary and secondary data in a single study of the implications of marriage structure for men's attitudes to women in the workplace

In order to understand the implications of marriage structure, Sreedhari, Chugh, and Brief (2014) conducted a total of five studies combining the analyses of secondary data from US and UK survey sources with quasi-experiments on managers and undergraduate students. The secondary analyses were based on:

1. data from the 1996 General Social Survey (GSS), a US national probability survey of adults, focusing on the attitudes of 282 heterosexual married men and analysing items that asked them to indicate their level of agreement/disagreement to questions such as: 'wife should help husband's career first' using a four-point Likert scale, correlating these with the predictor variable 'marriage structure', classifying respondents according to 'traditional' (wife not employed), 'semi traditional' (wife works part-time), and 'dual earner' marriage structure.

2. data from two 2002 surveys, the GSS and the National Organizations Survey (NOS). For the NOS, the employers of some GSS respondents were contacted and asked about employment practices in their firms. Using data from the two surveys enabled organization-level data and responses from individuals to be linked, resulting in a sample of 89 full-time male employees and focusing on the variable 'perceived smoothness of workplace operations' and its correlation with the same predictor variable of 'marriage structure'.

The results from both of these studies indicated that marriage structures predicted how egalitarian men are, those in traditional marriages being more likely to hold negative attitudes toward women in their workplace.

The researchers then conducted a controlled quasi-experiment based on a recruitment scenario on 89 male undergraduate students, which indicated that men from traditional marriages were less attracted to organizations with female leaders. This was followed by another quasi-experiment, this time involving a convenience sample of 232 managers recruited from a US accounting organization, to examine whether men in traditional marriage structures were more likely to behave in ways that would prevent women in the organization advancing in their careers. This involved an online organizational simulation (see Chapter 12), in which the gender of the potential leader was manipulated. The fifth and final study sought to establish whether the attitudes of men who were single would change their attitudes to those of women in the workplace once they were married. The researchers also wanted to test whether these findings would generalize to a non-US sample. They therefore used data relating to a sample of 304 men from the 1991 and 1993 British Household Panel Survey (BHPS). The sample was comprised of men who were single in the first wave of data collection but had married by the time of the second data collection point. The findings from all five of the studies carried out by Sreedhari, Chugh, and Brief (2014) showed that men in traditional marriages tend to hold negative views towards the presence of women in the workplace.

Archive (see section on 'Accessing the UK Data Archive' below), for a tiny fraction of the resources involved in carrying out a data collection exercise yourself.

- *High-quality data.* Many of the datasets that are employed most frequently for secondary analysis are of extremely high quality. By this we mean several things. First, the sampling procedures have been rigorous, in most cases resulting in samples that are as close to being representative as one is likely to achieve. While the organizations responsible for these studies suffer the same problems of survey non-response as anybody else, well-established procedures are usually in place for following up non-respondents and thereby keeping this problem to a minimum. Secondly, the samples are often national samples or at least cover a wide variety of regions. In addition, some datasets enable cross-national comparison (see Research in focus 14.4). The degree of geographical spread and the sample size of such datasets are invariably attained only in research that attracts quite substantial resources. It is certainly inconceivable that student projects could even get close to the coverage that such datasets attain. Thirdly, many datasets have been generated by highly experienced researchers and, in the case of some of the large datasets, such as the WERS (see Research in focus 3.14) and the LFS (see Research in focus 14.7), the data have been gathered by research organizations that have developed structures and control procedures to check on the quality of the emerging data. Some large datasets that are suitable for secondary analysis are described in Table 14.1.

Table 14.1

Large UK and European datasets suitable for secondary analysis		
Title	Dataset details	Topics covered
Business Register and Employment Survey (BRES)	Produces UK annual employment statistics and collects data on local units and business structures to update the Inter-Departmental Business Register, which is used as a sampling frame in many surveys. Survey conducted annually and sample size is approximately 82,000. Accessed via the Office for National Statistics and Nomis official labour market statistics website: ***www.nomisweb.co.uk*** (accessed 29 October 2014)	Data are collected on the number of jobs by geographical location, detailed industrial activity (SIC code), and whether full- or part-time.
Understanding Society	This survey builds on 18 years of the British Household Panel Survey (BHPS), which it replaced in 2009/10. Like the BHPS, which started in 1991, the Understanding Society survey uses interviews and questionnaires and follows the same nationally representative sample of individuals within a household, but is based on a much larger panel of 40,000 households. See ***www.understandingsociety.org.uk*** (accessed 29 October 2014)	Household organization; labour market behaviour; income and wealth; housing; health; and socio-economic values.

Table 14.1

Continued

Title	Dataset details	Topics covered
British Social Attitudes (BSA) survey	More or less annual survey since 1983 of a representative sample aged 18 and over by interview and questionnaire. Each survey comprises an hour-long interview and a self-completion questionnaire. Accessible through the National Centre for Social Research at: *www.natcen.ac.uk/our-research/research/british-social-attitudes/*(accessed 29 October 2014)	Covers wide range of areas of social attitudes and behaviour. The survey focuses mainly on people's attitudes, but also collects details of their behaviour patterns, household circumstances, and work.
European Community Studies and Eurobarometer	Since the early 1970s, public opinion surveys have been conducted on behalf of the European Commission at least twice a year in all member states of the European Union. The Eurobarometer series began in 1974. It comprises individual face-to-face interviews with national samples and is conducted biannually, in spring and autumn. Accessible through European Commission website at: *ec.europa.eu/public_opinion/index_en.htm* (accessed 29 October 2014)	Cross-national comparison of wide range of social and political issues, including European integration; life satisfaction; social goals; currency issues; working conditions; and travel.
European Working Conditions Survey (EWCS)	A cross-sectional survey conducted every five years since 1990 by the European Foundation for the Improvement of Living and Working Conditions (Eurofound). The fifth survey, of nearly 44,000 workers, was conducted in 2010 and covered 34 countries. Accessible via the European Working Conditions Observatory at: *www.eurofound.europa.eu/working/surveys/*	Areas covered include precarious employment, leadership styles and worker participation as well as the general job context, working time, work organization, pay, work-related health risks, cognitive and psychosocial factors, work-life balance and access to training. Questions were also asked about the effects of the economic downturn on working conditions.
International Social Survey Programme (ISSP)	Annual programme since 1983 based on cross-national collaboration covering survey topics important for social science research. Accessible through the GESIS Leibniz Institute for the Social Sciences at: *www.gesis.org/en/issp/issp-home/*(accessed 29 October 2014)	Attitudes towards legal systems and the economy. Covers special topics, including work orientations (see Research in focus 14.4); the environment; and national identity.
Labour Force Survey (LFS)	Largest regular household survey in the UK. Biennial interviews, 1973–83, annual interviews, 1984–91, comprising a quarterly survey of around 15,000 addresses per quarter and an additional survey in March–May; since 1991, quarterly survey of around 60,000 addresses. Since 1998, core questions have also been administered in member states of the European Union. Accessible via UK Data Service at: *ukdataservice.ac.uk/*(accessed 29 October 2014)	Covers hours worked, job search methods, training, and personal details, such as nationality and gender.
Office for National Statistics (ONS) Opinions and Lifestyle Survey	Survey carried out eight times a year since 1990 and monthly since 2005 using face-to-face structured interviews on a sample of just under 2000 people. Uses short, simple sets of questions to gain an impression of public attitudes concerning topics that change frequently. Accessible via UK Data Service at: *ukdataservice.ac.uk/*(accessed 29 October 2014)	Covers core demographic questions about respondents plus questions that change from month to month about topics that change frequently—e.g. food safety, eating behaviour, personal finance, sports participation, Internet access, human rights, AIDS awareness.

Table 14.1

Continued

Title	Dataset details	Topics covered
Population Census (UK)	A simple questionnaire survey of the population of England and Wales held every ten years since 1801. The most recent Census was held in 2011 and the one before that in 2001. It can be accessed via the Office for National Statistics and Nomis, official labour market statistics website: *http://www.nomisweb.co.uk/ census/2011* (accessed 29 October 2014)	Contains information about households and individuals covering topics as diverse as age, gender, occupation, qualifications, ethnicity, social class, employment, family structure, amenities, and tenure.
Annual Survey of Hours and Earnings (ASHE)	The most comprehensive source of earnings information in the UK, conducted annually since 1970 and surveying the earnings of employees. Reports are free to view or download from the UK National Statistics Publication Hub web site at: *www.statistics.gov.uk/hub/index.html* (accessed 29 October 2014)	Looks at levels, composition, and distribution of earnings and details of hours worked, broken down by industry, occupation, age group, and gender.
Workplace Employment Relations Survey (WERS)	This survey has been carried out in 1980, 1984, 1990, 1998, 2004, and 2011. The sample comprises workplaces where interviews are carried out with managers and worker representatives, and questionnaires administered to employees. Accessible through UK Data Service at: *ukdataservice. ac.uk/*(accessed 29 October 2014)	Wide range of areas covered, including: pay determination; recruitment and training; equal opportunities; workplace change; work attitudes; management organization; and employee representation.

Research in focus 14.4
Cross-national comparison of work orientations: an example of a secondary dataset

The International Social Survey Programme (ISSP) conducted three surveys focusing on the topic of work orientations, first in 1989, then in 1997, and again in 2005. 32 countries participated in the 2005 survey. The survey uses mail, written, or oral survey with a standardized questionnaire and focuses on respondents' general attitudes towards work and leisure, work organization, and work content. Opinions were elicited on such issues as: preferred time budget for selected activities such as work, leisure time etc.; work orientation; importance of selected demands of a job (scale); preference for being self-employed or being an employee, working in a small or in a large firm, and working in private business or civil service; advantages of employee status (greater job security and lower impairment of the family life); importance of unions for job security and working conditions of employee; preference for full-time employment or part-time employment; preference for more work (and money) or for reduction in working hours. Demographic variables include age, sex, education, marital status, personal and family income, employment status, household size and composition, occupation, religion and church attendance, social class, union membership, political party, voting history, size of community, region, and ethnicity. A fourth survey is planned for 2015 and the dataset can be accessed via the International Social Survey Programme Data Archive: *www.gesis.org/en/issp/issp-home/*

- *Opportunity for longitudinal analysis*. Partly linked to the last point is the fact that secondary analysis can offer the opportunity for longitudinal research, which, as noted in Chapter 3, is rather rare in business and management research because of the time and cost involved. Sometimes, as with the WERS, a panel design has been employed and it is possible to chart trends and connections over time. Such data are sometimes analysed cross-sectionally, but there are obviously opportunities for longitudinal analysis as well. Also, with datasets such as the LFS, where similar data are collected over time, usually because certain interview questions are recycled each year, trends (such as changes in working time or shifting patterns of employment) can be identified over time. With such datasets, respondents differ from year to year so that causal inferences over time cannot be readily established, but

nonetheless it is still possible to gauge trends. For example, although the study by Knight and Latreille (2000) was confined to use of the 1998 WERS data (see Research in focus 14.5), the authors made frequent comparison with analyses from the 1990 WERS data to show that there had been relatively little change in patterns and rates of disciplinary sanctions and dismissals and complaints to employment tribunals during this time period. Similarly, a study by Addison and Belfield (2000) used data from the 1998 WERS to replicate research done by other researchers who had used data from the 1990 WERS in order to test whether or not efforts to boost employee participation have had any effect. Undoubtedly, the publication of findings from WERS 2011 will have enabled researchers to compare data from the most recent study with data from previous iterations of the survey.

Research in focus 14.5
Unfair dismissal complaints and employment tribunals: an example of secondary analysis using the WERS data

Knight and Latreille (2000) used the 1998 Workplace Employee Relations Survey (WERS) data to investigate the incidence of disciplinary sanctions, dismissals, and unfair dismissal complaints made to UK employment tribunals. Using the management respondent dataset, their analysis is based on analysis of the following dependent variables:

1. the disciplinary sanction rate per 100 employees;

2. the dismissal rate per 100 employees; and

3. the incidence of claims for unfair dismissal during the twelve months preceding the survey.

In a consideration of disciplinary sanction rates, analysis of the WERS data revealed that the rate of disciplinary sanction is lower among part-time and female workers. This confirms findings of other researchers (for example, P. Edwards 1995), which suggested that women and part-time workers are more compliant to work discipline because of shorter tenure and lower pay. Knight and Latreille's findings show that the probability of dismissal is highest in workplaces with higher proportions of manual workers who are employed in routine and unskilled jobs. They also found that rates of dismissal are higher in workplaces where a greater proportion of younger workers is employed. These findings also confirm the findings of other researchers, which suggest that discipline and dismissal rates will be higher in workplaces where there is a high proportion of manual and less skilled workers because the costs of hiring and firing are lower compared with skilled employees. Finally, in workplaces where union membership is high, there is a significantly lower rate of dismissals, suggesting that unions protect their members from discipline and dismissal. In terms of the incidence of employment tribunal applications for unfair dismissal, the researchers found similar patterns: that the incidence of tribunal applications is higher in workplaces where there is a higher proportion of manual workers and in larger workplaces. The reasons for this latter finding, however, may relate to a number of factors, not least that there are likely to be more dismissals in larger workplaces and therefore more occasions on which employees are likely to feel sufficiently aggrieved to make an application to an employment tribunal. This highlights some of the limitations of the WERS data, from which it is not possible to establish the number of unfair dismissal claims brought at each workplace.

- *Subgroup or subset analysis*. When large samples are the source of data (as in the WERS), there is the opportunity to study what can often be quite sizeable subgroups of individuals or subsets of questions. Very often, in order to study specialized categories of individuals, small, localized studies are the only feasible way forward because of costs. However, large datasets can frequently yield quite large nationally representative samples of specialized categories of individuals, such as workers in a particular industry or occupation or with a particular set of personal characteristics. These can form the basis for representative sampling of individuals. Similarly, when a large-scale survey covers several topic areas, analysis may involve focusing on a smaller subset of questions that are covered by the survey. For example, Addison and Belfield (2000) were interested in the effects of European works councils on organizational performance and employee attitudes. They therefore analysed the responses from just *one* question in the 1998 WERS, which related to the status of these new institutional arrangements.

- *Opportunity for cross-cultural analysis*. Cross-cultural research has considerable appeal at a time when social scientists are more attuned to the processes associated with globalization and to cultural differences, though it is easy to forget that many findings should not be taken to apply to countries other than the one in which the research was conducted.

However, cross-cultural research presents barriers to the social scientist. There are obvious barriers to do with the cost and practical difficulties of doing research in a different country, especially when language and cultural differences are likely to be significant. The secondary analysis of comparable data from two or more countries provides one possible model for conducting cross-cultural research. The ISSP is explicitly concerned with bringing together findings from existing social science surveys from different countries and contexts. An example of the kind of cross-cultural analysis the programme has produced is given in Research in focus 14.4. Another example to illustrate how data from more than one country can be compared is a study by Coutrot (1998), in which he compared the industrial relations systems of France and the UK through statistical analysis of two broadly similar datasets—WERS 1990 and Relations Professionnelles et Négociations d'Entreprise (REPONSE) 1992 (a large-scale survey that covers similar issues to WERS and is based on interviews with managers and employee representatives in France). However, in order for a cross-cultural analysis to be conducted, some coordination is necessary so that the questions asked are comparable. Differences between countries in the definitions used and the criteria for inclusion can make this difficult, as the example relating to the use of official statistics, provided by Jackie Davies (2001; see Research in focus 14.6), illustrates.

Research in focus 14.6
Difficulties in making cross-cultural comparisons using official statistics

Jackie Davies (2001) carried out an international comparison of labour disputes and stoppages through strike action in twenty-three OECD countries between 1990 and 1999 using statistical data collected at a national level. However, the article is careful to point out the limitations of such an analysis for the following reasons:

- *Voluntary notification*. In most of the countries governments rely on employers notifying them of any disputes, which they are then able to confirm through media reports.

- *Fail to measure full effects*. None of the countries records the full effects of stoppages at work—for example, measured in terms of lost working time in companies that are not involved in the dispute but are unable to work because of a shortage of materials caused by the strike.

- *Different thresholds for inclusion*. The countries differ in the criteria they use to determine when a stoppage is entered into the statistics. In the UK, for example, disputes involving fewer than ten employees or lasting less than one day are excluded from the recorded figures. In some countries, the thresholds for inclusion are particularly high. For example, in the USA records include only disputes involving more than 1000 workers. This can make comparison of strike rates between countries particularly problematic.

- *Exclusion of certain industrial sectors.* Some of the countries exclude the effects of disputes in certain sectors—for example, Portugal omits public-sector and general strikes.

- *Changes in the way figures are recorded.* For example, France has changed the way it records lost working days, thus making it difficult to make a comparison over time.

- *Indirectly involved workers.* There are differences between the countries in their attempts to record those workers who are indirectly involved in a stoppage but who are unable to work because others at their workplace are on strike. Half of the countries, including France, the Netherlands, and New Zealand, attempt to include these workers in the statistics, but the other half, including Italy and Japan, do not.

- *Dispute rates affected by small number of very large strikes.* Some countries can appear to have very high labour dispute rates in one particular year because of one strike involving a large number of workers. In France, for example, there was a strike in 1995 involving the whole public sector. Some of these difficulties can be overcome by making comparisons over several years.

These differences lead some countries, such as the USA or Japan, to record a lower number of working days lost through labour disputes than, say, the UK or Germany, simply because of the different methods used for compiling statistics in the individual countries. This means that cross-cultural comparisons using nationally collected statistics need to be made with a degree of caution.

- *More time for data analysis.* Precisely because data collection is time-consuming, the analysis of data is often squeezed. It is easy to perceive the data collection as the difficult phase and to take the view that the analysis of data is relatively straightforward. This is not the case. Working out what to make of your data is no easy matter and requires considerable thought and often a preparedness to consider learning about unfamiliar techniques of data analysis. While secondary analysis invariably entails a lot of data management—partly so that you can get to know the data and partly so that you can get it into a form that you need (and this phase should not be underestimated)—the fact that you are freed from having to collect fresh data means that your approach to the analysis of data can be more considered than perhaps it might otherwise have been.

- *Reanalysis may offer new interpretations.* It is easy to take the view that, once a set of data has been analysed, the data have in some sense been drained of further insight. What, in other words, could possibly be gained by going over the same data that someone else has analysed? In fact, data can be analysed in so many different ways that it is very unusual for the range of possible analyses to be exhausted. Several possibilities can be envisaged. First, a secondary analyst may decide to consider the impact of a certain variable on the relationships between variables of interest. Such a possibility may not have been envisaged by the initial researchers. Secondly, the arrival of new theoretical ideas may suggest analyses that could not have been conceived of by the original researchers. In other words, the arrival of such new theoretical directions may prompt a reconsideration of the relevance of the data. Thirdly, an alternative method of quantitative data analysis may be employed which offers the prospect of a rather different interpretation of the data. Fourthly (and related to the last point), new methods of quantitative data analysis, such as meta-analysis (see Key concept 14.9 and Research in focus 14.10), are continuously emerging. As awareness of such techniques spreads, and their potential relevance is recognized, researchers become interested in applying them to other datasets.

- *The wider obligations of the business researcher.* For all types of business research, research participants give up some of their time, usually for no reward. It is not unreasonable that the participants should expect that the data that they participate in generating should be mined to their fullest extent. However, much business research is chronically under-analysed. Primary researchers may feel they want to analyse only data relating to central research questions, or lose interest as a new set of research questions interpose themselves into their imagination. Making data available for secondary analysis enhances the possibility that fuller use will be made of the data.

Telling it like it is
Using secondary analysis in a small-scale research project

Tore's research project involved secondary analysis of data about the social networks of university students. As he explained: 'I had a lot of data [about] social network involving real people. A lot of the data in the literature is based on power lines, computer networks and all this kind of stuff where people do not have much social interaction or human interaction so I thought, "Well, I have a whole lot of data involving real human interaction." So I thought it would be interesting to have a look at this data. So I spoke with my supervisor and he was very interested and then that's how the project got started.'

Tore's secondary analysis focused on data that formed part of a website that he had designed and run during the second year of his degree for students to socialize with one another. 'This data was taken from a database from the web site that included profiles of students. The profiles had variables such as age, sex, gender, what course they attended and then it also had messages sent between them. There were 1,284 students on the website and there were over 60,000 messages that had been sent between them. So I could measure interaction between them.'

Tore's experience is valuable because it shows how a research project need not necessarily involve the collection of primary data. His experience is also relatively unusual because, although it involves analysis of data that were not collected for the purpose of the research, he was the person who collected the data, even though he did not at the time consider using it for the purposes of research. It is more usual for secondary data analysis to involve the use of data collected by a third party. One of the big advantages for Tore in this situation was that he did not have to do anything to gain access or permission to use the data, since he was already in possession of the dataset.

Limitations of secondary analysis

The foregoing list of benefits of secondary analysis sounds almost too good to be true. In fact, there are not very many limitations, but the following warrant some attention.

- *Lack of familiarity with data*. When you collect your own data, when the dataset is generated, it is hardly surprising that you are very familiar with the structure and contours of your data. However, with data collected by others, a period of familiarization is necessary. You have to get to grips with the range of variables, the ways in which the variables have been coded, and various aspects of the organization of the data. The period of familiarization can be quite substantial with large complex datasets and should not be underestimated.

- *Complexity of the data*. Some of the best-known datasets that are employed for secondary analysis, such as the WERS, are very large in the sense of having large numbers of both respondents and variables. Sometimes, the sheer volume of data can present problems with the management of the information at hand, and, again, a period of acclimatization may be required.

Also, some of the most prominent datasets that have been employed for secondary analysis are known as *hierarchical* datasets, such as the WERS. The difficulty here is that the data are collected and presented at the level of both the organization and the individual, as well as other levels. The secondary analyst must decide which level of analysis is going to be employed. If the decision is to analyse individual-level data, the individual-level data must then be extracted from the dataset. Different data will apply to each level. Thus, at the organizational level, the WERS provides data on such variables as number of employees and level of ownership, while, at the individual level, data on age, qualifications, and salary level can be found. For example, Hoque (2003) was interested in the impact of Investors in People (IiP) accreditation on workplace training practice. He used data from the 1998 WERS managers' survey to extract organization-level data to build up a profile of workplaces that have IiP accreditation. However, in order to evaluate the impact of IiP accreditation on training practice, Hoque relied on individual-level data, in the form of data about training activity taken from the survey of employees. These included questions about the number of days spent on training that were paid for or organized by the employer and whether or not the employee had, in the previous twelve months, discussed his or her training needs with his or her supervisor. He used these data to draw conclusions at the level of the organization, and to make comparisons of the effectiveness of training practice in accredited versus non-accredited workplaces.

- *No control over data quality*. The point has been made on several occasions that secondary analysis offers the opportunity for students and others to examine data of far higher quality than they could collect themselves. However, this point applies mainly to datasets from a regulated source such as the UK Data Service (see Table 14.1). These tend to be commissioned by a government department and conducted by researchers who are regarded as independent or at least somewhat distanced from the issues that are being investigated, such as academics working for a university research unit. While the quality of data should never be taken for granted, in the case of such datasets it is reasonably assured, though that is not to say that the data will necessarily meet all of a prospective secondary analyst's needs, since they may not have been collected on an aspect of a topic that would have been of considerable interest. With other datasets, somewhat more caution may be necessary in connection with assessment of

data quality. This may be of particular concern when using data that are the result of commercially commissioned research, as is the case in market research or when using surveys that have been conducted in-house by a company that wants, for example, to measure the effectiveness of its HRM strategy.

- *Absence of key variables*. Because secondary analysis entails the analysis of data collected by others for their own purposes, it may be that one or more key variables may not be present. You may, for example, want to examine whether or not a relationship between two variables holds when one or more *other* variables are taken into account. Such an analysis is known as **multivariate analysis**, an area that will be touched on in Chapter 15. The inability to examine the significance or otherwise of a theoretically important variable can be frustrating and can arise when, for example, a theoretical approach that has emerged since the collection of the data suggests its importance. This is also a drawback in meta-analysis (Key concept 14.9 and Research in focus 14.10), sometimes making it difficult for researchers to generate unambiguous conclusions as a result of the analysis). Obviously, when researchers collect primary data themselves, the prospect of this happening should be less pronounced.

Research in focus 14.7
Age and work-related health: methodological issues involved in secondary analysis using the Labour Force Survey

Davies, Jones, and Lloyd-Williams (2014) used data from the UK Labour Force Survey (LFS) to consider two methodological issues related to age and work-related health. Their first point is that the LFS is unusual in asking questions relating to health of people who are not in employment. This enables a more representative analysis than through focusing only on people currently in work. Data from LFS also enables comparison between work-related health problems that arise from the person's current job with those arising from previous employment. The LFS data are also based on self-reporting, which relies on 'individuals' perception of the attribution of an illness being caused or made worse by their occupation, rather than verification of work attribution made by a medical practitioner' (Davies, Jones, and Lloyd-Williams, 2014: 4). While the researchers acknowledge that this is a subjective measure which may result in reporting bias, the under-reporting of work-related health data by employers makes these supposedly more objective measures equally problematic. The LFS data thus enable better understanding of the health advantages and disadvantages associated with government policies to encourage people to work longer.

Accessing the UK Data Archive

For researchers based in the UK, the UK Data Archive is likely to be your main source of quantitative data for secondary analysis. Containing over 4000 datasets, the Archive is the largest collection of accessible digital data on social and economic topics in the UK. Data are acquired from academic, commercial, and government sources and preserved and made available for further analysis.

Access to the Archive's holdings is provided to all academic researchers unless restrictions have been placed on the dataset by the owners. In addition to UK cross-sectoral studies from academic, government, and commercial sources, the Archive holds time series data, major longitudinal studies, panel surveys, and major cross-sectional studies. Data holdings include: UK Census data; Office for National Statistics (ONS) Omnibus Survey; Labour Force Survey (LFS); and British Social Attitudes (BSA). Data are made available over the network, on CD-ROM, and on other media. The Archive can also be used to locate and acquire data from other archives within Europe and worldwide, using a series of reciprocal agreements with other institutions. By far the most straightforward route to find out whether or not the Archive contains data on the topic you are interested in is by going to the UK Data Service's online catalogue, 'Discover', which provides a single point of access to data for social and economic researchers. It can be accessed by going to the home page at: *ukdataservice.ac.uk/* (accessed 29 October 2014)

Enter your terms into the box and click 'Search' (see Plate 14.1). You can use Boolean logic search terms AND, NOT, OR, to refine your search and combine search terms with filters. For example, we asked for studies with the keywords 'consumers' and 'technolog*' (* is used as a 'wild card' in searches so that it covers 'technolo*gy*', 'techno*logical*', 'technolo*gies*', etc.) found anywhere in the study description. We refined the search using the following filters: **Type** 'data collections', **Subject** 'Employment and labour' and **Date** 2010–2014. This resulted in nine studies being found (see Plate 14.2). We selected Study Number SN 6676 which is described in the title as 'Understanding Society: Waves 1-3 2009-2011', and selected **Full record**, which provided a 2-page abstract of the study, including information about the sponsors; sampling details; method of data collection; main topics of the survey; and information about publications deriving from the study. At the bottom of this page is a further section on administrative and access information, which informs you of any special conditions relating to access. With the one we specified, we are told that because the data 'are more sensitive and/or pose a higher risk of disclosure' there are access restrictions which mean that data cannot be downloaded except by registration as a Secure User, which would normally be a professional researcher, rather than a student or member of the public. But for others, such as the Labour Force Survey, access to data is via registration or by setting up an account that will allow you to download data. You will need to find out if there is an administrative charge for receiving the data, but it is likely that, if you are a student at or a member of staff in a UK institution of higher education, there will be no charge. A small number of quantitative and qualitative datasets, including World Bank macrodata, are also available without registration or authentication via the UK Data Service Data Open Access Policy, including some that can be used as a teaching resource. See the website for more details.

Information about searching for qualitative data for the purpose of conducting a secondary analysis can be found in Chapter 24.

Table 14.1 lists several large datasets that are accessible to students and would repay further investigation in terms of their potential use in the context of research questions in which you might be interested.

In addition to the government-sponsored datasets available via the UK Data Service, there are some commercial sources of business information that can be used for secondary analysis. Target Group Index (TGI) is one of the largest commercially produced continuous consumer surveys conducted in Great Britain. The survey covers the ownership, level, and frequency of purchase and expenditure on most consumer products and services. It also covers information on respondents' media habits—that is, what they read, listen to, or watch. An annual survey is carried out among 25,000 adults nationwide. Data are available in two formats—hard copy (thirty-four volumes of data categorized by product group) and online. However, although some of the older TGI survey data can be accessed from libraries accessing these kinds of data is likely to prove prohibitively expensive for a student researcher.

Archival proxies and meta-analysis

However, it need not necessarily be the case that secondary analysis entails the analysis of primary data collected by other researchers, as the discussion of the use of archival proxies in strategic management (Research in focus 14.8) illustrates. Another context in which secondary analysis of other researchers' data may be carried out is through meta-analysis of existing research studies. With this method, the secondary researcher analyses data provided in articles that relate to the research question(s) of interest. See Key concept 14.9 and Research in focus 14.10.

Plate 14.1

The UK Data Service 'Discover' Catalogue

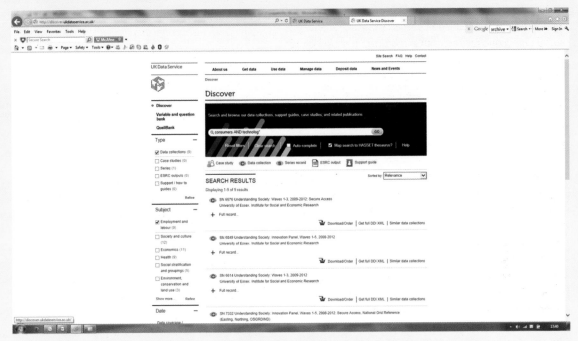

Webpage created for the UK Data Service, an ESRC-funded resource. Reproduced with permission from the University of Essex. The page is available online at discover.ukdataservice.ac.uk.

Plate 14.2

Results of a search

Research in focus 14.8
The use of archival proxies in the field of strategic management

In the field of strategic management, considerable use is made of *archival proxies*, that is, quantitative data collected by organizations that can be used to represent an underlying theoretical construct. Such data are routinely collected by firms and are usually publicly accessible through such outlets as company reports. Ketchen et al. (2012) have considered how far such proxy measures (which are are a form of *unobtrusive measure*—Key concept 14.12) can be used as valid indicators of underlying concepts. In the strategic management field, the issue is of considerable importance because their use has been increasing since the 1980s while the use of questionnaires and laboratory experiments has declined (Boyd et al. 2012). Ketchen et al. consider three archival proxy measures: research and development intensity, patent counts, and patent citations. An examination of the use of these proxies in two prominent journals—*Academy of Management Journal and Strategic Management Journal*—shows that they have been used to represent quite a wide variety of theoretical constructs. For example, patent counts have been used to indicate constructs as diverse as the quantity of innovations carried out by a firm and a firm's technological capabilities. Ketchen et al. propose that the former use is not unreasonable and has face validity but the latter use is stretching its meaning, since, as the authors observe, applying for a patent does not necessarily mean that a firm has the capacity to develop the technology. Similarly, R&D intensity can usefully be regarded as a reasonable measure of some underlying constructs such as 'technological capabilities', but others have treated it as a measure of innovations and innovativeness, which seems less acceptable since whether a firm has the capacity to innovate is a different issue from the amount of money spent on research and development. While the discussion by Ketchen et al. does not depart from a consideration of the basic issue of the face validity of these measures, it provides an instructive warning about the need to ensure a reasonable correspondence between concepts and measures.

Key concept 14.9
What is meta-analysis?

Meta-analysis involves summarizing the results of a large number of quantitative studies and conducting various analytical tests to show whether or not a particular variable has an effect. This provides a means whereby the results of large numbers of quantitative studies of a particular topic can be summarized and compared. The aim of this approach is to establish whether or not a particular variable has a certain effect by comparing the results of different studies. Meta-analysis thus involves pooling the results from various studies in order to estimate an overall effect by correcting the various sampling and non-sampling errors that may arise in relation to a particular study. In a sense, a meta-analysis lies between two kinds of activity covered in this book: doing a literature review of existing studies in an area in which you are interested (the focus of Chapter 5), and conducting a secondary analysis of other researchers' data as has been discussed above. However, the technique relies on all the relevant information being available for each of the studies examined. Since not all the same information relating to methods of study and sample size is included in published papers, meta-analysis is not always feasible. One particular problem that meta-analysts face is known as the 'file drawer problem', whereby research that does not generate interesting publishable findings tends to be filed away and never sees the light of day. This tendency almost certainly creates a bias in meta-analytic reviews, since findings that fail to support a hypothesis or are equivocal in their implications may be less likely to be published.

Research in focus 14.10
A meta-analysis of the impact of leadership interventions

A meta-analysis conducted by Avolio et al. (2009) sought to examine the research question: 'do leadership interventions have the intended impact and if so to what degree?' This is a significant question, given the attention that is often lavished on the concept of leadership and the amounts of money spent on training leaders to exhibit certain kinds of behaviour. Avolio et al. wanted to include in their review all experimental and quasi-experimental studies of leadership interventions. This meant that all cross-sectional design studies that addressed leadership and leadership interventions did not qualify, as they do not involve an intervention in which there is a manipulation of the independent variable. The authors' search for a comprehensive set of studies involved the following procedures:

1. A search of eighteen electronic databases using 124 keywords and phrases.

2. An examination of the bibliographies of all studies produced through the electronic database searches and an examination of the bibliographies of previous meta-analyses in the field.

3. Emails to 670 leadership researchers asking them to review a proposed list of studies.

4. A manual search of leadership handbooks and other books.

This search process yielded over 500 studies, which were gradually trimmed down to 200 studies that met the authors' criteria. The main reason for exclusion was that the research was not an intervention study. Interestingly, of the 200 studies, 16 per cent were unpublished, suggesting that meta-analyses and other kinds of review that are based exclusively on published research may be missing a significant number of studies, and this may be a source of bias. The authors found a strong relationship between leadership interventions and various kinds of outcomes such as task performance. In other words, leadership interventions do have a significant impact on various kinds of dependent variable.

Official statistics

The analysis of official statistics has been a feature of business research for many years. Agencies of the state, in the course of their business, are required to keep a record of their areas of activity. When these records are aggregated, they form the official statistics in an area of activity. In the UK, the Office for National Statistics publishes data that form the basis for the level of unemployment (also known as the 'claimant count'). This is just one, as it happens high-profile, set of statistics that can be subsumed under the general category of 'official statistics'. Such statistics offer considerable potential for business researchers. We could imagine such official statistics offering the researcher certain advantages over some other forms of quantitative data, such as data based on surveys.

- The data have already been collected. Therefore, as with other kinds of secondary analysis of data (see above), considerable time and expense may be saved. Also, the data may not be based on samples, so that a complete picture can be obtained.

- Since the people who are the source of the data are not being asked questions that are part of a research project, the problem of *reactivity* will be much less pronounced than when data are collected by interview or questionnaire.

- There is the prospect of analysing the data both cross-sectionally and longitudinally. When analysing the data cross-sectionally, we could examine employment rates (in addition to unemployment rates) in terms of such standard variables as social class, income, ethnicity, age, gender, and region. Such analyses allow us to search for the factors that are associated with employment. Also, we can analyse the data over time.

Precisely because the data are compiled over many years, it is possible to chart trends over time and perhaps to relate these to wider social changes.

- There is the prospect as well of cross-cultural analysis, since the official statistics from different nation-states can be compared for a specific area of activity.

However, readers who recall the discussion of convergent validity introduced in Chapter 7 will already be on their guard. The official statistics concerned with an area of social life such as employment can be very misleading, because they record only those individuals who are processed by the agencies that have the responsibility for compiling the statistics. In addition, the process whereby official statistics are generated involves an element of interpretation. As the example in Research in focus 14.6 illustrates, government agencies will vary in terms of how they record information. In the case of labour disputes, this means that a substantial number of disputes are likely to go unrecorded as a result either of not being reported or of not being recognized as a labour dispute according to the criteria used by the agency. This level of unrecorded activity is sometimes referred to in relation to the field of crime (which has been one of the main areas for discussions about the uses and limitations of official statistics) as 'the dark figure' (Coleman and Moynihan 1996). Nor can the example of labour disputes be regarded as alone in this connection. To push the point even further, the deficiencies of official statistics also extend to the recording of levels of employment and unemployment. For example, the 'claimant count', which is used to gain a picture each month of the level of unemployment, may misrepresent the 'real' level of unemployment: people who are unemployed but who do not claim benefits or whose claim is disallowed will not be counted in the statistics, while those who form part of the claimant count but who work in part of what is known as the 'black' or 'informal' economy (and who therefore are not really unemployed) *will* be included in the unemployment statistics.

A great deal of national and cross-national official statistical information can be obtained via Internet sources. The UK National Statistics Publication Hub is the gateway to official statistics reflecting the economy, population, and society at national and local level, publishing summary stories and detailed data releases free of charge, including statistical information relating to various aspects of labour-market activity in the UK. Reports such as *Labour Market Trends* and *Social Trends* provide aggregated results based on this type of large-scale survey

data. The website addresses for these gateways are given below: *www.statistics.gov.uk/hub/index.html* (accessed 29 October 2014)

Finally, Eurostat, the statistics website of the European Union, provides an additional useful source of official documents and statistics relating to European Union affairs and European integration. The website can be found at: *epp.eurostat.ec.europa.eu/portal/page/portal/eurostat/home* (accessed 29 October 2014)

Reliability and validity

Issues of reliability and validity seem to loom large in these considerations. Reliability seems to be jeopardized because definitions and policies regarding the phenomena to be counted vary over time, as the example of the different definitions of labour disputes used by Organization for Economic Cooperation and Development (OECD) nations given by Jackie Davies (2001) effectively illustrates (see Research in focus 14.6). The problem for the reliability of such statistics is that variations over time in levels of labour dispute may be due not to variations in the level of workplace conflict but to variations in the propensity to expend resources in recording these events. Also, there may be changes over time in the definitions of labour dispute or in the propensity of employers to report disputes to government. Such changes will clearly affect the degree to which fluctuations in the rate of occurrence of labour disputes reflect 'real' fluctuations in the rate of incidence. To the extent that such factors operate, the reliability of the data will be adversely affected and, as a result, validity will be similarly impaired.

Also, the problems with official statistics extend to the examination of the variables with which the rate of occurrence is associated. For example, it might be assumed that, if an examination of differences in labour disputes demonstrates that the rate varies by sector—for example, with industries such as manufacturing and transport having consistently high strike rates, whereas sectors like agriculture have very low ones—this implies that the industrial sector is related to labour militancy leading to strike action. There are two problems with drawing such an inference. First, there is an analytic difficulty known as the **ecological fallacy** (see Key concept 14.11). Secondly, even if we could ignore the problem of the ecological fallacy (which we cannot, of course), we would still be faced with an issue that is related to the matter of validity. Variations between industrial sectors may be a product of factors other than the difference in their propensity to take strike action. Instead, the variations may

Key concept 14.11
What is the ecological fallacy?

The ecological fallacy is the error of assuming that inferences about individuals or organizations can be made from findings relating to aggregate data. For example, official statistics might demonstrate a positive relationship between size of firm and the number of labour disputes involving strike action. Such a finding could be taken to imply that employees in larger firms are more likely than those in small firms to take strike action. However, it would be wrong to draw such an inference about individual firms or groups of employees from aggregate data. A particular large firm may show quite low levels of strike activity, while a particular small firm might show a high level. The fallacy can arise for several reasons—the reason highlighted in this case being that it may not be the size of the firm that is responsible for the level of strike activity.

be due to such factors as variations in the average rates of pay and the terms and conditions of employment in different industrial sectors; likelihood of employers in different industrial sectors to report a dispute; differences in the number of employees working in these sectors; variation in the average number of people employed by organizations in different sectors; differences in the level of union membership and union activity; and variations in the effectiveness of formal communication systems.

Condemning and resurrecting official statistics

Criticism of the use of various kinds of official statistics in the social sciences has drawn attention to these problems. Instead, it was recommended that researchers should turn their attention to the investigation of the organizational processes that produce the various deficiencies identified by the various writers. The effect of this view was to consign official statistics to the sidelines of business research so that it became an object of research interest rather than a potential source of data, although research based on official statistics continued in certain quarters. It would also be wrong to think that critique was the sole reason for the neglect of official statistics during this period. The fact that official statistics, because they are a sideline for many state agencies, are invariably not tailored to the needs of business and management researchers can be considered a further limitation. In other words, it may be that the definitions of apparently similar or identical terms (such as labour disputes or working at home) employed by those responsible for compiling official statistics may not be commensurate with the definitions employed by business and management researchers. However, others have argued that the flaws in many of the official statistics

are probably no worse than the errors that occur in much measurement deriving from methods such as social surveys based on questionnaires and structured interviews (Bulmer 1980). Indeed, some forms of official statistics, such as population census data, are probably very accurate by almost any set of criteria.

A further criticism of the rejection of various forms of official statistics is that it seems to imply that quantitative data compiled by business researchers are somehow error-free, or at least superior. However, as we have seen in previous chapters, while business and management researchers do their best to reduce the amount of error in their measurement of key concepts (such as through the standardization of the asking of questions and the recording of answers in survey research), it is not the case that the various measures that are derived are free of error. All social measurement is prone to error; what is crucial is taking steps to keep that error to a minimum. Therefore, to reject official statistics because they contain errors is misleading if in fact all measurement in business research contains errors. It is clear that the wholesale rejection of official statistics by many researchers has been tempered. While there is widespread recognition and acknowledgement that problems remain with certain forms of official statistics, each set of statistics has to be evaluated on its own merits for the purposes of business and management research.

Official statistics as a form of unobtrusive measure

One of the most compelling and frequently cited cases for the continued use of official statistics is that they can be considered a form of unobtrusive measure, although nowadays many writers prefer to use the term

Key concept 14.12
What are unobtrusive measures?

An unobtrusive measure is 'any method of observation that directly removes the observer from the set of interactions or events being studied' (Denzin 1970). Webb et al. (1966) distinguished four main types of such observation:

1. *Physical traces*. These are the 'signs left behind by a group' and include such things as graffiti and rubbish.

2. *Archive materials*. This category includes statistics collected by governmental and non-governmental organizations, such as diaries, the mass media, and historical records. See Research in focus 14.8 for a discussion of such data.

3. *Simple observation*. This refers to 'situations in which the observer has no control over the behaviour or sign in question, and plays an unobserved, passive, and non-intrusive role in the research situation' (Webb et al. 1966: 112).

4. *Contrived observation*. This is the same as simple observation, but the observer either actively varies the setting in some way (but without jeopardizing the unobtrusive quality of the observation) or employs hidden hardware to record observations, such as video cameras.

Official statistics would be subsumed under Category 2, as would content analysis of media of the kind described in Chapter 13. However, a content analysis such as that described in Research in focus 13.9 would not be considered an example of an unobtrusive measure, because the material being content analysed (workplace ethnographies) derives from studies in which the data were generated in an obtrusive fashion. Structured observation of the kind covered in Chapter 12 will typically not fall into Categories 3 and 4, because the observer is usually known to those being observed. However, field stimulations, such as the mystery shopper example described in Research in focus 12.10, are an example of contrived observation. In this case, the mystery shoppers were not known by travel agents to be researchers and they actively varied the situation through communication of their specific holiday requirements in order to elicit travel agents' recommendations.

It is important to realize that Webb et al. (1966) were not intending that unobtrusive methods should supplant conventional methods. Instead, they argued that the problem they were identifying was the almost exclusive reliance upon methods that were likely to be affected by reactivity. Webb et al. argued for greater 'triangulation' (see Key concept 17.6) in social research, whereby conventional (reactive) and unobtrusive (non-reactive) methods would be employed in conjunction. For example, they wrote that they were providing an inventory of unobtrusive methods, 'because they demonstrate ways in which the investigator may shore up reactive infirmities of the interview and questionnaire' (1966: 174).

It is worth noting that unobtrusive methods or measures encapsulate at least two kinds of ways of thinking about the process of capturing data. First, many so-called unobtrusive measures are in fact *sources* of data, such as graffiti, diaries, media articles, and official statistics. Such sources require analysis in order to be rendered interesting to a business school audience. Secondly, such measures include *methods* of data collection, such as simple and contrived observation. While the data generated by such methods of data collection also require analysis, the data have to be produced by the methods. The data are not simply out there awaiting analysis in the way in which diaries or newspaper articles are (although, of course, a great deal of detective work is often necessary to unearth such sources). This means that neither of the terms 'unobtrusive methods' or 'unobtrusive measures' captures the variety of forms terribly well. A further disadvantage of the term 'unobtrusive measure' is that it seems to imply a connection to quantitative research alone, whereas certain approaches employed by qualitative researchers may qualify as unobtrusive methods.

R. M. Lee (2000) has developed a classification of unobtrusive methods that differs slightly from that of Webb et al. (1996). He distinguishes the following kinds of data:

1. *Found data*. This category corresponds more or less exactly to physical traces.

2. *Captured data*. This category comprises both *simple observation* and *contrived observation*.

3. *Retrieved data: running records*. This category would include, for example, company information that is held in a national database such as by Companies House in the UK, where records can be examined over quite long periods so that changes can be explored. He also includes in this category such things as job advertisements.

4. *Retrieved data: personal and episodic records*. With this category, Lee has in mind three kinds of data: **personal documents** (letters, diaries, memoirs), visual images in the mass media (for example, newspaper photographs and advertisements), and 'documents produced through "institutional discovery" procedures' (R. M. Lee 2000: 87) (for example, reports of inquiries into factors that led to a disaster; see Research in Focus 23.4 for an example).

5. Lee also distinguishes *records produced through the Internet*, especially the various forms of computer-mediated communication such as email and various kinds of social network. In the years since Lee wrote, blogs have become another kind.

Many of these different kinds of data are encountered elsewhere in this book, e.g. personal documents in Chapter 23 and computer-mediated communications in Chapters 23 and 28. Each of the different types that Webb et al. and Lee identify pose distinctive questions in terms of issues such as the reliability of the evidence and the ethical issues involved.

An interesting use of unobtrusive methods can be found in Chatterjee and Hambrick's (2007) research on narcissistic CEOs. Rather than use one of the standard questionnaire inventories that have been devised to measure narcissism, the researchers used five unobtrusive indicators that they felt captured the sense of superiority and self-absorption that typifies this personality type:

(1) the prominence of the CEO's photograph in the company's annual report; (2) the CEO's prominence in the company's press releases; (3) the CEO's use of first-person singular pronouns in interviews; (4) the CEO's cash compensation divided by that of the second-highest-paid executive in the firm; and (5) the CEO's non-cash compensation divided by that of the second-highest-paid executive in the firm.

(Chatterjee and Hambrick 2007: 363)

All of these indicators are unobtrusive in that the data do not entail the involvement of the CEOs. In Lee's (2000) terms, they are largely 'retrieved data'. From the point of view of the reader, the credibility of these indicators rests or falls on how far the researchers are convincing in the case that they make for their use as measures of narcissism.

unobtrusive methods (R. M. Lee 2000). This term is derived from the notion of 'unobtrusive measure' coined by Webb et al. (1966). In a highly influential book, Webb et al. argued that social researchers are excessively reliant on measures of social phenomena deriving from methods of data collection that are prone to *reactivity* (see Research in focus 3.8 and Key concept 12.8, where this idea is introduced). This means that, whenever people know that they are participating in a study (which is invariably the case with methods of data collection such as structured interviewing, self-completion questionnaire, and structured observation), a component of their replies or behaviour is likely to be influenced by their knowledge that they are being investigated. In other words, their answers to questions or the behaviour they exhibit may be untypical.

Official statistics fit fairly squarely in the second of the four types of unobtrusive measures outlined in Key concept 14.12. As noted in the box, this second grouping covers a very wide range of sources of data, which includes statistics generated by organizations that are not agencies of the state. This is a useful reminder that potentially interesting statistical data are frequently compiled by a wide range of organizations, such as market research agencies. There may be greater potential for searching out and mining statistical data produced by organizations that are relatively independent of the state.

Key points

- Secondary analysis of existing data offers the prospect of being able to explore research questions of interest to you without having to go through the process of collecting the data yourself.

- Very often, secondary analysis offers the opportunity of being able to employ high-quality datasets that are based on large, reasonably representative samples.

- Secondary analysis presents few disadvantages.

- The analysis of official statistics may be thought of as a special form of secondary analysis but one that is more controversial because of the unease about the reliability and validity of certain types of official data, especially those relating to unemployment and labour disputes.

- Some forms of official statistics are much less prone to errors, but there remains the possible problem of divergences of definition between compilers of such data and business researchers.

- Official statistics represent a form of unobtrusive method and enjoy certain advantages (especially lack of reactivity) because of that.

Questions for review

- What is secondary analysis?

Other researchers' data

- Outline the main advantages and limitations of secondary analysis of other researchers' data.

- Does the possibility of conducting a secondary analysis apply only to quantitative data produced by other researchers?

Official statistics

- Why have many business researchers been sceptical about the use of official statistics for research purposes?

- How justified is their scepticism?

- What reliability and validity issues do official statistics pose?

- What are unobtrusive methods or measures? What is the chief advantage of such methods?

Online Resource Centre

www.oxfordtextbooks.co.uk/orc/brymanbrm4e/

Visit the Interactive Research Guide that accompanies this book to complete an exercise in Secondary Analysis and Official Statistics.

15

Quantitative data analysis

Chapter outline

In this chapter, some of the basic but nonetheless most frequently used methods for analysing quantitative data will be presented. In order to illustrate the use of the methods of data analysis, a small imaginary set of data based on attendance at a gym is used. It is the kind of small research project that would be feasible for most students doing undergraduate research projects for a dissertation or similar exercise. The chapter explores:

- the importance of *not* leaving considerations of how you will analyse your quantitative data until after you have collected all your data; you should be aware of the ways in which you would like to analyse your data from the earliest stage of your research;

- the distinctions between the different kinds of variable that can be generated in quantitative research; knowing how to distinguish types of variables is crucial so that you appreciate which methods of analysis can be applied when you examine variables and relationships between them;

- methods for analysing a single variable at a time (*univariate analysis*);

- methods for analysing relationships between variables (*bivariate analysis*);

- the analysis of relationships between three or more variables (*multivariate analysis*).

Introduction

In this chapter, some very basic techniques for analysing quantitative data will be examined. In Chapter 16, the ways in which these techniques can be implemented using sophisticated computer software will be introduced. The software is known as IBM SPSS and the version discussed in Chapter 16 is Release 22. The formulae that underpin the techniques discussed in this chapter will not be presented here, since the necessary calculations can easily be carried out by using SPSS. Two chapters cannot do justice to these topics and readers are advised to move on as soon as possible to books that provide more detailed and advanced treatments (e.g. Bryman and Cramer 2011).

Before beginning this exposition of techniques, we would like to give you advance warning of one of the biggest mistakes that people make about quantitative data analysis:

> I don't have to concern myself with how I'm going to analyse my survey data until after I've collected my data. I'll leave thinking about it till then, because it doesn't impinge on how I collect my data.

This is a common error that arises because quantitative data analysis looks like a distinct phase that occurs after the

data have been collected (see, for example, Figure 7.1, in which the analysis of quantitative data is depicted as a late step—number 9—in quantitative research). Quantitative data analysis is indeed something that occurs typically at a late stage in the overall process and is also a distinct stage.

However, that does not mean that you should not be considering how you will analyse your data until then. In fact, you should be fully aware of what techniques you will apply at a fairly early stage—for example, when you are designing your questionnaire, observation schedule, coding frame, or whatever. The two main reasons for this are as follows.

1. You cannot apply just any technique to any variable. Techniques have to be appropriately matched to the types of variables that you have created through your research. This means that you must be fully conversant with the ways in which different types of variable are classified.

2. The size and nature of your sample are likely to impose limitations on the kinds of techniques you can use (see the section on 'Kind of analysis' in Chapter 8).

In other words, you need to be aware that decisions that you make at quite an early stage in the research process, such as the kinds of data you collect and the size of your sample, will have implications for the sorts of analysis that you will be able to conduct.

A small research project

This discussion of quantitative data analysis will be based upon an imaginary piece of research carried out by an undergraduate marketing student for a dissertation. The student in question is interested in the role of the sport and leisure industry and in particular, because of her own enthusiasm for leisure clubs and gyms, in the ways in which such venues are used and people's reasons for joining them. She has read an article that suggests that participant involvement in adult fitness programmes is associated with their attitudinal loyalty, comprising investment of time and money, social pressure from significant others, and internalization or commitment to the fitness regime (Park 1996). She intends to use this theory as a framework for her findings. The student is also interested in issues relating to gender and body image and she suspects that men and women will differ in their reasons for going to a gym and the kinds of activities in which they engage in the gym. Her final issue of interest relates to the importance of age in determining gym involvement. In particular, she has discovered that previous research has shown that older people tend to show higher levels of attitudinal loyalty to recreational activities more generally and she wants to find out if this finding also applies to involvement in leisure clubs and gyms.

She secures the agreement of a gym close to her home to contact a sample of its members by post. The gym has 1200 members and she decides to take a simple random sample of 10 per cent of the membership (that is, 120 members). She sends out postal questionnaires to members of the sample with a covering letter testifying to the gym's support of her research. One thing she wants to know is how much time people spend on each of the three main classes of activity in the gym: cardiovascular equipment, weights equipment, and exercises. She defines each of these carefully in the covering letter and asks members of the sample to keep a note of how long they spend on each of the three activities on their next visit. They are then requested to return the questionnaires to her in a prepaid reply envelope. She ends up with a sample of ninety questionnaires—a response rate of 75 per cent.

Part of the questionnaire is presented in Tips and skills 'A completed and processed questionnaire' and has been completed by a respondent and coded by the student. The entire questionnaire runs to four pages, but only twelve of the questions are provided here. Many of the questions (1, 3, 4, 5, 6, 7, 8, and 9) are pre-coded, and the student simply has to circle the code to the far right of the question under the column 'code'. With the remainder of the questions, specific figures are requested, and the student simply transfers the relevant figure to the code column.

Tips and skills
A completed and processed questionnaire

Questionnaire   Code

1. Are you male or female (please tick)?

    Male _✓_ Female ____   ① 2

2. How old are you?

    _21_ years   *21*

3. Which of the following best describes your *main* reason for going to the gym? (please tick *one* only)

		Code
Relaxation	____	1
Maintain or improve fitness	✓	②
Lose weight	____	3
Meet others	____	4
Build strength	____	5
Other (please specify)	____	6

4. When you go to the gym, how often do you use the cardiovascular equipment (jogger, step machine, bike, rower)? (please tick)

Always	✓	①
Usually	⎯	2
Rarely	⎯	3
Never	⎯	4

5. When you go to the gym, how often do you use the weights machines (including free weights)? (please tick)

Always	✓	①
Usually	⎯	2
Rarely	⎯	3
Never	⎯	4

6. How frequently do you usually go to the gym? (please tick)

Every day	⎯	1
4–6 days a week	⎯	2
2 or 3 days a week	✓	③
Once a week	⎯	4
2 or 3 times a month	⎯	5
Once a month	⎯	6
Less than once a month	⎯	7

7. Are you usually accompanied when you go to the gym or do you usually go on your own? (please tick *one* only)

On my own	✓	①
With a friend	⎯	2
With a partner/spouse	⎯	3

8. Do you have sources of regular exercise other than the gym?

Yes ⎯⎯ No ✓   1 ②

*If you have answered **No** to this question, please proceed to question **10***

9. If you have replied **Yes** to question **8**, please indicate the *main* source of regular exercise in the last six months from this list. (please tick *one* only)

Sport	⎯	1
Cycling on the road	⎯	2
Jogging	⎯	3
Long walks	⎯	4
Other (please specify)	⎯	5

10. During your last visit to the gym, how many minutes did you spend on the cardiovascular equipment (jogger, step machine, bike, rower)?

_**33**_ minutes   *33*

11. During your last visit to the gym, how many minutes did you spend on the weights machines (including free weights)?

_**17**_ minutes   *17*

12. During your last visit to the gym, how many minutes did you spend on other activities (e.g. stretching exercises)?

_**5**_ minutes   *5*

Missing data

The data for all ninety respondents are presented in Tips and skills 'Gym survey data'. Each of the twelve questions is known for the time being as a variable number (var00001, etc.). The variable number is a default number that is imposed by SPSS, the statistical package that is described in Chapter 16. Each variable number corresponds to the question number in Tips and skills 'A completed and processed questionnaire' (i.e. var00001 is question 1, var00002 is question 2, etc.). In the management of data, an important issue arises as to how to handle 'missing data'. Missing data arise when respondents fail to reply to a question—either by accident or because they do not want to answer the question. Thus, respondent 24 has failed to answer question 2, which is concerned with age. This has been coded as a zero (0) and it will be important to ensure that the computer software is notified of this fact, since it needs to be taken into account during the analysis. Also, question 9 has a large number of zeros: many people did not answer it, because they have been filtered out by the previous question (that is, they do not have other sources of regular exercise). These have also been coded as zero to denote missing data, though strictly speaking their failure to reply is more indicative of the question not being applicable to them. Note also, that there are zeros for var00010, var00011, and var00012. However, these do *not* denote missing data but that the respondent spends 0 minutes on the activity in question. Everyone has answered questions 10, 11, and 12, so there are in fact no missing data for these variables. If there had been missing data, it would be necessary to code missing data with a number that could not also be a true figure. For example, nobody has spent 99 minutes on these activities, so this might be an appropriate number, as it is easy to remember and could not be read by the computer as anything other than missing data.

Tips and skills
Gym survey data

var00001	var00002	var00003	var00004	var00005	var00006	var00007	var00008	var00009	var00010	var00011	var00012
1	21	2	1	1	3	1	2	0	33	17	5
2	44	1	3	1	4	3	1	2	10	23	10
2	19	3	1	2	2	1	1	1	27	18	12
2	27	3	2	1	2	1	2	0	30	17	3
1	57	2	1	3	2	3	1	4	22	0	15
2	27	3	1	1	3	1	1	3	34	17	0
1	39	5	2	1	5	1	1	5	17	48	10
2	36	3	1	2	2	2	1	1	25	18	7
1	37	2	1	1	3	1	2	0	34	15	0
2	51	2	2	2	4	3	2	0	16	18	11
1	24	5	2	1	3	1	1	1	0	42	16
2	29	2	1	2	3	1	2	0	34	22	12
1	20	5	1	1	2	1	2	0	22	31	7
2	22	2	1	3	4	2	1	3	37	14	12
2	46	3	1	1	5	2	2	0	26	9	4
2	41	3	1	2	2	3	1	4	22	7	10
1	25	5	1	1	3	1	1	1	21	29	4
2	46	3	1	2	4	2	1	4	18	8	11
1	30	3	1	1	5	1	2	0	23	9	6
1	25	5	2	1	3	1	1	1	23	19	0
2	24	2	1	1	3	2	1	2	20	7	6

var00001	var00002	var00003	var00004	var00005	var00006	var00007	var00008	var00009	var00010	var00011	var00012
2	39	1	2	3	5	1	2	0	17	0	9
1	44	3	1	1	3	2	1	2	22	8	5
1	0	1	2	2	4	2	1	4	15	10	4
2	18	3	1	2	3	1	2	1	18	7	10
1	41	3	1	1	3	1	2	0	34	10	4
2	38	2	1	2	5	3	1	2	24	14	10
1	25	2	1	1	2	1	2	0	48	22	7
1	41	5	2	1	3	1	1	2	17	27	0
2	30	3	1	1	2	2	2	0	32	13	10
2	29	3	1	3	2	1	2	0	31	0	7
2	42	1	2	2	4	2	1	4	17	14	6
1	31	2	1	1	2	1	2	0	49	21	2
2	25	3	1	1	2	3	2	0	30	17	15
1	46	3	1	1	3	1	1	3	32	10	5
1	24	5	2	1	4	1	1	2	0	36	11
2	34	3	1	1	3	2	1	4	27	14	12
2	50	2	1	2	2	3	2	0	28	8	6
1	28	5	1	1	3	2	1	1	26	22	8
2	30	3	1	1	2	1	1	4	21	9	12
1	27	2	1	1	2	1	1	3	64	15	8
2	27	2	1	2	4	2	1	4	22	10	7
1	36	5	1	1	3	2	2	0	21	24	0
2	43	3	1	1	4	1	2	0	25	13	8
1	34	2	1	1	3	2	1	1	45	15	6
2	27	3	1	1	2	1	1	4	33	10	9
2	38	2	1	3	4	2	2	0	23	0	16
1	28	2	1	1	3	3	1	2	38	13	5
1	44	5	1	1	2	1	2	0	27	19	7
2	31	3	1	2	3	2	2	0	32	11	5
2	23	2	1	1	4	2	1	1	33	18	8
1	45	3	1	1	3	1	1	2	26	10	7
2	34	3	1	2	2	3	2	0	36	8	12
1	27	3	1	1	2	3	1	3	42	13	6
2	40	3	1	1	2	2	1	4	26	9	10
2	24	2	1	1	2	1	1	2	22	10	9
1	37	2	1	1	5	2	2	0	21	11	0
1	22	5	1	1	4	1	1	1	23	17	6
2	31	3	1	2	3	1	1	4	40	16	12
1	37	2	1	1	2	3	2	0	54	12	3
2	33	1	2	2	4	2	2	0	17	10	5
1	23	5	1	1	3	1	1	1	41	27	8
1	28	3	1	1	3	3	2	0	27	11	8
2	29	2	1	2	5	2	1	2	24	9	9
2	43	3	1	1	2	1	2	0	36	17	12
1	28	5	1	1	3	1	1	1	22	15	4
1	48	2	1	1	5	1	1	4	25	11	7
2	32	2	2	2	4	2	2	0	27	13	11
1	28	5	1	1	2	2	2	0	15	23	7

var00001	var00002	var00003	var00004	var00005	var00006	var00007	var00008	var00009	var00010	var00011	var00012
2	23	2	1	1	5	1	1	4	14	11	5
2	43	2	1	2	5	1	2	0	18	7	3
1	28	2	1	1	4	3	1	2	34	18	8
2	23	3	1	1	2	1	2	0	37	17	17
2	36	1	2	2	4	2	1	4	18	12	4
1	50	2	1	1	3	1	1	2	28	14	3
1	37	3	1	1	2	2	2	0	26	14	9
2	41	3	1	1	2	1	1	4	24	11	4
1	26	5	2	1	5	1	1	1	23	19	8
2	28	3	1	1	4	1	2	0	27	12	4
2	35	2	1	1	3	1	1	1	28	14	0
1	28	5	1	1	2	1	1	2	20	24	12
2	36	2	1	1	3	2	2	0	26	9	14
2	29	3	1	1	4	1	1	4	23	13	4
1	34	1	2	2	4	2	1	0	24	12	3
1	53	2	1	1	3	3	1	1	32	17	6
2	30	3	1	1	4	1	2	0	24	10	9
1	43	2	1	1	2	1	1	2	24	14	10
2	26	5	2	1	4	1	1	1	16	23	7
2	44	1	1	1	4	2	2	0	27	18	6
1	45	1	2	2	3	3	2	0	20	14	5

Types of variable

One of the things that might strike you when you look at the questions is that the kinds of information that you receive varies by question. Some of the questions call for answers in terms of real numbers: questions 2, 10, 11, and 12. Questions 1 and 8 yield either/or answers and are therefore in the form of dichotomies. The rest of the questions take the form of lists of categories, but there are differences between these too. Some of the questions are in terms of answers that are rank ordered: questions 4, 5, and 6. Thus we can say in the case of question 6 that the category 'every day' implies greater frequency than '4–6 days a week', which in turn implies greater frequency than '2 or 3 days a week', and so on. However, in the case of questions 3, 7, and 9, the categories are *not* capable of being rank ordered. We

cannot say in the case of question 3 that 'relaxation' is more of something than 'maintain or improve fitness' or 'lose weight'.

These considerations lead to a classification of the different types of variable that are generated in the course of research. The four main types are:

- **Interval variables/ratio variables** are variables where the distances between the categories are identical across the range of categories. In the case of variables var00010 and var00011, the distance between the categories is 1 minute. Thus, a person may spend 32 minutes on cardiovascular equipment, which is 1 minute more than someone who spends 31 minutes on this equipment. That difference is the same as the difference between someone who spends 8 minutes and another who spends 9 minutes on the equipment. This is the highest level of measurement and a very wide range of techniques of analysis can be applied to interval/ratio variables. There is, in fact, a distinction between interval and ratio variables, in that the latter are interval variables with a fixed zero point. However, since most ratio variables exhibit this quality in business research (for example, income, age, number of employees, revenue), they are not being distinguished here.

- **Ordinal variables** are variables whose categories can be rank ordered (as in the case of interval/ratio variables) but the distances between the categories are not equal across the range. Thus, in the case of question 6, the difference between the category 'every day' and '4–6 days a week' is not the same as the difference between '4–6 days a week' and '2 or 3 days a week', and so on. Nonetheless, we can say that 'every day' is more frequent than '4–6 days a week', which is more frequent than '2 or 3 days a week', etc. You should also bear in mind that, if you subsequently group an interval/ratio variable such as var00002, which refers to people's ages, into categories (e.g. 20 and under; 21–30; 31–40; 41–50; 51 and over), you are transforming it into an ordinal variable.

- **Nominal variables**, also known as *categorical variables*, comprise categories that cannot be rank ordered.

As noted previously, we cannot say in the case of question 3 that 'relaxation' is more of something than 'maintain or improve fitness' or 'lose weight'.

- **Dichotomous variables** contain data that have only two categories (for example, gender). Their position in relation to the other types is slightly ambiguous, as they have only one interval. They therefore can be considered as having attributes of the other three types of variable. They look as though they are nominal variables, but because they have only one interval they are sometimes treated as ordinal variables. However, it is probably safest to treat them for most purposes as if they were ordinary nominal variables.

The four main types of variable and illustrations of them from the gym survey are provided in Table 15.1.

Multiple-indicator (or multiple-item) measures of concepts, such as Likert scales (see Research in focus 7.3), produce strictly speaking ordinal variables. However, many writers argue that they can be treated as though they produce interval/ratio variables, because of the relatively large number of categories they generate. For a brief discussion of this issue, see Bryman and Cramer (2011), who distinguish between 'true' interval/ratio variables and those produced by multiple-indicator measures (2011: 71–3).

Figure 15.1 provides guidance about how to identify variables of each type.

Table 15.1

Types of variable

Type	Description	Examples in gym study	Variable name in SPSS (see Chapter 16)
Interval/ratio	Variables where the distances between the categories are identical across the range	var00002	age
		var00010	cardmins
		var00011	weimins
		var00012	othmins
Ordinal	Variables whose categories can be rank ordered but where the distances between the categories are not equal across the range	var00004	carduse
		var00005	weiuse
		var00006	frequent
Nominal	Variables whose categories cannot be rank ordered; also known as *categorical*	var00003	reasons
		var00007	accomp
		var00009	exercise
Dichotomous	Variables containing data that have only two categories	var00001	gender
		var00008	othsourc

Figure 15.1

Deciding how to categorize a variable

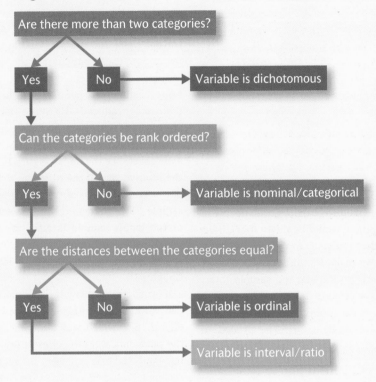

Univariate analysis

Univariate analysis refers to the analysis of one variable at a time. In this section, the commonest approaches will be outlined.

Frequency tables

A **frequency table** provides the number of people and the percentage belonging to each of the categories for the

Table 15.2

Frequency table showing reasons for visiting the gym		
Reason	*n*	%
Relaxation	9	10
Maintain or improve fitness	31	34
Lose weight	33	37
Build strength	17	19
TOTAL	90	100

variable in question. It can be used in relation to all of the different types of variable. An example of a frequency table is provided for var00003 in Table 15.2. Notice that nobody chose two of the possible choices of answer—'meet others' and 'other'—so these are not included in the table. The table shows, for example, that 33 members of the sample go the gym to lose weight and that they represent 37 per cent (percentages are often rounded up and down in frequency tables) of the entire sample. The procedure for generating a frequency table with SPSS is described in Chapter 16.

If an interval/ratio variable (such as people's ages) is to be presented in a frequency table format, it is invariably the case that the categories will need to be grouped. When grouping in this way, take care to ensure that the categories you create do not overlap (for example, like this: 20–30, 30–40, 40–50, etc.). An example of a frequency table for an interval/ratio variable is shown in Table 15.3: it provides a frequency

Table 15.3

| Frequency table showing ages of gym members | | |
Age	*n*	%
20 and under	3	3
21–30	39	44
31–40	23	26
41–50	21	24
51 and over	3	3
TOTAL	89	100

table for var00002, which is concerned with the ages of those visiting the gym. If we did not group people in terms of age ranges, there would be thirty-four different categories, which is too many to take in. By creating five categories, we make the distribution of ages easier to comprehend. Notice that the sample totals 89 and that the percentages are based on a total of 89 rather than 90. This is because this variable contains one missing value (respondent 24). The procedure for grouping respondents with SPSS is described in Chapter 16.

Diagrams

Diagrams are among the most frequently used methods of displaying quantitative data. Their chief advantage is that they are relatively easy to interpret and understand. If you are working with nominal or ordinal variables, the *bar chart* and the *pie chart* are two of the easiest methods to use. A bar chart of the same data presented in Table 15.2 is presented in Figure 15.2. Each bar represents the number of people falling in each category. This figure was produced with SPSS. The procedure for generating a bar chart with SPSS is described in Chapter 16.

Another way of displaying the same data is through a pie chart, like the one in Figure 15.3. This also shows the relative size of the different categories but brings out as well the size of each slice relative to the total sample. The percentage that each slice represents of the whole sample is also given in this diagram, which was also produced with SPSS. The procedure for generating a pie chart with SPSS is described in Chapter 16.

If you are displaying an interval/ratio variable, like var00002, a *histogram* is likely to be employed. Figure 15.4, which was also generated by SPSS, uses the same data and categories as Table 15.3. As with the bar chart, the bars represent the relative size of each of

Figure 15.2

Bar chart showing the main reasons for visiting the gym (SPSS output)

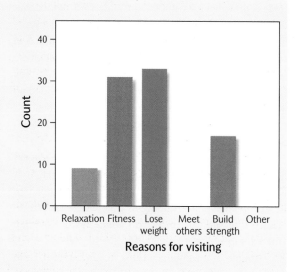

Figure 15.3

Pie chart showing the main reasons for visiting the gym (SPSS output)

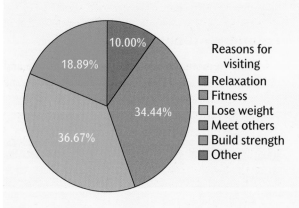

Figure 15.4

Histogram showing the ages of gym visitors (SPSS output)

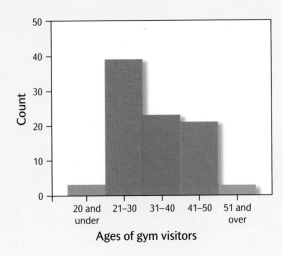

Ages of gym visitors

pressure on the mean, by taking the mid-point of a distribution the median is not affected in this way. The median is derived by arraying all the values in a distribution from the smallest to the largest and then finding the middle point. If there is an even number of values, the median is calculated by taking the mean of the two middle numbers of the distribution. In the case of var00002, the median is 31. This is slightly lower than the mean, in part because some considerably older members (especially respondents 5 and 10) inflate the mean slightly. The median can be employed in relation to both interval/ratio and ordinal variables.

- *Mode*. The **mode** is the value that occurs most frequently in a distribution. The mode for var00002 is 28. The mode can be employed in relation to all types of variable.

The procedure for generating the mean, median, and mode with SPSS is described in Chapter 16.

Measures of dispersion

The amount of variation in a sample can be just as interesting as providing estimates of the typical value of a distribution. For one thing, it becomes possible to draw contrasts between comparable distributions of values. For example, is there more or less variability in the amount of time spent on cardiovascular equipment as compared to weights machines?

The most obvious way of measuring dispersion is by the **range**. This is simply the difference between the maximum and the minimum value in a distribution of values associated with an interval/ratio variable. We find that the range for the two types of equipment is 64 minutes for the cardiovascular equipment and 48 minutes for the weights machines. This suggests that there is more variability in the amount of time spent on the former. However, like the mean, the range is influenced by outliers, such as respondent 60 in the case of var00010.

Another **measure of dispersion** is the **standard deviation**, which is essentially the average amount of variation around the mean. Although the calculation is somewhat more complicated than this, the standard deviation is calculated by taking the difference between each value in a distribution and the mean and then dividing the total of the differences by the number of values. The standard deviation for var00010 is 9.9 minutes and for var00011 it is 8 minutes. Thus, not only is the average amount of time spent on the cardiovascular equipment

the age bands. However, note that, with the histogram, there is no space between the bars, whereas there is a space between the bars of a bar chart. Histograms are produced for interval/ratio variables, whereas bar charts are produced for nominal and ordinal variables. The procedure for generating a histogram with SPSS is described in Chapter 16.

Measures of central tendency

Measures of central tendency encapsulate in one figure a value that is typical for a **distribution of values**. In effect, we are seeking out an average for a distribution, but, in quantitative data analysis, three different forms of average are recognized.

- *Arithmetic mean*. This is the average as we understand it in everyday use—that is, we sum all the values in a distribution and then divide by the number of values. Thus, the arithmetic mean (or more simply the *mean*) for var00002 is 33.6, meaning that the average age of gym visitors is nearly 34 years of age. The mean should be employed only in relation to interval/ratio variables, though it is not uncommon to see it being used for ordinal variables as well.

- *Median*. The **median** is the mid-point in a distribution of values. Whereas the mean is vulnerable to **outliers** (extreme values at either end of the distribution), which will exert considerable upwards or downwards

Figure 15.5

A boxplot for the number of minutes spent on the last visit to the gym

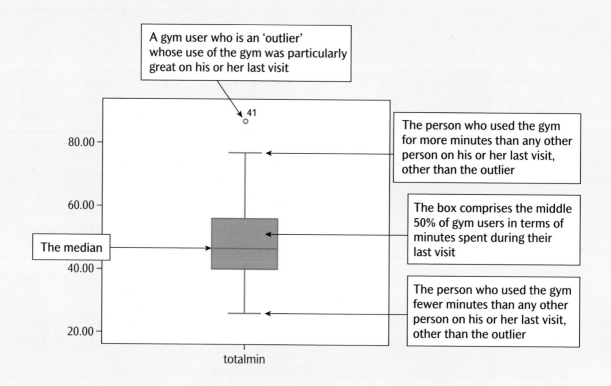

A gym user who is an 'outlier' whose use of the gym was particularly great on his or her last visit

The person who used the gym for more minutes than any other person on his or her last visit, other than the outlier

The box comprises the middle 50% of gym users in terms of minutes spent during their last visit

The median

The person who used the gym fewer minutes than any other person on his or her last visit, other than the outlier

higher than for the weights equipment; the standard deviation is greater too. The standard deviation is also affected by outliers, but, unlike the range, their impact is offset by dividing by the number of values in the distribution. The procedure for generating the standard deviation with SPSS is described in Chapter 16.

A type of figure that has become popular for displaying interval/ratio variables is the *boxplot* (see Figure 15.5). This form of display provides an indication of both central tendency (the median) and dispersion (the range). It also indicates whether there are any outliers. Figure 15.5 displays a boxplot for the total number of minutes users spent during their last gym visit. There is an outlier—case number 41, who spent a total of 87 minutes in the gym. The box represents the middle 50 per cent of users. The upper line of the box indicates the greatest use of the gym

within the 50 per cent and the lower line of the box represents the least use of the gym within the 50 per cent. The line going across the box indicates the median. The line going upwards from the box goes up to the person whose use of the gym was greater than any other user, other than case number 41. The line going downwards from the box goes down to the person whose use of the gym was lower than that of any other user. Boxplots are useful because they display both central tendency and dispersion. They vary in their shape depending on whether cases tend to be high or low in relation to the median. With Figure 15.5, the box and the median are closer to the bottom end of the distribution, suggesting less variation among gym users below the median. There is more variation above the median. The procedure for generating the boxplot with SPSS is described in Chapter 16.

Bivariate analysis

Bivariate analysis is concerned with the analysis of two variables at a time in order to uncover whether or not the two variables are related. Exploring relationships between variables means searching for evidence that the variation in one variable coincides with variation in another variable. A variety of techniques is available for examining relationships, but their use depends on the nature of the two variables being analysed. Figure 15.6 attempts to portray the main types of bivariate analysis according to the types of variable involved.

Relationships not causality

An important point to bear in mind about all of the methods for analysing relationships between variables is that it is precisely **relationships** that they uncover. As was noted in Chapter 3 in relation to cross-sectional designs, this means that you cannot infer that one variable causes another. Indeed, there are cases when what appears to be a causal influence working in one direction actually works in the other way. An interesting example of this problem

of causal direction will be presented later in the book in Chapter 27. The example shows that Sutton and Rafaeli (1988) expected to find a causal relationship between the display of positive emotions (for example, smiling or friendliness) on the part of checkout staff in retail outlets and sales in those outlets. In other words, the display of positive emotions was deemed to have a causal influence on levels of retail sales. In fact, the relationship was found to be the other way round: levels of retail sales exerted a causal influence on the display of emotions (see Research in focus 27.9 for more detailed explanation of this study).

Sometimes, we may feel confident that we can infer a causal direction when a relationship between two variables is discerned—for example, if we find that age and voting behaviour are related. It is impossible for the way people vote to influence their age, so, if we do find the two variables to be related, we can infer with complete confidence that age is the independent variable. It is not uncommon for researchers, when analysing their data, to draw inferences about causal direction based on their assumptions about the likely

Figure 15.6

Methods of bivariate analysis

	Nominal	Ordinal	Interval/ratio	Dichotomous
Nominal	Contingency table + chi-square (χ^2) + Cramér's V	Contingency table + chi-square (χ^2) + Cramér's V	Contingency table + chi-square (χ^2) + Cramér's V If the interval/ratio variable can be identified as the dependent variable, compare means + eta	Contingency table + chi-square (χ^2) + Cramér's V
Ordinal	Contingency table + chi-square (χ^2) + Cramér's V	Spearman's rho (ρ)	Spearman's rho (ρ)	Spearman's rho (ρ)
Interval/ratio	Contingency table + chi-square (χ^2) + Cramér's V If the interval/ratio variable can be identified as the dependent variable, compare means + eta	Spearman's rho (ρ)	Pearson's r	Spearman's rho (ρ)
Dichotomous	Contingency table + chi-square (χ^2) + Cramér's V	Spearman's rho (ρ)	Spearman's rho (ρ)	phi (ϕ)

Table 15.4

Contingency table showing the relationship between gender and reasons for visiting the gym

Reasons	Gender			
	Male		Female	
	No.	%	No.	%
Relaxation	3	7	6	13
Fitness	15	36	16	33
Lose weight	8	19	25	52
Build strength	16	38	1	2
TOTAL	42		48	

Note: $\chi^2 = 22.726$ $p < 0.0001$.

causal direction among related variables, as Sutton and Rafaeli (1988) did in their study. Although such inferences may be based on sound reasoning, they can only be inferences, and there is the possibility that the real pattern of causal direction is the opposite of that which is anticipated.

Contingency tables

Contingency tables are probably the most flexible of all methods of analysing relationships in that they can be employed in relation to any pair of variables, though they are not the most efficient method for some pairs, which is the reason why the method is not recommended in all the cells in Figure 15.6. A contingency table is like a frequency table but it allows two variables to be simultaneously analysed so that relationships between the two variables can be examined. It is normal for contingency tables to include percentages, since these make the tables easier to interpret. Table 15.4 examines the relationship between two variables from the gym survey: gender and reasons for visiting the gym. The percentages are *column percentages*—that is, they calculate the number in each **cell** as a percentage of the total number in that column. Thus, to take the top left-hand cell, the three men who go to the gym for relaxation are 7 per cent of all 42 men in the sample. Users of contingency tables often present the presumed independent variable (if one can in fact be presumed) as the column variable and the presumed dependent variable as the row variable. In this case, we are presuming that gender influences reasons for going to the gym. In fact, we know that going to the gym cannot influence gender. In such circumstances, it is column rather than row percentages that will be required. The

procedure for generating a contingency table with SPSS is described in Chapter 16.

Contingency tables are generated so that patterns of association can be searched for. In this case, we can see clear gender differences in reasons for visiting the gym. As our student anticipated, females are much more likely than men to go to the gym to lose weight. They are also somewhat more likely to go to the gym for relaxation. By contrast, men are much more likely to go to the gym to build strength. There is little difference between the two genders in terms of fitness as a reason.

Pearson's *r*

Pearson's *r* is a method for examining relationships between interval/ratio variables. The chief features of this method are as follows:

- the coefficient will almost certainly lie between 0 (zero or no relationship between the two variables) and 1 (a perfect relationship)—this indicates the *strength* of a relationship;

- the closer the coefficient is to 1, the stronger the relationship; the closer it is to 0, the weaker the relationship;

- the coefficient will be either positive or negative—this indicates the *direction* of a relationship.

To illustrate these features consider Tips and skills 'Imaginary data from five variables to show different types of relationship', which gives imaginary data for five variables, and the scatter diagrams in Figures 15.7–15.10, which look at the relationship between pairs of interval/ratio variables. The scatter diagram for variables 1 and 2 is presented in Figure 15.7 and shows a perfect **positive relationship**, which would have a Pearson's *r* correlation of 1. This means that, as one variable increases, the other variable increases by the same amount and that no other variable is related to either of them. If the correlation was below 1, it would mean that variable 1 is related to at least one other variable as well as to variable 2.

The scatter diagram for variables 2 and 3 (see Figure 15.8) shows a perfect **negative relationship**, which would have a Pearson's *r* correlation of –1. This means that, as one variable increases, the other variable decreases and that no other variable is related to either of them.

If there was no or virtually no correlation between the variables, there would be no apparent pattern to the markers in the scatter diagram. This is the case with the relationship between variables 2 and 5. The correlation is virtually zero at – 0.041. This means that the variation

Figure 15.7

Scatter diagram showing a perfect positive relationship

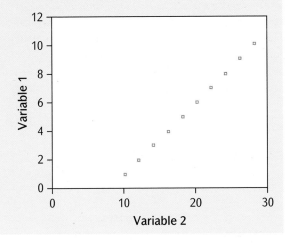

Figure 15.8

Scatter diagram showing a perfect negative relationship

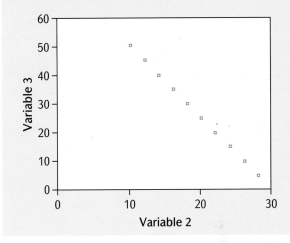

in each variable is associated with other variables than the ones present in this analysis. Figure 15.9 shows the appropriate scatter diagram.

If a relationship is strong, a clear patterning to the variables will be evident. This is the case with variables 2 and 4, whose scatter diagram appears in Figure 15.10. There is clearly a positive relationship, and in fact the Pearson's r value is + 0.88 (usually, positive correlations

are presented without the + sign). This means that the variation in the two variables is very closely connected, but that there is some influence of other variables in the extent to which they vary.

Going back to the gym survey, we find that the correlation between age (var00002) and the amount of time spent on weights equipment (var00011) is – 0.27, implying a weak negative relationship. This suggests that there

Tips and skills
Imaginary data from five variables to show different types of relationship

| Variables | | | | |
1	2	3	4	5
1	10	50	7	9
2	12	45	13	23
3	14	40	18	7
4	16	35	14	15
5	18	30	16	6
6	20	25	23	22
7	22	20	19	12
8	24	15	24	8
9	26	10	22	18
10	28	5	24	10

Figure 15.9

Scatter diagram showing two variables that are not related

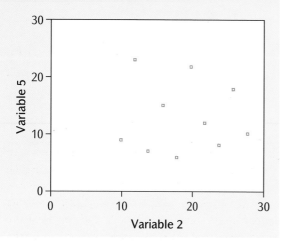

Figure 15.10

Scatter diagram showing a strong positive relationship

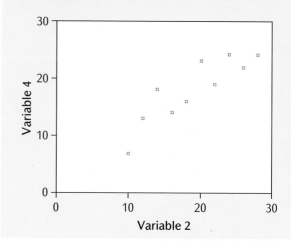

is a tendency such that, the older a person is, the less likely he or she is to spend much time on such equipment, but that other variables clearly influence the amount of time spent on this activity.

In order to be able to use Pearson's *r*, the relationship between the two variables must be broadly *linear*—that is, when plotted on a scatter diagram, the values of the two variables approximate to a straight line (even though they may be scattered, as in Figure 15.10) and do not curve. Therefore, plotting a scatter diagram before using Pearson's *r* is important, in order to determine that the nature of the relationship between a pair of variables does not violate the assumptions being made when this method of correlation is employed.

If you square a value of Pearson's *r*, you can derive a further useful statistic—namely the *coefficient of determination*, which expresses how much of the variation in one variable is due to the other variable. Thus, if *r* is −0.27, r^2 is 0.0729. We can then express this as a percentage by multiplying r^2 by 100. The product of this exercise is 7 per cent. This means that just 7 per cent of the variation in the use of cardiovascular equipment is accounted for by age. The coefficient of determination is a useful adjunct to the interpretation of correlation information.

The procedures for generating Pearson's *r* and scatter diagrams with SPSS are described in Chapter 16.

Spearman's rho

Spearman's rho, which is often represented with the Greek letter ρ, is designed for the use of pairs of ordinal

variables, but is also used, as suggested by Figure 15.6, when one variable is ordinal and the other is interval/ratio. It is exactly the same as Pearson's *r* in terms of the outcome of calculating it, in that the computed value of rho will be either positive or negative and will vary between 0 and 1. If we look at the gym study, there are three ordinal variables: var00004, var00005, and var00006 (see Table 15.1). If we use Spearman's rho to calculate the correlation between the first two variables, we find that the correlation between var00004 and var00005—frequency of use of the cardiovascular and weights equipment—is low at 0.2. A slightly stronger relationship is found between var00006 (frequency of going to the gym) and var00010 (amount of time spent on the cardiovascular equipment), which is 0.4. Note that the latter variable is an interval/ratio variable. When confronted with a situation in which we want to calculate the correlation between an ordinal and an interval/ratio variable, we cannot use Pearson's *r*, because both variables must be at the interval/ratio level of measurement. Instead, we must use Spearman's rho (see Figure 15.6). The procedure for generating Spearman's rho with SPSS is described in Chapter 16.

Phi and Cramér's *V*

Phi (φ) and **Cramér's** *V* are two closely related statistics. The phi coefficient is used for the analysis of the relationship between two dichotomous variables. Like Pearson's *r*, it results in a computed statistic that varies between 0 and +1 or −1. The correlation between var00001 (gender) and var00008 (other sources of regular exercise) is 0.24,

Table 15.5

Comparing subgroup means: time spent on cardiovascular equipment by reasons for going to the gym					
Time	Reasons				
	Relaxation	Fitness	Lose weight	Build strength	Total
Mean number of minutes spent on cardiovascular equipment	18.33	30.55	28.36	19.65	26.47
n	9	31	33	17	90

implying that males are somewhat more likely than females to have other sources of regular exercise, though the relationship is weak.

Cramér's *V* uses a similar formula to phi and can be employed with nominal variables (see Figure 15.6). However, this statistic can take on only a positive value, so that it can give an indication only of the strength of the relationship between two variables, not of the direction. The value of Cramér's *V* associated with the analysis presented in Table 15.4 is 0.50. This suggests a moderate relationship between the two variables. Cramér's *V* is usually reported along with a contingency table and a **chi-square test** (see section on 'The chi-square test' below. It is not normally presented on its own. The procedure for generating phi and Cramér's *V* with SPSS is described in Chapter 16.

Comparing means and eta

If you need to examine the relationship between an interval/ratio variable and a nominal variable, and if the latter can be relatively unambiguously identified as the independent variable, a potentially fruitful approach is to compare the means of the interval/ratio variable for each subgroup of the nominal variable.

As an example, consider Table 15.5, which presents the mean number of minutes spent on cardiovascular equipment (var00010) for each of the four categories of reasons for going to the gym (var00003). The means suggest that people who go to the gym for fitness or to lose weight spend considerably more time on this equipment than people who go to the gym to relax or to build strength.

This procedure is often accompanied by a test of association between variables called **eta** (η). This statistic expresses the level of association between the two variables and, like Cramér's *V*, will always be positive. The level of eta for the data in Table 15.5 is 0.48. This suggests a moderate relationship between the two variables. Eta-squared expresses the amount of variation in the interval/ratio variable that is due to the nominal variable. In the case of this example, eta-squared is 22 per cent. Eta is a very flexible method for exploring the relationship between two variables, because it can be employed when one variable is nominal and the other interval/ratio. Also, it does not make the assumption that the relationship between variables is linear. The procedure for comparing means and for generating eta with SPSS is described in Chapter 16.

Multivariate analysis

Multivariate analysis entails the simultaneous analysis of three or more variables. This is quite an advanced topic, and it is recommended that readers examine a textbook on quantitative data analysis for an exposition of techniques (e.g. Bryman and Cramer 2011). There are three main contexts within which multivariate analysis might be employed.

Could the relationship be spurious?

In order for a relationship between two variables to be established, not only must there be evidence that there is a relationship but the relationship must be shown to be *non-spurious*. A **spurious relationship** exists when there appears to be a relationship between two variables, but the relationship is not real: it is being produced because each variable is itself related to a third variable. For example, if we find a relationship in a firm between employees' levels of organizational commitment and job satisfaction, we might ask: could the relationship be an artefact of the leadership style of respondents' immediate managers (see Figure 15.11)? The more committed people are to their organization, the more job satisfaction they are likely to exhibit. However, whether leaders are considerate to their subordinates or not is likely to influence both organizational commitment *and* job satisfaction. If leadership style were found to be producing the apparent relationship between organizational commitment and job satisfaction, we would conclude that the relationship is spurious. In this case, the variable of leadership style would be known as a **confounding variable**.

An interesting possible case of a spurious relationship was highlighted in a very short report in *The Times* (1 October 1999, p. 2) of some medical findings. The article noted that there is evidence to suggest that women on hormone replacement therapy (HRT) have lower levels of heart disease than those not on this form of therapy. The article cites Swedish findings that suggest that the relationship may be due to the fact that women who choose to start the therapy are 'thinner, richer and healthier' than those who do not. These background factors would seem to affect both the likelihood of taking HRT *and* the likelihood of getting heart disease. A further illustration in connection with a health-related issue comes from another *Times* article (Hawkes 2003), which reports a relationship among men between frequency of shaving and likelihood of a heart attack or stroke. The reason appears to be that each of the variables (frequency of shaving and vulnerability to a heart attack or stroke) is affected by lifestyle and hormonal factors.

Could there be an intervening variable?

Let us say that we do not find that the relationship is spurious; we might ask *why* there is a relationship between two variables. For example, there have been several studies that have explored the relationship between an organization's market orientation and its business performance. However, the mixed nature of the findings to have emerged from these studies led Piercy, Harris, and Lane (2002) to suggest that there is a more complex relationship between these two variables than previous studies have assumed. In particular, they speculated that higher levels of market orientation are associated with higher levels of employee motivation, satisfaction, and commitment, which in turn leads to enhanced organizational performance. Employee attitudes are thus an **intervening variable**:

$$\begin{array}{ccccc} \text{market} & \rightarrow & \text{employee} & \rightarrow & \text{organizational} \\ \text{orientation} & & \text{attitudes} & & \text{performance} \end{array}$$

An intervening variable allows us to answer questions about the bivariate relationship between variables. It suggests that the relationship between the two variables is not a direct one, since the impact of market orientation on organizational performance is viewed as occurring via employee attitudes.

Figure 15.11

A spurious relationship

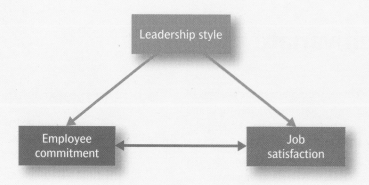

Table 15.6

Contingency table showing the relationship between age and whether or not gym visitors have other sources of regular exercise (%)			
Other source of exercise	Age		
	30 and under	31–40	41 and over
Other source	64	43	58
No other source	36	57	42
n	42	23	24

Could a third variable moderate the relationship?

We might ask a question like: does the relationship between two variables hold for men but not for women? If it does, the relationship is said to be moderated by gender. We might ask in the gym study, for example, if the relationship between

age and whether visitors have other sources of regular exercise (var00008) is moderated by gender. This would imply that, if we find a pattern relating age to other sources of exercise, that pattern will vary by gender. Table 15.6 shows the relationship between age and other sources of exercise. In this table, age has been broken down into just three age bands to make the table easier to read. The table suggests that the 31–40 age group is less likely to have other sources of regular exercise than the 30 and under and 41 and over age groups. However, Table 15.7, which breaks the relationship down by gender, suggests that the pattern for males and females is somewhat different. Among males, the pattern shown in Table 15.6 is very pronounced, but for females the likelihood of having other sources of exercise declines with gender. It would seem that the relationship between age and other sources of exercise is a **moderated relationship** because it is moderated by gender. This example illustrates the way in which contingency tables can be employed for multivariate analysis. However, there is a wide variety of other techniques (Bryman and Cramer 2011: Chapter 10). The procedure for conducting such an analysis with SPSS is described in Chapter 16.

Statistical significance

One difficulty with working on data deriving from a sample is that there is often the lingering worry that, even though you have employed a probability sampling procedure (as in the gym survey), your findings will not be generalizable to the population from which the sample was drawn. As we saw in Chapter 8, there is always

the possibility that **sampling error** (difference between the population and the sample that you have selected) has occurred, even when probability sampling procedures have been followed. If this happens, the sample will be unrepresentative of the wider population and therefore any findings will be invalid. To make matters

Table 15.7

Contingency table showing the relationship between age and whether or not gym visitors have other sources of regular exercise for males and females (%)						
Other source of exercise	Gender					
	Male			Female		
	30 and under	31–40	41 and over	30 and under	31–40	41 and over
Other source	70	33	75	59	50	42
No other source	30	67	25	41	50	58
n	20	9	12	22	14	12

worse, there is no feasible way of finding out whether or not they do in fact apply to the population! What you can do is provide an indication of how confident you can be in your findings. This is where **statistical significance** and the various tests of statistical significance come in.

We need to know how confident we can be that our findings can be generalized to the population from which that sample was selected. Since we cannot be absolutely certain that a finding based on a sample will also be found in the population, we need a technique that allows us to establish how confident we can be that the finding exists in the population and what risk we are taking in inferring that the finding exists in the population. These two elements—confidence and risk—lie at the heart of tests of statistical significance (see Key concept 15.1). However, it is important to appreciate that tests of statistical significance can be employed only in relation to samples that have been drawn using probability sampling. The process of inferring findings from a probability sample to the population from which it was selected is known as statistical inference.

In Chapter 8 (see Tips and skills 'Generalizing from a random sample to the population'), in the context of the discussion of the standard error of the mean, we began to get an appreciation of the ideas behind statistical significance. For example, we know that the mean age of the gym sample is 33.6. Using the concept of the standard error of the mean, we can calculate that we can be 95 per cent confident that the population mean lies between 31.72 and 35.47. This suggests that we can determine in broad outline the degree of confidence that we can have in a sample mean.

In the rest of this section, we will look at the tests that are available for determining the degree of confidence we can have in our findings when we explore relationships between variables. All of the tests have a common structure.

- *Set up a null hypothesis*. A **null hypothesis** stipulates that two variables are not related in the population—for example, that there is *no* relationship between gender and visiting the gym in the population from which the sample was selected.

- *Establish the level of statistical significance that you find acceptable*. This is essentially a measure of the degree of risk that you might reject the null hypothesis (implying that there *is* a relationship in the population) when you should support it (implying that there is no relationship in the population). Levels of statistical significance are expressed as probability levels—that is, the probability of rejecting the null hypothesis when you should be confirming it. See Key concept 15.2 on this issue. The convention among most business researchers is that the maximum level of statistical significance that is acceptable is $p < 0.05$, which implies that there are fewer than 5 chances in 100 that you could have a sample that shows a relationship when there is not one in the population.

- *Determine the statistical significance of your findings* (that is, use a statistical test such as chi-square—see section on 'The chi-square test' below).

- If your findings are statistically significant at the 0.05 level—so that the risk of getting a relationship as strong as the one you have found when there is *no* relationship in the population is no higher than 5 in 100—you would *reject* the null hypothesis. Therefore, you are implying that the results are unlikely to have occurred by *chance*.

Key concept 15.1
What is a test of statistical significance?

A test of statistical significance allows the analyst to estimate how confident he or she can be that the results deriving from a study based on a randomly selected sample are generalizable to the population from which the sample was drawn. When examining statistical significance in relation to the relationship between two variables, it also tells us about the risk of concluding that there is in fact a relationship in the population when there is no such relationship in the population. If an analysis reveals a statistically significant finding, this does not mean that the finding is intrinsically significant or important. The word 'significant' seems to imply importance. However, statistical significance is solely concerned with the confidence researchers can have in their findings. It does not mean that a statistically significant finding is substantively significant.

Key concept 15.2
What is the level of statistical significance?

The level of statistical significance is the level of risk that you are prepared to take that you are inferring that there is a relationship between two variables in the population from which the sample was taken when in fact no such relationship exists. The maximum level of risk that is conventionally taken in business research is to say that there are up to 5 chances in 100 that we might be falsely concluding that there is a relationship when there is not one in the population from which the sample was taken. This means that, if we drew 100 samples, we are recognizing that as many as 5 of them might exhibit a relationship when there is not one in the population. Our sample might be one of those 5, but the risk is fairly small. This significance level is denoted by $p < 0.05$ (p means *probability*). If we accepted a significance level of $p < 0.1$, we would be accepting the possibility that as many as 10 in 100 samples might show a relationship where none exists in the population. In this case, there is a greater risk than with $p < 0.05$ that we might have a sample that implies a relationship when there is not one in the population, since the probability of our having such a sample is greater when the risk is 1 in 10 (10 out of 100 when $p < 0.1$) than when the risk is 1 in 20 (5 out of 100 when $p < 0.05$). Therefore, we would have greater confidence when the risk of falsely inferring that there is a relationship between 2 variables is 1 in 20, as against 1 in 10. But, if you want a more stringent test, perhaps because you are worried about the use that might be made of your results, you might choose the $p < 0.01$ level. This means that you are prepared to accept as your level of risk a probability of only 1 in 100 that the results could have arisen by chance (that is, due to sampling error). Therefore, if the results, following administration of a test, show that a relationship is statistically significant at the $p < 0.05$ level, but *not* the $p < 0.01$ level, you would have to confirm the null hypothesis.

There are in fact two types of error that can be made when inferring statistical significance. These errors are known as Type I and Type II errors (see Figure 15.12). A Type I error occurs when you reject the null hypothesis when it should in fact be confirmed. This means that your results have arisen by chance and you are falsely concluding that there is a relationship in the population when there is not one. Using a $p < 0.05$ level of significance means that we are more likely to make a Type I error than when using a $p < 0.01$ level of significance.

Figure 15.12

Type I and Type II errors

	Error	
	Type I (risk of rejecting the null hypothesis when it should be confirmed)	**Type II** (risk of confirming the null hypothesis when it should be rejected)
0.05	Greater risk	Lower risk
0.01	Lower risk	Greater risk

p level

This is because with 0.01 there is less chance of falsely rejecting the null hypothesis. However, in doing so, you increase the chance of making a Type II error (accepting the null hypothesis when you should reject it). This is because you are more likely to confirm the null hypothesis when the significance level is 0.01 (1 in 100) than when it is 0.05 (1 in 20).

The chi-square test

The chi-square (χ^2) test is applied to contingency tables like Table 15.4. It allows us to establish how confident we can be that there is a relationship between the two variables in the population. The test works by calculating for each cell in the table an expected frequency or value—that is, one that would occur on the basis of chance alone. The chi-square value, which in Table 15.4 is 22.726, is produced by calculating the differences between the actual and expected values for each cell in the table and then summing those differences (it is slightly more complicated than this, but the details need not concern us here). The chi-square value means nothing on its own and can be meaningfully interpreted only in relation to its associated level of statistical significance, which in this case is $p < 0.0001$. This means that there is only 1 chance in 10,000 of falsely rejecting the null hypothesis (that is, inferring that there is a relationship in the population when there is no such relationship in the population). You could be extremely confident that there is a relationship between gender and reasons for visiting the gym among all gym members, since the chance that you have obtained a sample that shows a relationship when there is no relationship among all gym members is 1 in 10,000.

Whether or not a chi-square value achieves statistical significance depends not just on its magnitude but also on the number of categories of the two variables being analysed. This latter issue is governed by what is known as the 'degrees of freedom' associated with the table. The number of degrees of freedom is governed by the simple formula:

Number of degrees of freedom
= (number of columns −1) (number of rows −1).

In the case of Table 15.4, this will be $(2-1)(4-1)$—that is, 3. In other words, the chi-square value that is arrived at is affected by the size of the table, and this is taken into account when deciding whether the chi-square value is statistically significant or not. The procedure for generating chi-square in conjunction with a contingency table with SPSS is described in Chapter 16.

Correlation and statistical significance

Examining the statistical significance of a computed correlation coefficient, which is based on a randomly selected sample, provides information about the likelihood that the coefficient will be found in the population from which the sample was taken. Thus, if we find a correlation of −0.62, what is the likelihood that a relationship of at least that size exists in the population? This tells us if the relationship could have arisen by chance.

If the correlation coefficient r is −0.62 and the significance level is $p < 0.05$, we can reject the null hypothesis that there is no relationship in the population. We can infer that there are only 5 chances in 100 that a correlation of at least −0.62 could have arisen by chance alone. You *could* have 1 of the 5 samples in 100 that shows a relationship when there is not one in the population, but the degree of risk is reasonably small. If, say, it was found that $r = -0.62$ and $p < 0.1$, there could be as many as 10 chances in 100 that there is no correlation in the population. This would *not* be an acceptable level of risk for most purposes. It would mean that in as many as 1 sample in 10 we might find a correlation of −0.62 or above when there is not a correlation in the population. If $r = -0.62$ and $p < 0.001$, there is only 1 chance in 1000 that no correlation exists in the population. There would be a very low level of risk if you inferred that the correlation had not arisen by chance.

Whether a correlation coefficient is statistically significant or not will be affected by two factors:

1. the size of the computed coefficient; and

2. the size of the sample.

This second factor may appear surprising. Basically, the larger a sample, the more likely it is that a computed correlation coefficient will be found to be statistically significant. Thus, even though the correlation between age and the amount of time spent on weights machines in the gym survey was found to be just −0.27, which is a fairly weak relationship, it is statistically significant at the $p < 0.01$ level. This means that there is only 1 chance in 100 that there is no relationship in the population. Because the question of whether or not a correlation coefficient is statistically significant depends so much on the sample size, it is important to realize that you should always examine *both* the correlation coefficient *and* the significance level. You should not examine one at the expense of the other.

This treatment of correlation and statistical significance applies to both Pearson's r and Spearman's rho.

A similar interpretation can also be applied to phi and Cramér's *V*. SPSS automatically produces information regarding statistical significance when Pearson's *r*, Spearman's rho, phi, and Cramér's *V* are generated.

Comparing means and statistical significance

A test of statistical significance can also be applied to the comparison of means that was carried out in Table 15.5. This procedure entails treating the total amount of variation in the dependent variable—amount of time spent on cardiovascular equipment—as made up of two types: variation *within* the four subgroups that make up the independent variable, and variation *between* them. The latter is often called the *explained variance* and the former the *error variance*. A test of statistical significance for the comparison of means entails relating the two types of variance to form what is known as the *F* statistic. This statistic expresses the amount of explained variance in relation to the amount of error variance. In the case of the data in Table 15.5, the resulting *F* statistic is statistically significant at the $p < 0.001$ level. This finding suggests that there is only 1 chance in 1000 that there is no relationship between the two variables among all gym members. SPSS produces information regarding the *F* statistic and its statistical significance if the procedures described in Chapter 16 are followed.

Checklist

Doing and writing up quantitative data analysis

○ Have you answered your research questions?

○ Have you made sure that you have presented only analyses that are relevant to your research questions?

○ Have you made sure that you have taken into account the nature of the variable(s) being analysed when using a particular technique (that is, whether nominal, ordinal, interval/ratio, or dichotomous)?

○ Have you used the most appropriate and powerful techniques for answering your research questions?

○ If your sample has *not* been randomly selected, have you made sure that you have not made inferences about a population (or at least, if you have done so, have you outlined the limitations of making such an inference)?

○ If your data are based on a cross-sectional design, have you resisted making unsustainable inferences about causality?

○ Have you remembered to code any missing data?

○ Have you commented on all the analyses you present?

○ Have you gone beyond univariate analysis and conducted at least some bivariate analyses?

○ If you have used a Likert scale with reversed items, have you remembered to reverse the coding of them?

Key points

- You need to think about your data analysis before you begin designing your research instruments.

- Techniques of data analysis are applicable to some types of variable and not others. You need to know the difference between nominal, ordinal, interval/ratio, and dichotomous variables.

- You need to think about the kinds of data you are collecting and the implications your decisions will have for the sorts of techniques you will be able to employ.

- Become familiar with computer software such as SPSS before you begin designing your research instruments, because it is advisable to be aware at an early stage of difficulties you might have in presenting your data in SPSS.

- Make sure you are thoroughly familiar with the techniques introduced in this chapter and when you can and cannot use them.

- The basic message, then, is not to leave these considerations until your data have been collected, tempting though it may be.

- Do not confuse statistical significance with substantive significance.

Questions for review

- At what stage should you begin to think about the kinds of data analysis you need to conduct?

- What are missing data and why do they arise?

Types of variable

- What are the differences between the four types of variable outlined in this chapter: interval/ratio; ordinal; nominal; and dichotomous?

- Why is it important to be able to distinguish between the four types of variable?

- Imagine the kinds of answers you would receive if you administered the following four questions in an interview survey. What kind of variable would each question generate: dichotomous; nominal; ordinal; or interval/ratio?

    1. Do you enjoy going shopping?

        Yes ____

        No ____

    2. How many times have you shopped in the last month? Please write in the number of occasions below.

        ____

    3. For which kinds of items do you most enjoy shopping? Please tick one only.

        Clothes (including shoes) ____

        Food ____

        Things for the house ____

        Presents ____

        Entertainment (CDs, videos, etc.) ____

4. How important is it to you to buy clothes with designer labels?

Very important   ____

Fairly important   ____

Not very important   ____

Not at all important   ____

Univariate analysis

● What is an outlier and why might one have an adverse effect on the mean and the range?

● In conjunction with which measure of central tendency would you expect to report the standard deviation: the mean; the median; or the mode?

Bivariate analysis

● Can you infer causality from bivariate analysis?

● Why are percentages crucial when presenting contingency tables?

● In what circumstances would you use each of the following: Pearson's *r*; Spearman's rho; phi; Cramér's *V*; eta?

Multivariate analysis

● What is a spurious relationship?

● What is an intervening variable?

● What does it mean to say that a relationship is moderated?

Statistical significance

● What does statistical significance mean and how does it differ from substantive significance?

● What is a significance level?

● What does the chi-square test achieve?

● What does it mean to say that a correlation of 0.42 is statistically significant at $p < 0.05$?

....

Online Resource Centre
www.oxfordtextbooks.co.uk/orc/brymanbrm4e/

Visit the Interactive Research Guide that accompanies this book to complete an exercise in Quantitative Data Analysis.

....

16

Using IBM SPSS statistics

Chapter outline

In order to implement the techniques that you learned in Chapter 15, you would need to do either of two things: learn the underlying formula for each technique and apply your data to it, or use computer software to analyse your data. The latter is the approach chosen in this book for two main reasons.

- It is closer to the way in which quantitative data analysis is carried out in real research nowadays.
- It helps to equip you with a useful transferable skill.

You will be learning IBM SPSS Statistics, which is the most widely used package of computer software for doing this kind of analysis. It is relatively straightforward to use. We will be continuing to refer to the techniques introduced in Chapter 15 and will continue to use the gym survey as an example.

This chapter largely operates in parallel to Chapter 15, so that you can see the links between the techniques learned there and the use of SPSS to implement them.

Introduction

This chapter aims to provide a familiarity with some basic aspects of SPSS for Windows, which is possibly the most widely used computer software for the analysis of quantitative data for social scientists. SPSS, which originally was short for Statistical Package for the Social Sciences, has been in existence since the mid-1960s and over the years has undergone many revisions, particularly since the arrival of personal computers. It is now known as IBM SPSS Statistics and the version that was used in preparing this chapter was Release 22. The gym survey used in Chapter 15 will be employed to illustrate SPSS operations and methods of analysis. The aim of this chapter is to introduce ways of using SPSS to implement the methods of analysis discussed in Chapter 15.

SPSS operations will be presented in **bold**, for example, **Variable Name:** and **Analyze**. Names given to variables in the course of using SPSS will be presented in ***bold italics***, e.g. ***gender*** and ***reasons***. Labels given to values or to variables are also in bold but in a different font, e.g. **reasons for visiting** and **male**. Tips and skills 'Basic operations in SPSS' presents a list summarizing these. One further element in the presentation is that a right-pointing arrow (→) will be used to denote 'click once with the left-hand button of your mouse'. This action is employed to make selections and for similar activities.

Tips and skills
Basic operations in SPSS

- The **SPSS Data Editor**. This is the sphere of SPSS into which data are entered and subsequently edited and defined. It is made up of two screens: the **Data Viewer** and the **Variable Viewer**. You move between these two viewers by selecting the appropriate tab at the bottom of the screen.
- The **Data Viewer**. This is the spreadsheet into which your data are entered. When you start up SPSS, the **Data Viewer** will be facing you.
- The **Variable Viewer**. This is another spreadsheet, but this one displays information about each of the variables and allows you to change that information. It is the platform from which you provide for each variable such information as: the variable name; a variable label; and value labels (see below).

- The **Output Viewer**. When you perform an analysis or produce a diagram (called a 'chart' in SPSS), your output will be deposited here. The **Output Viewer** superimposes itself over the **Data Editor** after an analysis has been performed or a chart generated.

- A **Variable Name**. This is the name that you give to a variable, e.g. *gender*. The name must be no more than eight characters. Until you give a variable a name, it will be referred to as *var00001*, etc. When the variable has been given a name, it will appear in the column for that variable in the Data View window. It is generated from the **Variable Viewer**.

- A **Variable Label**. This is a label that you can give to a variable but which is not restricted to eight characters. Spaces can be used, e.g. **reasons for visiting**. The Label will appear in any output you generate. It is generated from the **Variable Viewer**.

- A **Value Label**. This is a label that you can attach to a code that has been used when entering data for all types of variables other than interval/ratio variables. Thus, for var00001, we would attach the label 'male' to 1 and 'female' to 2. When you generate output, such as a frequency table or chart, the labels for each value will be presented. This makes the interpretation of output easier. It is generated from the **Variable Viewer**.

- **Missing Values.** When you do not have data for a particular variable when entering data for a case, you must specify how you are denoting missing values for that variable. Missing values are generated from the **Variable Viewer**.

- **Recode**. A procedure that allows codes or numbers to be changed. It is especially helpful when you need to combine groups of people—for example, when producing age bands.

- **Compute**. A procedure that allows you to combine two or more variables to form a new variable.

- **Analyze**. This is the point on the menu bar above the **Data Editor** from which you choose (via a dropdown menu) which method of analysis you want to select. Note that, whenever an item on a menu appears with a right-pointing arrowhead after it, this means that, if you select that option, a further menu will follow on.

- **Graphs**. This is the point on the menu bar above the **Data Editor** from which you choose (via a drop-down menu) which chart you want to select.

- **Chart Editor**. When you produce a graph, you can edit it with the **Chart Editor**. To activate this editor, double-click anywhere in the graph. A small chart editor window will appear and your main graph will appear opaque until you exit the Editor. From the Editor, you can make various changes and enhancements to your graph.

Getting started in SPSS

Beginning SPSS

To start SPSS, double-click on the **PASW Statistics** icon on your computer screen. If there is no icon, → the Start button in the bottom left-hand corner of your screen. From the menu of programs, → **SPSS Inc**. A follow-on menu will appear, from which you should select **PASW Statistics 18**. When SPSS loads, you *may* be faced with an opening dialog box with the title 'What do you want to do?' and a list of options. Many users prefer to disable this opening box. It is not important in relation to the following exposition, so → **Cancel**. You will then be faced with the **SPSS Data Editor**. This is made up of two components: **Data View** and **Variable View**. In the following discussion, these two screens are referred to as the **Data Viewer** and the **Variable Viewer**. You move between these two viewers by selecting the appropriate tab at the bottom of the screen. The **Data Viewer** is in the form of a spreadsheet grid into which you enter your data. The columns represent *variables*—in other words, information about characteristics of each person in the gym study sample. Until data are entered and names are given to variables, each column simply has **var** as its heading. The rows represent *cases*, which can be people (as in the example you will be working through) or any unit of analysis. Each block in the grid is referred to as a 'cell'. Note also that when the data are in the SPSS spreadsheet, they will look different; for example, 1 will be 1.00.

Entering data in the Data Viewer

To input the data into the **Data Viewer**, make sure that the top left-hand cell in the grid is highlighted (see Plate 16.1). If it is not highlighted, simply click once in that cell. Then, type the appropriate figure for that cell—that is, 1. This number goes directly into that cell and into the box beneath the toolbar. As an alternative to using the mouse, many people find it easier to use the arrow keys on their keyboard to move from cell to cell. If you make a mistake at any point, simply click once in the cell in question, type in the correct value, and click once more in that cell. When you have finished, you should end up in the bottom right-hand cell of what will be a perfect rectangle of data.

Plate 16.2 shows the **Data Viewer** with the data from the gym survey entered (though only part of the set of data is visible, in that only the first thirty-three respondents are visible). The first row of data contains the coded answers from the completed questionnaire in Chapter 15 (see Tips and skills 'A completed and processed questionnaire' in Chapter 15).

In order to proceed further, you will find that SPSS works in the following typical sequence for defining variables and analysing your data.

1. You make a selection from the menu bar at the top of the screen, e.g. → **A**nalyze.

2. From the menu that will appear, make a selection, e.g. → **D**escriptive Statistics.

3. This will bring up a *dialog box* into which you will usually inform SPSS of what you are trying to do—e.g. which variables are to be analysed.

Plate 16.1

The SPSS Data Viewer

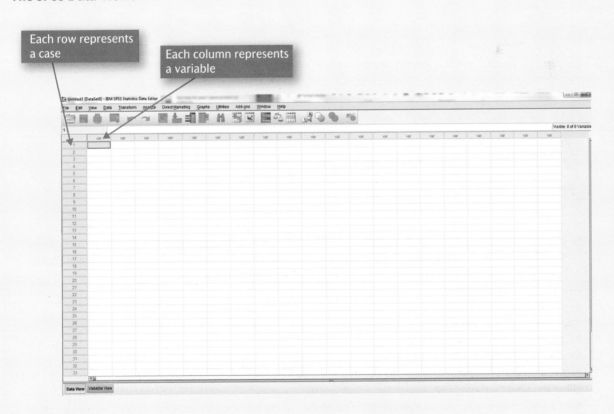

Each row represents a case

Each column represents a variable

Plate 16.2

The Data Viewer with 'gym study' data entered

This row shows the data for the first person who answered the Gym Survey questionnaire

	var00001	var00002	var00003	var00004	var00005	var00006	var00007	var00008	var00009	var00010	var00011	var00012	var	v
1	1.00	21.00	2.00	1.00	1.00	3.00	1.00	2.00	.00	33.00	17.00	5.00		
2	2.00	44.00	1.00	3.00	1.00	4.00	3.00	1.00	2.00	10.00	23.00	10.00		
3	2.00	19.00	3.00	1.00	2.00	2.00	1.00	1.00	1.00	27.00	18.00	12.00		
4	2.00	27.00	3.00	2.00	1.00	2.00	1.00	2.00	.00	30.00	17.00	3.00		
5	1.00	57.00	2.00	1.00	3.00	2.00	3.00	1.00	4.00	22.00	.00	15.00		
6	2.00	27.00	3.00	1.00	1.00	3.00	1.00	1.00	3.00	34.00	17.00	.00		
7	1.00	39.00	5.00	2.00	1.00	5.00	1.00	1.00	5.00	17.00	48.00	10.00		
8	2.00	36.00	3.00	1.00	2.00	2.00	2.00	1.00	1.00	25.00	18.00	7.00		
9	1.00	37.00	2.00	1.00	1.00	3.00	1.00	2.00	.00	34.00	15.00	.00		
10	2.00	51.00	2.00	2.00	2.00	4.00	3.00	2.00	.00	16.00	18.00	11.00		
11	1.00	24.00	5.00	2.00	1.00	3.00	1.00	1.00	1.00	.00	42.00	16.00		
12	2.00	29.00	2.00	1.00	2.00	3.00	1.00	2.00	.00	34.00	22.00	12.00		
13	1.00	20.00	5.00	1.00	1.00	2.00	1.00	2.00	.00	22.00	31.00	7.00		
14	2.00	22.00	2.00	1.00	3.00	4.00	2.00	1.00	3.00	37.00	14.00	12.00		
15	2.00	46.00	3.00	1.00	1.00	5.00	2.00	2.00	.00	26.00	9.00	4.00		
16	2.00	41.00	3.00	1.00	2.00	2.00	3.00	1.00	4.00	22.00	7.00	10.00		
17	1.00	25.00	5.00	1.00	1.00	3.00	1.00	1.00	1.00	21.00	29.00	4.00		
18	2.00	46.00	3.00	1.00	2.00	4.00	2.00	1.00	4.00	18.00	8.00	11.00		
19	1.00	30.00	3.00	1.00	1.00	5.00	1.00	2.00	.00	23.00	9.00	6.00		
20	1.00	25.00	5.00	2.00	1.00	3.00	1.00	1.00	1.00	23.00	19.00	.00		
21	2.00	24.00	2.00	1.00	1.00	3.00	2.00	1.00	2.00	20.00	7.00	6.00		
22	2.00	39.00	1.00	2.00	3.00	5.00	1.00	2.00	.00	17.00	.00	9.00		
23	1.00	44.00	3.00	1.00	1.00	3.00	2.00	1.00	2.00	22.00	8.00	5.00		
24	1.00	.00	1.00	2.00	2.00	4.00	2.00	1.00	4.00	15.00	10.00	4.00		
25	2.00	18.00	3.00	1.00	2.00	3.00	1.00	2.00	1.00	18.00	7.00	10.00		
26	1.00	41.00	3.00	1.00	1.00	3.00	1.00	2.00	.00	34.00	10.00	4.00		
27	2.00	38.00	2.00	1.00	2.00	5.00	3.00	1.00	2.00	24.00	14.00	10.00		
28	1.00	25.00	2.00	1.00	1.00	2.00	1.00	2.00	.00	48.00	22.00	7.00		
29	1.00	41.00	5.00	2.00	1.00	3.00	1.00	1.00	2.00	17.00	27.00	.00		
30	2.00	30.00	3.00	1.00	1.00	2.00	2.00	2.00	.00	32.00	13.00	10.00		
31	2.00	29.00	3.00	1.00	3.00	2.00	1.00	2.00	.00	31.00	.00	7.00		
32	2.00	42.00	1.00	2.00	2.00	4.00	2.00	1.00	4.00	17.00	14.00	6.00		
33	1.00	31.00	2.00	1.00	1.00	2.00	1.00	2.00	.00	49.00	21.00	2.00		

Data View Variable View

4. Very often, you then need to convey further information and to do this you have to → a button that will bring up what is called, following Bryman and Cramer (2011), a *sub-dialog box*.

5. You then provide the information in the sub-dialog box and then go back to the dialog box. Sometimes, you will need to bring up a further sub-dialog box and then go back to the dialog box.

When you have finished going through the entire procedure, → **OK**. The toolbar beneath the menu bar allows shortcut access to certain SPSS operations.

Defining variables: variable names, missing values, variable labels, and value labels

Once you have finished entering your data, you need to define your variables. The following steps will allow you to do this:

1. → the **Variable View** tab at the bottom of the **Data Viewer** (opens the **Variable Viewer** shown in Plate 16.3).

2. To provide a variable name, click on the current variable name (e.g. *var00003*) and type the name you

Plate 16.3

The Variable Viewer

> To create **Missing Values** for **var00003**, click here. A little button with 3 dots will appear.

File Edit View Data Transform Analyze Direct Marketing Graphs Utilities Add-ons Window Help

	Name	Type	Width	Decimals	Label	Values	Missing	Columns	Align	Measure	Role
1	var00001	Numeric	8	2		None	None	8	Right	Scale	Input
2	var00002	Numeric	8	2		None	None	8	Right	Scale	Input
3	var00003	Numeric	8	2		None	None	8	Right	Scale	Input
4	var00004	Numeric	8	2		None	None	8	Right	Scale	Input
5	var00005	Numeric	8	2		None	None	8	Right	Scale	Input
6	var00006	Numeric	8	2		None	None	8	Right	Scale	Input
7	var00007	Numeric	8	2		None	None	8	Right	Scale	Input
8	var00008	Numeric	8	2		None	None	8	Right	Scale	Input
9	var00009	Numeric	8	2		None	None	8	Right	Scale	Input
10	var00010	Numeric	8	2		None	None	8	Right	Scale	Input
11	var00011	Numeric	8	2		None	None	8	Right	Scale	Input
12	var00012	Numeric	8	2		None	None	8	Right	Scale	Input
13											

want to give it (e.g. *reasons*). Remember that this name must be no more than eight characters and you *cannot* use spaces.

3. You can then give your variable a more detailed name, known in SPSS as a variable label. To do this, → cell in the **Label** column relating to the variable for which you want to supply a variable label. Then, simply type in the variable label (i.e. **reasons for visiting**).

4. Then you will need to provide 'value labels' for variables that have been given codes. The procedure generally applies to variables that are not interval/ratio variables. The latter, which are numeric variables, do not need to be coded (unless you are grouping them in some way). To assign value labels, → in the **Values** column relating to the variable you are working on. A small button with three dots on it will appear. → the button. The **Value Labels** dialog box will appear (see Plate 16.4). → the box to the right of **Value** and begin to define the value labels. To do this, enter the value (e.g. **1**) in the area to the right of **Value** and then the value label (e.g. **relaxation**) in the area to the right of **Label**. Then → **Add**. Do this for each value. When you have finished → **OK**.

5. You will then need to inform SPSS of the value that you have nominated for each variable to indicate a missing value. In the case of *reasons*, the value is 0 (zero). To assign the missing value, → the cell for this variable in the **Missing** column. Again, → the button that will appear with three dots on it. This will generate the **Missing Values** dialog box (see Plate 16.5). In the **Missing Values** dialog box, enter the missing value (**0**) below <u>D</u>iscrete missing values: and then → **OK**.

In order to simplify the following presentation, *reasons* will be the only variable for which a variable label will be defined.

Recoding variables

Sometimes you need to recode variables—for example, when you want to group people. You would need to do this in order to produce a table like Table 15.3 for an interval/ratio variable like **var00002**, which we will give the variable name *age*. SPSS offers two choices: you can recode *age* so that it will be changed in the Data Viewer, or you can keep *age* as it is and create a new variable. This latter option is desirable whenever you want to preserve

Plate 16.4

The Value Labels dialog box

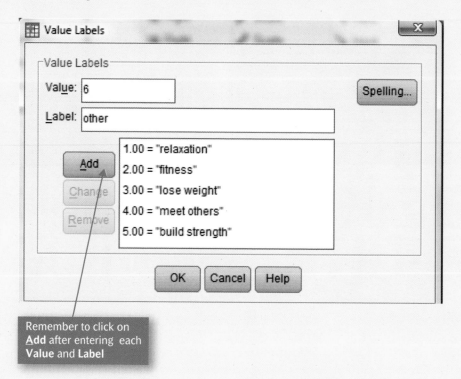

Remember to click on **Add** after entering each **Value** and **Label**

Plate 16.5

The Missing Values dialog box

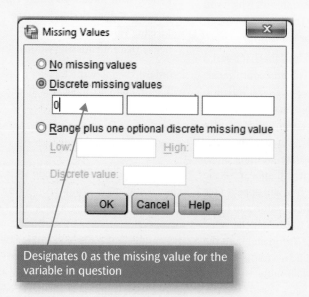

Designates 0 as the missing value for the variable in question

Plate 16.6

The Recode into Different Variables dialog box

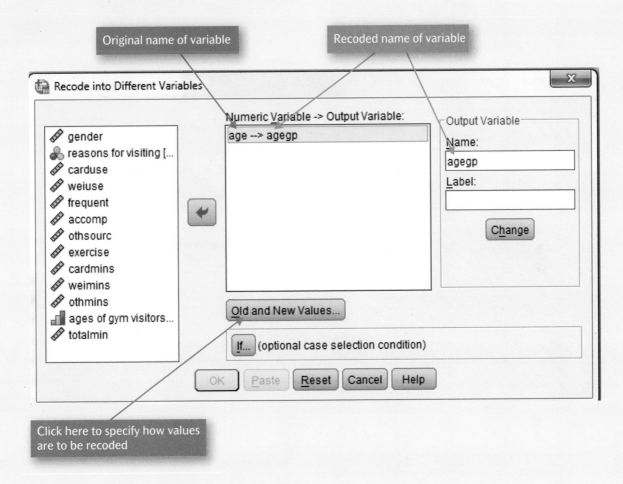

the variable in question as well as create a new one. Since we may want to carry out analyses involving **age** as an interval/ratio variable, we will recode it so that a new variable, which we will call **agegp**, for **age** groups, will be created. The aim of the following operations is to create a new variable—**agegp**—which will comprise five age bands, as in Table 15.3.

1. →**Transform** → **Recode** → **Into Different Variables** . . . [opens **Recode into Different Variables** dialog box shown in Plate 16.6]

2. → **age** → [puts **age** in **Numeric Variable** –> **Output Variable:** box] → box beneath **Output Variable Name:**

and type **agegp** → **Change** [puts **agegp** in the **Numeric Variable** –> **Output Variable:** box] → **Old and New Values** . . . [opens **Recode into Different Variables: Old and New Values** sub-dialog box shown in Plate 16.7]

3. → the circle by **System- or user-missing** and by **System-missing** under **New Value**, if you have missing values for a variable, which is the case for this variable

4. → circle by **Range, LOWEST through value:** and type **20** in the box → box by **Value** under **New Value** and type **1** → **Add** [the new value will appear in the **Old** –> **New:** box]

Plate 16.7

The Recode into Different Variables: Old and New Values sub-dialog box

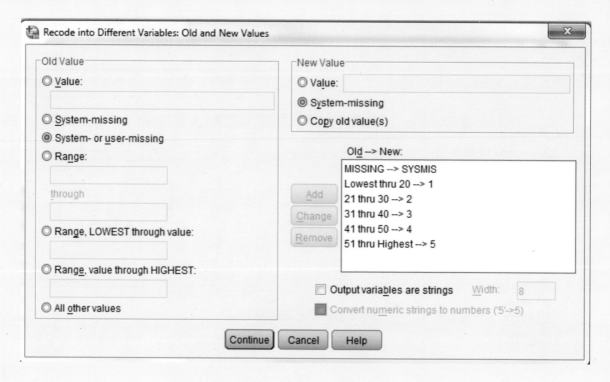

5. → first box by **Range:** and type **21** and in box after **through** type **30** → box by **Value** under **New Value** and type **2** → **Add**

6. → first box by **Range:** and type **31** and in box after **through** type **40** → box by **Value** under **New Value** and type **3** → **Add**

7. → first box by **Range:** and type **41** and in box after **through** type **50** → box by **Value** under **New Value** and type **4** → **Add**

8. → circle by **Range, value through HIGHEST** and type **51** in the box → box by **Value** in **New Value** and type **5** → **Add** → **Continue** [closes the **Recode into Different Variables: Old and New Values** sub-dialog box shown in Plate 16.7 and returns you to the **Recode into Different Variables** dialog box shown in Plate 16.6]

9. → **OK**

The new variable **agegp** will be created and will appear in the **Data Viewer**. You would then need to generate **value labels** for the five age bands and possibly a **variable label** using the approach described above.

Computing a new variable

A person's total amount of time spent in the gym is made up of three variables: *cardmins*, *weimins*, and *othmins*. If we add these up, we should arrive at the total number of minutes spent on activities in the gym. In so doing, we will create a new variable *totalmin*. To do this, this procedure should be followed:

1. → **Transform** → **Compute** . . . [opens the **Compute Variable** dialog box shown in Plate 16.8]

2. under **Target Variable:** type *totalmin*

3. from the list of variables at the left, → *cardmins* [→] [puts *cardmins* in box beneath **Numeric Expression:**] → +button → *weimins* [→] [puts *weimins* after + sign] → +button; → *othmins* [→] [puts *othmins* after + sign]

4. → **OK**

The new variable *totalmin* will be created and will appear in the **Data Editor**.

Now at last, we can begin to analyse the data!

Plate 16.8

The Compute Variable dialog box

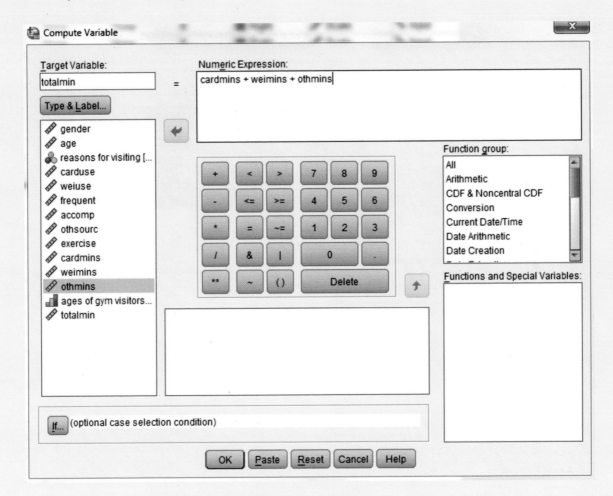

Data analysis with SPSS

Generating a frequency table

To produce a frequency table like the one in Table 15.2:

1. → **Analyze** → **Descriptive Statistics** → **Frequencies** . . . [opens the **Frequencies** dialog box shown in Plate 16.9]

2. → **reasons for visiting** → [puts **reasons for visiting** in **Variable[s]:** box]

3. → **OK**

The table will appear in the **Output Viewer** (see Plate 16.10).

Note that in the Frequencies dialog box, variables that have been assigned labels will appear in terms of their variable labels, but those that have not been assigned labels will appear in terms of their variable names. This is a feature of all dialog boxes produced via Analyze and Graphs (see below).

Plate 16.9

The Frequencies dialog box

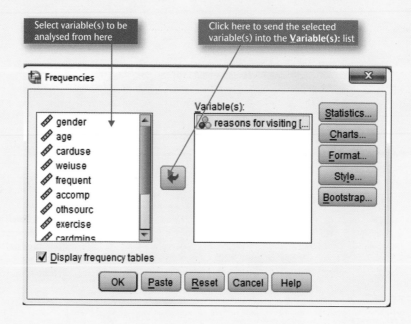

Plate 16.10

The Output Viewer with Frequency table

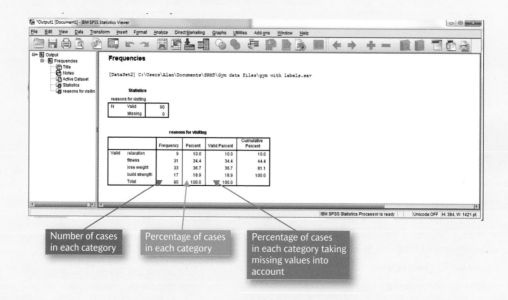

Plate 16.11

Creating a bar chart with the Chart Builder

The define simple bar: Summaries for groups of cases sub-dialog box

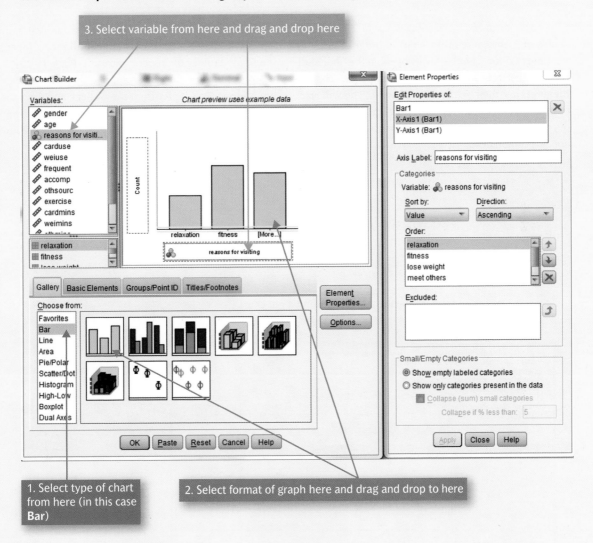

3. Select variable from here and drag and drop here

1. Select type of chart from here (in this case **Bar**)

2. Select format of graph here and drag and drop to here

Generating a bar chart

To produce a bar chart like the one in Figure 15.2:

1. → **Graphs** → **Chart Builder** . . . [opens **Chart Builder** dialog box shown in Plate 16.11]

2. → **Bar** below **Choose from:** and then → the simple bar format in the top left-hand corner of the **Gallery** and drag and drop it into the area above it. Then → *age* and drag and drop in the same way as for a bar chart.

3. → **reasons for visiting** from below **Variables:** and drag and drop into area marked in blue **X-Axis?**

4. → **OK**

Generating a pie chart

To produce a pie chart like the one in Figure 15.3:

1. → **Graphs** → **Chart Builder** . . . [opens the **Chart Builder** dialog box shown in Plate 16.12] → **Pie/Polar**

below **Choose from:** and then → the pie chart format in the top left-hand corner of the **Gallery** and drag and drop it into the area above it.

2. → **reasons for visiting** from below **Variables:** and drag and drop into area marked in blue **Slice by?**]

3. → **OK**

In order to include percentages, as in Figure 15.3, *double-click* anywhere in the chart in order to bring up the **Chart Editor.** The chart will appear in the **Chart Editor** and the main figure will become opaque. Then → **Elements** and then → **Show Data Labels**. This will place percentages in each slice as a default. If you want the frequencies, → **Count** in the **Properties** sub-dialog box that appears simultaneously (see Plate 16.12).

Your chart will be in colour, but, if you have access only to a monochrome printer, you can change your pie chart into patterns, which allows the slices to be clearer. This can be done through the **Chart Editor.**

Generating a histogram

In order to generate a histogram for an interval/ratio variable like *age*, → **Graphs** → **Chart Builder** . . . [opens the Chart Builder dialog box shown in Plate 16.12] → **Histogram** below **Choose from:** and then → the histogram format you prefer from the **Gallery** and drag and drop it into the area above it. Then → *age* and drag and drop it in the same way as for a bar chart. This procedure will generate a histogram whose age bands are defined

Plate 16.12

Creating a pie chart with the Chart Builder and Properties box

The chart editor and the properties box for editing a pie chart

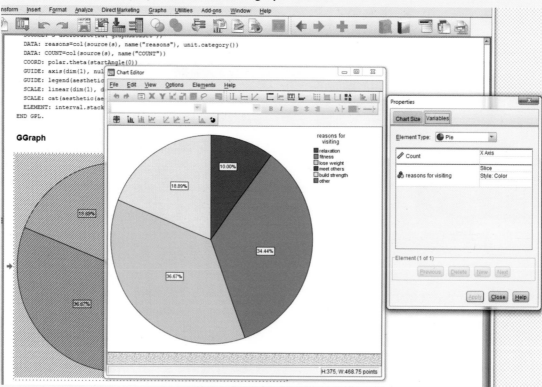

by the software. By double-clicking on the diagram, the histogram can be edited using the **Chart Editor**.

Generating the arithmetic mean, median, standard deviation, range, and boxplots

To produce the mean, median, standard deviation, and the range for an interval/ratio variable such as *age*, the following steps should be followed:

1. → **Analyze** → **Descriptive Statistics** → **Explore** . . . [opens the **Explore** dialog box]

2. → *age* → ▼ to the left of **Dependent List:** [puts *age* in the **Dependent List:** box] → **Statistics** under **Display** → **OK**

The output will also include the 95 per cent confidence interval for the mean, which is based on the standard error of the mean. The output can be found in Table 16.1. If you select **Plots . . .**, the **Explore: Plots** sub-dialog box will

come up and you can elect to generate a histogram. To do this, you will need to select either **Both** or **Plots** under **Display** on the **Explore** dialog box. In addition, selecting **Both** or **Plots** will produce two further types of figure, one of which is a boxplot, which was covered in Chapter 15.

Generating a contingency table, chi-square, and Cramér's *V*

In order to generate a contingency table, like that in Table 15.4, along with a chi-square test and Cramér's *V*, use the following procedure:

1. → **Analyze** → **Descriptive Statistics** → **Crosstabs** . . . [opens the **Crosstabs** dialog box shown in Plate 16.13]

2. → **reasons for visiting** → ▼ by **Row[s]** [reasons for visiting will appear in the **Row[s]:** box] → *gender* → ▼ by **Column[s]:** [*gender* will appear in the **Column[s]:** box] → **Cells** . . . [opens **Cross-tabs: Cell Display** sub-dialog box shown in Plate 16.14]

Table 16.1

Explore output for *age* (SPSS output)

Explore

Case Processing Summary

	Cases					
	Valid		Missing		Total	
	N	Percent	N	Percent	N	Percent
age	89	98.9%	1	1.1%	90	100.0%

Descriptives

			Statistic	Std. Error
age	Mean		33.5955	.94197
	95% Confidence Interval for Mean	Lower Bound	31.7235	
		Upper Bound	35.4675	
	5% Trimmed Mean		33.3159	
	Median		31.0000	
	Variance		78.971	
	Std. Deviation		8.88656	
	Minimum		18.00	
	Maximum		57.00	
	Range		39.00	
	Interquartile Range		14.00	
	Skewness		.446	.255
	Kurtosis		−.645	.506

Plate 16.13

The Crosstabs dialog box

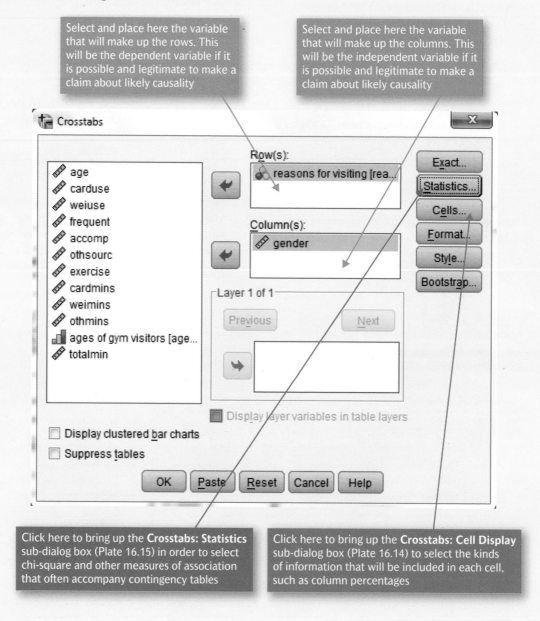

Select and place here the variable that will make up the rows. This will be the dependent variable if it is possible and legitimate to make a claim about likely causality

Select and place here the variable that will make up the columns. This will be the independent variable if it is possible and legitimate to make a claim about likely causality

Click here to bring up the **Crosstabs: Statistics** sub-dialog box (Plate 16.15) in order to select chi-square and other measures of association that often accompany contingency tables

Click here to bring up the **Crosstabs: Cell Display** sub-dialog box (Plate 16.14) to select the kinds of information that will be included in each cell, such as column percentages

3. Make sure **Observed** in the **Counts** box has been selected. Make sure **Column** under **Percentages** has been selected. If either of these has not been selected, simply click at the relevant point. → **Continue** [closes

Crosstabs: Cell Display sub-dialog box and returns you to the **Crosstabs** dialog box shown in Plate 16.13]

4. → **Statistics** . . . [opens the **Crosstabs: Statistics** sub-dialog box shown in Plate 16.15]

Plate 16.14

The Crosstabs: Cell Display sub-dialog box

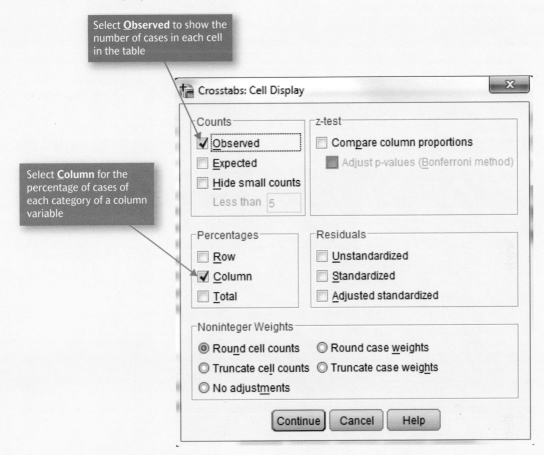

Select **Observed** to show the number of cases in each cell in the table

Select **Column** for the percentage of cases of each category of a column variable

5. → **Chi-square** → **Phi and Cramér's *V*** → **Continue** [closes **Crosstabs: Statistics** sub-dialog box and returns you to the **Crosstabs** dialog box shown in Plate 16.13]

6. → **OK**

The resulting output can be found in Table 16.2.

If you have a table with two dichotomous variables, you would use the same sequence of steps to produce phi.

Generating Pearson's *r* and Spearman's rho

To produce Pearson's *r* in order to find the correlations between *age*, *cardmins*, and *weimins*, follow these steps:

1. → **Analyze** → **Correlate** → **Bivariate** . . . [opens **Bivariate Correlations** dialog box shown in Plate 16.16]

2. → *age* → [→] → *cardmins* → [→] → *weimins* → [→] [*age*, *cardmins*, and *weimins* should now be in the **Variables:** box] → **Pearson** [*if* not already selected] → **OK**

The resulting output is in Table 16.3.

To produce correlations with Spearman's rho, follow the same procedure, but, instead of selecting **Pearson**, you should → **Spearman** instead.

Generating scatter diagrams

Scatter diagrams, known as *scatterplots* in SPSS, are produced in the following way. Let us say that we want to plot the relationship between *age* and *cardmins*. There is a convention that, if one variable can be identified as likely to be the independent variable, it should be placed on the *x* axis—that is, the horizontal axis. Since *age* is

Table 16.2

Contingency table for *reasons for visiting* by *gender* (SPSS output)

Crosstabs

Case Processing Summary

	Cases					
	Valid		Missing		Total	
	N	Percent	N	Percent	N	Percent
reasons for visiting * gender	90	100.0%	0	0.0%	90	100.0%

reasons for visiting * gender Crosstabulation

			gender		
			Male	Female	Total
reasons for visiting	relaxation	Count	3	6	9
		% within gender	7.1%	12.5%	10.0%
	fitness	Count	15	16	31
		% within gender	35.7%	33.3%	34.4%
	lose weight	Count	8	25	33
		% within gender	19.0%	52.1%	36.7%
	build strength	Count	16	1	17
		% within gender	38.1%	2.1%	18.9%
Total		Count	42	48	90
		% within gender	100.0%	100.0%	100.0%

Chi-Square Tests

	Value	df	Asymp. Sig. (2-sided)
Pearson Chi-Square	22.726[a]	3	.000
Likelihood Ratio	25.805	3	.000
Linear-by-Linear Association	9.716	1	.002
N of Valid Cases	90		

[a] 2 cells (25.0%) have expected count less than 5. The minimum expected count is 4.20.

Symmetric Measures

		Value	Approx. Sig.
Nominal by Nominal	Phi	.503	.000
	Cramer's V	.503	.000
N of Valid Cases		90	

Plate 16.15

The Crosstabs: Statistics sub-dialog box

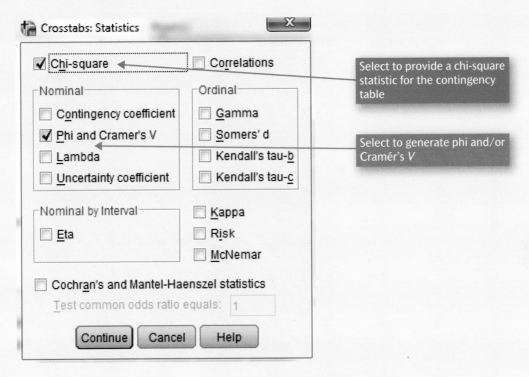

Select to provide a chi-square statistic for the contingency table

Select to generate phi and/or Cramér's *V*

Table 16.3

Correlations output for *age*, *weimins*, and *cardmins* (SPSS output)

Correlations

Correlations

		age	cardmins	weimins
age	Pearson Correlation	1	−.109	−.273**
	Sig. (2-tailed)		.311	.010
	N	89	89	89
cardmins	Pearson Correlation	−.109	1	−.161
	Sig. (2-tailed)	.311		.130
	N	89	90	90
weimins	Pearson Correlation	−.273**	−.161	1
	Sig. (2-tailed)	.010	.130	
	N	89	90	90

**. Correlation is significant at the 0.01 level (2-tailed).

Figure 16.1

Scatter diagram showing the relationship between *age* and *cardmins* (SPSS output)

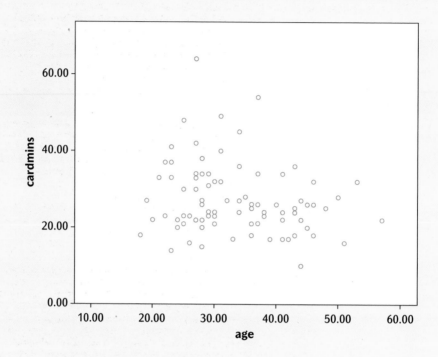

bound to be the independent variable, we would follow these steps:

1. → **Graphs** → **Chart Builder** [opens the **Chart Builder** dialog box shown in Plate 16.17]

2. → **Scatter/Dot** from below **Choose from:**. Then select from the scatter diagram formats, the basic format which is in the top left-hand corner and drag and drop into the area above the scatter diagram formats

3. → *cardmins* and drag and drop into area designated **Y-Axis?** and → *age* and drag and drop into area designated **X-Axis?** (see Plate 16.17)

A default scatter diagram is shown in Figure 16.1. The scatter diagram can then be edited by bringing up the **Chart Editor** by double-clicking with the left-hand button anywhere in the diagram. For example, the type and size of the markers can be changed by clicking anywhere in the chart in the **Chart Editor**. This brings up a **Properties** sub-dialog box, which allows a variety of changes to

the appearance of the diagram, such as colour and the nature of the points on the plot.

Comparing means and eta

To produce a table like Table 15.5, these steps should be followed:

1. → **Analyze** → **Compare Means** → **Means** . . . [opens the **Means** dialog box shown in Plate 16.18]

2. → *cardmins* → ⬇ to the left of **Dependent List:** [puts *cardmins* in the **Dependent List:** box] → **reasons for visiting** → ⬇ to the left of **Independent List:** [puts **reasons for visiting** in the **Independent List:box**]→ **Options** . . . [opens the **Means: Options** sub-dialog box]

3. → **Anova table and eta** underneath **Statistics for First Layer** → **Continue** [closes the **Means: Options** sub-dialog box and returns you to the **Means** dialog box shown in Plate 16.18] → **OK**

Plate 16.16

The Bivariate Correlations dialog box

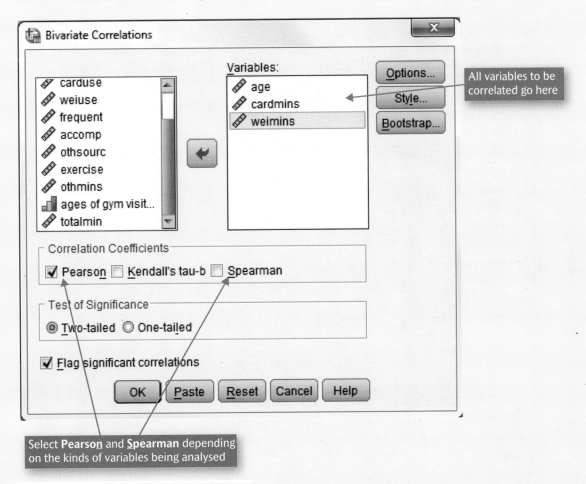

Generating a contingency table with three variables

To create a table like that in Table 15.7, you would need to follow these steps:

1. → **Analyze** → **Descriptive Statistics** → **Crosstabs** . . . [opens the **Crosstabs** dialog box shown in Plate 16.13]

2. → *othsourc* → **Independent List:** by **Row[s]** [oth-sourc will appear in the **Row[s]:** box]

3. → *age3* [this is the name we gave when we created a new variable with *age* recoded into three categories] → **Independent List:** by **Column[s]:** [*age3* will appear in the **Column[s]:** box] → *gender* → **Independent List:**

beneath **Previous** [*gender* will appear in the box underneath **Layer 1 of 1**] → **Cells** [opens **Crosstabs: Cell Display** sub-dialog box shown in Plate 16.14]

4. Make sure **Observed** in the **Counts** box has been selected. Make sure **Column** under **Percentages** has been selected. If either of these has not been selected, simply click at the relevant point. → **Continue** [closes **Crosstabs: Cell Display** sub-dialog box and returns you to the **Crosstabs** dialog box shown in Plate 16.13]

5. → **OK**

The resulting table will look somewhat different from Table 15.7 in that gender will appear as a row rather than as a column variable.

Plate 16.17

Creating a scatter diagram with the Chart Builder

The simple scatterlot sub-dialog box

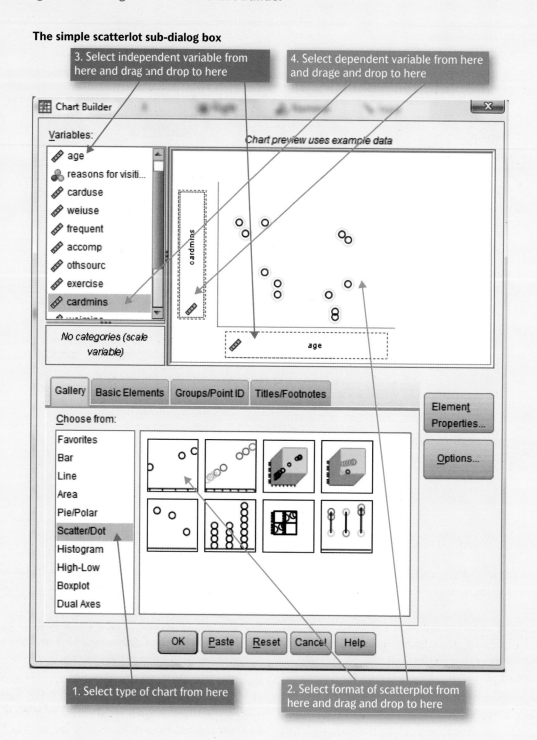

3. Select independent variable from here and drag and drop to here

4. Select dependent variable from here and drage and drop to here

1. Select type of chart from here

2. Select format of scatterplot from here and drag and drop to here

Plate 16.18

The Means dialog box

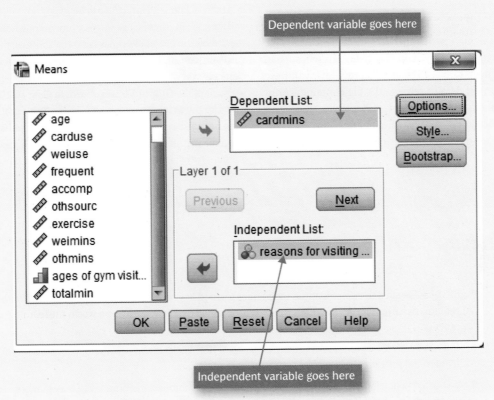

Dependent variable goes here

Independent variable goes here

Further operations in SPSS

Saving your data

You will need to save your data for future use. To do this, make sure that the **Data Editor** is the active window. Then,

→ **File** → **Save As** . . .

The **Save Data As** dialog box will then appear. You will need to provide a name for your data, which will be placed after **File name:** We called the file 'gym study'. You also need to decide where you are going to save the data—for example, onto a memory stick. To

select the destination drive, → the downward pointing arrow to the left of **Look in** and then select the drive and folder into which you want to place your data. Then → **Save**.

Remember that this procedure saves your data *and* any other work you have done on your data—for example, value labels and recoded variables. If you subsequently use the data again and do more work on your data, such as creating a new variable, you will need to save the data again or the new work will be lost. SPSS will give you a choice of renaming your data, in which case you will have two files of data (one with the original data and one with any changes), or keeping the same name, in which case the file will be changed and the existing name retained.

Retrieving your data

When you want to retrieve the data file you have created, → **File** → **Open** . . . The **Open File** dialog box will appear. You then need to go to the location in which you have deposited your data to retrieve the file containing your data and then → **Open** → **Data** . . . A shortcut alternative to this procedure is to → the first button on the toolbar (it looks like an open file), which brings up the **Open File** dialog box.

Printing output

To print all the output in the **SPSS Output Viewer**, make sure that the **Output 1—SPSS Viewer** is the active window and then → **File** → **Print** . . . The **Print** dialog box will appear and then → **OK**. To print just some of your output, hold down the Ctrl button on your keyboard and click once on the parts you want to print. The easiest way to do this is to select all the elements you want in the output summary in the left-hand segment of the **Output Viewer** shown in Plate 16.10. Then bring up the **Print** dialog box. When the **Print** dialog box appears, make sure **Selection** under **Print range** has been selected. The third button on the toolbar (which appears as a printer) provides a shortcut to the **Print** dialog box.

Key points

- SPSS can be used to implement the techniques learned in Chapter 15, but learning new software requires perseverance and at times the results obtained may not seem to be worth the learning process.

- But it is worth it—it would take you far longer to perform calculations on a sample of around 100 than to learn the software.

- If you find yourself moving into much more advanced techniques, the time saved is even more substantial, particularly with large samples.

- It is better to become familiar with SPSS before you begin designing your research instruments, so you are aware of difficulties you might have in presenting your data in SPSS at an early stage.

Questions for review

Getting started in SPSS

- Outline the differences between variable names, variable labels, and value labels.

- In what circumstances might you want to recode a variable?

- In what circumstances might you want to create a new variable?

Data analysis with SPSS

Using the gym survey data, create:

- a frequency table for *exercise*;

- a bar chart and pie chart for *exercise* and compare their usefulness;

- a histogram for *cardmins*;

- measures of central tendency and dispersion for *cardmins*;

- a contingency table and chi-square test for *exercise* and *gender*;

- Pearson's *r* for **age** and **cardmins**;
- Spearman's rho for **carduse** and **weiuse**;
- a scatter diagram for **age** and **cardmins**;
- a comparing means analysis for **totalmin** and **reasons for visiting**.

Online Resource Centre

www.oxfordtextbooks.co.uk/orc/brymansrm4e/

Visit the Interactive Research Guide that accompanies this book to complete an exercise in Using IBM SPSS.

Part Three
Qualitative research

Part Three of this book is concerned with qualitative research. Chapter 17 sets the scene by exploring the main features of this research strategy. Chapter 18 discusses sampling in qualitative research and in particular the notion of purposive sampling. Chapter 19 deals with ethnography and participant observation, which are among the main ways of collecting qualitative data. Chapter 20 is concerned with the kind of interviewing that is carried out in qualitative research. Chapter 21 addresses the focus group method, a technique that allows groups of people to be interviewed. Chapter 22 explores approaches to the study of language in business research, including conversation analysis and discourse analysis. Chapter 23 explores the types of documents which qualitative researchers tend to be concerned with, and approaches to examining them. Chapter 24 examines different approaches to qualitative data analysis and offers advice on how it can be carried out. Chapter 25 shows you how to use computer software in the form of NVivo to conduct the kind of analysis discussed in Chapter 24.

These chapters will provide you with the essential tools for doing qualitative research. They will take you from the general issues to do with the generic features of qualitative research to the practical issues of conducting your own observational studies or interviews and analysing your own data.

17

The nature of qualitative research

Chapter outline

Qualitative research is a research strategy that usually emphasizes words rather than quantification in the collection and analysis of data. As a research strategy it is inductivist, constructionist, and interpretivist, but qualitative researchers do not always subscribe to all of these intellectual positions. This chapter is concerned with outlining the main features of qualitative research, which is an established approach to business research. The chapter explores:

- the main steps in qualitative research: delineating the sequence of stages in qualitative research is more controversial than with quantitative research, because it exhibits somewhat less codification of the research process;

- the relationship between theory and research;

- the nature of concepts in qualitative research and their differences from concepts in quantitative research;

- how far reliability and validity are appropriate criteria for qualitative researchers and whether or not alternative criteria that are more tailored to the research strategy are necessary;

- the main preoccupations of qualitative researchers; five areas are identified in terms of an emphasis on: seeing through the eyes of research participants; description and context; process; flexibility and lack of structure; and concepts and theory as outcomes of the research process;

- some common criticisms of qualitative research;

- the main contrasts between qualitative and quantitative research;

- the stance of feminist researchers on qualitative research.

Introduction

We began Chapter 7 by noting that *quantitative* research had been outlined in Chapter 2 as a distinctive research strategy. Much the same kind of general point can be made in relation to *qualitative* research. In Chapter 2 it was suggested that qualitative research differs from quantitative research in several ways. Most obviously, qualitative research tends to be concerned with words rather than numbers, but three further features are particularly noteworthy:

- an inductive view of the relationship between theory and research, whereby the former is generated out of the latter;

- an epistemological position described as interpretivist, meaning that, in contrast to the adoption of a natural scientific model in quantitative research, the stress is on the understanding of the social world through an examination of the interpretation of that world by its participants; and

- an ontological position described as constructionist, which implies that social properties are outcomes of the interactions between individuals, rather than phenomena 'out there' and separate from those involved in their construction.

As Bryman and Burgess (1999) observe, although there has been a proliferation of writings on qualitative research since the 1970s, stipulating what it is and is not as a distinct research strategy is by no means straightforward. They propose three reasons for this uncertainty.

- As a term, 'qualitative research' is sometimes taken to imply an approach to business research in which quantitative data are not collected or generated. Many writers on qualitative research are critical of such a rendition of qualitative research, because (as we will see) the distinctiveness of qualitative research does not reside solely in the absence of numbers.

Key concept 17.1
Four traditions of qualitative research

Gubrium and Holstein (1997) suggest four traditions of qualitative research.

- *Naturalism*: seeks to understand social reality in its own terms; 'as it really is'; provides rich descriptions of people and interaction in natural settings.

- *Ethnomethodology*: seeks to understand how social order is created through talk and interaction; has a naturalistic orientation.

- *Emotionalism*: exhibits a concern with subjectivity and gaining access to 'inside' experience; concern with the inner reality of humans.

- *Postmodernism*: has an emphasis on 'method talk'; sensitive to the different ways social reality can be constructed. For a definition of postmodernism, see Key concept 17.2.

We encountered the term *naturalism* in Key concept 3.4. The use of the term here is more or less the same as the second meaning referred to in Key concept 3.4. The naturalist tradition has probably been the most common one over the years. The second tradition, ethnomethodology, will be encountered in Chapter 22, when we will be looking at an approach to the collection of qualitative data known as **conversation analysis**. The more recent postmodern standpoint informs some recent forms of reflexive ethnographic writing (see Chapters 19 and 29). The third tradition—emotionalism—has not become the focus of a significant stream of research and will not be emphasized in this book. However, the presence of these four contrasting traditions points to the difficulty of creating a definitive account of what qualitative research is and is not.

- Such writers as Gubrium and Holstein (1997) have suggested that several traditions in qualitative research can be identified (see Key concept 17.1).

- Sometimes, qualitative research is discussed in terms of the ways in which it differs from quantitative research. A potential problem with this tactic is that it means that qualitative research ends up being addressed in terms of what quantitative research is *not*.

Silverman (1993) has been critical of accounts of qualitative research that do not acknowledge the variety of forms that the research strategy can take. Others, such as Denzin and Lincoln (2005), have argued that qualitative research has evolved over time into a series of distinct phases or 'moments'. In other words, writers such as Silverman are critical of attempts to specify the nature of qualitative research as a general approach. However, unless we can talk to a certain degree about the nature of qualitative research, it is difficult to see how it is possible to refer to qualitative research as a distinctive research strategy. In much the same way that in Chapter 7 it was recognized that quantitative researchers use different research designs, in writing about the characteristics of qualitative research we need to be sensitive to the different orientations of qualitative researchers. Without a sense of what is common to many if not most studies that are described as qualitative, the very notion of qualitative research would be rendered problematic. Yet it is clear that, for many social scientists, it is a helpful and meaningful category that can be seen in a variety of ways. Examples are the arrival of specialist journals, such as *Qualitative Research in Organizations and Management* and *Qualitative Inquiry*; texts on qualitative research (e.g. Silverman 1993, 2000; Seale 1999); a huge *Handbook of Qualitative Research* (Denzin and Lincoln 2000); and a series of books on different facets of qualitative research (the Sage Qualitative Research Methods Series).

Several reasons might be proposed for the unease among some writers about specifying the nature of qualitative research. First, qualitative research subsumes several diverse research methods that differ from each other considerably. The following are the main research methods associated with qualitative research.

- *Ethnography/participant observation*. While some caution is advisable in treating ethnography and participant observation as synonyms, they refer to similar approaches to data collection in which the researcher is immersed in a social setting for some time in order to observe and listen with a view to gaining an appreciation of the culture of a social group. These methods have been used in Dalton's (1959) study of managerial work in the USA and Lupton's (1963) exploration of shopfloor factory life and restriction of output in England.

- *Qualitative interviewing*. This is a very broad term to describe a wide range of interviewing styles (see Key concept 9.2 for an introduction). Moreover, qualitative researchers employing ethnography or participant observation typically engage in a substantial amount of qualitative interviewing.

- *Focus groups* (see Key concept 9.2).

- *Language-based approaches to the collection of qualitative data*, such as discourse and conversation analysis.

- *The collection and qualitative analysis of texts and documents*.

Each of these approaches to data collection will be examined in Part Three. As noted above, researchers employing ethnography or participant observation frequently conduct qualitative interviews. However, they also often collect and analyse texts and documents as well. Thus, there is considerable variability in the collection of data among studies that are deemed to be qualitative. Of course, quantitative research also subsumes several different methods of data collection (these were covered in Part Two), but the inclusion of methods concerned with the analysis of language as a form of qualitative research implies somewhat greater variability.

A second reason why there is some resistance to specifying the nature of qualitative research is that the connection between theory and research is more ambiguous than in quantitative research. With the latter research strategy, theoretical issues drive the formulation of a research question, which in turn drives the collection and analysis of data. Findings then feed back into the relevant theory. In qualitative research, theory is supposed to be an outcome of an investigation rather than something that precedes it. However, some writers, like Silverman (1993: 24), have argued that such a depiction of qualitative research is 'out of tune with the greater sophistication of contemporary field research design, born out of accumulated knowledge of interaction and greater concern with issues of reliability and validity'. Nonetheless, qualitative research is more usually regarded as denoting an approach in which theory and categorization emerge out of the collection and analysis of data. The more general point being made is that such a difference within qualitative research may account for the unease about depicting the research strategy in terms of a set of stages.

Key concept 17.2
What is postmodernism?

Postmodernism is extremely difficult to pin down. Part of the problem is that, as an approach, postmodernism is at least two things. One is that it is a perspective on the nature of modern society and culture. The other, and more relevant, aspect for this book is that it represents a way of thinking about and representing the nature of the social sciences and their claims to knowledge. In particular, it is a distinctive sensitivity regarding the representation of social scientific findings. Postmodernists tend to be deeply suspicious of notions that imply that it is possible to arrive at a definitive version of any reality. Reports of findings are viewed as versions of an external reality, so that the key issue becomes one of the plausibility of those versions rather than whether they are right or wrong in any absolute sense. Typically, writers of a postmodernist persuasion have less to say about data collection issues than about the writing and representation of social science findings, though it is probably the case that they are more sympathetic to qualitative than quantitative research (Alvesson 2002). Indeed, postmodernists have probably been most influential in qualitative research when discussing the nature of ethnographic accounts and questioning the ethnographer's implicit claim that he or she has provided a definitive account of a society. This thinking can be discerned in Van Maanen's (1988) implicit critique of 'realist tales' (see Key concept 19.17).

Postmodernists tend to emphasize the notion of **reflexivity** (see Chapter 29), which highlights the significance of the researcher in the research process and consequently the tentativeness of any findings presented (since the researcher is always implicated in his or her findings). As this account of postmodernism implies, postmodernists are critical of any view of research that implies that there are or can be accepted foundations to knowledge, as is suggested by positivists (see Key concept 2.7). Postmodernism problematizes and questions our capacity to know anything. Views vary on postmodernism's current appeal. Matthewman and Hoey (2006) depict its influence as having waned to a significant extent, while Bloland (2005) argues that it has had an impact on thinking in many fields and that this is especially noticeable among those who do not identify themselves as postmodernists.

The main steps in qualitative research

The sequence outlined in Figure 17.1 provides a representation of how the qualitative research process can be visualized. In order to illustrate these steps, a study by Ladge et al. (2012) of identity transitions among women professionals in early pregnancy will be used.

- *Step 1. General research questions* (see Thinking deeply 17.3). Ladge et al.'s (2012) study focused on how professional women in pregnancy experience identity changes. Their theoretical interest, as they explain, 'is in understanding how a life-altering change in an individual's nonwork self often instigates a need to reorient his/her work identity' (Ladge et al. 2012: 1450). They therefore chose to focus on professional women who were in the early stages of their first pregnancy, asserting that these women start to explore and enact the identity of motherhood long before the child is born. Through this, Ladge et al. (2012) make a theoretical contribution to understanding how work and nonwork

identities coevolve in 'liminal periods', when identity is in flux. Drawing on the identity literature, they assume that this liminal period will be characterised by 'feelings of ambiguity, openness, disorientation, self-questioning and indeterminacy' (Ladge et al. 2012: 1451), as women are no longer fully connected to their old professional identity and are anticipating a new identity where they will be mothers and professionals. This led the researchers towards the development of their research goal which was to 'study women's experiences of the liminal period of pregnancy as they develop their new maternal identity and begin reconstructing their professional identity in light of impending motherhood' (Ladge et al. 2012: 1453). A set of general questions including 'How do women manage their work identity while pregnant?' guided the research, 'but as we moved through the data, we were open to making adjustments to these questions … based on our own

Figure 17.1

An outline of the main steps of qualitative research

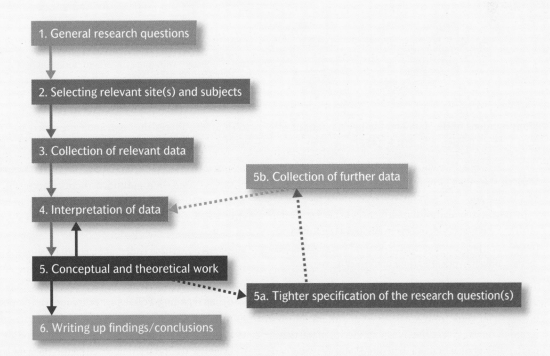

Thinking deeply 17.3
Research questions in qualitative research

Research questions in qualitative research are stated with varying degrees of explicitness. Sometimes, the research question is embedded within a general statement about the orientation of an article. Other studies are more explicit in stating research questions. Ashforth et al. (2007) were interested in the phenomenon of 'dirty work', a term that refers to work that is tainted 'physically, socially or morally' (E. C. Hughes 1958: 122; quoted in Ashforth et al. 2007: 149). They conducted semi-structured interviews with managers in eighteen such occupations in order to explore how the work is 'normalized'—that is, how they develop ways of dealing with or reducing the significance of the taint of dirty work. After a discussion of the literature and their view of its implications for their own work, they write:

> In summary, our research questions were:
> *Research Question 1. What normalization challenges do managers in dirty work occupations face?*
> *Research Question 2. What tactics do managers report using to normalize dirty work?*
>
> (Ashforth et al. 2007: 151; emphasis in original)

One factor that may affect the degree of explicitness with which research questions are stated is the outlet in which the research is published. Ashforth et al. (2007) published this article in the *Academy of Management Journal*, which in the past has tended to publish mainly empirical articles deriving from quantitative research. It may be that Ashforth et al. chose this format for presenting their research questions so that it would exhibit some of the characteristics of research questions or hypotheses in quantitative research that tend to be stated explicitly. Another article in the same issue also stated its research questions very explicitly, though not in the same way.

> Thus two research questions guided this article: (1) What conditions trigger organizational stakeholders and leaders to engage in sensemaking activities? and (2) What conditions enable sensegiving on the part of stakeholders and leaders motivated to engage in sensemaking activities?
>
> (Maitlis and Lawrence 2007: 59)

The researchers investigated these two research questions by collecting qualitative data from semi-structured interviews, observation, and examination of documents in connection with three British symphony orchestras.

interpretations of the data and the interpretations of respondents' (Ladge et al. 2012: 1455).

- *Step 2. Selecting relevant site(s) and subjects.* The first stage of the project involved a pilot study of ten interviews with pregnant women who were either pregnant with their first child or within six months of having given birth to their first child. Interviewees had a minimum of three years' professional experience and were planning on returning to work after their maternity leave.

- *Step 3. Collection of relevant data.* The researchers justify their choice of qualitative research methods as a response to calls from work-life scholars for more research that explores the lived experience of participants, their choice of semi-structured interview methods enabling the exploration of women's work experience while pregnant. Interviews were between 60 and 90 minutes' duration and were taped and transcribed verbatim.

- *Step 4. Interpretation of data.* Ladge et al. describe their study as based on a grounded theory approach. The process of analysis began by developing a set of codes that emerged inductively from the interviews. The three researchers worked together to develop shared agreement on these codes, each coding a subset of the transcripts independently and then meeting up to compare and consolidate, returning to the literature and then recoding. Following techniques developed by Strauss and Corbin (1990), they went through several cycles of this process. Eventually, 'after coding 29 interviews, we felt we had reached the point of theoretical saturation because no new codes were being generated' (Ladge, et al., 2012: 1456).

- *Step 5. Conceptual and theoretical work.* Consistent with their grounded theory approach, Ladge et al. describe their goal as to expand knowledge about liminal periods and to build new theory about identity transitions. The researchers therefore develop a theoretical model (in the form of a detailed flow diagram) to illustrate the experiences of identity transitions in liminal periods. In this model, pregnancy is labelled as a 'triggering event' that evokes identity uncertainty. The emphasis in this model is on explaining the process of identity transition as it unfolds in the liminal period.

- *Step 5a. Tighter specification of the research question(s), and Step 5b. Collection of further data.* Having done the pilot study, Ladge et al. refined their definition of the population being studied, their theoretical frame, and the questions that comprised the interview protocol. The extent of these changes illustrates the extent to which qualitative researchers are flexible in their approach to study, changing direction in the course of the investigation, a point which we will return to later in this chapter. They explain: 'we learned from the pilot study that we needed to focus on a precise segment of working women ... Thus, we decided to focus our attention on women who had at least three years professional experience'. The women in this second sample held a variety of professional occupations, including manager, lawyer, and college professor. Through analysis of the interview transcripts from the pilot study, the researchers returned to the literature on identity transitions 'and recognized that pregnancy represents a liminal space. Thus, we modified our full study to focus exclusively on pregnant women, excluding those who had given birth' (Ladge et al. 2012: 1453–1454). They then interviewed a further 25 women based on these refined sampling criteria. A snowball sampling technique was used to identify participants in the main study. Initially this involved publicising the study via University alumni and professional networks. Although they do not make this explicit, all of the interviews appear to have been conducted in the United States, where the three researchers are based. Ladge et al. give much more detail about the interview

questions they asked in the main study than they do for the pilot. Questions covered three main themes. The first set asked participants to share thoughts and ideals related to work and pregnancy in light of their backgrounds—an example would be 'What aspects of your youth and history have formulated your views of motherhood?' A second set probed women's experiences of pregnancy and work, e.g. 'Tell the story about when you first found out that you were pregnant'. A third group of questions explored women's specific experiences in the workplace related to their pregnancy and their strategies for managing pregnancy in the workplace. Such a strategy is frequently referred to as *iterative*: the stages of data collection and analysis take place in parallel, as initial stages of data collection and analysis are used to refine subsequent phases of data collection and analysis.

- *Step 6. Writing up findings/conclusions.* There is no real difference between the significance of writing up in quantitative research and qualitative research, so that exactly the same points made in relation to Step 11 in Figure 7.1 apply here. An audience has to be convinced about the credibility and significance of the interpretations offered. Researchers are not and cannot be simply conduits for the things they see and the words they hear. The salience of what researchers have seen and heard has to be impressed on the audience. Ladge et al. do this by making clear the theoretical and practical implications of their study. They also suggest how the findings from this study may be generalizable to other situations where a future nonwork role has an impact on one's work role, such as when a manager finds himself with responsibilities to care for an aging parent. The practical implications arising from the study relate to the role of organizations in more proactively supporting women during pregnancy, 'as they wrestle with conceptualizing possible selves' (Ladge et al. 2012: 1467), rather than providing work-life support for working mothers when they return to work after the baby is born.

Two distinctive aspects of the sequence of steps in qualitative research are the related issues of theory and concepts, issues to which we now turn.

Theory and research

Most qualitative researchers when writing about their craft emphasize a preference for treating theory as something that emerges out of the collection and analysis of data.

For example, Marshall (1984) describes her approach to the analysis of research data on women managers' career histories as 'immersion', clearly derived from an inductive approach, as explained in Chapter 2. This involves trying to appreciate inherent patterns rather than to impose preconceived ideas on the data. For Marshall (1981), in the early stages of data analysis impressions seem to dominate, but at this point, although there is a sense that something is coming out of the data, it is not clear what. At the same time Marshall explains 'there is a kind of fear that *nothing* is going to come out of the research and that I'm going to be left with a pile of tapes and nothing to say at the end' (1981: 396). Structuring the data involves picking certain things out and putting them under some headings, but again Marshall states: 'I'm a bit unsure about this, because this seems to *rob* the individual case of its wholeness. So I have to compensate for parcelling out little bits of a person and putting them under different categories and headings, and try to appreciate the wholeness of each person as well' (1981: 396). The final stage involves a lot of attention; it demands mental space in order to allow insights to emerge from an unconscious level so that connections can be made at lots of different levels. Towards the end of the analysis there comes a point that Marshall describes as feeling almost overloaded and things needing to be brought together into a structure. At this point 'it's almost like having the *essence* of things that I can always fall back on now, so it does become more solid and understandable. That feeling gives me confidence that I can put it together' (1981: 398). As will be seen in Chapter 24, practitioners of grounded theory stress the importance of allowing theoretical ideas to emerge

out of one's data. But some qualitative researchers argue that qualitative data can and should have an important role in relation to the *testing* of theories as well. Silverman (1993) has argued that in more recent times qualitative researchers have become increasingly interested in the testing of theories and that this is a reflection of the growing maturity of the strategy. Certainly, there is no reason why qualitative research cannot be employed in order to test theories that are specified in advance of data collection. In any case, much qualitative research involves testing theories in the course of the research process. So, in Figure 17.1, the loop back from Step 5a 'Tighter specification of the research question(s)' to Step 5b 'Collection of further data' implies that a theoretical position may emerge in the course of research and may spur the collection of further data to test that theory. This kind of oscillation between testing emerging theories and collecting data is a particularly prominent feature of grounded theory. It is presented as a dashed line in Figure 17.1, because it is not as necessary a feature of the process of qualitative research as the other steps.

One key point that is implied by Figure 17.1 is that the typical sequence of steps in qualitative research entails the generation of theories rather than the testing of theories that are specified at the outset. Silverman (1993) is undoubtedly correct that pre-specified theories *can be* and sometimes *are* tested with qualitative data, but the generation of theory tends to be the preferred approach.

Concepts in qualitative research

A central feature of Chapter 7 was the discussion of concepts and their measurement. For most qualitative researchers, developing measures of concepts will not be a significant consideration, but concepts are very much part of the landscape in qualitative research. However, the way in which concepts are developed and employed is often rather different from that implied in the quantitative research strategy. Blumer's (1954) distinction between 'definitive' and 'sensitizing' concepts captures aspects of the different ways in which concepts are thought about.

Blumer (1954) argued stridently against the use of definitive concepts in social research. The idea of definitive concepts is typified by the way in which, in quantitative research, a concept, once developed, becomes fixed

through the elaboration of indicators. For Blumer, such an approach entailed the application of a straitjacket on the social world, because the concept in question comes to be seen exclusively in terms of the indicators that have been developed for it. Fine nuances in the form that the concept can assume or alternative ways of viewing the concept and its manifestations are sidelined. In other words, definitive concepts are excessively concerned with what is common to the phenomena that the concept is supposed to subsume rather than with variety. Instead, Blumer recommended that social researchers should recognize that the concepts they use are sensitizing concepts in that they provide 'a general sense of reference and guidance in approaching empirical instances' (1954: 7).

Research in focus 17.4
The emergence of a concept in qualitative research: 'emotional labour'

Hochschild's (1983) idea of emotional labour—labour that 'requires one to induce or suppress feelings in order to sustain the outward countenance that produces the proper state of mind in others' (1983: 7)—has become a very influential concept in the sociology of work and in the developing area of the sociology of emotions. Somewhat ironically for a predominantly qualitative study, Hochschild's initial conceptualization appears to have emerged from a questionnaire she distributed to 261 university students. Within the questionnaire were two requests: 'Describe a real situation that was important to you in which you experienced a deep emotion' and 'Describe as fully and concretely as possible a real situation that was important to you in which you either changed the situation to fit your feelings or changed your feelings to fit the situation' (1983: 13). Thus, although a self-completion questionnaire was employed, the resulting data were qualitative. The data were analysed in terms of the idea of emotion *work*, which is the same as emotional labour but occurs in a private context. Emotional labour is essentially emotion work that is performed as part of one's paid employment. In order to develop the idea of emotional labour, Hochschild looked to the world of work. The main occupation she studied was the flight attendant. Several sources of data on emotional labour among flight attendants were used. She gained access to Delta Airlines, a large American airline, and she

- watched sessions for training attendants and had many conversations with both trainees and experienced attendants during the sessions;
- interviewed various personnel, such as managers in various sections, and advertising agents;
- examined Delta advertisements spanning thirty years;
- observed the flight attendant recruitment process at Pan American Airways, since she had not been allowed to do this at Delta;
- conducted 'open-ended interviews lasting three to five hours each with thirty flight attendants in the San Francisco Bay Area' (1983: 15).

As a contrasting occupational group that is also involved in emotional labour, she also interviewed five debt-collectors. In her book, she explores such topics as the human costs of emotional labour and the issue of gender in relation to it. It is clear that Hochschild's concept of emotional labour began as a somewhat imprecise idea that emerged out of a concern with emotion work and that was gradually developed in order to address its wider significance.

The concept has been picked up by other qualitative researchers in management and organization studies. For example, Leidner (1993) has explored, through ethnographic studies of a McDonald's restaurant and an insurance company, the ways in which organizations seek to 'routinize' the display of emotional labour.

As the example in Research in focus 17.4 suggests, the researcher frequently starts out with a broad outline of a concept, which is revised and narrowed during the course of data collection. Subsequent researchers may take up and revise the concept and use it in different organizational contexts or in relation to different research questions.

Reliability and validity in qualitative research

In Chapters 3 and 7 it was noted that reliability and validity are important criteria in establishing and assessing the quality of research for the quantitative researcher. However, there has been discussion among qualitative researchers concerning the relevance of reliability and validity for qualitative research. Even writers who do take the view that the criteria are relevant have considered the possibility that the meanings of the terms need to be altered. For example, the issue of measurement validity almost by definition seems to carry connotations of measurement. Since measurement is not a major preoccupation among qualitative researchers, the issue of validity would seem to have little bearing on such studies. As foreshadowed briefly in Chapter 3, a number of stances have been taken by qualitative researchers in relation to these issues.

Adapting reliability and validity for qualitative research

One stance is to assimilate reliability and validity into qualitative research with little change of meaning other than playing down the salience of measurement issues. Mason (1996), for example, argues that reliability, validity, and generalizability (which is the main component of external validity; see Chapter 3) 'are different kinds of measures of the quality, rigour and wider potential of research, which are achieved according to certain methodological and disciplinary conventions and principles' (1996: 21). She sticks closely to the meaning that these criteria have in quantitative research, where they have been largely developed. Thus, validity refers to whether 'you are observing, identifying, or "measuring" what you say you are' (1996: 24). LeCompte and Goetz (1982) and Kirk and Miller (1986) also write about reliability and validity in relation to qualitative research but invest the terms with a somewhat different meaning from Mason. LeCompte and Goetz write about the following:

- *External reliability*, by which they mean the degree to which a study can be replicated. This is a difficult criterion to meet in qualitative research, since, as LeCompte and Goetz recognize, it is impossible to 'freeze' a social setting and the circumstances of an initial study to make it replicable in the sense in which the term is usually employed (see Chapter 7). However, they suggest several strategies that can be introduced in order to approach the requirements of external reliability. For example, they suggest that a qualitative researcher replicating ethnographic research needs to adopt a similar social role to that adopted by the original researcher. Otherwise what a researcher conducting a replication sees and hears will not be comparable to the original research.
- *Internal reliability*, by which they mean whether or not, when there is more than one observer, members of the research team agree about what they see and hear.

This is a similar notion to *inter-observer consistency* (see Key concept 12.7).

- *Internal validity*, by which they mean whether or not there is a good match between researchers' observations and the theoretical ideas they develop. LeCompte and Goetz argue that internal validity tends to be a strength of qualitative research, particularly ethnographic research, because the prolonged participation in the social life of a group over a long period of time allows the researcher to ensure a high level of congruence between concepts and observations.
- *External validity*, which refers to the degree to which findings can be generalized across social settings. LeCompte and Goetz argue that, unlike internal validity, external validity represents a problem for qualitative researchers because of their tendency to use case studies and small samples.

As this suggests, qualitative researchers have tended to use the terms reliability and validity in similar ways to quantitative researchers when seeking to develop criteria for assessing research.

Alternative criteria for evaluating qualitative research

However, some writers have suggested that qualitative studies should be evaluated according to quite different criteria from those used by quantitative researchers. Lincoln and Guba (1985) and Guba and Lincoln (1994) propose that it is necessary to specify terms and ways of establishing and assessing the quality of qualitative research that provide an alternative to reliability and validity. They propose two primary criteria for assessing a qualitative study: *trustworthiness* and *authenticity*.

Trustworthiness is made up of four criteria, each of which has an equivalent criterion in quantitative research:

- *credibility*, which parallels internal validity;
- *transferability*, which parallels external validity;
- *dependability*, which parallels reliability;
- *confirmability*, which parallels objectivity.

A major reason for Guba and Lincoln's unease about the simple application of reliability and validity standards to qualitative research is that the criteria presuppose that a single absolute account of social reality is feasible. In other words, they are critical of the view (described in Chapter 2 as *realist*) that there are absolute truths about the social world that it is the job of the social scientist to reveal. Instead, they argue that there can be more than one and possibly several accounts.

Credibility

The significance of this stress on multiple accounts of social reality is especially evident in the trustworthiness criterion of *credibility*. After all, if there can be several possible accounts of an aspect of social reality, it is the plausibility or credibility of the account that a researcher arrives at that is going to determine its acceptability to others. The establishment of the credibility of findings entails both ensuring that research is carried out according to the canons of good practice *and* submitting research findings to the members of the social world who were studied for confirmation that the investigator has correctly understood that social world. This latter technique is often referred to as **respondent validation** or *member validation* (see Key concept 17.5). Another technique Guba and Lincoln recommend is **triangulation** (see Key concept 17.6).

Key concept 17.5
What is respondent validation?

Respondent validation, which is also sometimes called *member validation*, is a process whereby a researcher provides the people on whom he or she has conducted research with an account of his or her findings. The aim of the exercise is to seek corroboration or otherwise of the account that the researcher has arrived at. Respondent validation has been particularly popular among qualitative researchers, because they frequently want to ensure that there is a good correspondence between their findings and the perspectives and experiences of their research participants. The form that respondent validation can assume varies. There are several forms:

- The researcher provides each research participant with an account of what he or she has said to the researcher in an interview and conversations, or of what the researcher observed by watching that person in the course of an observational study. For example, Marshall (1995) wanted to tell the stories of a small group of women managers who had left or were leaving senior organization positions, from these women's points of view. To achieve this she met with each manager, for between one-and-a-half and two hours, and asked her to tell her story. Marshall stated that she would be happy to discuss her own views and experiences if relevant. Once the story had been transcribed, she wrote an initial draft of the woman's story and invited the manager to read it.

- The researcher feeds back to a group of people or an organization his or her impressions and findings in relation to that group or organization. In Marshall's (1995) research, after reading the case the respondent then met Marshall again, or exchanged letters and phone calls, to develop the case to their mutual satisfaction. Most of the women were generally happy with the drafts but wanted minor amendments. Marshall revised the stories, taking research participants' comments into account. She states that, ultimately, the woman manager had the right of veto over what appeared in 'her' chapter of the book that Marshall wrote.

Later, all participants were invited to a one-day **collaborative enquiry** workshop, in which they jointly reviewed their experiences of employment and discussed issues of mutual interest.

In each case, the goal is to seek confirmation that the researcher's findings and impressions are congruent with the views of those on whom the research was conducted and to seek out areas where there is a lack of correspondence and the reasons for it. However, the idea is not without practical difficulties.

- Respondent validation may occasion defensive reactions on the part of research participants and even censorship. Marshall was willing to accept this as a consequence of her collaborative approach. Hence one participant decided that her story made her too identifiable and vulnerable. Even though her reasons for this were highly relevant to the research, as they centred on the difficulties of establishing a positive, accepted identity as a lesbian manager, Marshall agreed only to write a brief account of 'Ruth's' experience, in a chapter amounting only to six pages.

- It is highly questionable whether research participants can validate a researcher's analysis, since this entails inferences being made for an audience of business researchers. This means that, even though these methods

(continued)

may receive a corroborative response, the researcher still has to make a further leap, through developing concepts and theories that provide a framework for publication. Marshall was therefore careful to define the boundaries between data over which participants had a right of veto (the stories) and other material over which she wished to retain control, to put her own views and pursue her 'more academic concerns' (1995: 336), stressing from the outset that she would want to be able to use this in her publications.

Respondent validation can provide a means of confirming the validity of individual accounts. It can also help to redress the power imbalance between researcher and researched by providing the participants with a degree of authority in relation to the writing of the final research account. However, a distinction must be made between seeking validation from individuals and seeking validation from organizations, or—as is more likely—key groupings within organizations, such as senior managers. The latter option, by giving powerful groups within the organization control over the research, can introduce particular problems of censorship.

Transferability

As qualitative research typically entails the intensive study of a small group, or of individuals sharing certain characteristics (that is, depth rather than the breadth that is a preoccupation in quantitative research), qualitative findings tend to be orientated to the contextual uniqueness and significance of the aspect of the social world being studied. As Guba and Lincoln put it, whether or not findings 'hold in some other context, or even in the same context at some other time, is an empirical issue' (Lincoln and Guba 1985: 316). Instead, qualitative researchers are encouraged to produce what Geertz (1973) calls **thick description**—that is, rich accounts of the details of a culture. Guba and Lincoln argue that a thick description provides others with what they refer to as a database for making judgements about the possible transferability of findings to other milieux.

Key concept 17.6
What is triangulation?

Triangulation involves using more than one method or source of data in the study of social phenomena. The triangulation metaphor is taken from navigation and military strategy, where it refers to the process whereby multiple reference points are used to locate an object's exact position. The term has been used more broadly by Denzin (1970: 310) to refer to an approach that uses 'multiple observers, theoretical perspectives, sources of data, and methodologies', but the emphasis has tended to be on methods of investigation and sources of data. One of the reasons for the advocacy by Webb et al. (1966) of greater use of unobtrusive methods was their potential in relation to a strategy of triangulation. Triangulation can operate within and across research strategies. It was originally conceptualized by Webb et al. (1966) as an approach to the development of measures of concepts, whereby more than one method would be employed in the development of measures, resulting in greater confidence in findings. As such, triangulation was very much associated with a quantitative research strategy. However, triangulation can also take place within a qualitative research strategy. In fact, ethnographers often check out their observations with interview questions to determine whether they might have misunderstood what they had seen. Increasingly, triangulation is also being used to refer to a process of cross-checking findings deriving from both quantitative and qualitative research (Deacon, Bryman, and Fenton 1998). For example, Kanter (1977) draws attention to the triangulation of methods that characterized her approach, stating, 'I used each source of data, and each informant, as a check against the others' (1977: 337). She suggests that 'a combination of methods . . . emerges as the most valid and reliable way to develop understanding of such a complex social reality as the corporation' (1977: 337).

In addition to allowing the cross-checking of qualitative data, the use of quantitative and qualitative research in conjunction may allow access to different levels of reality. However, triangulation is just one way of thinking about the integration of these two research strategies; this is discussed in depth in Chapter 27.

Dependability

As a parallel to reliability in quantitative research, Guba and Lincoln propose the idea of dependability and argue that, to establish the merit of research in terms of this criterion of trustworthiness, researchers should adopt an 'auditing' approach. This entails ensuring that complete records are kept of all phases of the research process—problem formulation, selection of research participants, fieldwork notes, interview transcripts, data analysis decisions—in an accessible manner. Peers would then act as auditors, possibly during the course of the research and certainly at the end, to establish how far proper procedures are being and have been followed. This would include assessing the degree to which theoretical inferences can be justified. Auditing has not become a popular approach to enhancing the dependability of qualitative business research, partly because of some of the problems that are associated with it. One is that it is very demanding for the auditors, bearing in mind that qualitative research frequently generates extremely large datasets, and it may be that this is a major reason why it has not become a pervasive approach to validation.

Confirmability

Confirmability is concerned with ensuring that, while recognizing that complete objectivity is impossible in business research, the researcher can be shown to have acted in good faith; in other words, it should be apparent that he or she has not overtly allowed personal values or theoretical inclinations manifestly to sway the conduct of the research and findings deriving from it. Guba and Lincoln propose that establishing confirmability should be one of the objectives of auditors.

Authenticity

In addition to these four trustworthiness criteria, Guba and Lincoln suggest criteria of *authenticity*. These criteria raise a wider set of issues concerning the wider political impact of research. These are the criteria.

- *Fairness*. Does the research fairly represent different viewpoints among members of the social setting? For example, according to Starbuck (1981) one of the most serious deficiencies of the early (1963–72) Aston studies stems from the fact that the data about contexts and structures were collected primarily through interviews with senior managers. The first wave of interviews (1962–4) was conducted with chief executives and heads of departments, whereas the second set of interviews involved just one (senior) executive in the organization. Starbuck suggests that the data thus represent managerial perceptions and exclude the perceptions of other stakeholders, including first-line workers, customers, and suppliers.

- *Ontological authenticity*. Does the research help members to arrive at a better understanding of their social milieu?

- *Educative authenticity*. Does the research help members to appreciate better the perspectives of other members of their social setting?

- *Catalytic authenticity*. Has the research acted as an impetus to members to engage in action to change their circumstances?

- *Tactical authenticity*. Has the research empowered members to take the steps necessary for engaging in action?

These authenticity criteria are thought-provoking but have not been influential, and their emphasis on the wider impact of research is controversial. However, the main point of discussing Guba and Lincoln's ideas is that these authors differ from such writers as LeCompte and Goetz in seeking criteria for evaluating qualitative research that represent a departure from those employed by quantitative researchers. The authenticity criteria also have certain points of affinity with **action research**, which will be discussed later in this chapter.

The issue of research quality in relation to qualitative investigations has become a rather contested area in recent years, with several schemes of criteria being proposed as possible alternatives to reliability and validity as criteria and to such schemes as Lincoln and Guba's list. For example, Yardley (2000) has proposed the following four criteria:

- *Sensitivity to context*: sensitivity not just to the context of the social setting in which the research is conducted but also to potentially relevant theoretical positions and ethical issues.

- *Commitment and rigour*: substantial engagement with the subject matter, having the necessary skills, and through data collection and analysis.

- *Transparency and coherence*: research methods clearly specified, a clearly articulated argument, and a reflexive stance (see Chapter 29 for a discussion of reflexivity).

- *Impact and importance*: importance of having an impact on and significance for theory, for the community on which the research is conducted, and for practitioners.

When compiling these criteria, Yardley had in mind health researchers who are likely to emphasize the impact of a study, but this emphasis can also be seen clearly in business research, as discussed in Chapter 2. The emphasis on impact probably accounts for the presence of the last of these four criteria—impact and importance—which has some affinities with Lincoln and Guba's authenticity criteria.

Even though qualitative researchers have sought to make progress in formulating quality criteria appropriate to their approach, this has not necessarily had an impact on the reception of their research. Pratt (2008) has shown that many qualitative researchers believe that their work continues to be judged by the criteria associated with validity and reliability that were introduced in Chapter 3, which tend to be viewed as more appropriate to quantitative research. This tendency has implications for the nature of the research that gets published in academic journals, in that it gives an advantage to those researchers working within a quantitative research tradition. In other words, although qualitative researchers have sought to develop what they deem to be appropriate criteria, the impact on evaluation of research is not as great as might be expected.

Overview of the issue of criteria

There is a recognition—albeit to varying degrees—that a simple application of the quantitative researcher's criteria of reliability and validity to qualitative research is not desirable, but writers vary in the degree to which they propose a complete overhaul of those criteria. Nor do the three positions outlined above represent the full range of possible stances on this issue (Hammersley 1992a; Seale 1999). To a large extent, the differences between the three positions reflect divergences in the degree to which a realist position is broadly accepted or rejected. Writers on qualitative research who apply the ideas of reliability and validity with little if any adaptation broadly position themselves as realists—that is, as saying that social reality can be captured by qualitative researchers through their concepts and theories. Lincoln and Guba reject this view, arguing instead that qualitative researchers' concepts and theories are representations and that there may, therefore, be other equally credible representations of the same phenomena. Hammersley's position occupies a middle ground in terms of the axis, with realism at one end and anti-realism at the other, in that, while acknowledging the existence of social phenomena that are part of an external reality, he disavows any suggestion that it is possible to reproduce that reality for the audiences of social scientific endeavour. Most qualitative researchers nowadays probably operate around the midpoint on this realism axis, though without necessarily endorsing Hammersley's views. Typically, they treat their accounts as one of a number of possible representations, rather than as definitive versions of social reality. They also bolster those accounts through some of the strategies advocated by Lincoln and Guba, such as thick descriptions, respondent validation exercises, and triangulation.

The main preoccupations of qualitative researchers

As noted in Chapter 7, quantitative and qualitative research exhibit a set of distinctive but contrasting preoccupations. These preoccupations reflect epistemologically grounded beliefs about what constitutes acceptable knowledge. In Chapter 2 it was suggested that, at the level of epistemology, whereas quantitative research is profoundly influenced by a natural science approach of what should count as acceptable knowledge, qualitative researchers are more influenced by *interpretivism* (see Key concept 2.10). This position is the product of the confluence of three related stances: Weber's notion of *Verstehen*; symbolic interactionism; and phenomenology. In this section, five distinctive preoccupations among qualitative researchers will be outlined and examined.

Seeing through the eyes of the people being studied

An underlying premise of many qualitative researchers is that the subject matter of the social sciences (that is, people and their social world) does differ from the subject matter of the natural sciences. A key difference is that the objects of analysis of the natural sciences (atoms, molecules, gases, chemicals, metals, and so on) cannot attribute meaning to events and to their environment. However, people *do*. This argument is especially evident in the work of Schutz (1962) and can particularly be seen in the passage quoted in Chapter 2, where Schutz draws attention to the fact that, unlike the objects of the natural sciences, the objects of the social sciences—people—are

Research in focus 17.7
Gaining an insider view of strategic change

In their study of strategic change in a university, Gioia et al. (1994) describe themselves as adopting an interpretative approach to the research in attempting 'to represent the experience and interpretations of informants without giving precedence to prior theoretical views that might not be appropriate' (1994: 367). To this end, they give priority to the insider's perspective, to counterbalance the arrogant stance that they suggest organizational researchers tend to adopt towards their subjects of study. However, they also recognize the limitations of this reliance on informant views, which do not address the 'dimensions or structure of phenomena' (1994: 367). They therefore juxtapose this first-hand account with a grounded theoretical analysis of the case, to develop a triangulated approach.

Similarly, in another study of strategic change, Harfield and Hamilton (1997) suggest that the majority of research in strategic management has adopted a detached, outsider approach, which is 'bound up in a straightjacket of "dated" organizational concepts and "multivariate statistical methodology"' (1997: 61, quoting Bettis 1991). As an alternative, they seek to accommodate managers' experiences by using the storytelling method, in the belief that this will have greater relevance to other managers in dealing with rapidly changing environments. They suggest that an interpretative methodology enables strategy to be presented as a continually unfolding experience, and not, as much of the traditional view of strategy explains it, as an end point or destination.

These examples illustrate how some strategic management researchers suggest that qualitative approaches provide an important complement to the explanations enabled by statistical methods that tend to be used within this field.

capable of attributing meaning to their environment. Consequently, many qualitative researchers have suggested that a methodology is required for studying people that reflects these differences between people and the objects of the natural sciences. As a result, many qualitative researchers express a commitment to viewing events and the social world through the eyes of the people that they study. The social world must be interpreted from the perspective of the people being studied, rather than as though those subjects were incapable of their own reflections on the social world. The epistemology underlying qualitative research has been expressed by the authors of one widely read text as involving two central tenets: '(1) . . . face-to-face interaction is the fullest condition of participating in the mind of another human being, and (2) . . . you must participate in the mind of another human being (in sociological terms, "take the role of the other") to acquire social knowledge' (Lofland and Lofland 1995: 16). Examples of this approach are given in Research in focus 17.7.

It is not surprising, therefore, that many researchers make claims in their reports of their investigations about having sought to take the views of the people they studied as the point of departure (see Research in focus 17.8). This tendency reveals itself in frequent references to empathy and seeing through others' eyes. Here are some examples.

- Nichols and Beynon (1977) wanted to understand the working lives of workers, foremen, and managers at 'ChemCo', a British-owned multinational chemical producer, from a Marxist perspective. Nichols and Beynon suggest that theory 'fails to connect with the lives that people lead, whereas most descriptive social surveys too often fail to grasp the structure of social relations and the sense which people make of them. It is almost as if another way of writing has to be developed; something which "tells it like it is," even though in any simple sense this is not possible' (1977: 2).

- Marshall (1984) describes herself as an 'interpreter' rather than a manipulator of data, 'concerned with capturing other people's meanings rather than testing hypotheses' (1984: 116).

- Jackall (1988), in his ethnographic study of bureaucracy and morality in large corporations, seeks to generate an understanding of 'how men and women in business actually experience their work' (1988: 5), in order to ascertain its moral salience for them.

- Casey (1995) acknowledges that her study interprets and analyses the speech of her interviewees, albeit highly selectively, and thereby does to some extent attempt to '"give voice" to other voices' (1995: 203), even though the selection of data was based on her own interpretation as an academic researcher.

The preference for seeing through the eyes of the people studied in qualitative research is often accompanied by the closely related goal of seeking to probe beneath surface appearances. After all, if you take the position of the people you are studying, the prospect is raised that they might view things differently from the way an outsider with little direct contact might have expected. This stance reveals itself in:

- Dalton's (1959) research study of the informal organization, which found that the boundaries between unofficial reward obtained through expense accounting, and organizational theft, or pilfering, were defined quite differently by individual managers, depending on their position within the hierarchy;

- the work of Collinson (1992a), who found that shop-floor workers at 'Slavs' dealt with their occupational status partly by channelling their personal ambitions and energies outside the workplace into the alternative domains of family and home, investing in 'the self-sacrificing role of parental breadwinner' (1992a: 185);

- Marshall's (1984) study of women in management, which showed that this issue could not be understood without taking into account the wider social context, including society's values about work, and the way of life in large organizations, in order to make sense of the kinds of job roles that women in employment adopt;

- Ram's (1994) study of management in small firms, which showed that workers were not just controlled through direct supervision and intensive working methods, as previous studies had suggested. Using ethnographic methods, Ram was able to pick up on a variety of largely informal negotiating processes, whereby employees negotiated a 'fair' rate for the job, taking into account considerations such as the time of the year, the type of work, caste, and culture.

The empathetic stance of seeking to see through the eyes of one's research participants is very much in tune with interpretivism and demonstrates well the epistemological links with phenomenology, symbolic interactionism, and *Verstehen*. However, it is not without practical problems. For example: the risk of 'going native' and losing sight of what you are studying (see Key concept 19.9); the problem of how far the researcher should go, such as the potential problem of participating in illegal or dangerous activities; and the possibility that the researcher will be able to see through the eyes of only some of the people who form part of a social scene but not others, such as only people of the same gender.

Description and the emphasis on context

Qualitative researchers are more inclined than quantitative researchers to provide a great deal of descriptive detail when reporting their research. This is not to say that they are exclusively concerned with description. They *are* concerned with explanation, and indeed the extent to which qualitative researchers ask 'Why?' questions is frequently understated. In addition, more critical or radical qualitative researchers are often concerned with understanding the political and economic interests that inform organizational actions, in order to enhance the possibilities for changing them. For example, in her ethnography of a multinational corporation, Casey (1995) describes herself as concerned with understanding dominant social constructions about work, the self, and society, in the hope that this might increase the likelihood of societal transformation.

Many qualitative studies provide a detailed account of what goes on in the setting being investigated. Very often qualitative studies seem to be full of apparently trivial details. However, these details are frequently important for the qualitative researcher, because of their significance for their subjects and also because the details provide an account of the context within which people's behaviour takes place. It was with this point in mind that Geertz (1973) recommended the provision of thick descriptions of social settings, events, and often individuals. As a result of this emphasis on description, qualitative studies are often full of detailed information about the social worlds being examined. On the surface, some of this detail may appear irrelevant, and, indeed, there is a risk of the researcher becoming too embroiled in descriptive detail. Lofland and Lofland (1995: 164–5), for example, warn against the sin of what they call 'descriptive excess' in qualitative research, whereby the amount of detail overwhelms or inhibits the analysis of data.

One of the main reasons why qualitative researchers are keen to provide considerable descriptive detail is that they typically emphasize the importance of the contextual understanding of social behaviour. This means that behaviour and values must be understood in the situations where they arise. This recommendation means that we cannot understand the behaviour of members of a social group other than in terms of the specific environment in which they operate. In this way, behaviour that may appear odd or irrational can make perfect sense when we understand the particular context within which that behaviour takes place. The emphasis on context in qualitative research goes back to many of the classic studies in social anthropology, which often demonstrated how a particular practice, such as the magical ritual that may accompany the sowing of seeds, made little sense unless we understand the belief systems of that society. One of the chief reasons for the emphasis on descriptive detail is that it is often precisely this detail that provides the mapping of context in terms of which behaviour is understood. The propensity for description can also be interpreted as a manifestation of the naturalism that pervades much qualitative research (see Key concept 3.4 and Key concept 17.1), because it places a premium on detailed, rich descriptions of social settings.

Emphasis on process

Qualitative research tends to view social life in terms of processes. This tendency reveals itself in a number of ways. One of the main ways is that there is often a concern to show how events and patterns unfold over time. As a result, qualitative evidence often conveys a strong sense of change and flux. As Pettigrew (1997: 338) explains, process is 'a sequence of individual and collective events, actions, and activities unfolding over time in context'. This includes understanding how the past history of an organization shapes the present reality and how the 'interchange between agents and contexts occurs over time and is cumulative' (Pettigrew 1997: 339). This aspect of

qualitative research is recognized in the distinction that is sometimes made between variance and process theories in organizational life (Mohr 1982; Langley 2009). With the former, the goal is to express explanations of organizational characteristics and events in terms of connections between independent and dependent variables. In contrast, process theories 'provide explanations in terms of patterns in events, activities, and choices over time' (Langley 2009: 409). As Langley observes, time is a key ingredient of organizational life, so *not* taking it into account (as variance theory does) is to miss out on something that is core to organizational reality.

Qualitative research based on ethnographic methods is particularly associated with this emphasis on process. It is the element of participant observation, a key feature of ethnography, that is especially instrumental in generating this feature. Ethnographers are typically immersed in a social setting for a long time—sometimes years, as in Michel's (2011) study of Wall Street bankers (Research in focus 19.2). Consequently, they are able to observe the ways in which events develop over time or the ways in which the different elements of a social system (values, beliefs, behaviour, and so on) interconnect. Such findings can inject a sense of process by seeing social life in terms of streams of interdependent events and elements (see Research in focus 17.8 for an example).

This is not to say, however, that ethnographers are the only qualitative researchers who inject a sense of process into our understanding of social life. It can also be achieved through semi-structured and unstructured

Research in focus 17.8
Process in strike action

D. Waddington (1994) describes his experiences of participant observation of a strike at the Ansells brewery in Birmingham in the 1980s. As a participant observer, he was involved in 'attending picket lines, mass meetings and planning discussions, and accompanying the strikers of flying picketing and intelligence gathering manoeuvres' (1994: 113). In addition to observation, he carried out informal interviews and linked these data to other sources, such as 'material deriving from newspaper archives, company and trade union documents, letters and richly detailed minutes of trade-union management meetings' (1994: 115). As a result, he was able to show 'how the contemporary beliefs, values and attitudes of the workforce, and the mutual feelings of animosity and distrust between employees and management, were shaped by a sequence of historical events stretching back over 20 years' (1994: 115). We can see in this example the development of a sense of process in three ways: through observation of the strike over its entirety, so that developments and interconnections between events could be brought out; through connecting these events with historical and other data, so that the links between the strike and previous and other events and actions could be outlined; and through the sketching of the context (in the form of the past, as well as current beliefs and values) and its links with behaviour during the strike.

interviewing, by asking participants to reflect on the processes leading up to or following on from an event.

The life history approach is another form of qualitative research. This technique takes as research data accounts of individuals about their lives or specific areas of their social world. Accounts focus on the relationship between the individual and his or her social context. G. Jones (1983) suggests that the life history approach is useful as a means of researching organizational socialization and career development. This involves leading individuals through an account of their organizational careers and asking them to chart out significant events through which they came to an understanding of their social organizational context.

Flexibility and limited structure

Many qualitative researchers are disdainful of approaches to research that entail the imposition of predetermined formats on the social world. This position is largely to do with the preference for seeing through the eyes of the people being studied. After all, if a structured method of data collection is employed, since this is bound to be the product of an investigator's ruminations about the object of enquiry, certain decisions must have been made about what he or she expects to find and about the nature of the social reality that is to be encountered. Therefore, the researcher is limited in the degree to which he or she can genuinely adopt the world view of the people being studied. Consequently, most qualitative researchers prefer a research orientation that entails as little prior contamination of the social world as possible. To do otherwise risks imposing an inappropriate frame of reference on people. Keeping structure to a minimum is supposed to enhance the

opportunity of genuinely revealing the perspectives of the people you are studying. Also, in the process, aspects of people's social world that are particularly important to them, but that might not even have crossed the mind of a researcher unacquainted with it, are more likely to be forthcoming. As a result, qualitative research tends to be a strategy that tries not to delimit areas of enquiry too much and to ask fairly general rather than specific research questions (see Figure 17.1).

Owing to the preference for a loosely structured approach to the collection of data, qualitative researchers adopt methods of research that do not require the investigator to develop highly specific research questions in advance and therefore to devise instruments specifically for those questions to be answered. Ethnography, with its emphasis on participant observation, is particularly well suited to this orientation. It allows researchers to submerge themselves in a social setting with a fairly general research focus in mind and gradually to formulate a narrower emphasis by making as many observations of that setting as possible. They can then formulate more specific research questions out of their collected data. Similarly, interviewing is an extremely prominent method in the qualitative researcher's armoury, but it is not of the kind we encountered in the course of most of Chapter 9—namely, the structured interview. Instead, qualitative researchers prefer less structured approaches to interviewing, as we will see in Chapter 20. Blumer's (1954) argument for sensitizing rather than definitive concepts (that is, the kind employed by quantitative researchers) is symptomatic of the preference for a more open-ended, and hence less structured, approach. Some researchers have argued that this is more likely to lead to research that is interesting, in terms of standing out in some way from other

Thinking deeply 17.9
Is qualitative research more 'interesting'?

The *Academy of Management Journal* featured a discussion in which editors and invited contributors pondered on what makes research interesting (Bartunek, Rynes, and Ireland 2006). The discussion was prompted by a survey that found that, while articles in the journal were considered to be technically highly competent, they did not find very many of the papers to be interesting in terms of engaging readers' attention or challenging commonly held assumptions about a subject. This prompted the journal editors to try to expand the remit of the journal to include research that develops theory in addition to research that tests or extends it (see discussion of deductive and inductive research strategies in Chapter 2). In terms of being interesting, Barley (2006) argues that qualitative researchers have greater potential to produce interesting papers because, unlike quantitative researchers, they have 'already departed from mainstream methods, [and] have less to lose by studying odd topics and taking theoretical risks' (Barley 2006: 19).

Key concept 17.10
What are first and second-order concepts?

Gioia et al. (2012) describe their approach to developing concepts and building theory through data which they developed in the course of their research practice over more than 20 years. This is based on a systematic two-stage process involving:

First-order analysis: using informant-centric terms and codes;

Second-order analysis: using researcher-centric concepts, themes and dimensions.

While this distinction bears close relation to grounded theory, first-order analysis sharing many characteristics with open coding, and second-order analysis being closely related to the development of categories (see Chapter 24), the next stage involves developing the data into a 'data structure', a visual map illustrating the progression from raw data to terms and themes, which forces researchers to think about their data theoretically. This systematic approach enabled Gioia et al. to demonstrate the rigorous nature of their conceptual and theory development in a way which was convincing to reviewers less familiar with a qualitative approach. However, the first-/second-order distinction has now become so prevalent in qualitative business and management research that Gioia et al. suggest it may be being overused and treated as a template, as data structure formats from previously published work are simply reproduced. They caution against this 'cookbook' approach because it goes against the use of this methodology, which must be open to innovation in order to remain effective.

studies and changing the way that we think about the social world (see Thinking deeply 17.9).

An advantage of the unstructured nature of most qualitative enquiry (that is, in addition to gaining access to people's world views) is that it offers the prospect of flexibility. The researcher can change direction in the course of his or her investigation much more easily than in quantitative research, which tends to have a built-in momentum once the data collection is under way: if you send out hundreds of postal questionnaires and realize after you have started to get some back that there is an issue that you would have liked to investigate, you are not going to find it easy to retrieve the situation. Structured interviewing and structured observation can involve some flexibility, but the requirement to make interviews as comparable as possible for survey investigations limits the extent to which this can happen.

Concepts and theory grounded in data

For qualitative researchers, concepts and theories are usually inductively arrived at from the data that are collected through a process of development (see Research in focus 17.4). In recent years, attempts have been made to enhance the transparency surrounding this process and to introduce greater rigour into this aspect of qualitative research (see Key concept 17.10).

Not just words

In recent years qualitative business researchers have become increasingly interested in analysing visual as well as linguistic meaning. Prior to this, the analysis of visual data in business research was relatively uncommon (Meyer 1991; Holliday 2001). However, this is now changing, partly because of a growing interest in visual analysis across the social sciences (Banks 2001; Pink 2001; Rose 2001). A distinction can be made between the use of visual materials that are *extant* and those produced more or less exclusively for the purposes of research. The former will be discussed in more detail in Chapter 23 and include such artefacts as company annual reports and product advertisements. Research in focus 17.11 involves the use of research-driven visual images in the form of photographs. Such images may be taken either by the researcher or by research participants themselves. In either case, the images may be used as a basis for what is often referred to as **photo-elicitation** (Key concept 9.10 and Research in focus 9.11). Photo-elicitation can be used with extant images too, as will be shown in Chapter 23.

Photographs produced as part of fieldwork may be taken by the researcher and analysed alongside other types of documents containing written words, such as interview transcripts, as in the study of business process re-engineering by Buchanan (2001). Sometimes the use of photographs and other visual records is not built into the researcher's plans at the outset. For example,

Cockburn and Ormrod (1993) did not initially intend to use photographs in their case studies of firms manufacturing and selling microwave ovens, but Cockburn was impeded in writing by 'repetitive strain injury' from many years of typing, so she decided to return to the research sites with a camera as a way of creating a narrative that could run parallel to their interview data. By contrast, Buchanan (2001), in his study of the introduction of business process re-engineering in Leicester General Hospital, included photography from the outset as part of the battery of data collection techniques he employed. As part of his focus on getting a sense of the 'patient trail', over 150 transparency slides were taken. Buchanan (2001: 151) argues that using photographs in conjunction with other methods of data collection helps the organizational researcher

- to develop a richer understanding of organizational processes;
- to capture data not disclosed in interview;
- to reveal to staff aspects of work in other sections of the organization with which they have little or no regular contact;
- to offer a novel channel for respondent validation of data; and
- to involve staff in debate concerning the implications of research findings for organization process redesign and improvement.

The distinction between extant and research-driven visual materials is not entirely satisfactory. For example, when research participants are asked to discuss items in their photograph collections, this is similar to asking participants to take photographs and then discuss the images that are taken, as in the study of aesthetics conducted by S. Warren (2002, 2005, Research in focus 17.11). Warren's study involved giving a camera to employees in a website design department of a global IT company located in a rural location in the south of England and asking them to take photographs that would 'show' how it 'felt' to work there. Plates 17.1–17.3 show three photographs taken by respondents. Plate 17.1 is a photograph of a cup of tea from a vending machine. When the respondent was asked why he had taken this particular picture, he raised issues concerning his dissatisfaction with the amount of money that had been spent on the office at the expense of other things that were more important to employees. Plate 17.2 shows a meeting room that was photographed by a respondent who found it to be an escape and a contrast from the normal work environment. However, Warren argues that in her study the use of photographs did not primarily entail analysis of their content. Instead the photographs formed part of a data-generating triangle involving the image, respondent, and researcher, focusing on the reasons why they were taken. Plate 17.3 provides a good illustration of this, since the blurred nature of this photograph of the office space means it would be difficult to distinguish the

Plate 17.1

'Cup of tea from vending machine'

Copyright Samantha Warren. Reproduced with thanks.

Plate 17.2

'Thinktank: aestheticized meeting room'

Copyright Samantha Warren. Reproduced with thanks.

content at all without the account provided by the respondent, who explains that they were trying to capture the 'busyness' and 'colour' that defined the atmosphere of the workplace. Warren also notes that photographs such as this one show how intangible emotional concepts that are hard to communicate through language can be conveyed through the use of images.

Two recent reviews (Bell and Davison 2013, Meyer et al. 2013) highlight the growing interest of qualitative researchers in the visual dimension of business and

Plate 17.3

'Blurred view of office space'

Copyright Samantha Warren. Reproduced with thanks.

management. Both draw attention to the role of the linguistic turn (see Chapter 22) in emphasising the importance of language in constituting meaning, suggesting that this has become limiting. They highlight the unique aspects of the visual in contrast to linguistic meaning, including aesthetic attributes and the mimetic potential to induce immediate, memorable effects on audiences. In addition to the various kinds of secondary documents that can provide sources of visual data, such as annual reports and company archives, which will be discussed in Chapter 23, visual material can be generated through the research process, for example by the researcher or research participants taking photographs. Meyer et al. (2013) provide an overview of how visuals have been integrated into qualitative organizational research and identify five ideal-typical approaches:

- *Archaeological:* based on analysis of visual artefacts in which socially constructed meaning is embodied; Davison's (2009) study of iconography in a UK bank (Research in focus 23.9) provides an example;

- *Practice:* involving the study of visual artefacts in situ, including how they are used by social actors in various processes of organizing; an example is Bell's (2012) study of visual expression of change and loss surrounding the closure of a car manufacturing plant (Research in focus 19.16);

- *Strategic:* this builds on psychological, linguistic or semiotic theory and involves the use of visual methods to elicit desired responses from audiences; an example is the study of change by Broussine and Vince (1996), where they asked managers to draw pictures;

- *Dialogical:* this type of research uses visuals as a form of communication between the researcher and the field, such as through the use of projective techniques, pictorial and photo-elicitation (see Chapter 9). An example would be Warren's study of aesthetic experiences of employees in a global IT firm (Research in focus 17.11);

- *Documenting:* this involves the use of visual artifacts as a form of field notes to document the research process; examples include Buchanan's (1998) study of the hospital patient trail (Research in focus 9.11) and Bryman's use of photographs in researching Disneyization (Research in focus 19.14).

However, Meyer et al. (2013) suggest there is still some way to go before the inclusion of visual data in empirical analyses becomes the norm rather than the exception. A useful source of information about these developments is the International Network for Visual Studies in Organizations, *in*Visio, which is dedicated to bringing together researchers, practitioners, and artists to explore the visual dimensions of business, management, and organizational life. The website contains information about studies that use visual methods, and details of workshops and events. It can be found at:

http://moodle.in-visio.org/ (accessed 31 October 2014)

Research in focus 17.11
An example of visual research

Dialogical visual research (Meyer et al. 2013) involves using visual artefacts as a means of communication between the researcher and research participants. S. Warren (2002) used photographs to explore the aesthetic dimension of organization. Warren was prompted to use visual methods because she was convinced that 'in order to explore the relationship between the feel, sights, smells, and even the tastes of the organizational setting . . . a more "sensually complete" methodology' (2002: 230) was required in order to record things that could not be spoken or written down. Her case study was the website design department of a global IT company, where she carried out participant observation, taking photographs of the physical environment of the workplace. She also gave the camera to her respondents, asking them to show her 'how it feels to work here'. She claims that 'the photographs make an interesting data set in their own right regarding the ways in which the respondents chose to define their work environments, what they felt to be worthy (and not worthy) of photographing, and the individual and sometimes innovative ways they framed their subjects' (2002: 232). The photographs were then discussed in the context of an interview conversation with the respondent. Warren suggests that the photographs added to the richness of data gathered through their imagery, which she argues was used by respondents to give an emotional sense of the work environment. She concludes, 'the choice of what to photograph and how to place it within the frame are inextricably bound up with the visual culture of the photographer and his or her intentions and motives' (2002: 236).

Tips and skills
Copyright and photographs

Pink (2001) emphasizes the importance of checking the legal position regarding publishing photographs that you have produced yourself for research purposes. Under UK law, researchers usually own the copyright of photographs they have produced themselves. However, if you are taking photographs of other people, you should gain at least their verbal, and possibly their written, permission before publishing or displaying the photograph in a public forum. In addition, if you are using photographs that have been produced by someone else, you need to check who owns the copyright and seek their permission to reproduce it, for which a fee may be payable. S. Warren (2009) points out that for visual researchers conducting organizational research care is needed to ensure that rights associated with copyright images such as logos are not infringed. What is and is not a copyright image is not always obvious. Alan Bryman (1995, 2004b) was unable to use any photographs taken in Disney theme parks, because it is not just the characters whose images are covered by copyright (for example, Donald Duck) but also the buildings, which are often just as iconic and memorable.

More information on the legal position regarding copyright of photographs in the UK can be found at the following websites, where links to other national copyright sites can also be found:

www.copyrightservice.co.uk (accessed 31 October 2014)

Finally, visual research methods raise especially difficult issues of ethics, an area that is explored in Chapter 6. The Visual Sociology Group, a study group of the British Sociological Association (BSA), has produced a statement of ethical practice for researchers using visual methods:

www.visualsociology.org.uk/about/ethical_statement.php (accessed 30 October 2014)

This is a useful statement, which draws on the BSA's *Statement of Ethical Practice*, referred to in Chapter 6. Here are some statements of ethical practice that are recommended:

Researchers may want to discuss the status of the images with participants in order to clearly explain the dissemination strategy of the research project. In certain circumstances, they may want to create a written or verbal contract guaranteeing the participants ownership of the images produced. Under UK law copyright can be waived by participants and given to the researcher(s); however it is recommended that researchers read the current legislation or seek legal advice if taking this option (please note that the date of the creation of the image affects the legal status).

The critique of qualitative research

In a similar way to the criticisms that have been levelled at quantitative research mainly by qualitative researchers, a parallel critique has been built up of qualitative research. These are some of the more common issues raised.

Qualitative research is too subjective

Quantitative researchers sometimes criticize qualitative research as being too impressionistic and subjective. By these criticisms they usually mean that qualitative findings rely too much on the researcher's often unsystematic views about what is significant and important, and also upon the close personal relationships that the researcher frequently strikes up with the people studied. Precisely because qualitative research often begins in a relatively open-ended way and entails a gradual narrowing-down of research questions or problems, the consumer of the writings deriving from the research is given few clues as to why one area was the chosen area upon which attention was focused rather than another. By contrast, quantitative researchers point to the tendency for the problem formulation stage in their work to be more explicitly stated in terms of such matters as the existing literature on that topic and key theoretical ideas.

Difficult to replicate

Quantitative researchers also often argue that these tendencies are made more problematic because of the difficulty of replicating a qualitative study, although replication is by no means a straightforward matter regardless of this particular issue (see Chapter 7). Precisely because it is unstructured and reliant upon the qualitative researcher's ingenuity, it is almost impossible to conduct a true replication, since there are hardly any standard procedures to be followed. In qualitative research, the investigator him or herself is the main instrument of data collection, so that what is observed and heard and also what the researcher decides to concentrate upon is very much a product of his or her preferences. There are several possible components of this criticism: what qualitative researchers (especially perhaps in ethnography) choose to focus upon while in the field is a product of what strikes them as significant, whereas other researchers are likely to empathize with other issues; the responses of participants (people being observed or interviewed) to qualitative researchers are likely to be affected by the characteristics of the researcher (personality, age, gender, and so on); and, because of the unstructured nature of qualitative data, interpretation will be profoundly influenced by the subjective leanings of a researcher. Because of such factors it is difficult to replicate qualitative findings. The difficulties ethnographers experience when they revisit grounds previously trodden by another researcher (often referred to as a 'restudy') do not inspire confidence in the replicability of qualitative research (Bryman 1994).

Problems of generalization

It is often suggested that the scope of the findings of qualitative investigations is restricted. When participant observation is used or when unstructured interviews are conducted with a small number of individuals in a certain organization or locality, they argue that it is impossible to know how the findings can be generalized to other settings. How can just one or two cases be representative of all cases? In other words, can we really treat Perlow's (1997; see Key concept 19.1) research on the time and the work–life balance of software engineers in a high-tech corporation in the USA as representative of all software engineers; or Ladge et al.'s (2012) research on pregnant women professionals as representative of the identity transition experiences of women working in non-professional occupations? In the case of research based on interviews rather than participation, can we treat interviewees who have not been selected through a probability procedure or even quota sampling as representative? Are Watson's

(1994a) managers typical of all managers working within the telecommunications industry, or are Ram's (1994; see Research in focus 19.5) small-firm case studies in the West Midlands typical of small firms elsewhere?

The answer in all these cases is, of course, emphatically 'no'. A case study is not a sample of one drawn from a known population. Similarly, the people who are interviewed in qualitative research are not meant to be representative of a population and indeed, in some cases, like managers, we may find it more or less impossible to enumerate the population in any precise manner. Instead, the findings of qualitative research are to generalize to theory rather than to populations. It is 'the cogency of the theoretical reasoning' (J. C. Mitchell 1983: 207), rather than statistical criteria, that is decisive in considering the generalizability of the findings of qualitative research. In other words, it is the quality of the theoretical inferences that are made out of qualitative data that is crucial to the assessment of generalization.

These three criticisms reflect many of the preoccupations of quantitative research that were discussed in Chapter 7. A further criticism that is often made of qualitative research, but that is perhaps less influenced by quantitative research criteria, is the suggestion that qualitative research frequently lacks transparency in how the research was conducted.

Lack of transparency

It is sometimes difficult to establish from qualitative research what the researcher actually *did* and how he or she arrived at the study's conclusions. For example, qualitative research reports are sometimes unclear about such matters as how people were chosen for observation or interview. This deficiency contrasts sharply with the sometimes laborious accounts of sampling procedures in reports of quantitative research. However, it does not seem plausible to suggest that outlining in some detail the ways in which research participants are selected constitutes the application of quantitative research criteria. Readers have a right to know to what extent research participants were selected to correspond to a wide range of people. Also, the process of qualitative data analysis is frequently unclear (see Bryman and Burgess 1994a). It is often not obvious how the analysis was conducted—in other words, what the researcher was actually doing when the data were analysed and therefore how the study's conclusions were arrived at. These issues of lack of transparency are being addressed (see Thinking deeply 17.12), but not always in ways that are consistent with the principles of qualitative research.

Thinking deeply 17.12
A quantitative review of qualitative research in management and business

Bluhm et al. (2011) conducted a quantitative review of 198 articles based on qualitative research published in leading US and European management journals over a ten-year period (1998–2008). They assert that support for qualitative research grew in this period and that overall quality standards rose, a trend they attribute to greater standardization and increased scientific and methodological rigour and validity. The authors identify the most common theoretical purpose of these articles as theory elaboration and theory generation. In terms of research design, most (59 per cent) used more than one method of data collection, with interviewing being by far the most popular method used. One interesting finding to emerge from the review was that studies using novel or innovative qualitative methods, such as focus groups or diaries, tend to be cited more often than those that use conventional research designs. The authors therefore recommend greater use of innovative qualitative techniques by drawing on methods used in other disciplines, such as sociology or linguistics. The authors used a combination of quantitative content analysis (see Chapter 13) and citation analysis in their review which they argue enabled them to 'draw precise conclusions and make more accurate comparisons' (Bluhm et al. 2011: 1872). However, their application of positivist quality criteria, such as removal of researcher bias and replicability, could be seen as a somewhat contradictory and inappropriate imposition of quantitative standards of evaluation on qualitative research.

Is it always like this?

This was a heading that was employed in Chapter 7 in relation to quantitative research, but it is perhaps less easy to answer in relation to qualitative research. To a large extent, this is because qualitative research is less codified than quantitative research—that is, it is less influenced by strict guidelines and directions about how to go about data collection and analysis. For example, Dalton (1964) (see Chapter 19) explains that no explicit hypotheses formed the basis for his participant-observational study of managerial work, for three reasons. First, he was not able to be sure what was relevant until he had gained 'some intimacy with the situation'; secondly, once uttered, a hypothesis becomes somewhat 'obligatory'; and, thirdly, there is a danger that the hypothesis carries a quasi-scientific status. Instead he worked on the basis of 'hunches', which guided him through the research.

As a result, accounts of qualitative research are frequently less prescriptive in tone than those encountered in relation to quantitative research. Instead, they often exhibit more of a descriptive tenor, outlining the different ways qualitative researchers have gone about research or suggesting alternative ways of conducting research or analysis based on the writer's own experiences or those of others. To a large extent, this picture is changing, in that there is a growing number of books and articles that seek to make clear-cut recommendations about how qualitative research should be carried out (see Thinking deeply 17.12 for an illustration of this type of standardizing approach).

However, if we look at some of the preoccupations of qualitative research that were described above, we can see certain ways in which there are departures from the practices that are implied by these preoccupations. One of the main departures is that qualitative research is sometimes a lot more focused than is implied by the suggestion that the researcher begins with general research questions and narrows it down so that theory and concepts are arrived at during and after the data collection. There is no *necessary* reason why qualitative research cannot be employed to investigate a specific research problem. A related way in which qualitative research differs from the standard model is in connection with the notion of a lack of structure in approaches to collecting and analysing data. As will be seen in Chapter 22, such techniques as conversation analysis entail the application of a highly codified method for analysing talk.

Moreover, the use of computer-assisted qualitative data analysis software (CAQDAS), which will be the subject of Chapter 25, has led to greater transparency in the procedures used for analysing qualitative data. This may lead to more codification in qualitative data analysis than has previously been the case.

Some contrasts between quantitative and qualitative research

Several writers have explored the contrasts between quantitative and qualitative research by devising tables that allow the differences to be brought out (e.g. Halfpenny 1979; Bryman 1988a; Hammersley 1992b). Table 17.1 attempts to draw out the chief contrasting features.

- *Numbers vs Words*. Quantitative researchers are often portrayed as preoccupied with applying measurement procedures to social life, while qualitative researchers are seen as using words in the presentation of analyses of society, although, as we have emphasized, qualitative researchers are also concerned with the analysis of visual data.
- *Point of view of researcher vs Points of view of participants*. In quantitative research, the investigator is in the driving seat. The set of concerns that he or she brings to an investigation structures the investigation. In qualitative research, the perspective of those being studied—what they see as important and significant—provides the point of orientation.
- *Researcher is distant vs Researcher is close*. In quantitative research, researchers are uninvolved with their subjects and in some cases, as in research based on postal questionnaires or on hired interviewers, may have no contact with them at all. Sometimes, this lack of a relationship with the subjects of an investigation is regarded as desirable by quantitative researchers, because they feel that their objectivity might be compromised if they become too involved with the people they study. The qualitative researcher seeks close

Table 17.1

Some common contrasts between quantitative and qualitative research	
Quantitative	Qualitative
Numbers	Words
Point of view of researcher	Points of view of participants
Researcher distant	Researcher close
Theory testing	Theory emergent
Static	Process
Structured	Unstructured
Generalization	Contextual understanding
Hard, reliable data	Rich, deep data
Macro	Micro
Behaviour	Meaning
Artificial settings	Natural settings

involvement with the people being investigated, so that he or she can genuinely understand the world through their eyes.

- *Theory and concepts tested in research vs Theory and concepts emergent from data.* Quantitative researchers typically bring a set of concepts to bear on the research instruments being employed, so that theoretical work precedes the collection of data, whereas in qualitative research concepts and theoretical elaboration emerge out of data collection.

- *Static vs Process.* Quantitative research is frequently depicted as presenting a static image of social reality with its emphasis on relationships between variables. Change and connections between events over time tend not to surface, other than in a mechanistic fashion. Qualitative research is often depicted as attuned to the unfolding of events over time and to the interconnections between the actions of participants of social settings.

- *Structured vs Unstructured.* Quantitative research is typically highly structured, so that the investigator is able to examine the precise concepts and issues that are the focus of the study; in qualitative research the approach is invariably unstructured, so that the possibility of getting at actors' meanings and of concepts emerging out of data collection is enhanced.

- *Generalization vs Contextual understanding.* Whereas quantitative researchers want their findings to be generalizable to the relevant population, the qualitative researcher seeks an understanding of behaviour, values, beliefs, and so on in terms of the context in which the research is conducted.

- *Hard, reliable data vs Rich, deep data.* Quantitative data are often depicted as 'hard' in the sense of being robust and unambiguous, owing to the precision offered by measurement. Qualitative researchers claim, by contrast, that their contextual approach and their often prolonged involvement in a setting engender rich data.

- *Macro vs Micro.* Quantitative researchers are often depicted as involved in uncovering large-scale social trends and connections between variables, whereas qualitative researchers are seen as concerned with small-scale aspects of social reality, such as interaction.

- *Behaviour vs Meaning.* It is sometimes suggested that the quantitative researcher is concerned with people's behaviour and the qualitative researcher with the meaning of action.

- *Artificial settings vs Natural settings.* Whereas quantitative researchers conduct research in a contrived context, qualitative researchers investigate people in natural environments.

However, as we will see in Chapter 26, while these contrasts depict reasonably well the differences between quantitative and qualitative research, they should not be viewed as constituting hard and fast distinctions. These issues will be returned to in the next three chapters.

Some similarities between quantitative and qualitative research

It is also worth bearing in mind the ways in which quantitative and qualitative research are *similar* rather than different, as Hardy and Bryman (2004) have pointed out. They draw attention to the following points:

- *Both are concerned with data reduction.* Both quantitative and qualitative researchers collect large amounts of data. These large amounts of data represent a problem for researchers, because they then have to distil the data. By reducing the amount of data, they can then begin to make sense of it. In quantitative research, the process of data reduction takes the form of statistical analysis—something like a mean or frequency table is a way of reducing the amount of data on large numbers of people. In qualitative data analysis, as will be seen in Chapter 24, qualitative researchers develop concepts out of their often rich data.

- *Both are concerned with answering research questions.* Although the nature of the kinds of research questions asked in quantitative and qualitative research are typically different (more specific in quantitative research, more open-ended in qualitative research), they are both fundamentally concerned with answering questions about the nature of social reality.

- *Both are concerned with relating data analysis to the research literature.* Both quantitative and qualitative researchers are typically concerned to relate their findings to points thrown up by the literature relating to the topics on which they work. In other words, the researcher's findings take on significance in large part when they are related to the literature.

- *Both are concerned with variation.* In different ways, both quantitative and qualitative researchers seek to uncover variation and then to represent the variation that they uncover. This means that both groups of researchers are keen to explore how organizations (or whatever the unit of analysis is) differ and to explore some of the factors connected to that variation, although, once again, the *form* that variation takes differs.

- *Both treat frequency as a springboard for analysis.* In quantitative research, frequency is a core outcome of collecting data, as the investigator typically wants to reveal the relative frequency with which certain types of behaviour occur or how many newspaper articles emphasize a certain issue. In qualitative research, issues of frequency arise in the fact that, in reports of findings in publications, such terms as 'often' or 'most' are commonly employed. Also, when analysing qualitative data, the frequency with which certain themes occur commonly acts as a catalyst for which ones tend to be emphasized when writing up findings.

- *Both seek to ensure that deliberate distortion does not occur.* Very few business researchers nowadays subscribe to the view that it is possible to be an entirely objective and dispassionate student of organizational life. Further, sometimes researchers can be partisan (Chapter 6). However, that does not imply that 'anything goes'. In particular, researchers seek to ensure that 'wilful bias' (Hammersley and Gomm 2000) or what Hardy and Bryman (2004: 7) call 'consciously motivated misrepresentation' does not occur.

- *Both argue for the importance of transparency.* Both quantitative and qualitative researchers seek to be clear about their research procedures and how their findings were arrived at. This allows others to judge the quality and importance of their work. In the past, it has sometimes been suggested that qualitative researchers could be opaque about how they went about their investigations, but increasingly transparency is an expectation.

- *Both must address the question of error.* In Chapter 9, readers were introduced to the significance of error for quantitative research (or, more specifically, survey research) and what steps are taken to reduce its likelihood. For the quantitative researcher, error must be reduced as far as possible so that variation that is uncovered is real variation and not the product of problems with how questions are asked or how research instruments are administered. In qualitative research, the investigator seeks to reduce error by ensuring that, for example, there is a good fit between his or her concepts and the evidence that has been amassed.

- *Research methods should be appropriate to the research questions.* This is not addressed by Hardy and Bryman (2004), but a further issue is that both groups of researchers seek to ensure that, when they specify research questions, they select research methods and approaches to the analysis of data that are appropriate to those questions.

These tend to be rather general points of similarity, but they are an important corrective to any view that portrays the two approaches as completely different. There *are* differences between quantitative and qualitative research but that is not to say that there are no points of similarity.

Researcher–subject relationships

A further difference between quantitative and qualitative research arises from the way that qualitative researchers relate to their research subjects. Qualitative researchers tend to take greater account of the power relations that exist between the researcher him or herself and the people who are the subject of study. This has led to the development of several qualitative approaches that enable research subjects to play a more active part in designing the research and to influence the outcomes of the process. **Action research**, feminism, and collaborative and participative forms of enquiry all fall into this category. We will consider the main features of each of these approaches and explore the implications that they have for researcher–subject relationships.

Action research

There is no single type of action research, but broadly it can be defined as an approach in which the action researcher and a client collaborate in the diagnosis of a

Research in focus 17.13
Action research

Participatory action research can be seen as an emergent process to the extent that it may not even begin as explicitly participatory. Based on their involvement with the US-based multinational Xerox corporation, Greenwood, Whyte, and Harkavy (1993) propose that the aim of participatory action research is to encourage continuous learning on the part of researchers and the members of the organization.

The case began as a 'fairly conventional consulting program' (1993: 181). However, in response to declining market share and profits, the company implemented a competitive benchmarking programme that threatened major job losses. This led to a participatory action research project that focused on socio-technical change processes. The project involved management and union officials working together with researchers, drawing on theories and ideas from a variety of fields. The team learned how to address the internal cost accounting procedures that 'could lead management to make decisions adverse to the economic interests of both company and workers' (1993: 183).

Greenwood and his colleagues say little about how the shift from consulting programme to action research project was negotiated. However, they do say that a sense of organizational crisis was important in precipitating this shift. This in part depends on organizational leaders being willing to take risks and allow action researchers to engage in processes that senior management does not control.

problem and in the development of a solution based on the diagnosis. A common theme among business researchers is that action research output results from 'involvement with members of an organization' over a matter of 'genuine concern to them' (Eden and Huxham 1996: 75). Many writers therefore stress the need for action research to be useful to the practitioner and suggest it should provide a means of empowering participants. For an example of action research, see Research in focus 17.13.

Action research is defined by Argyris, Putnam, and Smith (1985) as follows:

- Experiments are on real problems within an organization and are designed to assist in their solution.

- This involves an iterative process of problem identification, planning, action, and evaluation.

- Action research leads eventually to re-education, changing patterns of thinking, and action. This depends on the participation of research subjects (who are often referred to in action research as clients) in identifying new courses of action.

- It is intended to contribute both to academic theory and practical action.

Eden and Huxham (1996) define the characteristics of action research in terms of outcomes and processes. Good and effective action research should have the following outcomes:

- It should have implications that relate to situations other than the one that is studied.

- As well as being usable in everyday life, action research should also be concerned with theory.

- It should lead to the generation of emergent or grounded theory, which emanates from the data in gradual incremental steps.

- Action researchers must recognize that their findings will have practical implications and they should be clear about what they expect participants to take away from the project.

- The collection of data is likely to be involved in the formulation of the diagnosis of a problem and in the evaluation of a problem. Data collection methods can include keeping a diary of subjective impressions, a collection of documents relating to a situation, observation notes of meetings, questionnaire surveys, interviews, audio or video recordings of meetings, and written descriptions of meetings or interviews (which may be given to participants for them to validate or amend). In action research, the investigator becomes part of the field of study, and, as with participant observation, this has its own attendant problems. In their action research study of an outpatient health centre, Ramirez and Bartunek (1989) suggest that they were involved in dilemmas that related to conflicting organizational roles, which led to conflict over researcher loyalties. This affected how the action researcher (who was an internal consultant) was seen, as rumours were spread in order to discredit the action researcher by suggesting that she was using the project

Thinking deeply 17.14
Feminist research in business and management

Organizational research has typically been pursued from a male-orientated perspective, which, according to Wilson (1995), regards men and women as alike and fails to consider gender as a significant variable within organizational processes. To illustrate this, Wilson cites the example of the Hawthorne studies (see also Research in focus 3.8), which involved the observational study of a group of female employees in the 'test room' and a group of male employees in the 'bank wiring room'. 'The men were observed under normal working conditions while the female group was pressured, by male supervisors, into an experimental situation. Despite the fact that output was increased by the women and restricted by the men, the overall findings were presented as an explanation of the behaviour of employees *per se*' (1995: 1–2). Other studies have tended to treat women as entirely peripheral to organizational life. This bias is particularly evident in the study of management. As the majority of managers are men, studies of management have mainly focused on observation of male managers. Therefore, recommendations about what makes effective management often erroneously assume that better managers are more masculine, reinforcing this masculine gender stereotype. Despite the growth of feminist research in various disciplines, much of this has occurred outside the boundaries of business research. If, as Wilson suggests, we need to 'see reality differently' and reformulate the way in which work organizations are understood, feminist methods provide a means whereby male-orientated values can be exposed and challenged.

to set up a favourable position within the organization for herself.

Action research is criticized, in a similar way to other qualitative methods, for its lack of repeatability and consequent lack of rigour and for concentrating too much on organizational action at the expense of research findings. In their defence, action researchers claim that involvement with practitioners concerning issues that are important to them provides a richness of insight that cannot be gained in other ways. It is also claimed that theory generated from action research is 'grounded in action' (Eden and Huxham 1996), thereby overcoming some of the difficulties of relying on talk as a source of data, instead of action or overt behaviour.

One of the techniques used by action researchers is **cognitive mapping**, because the maps can be used as a problem-solving device by researchers, who work interactively with managers to address a particular organizational issue. The method draws on personal construct theory (Kelly 1955), which also informs the use of repertory grid technique (see Chapter 9), and is based on the assumption that people are actively engaged in constructing models, hypotheses, or representations that enable them to make sense of the world around them. While cognitive maps can be seen as models of cognition, their primary function is as a tool for reflective thinking about a problem that enables steps to be taken towards its solution. The mapping process involves carrying out either group or individual interviews with participants to understand the person's individual construct system and

work out how this affects a particular decision-making 'goal' (Eden 1988). These data are then put into a map-like diagram that reflects the relationship between the concepts and represents how the problem is understood.

Action research should not be confused with *evaluation research* (see Key concept 3.10), which usually denotes the study of the impact of an intervention, such as a new social policy or a new innovation in organizations.

Feminism and qualitative research

A further dimension to add to this discussion is that in the view of some writers, qualitative research is associated with a feminist sensitivity, and that, by implication, quantitative research is viewed as incompatible with feminism. Moreover, feminist research could be seen as having a particularly important role to play in relation to business research, which has typically been pursued from a masculine perspective (see Thinking deeply 17.14). The bias towards a masculine perspective in business research could also be related to the dominance of quantitative methods, which are regarded as 'hard' or 'masculine', rather than qualitative methods, which are seen as 'soft' and lacking in concreteness (Gherardi and Turner 1987).

The notion that there is an affinity between feminism and qualitative research has at least two main components to it: a view that quantitative research is inherently incompatible with feminism, and a view that qualitative research provides greater opportunity for a feminist sensitivity to come to the fore. Quantitative research is frequently viewed as incompatible with feminism for the following reasons:

- According to Mies (1993), quantitative research suppresses the voices of women either by ignoring them or by submerging them in a torrent of facts and statistics.

- The criteria of valid knowledge associated with quantitative research are ones that turn women, when they are the focus of research, into objects. This means that women are again subjected to exploitation, in that knowledge and experience are extracted from them with nothing in return, even when the research is conducted by women (Mies 1993).

- The emphasis on controlling variables further exacerbates this last problem, and indeed the very idea of control is viewed as a masculine approach.

- The use of predetermined categories in quantitative research results in an emphasis on what is already known and consequently in 'the silencing of women's own voices' (Maynard 1998: 128).

- The criteria of valid knowledge associated with quantitative research also mean that women are to be researched in a value-neutral way, when in fact the goals of feminist research should be to conduct research specifically *for* women.

- It is sometimes suggested that the quest for universal laws is inconsistent with feminisms's emphasis on the situated nature of social reality, which is seen as embedded in the various social identities (based on gender, ethnicity, sexual orientation, class, etc.) that are unique to individuals (Miner-Rubino, Jayaratne, and Konik, 2007).

By contrast, qualitative research was viewed by many feminists as either more compatible with feminism's central tenets or as more capable of being adapted to those tenets. In contrast to quantitative research, qualitative research allows:

- women's voices to be heard;

- exploitation to be reduced by giving as well as by receiving in the course of fieldwork;

- women *not* to be treated as objects to be controlled by the researcher's technical procedures; and

- the emancipatory goals of feminism to be realized.

How qualitative research achieves these goals will be addressed particularly in the next three chapters, since the issues and arguments vary from one method to the other. The issue of qualitative research providing the opportunity for a feminist approach has different aspects when looking at ethnography, qualitative interviewing, and focus groups. However, business research has a tendency towards gender-blindness in terms of the way that research topics are defined. For example, Mirchandani (1999) observes that much of the research on women's experiences of entrepreneurship focuses on identifying similarities and differences between female and male business-owners, and on providing explanations of these differences. She argues that, although this is useful in compensating for the exclusion of women in earlier studies, it does not explain why entrepreneurship is defined and understood only in terms of the behaviour of men. Mirchandani argues that the construction of the category of 'the female entrepreneur' prioritizes gender over other important aspects of identity, such as social stratification, business ownership, organizational structure, and industry, that need to be explored in relation to female *and* male business-owners. Some business researchers have sought to adopt a feminist approach (see Research in focus 17.15). However, there has been a softening of attitude among some feminist writers towards quantitative research in recent years which can be summarised as follows:

- There is a recognition that many of the worst excesses of discrimination against women might not have come to light so clearly were it not for the collection and analysis of statistics revealing discrimination (Maynard 1994; Oakley 1998). The presence of factual evidence of this kind has allowed the case for equal opportunities legislation to be made much more sharply, although, needless to say, there is much more that still needs to be done.

- Qualitative research can be enlisted as an aid to implementing social change for feminists. Miner-Rubino, Jayaratne, and Konik (2007) suggest that knowledge about the distribution of attitudes and behaviours in a sample can be used to establish the most appropriate course of action for social change.

- As Jayaratne and Stewart (1991) and Maynard (1994, 1998) have pointed out, at the very least it is difficult to see why feminist research that combines quantitative and qualitative research would be incompatible with the feminist cause.

- There has also been a recognition of the fact that qualitative research is not *ipso facto* feminist in orientation. If, for example, ethnography, which is covered in the next chapter, provided for a feminist sensitivity, we would expect subjects such as social anthropology, which have been virtually founded on the approach, to be almost inherently feminist, which is patently not the case (Reinharz 1992: 47–8). If this is so, the question

Research in focus 17.15
A feminist analysis of embodied identity at work

The subject of embodied identities at work has attracted interest from feminist researchers, who see feminist theories as key to understanding how bodies, and in particular women's bodies, are understood in the workplace. Trethewey (1999), who is a Foucauldian feminist, interviewed nineteen professional women about their definitions and experiences of their professional bodies using the friendship model of interviewing (Oakley 1981), explained in Chapter 20. Trethewey explains: 'I felt more comfortable approaching the participants as friends rather than as subjects or data. I have since formed friendships with several of the participants, have joined the reading group of another participant, and was invited to participate in a local women's mentoring committee by yet another participant' (1999: 427). This shows how feminist researchers seek to break down the boundaries between the researcher and (female) research participants as a means of trying to make the research relationship more equal.

of appropriate approaches to feminist research would seem to reside in the *application* of methods rather than something that is inherent in them. Consequently, some writers have preferred to write about *feminist research practice* rather than about *feminist methods* (Maynard 1998: 128).

Collaborative and participatory research

Like action research and some kinds of feminist research, collaborative and participatory researchers assume that research should be driven by practical outcomes rather than by theoretical understanding. However, the distinguishing feature of collaborative research is that it assumes members of the organization being studied should actively participate in the research process and also benefit from it. Collaborative methods are seen as particularly important in researching groups such as children who would otherwise be at a particular power disadvantage in dealing with researchers. Collaborative research can be seen as a form of respondent validation (see Key concept 17.5) by attempting to redistribute power between the researcher and research participants. P. Park (1999) describes participatory research as focused on disempowered groups that can be helped through research that addresses problems related to their welfare in an organized way. The researcher should ideally be someone who is familiar with the community and committed to working towards improving their conditions. This, he argues, is what differentiates participatory researchers from other types of action researchers who are concerned only with solving problems of a job-related nature. This is similar to critical or emancipatory action research (Zuber-Skerritt 1996), which is a form of collaborative enquiry engaged in by

practitioners who want to explore a problem or issue in relation to their own practice.

An important milestone in the development of these research traditions was the publication of a book by Reason and Rowan (1981), which brought together writers from these traditions and argued for the legitimacy of a 'new paradigm' of research based on increased participation and collaboration with research subjects. (For an example of the kind of research that this book encouraged, see Research in focus 17.16.) This set of perspectives broadly defined research as a two-way process whereby the researcher becomes involved in the participant's world and the practitioner gets involved in the generation of research outputs. At its most radical, this leads to cooperative enquiry, where all those involved are both co-researchers and co-subjects (Reason 1999).

Collaborative methods of enquiry stem from a desire to challenge the conventional methods whereby knowledge is constructed in the social sciences. This involves challenging the monopoly, traditionally held by universities, over the processes and outcomes of research and offering a more democratic alternative whereby research participants are treated as active agents rather than as passive subjects. It is about doing research 'with people' rather than 'on people' (Heron and Reason 2000). It also seeks to acknowledge that the motivation to do research is related to our own personal needs for development, change, and learning (Reason and Marshall 1987) and that research often involves personal growth (see Research in focus 17.16 for an illustration).

Postcolonial and indigenous research

A further way in which researcher-subject relationships have been challenged in recent years is through

Research in focus 17.16
Collaborative enquiry into workplace diversity

In order to consider the resources necessary to support an increasingly diverse workforce, Bond and Pyle (1998) used a social ecological perspective in order to suggest that the environment, and in particular the distribution of resources, exerts a powerful influence on human behaviour. Their observations are based on an organizational case study called 'Chemical Products', where they used a collaborative enquiry process. They explain:

> We chose a collaborative inquiry process because of our ecologically-driven belief that organization members are not only in the best position to answer questions about their own setting, but they are also the most knowledgeable about what questions to ask, how to ask the questions, and how to understand participants' responses. To facilitate such a participative process, we worked closely with the HR Manager and her staff. After getting approval for the project from the President, we reviewed goals with the Unit Managers Group. We then established a Steering Team to guide the Workplace Chemistry Project. We clarified project goals with other existing groups such as the cross-department People Team. These meetings were followed by thirty-six in-depth interviews, participant observation of meetings, and a series of feedback sessions.
>
> (Bond and Pyle 1998: 597)

postcolonialist critique of practices of social scientific knowledge production, which are based on a conception of research which developed in the countries of Europe and North America that was subsequently exported to the global South. This relies on the assertion that 'social science can have only one, universal, body of concepts and methods, the one created in the global North' (Connell 2007: ix). Writers like Connell challenge this by exposing the hidden biases contained within theories produced from within the global North which claim universal relevance based on the assumption that 'all societies are knowable, and they are knowable in the same way and from the same point of view' (Connell 2007: 44). Such an approach is suggested to be inherently colonizing, involving the abandonment of local cultural knowledge and the imposition of discourses of scientific research that are claimed to be neutral but that involve the assertion of imperialist neocolonial power relations of oppression and domination. This can be seen from the ways in which scientific research has been used as a tool of colonialist exploitation; for example, Prasad (2003) points out that ethnography (see Chapter 19) was used in the nineteenth and early twentieth centuries by imperialist European powers of Britain, France, and the Netherlands, to gather data about Asian and African cultures which enabled their subjugation and explanation, 'by carving out identities of the Western self and the non-Western Other, and by delineating relationships between them through

a series of hierarchical oppositional categories' (Prasad 2003: 155). She argues that the concept of the ethnographic imagination, based on discourses of primitivism, orientalism, and tropicalization, which the colonial project entailed, can still be seen in many recent ethnographic accounts of fieldwork which celebrate risky adventures in 'foreign' lands.

These critiques have opened up spaces for the construction of alternative approaches to knowledge production, in the form of indigenous methodologies, a term which invites exploration of methods that enable the voices of colonized peoples to be heard, in addition to non-human interests related to ecosystems (Tuhiwai Smith, 1999). Informed by feminist approaches to research, indigenous methodologies seek to disrupt established relationships between (mostly non-indigenous) researchers and indigenous peoples and enable them to find their own academic voice and identity; the focus is thus on the ethics of research and the implications for communities of research. These ideas are potentially highly significant in understanding globalization and its effects in fields such as international and comparative management and business. For example, Jack and Westwood (2006) use ideas from postcolonialism to argue that researchers in these fields, even those committed to qualitative methods, have been slow to acknowledge the political nature of research in reflecting the interests and values of the researcher. They propose an alternative, in the form of a postcolonial

Research in focus 17.17
Indigenous ways of understanding leadership

Warner and Grint (2006) explore Native American traditions of leadership which they assert can displace the imperialist foundations of the American approach to studying this subject and open up alternatives. However, one of the challenges they faced in this project related to the dominance of the English language, and the difficulty of translating meanings from indigenous cultural contexts: 'when discussing leadership with American Indians whose second language is English, the first author sought to have them give their own tribal word for "leader"' (Warner and Grint 2006: 231). This prompted discussion of numerous terms related to leadership, which the authors found very difficult to translate in a way which preserved their cultural meaning. A key characteristic of their research involved an obligation actively to work with research subjects to question the methods and processes of research, including the reliance on observation and the privileging of the written word, and to question what is actually meant by 'leadership'. They conclude 'that we need more studies of [Native American] leadership by insiders not simply of insiders if we are ever to get beyond a superficial comprehension of the "other"' (Warner and Grint 2006: 240).

epistemology which enables the universalizing tendencies of Western knowledge systems, which construct and legitimate the dominance of the West as a source of knowledge about international business, to be resisted. Research in focus 17.17 provides an example of how these ideas have also been applied in the field of leadership.

Key points

- There is disagreement over what precisely qualitative research is.

- Qualitative research does not lend itself to the delineation of a clear set of linear steps.

- It tends to be a more open-ended research strategy than is typically the case with quantitative research.

- Theories and concepts are viewed as outcomes of the research process.

- Visual materials, such as photographs and video, have attracted considerable interest among qualitative business researchers in recent years, not just as adjuncts to data collection but as objects of interest in their own right.

- There is considerable unease about the simple application of the reliability and validity criteria associated with quantitative research to qualitative research. Indeed, some writers prefer to use alternative criteria that have parallels with reliability and validity.

- Action research is an approach in which the researcher and a client collaborate in the diagnosis of a problem and in the development of a solution to the problem based on the diagnosis. It is connected with the method of cognitive mapping.

- Most qualitative researchers reveal a preference for seeing through the eyes of research participants.

- Several writers have depicted qualitative research as having a far greater affinity with a feminist standpoint than quantitative research.

- Action research, feminism, collaborative and indigenous methods of enquiry have changed the relationship between researchers and the research subjects.

Questions for review

- What are some of the difficulties with providing a general account of the nature of qualitative research?
- Outline some of the traditions of qualitative research.
- What are some of the main research methods associated with qualitative research?

The main steps in qualitative research

- Does a research question in qualitative research have the same significance and characteristics as in quantitative research?

Theory and research

- Is the approach to theory in qualitative research inductive or deductive?

Concepts in qualitative research

- What is the difference between definitive and sensitizing concepts?

Reliability and validity in qualitative research

- How have some writers adapted the notions of reliability and validity to qualitative research?
- Why have some writers sought alternative criteria for the evaluation of qualitative research?
- Evaluate Lincoln and Guba's criteria.
- What is respondent validation?
- What is triangulation?

The main preoccupations of qualitative researchers

- Outline the main preoccupations of qualitative researchers.
- How do these preoccupations differ from those of quantitative researchers, which were considered in Chapter 7?

The critique of qualitative research

- What are some of the main criticisms that are frequently levelled at qualitative research?
- To what extent do these criticisms reflect the preoccupations of quantitative research?

Is it always like this?

- Can qualitative research be employed in relation to hypothesis testing?

Some contrasts and similarities between quantitative and qualitative research

- 'The difference between quantitative and qualitative research revolves entirely around the concern with numbers in the former and with words in the latter.' How far do you agree with this statement?

Researcher–subject relationships

- What is action research?
- Is there a role for feminist research in the study of business and management?

- How have collaborative approaches to qualitative research changed the relationship between the researcher and research subjects?
- What are the distinguishing features of indigenous and postcolonial methodologies and how can they be applied in business research?

Online Resource Centre

www.oxfordtextbooks.co.uk/orc/brymanbrm4e/

Visit the Interactive Research Guide that accompanies this book to complete an exercise in The Nature of Qualitative Research.

18

Sampling in qualitative research

Chapter outline

This chapter outlines some of the main ways of thinking about conducting sampling in qualitative research. Whereas, in survey research, there is an emphasis on probability sampling, qualitative researchers tend to emphasize the importance of *purposive sampling* for their work. Purposive sampling places the investigator's research questions at the heart of the sampling considerations. This chapter explores:

- the significance of a consideration of levels of sampling;
- the nature of purposive sampling and the reasons for the emphasis on it among many qualitative researchers;
- theoretical sampling, which is a key ingredient of the grounded theory approach, and the nature of theoretical saturation, which is one of the main elements of this sampling strategy;
- the importance of not assuming that theoretical and purposive sampling are the same thing;
- the generic purposive sampling approach as a means of distinguishing theoretical sampling from purposive sampling in general;
- the use of more than one sampling approach in qualitative research.

Introduction

In much the same way that, in quantitative research, the discussion of sampling revolves around **probability sampling**, discussions of sampling in qualitative research tend to revolve around the notion of **purposive sampling** (see Key concept 18.1). This type of sampling is essentially to do with the selection of units (which may be people, organizations, documents, departments, and so on), with direct reference to the research questions being asked. The idea is that the research questions should give an indication of what units need to be sampled. Research questions are likely to provide guidelines as to what categories of people (or whatever the unit of analysis is) need to be the focus of attention and therefore sampled. In this chapter, purposive sampling will act as the master concept around which different sampling approaches in qualitative research can be distinguished.

Probability sampling may be used in qualitative research, though it is more likely to occur in interview-based rather than in ethnographic qualitative studies. There is no obvious rule of thumb that might be used to help the qualitative researcher in deciding when it might be appropriate to employ probability sampling, but two criteria might be envisaged. First, if it is highly significant or important for the qualitative researcher to be able to generalize to a wider population, probability sampling is likely to be a more compelling sampling approach. This might occur when the audience for one's work is one for whom generalizability in the traditional sense of the word is important. Second, if the research questions do not suggest that particular categories of people (or whatever the unit of analysis is) should be sampled, there may be a case for sampling randomly.

However, in many cases, probability sampling is not feasible, because of the constraints of ongoing fieldwork and also because it can be difficult and often impossible to map 'the population' from which a random sample might be taken—that is, to create a sampling frame. However, the reason why qualitative researchers rarely seek to generate random samples is not due to these technical constraints but because, like researchers basing their investigations on qualitative interviewing, they typically want to ensure that they gain access to as wide a range of individuals relevant to their research questions as possible, so that many different perspectives and ranges of activity are the focus of attention.

Key concept 18.1
What is purposive sampling?

Purposive sampling is a non-probability form of sampling. The researcher does not seek to sample research participants on a random basis. The goal of purposive sampling is to sample cases/participants in a strategic way, so that those sampled are relevant to the research questions that are being posed. Very often, the researcher will want to sample in order to ensure that there is a good deal of variety in the resulting sample, so that sample members differ from each other in terms of key characteristics relevant to the research question. Because it is a non-probability sampling approach, purposive sampling does not allow the researcher to generalize to a population. Although a purposive sample is not a random sample, it is not a convenience sample either (see Chapter 8 on convenience sampling). A convenience sample is simply available by chance to the researcher, whereas in purposive sampling the researcher samples with his or her research goals in mind. In purposive sampling, sites, such as organizations, and people (or whatever the unit of analysis is) within sites are selected because of their relevance to the research questions. The researcher needs to be clear in his or her mind what the criteria are that will be relevant to the inclusion or exclusion of units of analysis (whether the 'units' are sites, people, or something else). Examples of purposive sampling in qualitative research are theoretical sampling (see Key concept 18.3) and **snowball sampling** (see Research in focus 18.6 for an example). In quantitative research, quota sampling is a form of purposive sampling procedure.

Levels of sampling

Writers on sampling in qualitative research sometimes provide lists of the different sampling approaches that may be found (see Key concept 18.2 for some of the main types that are frequently identified). While these are useful, they sometimes intermingle two different levels of sampling, an issue that is particularly relevant to the consideration of sampling in qualitative research based on single case study or multiple case study designs. With such research designs, the researcher must first select the case or cases; subsequently, the researcher must sample units within the case. When sampling contexts or cases, qualitative researchers have a number of principles of purposive sampling on which to draw. To a significant extent, the ideas and principles behind these were introduced in Chapter 3 in connection with the different types of case, particularly following Yin's (2009) classification.

An example is a study by Pringle (1988) of power relations and secretarial work. This study involved interviews with secretarial students and with a range of workers, both secretarial and non-secretarial, in a variety of Australian workplaces. The first stage of this process involved groups of three secretarial students who were interviewed for 20–30 minutes about their course. A smaller sample ($n = 30$) were interviewed again near the end of their course and then followed into the workforce. Fifteen were interviewed a third time individually at home and asked

to reflect on the value of their course. The second stage of interviews was carried out in a representative range of workplaces. 'Of 244 interviews 72 were with employees in the public sector, 32 with unions, 92 with large corporations and 44 with small companies, agencies and partnerships' (Pringle 1988: 268). A breakdown of interviewees by occupation is given in Table 18.1.

Table 18.1

A stratified interview sample		
Interviewees by occupation	Number	%
Top and middle management	54	22
Lower management	22	9
Administrative	18	7.5
Supervisory	9	3.5
Personal assistant	3	1.5
Secretary (1 boss)	67	27.5
Secretary (2+ bosses)	29	12
Word processor/typist	22	9
Clerical assistant	20	8
Total	244	100

Source: adapted from Pringle (1988).

Key concept 18.2
Some purposive sampling approaches

The following is a list of some prominent types of purposive sample that have been identified by writers such as Patton (1990) and Palys (2008):

1. *Extreme or deviant case sampling*. Sampling cases that are unusual or that are unusually at the far end(s) of a particular dimension of interest.

2. *Typical case sampling*. Sampling a case because it exemplifies a dimension of interest.

3. *Critical case sampling*. Sampling a crucial case that permits a logical inference about the phenomenon of interest—for example, a case might be chosen precisely because it is anticipated that it might allow a theory to be tested.

4. *Maximum variation sampling*. Sampling to ensure as wide a variation as possible in terms of the dimension of interest.

5. *Criterion sampling*. Sampling all units (cases or individuals) that meet a particular criterion.

6. *Theoretical sampling*. See Key concept 18.3.

7. *Snowball sampling*. See Research in focus 18.6.

8. *Opportunistic sampling*. Capitalizing on opportunities to collect data from certain individuals, contact with whom is largely unforeseen but who may provide data relevant to the research question.

9. *Stratified purposive sampling*. Sampling of usually typical cases or individuals within subgroups of interest.

The first three purposive sampling approaches are ones that are particularly likely to be employed in connection with the selection of cases or contexts. The others are likely to be used in connection with the sampling of individuals as well as cases or contexts.

Purposive sampling

Most sampling in qualitative research entails purposive sampling of some kind. What links the various kinds of purposive sampling approach is that the sampling is conducted with reference to the goals of the research, so that units of analysis are selected in terms of criteria that will allow the research questions to be answered. This term is explained in Key concept 18.1.

In order to contextualize the discussion, we will draw on two useful distinctions that have been employed in relation to purposive sampling. First, Teddlie and Yu (2007) distinguish a sampling approach that they refer to as sequential sampling, which implies a distinction between sequential and non-sequential approaches. Non-sequential approaches to sampling might be termed 'fixed sampling strategies'. With a sequential approach, sampling is an evolving process in that the researcher usually begins with an initial sample and gradually adds to the sample as befits the research questions. Units are selected by virtue of their relevance to the research

questions, and the sample is gradually added to as the investigation evolves. With a fixed purposive sampling strategy, the sample is more or less established at the outset of the research, and there is little or no adding to the sample as the research proceeds. The research questions guide the sampling approach, but the sample is more or less fixed early on in the research process. Second, Hood (2007) distinguishes between *a priori* and contingent sampling approaches. A purposive sampling approach is contingent when the criteria for sampling units of analysis evolve over the course of the research. The research questions again guide the sampling of participants, but the relevant sampling criteria shift over the course of the research as the research questions change or multiply. With an *a priori* purposive sample, the criteria for selecting participants are established at the outset of the research. The criteria will again be ones that are designed to answer the research questions, but the criteria do not evolve as the research progresses.

Telling it like it is
Purposive sampling in a student's research project

Karen's experience of semi-structured interviewing shows how interviewees may be selected purposively on the basis of their likely ability to contribute to theoretical understanding of a subject. As she explained: 'I wanted people who knew something about person–culture fit. I wanted people who were involved in the recruitment process and so I used my own contacts from within the organization, which then obviously brings up a possible element of bias, I suppose, because I didn't choose them by any random means. I chose them because I knew that they were already involved in it. The reason for that was that I wanted people who had opinions on it, whichever they were, so that I could really explore the ideas with them'.

Theoretical sampling

One form of purposive sampling is **theoretical sampling** (see Key concept 18.3), advocated by Glaser and Strauss (1967) and Strauss and Corbin (1998) in the context of an approach to qualitative data analysis they developed known as **grounded theory**. In Glaser and Strauss's view, because of its reliance on statistical rather than theoretical criteria, probability sampling is not appropriate to qualitative research. Theoretical sampling is meant to be an alternative strategy. As they put it: 'Theoretical sampling is done in order to discover categories and their properties and to suggest the inter-relationships into a theory. Statistical sampling is done to obtain accurate evidence on distributions of people among categories to be used in descriptions and verifications' (Glaser and Strauss 1967: 62). What distinguishes theoretical sampling from other sampling approaches is the emphasis on the selection of cases and units with reference to the quest for the generation of a theoretical understanding. Figure 18.1 outlines the main steps in theoretical sampling.

In grounded theory, you carry on collecting data (observing, interviewing, collecting documents) through theoretical sampling until **theoretical saturation** (see Key concept 18.4) has been achieved. This means that successive interviews/observations have both formed the basis for the creation of a category and confirmed its importance and

Key concept 18.3
What is theoretical sampling?

According to Glaser and Strauss (1967: 45), theoretical sampling 'is the process of data collection for generating theory whereby the analyst jointly collects, codes, and analyzes his data and decides what data to collect next and where to find them, in order to develop his theory as it emerges. The process of data collection is *controlled* by the emerging theory, whether substantive or formal.' This definition conveys a crucial characteristic of theoretical sampling—namely, that it is an ongoing process rather than a distinct and single stage, as it is, for example, in probability sampling. Moreover, it is important to realize that it is not just people who are the 'objects' of sampling, as can be seen in a more recent definition: 'Data gathering driven by concepts derived from the evolving theory and based on the concept of "making comparisons," whose purpose is to go to places, people, or events that will maximize opportunities to discover variations among concepts and to densify categories in terms of their properties and dimensions' (Strauss and Corbin 1998: 201). For Charmaz (2000: 519), theoretical sampling is a 'defining property of grounded theory' and is concerned with the refinement of the theoretical categories that emerge in the course of analysing data that have been collected, rather than boosting sample size. Theoretical sampling differs from generic purposive sampling, which is outlined below, in that its practitioners emphasize using it to provide a springboard for the generation of theory and the refinement of theoretical categories. It is iterative in the sense that it is not a one-off but an ongoing process that entails several stages. It emphasizes **theoretical saturation** (see Key concept 18.4) as a criterion for deciding when to cease collecting new data on a particular theoretical idea and to move on to the investigation of some ramifications of the emerging theory.

Figure 18.1

The process of theoretical sampling

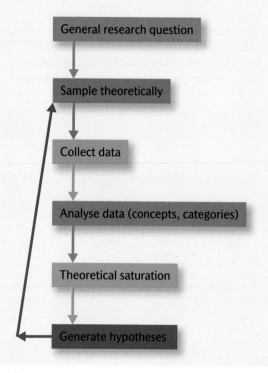

General research question
↓
Sample theoretically
↓
Collect data
↓
Analyse data (concepts, categories)
↓
Theoretical saturation
↓
Generate hypotheses

there is no need to continue with data collection in relation to that category or cluster of categories; instead, the researcher should move on and generate hypotheses out of the categories that are building up and then move on to collecting data in relation to these hypotheses. As Charmaz (2006) puts it, when new data no longer stimulate new theoretical understandings or new dimensions of the principal

theoretical categories, the relevant categories are saturated. Proponents of grounded theory argue that there is a great deal of redundancy in statistical sampling. For example, committing yourself to interviewing x per cent of an organization's members may mean that you end up wasting time and resources because you could have confirmed the significance of a concept and/or its connections with other concepts by using a much smaller sample. Instead, grounded theory advocates that you sample in terms of what is relevant to and meaningful for your theory. The key is to ensure you sample so as to test your emerging theoretical ideas. The approach is supposed to be an iterative one—that is, one in which there is a movement backwards and forwards between sampling and theoretical reflection, but it may be that the researcher feels that his or her categories achieve theoretical saturation (see Key concept 18.4) at a relatively early stage. For example, for their research on organization dress, referred to in Research in focus 20.8, Rafaeli et al. (1997: 14) initially 'identified a stratified random sample of 20 people from the population of full-time, permanent administrative employees in the organization' (1997: 13–14). They then evaluated their data 'after completing interviews with the 20 individuals selected and concluded that, because we had reached theoretical saturation (Glaser and Strauss 1967), no additional interviews were necessary'. The use of theoretical saturation as a criterion for deciding when to cease further sampling does not necessarily imply that a theoretical sampling approach has been employed. This is suggested by the quotation from Rafaeli et al., where there is no suggestion of an iterative movement between sampling and theory development. What we see here is an approach that is more redolent of what we call below a generic purposive sampling approach than of theoretical sampling.

Key concept 18.4
What is theoretical saturation?

The key idea is that you carry on sampling theoretically until a category has been saturated with data. 'This means, until (*a*) no new or relevant data seem to be emerging regarding a category, (*b*) the category is well developed in terms of its properties and dimensions demonstrating variation, and (*c*) the relationships among categories are well established and validated' (Strauss and Corbin 1998: 212). In the language of grounded theory, a category operates at a somewhat higher level of abstraction than a concept in that it may group together several concepts that have common features denoted by the category. Saturation does not mean, as is sometimes suggested, that the researcher develops a sense of déjà vu when listening to what people say in interviews but that new data no longer suggest new insights into an emergent theory or no longer suggest new dimensions of theoretical categories.

Research in focus 18.5
An example of theoretical sampling

Treviño et al. (2014) conducted an interview study of forty ethics and compliance officers in order to address research questions relating to the origins of the role in the officers' respective organizations and the nature of their work. Initially, they sampled a varied group of officers, so that their initial sampling approach was influenced by purposive sampling. Then they used the insights gleaned from their early examination of their data to establish who to interview next. Thus, their initial analysis of their data from the first sampling phase influenced which officers should be interviewed next in order to flesh out and elaborate their emerging theoretical understanding of the data.

A sampling approach that is more in tune with Glaser and Strauss's (1967) idea of theoretical sampling is provided by Treviño et al. (2014) in their study of ethics and compliance officers (see Research in focus 18.5). The chief virtue of theoretical sampling is that the emphasis is upon using theoretical reflection on data as the guide to whether more data are needed. It therefore places a premium on theorizing rather than the statistical adequacy of a sample, which may be a limited guide to sample selection in many instances. However, O'Reilly and Parker (2013) argue that the notion of theoretical saturation has become overused in qualitative research in generic ways that do not respect the true meaning of the term or the diversity of qualitative research methods. Crucially, they distinguish between data saturation, which is when sampling continues until no new findings are generated, and theoretical saturation, which involves continuing to sample until conceptual categories are fully developed and relationships between them are accounted for. This latter usage is integral to the approach of grounded theory, which will be examined in greater detail in the context of qualitative data analysis in Chapter 24. O'Reilly and Parker are also critical of the lack of transparency that surrounds the notion of saturation, as researchers rarely explain in a transparent way how this was achieved. Further, in the context of inductive research, they suggest that data saturation may be an unrealistic target, as the number of themes emerging from a dataset is potentially limitless.

Generic purposive sampling

Hood (2007: 152) has usefully pointed out that there is a tendency among many writers and researchers to 'identify all things qualitative with "grounded theory"'. This is particularly the case with the notion of theoretical sampling, which is often treated as synonymous with purposive sampling when in fact it is one form of purposive sampling (see Key concept 18.3). Hood usefully contrasts grounded theory with what she calls a 'generic inductive qualitative model', which is relatively open-ended and emphasizes the generation of concepts and theories but does not entail (among other things) the iterative style of grounded theory. Sampling considerations are particularly prominent in this contrast between grounded theory and the generic inductive qualitative model. Whereas, as we have seen, theoretical sampling is a sequential sampling process whereby sampling is conducted in order to develop theoretical categories and inferences, in the generic inductive qualitative model, sampling is conducted purposively but not necessarily with regard to the generation of theory and theoretical categories. We are going to call this sampling approach *generic purposive sampling*, a category that subsumes several of the sampling strategies identified in Key concept 18.2, though not theoretical sampling. Generic purposive sampling may be employed in a sequential or in a fixed manner and the criteria for selecting cases or individuals may be formed *a priori* (for example, socio-demographic criteria) or be contingent or a mixture of both. In most of the examples discussed in this book, generic purposive sampling is fixed and *a priori*. However, the criteria employed are ones that are informed by the research questions. When using a generic purposive sampling approach with respect to the selection of cases or contexts, the researcher establishes criteria concerning the kinds of cases needed to address the research questions, identifies appropriate cases, and then samples from those cases that have been identified. When contexts are being sampled, it is common for some form of generic purposive sampling to be employed.

In business research, generic purposive sampling is often used to gain an insight into a wide range of roles within an organization. For example, Casey (1995) describes how she interviewed sixty people during her research at the Hephaestus Corporation, in an effort

Telling it like it is
Stratified sampling in a student's research project

Lucie's interview sampling strategy within the institute was based on stratified sampling to gain an impression of views of enterprise at different levels of the organization. 'There aren't that many staff in the institute and the main people basically oversee everything, so they knew everything. So I interviewed the Director and the Administrator, because they were the people that I was dealing with, so they were the easiest to access for an interview I suppose. And . . . then I interviewed a few people who worked as temps just to get their perspective, because obviously the Director and the Administrator, they'd be very positive about their institute. So I wanted to get a smaller person's—if that's the right word—perspective on the institute as well, to see whether that was how it was really run.'

to gain a wide sample of occupation, rank, tenure, and demographic features such as gender, race, ethnicity, and regional origin. She goes on to describe how interviewees came from a variety of occupational groupings, including engineers, computer professionals, scientists, technical analysts, financial analysts, administrators, managers, and manufacturing workers. Finally, some individuals were chosen on the basis of their strategic importance within the team or division, including the Vice-President, a union representative, a new entry employee, and a returned retiree. The primary stratifying criteria then were occupational and strategic level.

Generic purposive sampling (or variations of it) is often employed in relation to the selection of participants. For their study of the meaning of work–life balance issues for trade union representatives in two sectors (retailing and media), Rigby and O'Brien-Smith (2010) selected a purposive sample based on three criteria: making sure that representatives were at each of three levels (national officials, full-time officials, and lay representatives); union respondents were at 'better organised workplaces' (2010: 206); and there was variety in the geographical location of the representatives who were interviewed. Finally, for the research referred to in Research in focus 20.9, the authors purposively sampled employees from each of six quite different organizations. They write: 'We aimed for diversity in terms of age, organization and occupation, and approximately equal numbers of men and women. Our assumption was that this would maximize the likelihood of accessing variation and highlight any common core of experience more than a homogeneous sample would' (Bosley et al. 2009: 1499). What we see in all these examples is a quest for appropriate samples in terms of the research questions in which the researcher is interested.

Snowball sampling

In certain respects, snowball sampling is a form of convenience sample, but it is worth distinguishing because it has attracted quite a lot of attention over the years. With this approach to sampling, the researcher makes initial contact with a small group of people who are relevant to the research topic and then uses these to establish contacts with others. Bryman used an approach like this to create a sample of British visitors to Disney theme parks (Bryman 1999). Another example of snowball sampling is given in the study by Venter, Boshoff, and Maas (2005) (see Research in focus 18.6), where this technique was used to identify owner-managers and successors of small and medium-sized family businesses in South Africa. A snowball sample is in no sense random, because there is no way of knowing the precise extent of the population from which it would have to be drawn. In other words, there is no accessible sampling frame for the population from which the sample is to be taken, and the difficulty of creating such a sampling frame means that such an approach is the only feasible one. Moreover, even if one could create a sampling frame of strategic decision-makers or of British visitors to Disney theme parks, it would almost certainly be inaccurate straight away, because this is a shifting population. People will constantly be becoming and ceasing to be associated with the decision-making network, while new theme park visitors are arriving all the time. The problem with snowball sampling is that it is very unlikely that the sample will be representative of the population, though, as we have just suggested, the very notion of a population may be problematic in some circumstances. However, by and large, snowball sampling is used not within a quantitative research strategy, but within a qualitative one: both Franwick's and Bryman's studies

Research in focus 18.6
A snowball sample

Venter, Boshoff, and Maas (2005) were interested in factors that influence the succession process in small and medium-sized family businesses. Their initial intention was to obtain access to a mailing list of small and medium-sized family businesses in South Africa from banks and other large organizations that had family businesses as clients. This would then have formed the basis of their sample. However, these large organizations declined to share their client information with the research team which instead used snowball sampling. This involved research associates, who were employed in different regions of the country, contacting small and medium-sized businesses with the aim of identifying those that were family businesses. Potential respondents were then asked to refer the researchers on to other family businesses that they knew about. As the researchers explain, 'following up on referrals proved to be the most effective approach and eventually yielded the majority of the potential respondents listed on the sampling frame' (2005: 291). A questionnaire survey was then mailed to 2458 respondents, comprising current owner-managers, potential successors, successors, and retiring owner-managers in 1038 family businesses, and a total of 332 usable questionnaires were returned.

were carried out within a predominantly qualitative research framework. Concerns about external validity and the ability to generalize do not loom as large within a qualitative research strategy as they do in a quantitative research one (see Chapters 7 and 17). In qualitative research, the orientation to sampling is more likely to be guided by a preference for *theoretical sampling* than with the kind of statistical sampling that has been the focus of this chapter. There is a much better 'fit' between snowball sampling and the theoretical sampling strategy of qualitative research than with the statistical sampling approach of quantitative research. This is not to suggest that snowball sampling is entirely irrelevant to quantitative research: when the researcher needs to focus upon or to reflect relationships between people, tracing connections through snowball sampling may be a better approach than conventional probability sampling (J. S. Coleman 1958).

Snowball sampling is a sampling technique in which the researcher samples initially a small group of people relevant to the research questions, and these sampled participants propose other participants who have had the experience or characteristics relevant to the research. These participants will then suggest others and so on. As noted in Chapter 8, it is sometimes (though rarely) used in survey research when probability sampling is more or less impossible. It is also sometimes recommended when networks of individuals are the focus of attention (Coleman 1958). In fact, Noy (2008) points out that snowball sampling is frequently presented as a strategy to be employed when probability sampling is impossible or not feasible—for example, when trying

to sample hard-to-reach populations because of the absence of a sampling frame. This is often how it is represented in discussions of its use in survey research and sometimes in qualitative research too (see Research in focus 18.6). However, Noy observes that one advantage the technique offers is that it is able simultaneously to capitalize on and to reveal the connectedness of individuals in networks.

The sampling of informants in ethnographic research is sometimes a combination of opportunistic sampling and snowball sampling. Much of the time ethnographers are forced to gather information from whatever sources are available to them. Very often they face opposition or at least indifference to their research and are relieved to glean information or views from whoever is prepared to divulge such details. An example of opportunistic sampling is provided by Jackall (1988), who went into several large organizations in order to study how bureaucracy shapes moral consciousness. Analysis of the occupational ethics of corporate managers was based on core data of 143 intensive, semi-structured interviews with managers at every level of the organization. This formed the basis for selection of a smaller stratified group of twelve managers, who were reinterviewed several times and asked to interpret materials that Jackall was collecting. However, as the study progressed Jackall realized that an investigation of organizational morality should also explore managerial dissenters, or 'whistleblowers'—individuals who had taken stands against their organizations on grounds that they defined as moral. Between 1982 and 1988, Jackall conducted case studies of these dissenters, interviewing eighteen 'whistleblowers' and reviewing large amounts of documentary evidence. In order to explore managerial morality further, he then presented these cases to the stratified group of twelve managers, and asked them 'to assess the dissenters' actions and motives by their own standards' (1988: 206).

Sample size

One of the problems that the qualitative researcher faces is that it can be difficult to establish at the outset how many people will be interviewed if theoretical considerations guide selection. It is impossible to know, for example, how many people should be interviewed before theoretical saturation has been achieved. To a certain extent, this is not helped by the fact that the criteria for recognizing or establishing when or whether saturation has been achieved are rarely articulated in detail (Guest et al. 2006). Also, as an investigation proceeds, it may become apparent that groups will need to be interviewed who were not anticipated at the outset. Morse (2004a) gives the example of a study of sudden infant death syndrome, which was initially to focus on parents but which, as a result of interviews with them, had to be broadened to include professionals. This necessity arose because parents' accounts flagged the importance of there being uncertainty about which groups of professionals had primary responsibility in such circumstances. With probability sampling, such considerations can be specified, taking into account the size of the population and time and cost constraints.

As a rule of thumb, however, the broader the scope of a qualitative study and the more comparisons between groups in the sample that are required, the more interviews will need to be carried out (Warren 2002; Morse 2004b). Taking the second of these two criteria, if several comparisons are likely to be wanted—between males and females, different age groups, different types of research participants in terms of locally relevant factors—a larger sample is likely to be necessary. Also, in a study of the experience of relationship breakdown, fewer respondents are likely to be necessary if the emphasis is on those who have been formally married as opposed to the more general category of being in a relationship. Nonetheless, Warren (2002: 99) makes the interesting remark that, for a qualitative interview study to be published, the minimum number of interviews required seems to be between twenty and thirty. This suggests that, although there is an emphasis on the importance of sampling purposively in qualitative research, minimum levels of acceptability operate, although there are almost certainly exceptions to Warren's rule (for example, very intensive interviews of the kind conducted in life story interviews, where there may be just one or two interviewees). Moreover, by no means all practitioners would agree with Warren's figure. Gerson and Horowitz (2002: 223) write that 'fewer than 60 interviews cannot support convincing conclusions and more than 150 produce too much material to analyse effectively and expeditiously'. The differences between these authors' views suggest how difficult it can be to try to specify minimum sample sizes (see also Guest et al. (2006) and Mason (2010) for other summaries of some researchers' suggestions on this issue). The size of sample that is able to support convincing conclusions is likely to vary somewhat from situation to situation in purposive sampling terms, and qualitative researchers have to recognize that they are engaged in a delicate balancing act:

> In general, sample sizes in qualitative research should not be so small as to make it difficult to achieve data saturation, theoretical saturation, or informational redundancy. At the same time, the sample should not be so large that it is difficult to undertake a deep, case-oriented analysis.
>
> (Onwuegbuzie and Collins 2007: 289)

Given the ranges of opinion about appropriate sample sizes, it is not surprising that, when Mason (2010) examined the abstracts of doctoral theses derived from interview-based qualitative research in Great Britain and Ireland, he found that the 560 theses varied in sample size from 1 to 95, with a mean of 31 and a median of 28. The difference between the mean and median suggests that the mean is being inflated by some rather large samples. Mason refers to a study that reviewed 50 grounded theory-based research articles, which found sample sizes to vary between 5 and 350.

It is also likely that the orientation of the researchers and the purposes of their research will be significant.

What is likely to be crucial is to justify rigorously any sample size. In other words, rather than rely on others' impressions of suitable sample sizes in qualitative research, it is almost certainly better to be clear about the sampling method you employed, why you used it, and why the sample size you achieved is appropriate. It may be that the reason why you feel that a sample of a certain size is adequate is because you feel you have achieved theoretical saturation, a term that, while strongly linked to grounded theory, is often used by researchers operating within a variety of approaches. If saturation is the criterion for sample size, specifying minima or maxima for sample sizes is pointless. Essentially, the criterion for sample size is whatever it takes to achieve saturation. The problem is that, as several writers observe (e.g. Guest et al. 2006; Mason 2010), saturation is often *claimed* but not justified or explained (Bowen 2008). See Thinking deeply 18.7 for more on this issue.

Related to this issue is that you need to be sure that you do not generalize inappropriately from your data. Onwuegbuzie and Leech (2010) observe that for the most part there are two kinds of generalization that may be inferred from a qualitative study. One is analytic generalization, which is much the same as theoretical generalization (J. C. Mitchell 1983) which refers to the credibility of the theoretical inferences that the researcher draws from his or her findings. The

Telling it like it is
How many interviews in a student research project?

One of the questions that we are often asked by students at postgraduate as well as undergraduate level is how many interviews they should do for their research project. As Tom explained: 'I think this is one of the key questions that people ask. You say "What's the minimum number of interviews I have to do to make this project viable?" [*chuckles*] and my tutor did say that because I'd decided to cut myself free from the bounds of positivism I could just do one interview if I wanted to and that would be quite legitimate. I didn't quite feel up to doing that. I think there were about 40 people [who] worked in this call centre, so I kind of felt I needed to get a reasonable feel for what life was like there so I did eight interviews but it wasn't very scientific.'

This is also an area where practice varies from one university business school to another, depending on the word limit set for the dissertation, time available, credit weighting of the dissertation within the degree course as a whole, the attitudes of those people who are running the course, and the expectations of your supervisor. So you should definitely refer to the advice given by your own university on this. However, it is useful to compare the experiences of some of the undergraduate students we interviewed.

Chris did four interviews with three female managers and the head of diversity who was also a woman. He audio-recorded them and then listened to them a number of times, looking for patterns in what each interviewee was saying and writing down 'bits and pieces of it'.

Angharad did ten interviews each lasting about half an hour with women managers in one department of a public-sector organization. She took notes and audio-recorded them and transcribed them afterwards.

Nirwanthi carried out seven interviews with managers in one company. She audio-recorded them and took notes as well. She had to conduct two of the interviews in the Sri Lankan language of Sinhala, 'because it was easier for the employees to speak to me in Sinhala rather than in English', later translating these into English. She then listened to each interview once or twice, making more notes and summarizing them.

Karen did fifteen interviews with managers in one organization, each lasting one hour, taking notes throughout.

As the above summaries illustrate, there is quite a difference in the number of interviews carried out by each of these students. However, it is important not to place too much emphasis on our sample, which is not statistically representative of the entire population of business school students in the UK. It is also important to note that the expectations for postgraduate student dissertations may be higher than those for undergraduates.

Thinking deeply 18.7
Saturation and sample size

As noted in the text, it is very difficult to know in advance how many interviews you need to conduct if theoretical saturation (see Key concept 18.4) is employed as a principle for assessing the adequacy of a sample. Further, the criteria for deciding when theoretical saturation has been achieved are more or less absent. In their study of Ethics and Compliance Officers which was referred to in Research in focus 18.5, Treviño et al. (2014) found that after their thirtieth interview only one new code was generated and after the thirty-fifth interview no new codes were arrived at. Therefore, in this case, the last ten interviews (there were forty in total) hardly generated any new theoretical insights at all. This finding should not be taken as a rule of thumb as it may not apply in other instances, but it does suggest that saturation may be achieved earlier than might be anticipated.

other they call 'case-to-case transfer', which refers to making generalizations from one case to another case that is broadly similar. This is more or less the same as the notion of *moderatum* generalization suggested by M. Williams (2000: 215) who has argued that, in many cases, qualitative researchers are in a position to produce what he calls *moderatum* generalizations—that is, ones in which aspects of the focus of enquiry (e.g. a small network of female entrepreneurs, a big data processing firm) 'can be seen to be instances of a broader set of recognizable features'. In addition, Williams argues that not only is it the case that qualitative researchers *can* make such generalizations but that in fact they often *do* make them. Thus, when generating findings relating to a firm that processes big data, a researcher is likely to draw comparisons with findings by other researchers relating to comparable organizations (e.g. information technology firms). When forging such comparisons and linkages, the researcher is engaging in *moderatum* generalization. *Moderatum* generalizations will always be limited and somewhat more tentative than those associated with statistical

generalizations of the kind associated with probability sampling (see Chapter 8). On the other hand, they do permit an element of generalization and help to counter the view that generalization beyond the immediate evidence and the case is impossible in qualitative research. Generalization to a population may be legitimate when a probability sampling procedure has been employed. Onwuegbuzie and Leech analysed all 125 empirical articles that had been published in the *Qualitative Report*, an academic journal that has been in publication since 1990. They found that 29.6 per cent of the articles contained generalizations that illegitimately went beyond the sample participants. In other words, just under one-third of articles made inferences to a population beyond the study's participants. As the authors note, when this occurs, there is an inconsistency between the design of the research and the interpretations that are made about the resulting data. There is clearly a lesson here about the need to be clear about what you can and cannot infer from a sample of any kind, something that applies to sampling in quantitative research too.

Not just people

Sampling is not just about people but also about sampling other things. For one thing, principles of purposive sampling can be applied to such things as documents, in much the same way that probability sampling can be applied to different kinds of phenomena to generate a representative sample. However, there is another dimension to sampling

in qualitative research that is worth bearing in mind. This is to do with needing to sample the different contexts within which interviewing or observation take place. Writing about ethnographic research, Hammersley and Atkinson (1995) mention time and context as units that need to be considered in the context of sampling. Attending to *time* means that the ethnographer must make sure that people or events are observed at different times of the day and different days of the week. To do otherwise risks drawing inferences about certain people's behaviour or about events that are valid only for mornings or for weekdays rather than weekends. It is impossible to be an ethnographer all the time for several reasons: need to take time out to write up notes; other commitments (work or domestic); and body imperatives (eating, sleeping, and so on). When the group in question operates a different cycle from the ethnographer's normal regime (such as night shifts in a factory or hospital), the requirement to time sample may necessitate a considerable change of habit. Delbridge (1998), for example, describes how tired he felt after a day making windscreen wipers or circuit boards for televisions. In addition, he explains that 'there was real pressure and intensity during the fieldwork, particularly during the early stages when I was negotiating my informal access and acceptance into the group. I developed a nervous tic in my cheek during the first two weeks, something I have never experienced before or since' (1998: 19).

It can also be important to sample in terms of *context*. People's behaviour is influenced by contextual factors, so that it is important to ensure that such behaviour is observed in a variety of locations. For example, in his study of masculinity and workplace culture in a lorry-making factory in the north-west of England, Collinson (1992a) draws attention to the ways in which shopfloor workers resist managerial control by spending time chatting and joking. By spending time with workers during lunch and unofficial breaks, in the toilet, the canteen, the car park, on the works' bus, in the pub, and occasionally in people's homes, Collinson was able to explore these cultural practices in far more detail than if he had confined his study and himself to observing practices within formal workplace settings.

 # Using more than one sampling approach

Purposive sampling often involves more than one of the approaches outlined above. For example, it is quite common for snowball sampling to be preceded by another form of purposive sampling. This process can entail sampling initial participants without using a snowball approach and then using these initial contacts to broaden out through a snowballing method. Thus, in their study of the role of power in the branding of a tourist destination—the Gold Coast in Australia—Marzano and Scott (2009) initially purposively sampled key stakeholders in the branding process. These were individuals who had key roles in the agencies responsible for and with an interest in the branding of this tourist destination. As a result of the snowballing process, people such as senior managers in hotels and theme parks were also identified and became candidates for inclusion in the research, which was conducted by semi-structured interview.

A further sense in which more than one sampling approach may be employed is when researchers try to introduce an element of purposiveness into a snowball sample. For example, Marshall (1984) describes how, in order to identify her sample of thirty women managers, she would first make a contact within a particular company (sometimes a woman manager and sometimes a helpful member of the personnel department) and then ask him or her to suggest other potential interviewees. However, Marshall also made a number of decisions in advance of her study about the type of participants she was interested in. First, she decided to interview only in and around London, to reduce the significance of whether or not managers were geographically mobile; secondly, to impose an upper age limit of 45 years, to reduce the potential differences between generations; thirdly, to contact several people in each company to provide a guide to the influence of the company; and, fourthly, to restrict the number of personnel managers in the sample, to avoid weighting her sample towards this 'traditional stronghold of female employment' (1984: 115). Her approach thus also involved an element of *a priori* purposive sampling.

There is evidence of a quest for both purposiveness and representativeness in these studies. With the work of Marshall the purposiveness reveals itself mainly in the search for women managers with appropriate characteristics; in the case of Marzano and Scott's research, the purposive sample was boosted through subsequent snowball sampling. At the same time, there is a strong sense of wanting to generate a sample with at least a semblance of representativeness. This is quite an interesting development, since sampling in qualitative research, as we have seen, is primarily associated with purposive sampling. At the same time, it raises an interesting question that may at least in part lie behind the use of representativeness in these studies. Given that, when you sample purposively, in many cases several individuals (or whatever the unit of analysis is) will be eligible for inclusion, how do you decide which one or ones to include? In other words, if your research questions direct you to select a subsample that has criteria *a* and *b* and another subsample that has criteria *a* and *c*, so that you can compare them, how do you choose between the individuals who meet each of the two pairs of criteria? Sampling for at least a modicum of representativeness, as these researchers appear to have done, may be one way of making such a decision.

Key points

- Purposive sampling is the fundamental principle for selecting cases and individuals in qualitative research.

- Purposive sampling places the investigation's research questions at the forefront of sampling considerations.

- It is important to bear in mind that purposive sampling will entail considerations of the levels at which sampling needs to take place.

- It is important to distinguish between theoretical sampling and the generic purposive sampling approach, as they are sometimes treated synonymously.

- Theoretical saturation is a useful principle for making decisions about sample size, but there is evidence that it is often claimed rather than demonstrated.

Questions for review

- How does purposive sampling differ from probability sampling and why do many qualitative researchers prefer to use the former?

- In what circumstances might you employ snowball sampling?

Levels of sampling

- Why might it be significant to distinguish between the different levels at which sampling can take place in a qualitative research project?

Purposive sampling

- Why is theoretical sampling such an important facet of grounded theory?

- How does theoretical sampling differ from the generic purposive sampling approach?

- Why is theoretical saturation such an important ingredient of theoretical sampling?

- What are the main reasons for considering the use of snowball sampling?

Sample size

- Why do writers seem to disagree so much on what is a minimum acceptable sample size in qualitative research?

- To what extent does theoretical sampling assist the qualitative researcher in making decisions about sample size?

Not just people

● Why might it be important to remember in purposive sampling that it is not just people who are candidates for consideration in sampling issues?

Using more than one sampling approach

● How might it be useful to select people purposively following a survey?

Online Resource Centre
www.oxfordtextbooks.co.uk/orc/brymansrm4e/

Visit the Interactive Research Guide that accompanies this book to complete an exercise in Research Designs.

19

Ethnography and participant observation

Chapter outline

Ethnography and participant observation entail the extended involvement of the researcher in the social life of those he or she studies (see Key concept 19.1). However, the former term is also frequently taken to refer to the written output of that research. This chapter explores:

- the problems of gaining access to different settings and some suggestions about how they might be overcome;
- the issue of whether or not a covert role is practicable and acceptable;
- the role of key informants and gatekeepers for the ethnographer;
- the different kinds of roles that ethnographers can assume in the course of their fieldwork;
- the role of field notes in ethnography and the variety of forms they can assume;
- bringing ethnography to an end.

Introduction

Discussions about the merits and limitations of participant observation have been a fairly standard ingredient in textbooks on business research for many years. However, writers on research methods increasingly prefer to write about 'ethnography' rather than 'participant observation'. It is difficult to date the point at which this change of terminology (though it is more than just this) occurred, but sometime in the 1970s ethnography began to become the preferred term. Prior to that, ethnography was primarily associated with social anthropological research, whereby the investigator visits a (usually) foreign land, gains access to a group (for example, a tribe or village), spends a considerable amount of time (often many years) with that group with the aim of uncovering its culture, watches and listens to what people say and do, engages people in conversations to probe specific issues of interest, takes copious field notes, and returns home to write up the fruits of his or her labours.

Ethnography could be viewed as a simple process of joining a group, watching what goes on, making some notes, and writing it all up. In fact, ethnography is nowhere nearly as straightforward as this implies. This chapter will outline some of the main decision areas that confront ethnographers, along with some of the many contingencies they face. However, it is not easy to generalize about the ethnographic research process in such a way as to provide definitive recommendations about research practice. As prefigured at the end of the previous chapter, the diversity of experiences that confront ethnographers and the variety of ways in which they deal with them does not readily permit clear-cut generalizations. The following comment in a book on ethnography makes this point well.

> Every field situation *is* different and initial luck in meeting good informants, being in the right place at the right time and striking the right note in relationships may be just as important as skill in technique. Indeed, many successful episodes in the field do come about through good luck as much as through sophisticated planning, and many unsuccessful episodes are due as much to bad luck as to bad judgement.
>
> (Sarsby 1984: 96)

However, this statement should not be taken to imply that forethought and an awareness of alternative ways of doing things are irrelevant. It is with this kind of issue that the rest of this chapter will be concerned. However, issues to do with the conduct of interviews by ethnographers will be reserved for Chapter 20.

Organizational ethnography

Ethnography has also become a 'label of choice' for many researchers working in professional and applied fields. Among these are business researchers who have imported the methods and many of the conventions of ethnography into the study of organizational settings. Rosen (1991) understands organizational ethnography to be distinctive because it is concerned with social relations that are related to certain goal-directed activities. He suggests that the rules, strategies, and meanings within a structured work situation are different from those that affect other areas of social life. An ethnographic approach implies intense researcher involvement in the day-to-day running of an organization, so that the researcher can understand it from an insider's point of view. In order to become immersed in other people's realities, organizational ethnographers, like their anthropological predecessors, engage in fieldwork that tends to commit them to a period of time spent in the organization, or a long stay 'in the field'.

Many of these studies draw attention to the similarities between ethnography and participant observation (see Key concept 19.1 for an explanation of the relationship between these terms). Industrial sociologists working

Key concept 19.1
What are ethnography and participant observation?

Definitions of ethnography and participant observation are difficult to distinguish. Both draw attention to the fact that the participant observer/ethnographer immerses him or herself in a group for an extended period of time, observing behaviour, listening to what is said in conversations both between others and with the fieldworker, and asking questions. It is possible that the term 'ethnography' is sometimes preferred, because 'participant observation' seems to imply just observation, though in practice participant observers do more than simply observe. Typically, participant observers and ethnographers will gather further data through interviews and the collection of documents. It may be that the apparent emphasis on observation in the term 'participant observation' has meant that an apparently more inclusive term is preferable, even though it is generally recognized that the method entails a wide range of methods of data collection and sources. Ethnography is also sometimes taken to refer to a study in which participant observation is the prevalent research method but that also has a specific focus on the culture of the group in which the ethnographer is immersed.

However, the term 'ethnography' has an additional meaning, in that it frequently simultaneously refers to both a method of research of the kind outlined above *and* the written product of that research. Indeed, 'ethnography' frequently denotes both a research process and the written outcome of the research. A typical account of the ethnographic research process is provided by Perlow (1997), in her study of work–life issues in post-industrial American corporations.

> I spent much of each day wandering around, talking to people and observing their daily activities. I had an office in the same corridor, where I would type my field notes on a laptop computer. Even when typing notes, I left my office door open. I sat facing the door, looking up when people walked by, inviting conversation if an engineer or manager chose to enter.
>
> In addition to being present and available to talk to the engineers, I conducted interviews and attended meetings . . . Later, I shadowed engineers . . . to get a sense of how they accomplished their work. Moreover, I sat for hours in each of the software labs observing and talking to the engineers at work and listening to the 'natural' interactions that occurred in the labs.
>
> (1997: 143)

As part of this research was about the relationship between work and home domains, Perlow also wanted to understand the engineers' lives outside work. She therefore asked the married engineers to let her visit their homes and interview their spouses. Finally, Perlow describes how she participated in many social events during the fieldwork; she went to lunch with the engineers on a regular basis, joined them for 'happy hour' on Friday nights at one of the bars downtown, went with them on a three-day bus trip to New York city, and attended official celebrations organized by the company.

Perlow also describes how she adopted the role of confidante:

> It was my job to listen, regardless of what I was doing or how I was feeling, I made myself available when the engineers wanted to tell me something. I found myself privy to many unsolicited conversations whether engineers had something specific they felt I should know or they were simply looking for a break in their work and wanted someone to chat with.
>
> (1997: 146)

out of the Chicago School were followed by a group of writers who studied UK-based work organizations and relied heavily on the traditional ethnographic method of participant observation. These studies, which sometimes involved taking jobs in the research sites, included:

- D. Roy (1958), who spent two months working as a machine operator in the 'clicking room' of a factory in Chicago. The same factory was later used as a research setting by Burawoy (1979), who also worked as a machine operator for ten months in the same plant.

- Lupton (1963), who became a participant-observer in Manchester factories in order to explore processes of work group influence on production levels. Lupton compared an engineering plant in which 'fiddles' were prevalent with a clothing factory where these practices were absent.

- Beynon (1975), who over a period of five years studied the Ford Motor Company's Halewood assembly plant in Liverpool to produce an account of factory life that described the process whereby people became shop stewards, the way they understood the job, and the kinds of pressures they experienced. This study also involved understanding the experience of people who worked on the assembly lines and the way they made sense of industrial politics.

The tradition of participant observation continues through more recent studies such as Lok and de Rond's (2013) 199-day ethnographic study of the Cambridge University Boat Race, which focuses on the institutional practices of the Club which determine how crew are selected to participate in the race. As they explain: 'true to the ethnographic tradition one of us spent an entire Boat Race season (September 9, 2006, to April 7, 2007) with the squad full-time. The researcher joined the squad for their daily training sessions, sat in on all coaches' meetings, and socialized with the squad and coaches outside of training hours.' When the squad trained off-site 'he traveled with them, slept in their rooms, worked along side them in rigging boats, loading equipment, driving club vans, mopping floors, cooking breakfast and studying video footage of water outings and past boat races' (Lok and de Rond 2013: 192).

Since the 1980s the popularity of organizational culture as a concept has meant that ethnographic methods have enjoyed something of a revival within business and management research. Ethnography, which denotes the practice of writing (*graphy*) about people and cultures (*ethno*), has provided researchers with an obvious method for understanding work organizations as cultural entities. Studies that focus on the construction of cultural norms, expressions of organizational values, and patterns of workplace behaviour include:

- Kunda's (1992) study of a high-technology company, 'Lyndsville Tech', in Silicon Valley, USA.

- Watson's (1994a) account of managerial identity in a UK-based telecommunications firm.

- Casey's (1995) exploration of new-product development workers in an American-based multinational corporation.

- Delbridge's (1998) study of the impact of new manufacturing techniques on workers in a Japanese-owned consumer electronics plant, 'Nippon CTV', and a European-owned automotive components supplier, 'Valleyco'.

- Michel's (2011) nine-year study of Wall Street investment bankers' practices of habitual overwork and the effects this has on their bodies (Research in focus 19.2).

Research in focus 19.2
An example of an organizational ethnography lasting 9 years

Michel's (2011) ethnography of investment banks focuses on Wall Street investment bankers' bodies, including how they are adversely affected by their intense working conditions and why they engage in habitual overwork which causes such strain on their bodies, even though they have a high degree of autonomy and ability to control their workload. Her nine-year study of two investment banking departments involved tracking four cohorts of employees, two in each bank, from the point of joining and for as long as they stayed with the bank. Michel is very detailed in her description of the data collection process that formed the basis for her study:

Participant and non-participant observation: over two years, about 7000 hours in years 1–2 of the study;

Semi-structured formal interviews: 136 (30–45 minutes in length) in year 2 of the study, followed by almost 500 1–3 hour follow-up interviews in years 3–9 of the study;

Informal interviews: 200, based on themes evolving from the study.

The banks were highly restrictive in terms of how they allowed Michel to use the data, not allowing her to reveal the size of the cohorts or the dates of the study, and not allowing her to audio-record the interviews. Although nine years is an unusually long time for an ethnographic study to continue, this longitudinal aspect of the study enabled Michel to track long-term physical and mental health problems experienced by the bankers and to trace how this caused them to reevaluate their relationships to their bodies and their careers.

Tips and skills
Micro-ethnography

If you are doing research for an undergraduate project or Master's dissertation, it is unlikely that you will be able to conduct a full-scale ethnography, because this would almost certainly involve you spending a considerable period of time in an organizational setting. Nevertheless, it may be possible for you to carry out a form of *micro-ethnography* (Wolcott 1995). This involves focusing on a particular aspect of an organizational culture, such as the way the organization has implemented TQM, and showing how the culture is reflected through this managerial initiative. A shorter period of time (from a couple of weeks to a few months) could be spent in the organization—on either a full-time or a part-time basis—to achieve this more closely defined cultural understanding.

Telling it like it is
Participant observation in a student research project

Lucie felt that participant observation would enable her to gain an insider perspective on the process of constructing entrepreneurial identity among university students. Being a university student herself, she was in a good position to be able to try to view these events through the eyes of the people she was studying and to be accepted into the research setting. So she made arrangements to attend some of the events and workshops that were intended to help university students to develop entrepreneurial behaviour. As Lucie explained, this meant 'I could get the feel of how the organizers were trying to present enterprise to me as a student. I could get first-hand experience of it and embrace what they were trying to say.'

However, Lucie found the pressures associated with ethnographic participant observation significant. 'Because I was trying to research this, I don't know if I was looking at things a bit too deeply and not just kind of taking it for what it was. I found myself looking around and trying to kind of gauge other people's reactions as well, so I don't know if I sat there and did it as much as kind of just sitting there and taking everything in really. It was quite difficult. I was trying to write everything down because they didn't want me to tape record anything so I had to take notes and I didn't want to miss anything. So it was quite difficult really to decide "Is that important or is that irrelevant?" and it got a bit kind of confusing at times. It was quite a lot of information to take in I suppose.'

Global and multisite ethnography

A defining feature of a classic approach to ethnography is the way that the researcher concentrates on the specific social processes within one particular community. This means that there is a tendency to overlook the context within which that particular community operates. This is particularly important in organizational ethnography because the culture of a particular workgroup or company can be understood only in relation to the cultural context in which it is located. Moreover, it is often difficult to set boundaries around the particular community that is being studied, especially in cases where the organization being studied is part of a multinational corporation. Traditionally, these boundaries were determined by place—the ethnographer travelled to the place where the community was located and studied what he or she found there. However, organizations are increasingly distributed over a wide geographical area, and this too makes it difficult to determine the focus of study. This has given rise to new forms of ethnographic research which are not dependent on place, in the form of multi-site and global ethnography.

Global ethnography focuses on the way that particular cultures are affected by globalization, leading to the dissolution of traditional ways of working (Burawoy et al. 2000). The global ethnographer seeks to gain insight into the lived experience of globalization through the study of such diverse groups as job-hopping Irish software engineers or Indian nurses working in the United States. This shift in emphasis opens up significant opportunities for organizational ethnographers to study such things as the effects of advances in telecommunications and information technologies on working practices and to explore how work has become less dependent on physical location. Global ethnography thus extends the tradition of ethnographic studies of industrial and large bureaucratic organizations that was started by such writers as Beynon (1975) and continued by Casey (1995), who studied social settings with relatively fixed boundaries.

Related to global ethnography is the concept of multi-site ethnography, in which the same kind of close attention is devoted to phenomena as in conventional ethnography (Prasad and Prasad 2009). In such studies 'the researcher does not confine his/her observations and analysis to a single organization or location but follows specific social phenomena as they travel between different actors and networks in multiple institutional domains' (Prasad et al. 2011: 707). As with global ethnography, there is a recognition that organizations have permeable boundaries and are influenced by other organizations and institutions, and so there is a need to move beyond single sites and locations and to reconnect local meaning-making practices with 'wider social events and mindsets' (Prasad et al. 2011: 707). These authors were influenced by Marcus (1999) in suggesting the strategy of 'following', as a distinguishing feature of such research, tracking 'people (e.g. expatriate managers, minority executives, female bond traders, etc.), products (e.g. coffee, sushi, T-shirts, etc.), conflicts (over resources or social issues), life-histories, laws, policies, and an array of discourses as they wind in and out of multiple organizational locations' (Prasad et al. 2011: 708; Research in focus 19.3).

Research in focus 19.3
A multi-site ethnography of diversity management

Prasad et al. (2011) conducted a four-year long multi-sited ethnography of six organizations from the Canadian petroleum and insurance industries. Their focus was on the workplace diversity management programmes that had been implemented in these organizations, and on the discourse of fashion that had shaped the implementation process. In each of the six organizations, three components of data collection were involved:

1. Ethnographic observations: primarily this involved observing diversity training sessions, internal meetings, a diversity conference, and diversity training for HR professionals delivered by external consultants;

2. In-depth ethnographic interviews: with diversity consultants and trainers, personnel and HR directors, diversity managers, and participants in diversity workshops:

3. Examination of documents: related to the diversity management process, including brochures, videos, training exercises, and cases.

What is interesting about this study is that the focus on fashion relies on understanding the relationships between fashion setters and followers, which a multi-site ethnographic approach enables more effectively than a single-site approach.

Access

One of the key and yet most difficult steps in ethnography is gaining access to a social setting that is relevant to the research problem in which you are interested. The way in which access is approached differs according to whether the setting is a relatively open one or a relatively closed one (Bell 1969). The majority of organizational ethnography is done in predominantly closed or non-public settings of various kinds, such as factories or offices. The negotiation of access involves gaining permission to enter these privately managed spaces or situations. Gaining access to organizations can initially be a very formal process involving a lengthy sequence of letter writing and meetings, in order to deal with managerial concerns about your goals. However, the distinction between open and closed settings is not a hard-and-fast one. Organizations also have a highly public character, made visible through marketing and public-relations activities.

Buchanan, Boddy, and McCalman (1988) suggest that researchers should adopt an opportunistic approach towards fieldwork in organizations, balancing what is desirable against what is possible. 'The research timetable must therefore take into account the possibility that access will not be automatic and instant, but may take weeks and months of meetings and correspondence to achieve' (1988: 56). As Van Maanen and Kolb (1985: 11)

observe, 'gaining access to most organizations is not a matter to be taken lightly but one that involves some combination of strategic planning, hard work and dumb luck'. Sometimes, ethnographers will be able to have their paths smoothed by individuals who act as both sponsor and gatekeeper. Some of the most influential organizational research relationships are those made with senior management, who may act as 'gatekeepers' to the research setting. Gaining access is also sometimes seen as a process of exchange whereby the organizational ethnographer cannot expect to get something out, in the form of data, without giving something in return, often in the form of their physical, mental, or emotional labour. Often, access is built on the researcher's previous employment through which they have developed relationships with gatekeepers. For example, Michel's (2011) access to investment banks was enabled by the fact that she had been an associate at a Wall Street bank before entering academic life. This enabled her to cultivate relationships that were the basis for her nine-year ethnographic study. Similarly, Zhang and Spicer's (2014: 744) ten-month ethnographic study of the production of hierarchical space was enabled by the first author's former employment in a 'large tax authority in a coastal metropolis in eastern China… By courtesy of his former colleagues, he was granted otherwise rare research access to the organization'.

In selecting a particular social setting to act as a case study in which to conduct an ethnographic investigation, the researcher may employ several criteria. These criteria should be determined by the general research area in which he or she is interested. Very often a number of potential cases (and sometimes very many) will be relevant to your research problem. Hence, during his year of participant observation at ZTC Ryland, Watson (1994a) used to joke with managers about the fact that he had chosen the company for the study because of its convenient location, just a twenty-minute walk from his house. The other reason he gave for choosing the company as a research site was because management had been involved in a succession of change initiatives associated with the development of a 'strong' corporate culture. These policies had been informed by the advice of consultants who were academics, providing Watson with potential insight into the processes whereby managerial ideas about culture building were transferred into practice.

You may also choose a certain case because of its 'fit' with your research questions, but there are no guarantees of success, as Van Maanen and Kolb's remark suggests. Sometimes, sheer perseverance pays off. Leidner (1993) was determined that one of the organizations in which she conducted ethnographic research on the routinization of service work should be McDonald's. She writes:

> I knew from the beginning that I wanted one of the case studies to be of McDonald's. The company was a pioneer and exemplar of routinized interaction, and since it was locally based, it seemed like the perfect place to start. McDonald's had other ideas, however, and only after tenacious pestering and persuasion did I overcome corporate employees' polite demurrals, couched in terms of protecting proprietary information and the company's image.
>
> (Leidner 1993: 234–5)

This kind of determination is necessary for any instance in which you want to study a specific organization, where rejection is likely to require a complete rethink.

However, with many research questions, several potential cases are likely to meet your criteria. Organizational researchers use a range of tactics, many of which may seem rather unsystematic, but they are worth drawing attention to.

Telling it like it is
Gaining research access through family or friends

In setting up a research project, it is important to make use of whatever practical resources and personal contacts are available to you, providing that you are working within ethical guidelines (see Chapter 6). Nirwanthi and Angharad both made use of family members who helped to facilitate their research access to organizations, whereas Tom had a friend who was the manager where he carried out his research project.

Nirwanthi's father is a director of the company that she used for her research project. As she explained, this meant that 'I knew that I would have access to all the departments of the company'. However, she was also aware that her use of this personal contact might jeopardize the validity of her findings. 'I discussed it with my supervisor because I was telling him that I would try to keep it as structured as possible but there would be some employees who would recognize me and would know me because of my father and my involvement as well in the company. So I have acknowledged that in my research, saying that it could have influenced some of the data.'

Angharad was advised by her university lecturers to 'go for somewhere where you're likely to be able to get access' and Angharad felt that a public-sector organization would probably be more receptive to requests from students to do research. Since her mother works for a county council organization, she was able to put Angharad in contact with the human resources manager, and Angharad negotiated her access from there. 'Apart from providing the first name to contact, my mum didn't really do anything else and have any other involvement. So it wasn't the same as sort of like I was just going in with my mum. It was kind of separate. I mean it was in her department so she was there, but I wouldn't have liked it if it had looked like I was clinging to my mum and my mum was organizing it.'

(continued)

Tom's friend managed a call centre run by a local government authority, which, he explained, is quite unusual, since 'the majority of call centres are managed in the private sector and almost all the literature that's been published is about call centres in the private sector, so that seemed to be another dimension to this study in looking at different ways of running call centres. I negotiated access through this contact. I'm not quite sure how I'd have gone about it if I hadn't had that contact. I think the majority of people on my course either did research in their own workplace or did research which wasn't specific to one organization or they had some sort of contact like I did. I'm sure you could just approach people cold, but it's a lot easier if you've got a link.'

- Use friends, contacts, colleagues, academics to help you gain access; provided the organization is relevant to your research question, the route should not matter.

- Try to get the support of someone within the organization who will act as your champion. This person may be prepared to vouch for you and the value of your research. Such people are placed in the role of 'sponsors'.

- Usually you will need to get access through top management/senior executives. Even though you may secure a certain level of agreement lower down the hierarchy, you will usually need clearance from them. Such senior people act as 'gatekeepers'.

- Offer something in return (for example, a report). This helps to create a sense of being *trustworthy*. However, this strategy also carries risks, in that it may turn you into a cheap consultant and may invite restrictions on your activities, such as insistence on seeing what you write or restrictions on who is willing to talk to you. For example, Milkman (1997) in her study of General Motors (see Research in focus 19.4) found that,

although her research approach gained her legitimacy in the eyes of management, it stimulated scepticism and lack of trust among the workers.

- Provide a clear explanation of your aims and methods and be prepared to deal with concerns. Suggest a meeting at which you can deal with worries and provide an explanation of what you intend to do in terms that can readily be understood by others.

- Be prepared to negotiate—you will want complete access but it is unlikely you will be given a *carte blanche*. Milkman (1997) describes how, in negotiating access to the General Motors automobile assembly plant, the promise to produce 'hard', quantitative data to management, through survey research, was what eventually secured the researchers' access to the plant—even though she had no previous experience in designing or conducting surveys!

- Be reasonably honest about the amount of people's time you are likely to take up. This is a question you will almost certainly be asked if you are seeking access to commercial organizations and probably many not-for-profit ones too.

Research in focus 19.4
Finding a working role in the organization

Being an organizational ethnographer involves managing the impressions others have of you by developing a role that helps you to blend into a particular organizational setting. One way of doing this is by developing a working role, some examples of which can be found in Table 19.1. The first possibility involves the ethnographer casting him or herself in the role of a management consultant. This involves being seen as a credible outsider, as someone who can be trusted and allowed to develop close relationships with management. Watson (1994*a*) illustrates how he used this role to gain access to and credibility within the organization. He agreed that his year-long access to the company would result in the development of a scheme identifying and expressing the competencies that the company could use in selecting and developing its future managers. However, there may be dangers in becoming too closely identified with managerial groupings, as this can cut off access to potentially valuable informants in other non-managerial roles within the organization. For example, Milkman (1997) describes how the very fact that she had legitimacy with both management and the union at General Motors rendered her untrustworthy in the eyes of workers whom she was most interested in studying. This was because, 'in the intensely political world of the factory, academic researchers were an entirely unknown quantity and could only be understood as servicing someone else's immediate interests' (1997: 192).

A second option involves becoming a confidant. Dalton (1959), for example, describes how a female secretary helped him to obtain confidential data about managerial salaries. In exchange, she asked Dalton, given his sociological training, to provide her with some relationship counselling to help her to work out the feelings she held towards a man she was seriously dating. Dalton obliged, in exchange for the data; the secretary married the man within a year. Similarly, Casey (1995: 203) describes how she was accorded the roles of witness, scribe, analyst, and therapist. She did not discourage the therapeutic role, as it gave her access to considerable data and insights and 'provided some catharsis for employees' who were trying to make sense of their organizational lives. M. Parker (2000) suggests the role of the confidant is the most productive one for revealing insights into the politics of the particular organization. He describes how his interviewees saw him as someone who would listen to their problems when others wouldn't. D. Fletcher (2002) describes how she adopted a role as 'emotional-nurturer' in her study of a small engineering company. The gendered understandings that defined her fieldwork interactions in a masculine organizational setting led her subconsciously to 'choose' this role as a way of responding to her feelings of 'femaleness' and difference. She explains that she felt 'out of place and "different"' (2002: 430) and so, in order to try to gain acceptance and gain access within the organization, she assigned herself to non-threatening and menial tasks, such as photocopying and filing, and 'provided positive stroking concerning job/marital problems' (2002: 411). In this way Fletcher describes how she 'tried to create a non-threatening comfort zone in which people could have a break from work and talk about their work' (2002: 412). However, Fletcher also explains that she felt that something of herself was 'lost' through this process, making her sometimes tired, depressed, and frustrated, as 'constantly providing emotional nurture is exhausting and neverending' (2002: 414).

A third potential role involves the researcher becoming an apprentice, adopting a more active work role in the setting. For example, Sharpe (1997) describes how she gained insider status by taking up employment as a shopfloor worker in a Japanese car manufacturing company on a six-month student job placement contract. She explains: 'by immersing myself in the shopfloor life, I believed I would be able to offer a richer, reflexive understanding of social processes and dynamics than if I took a more conventional approach of research as an outsider or distant observer' (1997: 230).

'Hanging around' is another common access strategy. As a strategy, it typically entails either loitering in an area until you are noticed or gradually becoming incorporated into or asking to join a group. For example, as well as interviewing shop stewards who represented assembly-line workers and a selection of workers from each of the four main production departments, Beynon (1975) spent a day each week at the Ford plant observing and listening to the shop stewards 'as they negotiated, argued and discussed issues amongst themselves and with their members' (1975: 13). He describes how he 'sat at tables in the canteens and at benches around the coffee-vending machines at break times' and 'talked with workers as they queued up for their dinner, for buses or to clock their cards at the beginning and the end of every day' (1975: 13). Similarly, Casey, in her study of a group of professional workers at the multinational 'Hephaestus' Corporation, tells how she 'spent a great deal of time lingering around individual people' (1995: 201). Similarly,

M. Parker (2000: 236) describes how he spent time waiting 'outside managers' offices, often for long periods of time, and wandering around the factory or offices' just to collect small details or fragments of data.

Sometimes, as research relationships evolve, they come to a point where a degree of informal interaction becomes significant in developing insider status. For example, Heyes (1997), whose research took place inside a chemical plant, lists the many social aspects of organizational life in which he was eventually involved, including 'general conversation, banter, smoke breaks' and rituals such as 'the take-away meals which were consumed on the weekend night-shift' (1997: 69).

As these anecdotes suggest, gaining access to social settings is a crucial first step in ethnographic research, in that, without access, your research plans will be halted in their tracks. As Ram (1994) illustrates in his study of employment relations in small firms (see Research in focus 19.5), attention to cultural context and local

Research in focus 19.5
A complete participant?

One of the aims of Ram's (1994) ethnographic study of employment relations in small firms was to consider some of the ways in which employees and employers negotiated the labour process.

However, just getting into clothing companies in the West Midlands, which formed the focus of his study, was known to be 'notoriously difficult' (1994: 26). In order to gain access to the three clothing firms that formed the basis for his study, Ram relied on his family and community connections to establish the trust necessary for him to 'tap into the workplace culture' (1994: 23). Being able to speak fluent Punjabi was essential to understanding people in the workplace, but equally important for Ram in becoming an 'insider' was being able to understand how the shopfloor manufacturing industry culture worked. Crucial to this was his own first-hand experience of the clothing industry. Ram describes himself as having been involved in the clothing trade for most of his life.

> My two elder sisters and one younger sister are married into clothing families, where they work as sewing machinists and assist in the management of the in-laws' firms. My elder brother runs a clothing manufacturing business with a cousin . . . My younger brother is in charge of the family-owned warehouse.
>
> (1994: 24)

Ram adopted an 'opportunistic' approach to the fieldwork, relying on his friends and relatives and on his personal background as a member of a 'respected' family in the local Asian community. Ram's own father was in charge of 'Company A', which formed one of Ram's case studies. In addition, Ram himself had worked for this company either full- or part-time, 'since it came into being' (1994: 30). He had the power to 'sign cheques, purchase stock, make use of the firm's equipment and give instructions to the company's workers' (1994: 30), and during one period of the fieldwork his father went on holiday, leaving Ram and his younger brother to run the firm. However, despite his apparent role as a total participant, it was hard for Ram to talk to the shopfloor machinists, who were mostly women, because of the customary regulation of gender relationships within Asian society. He therefore used a chaperone, a senior female machinist, who accompanied him when he questioned individual female operatives.

norms and values can be important considerations when seeking access to closed settings. Gender can also be an important dynamic when negotiating access to many male-dominated organizational settings (see Research in focus 19.13). In summary, gaining access is often fraught with difficulties. Therefore this discussion of access strategies can be only a starting point in knowing what kinds of approach can be considered.

However, opportunities for access can also arise from studying contexts with which the researcher is already involved as a complete participant—for example, through being employed in the organization he or she intends to study. Spradley and McCurdy (1972) suggest that the ethnographer's own place of work may even have special advantages as a research site, such as ease of access and already formed relationships with key informants. This may make the time needed to conduct the research shorter. However, this ethnographic approach is not without its own difficulties: the more familiar you

are with a social situation, the less you may be able to recognize the tacit cultural rules that are at work. Alvesson (2003) uses the term self-ethnography to refer to a particular type of ethnographic study based on settings with which the researcher is highly familiar, such as universities, which he argues offer particular advantages in terms of gaining research access, understanding the culture, and managing the time demands associated with qualitative research. Brannick and Coghlan (2007) refer to this as 'insider research' (see Chapter 2).

Overt versus covert?

One way to ease the access problem is to assume a *covert* role—in other words, not to disclose the fact that you are a researcher. This strategy obviates the need to negotiate access to organizations or to explain why you want to intrude into people's lives and make them objects of study. As we have seen, seeking access is a

Key concept 19.6
What is the covert role in ethnography?

Advantages

- *There is no problem of access*. Adopting a covert role largely gets around the access problem, because the researcher does not have to seek permission to gain entry to a social setting or organization.

- *Reactivity is not a problem*. Using a covert role also reduces reactivity (see Key concept 12.8), because participants do not know the person conducting the study is a researcher. Therefore, they are less likely to adjust their behaviour because of the researcher's presence.

Disadvantages

- *The problem of taking notes*. As Ditton (1977; see Research in focus 19.7) discovered, it is difficult and probably in some circumstances impossible to take notes when people do not realize you are conducting research. As we will see below, notes are very important to an ethnographer, and it is too risky to rely exclusively on your memory.

- *The problem of not being able to use other methods*. Ethnography entails the use of several methods, but, if the researcher is in a covert role, it is difficult to steer conversations in a certain direction for fear of detection and it is essentially impossible to engage in interviewing.

- *Anxiety*. The ethnographer is under constant threat of having his or her cover blown. Ethnography is frequently a stressful research method, and the worries about detection can add to those anxieties. Moreover, if the ethnographer is found out, the whole research project may be jeopardized.

- *Ethical problems*. Covert observation transgresses two important ethical tenets: it does not provide participants with the opportunity for 'informed consent' (whereby they can agree or disagree to participate on the basis of information supplied to them) and it entails deception. It can also be taken to be a violation of the principle of privacy. Also, many writers take the view that, in addition to being potentially damaging to research participants, it can also harm the practice of research, because of fears about social researchers being identified by the public as snoopers or voyeurs if they are found out. Ethical issues are considered in greater detail in Chapter 6.

However, as the main text points out, in some circumstances the overt/covert distinction may be a matter of degree.

highly fraught business, and the adoption of a covert role removes some of these difficulties. An outline of the advantages and disadvantages of covert ethnography is given in Key concept 19.6.

Covert ethnography is relatively uncommon within studies of management and business. An exception is Dalton's (1959) classic study of managers, *Men Who Manage*, which focused on the gap between official and unofficial action. Dalton describes how, in setting up access, he made no formal approach to the top management of any of the four firms he studied in the heavily industrialized area of 'Mobile Acres' in the USA. He relied instead on his status as an employee in two of the firms he studied and relied primarily on the method of covert participant observation. Describing some of the difficulties associated with his covert research role, Dalton draws attention to the problem of 'knowing too much', describing how his situation became more sensitive as he acquired more unofficial information about practices such as 'pilfering' (employee theft of materials).

Dalton describes his work role as giving him 'great freedom of movement and wide contacts' (1959: 278) within the firm. However, it is not clear from his accounts to what extent people in the firms actually knew what he was doing. Dalton draws attention to the importance of 'intimates', trusted individuals who gave information and aid to the research process. This circle of individuals had shown over a period of about three years that 'they could be counted on not to jeopardize the study' (Dalton 1964: 66) and did not pry too much into the information that he was getting from others. As far as these intimates were concerned, therefore, it is not clear to what extent they encountered his research role as truly covert.

In another classic study, Donald Roy (1958) was similarly oblique with his co-workers about why he was working at the factory. Working under the pseudonym 'Danelly', he describes how workers knew that he had been attending 'college' but 'the specific course of study remained somewhat obscure' (1958: 164) to them. In

Research in focus 19.7
An example of the perils of covert observation: the case of field notes in the lavatory

Ditton's (1977) research on 'fiddling' in a bakery provides an interesting case of the practical difficulties of taking notes during covert observation, as well as an illustration of an ethnographer who shifted his position from covert to overt observation at least in part because of those difficulties:

> Nevertheless, I *was* able to develop personal covert participant–observation skills. Right from the start, I found it impossible to keep everything that I wanted to remember in my head until the end of the working day . . . and so had to take rough notes as I was going along. But I was stuck 'on the line', and had nowhere to retire to privately to jot things down. Eventually, the wheeze of using innocently provided lavatory cubicles occurred to me. Looking back, all my notes for that third summer were on Bronco toilet paper! Apart from the awkward tendency for pencilled notes to be self-erasing from hard toilet paper . . . my frequent requests for 'time out' after interesting happenings or conversations in the bakehouse and the amount of time I was spending in the lavatory began to get noticed. I had to pacify some genuinely concerned work-mates, give up totally undercover operations, and 'come out' as an observer—albeit in a limited way. I eventually began to scribble notes more openly, but still not in front of people when they were talking. When questioned about this, as I was occasionally, I coyly said that I was writing things down that occurred to me about 'my studies'.

> (1977: 5)

answer to the question 'Why are you working here?', Roy stressed the importance of working 'lots of overtime' and this, according to Roy, seemed to 'suffice' for the workers.

However, the overt versus covert distinction is not without problems. For example, while an ethnographer may seek access through an overt route, there may be many people with whom he or she comes into contact who will not be aware of the ethnographer's status as a researcher. Also, some ethnographers move between the two roles (see Research in focus 19.7).

Another interesting case is provided by Glucksmann (1994), who in the 1970s left her academic post to work on a factory assembly line to explore the reasons why feminism appeared not to be relevant to working-class women. In a sense, she was a covert observer, but her motives for the research were primarily political, and she says that, at the time she was undertaking the research, she had no intention of writing the book that subsequently appeared and that was published under a pseudonym (Cavendish 1982). After the book's publication, it was treated as an example of ethnographic research. Was she an overt or a covert observer (or neither or both)? Whichever description applies, this is an interesting case of what might be termed *retrospective ethnography*.

Ethnographers are far more likely to be in an overt role than a covert one. Some of the reasons for this situation are extremely practical. For example, Freeman (2000) explains that being white and American made it impossible for her to adopt a covert role in her study of data entry workers in Barbados, and company production demands and limited space made it impossible for her to work on an unpaid temporary basis. However, as Key concept 19.6 reveals, the reasons for the preference of most ethnographers for an overt role are to do with ethical considerations. Because of the ethical problems that beset covert research (and indeed some of the practical difficulties), the bulk of the discussion of access issues that follows will focus upon ethnographers seeking to employ an overt role.

Ongoing access

Negotiation of access does not finish when you have made contact and gained an entrée to the organization. You still need access to *people*. Simply because you have gained access to an organization does not mean that you will have an easy passage through it. Securing access is in many ways an ongoing activity, which takes considerable effort and time. This is likely to prove a particular problem in closed contexts such as organizations, as Delbridge (1998) effectively illustrates when describing his attempts to become integrated as a worker on the shopfloor of a factory sited in a small Welsh valley community. At first,

'I stood out like a sore thumb, I was even noticed and looked at in the street'. However, 'my actual participation in the tasks which faced the workers helped to break down the barriers and several people approached me over the weeks and told me that when they actually saw me sitting there alongside them day after day they began to have some respect for what I was doing' (1998: 19).

Even so, there are various concerns that group members may have, and these will affect the level of ongoing access that you are able to achieve.

- People will have suspicions about you, perhaps seeing you as an instrument of top management (it is very common for members of organizations to believe that researchers are placed there to check up on them or even to mistake them for other people). For example, Roethlisberger and Dickson (1939) describe how one of the interviewers in the Hawthorne studies was mistaken for a rate setter.

> There was a buzz of conversation and the men seemed to be working at great speed. Suddenly there was a sharp hissing sound. The conversation died away, and there was a noticeable slowing up in the work pace. The interviewer later discovered from an acquaintance in the department that he had been mistaken for a rate setter. One of the workmen, who acted as a lookout, had stepped on a valve releasing compressed air, a prearranged signal for slowing down.
>
> (Roethlisberger and Dickson 1939: 386)

- Another example is provided by Freeman (2000), who found that her research access was halted because of fears that she was a corporate spy, sent by a competitor organization to poach members of the workforce.

- People will worry that what they say or do may get back to bosses or to colleagues. Van Maanen (1991a) notes from his research on the police that, when conducting ethnographic research among officers, you are likely to observe activities that may be deeply discrediting and even illegal. Your credibility among police officers will be determined by your reactions to situations and events that are known to be difficult for individuals.

- If they have these worries, they may go along with your research, but in fact sabotage it, engaging in deceptions, misinformation, and not allowing access to 'back regions' (Goffman 1959).

There are four things you can do to smooth the path of ongoing access.

- Play up your credentials—past work and experience; your knowledge of the organization and/or its sector; understanding of their problems—and be prepared for tests of either competence or credibility. For example, Perlow (1997) observes that a critical factor in gaining the support of engineers at the Ditto corporation was that she came from the Massachusetts Institute of Technology (MIT), as 'there is no institution that the engineers we studied hold in higher regard' (1997: 142).

- Pass tests—be non-judgemental when things are said to you about informal activities or about the organization; make sure information given to you does not get back to others, whether bosses or peers. M. Parker (2000) describes how, when at the end of his fieldwork he submitted his report to management, an uncomplimentary comment about the Managing Director was traced back to an insufficiently anonymized source. Parker subsequently came in for a humiliating grilling from three of the company directors. He claims that this event probably damaged the manager's reputation in the organization, and his trust in him.

- You may need a role—if your research involves quite a lot of participant observation, the role will be related to your position within the organization (see Research in focus 19.4). Otherwise, you will need to construct a 'front', as Ditton (1977; see Research in focus 19.7) did when referring to 'his studies'. This will involve thinking about your dress and your explanations about what you are doing there, and possibly helping out occasionally with work or offering advice. Make sure you have thought about ways in which people's suspicions can be allayed and do not behave ambiguously or inconsistently.

- Be prepared for changes in circumstances that may affect your access, such as changes of senior management.

Key informants

One aspect of having sponsors or gatekeepers who smooth access for the ethnographer is that they may become *key informants* in the course of the subsequent fieldwork. The ethnographer relies a lot on informants, but certain informants may become particularly important to the research. They often develop an appreciation of the research and direct the ethnographer to situations, events, or people likely to be helpful to the progress of the investigation.

An example is provided by Kanter (1977), who describes the relationships she developed with a small group of people with whom she worked closely at Indsco Corporation.

'These people were largely in functions where they were well placed to see a large number of people in a large number of levels . . . They could tell me about the history of the company and a variety of experiences in the organization as well as provide information about the issues in their own careers. I could also use them to check out stories I gathered elsewhere' (1977: 336). Similarly, Collinson (1992*b*) describes how being a man researching equal opportunities sometimes resulted in research respondents withholding cooperation. He describes how the identification of key women informants, who were prepared to assist the 'young lad from the university', was crucial in providing him with 'insider' information. One woman trade unionist in particular provided extensive help with the project. Collinson and the woman trade unionist developed 'a much closer and mutually supportive working relationship than would usually be the case between researcher and respondents' (1992*b*: 115). This provided him with 'deeper insight into the difficulties faced by women in employment and within the trade union movement' (1992*b*: 115) and greater understanding of the problems of managing work and home.

In summary, key informants can clearly be of great help to the ethnographer and frequently provide a support that helps with the stress of fieldwork. However, it also needs to be borne in mind that they carry risks in that the ethnographer may develop an undue reliance on the key informant, and, rather than seeing social reality through the eyes of members of the social setting, the researcher is seeing social reality through the eyes of the key informant.

The ethnographer will encounter many other people who will also act as informants. Their accounts may be solicited or unsolicited (Hammersley and Atkinson 1995). Some researchers prefer the latter, because of its greater spontaneity and naturalism. Very often, research participants develop a sense of the kinds of events the ethnographer wants to see or encounters that it would be beneficial to be present at. Such unsolicited sources of information are highly attractive to the ethnographer because of their relative spontaneity, although, as Hammersley and Atkinson (1995: 130–1) observe, they may on occasions be staged for the ethnographer's benefit. Solicited accounts can occur in two ways: by interview (see Chapter 20) or by casual questioning during conversations (though in ethnographic research the boundary between an interview and a conversation is by no means clear-cut, as Burgess (1984) makes clear). When the ethnographer needs specific information concerning an issue that is not amenable to direct observation or that is not cropping up during 'natural' conversations, solicited accounts are likely to be the only way forward.

 # Roles for ethnographers

Related to the issue of ongoing access (or relationships in the field, as it is sometimes called) is the question of the kind of role the ethnographer adopts in relation to the social setting and its members. Several schemes have been devised by writers on research methods to describe the various roles that can be and have been adopted by ethnographers. One of the most widely cited schemes is Gold's (1958) classification of participant observer roles, which can be arrayed on a continuum of degrees of involvement with and detachment from members of the social setting (see Figure 19.1). There are four roles.

- *Complete participant.* According to Gold, the complete participant is a fully functioning member of the social setting and his or her true identity is not known to members. As such, the complete participant is a covert observer, like D. Roy (1958) and Dalton (1959).

- *Participant-as-observer.* This role is the same as the complete participant one, but members of the social setting are aware of the researcher's status as a researcher. The ethnographer is engaged in regular interaction with people and participates in their daily lives and is open about their research. In organizational ethnography this frequently involves taking up either paid or unpaid employment in the research setting, as did Delbridge (1998) in his study of contemporary manufacturing under TQM and Sharpe (1997) in her study of Japanese work practices in a UK-based car manufacturing plant.

- *Observer-as-participant.* In this role, the researcher is mainly an interviewer. There is some observation, but very little of it involves any participation. Many of the studies covered in Chapter 20 are of this type. Prasad's (1993) study of the effects of computerization of work, described in Research in focus 20.3, also fits into this category, as her research relied on structured periods of observation during which she would watch the staff

Figure 19.1

Gold's classification of participant observer roles

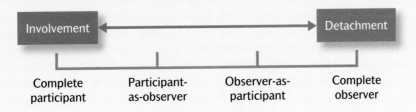

| Involvement | ⟷ | Detachment |

Complete participant   Participant-as-observer   Observer-as-participant   Complete observer

at work and document these observations, only helping out occasionally on the reception desk when it was particularly busy. See Research in focus 19.8 for a further illustration.

- *Complete observer*. The researcher does not interact with people. According to Gold, people do not have to take the researcher into account. This kind of role relies on forms of observation that are unobtrusive in character. For example, in studies at the Western Electric Company's Hawthorne plant, investigators spent a total of six months observing the informal social relationships between operators in the Bank Wiring Observation Room. Investigations involved an observer, who maintained a role as 'disinterested spectator' with the aim of observing and describing what was going on. Observation involved certain general rules: the investigator should not give orders or answer any questions that necessitated the assumption of authority; he should not enter voluntarily into any argument and generally should remain as non-committal as possible; he should not force himself into any conversation or

appear anxious to overhear; he should never violate confidences or give information to supervisors; and he should not by his manner of speech or behaviour 'set himself off from the group' (Roethlisberger and Dickson 1939: 388–9).

However, most writers would take the view that, since ethnography entails immersion in a social setting and fairly prolonged involvement, the complete observer role should not be considered as participant observation or ethnography at all, since participation is likely to be more or less entirely missing. Some writers might also question whether research based on the observer-as-participant role can genuinely be regarded as ethnography, but, since it is likely that certain situations are unlikely to be amenable to the immersion that is a key ingredient of the method, it could be argued that to dismiss it totally as an approach to ethnography is rather restrictive. It is significant in this context that Gold referred to the four roles in relation to conducting 'fieldwork', which has the potential for a broader meaning than either participant observation or ethnography.

Research in focus 19.8
An example of observer-as-participant in the Magic Kingdom

An illustration of research that comes very close to the observer-as-participant role is Raz's (1999) study of Tokyo Disneyland. His main sources of data were: many visits to the theme park, including being part of several official and unofficial tours; interviews with current and former employees; a textual analysis of company guidebooks; and an examination of the reception of the park by visitors through a focus group. Raz's goal was to explore the meeting place of the forces of globalization, in the form of the familiar themes associated with the Disney company, and forces of the 'local', in the form of the distinctive character of Japanese culture. He draws on ideas such as 'globalization' in order to develop an understanding of the ways in which the combination of global and local forces is played out, and on Hochschild's (1983) concept of 'emotional labour' (see Research in focus 17.4) to develop an appreciation of the world of work for the Disney employee.

Key concept 19.9
What is 'going native'?

'Going native' refers to a plight that is supposed sometimes to afflict ethnographers when they lose their sense of being a researcher and become wrapped up in the world view of the people they are studying. The prolonged immersion of ethnographers in the lives of the people they study, coupled with the commitment to seeing the social world through their eyes, lie behind the risk and actuality of going native. Going native is a potential problem for several reasons but especially because the ethnographer can lose sight of his or her position as a researcher and therefore find it difficult to develop a socially scientific angle on the collection and analysis of data.

Each role carries its own advantages and risks. The issues concerning being a complete participant were covered in Key concept 19.5. According to Gold, the participant-as-observer role carries the risk of over-identification and hence of 'going native' (see Key concept 19.9), but offers the opportunity to get close to people. Gold argues that the observer-as-participant role carries the risk of not understanding the social setting and people in it sufficiently and therefore of making incorrect inferences. The complete observer role shares with complete participation the removal of the possible problem of reactivity, but it carries even further risks than the observer-as-participant role of failing to understand situations.

Gans (1968) has devised a classification of participant observer roles, but he views these as roles that will coexist in any project. In other words, the three roles he outlines will be employed at different times in the course of ethnographic research and for different purposes. The three roles are:

- *total participant*, in which the ethnographer is completely involved in a certain situation and has to resume a researcher stance once the situation has unfolded and then write down notes;

- *researcher–participant*, whereby the ethnographer participates in a situation but is only semi-involved, so that he or she can function fully as a researcher in the course of the situation;

- *total researcher*, which entails observation without involvement in the situation, as in attendance at a public meeting or watching what is going on in a bar; when in this role, the researcher does not participate in the flow of events.

The advantage of Gans's classification is that, like Gold's, it reflects degrees of involvement and detachment, but it deals only with overt observation and recognizes that ethnographers do not typically adopt a single role throughout their dealings. For example, looking at the research process described by Ram (1994; see Research in focus 19.5), it is clear that in one sense Ram was a total participant, running the firm, speaking Punjabi, and having first-hand experience of the clothing industry. However, in relation to the women shopfloor machinists, he was a total researcher, unable, because of the customary regulation of gender relationships in Asian society, to participate in the flow of events.

Table 19.1 outlines some of the working roles that organizational ethnographers take on in order to secure access to closed settings. However, it is evident from the table and the organizational ethnographies referred to in this chapter that more than one role may be involved in a particular setting. Holliday (1995), who took on the role of the apprentice, accounts for the value of her labour in exchange for access, which she estimates to have cost her approximately £2500. Some more examples of working roles are given in Research in focus 19.4.

Clearly these three organizational roles are overlapping, and more than one may be adopted in a particular setting. They are also likely to change over time as the fieldwork progresses. It is arguably the case that, even if it were possible to adopt a single ethnographic role over the entire course of a project, it is likely that it would be undesirable, because there would be a lack of flexibility in handling situations and people, and risks of excessive involvement (and hence going native) or detachment would loom large. This is a criticism that was levelled at Beynon (1975) in his ethnographic study of *Working for Ford* (see Research in focus 19.10). The issue of the kind of role(s) the ethnographer adopts is therefore of considerable significance, because it has implications for field relationships in the various situations that are encountered.

The kind of role adopted by an ethnographer is likely to have implications for his or her capacity to penetrate the surface layers of an organization. One of the strengths of organizational ethnography is that it offers the prospect of being able to find out what an organization is 'really' like, as opposed to how it formally depicts itself. For

Table 19.1

Three roles for organizational ethnographers

	Ethnographer's role		
	Consultant	Apprentice	Confidant
Characteristics	Competent, knowledgeable, professional	Naïve, unthreatening, personable	Mature, attentive, trustworthy
	A credible outsider who secures the trust of management	A younger person who can make him or herself useful within the organization	An impartial outsider who is able to listen to people's problems
	Exchange of access for knowledge or information, often in the form of a written report or verbal presentation	Exchange of access for productive labour	Exchange of access for psycho-social support or therapy
Examples	Ram (1994)	Dalton (1959)	Collinson (1992*a*)
	Watson (1994a)	Casey (1995)	Crang (1994)
	Holliday (1995)	Perlow (1997)	Holliday (1995)
	Parker (2000)	Freeman (2000)	Sharpe (1997)
		Parker (2000)	Delbridge (1998)
			Fletcher (2002)

example, Michael Humphreys conducted ethnographic research in the UK headquarters of a US bank referred to pseudonymously as Credit Line (Humphreys and Watson 2009). He was aware of the firm's commitment to corporate social responsibility but became increasingly aware that, although people working in the organization were publicly enthusiastic about its ethical stance, many were privately sceptical about the firm's actual commitment. For example, he quotes one employee (Charity) as saying: 'My problem is that, in this organization, corporate social responsibility is a sham—it's just rhetoric—I mean how can we call ourselves responsible when we give credit cards to poor people and charge them 30 per cent APR [annual percentage rate] just because they are high

risk?' (Humphreys and Watson 2009: 50). For employees to divulge such private views, which cast doubt on the integrity of their organization, the ethnographer will probably need to be closer to the confidant role referred to in Table 19.1, since it requires the organizational participants to be confident about sharing their private views, which could lead to them being censured by senior managers.

Active or passive?

A further issue that is raised about any situation in which the ethnographer participates is the degree to which he or she should be or can be an active or a passive participant

Research in focus 19.10
An example of going native

In the preface to the second edition of his classic study *Working for Ford* (1975: 11–12), Beynon describes how he was criticized by reviewers for 'going native' following publication of the first edition of the book. It was suggested that he had become a spokesperson for the Ford factory workers, and his emotional involvement was seen as having gone a stage too far. He was accused of having a 'prolonged love affair' with 'foul mouthed shop stewards' and of having used the 'picturesque language of Billingsgate' in his 'confused, chatty, repetitive and ungrammatical' book, which was dismissed by one source as being of 'doubtful value as an objective sociological study'. The accuracy and validity of Beynon's account of working life at the Ford factory were thus called into question, and the study was dismissed by some as subjective, naïve reportage.

(Van Maanen 1978). Even when the ethnographer is in an observer-as-participant role, there may be contexts in which either participation is unavoidable or a compulsion to join in a limited way may be felt. For example, Fine's (1996) research on the work of chefs in restaurants was carried out largely by semi-structured interview. In spite of his limited participation, he found himself involved in washing up in the kitchens to help out during busy periods. Sometimes ethnographers may *feel* they have no choice but to get involved, because a failure to participate actively might indicate to members of the social setting a lack of commitment and lead to a loss of credibility. Another example is provided by Holliday (1995), who describes how in smaller organizations active work-role participation is more likely to be expected of the ethnographer than in larger companies where there is more space to 'hang around'. She describes how at FranTech she was given 'a variety of jobs, from typing and answering the telephone to "managerial" tasks such as auditing the production schedule and writing procedures for the BS5750' (Holliday 1995: 27). Similarly Ram (1994; see Research in focus 19.5), in his study of family-owned and managed firms in the West Midlands clothing industry, talks about helping with social security queries, housing issues, and passport problems, advising on higher education, and even tying turbans while in the field. However, the pressure to get involved raises ethical considerations, as the ethnographer may be asked to participate in an activity that involves a degree of deception or even illegal activity (see Chapter 6 for more on ethical considerations).

Ethnography also includes the use of non-observational methods and sources such as interviewing and documents. For example, Lok and de Ronde's (2013) ethnography of the Cambridge University Boat Club involved the ethnographer being copied in on all email correspondence between the squad and coaches, generating a total of around 150 emails. This, in addition to archival data including a log book kept by former club captains, and media post-race reports, formed the basis for their analysis of 'practice breakdowns', where things did not go as anticipated for crew members. Similarly, Zhang and Spicer (2014), in their study of a Chinese bureaucracy, used visual methods, taking photographs and also asking participants to take photographs of aspects of the building they felt strongly about, in addition to more traditional ethnographic methods such as field notes and interviews.

Shadowing

A form of observation that has affinities with the notion of passive participant observation and which may be feasible for some students when doing research for their dissertations is the notion of *shadowing*, which McDonald (2005) used in her study of team leaders in a high-tech organization. She defines shadowing as 'a research technique which involves a researcher closely following a member of an organization over an extended period of time' (2005: 456). This includes shadowing him or her at meetings as well as time spent writing at his or her desk. Although shadowing need not necessarily form part of an ethnographic study—it could also be used as a stand-alone method—it does bear some similarity to the kinds of participant observation that ethnographers typically engage in. In addition to following the member of the organization throughout his or her working day, the researcher also asks him or her questions about what he or she is doing: 'some of the questions will be for clarification, such as what was being said on the other end of a phone call, or what a departmental joke means. Other questions will be intended to reveal purpose, such as why a particular line of argument was pursued in a meeting, or what the current operational priorities are' (2005: 456). During this process, the researcher will also write field notes (for more on field notes, see Tips and skills 'Writing field notes') recording the times and subject of conversation and the body language and moods of the person being shadowed. McDonald claims that one of the advantages of shadowing is that, rather than relying on an individual's account of his or her role in an organization, it enables the researcher to view the behaviour directly. Also, as Czarniawska (2007) points out, shadowing is likely to involve mobility, so that the researcher is able to view the work of the person being shadowed in a variety of contexts. Czarniawska (2014) has also pointed out that this represents an important advantage of shadowing over traditional participant observation, which assumed that people remain in the same location most of the time.

McDonald also lists a number of practical recommendations for shadowing, which are broadly similar to those given to ethnographers:

- *never go in cold:* spend time getting to know the organization and the person you intend to shadow beforehand;

- *use a small,* hardback notebook rather than a digital recorder, which is less practical for shadowing;

- *write down as much as you can,* including descriptions of settings, meaning of acronyms, your first impressions of people, your emotional reaction to situations;

- *find a mentor* who is not part of the organization to talk to about your research;

- *make a daily audio dump* recording your thoughts at the end of the work day, which will help you to understand your notes when you go back to them later;

- *plan your data management* before you go into the field.

Gill, Barbour, and Dean (2014) have gone further by drawing up a list of ten recommendations which are outlined in terms of three phases. First, there is the 'arriving phase' during which the shadower should attend to a range of initial pre-fieldwork issues such as negotiating with the shadowee what areas of organizational activity can be subjected to the shadowing method. Second, there is the shadowing phase itself, during which the shadower should consider such issues as different note-taking strategies and learning the behvioural rules suggested by the organizational culture so that these are not transgressed. Third, there is the 'leaving' phase during which the shadower has to consider how best to make an acceptable exit and to do so in a way that will allow some ongoing contact, for example, so that the shadowee might appraise items written by the shadower.

Urban and Quinlan's (2014: 47) experiences of shadowing in Canadian health care organizations suggests that the method, as they put it, is 'not for the faint of heart'. The sometimes frantic world of nurses and the ethical dilemmas that are regularly faced (since informed consent cannot be continually negotiated with those with whom shadowees come into contact) suggest that the method can be a difficult one to implement.

Field notes

Because of the frailties of human memory, ethnographers have to take notes based on their observations. These should be fairly detailed summaries of events and behaviour and the researcher's initial reflections on them. The notes need to specify key dimensions of whatever is observed or heard. There are some general principles.

- Write down notes, however brief, as quickly as possible after seeing or hearing something interesting.

- Write up full field notes at the very latest at the end of the day and include such details as location, who was involved, what prompted the exchange, date and time of the day, etc.

- People may prefer to use a digital recorder to record initial notes, but this may create a problem of needing to transcribe a lot of speech.

- Notes must be vivid and clear—you should not have to ask at a later date, 'What did I mean by that?'

- You need to take copious notes, so, if in doubt, write it down. The notes may be of different types (see the section on 'Types of field notes' below).

Obviously, it can be very useful to take your notes down straight away—that is, as soon as something interesting happens. However, wandering around with a notebook and pencil in hand and scribbling notes down on a continuous basis runs the risk of making people self-conscious. It may be necessary, therefore, to develop strategies of taking small amounts of time out, though hopefully without generating the anxieties Ditton (1977) appears to have occasioned (see Research in focus 19.7). Keeping field notes on top of the demands of being an observer in organizations requires energy and dedication. For example, in their participant observation study of the Cambridge University Boat Race, Lok and de Rond (2013: 192) describe how at the end of each day the ethnographer 'transcribed each day's extensive fieldnotes', a potentially demanding task in addition to training for the race.

To some extent, strategies for taking field notes will be affected by the degree to which the ethnographer enters the field with clearly delineated research questions. As noted in Chapter 17, most qualitative research adopts a general approach of beginning with general research questions (as specifically implied by Figure 17.1), but there is considerable variation in the degree to which this is the case. Obviously, when there is some specificity to a research question, ethnographers have to orient their observations to that research focus, but at the same time maintain a fairly open mind so that the element of flexibility that is such a strength of a qualitative research strategy is not eroded. Ditton (see Research in focus 19.7) provides an illustration of a very open-ended approach when he writes that his research 'was not set up to answer any empirical questions' (1977: 11).

Similarly, Kunda (1992) describes how he was swamped with information, partly because he did not seek to define his focus of study. His interest in any event that was occurring at the time led to the generation of a vast quantity of data. During his year in the field he 'generated thousands of pages of fieldnotes and interview transcripts (produced each day from the fragmented notes hastily scribbled during and between events and interviews), collections of archival material, computer output, newsletters, papers, memos, brochures, posters, textbooks, and assorted leftovers' (1992: 237). This period of open-endedness usually cannot last long, because there is the temptation to try to record the details of absolutely everything, which can be very trying. Usually the ethnographer will begin to narrow down the focus of his or her research and to match observations to the emerging research focus. Hence, M. Parker (2000: 239) describes how, as each case study progressed, he began to focus down on certain key issues and ideas that began to guide his interviews and observation. This was partly a result of feeling the need to develop a framework that could enable him to cope with the 'huge quantity of ideas' and 'incoherent impressions' that he had generated. This approach is implied by the sequence suggested by Figure 17.1.

For most ethnographers, the main equipment with which they will need to supply themselves in the course of observation will be a notepad and pen (see, e.g., Armstrong 1993: 28). A digital recorder can be another useful addition to one's hardware, but, as suggested above, it is likely to increase radically the amount of transcription and is possibly more obtrusive than writing notes. Most ethnographers report that after a period of time they become less obtrusive to participants in social settings, who become familiar with their presence (e.g. Atkinson 1981: 128). Speaking into a digital recorder may rekindle an awareness of the ethnographer's presence. Also, in shops, offices, and factories it may be difficult to use without the availability of an interview room, because of the impact of extraneous noise.

Types of field notes

Some writers have found it useful to classify the types of field notes that are generated in the process of conducting an ethnography. The following classification is based on the similar categories suggested by Lofland and Lofland (1995) and Sanjek (1990).

- *Mental notes*: particularly useful when it is inappropriate to be seen taking notes.

- *Jotted notes* (also called *scratch notes*): very brief notes written down on pieces of paper or in small notebooks to jog one's memory about events that should be written up later. Lofland and Lofland (1995: 90) refer to these as being made up of 'little phrases, quotes, key words, and the like'. They need to be jotted down inconspicuously, preferably out of sight, since detailed note-taking in front of people may make them self-conscious. Crang (1994) refers to his use of scratch notes in his study of waiting staff in a restaurant (see Research in focus 19.11).

- *Full field notes*: as soon as possible, make detailed notes, which will be your main data source. They

Research in focus 19.11
Writing field notes

Crang (1994) describes how, while working as a part-time waiter in a restaurant, Smoky Joe's, in the south-east of England, he decided to become a participant observer and started to take field notes about his workplace setting.

> Field notes were taken on my order pad when possible (this was not easy when very busy, so then I wrote single word 'scratch notes' and elaborated them in the break period at the end of the shift), and these were written from to produce shift-by-shift research diary entries (usually written through the morning after a shift, given that the evening rarely finished before 1.30 am). The latter included initial notes of 'factual detail' (that is, an expansion of field notes), followed by deliberately speculative reflections on these.
>
> (1994: 676)

Crang's flexible strategy for taking field notes thus combines different types of notes that result in the eventual production of a research diary. Through them he describes the social relations with customers that helped to distinguish Smoky's from its competitors. Waiting staff were encouraged to 'put on a show'; and their uniform, a waistcoat and bowler hat, according to Crang, more closely resembled a costume. In his research diary Crang relates the 'Tale of Dolly's socks', which illustrates the complex nature of the roles played by waiting staff.

> As I've often noted, socks are a big thing here. Wearing what are called 'jazzy' socks is pretty much compulsory and nearly all the competitions recently have had socks as their prizes! It's part of the 'fun atmosphere' don't you know. Dolly wears an extra pair of socks pinned to the back of her waistcoat, which she changes every night. Last night I finally asked her why. Oddly it felt silly to ask; it seems sensible in the context of Smoky's. Anyhow, she said she began when she won a pair, as a bit of a piss-take about Mark [the manager] going on about socks. But . . . Dolly always talks and laughs about them with her tables, and the socks are a talking point; she gets great tips. But Mark thinks they are a great idea; he wants her to take the piss a bit. So laughing at his idea is actually part of the fun itself, and can't escape that. It becomes part of the atmosphere, the service, to laugh at that service. Dolly tells her customers what she told me, about Mark saying to wear jazzy socks but not saying where, and so distances herself from the idea, but she also sells Smoky's as a fun, lively place by 'rebelling' and I think she wants to . . .
>
> (1994: 699).

should be written at the end of the day or sooner if possible. Write as promptly and as fully as possible. Write down information about events, people, conversations, etc. Write down initial ideas about interpretation. Record impressions and feelings.

The content of field notes is often to do with the ethnographer as well as the social setting being observed. For example, when Holliday (1995) describes the emotions associated with her fieldwork experience, she draws attention to her prevailing fear of incompetence, her concern about being liked, and her anxiety about whether or not to disagree with or challenge people. Precisely because they record the quotidian as observed and experienced by ethnographers, it is here that the ethnographer comes to the surface. In the finished work—the ethnography in the sense of a written account of a group and its culture—the ethnographer is frequently written out of the picture (Van Maanen 1988). A major difference here is that field notes are invariably for personal consumption (Coffey 1999), whereas the written ethnography is for public consumption and has to be presented as a definitive account of the social setting and culture in question. To keep on allowing the ethnographer to surface in the text risks conveying a sense of the account as an artifice rather than an authoritative chronicle. This issue will be addressed in further detail in Chapter 29.

Bringing ethnographic fieldwork to an end

Knowing when to stop is not an easy or straightforward matter in ethnography. Because of its unstructured nature and the absence of specific hypotheses to be tested (other than those that might emerge during data collection and analysis), there is a tendency for ethnographic research to lack a sense of an obvious end point. Traditions within anthropology have dictated that long-term continuous fieldwork should usually consist of a period of twelve months, so as to enable the study of a culture through a full seasonal cycle of activity (C. A. Davies 1999). These conventions apply to a lesser extent within organizational ethnography, where a 'long stay' in the field is still seen as crucial to securing 'insider' status (see Thinking deeply 19.15 for a discussion of these issues). At some point, however, ethnographic research does come to an end! In organizational research it is likely that a deadline for data collection will be negotiated at the outset. Buchanan, Boddy, and McCalman (1988) recommend that leaving the research site, or 'getting out', is handled in such a way as to leave the door open to the possibility of future research or fieldwork visits. At this stage it is useful to confirm the conclusion of the research in writing, thanking staff for their cooperation. Sometimes, the rhythms of the ethnographer's occupational career or personal and family life will necessitate withdrawal from the field, or research funding commitments will bring fieldwork to a close. Such factors include: the end of a period of sabbatical leave; the need to write up and submit a doctoral thesis by a certain date; or funding for research drawing to a close.

Ethnographic research can be highly stressful for many reasons: the nature of the topic, which may place the fieldworker in stressful situations; the marginality of the researcher in the social setting and the need constantly to manage a front; and the prolonged absence from one's normal life that is often necessary. The ethnographer may feel that he or she has simply had enough. A further possibility that may start to bring about moves to bring fieldwork to a close is that the ethnographer may begin to feel that the research questions on which he or she has decided to concentrate are answered, so that there are no new data worth generating. The ethnographer may even feel a strong sense of *déjà vu* towards the end of data collection. Altheide (1980: 310) has written that his decision to leave the various news organizations in which he had conducted ethnographic research was often motivated by 'the recurrence of familiar situations and the feeling that little worthwhile was being revealed'. In the language of grounded theory, all the researcher's categories are thoroughly *saturated*, although Glaser and Strauss's (1967) approach would invite you to be certain that there are no new questions to be asked of the area you are investigating, or no new comparisons to be made.

The reasons for bringing ethnographic research to a close can involve a wide range of factors from the personal to matters of research design. Whatever the reason, disengagement has to be *managed*. For one thing, this means that promises must be kept, so that, if you promised a report to an organization as a condition of entry, that promise should not be forgotten. It also means that ethnographers must provide good explanations for their departure. Members of a social setting always know that the researcher is a temporary fixture, but over a long period of time, and especially if there was genuine participation in activities within that setting, people may forget that the ethnographer's presence is finite. The farewells have to be managed and in an orderly fashion.

Also, the ethnographer's *ethical* commitments must not be forgotten, such as the need to ensure that persons and settings are anonymized. It is common practice within organizational ethnography to change the name of a company in order to protect the anonymity of the organization, as well as the names of individuals who participated in the study—even place names and locations may be changed. For example, Dalton (1959) protected the anonymity of his 'intimates' or informants by changing the place names and locations associated with the study. He also declined to disclose the nature of his formal work roles at Milo and Fruhling, as he felt this would endanger the exposure of 'intimates' to their superiors. Whatever happens, it is wise to reach an agreement with senior members of the organization before disclosing the identity of an organization, and it may be less threatening for senior managers and employers if the researcher offers anonymity as an explicit aspect of the access agreement.

Michael Humphreys, in his research on Credit Line, which was referred to above, went even further in his desire for organizational participants to remain anonymous (Humphreys and Watson 2009). He became aware that the gulf between the company's public position on corporate social responsibility and the private views of many staff about that position presented him with an ethical dilemma in that he clearly needed to protect their anonymity so that they would not get into trouble with the firm. The words of 'Charity' are quoted in this chapter, but Charity is not a pseudonym, the usual tactic used by researchers to preserve the identity of their informants. 'Charity' is a composite person rather than a real person. Her views and words are in fact an aggregation of those of several employees who expressed identical or similar positions.

 # Feminist and institutional ethnography

In this section we will review some of the central debates within feminist research and relate them to the ethnographic tradition. There are several examples of ethnographies done by women and of women's work (e.g. Cavendish 1982; Westwood 1984; see also Research in focus 19.12; Research in focus 19.16), but few ethnographic studies are informed by feminist tenets of the kind outlined in Chapter 17.

Reinharz (1992) sees feminist ethnography as significant in terms of feminism, because:

- it documents women's lives and activities, which were previously largely seen as marginal and subsidiary to men's;

- it understands women from their perspective, so that the tendency that 'trivializes females' activities and

Research in focus 19.12
An ethnography of work from a woman's perspective

In her study of women employed in unskilled, manual jobs in Britain, Pollert (1981) set out to understand the lived experience of working under modern capitalism from a woman's perspective. The study is based on informal interviews and observation on the shopfloor of a Bristol tobacco factory in 1972. 'It is a glimpse into the everyday working lives of the young girls and older women who worked there: about how they got on with their jobs, their bosses and each other—and in a background sense, their boyfriends, their husbands and their families—and how all these strands wove together into their experience and consciousness' (1981: 6).

Pollert was not employed in the factory and was open about her status as a researcher. In this sense her role was one of observer-as-participant, according to Gold's classification scheme. Being a female researcher was, according to Pollert, vitally important to the study and an important factor in breaking down barriers with women workers. However, while she was a woman among women, she was also middle-class, had a middle-class accent, and was not there to earn money—factors that clearly set her apart from the women. To begin with she was 'naturally scrutinized with a mixture of hostility, suspicion and curiosity' (1981: 7) and was called upon to answer more questions than she asked. In managing to break down some of these barriers, Pollert explains that she tried to be open with her opinions, in wanting to argue with and challenge attitudes as well as to learn, and not to set herself up as a 'reporter' who was interested in 'how the masses think'. Interestingly, unlike many male organizational ethnographers, Pollert kept a degree of social distance from her research subjects, having very little direct involvement with home, community, and social life. 'It was simply not on to suggest we meet for a drink in a pub, the normal "neutral" meeting-place for men.' Instead, what she learned about home and social life was filtered through factory experience.

Pollert's research goes some of the way towards being what could be described as a feminist ethnography (she focuses on the working lives of women and seeks to understand the women from their own perspective and in their own context). However, as Pollert managed the power relations between herself and the women mainly as a one-way process, the study does not conform to the ideals of feminist ethnography in this respect.

thoughts, or interprets them from the standpoint of men in the society or of the male researcher' (1992: 52) is mitigated; and

- it understands women in context.

However, such commitments and practices go only part of the way. Of great significance to feminist researchers is the question of whether or not the research allows for a non-exploitative relationship between researcher and researched. One of the main elements of such a strategy is that the ethnographer does not treat the relationship as a one-way process of extracting information from others, but actually provides something in return. However, Stacey (1988) argues, on the basis of her fieldwork experience, that the various situations she encountered as a feminist ethnographer placed her

in situations of inauthenticity, dissimilitude, and potential, perhaps inevitable, betrayal situations that I now believe are inherent in fieldwork method. For

no matter how welcome, even enjoyable the fieldworker's presence may appear to 'natives', fieldwork represents an intrusion and intervention into a system of relationships, a system of relationships that the researcher is far freer to leave.

(1988: 23)

Stacey also argues that, when the research is written up, it is the feminist ethnographer's interpretations and judgements that come through and have authority.

However, Reinharz (1992: 74–5) argues that, although ethnographic fieldwork relationships may sometimes *seem* manipulative, a clear undercurrent of reciprocity often lies beneath them. The researcher, in other words, may offer help or advice to her research participants, or she may be exhibiting reciprocity by giving a public airing to normally marginalized voices (although the ethnographer is always the mouthpiece for such voices and may be imposing a particular 'spin' on them). Moreover,

Research in focus 19.13
'Not one of the guys': ethnography in a male-dominated setting

The male-dominated nature of many business and management fieldwork settings such as factory shopfloors or management boardrooms means that gender and sexuality can often be important and highly visible dynamics in fieldwork encounters. Several organizational ethnographies, such as Dalton (1959), Collinson (1992*a*), and Watson (1994*a*), have focused on the masculine nature of these organizational settings—for example, Collinson (1992*a*) writes about the collectivist, masculine practices of 'piss taking' and swearing on the shopfloor, and Watson drawing attention to the jokes and 'dirty talking' that reinforced his inclusion among managers at ZTC Ryland.

The emphasis on jokes, humour, swearing, and 'becoming one of the lads' could be interpreted as demonstrating that the male ethnographer has privileged 'insider' status to a masculine subculture and is, as a result, able to produce an ethnography that is more valid. However, E. Bell (1999) argues that it would be wrong to assume that an ethnographer's ability to participate in masculine practices necessarily confirms their status as an insider. Even though female organizational ethnographers experience masculine organizational settings in a way that confirms their 'difference' and can make them feel uncomfortable, for example, through constant exposure to pornographic images on the wall (D. Fletcher 2002) or not having access to any women's toilets (Bell 1999), it should not be assumed that this precludes them from gaining access or acceptance. Neither, argues D. Fletcher (2002), should a feminist epistemology be adopted—for example, which attributes to women a special ability to recognize and engage with emotions in the fieldwork setting. Instead, gender can be seen as a dynamic characteristic of the researcher's identity (C. Warren 1988) that changes over time as the role of the researcher is negotiated. Bell (1999) argues that it is necessary to challenge some of these stereotypical gendered assumptions and instead focus on the dynamic complexity of gendered fieldwork relationships.

it seems extreme to abandon feminist ethnography on the grounds that the ethnographer cannot fulfil all possible obligations simultaneously. Indeed, this would be a recipe for the abandonment of all research, feminist or otherwise. What is also crucial is transparency—transparency in the feminist ethnographer's dealings with the women she studies and transparency in the account of the research process.

Institutional ethnography provides an illustration of what feminist ethnography looks like, and how it differs from other types of ethnographic inquiry. This involves treating people's experience not as 'the topic or object of interest, but as "entry" into the social relations of the setting' (Campbell 1998: 57). The purpose then is to give people whose lives are subject to ruling relations access

to knowledge about themselves which gives them the opportunity to act on the basis of this. Campbell's study of Total Quality Management in a health care organization provides an example of how institutional ethnography is used to study organizations. As she writes: 'I was not entering [the field] as a naïve observer working in a naturalist mode, nor was I looking for theory to arise out of the data, as a grounded theorist might' (Campbell 1998: 58). Instead, she used a discursive approach to focus on the local experiential knowing of nurses, and to explore how this was subordinated to managerial ruling practices which undermined their care-giving and professionalism. Hence institutional ethnography involves taking the standpoint of those being ruled, and exposing the social relations that shape their experience.

Visual ethnography

The term 'visual ethnography' is becoming increasingly popular (e.g. Peñaloza 1999; Pink 2001), however, it is sometimes used in a way that does not imply the kind of

sustained immersion in a social setting that has been taken in this chapter to be a feature of ethnography. Sometimes the term is used to include interviews of the kind covered in Chapter 20 in which visual materials feature prominently. An example of visual ethnography is provided by Peñaloza (2000), a marketing researcher, who was interested in how the cultural meaning of the American West is produced through the activities of cattle trade shows. She suggests that the rich imagery of the American West, reflected by such examples as Marlboro cigarettes, Wrangler jeans, and Jeep Cherokees, is represented through the trade show where animals are bought and sold, but also where the culture of the American West is enacted and celebrated. In addition to participant observation and in-depth interviewing, her ethnographic study incorporated 550 photographs taken at the shows over a six-year period. These were mainly photographs of the events—including cattle sales, breed shows, and rodeos. As a visible record of people and activities, the photographs helped Peñaloza to build up a profile of the race/ethnicity and sex of attendees at particular events and of the type of activities that were involved in the show.

In the discussion that follows, we will emphasize photographs, mainly because they are the visual medium that has received the greatest attention. There are a number of ways in which photographs have been employed by qualitative researchers:

- as an *aide-mémoire* in the course of fieldwork, in which context the images essentially become components of the ethnographer's field notes; Alan Bryman's research on Disneyization in Research in focus 19.14 provides an example;

- as a source of data in their own right and not simply as adjuncts to the ethnographer's field notes, as in Bell's research focusing on visual messages of death and loss

following the closure of a car factory (Research in focus 19.16);

- as prompts for discussion by research participants. Sometimes the photographs may be extant, and this kind of context will be examined in Chapter 23. In other contexts, the discussions may be based on photographs taken by the ethnographer or by research participants more or less exclusively for the purposes of the investigation, such as in the study of aesthetics by S. Warren (2002, 2005; Research in focus 17.11). In the case of photographs that are taken by research participants that form the basis for an interview or discussion, Pink (2004: 399) writes: 'By working with informants to produce images that are meaningful for them we can gain insights into their visual cultures and into what is important for them as individuals living in particular localities.'

Pink (2001) draws attention to two different ways in which visual images have been conceptualized in social research. She calls these *realist* and *reflexive* approaches. The latter approach to the visual is frequently collaborative, in the sense that research participants may be involved in decisions about what photographs should be taken and then how they should be interpreted. Further, there is recognition of the fluidity of the meaning of images, implying that they can never be fixed and will always be viewed by different people in different ways. For example, in Bell's (2012) study of the closure of a Jaguar car manufacturing plant (Research in focus 19.16), she analysed the positionality of the person who took the photograph or produced the image, as well as the content of the photograph itself.

Research in focus 19.14
Researching Disneyization

In recent years, one of the authors of this book, Alan Bryman, has been interested in something that he calls 'Disneyization', which is the process by which the principles associated with Disney theme parks have permeated many aspects of modern society and economy. In his book on this subject (Bryman 2004*b*) he included several photographs that illustrated these processes. In addition, the photographs were very helpful in acting as reminders of contexts that revealed the process of Disneyization. This was especially the case with an article on the Disneyization of McDonald's (Bryman 2003). The article included a discussion of the case of a themed McDonald's in Chicago that was based on rock 'n' roll. Alan had visited Chicago a year previously to give a paper at a conference and took the opportunity to take some photographs of the restaurant. These images were very helpful in remembering the restaurant, although he did not use them for illustrative purposes in either the book or the article. Two of the images are presented here—Plate 19.1 shows the restaurant's exterior against the Chicago skyline and Plate 19.2 shows statues of three members of the Beatles, which were among the many artefacts that contributed to the musical theme.

Plate 19.1

Disneyization in pictures: a themed McDonald's

Plate 19.2

Disneyization in pictures: The Beatles in the themed McDonald's

Key concept 19.15
What is visual ethnography?

In addition to field notes, changing technologies have opened up greater potential for the use of photography, video, and hypermedia as methods of data collection in ethnographic research. Pink (2001) distinguishes between scientific–realist approaches to the use of visual methods in ethnographic research, which suggest visual images are a way of observing and recording reality, and reflexive approaches, which involve exploring how informants and ethnographers experience their social setting. She also argues that, while visual images should be accorded higher status in the generation of ethnographic knowledge, they should not be seen as a replacement for data that rely on the written or spoken word. 'Thus visual images, objects, descriptions should be incorporated when it is appropriate, opportune or enlightening to do so' (2001: 5). Visual ethnography often involves the ethnographer taking photographs or making video recordings of research participants in their social setting. Pink suggests that this has the advantage of being an activity that is more visible and comprehensible to participants, in contrast to field note writing, which is a relatively solitary activity. Analysis focuses on interpreting the meaning of these visual images within their cultural context. Photographs and video footage can also provide a basis for interviewing members of a social group about their social setting and culture in a similar way to photo-elicitation, described in Chapter 9. Finally, visual ethnography can also include the analysis of visual images in the form of documents containing photographs or artwork that are collected by the ethnographer during his or her involvement in the research setting. We will return to these issues at the end of this chapter and in Chapter 23.

These various examples of the use of visual materials give a sense that they have great potential for ethnographers and qualitative researchers more generally. However, their growing popularity should not entice readers into thinking that visual methods should necessarily be incorporated into their investigations: their use must be relevant to the research questions being asked. As sources of data, visual research methods require an ability on

Research in focus 19.16
Images of organizational death and loss

Photographs and artistic images have also been used by Emma Bell to understand reactions to events surrounding the closure of a Jaguar car manufacturing plant in the UK city of Coventry (Bell 2012). She first became aware of the role of visual images in communicating messages about the closure when an image was published in the local newspaper featuring a Jaguar E-Type vehicle with the letters 'RIP JAG' written across the front of the vehicle, accompanied by a story about the decision of the Ford Motor Company to close the Coventry manufacturing site. She studied the huge collection of extant images in Jaguar company archives, which included artworks and professional photographs that focused on the aesthetics of the product and celebrated the labour process surrounding its production. Through this she became aware of the significance of the visual in constructing organizational memory and narrating a story about the organization's past. Participant observation at the site led to the discovery and analysis of a number of other extant images that had been created by employees in response to the announcement of closure, including one that had been produced by the Transport and General Workers Union as part of its campaign against the closure, featuring Uncle Sam, wearing a hat displaying the Ford logo, murdering the Jaguar cat with a knife. She also analysed more than 600 photographs of the manufacturing plant that were taken by the organization's picture archivist in the last days before car production ceased. Plates 19.3 and Plate 19.4 are two of them. The pictures of Jaguar cars on the walls of the staff break area in Plate 19.3 confirm the significance of the visual in the work identities of employees. The lack of people or cars contained with the images communicates and commemorates the loss of what made the workplace distinctive. The findings from the case led her to conclude that the visual constitutes a vital resource in the construction of organizational memory that enables dominant organizational narratives to be contested and alternatives to be constructed.

Plate 19.3

'An empty staff break area on the last day of production'

Copyright Karam Ram and Jaguar Heritage. Reproduced with thanks.

Plate 19.4

'After the last car has left the track'

Copyright Karam Ram and Jaguar Heritage. Reproduced with thanks.

the part of the researcher to 'read' images in a manner that is sensitive to the context in which they were generated; the potential for multiple meanings that may need to be worked through with research participants; and, where the researcher is the source of the images, the significance of his or her own social position. In other words, the analyst of visual materials needs to be sceptical about the notion that a photograph provides an unproblematic depiction of reality (Bell and Davison 2013). In addition, researchers will usually include non-visual research methods in their investigations (such as interviews). This leads to the question of the relative significance of words and images in the analysis of data and the presentation of findings. Since words are the traditional medium, it is easy to slip into seeing the visual as ancillary.

However, at the same time, Pink (2004) reminds us that visual research methods are never purely visual. There are two aspects to this point. First, as Pink points out, visual research methods are usually accompanied by other (often traditional) research methods such as interviewing and observation. Second, the visual is almost always accompanied by the non-visual—words—which is the medium of expression for both the research participants and the researchers themselves.

Writing ethnography

In addition to being a way of doing research, the label 'ethnography' is also used describe the end result or written product of such studies. Since the 1980s, there has been an interest not just in how ethnography is carried out in the field but also in the rhetorical conventions used to produce ethnographic texts.

Ethnographic texts are designed to convince readers of the *reality* of the events and situations described and the plausibility of the analyst's explanations. The ethnographic text must not simply present a set of findings: it must provide an 'authoritative' account of the group or culture in question. In other words, the ethnographer must convince us that he or she has arrived at an account of social reality that has strong claims to truth.

The ethnographic text is permeated by stylistic and rhetorical devices whereby the reader is persuaded to enter into a shared framework of facts and interpretations, observations and reflections. Just like the scientific paper and the kind of approach to writing found in reporting quantitative business research, the ethnographer typically works within a writing strategy that is imbued with *realism*. This simply means that the researcher presents an authoritative, dispassionate account that represents an external, objective reality. In this respect, there is little difference between the writing styles of quantitative and qualitative researchers. Van Maanen (1988) calls ethnography texts that conform to these characteristics *realist tales*. These are the most common type of ethnographic writing, though he distinguishes other types (see Key concept 19.17). However, the *form* that this realism takes differs. Van Maanen distinguishes four characteristics of

realist tales: experiential authority; typical forms; the native's point of view; and interpretative omnipotence. Realist tales are prevalent in business research writing (see Research in focus 19.18).

Experiential authority

Just as in much quantitative research writing, the author disappears from view. We are told what members of a group say and do, and they are the only people directly visible in the text. The author provides a narrative in which he or she is no longer to be seen. As a result, an impression is conveyed that the findings presented are what any reasonable, similarly placed researcher would have found. As readers, we have to accept that this is what the ethnographer saw and heard while working as a participant observer or whatever. The personal subjectivity of the author/ethnographer is essentially played down by this strategy. The possibility that the fieldworker may have his or her own biases or may have become too involved with the people being studied is suppressed. To this end, when writing up the results of their ethnographic work, authors play up their academic credentials and qualifications, their previous experience, and so on. All this enhances the degree to which it appears the author's account can be relied upon. The author/ethnographer can then appear as a reliable witness.

A further element of experiential authority is that, when describing their methods, ethnographers invariably make a great deal of the intensiveness of the research that they carried out—they spent so many months in the field, had conversations and interviews with countless individuals, worked hard to establish rapport, and so on. These features are also added to by drawing the reader's attention to such hardships as the inconvenience of the fieldwork—the danger, the poor food, the disruptive effect on normal life, the feelings of isolation and loneliness, and so on.

Also worth mentioning are the extensive quotations from conversations and interviews that invariably form part of the ethnographic report. These are also obviously important ingredients of the author's use of *evidence* to support points. However, they are a mechanism for establishing the credibility of the report in that they demonstrate the author's ability to encourage people to talk and so demonstrate that he or she achieved rapport with them. The copious descriptive details—of places, patterns of behaviour, contexts, and so on—can also be viewed as a means of piling on the sense of the author being an ideally placed witness for all the findings that have been uncovered.

Typical forms

The author often writes about typical forms of institutions or of patterns of behaviour. What is happening here is that the author is generalizing about a number of recurring features of the group in question to create a typical form that that feature takes. He or she may use examples based on particular incidents or people, but basically the emphasis is on the general. For example, in Watson's (1994a) conclusion to his ethnographic study of managers in a UK telecommunications company, cited several times in this book, we encounter the following statement:

> The image which has taken shape is one of management as essentially and inherently a social and moral activity; one whose greatest successes in efficiently and effectively producing goods and services is likely to come through building organisational patterns, cultures and understandings based on relationships of mutual trust and shared obligation among people involved with the organisation.
>
> (1994a: 223)

The study is thus meant to portray managers in general, and individuals are important only in so far as they represent such general tendencies.

Key concept 19.17
Three forms of ethnographic writing

Van Maanen (1988) has distinguished three major types of ethnographic writing:

- *Realist tales*: apparently definitive, confident, and dispassionate third-person accounts of a culture and of the behaviour of members of that culture. This is the most prevalent form of ethnographic writing.

- *Confessional tales*: personalized accounts in which the ethnographer is fully implicated in the data-gathering and writing-up processes. These are warts-and-all accounts of the trials and tribulations of doing ethnography. They have become more prominent since the 1970s and reflect a growing emphasis on reflexivity in qualitative research in particular. In the edited volume *Doing Research in Organizations* (Bryman 1988b), several of the contributors provide inside accounts of doing qualitative research in industrial enterprises. Beynon (1988), for example, describes how his account, published in *Working for Ford* (1975), of how a dead man was left lying on the factory floor for ten minutes while the line continued to run provoked a response from the Ford Motor Company, which sought to discredit his research. As this example illustrates, confessional tales are more concerned with detailing how research was carried out than with presenting findings. Very often the confessional tale is told in a particular context (such as an invited chapter in a book of similar tales), but the main findings are written up in realist tale form.

- *Impressionist tales*: accounts that place a heavy emphasis on 'words, metaphors, phrasings, and . . . the expansive recall of fieldwork experience' (Van Maanen 1988: 102). There is a heavy emphasis on stories of dramatic events that provide 'a representational means of cracking open the culture and the fieldworker's way of knowing it' (1988: 102). However, as Van Maanen notes, impressionist tales 'are typically enclosed within realist, or perhaps more frequently, confessional tales' (1988: 106).

Research in focus 19.18
Realism in organizational ethnography

Many organizational ethnographies tend to be written as realist tales (see Key concept 19.17) and narrated dispassionately in order to reinforce the authenticity of the account. Typically, the author is absent from the text, or is a minor character in the story, and methods are revealed only at the end, in the form of a 'confessional' chapter or appendix, where the ethnographer 'reveals his hand' (Watson 1994*a*) by disclosing personal details about the fieldwork experience. However, this is not to say that organizational ethnographers are unaware of the representational difficulties caused by such an approach to writing. Consider, for example, the first few sentences of the methodological appendix that is provided by Kunda (1992) in the book *Engineering Culture: Control and Commitment in a High-Tech Corporation*.

> This study belongs to the genre known as 'ethnographic realism'. This identification says much about presentational style, little about the actual research process. The descriptive style of this genre presents an author functioning more or less as a fly on the wall in the course of his sojourn in the field—an objective, unseen observer following well-defined procedures for data collection and verification. It requires no great insight, however, to recognize that ethnographic realism is a distortion of convenience. Fieldwork, as all who have engaged in it will testify, is an intensely personal and subjective process, and there are probably at least as many 'methods' as there are fieldworkers.
>
> (Kunda 1992: 229).

Kunda questions the extent to which the ethnographer is an objective observer, suggesting instead that he or she experiences organizational life from a situated position as an insider. He implies that it is, therefore, impossible for ethnographers to distance themselves from the fieldwork experience. However, despite this recognition of the need for greater 'reflexivity' within organizational ethnography, only a few organizational ethnographies are actually written in the first person, with the researcher as a main character who is telling the story. Even in cases when this does occur, the main character narrative tends to be located peripherally, in the appendices or footnotes of an article or book (Hatch 1996), such as Kunda himself has done.

The point has been made several times that one of the distinguishing features of much qualitative research is the commitment to seeing through the eyes of the people being studied. This is an important feature for qualitative researchers, because it is part of a strategy of getting at the meaning of social reality from the perspective of those studied. However, it also represents an important element in creating a sense of authoritativeness on the part of the ethnographer. After all, claiming that he or she takes the native's point of view and sees through the native's eyes means that he or she is in an excellent position to speak authoritatively about the group in question. The very fact that the ethnographer has taken the native's point of view testifies to the fact that he or she is well placed to write definitively about the group in question. Realist tales frequently include numerous references to the steps taken by the ethnographer to get close to the people studied and his or her success in this regard. Thus, in her study of Afro-Caribbean women working in high-tech informatics, Freeman (2000) writes about the small group of six women at Multitext who became the focus of more intense, long-term data collection:

> After many Sunday lunches, picnics, church services, birthday celebrations, and family outings, I got to know these few women better, seeing them not only as workers but also as members of families, as partners in complex relationships, as mothers, as daughters, as co-workers, and as friends. We spent time together in my rented flat, and in their wood and 'wall house' homes, cooking and eating meals together, sometimes watching videos as we talked. I persuaded them, on rare occasions, to picnic at the beach, and they took me to their churches and fetes and on special outings—to the circus, to the calypso contests, and to national sites enjoyed by tourists and locals alike. Sometimes we went shopping, and sometimes we bought ice cream after work.
>
> (2000: 17)

When writing up an ethnography in the realist style, the author rarely presents possible alternative interpretations of an event or pattern of behaviour. Instead, the phenomenon in question is presented as having a single meaning or significance, which the fieldworker alone has cracked. Indeed, the evidence provided is carefully marshalled to support the singular interpretation that is placed on the event or pattern of behaviour. We are presented with an inevitability. It seems obvious or inevitable that someone would draw the inferences that the author has drawn when faced with such clear-cut evidence.

These four characteristics of realist tales imply that what the researcher did *qua* researcher is only one part of creating a sense of having figured out the nature of a culture. It is also very much to do with how the researcher represents what he or she did through writing about ethnography. From a postmodernist perspective (Key concept 17.2), any realist tale is merely one 'spin'—that is, one version—which can be or has been formulated in relation to the culture in question.

Van Maanen (1996) has suggested that 'in these textually sophisticated times, few argue that a research report is anything more (or, certainly, anything less) than a framework- or paradigm-dependent document, crafted and shaped within the rules and conventions of a particular research community, some articulated (and

written in the back of research journals) and some tacitly understood' (1996: 376). This statement is linked to the influence of postmodernism (Key concept 17.2) and the linguistic turn within the social sciences (Key concept 19.19). This has led to a particular interest in the claims to ethnographic authority inscribed into ethnographic texts (Clifford 1983). The ethnographic text 'presumes a world out there (the real) that can be captured by a "knowing" author through the careful transcription and analysis of field materials (interviews, notes, etc.)' (Denzin 1994: 296). Postmodernism problematizes such accounts and their authority to represent a reality because there 'can never be a final, accurate representation of what was meant or said, only different textual representations of different experiences' (Denzin 1994: 296). This has led to an interest in the ways in which privilege is conveyed in ethnographic texts and how voices, particularly of marginal groups, are suppressed.

These concerns have led to the development of new forms of writing such as auto-ethnography (see Key concept 19.20).

The concerns within these and other traditions (including postmodernism) have led to experiments in writing ethnography (Richardson 1994) that involve the identity of the ethnographer being written into the text (see Research in focus 19.21). An example is the use of a 'dialogic' form of writing that seeks to raise the profile of

Key concept 19.19
What is the linguistic turn?

Postmodernism can also be seen as the stimulus for the linguistic turn in the social sciences. The linguistic turn is based on the idea that language shapes our understanding of the world. Moreover, because knowledge is constructed through language, and language can never create an objective representation of external reality, meaning is uncontrollable and undiscoverable. This leads to a rejection of positivist scientists' claims to be able to produce reliable knowledge through a neutral process of exploration. Postmodernists argue that knowledge is never neutral and is constantly open to revision. They reject what they see as scientific 'grand' or 'meta' narratives that seek to explain the world from an objective viewpoint. Scientific investigation is thus suggested by postmodernists to be nothing more than a type of 'language game' (Rorty 1979) used by this particular community to produce localized understandings.

Postmodernists have also suggested that certain methods can be more easily adapted to the linguistic turn, in particular ethnography, because it can be used to deconstruct claims to represent reality and can provide alternative versions of reality that attempt to blur the boundary between 'fact' and 'fiction' (Linstead 1993). Auto-ethnography (see Key concept 19.20) can be seen as an attempt to modify the way we use language in research that reflects the linguistic turn. These new forms of writing are sometimes described as being part of the *narrative* turn that seeks to expose the 'fiction' of ethnographic writing by deconstructing its conventions. The narrative turn involves the use of different writing styles that do not involve the creation of ethnographic authority (Woolgar 1988*b*) and instead encourage a number of perspectives to be represented.

Key concept 19.20
What is auto-ethnography?

One of the ways in which more reflexive, narrative forms of ethnographic writing have been cultivated is through the emerging cross-disciplinary genre of auto-ethnography. This relates to the interest of anthropologists in auto-anthropology (Strathern 1987), which is an autobiographical form of research that is concerned with researching settings where the cultural backgrounds of the observer and observed are shared. Auto-ethnography involves the writing of a highly personalized text in which the personal is related to the cultural and the political in a way that claims the conventions associated with literary writing. However, it is difficult to summarize what auto-ethnography is about, precisely because its purpose is to challenge the conventions of social scientific writing by blurring the boundaries of genre that separate art and science, a practice that has come to be known as 'genre bending'. A recent example of this is a book by Ellis (2004) entitled *The Ethnographic I: A Methodological Novel about Teaching and Doing Autoethnography*, which uses a fictitious account of her teaching a graduate course on auto-ethnography as the basis for discussion of doing and writing auto-ethnography. This involves blending the highly personalized accounts of her own and her students' lives with methodological discussions in a way that has come to be labelled as 'creative non-fiction'. Crucial to the auto-ethnographic style of writing is the focus on 'creating a palpable emotional experience' (Holman Jones 2005: 767) for readers so that they experience the narrative 'as if it were happening to them' (Ellis 2004: 116). Although there are few signs so far of auto-ethnography having been imported into the study of management and business, one example is found in a book by Goodall (1994) entitled *Casing a Promised Land: The Autobiography of an Organizational Detective as Cultural Ethnographer*, which describes the adventures of an organization communication specialist who enters a variety of organizational settings and, like a detective, looks for clues in order to understand them. Watson (2000) has argued that ethnographic research accounts can be written in a way that bridges the genres of creative writing and social science, calling this 'ethnographic fiction science'. One of the challenges for many social science researchers is that this entails having the skills of a fiction writer as well as the abilities of a researcher, which is a demanding combination that their experience may not have prepared them for.

Research in focus 19.21
Identity and ethnographic writing

In her study of everyday life on the shopfloor of a Japanese factory, Kondo (1990) provides an example of ethnographic writing in which the self is central to the account. Kondo describes how, as a Japanese–American academic studying Japanese factory life, she had to learn how to act and behave as a Japanese woman: 'My first nine months of fieldwork were characterised by an attempt to reduce the distance between expectation and inadequate reality, as my informants and I conspired to rewrite my identity as Japanese' (1990: 25). Her sense of self and identity was thereby mediated 'by the experiences, relations and interactions of her fieldwork' (Coffey 1999: 24).

Writing partly in the first person, Kondo seeks to reveal her identity through the text in order to emphasize the point that the ethnographic text is constructed through the stance assumed in relation to the observed. For example she states: 'what I write is no mere academic exercise; for me it matters, and matters deeply' (Kondo 1990: 302).

Kondo is also critical of conventional ethnographic writing, which 'sandwiches the "data" into the body of the book, leaving "theory" for the beginning and the end' (1990: 304). Instead she 'scatters' theoretical discussion 'in different parts of the text, and the "ethnographic" vignettes and anecdotes are marshaled analytically' (1990: 304).

Kondo's work thus provides an example of a contemporary organizational ethnography that seeks to achieve a postmodern reflexivity, partly through exploration of experimental writing strategies.

the multiplicity of voices that can be heard in the course of fieldwork. As Lincoln and Denzin (1994: 584) put it: 'Slowly it dawns on us that there may . . . be . . . not one "voice," but polyvocality; not one story, but many tales, dramas, pieces of fiction, fables, memories, histories, autobiographies, poems, and other texts to inform our sense of lifeways, to extend our understandings of the Other.' This postmodern preference for seeking out multiple voices and

for turning the ethnographer into a 'bit player' reflects the mistrust among postmodernists of 'meta-narratives'—that is, positions or grand accounts that implicitly make claims about absolute truths and that therefore rule out the possibility of alternative versions of reality. On the other hand, 'mini-narratives, micronarratives, local narratives are just stories that make no truth claims and are therefore more acceptable to postmodernists' (Rosenau 1992: p. xiii).

Key points

- Ethnography is a term that refers to both a method and the written product of research based on that method.

- The ethnographer is typically a participant observer who also uses non-observational methods and sources such as interviewing and documents.

- The ethnographer may adopt an overt or a covert role, but the latter carries ethical difficulties.

- The negotiation of access to a social setting can be a lengthy process. It may depend on establishing an exchange relationship.

- Key informants frequently play an important role for the ethnographer, but care is needed to ensure that their impact on the direction of research is not excessive.

- There are several different ways of classifying the kinds of role that the ethnographer may assume. These are not necessarily mutually exclusive.

- Field notes are important for prompting the ethnographer's memory.

- Feminist ethnography is relatively unusual in business research but the methodology of institutional ethnography shows how it can be applied.

- Visual ethnography is of growing interest in business research but this sometimes differs from how ethnography is traditionally understood.

Questions for review

- Is it possible to distinguish ethnography and participant observation?

- How does participant observation differ from structured observation?

Organizational ethnography

- To what extent do participant observation and ethnography rely solely on observation?

- What distinguishes organizational ethnography from other forms of ethnography?

Access

- 'Covert ethnography obviates the need to gain access to inaccessible settings and therefore has much to recommend it.' Discuss.

- Examine some articles in business and management journals in which ethnography and participant observation figure strongly. Was the researcher in an overt or a covert role? How was access achieved?

- Does the problem of access finish once access to a chosen setting has been achieved?

- What might be the role of key informants in ethnographic research? Is there anything to be concerned about when using them?

Roles for ethnographers

- Compare Gold's and Gans's schemes for classifying participant observer roles.

- What is meant by 'going native'?

- Should ethnographers be active or passive in the settings in which they conduct research?

- How does shadowing differ from participant observation and do the differences matter?

Field notes

- Why are field notes important for ethnographers?

- Why is it useful to distinguish between different types of field notes?

Bringing ethnographic fieldwork to an end

- How do you decide when to complete the data collection phase in ethnographic research?

Feminist and institutional ethnography

- What are the main ingredients of feminist and institutional ethnography?

Visual ethnography

- What role can visual materials play in ethnography?

- What distinguishes visual ethnography from other research methods that focus on visual data?

Writing ethnography

- How far is it true to say that ethnographic writing is typically imbued with realism?

- What forms of ethnographic writing other than realist tales can be found?

- What are the main characteristics of realist tales?

- What are the implications of the linguistic turn for ethnographic writing?

....

Online Resource Centre

www.oxfordtextbooks.co.uk/orc/brymanbrm4e/

Visit the Interactive Research Guide that accompanies this book to complete an exercise in Ethnography and Participant Observation.

....

20

Interviewing in qualitative research

Chapter outline

This chapter is concerned with the interview in qualitative research. The term *qualitative interview* is often used to capture the different types of interview that are used in qualitative research. Such interviews tend to be far less structured than the kind of interview associated with survey research, which was discussed in Chapter 9 in terms of structured interviewing. This chapter is concerned with individual interviews in qualitative research; the focus group method, which is a form of interview but with several people, is discussed in Chapter 21. The two forms of qualitative interviewing discussed in this chapter are unstructured and semi-structured interviewing. The chapter explores:

- the differences between structured interviewing and qualitative interviewing;
- the main characteristics of and differences between unstructured and semi-structured interviewing; this entails a recognition that the two terms refer to extremes and that in practice a wide range of interviews with differing degrees of structure lie between the extremes;
- how to devise and use an interview guide for semi-structured interviewing;
- the kinds of question that can be asked in an interview guide;
- the importance of audio-recording and transcribing qualitative interviews;
- the significance of qualitative interviewing in feminist research;
- the advantages and disadvantages of qualitative interviewing relative to participant observation.

Introduction

The interview is probably the most widely employed method in qualitative research. Of course, as we have seen in Chapter 19, ethnography usually involves a substantial amount of interviewing, and this factor undoubtedly contributes to the widespread use of the interview by qualitative researchers. However, it is the flexibility of the interview that makes it so attractive. Since ethnography entails an extended period of participant observation, which is very disruptive for researchers because of the sustained absence(s) required from work and/or family life, research based more or less exclusively on interviews is a highly attractive alternative for the collection of qualitative data. Interviewing, the transcription of interviews, and the analysis of transcripts are all very time-consuming, but they can be more readily accommodated into researchers' personal lives.

In Key concept 9.2 several types of interview were briefly outlined. The bulk of the types outlined there—other than the structured interview and the standardized interview—are ones associated with qualitative research. *Focus groups* and *group interviewing* will be examined in Chapter 21 and the remaining forms of interview associated with qualitative research will be explored at various points in this chapter. However, in spite of the apparent proliferation of terms describing types of interview in qualitative research, the two main types are the *unstructured interview* and the *semi-structured interview*. Researchers sometimes employ the term *qualitative interview* to encapsulate these two types of interview. There is clearly the potential for considerable confusion here, but the types and definitions offered in Key concept 9.2 are meant to inject a degree of consistency of terminology. One final point to note at the outset is that, in qualitative research, no single interview stands alone. 'It has meaning to the researcher only in terms of other interviews and observations' (Whyte 1953: 22).

Telling it like it is
Intensive interviewing

Sometimes the conditions of research access combined with other university commitments mean that students have to adopt an intensive approach to interviewing. For Angharad and Chris this meant they carried out all of their interviews over a short time period of just one day. For Angharad this was a matter of making the most of the opportunity that she had been granted, although she conceded: 'I was very tired by the end of the day, trying to take all that information in and stay on the ball.' Although these practical constraints sometimes just have to be worked with, it is important to recognize that interviewing can be quite a stressful and tiring activity, and doing a large number of interviews in one day particularly so. This makes it even more important to have considered the issues covered in this chapter before doing your interviews.

In Chris's case, practical constraints also affected the time in which he conducted the interviews. 'I did all the interviews on the same day, which was a matter of convenience because I was coming from Birmingham to London so I didn't really have the budget to make several journeys but looking back on it, it might have been a good idea to say, "Right. Well, I did the first one. These are the questions I asked. These are the responses. That's an interesting response," or, "I didn't get quite what I'd expect there. Let me tailor the question or maybe the questions. Go and change it slightly." ' Chris acknowledges that, if he had piloted and pre-tested his questions (see Chapter 11), this might have enhanced the overall quality of his data. However, although he carried out the interviews in a short time period, Chris had already built up relationships with his interviewees beforehand as a result of his internship. As he explained, 'I'd known all of them for at least eight weeks so I suppose that would have obviously had an effect on the style of conversation that I had with them in the interviews as opposed to somebody I'd interviewed without knowing them beforehand. I'm sure that did have an effect and it meant that some of the questions I asked were more personal because I had background about what they'd done, families, that kind of thing. And they brought that kind of thing into the interviews. Whether somebody who didn't know me would have been so happy to do that, I don't know.'

Differences between the structured interview and the qualitative interview

Qualitative interviewing is usually very different from interviewing in quantitative research in a number of ways.

- The approach tends to be much less structured in qualitative research. In quantitative research, the approach is structured to maximize the reliability and validity of measurement of key concepts. It is also more structured because the researcher has a clearly specified set of research questions that are to be investigated. The structured interview is designed to answer these questions. Instead, in qualitative research, there is an emphasis on greater generality in the formulation of initial research ideas and on interviewees' own perspectives.

- In qualitative interviewing, there is much greater interest in the interviewee's point of view; in quantitative research, the interview reflects the researcher's concerns. This contrast is a direct outcome of the previously mentioned one. For example, Ram (1994) describes his qualitative interviewing style as owing little to the 'textbook' approach, which 'exhorts the interviewer to remain aloof while seeking to extract information from the respondent' (1994: 32), as it would have been 'absurd and counter-productive' to assume this degree of social distance from family and friends whom he had known for years.

- In qualitative interviewing, 'rambling' or going off at tangents is often encouraged—it gives insight into what the interviewee sees as relevant and important; in quantitative research, it is usually regarded as a nuisance and discouraged.

- In qualitative interviewing, interviewers can depart significantly from any schedule or guide that is being used. They can ask new questions that follow up interviewees' replies and can vary the order of questions and even the wording of questions. In quantitative research, none of these things should be done, because they will compromise the standardization of the interview process and hence the reliability and validity of measurement.

- As a result, qualitative interviewing tends to be flexible (see Research in focus 20.2 for an example), responding to the direction in which interviewees take the interview and perhaps adjusting the emphases in the research as a result of significant issues that emerge in the course of interviews. By contrast, structured interviews are typically inflexible, because of

the need to standardize the way in which each interviewee is dealt with.

- In qualitative interviewing, the researcher wants rich, detailed answers; in quantitative research, the interview is supposed to generate answers that can be coded and processed quickly.

- In qualitative interviewing, the interviewee may be interviewed on more than one and sometimes even several occasions. In quantitative research, unless the research is longitudinal in character, the person will be interviewed on one occasion only.

 # Asking questions in the qualitative interview

Qualitative interviewing varies a great deal in the approach taken by the interviewer. The two major types were mentioned at the beginning of the chapter.

- The almost totally *unstructured interview*. Here the researcher uses at most an *aide-mémoire* as a brief set of prompts to him or herself to deal with a certain range of topics. There may be just a single question that the interviewer asks, and the interviewee is then allowed to respond freely, with the interviewer simply responding to points that seem worthy of being followed up. Unstructured interviewing tends to be very similar in character to a conversation (Burgess 1984). Dalton (1959) refers to the importance of 'conversational interviewing' as the basis for his data collection strategy. These are not interviews in the usual sense, but a series of broken and incomplete conversations that, when written up, may, according to Dalton, be 'tied together as one statement' (1959: 280). Conversational interviews are characterized by being precipitated by events. In some instances, these were prompted by Dalton, who asked managers at the end of an important meeting an open-ended question like 'How did things go?', but in others they were simply the result of overheard exchanges in shops or offices. See Research in focus 20.1 for another illustration of an unstructured interview style.

- A *semi-structured interview*. The researcher has a list of questions on fairly specific topics to be covered, often referred to as an *interview guide*, but the interviewee has a great deal of leeway in how to reply. Questions may not follow on exactly in the way outlined on the

schedule. Questions that are not included in the guide may be asked as the interviewer picks up on things said by interviewees. But, by and large, all the questions will be asked and a similar wording will be used from interviewee to interviewee. For example, Willman et al. (2002) carried out semi-structured interviews with traders in financial markets in London. The interviews covered a range of issues, including motivations, emotions, trading strategies, and questions about organizational culture. They also included questions about control incentives and management style. In this analysis, the researchers focused on sections of the interview that dealt with the aversion to and seeking of risk; this formed the basis for their conclusion that traders focus on avoiding losses rather than making gains. Research in focus 20.2 provides a further example of these features.

In both cases, the interview process is *flexible*. Also, the emphasis must be on how the interviewee frames and understands issues and events—that is, what the interviewee views as important in explaining and understanding events, patterns, and forms of behaviour. Thus, Leidner (1993) describes the interviewing she carried out in a McDonald's restaurant as involving a degree of structure, but adds that the interviews also 'allowed room to pursue topics of particular interest to the workers' (1993: 238). Milkman (1997), in her study of auto workers at General Motors, describes how in the second stage of her research she interviewed a total of thirty buyout takers and workers, using a 'very general interview guide', trying to be as casual as she could, and

Research in focus 20.1
An example of unstructured interviewing

Whyte (1953) presents an example of a 'non-directive', or unstructured, interview conducted in 1952 during a one-day visit to the Chicago plant of the Inland Steel Container Company. The aim of this interview was to catch up with developments in union–management relations that had taken place since his previous visit to the plant and since Whyte's publication of a book on this subject. Whyte suggests that the book had been received favourably at the plant, as it showed management and union officials in a positive light. Publication was marked by a public meeting, and every worker in the plant had been presented with a copy. This, in Whyte's view, helped to ensure positive rapport with the respondent on the day in question.

The interview was with Columbus Gary, vice-president of the union and chairman of its grievance committee. It was held in the management conference room of the plant. Whyte explains: 'Gary was neither a complete stranger to me nor a close acquaintance.' He goes on to suggest that he had no problem in establishing rapport with Gary, stating that Gary 'was willing to tell me anything I wanted to know' (1953: 16). Then follows a section of the verbatim interview with Gary, for which Whyte provides a commentary that involves analysing his own interviewing technique, including such 'mistakes' as presenting a leading question.

Although Whyte suggests that he was following the 'rules' of non-directive interviewing (by concentrating on listening, not interrupting or arguing with the informant, and periodically restating what had been said), he also suggests that in certain important respects he was not. In particular, Whyte attempted to direct Gary towards an account of the social process. Specifically, how did the problem come to the attention of the person concerned, and what were the steps involved in the action taken?

> Right at the outset I sought to move him from a statement of sentiments to an account of interpersonal events. I was interested not only in what happened at a particular time, but in how that event related to others that took place before or afterwards. For all these events I wanted answers to the question: Who did what, with whom, and where?
>
> (1953: 21–2)

Whyte concludes that the interviewer must learn to recognize the difference between a statement of substance and an account of process in order to be able to guide an informant from one to the other. This enables the reconstruction of events by asking interviewees to consider how a sequence of events evolved. Therefore, we can see that, although Whyte describes his approach to organizational interviewing as non-directive, it is not as unstructured as it at first seems.

never discouraging anyone from going off on tangents. Most interviews were with individuals. However, in a few cases workers invited their friends from the plant as well. Milkman claims that 'these turned out to be among the best interviews, since they developed a group dynamic in which my presence often became marginal' (1997: 198). In an interview study of secretarial work involving almost 500 office workers, Pringle (1988) followed an oral history format. She explains:

> We did not restrict the subject matter to work. Initially people were asked to start by talking about a typical day . . . Over time, our interests shifted or became more focused on the relation between different parts

> of their lives, on home and family, and their views on a range of political and social issues, and on their notions of a 'good boss' and 'good secretary'.
>
> (1988: 270)

Once again, we must remember that qualitative research is *not* quantitative research with the numbers missing. The kinds of interviewing carried out in qualitative research are typical also of *life history* and *oral history* interviewing (see the section on this topic below).

The two different types of interview in qualitative research are extremes, and there is quite a lot of variability between them, but most qualitative interviews

Research in focus 20.2
Flexibility in semi-structured interviewing

Between February and April 1990, Prasad (1993) interviewed thirty-four employees as part of her study of computerization at the Paragon Corporation. Interviews focused on understanding employees' experiences of computerized work. Each one lasted between forty-five minutes and one-and-a-half hours and was 'semi-structured'. Prasad explains that in some cases the interviews corroborated her own assessment of the situation, while in others they offered a different interpretation that helped her to rethink her analysis. This meant that 'there was no one set of questions administered to all interviewees and no specific sequencing of the issues raised' (1993: 1408). She writes that the interviews were informed by the idea of 'grand tour' and 'mini tour' questions (Spradley and McCurdy 1972).

> The broad and exploratory grand tour questions gave the interviews focus and were developed keeping my research interests in mind. For the most part, grand tour questions got interviewees talking about aspects of computerization and related organizational issues. If the interviewee touched on something that was closely connected with the symbolism of computers or seemed particularly concerned about certain aspects of computerization, I pursued those areas through the use of more specific and detailed mini tour questions.
>
> (Prasad 1993: 1409)

are close to one type or the other. In neither case does the interviewer slavishly follow a schedule, as is done in quantitative research interviewing; but in semi-structured interviews the interviewer does follow a script to a certain extent. The choice of whether to veer towards one type rather than the other is likely to be affected by a variety of factors.

- If it is important to the researcher to gain a genuine understanding of the world views of members of a social setting or of people sharing common attributes,

an unstructured interviewing approach may be preferable. With a more unstructured approach, the researcher is less likely to come at participants' world views with presuppositions or expectations and is more likely to see things as the participants see them.

- If the researcher is beginning the investigation with a fairly clear focus, rather than a very general notion of wanting to do research on a topic, it is likely that the interviews will be semi-structured ones, so that the more specific issues can be addressed. More

Telling it like it is
Semi-structured interviewing

Lucie carried out informal interviews with fifteen other students who were on the entrepreneurship courses she attended. She did not audio-record these interviews but took notes on what interviewees said. She then interviewed four of the staff at the institute. Lucie audio-recorded and later transcribed these interviews. She explained that her approach to interviewing as semi-structured. 'I knew kind of what I wanted to find out. I wanted to know what types of enterprise they were trying to encourage because part way through my research it was clear that there wasn't really a good definition of enterprise and no one really knew what enterprise was. Even the students attending didn't really know what it was. So I wanted to kind of clarify this, I suppose, through the students and through the institute, what they thought enterprise was and what they were hoping to gain out of that. It wasn't really like a structured interview. It was kind of a semi-structured interview so they could kind of talk about what they were experiencing and what they wanted out of the course and things. So it wasn't really like I had structured questions, but I just knew the areas I wanted them to talk about.'

Tips and skills
Learning how to interview by watching films

If you have never done any qualitative interviewing before, a useful way of familiarizing yourself with the method and the techniques involved is by watching films that sensitize you to some of the issues involved in naturalistic inquiry. Saldaña (2009) recommends several popular films that he suggests simulate the kinds of real-world dilemmas and human interaction that researchers commonly face in their practice. For qualitiative interviewing, his recommendations include *Kinsey* (2004), a film about the controversial biologist Dr Alfred Kinsey, who studied sexual behaviour in the United States in the 1940s and 1950s. Kinsey used a combination of structured and semi-structured interviews, observation, and participational methods. The film provides insight into the issues involved in researching a highly sensitive topic and the influence of the researcher's personal values (see Chapter 2) on his choice of research subject. Saldaña also recommends *The Matrix* (1999) to gain insight into the concepts of epistemology and ontology and *The Truman Show* (1998) to illustrate the principles of participant observation (see Chapter 19) and the ethical issues (see Chapter 6) entailed in acting without having obtained someone's informed consent.

structure is also likely to be imposed when the researcher has a clear idea of how the data will be analysed. In the case of using interviews to generate data about critical incidents (see Research in focus 20.3), a set of subject themes can be used to guide respondents who are asked to recall examples of specific events that illustrate each theme.

- If more than one person is to carry out the fieldwork, in order to ensure a modicum of comparability of interviewing style it is likely that semi-structured interviewing will be preferred. See Research in focus 20.2 for an example.

- If you are doing multiple case study research, you are likely to find that you will need some structure in order to ensure cross-case comparability. Certainly, all Bryman's qualitative research on different kinds of organization has entailed semi-structured interviewing, and it is not a coincidence that this is because most

Research in focus 20.3
An example of critical incident technique

Curran and Blackburn (1994) used a critical incident approach to examine the relationships between small and large businesses and their local economies. This involved focusing on particular events as a means of exploring how small business owner-managers related to their social and economic community. Forty-five owner-managers from a diverse range of businesses, including computer services, employment, secretarial and training agencies, and garages and vehicle repairers, were interviewed about a range of critical incidents that they had experienced over the previous two years. Five themes were selected as a basis for exploring how owners articulate with their environments: customers and the market; investment and finance; co-directors and partners; family and kinship; and local authority connections and involvements. Respondents were sent the list of potential themes for discussion prior to the interview. This was a way of encouraging more detailed narratives than would have been possible if the subjects were first raised in the interview. Each theme was introduced by the interviewer, who gave a general preamble. For example, in the case of gaining or losing a major customer the interviewer would say:

> The success of any business greatly depends on its customers. Most businesses lose or gain a major customer from time to time and this can create problems—especially losing an important customer. We would like you to highlight any people who were involved, consulted or who helped you in this situation.
>
> (1994: 107)

If the respondent had experienced an event like this in the previous two years, he or she was asked to talk through what happened, how he or she had coped, and with whom he or she had discussed the event. Curran and Blackburn found that losing a major customer sometimes led owner-managers to seek outside help to resolve the problem; on other occasions they chose to deal with the problem themselves without any outside help. Critical incidents also revealed the conflicting pressures, particularly for female owner-managers, in managing business and family life. One explained how she had worked up to the last possible moment before she went into labour for the birth of one of her children:

> I was doing someone's wages when I went into labour and this poor man kept looking at me and saying 'Don't you think you'd better go now?' and I said 'No it's all right, I'll just finish the wages . . . Oh dear! Hang on a minute' [indicating a response to a pain contraction].
>
> (Owner-manager, employment agency, Suffolk; Curran and Blackburn 1994: 112)

The researchers suggest that critical incident analysis enables increased understanding of the reasons why owner-managers use links outside the business. They conclude that owner-managers tend to have relatively small networks and few external contacts such as accountants and bank managers. In addition, owner-managers rarely use non-economic contacts based on family, kinship, or social groupings for business information or advice. This example is illustrative of a more qualitative application of the critical incident technique than was used in the classic study of job satisfaction by Herzberg, Mausner, and Snyderman (1959) discussed in Chapter 9.

of it has been multiple case study research (e.g. Bryman, Haslam, and Webb 1994; Bryman, Gillingwater, and McGuinness 1996).

In business research there are some additional considerations that relate to qualitative interviewing. Interviewing managers often raises specific issues; the status and power held, particularly at a senior level, mean that gaining access to this group of people can be extremely difficult, and arranging a mutually convenient time in which to conduct an interview, which may last several hours, even more so. Given the number of outside requests for information and assistance that most managers receive, it is particularly important to structure a request for interview in a way that is most likely to lead to a favourable response. A request for interview may be made either by letter or by telephone. Healey and Rawlinson (1993) recommend a dual approach: first make a telephone call, 'fishing' for a named person who is most likely to be appropriate for the interview, then follow this up with an introductory letter. In the letter, it may be appropriate to enclose a short outline of the nature and purpose of the project and an indication of how the findings might be useful to the respondent. If the research is supported by a high-profile sponsoring organization (for example, a company or university business school), it may be worth enclosing a letter from a senior person within this organization endorsing the aims of the research. Finally, a telephone call made a few days

after receipt of the letter can provide an opportunity for the researcher to deal with any queries the manager may have. The most important thing to remember, however, is that 'polite persistence' is often crucial (Healey and Rawlinson 1993).

Interviewing within organizations also involves encroaching on an individual's work time, and in some cases it may not be possible to take people away from their work during the hours of their employment. Managers may be unwilling to grant lower-level employees the time away from productive activity that is needed to conduct an interview, or there may simply be no one available to cover their duties. When employees are paid on an hourly basis, this becomes a particularly important issue. For example, in her research into work roles in restaurants, Elaine Hall (1993) wanted to interview a sample of the servers (waiters and waitresses) who worked in the five selected restaurants. To do this, she had to approach servers on duty to schedule individual interviews for off-duty times, usually before or after their work shift. This relied on servers' willingness to devote an hour of their unpaid time to this task.

However, sometimes managers demonstrate a willingness to enable the interview process despite the cost implications. For example, Freeman (2000) describes how one of the companies involved in the research provided release time for managers and workers so that she could interview them on company premises. Similarly,

Bell, Taylor, and Thorpe (2001) were able to conduct a group interview with employees in one plant because the section manager and his team agreed to cease production for a period of time, in order to allow the interview to take place. However, this is not to suggest that it is only the interviewer who benefits from the interview process. Some interviewees, particularly senior managers, may welcome the opportunity to offload issues and concerns or think through a problem in a structured way, particularly if they are able to see a copy of the transcript afterwards. In these instances the interview is very much a two-way process, with both parties gaining something beneficial from it.

Preparing an interview guide

The idea of an interview guide is much less specific than the notion of a structured interview schedule. In fact, the term can be employed to refer to the brief list of memory prompts of areas to be covered that is often employed in unstructured interviewing or to the somewhat more structured list of issues to be addressed or questions to be asked in semi-structured interviewing. Moreover, an interview guide does not necessarily have to comprise written words; instead it can take the form of a series of visual prompts related to a subject (see Research in focus 20.4). Researchers may offer to provide a copy of the interview guide or schedule to interested readers on request. This can help to strengthen the dependability of the research (see Chapter 17). What is crucial is that the questioning allows interviewers to glean the ways in which research participants view their social world and that there is flexibility in the conduct of the interviews. The latter is as much if not more to do with the conduct of the interview than with the nature of the interview guide as such.

In preparing for qualitative interviews, Lofland and Lofland (1995: 78) suggest asking yourself the question 'Just what about this thing is puzzling me?' This can be applied to each of the research questions you have generated or it may be a mechanism for generating some research questions. They suggest that your puzzlement can be stimulated by various activities: random thoughts in different contexts, which are then written down as quickly as possible; discussions with colleagues, friends, and relatives; and, of course, the existing literature on the topic. The formulation of the research question(s) should not be so specific that alternative avenues of enquiry that might arise during the collection of fieldwork data are closed off. Such premature closure of your research focus would be inconsistent with the process of qualitative research (see Figure 17.1), with the emphasis on the world view of the people you will be interviewing, and with the approaches to qualitative data analysis such as grounded theory that emphasize the importance of not starting out with too many preconceptions (see Chapter 24). Gradually, an order and structure will begin to emerge in your meanderings around your research question(s) and will form the basis for your interview guide.

You should also consider 'What do I need to know in order to answer each of the research questions I am interested in?' This means trying to get an appreciation

Tips and skills
Where to conduct an interview?

Finding a quiet, private space in which to conduct an interview uninterrupted can be one of the most difficult tasks for the qualitative researcher. Many organizations will struggle to find you a spare room that is not being used and is even remotely suitable. Think carefully before agreeing to interview someone in his or her own office; are there likely to be frequent telephone calls or interruptions that make the interview difficult? Also, traffic, aircraft, or machinery can contribute to background noise that can make the audio-recorded speech inaudible. It is a good idea to spend some time in the room prior to the interview; do a speech recording to test the acoustics of the room and carefully position the furniture; if there is noise from outside the room, think about closing doors or windows. Similarly, you may wish to turn off a noisy heater. Position the microphone as near to your interviewees as possible and make sure that they are unlikely to knock it. You will, of course, need to balance these issues against the comfort and convenience of your interviewee (it would not be feasible to insist on having all the windows closed in a hot factory in the middle of summer!). But do not be afraid to explain what you need in order to conduct the interview, even though you may have to be prepared to compromise when it comes to actually getting it.

Tips and skills
Multiple interviewers

Bechhofer, Elliott, and McCrone (1984) claim there are advantages to having more than one interviewer to interview each respondent. In their study, this nearly always meant having two interviewers, but in one instance three interviewers were involved. They explain: 'After the customary introductory pleasantries and opening remarks, one person would take up the interview, making only brief notes as it went on. The other would take extensive notes, carefully observe the reactions of the respondent and the other interviewer, nod sagely from time to time, or grunt in the way of interviewers. The "passive" interviewer could thus assess the overall development of the interview, keep an eye on topics to be covered, and await the appropriate moment to take over' (Bechhofer, Elliott, and McCrone 1984: 97). The passive interviewer could intervene at any point at which he or she felt an issue needed to be probed further or felt the questioning needed a change of direction. It was also possible for the two interviewers to debate a point between themselves, as a means of drawing the interviewee into the discussion, but with less risk of antagonizing him or her than if he or she was the focus of the debate. Finally, the use of two interviewers enables the incorporation of different styles of questioning, as one interviewer can play the 'hard' role in asking difficult questions while the other can play a softer, more supportive one.

The use of multiple interviewers also contributed to a more informal atmosphere, akin to a discussion between three people rather than an exchange between two persons. However, they acknowledge that some respondents might find talking to two interviewers intimidating and that it might be inappropriate for some social groups. They claim it works best 'in what one might call "collegial" situations; a small group carrying out an investigation, doing the interviewing themselves and in constant touch with each other' (1984: 98). There are also disadvantages in terms of the time cost involved in having two interviewers attending each interview. They further highlight the importance of sensitivity; both interviewers need to be sensitive to each other, and to be able to read each others' conversational cues and respond to them.

Research in focus 20.4
Photo-interviewing in a study of consumer behaviour

Hurworth (2003) suggests some ways that photographs can be integrated into the interviewing process (see also discussion of photo-elicitation in Chapter 9). Showing an interviewee a photo can help him or her recall events from the past, articulate abstract concepts, or express complex emotions. Photographs also have advantages in overcoming interviewees' discomfort in being interviewed and can encourage them to discuss issues in more detail.

Heisley and Levy (1991) used photo-interviewing in a study of consumer behaviour related to family meals. They met each family and took photographs of them preparing and consuming dinner as a family. The researchers edited the photographs into a chronological set that represented the main events of the evening and the family members involved. Next, the informants were interviewed and asked to 'tell me whatever you think about when you look at [these photographs]' (Heisley and Levy 1991: 263). Finally, informants were shown the photographs again, accompanied by an audio recording of the first interview, and asked to comment on the data generated. One of the findings from the study related to how interviewees commented on the consumer products in the photograph, such as furnishings and table utensils, their responses highlighting how these objects are embedded in social relationships—for example, fondue sets as wedding gifts. They conclude: 'A photograph motivates people to provide a perspective of action, to explain what lies behind the pictures, and to relate how the frozen moment relates to the reality as they see it' (Heisley and Levy 1991: 269).

of what the interviewee sees as significant and important in relation to each of your topic areas. Thus, your questioning will need to cover the areas that you need but from the perspective of your interviewees. This means that, even though qualitative research is predominantly unstructured, it is rarely so unstructured that the researcher cannot at least specify a research focus.

Some basic elements in the preparation of your interview guide will be:

- create a certain amount of order on the topic areas, so that your questions about them flow reasonably well, but be prepared to alter the order of questions during the actual interview;

- formulate interview questions or topics in a way that will help you to answer your research questions (but try not to make them too specific);

- try to use a language that is comprehensible and relevant to the people you are interviewing;

- just as in interviewing in quantitative research, do not ask leading questions;

- remember to ensure that you ask or record 'facesheet' information of a general kind (name, age, gender, etc.) and a specific kind (position in company, number of years employed, number of years involved in a group, etc.), because such information is useful for contextualizing people's answers.

There are some practical details to attend to before the interview.

- Make sure you are familiar with the setting in which the interviewee works, lives, or engages in the behaviour of interest to you. This will help you to understand what he or she is saying in the interviewee's own terms.

- Get hold of a good digital audio recorder. Qualitative researchers nearly always audio-record and then transcribe their interviews. This procedure is important for the detailed analysis required in qualitative research and to ensure that the interviewees' answers are captured in their own terms. If you are taking notes, it is easy to lose the phrases and language used. Also, because the interviewer is supposed not to be following a strictly formulated schedule of questions of the kind used in structured interviewing, he or she will need to be responsive to the interviewee's answers so that it is possible to follow them up. A good microphone is highly desirable, because many interviews are let down by poor recording.

- Make sure as far as possible that the interview takes place in a setting that is quiet (so there is little or no outside noise that might affect the quality of the audio recording) and private (so the interviewee does not have to worry about being overheard).

- Prepare yourself for the interview by cultivating as many of the criteria of a quality interviewer suggested by Kvale (see Tips and skills 'Criteria of a successful interviewer') as possible.

After the interview, make notes about:

- how the interview went (was interviewee talkative, cooperative, nervous, well dressed/scruffy, etc.?);

- where the interview took place;

Tips and skills
Criteria of a successful interviewer

Kvale (1996) has proposed a list of ten criteria of a successful interviewer.

1. *Knowledgeable*: is thoroughly familiar with the focus of the interview; pilot interviews of the kind used in survey interviewing can be useful here.

2. *Structuring*: gives purpose for interview; rounds it off; asks whether interviewee has questions.

3. *Clear*: asks simple, easy, short questions; no jargon.

4. *Gentle*: lets people finish; gives them time to think; tolerates pauses.

5. *Sensitive*: listens attentively to what is said and how it is said; is empathetic in dealing with the interviewee.

6. *Open*: responds to what is important to interviewee and is flexible.

7. *Steering*: knows what he or she wants to find out.

8. *Critical*: is prepared to challenge what is said—for example, dealing with inconsistencies in interviewees' replies.

9. *Remembering*: relates what is said to what has previously been said.

10. *Interpreting*: clarifies and extends meanings of interviewees' statements, but without imposing meaning on them.

To Kvale's list we would add the following.

- *Balanced*: does not talk too much, which may make the interviewee passive, and does not talk too little, which may result in the interviewee feeling he or she is not talking along the right lines.

- *Ethically sensitive*: is sensitive to the ethical dimension of interviewing, ensuring the interviewee appreciates what the research is about, its purposes, and that his or her answers will be treated confidentially.

- any other feelings about the interview (did it open up new avenues of interest?);

- the setting (busy/quiet, many/few other people in the vicinity, new/old buildings, use of computers).

These various guidelines suggest the series of steps in formulating questions for an interview guide in qualitative research presented in Figure 20.1.

Figure 20.1

Formulating questions for an interview guide

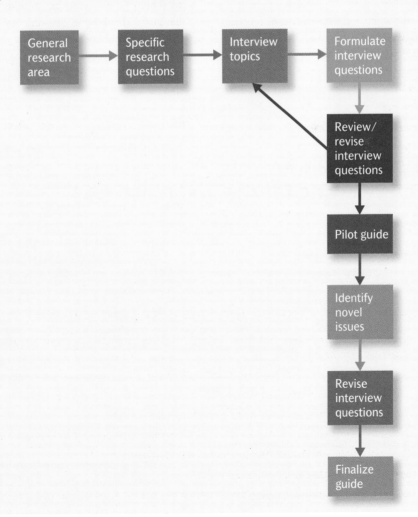

Kinds of questions

The kinds of question asked in qualitative interviews are highly variable. Kvale (1996) has suggested nine different kinds of question. Most interviews will contain virtually all of them, although interviews that rely on lists of topics are likely to follow a somewhat looser format. Kvale's nine types of question are as follows.

1. *Introducing questions*: 'Please tell me about when your interest in X first began'; 'Have you ever . . . ?'; 'Why did you go to . . . ?'

2. *Follow-up questions*: getting the interviewee to elaborate his or her answer, such as 'Could you say some more about that?'; 'What do you mean by that . . . ?'; 'Can you give me an example . . . ?'; even 'Yeeees?'

3. *Probing questions*: following up what has been said through direct questioning.

4. *Specifying questions*: 'What did you do then?'; 'How did X react to what you said?'

5. *Direct questions*: 'Do you find it easy to keep smiling when serving customers?'; 'Are you happy with the amount of on-the-job training you have received?' Such questions are perhaps best left until towards the end of the interview, in order not to influence the direction of the interview too much.

6. *Indirect questions*: 'What do most people round here think of the ways that management treats its staff?', perhaps followed up by 'Is that the way you feel too?', in order to get at the individual's own view.

7. *Structuring questions*: 'I would now like to move on to a different topic.'

8. *Silence*: allow pauses to signal that you want to give the interviewee the opportunity to reflect and amplify an answer.

9. *Interpreting questions*: 'Do you mean that your leadership role has had to change from one of encouraging others to a more directive one?'; 'Is it fair to say that you don't mind being friendly towards customers most of the time, but when they are unpleasant or demanding you find it more difficult?'

In their study of ethics and compliance officers, Treviño et al. (2014) used a final question that does not fit easily in any of these categories. This is a 'what do you think I should have asked you about that I haven't' question. They asked: 'If I really want to understand your role what should I have asked that I didn't?' (Treviño et al. 2014: 204). This kind of question is worth considering as a means of catching perspectives that your other question failed to reveal but which may be very significant to the interviewee.

Tips and skills
Interviewing for the first time

The prospect of doing your first interview can be daunting. Also, it is easy to make some fundamental mistakes when you begin interviewing. An American study of postgraduates' experiences of a lengthy interview training course showed that novice interviewers were easily thrown out by a number of events or experiences in the course of the interview (Roulston, DeMarrais, and Lewis 2003). The researchers' findings suggest five challenges that are worth bearing in mind when approaching your first interview(s).

1. *Unexpected interviewee behaviour or environmental problems*. These inexperienced interviewers were easily discomforted by responses or behaviour on the part of the interviewees or by problems such as noise in the vicinity of the interview. When you go into the interview, bear in mind that things may not go according to plan. Interviewees may say things that you find surprising or shocking. Equally, there can be many distractions close to where the interview takes place. You clearly cannot plan for or control these things, but you can bear in mind that they might happen and try to limit their impact on you and on the course of the interview.

2. *Intrusion of own biases and expectations*. Roulston et al. report that some of the trainees were surprised when they read their own transcripts at how their own biases and expectations were evident in the ways they asked questions and followed up on replies.

3. *Maintaining focus in asking questions*. Students reported that they sometimes had difficulty probing answers, asking follow-up questions, and clarifying questions in a way that did not lose sight of the research topic and what the questions were getting at.

4. *Dealing with sensitive issues.* Some students asked questions that caused interviewees to become upset, and this response could have an adverse effect on the conduct of the interview. However, most students felt that they coped reasonably well with such emotionally charged situations.

5. *Transcription.* Many reported finding transcription difficult and time-consuming—more so than they had imagined.

There are, of course, many other possible issues that impinge on first-time interviewees. Many do not go away either, no matter how experienced you are. It is very difficult to know how to deal with some of these contingencies. However, it is worth bearing in mind that they do arise and that their impact may be greatest when you have less interviewing experience.

As this list suggests, one of the main ingredients of the interview is listening—being very attentive to what the interviewee is saying or even not saying. It means that the interviewer is active without being too intrusive—a difficult balance. But it also means that, just because the interview is being audio-recorded (the generally recommended practice whenever it is feasible), the interviewer cannot take things easy. In fact, an interviewer must be very attuned and responsive to what the interviewee is saying and doing. This is also important because something like body language may indicate that the interviewee is becoming uneasy or anxious about a line of questioning. An ethically sensitive interviewer will not want to place undue pressure on the person he or she is talking to and will need to be prepared to cut short that line of questioning if it is clearly a source of concern.

Remember as well that in interviews you are going to ask about different kinds of things, such as:

- values: of interviewee, of group, of organization;
- beliefs: of interviewee, of others, of group;
- behaviour: of interviewee, of others;
- formal and informal roles: of interviewee, of others;
- relationships: of interviewee, of others;
- places and locales;

- emotions: particularly of the interviewee, but also possibly of others;
- encounters;
- stories.

Try to vary the questioning in terms of types of question (as suggested by Kvale's nine types, which were outlined above) *and* the types of phenomena you ask about. Finally, you must think about how to end interviews satisfactorily, making sure that your interviewees have had a chance to comment fully on the topic concerned and giving them the opportunity to raise any issues that they think you have overlooked in your questions. The closing moments of an interview also provide an opportunity to include a final 'catch-all' question. Journalists sometimes refer to this as the 'doorknob question', since it is asked at the end, when rapport has been established and the interviewee has relaxed into the situation. This type of closing question tends to be directive—for example, 'If you were advising the organization on this subject, what are the main changes or improvements that you would recommend?' or 'From your experience in this area, what advice would you offer to other managers facing similar problems?' This encourages the interviewee to comment on specific issues and to put forward a personal opinion.

Tips and skills
Interviewees and distance

Sometimes you may need to contact interviewees who are a long way from you—perhaps even abroad. While interviewing in qualitative research is usually of the face-to-face kind, time and money restrictions may mean that you will need to interview such people in a less personal context. There are several possibilities. One is telephone interviewing. The cost of a telephone interview is much less than the cost involved in travelling long distances. Such interviewing is touched on in the context of the structured interview in Chapter 9. Other possibilities are the online interview, in which the interview is conducted by email, or the Skype interview. These methods are described in Chapter 28.

Telling it like it is
Learning how to interview

Karen found that through the experience of doing a research project involving qualitative interviewing she had acquired a new and potentially transferable skill. 'I learned a lot through the interviews that I did about how to probe and to get what you want out of it. You can so easily just go into an interview and just sit there and listen to what they're saying and then you go out and think, "Actually they didn't give me anything that I wanted. They just talked at me." But you need to balance that with not actually telling them what you want to know, but just sort of guiding them towards it so that you can achieve the objectives that you've got. That's another skill that I wouldn't say I've managed to learn completely, but I think it's something that you pick up and you can get better at through doing this sort of research. Since then I've done quite a lot of sort of client-based consultancy projects and I think this is definitely one of the main skills I applied there. Having it clear in your own mind what you want to get and asking the questions in a way that can get what you want without leading people to tell you what you want to hear.'

Using an interview guide: an example

Research in focus 20.5 is taken from an interview from Bryman's (1999) study of visitors to Disney theme parks. The study was briefly mentioned in Chapter 18 as an example of a snowball sampling procedure. The interviews were concerned to elicit visitors' interpretations of the parks that had been visited. The interview is with a man who was in his sixties and his wife who was two years younger. They had visited Walt Disney World in Orlando, Florida, and were very enthusiastic about their visit.

Research in focus 20.5
Part of the transcript of a semi-structured interview

Interviewer	OK. What were your views or feelings about the presentation of different cultures, as shown in, for example, Jungle Cruise or It's a Small World at the Magic Kingdom or in World Showcase at Epcot?
Wife	Well, I thought the different countries at Epcot were wonderful, but I need to say more than that, don't I?
Husband	They were very good and some were better than others, but that was down to the host countries themselves really, as I suppose each of the countries represented would have been responsible for their own part, so that's nothing to do with Disney, I wouldn't have thought. I mean some of the landmarks were hard to recognize for what they were supposed to be, but some were very well done. Britain was OK, but there was only a pub and a Welsh shop there really, whereas some of the other pavilions, as I think they were called, were good ambassadors for the countries they represented. China, for example, had an excellent 360 degree film showing parts of China and I found that very interesting.
Interviewer	Did you think there was anything lacking about the content?
Husband	Well I did notice that there weren't many black people at World Showcase, particularly the American Adventure. Now whether we were there on an unusual day in that respect I don't know, but we saw plenty of black Americans in the Magic Kingdom and other places, but very few if any in that World Showcase. And there was certainly little mention of black history in the American Adventure presentation, so maybe they felt alienated by that, I don't know, but they were noticeable by their absence.

Interviewer	So did you think there were any special emphases?
Husband	Well thinking about it now, because I hadn't really given this any consideration before you started asking about it, but thinking about it now, it was only really representative of the developed world, you know, Britain, America, Japan, world leaders many of them in technology, and there was nothing of the Third World there. Maybe that's their own fault, maybe they were asked to participate and didn't, but now that I think about it, that does come to me. What do you think, love?
Wife	Well, like you, I hadn't thought of it like that before, but I agree with you.

The sequence begins with the interviewer asking what would be considered a 'direct question' in terms of the list of nine question types suggested by Kvale (1996) and outlined above. The replies are very bland and do little more than reflect the interviewees' positive feelings about their visit to Disney World. The wife acknowledges this when she says 'but I need to say more than that, don't I?' Interviewees frequently know that they are expected to be expansive in their answers. This sequence occurred around halfway through the interview, so the interviewees were primed by then into realizing that more details were expected. There is almost a tinge of embarrassment that the answer has been so brief and unilluminating. The husband's answer is more expansive but not particularly enlightening.

There then follows the first of two important prompts by the interviewer. The husband's response is more interesting in that he now begins to answer in terms of the possibility that black people were under-represented in such attractions as the American Adventure, which tells the story of America through tableaux and films via a debate between two audio-animatronic figures—Mark Twain and Benjamin Franklin. The second prompt yields further useful reflection, this time carrying the implication that Third World countries are under-represented in the World Showcase in the Epcot Centre. The couple are clearly aware that it is the prompting that has made them provide these reflections when they say: 'Well thinking about it now, because I hadn't really given this any consideration before you started asking about it' and 'Well, like you, I hadn't thought of it like that before'. This is the whole point of prompting—to get the interviewee to think more about the topic and to provide the opportunity for a more detailed response. It is not a leading question, since the interviewees were not being asked, 'Do you think that the Disney company fails to recognize the significance of Black history (or ignores the Third World) in its presentation of different cultures?' There is no doubt that it is the prompts that elicit the more interesting replies, but that is precisely their role.

Tips and skills
Why you should record and transcribe interviews

With approaches that entail detailed attention to language, such as conversation analysis and discourse analysis (see Chapter 22), the recording of conversations and interviews is to all intents and purposes mandatory. However, researchers who use qualitative interviews and focus groups (see Chapter 21) also tend to record and then transcribe interviews. Heritage (1984: 238) suggests that the procedure of recording and transcribing interviews has the following advantages.

* It helps to correct the natural limitations of our memories and of the intuitive glosses that we might place on what people say in interviews.
* It allows more thorough examination of what people say.
* It permits repeated examinations of the interviewees' answers.
* It opens up the data to public scrutiny by other researchers, who can evaluate the analysis that is carried out by the original researchers of the data (that is, a secondary analysis).
* It therefore helps to counter accusations that an analysis might have been influenced by a researcher's values or biases.

(continued)

- It allows the data to be reused in other ways from those intended by the original researcher—for example, in the light of new theoretical ideas or analytic strategies.

However, it has to be recognized that the procedure is very time-consuming. It also requires good equipment, usually in the form of a digital audio recorder and microphone. Transcription also very quickly results in a daunting pile of paper. Also, recording equipment may be daunting for interviewees.

It is also worth bearing in mind that, in our experience, focus group research, which is the subject of Chapter 21, can be difficult to transcribe. This is because people in the discussions often talk over each other, in spite of warnings by the **moderator** not to do so. Even a high-quality microphone will not readily deal with this issue. One possibility is to video-record, as well as audio-record. However, this is likely to be beyond the means of most students and also requires a very suitable environment for the focus group. The possible problems of transcription should be borne in mind if you are considering using a focus group.

Recording and transcription

We have already made the point on several occasions that, in qualitative research, the interview is usually audio-recorded and transcribed whenever possible (see Tips and skills 'Why you should record and transcribe interviews'). Qualitative researchers are frequently interested not just in *what* people say but also in the *way* that they say it. If this aspect is to be fully woven into an analysis, it is necessary for a complete account of the series of exchanges in an interview to be available. Also, because the interviewer is supposed to be highly alert to what is being said—following up interesting points made, prompting and probing where necessary, drawing attention to any inconsistencies in the interviewee's answers—it is best if he or she is not distracted by having to concentrate on getting down notes on what is said.

As with just about everything in conducting business research, there is a cost, in that the use of a digital audio recorder may disconcert respondents, who become self-conscious or alarmed at the prospect of their words being preserved. Most people accede to the request for the interview to be audio-recorded, though it is not uncommon for a small number to refuse (see Research in focus 20.6). When faced with refusal, you should still go ahead with the interview, as it is highly likely that useful information will still be forthcoming. For example, Prasad (1993; see Research in focus 20.2) recounts that, in the few

Research in focus 20.6
Getting it recorded and transcribed: an illustration of two problems

Rafaeli et al. (1997) conducted semi-structured interviews with twenty female administrators in a university business school in order to study the significance of dress at the workplace. They write:

> Everyone we contacted agreed to participate. Interviews took place in participants' offices or in a school lounge and lasted between 45 minutes and three hours. We recorded and transcribed all but two interviews: 1 participant refused to be taped, and the tape recorder malfunctioned during another interview. For interviews not taped, we recorded detailed notes. We assured all participants that their responses would remain confidential and anonymous and hired an outside contractor to transcribe the interviews.
>
> (1997: 14)

Even though overall this interview study was highly successful, generating eighteen interviews that were recorded and transcribed, it does show two kinds of problems qualitative interviewers can face—namely, hardware malfunctions and refusals to be recorded.

Tips and skills
Transcribing interviews

If you are doing research for a project or dissertation, you may not have the resources to pay for professional transcription, and, unless you are an accurate touch typist, it may take you longer than the suggested five to six hours per hour of speech. The important thing to bear in mind is that you must allow sufficient time for transcription and be realistic about how many interviews you are going to be able to transcribe in the time available.

instances where employees at Paragon indicated discomfort with being recorded, she took notes during the interview and wrote these up after the session. The summary notes were then shown to the interviewee, who evaluated their accuracy. This advice also applies to cases of recorder malfunction (again see Research in focus 20.6). Among those who do agree to be audio-recorded, there will be some who will not get over their alarm at being confronted with a microphone. As a result, some interviews may not be as interesting as you might have hoped. In qualitative research, there is often quite a large amount of variation in the amount of time that interviews take. For example, in Milkman's (1997) study of technological change at General Motors, the length of the interviews ranged between forty-five minutes and four hours. Similarly, Marshall's (1995) (see Key concept 17.5) research involved interviews with women managers that lasted between one-and-a-half and two hours. It should not be assumed that shorter interviews are necessarily inferior to longer ones, but very short ones that are a product of interviewee non-cooperation or anxiety about being audio-recorded are likely to be less useful. In the extreme, when an interview has produced very little of significance, it may not be worth the time and cost of transcription. Thankfully, such occasions are relatively unusual. If people do agree to be interviewed, they usually do so in a cooperative way and loosen up after initial anxiety about the microphone. As a result, even short interviews are often quite revealing.

The problem with transcribing interviews is that it is very time-consuming. Pettigrew (1985) notes that his interviews at Imperial Chemical Industries (ICI) produced around 500 hours of audio-recorded information for analysis, which were either completely transcribed or coded onto 8×5 inch cards according to predetermined and emergent categories. Similarly, in their study of traders and managers in four investment banks, Willman et al. (2002) interviewed 118 traders and trader-managers and 10 senior managers. Interviews averaged one hour in duration, and they were all recorded and transcripts were produced. It is best to allow around five to six hours

for transcription for every hour of speech. Also, transcription yields vast amounts of paper, which you will need to wade through when analysing the data. Prasad (1993) reports that her 34 interviews on computerization (see Research in focus 20.2) generated nearly 800 pages of interview transcripts that needed to be analysed, in addition to over 1800 pages of field notes from observations. It is clear, therefore, that while transcription has the advantage of keeping intact the interviewee's (and interviewer's) words, it does so by piling up the amount of text to be analysed. It is no wonder that writers such as Lofland and Lofland (1995) advise that the analysis of qualitative data is not left until all the interviews have been completed and transcribed. To procrastinate may give the researcher the impression that he or she faces a monumental task. Also, there are good grounds for making analysis an ongoing activity, because it allows the researcher to be more aware of emerging themes that he or she may want to ask about in a more direct way in later interviews. Ongoing analysis is also very much recommended by proponents of approaches to qualitative data analysis such as grounded theory (see Chapter 24).

It is easy to take the view that transcription is a relatively unproblematic translation of the spoken into the written word. However, given the reliance on transcripts in qualitative research based on interviews, the issue should not be taken lightly. The first question to consider is whether to do the transcription yourself, or to use secretarial assistance. Transcribers need to be trained in much the same way that interviewers do. Moreover, even among experienced transcribers, errors can creep in. For example, Spender (1989) describes how, of the thirty-four interviews in his sample, twenty-five were transcribed. During the exploratory stages of the research this was done by assistants. However, this proved unsatisfactory, as 'there are important data in the respondent's intonations, hesitations, etc. which need to be available'. He concluded that 'the recording can help to recapture the actual data, which is neither the recording, nor the transcript, but the researcher's experience of the interview in its own context' (1989: 82). Poland (1995) has

Tips and skills
Conventions when using direct quotations from an interview

When you are transcribing an interview, it is important that the written text reproduces exactly what the interviewee said, word for word. For this reason, if there are parts of the interview that you cannot hear properly on the recording, do not be tempted to guess or make them up. Instead indicate in your transcript that there is a missing word or phrase, for example by using the convention {???}. This helps to give the reader confidence in your data collection process. However, people rarely speak in fully formed sentences. They often repeat themselves and they may have verbal 'tics' in the form of a common word or phrase that is repeated either through habit or just because they like it! So when it comes to writing up your research, when you will probably wish to quote directly from the interview transcripts, you may want to edit out some of these digressions for the sake of length and ease of understanding. However, you must make sure that you do not paraphrase the words of the speaker and then claim these as the actual words that were spoken because this is misleading, and there is always the possibility that someone reading your work might suspect that people did not really speak in such a fluent way. The use of certain conventions when quoting from an interview transcript helps to overcome these problems.

- Use quotation marks to indicate that this is a direct quotation or indicate this by consistently setting quotes so they stand out from the main body of text—for example, by indenting them or by using a different font, in a similar way to how you would quote at length from a book. This makes it immediately apparent to the reader that this is a direct quotation, and it enables you to differentiate between your presentation of the data and your analysis of it.

- If it is appropriate in relation to ethical considerations (see Chapter 6), indicate who is speaking in the quotation, either introducing the speaker before the quotation by saying something like 'As John put it,' or 'Anne explained her reasons for this', or attribute the quotation to the interviewee immediately afterwards, for example by writing his or her pseudonym or [Interviewee 1] in square brackets.

- If you wish to quote the first sentence from a section of speech and then a sentence or two further on from the transcript, use the convention of three consecutive dots to indicate the break point.

- If an interviewee omits a word from a sentence that is a grammatical omission or if the interviewee refers to a subject in a way that does not make its meaning clear and you need to provide readers with more contextual information so that they can understand the quote, use the convention of parentheses or square brackets in which you insert the words you have added.

- Finally, one of the most difficult things about presenting interview data as part of your analysis is that it can take some effort and perseverance to create a smooth flow to the text because of the switches between your 'voice', as the researcher, and the 'voices' of the interviewees, which can make the text seem quite fragmented. For this reason it is important to introduce direct quotes before you present them and then take a sentence or two of your analysis to explain in your own words how you have interpreted them. In this way you construct a narrative that guides the reader through your data and shows why you have chosen the particular quotations you have as illustrative of particular themes or concepts.

These conventions are applied in the example that follows, which is taken from an article that reports the findings from an interview study of Irish women entering the labour force (Collins and Wickham 2004; see Research in focus 3.20). As this study involved interviewing the women on more than one occasion, the authors also included specification of whether this was the first or second interview at the end of each quotation.

> Grace still hopes to move out of retail work and plans to start a bed and breakfast business:
>
> I am aiming (to) leave the retailing industry completely . . . and I work in (an area of Dublin) which is logistically quite far from where I live and people say to me 'would you not get a transfer' . . . and I say why would I transfer from the devil to the deep blue sea. I'd want to move into something completely different . . . I'd hate to think that was my only ambition to get the company to move me to a different store. (First interview)

provided some fascinating examples of mistakes in transcription that can be the result of many different factors (mishearing, fatigue, carelessness). For example, one transcript contained the following passage:

> I think unless we want to become like other countries, where people have, you know, democratic freedoms . . .

But the actual words on the audio recording were:

> I think unless we want to become like other countries, where people have no democratic freedoms . . .
>
> (Poland 1995: 294)

Steps clearly need to be taken to check on the quality of transcription.

Flexibility in the interview

One further point to bear in mind is that you need to be generally flexible in your approach to interviewing in qualitative research. This advice is not just to do with needing to be responsive to what interviewees say to you and following up interesting points that they make. Such flexibility *is* important and is an important reminder that, with semi-structured interviewing, you should not turn the interview into a kind of structured interview but with open questions. Flexibility is important in such areas as varying the order of questions, following up leads, and clearing up inconsistencies in answers. Flexibility is important in other respects, such as coping with audio recording equipment breakdown and refusals by interviewees to allow a recording to take place (see Research in focus 20.6). A further element is that interviewers often find that, as soon as they switch off their audio recorders, the interviewee continues to ruminate on the topic of interest and frequently will say more interesting things than in the interview. It is usually not feasible to switch the machine back on again, so try to take some notes, either while the person is talking or as soon as possible after the interview. Such 'unsolicited accounts' can often be the source of revealing information or views (Hammersley and Atkinson 1995). This is certainly what M. Parker (2000) found in connection with his research on three British organizations—a National Health Service District Health Authority, a building society, and a manufacturing company—which was based primarily on semi-structured interviews: 'Indeed, some of the most valuable parts of the interview took place after the tape had been switched off, the closing intimacies of the conversation being prefixed with a silent or explicit "Well, if you want to know what I really think . . .". Needless to say, a visit to the toilet to write up as much as I could remember followed almost immediately' (2000: 236).

Telephone interviewing

Telephone interviewing is quite common in survey research, as noted in Chapter 9. However, it has not been used a great deal in qualitative research. It is likely to have certain benefits when compared to face-to-face qualitative interviewing. One of these is cost, since it will be much cheaper to conduct qualitative interviews by telephone, just as it is with survey interviewing. It is likely to be especially useful for hard-to-reach groups and when interviewer safety is a consideration. Further, it may be that asking sensitive questions by telephone will be more effective, since interviewees may be less distressed about answering when the interviewer is not physically present. It may also be that in organizations where the telephone is a core means of service delivery, such as call centres, or organizations located overseas, the use of telephone interviewing as a research method may be more appropriate and more practical. For example, Patwardhan,

Tips and skills
Transcribing sections of an interview

Some interviews or at least large portions of them are sometimes not very useful, perhaps because interviewees are reticent or their answers are not as relevant to your research topic as you had hoped. There seems little point in transcribing material that you know is unlikely to be fruitful. It may be that, for many of your interviews, it would be better to listen to them closely first, at least once or more usually twice, and then transcribe only those portions that you think are useful or relevant. However, this may mean that you miss certain things or that you have to go back to the recordings at a later stage in your analysis to try to find something that emerges as significant only later on.

Telling it like it is
To transcribe or not to transcribe?

Angharad decided to transcribe all ten of her interviews in their entirety, as she explains in this extract from our interview with her.

Emma: Uh-huh. And did you record the interviews or take notes? How did you deal with it?

Angharad: I took notes, but I recorded all the interviews as well and transcribed all of those.

Emma: Right.

Angharad: I only took notes just in case it didn't work.

Emma: Yes, that's always a good idea. And in terms of the transcription, that's quite a big job. How did you find that?

Angharad: Horrible! It was horrible! It was a mission, but I was so glad that I did it actually because it made actually writing up the analysis and the research and thinking about it so much easier when you've got it in front of you rather than if I'd had to sit there and listen to the tapes over and over again. I think it would have been a lot more difficult.

Emma: Hmmm. I mean it is a time-consuming business as well. How long did it take you?

Angharad: I did it over Christmas—not actually on Christmas Day! [*chuckles*]—but I'd say it probably took me a week pretty much solidly to write them all up.

Lucie also found the process of transcribing her interviews to be very time-consuming, but she did also see benefits in the process: 'It was quite tedious because you have to write down everything that they say, even the kind of things that you know you won't be using. And I'm not a touch-typist or anything, so I had to like go back and listen over again. It took a long time. It would take three times the amount of time of the interview to transcribe it. Even longer actually! But it was quite useful because listening over again you pick up on things that you didn't pick up initially, but I didn't know if it was me reading into it too much because I'd heard it so many times. I was like "Oh, that's interesting!" and "What did she mean by that?" So I thought it was useful in that sense, but it was quite a long process'.

Karen, on the other hand, did not transcribe any of her fifteen interviews. Instead she took detailed notes that included some direct quotes from her interviewees. She explained: 'I think, looking back on it, I would have liked to have either had somebody else sitting in on the interview with me or to have an audio-recorder, but at the time it just wasn't possible. You just sort of grabbed a bit of time when you had it. I did some over the lunch hour and some sort of, you know, early in the morning when people had just got into work. It was just when I could actually get hold of people, but I think, looking back when I went back to some of my scripts I was sort of like you know, "What exactly did I mean there?" But I'd written down quotes, which I think was the most important thing because I'd captured exactly what some people said.'

Our final example is Tom, who transcribed the majority of his interviews but did not transcribe sections that he judged were unlikely to be useful: 'I didn't actually transcribe everything that was said to me because sometimes people would go off on a big explanation of technical procedures in the call centre, which I knew wasn't going to answer any of my research questions because I wasn't interested in making any technical recommendations about the organization of the work and so when people started going on into kind of procedures and how they prioritized calls I thought "There's no point in me transcribing this because it's not going to help me in any way." So I was a bit selective although I still had to transcribe most of it.'

Noble, and Nishihara (2009) were interested in the use of strategic deception by call centre operators to develop relationships with consumers, through such tactics as giving a Western 'pseudo name' (2009: 321), or pretending that the call centre was in a location in the USA or UK rather than in India. They carried out twelve face-to-face and nine telephone interviews with call centre operators who worked for a health care financial service company

Tips and skills
Digital audio recording and
speech-recognition software

Digital voice recording means that interviews can be played back over and over again (for example, to try to catch a word that is difficult to hear). Files are transferred from the recorder to a computer following the interview and can also be played back—for example, on an MP3 player or via speakers connected to a computer. Digital voice recorders are also extremely small, easy to use, light, and portable, making them unobtrusive in a research interview and easy to carry.

Digital recording also enables the use of digital editing programs to adjust recording levels, adjust volume between different speakers, reduce background noise, extract information to protect anonymity, or cut out unwanted sections of recording (Stockdale 2002). There is also transcription software available that allows you to insert tags that show up in the transcribed text. When reading the transcript, you can click the tag and listen to the appropriate section of the audio recording. However, there are certain disadvantages. First, there is the cost of the digital recorder, and you will probably also need an external microphone, because the internal microphones are often of insufficient quality. Secondly, the files take up a considerable amount of computer memory—for example, a one-hour interview, recorded in mono format, can consume around 6MB of memory. This can be partly overcome by using a compression scheme that reduces the size of the file. Third, there is the risk of inadvertently deleting the file. Finally, the technology is still quite new and rapidly changing, so there are various systems on the market and choosing which one to commit to can be difficult.

There are a number of speech-recognition or voice-to-text software packages emerging, which claim to enable automatic transcription. Given the time-consuming nature of manual transcription, this superficially might seem very attractive, although they require a great deal of perseverance so that the software becomes accustomed to the speaker's voice. Harlow et al. (2003) describe how this was used to assist older participants in telling their life stories. The researchers used a digital audio recorder and headset microphone to interface with a personal computer on which a speech-recognition software program had been installed. The use of speech-recognition software requires the interviewee to complete an initial speech training. This provides the computer with a sample of his or her speech, which it uses to recognize the rest of the interview. This took twenty-five minutes at the start of each interview and involved the interviewee reading sixteen pages of written text into the recorder. The main challenge arose from having to correct the machine-generated text so that it matched the audio recording. This involved having to retype words or whole phrases that the software program had misinterpreted. The researchers note 'almost always the software program would get confused if people talked in asides. This was problematic as most if not all interviewees had occasions when they would start a sentence and then diverge and start talking in an aside' (Harlow et al. 2003: 399). The editing process averaged a staggering seven minutes per one minute of audio. As Harlow notes, 'someone with good typing skills could actually have transcribed the stories in less time than it took me to correct them' (Harlow et al. 2003: 404). To an extent, these difficulties can be overcome by 'vocabulary building', gradually correcting words that the computer gets wrong, but this has to be done using the voice of the original speaker, which is problematic in an interview study. Speech-recognition software thus might seem very attractive, but its effectiveness is limited in translating naturally occurring speech, with all its quick asides and lack of punctuation, into written text. However, the technology is developing fast, and it is reported that later versions of the software may require less voice training time. Some researchers have adapted to the use of speech-recognition software and the difficulty of getting interviewees voice-trained for the software by using their own voices to speak back all of the recording into the microphone so that their speech alone is processed by the software. They use a headset to listen to the recording and simultaneously speak what is said into the microphone, though it is necessary to keep on stopping and starting the recording that is being listened to.

Tips and skills
Translating interview data

As more and more business and management research is conducted from international or cross-cultural perspectives, this raises potential language and translation problems associated with collecting data in a language other than English and then translating it into English for the purposes of reporting it in a journal article or writing a dissertation. Xian (2008) argues that much of the discussion about this issue to date has been positivistic in orientation, seeing translation purely as a technical exercise rather than an interpretative process. Instead she argues that interview translation is based on the negotiation of cultural differences between the interviewer and the interviewee. Drawing on her study of Chinese women's narratives, she suggests that 'the translation process constitutes a (re)construction of the social reality of a culture in a different language, in which the translator interacts with the data, actively interpreting social concepts and meanings' (2008: 233). Xian identifies three types of problem associated with translating interview data:

1. *Linguistic.* This includes situations where interviewees use words for which there is no equivalent in English, or grammatical structures that cannot be translated easily.

2. *Sociocultural.* This includes difficulties associated with translating idioms or proverbs from one language to another that rely on socio-historical knowledge for their meaning. Xian recommends the use of footnotes to provide the contextual understanding through which the translation can be made meaningful. However, Xian is cautious about back-translating the transcript into the primary language and asking interviewees to verify the back-translation because of concern that they would just not be able to recognize their own accounts.

3. *Methodological.* Taking a postmodern perspective (see Chapter 29), Xian argues that translation is a process that involves the translator imposing his or her authority on the foreign culture. Instead she recommends a more reflexive approach that involves acknowledging and working with the difficulties associated with translation and not allowing silences to be overlooked.

Translation, she concludes, is therefore a sensemaking process that involves the translator's knowledge, social background, and personal experience.

in India in order qualitatively to explore the types of deception used with Western consumers. The authors state that the decision to carry out face-to-face versus telephone interviews was made purely for practical reasons; international telephone interviews made from the USA where the researchers worked were the second choice in cases where it was not possible to meet the interviewee face to face. However, it may be argued that, because call centre workers use the telephone as their main medium of communication with consumers, they might be more comfortable participating in a telephone interview study

than other groups of employees. Furthermore, since this study focused on ethically sensitive practices—that is, call centre workers lying to consumers, and the training given by the company to support these deceptive practices—it could be that the lack of physical proximity between the researcher and the participants enabled by telephone interviewing increased the employees' sense of anonymity and encouraged them to participate in the study.

Certain issues about the use of telephone interviewing in qualitative research need to be borne in mind. Most obviously, it will not be appropriate to some

Tips and skills
Keeping the recorder going

Since interviewees sometimes 'open up' at the end of the interview, perhaps just when the audio recorder has been switched off, there are good grounds for suggesting that you should keep it switched on for as long as possible. So, when you are winding the interview down, don't switch off the recorder immediately.

groups of interviewees, such as those with no or limited access to telephones. Secondly, it is unlikely to work well with very long interviews. It is much easier for the interviewee to terminate a telephone interview than one conducted in person. This is especially significant for qualitative interviews, which are often time-consuming for interviewees. Thirdly, it is not possible to observe body language to see how interviewees respond in a physical sense to questions. Body language may be important, because through it the interviewer may be able to discern such things as discomfort, puzzlement, or confusion. It should also be borne in mind that there can be technical difficulties with recording telephone interviews. Special equipment may be needed, and there is always the possibility that the line will be poor. Increasingly, researchers are using Skype as an alternative to telephone interviewing; this will be covered in Chapter 28.

Life history and oral history interviews

Two special forms of the kind of interview associated with qualitative research are *life history* and *oral history* interviews.

The life history interview is associated with the **life history method**, where it is often combined with various kinds of personal documents such as diaries, photographs, and letters. This method is also referred to as the biographical method. A life history interview is a kind of unstructured interview covering the totality of an individual's life. It documents 'the inner experience of individuals, how they interpret, understand, and define the world around them' (Faraday and Plummer 1979: 776).

Life history methodology is useful in situations when the researcher is attempting to understand the complex processes whereby people make sense of their organizational reality. Musson (1998) suggests that it can provide answers to such research questions as: How does socialization take place in organizations? How are organizational careers created and maintained? How do certain managerial styles come to be accepted as natural? What influence do leaders and founders have on organizational culture?

Despite the suggested relevance of life history interviews to organizational research, there has been only a trickle of empirical studies that have used this approach over the years. Bowen and Hisrich (1986) suggest that a very 'uneven picture' emerges of the female entrepreneur owing to a lack of published research. The few studies that exist tend to employ 'very small samples' and 'seldom attempt to be representative' (1986: 404). They suggest that longitudinal studies following the careers of entrepreneurs over time would enable development of a life cycle conception of the careers of female entrepreneurs and they recommend the use of a life history approach.

The life history method has tended to suffer because of an erroneous treatment of the life in question as a sample of one and hence of limited generalizability. However, it has clear strengths from the point of view of the qualitative researcher: its unambiguous emphasis on the point of view of the life in question and a clear commitment to the processual aspects of social life, showing how events unfold and interrelate in people's lives. The terms *life history* and *life story* are sometimes employed interchangeably, but R. L. Miller (2000: 19) suggests that the latter is an account someone gives about his or her life and that a life history dovetails a life story with other sources, such as diaries and letters (of the kind discussed in Chapter 23).

An example of the life history interview approach in organizational research is provided by Musson in the context of her research on how general medical practitioners in the UK experienced and understood the 1990 health care reforms. As the research progressed, it became apparent to Musson that life histories of key actors were significant in the way that changes were understood and experienced.

> I directed the storytelling process to a large extent by asking individuals to tell me about when and how their understanding of the purpose of the organization shifted . . . These stories differed from focusing on the history of an individual's marital difficulties, to telling me a story about an individual patient and the way she was treated by the GPs in the practice . . . Likewise, I asked people to tell me about their lives

Research in focus 20.7
Constructionism in a life history study of occupational careers

In an article on the concept of occupational career by Bosley, Arnold, and Cohen (2009), an explicitly constructionist stance was taken. Rather than viewing careers as a relatively fixed series of stages through which people progress, Bosley et al. researched careers as social constructions that are highly contingent on a series of experiences and on other individuals who influence the occupational directions that people take. As the authors put it: 'career is seen as social practice, constituted by actors themselves in and through their relationships with others, and as they move through time and space. It is an iterative and on-going process' (2009: 1498). The authors employed a life story method in which twenty-eight employees were interviewed. The interviews 'elicited participants' accounts of their careers from school-leaving to present day. Describing encounters with helpers in the context of preceding and subsequent events enabled participants to recall and identify significant career helpers and the role played by helpers in shaping their careers' (2009: 1499). For each interviewee, a narrative account was generated that portrayed each interviewee's career in terms of contacts, relationships, and encounters that shaped his or her career direction. Out of these narratives, the authors forged a typology of career shaping roles: adviser, informant, witness, gatekeeper, and intermediary. Each role is associated with a different kind of impact on employees' career trajectories and decision-making. The authors write: 'shaping encounters served as a vehicle through which participants negotiated with and navigated through the structural environments in which they were situated' (2009: 1515). The constructionism associated with this research lies in its emphasis on interviewees, and the events and people that were significant in the course and direction of their careers.

---

in previous organizations and how they had experienced these; what they had found rewarding, constraining or difficult to make sense of, and how this differed in their current organization. Again, the open ended structure of the narratives allowed people to introduce subjects of major importance to them.

(Musson 1998: 16)

Miller suggests there has been a resurgence of interest in recent years, and Chamberlayne, Bornat, and Wengraf (2000) argue that there has been a recent 'turn to biographical methods'. To a large extent, the revival of the approach derives from a growth of interest in the role and significance of agency in social life. The revival is largely associated with the growing use of life story interviews and especially in association with *narrative analysis* (see Chapter 22). The growing use of such interviews has come to be associated less and less with the study of a single life (or indeed just one or two lives) and increasingly with the study of several lives (see Research in focus 20.7 for an example).

Plummer (2001) draws a useful distinction between three types of life story:

1. *Naturalistic life stories*. These are life stories that occur whenever people reminisce or write autobiographies, or when job applicants write out letters of application and are interviewed.

2. *Researched life stories*. These are life stories that are solicited by researchers with a social scientific purpose in mind. Most research based on life history/story interviews are of this kind.

3. *Reflexive and recursive life stories*. This recognizes that the life story is always a construction in which the interviewer is implicated. An *oral history* interview is usually somewhat more specific in tone in that the subject is asked to reflect upon specific events or periods in the past. It too is sometimes combined with other sources, such as documents. The chief problem with the oral history interview (which it shares with the life history interview) is the possibility of bias introduced by memory lapses and distortions (Grele 1998). On the other hand, oral history testimonies have allowed the voices to come through of groups that are typically marginalized in historical research (a point that also applies to life history interviews), either because of their lack of power or because they are typically regarded as unexceptional (Samuel 1976).

Feminist research and interviewing in qualitative research

Unstructured and semi-structured interviewing have become prominent methods of data gathering within a feminist research framework. In part, this is a reflection of the preference for qualitative research among feminist researchers, but it also reflects a view that the kind of interview with which qualitative research is associated allows many of the goals of feminist research to be realized. Indeed, the view has been expressed that, 'Whilst several brave women in the 1980s defended quantitative methods, it is nonetheless still the case that not just qualitative methods, but the in-depth face-to-face interview has become the paradigmatic "feminist method"' (Kelly, Burton, and Regan 1994: 34). This comment is enlightening because it implies that it is not simply that qualitative research is seen by many writers and researchers as more consistent with a feminist position than quantitative research, but that specifically qualitative interviewing is seen as especially appropriate. The point that is being made here is not necessarily that such interviewing is somehow more in tune with feminist values than, say, ethnography (especially since it is often an ingredient of ethnographic research). Instead, it could be that the intensive and time-consuming nature of ethnography means that, although it has great potential as an approach to feminist research (see Chapter 19), qualitative interviewing is often preferred because it is usually less invasive in these respects.

However, it is specifically interviewing of the kind conducted in qualitative research that is seen as having potential for a feminist approach, not the structured interview with which survey research is associated. Why might one type of interview be consistent with a sensitivity to feminism and the other not? In a frequently cited article, Oakley outlines the following points about the standard survey interview.

- It is a one-way process—the interviewer extracts information or views from the interviewee.
- The interviewer offers nothing in return for the extraction of information. For example, interviewers using a structured interview do not offer information or their own views if asked. Indeed, they are typically advised not to do such things because of worries about contaminating their respondents' answers.
- The interviewer–interviewee relationship is a form of hierarchical or power relationship. Interviewers arrogate to themselves the right to ask questions, implicitly placing their interviewees in a position of subservience or inferiority.
- The element of power is also revealed by the fact that the structured interview seeks out information from the perspective of the researcher.
- Because of these points, the standard survey interview is inconsistent with feminism when women interview other women. This view arises because it is seen as indefensible for women to 'use' other women in these ways.

Instead of this framework for conducting interviews, feminist researchers advocate one that establishes:

- a high level of rapport between interviewer and interviewee;
- a high degree of reciprocity on the part of the interviewer;
- the perspective of the women being interviewed;
- a non-hierarchical relationship.

In connection with the reciprocity that she advocates, Oakley noted, for example, that in her research on the transition to motherhood, she was frequently asked questions by her respondents. She argues that it was ethically indefensible for a feminist not to answer when confronted with questions of a certain kind. For Oakley, therefore, the qualitative interview was viewed as a means of resolving the dilemmas that she encountered as a feminist interviewing other women. However, as noted in previous chapters, while this broad adherence to a set of principles for interviewing in feminist research continues, it has been tempered by a greater recognition of the possible value of quantitative research.

An interesting dilemma that is perhaps not so easily resolved is the question of what feminist researchers should do when their own 'understandings and interpretations of women's accounts would either not be shared by some of them [i.e. the research participants], and/or represent a form of challenge or threat to their perceptions, choices and coping strategies' (Kelly, Burton, and Regan 1994: 37). It is the first type of situation that we will examine, at least in part, because while it is of particular significance to feminist researchers, its implications are somewhat broader. It raises the tricky question of how far the commitment of seeing through the eyes of the people you study can and/or should be stretched. Two examples are relevant here. Reinharz (1992: 28–9) cites the case of an American study by M. Andersen (1981), who interviewed twenty 'corporate wives', who came across as happy with their lot and were supportive of feminism only in relation to employment discrimination. Andersen interpreted their responses to her questions as indicative of 'false consciousness'—in other words, she did not really believe her interviewees. When Andersen wrote an article on her findings, the women wrote a letter rejecting her account, affirming that women can be fulfilled as wives and mothers. A similar situation confronted Millen (1997) when she interviewed thirty-two British female scientists using 'semi-structured, in-depth individual interviewing' (1997: 4.6). As Millen puts it:

> There was a tension between my interpretation of their reported experience as sex-based, and the meaning the participants themselves tended to attribute to their experience, since the majority of respondents did not analyse these experiences in terms of patriarchy or sex–gender systems, but considered them to be individualised, or as 'just something that had to be coped with' . . . From my external, academically privileged vantage point, it is clear that sexism pervades these professions, and that men are assumed from the start by other scientists to be competent scientists of status whilst women have to prove themselves, overcome the barrier of their difference before they are accepted. These women, on the other hand, did not generally view their interactions in terms of gendered social systems. There is therefore a tension between their characterisation of their experience and my interpretation of it . . .
>
> (1997: 5.6, 5.9)

Three interesting issues are thrown up by these two accounts. First, how can such a situation arise? This is an issue that pervades qualitative research that makes claims to reveal social reality as viewed by members of the setting in question. If researchers are genuinely seeing through others' eyes, the 'tension' to which Millen refers should not arise. However, it clearly can and does, and this strongly suggests that qualitative researchers are more affected by their own perspectives and research questions when collecting and analysing data than might be expected from textbook accounts of the research process. Secondly, there is the question of how to handle such a 'tension'—that is, how do you reconcile the two accounts? M. Andersen's (1981) solution to the tension she encountered was to reinterpret her findings in terms of the conditions that engender the contentment she uncovered. Thirdly, given that feminist research is often concerned with wider political goals of emancipation, a tension between participants' world views and the researcher's position raises moral questions about the appropriateness of imposing an interpretation that is not shared by research participants themselves. Such an imposition could hardly be regarded as consistent with the principle of a non-hierarchical relationship in the interview situation.

Therefore, while qualitative interviewing has become a highly popular research method for feminist researchers because of its malleability into a form that can support the principles of feminism, interesting questions are raised in terms of the relationship between researchers' and participants' accounts. Such questions have a significance generally for the conduct of qualitative research.

Qualitative interviewing versus participant observation

The aim of this section is to compare the merits and limitations of interviewing in qualitative research with those of participant observation. These are probably the two most prominent methods of data collection in qualitative research, so there is some virtue in assessing their strengths, a debate that was first begun many years ago (Becker and Geer 1957a, b; Trow 1957). In this section, interviewing is being compared to participant observation rather than ethnography, because the latter invariably entails a significant amount of interviewing. So too

does participant observation, but in this discussion we will be following the principle that we outlined in Key concept 19.1—namely, that the term will be employed to refer to the specifically observational activities in which the participant observer engages. As noted in Key concept 19.1, the term 'ethnography' is being reserved for the wide range of data collection activities in which ethnographers engage—one of which is participant observation—along with the written account that is a product of those activities.

Advantages of participant observation in comparison to qualitative interviewing

Seeing through others' eyes

As noted in Chapters 2 and 17, this is one of the main tenets of qualitative research, but, on the face of it, the participant observer would seem to be better placed for gaining a foothold on social reality in this way. The researcher's prolonged immersion in a social setting would seem to make him or her better equipped to see as others see. The participant observer is in much closer contact with people for a longer period of time; also, he or she participates in many of the same kinds of activity as the members of the social setting being studied. Research that relies on interviewing alone is likely to entail much more fleeting contacts, though in qualitative research interviews can last many hours and reinterviewing is not unusual.

Learning the native language

Becker and Geer (1957a) argued that the participant observer is in the same position as a social anthropologist visiting a distant land, in that, in order to understand a culture, the language must be learned. However, it is not simply the formal language that must be understood in the case of the kinds of business research in which a participant observer in a complex organization engages. It is also very often the 'argot'—the special uses of words and slang that are important to penetrate that culture. Such an understanding is arrived at through the observation of language use.

The taken for granted

Although much important information can be obtained through interviews, some kinds of data cannot be captured through this particular research method. The interview relies primarily on verbal behavior, so matters that interviewees take for granted are less likely to surface than in participant observation, where implicit features in social life are more likely to be revealed as a result of the observer's continued presence and because of the ability to observe behaviour rather than just to rely on what is said. For example, few interviewees will be able accurately to recollect the dynamics of a meeting involving several people—they may remember parts of what was said, and the nature of the problem under discussion, but are unlikely to recollect how decisions evolved as part of a social process (Whyte 1953), so for this researchers must continue to rely on observation.

Deviant and hidden activities

Much of what we know about patterns of resistance at work, industrial sabotage, and other criminal or deviant activity within organizations has been gleaned from participant observation. For example, Linstead's (1985) account of the practical jokes, general kidding, and games played by bakery workers was obtained through participant observation. Similarly, Collinson's (1988) analysis of humour in the context of a male-dominated workplace (see also Chapter 19) relied partly on non-participant observation to obtain data about the daily jibes, socialization rituals, and initiation ceremonies that characterized daily life on the shopfloor at Slavs. These are areas that insiders are likely to be reluctant to talk about in an interview context alone. Understanding is again likely to come through prolonged interaction. Ethnographers conducting participant observation are more likely to place themselves in situations in which their continued involvement allows them gradually to infiltrate such social worlds and to insinuate themselves into the lives of people who might be sensitive to outsiders.

Sensitivity to context

The participant observer's extensive contact with a social setting allows the context of people's behaviour to be mapped out fully. The participant observer interacts with people in a variety of situations and possibly roles, so that the links between behaviour and context can be forged.

Encountering the unexpected and flexibility

It may be that, because of the unstructured nature of participant observation, it is more likely to uncover unexpected topics or issues. Except with the most unstructured forms of interview, the interview process is likely to entail some degree of closure as the interview guide is put together, which may blinker the researcher slightly. Also, participant observation may be more flexible because of the tendency for interviewers to instil an element of comparability (and hence a modicum of structure) in their questioning of different people. Ditton's (1977) decision at a very late stage in the data collection process to focus on pilferage in the bakery in which he was a participant observer is an example of this feature.

Naturalistic emphasis

Participant observation has the potential to come closer to a naturalistic emphasis, because the qualitative researcher confronts members of a social setting in their natural environments. Interviewing, because of its nature as a disruption of members' normal flow of events, even when it is at its most informal, is less amenable to this feature.

It is unsurprising, therefore, that, when referring to naturalism as a tradition in qualitative research, Gubrium and Holstein (1997) (see Key concept 17.1) largely refer to studies in which participant observation was a prominent component (e.g. Whyte 1955).

Advantages of qualitative interviewing in comparison to participant observation

Issues resistant to observation

It is likely that there is a wide range of issues that are simply not amenable to observation, so that asking people about them represents the only viable means of finding out about them within a qualitative research strategy. For example, in Emma Bell's (2001) research on payment systems in the chemical industry, it was not really possible to explore the systems and rules whereby payments were made by observing shopfloor practices, although the latter was very useful in gaining an understanding of the cultural context in which payment systems were located. For most workers, payment is an issue that surfaces through consideration of issues that relate to the 'effort-bargain', and this understanding was more readily accessed through interviews.

Reconstruction of events

Qualitative research frequently entails the reconstruction of events by asking interviewees to think back over how a certain series of events unfolded in relation to a current situation. An example is Pettigrew's (1985) research on ICI, which entailed interviewing about contemporaneous events but also included 'retrospective interviewing', as Pettigrew defines it (see Research in focus 3.16). This reconstruction of events is something that cannot be accomplished through participant observation alone.

Ethical considerations

There are certain areas that could be observed—albeit indirectly through hidden hardware such as a microphone—but to do so would raise ethical considerations. For example, Ditton (1977) never disclosed to his fellow workers in the bakery that he was interested in pilferage, although he did seek to protect their anonymity by omitting names and changing other irrelevant facts in the published study. He goes on to claim that he could not have disclosed his interest in pilferage, partly because he did not decide to concentrate on this subject until some time after the conclusion of the study. However, in this case, participant observation does raise ethical issues relating to the observation of criminal activity and the extent to which the researcher actively participates in it.

Reactive effects

The question of reactive effects is by no means a straightforward matter. As with structured observation (see Chapter 12), it might be anticipated that the presence of a participant observer would result in reactive effects (see Key concept 12.8). People's knowledge of the fact that they are being observed may make them behave less naturally. However, participant observers, like researchers using structured observation, typically find that people become accustomed to their presence and begin to behave more naturally the longer they are around. Indeed, members of social settings sometimes express surprise when participant observers announce their imminent departure when they are on the verge of disengagement. Interviewers clearly do not suffer from the same kind of problem, but it could be argued that the unnatural character of the interview encounter can also be regarded as a context within which reactive effects may emerge. Participant observation also suffers from the related problem of observers disturbing the very situation being studied, because conversations and interactions will occur in conjunction with the observer that otherwise would not happen. This is by no means an easy issue to resolve and it seems likely that both participant observation and qualitative interviewing set in motion reactive effects but of different kinds.

Less intrusive in people's lives

Participant observation can be very intrusive in people's lives in that the observer is likely to take up a lot more of their time than in an interview. Interviews in qualitative research can sometimes be very long and reinterviewing is not uncommon, but the impact on people's time will probably be less than having to take observers into account on a regular basis, though it is likely that this feature will vary from situation to situation. Participant observation is likely to be especially intrusive in terms of the amount of people's time taken up when it is in organizational settings. In work organizations, there is a risk that the rhythms of work lives will be disrupted.

Longitudinal research easier

One of the advantages of participant observation is that it is inherently longitudinal in character, because the observer is present in a social setting for a period of time. As a result, change and connections between events can be observed. However, there are limits to the amount of time that participant observers can devote to being away from their normal routines. Consequently, participant observation does not usually extend much beyond two to three years in duration. When participant observation is being conducted into an area of research that is episodic rather than requiring continued observation, a longer time period may be feasible. Pettigrew's (1985) research at ICI combined interviewing in late 1975, 1976, and early 1977, the latter parts of 1980 and early 1981, and again in 1982, with his interventions into the company as a consultant. During that period 134 people were interviewed from the ICI corporate headquarters and the four divisions under study. Several of these individuals were interviewed more than once, and the total number of research interviews amounted to 175. Kanter (1977) employed a similar strategy combining consultant activity with research over a five-year period. Research in focus 20.8 gives an example of a longitudinal telephone interview study that, although it took place over a shorter six-month time period, traced a period of dramatic change following the closure of a car plant that marked the loss of the last remaining British-owned car manufacturer. In summary, interviewing can be carried out within a longitudinal research design somewhat more easily, because repeat interviews may be easier to organize than repeat visits to participant observers' research settings, though the latter is not impossible. Following up interviewees on several occasions is likely to be easier than returning to research sites on a regular basis.

Greater breadth of coverage

In participant observation, the researcher is invariably constrained in his or her interactions and observations to a fairly restricted range of people, incidents, and localities. Participant observation in a large organization, for example, is likely to mean that knowledge of that organization beyond the confines of the department or section in which the observation is carried out is not likely to be very extensive. Interviewing can allow access to a wider variety of people and situations.

Specific focus

As noted in Chapter 17, qualitative research sometimes begins with a specific focus, and indeed Silverman (1993) has been critical of the notion that it should be regarded as an open-ended form of research. Qualitative interviewing would seem to be better suited to such a situation, since the interview can be directed at that focus and its associated research questions. Thus, the research by Bryman and his colleagues on the police had a very specific research focus in line with its Home Office funding— namely, conceptions of leadership among police officers (Bryman, Stephens, and A Campo 1996). The bulk of the data gathering was in two police forces and entailed the interviewing of police officers at all levels using a semi-structured interview guide. As it had such a clear focus, it was more appropriate to conduct the research by interview rather than participant observation, since issues to

Research in focus 20.8
A longitudinal interview study

Following the closure of the MG Rover car plant at Longbridge in the UK Midlands in April 2005, the Work Foundation embarked on a study commissioned by BBC Radio 4 to explore what happened to the workers following the job losses. The interview study was also the basis for a series of three radio programmes broadcast in 2006 to mark the first anniversary of the closure. The aims of the research were to find out if former MG Rover workers had found 'good' jobs or whether they had been forced to accept 'bad' jobs in an already economically disadvantaged region. The researchers also wanted to trace the effects of unemployment on those who had been unable to find jobs, on the workers themselves, their families, and their communities. Letters were sent to all ex-MG Rover workers inviting them to participate in the study, which would involve being interviewed by telephone. There were two waves of data collection: the first was in July 2005, when 273 telephone interviews were conducted with ex-MG Rover workers; the second, in December 2005, involved 232 telephone interviews with the same group (consisting of 83 per cent of the original sample). Although by the second wave of study nearly two-thirds of the sample had been re-employed, many of them were in 'bad' jobs. The researchers conclude that 'as a nation we must learn to proactively and effectively support those affected by structural change in the economy' (Armstrong 2006: 37).

do with leadership notions may not crop up on a regular basis, which would make observation a very extravagant method of data collection.

Overview

When Becker and Geer (1957a: 28) proclaimed over fifty years ago that the 'most complete form of the sociological datum . . . is the form in which the participant observer gathers it', Trow (1957: 33) reprimanded them for making such a universal claim and argued that 'the problem under investigation properly dictates the methods of investigation'. The latter view is very much the one taken in this book. Research methods are appropriate to researching some issues and areas but not others. This discussion of the merits and limitations of participant observation and qualitative interviews is meant simply to

draw attention to some of the considerations that might be taken into account if there is a genuine opportunity to use one or the other in a study.

Equally, and to repeat an earlier point, the comparison is a somewhat artificial exercise, because participant observation is usually carried out as part of ethnographic research and as such it is usually accompanied by interviewing as well as other methods. In other words, participant observers frequently buttress their observations with methods of data collection that allow them access to important areas that are not amenable to observation. However, the aim of the comparison was to provide a kind of balance sheet in considering the strengths and limitations of a reliance on either participant observation or qualitative interview alone. Its aim is to draw attention to some of the factors that might be taken into account in deciding how to plan a study and even how to evaluate existing research.

Checklist

Issues to consider for your qualitative interview

○ Have you devised a clear and comprehensive/informative way of introducing the research to interviewees?

○ Does your interview guide clearly relate to your research questions?

○ Have you piloted the guide with some appropriate respondents?

○ Have you thought about what you will do if your interviewee does not turn up for the interview?

○ Does the guide contain a good mixture of different kinds of questions, such as probing, specifying, and direct questions?

○ Have you ensured that interviews will allow novel or unexpected themes and issues to arise?

○ Is your language in the questions clear, comprehensible, and free of unnecessary jargon?

○ Are your questions relevant to the people you are proposing to interview?

○ Does your interview guide include requests for information about the interviewee, such as his or her age, work experience, position in the firm?

○ Have your questions been designed to elicit reflective discussions, so that interviewees are not tempted to answer in 'yes' or 'no' terms?

○ Do your questions offer a real prospect of seeing the world from your interviewees' point of view rather than imposing your own frame of reference on them?

○ Are you familiar with the setting(s) in which the interviews will take place?

○ Are you thoroughly familiar with and have you tested your recording equipment?

○ Have you thought about how you will present yourself in the interview, such as how you will be dressed?

○ Have you thought about how you will go about putting into operation the skills that make a good interviewer (see Tips and skills 'Criteria of a successful interviewer')?

Key points

- Interviewing in qualitative research is typically of the unstructured or semi-structured kind.

- In qualitative research, interviewing may be the sole method in an investigation or may be used as part of an ethnographic study, or indeed in tandem with another qualitative method.

- Qualitative interviewing is meant to be flexible and to seek out the world views of research participants.

- If an interview guide is employed, it should not be too structured in its application and should allow some flexibility in the asking of questions.

- The qualitative interview should be audio-recorded and then transcribed.

- As with ethnographic research, investigations using qualitative interviews tend not to employ random sampling to select participants.

- The qualitative interview has become an extremely popular method of data collection in feminist studies.

- Whether to use participant observation or qualitative interviews depends in large part on their relative suitability to the research questions being addressed. However, it must also be borne in mind that participant observers invariably conduct some interviews in the course of their investigations.

Questions for review

Differences between the structured interview and the qualitative interview

- How does qualitative interviewing differ from structured interviewing?

Asking questions in the qualitative interview

- What kinds of skill does the interviewer need to develop in qualitative interviewing?

- What kinds of consideration need to be borne in mind when preparing an interview guide?

- What are the differences between unstructured and semi-structured interviewing?

- Could semi-structured interviewing stand in the way of flexibility in qualitative research?

- What kinds of question might be asked in an interview guide?

- Why is it important to record and transcribe qualitative interviews?

Life history and oral history interviews

- What are the differences between life history and oral history interviews?

Feminist research and interviewing in qualitative research

- Why has the qualitative interview become such a prominent research method for feminist researchers?

- What dilemmas might be posed for feminist researchers using qualitative interviewing?

Qualitative interviewing versus participant observation

- Outline the relative advantages and disadvantages of qualitative interviewing and participant observation.

- Does one method seem more in tune with the preoccupations of qualitative researchers than the other?

Online Resource Centre

www.oxfordtextbooks.co.uk/orc/brymanbrm4e/

Visit the Interactive Research Guide that accompanies this book to complete an exercise in Interviewing in Qualitative Research.

21

Focus groups

Chapter outline

The focus group method is an interview with several people on a specific topic or issue. This chapter explores:

- the possible reasons for preferring focus group interviews to individual interviews of the kind discussed in Chapter 20;

- the role of focus groups in market research;

- how focus groups should be conducted in terms of such features as the need for recording, the number and size of groups, how participants can be selected, and how direct the questioning should be;

- the significance of interaction between participants in focus group discussions;

- the suggestion that the focus group method fits particularly well with a feminist research approach;

- some practical difficulties with focus group sessions, such as the possible loss of control over proceedings and the potential for unwanted group effects.

Introduction

We are used to thinking of the interview as something that involves an interviewer and one interviewee. Most textbooks reinforce this perception by concentrating on individual interviews. The focus group technique is a method of interviewing that involves more than one, usually at least four, interviewees. Essentially it is a group interview. Some authors draw a distinction between focus group and group interview techniques. Three reasons are sometimes put forward to suggest a distinction.

- Focus groups typically emphasize a specific theme or topic that is explored in depth, whereas group interviews often span very widely.

- Sometimes group interviews are carried out so that the researcher is able to save time and money by carrying out interviews with a number of individuals simultaneously. However, focus groups are not carried out for this reason.

- The focus group practitioner is invariably interested in the ways in which individuals discuss a certain issue *as members of a group*, rather than simply as individuals. In other words, with a focus group the researcher will be interested in such things as how people respond to each other's views and build up a view out of the interaction that takes place within the group.

However, the distinction between the focus group method and the group interview is by no means clear-cut, and the two terms are frequently employed interchangeably. Boddy (2005) suggests that the confusion is even broader than this, and also includes terms such as the 'nominal group interview', making it difficult for researchers to talk to each other in a common language. Nonetheless, the definition proposed in Key concept 21.1 provides a starting point.

Most focus group researchers undertake their work within the traditions of qualitative research. This means that they are explicitly concerned to reveal how the group participants view the issues with which they are confronted; therefore the researcher will aim to provide a fairly unstructured setting for the extraction of their views and perspectives. The person who runs the focus group session is usually called the **moderator** or facilitator, and he or she will be expected to guide the session but not to be too intrusive.

Another general point about the focus group method is that, although it has been used for many years in market research to test reactions to products and to advertising initiatives, it has more recently been developed for a wider variety of purposes. Hence focus groups are now used by politicians, not only quantitatively to predict the outcome of an election, but also qualitatively to shape their policies and images. Cowley (2000) reports that one politician used focus group research to determine that he should be filmed only from one side of his face, and he should be made to look older in order to increase voter support. Focus groups are used by film-makers to

Key concept 21.1
What is the focus group method?

The focus group method is a form of group interview in which there are several participants (in addition to the moderator/facilitator); there is an emphasis in the questioning on a particular fairly tightly defined topic; and the accent is upon interaction within the group and the joint construction of meaning. As such, the focus group contains elements of two methods: the group interview, in which several people discuss a number of topics; and what has been called a *focused interview*, in which interviewees are selected because they 'are known to have been involved in a particular situation' (Merton, Fiske, and Kendall 1956: 3) and are asked about that involvement. The focused interview may be administered to individuals or to groups. Thus, the focus group method appends to the focused interview the element of interaction within groups as an area of interest and is more focused than the group interview.

determine the end of a major film run, by art entrepreneurs to determine what paintings will sell, and by CEOs to test corporate communications. However, the popularization of the focus group method may have disadvantages for business and management researchers. For example, Blackburn and Stokes (2000) in their study of small businesses suggest that it was more difficult to convince research audiences of the significance of their focus group research, partly because of the proliferation of the use of focus groups by political parties. Similarly, Cowley (2000) suggests that, in order to distinguish research based on 'strategic qualitative market research focus groups' from research that is done by those who simply decide 'they can run' focus groups, despite their lack of experience, a professional code of conduct is needed. However, it must be remembered that, while the use of focus groups is becoming more widespread, it is by no means a new technique, as it has a long-established use in various forms of research. Based on his experience of academic and market research in an international context, Boddy (2005) distinguishes between the 'focus group interview' and the 'focus group discussion'. The focus group discussion is loosely directed by a facilitator

and involves a group of people who are brought together to discuss a subject of interest with the other members of the group; this can include argument and disagreement but is generally conducted in an open, friendly manner. The focus group interview is more closely controlled by the facilitator and discussion is mainly between the facilitator and the group, rather than between participants. Group members may use hand-held electronic devices to select their preferences and 'mini-questionnaires' may also be used. The focus group interview is more associated with market research, rather than with qualitative research of the kind we are discussing here.

One final point to make is that there is growing interest in the use of online focus groups, which will be covered in the context of Internet-based research methods in Chapter 28. There is evidence that, although they tend to be shorter than comparable face-to-face focus groups, they can generate a considerable amount of relevant data for the researcher (Reid and Reid 2005). When this is viewed in relation to the saving in travel time and cost for both researchers and participants, it is clear that this is a variation on the method that is likely to be used more in the future.

Uses of focus groups

What are the uses of the focus group method? In many ways its uses are bound up with the uses of qualitative research in general, but, over and above these, the following points can be registered:

- The original idea for the focus group—the focused interview—was that people who were known to have

had a certain experience could be interviewed in a relatively unstructured way about that experience. The bulk of the discussion by Merton, Fiske, and Kendall (1956) of the notion of the focused interview was in terms of individual interviews, but their book also considered the extension of the method into group interview contexts. Subsequently, the focus group has become a popular method for researchers examining the ways in which people in conjunction with one another construe the general topics in which the researcher is interested. In management and business, early use of the focus group technique was also seen as a way of helping individuals to define problems and work together to identify potential solutions (Hutt 1979). The dynamics of group discussion could lead individuals to define business problems in new and innovative ways and to stimulate creative ideas for their solution.

- The technique allows the researcher to develop an understanding about *why* people feel the way they do. In a normal individual interview the interviewee is often asked about his or her reasons for holding a particular view, but the focus group approach offers the opportunity of allowing people to probe each other's reasons for holding a certain view. This can be more interesting than the sometimes predictable question-followed-by-answer approach of normal interviews. For one thing, an individual may answer in a certain way during a focus group, but, as he or she listens to others' answers, he or she may want to qualify or modify a view; or alternatively may want to voice agreement to something that he or she probably would not have thought of without the opportunity of hearing the views of others. These possibilities mean that focus groups may also be very helpful in the elicitation of a wide variety of views in relation to a particular issue.

- In focus groups, participants are able to bring to the fore issues in relation to a topic that they deem to be important and significant. This is clearly an aim of individual interviews too, but, because the moderator has to relinquish a certain amount of control to the participants, the issues that concern them can surface. This is clearly an important consideration in the context of qualitative research, since the viewpoints of the people being studied are an important point of departure.

- In conventional one-to-one interviewing, interviewees are rarely challenged; they might say things that are inconsistent with earlier replies or that patently could not be true, but we are often reluctant to point out such deficiencies. In the context of a focus group, individuals will often argue with each other and challenge each other's views. This process of arguing means that the researcher may stand a chance of ending up with more realistic accounts of what people think, because they are forced to think about and possibly revise their views.

- The focus group offers the researcher the opportunity to study the ways in which individuals collectively make sense of a phenomenon and construct meanings around it. It is a central tenet of such theoretical positions as symbolic interactionism that the process of coming to terms with (that is, understanding) social phenomena is not undertaken by individuals in isolation from each other. Instead, it is something that occurs in interaction and discussion with others. In this sense, therefore, focus groups reflect the processes through which meaning is constructed in everyday life and to that extent can be regarded as more naturalistic (see Key concept 3.4 on the idea of naturalism) than individual interviews (Wilkinson 1998).

As we mentioned in the Introduction, focus groups have been used extensively in market research for many years, where the method is employed for such purposes as testing responses to new products and advertising initiatives. According to the UK Association of Qualitative Market Research Practitioners, focus groups represent the most commonly used research method in market research; see the Association for Qualitative Research for more on this: *www.aqrp.co.uk* (accessed 1 November 2014)

Focus groups typically involve groups of six to twelve consumers, who are brought together to discuss their reactions to new products, packaging, advertisements, or promotions. In fact there is a large literature within market research to do with the practices that are associated with focus group research and their implementation (e.g. Calder 1977).

However, the use of focus group methods in market research has attracted its fair share of controversy. Some researchers have suggested that it is a weaker method than, say, experiments or surveys (to name two research approaches that are common in market research). The most frequently mentioned problem is the perceived lack of generalizability—results are not always a reliable indicator of the reactions of the wider population. Criticism is also made of the unsystematic nature of the sample, which is not as rigorous as probability sampling (see Chapter 8). For example, Sudman and Blair (1999: 272) have suggested that, although the focus group method is an excellent tool for gaining insight about markets, 'it should be evident that a group of 10 or so people chosen haphazardly at a single location cannot be expected to reflect the total population of consumers'. A further difficulty stems from the lack of realism associated with focus groups. Participants may be given written or verbal descriptions of a product, or an artist's sketch, but this bears little relation to the real-life experience of choosing a product in a competitive context. Criticisms also stem from problems of reliability. This relates to the role of the moderator and the suggestion that there can be variation in the interpretation of transcripts. Fern (2001) has provided a rebuttal of these criticisms by arguing that the generalizability of focus group findings, as with other research methods, depends on the scale of the sample—a two-group study may have limited generalizability but a 32-group study is another matter. He also defends the reliability of focus groups, suggesting that representativeness can be achieved by stratifying the population and drawing random samples from each stratum. Fern suggests that greater reliability can be gained by using different moderators with different backgrounds (for example, male and female) to conduct group discussions on a relevant topic (for example, gender). The results from each group can then be compared for consistency of interpretation. Overall, however, what seems puzzling is that market researchers are attempting to defend their use of focus group methods in terms of quantitative rather than qualitative criteria; this is mainly because they are being criticized in terms of quantitative research criteria.

Conducting focus groups

There are a number of practical aspects of the conduct of focus group research that require some discussion.

Recording and transcription

As with interviewing for qualitative research, the focus group session will work best if it is recorded and subsequently transcribed. The following reasons are often used to explain this preference:

- One reason is the simple difficulty of writing down not only exactly what people say but also who says it. In an individual interview you might be able to ask the respondent to hold on while you write something down, but to do this in the context of an interview involving several people would be extremely disruptive.

- The researcher will be interested in who expresses views within the group, such as whether certain individuals seem to act as opinion leaders or dominate the discussion. This also means that there is an interest in ranges of opinions within groups; for example, in a session, does most of the range of opinion derive from just one or two people or from most of the people in the group?

- A major reason for conducting focus group research is the fact that it is possible to study the processes whereby meaning is collectively constructed within each session (see above). It would be very difficult to do this by taking notes, because of the need to keep track of *who says* what (see also previous point). If this element is lost, the dynamics of the focus group session would also be lost, and a major rationale for doing focus group interviews rather than individual ones would be undermined.

- Like all qualitative researchers, the focus group practitioner will be interested in not just what people say but *how* they say it—for example, the particular language that they employ. There is every chance that the nuances of language will be lost if the researcher has to rely on notes.

It should be borne in mind that transcribing focus group sessions is more complicated and hence more time-consuming than transcribing traditional interview recordings. This is because you need to take account of *who* is talking in the session, as well as what is said. This is sometimes difficult, since people's voices are not always easy to distinguish. Also, people sometimes talk over each other, which can make transcription even more difficult. In addition, it is extremely important to ensure that you equip yourself with a very high-quality microphone, which is capable of picking up voices, some of which may be quite faint, from many directions. Focus group transcripts always seem to have more missing bits owing to lack of audibility than transcripts from conventional interviews.

A recent development in market research has involved the introduction of virtual or online focus groups, who interact with each other via computer. This overcomes some of the problems associated with recording what goes on in focus groups, but it also raises difficulties. Virtual focus groups are addressed in Chapter 28.

Tips and skills
Transcribing focus group interviews

In Chapter 20, we provided the practical tip that it may not always be desirable or feasible to transcribe the whole of the interview. The same applies to focus group research, which is often more difficult and time-consuming to transcribe than personal interview recordings because of the number of speakers who are involved. The suggestions we made in Chapter 20 in relation to transcribing sections of an interview therefore apply equally well to focus group recordings.

How many groups?

How many groups do you need? Table 21.1 provides an example detailing the composition of a sequence of focus groups that was designed to reflect the impact of the local socio-economic context on small business owner-managers. This was a longitudinal focus group study, so the groups met on several occasions during an eighteen-month period (see Research in focus 21.2). There is a good deal of variation in the numbers of focus groups that are used in any particular study, with the norm being somewhere between twelve and fifteen. However, much lower numbers are not uncommon. Chan et al. (2012) conducted focus group research into the management of stress among expatriate Hong Kong construction professionals in mainland China and held just six groups. Four were from different parts of mainland China, one was a group of Hong Kong professionals who had repatriated from China, and one was group of Hong Kong professionals without expatriate experience.

Clearly, it is unlikely that just one group will suffice the needs of the researcher, since there is always the possibility that the responses are particular to that one group. Obviously, time and resources will be a factor, but there are strong arguments for saying that too many groups will be a waste of time. Calder (1977) proposes that, when the moderator reaches the point that he or she is able to anticipate fairly accurately what the next group is going to say, then there are probably enough groups already. This notion is very similar to the *theoretical saturation* criterion that was briefly introduced in Key concept 18.4. In other words, once your major analytic categories have been saturated, there seems little point in continuing, and so it would be appropriate to bring data collection to a halt. For their study of audience discussion programmes, Livingstone and Lunt (1994: 181) used this criterion: 'The number of focus groups was determined by continuing until comments and patterns began to repeat and little new material was generated.' When this point of theoretical saturation is reached, as an alternative to terminating data collection, there may be a case for moving on to an extension of the issues that have been raised in the focus group sessions that have been carried out.

One factor that may affect the number of groups is whether the researcher feels that the kinds and range of views are likely to be affected by socio-demographic factors such as age, gender, class, and so on. Many focus group researchers like to use stratifying criteria such as these to ensure that groups with a wide range of features will be included. If so, a larger number of groups may be required to reflect the criteria. In connection with the research described in Research in focus 21.2, Blackburn and Stokes (2000) explain that the composition of the

Tips and skills
Number of focus groups

Focus groups take a long time to arrange, and it takes a long time to transcribe the recordings that are made. It is likely that students will not be able to include as many focus group sessions for projects or dissertations as the studies cited in this chapter. You will, therefore, need to make do with a smaller number of groups in most instances. Make sure you are able to justify the number of groups you have chosen and why your data are still significant.

groups was stratified according to business and personal criteria, including gender. A range of business sectors was represented within the focus groups, including manufacturing, construction, and services. Small businesses were defined quite broadly in terms of certain turnover parameters—from a minimum of £50,000 to a maximum of £3,000,000. However, it may be that high levels of diversity are not anticipated in connection with some topics, in which case a large number of groups could represent an unnecessary expense.

One further point to bear in mind when considering the number of groups is that more groups will increase the complexity of your analysis. For example, Schlesinger et al. (1992: 29) report that the fourteen audio-recorded sessions they organized produced over 1400 pages of transcription. This pile of paper was accumulated from discussions in each group of an average of one hour for each of the four screenings that session participants were shown. Although this means that the sessions were longer than is normally the case, it does demonstrate that the amount of data to analyse can be very large, even though a total of fourteen sessions may not sound like a lot to someone unfamiliar with the workings of the method.

Size of groups

How large should groups be? Morgan (1998a) suggests that the typical group size is six to ten members, although in their study of small business owner-managers Blackburn and Stokes (2000) found that discussion in groups of more than eight was difficult to manage, so, as the research progressed, they scaled down the number of participants who were invited on each occasion. One major problem faced by focus group practitioners is people who agree to participate but who do not turn up on the day.

It is almost impossible to control for 'no-shows' other than consciously over-recruiting, a strategy that is sometimes recommended (e.g. Wilkinson 1999a: 188).

In their research into small businesses, Blackburn and Stokes (2000) found that recruiting business-owners to attend a group discussion at a pre-set date and venue away from their business context proved to be a time-consuming process (see Research in focus 21.2). The acceptance rate to invitations was as low as one to ten, and the exercise of ensuring attendance involved a great number of telephone calls to ensure a broad spread of participants. However, after participants had attended one focus group and had got to know each other and exchanged business cards, they were more likely to attend a second time, as they were keen to hear how each other's businesses were developing. Overall the researchers found it very difficult to predict the 'no-show' rate. This meant that the size of their focus groups varied considerably, from three to ten (see Table 21.1). Blackburn and Stokes acknowledge that there were likely to be quite different dynamics in the different-sized groups; in particular, in the smaller groups greater demands were made on each participant to contribute more.

Almost the opposite problem was faced by Milkman (1997) in her study of auto factory workers at the General Motors plant in New Jersey. Milkman and a colleague conducted three focus group discussions at the plant—two with production workers and one with skilled trades workers. Each discussion was held in a conference room inside the plant during regular working hours, lasted around two hours, and was audio-recorded and transcribed. Workers were selected randomly from the plant roster and they were paid their normal wage for the time spent in discussion. This, according to Milkman, 'ensured perfect attendance', but it also 'underscored the project's

Table 21.1

Location and attendees from five focus groups				
Location	Number of participants in each focus group			
	Sept. 1997	Mar. 1998	Nov. 1998	Mar. 1999
Reading	10	5	6	6
London	8	3	6	5
Kidderminster	7	7	3	6
Manchester	5	5	5	7
Glasgow/Hartlepool	6	6	–	–
TOTAL	36	26	26	30

Source: adapted from Blackburn and Stokes (2000).

official status' (1997: 195). She suspects that this made some participants suspicious and less inclined to speak freely.

Morgan (1998a) recommends smaller groups when participants are likely to have a lot to say on the research topic. This is likely to occur when participants are very involved in or emotionally preoccupied with the topic. He also suggests smaller groups when topics are controversial or complex and when gleaning participants' personal accounts is a major goal. Morgan recommends larger groups when involvement with a topic is likely to be low or when the researcher wants 'to hear numerous brief suggestions' (1998a: 75). However, we are not convinced that larger groups are necessarily superior for topics in which participants have little involvement, since it may be more difficult to stimulate discussion in such a context. Larger groups may make it even more difficult if people are rather diffident about talking about a topic about which they know little or have little experience. This was a potential problem in Blackburn and Stokes's (2000) study, where external information, such as government proposals on late-payment legislation, formed the basis for discussion. However, in these instances, the researchers found that participants relied more heavily on their own personal experiences and provided detailed accounts of payment practices in their industry.

Research in focus 21.2
Focus groups in small business research

Blackburn and Stokes (2000) used focus groups in their research into UK small firms across a range of sectors. Their decision was partly driven by a concern that much research into small firms has revealed little about the motivations, rationales, and experiences of business owner-managers. For this, more qualitative research is required, and focus groups were seen as a means through which the culturally different world of the owner-manager can be encountered on a more equal basis.

One of the aims of the focus groups was to capture the immediate reactions of business owners to government statements and the launch of new initiatives. Focus groups were held on four occasions at six-monthly intervals (see Table 21.1) in order to compare their initial reactions with later, more considered views.

Each focus group had three main objectives:

- to generate data on owner-managers' experiences of and reasons for running a business;
- to seek their views about the current business environment, including government policy;
- to explore how they see their world as business owner-managers and how they approach issues such as succession planning and finding new customers.

Focus groups were held in locations across the UK, based on the assumption that experiences would be different in particular local environments and socio-economic contexts. 'Whilst it is accepted that these focus groups cannot aim to be truly *representative* of the small business population as a whole, it was important to ensure that the results could be *illustrative* of the possible regional and sectoral variations and therefore provide a limited level of generalizability for the results' (2000: 51). Potential participants were identified using local business directories. The incentive they were offered was primarily social—participants would get the chance to meet other business owners and exchange experiences. The researchers also offered to pay for participants' expenses.

The meetings were held in the offices of a sponsor, a chartered accountancy practice. Blackburn and Stokes acknowledge that this location might have been a deterrent for business owners, presumably as it may be associated with taxation, but they argue that the impact of this possibility was minimized by informing business owners of the location only once they had agreed to participate!

Each moderator was accompanied by an assistant, who organized the layout of the room, took responsibility for audio-recording the event, and took notes to capture non-verbal signals and nuances. Room size constraints meant that the researchers decided against video recording.

Prior to the study, one of the concerns that the researchers had was about the extent to which business owners would be prepared to share the detail of their specific cases in a group setting. As the extract in Tips and skills 'Extract from a focus group discussion showing no moderator involvement' suggests, this proved not to be a problem: 'any reservations we had that business owners would be reluctant to open up in front of their peers . . . were not borne out' (2000: 60).

The study also raised some ethical issues. In particular, although the researchers changed the names of participants in order to ensure their confidentiality, when the research was published, the research unit that had commissioned the research was approached by the media, seeking names and telephone numbers of the participants, to speak to them directly. Blackburn and Stokes contacted the focus group participants and asked them if they were willing to talk to the press. Only if they were willing were their details passed on to the journalist.

Level of moderator involvement

How involved should the moderator/facilitator be? In qualitative research, the aim is to get at the perspectives of those being studied. Consequently, the approach should not be intrusive and structured. Therefore, there is a tendency for researchers to use a fairly small number of very general questions to guide the focus group session. Moreover, there is a further tendency for moderators to allow quite a lot of latitude to participants, so that the discussion can range fairly widely. Tips and skills 'Extract from a focus group discussion showing no moderator involvement' provides an example of this. In this instance, three quite different opinions emerge in relation to the issue of succession planning without any moderator prompting. Obviously, if the discussion goes off at a total tangent, it may be necessary to refocus the participants' attention, but even then it may be necessary to be careful, because what may appear to be digressions may in fact reveal something of interest to the group participants. The advantage of allowing a fairly free rein to the discussion is that the researcher stands a better chance of getting access to what individuals see as important or interesting. On the other hand, too much totally irrelevant discussion may prove too unproductive, especially in the commercial environment of market research. It is not surprising, therefore, that, as Wilkinson (1999*a*) observes, some writers on focus groups perceive the possibility that participants come to take over the running of a session from the moderator as a problem and offer advice on how to reassert control (e.g. Krueger 1988).

Tips and skills
Extract from a focus group discussion showing no moderator involvement

Michael . . . --- talking about your family taking over the business—that's something I wouldn't do with my family because I don't think they've got the fire. I just don't think my daughters have got the same fire as I've got.

Mike You're forcing them down a particular channel—there are so many things they can do . . . I think that they may or may not have the right qualities to do that—they may wish to go out and do other things . . . plus you might think that in giving them a thriving business you're spoiling them so I just think this whole family business thing is an absolute can of worms.

Gary If they're in it already though it's a different situation.

Mike . . . Well I accept that . . . my exit strategy is that at some point I've got to sell the business and I think the management team realise that. So they know when we're discussing share options there's only one point—you know we were discussing what's the point in owning shares in a private business—there is only one point when it is worth it and that's when the business is sold. So what it is, is when the business is sold they get a share of the benefit—so that's the sort of logic there.

(Blackburn and Stokes 2000: 60)

Tips and skills
Extract from a focus group discussion showing some moderator involvement

Moderator	Has anyone other than Gary taken advice on exit routes?
Lilian	We took advice when we made our plan in the first place about moving ourselves away from the front end of the business. How we geared our pension schemes . . .
Mike	I've taken advice and their advice was you need to be bigger . . . to make the amount of money you need to actually walk away from it . . . I'm in the process of doing that . . .
Marina	We started this actually about two years ago and we have taken advice and put plans into place. I do believe it is very important to have those plans and the correct ones. They always advise you to get bigger and you have to be a certain size . . .

(Blackburn and Stokes 2000: 59)

One way in which the moderator may need to be involved is in responding to specific points that are of potential interest to the research questions but that are not picked up by other participants. In Tips and skills 'Extract from a focus group discussion showing some moderator involvement', which is also taken from the study of small business owner-managers (Blackburn and Stokes 2000), the moderator provides a prompt to guide the discussion of planned business succession to find out if any of the participants have taken advice on this issue. This encourages the group to share their experiences.

Clearly, the moderator has to straddle two positions: allowing the discussion to flow freely and intervening to bring out especially salient issues, particularly when group participants do not do so. This is not an easy conundrum to resolve and each tactic—intervention and non-intervention—carries risks. The best advice is to err on the side of minimal intervention—other than to start the group on a fresh set of issues—but to intervene when the group is struggling in its discussions or when it has not alighted on something that is said in the course of the session that appears significant for the research topic. Kandola (2012) usefully recommends tactics to keep the discussion flowing, such as acknowledging what has been said, summarizing and stimulating reflection on what has been said, and allowing adequate time for participants to speak. Equally, she recommends that the moderator should avoid certain forms of intervention, notably agreeing or disagreeing, expressing personal opinions, and interrupting. She also cautions against the use of bodily responses like frowning, looking distracted, fidgeting, and shaking one's head (nodding is recommended, though we would recommend caution here as nodding can be interpreted by participants as agreement).

One of the challenges for focus group moderators is ensuring that there is a good level of participation among members. Getting equal participation is unrealistic but it is clearly preferable for all group members to participate to a reasonable degree. One technique she suggests as a means of stimulating participation is writing comments that arise in the course of a discussion onto a flipchart. Chan et al. (2012) wrote comments onto a board when they conducted focus group research into the management of stress among expatriate Hong Kong construction professionals in mainland China. The moderator noted points made by participants, which allowed them to reflect on what had been said and acted as a stimulus to further discussion. As Chan et al. observe, doing this also proffered the opportunity for participants to check on the researchers' emerging understanding. However, Kandola cautions that as far as possible, participants' own language should be employed when making such notes so that the researchers' own understandings are not imposed.

Selecting participants

So who should participate in a focus group? This depends on who will find the topic relevant and who can represent specific occupational or organizational groupings that have an interest in the topic concerned. Usually, a wide range of organizational members or stakeholders from different organizations is required, but they are organized into separate groups in terms of stratifying criteria, such as age, gender, occupation, profession, hierarchical position within the organization, or length of service. Participants for each group can then be selected randomly or through some kind of snowball sampling method. The aim is to establish whether or not there is any systematic variation in the ways in which different groups discuss a matter.

A further issue in relation to the selection of group participants is whether to select people who are unknown to each other (for example, members of the same professional association or employees from different divisions within the same organization) or to use natural groupings (for example, co-workers or students on the same course). Some researchers prefer to exclude people who know each other on the grounds that pre-existing styles of interaction or status differences may contaminate the session. Not all writers accept this rule of thumb. Some prefer to select natural groups whenever possible. For example, in marketing research, companies like Procter & Gamble tend to go back repeatedly to the same pool from which they draw focus groups (Kiely 1998).

However, opting for a strategy of recruiting people entirely from natural groups is not always feasible, because of difficulties of securing participation. For example, it is not always feasible to remove a number of employees from work activity at the same time; in such cases other strategies of selection may have to be used. Morgan (1998a) suggests that one problem with using natural groups is that people who know each other well are likely to operate with taken-for-granted assumptions that they feel do not need to be brought to the fore. He suggests that, if it is important for the researcher to bring out such assumptions, groups of strangers are likely to work better. On the other hand, if the focus group is intended to explore collective understandings or shared meanings held within a work group, this can be achieved more readily by using participants who are all members of the same group.

Asking questions

An issue that is close to the question of the degree of involvement on the part of the moderator is the matter of how far there should be a set of questions that must be addressed. This issue is very similar to the considerations about how unstructured an interview should be in qualitative interviewing (see Chapter 20). Some researchers prefer to use just one or two very general questions to stimulate discussion, with the moderator intervening as necessary along the lines outlined above.

However, other researchers prefer to inject somewhat more structure into the organization of the focus group sessions. A clear example of this is the research on small business owner-managers, in which moderators worked with a topic agenda with times allocated to the discussion of each topic (see Figure 21.1). Opening questions were designed to generate initial reactions in a relatively open-ended way, to put the owner-managers at ease, and to get them talking as soon as possible in an informal manner. Then the moderator moved the discussion on to the substantive issues of trading climate, challenges in the business environment, government policies, and business succession and exit strategies. Such a general approach to questioning, which is fairly common in focus group research, allows the researcher to navigate the channel between, on the one side, addressing the research questions and ensuring comparability between sessions, and, on the other side, allowing participants to raise issues they see as significant and in their own terms.

Clearly, there are different questioning strategies and approaches to moderating focus group sessions. Most seem to lie somewhere in between the rather open-ended approach employed by Tyler and Cohen (2010) (see Research in focus 21.3) and the somewhat more structured one used by Blackburn and Stokes (2000) (see Research in focus 21.2). There is probably no one best way, and the style of questioning and moderating is likely to be affected by various factors, such as the nature of the research topic (for example, is it one that the researcher already knows a lot about, in which case a modicum of structure is feasible?) and levels of interest and/or knowledge among participants in the research (for example, a low level of participant interest may require a somewhat more structured approach). Kandola (2012) recommends asking for examples and further elaboration as a means of stimulating further discussion that may allow amplification of key points. Whichever strategy of questioning is employed, the focus group researcher should generally be prepared to allow at least some discussion that departs from the interview guide, since such debate may provide new and unexpected insights. A more structured approach to questioning might inhibit such spontaneity, but it is unlikely to remove it altogether.

Beginning and finishing

It is recommended that focus group sessions begin with an introduction, whereby the moderators thank people for coming and introduce themselves, the

Figure 21.1

An example of a topic agenda for a small business owner-manager focus group

Topic Agenda

1. **Introduction (15 mins.)**
   Introduce the research team and roles
   Aim and format of the focus group
   Conventions (confidentiality, speak one at a time, recordings, everybody's **views, open debate, report of proceedings**)
   Personal introduction of participants and their businesses

2. **Discussion Topics**
   (i)   *Current trading climate* (15 mins.)
         (e.g. comparative order levels)
   (ii) *Main challenges in the business environment* (20 mins.)
         (e.g. exchange rates, recruitment, raising money)
   (iii) *Government policies and small firms* (20 mins.)
         (e.g. the minimum wage, entry into the Euro)
   (iv) *Topical issues* (20 mins.)
         (e.g. business succession and exit strategies)

3. **Summing Up**
   Thanks for participation and report back
   Invite back to next event in six months
   Reimburse expenses

4. **Lunch**
   Sandwiches and drinks
   Close

goals of the research are briefly outlined, the reasons for recording the session are given, and the format of the focus group session is sketched out. It is also important to present some of the conventions of focus group participation, such as only one person should speak at a time (perhaps explaining the problems that occur with recordings when people speak over each other); that all data will be treated confidentially and anonymized; that the session is open and everyone's views are important; and the amount of time that will be taken up. During the introduction phase, focus group researchers also often ask participants to fill in forms providing basic socio-demographic information about themselves, such as age, gender, and occupation. Participants should then be encouraged to introduce themselves and to write out their first names on a badge or card placed in front of them, so that everyone's name is known.

At the end the moderators should thank the group members for their participation and explain briefly what will happen to the data they have supplied. If a further session is to be arranged, steps should be taken to coordinate this.

Group interaction in focus group sessions

Kitzinger (1994) has observed that reports of focus group research frequently do not take into account interaction within the group. This is surprising because it is precisely the operation of social interaction and its forms and impact that would seem to distinguish the focus group session from the individual interview. Yet, as Kitzinger observes, very few publications based on focus group research cite or draw inferences from patterns of interaction within the group. Wilkinson (1998) reviewed over 200 studies based on focus groups published between 1946 and 1996. She concluded: 'Focus group data is most commonly presented as if it were one-to-one interview data, with interactions between group participants rarely reported, let alone analysed' (1998: 112).

Interactions between focus group participants may be either complementary or argumentative (Kitzinger 1994). The former brings out the elements of the social world that provide participants' own frameworks of understanding, so that agreement emerges in people's minds. In the example in Tips and skills 'Extract from a focus group discussion showing some moderator involvement', the first part of the discussion demonstrates broad agreement between Michael and Mike about the issues involved in handing over the business to a family member, with Mike building on the preceding remarks made by Michael. This complementary interaction is then interrupted by Gary, who suggests that this depends on whether or not the family member is actively involved in the day-to-day running of the business. This more argumentative interaction leads Mike to revert to an alternative exit strategy—one that relies ultimately on selling the business.

However, as Kitzinger suggests, arguments in focus groups can be equally revealing. She suggests that moderators can play an important role in identifying differences of opinion and exploring with participants the factors that may lie behind them. Disagreement can provide participants with the opportunity to revise their opinions or to think more about the reasons why they hold the view that they do. As Kitzinger argues, drawing attention to patterns of interaction within focus groups allows the researcher to determine how group participants view the issues with which they are confronted in their own terms. The posing of questions by, and agreement and disagreement among, participants helps to bring out their own stances on these issues. The resolution of disagreements also helps to force participants to express the grounds on which they hold particular views.

The focus group as a feminist method

The use of focus groups by feminist researchers has grown considerably in recent years, and Wilkinson (1998, 1999b) has argued that it has great potential in this regard. Three aspects of the method stand out in terms of their compatibility with the ethics and politics of feminism:

- Focus group research is less artificial than many other methods, because, in emphasizing group interaction, which is a normal part of social life, it does not suffer from the problem of gleaning information in an unnatural situation. Moreover, the tendency of many focus group researchers to recruit participants from naturally occurring groups underpins the lower level of artificiality of the method, since people are able to discuss in situations that are quite normal for them. As a result, there is greater opportunity to derive understandings that chime with the 'lived experience' of women. However, not all writers accept the contention that focus groups are more naturalistic than individual interviews. Even when natural groups are used, gathering people to discuss a certain topic (such as a television advertisement) is not inherently naturalistic, because the social setting is to a significant extent contrived (Morrison 1998: 154–5).

Indeed, completing questionnaires or being interviewed may appear more natural, because such instruments are fairly commonplace, whereas being asked to discuss in a group an issue not necessarily of one's choosing is less so.

- Feminist researchers have expressed a preference for methods that avoid *decontextualization*—that is, that successfully study the individual within a social context. The tendency for most methods to treat the individual as a separate entity devoid of a social context is disliked by many feminist researchers, who prefer to analyse 'the self as relational or as socially constructed' (Wilkinson 1999b: 229–30). Because the individual is very much part of a group in the focus group method, this tendency towards decontextualization is avoided.

- As we have seen in previous chapters, feminist researchers are suspicious of research methods that are exploitative and create a power relationship between the female researcher and the female respondent. Wilkinson observes that the risk of this occurring is greatly reduced, because focus group participants are able to take over much of the direction of

Research in focus 21.3
A less structured approach to focus group interviewing

Tyler and Cohen (2010) used a combination of focus groups and interviews with women working in diverse roles in a university setting, to explore how gender is materialized through workspace. Their research was inspired by the work of a contemporary video artist, Sofia Hulten, called *Grey Area,* which features the artist in a grey suit hiding in various places in an office and eventually getting inside a bin liner, in a gesture of throwing herself away. Their interest in this topic was also prompted by personal experiences at work, where they were criticised by a female colleague for displaying pictures of their family and children's drawings in their office because it portrayed them in stereotypically gendered ways. They therefore used still images from Grey Area as the basis for focus groups and individual interviews with women, to discuss their lived, embodied experiences of the workplace. Their convenience sample relied on posting an invitation on the website of the university where they both worked, inviting participation in the study. They ran three focus groups, each held a week apart: 9 participants, duration 80 minutes, 22 pages of transcript; 11 participants, duration 70 minutes, 20 pages of transcript; and 10 participants, duration 90 minutes, 24 pages of transcript.

They describe the method used in focus groups as follows:

> We used printed colour sheets of stills from *Grey Area* as a starting point for the focus groups ... laying the room out so that participants sat around a large table facing each other, with an A3 sheet of the stills in front of them. We were loosely guided by an interview schedule, in which we asked the women taking part to reflect on the images and on how they might relate (if at all) to their own experiences of the workplace, and of their own workspace. We asked participants about their first impressions, if there were any images in the sequence that struck them as particularly interesting or important, and why. We then talked about how the images made them feel, and about how they thought the woman in the video might be feeling. At various points, we focused on the theme of hiding, and particularly on the woman throwing herself away at the end of the sequence. We also had lengthy discussions in each group about why the video is called *Grey Area*, and about what greyness connotes in relation to gender, identity and workspace. In each of the sessions, participants asked questions of themselves, of us and of each other.
>
> (Tyler and Cohen 2010: 183)

The focus groups were facilitated by the two researchers together with a part-time researcher and a research student. This enabled them to delegate responsibility for the recording equipment and taking notes, leaving them free to concentrate on the discussion. Following iterative analysis of the focus group transcripts, they developed an interview schedule which formed the basis for individual follow-up interviews with 23 of the women who had participated in the focus groups, in addition to a further 24 other women who volunteered to participate. The researchers' choice of artwork as a prompt for these discussions sought to 'move' participants and to encourage them to reflect on their experiences in ways which they might otherwise struggle to articulate.

the session from the moderator. Indeed, they may even subvert the goals of the session in ways that could be of considerable interest to the moderator. As a result, participants' points of view are much more likely to be revealed than in a traditional interview.

Wilkinson does not argue that focus groups or indeed any method can be described as inherently feminist.

Instead, she argues that, because of these three features and when employed with a sensitivity towards feminist concerns, the focus group method has considerable potential as a tool of feminist research. Tyler and Cohen's (2010) study of women's embodied experiences of the workplace (Research in focus 21.3) provides an example of this.

Research in focus 21.4
Using focus groups in a study of female entrepreneurs

In a qualitative analysis of female entrepreneurs' accounts of their role, Buttner (2001) used the focus group method to explore the leadership and management style of women entrepreneurs in their own organizations. Although the study was exploratory, 'designed to capture the women's "voice" as they spoke about their role in their businesses' (2001: 258), a structured interview protocol was used. One hundred and twenty-nine women entrepreneurs from twelve research sites across the United States participated in the focus groups, and the results were video-recorded and transcribed. One of the interesting things about the way that the data in this study were analysed and presented is that the frequency of comments was recorded in addition to the content. This was achieved with the aid of a qualitative analysis software package of the kind discussed in Chapter 25. In reporting the results of the focus groups, in addition to using direct quotes of the focus group participants, Buttner (2001) also records the number or proportion of the women in her sample who made comments about a particular issue. This helps to add strength to her argument and is an example of how qualitative researchers sometimes undertake a limited amount of quantification of their data (an issue that we will discuss in more depth in Chapter 26).

The kinds of argument put forward regarding the fit between the focus group method and feminist research have been extended to suggest they may have a further role in allowing the voices of highly marginalized groups of women to surface. Madriz (2000: 843) argues that, for a group such as lower-socio-economic-class women of colour, focus groups constitute a relatively rare opportunity for them to 'empower themselves by making sense of their experience of vulnerability and subjugation'. Research in focus 21.4 provides an example of some research that uses focus groups to study women, although this study does not claim to be feminist research, and it involves studying women who are relatively powerful

(running successful businesses and employing other staff) rather than powerless. However, Buttner's (2001) use of focus group methods could be seen as supportive of the feminist emphasis on methods that seek to avoid decontextualizing research subjects, since her study is interested in developing understanding of women entrepreneurs in a relational context, based on earlier research into gender that suggests women's identities are based on an ability to make and maintain relationships with others. Focus groups could therefore be seen as a way for female entrepreneurs to make sense of their relationships with employees, suppliers, and clients through talking to other women who had similar experiences.

Limitations of focus groups

Focus groups clearly have considerable potential for research questions in which the processes through which meaning is jointly constructed are likely to be of particular interest. Indeed, it may be that even when this is not a prominent emphasis, the use of the focus group method may be appropriate and even advantageous, since it allows participants' perspectives—an important feature of much qualitative research (see Chapter 17)—to be revealed in ways that are different from individual interviews (for example, through discussion, participants' questions, arguments, and so on). It also offers considerable potential for feminist researchers. What, then, might be its chief limitations?

- The researcher probably has less control over proceedings than with the individual interview. As we have seen, by no means all writers on focus groups perceive this as a disadvantage, and indeed feminist researchers often see it as an advantage. However, the question of control raises issues for researchers of how far they can allow a focus group to 'take over' the running of proceedings. There is clearly a delicate balance to be taken into account over how involved moderators should be and how far a set of prompts or questions should influence the conduct of a focus group, as some of the earlier discussions have suggested. What is not

Research in focus 21.5
Group conformity and the focus group method

Asch's (1951) laboratory studies into individual conformity to group norms provide us with an indication of the risks that are associated with focus groups. One experiment involved seven men who were brought together as a group and seated at a table. The men were told that they were participating in a study on visual perception. However, only one of the men was a real participant; the rest were 'actors' paid by Asch to participate. The group was shown a series of lines and asked to judge which were equal in length.

However, the actor-participants had been instructed to lie about which of the lines was equal. Despite the obviousness of the task, in most of the trials that Asch conducted the individual subject conceded to the group judgement, rather than giving the response he or she judged to be correct. The research showed that it was difficult for individuals to express their opinions when they contradict the views of other group members.

These findings have obvious implications for the conduct of focus groups, particularly since Asch also found that conformity increased when group members had to continue working together in the future—a distinct possibility within organizational research. However, Asch also found that conformity decreased when subjects were not face to face.

clear is the degree to which it is appropriate to surrender control of a focus group to its participants, especially when there is a reasonably explicit set of research questions to be answered, as is commonly the case, for example, in funded research.

- The data are difficult to analyse. A huge amount of data can be very quickly produced. Developing a strategy of analysis that incorporates both themes in what people say and patterns of interaction is not easy. Also, as previously pointed out, focus group recordings are particularly prone to inaudible elements, which affects transcription.

- They are difficult to organize. Not only do you have to secure the agreement of people to participate in your study; you also need to persuade them to turn up at a particular time. Small inducements, such as payment of expenses or provision of lunch, are sometimes made to induce participation, but nonetheless it is common for people not to turn up.

- The recordings are probably more time-consuming to transcribe than equivalent recordings of individual interviews, because of variations in voice pitch and the need to take account of who says what.

- There are possible problems of group effects. This includes the obvious problem of dealing with reticent speakers and with those who hog the stage! In this respect, they are a bit like tutorials. Krueger (1998) suggests in relation to the problem of overly prominent

participants that the moderator should make clear to the speaker and other group participants that other people's views are definitely required; for example, he suggests saying something like: 'That's one point of view. Does anyone have another point of view?' (1998: 59). As for those who do not speak very much, it is recommended that they are actively encouraged to say something. Also, as the well-known Asch experiments showed (see Research in focus 21.5), an emerging group view may mean that a perfectly legitimate perspective held by just one individual may be suppressed. There is also evidence that, as a group comes to share a certain point of view, group members come to think uncritically about it and to develop almost irrational attachments to it (Janis 1982). It is not known how far such group effects have an adverse impact on focus group findings, but it is clear that they cannot be entirely ignored. In this context, it would be interesting to know how far agreement among focus group participants is more frequently encountered than disagreement (we have a hunch that it is), since the effects to which both Asch and Janis referred would lead us to expect more agreement than disagreement in focus group discussions. Related to this, in group contexts participants may be more prone to expressing culturally expected views than in individual interviews.

- Madriz (2000) proposes that there are circumstances when focus groups may not be appropriate because of their potential for causing discomfort among participants. When such discomfort might arise, individual interviews are likely to be preferable. Situations in which unease might be occasioned are when intimate details of private lives need to be revealed; when participants may not be comfortable in each other's presence (for example, bringing together people in a hierarchical relationship to each other); and when participants are likely to disagree profoundly with each other.

Checklist

Issues to consider for your focus group

○ Have you devised a clear and comprehensive way of introducing the research to participants?

○ Do the questions or topics you have devised allow you to answer all your research questions?

○ Have you piloted the guide with some appropriate respondents?

○ Have you devised a strategy for encouraging respondents to turn up for the focus group meeting?

○ Have you thought about what you will do if some participants do not turn up for the session?

○ Have you ensured that interviews will allow novel or unexpected themes and issues to arise?

○ Is your language in the questions clear and comprehensible?

○ Are your questions relevant to the people who are participating in the focus groups?

○ Have your questions been designed to elicit reflective discussions so that participants are not tempted to answer in 'yes' or 'no' terms?

○ Have your questions been designed to encourage group interaction and discussion?

○ Do your questions offer a real prospect of seeing the world from your interviewees' point of view rather than imposing your own frame of reference on them?

○ Are you familiar with the setting(s) in which the interview will take place?

○ Are you thoroughly familiar with and have you tested your recording or audio-visual equipment?

○ Have you thought about how you will present yourself in the session, such as how you will be dressed?

○ Have you devised a strategy for dealing with silences?

○ Have you devised a strategy for dealing with participants who are reluctant to speak?

○ Have you devised a strategy for dealing with participants who speak too much and hog the discussion?

○ Do you have a strategy for how far you are going to intervene in the focus group discussion?

○ Do you have a strategy for dealing with the focus group if the discussion goes off at a tangent?

○ Have you tested out any aids that you are going to present to focus group participants (e.g. visual aids, segments of film, case studies)?

Key points

- The focus group is a group interview that is concerned with exploring a certain topic.

- The moderator generally tries to provide a relatively free rein to the discussion. However, there may be contexts in which it is necessary to ask fairly specific questions, especially when cross-group comparability is an issue.

- There is concern with the joint production of meaning.

- Focus group discussions need to be recorded and transcribed.

- There are several issues concerning the recruitment of focus group participants—in particular, whether to use natural groupings or to employ stratifying criteria.

- Group interaction is an important component of discussions.

- Some writers view focus groups as well suited to a feminist standpoint.

Questions for review

- Why might it be useful to distinguish between a focus group and a group interview?

Uses of focus groups

- What advantages might the focus group method offer in contrast to an individual qualitative interview?

Conducting focus groups

- How involved should the moderator be?

- Why is it necessary to record and transcribe focus group sessions?

- Are there any circumstances in which it might be a good idea to select participants who know each other?

- What might be the advantages and disadvantages of using an interview guide in focus group sessions?

Group interaction in focus group sessions

- Why might it be important to treat group interaction as an important issue when analysing focus group data?

The focus group as a feminist method

- Evaluate the argument that the focus group can be viewed as a feminist method.

- To what extent are focus groups a naturalistic approach to data collection?

Limitations of focus groups

- Does the potential for the loss of control over proceedings and group effects damage the potential utility of the focus group as a method?

- How far do the greater problems of transcription and difficulty of analysis undermine the potential of focus groups?

Online Resource Centre

[www.oxfordtextbooks.co.uk/orc/brymanbrm4e/]

Visit the Interactive Research Guide that accompanies this book to complete an exercise in Focus Groups.

22

Language in qualitative research

Chapter outline

This chapter is concerned with approaches to the examination of language, including conversation analysis and discourse analysis. For the practitioners of these approaches, language is an object of interest in its own right and not simply a resource through which research participants communicate with researchers. The chapter explores:

- fine-grained approaches to analysis, including conversation and discourse analysis, that focus in detail on the way that language is used, especially in conversation and dialogue;
- analytical approaches that explore the use of specific literary devices, including narrative and rhetoric, to create meaning in social situations through the use of language;
- approaches that seek to contextualize the use of language by analysing the historical and social circumstances in which it is produced, treating **texts** (see Chapter 23 for a discussion of the term 'text') as interrelated to each other and dependent on context.

Introduction

Language is bound to be of importance for organizational researchers. It is, after all, through language that we ask people questions in interviews and through which the questions are answered. Language is also central to the structuring of organizations, if only because people in work organizations rely so heavily on talk—in meetings, on the telephone, in the cafeteria—in order to accomplish their everyday business. It is through language that people in organizations exchange information, skills, services, and resources and make sense of their situation through interaction with each other. Furthermore, within managerial work a remarkably high emphasis is placed on verbal interaction, as findings from various research studies have suggested. For example, Mintzberg's (1973) study reports that verbal contacts, face to face and on the telephone, accounted for 75 per cent of senior managers' time and 67 per cent of their activities (see Chapter 12 for a more detailed explanation of Mintzberg's study). Other studies have shown that between 57 and 89 per cent of

managerial time is spent in verbal interaction (Boden 1994). The role of the organizational researcher who focuses on language is to explore the nature of the relationship between language and action in these instances.

What is crucial about the approaches discussed in this chapter is that, unlike traditional views of the role of language in business research, they treat language as a topic rather than as a resource (admittedly a cliché phrase). This means that language is treated as significantly more than a medium through which the business of research is conducted (such as asking questions in interviews). It becomes a focus of attention in its own right. This implies that language is not just seen as reflective of what goes on in an organization; instead, language and organization become one and the same. This means, for example, that as soon as managers in a public-sector organization start to talk of their client groups as 'customers', a whole new way of defining the organization's purpose and activities is introduced.

Fine-grained approaches

The first part of this chapter examines two fine-grained approaches that treat language as their central focal points—conversation analysis (CA) and discourse

analysis (DA). Fine-grained approaches focus on language in use, in conversation or in dialogue, and seek to examine talk in order to understand its organizing properties—in other words, the rules and structures that determine what people say in a given interaction. Both CA and DA are predominantly concerned with capturing and analysing language as it is used in a particular moment rather than over a period of time. While CA and DA do not exhaust the range of possibilities for studying language as a topic, they do represent two of the most prominent fine-grained approaches. Each has evolved a technical vocabulary and set of techniques. The first part of this chapter will outline some of the basic elements of each of them and draw attention to some contrasting features.

Conversation analysis

The roots of CA lie in ethnomethodology, a sociological position developed in the USA under the general tutelage of Harold Garfinkel and Harvey Sacks, though it is the latter with whom CA is most associated. Ethnomethodology takes as its basic focus of attention 'practical, common-sense reasoning' in everyday life and as such is fundamentally concerned with the notion of social life as an accomplishment. Social order is seen not as a pre-existing force constraining individual action, but as something that is worked at and accomplished through interaction. Contrary to what its name implies, ethnomethodology is *not* a research methodology; it is the study of the methods employed in everyday life though which social order is accomplished.

Two ideas are particularly central to ethnomethodology and find clear expression in CA: indexicality and reflexivity. Indexicality means that the meaning of an act, which in CA essentially means spoken words or utterances including pauses and sounds, depends upon the context in which it is used. Reflexivity means that spoken words are constitutive of the social world in which they are located; in other words, the principle of reflexivity in ethnomethodology means that talk is not a 'mere' representation of the social world, so that it does much more than just stand for something else. In these ways, ethnomethodology fits fairly squarely with two

aspects of qualitative research—the preference for a contextual understanding of action (see Chapter 17) and an ontological position associated with constructionism (see Chapter 2).

In the years following its initial introduction into sociology, ethnomethodological research split into two camps. One entailed drawing on traditional social research methods, albeit in perhaps a somewhat altered form, and on ethnography in particular (e.g. Cicourel 1968). The other, which is mainly associated with Sacks and his co-workers (e.g. Sacks, Schegloff, and Jefferson 1974), sought to conduct fine-grained analyses of talk in naturally occurring situations. Moreover, it is not just talk in itself that is the object of interest but talk as it occurs in and through social interaction. CA concerns itself with the organization of such talk in the context of interaction (see Key concept 22.1). In order to conduct such investigations, a premium was placed on the recording of naturally occurring conversations and their transcription for the purpose of intensive analysis of the sequences of interaction revealed in the subsequent transcripts. As such, CA is a multifaceted approach—part theory, part method of data acquisition, part method of analysis. The predilection for the analysis of talk gleaned from naturally occurring situations suggests that CA chimes with another preoccupation among qualitative researchers—namely, a commitment to naturalism (see Key concept 3.4 and Key concept 17.1).

As the definition in Key concept 22.1 and the preceding discussion suggest, CA takes from ethnomethodology a concern with the production of social order through and in the course of social interaction, but takes conversation as the basic form through which that social order is achieved. The element of indexicality is also evident, in that practitioners of CA argue that the meaning of words is contextually grounded, while the commitment to reflexivity is revealed in the view that talk is constitutive of the social context in which it occurs.

Conversation analysts have developed a variety of procedures for the study of talk in interaction. Psathas

Key concept 22.1
What is conversation analysis?

Conversation analysis (CA) is the fine-grained analysis of talk as it occurs in interaction in naturally occurring situations. The talk is usually recorded and transcribed so that the detailed analyses can be carried out. These analyses are concerned with uncovering the underlying structures of talk in interaction and as such with the achievement of order through interaction.

(1995: 1) has described them as 'rigorous, systematic procedures' that can 'provide reproducible results'. Such a framework smacks of the commitment to the codification of procedures that generate valid, reliable, and replicable findings that are a feature of quantitative research. It is not surprising, therefore, that CA is sometimes described as having a positivist orientation. Thus, a cluster of features that are broadly in tune with qualitative research (contextual, naturalistic, studying the social world in its own terms and without prior theoretical commitments) are married to traits that are resonant of quantitative research. However, the emphasis on context in CA is somewhat at variance with the way in which contextual understanding is normally conceptualized in qualitative research. For CA practitioners, context refers to the specific here-and-now context of immediately preceding talk, whereas for most qualitative researchers it has a much wider set of resonances, which has to do with an appreciation of such things as the culture of the group within which action occurs. In other words, action is to be understood in terms of the values, beliefs, and typical modes of behaviour of that group. This is precisely the kind of attribution from which CA practitioners are keen to refrain. It is no wonder, therefore, that writers like

Gubrium and Holstein (1997) treat it as a separate tradition within qualitative research (see Key concept 17.1), while Silverman (1993) finds it difficult to fit CA into broad descriptions of the nature of qualitative research.

Conversation analysts study talk in a range of institutional settings, such as television news interviews, courtroom trials, and clinical interaction. Boden (1994) uses CA to explore how talk influences organizational structures. She highlights the importance of formal and informal meetings, which she sees as involving sequences of talk that enable people to transmit information, make decisions, and sort out misunderstandings. She suggests CA can provide a means of understanding these interactional contexts, by looking at the way talk is organized in meetings. A further example of CA in management meetings is provided by Gibson (2005), who analyses the effects of hierarchical and horizontal networks on managers' participation shifts (see Research in focus 22.2).

Heritage (1984, 1987) has proposed that CA is governed by three basic assumptions.

- *Talk is structured.* Talk comprises invariant patterns—that is, it is structured. Participants are implicitly aware of the rules that underpin these patterns. As a

Research in focus 22.2
A conversation analysis of the impact of networks on managers' participation in meetings

Gibson's (2005) research focused on social networks within organizations, but unusually he was also interested in how these networks affected interactional behaviour. In order to explore this he combined the methods of network analysts, which involved a questionnaire survey focusing on identifying patterns of friendship, co-working, socializing influence, and respect, with the methods of CA based on analysis of 37,309 observations of speaking taken from the observation of 75 meetings involving 10 groups of managers.

His focus was on identifying patterns of participation, and specifically 'participation shifts' which determine who speaks and who is the target of the verbal exchange according to **turn-taking** rules. This CA enabled statistical analysis of participation shifts, which were compared against the data concerning social networks, including hierarchical (superior–subordinate) and horizontal (friendship and co-working) relationships. Gibson observes that, although conversation analysts are generally sceptical of quantification, this can be a useful way of obtaining 'information on the larger sequential context in which a particular event occurs' (2005: 1566).

Among the findings arising from the study was that superiors were unlikely to reply when addressed by subordinates, and subordinates use more qualifiers when addressing their superiors and were unlikely to move conversation away from superiors when they had the floor. Gibson concludes that this mixed-method research design (see Chapter 27) also enabled a temporal dimension to be reflected, the network analysis providing 'snapshot complexity but no temporal definition' and the CA capturing 'snapshot simplicity . . . but tremendous temporal complexity' (2005: 1590).

result, conversation analysts eschew attempts to infer the motivations of speakers from what they say or to ascribe their talk to personal characteristics. Such information is unnecessary, since the conversation analyst is orientated to the underlying structures of action, as revealed in talk.

- *Talk is forged contextually*. Action is revealed in talk, and as such talk must be analysed in terms of its context. This means that we must seek to understand what someone says in terms of the talk that has preceded it and that therefore talk is viewed as exhibiting patterned sequences.

- *Analysis is grounded in data*. Conversation analysts shun prior theoretical schemes and instead argue that characteristics of talk and of the constitutive nature of social order in each empirical instance must be induced out of data. Heritage (1987: 258) has written: 'It is assumed that social actions work in *detail* and hence that the specific details of interaction cannot simply be ignored as insignificant without damaging the prospects for coherent and effective analyses.' This assumption represents a manifesto for the emphasis on fine-grained details (including length of pauses, prolongation of sounds, and so on) that is the hallmark of CA.

As the third of the three assumptions associated with CA indicates, the approach requires the analyst to produce detailed transcripts of natural conversation that includes all the pauses, interruptions, and intonations used by speakers. Some of the basic notational symbols employed in CA are listed below.

- A figure in parentheses is used to indicate the length of a period of silence, usually measured in tenths of one second. Thus, (0.3) signals three-tenths of a second of silence.

- Punctuation marks, such as an exclamation mark, are used to capture characteristics of speech delivery rather than grammatical notation.

- Italics are indicative of an emphasis in the speaker's delivery of a word.

- A hyphen represents a cut-off of a prior word or syllable, which may arise because a speaker is interrupted by someone else.

- Brackets indicate the point at which simultaneous speech overlaps—for example when more than one speaker talks at the same time.

- A colon in the middle of a word indicates that the sound that occurs directly before the colon is prolonged (e.g. we:ll). More than one colon means further prolongation (e.g. : : : :).

- .hh h's preceded by a dot indicate an intake of breath. If no dot is present, it means breathing out.

- (.) Indicates a very slight pause.

The attention to detail in CA is very striking and represents a clear difference from the way in which talk is normally treated by social researchers in their transcription conventions when analysing qualitative interviews. It has sometimes been suggested that CA fails to capture body movements, but in recent times the use of video recordings, as in the analysis of the public lectures of management gurus by Greatbatch and Clark (2003; see Research in focus 22.3), has supplemented its tool kit of methods (e.g. Heath 1997). Attention to fine details is thus an essential ingredient of CA work. Pauses and

Research in focus 22.3
A conversation analysis of the public lectures of management gurus

Greatbatch and Clark (2003) used CA to analyse the public lectures of management gurus to try to find out how they used their appearance on the international lecture circuit to disseminate ideas and build their personal reputations with audiences. Their analysis was based on commercially produced video recordings of lectures conducted by Tom Peters, Rosabeth Moss Kanter, Peter Senge, and Gary Hamel, and their focus was on the occurrence of collective audience laughter. The use of video recordings enabled them to track gestures and gaze direction, as well as the details of the management gurus' speech. Greatbatch and Clark note that previous CA research on public speaking indicates that 'collective audience responses, such as applause and laughter, are not simply spontaneous reactions to the messages that evoke them' (2003: 1520). Instead, audiences will generally

(continued)

clap or laugh at public speakers' remarks only if they feel that other members of the audience will also do so. Crucial to enabling this is the speaker providing clear completion points in a speech sequence so that audience members can coordinate their actions, and also using non-verbal techniques, including comedic gestures, that 'invite' the audience to respond. For example, on one occasion, Tom Peters 'suddenly leans forward, glares at a section of the audience and speaks louder as he adopts a "mock angry" tone' (2003: 1530). The authors also note that the gurus use humour to refer to aspects of organizational life with which their audience is likely to identify, such as the difficulties of dealing with slow bureaucratic organizations, rather than to convey their core ideas. This is because the latter use of humour might cause the audience members to feel threatened or inadequate because they are unlikely to be using the ideas and therefore to feel unable to join in with the joke.

emphases are not to be regarded as incidental or of little significance in terms of what the speaker is trying to achieve; instead, they are part of 'the specific details of interaction [that] cannot simply be ignored as insignificant', as Heritage (1987: 248) puts it.

The gradual accumulation of detailed analyses of talk in interaction has resulted in recognition of recurring features in the way that talk is organized. These features can be regarded as tools that can be applied to sequences of conversation. One of the most basic ideas in CA is the notion that one of the ways in which order is achieved in everyday conversation is through turn-taking. This is a particularly important tool of CA, because it illustrates that talk depends on shared codes. If such codes did not exist, there would not be smooth transitions in conversation. In other words, there must be codes for indicating the ends of utterances.

One of the ways in which turn-taking is revealed is through the examination of **adjacency pairs**. The idea of the adjacency pair draws attention to the well-attested tendency for some kinds of activity as revealed in talk to involve two linked phases: a question followed by an answer; an invitation followed by a response (accept/decline); or a greeting followed by a returned greeting. The first phase invariably implies that the other part of the adjacency pair will be forthcoming—for example, that an invitation will be responded to. The second phase is of interest to the conversation analyst not just because it becomes a springboard for a response in its own right but because compliance with the putative normative structure of the pairing indicates an appreciation of how one is supposed to respond to the initial phase. In this way, 'intersubjective understandings' are continuously reinforced (Heritage 1987: 259–60). This is not to imply that the second phase will *always* follow the first; indeed, the response to a failure to comply with the expected response is itself the focus of attention by conversation analysts.

A further tool employed in CA is the account. The important feature to note about the treatment of accounts in CA is that they are analysed in context—that is, the form that they assume is handled as being occasioned by the speech act that precedes it. Moreover, in CA, accounts are not unusual phenomena to be deployed when things go wrong but are intrinsic to talk in a variety of situations. It is striking that many accounts are in essence simply a description or expression of a state of affairs. However, this review of CA can only scratch the surface of an approach that has developed a highly sophisticated way of studying talk in interaction.

The insistence of conversation analysts that it is important to locate understanding in terms of sequences of talk, and therefore to avoid making extraneous inferences about the meanings of that talk, marks CA as representing a somewhat different approach from much qualitative research. As we have seen in previous chapters, qualitative researchers often claim (perhaps erroneously from the perspective of CA) that they seek to achieve understanding from the perspective of those being studied. Conversation analysts claim to do this only in so far as that understanding can be revealed in the specific contexts of talk. To import elements that are not specifically grounded in the here and now of what has just been said during a conversation risks the implanting of understanding that is not grounded in participants' own terms (Schegloff 1997). Boden (1994), for example, points out that her concern is not automatically with 'typical' variables such as age, race, class, or gender, nor does she assume organizational structure or size as an important starting point for analysis. The status of the speaker is not assumed to dictate the talk; instead, the point of interest for her as a conversation analyst is on how 'aspects of biography and social structure are made relevant in particular talk settings' (1994: 77).

Two points seem relevant here. First, this is a somewhat limiting stance, in that it means that the attribution of motives and meanings as a result of an in-depth understanding of a culture is illegitimate. While an interpretative understanding of social action carries risks of misunderstanding, an approach that prohibits such speculation is potentially restrictive. Secondly, CA is contextual in that it locates understanding in the sequences of talk. However, for the participants of an exchange, much of their talk is informed by their mutual knowledge of contexts. The analyst is restricted from taking those additional components of the context into account if they are not specifically part of the organization of talk. Again, this admonition seems to restrict the analyst more than is desirable in many circumstances and to consign CA to a range of research questions that are amenable solely to the location of meaning in talk alone. On the other hand, CA reduces the risk about making unwarranted speculations about what is happening in social interaction and has contributed much to our understanding of the accomplishment of social order, which is one of the classic concerns of social theory.

Discourse analysis

Unlike CA, DA is an approach to language that can be applied to forms of communication other than talk. As such, it can be and has been applied to other types of texts, such as company mission statements, websites, or email messages, and in this respect it is more flexible than CA. Moreover, in DA there is much less of an emphasis on naturally occurring talk, so that talk in research interviews can be a legitimate target for analysis. However, DA should not be treated totally in opposition or contradistinction to CA, since it incorporates insights from it.

Unlike CA, which by and large reveals a uniformity based on an orthodoxy associated with certain classic statements concerning its core practices (e.g. Sacks, Schegloff, and Jefferson 1974), there are several different approaches that are labelled as DA (Potter 1997).

The version that is to be discussed in this section is one that is associated with such writers as Potter (1997), Potter and Wetherell (1987, 1994), Billig (1992), and Gilbert and Mulkay (1984). It is to be differentiated from critical discourse analysis (CDA), which is associated with writers such as Fairclough (1992, 1995, 2003), Hardy (2001), and Phillips and Hardy (2002), and which will be dealt with later in this chapter. The version of DA that we are concerned with here (see Key concept 22.4) has been described as exhibiting two distinctive features at the level of epistemology and ontology (Potter 1997).

- It is *anti-realist*: in other words, it denies that there is an external reality awaiting a definitive portrayal by the researcher and it therefore disavows the notion that any researcher can arrive at a privileged account of the aspect of the social world being investigated. Some discourse analysts, however, adopt a stance that is closer to a realist position, but most seem to be anti-realist in orientation.

- It is *constructionist*: in other words, the emphasis is placed on the versions of reality propounded by members of the social setting being investigated and on the fashioning of that reality through their renditions of it (see Key concept 2.12). More specifically, the constructionist emphasis entails a recognition that discourse entails a selection from many viable renditions and that in the process a particular depiction of reality is built up.

Thus, discourse is not simply a neutral device for imparting meaning. People seek to accomplish things when they talk or when they write; DA is concerned with the strategies they employ in trying to create different kinds

Key concept 22.4
What is discourse analysis?

The version of DA described in this section is one that has been of particular interest to social scientists; it can be applied to both naturally occurring and contrived forms of talk and to texts. According to Potter (1997), DA 'emphasizes the way versions of the world, of society, events and inner psychological worlds are produced in discourse' (1997: 146).

This definition of DA means that discourse is not just a mirror on the social world around us but in many ways plays a key role in producing that world. *How* we say things—our phrases, our emphases, the things we leave out—is meant to accomplish certain effects in others. In so doing, we have an impact on others' perceptions and understandings and as such on their and our reality.

of effect. This version of DA is, therefore, action orientated—that is, is a way of getting things done. This is revealed in three basic discourse-analytic questions:

1. What is this discourse doing?
2. How is this discourse constructed to make this happen?
3. What resources are available to perform this activity?

(Potter 2004: 609)

In addition, DA shares with CA a preference for locating contextual understanding in terms of the situational specifics of talk. As Potter (1997: 158) puts it, discourse analysts prefer to avoid making reference in their analyses to what he refers to as 'ethnographic particulars' and argues that instead they prefer 'to see things as things that are worked up, attended to and made relevant in interaction rather than being external determinants'. However, DA practitioners are less committed to this principle than conversation analysts, in that the former sometimes show a greater preparedness to make reference to 'ethnographic particulars'.

Discourse analysts resist the idea of a codification of their practices and indeed argue that such a codification is probably impossible. Instead, they prefer to see their style of research as an 'analytic mentality' and as such as 'a craft skill, more like bike riding or chicken sexing than following the recipe for a mild chicken rogan josh' (Potter 1997: 147–8). One useful point of departure for DA research that has been suggested by Gill (1996), following Widdicombe (1993), is to treat the way that something is said as being 'a solution to a problem' (Widdicombe 1993: 97, quoted in Gill 1996: 146). Gill (2000) also suggests adopting a posture of 'sceptical reading'. This means searching for a purpose lurking behind the ways that something is said or presented. Gill has also proposed that DA can usefully be thought of as comprising four main themes, which are outlined in Thinking deeply 22.5.

The bulk of the exposition of DA that follows is based on three studies:

- research into the discourses applied to unemployed older workers in Australia (Ainsworth and Hardy 2009);
- a study of MBA students' use of role models in professional identity formation (Kelan and Mah 2014);
- an analysis of corporate social responsibility in the context of the web pages of an oil producing and refining company (Coupland 2005).

The first study, by Ainsworth and Hardy (2009; see Research in focus 22.6), shows how discourses of the mind and body are used to discipline unemployed older workers in a way that is disempowering; the second study, by Kelan and Mah (2014; see Research in focus 22.7), provides an illustration of how the notion of interpretative repertoires can be used to understand gendered processes of identity formation among MBA students; finally, in the study of company websites by Coupland (2005; see Research in focus 22.8), discourse analysis is applied to understand how constructions of corporate social responsibility are made plausible and legitimate in the context of company websites.

A further element to be sensitive to is that, as Gill (1996), following Billig (1991), suggests, what is said is always a way of *not* saying something else. In other words, either total silence on a topic, or formulating an argument in a conversation or article in one way rather than in another way, is a crucial component of seeing discourse as a solution to a problem. For example, Ainsworth and Hardy (2009) argue that discourse shapes the rules that determine how we speak and act

Tips and skills
Using existing material

As some of the examples of DA illustrate, you may be able to use the technique to illuminate issues of interest to you based on materials that are in the public domain, such as speeches. In many cases, these will be available in electronic form. This means that you do not have to put a lot of effort into the collection of data, though it will be necessary to seek out the materials. Instead, you can give greater emphasis to analysing the materials using the DA approach. Research in focus 22.6 provides an example of a study that relied exclusively on publicly available written texts.

Thinking deeply 22.5
Four themes in discourse analysis

Gill (2000) has drawn attention to four prominent themes in DA.

1. *Discourse is a topic*. This means that discourse is a focus of enquiry itself and not just a means of gaining access to aspects of social reality that lie behind it. This view contrasts with a traditional research interview in which language is a way of revealing what interviewees think about a topic or their behaviour and the reasons for that behaviour.

2. *Language is constructive*. This means that discourse is a way of constituting a particular view of social reality. Moreover, in rendering that view, choices are made regarding the most appropriate way of presenting it, and these will reflect the disposition of the person responsible for devising it.

3. *Discourse is a form of action*. As Gill (2000: 175) puts it, language is viewed 'as a practice in its own right'. Language is a way of accomplishing acts, such as attributing blame, presenting oneself in a particular way, or getting an argument across. Moreover, a person's discourse is affected by the context that he or she is confronting. Thus, your account of your reasons for wanting a job may vary according to whether you are addressing interviewers in a job interview, members of your family, or friends.

4. *Discourse is rhetorically organized*. This means that DA practitioners recognize that discourse is concerned with 'establishing one version of the world in the face of competing versions' (Gill 2000: 176). In other words, there is a recognition that we want to persuade others when we present a version of events or state a position on an issue.

Research in focus 22.6
The application of mind and body discourses to older workers

Ainsworth and Hardy (2009) studied the discourses pertaining to the employment of older workers through a discursive analysis of a parliamentary inquiry in Australia, which was set up to examine the barriers that older unemployed workers face in regaining employment. The inquiry lasted just over a year (1998–9) and comprised a series of written submissions and public hearings held throughout Australia, where employee and lobby groups, unions, government representatives, and private individuals were invited to appear. A final report was then published in 2000 on the findings of the inquiry. One of the reasons for selecting the inquiry as a research site was because of the accessibility, volume, and range of available texts relating to it, which included media releases, written submissions, and more than 1000 pages of oral evidence and testimony relating to the public hearings, which had been transcribed verbatim. There was the further advantage that many of these documents could be obtained from the government website. Ainsworth and Hardy (2009) claim that, because these 'naturally occurring' texts were generated independently of the researcher, they have the advantage of not being subject to **reactive effect** and provided very useful materials for systematic analysis.

The authors identify two discourses in the texts:

1. *physical discourses relating to the body*: which portray ageing as a process of inevitable decline;

2. *discourses of the mind*: which psychologize and individualize the problem of unemployment.

They further argue that, while these discourses have separate effects, their consequences for identity formation are even greater when brought together through a normative 'mechanism of grief', which encourages older unemployed workers to make use of labour market interventions that help them to accept their loss of

(continued)

employment rather than locate permanent job opportunities. Unemployed older workers were thus advised to 'manage the grief' associated with their loss of employment and to 'resolve the anger' that they felt in relation to job loss because this was deemed 'unhealthy' and claimed to be harming their chances of re-employment. The personal stories told by unemployed older workers were thereby discursively regulated through retelling and reframing by others in a way that deflected responsibility away from government agencies or employers. The authors conclude that, 'rather than provide space for resistance, the intersection of these discourses disempowers an already disadvantaged group' (Ainsworth and Hardy 2009: 1200).

in relation to a given topic, in a way that gives certain actors more legitimacy and rights to commentate than others. They found that discourses that represent the physical process of human ageing as a process of inevitable decline and discourses of the mind that focus on psychologizing feelings of loss and anger associated with job losses were used to marginalize older workers and to exclude them from the labour market. Formulating understandings of unemployment in this way thus discourages collective acknowledgement of responsibility for the problem of older worker unemployment and

invites older unemployed people to accept their disempowered situation. This example illustrates the potential for discourses to affect the power relations between social actors, a point to which we will return at the end of this chapter in the section on 'critical discourse analysis'.

Potter and Wetherell (1994) suggest that there are two tendencies within DA, although they acknowledge that the distinction is somewhat artificial. One is the identification of 'the general resources that are used to construct discourse and enable the performance of particular actions' (1994: 48–9), which is concerned

Research in focus 22.7
Interpretative repertoires in the identification of role models by MBA students

Kelan and Mah (2014) were interested in how MBA students construct a professional self identity, and in particular their identification of gendered role models. Their interest in this topic arose from previous research findings which suggested that women managers struggle to find examples of women leaders with whom they can identify. They conducted 20 in-depth interviews with full-time MBA students at an elite British business school, ten of whom were men and ten women, each interview lasting between 45 and 110 minutes. The researchers also used visual methods to encourage interviewees' engagement with this topic; their questions related to a person the interviewee admired, as follows:

'We asked you to bring along a picture of a person in business you admire. Who have you chosen? What do you admire in this person?'

(Kelan and Mah, 2014: 94)

Although only half of the interviewees actually brought a photo of a person they admired, asking interviewees to bring along a picture to the interview helped ensure they had thought about this in advance. All of the male interviewees selected men as the people they admired, whereas the female interviewees selected men and women. Through their analysis, Kelan and Mah identified two interpretative repertoires, comprised of common tropes of language which interviewees used to talk about the person they admire: the 'idealization' repertoire and the 'admiration' repertoire. They found significant differences between men and women MBA students in their study in terms of the way students used these two interpretative repertoires to construct a professional self-identity. Their findings showed that the interpretative repertoire of idealization was used by all the male MBA students, whereas the repertoire of admiration was used almost exclusively by the women students when talking about women they admired.

Research in focus 22.8
Repertoires of corporate social responsibility

In a study of corporate social responsibility (CSR) on the Web, Coupland's (2005) research design was founded on the premise that websites involve language games whose success relies on their persuasiveness 'in the light of available, alternative, versions of company behaviour' (2005: 357). Her focus was on repertoires of argumentation concerning CSR found on the websites of four multinational organizations in the petrochemical industry. This industry was selected because the nature of the activities of these organizations locates them within environmental debates. The aim of the study was to identify the argumentation repertoires that are used by the organizations to describe their socially responsible activities.

The websites were monitored over a six-month period, and major changes were noted. Using the websites' own search engines, keyword searches were conducted relating to 'social responsibility'. These searches resulted in several hundred hits from the four websites. The data were grouped into themes, or repertoires (Potter and Wetherell 1987), that emerged as supportive of corporate claims to socially responsible activities (Coupland 2005: 358). The aim of this analysis was to 'make an account of devices, or procedures, that contribute to the sense that discourses are literally describing the world' (2005: 358). Analysis of the content of company websites led Coupland to identify four interdependent repertoires of social responsibility:

* *Societal legitimation*. The main purpose of this rhetoric was to account for the organization's attention to issues beyond being focused on profit.

* *Responsible legitimation*. Three themes of responsibility were identified, first in relation to the 'business case' for CSR, second in relation to balancing the competing demands of shareholders and other stakeholders, and third in relation to the law of the country of operation.

* *Other de-legitimation*: This repertoire involved questioning of some pressure groups and acknowledgement of CSR as a passing trend about which there is little consensus.

* *Context-specific legitimation*: This repertoire relates to the genre of communication—the website. Hence producers of website content used titles that positioned the issues as 'vague, generalized, notions, which existed as separate from the company' (2005: 362).

Coupland describes these repertoires as 'virtuous circles' because of their interdependent nature. Coupland concedes that the study of website discourses involves bracketing material and social practices; in other words, what an organization says about CSR may be quite different from what it actually does. However, the importance of websites as a genre of communication renders them an important source in the study of organizational identity formation.

---

with identifying *interpretative repertoires*. The other is concerned to identify 'the detailed procedures through which versions are constructed and made to look factual' (1994: 49). We will now explore these two strands of DA.

In order to illustrate the idea of an **interpretative repertoire**, a study of professional role models adopted by MBA students will be referred to (see Research in focus 22.7). Another example of the use of repertoires can be seen in the study by Coupland (2005) of corporate social responsibility on the Web. This research is outlined in Research in focus 22.8.

Kelan and Mah (2014: 93) define the interpretative repertoire as 'a repeatedly encountered construction

employed in sensemaking. It is a repertoire because only a limited number of terms are used'. They go on to say that these common-sense units of understanding have 'an "off-the-shelf" character and can be used flexibly to make a point in any given situation'. They identify two interpretative repertoires that reflect the ways that individuals talked about people in business whom they admire.

* *The idealization repertoire*. This is comprised of respondents' talk about people who are business founders or very senior in organizations, such as CEOs. Themes include 'being self-made', having achieved

success through hard work and perseverance, and 'being authentic'. This is illustrated by one of their respondents, Luke, who talks about the person he admires in these terms, stating:

> He got a football scholarship to school (…) and started up a load of car dealerships. And made kind of five or six hundred million dollars by the time he was fifty (…) it's that sort of completely self-made, incredibly sharp (…) he's got very high levels of integrity, you know, what you see is what you get.
>
> (Kelan and Mah 2014: 96).

While the themes of being self-made and being authentic might seem contradictory, Kelan and Mah suggest that they justify and balance the two ideals of 'wealth, status and power' and 'integrity, passion and being true to the self'. They then go on to contrast this with:

- *The admiration repertoire*. This is characterised by ambivalence and caveats in talking about the admired person, such as the 'Superwoman' who appears to do it all. This includes talk about their not-admired characteristics (neutral or negative), as well as the positive traits of the individual. It thereby involves more critical evaluation of the person with whom one identifies. For example:

> 'Frances: 'I like her' 'cause she's a woman who's basically lived her life according to her own values (…) I was always a bit suspicious that she'd be a bit of a fraud. Until I actually saw her speak (…) And then I realized that she's just very, very open, you know, and what you see is what there is.'
>
> (Kelan and Mah 2014: 98).

A key difference then between the second and the first interpretative repertoire is that the admiration repertoire contains much greater ambivalence, reflecting tensions and suspicions about whether a person such as this could really exist. The notion of the interpretative repertoire is interesting because it brings out the idea that belief and action take place within templates that guide and influence the writer or speaker. However, the interpretative repertoires identified by Kelan and Mah (2014) and Coupland (2005) by no means exhaust the range of possibilities of analysis, as the advantages of the notion of interpretative repertoires stem primarily from

its flexibility in accounting for a diverse range of social practices. Hence, Potter and Wetherell (1987) suggest that repertoires are available to people with many different social group memberships. They also point out that there is no need to attempt to find consensus with regard to repertoires—because they are used to perform different sorts of accounting tasks, individuals are able to draw upon a variety of repertoires in different situations. Finally, they emphasize that 'the concept of repertoire is but one component in a systematic approach to the study of discourse' (Potter and Wetherell 1987: 157), one that in a few years' time may be developed further or even discarded.

In discourse analytic research there is also an emphasis on the resources that are employed in conveying allegedly factual knowledge—or what Potter and Wetherell (1994) might describe as *quantification rhetoric*, by which is meant the ways in which numerical and non-numerical statements are made to support or refute arguments. Instead, the texts largely consist of general statements, claims, and conclusions. This is interesting, given the importance of quantification in everyday life and the tendency for many social scientists to make use of this strategy themselves (John 1992).

A number of further characteristics apply to DA. Some of the most important are presented in the list that follows.

- *Reading the detail*: discourse analysts incorporate the CA preference for attention to the details of discourse.
- *Looking for rhetorical detail*: attention to rhetorical detail entails a sensitivity to the ways in which arguments are constructed.
- *Looking for accountability*: discourse analysts draw on CA practitioners' interest in and approach to accounts. From the point of view of both CA and DA, discourse can and should be regarded as accounts. For DA practitioners, the search for accountability entails attending to the details through which these accounts are constructed.
- *Cross-referencing discourse studies*: Potter and Wetherell suggest that reading other discourse studies is itself an important activity. First, it helps to sharpen the analytic mentality at the heart of DA. Secondly, other studies often provide insights that are suggestive for one's own data.

As this discussion of DA has emphasized on several occasions, DA draws on insights from CA. Particularly when analysing strings of talk, DA draws on conversation analytic insights into the ways in which interaction is realized in and through talk in interaction, but it is more flexible than CA in terms of the kinds of texts that are analysed, including various kinds of documents and research interviews, in addition to naturally occurring conversation in their work. The CA injunction to focus on the talk itself and the ways in which intersubjective meaning is accomplished in sequences of talk are also incorporated into DA. DA, however, to a greater extent than CA, permits the intrusion of understandings of what is going on that are not specific to the immediacy of previous utterances. For their part, discourse analysts object to the restriction that this injunction imposes, because it means that conversation analysts 'rarely raise their eyes from the next turn in the conversation, and, further, this is not an entire conversation or sizeable slice of social life but usually a tiny fragment' (Wetherell 1998: 402). Thus, for discourse analysts, phenomena such as interpretative repertoires are very much part of the context within which talk occurs, whereas in CA they are inadmissible evidence. But it is here that we see the dilemma for the discourse analyst, for, in seeking to admit a broader sense of context (such as attention to interpretative repertoires

in operation) while wanting to stick close to the conversation analysts' distaste for ethnographic particulars, they are faced with the uncertainty of just how far to go in allowing the inclusion of conversationally extraneous factors.

Hence, fine-grained approaches such as CA and DA have been criticized for being too narrow in focus or not sufficiently sensitive to context. The anti-realist inclination of many DA practitioners has been a source of controversy, because the emphasis on representational practices through discourses sidelines any notion of a pre-existing material reality that can constrain individual agency. Reality becomes little more than that which is constituted in and through discourse. This lack of attention to a material reality that lies behind and underpins discourse has proved too abstracted for some social researchers and theorists. This is an issue that will be returned to at the end of this chapter, when we examine critical discourse analysis. The main point to note at this stage is that, while many DA practitioners are anti-realist, an alternative realist or critical realist position in relation to discourse is also feasible.

Narrative analysis

Narrative analysis is an approach to the elicitation and analysis of language that is sensitive to the sense of temporal sequence that people, as tellers of stories about their lives or events around them, detect in their lives and surrounding episodes and inject into their accounts. Proponents of narrative analysis argue that most approaches to the collection and analysis of data neglect the fact that people perceive their lives in terms of continuity and process, and that attempts to understand social life that are not attuned to this feature neglect the perspective of those being studied. Life history research (see Chapter 20) is an obvious location for the application of a narrative analysis, but its use can be much broader than this. Mishler (1986: 77), for example, has argued for greater interest in 'elicited personal narratives'. In his view, and that of many others, the answers that people provide, in particular in qualitative interviews, can be viewed as stories that are potential fodder for a narrative analysis. In other words, narrative analysis relates not just to the life span but also to accounts relating to episodes and to the interconnections between them. Some researchers apply narrative analysis to interview accounts (e.g. Riessman

1993), while others deliberately ask people to recount stories (e.g. R. L. Miller 2000). A further type of qualitative analysis that is related to narrative relates to the analysis of organizations as a dramatic performance like a stage play (see Research in focus 22.15).

Coffey and Atkinson (1996) argue that a narrative should be viewed in terms of the functions that the narrative serves for the teller. The aim of narrative interviews is to elicit interviewees' reconstructed accounts of connections between events and between events and contexts. A narrative analysis will then entail a seeking-out of the forms and functions of narrative. R. L. Miller (2000) proposes that narrative interviews in life story or biographical research are far more concerned with eliciting the interviewee's perspective as revealed in the telling of the story of his or her life or family than with the facts of that life. There is a concern with how that perspective changes in relation to different contexts. The interviewer is very much a part of the process, in that he or she is fully implicated in the construction of the story for the interviewee.

Narrative analysis has made significant inroads into business research in recent years (Czarniawska 1998;

Research in focus 22.9
The narrative styles of managers and workers

Beech (2000) analysed the stories told by managers and workers in three organizations that were implementing culture change and from this he identified six factors that were related to four underlying narrative styles that are typified in the following examples:

- *Heroic director*. This narrative is characterized by a problem that is solved by the heroic individual actions of a senior manager.
- *Romantic ward manager*. In this narrative the lead character asks the organization for help but is refused. Despite encountering a series of organizational obstacles, he or she keeps trying to build a positive future.
- *Tragic skilled worker*. This narrative involves the central figure who seeks to fulfil his or her organizational duty but is not listened to by the holders of power. The impossibility of the situation leads to failure and he or she pays the cost personally.
- *Ironic response to HRM*. In this narrative managerial intentions produce the opposite effect from what was intended because they do not take into account the experience and common sense of those who are managed.

Beech argues that, rather than being fixed in a single style category, managers' and workers' use of different narrative styles is dependent on their social circumstances.

Boje 2001; see also Research in focus 22.11). For the organizational researcher, narrative analysis can prove extremely helpful in providing a springboard for understanding what Weick (1995) has termed 'organizational sense making'. In one of the best-known studies using a narrative approach, Boje (1991) analyses the types and uses of stories in an office supply firm based on his participant observation in the organization and interviews with key actors. Stories became a common focus of attention when researchers became interested in organizational culture in the 1980s, and this interest in organizational stories has continued, but they have tended to form just one of a number of aspects of culture in which researchers have been interested (for example, rituals

and mission statements). Thus, Boje (1991) provides an example of a strategic planning session in which, during a fairly brief interlude, a number of stories are recounted that serve the function of conveying to participants that printing was a different enterprise at the time of the stories in question from the current situation (see also Boje 2001: 118–21). For the CEO, the story helps participants to make sense of their current situation and conveys a sense of things being better now than they were in the past, at the time when the less than desirable features relating to printing orders pertained. In the process, the CEO is able to gain a certain amount of political advantage by portraying the current context in a more favourable light. The example in Research in

Research in focus 22.10
An example of narratives in a hospital

Brown (1998) has examined the competing narratives involved in the aftermath of the introduction of a hospital information support system (HISS) at a British hospital trust referred to as 'The City'. The IT implementation was largely seen as unsuccessful because of cost overruns and the absence of clear clinical benefits. Drawing on his interviews with key actors regarding the IT implementation and its aftermath, Brown presents three contrasting narratives—the ward narrative; the laboratory narrative; and the implementation team's narrative—thereby presenting the perspectives of the main groups of participants in the implementation.

The three contrasting narratives provide a very clear sense of the organization as a political arena in which groups and individuals contest the legitimacy of others' interpretations of events. Thus, 'the representations of each group's narrative are described as vehicles for establishing its altruistic motives for embarking on the project, and for attributing responsibility for what had come to be defined as a failing project to others' (Brown 1998: 49).

Thus, while the three groups had similar motivations for participating in the initiative, largely in terms of the espousal of an ethic of patient care, they had rather different latent motivations and interpretations of what went wrong. In terms of the former, whereas the ward narrative implied a latent motivation to save doctors' and nurses' time, the laboratory team emphasized the importance of retaining the existing IT systems, and the implementation team placed the accent on the possible advantages for their own careers, in large part by the increased level of dependence on their skills. In terms of the contrasting narratives of what went wrong, the ward narrative was to do with the failure of the implementation team to coordinate the initiative and meet deadlines, and the laboratory team emphasized the tendency for the implementation team not to listen or communicate. As for the implementation team, their diagnosis was to do with the ward staff failing to communicate their needs, lack of cooperation from the laboratory staff, and poorly written software.

focus 22.9 illustrates how narrative analysts focus on the identification of particular narrative styles that are commonly found within organizations.

The significance of narrative for understanding the internal politics of organizations is further indicated by the study referred to in Research in focus 22.10. As Brown (1998) notes in relation to this study, one of the advantages of narrative analysis in a context such as this is that it conveys a clear sense of an organization as an arena in which a variety of perspectives and viewpoints coexist, rather than a monolithic entity with a single voice. However, as Brown notes, his rendition of the three narratives of the implementation is itself a narrative. As such, it is either a compelling one or one that fails to convince us. This point presages the kind of issue that will receive more treatment in Chapter 29. In this sense, all research when it is written up entails a narrative analysis because the researcher/author always has a story to tell about his or her data (see Research in focus 22.11).

Research in focus 22.11
Narrative research in organizations

Rhodes and Brown (2005) conducted a review of the business and management literature on narrative analysis (one of which was the article in Research in focus 22.10). Their use of **narrative review** (see Chapter 5) is consistent with the focus of their review on a qualitative research method. They identify five principal research areas that narrative analysis has explored, assessing the theoretical value that each has added:

1. *sensemaking*: focuses on the role of stories as a device through which people make sense of organizational events;

2. *communication*: explores how narratives are used to create and maintain organizational culture and power structure;

3. *learning/change*: analyses how stories help people to learn and subjectively make sense of change;

4. *politics and power*: considers the role of shared narratives in the control of organizational meaning;

5. *identity and structuration*: focuses on the role of stories in creating and maintaining organizational identity.

They observe that this research has been beneficial to the field for several reasons. First, it has helped to focus attention on the temporal aspects of organizational life—how stories about organizational events express change and how the stories themselves change over time. Secondly, it stimulates reflection on the different and often divergent interpretations of organizational life. Thirdly, it draws attention to the role and significance of language in constructing organizational realities.

Rhetorical analysis

Related to narrative analysis is an approach that focuses on the importance of rhetorical devices as a means of communication and persuasion within management and organization. This includes analysis of classic rhetorical devices, such as argumentation, as well as various literary devices, including tropes such as metaphor, synecdoche, metonymy, and irony. Rhetoric and tropes are argued to be an unavoidable feature of organizational life (Oswick, Putnam, and Keenoy 2004). However, analyses often tend to focus on their role in communicating with large audiences. For example, Swales and Rogers (1995; see Research in focus 22.12) analysed corporate mission statements to demonstrate the importance of linguistic features in fostering organizational affiliation and identification. Rhetorical analysis has also been used to critique management fashions and management gurus by exploring how language is used to communicate ideas to global audiences (B. Jackson 2001) . Rhetorical analysis is also applied in the study of leadership, as another organizational context in which language is targeted at large audiences. For example, the study by Heracleous and Klaering (2014) described in Research in focus 22.13 analysed the rhetorical dynamics and metaphors used by the charismatic former CEO of Apple Inc., the late Steve Jobs, in communications with diverse audiences.

This study highlights the importance of rhetorical devices in provoking identification and commitment among listeners. It suggests that how a leader's message is

Research in focus 22.12
The rhetoric of corporate mission statements

Swales and Rogers (1995) use DA to explore how corporations project their philosophy through mission statements. From a collection of over 100 individual texts, they analyse a sample of 30 mission statements that reflect a diverse range of industries, organizational types, and countries of operation. They conclude that the content of these texts is 'pithy and up-beat', consisting of general statements with almost a total lack of 'support' such as examples, statistics, and so on. Mission statements 'tend to stress values, *positive* behaviour and guiding principles within the framework of the corporation's *announced* belief system and analysis' (1995: 227, emphasis in original).

Swales and Rogers show how mission statements use a number of linguistic features that are designed to foster affiliation and identification. Many use the rhetorical device of adopting the first-person-plural pronoun, 'we', to denote 'the employees of the corporation', rather than senior management or the corporation. In one instance they note that twenty-two of the sixty-six sentences in the document 'begin with the credo-like incantation "We believe . . ."' (1995: 234).

The second part of their research involved focusing on the mission statements of two well-known US companies—the Dana Corporation, a worldwide automotive parts supplier, and Honeywell, best known internationally for its temperature control systems.

In order to go beyond the surface of the text and explore the *framing content*, the researchers studied the companies' history, collected a wide range of documents, searched the business press, made site visits, and talked to key players. This enabled them to establish how mission statements get written and how they are perceived by their creators and users.

However, their original research plan also involved interviewing a stratified sample (see Chapter 8) of employees about their attitudes towards and uses of mission statements. This was not possible—'in both corporations, we were politely but firmly discouraged from such an ambition' (1995: 236)—because they were perceived as cultural outsiders.

Research in focus 22.13
The rhetorical construction of charismatic leadership

Heracleous and Klaering (2014) were interested in exploring the effect of rhetorical competence on charismatic leadership and whether leaders changed their rhetorical discourse in different contexts. Their empirical study of this question relied on an in-depth case study of Apple Inc. former CEO, the late Steve Jobs. A key aspect of charismatic leadership is suggested to involve the use of metaphors to communicate with followers. Their approach involved the analysis of three texts which were selected to represent temporal and contextual diversity and to reflect diversity in the leader's perceived 'ethos', or credibility in the situation:

1. A Securities and Exchange Commission (SEC) deposition by Steve Jobs given in 2008 concerning stock option backdating (119-page document comprising over 18,000 words), a situation of low ethos because Apple was being investigated for potential illegal practices;

2. A CNCB interview with Steve jobs regarding Apple's supplier shift from IBM to Intel conducted in 2005 (521 words), a situation of medium ethos where the leader was not particularly admired;

3. A discussion with Steve Jobs about media and technology in Wall Street Journal, 2010 (transcript length: 12,006 words), a situation of high ethos where the leader was being 'worshipped'.

One 500-word portion was selected for detailed analysis from each of the three texts, looking for central themes and the root metaphors employed. In addition to ethos, or speaker credibility, the researcher focused on two other aspects of rhetoric: 'logos', use of logic in arguments, and 'pathos', ability to ignite audience emotions.

framed, through the use of metaphors, rhythm, contrasts, and lists, is as important as what the speech is about in gaining commitment from followers. These 'tools for framing' define the form and construction of the message by providing vivid images for the audience. According to Heracleous and Klaering (2014), they include:

- *Pathos.* Here the speaker, Steve Jobs, attempts to evoke sympathy from the audience, by presenting himself as a human being rather than as the CEO of a successful multi-million dollar company, as the following extract from the SEC deposition illustrates:

> Steve Jobs: Well it was a tough situation, you know. It wasn't so much about the money... And as we've seen in the discussions of the past hour, I spent a lot of time trying to take care of people at Apple and to, you know, surprise and delight them with what a career at Apple could be... And I felt that the Board wasn't really doing the same with me... So I was hurt, I suppose would be the most accurate word... I had been working, you know, 4 years, 5 years of my life and not seeing my family very much and stuff and I just felt like there is nobody looking out for me here...
>
> (Heracleous and Klaering 2014: 141)

Through describing the Board of Director's lack of care for him, Steve Jobs invokes the rhetorical dynamic of pathos to evoke audience sympathy by portraying himself as 'a self-sacrificing businessman who places the company above his own interests' (Heracleous and Klaering 2014: 142). However, in the interview with the *Wall Street Journal*, where Steve Jobs is being interviewed as a respected expert and invited to share his wisdom, he draws on a much wider range of rhetorical techniques, including:

- *Metaphor.* Steve Jobs also uses root metaphors, such as the 'circle of life', as illustrated by the following extract:

> Steve Jobs: The way we've succeeded is by choosing what horses to ride really carefully, technically. We try to look for these technical vectors, that have a future and that are headed up and you know. Technology, different pieces of technology, kinda go in cycles, they have their springs and summers and autumns, and then they, you know, go to the graveyard of technology. So we try to pick things that are in their springs.

Research in focus 22.14
The rhetoric of marketing management textbooks

Another interesting application of rhetorical analysis is Hackley's (2003) rhetorical analysis of textbooks in the field of marketing management. Hackley notes that this field has spawned a huge number of books and that two publishers alone—Pearson Education and Macmillan—between them had over 200 titles in their UK catalogues in 2000. He explored the underlying rhetoric of a selection of these texts, including the work of leading figures such as Philip Kotler. Through his rhetorical exploration of these texts, Hackley uncovered several striking themes. He notes, for example, that 'theory' occupies a paradoxical position in these texts. It is both, as he puts it, 'aggrandized and despised' (2003: 1332). It is aggrandized because the texts typically indicate that they will cover key theories but then theory is knocked down because it is seen to be impractical and not likely, therefore, to provide guides to action. They frequently use other terms like 'tool', 'framework', and 'concept' rather than 'theory' because of its association with lofty ivory tower (and presumably irrelevant) reflection. Another rhetorical device noted is what Hackley calls 'bogus reflexivity', which occurs when the author of the marketing text notes limitations of typical work in the field but then proceeds to reaffirm the stance of much of that typical work. In other words, there is an acknowledgement of shortcomings, but those shortcomings are often held in abeyance so far as the writing of the text is concerned. For Hackley, the rhetorical examination of these texts provides an insight into managerialist ideology.

- Here, Steve Jobs is speaking in a context of high ethos, i.e. he has strong credibility and therefore he adopts a more entertaining and expansive rhetorical style, using the four seasons to describe products, with 'spring' referring to their birth, and 'graveyard' to describe their death. This 'circle of life' metaphor is also repeated in relation to the Apple company, which Jobs describes as 'on its way to oblivion', and then struggling for survival, before experiencing a rebirth.

Rhetorical analysis enables a focus on the persuasive acts that help to engender identification and foster co-operation within a group. For example, in the study by Swales and Rogers (1995) of corporate mission statements (see Research in focus 22.12), the researchers were especially interested in the way that mission statements were rhetorically designed to ensure maximum employee 'buy-in' and identification with the company.

However, they note that mission statements operate at a general and ambiguous level and deal mainly with abstractions. From the mission statements they analyse, they observe that there is an almost total absence of 'support' in the form of examples, quotations, or statistics. Swales and Rogers (1995: 227) note that verb forms used within the mission statements are predominantly present, imperative (for example, 'return to underwriting profit'), or purpose infinitive (for example, 'to provide a caring environment . . .'; 'to be the safest carrier'). The rhetorical devices that we have described in this section provide an important means whereby organizational researchers are able to explore and systematically analyse this use of language.

Research in focus 22.14 and Research in focus 22.15 provide some further examples of a rhetorical approach, though the latter is an extension of it, rather than an illustration as such.

Research in focus 22.15
Drama and executive action

Related to analyses of narrative and rhetoric is the notion of dramaturgy, as a method for analysing social action and people's explanations of social action. Building on the work of Goffman (1959) and the concept of impression management, dramaturgical analysis focuses on understanding the roles, scenes, scripts, and performances that people engage in as they interact with each other in a given setting.

Mangham's (1986) study of the executive function is based on the activities of a small group of managers as they think, talk, feel, and act on one afternoon during a boardroom discussion. Using a dramaturgical perspective, Mangham treats the processes whereby the executives interact with each other as 'performances', through which each member of the group asserts his power or status. The study focuses on just one short sequence of social activity, from which Mangham generates a series of 'readings' or interpretations of events. He explains:

> I have spent more hours of my life with these executives than I care to remember and recorded in one form or another thousands of lines of text. Out of this mass of material I have selected less than fifteen minutes and from these confused and confusing minutes I have shaped my presentation. A verbatim transcript of what was actually said—the entire repertoire of false starts, incomplete sentences, talkings over and the like—together with a detailed description of their non-verbal behaviour—the scratching, the fidgeting, the movement of feet, the twitching of brows, the coughs, stomach rumbles and so on—would fill several volumes and still be but a poor record of the actual scenes and exchanges.
>
> (1986: 153)

Mangham's analysis draws attention to the way that social actors construct their own power and status. This involves great skill in working with scripted roles combined with appropriate displays of emotion.

Context-sensitive approaches

The accusations levelled at fine-grained approaches, as too narrowly focused on language in use and insufficiently related to social and historical context, lead to consideration of approaches that seek to take into account to a greater extent factors that influence how language is produced, disseminated, and consumed. The approaches of narrative and rhetorical analysis can be considered to be more focused on the way that social reality is shaped through language. They can therefore be characterized as meso-level approaches (Alvesson and Kärreman 2000), being more sensitive to the context in which language is produced, concerned with finding generalizable patterns, and going beyond the detail of the text to a greater extent than fine-grained approaches. However, there is a further group of what Grant et al. (2004) describe as 'context-sensitive approaches' that take account of factors beyond the text itself. The most influential of these, in organizational research at least, is critical discourse analysis (CDA). The section that follows will introduce the theoretical approaches that underpin CDA and outline the basic framework and key concepts that CDA practitioners employ.

Critical discourse analysis

Critical discourse analysis emphasizes the role of language as a power resource that is related to ideology and socio-cultural change. It draws in particular on the theories and approaches of Foucault (1974, 1979, 1980), who sought to uncover the representational properties of discourse as a vehicle for the exercise of power based on the construction of disciplinary practices that enable the construction of the self-disciplining subject. The notion of discourse is, therefore, defined more broadly than in fine-grained approaches, as this summary by Phillips and Hardy (2002) illustrates.

> We define a discourse as an interrelated set of texts, and the practices of their production, dissemination, and reception, that brings an object into being (I. Parker 1992) . . . In other words, social reality is produced and made real through discourses, and social interactions cannot be fully understood without reference to the discourses that give them meaning. As discourse analysts, then, our task is to explore the relationship between discourse and reality.
>
> (Phillips and Hardy 2002: 3)

As the final part of this quote indicates, CDA practitioners are more receptive to the idea of a pre-existing material reality that constrains individual agency, and in particular to the epistemology of critical realism (see Key concept 2.8), arguing that discourses should be examined in relation to social structures, including the power relationships that are responsible for occasioning them (Reed 2000). Discourse is thus conceived as a 'generative mechanism' rather than as a self-referential sphere in which nothing of significance exists outside it, as Thinking deeply 22.16 explains.

In an organizational context, one of the things that CDA practitioners seek to trace is how discourses are constructed and maintained in relation to certain phenomena, such as globalization or strategic management (see Thinking deeply 22.17). Analysis seeks to reveal the meaning of a particular phenomenon by exploring how:

- the discourse has come to have a particular meaning today when forty or fifty years ago it may have had none or a quite different meaning;

- the discourse draws on and influences other discourses;

- the discourse is constructed through texts (such as academic articles or journalistic writing);

- the discourse gives meaning to social life and makes certain activities possible, desirable, or inevitable;

- particular actors draw on the discourse to legitimate their positions and actions (Phillips and Hardy 2002: 8).

As the second point in the above list indicates, discourses are conceived of as drawing on and influencing other discourses. So, for example, the discourse of globalization might affect discourses on new technology, free trade and liberalism, or corporate social responsibility. However, this is not always a complementary process, as in some cases discourses compete with each other for dominance in what is termed *dialogical struggle* (Keenoy, Oswick, and Grant 1997). An example of this can be seen in the analysis by Legge (1995) that traces the changing rhetorics of personnel management and HRM in the UK. Legge argues that 'the importance of HRM, and its apparent overshadowing of personnel management, lies just as much and (possibly more so) in its function

Thinking deeply 22.16
Critical realism and the discourse of organization

Fairclough (2005) argues that a version of CDA based on critical realism (see Key concept 2.8) is of particular value to organization studies, especially in relation to the study of organizational change. Fairclough is sceptical of the anti-realist assumptions of some discourse analysts who reject objectivist conceptions of organization as social structure in favour of seeing it as 'an interactive accomplishment' (2005: 917), according to a constructionist perspective (see Chapter 2). He quotes Mumby and Clair (1997) as typical of the latter position in saying 'we suggest that organizations exist only in so far as their members create them through discourse' (1997: 181).

Instead, Fairclough recommends an approach that centres on the tension between organizational discourse and organizational structure. Therefore, a critical realist approach to discourse analysis involves analysing not just the discourse *per se* but also its relationship to non-discoursal elements. This is particularly important in relation to the study of organizational change because, 'while change in discourse is a part of organizational change, and organizational change can often be understood partly in terms of the constructive effects of discourse on organizations, organizational change is not simply change in discourse' (2005: 931). Fairclough identifies four sets of organizational research issues that a critical realist approach to discourse analysis can address:

- *Emergence*: founded on the notion that 'new' organizational discourses emerge 'through "reweaving" relations between existing discourses' (2005: 932);

- *Hegemony*: focusing on how particular discourses become hegemonic in particular organizations and on 'how discourse figures within the strategies pursued by groups of social agents to change organizations in particular directions' (2005: 933);

- *Recontextualization*: involving identification of the principles through which 'external' discourses are internalized within particular organizations;

- *Operationalization*: focusing on how discourses are operationalized, transformed into new ways of acting and interacting, inculcated into new ways of being, or materialized, within organizations.

Thinking deeply 22.17
Critical discourse analysis and strategic management research

Phillips, Sewell, and Jaynes (2008) argue that there is potential for critical discourse analysis to be more widely applied in strategic management research. Using an example of a three-year case study of strategic change in a large banking and financial services institution, they show how the application of critical discourse analysis enables a focus on the way in which external discourses are imported into the organization. The authors did not confine themselves to written text but also conducted interviews and participant observation so that they 'were able to observe discursive practices as they unfolded' (Phillips, Sewell, and Jaynes 2008: 783). They show how discourses of 'Business' and 'Science' were used to legitimate the strategic change through drawing on modernist notions of rationality and progress in a way that portrayed the 'Transform' strategic change programme as natural and inevitable. This enabled any opposition to the programme to be characterized as an irrational response to scientifically derived facts. They further show how particular subject positions were authorized by the internal discourse, including 'Transform champions' and 'Transform trainees', showing how these limit appropriate conduct within the organization. Through extending their focus beyond official, written documents relating to the Transfom programme, the researchers were able to identify resistance to the authoritative discourse in the form of ironic and counter-narratives that they say they would not have picked up on had they relied on written documents alone.

as rhetoric about how employees should be managed to achieve competitive advantage than as a coherent new practice' (1995: p. xvi). This has the potential to give rise to a rhetoric–reality gap, in which discourses coexist and are translated into social practice in a variety of ways (Watson 1994a). CDA thus involves exploring why some meanings become privileged or taken for granted and others become marginalized. In other words, discourse does not just provide an account of what goes on in organizations; it is also a process whereby meaning is created. This involves asking 'who uses language, how, why and when' (Van Dijk 1997: 2).

Analysis of a particular *discursive event* is usually carried out according to a 'three-dimensional' framework, which proceeds as follows:

- examination of the actual content, structure, and meaning of the text under scrutiny (*the text dimension*);

- examination of the form of discursive interaction used to communicate meaning and beliefs (*the discursive practice dimension*);

- consideration of the social context in which the discursive event is taking place (*the social practice dimension*) (Grant et al. 2004: 11).

A further key concept within CDA is the notion of *intertextuality*, which draws attention to the notion of discourse as existing beyond the level of any particular discursive event on which analysis is focused. The notion of intertextuality thus enables a focus on the social and historical context in which discourse is embedded.

Overview

As the discussion in this chapter has emphasized, the different approaches to analysing language tend to draw on each other to a greater or lesser extent. Furthemore, DA, narrative, and critical discourse analysis are in some respects more flexible approaches to the study of language in business research than CA, because they are not solely concerned with the analysis of naturally occurring talk and enable a broader acknowledgement of the

socio-historical context within which language is located. Consequently, they encourage researchers to use methods such as interviews and participant observation, in addition to analysing written documents. For these reasons, discourse analysis has become increasingly popular as a method in business research in recent decades, and there is now a regular international conference dedicated to discursive approaches to organizational analysis as well as a handbook (Grant et al. 2004) and several journal special issues dedicated to the study of organizational discourses. As researchers who study discourse note, the focus on language in business research is perhaps not surprising, because language plays such a significant role in 'constructing, situating, facilitating and communicating the diverse cultural, institutional, political and socio-economic parameters of "organizational being"' (Grant, Keenoy, and Oswick 1998: 12).

One of the difficulties relating to discursive approaches concerns the anti-realist inclination of some DA researchers. This arises from the focus on representational practices—talk and written text—rather than on organizational action or behaviour. The lack of attention to a material reality that lies behind and underpins discourse has led some researchers to view the approach as too abstract. For example, writing from a critical realist position (see Key concept 2.8), M. I. Reed (2000) has argued that discourses should be examined in relation to social structures, such as power relationships, that are responsible for shaping discourses. Attention would additionally be focused on the ways in which discourses work through existing structures. Discourse is thereby conceived as a 'generative mechanism' rather than a self-referential sphere in which nothing of significance exists outside it. M. I. Reed (2000) provides an interesting example of such an alternative view:

> Discourses—such as the quantitatively based discourses of financial audit, quality control and risk management—are now seen as the generative mechanisms through which new regulatory regimes 'carried out' by rising expert groups—such as accountants, engineers and scientists—become established and legitimated in modern societies. What they represent is less important than what they do in facilitating a radical re-ordering of pre-existing institutional structures in favour of social groups who benefit from the upward mobility which such innovative regulatory regimes facilitate . . .
>
> (M. I. Reed 2000: 529)

As this passage suggests, while some DA practitioners are anti-realist, an alternative realist position in relation to discourse is possible. Such an alternative position is perhaps closer to the concerns of the business researcher than an anti-realist stance.

Furthermore, the extensive use of this term 'discourse' brings its own problems, because what different researchers understand the term discourse to mean varies considerably, and so does their approach to analysis. There is thus a danger, noted by Alvesson and Kärreman (2000), that the term 'discourse analysis' is too broad to be meaningful, authors treating the term as though it has a clear, broadly agreed-upon meaning, which, just from reading this chapter, you will be able to see it does not. Consequently, 'discourse sometimes comes close to standing for everything, and thus nothing' (Alvesson and Kärreman 2000: 1128). Building on this earlier article, Alvesson and Kärreman (2011) also warn that the privileging of discourse, and primarily of talk and language as the central force in organizational meaning-making, contributes towards a marginalization of the non-discursive, which includes the material, embodied and unarticulated. This builds on their earlier distinction between small 'd' discourse analysis, which is aligned with Potter and Wetherall's approach outlined earlier in this chapter, and big 'D' discourse analysis that draws on the work of Foucault and the critical approach, outlined in the previous section. They criticize small 'd' discourse analysts for an exclusionary focus on language that misses too much, and for mystifying agency through the vague definition of 'context'. They are also critical of big 'D' discourse analysis stating that 'any assessment and study of Discourse should be careful not to blow up Discourse to The Explanation, but rather to be sensitive to and curious about empirical indications that the constitutive powers of Discourse may be limited' (Alvesson and Kärreman 2011: 1133). However, the important thing to remember is that understanding how language is used is viewed by some researchers as crucial to understanding the social world, and the approaches examined in this chapter provide some tools through which language can be explored as a focus of attention in its own right.

Key points

- The approaches examined in this chapter take the position that language is itself a focus of interest, and not just a medium through which research participants communicate with each other or with researchers.
- Fine-grained approaches such as CA and DA focus in detail on the organizing properties of language and the rules and structures that determine what people say in a given interaction.
- CA is a highly detailed approach to the analysis of naturally occurring conversation and dialogue that uses systematic rules to reveal the underlying structures of language.
- DA is an anti-realist, constructionist approach for the analysis of language that conceives of discourse as a means of conveying meaning.
- Narrative analysis is an approach to the elicitation and analysis of language that is sensitive to the stories that people tell about their lives or events around them.
- Rhetorical analysis examines the use of persuasive forms of language that help to engender identification and foster cooperation within a group, focusing on the importance of rhetorical devices in this process.
- CDA conceives of a discourse as an interrelated set of texts and sees discourses as drawing on and influencing other discourses.
- CDA emphasizes the role of language as a power resource that is related to ideology and socio-cultural change.

Questions for review

- In what ways do fine-grained approaches to language differ from context-sensitive approaches?

Conversation analysis

- What three basic assumptions underpin the CA practitioner's approach?
- Why are notational symbols employed in CA?

Discourse analysis

- What is the significance of saying that DA is anti-realist and constructionist?
- What is an interpretative repertoire?

Narrative analysis

- What might be the main purpose of seeking to uncover organizational stories?
- How is it that the writing-up of research is in itself a process of narrative construction?

Rhetorical analysis

- List some of the main areas of business and management where rhetorical analysis has been applied and explain why rhetorical analysis is useful in understanding them.

Context-sensitive approaches

● What are the main criticisms made of fine-grained approaches?

Critical discourse analysis

● What key questions might a CDA practitioner ask in seeking to reveal the meaning of TQM discourses?

● Why is the notion of intertextuality important to CDA practitioners?

Online Resource Centre
[www.oxfordtextbooks.co.uk/orc/brymanbrm4e/]

Visit the Interactive Research Guide that accompanies this book to complete an exercise in Language in Qualitative Research.

23

Documents as sources of data

Chapter outline

The term 'documents' covers a very wide range of different sources. This chapter aims to reflect that variability by examining a range of documentary sources that have been or can be used in qualitative business research. In addition, the chapter touches on approaches to the analysis of such sources. The chapter explores:

- personal documents in both written form—such as diaries and letters—and visual form—such as photographs;

- public documents deriving, for example, from an inquiry or legal investigation;

- official documents deriving from organizational sources—such as company annual reports, policy documents, and internal memoranda;

- mass media outputs—such as newspaper articles;

- virtual outputs—such as Internet resources;

- the criteria for evaluating each of the above sources;

- how far readers of documents are active or passive consumers of documents;

- three approaches to the analysis of documents: qualitative content analysis; semiotics; and historical analysis.

Introduction

This chapter will be concerned with a fairly heterogeneous set of sources of data, such as letters, memos, diaries, autobiographies, internal reports, newspapers, magazines, and photographs. The emphasis is placed on documents that have not been produced at the request of a business researcher—instead, the objects that are the focus of this chapter are simply 'out there' waiting to be assembled and analysed. However, this is not to suggest that the fact that documents are available for the business researcher to work on renders them somehow less time-consuming or easier to deal with than collecting primary data. On the contrary, the search for documents relevant to your research can often be a frustrating and highly protracted process. Moreover, once they are collected, considerable interpretative skill is required to ascertain the meaning of the materials that have been uncovered.

In this chapter we will emphasize documents in the form of material that:

- can be read (though the term 'read' has to be understood in a somewhat looser fashion than is normally the case when we come to visual materials, such as photographs);

- has not been produced specifically for the purposes of research, although we will also refer to documents that have been generated by researchers;

- is preserved so that it becomes available for analysis; and

- is relevant to the concerns of the business researcher.

Documents have already been encountered in this book, albeit in a variety of contexts or guises. For example, the kinds of source upon which content analysis is often carried out are documents, such as newspaper articles. However, the emphasis in this chapter will be upon the use of documents in qualitative organizational research. A further way in which documents have previously surfaced was in the brief discussion in Key concept 14.12, which noted that archive materials are one form of unobtrusive measure. Indeed, this points to an often-noted advantage of using documents of the kind discussed in this chapter—namely, they are non-reactive. This means that, because they have not been created specifically for the purposes of business research, the possibility of a reactive effect can be largely discounted as a limitation on the validity of data.

In discussing the different kinds of documents used in the social sciences, John Scott (1990) has usefully distinguished between personal documents and official documents, and has further classified the latter in terms of private as opposed to state documents. These distinctions will be employed in much of the discussion that follows. A further set of important distinctions made by Scott relate to the criteria for assessing the quality of documents. He suggests (1990: 6) four criteria.

- *Authenticity*. Is the evidence genuine and of unquestionable origin?
- *Credibility*. Is the evidence free from error and distortion?

- *Representativeness*. Is the evidence typical of its kind, and, if not, is the extent of its untypicality known?
- *Meaning*. Is the evidence clear and comprehensible?

This is an extremely rigorous set of criteria against which documents might be gauged, and frequent reference to them will be made in the following discussion.

Personal documents

Personal documents such as diaries and letters may be used as the primary source of data within a qualitative study or alternatively as adjuncts to other methods, such as interviews or participant observation. Diaries and letters kept for reasons other than research purposes tend to be infrequently used by business researchers. However, there is scope for them to be used in the study of management, as the example of Schoneboom's use of 'workblogs' (Research in focus 23.1) illustrates. The emergence of workblogs over the past decade, in which individuals or loosely connected groups of workers articulate their feelings about work in a humorous, cynical way, has provided particular insight into call centre work, through blogs such as *Call Centre Confidential*, which documents the life of an anonymous team leader at an unidentified call centre, 'Next Stop Bombay': **http://callcentrediary.blogspot.co.uk/** (accessed 2 November 2014). Schoneboom (2011) suggests that although these accounts are written 'pseudonymously, and are often highly

fictionalised, they reveal employees' critical responses to the corporate cultures in which they are immersed' (Schoneboom 2011: 133); she sees such blog-based worker testimony as a form of creative resistance. However, perhaps because of the potential negative repercussions of workblogging, several bloggers have faced disciplinary action from their employers as a result of their exploits. Workbloggers have therefore become increasingly subtle in their approach, hiding work-related content within blogs that do not have an explicitly work-related theme. Consequently, bloggers are increasingly reluctant to enagage with researchers, and Schoneboom advises that posted content is 'harvested' quickly and regularly, as it can be taken down suddenly and often without warning. She adds that the emergence of Twitter and Facebook provides new opportunities for employees to talk about work. However, employer strategies of surveillance of employee Internet misbehaviour mean that this is continually shifting.

Research in focus 23.1
A study of online diaries written by white-collar workers

Schoneboom (2011) suggests that 'workblogs', which she defines as Internet-based employee diaries, provide a unique insight into the labour process from a worker perspective. Focusing on workblogs produced by white-collar workers in Greater Manchester and Lancashire in the North of England, she suggests that these virtual documents illustrate the countercultural values and creative aspirations of the bloggers, challenging the view of knowledge workers as atomized and apathetic, and instead showing them to be part of an organized and vocal movement. The anonymous bloggers were identified through a combination of snowball sampling and Internet searching. Using these methods, she identified 'bloggers who worked in white-collar office environments and who wrote

(continued)

critically about their work either as the primary topic of their blog or as an occasional theme' (Schoneboom 2011: 407). All six bloggers were aged between 20 and 40. Concentrating on bloggers in a specific geographical region enabled Schoneboom to study face-to-face interaction and local networking at 'blogmeets'. She complemented this with email and telephone interviews with the bloggers, in addition to analysis of archived material on the blogs, which she also contributed to in order to avoid being seen as 'lurking' (see Chapter 28). As she explains: 'through this I tried, as far as possible, to build a level of trust that allows me to assume that the bloggers involved in the study are being broadly honest about their occupation and are drawing artistic inspiration from real events' (Schoneboom 2011: 410). She also sought to build trust with the bloggers by referring them to her own online creative identity, in the form of a long-established personal website. A striking theme to emerge from all the blogs is a distain for managerialism, including management jargon, popular theories, and consultants. Interestingly, the bloggers also claimed to be doing well in their jobs, but simultaneously distanced themselves from the demands of the organization to work harder and seek promotion.

Another example of the use of personal documents in historical organizational research is given in Research in focus 23.2. In this study, Bloor (2002) analysed oral history tapes and transcripts from interviews carried out with Welsh miners in the 1970s. As Bloor comments, the main interest of these documents for the researcher 'lies in the fact that they describe events from the partisan standpoint of lived experience. They are thus a record of a local culture and of situated communal understandings of events' (2002: 93). Personal documents can also be used to trace the history of an organization through the letters and diaries of its founders. For example, the company archives of the chocolate manufacturer Cadbury are held at the Birmingham factory. The archives include diaries and letters documenting more than 100 years of history of the family firm. Many of these documents are held in private collections, making research access potentially difficult. However, it is likely that the use of personal diaries and letters in business and management

research will be confined largely to retrospective, historical analysis. A classic example of the use of letters to build up a historical picture of working life is provided by E. P. Thompson (1968) in his comprehensive and enormously detailed account of the making of the English working classes. Research for the book draws upon numerous data sources such as legal records, autobiographies, notes, pamphlets, newspapers, minutes of committee meetings, and letters. This latter data source includes 'correspondence preserved by Sir Joseph Radcliffe, the exceedingly active Huddersfield magistrate who received his knighthood in recognition of his services in bringing leading Yorkshire Luddites to trial' (1968: 941). However, the emergence of alternative forms of communication has undoubtedly limited the use of letters as a source of data, and it is likely that the use of email will mean that the role of letters as a potential source of documentary data will continue to decline.

Research in focus 23.2
Using oral histories in a historical study of safety risks in mining

In a study of industrial injury and safety threats in the coal-mining industry, Bloor (2002) used the oral history archive in the South Wales Miners' Library, focusing on 176 audiotaped oral history interviews conducted in 1973–4 (see Chapter 20 for a discussion of oral history interviews). He explains: 'the tapes describe experiences of pit and community going back before the First World War, and in some cases going back to the end of the 19th century' (Bloor 2002: 92). Bloor analysed the transcripts and untranscribed tapes for references to 'accidents' and 'disasters', photocopying relevant sections of the transcripts and transcribing relevant sections of the untranscribed tapes. He was interested in the way that miners acted as enforcers of pit safety regulations and in the role of the workforce's representatives, 'workmen inspectors', in reducing safety threats in pits between 1900 and 1947. Bloor argues that these documents have relevance for health and safety at work today by showing that collective health behaviour is driven by class struggle against management and government, whom the workers did not trust to ensure their own safety.

Another way that diaries can be used in qualitative research is as a method of data collection. In this instance, the diaries are produced specifically for the purpose of the research and the diarists are normally given some sort of topic guide to help them. They are different from quantitative diary studies (see Chapter 10), because a lesser degree of structure is imposed on the diarist. For example, Bowey and Thorpe (1986) were interested in exploring coal miners' attitudes to incentive schemes as part of a larger, multi-method study. Over a three-month period the miners were asked to keep a daily written record of their feelings, observations, and opinions about their life and work. The miners were given a large amount of scope in terms of what they wrote about in the diaries. In addition to writing about the bonus incentive scheme, they were invited to write about workplace relationships and matters relating to production. The researchers were thereby able to build up a picture of the operation of the incentive system that took into account the contextual features that framed its operation. The diaries were returned to the researchers each week, so that they could keep track of their development and write back to the diarist asking for clarification of specific points. Bowey and Thorpe claim that, in addition to aiding the analysis, this dialogue helped to encourage the diarists to keep writing in their diaries, because they felt that an interest was being taken in their work.

Whereas letters are a form of communication with other people, diarists invariably write for themselves. However, when they are written for wider consumption, diaries are difficult to distinguish from another kind of personal document—the autobiography. Like letters and diaries, autobiographies can be written at the request of the researcher, particularly in connection with life history studies (see Chapter 20 for a full explanation of the life history method). However, commercially published autobiographical sources can also be used for research purposes. For example, in the research into organizational culture carried out by Martin and Siehl (1983; see Research in focus 23.3), the authors relied extensively on a biography of the General Motors division manager, John DeLorean, written by J. P. Wright in 1979. Direct quotations and organizational stories from this source were analysed to build up a picture of the organizational counterculture that developed under DeLorean's influence.

Research in focus 23.3
Using biographical accounts in a study of organizational culture

In an article about organizational counterculture at General Motors (GM), Martin and Siehl (1983) draw on data from two sources:

1. E. Cray, *Chrome Colossus: General Motors and its Times* (1980)—a corporate history of GM.

2. J. P. Wright, *On a Clear Day You Can See General Motors* (1979)—an account of the activities of the influential manager John DeLorean at GM.

The first source was selected because it was the most current source at the time. It provides a detailed picture of the firm's dominant culture, and it includes some information that is critical of the firm. The second source was chosen because it is the most thorough published account of DeLorean's activities at GM. The two sources were supplemented by a number of interviews with present and former GM employees and by the use of other published books about the company.

An in-depth qualitative content analysis of the two books was conducted, and this was used as the basis for the interpretations, using direct quotations and stories from the two accounts.

Martin and Siehl note that a limitation of the two accounts is that they both focus primarily on the activities of 'relatively high ranking executives' without exploring 'how these activities were perceived by subordinates' (1983: 56).

They also note that, because Wright writes of DeLorean's experiences in the first person, the book is cited as representing DeLorean's point of view. However, they point out that DeLorean has disowned Wright's account, and it is highly likely that their opinions differ on some issues. They acknowledge that 'in such cases the book is probably more representative of Wright's opinions than DeLorean's, in spite of the former's use of the first person' (1983: 64).

When we evaluate personal documents, the *authenticity* criterion is clearly of considerable importance. Is the purported author of the letter or diary the real author? In the case of autobiographies, this has become a growing problem in recent years as a result of the increasing use of 'ghost' writers by the famous. In Martin and Siehl's (1983) study of organizational counterculture (see Research in focus 23.3), how can we be sure that interpretations of culture based on accounts of events and direct quotations from these biographical and historical sources are accurate? But the same is potentially true of other documents. Turning to the issue of *credibility*, John Scott (1990) observes that there are at least two major concerns with respect to personal documents: the factual accuracy of reports, and whether or not they report the true feelings of the writer. Scott recommends a strategy of healthy scepticism regarding the sincerity with which the writer reports his or her true feelings. Famous business people such as Richard Branson or Anita Roddick would be likely to be fully aware that their letters or diaries would be of considerable interest to others and might, therefore, have one eye firmly fixed on the degree to which they really revealed themselves in their writings, or alternatively would ensure that they conveyed a 'front' that they wanted to project. Authorized biographies and autobiographies have to be treated with similar caution, since they can frequently be exercises in reputation-building.

Representativeness is an additional concern for these materials. Surviving historical documents are relatively few in number, and they have been preserved only in relation to the most influential of companies, such as Cadbury, Unilever, or the Ford Foundation. Therefore, such historical documents are likely to be biased in terms of the organizations they represent. A further problem is the selective survival of documents like letters. Why do any survive at all and what proportion are damaged, lost, or thrown away? The question of *meaning* is often rendered problematic by such things as damage to letters and diaries, and the use by authors of abbreviations or codes that are difficult to decipher.

Public documents

The state is the source of a great deal of information of potential significance for business researchers. It produces a large amount of statistical information, some of which was touched on in Chapter 14. In addition to such quantitative data, the state is the source of a lot of textual material of potential interest, such as Acts of Parliament and official reports.

An interesting use of official documents is B. A. Turner's (1994) employment of the reports of public inquiries into three disasters, one of which—the fire at the Summerland Leisure Centre, Douglas, Isle of Man, in 1973—is particularly emphasized in his discussion. The report was published in 1974. Turner was primarily interested in the preconditions of the fire—the factors that were deemed by the inquiry to have led to the fire itself and the way in which the handling of the incident produced such disastrous consequences (fifty deaths). In his initial analysis, which was based on a grounded theory approach, Turner aimed to produce a theoretical account of the fire's preconditions. Turner describes the process for this and the other two public inquiry reports he examined as one of slowly going through the details of the report. He describes the process as follows:

> I asked, for each paragraph, what names or 'labels for ideas' I needed in order to identify those elements, events or notions which were of interest to me in my broad and initially very unfocused concern to develop a theory of disaster preconditions. I then recorded each name or concept label on the top of a 5 inch by 8 inch card, together with a note of the source paragraph, and added further paragraph references to the card as I encountered additional instances of the concept identified.
>
> (1994: 198)

He ended up with 182 of these cards, which provided the raw materials for building his theoretical model. Similar sources were employed by Weick (1990) in his study of the Tenerife plane crash in 1977, in that he used an official report of the Spanish Ministry of Transport and Communication and a further report by the US-based Airline Pilots Association.

A further example of this kind of study is provided by Gephart (1993), who based his analysis on naturally occurring retrospective and archival qualitative data, including public inquiry transcripts and proceedings, newspaper reports, and corporate and government documents (see Research in focus 23.4). This type of analysis, which uses publicly available data to analyse critical events or disasters, has been referred to as 'organizational post mortem' research (Orton 1997), and there is an increasing number of research studies in business and management that use this approach. Other examples include Vaughan's (1990) analysis of the space shuttle *Challenger* tragedy in 1986 and Orton's (1997) study of three critical events in the history of the US intelligence community. In the former, Vaughan used documents gathered by the Presidential Commission and reports and transcripts that related to the disaster; she also interviewed journalists and people responsible for regulating safety at NASA. Orton instead relied on organizational and presidential libraries, in particular the Ford Library, which contained over fourteen million original documents from the administration of President Ford. Familiarizing oneself with these kinds of research materials can be an extremely time-consuming activity, mainly because of the vastness and detail of documents associated with official events and inquiries, and this needs to be taken into account when planning to use such materials as a potential source of data. However, some researchers are selective in their use of documents associated with disasters and official inquiries, as the examples in Research in focus 23.5 illustrate.

In terms of John Scott's (1990) four criteria, such materials can certainly be seen as authentic and as having meaning (in the sense of being clear and comprehensible to the researcher), but the two other standards require somewhat greater consideration. The question of credibility raises the issue of whether or not the documentary source is biased. In other words, such documents can be interesting precisely because of the biases they reveal. Equally, this point suggests that caution is necessary in attempting to treat them as depictions of reality. The issue of representativeness is complicated in that materials like these are in a sense unique, and it is precisely their official or quasi-official character that makes them interesting in their own right. There is also, of course, the question of whether or not the case itself is representative, but in the context of qualitative research this is not a meaningful question, because no case can be representative in a statistical sense. The issue is one of establishing a cogent theoretical account and possibly examining that account in other contexts. B. A. Turner (1994) in fact examined three disasters and noted many common factors that were associated with behaviour in crisis situations.

Research in focus 23.4
Using public documents to analyse an organizational disaster

Gephart (1993) employed what he describes as a 'textual approach', using a variety of retrospective archival material in a way that treats researchers' observations and written documents as 'texts'. Two kinds of data were collected:

1. naturally occurring retrospective and archival qualitative data, including public inquiry transcripts and proceedings, newspaper reports, and corporate and government documents;

2. self-generated texts, including field notes describing inquiry events.

These texts were analysed in order to trace the life history of the focal event—a pipeline disaster—from the perspectives of a range of participants. The study sought to address the following research questions in the public inquiry context:

- What concepts and terms, or vocabularies, are used by organizational members in sensemaking about disasters?
- How do people use risk and blame concepts in disaster sensemaking?
- How are sensemaking practices used in the interpretation of disasters?
- What role do collective and individual interpretative schemes play in disaster sensemaking?

(continued)

The pipeline accident occurred in 1985 on the Western Pipe Lines system in Canada. A fireball erupted during attempts to control a leak of natural gas liquids, and two employees of the company died of burns. There followed a public inquiry in which the federal government energy board took evidence about the causes and consequences of the disaster. The public inquiry provided Gephart with a focus for his investigation through the series of texts that attempted to make sense of the disaster and tried publicly to attribute responsibility and blame.

Gephart attended the public inquiry throughout, informally interviewing managers, lawyers, and safety managers who were also attending the inquiry. This ethnographic aspect of his data collection resulted in 500 pages of field notes. These were combined with the other, naturally occurring, data used in the study, such as the official proceedings of the inquiry, and used to compile two electronically held databases:

1. a word processor database containing all the information from the transcripts, company documents, field notes, newspaper articles, and official report;

2. a textual database from the entire text of the inquiry proceedings.

Analysis, using a computer-based text retrieval program, focused on creating 'textual exhibits' 'that tell the story of the disaster and the inquiry using actual segments of text'; this enabled Gephart in his analysis to 'remain close to the raw data' and to illustrate its richness (1993: 1483). A set of keywords was then developed to reflect the way that participants saw concepts of risk, blame, and responsibility.

It was then possible to retrieve 'every occurrence of the keywords in the data' using the textual analysis software and to show these frequencies speaker by speaker. Gephart claims that the textual approach offers a way of uncovering practices and processes that generate and sustain organizational interpretations of events. The use of archival materials enables a longitudinal study of events, which in this case was complemented by the collection of primary ethnographic data.

Research in focus 23.5
Two separate uses of public documents to analyse the Stockwell shooting

Colville et al.'s (2013) analysis focuses on the 2005 Stockwell shooting, when specialist firearms officers from the London Metropolitan Police Service shot dead Jean Charles de Menezes in a tube train at Stockwell underground station because they suspected him of being a terrorist and carrying a bomb. Adopting a sensemaking perspective, Colville et al.'s primary data source is the report which followed the Official Inquiry into the shooting, conducted by the Independent Police Complaints Commission, the IPCC Stockwell One Report (2007). This, in combination with witness statements, voice recordings and CCTV footage, provided the basis for the 194-page report. The authors suggest that their ability to interpret the data was enhanced by the insider status of the third author, who was formerly a police officer with counter-terrorism experience. In contrast to other research on organizational disaster sensemaking, such as Gephart's (1993) and Turner's (1994), these researchers chose only to focus on this single report, rather than on multiple documents and media sources, as their analysis focused on the organizational/operational details of the incident and because this 'legally upheld document... in terms of its timelines and recorded explanations... [remains] uncontested' (Colville et al. 2013: 1206).

A completely separate analysis by Cornelissen et al. (2014) also takes a sensemaking approach to analysing the same incident. Cornelissen et al. used different documentary data sources from those used by Colville et al., including transcripts of the official inquest into the death of de Menezes. They assert that the data give insight into 'real-time sensemaking in the context of an unprecedented, complex and dynamic situation' (Cornelissen et al. 2014: 8).

Although it appears that these researchers were not aware of the other's interest in this subject (as they do not cite each others' articles), these studies illustrate remarkable consistency in the way this case has been analysed. Both analyses focus on the written logs of decisions taken by senior police officers on the day the incident happened, which give insight into events as they unfolded minute by minute. They also use similar theoretical concepts and focus on the framing of decisions that defined the situation, each highlighting different aspects of the process, e.g. novelty vs. emotion.

Organizational documents

This is a very heterogeneous group of sources that is of particular importance to the business and management researcher, not least because of the vast quantity of documentary information that is available within most organizations. Some of these documents are in the public domain, such as annual reports, mission statements, reports to shareholders, transcripts of chief executives' speeches, press releases, advertisements, and public-relations material in printed form and on the Web. Other documents are not (or may not be) in the public domain, such as company newsletters, organizational charts, external consultancy reports, minutes of meetings, memos, internal and external correspondence, manuals for new recruits, policy statements, company regulations, and so on. Such materials can provide the researcher with valuable background information about the company; they are, therefore, often used by organizational ethnographers as part of their investigations. Similarly, in case study research, documents can be used to build up a description of the organization and its history. Because documents can offer at least partial insights into past managerial decisions and actions, they can also be useful in building up a 'timeline', particularly in processual studies of organizational change (see Chapter 17 and Research in focus 17.8).

However, the difficulty of gaining access to some organizations means that some researchers have to rely on public-domain documents alone. Even if the researcher is an insider who has gained access to an organization, it may well be that certain documents that are not in the public domain will not be available to him or her. For his study of ICI, Pettigrew (1985; see Research in focus 3.16) was allowed access to company archives, so that, in addition to interviewing, he was allowed to examine 'materials on company strategy and personnel policy, documents relating to the birth and development of various company OD (organizational development) groups, files documenting the natural history of key organizational

changes, and information on the recruitment and training of internal OD consultants, and the use made of external OD consultants' (1985: 41). Such information can be very important for researchers conducting case studies of organizations using such methods as participant observation or (as in Pettigrew's case) qualitative interviews. Other writers have relied more or less exclusively on documents. For example, in B. A. Turner's (1994) study of large-scale disasters, his analysis relied entirely on the detailed accounts of action provided by the public inquiry records, and these formed the basis for his own written notes, which constituted his data documents.

Such documents need to be evaluated using Scott's four criteria. As with the materials considered in the previous section, documents deriving from private sources such as companies are likely to be authentic and meaningful, in the sense of being clear and comprehensible to the researcher, though this is not to suggest that the analyst of documents should be complacent. Issues of credibility and representativeness are likely to exercise the analyst of documents somewhat more. For instance, organizational documents that are in the public domain, such as company annual reports, may not be an accurate representation of how different organizational actors perceive the situations in which they are involved.

People who write organizational documents, such as managers, are likely to have a particular point of view that they want to get across. An interesting illustration of this simple observation is provided by a study of company documentation by Forster (1994). In the course of a study of career development issues in a major British retail company (referred to as TC), Forster carried out an extensive analysis of company documentation relating primarily to HRM issues, as well as interviews and a questionnaire survey. Because he was able to interview many of the authors of the documents about what they had written, 'both the accuracy of the documents and their authorship could be validated by the individuals who had produced them' (1994: 155). In other words, the authenticity of the documents was confirmed, and it would seem that credibility was verified as well. However, Forster also tells us that the documents showed up divergent interpretations among different groupings of key events and processes.

> One of the clearest themes to emerge was the apparently incompatible interpretations of the same events and processes among the three subgroups within the company—senior executives, HQ personnel staff and regional personnel managers . . . . These documents were not produced deliberately to distort or obscure events or processes being described, but their effect was to do precisely this.
>
> (1994: 160)

In other words, members of the different groupings expressed through the documents certain perspectives that reflected their positions in the organization.

Consequently, although authors of the documents could confirm the content of those documents, the latter could not be regarded as 'free from error and distortion', as John Scott puts it. Therefore, documents cannot be regarded as providing objective accounts of a state of affairs. They have to be interrogated and examined in the context of other sources of data. As Forster's case suggests, the different stances that are taken up by the authors of documents can be used as a platform for developing insights into the processes and factors that lie behind divergence. In this instance, the documents are interesting in bringing out the role and significance of subcultures within the organization.

Issues of representativeness are likely to loom large in most contexts of this kind. Did Forster have access to a totally comprehensive set of documents? It could be that some had been destroyed or that he was not allowed access to certain documents that were regarded as sensitive. Finally, gaining access to confidential or potentially sensitive documents within an organization, such as personnel files, as Dalton (1959) did (see Chapter 19), raises particular ethical issues, which have been discussed in Chapter 6.

 # Mass media outputs

Newspapers, magazines, television programmes, films, and other mass media are potential sources for business and management study. Of course, we have encountered these kinds of source before when exploring content analysis in Chapter 13. An example is given in Research in focus 23.6 of a study that relied exclusively on articles about a well-known business leader published in the popular press. In addition to exploring mass-media outputs using a quantitative form of data analysis such as content analysis, such sources can also be examined so that their qualitative nature is preserved. Typically, such analysis entails searching for themes in the sources that are examined, but see the discussion on analysing documents below for a more detailed examination of this issue.

Authenticity issues are sometimes difficult to ascertain in the case of mass-media outputs. While the outputs can usually be deemed to be genuine, the authorship of articles is often unclear (for example, editorials, some magazine articles), so that it is difficult to know if the account can be relied upon as being written by someone in a position to provide an accurate version.

Credibility is also frequently an issue, but in fact it is often the uncovering of error or distortion that is the objective of the analysis. For example, Jackson and Carter (1998) explored the constitution of management gurus through the analysis of a BBC management video featuring Frederick Herzberg giving a live lecture to an audience of UK managers on his Motivation–Hygiene theory. They compare this video with an earlier transmission of the lecture, which was shown on normal television in 1973, under the title 'Jumping for the Jelly Beans'. Comparison of the two versions reveals a number of differences between them; notably, in the video version a section subtitled 'KITA' (Herzberg's acronym for 'Kick in the Arse'), containing some offensive references including a joke about rape, has been edited out of the lecture. Jackson and Carter suggest that the reason for this careful editing relates to the need to maintain Herzberg's credibility as a management guru, ensuring that his image remains intact, despite the fact that the editing distorts the presentation of his ideas.

Representativeness is rarely an issue for analyses of newspaper or magazine articles, since the corpus from which a sample has been drawn is usually ascertainable, especially when a wide range of newspapers is employed. Finally, the evidence is usually clear and comprehensible but may require considerable awareness of contextual factors relating to the organization or company, such as information about share prices, movements of key personnel, and merger speculation.

Research in focus 23.6
Qualitative content analysis in leadership research

Chen and Meindl (1991) analysed articles in the popular press about Donald Burr, an entrepreneur who in 1980 started the low-cost US airline, People Express. Burr was widely revered as a charismatic leader because of the early success of his business and the high level of commitment exhibited by his staff. However, in 1984 the company began to founder, and it was taken over by a rival in 1987.

The researchers carried out two analyses of magazine and newspaper articles about Burr. The first followed traditional content analysis methods (of the kind described in Chapter 13); it involved identifying themes and then recording the frequency of their occurrence in the text. However, the second analysis was more interpretative; it involved identification of the metaphors used to describe Burr over the course of the airline's history. The first analysis sought to analyse Burr's image from the perspective of the *reader* of the news article, whereas the second analysis concentrated on gaining an impression from the point of view of the *writer*.

Articles were presented to a sample of seventy-five undergraduate business students, who were asked to write a description of Burr based on the materials they had just read. Fourteen different themes were extracted from the image descriptions and these were subjected to traditional content analysis to establish a pattern of frequency. The analysis revealed that the themes used to describe Burr varied according to the time period in the company's history that the articles covered. For example, when the company was doing well, Burr was seen as ambitious, fair, and caring, but when it was doing badly he was seen as determined and instrumental.

In the qualitative content analysis, Chen and Meindl (1991) focused on the journalists' descriptions of Burr (that is, the writers rather than the readers of the text):

> We screened, sentence by sentence, the same sampled journal articles that were presented to the respondents. Those words, phrases, or clauses that metaphorically described Burr's personality, his behaviours, or his impact were identified as metaphorical expressions. Altogether, 46 such expressions were identified.
>
> (1991: 539)

One of the most common metaphors uncovered was that of Burr as an unorthodox preacher who was visionary, charismatic, and dedicated to his mission, as these journalistic quotes illustrate:

> Within the new structure . . . Burr will go on preaching his unorthodox management approach.
>
> (1991: 550)

> Burr works hard when he talks. He paces, he sits; he stands; he throws out his arms; he condemns and praises, implores and jokes.
>
> (1991: 550)

The study found a high degree of correspondence between images constructed through metaphors and images constructed by the readers. This finding demonstrates the influence of the business press in constructing particular images of organizational leaders.

Visual documents

As we highlighted in Chapter 19, there is a growing interest in the visual in business and management research. While photographs are the most obvious manifestation of this trend (see Key concept 23.7), visual documents also encompass a wide range of graphic and artistic images, the visual content of websites, and video data including film and YouTube clips. Organizations are significant producers of visual documents, which tend to play an important role in constituting an organization's image and identity, and they have the advantage of often being publicly accessible and widely disseminated—for example, through websites, advertising, or newspaper reports. The example of Davison's (2009) study of the Bradford & Bingley bank illustrates the potential for analysis of corporate brand images (see Research in focus 23.8). With the vast amount of visual data that is now produced by organizations, including audio and video film data, there is considerable potential for organizational researchers to collect this type of data. Consequently, in recent years there has been a growth in the analysis of visual documents in business research, but, as we noted in Chapter 13, the potential of this data source has yet to be fully realized.

One of the main types of visual document that can be used as either a main or a supplementary data source alongside written or spoken words are photographs. As mentioned in Chapter 19, we make a distinction between photographs and other visual materials that are produced as part of fieldwork and those that are naturally occurring. An example of the analysis of photographs that are naturally occurring can be seen in research by Davison (2009). In this study, photographs found in company annual reports formed the basis of analysis (see Research in focus 23.8). An interesting example of the use of both naturally occurring and fieldwork-produced visual data is provided by Schwartzman (1993), who neatly and somewhat poignantly juxtaposes three photographs of the General Electric Hawthorne works that was the focus of the famous Hawthorne studies (see Research in focus 3.8): one contemporary image from the AT&T archives of one of the departments in which the studies were carried out (the Bank Wiring Observation Room); a 1987 photograph from the *Chicago Sun-Times* of the demolished Hawthorne works buildings; and a photograph taken of the Hawthorne Works Shopping Center that was built on the cleared land.

Key concept 23.7
Photographs in business research

Photographs may be used in a variety of ways in business research. While Chapter 19 and the present chapter discuss them in relation to qualitative research, they can also be used in quantitative research. For example, photographs can be the focus of **content analysis** (two examples of this from tourism studies are given in Chapter 13) or may be used as prompts in connection with **structured interviewing** (see Key concept 9.10 and Research in focus 9.11) or **experiments**. However, the growing interest in photographs and visual materials more generally has tended to come from qualitative researchers. There is an important distinction between the use of *extant* photographs that have not been produced for the research and *research-generated* photographs that have been produced by the researcher or at the researcher's request. Three common uses are:

1. *Illustrative.* Photographs may be used to do little more than illustrate points and thereby enliven what might otherwise be a rather dry discussion of findings. The examples given in Research in focus 19.14 are typical of this.

2. *As data.* Photographs may be viewed as data in their own right. Research-generated photographs can essentially be understood as part of the researcher's **field notes** (see, for example, the discussion of

research by Warren (2002) in Chapter 17). Extant photographs can be understood as a main source of data about the field in which the researcher is interested. The examples given in Research in focus 19.16 are in this category.

3. *As prompts*. Photographs may be used as prompts to entice people to talk about what is represented in them. Both research-driven photographs, such as in the example of S. Warren's (2002, 2005) study of organizational aesthetics discussed in Chapter 17 and Buchanan's (1998) study of change in a hospital (Research in focus 9.11), and extant photographs may be used in this way.

However, the photograph must not be taken at its face value when used as a research source; it is also necessary to have considerable additional knowledge of the social context to probe beneath the surface. Glossy photographs of happy, smiling employees in corporate brochures or newsletters, for example, might suggest that there is a gap between the photographic image of the company and the underlying reality as experienced at a day-to-day level. Scott sees the issue of *representativeness* as a particular problem for the analyst of photographs. As he suggests, the photographs that survive the passage of time—for example, in archives—are very unlikely to be representative. They are likely to have been subject to all sorts of hazards, such as damage and selective retention. Sensitivity to what is not photographed can reveal the 'mentality' of the person(s) behind the camera. What is clear is that the question of representativeness is much more fundamental than the issue of what survives, because it points to the way in which the selective survival of photographs may be constitutive of a reality that business owners and managers seek to fashion.

Research in focus 23.8
Analysing photographs in a study of brand identity in a UK bank

Davison's (2009) study of Bradford & Bingley shows how changes in lending and funding practices since its formation in the 1960s, which were indicative of shifts in the UK bank's ethos, were mirrored by changes in the visual iconography that the company used in its marketing campaigns and annual reporting documents. Davison traces the way that the iconography of the bowler hat, which formed an enduring part of the bank's brand identity, changed over time. Davison locates the icon of the bowler hat in popular culture, citing a diverse range of sources from film and television that have shaped its changing meaning. She thus argues that the bowler hat has been used as a symbol of class, as epitomized by the character John Steed in the 1960s UK TV series *The Avengers*; as a way of representing professionalism, as in the film *Men in Black* (1997); and to denote eroticism and entertainment, as when worn by Liza Minelli in the film *Cabaret* (1972). Two of the images from Davison's analysis are presented here. Plate 23.1 shows a relatively recent image from the company's website. Davison argues that, through the wearing of this item of traditionally male attire by a woman, the company seeks to shift the brand from its former values of masculine, anonymous, traditional, and reserved, to an identity that is more feminine, proactive, and seductive. Plate 23.2 shows a further use of the icon that is based on abstract representation in a manner that echoes the style of the artist Warhol. Davison states that 'here the icon of the bowler hat has been separated from its wearer to acquire a life and importance of its own in these repetitive stylised motifs' (Davison 2009: 897) in a way that provides memorability through repetition. Through this detailed reading of the visual meaning of the brand, Davison highlights its role and importance even in documents as apparently objective and numerically focused as the annual financial reports produced by banks.

(*continued*)

Plate 23.1

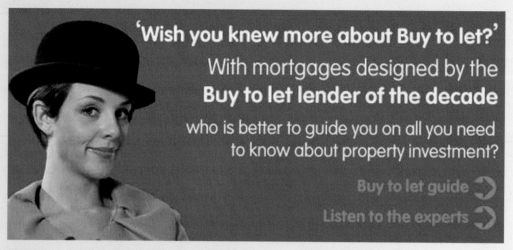

Plate 23.2

'Bradford & Bingley logo from 1990s "20 coloured bowler hats"'

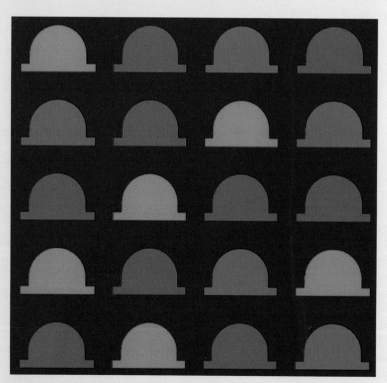

Virtual documents

There is one final type of document that ought to be mentioned—the documents that appear on the Internet. This is an area that is rapidly growing among business researchers because of the vastness of the Internet and its growing accessibility, which make it a likely source of documents for both quantitative and qualitative data analysis. Coupland's (2005) analysis of the websites of four multinational oil-producing and oil-refining organizations (see Research in focus 22.8) provides one example involving the analysis of virtual documents. Similarly, Ainsworth and Hardy (2009) analysed texts that were all obtained via a government website, including media releases, transcripts of public hearings, and reports (see Research in focus 22.6). A further example can be seen in Schoneboom's (2009) study of online 'workblogging' diaries (Research in focus 23.1).

There is clearly huge potential with the Internet as a source of documents, but John Scott's criteria need to be kept in mind. First, authenticity: anyone can set up a website, so that information and advice may be given by someone who is not an authority. Secondly, credibility: we need to be aware of possible distortions. For example, if we were studying advice about the purchase of shares,

it is known that websites have been set up encouraging people to buy or sell particular stocks held by the website authors, so that the prices of stocks can be manipulated. Thirdly, given the constant flux of the Internet, it is doubtful that we could ever know how representative websites on a certain topic are. An important consideration related to this issue stems from the dynamic nature of the content of websites, which may be updated on a weekly or even daily basis. It is particularly important, therefore, not only to record the date on which a website was consulted, but also to print out the relevant content in case it changes. Indeed, these changes may be important to the analysis; for example, Coupland's (2005) study monitored oil company websites for discourses of corporate social responsibility over a six-month period, noting any major changes in the discourse in this time period. Finally, websites are notorious for a kind of Webspeak, so that it may be difficult to comprehend what is being said without considerable insider knowledge. As the use of computers and in particular the Internet as a source of data is undoubtedly increasing, we will be returning to these issues and discussing them further in Chapter 28.

The world as text

There is one word that we have done our best to avoid using in the chapter so far—text. The word 'text' is frequently employed as a synonym for a term such as 'written document'. We have clearly strayed from this association, in that photographs and films have been touched upon. But, in relatively recent times, the word 'text' has been applied to an increasingly wide range of phenomena, so that theme parks, landscapes, heritage attractions, technologies, and a wide range of other objects are treated as texts out of which a 'reading' can be fashioned (e.g. Grint and Woolgar 1997). Thus, in Barthes's (1972) influential collection of essays, objects as varied as wrestling matches, Citroën cars, and striptease acts are submitted to readings. In a sense, therefore, just about everything can be treated as a text and perhaps as a document. Research

in focus 23.4 provides an example of textual analysis in management and business. In this study Gephart (1993) treats both the written documents and his own ethnographic field notes as texts, analysing them both using the same methods. The aim using this approach is 'to account for how a given text is made meaningful to readers', seeking 'to uncover the general conventions, interests and cultural practices' (1993: 1468) that enable meaning to be created. This approach is based on two assumptions: first, that the texts have the interpretations of their creators embedded in them and, second, that a text acquires meaning through 'its embeddedness in a multiplicity of discourses and texts' (1993: 1469). Gephart thus seeks to interpret the meaning of texts in relation to events, both of which constitute aspects of culture.

The reality of documents

An issue that has attracted attention relatively recently and that has implications for the interpretation of documents (the focus of the next section) is that of their status as a source of knowledge about reality. It is clearly tempting to assume that documents reveal something about an underlying social reality, so that the documents that an organization generates (minutes of meetings, newsletters, mission statements, job specifications, etc.) are viewed as representations of the reality of that organization. In other words, we might take the view that such documents tell us something about what goes on in that organization and will help us to uncover such things as its culture or ethos. According to such a view, documents are windows onto social and organizational realities.

However, some writers have expressed scepticism about the extent to which documents can be viewed in this way. Rather than view documents as ways of gaining access to an underlying reality, such writers as Atkinson and Coffey (2004) suggest that documents should be viewed as a distinct level of 'reality' in their own right. Atkinson and Coffey argue that documents should be examined in terms of, on the one hand, the context in which they were produced and, on the other hand, their implied readership. When viewed in this way, documents are significant for what they are supposed to accomplish and who they are written for. They are written in order to convey an impression, one that will be favourable to the author and those whom they represent. Moreover, any document should be viewed as linked to other documents, because invariably it refers to and/or is a response to other documents. Other documents form part of the context or background to the writing of a document. Atkinson and Coffey refer to the interconnectedness of documents as *inter-textuality*.

The minutes of a meeting in an organization might be the kind of document that would interest a business researcher. On the face of it, they are a record of such things as issues raised at the meeting; the discussion of those issues; views of the participants; and actions to be taken. As such, they might be deemed interesting for a business researcher for their ability to reveal such things as the culture of the organization or department responsible for the minutes, its preoccupations, and possible disputes among the meeting participants. However, precisely because the minutes are a document that is to be read not only by participants but also by others (members of other departments or other organizations; in the case of a UK public-sector organization, the minutes may be accessed by the public under the Freedom of Information Act), they are likely to be written with a view to prospective scrutiny by others in mind. Disagreements may be suppressed and actions to be taken may reflect a desire to demonstrate that important issues are to be addressed rather than because of a genuine desire to act on them. Also, the minutes are likely to be connected either explicitly or implicitly to other documents of that organization, such as previous minutes, mission statements, organizational regulations, and external documents (such as legislation). Further, following Atkinson and Coffey's suggestions, the minutes should be examined for the ways in which language is used to convey certain messages.

Atkinson and Coffey's central message is that documents have a distinctive **ontological** status, in that they form a separate reality, which the authors refer to as a 'documentary reality', and they should not be taken to be 'transparent representations' of an underlying organizational or social reality. They go on to write: 'We cannot . . . learn through written records alone how an organization actually operates day by day. Equally, we cannot treat records—however "official"—as firm evidence of what they report' (Atkinson and Coffey 2004: 58).

Atkinson and Coffey's central point is that documents need to be recognized for what they are—namely, texts written with distinctive purposes in mind, and not as simply reflecting reality. This means that if the researcher wishes to employ documents as a means of understanding aspects of an organization and its operations, it is likely that he or she will need to buttress an analysis of documents with other sources of data. An example of this relates to Vaughan's (1990) analysis of the Space Shuttle *Challenger* accident, mentioned earlier in this chapter. As Vaughan (2006) points out, examining documents such as Presidential Commission reports can be extremely illuminating about the kinds of issues that they emphasize and the kinds of ways in which the issues are framed. This is precisely the point that Atkinson and Coffey (2004) are making. Vaughan (2006) examined three Commission Reports: the *Challenger* report; the *Columbia* Accident Investigation Board Report, which dealt with another space shuttle disaster that took place in February 2003; and the 9/11 Commission Report. She shows that each report was shaped by a dominant frame, which was respectively: an 'accident investigation frame'; a 'sociological frame'; and a 'historical/war frame' (2006:

304). Further, she notes that the 9/11 report locates causation in what she calls 'regulatory failure' (2006: 300), which is to do with problems with the activities of the agencies charged with upholding national security. An effect of that attribution of causation is to absolve the president and to some extent US foreign policy of responsibility. This examination of documents implies that they can tell us about such things as how those responsible for reporting officially on major incidents construct the background and the causes of those incidents.

These documents are rhetorically designed to 'do something'. They are designed to assign moral and practical responsibility and to identify possible recommendations.

As Prior (2008) observes, documents are typically viewed by researchers as resources to be worked on in order for their substantive meaning to be unravelled, perhaps using techniques introduced in this chapter and in Chapters 14 and 26. At the same time, documents are written to get something done and as such are parts of chains of action that are potential research topics in their own right. This orientation to documents represents a shift in how they are conceived for research purposes. For many researchers, their content will continue to be the main focus of attention, but it is also important to be attuned to the significance of documents in terms of the parts they play in organizations and elsewhere.

Interpreting documents

Although it means straying into areas that are relevant to Chapter 24, this section will briefly consider the question of how to interpret documents qualitatively. Three possible approaches are outlined: qualitative content analysis; semiotics; and historical analysis. In addition to these, discourse analysis, which was covered in Chapter 22, has been employed as an approach for the analysis of documents.

Qualitative content analysis

This is probably the most prevalent approach to the qualitative analysis of documents, although in business research it remains less frequently used than quantitative content analysis (Insch, Moore, and Murphy 1997). It comprises a searching-out of underlying themes in the materials being analysed and can be discerned in several of the studies referred to earlier, such as Gephart (1993), Colville et al. (2013) and Cornelissen et al. (2014). A further example is provided in Chen and Meindl's (1991) study of the metaphors used to describe the entrepreneur and business leader Donald Burr (see Research in focus 23.6). Unlike quantitative content analysis, the processes through which the themes are extracted are usually left implicit. The extracted themes are usually illustrated—for example, with brief quotations from a newspaper article or magazine. The procedures adopted by B. A. Turner (1994) in connection with his research on the Summerland disaster are an example of the search for themes in texts, although Turner provided greater detail about what he did than is often the case.

Altheide (1996) has outlined an approach that he calls ethnographic content analysis (also called **qualitative**

content analysis), which he contrasts with quantitative content analysis of the kind outlined in Chapter 13. Altheide's approach (referred to by him as ECA) represents a codification of certain procedures that might be viewed as typical of the kind of qualitative content analysis on which many of the studies referred to so far are based. He describes his approach as differing from traditional quantitative content analysis, in that the researcher is constantly revising the themes or categories that are distilled from the examination of documents. As he puts it:

> ECA follows a recursive and reflexive movement between concept development- sampling-data, collection-data, coding-data, and analysis-interpretation. The aim is to be systematic and analytic but not rigid. Categories and variables initially guide the study, but others are allowed and expected to emerge during the study, including an orientation to *constant discovery* and *constant comparison* of relevant situations, settings, styles, images, meanings, and nuances.
>
> (Altheide 1996: 16; emphases in original)

Thus, with ECA there is much more movement back and forth between conceptualization, data collection, analysis, and interpretation than is the case with the kind of content analysis described in Chapter 13. Quantitative content analysis typically entails applying predefined categories to the sources; ECA employs some initial categorization, but there is greater potential for refinement of those categories and the generation of new ones.

Qualitative content analysis as a strategy for searching for themes in data lies at the heart of the coding approaches that are often employed in the analysis of qualitative data, such as grounded theory. This was the approach used by Colville et al. (2013) in their analysis of the Stockwell shooting of Jean Charles de Menezes in 2005 (Research in focus 23.5).

Semiotics

Semiotics is invariably referred to as the 'science of signs'. It is an approach to the analysis of symbols in everyday life and as such can be employed in relation not only to documentary sources but also to all kinds of other data because of its commitment to treating phenomena as texts. The main terms employed in semiotics are:

- the **sign**—that is, something that stands for something else;

- the sign is made up of: a *signifier* and the *signified*;

- the *signifier* is the thing that points to an underlying meaning (the term *sign vehicle* is sometimes used instead of *signifier*);

- the *signified* is the meaning to which the signifier points;

- a *denotative meaning* is the manifest or more obvious meaning of a signifier and as such indicates its function;

- a *sign-function* is an object that denotes a certain function;

- a *connotative meaning* is a meaning associated with a certain social context that is in addition to its denotative meaning;

- *polysemy* refers to a quality of signs—namely, that they are always capable of being interpreted in many ways;

- the *code* is the generalized meaning that interested parties may seek to instil in a sign; a code is sometimes also called a *sign system*.

Semiotic analysis focuses on the way that messages are communicated as systems of cultural meaning. It is based on semiotic theory, which suggests that the symbolic order of a culture is constructed and interpreted through a system of signs. A *sign* constitutes the relationship between the *signifier* (the recognizable word, sound, or picture that attracts our attention and communicates a particular message) and the *signified* (the message or concept itself). The link between the signifier and the signified is arbitrary; its meaning depends on the conventions held by groups of sign users about the mental concept (signified)

that the material object (signifier) is intended to represent. Barley (1983) provides the following example:

> As you drive toward me in your speeding car, I hold up my hand, palm out, intending an expression signifying the content, 'Stop while I cross the street.' From your vantage point behind the wheel, you wonder why I am so brash as to say hello from the middle of the crosswalk and you step on the gas. Obviously our conventions differ.
>
> (1983: 395–6)

This example places greater emphasis on the recipient of the message, who must actively interpret the signifier in order to establish its meaning by drawing on his or her cultural knowledge. The task of the researcher in semiotic analysis is to discover the rules that bind users of a sign together and enable them to make sense of their cultural world.

Signs contribute to systems of signification or *codes*, which provide a model for social action; these are composed of *denotative* and *connotative* elements. The denotative code represents meaning that is associated directly with the sign-vehicle itself, whereas the connotative code represents meaning that links the sign with its cultural context.

Despite the potential for applying semiotic analysis in the study of organizational cultures, its use has instead been mainly confined to studies of marketing and advertising. In advertising, semiotic analysis encourages recognition of the way that individuals interpret the same advertising message in slightly different ways. Combe and Crowther (2000) suggest, for example, that signs and symbols influence the positioning and repositioning of brands, such as Murphy's Irish stout, in recipients' minds. A further application of semiotic analysis in an organizational context is provided by Barley (1983) in his study of funeral work (see Research in focus 23.9).

Semiotics is concerned with uncovering the hidden meanings that reside in texts as broadly defined. Consider, by way of illustration, the curriculum vitae (CV) in academic life. The typical CV that an academic will produce contains such features as personal details; education; previous and current posts; administrative responsibilities and experience; teaching experience; research experience; research grants acquired; and publications. We can treat the CV as a system of interlocking signifiers that signify at the level of denotative meaning a summary of the individual's experience (its sign function) and at the connotative level an indication of an individual's value, particularly in connection with his or her prospective employability.

Research in focus 23.9
A semiotic analysis of a funeral business

Over a three-month period, Barley (1983) engaged in observation and conducted interviews in a US funeral home, with the intention of uncovering the signs used by funeral directors to make sense of their work. After interviewing funeral directors about various aspects of their work, including the history of the business, the layout and decor of the home, and the tasks involved in preparing a body or making a removal, Barley began to develop maps of connotative codes through which he saw funeral directors as striving to achieve the quality of 'naturalness' in the funeral scene by making arrangements in a way that they believe is least likely to disturb mourners. This might involve arranging the corpse in such a way as to convey the image of a restfully sleeping person or furnishing the funeral home in a way that simulates a comfortable living room, with coffee tables and comfortable chairs. Barley concludes that the funeral director's role relies on a system of signs or codes that create a subtle illusion of everyday life, in order to obscure the strangeness of death and thereby to reassure mourners.

Each CV is capable of being interpreted in different ways, as anyone who has ever sat in on a short-listing meeting for a lectureship can testify, and is therefore polysemic, but there is a code whereby certain attributes of CVs are seen as especially desirable and that are therefore less contentious in terms of the attribution of meaning. Indeed, applicants for posts know this latter point and devise their CVs to amplify the desired qualities so that the CV becomes an autobiographical practice for the presentation of self, as Miller and Morgan (1993) have suggested.

Research in focus 23.10 provides an illustration of a study from a semiotic perspective of Disneyland as a text. The chief strength of semiotics lies in its invitation to the analyst to try to see beyond and beneath the apparent ordinariness of everyday life and its manifestations. The main difficulty one often feels with the fruits of a semiotic analysis is that, although we are invariably given a compelling exposition of a facet of the quotidian, it is difficult to escape a sense of the arbitrariness of the analysis provided. However, in all probability this sensation is unfair to the approach, because the results of a semiotic analysis are probably no more arbitrary than any interpretation of documentary materials or any other data, such as a thematic, qualitative content analysis of the kind described in the previous section. Indeed, it would be surprising if we were not struck by a sense of arbitrariness in interpretation, in view of the principle of polysemy that lies at the heart of semiotics.

Research in focus 23.10
A semiotic Disneyland

Gottdiener (1982; 1997: 108–15) has proposed that Disneyland in Los Angeles, California, can be fruitfully analysed through a semiotic analysis. In so doing, he was treating Disneyland as a text. One component of his analysis is that Disneyland's meaning 'is revealed by its oppositions with the quotidian—the alienated everyday life of residents of L.A.' (1982: 148). He identifies through this principle nine *sign systems* that entail a contrast between the park and its surrounding environment: transportation; food; clothing; shelter; entertainment; social control; economics; politics; and family. Thus, the first of these sign systems—transportation—reveals a contrast between the Disneyland visitor as pedestrian (walk in a group; efficient mass transportation, which is fun) and as passenger (car is necessary; poor mass transportation; danger on the congested freeways). A further component of his analysis focuses on the **connotations** of the different 'lands' that make up the park. He suggests that each land is associated as a signifier with signifiers of capitalism, as follows:

- Frontierland—predatory capital;
- Adventureland—colonialism/imperialism;
- Tomorrowland—state capital;
- New Orleans—venture capital;
- Main Street—family capital. (1982: 156)

Historical analysis

Historical analysis is in this chapter because the kind of research that we are referring to in this section typically involves documents and other artefacts that can be used to trace the history of an organization or an industry. This can include letters and diaries of company founders and other members of the organization, financial reports, and records of meetings, which are often held in private or public archives for the purposes of historical study by researchers. However, historical analysis relates not just to the study of documents from the past but also to the methods that are used to interpret them. In recent years there has been a growing debate around the role of historical analysis in business research. There is a long-standing tradition in business research of studying the history of individual companies and industries, primarily through corporate archive research. However, some researchers have argued that business history has tended to be conducted from a relatively realist (see Chapter 2), or possibly even empiricist (see Key concept 2.3), perspective that suffers from a tendency towards 'myopic fact-collect[ing] without a method' (Kieser 1994: 612) involving 'a high degree of arbitrariness' (1994: 617) and a tailoring of 'facts to fit a preconceived theory' (1994: 617). I also suggested this to be a research strategy that is 'especially susceptible to ideologies' (1994: 617); and associated with 'inductively generated theories where causal mechanisms are either absent, implicit or used in an ad hoc manner' (1994: 618). In other words, business history has been accused of being an approach that does not use, or take account of recent developments in, historiographic methods (see Key concept 23.11 and Thinking deeply 23.12).

A more recent generation of business and management historians has instead taken inspiration from the work of White (1987). White argues that historical analysis is limited by a number of processes that make writing history akin to fiction—for example, in the choices the historian has to make as to which historical elements to focus on and which narrative style to use to order them. This has led to the development of a perspective on business and management history which sees it as a discourse and a narrative (see Chapter 22) that is actively constructed by historians and other social actors—including organizational leaders and managers, who often have a vested interest in promoting a particular view of the past in order to shape its role in the present life of the organization.

This has led some commentators to suggest that there has been a historic turn in management research, in the form of an attempt to write history back into management theory and in particular to acknowledge the socio-historical context within which management research is produced. This can be seen partly as a response to criticisms of business and management studies for having a tendency towards presentism, in which 'the present is often assumed to be a period of unprecedented change, heralding the dawning of a new age' (Booth and Rowlinson 2006: 6). As Booth and Rowlinson argue, this is often done without 'proper consideration of possible historical precedents' and is 'largely a rhetorical device for

Key concept 23.11
What is historiography?

Historiography is the study of historical method. It involves an examination of how history is conceived—for example, whether it utilizes a positivist or an interpretivist epistemology (see Chapter 2); how it is written—for example, what discourses are invoked and what narrative form is used (see Chapter 22); and how it is analysed—for example, does the historian frame the 'historical traces' in terms of a grand narrative or a competing histories approach. However, with few exceptions, historiography has not been widely discussed in business research.

A recent discussion of historiography (Taylor et al. 2009) attempts to take business historians to task for this lack of discussion. These authors argue that there is an implicit **epistemological** position in most business history writing. Some historians believe that it is 'risky' to talk and write openly about the status of data or analysis, because it might undermine the credibility of their arguments and conclusions and make their research easier to ignore. Taylor, Bell, and Cooke challenge this, and argue that, if historians were to be more open about their epistemological assumptions, then their research would actually become more credible. Instead, by ignoring the linguistic turn (see Key concept 19.19) in the social sciences and by refusing to talk about whether data and analysis reflect realities or construct them, business historians are writing in a way that gives an unrealistic sense of authenticity.

privileging an unbounded, extended present' (2006: 6). These ideas build on the earlier work of business scholars such as Kieser (1994), who argues that, despite the earlier importance of history to organization studies, it has now 'become extremely rare' for organizational researchers to draw on historical analysis (1994: 609). In arguing for a historical turn in business and management research, Kieser makes four main arguments:

1. *Understanding of contemporary organizations relies on having an awareness of how they developed historically.* Kieser (1994) uses the example of Hofstede's (1984) research into the influence of national cultural differences on organizational culture (see Chapter 2) and argues that these value differences are in fact rooted in historical development (Kieser 1994: 610).

2. *Historical analysis can reduce the ideological biases that are embedded in 'current "fashionable" trends in organization theory and practice'* (Kieser 1994: 610). Kieser's (1997) own work on 'rhetoric and myth in management fashion' details how management theory can reflect popular currents of thought (see also Abrahamson 1996). Historical analysis can also help to reveal ideological biases that lead to the popularization of one organizational theory over another (see Thinking deeply 23.13 for an example).

3. *Historical analysis enables interpretation of existing organizational arrangements as the result of intentional or implicit decisions made in the past rather than determined by objective laws.* Here the work of Henry Mintzberg and his colleagues is illustrative. Through a number of studies Mintzberg has examined the development of strategy over time to reveal that not all strategies are consciously developed but often arise out of a combination of spoken and unspoken assumptions that can be detected as patterns in a stream of action, whether the patterns are intended or are realized despite—or in the absence of—intentions (Mintzberg, Brunet, and Waters 1986: 4).

4. 'By confronting theories of organizational changes with historical development, these theories can be subjected to a more radical test than they have to pass when merely being confronted with data on short-run changes' (Kieser 1994: 612). Through a historical analysis of the realized strategies employed by McGill University in the period 1829–1980, Mintzberg and Rose (2003) call into question a number of the 'fundamental premises of strategic management' (2003: 270). They discovered that, 'amidst continual change in detail, there was remarkable stability in the aggregate, and nothing resembling quantum or revolutionary change in strategy ever occurred' (2003: 270). As this example illustrates, historical analysis enables the sometimes overly grand claims of management to be subjected to empirical scrutiny in a way that allows their validity to be assessed more rigorously.

Thinking deeply 23.12
Three arguments for a historical perspective in organization studies

Rowlinson (2004*a*: 8) outlines three arguments for a historical perspective in organization studies: factual, narrative, and archaeo-genealogical:

1. The *factual approach* can be seen as aligned with positivism in the argument that 'if organization studies were to take account of the facts revealed by history then a number of erroneous assumptions would be undermined' (2004*a*: 8). From this framework, history is viewed as 'a repository of facts which, so long as historians properly interpret them, can conveniently confirm or refute preferred or non-preferred theoretical positions' (2004*a*: 10).

2. The *narrative approach* suggests that history is not the skillfully crafted recounting of real, or factual, events from the past but a well-crafted story about the past that is constructed by the historian through the careful use of narrative. White (1987) exemplifies this approach by saying that 'all history is the study, not of past events that are gone for ever from perception, but rather of the "traces" of those events distilled into documents and monuments on one side, and the praxis of present social formations on the other. These

(continued)

"traces" are the raw materials of the historian's discourse, rather than the events themselves' (White 1987: 102, cited in Rowlinson 2004b: 10). This 'has shifted the emphasis away from seeing archival research as the historian's craft towards a view that it is the conventions and customs of writing that constitute the craft of history' (Rowlinson 2004b: 11).

3. The *archaeo-genealogical approach* is derived from the work of Foucault and his attempts to deconstruct the present through analyses of the past. In his archaeological phase, Foucault explored 'in language the sedimented evidence of the assumptions; the values; the common sense through which, for instance, a phenomenon such as madness could have one set of meanings in one era and a contradictory set of meanings in another' (Jacques 2010: 310). In his later genealogical phase Foucault examined 'the conditions under which the different ways of interpreting and evaluating ourselves have come to exist. The purpose of the genealogical method is to analyse and excavate the taken-for-granted' assumptions that define the present (Poutanen and Kovalainen 2010: 263). This method reframes 'the conduct of historical analysis to understand how it has transpired that the present has come to be accepted as inevitable or natural' (2010: 418).

Genealogical research has generated numerous studies in the field of business research, but, as Rowlinson (2004b: 13) contends, few of these accounts have involved archival research. A key exception to this is the work of Cooke (2003, 2006) (see Thinking deeply 23.13).

Thinking deeply 23.13
The influence of slavery and the cold war on management theory

In two journal articles, Bill Cooke (2003, 2006) demonstrates both the potential significance of reflective historical writing and the limited ways in which we tend to think about the history of management. In fact, as Cooke argues, there are multiple histories of management to add to the standard textbook accounts based around 'great men' such as Frederick Taylor or Elton Mayo.

In the first paper (Cooke 2003), he argues that we can find the roots of management theories and practices in nineteenth-century US cotton plantations staffed with slave labour. Cooke bases this argument on a close reading of primary and secondary sources—that is, both on contemporaneous accounts written by people living and working on the plantations and on academic analysis of the plantations. Using these sources, Cooke argues that management theorists have actively written out the shameful roots of many practices that we accept now as normal or rational. Cooke goes so far as to term this a 'denial', and such is the strength and clarity of his evidence and argument that it is difficult to argue against that conclusion.

In the second paper (Cooke 2006), his analysis of the roots of management practice focuses on the twentieth century, to a time of the cold war between the USA, the Soviet Union, and their various allies. Here Cooke works with a more traditional historical dataset, a series of letters between two men who contributed to the development of action research. The overall aim is similar, however, as the social, political, and ethical contexts of what we now take to be a rational, neutral managerial system are picked apart. Cooke's 'historicization' of action research suggests that one of the founders wanted to make it much more radical than the other, and that the more conservative version won out.

In common with many historians, Cooke does not spend a lot of time explaining his methods, but he is clear about his data sources and the uses he puts the data to. In this respect, Cooke's historical research can be seen as an example of reflexive, critical historical writing.

Despite the recent increase in historical analyses of business and management this remains a relatively marginal research field and it is rarely taught in undergraduate or postgraduate degree programmes. Cooke's research suggests one reason why this might be; Wolfram Cox and Hassard (2007) provide another. They suggest that management research and theory developed within modernism, leading to a focus on controlling and predicting future behaviour or events to make a better, more efficient world. Researchers therefore tend to concentrate on understanding the present to predict the future, forgetting about the past and its potential significance. However, recent interest in historical analysis, as indicated by the launch of a new journal, *Management & Organizational History*, in 2006, could be interpreted as a sign that this may be changing.

Checklist
Evaluating documents

Can you answer the following questions?

○ Who produced the document?

○ Why was the document produced?

○ Was the person or group that produced the document in a position to write authoritatively about the subject or issue?

○ Is the material genuine?

○ Did the person or group have an axe to grind and if so can you identify a particular slant?

○ Is the document typical of its kind and if not is it possible to establish how untypical it is and in what ways?

○ Is the meaning of the document clear?

○ Can you corroborate the events or accounts presented in the document?

○ Are there different interpretations of the document from the one you offer and if so what are they and why have you discounted them?

Key points

- Documents constitute a very heterogeneous set of sources of data, which include personal documents, official documents from both the state and private sources, and the mass media.

- Such materials can be the focus of both quantitative and qualitative enquiry, but the emphasis in this chapter has been upon the latter.

- Documents of the kinds considered may be in printed, visual, digital, or indeed any other retrievable format.

- For many writers, just about anything can be 'read' as a text.

- Criteria for evaluating the quality of documents are: authenticity; credibility; representativeness; and meaning. The relevance of these criteria varies somewhat according to the kind of document being assessed.

- There are several ways of analysing documents within qualitative research. In this chapter we have covered qualitative content analysis, semiotics, and historical analysis.

Questions for review

- What is meant by a document?

- What are John Scott's four criteria for assessing documents?

Personal documents

- Outline the different kinds of personal documents.

- How do they fare in terms of John Scott's criteria?

- What might be the role of personal documents in relation to the life history or biographical method?

- What uses can photographs have in business research?

Public documents

- What do the studies by Gephart, Turner, Colville et al. and Cornelissen et al. suggest in terms of the potential for business researchers to use official documents?

- How do such documents fare in terms of John Scott's criteria?

Organizational documents

- What kinds of documents might be obtained from organizational sources?

- How do such documents fare in terms of John Scott's criteria?

Mass media outputs

- What kinds of documents are mass media outputs?

- How do such documents fare in terms of John Scott's criteria?

Visual documents

- Name three ways that photographs can be used as a source of data in business research and explain the difference between them.

Virtual documents

- Do Internet documents and other virtual outputs raise special problems in terms of assessing them from the point of view of John Scott's criteria?

The world as text

- Can anything be treated as a text?

- What is the significance of audiences in connection with textual readings by academics?

The reality of documents

- To what extent can documents provide evidence that business researchers can use as data?

Interpreting documents

- How does qualitative content analysis differ from the kind of content analysis discussed in Chapter 13?

- What is a sign? How central is it to semiotics?

- What is the difference between denotative meaning and connotative meaning?

- What is historical analysis and how can it be applied in business research?

Online Resource Centre

www.oxfordtextbooks.co.uk/orc/brymanbrm4e/

Visit the Interactive Research Guide that accompanies this book to complete an exercise in Documents as Sources of Data.

24

Qualitative data analysis

Chapter outline

Because qualitative data deriving from interviews or participant observation typically take the form of a large corpus of unstructured textual material, they are not straightforward to analyse. Moreover, unlike quantitative data analysis, clear-cut rules about how qualitative data analysis should be carried out have not been developed. In this chapter, some general approaches to qualitative data analysis will be examined, along with *coding*, which is the main feature of most of these approaches. The chapter explores:

- **analytic induction** as a general strategy of qualitative data analysis;

- *grounded theory* as a general strategy of qualitative data analysis; this is probably the most prominent of the general approaches to qualitative data analysis; the chapter examines its main features, processes, and outcomes, along with some of the criticisms that are sometimes levelled at the approach;

- *coding* as a key process in grounded theory and in approaches to qualitative data analysis more generally; it is the focus of an extended discussion in terms of what it entails and some of the limitations of a reliance on coding;

- the criticism that is sometimes made of coding in relation to qualitative data—namely, that it tends to fragment data; the idea of *narrative analysis* is introduced as an approach to data analysis that is gaining a growing following and that does not result in data fragmentation;

- the possibility of conducting a secondary analysis of other researchers' qualitative data.

Introduction

One of the main difficulties with qualitative research is that it rapidly generates a large, cumbersome database because of its reliance on prose in the form of such media as field notes, interview transcripts, or documents. Miles (1979) has described qualitative data as an 'attractive nuisance', because of the attractiveness of its richness but the difficulty of finding analytic paths through that richness. The researcher must guard against being captivated by the richness of the data collected, so that there is a failure to give the data wider significance for the business community. In other words, it is crucial to guard against failing to carry out a genuine analysis. This means that you must protect yourself against the condition Lofland (1971: 18) once called 'analytic interruptus'.

Yet, finding a path through the thicket of prose that makes up your data is not an easy matter and is baffling to many researchers confronting such data for the first time. 'What do I do with it now?' is a common refrain. In large part, this is because, unlike the analysis of quantitative data, there are few well-established and widely accepted rules for the analysis of qualitative data. Although learning the techniques of quantitative data analysis may seem painful at the time,

they do give you an unambiguous set of rules about how to handle your data. You still have to interpret your analyses, but at least there are relatively clear rules for getting to that point. Qualitative data analysis has not reached this degree of codification of analytic procedures and many writers would argue that this is not necessarily desirable anyway (see Bryman and Burgess 1994b on this point). What *can* be provided are broad guidelines (Okely 1994), and it is in the spirit of this suggestion that this chapter has been written.

One of the most common ways of approaching qualitative data analysis is through conducting what is referred to as thematic analysis. However, unlike strategies such as grounded theory or critical discourse analysis, this is not an approach to analysis that has an identifiable heritage or that has been outlined in terms of a distinctive cluster of techniques. Indeed, the search for themes is an activity that can be discerned in many if not most approaches to qualitative data analysis, including grounded theory, critical discourse analysis, qualitative content analysis, and narrative analysis. Also, what business researchers mean when they talk about thematic analysis varies; for some a theme is more or less the same as a code (a term that will be

Telling it like it is
Generating large amounts of data and doing thematic analysis

Tom found that in one key respect his experience of doing a research project did tally with what he'd been led to expect from his reading—the tendency for qualitative research to generate large amounts of textual data that were difficult to analyse systematically. 'All textbooks say, don't they, that inexperienced researchers are likely to collect too much data and then not be able to process it all or analyse it all properly and it's true! [*laughs*] It's true! I certainly found it hard to process the amount of stuff that I'd collected.'

Lucie had a similar experience in her research project. 'It was really hard. It was probably the biggest part of my project. It just took me so long—the whole summer—because there was so much. I had to go through it all and try and look for the themes. I knew while I was doing it kind of what type of themes were emerging, so I went through the data looking for things to support that, but I had such a lot of data it was really difficult not to miss out anything and to try and get through all the data. It was really hard to pick out emerging themes—just going through the data was so difficult. At first I was a bit overwhelmed. I didn't really know how to do it. I hadn't carried out kind of qualitative research before, so I didn't really know how to approach it that well and I didn't really have a background in that because my undergraduate degree was in psychology so it was more quantitative, so I found it really difficult to kind of go through and also to be unbiased. Eventually I broke it down into the different themes and talked about those and used the data as evidence that supported what I was trying to say. The interview data was really useful because I could quote from it and what people said was really useful. They said it better than I could have said it. So I put that into my findings and analysis and quoted from their experiences of the courses and things like that.' Lucie also included the full transcripts of her interviews in an appendix.

explained later in this chapter), whereas for others it transcends any one code and is built up out of codes. Although the term 'thematic analysis' is not a widely used term in business and management research, the identification of themes from data is an important aspect of the analytical process in many studies. The study by Clarke et al. (2012) discussed in Chapter 1 provides an example.

This chapter has three main sections.

- *General strategies of qualitative data analysis*. In this section, we consider two approaches to data analysis—analytic induction and grounded theory.

- *Basic operations in qualitative data analysis*. This section builds on Chapter 23 and focuses on the steps, considerations, and problems that are associated with *coding*.

- *Narrative analysis*. This section explores an approach to qualitative data analysis, called narrative analysis, that has become popular among some researchers in the field of management and business.

In Chapter 24, the use of computers in qualitative data analysis will be outlined.

Tips and skills
Analysing data as part of an inductive research strategy

One of the things that we find in dealing with students who are analysing qualitative data is that they find it difficult to know how to deal with the emergence of themes in their data that do not relate to the theories they identified in their literature review. What typically happens is that, in the course of data collection involving semi-structured interviewing that encourages respondents to go into areas not covered in the interview schedule, some of the themes the student identifies within the dataset relate to literature that has been reviewed prior to the research, but the student also identifies interesting themes that do not. The student is then confused about how to deal with these new themes. Should they include them in their analysis, in which case they may need to go off and read a lot more literature on these subjects, or should they stick to the subject of their literature review, leaving themes that do not closely relate to it out of the analysis?

To an extent this dilemma is a logical outcome of using an inductive research strategy (see Chapter 2), in which data are collected to build theory rather than to test it. In inductive research, the data collected form the basis from which generalizable inferences are drawn. Inductive research is usually iterative, involving tracking back and forth between theory and data. This would suggest that the student should go back and read more theory to enable him or her to make sense of his or her data. But practical constraints can make this difficult. As we highlight in this chapter, qualitative data analysis can be very time-consuming, and students will probably be working towards writing up within a submission deadline, alongside other demands associated with being in their final year of study (see Chapter 29 for more on the need to start writing up early). The student is also likely to be dealing with constraints of length (see Chapter 29 also for more on this issue). By exploring more themes and dealing with an ever broader set of literature, there is a risk that the student ends up trying to cover too much within the dissertation, and their engagement with theory and analysis of the data consequently becomes too superficial.

Moreover, as we noted in Chapter 2, research is very rarely entirely inductive, and the process of reviewing the literature and reading about existing theory will almost certainly have informed the student's initial approach to data collection. In addition, within a dissertation project there is obviously less expectation on the researcher to develop or test theory, although in a few cases this does happen and it can lead to paper publication, often jointly with the dissertation supervisor. The main point to bear in mind is that it is important to try to achieve a balance here, and this is often a good point for the student to seek some advice from his or her supervisor.

General strategies of qualitative data analysis

This section considers two strategies of analysis—analytic induction and grounded theory. They are probably the most frequently cited approaches, though others do exist (e.g. R. Williams 1976; Hycner 1985). By a general strategy of qualitative data analysis, we simply mean a framework that is meant to guide the analysis of data. As we will see, one of the ways in which qualitative and quantitative data analysis sometimes differ is that, with the latter, analysis invariably occurs after your data have been collected. However, as noted in Chapter 17, general approaches such as grounded theory (and analytic induction) are often described as *iterative*—that is, there is a repetitive interplay between the collection and analysis of data. This means that analysis starts after some of the data have been collected and the implications of that analysis then shape the next steps in the data collection process. Consequently, while grounded

theory and analytic induction are described as strategies of analysis, they can also be viewed as strategies for the *collection* of data as well.

Analytic induction

The main steps in analytic induction are outlined in Figure 24.1. Analytic induction (see Key concept 24.1) begins with a rough definition of a research question, proceeds to a hypothetical explanation of that question, and then continues on to the collection of data (examination of cases). If a case that is inconsistent with the hypothesis is encountered, the analyst *either* redefines the hypothesis so as to exclude the deviant or negative case *or* reformulates the hypothesis and proceeds with further data collection. If the latter path is chosen, if a further deviant case is found, the

Telling it like it is
Getting support from your supervisor

When students reach the stage of analysing qualitative research for the first time, they can find the prospect quite daunting. As Karen explained: 'I had a lot of qualitative data from my interviews and a lot of sort of comments that I thought were really valuable, but I couldn't really work out how to actually analyse it. My tutor helped a lot at that point; he helped me to understand how to go about analysing it and pulling it all together.'

The supervisors we spoke to in preparing this edition of the book said that data analysis was an area that many students struggled with, some choosing qualitative methods of data collection because they saw this as an easier option, only to realize that the analysis of qualitative data is, if anything, more complex. Supervisors further commented that it was only in the very best projects where students were able coherently and clearly to analyse their data and explain how they had done it; in far more cases, students tended simply to describe the data rather than to analyse and interpret it. One supervisor also said that it was often only once students had reached the stage of analysing their data that the whole point of studying research methods suddenly began to make sense! All of this highlights the importance of taking time over qualitative data analysis and becoming skilled in undertaking it.

Figure 24.1

The process of analytic induction

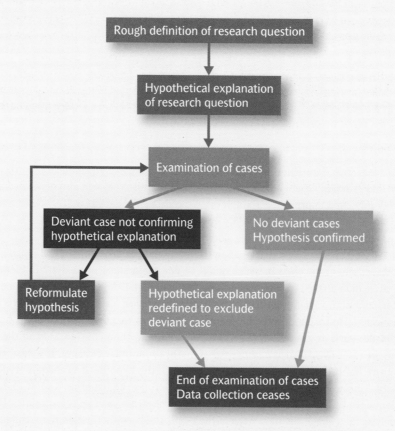

Key concept 24.1
What is analytic induction?

Analytic induction is an approach to the analysis of data in which the researcher seeks universal explanations of phenomena by pursuing the collection of data until no cases that are inconsistent with a hypothetical explanation (deviant or negative cases) of a phenomenon are found.

analyst must choose again between reformulation or redefinition. An example of analytic induction used in a study of corporate ecological responsiveness is given in Research in focus 24.2.

As this brief outline suggests, analytic induction is an extremely rigorous method of analysis, because encountering a single case that is inconsistent with a hypothesis is sufficient to necessitate further data collection or a reformulation of the hypothesis, and the selection of cases must be sufficiently diverse as to have adequately challenged the theory. This is reflected by Bansal and Roth's inclusion of Japanese companies in their

Research in focus 24.2
An example of the use of analytic induction

The aim of Bansal and Roth's (2000) research was to develop a robust model of the motives for corporate ecological responsiveness, or 'greening'. They chose an analytic induction approach because it enabled them to accommodate existing theories of corporate greening. This allowed them to begin by reviewing the literature in order to develop a set of hypotheses and then to move back and forth between data collection and theory generation.

From the data they developed a preliminary model of corporate ecological responsiveness as driven by legislation, stakeholder pressures, economic opportunities, and ethical motives. To test this model, data were collected from fifty-three firms in the UK and Japan. Theoretical sampling was used to select the case studies from sectors that faced a wide range of ecological issues. These included:

- food retailers—chosen because they were facing issues relating to the location of sites, the distribution of products, packaging, labelling, and recycling;
- subsidiaries of the British-based multinational P&O—chosen to assess the importance of internal organizational structure and culture in motivating a corporate environmental policy;
- auto manufacturers—a sample of five firms based in the UK;
- oil companies—involved in the extraction or refining of oil in the UK;
- Japan-based companies—a sample of ten companies chosen in order to challenge the emerging theory in a different cultural context.

Data sources included:

- interviews—a selection of key informants within the firms, chosen for their knowledge of the ecological initiatives of their firms;
- participant observation—of training seminars where environmental issues were discussed;
- public and private documents—including a newspaper search of the Reuters and Data Star databases, company accounts, annual reports, and corporate environmental reports.

Analysis involved an iterative process of collecting data from these sources, coding, developing, or refining emerging ideas, relating them to existing theory, and selecting further data for the next phase of analysis.

(*continued*)

Analysis focused on understanding why companies engaged in ecologically responsible initiatives. Three basic motives for ecological responsiveness were found:

1. competitiveness;
2. legitimation;
3. ecological responsibility.

Motives were also affected by three contextual dimensions, which influenced the dominant motivation of a firm. This led to the development of an advanced theoretical model that took the relationship between motives and context into account. By assessing the relationship between motives and context, Bansal and Roth suggest that it is possible to predict the kinds of ecological initiatives that firms will adopt.

The main weakness of the model, however, stems from the fact that Bansal and Roth were attempting to uncover a firm's motivations only after they had made the decision to act. This means that the research is subject to bias associated with retrospective accounts.

sample, in order to test their model of corporate ecological responsiveness in a different cultural context. Nor should the alternative of reformulating the hypothetical explanation be regarded as a soft option. The rigours of analytic induction have not endeared the approach to qualitative researchers, and most of the examples used in textbooks to illustrate analytic induction derive from the 1940s and early 1950s (Bryman and Burgess 1994a: 4); Bansal and Roth's (2000) work is unusual in being a relatively recent example.

Two further problems with analytic induction are worth noting. First, the final explanations that analytic induction arrives at specify the conditions that are *sufficient* for the phenomenon occurring but rarely specify the *necessary* conditions. This means that analytic induction may find out why companies with certain characteristics or in certain circumstances become ecologically responsive but it does not allow us to say why those particular companies became more responsive, rather than others in the same situation with the same

characteristics. Secondly, it does not provide useful guidelines (unlike grounded theory) as to how many cases need to be investigated before the absence of negative cases and the validity of the hypothetical explanation (whether reformulated or not) can be confirmed.

Grounded theory

Grounded theory (see Key concept 24.3) has become by far the most widely used framework for analysing qualitative data. The book that is the chief wellspring of the approach, *The Discovery of Grounded Theory: Strategies for Qualitative Research* by Barney G. Glaser and Anselm L. Strauss (published in 1967), must be one of the most widely cited books in the social sciences. However, providing a definitive account of the approach is by no means a straightforward matter, for the following reasons:

- Glaser and Strauss developed grounded theory along different paths after the publication of the above book.

Key concept 24.3
What is grounded theory?

In its most recent incarnation, grounded theory has been defined as 'theory that was derived from data, systematically gathered and analysed through the research process. In this method, data collection, analysis, and eventual theory stand in close relationship to one another' (Strauss and Corbin 1998: 12). Thus, two central features of grounded theory are that it is concerned with the development of theory out of data *and* that the approach is *iterative*, or *recursive*, as it is sometimes called, meaning that data collection and analysis proceed in tandem, repeatedly referring back to each other.

Glaser felt that the approach to grounded theory that Strauss was promoting (most notably in Strauss 1987 and Strauss and Corbin 1990) was too prescriptive and emphasized too much the development of concepts rather than of theories (Glaser 1992). However, because of the greater prominence of Strauss's writings, his version is largely the one followed in the exposition below. There is, however, considerable controversy about what grounded theory is and entails (Charmaz 2000).

- Straussian grounded theory has changed a great deal over the years. This is revealed in a constant addition to the tool chest of analytic devices that is revealed in his writings.

- Some writers have suggested that grounded theory is honoured more in the breach than in the observance, implying that claims are often made that grounded theory has been used but that evidence of this being the case is at best uncertain (Bryman 1988a: 85, 91; Locke 1996; Charmaz 2000). Sometimes the term is employed simply to imply that the analyst has grounded his or her theory in data. Grounded theory is more than this and refers to a set of procedures that are described below. Referencing academic publications is often part of a tactic of persuading readers of the legitimacy of one's work (Gilbert 1977), and this process can be discerned in the citation of grounded theory. Alternatively, researchers sometimes appear to have used just one or two features of grounded theory but refer to their having used the approach without qualification (Locke 1996).

Against such a background, writing about the essential ingredients of grounded theory is not an easy matter.

It is not going to be possible to describe here grounded theory in all its facets; instead, its main features will be outlined. In order to organize the exposition, we find it helpful to distinguish between *tools* and *outcomes* in grounded theory.

Tools of grounded theory

Some of the tools of grounded theory have been referred to in previous chapters. Their location is indicated in the list that follows.

- *Theoretical sampling*: see Key concept 18.3.
- *Coding*: the key process in grounded theory, whereby data are broken down into component parts, which are given names. It begins soon after the collection of initial data. As Charmaz (2000: 515) puts it: 'We grounded theorists code our emerging data as we

collect it ... Unlike quantitative research that requires data to fit into *preconceived* standardized codes, the researcher's interpretations of data shape his or her emergent codes in grounded theory' (emphasis in original). In grounded theory, different types or levels of coding are recognized (see Key concept 24.4).

- *Theoretical saturation*: see Key concept 18.4. Theoretical saturation is a process that relates to two phases in grounded theory: the coding of data (implying that you reach a point where there is no further point in reviewing your data to see how well they fit with your concepts or categories) and the collection of data (implying that, once a concept or category has been developed, you may wish to continue collecting data to determine its nature and operation but then reach a point where new data are no longer illuminating the concept).

- *Constant comparison*: an aspect of grounded theory that was prominent in Glaser and Strauss (1967) and that is often referred to as a significant phase by practitioners, but that seems to be an implicit, rather than an explicit, element in more recent writings. **Constant comparison** refers to a process of maintaining a close connection between data and conceptualization, so that the correspondence between concepts and categories with their indicators is not lost. More specifically, attention to the procedure of constant comparison enjoins the researcher constantly to compare phenomena being coded under a certain category so that a theoretical elaboration of that category can begin to emerge. Glaser and Strauss advised writing a memo (see below) on the category after a few phenomena had been coded. It also entails being sensitive to contrasts between the categories that are emerging.

Outcomes of grounded theory

The following are the products of different phases of grounded theory:

- *Concept(s)*—refers to labels given to discrete phenomena; concepts are referred to as the 'building blocks of theory' (Strauss and Corbin 1998: 101). The value of concepts is determined by their usefulness or utility. One criterion for deciding whether a concept is useful is that a useful concept will typically be found frequently, and members of the organization under study will be able to recognize it and relate it to

Key concept 24.4
Coding in grounded theory

Coding is one of the most central processes in grounded theory. It entails reviewing transcripts and/or field notes and giving labels (names) to component parts that seem to be of potential theoretical significance and/or that appear to be particularly salient within the social worlds of those being studied. As Charmaz (1983: 186) puts it: 'Codes . . . serve as shorthand devices to *label, separate, compile,* and *organize* data' (emphases in original). Coding is a somewhat different process from coding in relation to quantitative data, such as survey data. With the latter, coding is more or less solely a way of managing data, whereas in grounded theory, and indeed in approaches to qualitative data analysis that do not subscribe to the grounded theory approach, it is an important first step in the generation of theory. Coding in grounded theory is also somewhat more tentative than in relation to the generation of quantitative data, where there is a tendency to think of data and codes as very fixed. Coding in qualitative data analysis tends to be in a constant state of potential revision and fluidity. The data are treated as potential indicators of concepts and the indicators are *constantly compared* (see under 'Tools of grounded theory') for concepts they best fit with. As Strauss (1987: 25) put it: 'Many indicators (behavioral actions/events) are examined comparatively by the analyst who then "codes" them, naming them as indicators of a class of events/ behavioral actions.'

Strauss and Corbin (1990), drawing on their grounded theory approach, distinguish between three types of coding practice:

- *Open coding*: 'the process of breaking down, examining, comparing, conceptualizing and categorizing data' (1990: 61); this process of coding yields concepts, which are later to be grouped and turned into categories.

- *Axial coding*: 'a set of procedures whereby data are put back together in new ways after open coding, by making connections between categories' (1990: 96). This is done by linking codes to contexts, to consequences, to patterns of interaction, and to causes.

- *Selective coding*: 'the procedure of selecting the core category, systematically relating it to other categories, validating those relationships, and filling in categories that need further refinement and development' (1990: 116). A *core category* is the central issue or focus around which all other categories are integrated. It is what Strauss and Corbin call the storyline that frames your account.

The three types of coding are really different levels of coding and each relates to a different point in the elaboration of categories in grounded theory.

their experiences. Concepts are produced through *open coding* (see Key concept 24.4). Concepts can be recorded using concept cards (see Research in focus 24.5), through which incidents in the data can be recorded. An example of a concept card is provided in Figure 24.2.

- *Category, categories*—a concept that has been elaborated so that it is regarded as representing real-world phenomena. A category may subsume two or more concepts. As such, categories are at a higher level of abstraction than concepts. A category may become a *core category* around which the other categories pivot (see Key concept 24.4). The number of core categories may, in fact, be relatively few. For example, Martin and Turner (1986) give an example of one study in which from a large dataset and an initial 100 concepts, fewer

than 40 of these proved to be very useful and only 10 provided the basis for the final analysis.

- *Properties*: attributes or aspects of a category.

- *Hypotheses*: initial hunches about relationships between concepts.

- *Theory*: according to Strauss and Corbin (1998: 22), 'a set of well-developed categories . . . that are systematically related through statements of relationship to form a theoretical framework that explains some relevant social . . . or other phenomenon'. Since the inception of grounded theory, writings have pointed to two types or levels of theory: *substantive theory* and *formal theory*. The former relates to theory in a certain empirical instance or substantive area, such as occupational socialization. A formal theory is at a higher level of

Research in focus 24.5
Categories in grounded theory

Prasad (1993) used techniques of grounded theory to analyse the vast quantity of field notes and interview transcripts that were generated by her study (see Chapter 20). Using *concept cards* to identify important *concepts* in the data, she accumulated incidents, events, or pieces of conversation—*elements*—that related to a particular theme and put them together under a meaningful *label* on a concept card (see Figure 24.2). The initial aim of labels was to find a level of abstraction that was high enough to avoid creating a separate card for every element observed but low enough to ensure that the concept accurately represented the phenomenon.

Maintaining the concept cards was an iterative process that began early in the research process. New concepts were generated and further elements were added to the cards as more data were collected. Prasad then scanned the concept cards for relationships among elements on the same and different cards. She states that this led to the development of 'a new set of second-order cards that helped me make connections between certain symbolic representations of computerization and areas of organizational action' (1993: 1411).

Figure 24.2

An example of part of a concept card to show the symbolism of organizational turmoil related to work computerization

Data source	Organization member	Incident, quotation, opinion, event
Field notes No. 7, p. 3	Project manager	Discussing possible resistance to computers: 'Yes . . . we have got to pull out all our weapons to fight this thing out. But until we win . . . It's going to mean confusion.'
Interview No. 8, p. 23	Receptionist	Describing the first two weeks of computerization: 'What I hated was the anger and, well, the confusion. It was almost like my divorce all over again . . . blaming each other and mistakes every minute.'
Field notes No. 33, p. 24	Nurse supervisor	Official memo to trainers: 'We need to be well prepared for the next few weeks of chaos. Even the people you work with will not seem the same any more.'
Interview No. 24, pp. 8–9	Senior manager	'I finally know what army generals feel like . . . that's exactly what it was like. Fighting people all the time . . . the girls, the nurses, Joe, and the big brass at Paragon . . . and not knowing where the next attack would come from.'

Source: adapted from Prasad (1993).

abstraction and has a wider range of applicability to several substantive areas, such as socialization in a number of spheres, suggesting that higher-level processes are at work. The generation of formal theory requires data collection in contrasting settings.

The different elements are portrayed in Figure 24.3. As with all diagrams, this is a representation, and it is particularly so in the case of grounded theory, because the existence of different versions of the approach does not readily permit a more definitive rendition. Also, it is difficult to get across diagrammatically the iterative nature of grounded theory—in particular, its commitment to the idea that data collection and analysis occur in parallel. This is partly achieved in the diagram through the presence of arrows pointing in both directions in relation to certain steps. The figure implies the following:

- The researcher begins with a general research question (step 1).

Figure 24.3

Processes and outcomes in grounded theory

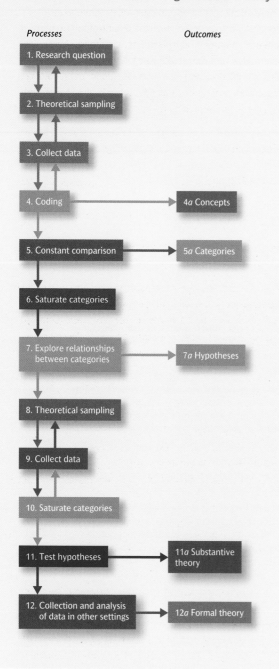

- There is a constant movement backwards and forwards between the first four steps, so that early coding suggests the need for new data, which results in the need to sample theoretically, and so on.

- Through a constant comparison of indicators and concepts (step 5), categories are generated (step 5b). The crucial issue is to ensure that there is a fit between indicators and concepts.

- Categories are saturated during the coding process (step 6).

- Relationships between categories are explored (step 7) in such a way that hypotheses about connections between categories emerge (step 7a).

- Further data are collected via theoretical sampling (steps 8 and 9).

- The collection of data is likely to be governed by the theoretical saturation principle (step 10) and by the testing of the emerging hypotheses (step 11), which leads to the specification of substantive theory (step 11a).

- The substantive theory is explored using grounded theory processes in relation to different settings from that in which it was generated (step 12), so that formal theory may be generated (step 12a). A formal theory will relate to more abstract categories, which are not specifically related to the research area in question.

Step 12 is relatively unusual in grounded theory, because researchers typically concentrate on a certain setting, although the study described in Research in focus 24.6 did examine other settings to explore the emerging concepts. A further way in which formal theory can be generated is through the use of existing theory and research in comparable settings.

Concepts and categories are perhaps the key elements in grounded theory. Indeed, it is sometimes suggested that, as a qualitative data analysis strategy, it works better for generating categories than theory. In part, this may be because studies purporting to use the approach often generate grounded *concepts* rather than grounded theory as such. Concepts and categories are nonetheless at the heart of the approach, and key processes such as coding, theoretical sampling, and theoretical saturation are designed to guide their generation.

Memos

One aid to the generation of concepts and categories is the *memo*. Memos in grounded theory are notes that researchers might write for themselves and for those with whom they work concerning such elements of grounded theory as coding or concepts. They serve as reminders

- Relevant people and/or incidents are theoretically sampled (step 2).

- Relevant data are collected (step 3).

- Data are coded (step 4), which at the level of open coding may generate concepts (step 4a).

Research in focus 24.6
Grounded theory in a study of a corporate spin-off

The research discussed here derives from a case study investigation of a corporate spin-off (referred to as 'Bozkinetic') from a large US company (referred to as 'Bozco') and the issue of how the organizational identity of the new organization changed in the course of the process of spinning it off. The findings are reported in Corley and Gioia (2004), and various aspects of the research methods employed are discussed in Gioia, Corley, and Hamilton (2012). Data collection and analysis took place in three distinct stages—before, during, and following the spin-off—and entailed semi-structured interviewing, examination of written and electronic documents, and non-participant observation of employees as they went about their work and during key meetings. The qualitative data analysis followed a classic grounded theory sequence of:

1. Open coding, whereby preliminary concepts were identified (often based on *in vivo* language) from the data and grouped;

2. Axial coding, whereby connections between the emergent themes were detected and grouped into higher-order conceptual categories;

3. Themes deriving from the axial coding were themselves grouped into theoretically fertile dimensions.

At the final stage, three 'aggregate' dimensions were proposed: triggers of identity ambiguity; change context; and leaders' responses to sense-giving imperative. We can take the first of these as an illustration.

Triggers of identity ambiguity were built up from three emergent themes derived at the axial coding stage referred to as 'change in social referents'; 'temporal identity discrepancies'; and 'construed external image discrepancies'. Each of these had been derived from an open coding process in which initial first-order concepts were identified. These were relatively low level in terms of theoretical elaboration but nonetheless pulled together key motifs in the data. 'Change in social referents', for example, was derived from three first-order concepts that the researchers described as:

- Loss of parent company as direct (internal) comparison;

- Shift in focus to comparisons with competitors;

- Media attention shifts away from Bozco to industry (Gioia et al. 2012: 21).

For each of the three emergent themes that were derived from the axial coding process, Corley and Gioia (2004) provided representative quotations. For example, a quotation from an executive vice-president that was indicative of 'Change in social referents' was:

> I think that instead of getting hung up on the fact that you want to be different than (Bozko) you are supposed to be differentiating yourself from your competition. Who cares if you are different from (Bozco)?
>
> (Corley and Gioia 2004: 188)

This quotation relates particularly well to the first-order concept of 'loss of parent company as direct (internal) comparison'. Thus, we see a process in which the aggregate dimension 'triggers of identity ambiguity' is derived as outlined in Figure 24.4. This sequence shows a gradual building up of theoretical level from relatively simple concepts that are closely tied to the interviewees' words (first-order concepts), to a bringing together of elements that are common to the underlying first-order concepts into a higher level of theoretical abstraction (second-order theme), which is combined with the two other second-order themes to produce a theoretical concept that operates at a high level of abstraction. By combining the theoretical concepts that were developed ('change in social referents'; 'temporal identity discrepancies'; and 'construed external image discrepancies') and specifying the temporal connections between them it was possible to build up a grounded theory of the process of organizational identity change (Corley and Gioia 2004: 185; Gioia et al. 2012: 23).

Figure 24.4

Producing a theoretical construct

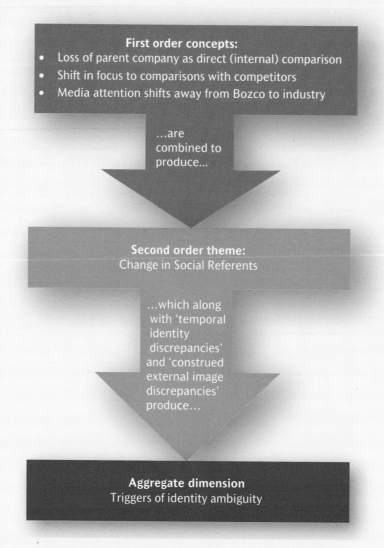

First order concepts:
- Loss of parent company as direct (internal) comparison
- Shift in focus to comparisons with competitors
- Media attention shifts away from Bozco to industry

...are combined to produce...

Second order theme:
Change in Social Referents

...which along with 'temporal identity discrepancies' and 'construed external image discrepancies' produce...

Aggregate dimension
Triggers of identity ambiguity

Source: based on Corley and Gioia (2004).

about what is meant by the terms being used and provide the building blocks for a certain amount of reflection. Memos are potentially very helpful to researchers in helping them to crystallize ideas and not to lose track of their thinking on various topics. An illustration of a memo from research in which Bryman was involved is provided in Research in focus 24.7.

Finding examples of grounded theory that reveal all its facets and stages is very difficult, and it is unsurprising that many expositions of grounded theory fall back on the original illustrations provided in Glaser and Strauss (1967). Many studies show some of its ingredients but not others. For example, Prasad's (1993) study of technological change (see Chapter 20, Research in focus 24.5, and Figure 24.2) certainly incorporates some of the features of a grounded theory approach, such as the use of concept cards to keep a record of coding, enabling a series of 'second-order' or core categories to

Research in focus 24.7
A memo

In the course of research into the bus industry that Bryman carried out with colleagues in the early 1990s (Bryman, Gillingwater, and McGuinness 1996), the researchers noticed that the managers they interviewed frequently referred to the notion that their companies had inherited features that derived from the running of those companies before deregulation. They often referred to the idea of inheriting characteristics that held them back in trying to meet the competitive environment they faced in the 1990s. As such, inheritance is what Strauss (1987) calls an *in vivo code* (one that derives from the language of people in the social context being studied), rather than what he calls *sociologically constructed codes*, which are labels employing the analyst's own terminology. The following memo outlines the concept of inheritance, provides some illustrative quotations, and suggests some properties of the concept.

Memo for Inheritance

Inheritance: many of our interviewees suggest that they have inherited certain company traits and traditions from the period prior to deregulation (i.e. pre-1985). It is a term that many of them themselves employed to denote company attributes that are not of their choosing but have survived from the pre-deregulation period. The key point about inheritance is that the inherited elements are seen by our interviewees as hindering their ability to respond to the changing environment of the post-deregulation era.

Inherited features include:

- expensive and often inappropriate fleets of vehicles and depots;
- the survival of attitudes and behaviour patterns, particularly among bus drivers, which are seen as inappropriate to the new environment (for example, lack of concern for customer service) and which hinder service innovation;
- high wage rates associated with the pre-deregulation era; means that new competitors can enter the market while paying drivers lower wages.

Sample comments:

> We *inherited* a very high cost structure because of deregulation. 75% of our staff were paid in terms of conditions affected by [rates prior to deregulation].
>
> (Commercial Director, Company B).

> I suppose another major weakness is that we are very tied by conditions and practices we've *inherited*.
>
> (Commercial Director, Company G).

> We have what we've *inherited* and we now have a massive surplus of double decks ... We have to go on operating those.
>
> (Managing Director, Company B).

Managing Director of Company E said the company had inherited staff who were steeped in pre-deregulation attitudes, which meant that 'we don't have a staff where the message is "the customer is number one". We don't have a staff where that is emblazoned on the hearts and minds of everyone, far from it.'

Pre/post-deregulation: interviewees make a contrast between the periods before and after deregulation to show how they have changed. This shows in a sense the *absence* of inherited features and their possible impact; can refer to how the impact of possibly inherited features was negated or offset. For example, *X* referring to the recent end of the three-week strike: 'there was no way we were going to give in to this sort of thing, this sort of blackmail. We just refused to move and the trade unions had never experienced that. It was all part of the change in culture following deregulation.'

Inheriting constraints: such as staff on high wage rates and with inappropriate attitudes.

Inheriting surplus capacity: such as too many buses or buses of the wrong size.

be generated. However, other tools of grounded theory, such as memos, were not used as part of this study. Similarly, although Gersick (1994) claims to have used a grounded theory approach in her study of the effects of time on organizational adaptation, her coding was based partly on themes that she was interested in prior to data collection, in addition to those that emerged during the interviews. Gersick's approach thus relied on isolating and coding statements from the interview transcripts that related to time and identifying themes among them.

It is clear that grounded theory provides qualitative researchers with tools and potential resources that can be employed in the analysis of qualitative data as well as in the research process as a whole. Constant comparison, theoretical sampling, coding, theoretical saturation, memos, and so on have crept into the discourse of research method without carrying with them the implication that a full-blooded grounded theory study has been conducted. O'Reilly et al. (2012) have been critical of what she calls the à la carte approach in which particular components of grounded theory are selected while others are ignored. She argues that this results in a number of problems: for example, a tendency for theoretical sampling not to be followed through properly, a tendency for the link between coding and data collection to become disrupted, and a tendency for coding not to be extended into the production of theory. However, it is also the case that grounded theory writers and researchers have produced a valuable set of techniques. It may be that picking just one or two of these does not make a genuine grounded theory study, but at the same time they may be valuable to those researchers who do not see themselves as committed to a fully-fledged grounded theory. Also, following through on all the steps in a grounded theory study can be very demanding in terms of the time required, so even when the aim is to conduct a grounded theory study, certain compromises have to be made in some instances.

Criticisms of grounded theory

In spite of the frequency with which it is cited and the frequent lip service paid to it, grounded theory is not without its limitations, of which the following can be briefly registered:

- Bulmer (1979) has questioned whether or not, as prescribed by the advocates of grounded theory, researchers can suspend their awareness of relevant theories or concepts until quite a late stage in the process of analysis. Business researchers are typically sensitive to the conceptual armoury of their disciplines, and it seems unlikely that this awareness can be put aside. Indeed, nowadays it is rarely accepted that theory-neutral observation is feasible. In other words, it is generally agreed that what we 'see' when we conduct research is conditioned by many factors, one of which is what we already know about the social world being studied (in terms both of social scientific conceptualizations and as members of society). Also, many writers might take the view that it is desirable that researchers are sensitive to existing conceptualizations, so that their investigations are focused and can build upon the work of others.

- Related to this first point is that, in many circumstances, researchers are required to spell out the possible implications of their planned investigation. For example, a lecturer making a bid for research funding or a student applying for funding for postgraduate research is usually required to demonstrate how his or her research will build upon what is already known or to demonstrate that he or she has a reasonably tightly defined research question, something that is also frequently disdained in grounded theory.

- There are practical difficulties with grounded theory. The time taken to transcribe audio recordings of interviews, for example, can make it difficult for researchers, especially when they have tight deadlines, to carry out a genuine grounded theory analysis with its constant interplay of data collection and conceptualization.

- It is somewhat doubtful whether grounded theory in many instances really results in *theory*. As previously suggested, it provides a rigorous approach to the generation of concepts, but it is often difficult to see what theory, in the sense of an explanation of something, is being put forward. Moreover, in spite of the frequent lip service paid to the generation of formal theory, most grounded theories are substantive in character; in other words, they pertain to the specific social phenomenon being researched and not to a broader range of phenomena (though, of course, they *may* have such broader applicability).

- In spite of the large amount written on grounded theory, but perhaps because of the many subtle changes in its presentation, it is still vague on certain points, such as the difference between concepts and categories. For example, while Strauss and Corbin (1998: 73) refer to theoretical sampling as 'sampling' on the basis of emerging *concepts*' (emphasis added), Charmaz (2000: 519) writes that it is used to 'develop our emerging *categories*' (emphasis added). The term 'categories' is increasingly being employed rather than 'concepts', but such inconsistent use of key terms is not helpful to people trying to understand the overall process.

- Grounded theory is very much associated with an approach to data analysis that invites researchers to fragment their data by coding the data into discrete chunks. However, in the eyes of some writers, this kind of activity results in a loss of a sense of context and of narrative flow (Coffey and Atkinson 1996), a point to which we will return below.

- The presence of competing accounts of the ingredients of grounded theory does not make it easy to characterize it or to establish how to use it. This situation has been made even more problematic by Charmaz's (2000) suggestion that most grounded theory is objectivist and that an alternative, constructionist (she calls it *constructivist*) approach is preferable. She argues that the grounded theory associated with Glaser, Strauss, and Corbin is objectivist in that it aims to uncover a reality that is external to social actors. She offers an alternative, constructionist version that 'assumes that people create and maintain meaningful worlds through dialectical processes of conferring meaning on their realities and acting within them ... Thus, social reality does not exist independent of human action' (Charmaz 2000: 521). Such a position stands in contrast to earlier grounded theory texts that 'imply' that categories and concepts inhere within the data, awaiting the researcher's discovery ... Instead, a constructivist approach recognizes that the categories, concepts, and theoretical level of an analysis emerge from the researcher's interaction within the field and questions about the data' (Charmaz 2000: 522). One difficulty here is that the two meanings of constructionism referred to in Key concept 2.12 seem to be conflated. The first quotation refers to constructionism as an ontological position in relating to social objects and categories; the second is a reference to constructionism in relation to the nature of knowledge of the social world. It is certainly fair to suggest that Glaser, Strauss, and Corbin in their various writings neglect the role of the researcher in the generation of knowledge, but it is not clear that they are indifferent to the notion that social reality exists independently of social actors. Strauss was, after all, the lead of the study referred to in Chapter 2 concerning the hospital as a negotiated order, which was used as an illustration of constructionism (Strauss et al. 1973). However, there is little doubt that there is considerable confusion currently about the nature of grounded theory. According to Partington (2000), there is little evidence of the successful application of Strauss and Corbin's (1990) grounded theory within management and business research. This is partly because of the greater difficulty in following this more prescriptive, proceduralized approach, which contrasts sharply with Glaser and Strauss's (1967) earlier emphasis on the development of insight based on open-minded sensitivity.

Nonetheless, grounded theory probably represents the most influential general strategy for conducting qualitative data analysis, though how far the approach is followed varies from study to study. Locke (2001) argues that grounded theory is particularly well suited to organizational research. She suggests that it is particularly good at the following:

- *Capturing complexity*. Grounded theory is good at capturing the complexity of contexts as action unfolds.

- *Linking with practice*. Grounded theory frequently facilitates an appreciation among organizational members of their situations. Such understanding can provide a helpful springboard for organizational action.

- *Facilitating theoretical work in substantive areas that have not been well researched by others*. As new forms of organizational or technological change emerge and become prominent in the business world, grounded theory is ideal for an open-ended research strategy that can then be employed for the generation of theory out of the resulting data.

- *Putting life into well-established fields*. Grounded theory can provide the basis for an alternative view of well-established fields, such as group effectiveness and leadership, through its open-ended approach to data collection followed by a rigorous approach to theoretical work.

In addition, many of grounded theory's core processes, such as coding, memos, and the very idea of allowing theoretical ideas to emerge out of one's data, have been hugely influential. Indeed, it is striking that one of the main developments in qualitative data analysis in recent years—computer-assisted qualitative data analysis—has implicitly promoted many of these processes, because the software programs have often been written with grounded theory in mind (Richards and Richards 1994; Lonkila 1995).

More on coding

Coding is the starting point for most forms of qualitative data analysis, including ethnography (see Research in focus 24.8 for an example). The principles involved have been well developed by writers on grounded theory and others. Some of the considerations in developing codes, some of which are derived from Lofland and Lofland (1995), are as follows:

- Of what general category is this item of data an instance?
- What does this item of data represent?
- What is this item of data about?
- Of what topic is this item of data an instance?
- What question about a topic does this item of data suggest?
- What sort of answer to a question about a topic does this item of data imply?
- What is happening here?
- What are people doing?
- What do people say they are doing?
- What kind of event is going on?

Research in focus 24.8
An example of ethnographic coding

Delbridge (1998) describes the process of analysing the hundreds of pages of handwritten field notes that described day-to-day events on the shopfloor of Valleyco and Nippon CTV as extremely challenging:

> Once the field notes were completed, I read through the first set from Valleyco and began to pick out themes which emerged from these notes. At first this consisted of noting any type of event, interaction or comment which occurred more than once. After generating a very long list of such instances, I then grouped these around a set of tentative themes which had begun to emerge. In the first round of reviewing the data, I identified about 150 key events or notes from my first month at Valleyco and labelled these under one or more of the nine themes. I then grouped the second month's notes from Valleyco within these themes and added to or amended the themes to cope with additional instances. I repeated these iterative loops on a weekly basis for the Nippon CTV notes until I have centred on thirteen issues which came from the data.
>
> (1998: 22)

The thirteen labels were:

QLTY	denoting systems of quality management;
SYS	the manufacturing system at the plants;
RELS	data regarding formal and informal relationships between actors;
UNTY	denoting issues of uncertainty and informality in the workplace;
CONT	issues of control and surveillance;
WORK	workers, their roles, and experiences;
COMM	communication issues and practices;
MGT	managers, their roles, and perspectives;
ACCOMM	issues of accommodation, indulgence, and resistance;
UNION	the role of unions in the workplace;
RES	issues pertaining to the research process;
COFACT	factual data on the companies involved;
JAP	data relating specifically to Japan and the Japanese.

It is interesting to note that, in starting to identify themes based on events, interactions, or comments that occurred 'more than once', Delbridge was attempting to make an initial judgement about the significance of the data based on frequency. However, it is not that unusual for qualitative researchers to engage in some kind of quantitative assessment of qualitative data, as Chapter 27 illustrates.

Steps and considerations in coding

The following steps and considerations need to be borne in mind in preparation for and during coding.

- *Code as soon as possible*. It is well worth coding as you go along, as grounded theory suggests. This may sharpen your understanding of your data and help with theoretical sampling. Also, it may help to alleviate the feeling of being swamped by your data, which may happen if you defer analysis entirely until the end of the data collection period. At the very least, you should ensure that, if your data collection involves recording interviews, you begin transcription at a relatively early stage.

- *Read through your initial set of transcripts, field notes, documents, etc.*, without taking any notes or considering an interpretation; perhaps at the end jot down a few general notes about what struck you as especially interesting, important, or significant.

- *Do it again*. Read through your data again, but this time begin to make marginal notes about significant remarks or observations. Make as many as possible. Initially, they will be very basic—perhaps keywords used by your respondents, names that you give to themes in the data. When you do this you are *coding*—generating an index of terms that will help you to interpret and theorize in relation to your data.

- *Review your codes*. Begin to review your codes, possibly in relation to your transcripts. Are you using two or more words or phrases to describe the same phenomenon? If so, remove one of them. Do some of your codes relate to concepts and categories in the existing literature? If so, might it be sensible to use these instead? Can you see any connections between the codes? Is there some evidence that respondents believe that one thing tends to be associated with or caused by something else? If so, how do you characterize and therefore code these connections?

- *Consider more general theoretical ideas in relation to codes and data*. At this point, you should be beginning to generate some general theoretical ideas about your data. Try to outline connections between concepts and categories you are developing. Consider in more detail how they relate to the existing literature. Develop hypotheses about the linkages you are making and go back to your data to see if they can be confirmed.

- Remember that any one item or slice of data can and often should be coded in more than one way.

- *Do not worry about generating what seem to be too many codes*—at least in the early stages of your analysis; some will be fruitful and others will not—the important thing is to be as inventive and imaginative as possible; you can worry about tidying things up later.

- *Keep coding in perspective*. Do not equate coding with analysis. It is part of your analysis, albeit an important one. It is a mechanism for thinking about the meaning of your data *and* for reducing the vast amount of data that you are facing (Huberman and Miles 1994). Miles and Huberman (1984) have developed several techniques for the display of data that have been coded through content analysis as a way of overcoming the difficulty of representing the complexity of qualitative analysis. One of the most important of these is the matrix format, which identifies constructs along one axis and occurrences along the other. This technique introduces an element of quantification into the qualitative analysis by drawing attention to the frequency of occurrences in the data. Another data display mechanism described by Gersick (1994) in her study of a new business venture is the timeline; this is used to represent the company's history, including major events and decisions, the time period over which they were implemented, and the eventual outcome of the actions. Whatever data display techniques you use, you must still interpret your findings. This means attending to issues such as the significance of your coded material for the lives of the people you are studying, forging interconnections between codes, and reflecting on the overall importance of your findings for the research questions and the research literature that have driven your data collection.

Turning data into fragments

The coding of such materials as interview transcripts has typically entailed writing marginal notes on them and gradually refining those notes into codes. In this way, portions of transcripts become seen as belonging to certain names or labels. In the past, this process was accompanied by cutting and pasting in the literal sense of using scissors and paste. It entailed cutting up one's transcripts into files of chunks of data, with each file representing a code. The process of cutting and pasting is useful for data retrieval, though it is always important to make sure that you have ways of identifying the origins of the chunk of text (for example, name, position, date). Word-processing programs allow this to be done in a way that does not rely on your cutting-and-pasting skills so much through the use of the 'find' function. Nowadays, computer-assisted qualitative data analysis software (CAQDAS) is increasingly used to perform these tasks (see Chapter 25).

There is no one correct approach to coding your data. As Key concept 24.4 suggests, grounded theory

Telling it like it is
Forming pre-analytical categories

From his literature review Chris had identified three main categories of explanation that women used to make sense of the unequal distribution of career opportunities between men and women. 'I classed them as individual, organizational, or societal. Individual reasons being for example: "I shouldn't" and "I'm not good enough". Organizational reasons being "well, you know, women shouldn't do that" and societal reasons such as saying "women have children, therefore they don't get on".' Chris's research questions were based on these three categories of explanation. This made the analysis of data a relatively straightforward task of categorizing interviewee responses. He explained that 'it was interesting hearing the responses to the questions. I was always able to go "right, that goes there and that goes there".'

Tips and skills
Coded text from the Disney project

Interviewer	OK. What were your views or feelings about the presentation of different cultures, as shown in, for example, Jungle Cruise or It's a Small World at the Magic Kingdom or in World Showcase at Epcot?	
Wife	Well, I thought the different countries at Epcot were wonderful, but I need to say more than that, don't I?	uncritical enthusiasm
Husband	They were very good and some were better than others, but that was down to the host countries themselves really, as I suppose each of the countries represented would have been responsible for their own part, so that's nothing to do with Disney, I wouldn't have thought.	not critical of Disney
	I mean some of the landmarks were hard to recognize for what they were supposed to be, but some were very well done. Britain was OK, but there was only a pub and a Welsh shop there really, whereas some of the other pavilions, as I think they were called, were good ambassadors for the countries they represented. China, for example, had an excellent 360 degree film showing parts of China and I found that very interesting.	content critique

aesthetic critique

Interviewer	Did you think there was anything lacking about the content?	
Husband	Well I did notice that there weren't many black people at World Showcase, particularly the American Adventure. Now whether we were there on an unusual day in that respect I don't know, but we saw plenty of black Americans in the Magic Kingdom and other places, but very few if any in that World Showcase.	visitors' ethnicity
	And there was certainly little mention of black history in the American Adventure presentation, so maybe they felt alienated by that, I don't know, but they were noticeable by their absence.	visitors' ethnicity

ethnicity critique

Interviewer	So did you think there were any special emphases?	
Husband	Well thinking about it now, because I hadn't really given this any consideration before you started asking about it, but thinking about it now, it was only really representative of the developed world, you know, Britain, America, Japan, world leaders many of them in technology, and there was nothing of the Third World there. Maybe that's their own fault, maybe they were asked to participate and didn't, but now that I think about it, that does come to me. What do you think, love?	nationality critique
Wife	Well, like you, I hadn't thought of it like that before, but I agree with you.	

conceives of different types of code. Coffey and Atkinson (1996) point to different levels of coding. These levels can be related to the passage from an interview that was previously encountered in Chapter 20 about the study of visitors to Disney theme parks. Tips and skills 'Coded text from the Disney project' shows some coded text from the Disney project, illustrating three coding levels.

- First there is a very basic coding, which, in the passage in Tips and skills 'Coded text from the Disney project', could be in terms of liking or disliking the Disney theme parks. However, such a coding scheme is unlikely to get us very far from an analytical vantage point.

- A second level comprises much more awareness of the content of what is said. Themes reflect much more the language the interviewee uses. We see much more the kinds of issues with which the interviewee is concerned. Examples might be 'developed world', 'black people', and 'black history'.

- A third level moves slightly away from a close association with what the respondent says and towards a concern with broad analytic themes. This is the way that the passage in Tips and skills 'Coded text from the Disney project' has been coded. Here the passage has been coded in terms of such features as whether a response is uncritically enthusiastic ('uncritical enthusiasm') or is not critical of the Disney Corporation ('not critical of Disney'); reveals comments made about typical visitors ('visitors' ethnicity'); and makes critical comments ('aesthetic critique'; 'ethnicity critique'; 'nationality critique'). Interestingly, the passage also reveals the potential for a code employed by Coffey and Atkinson (1996: 43–5) in

relation to one of their examples—namely, the use of a 'contrastive rhetoric'. This occurs when a person makes a point about something by comparing it to something else. This feature occurs when the husband makes a point about the representation of British culture, which in fact he regards as poor, by comparing it to that of China, which he regards as good. The poor showing of Britain is brought out by comparing it in a negative light to China. However, this coding category was not employed in relation to this research.

As Coffey and Atkinson (1996) observe, following Strauss and Corbin's account (1990) of grounded theory, codes should not be thought of purely as mechanisms for the fragmentation and retrieval of text. In other words, they can do more than simply manage the data you have gathered. If we ask about the properties and interconnections between codes, we may begin to see that some of them may be dimensions of a broader phenomenon. For example, as shown in Chapter 25, 'ethnicity critique' came to be seen as a dimension of 'ideology critique', along with 'class critique' and 'gender critique'. In this way, we can begin to map the more general or formal properties of concepts that are being developed.

Problems with coding

One of the most commonly mentioned criticisms of the coding approach to qualitative data analysis is the possible problem of losing the context of what is said. By plucking chunks of text out of the context within which they appeared, such as a particular interview transcript, the social setting can be lost.

Telling it like it is
A simple way to code

Angharad's supervisor recommended a fairly straightforward method for coding interview data that did not involve the use of computer-assisted qualitative analysis software, which would have been time-consuming to learn to use. He recommended that she should use a software program with which she was already very familiar. She said, 'It was actually really clever the idea that my tutor gave me, which was open up a Word document for different things that you can see across your data and cut and paste your data into it so that you can see what you've got basically and how much you've got in each for each idea. And some of them got merged and some of them I didn't like. That was a really clever idea and that was how I actually pulled out the themes from the data and then it was just a matter of writing it up.'

A second criticism of coding is that it results in a fragmentation of data, so that the narrative flow of what people say is lost (Coffey and Atkinson 1996). Sensitivity to this issue has been heightened by a growing interest in narrative analysis since the late 1980s (see Chapter 22). Riessman (1993) became concerned about the fragmentation of data that occurs as a result of coding themes when she came to analyse data she had collected through structured interviews on divorce and gender. She writes:

> Some [interviewees] developed long accounts of what had happened in their marriages to justify their divorces. I did not realize these were narratives until I struggled to code them. Applying traditional qualitative methods, I searched the texts for common thematic elements. But some individuals knotted together several themes into long accounts that had coherence and sequence, defying easy categorization. I found myself not wanting to fragment the long accounts into distinct thematic categories. There seemed to be a common structure beneath talk about a variety of topics. While I coded one interview, a respondent provided language for my trouble. As I have thought about it since, it was a 'click moment' in my biography as a narrative researcher.
>
> (Riessman 1993: p. vi)

'Riessman's account' is interesting because it suggests several possibilities: that the coding method of qualitative data analysis fragments data; that some forms of data may be unsuitable for the coding method; and that researchers can turn narrative analysis on themselves, since what she provides in this passage is precisely a narrative. Interest in narrative analysis certainly shows signs of growing, and in large part this trend parallels the revival of interest in the life history approach (see Chapter 20). Nonetheless, the coding method is unlikely to become less prominent, because of several factors: its widespread acceptance in the research community; the fact that not all analysts are interested in research questions that lend themselves to the elicitation of narratives; the influence of grounded theory and its associated techniques; and the growing use and acceptance of computer software for qualitative data analysis, which frequently invites a coding approach.

Regardless of which analytical strategy you employ, what you must not do is simply say: 'This is what my subjects said and did—isn't that incredibly interesting?' It may be reasonably interesting, but your work can acquire significance only when you theorize in relation to it. Many researchers are wary of this—they worry that, in the process of interpretation and theorizing, they may fail to do justice to what they have seen and heard; that they may contaminate their subjects' words and behaviour. This is a risk, but it has to be balanced against the fact that your findings acquire significance in our intellectual community only when you have reflected on, interpreted, and theorized your data. You are not there as a mere mouthpiece.

Telling it like it is
Interpreting and theorizing qualitative data

Angharad found the process of analysing her interview data difficult because she was uncomfortable about the way that coding required her to extract themes from their context, thereby lessening the emphasis on each individual's personal story. 'I found analysing the data quite hard because I did not like breaking down these stories that I'd been told. I felt like I wasn't doing it justice. I didn't like breaking it all up but I knew that I had to do it. Everything that had been said had been said within a context and to pull it out of that and cut bits out which I thought were important in people's stories. I just didn't like it. I did not like breaking down people's stories. It turned it from a story into data I suppose. Taking it out of context didn't do the stories and the women justice. I didn't want to commit and start deciding what was relevant and what wasn't and deciding what themes there were because that meant leaving bits out and I really didn't like leaving bits out. I felt everything I had was important. So it was just actually committing to do it and being ruthless as well. But then it also anonymized them a bit more. I could not have put stories in because the identity of the person would have been so obvious.'

An alternative way of analysing data that Angharad could have used to retain an emphasis on the integrity of each individual as a case is by using the life history method (see Chapter 20).

Thematic analysis

One of the most common approaches to qualitative data analysis entails what is often referred to as **thematic analysis**. However, unlike such strategies as grounded theory or critical discourse analysis, this is not an approach to analysis that has an identifiable heritage or that has been outlined in terms of a distinctive cluster of techniques. Indeed, the search for themes is an activity that can be discerned in many if not most approaches to qualitative data analysis, such as grounded theory, critical discourse analysis, qualitative content analysis, and narrative analysis. Also, for some writers a theme is more or less the same as a code, whereas for others it transcends any one code and is built up out of groups of codes. Key concept 24.9 provides some criteria for identifying what a theme is.

This does not appear to be a promising start, because, although qualitative researchers often claim to have employed thematic analysis, it is not an identifiable approach. Indeed, it did not appear as a separate section in the first three editions of this book! For example, Bosley et al. (2014: 1500) write that their interview transcripts 'were analysed using a thematic approach to identify common and/or recurring career shaper actions and interactions'.

One general strategy for assisting a thematic analysis of qualitative data is provided by Framework, an approach that has been developed at the National Centre for Social Research in the UK. Framework is described as a 'matrix based method for ordering and synthesising data' (Ritchie et al. 2003: 219). The idea is to construct an index of central themes and subthemes, which are then represented in a matrix that closely resembles an SPSS spreadsheet with its display of cases and variables. The themes and subthemes are essentially recurring motifs in the text that are then applied to the data. The themes and subthemes are the product of a thorough reading and rereading of the transcripts or field notes that make up the data. This framework is then applied to the data, which are organized initially into core themes, and the data are then displayed in terms of subthemes within the matrix and for each case. If we take the Disney project data described in Chapter 25, one of the main themes that was identified was 'ideological critique'. This theme can be viewed as having a number of subthemes—class critique; ethnicity critique; gender critique; and nationality critique. Figure 24.5 is a matrix that draws on the coded text in Tips and skills 'Coded text from the Disney project' and that would be used for representing the data

on the theme 'ideological critique'. The four subthemes are presented, and the idea is to place brief snippets from the data into the appropriate cell. Thus, the passage in Tips and skills 'Coded text from the Disney project' provides the data for the insertion of some material into two of the cells for Interviewee 4. It also specifies the location within the transcript of the snippet(s) that are included in the cell. Ritchie et al. advise that, when inserting material into cells, the researcher should:

1. indicate where in the transcript the fragment comes from (we have used the question number);

2. keep the language of the research participant as far as possible;

3. try not to insert too much quoted material; and

4. use abbreviations in cells so that cells do not become too full.

As its name implies, this approach is meant to provide a framework for the thematic analysis of qualitative data and provides one way of thinking about how to manage themes and data. It does not necessarily tell the user how to identify themes, which, as the authors suggest, are likely to reflect the analyst's awareness of recurring ideas and topics in the data.

When searching for themes, Ryan and Bernard (2003) recommend looking for:

- *repetitions*: topics that recur again and again;

- *indigenous typologies or categories*: local expressions that are either unfamiliar or used in an unfamiliar way;

- *metaphors and analogies*: the ways in which participants represent their thoughts in terms of metaphors or analogies (they give the example of people describing their marriage as like 'the Rock of Gibraltar');

- *transitions*: the ways in which topics shift in transcripts and other materials;

- *similarities and differences*: exploring how interviewees might discuss a topic in different ways or differ from each other in certain ways, or exploring whole texts such as transcripts and asking how they differ;

- *linguistic connectors*: examining the use of words like 'because' or 'since', because such terms point to causal connections in the minds of participants;

Figure 24.5

The framework approach to thematic analysis

Theme: Ideological critique

	Class critique	Ethnicity critique	Gender critique	Nationality critique
Interviewee 1				
Interviewee 2				
Interviewee 3				
Interviewee 4		'saw plenty of black Americans' in MK 'but few if any in that World Showcase'. 'Little mention of black history' (Q14)		World Showcase 'only really representative of the developed world' (Q14)
Interviewee 5				

Key concept 24.9
What is a theme?

In spite of its apparent frequency of use in the analysis of qualitative data (see main text), thematic analysis is a remarkably underdeveloped procedure, in that there are few specifications of its steps or ingredients. This is changing (e.g. Ryan and Bernard 2003; Braun and Clarke 2006), but, even so, what actually constitutes a theme is often not spelled out. By and large, we can say that a theme:

• is a category identified by the analyst through his/her data;

• relates to the analyst's research focus (and quite possibly the research questions);

• builds on codes identified in transcripts and/or field notes;

• provides the researcher with the basis for a theoretical understanding of his or her data that can make a theoretical contribution to the literature relating to the research focus.

- *missing data*: reflecting on what is *not* in the data by asking questions about what interviewees, for example, omit in their answers to questions;

- *theory-related material*: using social scientific concepts as a springboard for themes.

An emphasis on repetition is probably one of the most common criteria for establishing that a pattern within the data warrants being considered a theme. Repetition may refer to recurrence within a data source (for example, an interview transcript or document) or, as is more often the case, across data sources (for example, a corpus of interview transcripts or documents). However, repetition *per se* is an insufficient criterion for something to warrant being labelled a theme. Most importantly, it must be relevant to the investigation's research questions or research focus. In other words, simply because quite a large number of people who have been interviewed say much the same thing does not mean it warrants being considered a theme. The identification of a theme is a stage or two further on from coding data in terms of initial or open codes (Braun and Clarke 2006). In the research by Corley and Gioia (2004) referred to in Research in focus 24.6, themes were derived from 'first order concepts'. Figure 24.4 shows how the theme 'Change in social referents' was derived from three first-order concepts. This process requires the researcher to reflect on the initial codes that have been generated and to gain a sense of the continuities and linkages between them.

Notwithstanding its prominence as a means of conducting qualitative data analysis, thematic analysis lacks a clearly specified series of procedures. However, the framework approach and Ryan and Bernard's suggestions provide some pointers about how to begin and to organize such an analysis. It can be employed in relation to several of the different ways of analysing qualitative data covered in this book, such as grounded theory, narrative analysis, critical discourse analysis, and qualitative content analysis. It is this flexibility—the fact that it can be deployed with a wide variety of types of qualitative data and approaches to qualitative data analysis—that probably accounts for its popularity, in spite of the absence of a great deal of codification of its core procedures.

Secondary analysis of qualitative data

One final point to bear in mind is that this discussion of qualitative data analysis may have been presumed to be solely concerned with the analysis of data that the analyst has played a part in collecting. However, in recent years, secondary analysis of qualitative data has become a growing focus of discussion and interest. While the secondary analysis of quantitative data has been on the research agenda for many years (see Chapter 14), similar use of qualitative data has only recently come to the fore. The general idea of secondary analysis was addressed in Key concept 14.1.

There is no obvious reason why qualitative data cannot be the focus of secondary analysis, though such data do present certain problems that are not fully shared by quantitative data. The study in Research in focus 23.2 provides an example involving the secondary analysis of oral history interviews. The possible grounds for conducting a secondary analysis are more or less the same as those associated with quantitative data (see Chapter 14). With such considerations in mind, Qualidata, an archival resource centre, was created in the UK in 1994. The centre is concerned with 'locating, assessing and documenting qualitative data and arranging their deposit in suitable public archive repositories' (Corti, Foster, and Thompson 1995). Qualidata can be accessed via the UK Data Service's online catalogue, 'Discover', which provides a single point of access to data for social and economic researchers. It can be accessed via the home page at: **ukdataservice.ac.uk/** (accessed 2 November 2014)

An example involving secondary analysis of qualitative data is provided by Savage (2005), who analysed field notes that had been collected by Goldthorpe et al. in the *Affluent Worker* studies in the early 1960s, which he accessed through the Qualidata Archive. Savage argues that, although a huge amount of qualitative data was generated through the *Affluent Worker* studies, very little of this part of the research made its way into publication. Instead, the researchers focused on aspects of their data that could be quantified and consistently coded and 'a huge amount of evocative material was "left on the cutting room floor"' (Savage 2005: 932). Savage (2005) uses the field notes, which contain many verbatim quotes from respondent interviews, to argue that rereading the field notes with a contemporary understanding of issues of money, power, and status indicates that the respondents had different understandings of class from those of Goldthorpe et al. that the researchers did not pick up on, and this difference of understanding affected how the data were interpreted.

Qualidata's focus is on acquiring data collections created during the course of research projects from the Economic and Social Research Council's Research Programmes, from mixed methods research (see Chapter 27 for a definition), and from purely qualitative studies. Qualidata acknowledges certain difficulties with the reuse of qualitative data, such as the difficulty of making settings and people anonymous and the ethical problems involved in such reuse associated with promises of confidentiality. Also, Hammersley (1997) has suggested that reuse of qualitative data may be hindered by the secondary analyst's lack of an insider's understanding of the social context within which the data were produced. This possible difficulty may hinder the interpretation of data but would seem to be more of a problem with ethnographic field notes than with interview transcripts. Such problems even seem to afflict researchers revisiting their own data many years after the original research had been carried out (Mauthner, Parry, and Backett-Milburn 1998: 742). There are also distinctive ethical issues deriving from the fact that the original researcher(s) may not have obtained the consent of research participants for the analysis of data by others. This is a particular problem with qualitative data in view of the fact that it invariably contains detailed accounts of contexts and people that can make it difficult to conceal the identities of institutions and individuals in the presentation of raw data (as opposed to publications in which such concealment is usually feasible). Nonetheless, in spite of certain practical difficulties, secondary analysis offers rich opportunities not least because the tendency for qualitative researchers to generate large and unwieldy sets of data means that much of the material remains under-explored. Key concept 24.10 and Research in focus 24.11 illustrate meta-ethnography, which is an approach to secondary analysis, although rather than analysing data collected by others this involves synthesising the interpretations and explanations offered in other studies.

Key concept 24.10
What is meta-ethnography?

Meta-ethnography is a method that is used to achieve interpretative synthesis of qualitative research and other secondary sources. It can be used to synthesize and analyse information about a phenomenon that has been extensively studied. However, in contrast to meta-analysis in quantitative research (Key concept 14.9 and Research in focus 14.10), meta-ethnography 'refers not to developing overarching generalizations but, rather, translations of qualitative studies into one another' (Noblit and Hare 1988: 25). Meta-ethnography involves a series of seven phases that overlap and repeat as the synthesis progresses.

1. *Getting started*. This involves the researcher in identifying an intellectual interest that the qualitative research might inform by reading interpretative accounts.

2. *Deciding what is relevant to the initial interest*. Unlike positivists, interpretative researchers are not concerned with developing an exhaustive list of studies that might be included in the review. Instead the primary intent is to determine what accounts are likely to be credible and interesting to the intended audience for the synthesis.

3. *Reading the studies*. This involves the detailed, repeated reading of the studies, rather than moving to analysis of their characteristics.

4. *Determining how the studies are related*. This stage entails 'putting together' the various studies by determining the relationships between them and the metaphors used within them.

5. *Translating the studies into one another*. This phase is concerned with interpreting the meaning of studies in relation to each other: are they directly comparable or 'reciprocal' translations; do they stand in opposition to each other as 'refutational' translations; or do they, taken together, represent a line of argument that is neither 'reciprocal' nor 'refutational'?

6. *Synthesizing translations*. The researcher compares the different translations and shows how they relate to each other. This may involve grouping them into different types.

7. *Expressing the synthesis*. This involves translating the synthesis into a form that can be comprehended by the audience for which it is intended.

Crucial to this is that the synthesis focuses on the interpretations and explanations offered by studies that are included, rather than on the data that these studies are based on.

Research in focus 24.11
A meta-ethnography of research on the experiences of people with common mental disorders when they return to work

Andersen, Nielsen, and Brinkman (2012) used meta-ethnography as a method for synthesizing qualitative research concerned with the experiences of employees with common mental disorders (CMD) when they return to work (RTW). The synthesis was guided by three research questions:

1. What kinds of opportunities and obstacles do employees with CMD experience in relation to RTW?
2. What is the nature of the RTW process that they experience?
3. What is an optimal RTW intervention from their perspective?

Using keywords associated with each of the three main concepts—mental health (e.g. mental illness, depression, stress), work status (e.g. employability, sick leave, returning to work), and method (e.g. semi-structured interview, qualitative method, focus group)—six different online databases were searched for the period 1995–2011. This stage led to the identification of 4072 articles. Articles were included if they met the following conditions: a qualitative research method was used; research questions addressed both RTW and CMD; and the research was undertaken from the perspective of people with CMD. The initial stage of identifying relevance produced 64 articles and these were then examined in greater detail, resulting in just eight relevant studies. These studies were appraised for quality using 17 of the 18 quality criteria employed by the UK National Centre for Social Research. The authors elected to include in their synthesis studies that were of least 'medium' quality, resulting in eight studies being included in the final dataset of articles. These eight studies then became the focus of *data extraction*, that is, the process of identifying and summarizing key elements in each investigation. This number may seem like a rather small sample to end up with given that the initial trawl produced over 4000 articles, but this is a common outcome. The initial trawl is based entirely on the identification of articles through keywords and combinations of keywords. When the abstracts of these articles are examined it becomes clear that a great many are not relevant to the research questions and have to be excluded. When the remaining articles are examined in even greater detail (i.e. the entire article is read), there is a further loss of articles due to lack of relevance. There is then often a further reduction if articles are appraised for quality and some are found to be of insufficient quality. In the case of the synthesis by Andersen et al., no articles fell below the criterion of medium quality that they established. If they had relied on only articles that were of at least high quality, only three studies would have been the focus of the meta-ethnography.

For the actual synthesis method, the authors write that they mainly employed 'reciprocal translation analysis' (step 5 in Key concept 24.10). This process entailed examining all the articles in detail and inductively identifying what Andersen et al. call 'first-order concepts' and then developing higher-level 'second-order key concepts' out of these. For example, one of the five second-order key concepts associated with the RTW was called 'accommodations and social support', which was made up of three first-order concepts: gradual RTW, accommodations, and social support. The authors show that three articles provided evidence of the first of these three first-order concepts, five articles on the second, and four on the third. The articles were summarized in terms of the second-order key concepts. For example:

> The reviewed studies showed that reduced work hours alone were insufficient to secure RTW. Responsibilities and workload also needed to be increased gradually through relevant work accommodations (32, 36, 38, 39).
>
> (Andersen, Nielsen, and Brinkman 2012: 97–8)

The four numbers at the end of this quotation refer to the four studies that specifically identified that responsibilities and workload need to be increased gradually. The authors then describe their third-order interpretations of the findings from the second-order analysis. Andersen et al. arrive at two third-order interpretations of their examination of the key concepts: 'pre-illness conditions influence the RTW process' and an 'unfortunate lack of coordination between the different systems with which the employee is in contact during the RTW process' (Andersen, Nielsen, and Brinkman 2012: 100).

Key points

- The collection of qualitative data frequently results in the accumulation of a large volume of information.

- Qualitative data analysis is not governed by codified rules in the same way as quantitative data analysis.

- There are different approaches to qualitative data analysis, of which grounded theory is probably the most prominent.

- Coding is a key process in most qualitative data analysis strategies, but it is sometimes accused of fragmenting and decontextualizing text.

- Secondary analysis of qualitative data is becoming a more prominent activity than in the past.

Questions for review

- What is meant by suggesting that qualitative data are an 'attractive nuisance'?

General strategies of qualitative data analysis

- What are the main ingredients of analytic induction?

- What makes it a rigorous method?

- What are the main ingredients of grounded theory?

- What is the role of coding in grounded theory and what are the different types of coding?

- What is the role of memos in grounded theory?

- Charmaz has written that theoretical sampling 'represents' a defining property of grounded theory' (2000: 519). Why do you think she feels this to be the case?

- What are some of the main criticisms of grounded theory?

More on coding

- Is coding associated solely with grounded theory?

- What are the main steps in coding?

- To what extent does coding result in excessive fragmentation of data?

- To what extent does narrative analysis provide an alternative to data fragmentation?

Secondary analysis of qualitative data

- How feasible is it for researchers to analyse qualitative data collected by another researcher?

Online Resource Centre

www.oxfordtextbooks.co.uk/orc/brymanbrm4e/

Visit the Interactive Research Guide that accompanies this book to complete an exercise in Qualitative Data Analysis.

25

Computer-assisted qualitative data analysis: using NVivo

Chapter outline

One of the most significant developments in qualitative research since the middle of the 1980s is the emergence of software designed to assist in the analysis of qualitative data. This software is often referred to as computer-assisted (or computer-aided) qualitative data analysis software (CAQDAS). CAQDAS removes the clerical tasks associated with the manual coding and retrieving of data. There is no industry leader among the different programs. This chapter introduces NVivo, a widely-used CAQDAS package. This chapter explores:

* some of the debates about the desirability of CAQDAS;
* how to set up your research materials for analysis with NVivo;
* how to code using NVivo;
* how to retrieve coded text;
* how to create memos;
* basic computer operations in NVivo.

Introduction

One of the most notable developments in qualitative research in recent years has been the arrival of computer software that facilitates the analysis of qualitative data. Computer-assisted qualitative data analysis software, or CAQDAS as it is conventionally abbreviated, has been a growth area in terms of both the proliferation of programs that perform such analysis and the numbers of people using them. The term and its abbreviation were coined by Lee and Fielding (1991).

Most of the best-known programs are variations on the code-and-retrieve theme. This means that they allow the analyst to code text while working at the computer and to retrieve the coded text. Thus, if we code a large number of interviews, we can retrieve all those sequences of text to which a code (or combination of codes) was attached. This means that the computer takes over manual tasks associated with the coding process referred to in Chapter 24. Typically, the analyst would:

* go through a set of data marking sequences of text in terms of codes (coding); and
* for each code, collect together all sequences of text coded in a particular way (retrieving).

The computer takes over the physical task of writing marginal codes, making photocopies of transcripts or field notes, cutting out all chunks of text relating to a code, and pasting them together. CAQDAS does not automatically do these things: the researcher must still interpret the data, code it, and then retrieve the data, but the computer takes over the manual labour involved (wielding scissors and pasting small pieces of paper together, for example).

Is CAQDAS like quantitative data analysis software?

One of the comments often made about CAQDAS is that it does not and cannot help with decisions about the coding of textual materials or about the interpretation of findings (Sprokkereef et al. 1995; Weitzman and Miles 1995). However, this situation is no different from quantitative data analysis software. In quantitative research, the investigator sets out the crucial concepts and ideas in advance rather than generating them out of his or her data. Also, it would be wrong to represent the use of quantitative data analysis software such as SPSS as purely mechanical: once the analyses have been conducted, it is still necessary to interpret them. Indeed, the choice of variables and the techniques of analysis are areas in which a considerable amount of interpretative expertise is required. Creativity is required by both forms of software.

CAQDAS differs from the use of quantitative data analysis software largely in terms of the environment within which it operates.

No industry leader

With quantitative data analysis, SPSS is both widely known and widely used. It is not the only statistical software used by social researchers, but it is certainly dominant. It has competitors but SPSS is close to being the industry leader. No parallel situation exists with regard to CAQDAS.

In this chapter, we will introduce one of the best-known packages—NVivo.

Advice on qualitative data analysis software can be found at: *onlineqda.hud.ac.uk/Which_software/what_ packages_are_available/index.php* (accessed 4 November 2014)

Lack of universal agreement about the utility of CAQDAS

Unlike quantitative data analysis, in which the use of computer software is both widely accepted and to all intents and purposes a necessity, among qualitative data analysts its use is by no means universally embraced. There are several concerns.

- Some writers are concerned that the ease with which coded text can be quantified, either within qualitative data analysis packages or by importing coded information into quantitative data analysis packages such as SPSS, will mean that the temptation to quantify findings will prove irresistible. As a result, there is a concern that qualitative research will then be colonized by the reliability and validity criteria of quantitative research (Hesse-Biber 1995).

- It has been suggested that CAQDAS reinforces the tendency for the code-and-retrieve process that underpins most approaches to qualitative data analysis to result in a fragmentation of the textual materials on which researchers work (Weaver and Atkinson 1994). As a result, the narrative flow of interview transcripts and events recorded in field notes may be lost.

- It has also been suggested that the fragmentation process of coding text into chunks that are then retrieved and put together into groups of related fragments risks decontextualizing data (Buston 1997; Fielding and Lee 1998: 74). Having an awareness of context is crucial to many qualitative researchers and the prospect of this element being sidelined is unattractive.

- Catterall and Maclaran (1997) have argued that CAQDAS is not very suitable for focus group data because the code-and-retrieve function tends to result in a loss of the communication between participants. Many writers view the interaction that occurs in focus groups as an important feature of the method (Kitzinger 1994).

- Stanley and Temple (1995) have suggested that most of the coding and retrieval features are achievable through word-processing software. They show how this can be accomplished using Microsoft Word. The advantage of using such software is that it does not require a lengthy period of getting acquainted with it.

- Researchers working in teams may experience difficulties in coordinating the coding of text when different people are involved in this activity (Sprokkereef et al. 1995).

- Coffey, Holbrook, and Atkinson (1996) have argued that the style of qualitative data analysis enshrined in most CAQDAS software (including NVivo) is resulting in the emergence of a new orthodoxy. This arises because these programs presume a certain style of analysis—one based on coding and retrieving text—that owes a great deal to grounded theory. Coffey et al. argue that the emergence of a new orthodoxy is inconsistent with the growing experimentation with a variety of representational modes in qualitative research.

On the other hand, several writers are enthusiastic about CAQDAS software on a variety of grounds:

- Most obviously, CAQDAS can make the coding and retrieval process faster and more efficient.

- It has been suggested that new opportunities are offered. For example, Mangabeira (1995) has argued on the basis of her experience that her ability to relate her coded text to what are often referred to as 'facesheet variables' (sociodemographic and personal information such as age, title of job, number of years in school education) offered new opportunities in the process of analysing her data. Thus, CAQDAS may be helpful in the development of explanations.

- It is sometimes suggested that CAQDAS enhances the transparency of the process of qualitative data analysis. It is often noted that the ways in which qualitative data are analysed are unclear in reports of findings (Bryman and Burgess 1994*b*). CAQDAS may force researchers to be more explicit and reflective about the process of analysis.

- CAQDAS invites the analyst to think about codes that are developed in terms of 'trees' of interrelated ideas. This can be a useful feature, in that it urges the analyst to consider possible connections between codes.

- Writers like Silverman (1985) have commented on the tendency towards anecdotalism in much qualitative research—that is, the tendency to use quotations from interview transcripts or field notes but with little sense of the prevalence of the phenomenon they are supposed to exemplify. CAQDAS invariably offers the opportunity to count such things as the frequency with which a form of behaviour occurred or a viewpoint was expressed in interviews. However, some qualitative researchers perceive risks in the opportunity offered for quantification of findings.

- Paulus, Lester, and Britt (2013) suggest there are generational differences in researchers' attitudes to CAQDAS, with senior researchers in particular lacking exposure to CAQDAS use, and introductory methods textbooks on qualitative research tending to frame the use of technology tools as a 'discourse of caution' rather than a 'discourse of possibility' (Paulus, Lester and Britt 2013: 642) by focusing more on the limitations than on the potential advantages. They claim that this cautionary approach is based on an outdated understanding of what the software can and cannot do, and they urge researchers to embrace the affordances of this new technology.

To use or not to use CAQDAS? If you have a very small dataset it is probably not worth taking the time and trouble to navigate your way around new software, although if you think you may use it on a future occasion, making the effort may be worthwhile. It is also worth bearing in mind that learning new software does provide you with useful skills that may be transferable on a future occasion. If you do not have easy access to CAQDAS, it is likely to be too expensive for your personal purchase. By and large, we feel it is worthwhile, but you need to bear in mind some of the factors mentioned above in deciding whether or not to use it. It is also striking that the bulk of the references are pre-2000; see also the discussion of CAQDAS debates at: *onlineqda.hud.ac.uk/Intro_CAQDAS/software_debates.php* (accessed 16 July 2014)

In large part, this is because CAQDAS has become more accepted and because the main parameters of the debate have not changed significantly.

The rest of this chapter provides an introduction to NVivo. It is based on Bryman's study of visitors to Disney theme parks, where he used NVivo as a tool to assist him in the process of qualitative data analysis.

Learning NVivo

This explanation of NVivo and its functions addresses just its most basic features. There may be features not covered here that you would find useful in your own work, so try to explore it. There is a very good help facility, and tutorials have been included to assist learners. As in Chapter 16, → signifies 'click once with the left-hand button of your mouse'—that is, select.

On opening NVivo, you will be presented with a welcome screen (see Plate 25.1). This screen shows any existing NVivo projects and is the springboard for either opening one of the existing projects or starting a new one. If you are starting a new project, as in the example that follows, → **File** → **New**. The **New Project** dialog box appears and you are asked to provide a **Title** for your project. For this exercise, the title 'Disney Project1' was chosen. You are also asked to give a **Description** of the project, but this is optional. When you have done this, → **OK**.

You then need to import the documents you want to code. In this case, the documents are interview transcripts from the project on visitors to Disney theme parks, referred to in Chapter 24. Other kinds of documents can be imported, such as field notes. NVivo 10 can accept documents in both rich text and Word formats. To import the documents, → **Internals** (below **Sources** at the top of the **Navigation view**) → **External Data** tab on the **Ribbon** → **Documents** button on the **Find bar** [opens the **Import Internals** dialog box]

Plate 25.1

The opening screen

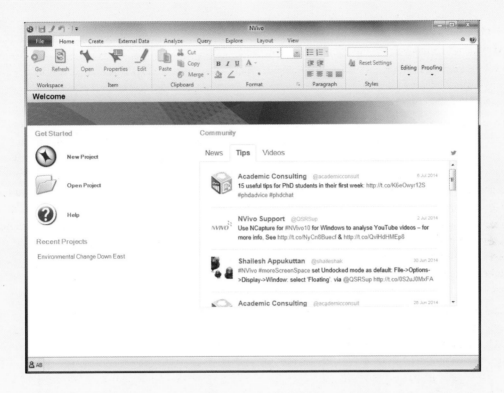

→ **Browse...** to locate the documents that are to be imported → the documents to be imported (you can hold down the Ctrl key to select several documents, or if you want to select all of them hold down the Ctrl key and tap the A key) → **Open**. (See Plate 25.2 for the series of steps.) The documents will then be visible in the Document Viewer. Once the documents have been imported, they can be read and edited. All you need to do is double-click on the ⬜ icon to the left of each interview in Viewer.

Coding

Coding your data is one of the key phases in the whole process of qualitative data analysis. For NVivo, coding is accomplished through *nodes* (see Key concept 25.1).

There are several ways of going about the coding process in NVivo. The approach Bryman took in relation to the coding of the Disney Project was to follow these steps:

1. Bryman read through the interviews both in printed form and in the Document Viewer (see Plate 25.3).

2. He worked out some codes that seemed relevant to the documents.

3. He went back into the documents and coded them using NVivo.

An alternative strategy is to code while browsing the documents.

Creating nodes

The nodes that Bryman used that were relevant to the passage in Tips and skills 'Coded text from the Disney project' (Chapter 24) are presented in Figure 25.1. Notice that there are two *non-hierarchical nodes* and three groups of *hierarchical nodes*. Prior to NVivo 9 and 10,

Plate 25.2

Stages in importing documents into NVivo

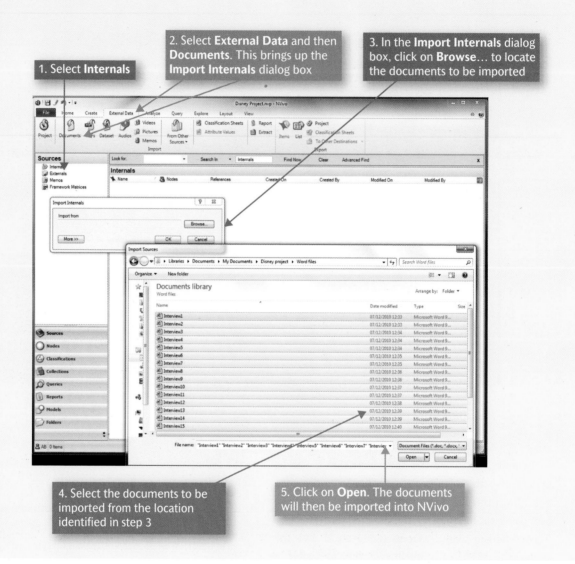

2. Select **External Data** and then **Documents**. This brings up the **Import Internals** dialog box

1. Select **Internals**

3. In the **Import Internals** dialog box, click on **Browse...** to locate the documents to be imported

4. Select the documents to be imported from the location identified in step 3

5. Click on **Open**. The documents will then be imported into NVivo

Key concept 25.1
What is a node?

NVivo's help system in earlier releases defined coding as 'the process of marking passages of text in a project's documents with *nodes*' (emphasis added). Nodes are, therefore, the route by which coding is undertaken. In turn, a node is defined in the latest release as 'a collection of references about a specific theme, place, person or other area of interest'. When a document has been coded, the node will incorporate references to those portions of documents in which the code appears. Once established, nodes can be changed or deleted.

Plate 25.3

The NVivo Workspace

The Document Viewer and its components

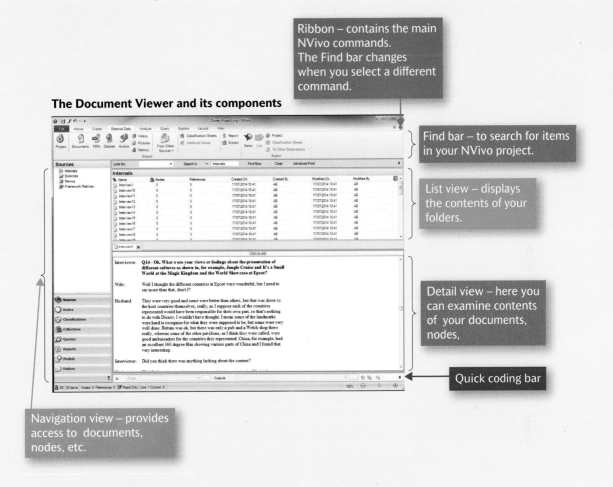

Ribbon – contains the main NVivo commands. The Find bar changes when you select a different command.

Find bar – to search for items in your NVivo project.

List view – displays the contents of your folders.

Detail view – here you can examine contents of your documents, nodes,

Quick coding bar

Navigation view – provides access to documents, nodes, etc.

when creating a node, the researcher chose between creating a 'free node 'or a 'tree node'. The latter is a node that is organized in a hierarchy of connected nodes, whereas free nodes were not organized in this way. This distinction was dropped in NVivo 9, and the software now assumes that a hierarchically-organized node is being created. Two points are crucial to note here for users of earlier releases of the software. First, the tendency now is not to refer to 'tree nodes' but to treat them as hierarchically organized nodes. Second, 'free nodes' (that is, nodes that are not hierarchically organized) can still be created—they are simply nodes without 'children', to use the latest NVivo terminology.

Notice that there are three groups of *hierarchically organized nodes* and two *non-hierarchically organized nodes* in

Figure 25.1. The nodes can be created in the following way.

Creating a non-hierarchically organized node

This sequence of steps demonstrates how to create the non-hierarchically organized node not critical of Disney.

1. While in the **Document Viewer** [the term used to describe the general screen shown in Plate 25.3] → **Create** in the Ribbon

2. → **Node** in the **Find bar** [opens the **New Node** dialog box—see Plate 25.4]

3. Enter the node **Name** [*not critical of Disney*] and a **Description** (this is optional)

4. → **OK**

Plate 25.4

Stages in creating a non-hierarchically organized node

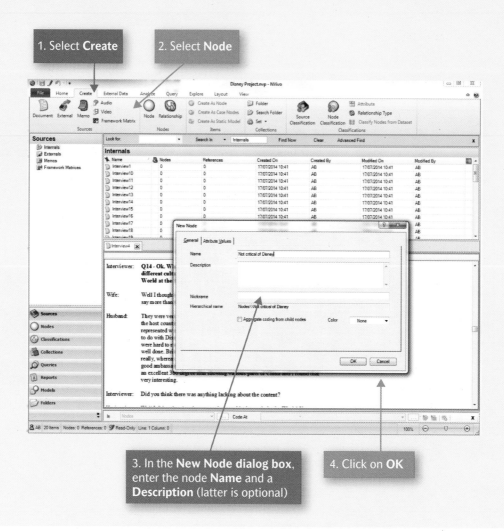

1. Select **Create**

2. Select **Node**

3. In the **New Node dialog box**, enter the node **Name** and a **Description** (latter is optional)

4. Click on **OK**

Creating hierarchically organized nodes

To create a hierarchically organized node, the initial process is exactly the same as with a non-hierarchically organized node. We will explain how to create the hierarchically organized node *Class critique*, which is a child of the hierarchically organized node *Ideological critique*, which is itself a child of the hierarchically organized node *Critique* (see Figure 25.1). The following steps will generate this node.

1. While in the **Document Viewer** → **Create** in the Ribbon

2. → **Node** in the **Find bar** [opens the **New Node** dialog box—see Plate 25.5]

3. Enter the node **Name** [*critique*] and a **Description** (the latter is optional)

4. → **OK**

5. → Critique in the list of nodes in the List viewer

6. → **Node** in the **Find bar** [opens the **New Node** dialog box—see Plate 25.5]

7. Enter the node **Name** [*Ideological critique*] and a **Description** (the latter is optional). This node will form a child of the hierarchically organized node

Figure 25.1

Nodes used in the Disney project

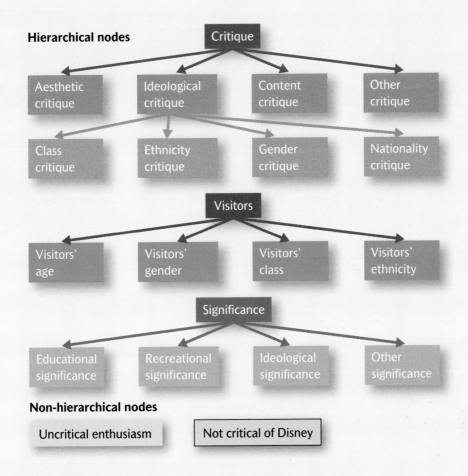

Hierarchical nodes

Critique

- Aesthetic critique
- Ideological critique
- Content critique
- Other critique

- Class critique
- Ethnicity critique
- Gender critique
- Nationality critique

Visitors

- Visitors' age
- Visitors' gender
- Visitors' class
- Visitors' ethnicity

Significance

- Educational significance
- Recreational significance
- Ideological significance
- Other significance

Non-hierarchical nodes

Uncritical enthusiasm

Not critical of Disney

[make sure that in Hierarchical name it reads **Nodes\\Critique**, as this will mean it is a child of **Critique**]. See Plate 25.5.

8. → *Ideological critique* in the list of nodes in the List viewer

9. → **Node** in the **Find bar** [opens the **New Node** dialog box—see Plate 25.5]

10. Enter the node **Name** [*Class critique*] and a **Description** (the latter is optional). This node will form a child of the hierarchically organized node [make sure that in Hierarchical name it reads **Nodes\\Critique**

Ideological critique, as this will mean it is a child of **Ideological critique**, which is itself a child of **Critique**]. See Plate 25.5.

11. → **OK**

Applying nodes in the coding process

Coding is carried out by applying nodes to segments of text. Once you have set up some nodes (and do remember you can add and alter them at any time), assuming that you are looking at a document in the viewer, you can highlight the area of the document that you want to code

Plate 25.5

Stages in creating a hierarchically organized node

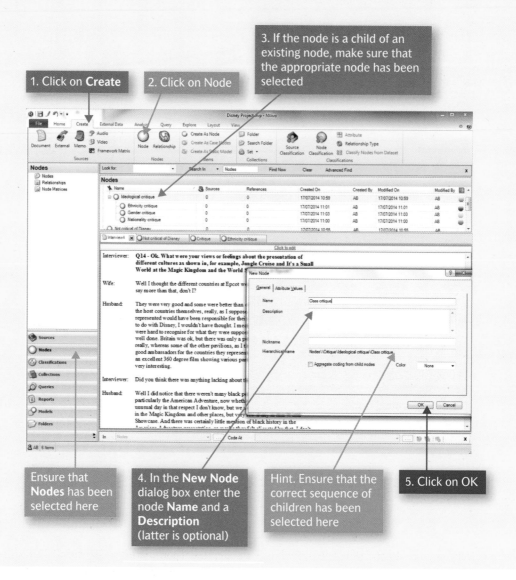

1. Click on **Create**

2. Click on Node

3. If the node is a child of an existing node, make sure that the appropriate node has been selected

Ensure that **Nodes** has been selected here

4. In the **New Node** dialog box enter the node **Name** and a **Description** (latter is optional)

Hint. Ensure that the correct sequence of children has been selected here

5. Click on OK

and then right-click on the mouse while holding the cursor over the highlighted text. Then, → **Code Selection** → **Code Selection at New Node**…. This opens the **New Node** dialog box. You can then create a new node in the manner outlined in the previous sections.

If the code you want to use has been created, one of the easiest ways of coding in NVivo is to drag and drop text into an existing code (see Plate 25.6). To do this, highlight the text to be coded and then, holding down the left-hand button, drag the text over to the appropriate node in the **List view**.

Another way is to highlight the text you want to code, right-click over the highlighted text, → **Code Selection** → **Code Selection at Existing Nodes**, which opens the **Select Project Items** dialog box (see Plate 25.7). Tick the node(s) you want to use. Thus, in the example in Plate 25.7, the tick by *Uncritical enthusiasm* will code the highlighted text at that node. If you also wanted to

Plate 25.6

Using drag and drop to code

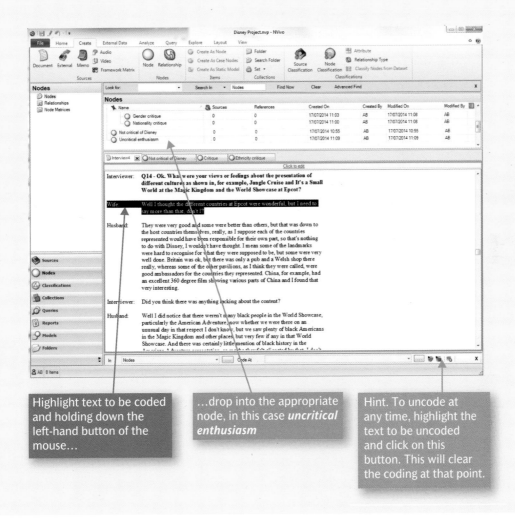

Highlight text to be coded and holding down the left-hand button of the mouse...

...drop into the appropriate node, in this case *uncritical enthusiasm*

Hint. To uncode at any time, highlight the text to be uncoded and click on this button. This will clear the coding at that point.

use a hierarchically organized node, you would need to find the appropriate parent in the list of nodes within the List view and then click on the plus to the left of it. To *uncode* at any point, simply highlight the passage to be uncoded, and → the button with a red cross in it in the Quick coding bar (see Plate 25.3). Alternatively, right-click on the highlighted text and → **Uncode**.

Coding stripes

It is very helpful to be able to see the areas of text that have been coded and the nodes applied to them. NVivo has a very useful aid to this called *coding stripes*. Selecting this facility allows you to see multicoloured stripes

that represent portions of coded text and the nodes used. Overlapping codes do not represent a problem.

To activate coding stripes, → **View** in the **Ribbon** and then → **Coding Stripes** in the **Find** bar → **Nodes Recently Coding**. Plate 25.8 shows these stripes. We can see that some segments have been coded at two or more nodes—such as *visitors' ethnicity* and *ethnicity critique*. All the nodes that have been used are clearly displayed.

Searching text

Once you have coded your data, however preliminary that may be, you will want to conduct searches of your data

Plate 25.7

Coding in NVivo

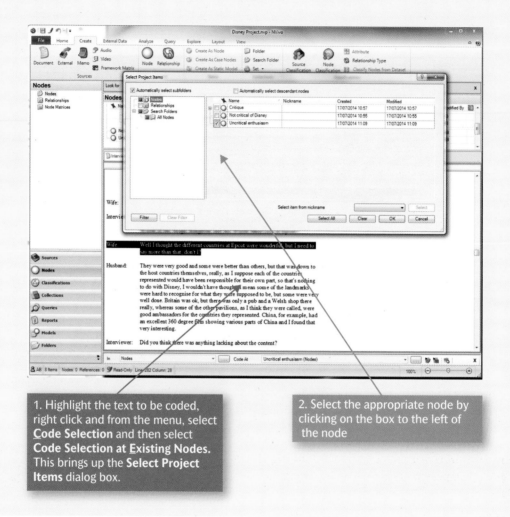

1. Highlight the text to be coded, right click and from the menu, select **Code Selection** and then select **Code Selection at Existing Nodes.** This brings up the **Select Project Items** dialog box.

2. Select the appropriate node by clicking on the box to the left of the node

at some point. A typical instance is that you are likely to want to retrieve all occurrences in your documents of a particular node. NVivo allows you very rapidly to trawl through all your documents so that you will end up with all text that was coded at a particular node in all of your documents. This is very easy to do in NVivo.

To search for occurrences of a single node

These steps describe how to conduct a search for sequences of text that have been coded in terms of the node *Ethnicity critique*. The stages are outlined in Plate 25.9.

1. While in the **Document Viewer** → **Nodes** in the **Navigation view**. This will bring up your list of nodes in the **List view**.

2. If you cannot find the parents of *Ethnicity critique* → on the little box with a + sign ⊞ 🔘 to the left of *Critique* [this brings up a list of all branches of the node *Critique*].

3. → on the + sign ⊞ 🔘 to the left of *Ideological critique* [this brings up a list of all branches of the node *Ideological critique*].

4. Double-click on *Ethnicity critique*.

Plate 25.8

Coding stripes

5. All instances of coded text at the node *Ethnicity critique* will appear at the bottom of the screen, as in Plate 25.9.

To search for text coded in terms of a free node, the process is simpler, in that you simply double-click on the relevant **Free Node** to generate all the text coded at that node.

To search for the intersection of two nodes

This section is concerned with searching for sequences of text that have been coded at two nodes: *aesthetic critique* and *not critical of Disney*. This type of search is known as a 'Boolean search'. It will locate text coded in terms of the two nodes together (that is, where they intersect), *not* text coded in terms of each of the two nodes. The following steps need to be followed:

1. In the **Document Viewer**, → **Queries** in the **Navigation view**

2. → **Query** on the **Find** bar

3. → 🔍 [opens the **Coding Query** dialog box as in Plate 25.10]

4. → **Coding Criteria** tab

5. → **Advanced** tab

6. In the **Define more criteria:** panel, → **Coded at** from the drop-down menu

7. → **Select**. You then need to choose the two nodes to be analysed from the **Select Project Items** dialog box

8. → Once the nodes have been selected, → **OK** which returns you to the **Coding Query** dialog box

9. In the **Coding Query** dialog box → **Add to List**

10. Make sure **AND** has been selected immediately below **Define more criteria:**

11. → **Run**

Plate 25.9

Stages in retrieving text from a hierarchically organized node

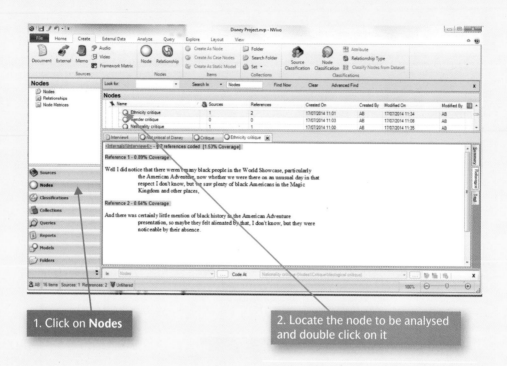

1. Click on **Nodes**

2. Locate the node to be analysed and double click on it

To search for specific text

NVivo can also perform searches for specific words or phrases, often referred to as 'strings' in computer jargon. For example, to search for **Magic Kingdom**, the following steps would need to be taken:

1. → **Home** on the **Ribbon**
2. → 🔍 [opens the **Find Content** dialog box in Plate 25.11]
3. Insert **Magic Kingdom** to the right of **Text**
4. To the right of **Look in**, make sure **Text** has been selected
5. → **Find Next**

Text searching can be useful for the identification of possible *in vivo* codes. You would then need to go back to the documents to create nodes to allow you to code in terms of any *in vivo* codes.

Output

To find the results of coding at a particular node, → the **Nodes** button in the bottom left. This will bring

up your node structure. Find the node that you are interested in and simply double-click on that node. This will bring up all text coded at that node along with information about which interview(s) the text comes from.

Memos

In Chapter 24, it was noted that one feature of the grounded theory approach to qualitative data analysis is the use of memos in which ideas and illustrations might be stored. Memos can be easily created in NVivo. The following steps, which are outlined in Plate 25.12, should be followed:

1. In the **Navigation View**, → **Sources**
2. Under **Sources** →**Memos**
3. →**Create** tab on the **Find bar** and then
4. →**Memo** [opens the **New Memo** dialog box shown in Plate 25.12]
5. To the right of **Name**, type in a name for the memo (e.g. **gender critique**). You can also provide a brief

Plate 25.10

The Coding Query dialog box (searching for the intersection of two nodes)

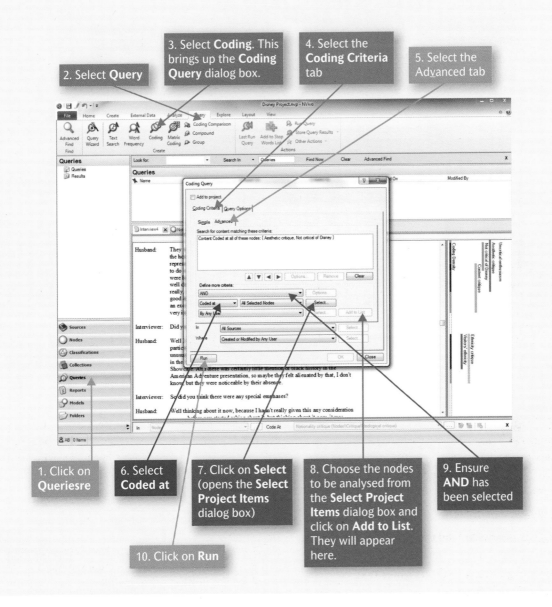

3. Select Coding. This brings up the **Coding Query** dialog box.

2. Select Query

4. Select the Coding Criteria tab

5. Select the Advanced tab

1. Click on Queriesre

6. Select Coded at

7. Click on Select (opens the Select Project Items dialog box)

8. Choose the nodes to be analysed from the Select Project Items dialog box and click on Add to List. They will appear here.

9. Ensure AND has been selected

10. Click on Run

description of the document in the window to the right of Description, as in Plate 25.12.

6. →**OK**

Saving an NVivo project

When you have finished working on your data, you will need to save it for future use. To do this, on the menu bar at the top, → **File** → **Save**. This will save all the work you have done. You will then be given the opportunity to exit NVivo or to create or open a project without worrying about losing all your hard work.

Opening an existing NVivo project

To retrieve a project you have created, at the Welcome screen, → **File** → **Open**. This opens the **Open Project**

Plate 25.11

The Find Content dialog box

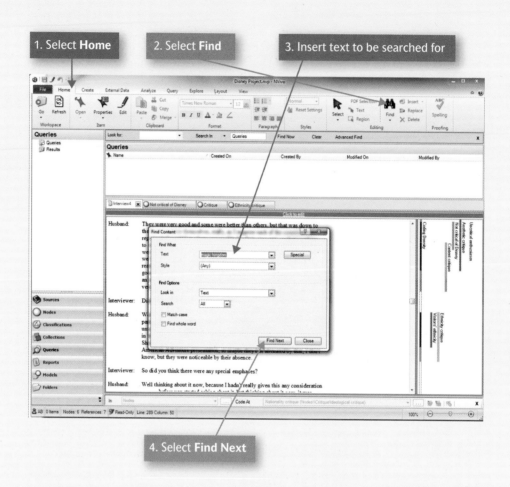

1. Select **Home**
2. Select **Find**
3. Insert text to be searched for
4. Select **Find Next**

dialog box. Search for and then select the project you want to work on. Then → **Open**.

Final thoughts

As with the chapter on SPSS (Chapter 16), a short chapter such as this can provide help only with the most basic features of the software. In so doing, we hope that it will have given students who may be uncertain about whether CAQDAS is for them an impression of what the software is like and a sense of its capabilities. Some readers may decide it is not for them and that the tried-and-tested scissors and paste will do the trick, but the software warrants serious consideration because of its power and flexibility.

Some useful online help in the use of NVivo can be found at the Online QDA website and the CAQDAS Networking Project website at: *http://onlineqda.hud. ac.uk/* (accessed 4 November 2014) *http://caqdas.soc. surrey.ac.uk/* (accessed 4 November 2014)

Plate 25.12

Stages in creating a memo

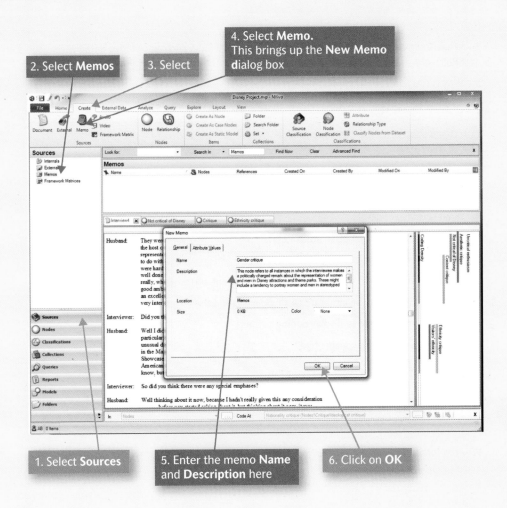

4. Select **Memo.**
This brings up the **New Memo** dialog box

2. Select **Memos**

3. Select

1. Select **Sources**

5. Enter the memo **Name** and **Description** here

6. Click on **OK**

Key points

- CAQDAS does not and cannot help with decisions about how to code qualitative data or how to interpret findings.

- CAQDAS can make many if not most of the clerical tasks associated with the manual coding and retrieving of data easier and faster.

- If you have a very small dataset, it is probably not worth the time and trouble navigating your way around a new software program.

- If you have a larger dataset, or are intending to use the software skills that you acquire on other research projects in the future, CAQDAS can be an invaluable tool.

Questions for review

Is CAQDAS like quantitative data analysis software?

- What are the main points of difference between CAQDAS and quantitative data analysis software like SPSS?

- Why is CAQDAS controversial?

- To what extent does CAQDAS help with qualitative data analysis?

Learning NVivo

- What is a node?

- What is the difference between a non-hierarchically organized node and a hierarchically organized node?

- What is *in vivo* coding?

- Do nodes have to be set up in advance?

- What is speed coding?

- In NVivo, what is the difference between a document and a memo?

- How do you go about searching for a single node and the intersection of two nodes?

- Why might it be useful to display coding stripes?

- How do you search for specific text?

Online Resource Centre
www.oxfordtextbooks.co.uk/orc/brymanbrm4e/

Visit the Interactive Research Guide that accompanies this book to complete an exercise in Computer-Assisted Qualitative Data Analysis: Using NVivo.

Part Four
Mixed methods research and other considerations

In Part Four, we will explore areas that transcend the quantitative/qualitative distinction. Chapter 26 invites readers to consider how useful the distinction is. This may seem a contrary thing to do, since this book has been organized around the quantitative/qualitative divide. However, the aim is to show that the distinction is not a hard-and-fast one. Chapter 27 considers the different ways in which quantitative and qualitative research can be combined. Such combinations are referred to as mixed methods research. Chapter 28 considers the growing possibilities for e-research and focuses on the use of the Internet both as a source of data and as a research method. Chapter 29 examines issues relating to the writing-up of business research and explores some features of good writing in both quantitative and qualitative research. This final chapter also offers advice to students faced with the often daunting prospect of writing up a student research project. It will also be helpful to those who have to do mini-projects as part of the coursework requirement associated with modules.

These chapters draw together certain issues from previous parts of the book but also address others that have been raised already, this time in much greater depth. In addition, they offer advice for those students who are confronted with the need to produce a lengthy piece of work, which is an increasingly common requirement.

26

Breaking down the quantitative/ qualitative divide

Chapter outline

This chapter is concerned with the degree to which the quantitative/qualitative divide should be regarded as a hard-and-fast one. It shows that, while there are many differences between the two research strategies, there are also many examples of research that transcend the distinction. One way in which this occurs is through research that combines quantitative and qualitative research, which is the focus of Chapter 27. The present chapter is concerned with points of overlap between them. This chapter explores:

- aspects of qualitative research that can contain elements of the natural science model;
- aspects of quantitative research that can contain elements of interpretivism;
- the idea that research methods are more independent of epistemological and ontological assumptions than is sometimes supposed;
- ways in which aspects of the quantitative/qualitative contrast sometimes break down;
- studies in which quantitative and qualitative research are employed in relation to each other, so that qualitative research is used to analyse quantitative research and vice versa;
- the use of quantification in qualitative research.

Introduction

With this book structured so far around the distinction between quantitative and qualitative research, it may appear perverse to raise the prospect that the distinction might be overblown at this stage. The distinction has been employed so far for two main reasons:

- There *are* differences between quantitative and qualitative research in terms of research strategy, and many researchers and writers on research methodology perceive this to be the case.

- It is a useful means of organizing research methods and approaches to data analysis.

However, while epistemological and ontological commitments may be associated with certain research methods—such as the often-cited links between a natural science epistemology (in particular, positivism) and survey research, or between an interpretivist epistemology (for example, phenomenology) and qualitative interviewing—the connections are not deterministic. In other words, while qualitative interviews may often reveal a predisposition towards or a reflection of an interpretivist and constructionist position, this is not always the case, as an early example suggested (see the discussion of the study by Hochschild (1983) in Chapter 2). This means that the connections that were posited in Chapter 2 between epistemology and ontology, on the one hand, and research method, on the other, are best thought of as tendencies rather than as definitive connections. Such connections were implied by the suggestion that within each of the two research strategies—quantitative and qualitative—there is a distinctive mix of epistemology, ontology, and research methods (see Table 2.1). However, we cannot say that the use of a structured interview or self-completion questionnaire *necessarily* implies a commitment to a natural scientific model or that ethnographic research *must* mean an interpretivist epistemology. We should not be surprised at this: after all, quantitative research teaches us that it is rarely the case that we find perfect associations between variables. We should not be surprised, therefore, that the practice of business research similarly lacks absolute determinism.

Research methods are much more free-floating than is sometimes supposed. A method of data collection such as participant observation can be employed in such a way that it is in tune with the tenets of constructionism, but equally it can be used in a manner that reveals an objectivist orientation. Also, it is easy to underemphasize the significance of practical considerations in the way in which business research is conducted (though look again at Figure 2.2). Conducting a study of humour and resistance on the shopfloor by postal questionnaire may not be totally impossible, but it is unlikely to succeed in terms of yielding valid answers to questions.

In the rest of this chapter, we will examine a variety of ways in which the contrast between quantitative and qualitative research should not be overdrawn.

The natural science model and qualitative research

One of the chief difficulties with the links that are frequently forged between issues of epistemology and matters of research method or technique is that they often entail a characterization of the natural sciences as necessarily or inherently positivist in orientation. There are three notable difficulties here.

- There is no agreement on the epistemological basis of the natural sciences. As noted in Chapter 2, such writers as Harré (1972) and Keat and Urry (1975) have argued that positivism is but one version of the nature of the natural sciences, *realism* being one alternative account (Bhaskar 1975).

- If we assume that the practices of natural scientists are those that are revealed in their written accounts of what they do (and most of the discussions of the nature of the natural sciences do assume this), we run into a problem because studies by social researchers of scientists' practices suggest that there is often a disparity between their work behaviour and their writings. Research by Gilbert and Mulkay (1984) suggested that the ways in which scientists talked about their work frequently revealed a different set of practices from those inscribed in their articles.

- As Platt (1981) has argued, a term like 'positivist' has to be treated in a circumspect way, because, while it does refer to a distinctive characterization of scientific enquiry (see Key concept 2.7), it is also frequently employed in a polemical way. When employed in this manner, it is rarely helpful, because the term is usually a characterization (a negative one) of the work of others rather than of one's own work.

Quite aside from the difficulty of addressing the natural science model and positivism, there are problems with associating them solely with quantitative research. Further, qualitative research frequently exhibits features that one would associate with a natural science model. This tendency is revealed in several ways:

- *Empiricist overtones*. Although empiricism (see Key concept 2.3) is typically associated with quantitative research, many writers on qualitative research display an equal emphasis on the importance of direct contact with social reality as the springboard for any investigation. Thus, writers on qualitative research frequently stress the importance of direct experience of social settings and fashioning an understanding of social worlds via that contact. The very idea that theory is to be grounded in data (see Chapter 24) seems to constitute a manifesto for empiricism, and it is unsurprising, therefore, that some writers claim to detect 'covert positivism' in qualitative research. Another way in which empiricist overtones are revealed is in the suggestion that social reality must be studied from the vantage point of research participants but that the only way to gain access to their interpretations is through extended contact with them, implying that meaning is accessible to the senses of researchers. The empiricism of qualitative research is perhaps most notable in conversation analysis, which was examined in Chapter 22. This is an approach that takes precise transcriptions of talk as its starting point and applies rules of analysis to such data. The analyst is actively discouraged from engaging in speculations about intention or context that might derive from an appreciation of the ethnographic particulars of the social setting.

- *A specific problem focus*. As noted in Chapter 17, qualitative research can be employed to investigate quite specific, tightly defined research questions of the kind normally associated with a natural science model of the research process.

- *Hypothesis- and theory-testing*. Following on from the previous point, qualitative researchers typically discuss hypothesis- and theory-testing in connection with hypotheses or theories generated in the course of conducting research, as in analytic induction or grounded theory. However, there is no obvious reason why this cannot occur in relation to previously specified hypotheses or theories. A. Scott's (1994) ethnographic study of British workers under HRM, for example, was designed to test the theory that British management was operating according to a 'new' model of industrial relations, based on a unitaristic view of organizational life, where workers and managers are seen to have a similar interest in the success of the firm. Scott wanted to test whether workers and managers in his case study firms actually shared similar interests or if they still adhered to ideas based on an 'old' industrial relations model founded on adversarial relationships. In the event, the research showed a complex picture, concluding that 'any cultural transformation of British management has only been partial, and the embrace of the "new IR" piecemeal' (A. Scott 1994: 131).

- *Realism*. Realism (see Key concept 2.8) is one way in which the epistemological basis of the natural sciences has been construed. It has entered into the social sciences in a number of ways, but one of the most significant of these is Bhaskar's (1989) notion of *critical realism*. This approach accepts neither a constructionist nor an objectivist ontology and instead takes the view that the 'social world is reproduced and transformed in daily life' (1989: 4). Social phenomena are produced by mechanisms that are real, but that are not directly accessible to observation and are discernible only through their effects. For critical realism the task of business research is to construct hypotheses about such mechanisms and to seek out their effects. Within business and management there is increasing interest in this ontological approach, which is undergoing something of an intellectual revitalization at the

moment (Reed 1997). Critical realism has also become popular in marketing research because it offers an alternative to the predominantly positivist paradigm in marketing (Easton 2002). Fleetwood (2005) suggests that critical realism offers a more fruitful alternative to postmodernism (see Key concept 17.2) for organization and management studies because it overcomes the ambiguity associated with postmodernism, which stems from 'ontological exaggeration' of the role of language in determining reality. Critical realists occupy a middle position between positivism and postmodernism by claiming that an entity can exist independently of our knowledge of it, while also asserting that access to the social world is always mediated and thus subjective. Critical realists also believe in the notion of material entities that are said to be real if they have an effect on behaviour. In addition to the empirical domain of observable events, there is a real domain 'in which generative mechanisms capable of producing patterns of events reside' (Tsang and Kwan 1999: 762). Fleetwood concludes: 'As many postmodernists come to realize that *critical* realism is absolutely opposed to the empirical or naïve realism of positivism, they have begun to realize that there may be some common ground between themselves and critical realists' (2005: 217). An example of the application of a critical realist perspective is provided by Research in focus 26.1. Porter's (1993) critical realist ethnography is also interesting in this connection (see Research in focus 26.2), because it demonstrates the use of ethnography in connection with an epistemological position that derives from the natural sciences. It also relates to the previous point in providing an illustration of hypothesis-testing qualitative research.

Research in focus 26.1
A critical realist study of a hospital merger

Kowalczyk (2004) carried out a study looking at the effects of a merger involving three hospitals informed by a critical realist perspective. She explains that critical realism enabled her to focus on changes made to the structure over time. Using Archer's (1995) concept of the 'morphogenetic cycle' to reflect the changes that occur when structure and agents interact, she applied this framework to understand how the three hospitals dealt with national guidelines set down by the UK government for the formation of NHS Trusts, which formed part of an attempted introduction of a more business-like culture. This study highlights two of the main benefits associated with critical realism, in enabling longitudinal analysis and allowing structural and cultural conditions to be seen as having an existence independent of social interaction. Agents are thus seen as choosing whether or not to apply the rules, rather than being wholly determined by them.

Research in focus 26.2
A critical realist ethnography

A critical realist stance was employed by Porter (1993) in connection with an ethnographic study in a large Irish hospital in which the author was employed for three months as a staff nurse. Porter's interest was in the possible role of racism in this setting. He suggests that racism and professionalism were in operation such that the latter tempered the effects of the former in the context of interactions between doctors and nurses. Thus, racism and professionalism were conceptualized as generative structures—that is, mechanisms—that could be productive of certain kinds of effect. Two hypotheses were proposed: that racism would play some part in the relationships between white staff and those from 'racialized minorities', and that the 'occupational situation would affect the way in which racism was expressed' (1993: 599). Porter found that racism was not a significant factor in relationships between members of racialized minorities and the other staff but did manifest itself behind the backs of the former in the form of racist remarks. Racism did not intrude into work relationships, because of the operation of the greater weight given to people's achievements and performance (such as qualifications and medical skills) rather than their ascriptive qualities (that is, 'race') when judging members of professions. The emphasis on values associated with professionalism counteracted the potential role of those associated with racism. Thus, 'racism can be seen as a tendency that is realised in certain circumstances, but exercised unrealised in others' (1993: 607). In terms of critical realism, one possible structural mechanism (racism) was countered by the operation of another structural mechanism (professional ideology).

In addition, writers on qualitative research sometimes distinguish stances on qualitative research that contain elements of both quantitative and qualitative research. R. L. Miller (2000), in connection with an examination of life history interviews (see Chapter 20), distinguishes three approaches to such research. One of these, which he calls 'neo-positivist', uses 'pre-existing networks of concepts... to make theoretically based predictions concerning people's experienced lives' (2000: 12). Therefore, one approach to the life history method, which is associated with qualitative rather than quantitative research, would seem to entail a theory-testing approach to the collection and analysis of qualitative data. A further illustration is Charmaz's (2000) suggestion that two approaches to grounded theory can be distinguished: objectivist and constructionist (she uses the term 'constructivist'). She argues that, in spite of the differences that developed between Glaser (1992) and Strauss (e.g. Strauss and Corbin 1998), both held to the view of an objective, external reality. In other words, in the eyes of both the major writers on grounded theory, there is a social world beyond the researcher, whose job it is to reveal its nature and functioning.

Quantitative research and interpretivism

Qualitative research would seem to have a monopoly of the ability to study meaning. Its proponents essentially claim that it is only through qualitative research that the world can be studied through the eyes of the people who are studied. As Platt (1981: 87) observes, this contention seems rather at odds with the widespread study of attitudes in surveys based on interviews and questionnaires. In fact, it would seem that quantitative researchers frequently address meanings. An example is the well-known concept of 'orientation to work' associated with the *Affluent Worker* research in the 1960s, which sought to uncover the nature and significance of the meanings that industrial workers bring with them to the workplace (Goldthorpe et al. 1968).

The widespread inclusion of questions about attitudes in surveys suggests that quantitative researchers are interested in matters of meaning. It might be objected that survey questions do not really tap issues of meaning because they are based on categories devised by the designers of the interview schedule or questionnaire. Two points are relevant here. First, in the absence of respondent validation exercises, the notion that qualitative research is more adept at gaining access to the point of view of those being studied than quantitative research is invariably assumed rather than demonstrated. Qualitative researchers frequently claim to have tapped into participants' world views because of, for example, their extensive participation in the daily round of those they study, the length of time they spent in the setting being studied, or the lengthy and intensive interviews conducted. However, the explicit demonstration that interpretative understanding has been accomplished—for example, through respondent validation (see Key concept 17.5)—is rarely undertaken. Secondly, if the design of attitude questions is based on prior questioning that seeks to bring out the range of possible attitudinal positions on an issue, as in the research discussed in Research in focus

11.3, attitudinal questions may be better able to gain access to meaning.

Also, as Marsh (1982) has pointed out, the practice in much survey research of asking respondents the reasons for their actions also implies that quantitative researchers are frequently concerned to uncover issues of meaning. For example, R. Stewart's (1967) diary study of how managers use their time (see Research in focus 10.4) focused on recording how much time was spent by each individual on different kinds of activity. However, Stewart followed up the diary study by sending each manager a summary of how he or she had spent his or her time, together with comparative figures for managers in similar jobs. Managers were then asked to comment on any unusual features in their figures and to explain individual and contextual reasons for these differences. Examples such as these further point to the possibility that the gulf between quantitative and qualitative research is not as wide as is sometimes supposed.

Quantitative research and constructionism

It was noted in Chapter 2 that one keynote of constructionism is a concern with issues of representation, as these play an important role in the construction of the social world. Qualitative content analysis has played an important role in developing just such an understanding, just as discourse analysis has in relation to the social construction of events and meanings in business leaders' speeches and mission statements. However, it is easy to forget that conventional quantitative content analysis can also be useful in this way.

Chen and Meindl's (1991) research into the entrepreneurial leadership of the founder of the low-cost US airline People Express, Donald Burr, referred to in Research in focus 23.6, provides an example of the combined use of quantitative and qualitative content analysis. Much of their understanding of Burr's leadership style was derived from qualitative content analysis, but they also employed a quantitative content analysis, 'identifying leader-charismatic themes, recording frequency, and analyzing trends' (1991: 530) using data from magazine and newspaper articles that focused on the company. However, rather than

simply content-analysing the articles themselves, the researchers involved seventy-two undergraduate business students, who were asked to read the new articles and write a description of Burr, as a person and as a CEO, based on the materials they had read. Content analysis was then conducted on the students' descriptions. This showed that the language used by the students to describe Burr changed as the performance of the company varied. Chen and Meindl conclude that images portrayed of Burr in the past interacted with indications of current performance to determine the reconstruction of the leader's image. In other words, instead of being rejected, old themes were modified and injected with new meaning. The second stage of the content analysis was more qualitative in nature. It involved qualitative content analysis of the actual newspaper articles in order to identify the metaphors used to describe Burr. The results of this analysis were broadly consistent with the first, thereby reinforcing the validity of the overall findings. More generally, this example shows how quantitative research can play a significant role in relation to a constructionist stance.

Epistemological and ontological considerations

If we review the argument so far, it is being suggested that:

- there are differences between quantitative and qualitative research in terms of their epistemological and ontological commitments; *but*

- the connection between research strategy, on the one hand, and epistemological and ontological commitments, on the other, is not deterministic. In other words, there is a tendency for quantitative and qualitative research to be associated with the epistemological and ontological positions outlined in Chapter 2 (for example, in Table 2.1), but the connections are not perfect.

However, some writers have suggested that research methods carry with them a cluster of epistemological and ontological commitments such that to elect to use a self-completion questionnaire is more or less simultaneously and inevitably to select a natural science model and an objectivist world view. Similarly, the use of participant observation is often taken to imply a commitment to interpretivism and constructionism. Such a view implies that research methods are imbued with specific clusters of epistemological and ontological commitments and can be seen in comments of the following kind: 'the choice and adequacy of a method embodies a variety of assumptions regarding the nature of knowledge and the methods through which that knowledge can be obtained, as well as a set of root assumptions about the nature of the phenomena to be investigated' (Morgan and Smircich 1980: 491). The difficulty with such a view is that, if we accept that there is no perfect correspondence between research strategy and matters of epistemology and ontology, the notion that a method is inherently or necessarily indicative of certain wider assumptions about knowledge and the nature of social reality begins to founder.

In business and management research, if Burrell and Morgan's (1979) influential 'four-paradigm' framework were consistently applied, one would expect to see a clear correspondence between the paradigm adopted (see Chapter 2) and the research methods used, in a manner similar to that illustrated by Hassard (see Chapter 2): the functionalist paradigm community using, for example, questionnaire surveys, and the interpretative paradigm community using, for example, ethnographic methods. In fact, research methods are much more 'free-floating' in terms of epistemology and ontology than this proposition suggests, and it is often not possible to uncover an unambiguous pattern linking the grounding of an article in one of the four paradigms with the research methods used. Furthermore, because of the dominance of mixed methods case study research in the business and management field, it is common for several methods to be used within the same research study. In summary, although there is undoubtedly a general tendency for specific paradigm communities to favour certain research methods, the reality is more complex than this picture at first suggests.

Problems with the quantitative/qualitative contrast

The contrasts between quantitative and qualitative research that were drawn in Chapter 17 suggest a somewhat hard-and-fast set of distinctions and differences (see, in particular, Table 17.1). However, there is a risk that this kind of representation tends to exaggerate the differences between them. A few of the distinctions will be examined to demonstrate this point.

Behaviour versus meaning

The distinction is sometimes drawn between a focus on behaviour and a focus on meanings. However, quantitative research frequently involves the study of meanings in the form of attitude scales (such as the Likert scaling technique) and other techniques. Qualitative researchers may feel that the tendency for attitude scales to be pre-formulated and imposed on research participants means that they do not really gain access to meanings. The key point being made here is that at the very least quantitative researchers frequently *try* to address meanings. Also, somewhat ironically, many of the techniques with which quantitative research is associated, most notably survey research based on questionnaires and interviews, have been shown to relate poorly to people's actual behaviour. Moreover, looking at the other side of the divide, qualitative research frequently, if not invariably, entails the examination of behaviour in context. Qualitative researchers often want to interpret people's behaviour in terms of the norms, values, and culture of the group or organization in question. In other words, quantitative and qualitative researchers are typically interested in both what people do and what they think, but they go about the investigation of these areas in different ways. Therefore, the degree to which the behaviour versus meaning contrast coincides with quantitative and qualitative research should not be overstated.

Theory tested in research versus emergent from data

A further related point is that the suggestion that theory and concepts are developed prior to undertaking a study in quantitative research is something of a caricature that is true only up to a point. It reflects a tendency to characterize quantitative research as driven by a theory-testing approach. However, while experimental investigations probably fit this model well, survey-based studies are often more exploratory than this view implies. Although concepts have to be measured, the nature of their inter-connections is frequently not specified in advance. Quantitative research is far less driven by a hypothesis-testing strategy than is frequently supposed. As a result, the analysis of quantitative data from social surveys is often more exploratory than is generally appreciated and consequently offers opportunities for the generation of theories and concepts (see Research in focus 26.3). As one American survey researcher has commented in relation to a large-scale survey he conducted in the 1950s, but that has much relevance today: 'There are so many questions which might be asked, so many correlations which can be run, so many ways in which the findings can be organized, and so few rules or precedents for making these choices that a thousand different studies could come out of the same data' (Davis 1964: 232).

The common depiction of quantitative research as solely an exercise in testing preformulated ideas fails to appreciate the degree to which findings frequently suggest new departures and theoretical contributions. Therefore, the suggestion that, unlike an interpretivist stance, quantitative research is concerned solely with the testing of ideas that have previously been formulated (such as hypotheses) fails to recognize the creative work that goes into the analysis of quantitative data and into the interpretation of findings (see Research in focus 26.3 for an example). Equally, as noted above, qualitative research can be used in relation to the testing of theories (see Research in focus 26.3 again for an example).

Research in focus 26.3
Inductive theory development using a quantitative dataset

Although deductive theory development based on hypothesis testing (see Chapter 2) is more commonly associated with quantitative research, and inductive theory development is more often associated with qualitative research, there are always exceptions to this general rule. For example, one of the authors of this book worked on a project involving quantitative secondary analysis on a dataset that had been collected by another organization. Since the data, which related to organizations that had been involved with the people management initiative Investors in People, had already been collected, statistical tests had to be run using the variables contained within the database. Fernández, Taylor, and Bell (2005) first decided how to analyse the data that they had negotiated access to—that is, which statistical tests to employ—and then they developed ideas about the likely relationships between variables for which data were available in the dataset. These ideas derived from their existing knowledge about the initiative, which was partly based on their previous qualitative research in this area (Bell, Taylor, and

Thorpe 2001, 2002), but it was also driven by the limitations and opportunities offered by the dataset that they had to work with.

More statistical tests were then developed based on interesting patterns that they observed in the data, and this informed the authors' theoretical development. For instance, the database contained information about the number of employees in companies involved with the IiP initiative at three stages: initial commitment (when the organization decided to get involved with the initiative), recognition (when they achieved the Standard), and revocation (when they stopped being involved with the Standard). From this they were able to test whether or not companies that 'upsized' (took on more employees) or 'downsized' (shed employees) were more likely to gain the IiP award. They were also able to test for the optimum duration of commitment (the period of time leading up to assessment), as the database is longitudinal. However, they were also constrained by the limitations of the dataset, which contained no information about why companies decide to revoke their involvement with IiP.

As Fernández, Taylor, and Bell (2005) were seeking to draw inferences out of these statistical observations, rather than trying to test theory through their analysis of the data, the research design was more inductive than deductive. This example illustrates that quantitative analysis is not always hypothesis-driven—it can also be led by the process of data analysis, particularly when conducting secondary analysis. Moreover, it also illustrates how quantitative analysis is an interpretative and creative process and statistical testing is not the end of the process, as the results have to be interpreted and understood in relation to other work that the researcher has read.

Initially Fernández, Taylor, and Bell wrote up their research without including any hypotheses, but they received negative responses from journal reviewers and editors because of this. So they rewrote their study to incorporate hypotheses based on the theory they had developed, that fitted the tests they had run. The experience of writing up this study thus illustrates the significance of conventions in research writing (see Chapter 29) that cannot be overlooked. It also suggests that, in writing up quantitative research, readers sometimes expect to see that certain conventions are associated with a deductive research strategy, even if the study entailed an approach where theory was emergent from the data.

Numbers versus words

Even perhaps this most basic element in the distinction between quantitative and qualitative research is not without problems. Qualitative researchers sometimes undertake a limited amount of quantification of their data. Silverman (1984, 1985) has argued that some quantification of findings from qualitative research can often help to uncover the generality of the phenomena being described. However, he warns that such quantification should reflect research participants' own ways of understanding their social world. Similarly, Miles and Huberman (1994), whose approach is commonly used in business and management research, recommend the use of a contact summary sheet as a means of recording themes that arise during a qualitative interview. Using the interview transcript, the researcher categorizes interview responses by theme, eventually generating a single-page summary of the interview. Not only does the contact summary sheet highlight the main concepts, themes, and issues, it also provides a record of their frequency of occurrence. Figure 26.1 illustrates an example of the contact summary sheet used by P. Stiles (2001) (this study is discussed in Chapter 9). This technique illustrates how qualitative interview data can be analysed in a way that involves a degree of quantification. In any case, it has often been noted that qualitative researchers engage in 'quasi-quantification' through the use of such terms as 'many', 'often', and 'some' (see below). All that is happening is that the researcher is injecting greater precision into such estimates of frequency.

Artificial versus natural

The artificial/natural contrast referred to in Table 17.1 can similarly be criticized. It is often assumed that because much quantitative research employs research instruments that are applied to the people being studied (questionnaires, structured interview schedules, structured observation schedules, and so on), it provides an artificial account of how the social world operates. Qualitative research is often viewed as more naturalistic (see Key concept 3.4 on naturalism). Ethnographic research in particular would seem to exhibit this quality, because the participant observer studies people in their normal social

Figure 26.1

A contact summary sheet to show interviewee interpretations of the role of boards of directors

Interviewee responses	Frequency
'The role of the board of directors is . . .'	
to be involved in strategy	32
to take responsibility for monitoring the health of the firm	20
to hire, appraise, and fire executives	7
to converse with shareholders/stakeholders	6
to ensure corporate renewal	5
to develop the corporate vision	5
to take responsibility for developing an ethical framework	4
to ensure corporate survival	3
to determine risk position	3
to lead strategic change	2
to review social responsibilities	2
to act as ambassadors for the firm	2
to understand current and forthcoming legislation	1
TOTAL	92

Source: adapted from P. Stiles (2001).

worlds and contexts—in other words, as they go about normal activities. However, when qualitative research is based on interviews (such as semi- and unstructured interviewing and focus groups), the depiction 'natural' is possibly less applicable. Interviews still have to be arranged and interviewees have to be taken away from activities that they would otherwise be engaged in, even when the interviewing style is of the more conversational kind. We know very little about interviewees' reactions to and feelings about being interviewed. M. Parker (2000), in describing his ethnographic role as a confidant (see Table 19.1), recounts a comment made by one of his interviewees: 'it's nice to have somebody to talk to and moan to you know. I try to talk to my wife like this but she doesn't listen' (2000: 237). While this interviewee clearly enjoyed being interviewed, it is likely that he was very conscious of the fact that he had been engaged in an interview rather than a conversation. The interview was clearly valuable in allowing this individual to express his concerns, but the point being made here is that the view that the methods associated with qualitative research are naturalistic is to exaggerate the contrast with the supposed artificiality of the research methods associated with quantitative research. Atkinson and Silverman (1997) have further suggested that qualitative researchers' obsession with the semi-structured interview as a naturalistic form of enquiry reflects a media-led societal trend towards confessional interviewing as a source of truth and meaning. They suggest that descriptive research of this nature is little different from chat shows or human interest journalism.

As noted in Chapter 21, focus group research is often described as more natural than qualitative interviewing because it emulates the way people discuss issues in real life. Natural groupings are often used to emphasize this element. However, whether or not this is how group participants view the nature of their participation is unclear. In particular, when it is borne in mind that people are sometimes strangers, have to travel to a site where the session takes place, are paid for their trouble, and frequently discuss topics they rarely if ever talk about, it is not hard to take the view that the naturalism of focus groups is assumed rather than demonstrated.

In participant observation, the researcher can be a source of interference that renders the research situation less natural than it might superficially appear to be. Whenever the ethnographer is in an overt role, a certain amount of reactivity is possible—even inevitable. It is difficult to estimate the degree to which the ethnographer represents an intrusive element that has an impact on what is found, but once again the naturalism of such research is often assumed rather than demonstrated, although it is admittedly likely that it will be less artificial than the methods associated with quantitative research. However, when the ethnographer also engages in interviewing (as opposed to casual conversations), the naturalistic quality is likely to be less pronounced.

These observations suggest that there are areas and examples of studies that lead us to question the degree to which the quantitative/qualitative contrast is a rigid one. Once again, this is not to suggest that the contrast is unhelpful, but that we should be wary of assuming that in writing and talking about quantitative and qualitative research we are referring to two absolutely divergent and inconsistent research strategies.

 # Reciprocal analysis

One further way in which the barriers between quantitative and qualitative research might be undermined is by virtue of developments in which each is used as an approach to analyse the other.

Qualitative analysis of quantitative data

There has been a growing interest in the examination of the writings of quantitative researchers using some of the methods associated with qualitative research. In part, this trend can be seen as an extension of the growth of interest among qualitative researchers in the writing of ethnography, which can be seen in such work as Van Maanen (1988) and Atkinson (1990). The attention to quantitative research is very much part of this trend because it reveals a concern in both cases with the notion that not only does the written account of research constitute the presentation of findings but it is also an attempt to persuade the reader of the credibility of those findings. This is true of the natural sciences too; for example, in relation to the research by Gilbert and Mulkay (1984) mentioned earlier in this chapter, it was shown that scientists employed an empiricist repertoire when writing up their findings. This writing strategy was used to show how proper procedures were followed in a systematic and linear way. However, Gilbert and Mulkay demonstrated that, when the scientists discussed in interviews how they did their research, it is clear that the process was suffused with the influence of factors to do with their personal biographies.

One way in which a qualitative research approach to quantitative research is manifested is through what Gephart (1988: 9) has called *ethnostatistics*, by which is meant 'the study of the construction, interpretation, and display of statistics in quantitative social research'. Gephart shows that there are a number of ways in which the idea of ethnostatistics can be realized, but it is with just one of these—approaching statistics as rhetoric— that we will be concerned here. Directing attention to the idea of statistics as rhetoric means becoming sensitive to the ways in which statistical arguments are deployed to bestow credibility on research for target audiences. More specifically, this means examining the language used in persuading audiences about the validity of research. Indeed, the very use of statistics themselves can be regarded as a rhetorical device because the use of quantification means that business research can bestow upon itself the appearance of a natural science and thereby achieve greater legitimacy and credibility by virtue of that association (McCartney 1970; John 1992). Some of the rhetorical strategies identified by analysts are presented in Key concept 29.4. However, the chief point being made here is that the nature of quantitative research can be illuminated by being approached from the vantage point of qualitative research.

Quantitative analysis of qualitative data

In Chapter 13, the research by Hodson (1996), which was based on the content analysis of workplace ethnographies, was given quite a lot of attention (see Research in focus 13.8). Essentially, Hodson's approach was to apply a quantitative research approach—in the form of content analysis—to qualitative research. This is a form of research that may have potential in other areas of business research in which ethnography has been a popular method, and as a result a good deal of ethnographic evidence has been built up. Hodson (1999) suggests that the study of social movements may be one such field; managerial fads and fashions may be yet another. Hodson's research is treated as a solution to the problem of making comparisons between ethnographic studies in a given area. One approach to synthesizing related qualitative studies is *meta-ethnography*, which is a qualitative research approach to such aggregation (Noblit and Hare 1988). However, whereas the practice of meta-ethnography is meant to be broadly in line with the goals of qualitative research, such as a commitment to interpretivism and a sensitivity to the social context, Hodson's approach is one that largely ignores contextual factors in order to explore relationships between variables that have been abstracted out of the ethnographies.

Certain key issues need to be resolved when conducting analyses of the kind carried out by Hodson. One relates to the issue of conducting an exhaustive literature search for suitable studies for possible inclusion. Hodson chose to analyse just books, rather than articles, because of the limited amount of information that can usually be included in the latter. Even then, criteria for the inclusion of a book needed to be stipulated. Hodson employed three: 'The criteria for inclusion were (*a*) the book had to be based on ethnographic methods of observation over a period of at least 6 months, (*b*) the observations had to be in a single organization, and (*c*) the book had to focus on at least one clearly identified group of workers' (1999: 22). The

application of these criteria resulted in the exclusion of 279 out of 365 books uncovered. A second crucial area relates to the coding of the studies, which was briefly covered in Research in focus 13.9. Hodson stresses the importance of having considerable knowledge of the subject area, adopting clear coding rules, and pilot testing the coding schedule. In addition, he recommends checking the *reliability* of coding by having 10 per cent of the documents coded by two people. The process of coding was time-consuming, in that Hodson calculates that each book-length ethnography took forty or more hours to code.

The approach has many attractions, not the least of which is the impossibility of a quantitative researcher being able to conduct investigations in such a varied set of organizations. Also, it means that more data of much greater depth can be used than can typically be gathered by quantitative researchers. It also allows hypotheses deriving from established theories to be tested, such as the 'technological implications' approach, which sees technologies as having impacts on the experience of work (Hodson 1996). However, the loss of a sense of social context is likely to be unattractive to many qualitative researchers.

However, of particular significance for this discussion is the remark that 'the fundamental contribution of the systematic analysis of documentary accounts is that it creates an analytic link between the in-depth accounts of professional observers and the statistical methods of quantitative researchers' (Hodson 1999: 68). In other words, the application of quantitative methods to qualitative research may provide a meeting ground for the two research strategies.

 # Quantification in qualitative research

As noted in Chapter 17, the numbers versus words contrast is perhaps the most basic in many people's minds when they think about the differences between quantitative and qualitative research. After all, it seems to relate in a most fundamental way to the very terms used to denote the two approaches that seem to imply the presence and absence of numbers. However, it is simply not the case that there is a complete absence of quantification in qualitative research. As we will see in Chapter 27, when qualitative researchers incorporate research methods associated with quantitative research into their investigations, a certain amount of quantification is injected into the research.

Quite aside from the issue of combining quantitative and qualitative research, three observations are worth making about quantification in the analysis and writing-up of qualitative data.

Thematic analysis

In Chapter 24, it was observed that one of the most common approaches to qualitative data analysis is undertaking a search for themes in transcripts or field notes. However, as Bryman and Burgess (1994*b*: 224) point out, the criteria employed in the identification of themes are often unclear. One possible factor that these authors suggest may be in operation is the frequency of the occurrence of certain incidents, words, phrases, and so on that denote a theme. In other words, a theme is more likely to be identified the more times the phenomenon it denotes occurs in the course of coding. This process may also account for the prominence given to some themes over others when writing up the fruits of qualitative data analysis. In other words, a kind of implicit quantification may be in operation that influences the identification of themes and the elevation of some themes over others.

Quasi-quantification in qualitative research

It has often been noted that qualitative researchers engage in 'quasi-quantification' through the use of terms such as 'many', 'frequently', 'rarely', 'often', and 'some'. In order to be able to make such allusions to quantity, the qualitative researcher should have some idea of the relative frequency of the phenomena being referred to. However, as expressions of quantities, they are imprecise, and it is often difficult to discern why they are being used at all. The alternative would seem to be to engage in a limited amount of quantification when it is appropriate, such as when an expression of quantity can bolster an argument. This point leads directly on to the next section.

Combating anecdotalism through limited quantification

One of the criticisms that is often levelled against qualitative research is that the publications on which it is based are often anecdotal, giving the reader little guidance as to the prevalence of the issue to which the anecdote refers. The widespread use of brief sequences of conversation, snippets from interview transcripts, and accounts of encounters between people provides little sense of the prevalence of whatever such items of evidence are supposed to indicate. There is the related risk that a particularly striking statement by someone or an unexpected activity may have more significance attached to it than might be warranted in terms of its frequency.

Perhaps at least partly in response to these problems, qualitative researchers sometimes undertake a limited amount of quantification of their data. Numbers can be used to give a fairly straightforward indication of the scale of the research project. Casey (1995), for example, explains that she interviewed sixty people during the course of her ethnographic study. However, numbers can also be used to interpret the significance of qualitative data. For example, in their research on concepts of leadership employed by British police officers, Bryman, Stephens, and A Campo (1996) counted the frequency with which certain leadership styles were cited in interview transcripts. This exercise allowed them to demonstrate that the kind of leadership preferred by police officers was different from what was in vogue among theorists of leadership at the time. Similarly, Gabriel (1998) describes how he studied organizational culture in a variety of organizations by collecting, during interviews, stories about the organizations in question. Computers and information technology were a particular focus of the stories elicited. Altogether 377 stories were collected in the course of 126 interviews in 5 organizations. Gabriel shows that the stories were of different types, such as: comic stories (which were usually a mechanism for disparagement of others); epic stories (survival against the odds); tragic stories (undeserved misfortune); gripes (personal injustices); and so on. He counted the number of each type: comic stories were the most numerous at 108; then epic stories (82); tragic stories (53); gripe stories (40); and so on. Themes in the stories were also counted, such as when they involved a leader, a personal trauma, an accident, and so forth. In all these cases, the types of stories and the themes could have been treated in an anecdotal way, but the use of such simple counting conveys a clear sense of their relative prevalence.

Exercises like these can be used to counter the suggestion that is sometimes made that the approach to presenting qualitative data can be too anecdotal, so that readers are given too little sense of the *extent* to which certain beliefs are held or a certain form of behaviour occurs. All that is happening in such cases is that the researcher is injecting greater precision into estimates of frequency than can be derived from quasi-quantification terms. Moreover, it is not inconceivable that there might be greater use of limited amounts of quantification in qualitative research in the future as a result of the use of computer-assisted qualitative data analysis software (CAQDAS). Most of the major software programs include a facility that allows the analyst to produce simple counts of such things as the frequency with which a word or a coded theme occurs. In many cases, they can also produce simple cross-tabulations—for example, relating the occurrence of a coded theme to gender. Writing when CAQDAS was used far less than it is today, Ragin and Becker (1989) concluded their review of the impact of microcomputers on sociologists' 'analytic habits' with the following remark: 'Thus, the microcomputer provides important technical means for new kinds of dialogues between ideas and evidence and, at the same time, provides a common technical ground for the meeting of qualitative and quantitative researchers' (1989: 54). Weaver and Atkinson (1994) further suggest that the introduction of CAQDAS may be bound up with attempts to make qualitative research more respectable within the scientific community and more acceptable to 'gatekeepers' of research—that is, funding bodies. The greater use of quantification by qualitative researchers may turn out to be one of the more significant areas for this 'meeting'.

Key points

- There are differences between quantitative and qualitative research, but it is important not to exaggerate them.
- The connections between epistemology and ontology, on the one hand, and research methods, on the other, are not deterministic.
- Qualitative research sometimes exhibits features normally associated with a natural science model.
- Quantitative research aims on occasions to engage with an interpretivist stance.
- Research methods are more autonomous in relation to epistemological commitments than is often appreciated.
- The artificial/natural contrast that is often an element in drawing a distinction between quantitative and qualitative research is frequently exaggerated.
- A quantitative research approach can be employed for the analysis of qualitative studies, and a qualitative research approach can be employed to examine the rhetoric of quantitative researchers.
- Some qualitative researchers employ quantification in their work.

Questions for review

The natural science model and qualitative research

- Are the natural sciences positivistic?
- To what extent can some qualitative research be deemed to exhibit the characteristics of a natural science model?

Quantitative research and interpretivism

- To what extent can some quantitative research be deemed to exhibit the characteristics of interpretivism?

Quantitative research and constructionism

- To what extent can some quantitative research be deemed to exhibit the characteristics of constructionism?

Epistemological and ontological considerations

- How far do research methods necessarily carry epistemological and ontological implications?

Problems with the quantitative/qualitative contrast

● Outline some of the ways in which the quantitative/qualitative contrast may not be as hard and fast as is often supposed.

Reciprocal analysis

● How have statistics been used to bestow credibility upon management and business research?

● How might Hodson's approach to the analysis of qualitative data be applied in business and management research?

Quantification in qualitative research

● How far is quantification a feature of qualitative research?

Online Resource Centre

www.oxfordtextbooks.co.uk/orc/brymanbrm4e/

Visit the Interactive Research Guide that accompanies this book to complete an exercise in Breaking Down the Quantitative/Qualitative Divide.

27

Mixed methods research: combining quantitative and qualitative research

Chapter outline

This chapter is concerned with mixed methods research—that is, research that combines quantitative and qualitative research. While this may seem a straightforward way of resolving and breaking down the divide between the two research strategies, it is not without controversy. Moreover, there may be practical difficulties associated with mixed methods research. This chapter explores:

- arguments against the combination of quantitative and qualitative research; two kinds of argument are distinguished and are referred to as the embedded methods argument and the paradigm argument;

- the suggestion that there are two versions of the debate about the possibility of combining quantitative and qualitative research: one that concentrates on methods of research and another that is concerned with epistemological issues;

- the different ways in which mixed methods research has been carried out;

- the need to recognize that mixed methods research is not inherently superior to research that employs a single research strategy.

Introduction

So far throughout the book an emphasis has been placed on the strengths and weaknesses of the research methods associated with quantitative and qualitative research. One possible response to this kind of recognition is to propose combining them. After all, such a strategy would seem to allow the various strengths to be capitalized upon and the weaknesses offset somewhat. However, not all writers on research methods agree that such integration is either desirable or feasible. On the other hand, it is probably the case that the amount of combined research has been increasing since the early 1980s and in business and management research combined research is particularly popular. Therefore, in discussing the combination of quantitative and qualitative research, this chapter will be concerned with three main issues:

1. an examination of the arguments against integrating quantitative and qualitative research;

2. the different ways in which quantitative and qualitative research have been combined;

3. an assessment of combined research, which asks if it is necessarily superior to investigations relying on just one research strategy and if there are any additional problems deriving from it.

The term *mixed methods research* is used as a simple shorthand to stand for research that integrates quantitative and qualitative research within a single project. Of course, there is research that, for example, combines structured interviewing with structured observation or ethnography with semi-structured interviewing. However, these instances of the combination of research methods are associated with just one research strategy. By mixed methods research we are referring to research that combines research methods that cross the two research strategies. In the first two editions of this book, we used the term **multi-strategy research** to describe investigations combining quantitative and qualitative research. However, 'mixed methods research' has increasingly become the preferred term, and in many ways better expresses the fact that, in many cases, using both quantitative and qualitative research should involve a mixing of the research methods involved and not just using them in tandem. In other words, the quantitative and the qualitative data deriving from mixed methods research should be mutually illuminating (Bryman 2006*a*, *b*). Indeed, mixed methods research has become something of a growth industry since the first edition of this book. Since *Business Research Methods* was first published in 2003, there have been numerous discussions of the approach, a handbook on it has been published followed by a second edition (Tashakkori and Teddlie 2003, 2010), and a *Journal of Mixed Methods Research* has begun life.

The argument against mixed methods research

The argument against mixed methods research tends to be based on either, and sometimes both, of two kinds of argument:

- the idea that research methods carry epistemological commitments; and
- the idea that quantitative and qualitative research are separate *paradigms*.

These two arguments will now be briefly reviewed.

The embedded methods argument

This first position, which was outlined in Chapter 26, implies that research methods are ineluctably rooted in epistemological and ontological commitments. Such a view of research methods can be discerned in statements like the following:

> every research tool or procedure is inextricably embedded in commitments to particular versions of the world and to knowing that world. To use a questionnaire, to use an attitude scale, to take the role of participant observer, to select a random sample, to measure rates of population growth, and so on, is to be involved in conceptions of the world which allow these instruments to be used for the purposes conceived.
>
> (Hughes 1990: 11)

According to such a position, the decision to employ, for example, participant observation is not simply about how to go about data collection but also a commitment to an epistemological position that is inimical to positivism and that is consistent with interpretivism.

This kind of view of research methods has led some writers to argue that mixed methods research is not feasible or even desirable. An ethnographer may collect questionnaire data to gain information about a slice of social life that is not amenable to participant observation, but this does not represent an integration of quantitative and qualitative research, because the epistemological positions in which the two methods are grounded constitute irreconcilable views about how social reality should be studied. J. K. Smith (1983) for example, argues that each of the two research strategies 'sponsors different procedures and has different epistemological implications', and therefore counsels researchers not to 'accept the unfounded assumption that the methods are complementary' (1983: 12, 13). Smith and Heshusius (1986) criticize the integration of research strategies, because it ignores the assumptions underlying research methods and transforms 'qualitative inquiry into a procedural variation of quantitative inquiry' (1986: 8).

The chief difficulty with the argument that writers like Smith present is that, as was noted in Chapter 26, the idea that research methods carry with them fixed epistemological and ontological implications is very difficult to sustain. They are capable of being put to a wide variety of tasks.

The paradigm argument

The paradigm argument was introduced in Chapter 2 in order to categorize some of the ontological and epistemological assumptions that are made in business research. It conceives of quantitative and qualitative research as *paradigms* (see Key concept 2.16) in which epistemological assumptions, values, and methods are inextricably intertwined and are incompatible between paradigms (e.g. Guba 1985; D. L. Morgan 1998*b*). Therefore, when researchers combine participant observation with a questionnaire, they are not really combining quantitative and qualitative research, since paradigms are incommensurable—that is, they are incompatible: the integration is only at a superficial level and within a single paradigm.

The problem with the paradigm argument is that it rests, as with the embedded methods argument, on contentions about the interconnectedness of method, and epistemology in particular, that cannot—in the case of business research—be demonstrated. Moreover, while Kuhn (1970) certainly argued that paradigms are incommensurable, it is by no means clear that quantitative and qualitative research are in fact paradigms. As suggested in Chapters 2 and 26, there are areas of overlap and commonality between them.

Two versions of the debate about quantitative and qualitative research

There would seem to be two different versions of the debate about the nature of quantitative and qualitative research, and these two different versions have implications in writers' minds about whether or not the two can be combined.

- An *epistemological version*, as in the embedded methods argument and the paradigm argument, sees quantitative and qualitative research as grounded in incompatible epistemological principles (and ontological ones too, but these tend not to be given as much attention). According to this version of their nature, mixed methods research is not possible.

- A *technical version*, which is the position taken by most researchers whose work is mentioned in the next section, gives greater prominence to the strengths of the data collection and data analysis techniques with which quantitative and qualitative research are each associated and sees these as capable of being fused. There is a

recognition that quantitative and qualitative research are each connected with distinctive epistemological and ontological assumptions, but the connections are not viewed as fixed and ineluctable. Research methods are perceived, unlike in the epistemological version of the debate, as autonomous. A research method from one research strategy is viewed as capable of being pressed into the service of another. Indeed, in some instances, as will be seen in the next section, the notion that there is a 'leading' research strategy in a mixed methods investigation may not even apply in some cases.

The technical version of the debate about the nature of quantitative and qualitative research essentially views the two research strategies as compatible. As a result, mixed methods research becomes both feasible and desirable. It is in that spirit that we now turn to a discussion of the ways in which quantitative and qualitative research can be combined.

The rise of mixed methods research

Mixed methods research has become an increasingly used and accepted approach to conducting business research and in the social sciences more generally. Bryman (2009) examined articles based on mixed methods research in the period 1994–2003 and found a threefold increase over that period. It has been the focus of a specialist handbook, which has gone into a second edition (Tashakkori and Teddlie 2003, 2010), and specialist journals, such as the *Journal of Mixed Methods Research*. In the field of marketing, Hanson and Grimmer (2005) found that nearly 9 per cent of all articles in three major marketing journals in the period 1993–2002 derived from mixed methods research, representing around 14 per cent of all empirical articles. An examination of the research methods used in the *Leadership Quarterly*, a journal that specializes in academic articles concerned with leadership and is based in the USA, found that over the first two decades of its existence (1990–2009), the proportion of empirical articles combining quantitative and qualitative research was around 12–13 per cent (Lowe and Gardner 2000; Gardner et al., 2010). Hummerinta-Peltomäki and Nummela (2006) examined four journals in the international

business field. They found that 17 per cent of all empirical articles derived from mixed methods research. Molina-Azorín (2009, 2012) found that 17 per cent of all empirical articles published in *Strategic Management Journal* between 1997 and 2006 were based on mixed methods research.

Thus, Bryman's (2009) research shows that there has been an increase in articles based on mixed methods research, while content analyses of the research methods used in such articles in the business and management field reveal that around 12–17 per cent are based on this methodological approach. This is somewhat higher than was found in an examination by Alise and Teddlie (2010) of articles published in journals in the following fields: psychology, sociology, nursing, and education. Alise and Teddlie found that 11 per cent of all empirical articles were based on mixed methods research, with education having a much larger proportion than the three other fields (24 per cent of all empirical articles, against 7, 5, and 9 per cent, respectively). These findings strongly suggest that mixed methods research has acquired credibility in the field of business studies and that it is

Telling it like it is
Using a mixed methods case study to overcome practical constraints

Lucie's study of entrepreneurial identity was based on a case study of a single organization, but her research design involved the use of quantitative and qualitative research methods. 'Within the case study I employed many different research methods—I carried out interviews, I participated and observed the courses that I attended and I carried out questionnaires and collected as much documentary data as I could. I thought this was all important to kind of get a fuller picture of how these institutes are run. So that was my research design really. It was a lot of different methods.'

Her choice of a mixed methods research approach was partly determined by practical constraints associated with the timing of her research project, which meant that she could not rely completely on the method of participant observation (see Chapter 19). 'Because of constraints of time I couldn't attend all the courses that had been run over the year because most of them had been carried out during the academic year and I was carrying out my dissertation over the summer so I could only attend about two of the different types of programmes. I wanted to get a feel of all the different types of programmes they run because there's some that are run to help students set up a business and there's some that are run to give them certain skills. So I wanted to kind of get a flavour of all of them. Because I couldn't attend all of them I thought it was important that I had to get the students' perspectives that had attended those programmes. So I had to interview them and send out questionnaires to those students and also try and get the perspective of the institute as well—kind of what they were trying to achieve and what kind of enterprise message they were trying to convey to students.'

being employed on a fairly regular basis as a distinctive research strategy.

In the three sections that follow, we examine some discussions about the nature of mixed methods research that have been a focus for writers concerned with these issues. The three foci are:

1. The priority and order through which quantitative research and qualitative research were carried out.

2. The different types of mixed methods design.

3. The purpose(s) of doing mixed methods research. This section will be structured in terms of a classification Bryman developed many years ago of the different ways in which mixed methods research has been undertaken (Bryman 1988*a*, 1992). The classification has been changed slightly from the one presented in his earlier publications.

Classifying mixed methods research in terms of priority and sequence

Several writers (e.g. D. L. Morgan 1998*b*, 2014) have distinguished various forms of mixed methods research in terms of two issues:

- *The priority decision*. How far is a qualitative or a quantitative method the principal data-gathering tool, or do they have equal weight?

- *The sequence decision*. Which method precedes which? In other words, does the qualitative method precede the quantitative one or vice versa, or is the

data collection associated with each method concurrent?

These criteria yield nine possible types (see Figure 27.1). In this classification, upper case indicates priority—for example, QUAL indicates that the qualitative component was the main data collection approach; lower case indicates a more subsidiary role—for example, qual. Arrows refer to the sequence—for example, QUAN→qual means that the collection of quantitative data was the

Figure 27.1

Classifying mixed methods research in terms of priority and sequence

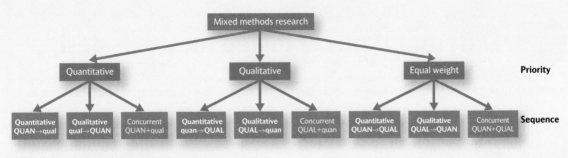

Capitals and lower case indicate priority

Arrows indicate sequence; + indicates concurrent

main data collection approach and that the collection of these quantitative data was undertaken before the qualitative data, which occupy a subsidiary role. The + simply means that the collection of the quantitative and the qualitative data was conducted more or less concurrently. One difficulty with this and related classifications that embellish it is that it is not always easy to establish issues of priority and sequence when reading the report of a study. However, it is useful as a way of thinking about fundamental aspects of the design of mixed methods studies.

Table 27.1 summarizes the percentages of mixed methods articles in four business research fields

(marketing, leadership, strategic management, and organizational behaviour) in terms of sequence and priority. The findings show that a clear tendency for mixed methods research in these fields to be sequential and for quantitative research to be the dominant partner in the conduct of the research. The latter finding almost certainly reflects a continued tendency for quantitative research to be the dominant research approach in fields such as these. Molina-Azorín and Cameron (2010) found that the typical article in *Strategic Management Journal* is qual→QUAN, which implies that qualitative research typically acts as preparation for the main phase of mixed

Table 27.1

Sequence and priority in mixed methods research articles in four business research fields				
	Nine marketing journals 2003–2009 (43 mixed methods articles) Based on Harrison and Reilly (2011)	Articles in *Leadership Quarterly* 2004–June 2012 (15 mixed methods articles) Based on Stentz et al. (2012)	Articles in *Strategic Management Journal* 2003–2009 (64 mixed methods articles) Based on Molina-Azorín and Cameron (2010)	Articles in *Journal of Organizational Behavior* 2003–2009 (20 mixed methods articles) Based on Molina-Azorín and Cameron (2010)
Sequence				
Sequential	79%	60%	95%	75%
Concurrent	19%[1]	33%[1]	5%	25%
Priority				
Quantitative	63%	47%	83%[2]	60%[2]
Qualitative	7%	20%	17%	40%
Equal weight	30%	33%		

[1]These figures do not add up to 100 because one study had both sequential and concurrent elements.

[2]The authors do not provide figures to distinguish between studies in which the quantitative or the qualitative research was dominant but do say that the quantitative component was the dominant one.

methods research which is quantitative in nature. Similarly, in connection with 45 mixed methods articles published in the field of international business studies, Hummerinta-Peltomäki and Nummela (2006) report that 27 of them were quite similar in that data were collected sequentially with the qualitative research preceding the quantitative phase. We suspect that this applies to the other fields referred to in Table 27.1 in view of the fact that they were all sequential and the quantitative component was dominant.

Different types of mixed methods design

Writers on mixed methods research have drawn on several of the distinctions outlined in the previous section to distinguish between different types of mixed methods design. Different ways of distinguishing them have been put forward by various writers, but the ones provided by Creswell and Plano Clark (2011) is probably the most commonly employed. They distinguish six designs, of which the four presented in Figure 27.2 are the most commonly referred to.

The Convergent Parallel Design entails the simultaneous collection of quantitative and qualitative data which have equal priority. The resulting analyses are then compared and/or merged to form an integrated whole. This kind of design tends to be associated with triangulation exercises, whereby the researcher aims to compare the two sets of findings, and also situations in which the researcher aims to offset the weaknesses of both quantitative and qualitative research by capitalizing on the strengths of both. The research by Stiles et al. (2001), which is discussed in Research in focus 9.9, provides an example of the use of this design.

The Exploratory Sequential Design entails the collection of qualitative data prior to the collection of quantitative data. It is associated with investigations in which the researcher wants to generate hypotheses or hunches, which can then be tested using quantitative research, and with investigations in which the aim is to develop research instruments such as questionnaire questions which can then be employed in a quantitative investigation. Another purpose is to follow up qualitative findings with quantitative research which allows the scope and generalizability of the qualitative findings to be assessed. Although Creswell and Plano Clark depict the quantitative element as typically having priority within this design, this is not always the case, such as when it has a largely handmaiden role in relation to the quantitative research. The research by Tripp et al. (2002) and by Deery et al. (2002; see also Research in focus 11.5) discussed later in this chapter provide examples of the use of this design.

The Explanatory Sequential Design entails the collection and analysis of quantitative data followed by the collection and analysis of qualitative data in order to elaborate or explain the quantitative findings. The need for such an approach can arise when the researcher feels that the broad patterns of relationships uncovered through quantitative research require an explanation which the quantitative data on their own are unable to supply or when further insight into the quantitative findings is required. Although Creswell and Plano Clark depict the quantitative element as typically having priority within this design, this is not always the case, such as when the explanation or elaboration to be provided by the qualitative findings is especially significant for the study's research questions. The research by Truss (2001) and Holmberg et al. (2008) discussed in Research in focus 2.16 provides examples of the use of this design. Although Figure 27.2 (c) implies that qualitative research is the priority approach, there are likely to be occasions when there is a strong quantitative research orientation and the qualitative research acts largely as a follow-up, in which case it will be the quantitative research that is the priority.

The Embedded Design can have either quantitative or qualitative research as the priority approach but draws on the other approach as well within the context of a study. The need for an Embedded Design can arise when the researcher needs to enhance either quantitative or qualitative research with the other approach. The phasing of the data collection may be simultaneous or sequential. The need for the design arises when the researcher feels that quantitative (or qualitative) research alone will be insufficient for understanding the phenomenon of interest. For example, the researcher may be interested in examining a research question principally using quantitative research but may have a subsidiary research question that is best addressed through qualitative research. The research by Perlow (1997, 1999; see also Chapter 17 and Key concept 19.1) discussed later in this chapter provides an example of the use of this design.

One of the issues that should emerge from this brief exposition of the different types of mixed methods design is that the choice of design is closely bound up with the

Figure 27.2

Four basic mixed methods designs

(a) Convergent Parallel Design

(b) Exploratory Sequential Design

(c) Explanatory Sequential Design

(d) Embedded Design

Source: Based on: Creswell and Plano Clark (2011)

anticipated use(s) of a mixed methods approach in the eyes of the researcher. Thus the choice of mixed methods design should be undertaken in tandem with the role that it is expected that mixed methods research will play.

Approaches to mixed methods research

The logic of triangulation

The idea of triangulation has been previously encountered in Key concept 17.6. When applied to the present context, it implies that the results of an investigation employing a method associated with one research strategy are cross-checked against the results of using a method associated with the other research strategy. It is an adaptation of the argument by writers such as Webb et al. (1966) that confidence in the findings deriving from a study using a quantitative research strategy can be enhanced by using more than one way of measuring a concept. For example, in their longitudinal study of culture in a governmental organization in the USA, Zamanou and Glaser (1994) collected different types of data in order to examine different aspects of organizational reality. By using survey, interview, and observational data, they were able to combine 'the specificity and accuracy of quantitative data with the ability to interpret idiosyncrasies and complex perceptions, provided by qualitative analysis' (1994: 478). Ratings on the 190 questionnaires were combined with data from the interviews, 76 of which were conducted before and 94 after the introduction of a communication intervention programme, which was designed to change the organizational culture. One of the researchers also became a participant observer in the organization for a period of two months. Zamanou and Glaser suggest that this triangulated approach enabled the collection of different types of data that related to different cultural elements, from values to material artefacts—something that other cultural researchers have found difficult to achieve.

As mentioned in Key concept 17.6, triangulation can also be associated with a quantitative strategy, as an approach to the development of multiple measures in order to improve confidence in findings (Webb et al. 1966); some writers have suggested that this kind of triangulation is declining in use. This can be demonstrated by reference to an article that has reviewed the methods used within business and management research. Scandura and Williams (2000) analysed all articles published in three top-ranking American journals, *Academy of Management Journal, Administrative Science Quarterly*, and the *Journal of Management*, over two time periods, 1985–7 and 1995–7. They were particularly interested in tracing changing practice in triangulation of methods and use of different measures of validity. A total of 614 articles was coded for the primary research methodologies they employed. The research showed that 'to publish in these three top-tier general management journals, researchers are increasingly employing research strategies and methodological approaches that compromise triangulation' (2000: 1259). A further finding indicated that internal, external, and construct validity had also declined during the period. They conclude that 'management research may be moving even further away from rigour' (2000: 1259), limiting the applicability of findings by failing to triangulate and using various designs in a programme of research in order to help counterbalance the strengths and weaknesses of each.

Another illustration of a study that uses a triangulation approach is an investigation by P. Stiles (2001) into the impact of boards of directors on corporate strategy. Stiles used a multi-method research design, which involved the following methods:

- *In-depth semi-structured interviews with 51 main board directors of UK public companies.* This was Stiles's primary means of collecting data. In order to develop a grounded understanding of board activities, he sought to allow directors 'to reveal their perceptions' (2001: 632). Pilot interviews, using a schedule based on analysis of existing literature, were carried out with five directors, and these were used to develop the final set of topics. Stiles also carried out a number of supplementary interviews with other stakeholders, which included a city journalist, a representative from the Consumers' Association, and a number of leading academics.

- *A questionnaire survey of 121 company secretaries.* Stiles's quantitative element in his research design relied on a questionnaire, which was sent to 900 members of the Institute of Company Secretaries and Administrators. This generated a response rate of 14 per cent. Had this been the main research method upon which the study relied, the low response rate would have called into question the external validity of the findings. However, Stiles points out that questionnaire results are used 'to support the main findings, which emerged from the qualitative data and . . . are meant to be illustrative rather than definitive' (2001: 633).

- *Four case studies of UK public limited companies, where several board members were interviewed, and secondary, archival data were collected.* Stiles chose four large UK businesses in which to test findings that emerged from data collected using his two preliminary research methods. The cases were chosen because they had strong reputations but had experienced periods of turbulence and change. Stiles claims that 'this buttressing of the original findings through testing in four different research sites affords a further element of triangulation into the study, with the new data from the case testing the validity and generality of the initial findings' (2001: 634). Validity was also improved through respondent validation (see Key concept 17.5), involving a draft of the findings being sent to the case companies on which individuals were invited to comment.

Stiles's main finding, that multiple perspectives are required in order to understand fully the nature of board activity, owes something to his research approach, which enabled exploration of the strategy-making role of the board and its multifunctional nature. In this research, the use of a triangulation strategy seems to have been planned by the researcher, and the two sets of results were broadly consistent. However, researchers may carry out mixed methods research for other purposes, but in the course of doing so discover that they have generated quantitative and qualitative findings on related issues, so that they can treat such overlapping findings as a triangulation exercise. Yauch and Steudel (2003: 467) provide an example of unplanned triangulation, in a study that was conducted 'to identify key cultural factors that aided or hindered a company's ability to successfully implement manufacturing cells'. They collected qualitative data in two case study firms that had recently introduced cellular manufacturing and also developed and administered in these firms a questionnaire instrument called the 'Organizational Culture Inventory'. The main goal of using both quantitative and qualitative research was to glean through the latter some of the factors that lay behind the patterns that were uncovered through the questionnaire. However, they also found that, while the two sets of data were congruent for one company, for the other they were not, prompting the researchers to explore possible reasons for the two sets of data to be inconsistent between the companies.

Whether planned or unplanned, when a triangulation exercise is undertaken, the possibility of a failure to corroborate findings always exists. This raises the issue of what approach should be taken towards inconsistent results. One approach is to treat one set of results as definitive. However, simply and often arbitrarily favouring one set of findings over another is not an ideal approach to reconciling conflicting findings deriving from a triangulation exercise.

Qualitative research facilitates quantitative research

There are several ways in which qualitative research can be used to guide quantitative research.

- *Providing hypotheses*. Because of its tendency towards an unstructured, open-ended approach to data collection, qualitative research is often very helpful as a source of hypotheses or hunches that can be subsequently tested using a quantitative research strategy.

An example is a study by Tripp et al. (2002) of revenge in the workplace. Initially, eighty-eight working MBA students in the USA were asked to give an account of two incidents in which the student or someone else had sought to gain revenge against another person. The revenge episodes were examined to establish the activities involved in taking revenge. The overriding finding was that the initial episode and the revenge should be in line with each other: there should be symmetry between them. This symmetry has two elements: symmetry of consequences—the revenge should do the same amount of harm as the original wrongdoing; and symmetry of method—the way in which revenge is exacted should resemble that involved in the initial harm that was done. Drawing on this distinction, the researchers conducted a second study, using an experimental design, to test their prediction, which emerged out of the qualitative study, that 'the symmetry of consequences will influence individual judgments of revenge [and] symmetry of method should shape individual judgments about revenge' (Tripp et al. 2002: 972–3). In fact, the experiment did not entirely support these expectations. When revenge is symmetric in terms of consequences, the experiment showed that the vengeful act is viewed more positively. This was in line with the researchers' expectations. However, symmetry of method operated in a manner contrary to their expectations: vengeful acts were viewed *more* harshly when they were symmetric with the original harmful act.

- *Aiding measurement*. The in-depth knowledge of social contexts acquired through qualitative research can be used to inform the design of survey questions for structured interviewing and self-completion questionnaires. In their study of work relationships in telephone call centres, Deery, Iverson, and Walsch (2002) analysed data from a questionnaire survey of 480 telephone service operators in 5 call centre locations in Melbourne and Sydney, Australia. The questionnaire was constructed following 'site visits and extensive discussions with focus groups of employees and meetings with shop stewards, team leaders and call centre managers' (2002: 481), and this helped the researchers to develop their understanding of the possible negative effects of this kind of work on the psychological well-being of employees. This preliminary, qualitative stage of the research, and the fact that the survey was endorsed both by the company and the union, may have contributed towards the high overall survey response rate of 88 per cent, a further benefit gained from the mixed methods research approach. Another example is given

Research in focus 27.1
Using qualitative data to inform quantitative measurement

Myers and Oetzel (2003) report the development and validation of a questionnaire measure of the concept of organizational assimilation using a mixed methods approach. Organizational assimilation is concerned with the degree to which individuals are integrated into the culture of an organization. The researchers' initial research question was to do with establishing the dimensions of organizational assimilation. Semi-structured interviews were conducted with thirteen members of organizations who were asked to describe their experiences of becoming assimilated into their organizations. The analysis of the answers yielded six dimensions:

- familiarity with others: getting to know people and interacting with them;
- acculturation: becoming acquainted with and absorbing the organizational culture;
- recognition: coming to feel that one's work is important in the organization;
- involvement with the organization: making a contribution to the organization through extra effort;
- job competency: becoming competent in one's work;
- adaptation and role negotiation: adapting to their organizational roles and adjusting to organizational expectations.

A questionnaire measure comprising sixty-one Likert-style items was then developed to reflect each of these six dimensions, with the respondent being asked to indicate strength of agreement or disagreement with each statement. For example, one of the items designed to indicate 'recognition' entailed indicating extent of agreement or disagreement with the statement 'My boss listens to my ideas' and for 'acculturation' one of the items was 'I know the values of my organization'. The researchers formulated some hypotheses to assess the construct validity of the measure. For example, they hypothesized that organizational assimilation will be:

- positively correlated with job satisfaction;
- positively correlated with organizational identification;
- negatively correlated with propensity to leave.

The face validity of the questionnaire was established by pre-testing it with two graduate students and two individuals from organizations that had participated in the research. Following some revisions to the wording, the questionnaires in which the measure of organizational assimilation was embedded were administered to individuals in the participating organizations. These hypotheses were confirmed so that the construct validity of the measure was established. In this study, qualitative research in the form of semi-structured interviewing was employed to explore the underlying meanings of the concept of organizational assimilation, and a questionnaire was then developed based on some of the insights gleaned from the analysis of the qualitative data.

in Research in focus 27.1, where qualitative interviews informed the design of a questionnaire measure of the concept of organizational assimilation.

Quantitative research facilitates qualitative research

One of the chief ways in which quantitative research can prepare the ground for qualitative research is through the selection of people to be interviewed, or companies to be selected as case studies. For example, Scase and Goffee (1989) used the results of their questionnaire survey of 374 UK managers (see Research in focus 3.15) to generate a smaller, representative sample of 80 managers for in-depth interviews. Similarly, in the research by Storey et al. (2002) on flexible employment (see Research in focus 27.2), the postal questionnaire survey of 2700 companies provided a basis for selection of 8 case study firms where the survey data had suggested there was an association between innovation and flexible employment. The case studies were then explored using a qualitative research strategy based on in-depth semi-structured interviewing

Research in focus 27.2
Using quantitative research to facilitate qualitative research

In a study that examined the relationship between increasing use of 'flexible employment contracts' and the incidence of product and process innovations, Storey et al. (2002) describe their use of two complementary research methods: (*a*) a postal survey and (*b*) eight case studies.

In the postal survey of 2700 companies, random sampling methods were used to select a representative cross-section of UK private-sector companies. Data collection in the case studies was used to help unpack some of the main findings from the survey. This second part of the research design relied on *theoretical sampling*; from the survey data the researchers identified instances of organizations where there was an association between high performance in innovation and various forms of flexible employment and outsourcing. They then approached these firms on the basis of their emerging theoretical focus and requested case study access, in order to explore some of the processes and rationales surrounding innovation and flexible employment in greater detail.

The case study part of the research then used in-depth semi-structured interviews, which were audio-recorded and transcribed. Interviewees were selected on the basis of snowball sampling, by moving from initial contacts to colleagues who were identified as 'important to the research'. In several cases, the researchers also carried out interviews in supplier and customer organizations in order to investigate external sources of knowledge and expertise. In total, fifty-seven interviews were conducted. However, Storey et al. do not explain how the decision to stop sampling was reached—that is, whether or not this was when theoretical saturation was achieved.

Findings from the large-scale survey suggest that in most firms the rhetoric of the strategic importance of innovation is not reflected by the proportion of resources devoted to it. Findings from both the survey and the case studies show that employers rarely use flexible working as a lever to achieve innovation; instead, the two phenomena are relatively decoupled at an organizational level. They conclude that an increase in the use of flexible labour has occurred in parallel with the greater emphasis on innovation, but that the pursuit of innovation has occurred independently of increased use of flexible employment contracts.

in order to investigate internal sources of knowledge and expertise within the organization.

Filling in the gaps

This approach to mixed methods research occurs when the researcher cannot rely on either a quantitative or a qualitative method alone and must buttress his or her findings with a method drawn from the other research strategy. Its most typical form is when ethnographers employ structured interviewing or possibly a self-completion questionnaire, because not everything they need to know about is accessible through participant observation. This kind of need can arise for several reasons, such as the need for information that is not accessible to observation or to qualitative interviewing (for example, systematic information about social backgrounds of people in a particular setting), or the difficulty of gaining access to certain groups of people. For example, Hochschild (1989) used quantitative analysis of time use in her study of working

couples with children to assess levels of participation in everyday domestic work. This formed the basis for her qualitative exploration based on interviews and observation of the gender strategies that working couples use (see Research in focus 27.3). Equally, qualitative methods may be used to provide important contextual information that supplements the findings from a larger quantitative study. For example, Zamanou and Glaser (1994) used semi-structured interviews and participant observation in order to help interpret and place in context the results of statistical analyses of the Organizational Culture Scale (OCS), which formed the basis for their questionnaire survey of culture change in a government organization. They state:

> the results of the OCS provided a quantitative description of the culture of the organization, but the study still lacked an exploration of the deeper, more subjective, and less observable layers of culture. Thus qualitative measures (i.e. interviews, observations)

Research in focus 27.3
Using quantitative data about time use to fill in the gaps in a qualitative study

Hochschild (1989) took a 'naturalistic approach' to understanding the way that working parents deal with the demands of work and home life. Together with her two 'associates', she interviewed fifty couples where both parents were in paid work; two-thirds of them were interviewed several times. She also interviewed forty-five other individuals, including baby-sitters, daycare workers, schoolteachers, traditional couples with small children, and divorcees who had formerly been part of two-job couples. The main part of her study was thus qualitative. However, she first carried out quantitative analysis of her respondents' time use, measuring how much time they spent working and on domestic tasks using a short questionnaire sent to every thirteenth name from the personnel list of a large corporation. This quantitative aspect of Hochschild's research design enabled her to gain information that was not accessible from interview data alone. Although it would have been possible to collect information about time use through observational methods, this would have been very time-consuming. At the end of the questionnaire, respondents were asked if they were willing to volunteer to be interviewed. This sample then formed the basis for the qualitative aspect of the study.

were combined with the questionnaire results to illustrate the quantitative findings and to provide an examination of the depth of the culture.

(1994: 479)

Static and processual features

One of the contrasts suggested by Table 17.1 is that, whereas quantitative research tends to bring out a static picture of social life, qualitative research is more processual. The term 'static' can easily be viewed in a rather negative light. In fact, it is very valuable on many occasions to uncover regularities, and it is often the identification of such regularities that allows a processual analysis to proceed. A mixed methods research approach offers the prospect of being able to combine both elements.

For example, Zamanou and Glaser (1994) wanted to explore the impact of a communication intervention programme designed to change the culture of a governmental organization from hierarchical and authoritarian to participative and involved. They argue that the study of organizational culture lends itself to a mixed methods research approach because different methods can be used to capture different cultural elements and processes. In addition, as we mentioned in Chapter 17, a longitudinal research design can enable understanding of events over time (see Research in focus 19.2). The questionnaire survey used by Zamanou and Glaser provided a static picture of the organizational culture prior to the intervention (Time 1) and again after it had ended (Time 2). It was

hypothesized that ratings on scales such as teamwork, morale, and involvement would be significantly higher after the intervention than before it. Interviews were then used to explore employees' perceptions of culture in more detail, asking them to describe cultural incidents, events, and stories that had helped to form their perceptions. However, it is not only qualitative research that can incorporate processual analysis. Quantitative diary study research by R. Stewart (1967) analysed the way in which 160 managers spent their time during a four-week period in order to discover similarities and differences in their use of time and the reasons for them (see Research in focus 10.4). In focusing on managerial activity over a period of time, this study provided a dynamic, rather than a static, analysis of what managers actually do.

Research issues and participants' perspectives

Sometimes, researchers want to gather two kinds of data: qualitative data that will allow them to gain access to the perspectives of the people they are studying; and quantitative data that will allow them to explore specific issues in which they are interested. When this occurs, they are seeking to explore an area in both ways, so that they can both adopt an unstructured approach to data collection in which participants' meanings are the focus of attention and investigate a specific set of issues through the more structured approach of quantitative research. An example of this is Milkman's (1997) study of a General Motors car manufacturing plant in the USA, referred to in Chapter 19.

Milkman was interested in the nature of the labour process in the late twentieth century and whether or not new factory conditions were markedly different for car workers from the negative portrayals of such work in the 1950s and early 1960s (e.g. Blauner 1964). As such, she was interested in the meaning of industrial work. She employed semi-structured interviews and focus groups with car production workers to elicit data relevant to this aspect of her work. However, in addition she had some specific interests in a 'buyout' plan that the company's management introduced in the mid-1980s after it had initiated a variety of changes to work practices. The plan gave workers the opportunity to give up their jobs for a substantial cash payment. In 1988, Milkman carried out a questionnaire survey of workers who had taken up the company's buyout offer. These workers were surveyed again the following year and in 1991. The reason for the surveys was that Milkman had some very specific interests in the buyout scheme, such as reasons for taking the buyout, how they had fared since leaving General Motors, how they felt about their current employment, and differences between social groups (in particular, different ethnic groups) in current earnings relative to those at General Motors.

The problem of generality

As noted in Chapter 26, a problem that is often referred to by critics of qualitative research is that the tendency for findings to be presented in an anecdotal fashion is frequently frustrating, since we are given little sense of the relative importance of the themes identified. Silverman (1984, 1985) has argued that some quantification of findings from qualitative research can often help to uncover the generality of the phenomena being described.

In addition, the combined use of qualitative and quantitative research methods represents a common pattern in case study research in business and management, used by researchers in order to enhance the generality of their findings. An illustration of this tendency is given in Research in focus 27.4, where Kanter (1977) describes the diverse range of methods that she used in her case study of a single organization, Indsco Supply Corporation. Even though the fieldwork was undertaken in just one company and the case constituted a focus of interest in its own right, Kanter claims that its findings are typical of other large corporations. However, it is more than coincidental that she makes this claim only after having accounted in some detail for the complex set of methods that were involved in her mixed methods research approach.

Other studies have attempted to counter the criticism of anecdotalism that is levelled at qualitative research by introducing a quantitative aspect into their analysis. These include Bryman, Stephens, and A Campo's (1996) study of leadership in the British police force and Gabriel's 1998 study of organizational culture (see Chapter 26), both of which calculate the frequency of themes in order to provide a sense of their relative importance. However, Silverman warns that such quantification should reflect research participants' own ways of understanding their social world. If this occurs, the quantification is more consistent with the goals of qualitative research.

Qualitative research may facilitate the interpretation of the relationship between variables

One of the problems that frequently confront quantitative researchers is how to explain relationships between variables. One strategy is to look for what is called an intervening variable, which is influenced by the independent variable but which in turn has an effect on the dependent variable. Thus, if we find a relationship between gender and small business ownership, we might propose that entrepreneurial attitude is one factor behind the relationship implying:

> gender → entrepreneurial attitude → small business ownership.

This sequence implies that the variable of gender has an impact on how an individual feels about taking on an entrepreneurial role and becoming committed to the ideals associated with it (for example, belief in economic self-advancement, individualism, self-reliance, and a strong work ethic), which in turn has implications for the kinds of choices they make within the labour market. However, an alternative approach might be to seek to explore the relationship between the variables further by conducting a qualitative investigation of the ways in which entrepreneurial work is situated within gendered processes that are embedded within society (Mirchandani 1999). This would involve challenging the sequence of these variables, drawing attention to the gendered nature of entrepreneurial values.

Truss (2001) argues that more qualitative research is needed in order to increase our understanding of the link between HRM and organizational performance (see Research in focus 27.5). She suggests that many existing studies rely on a single informant in each organization and focus on financial performance, rather than on a broader range of outcome variables. In contrast,

Research in focus 27.4
A mixed methods case study

Kanter (1977) describes her research at Indsco as a 'case study of a single organization'. Kanter describes how, over a five-year period, she spent time as a consultant, participant-observer, and researcher at Indsco Supply Corporation. Her sources of data included:

- a postal questionnaire survey, taking 2–3 hours to complete, of 205 sales workers and managers out of a population of 350;
- semi-structured interviews with the first 20 women to enter the sales force;
- access to a survey of employees on attitudes towards promotion;
- content analysis of 100 performance appraisal forms;
- group discussions with employees—from managers to secretaries, recorded verbatim;
- participation in meetings;
- participant observation in training programmes;
- internal reports, memoranda, and public documents relating to personnel policies;
- conversations in offices, at social gatherings, or in people's homes.

Overall, Kanter suggests that she spent over 120 personal contact days on-site, and the number of people with whom she held conversations was well over 120. A further 500 people participated in written surveys—the primary source of quantitative data used in the study. Kanter draws attention to the potential for *generalizability* from a single case, by suggesting that 'the case provided material out of which to generate the concepts and flesh for giving meaning to the abstract propositions I was developing' (1977: 332).

Although Kanter does not claim statistical generalizability for her data, she does draw attention to the way that she used the data from the case to generate concepts that could be transferred to other organizational contexts. Hence she states that, after having formulated her initial impressions about Indsco, she had conversations with informants in three other large corporations 'in order to satisfy myself that Indsco . . . was not particularly unique in the relationships I observed. I learned that Indsco, indeed, was typical, and its story could be that of many large corporations' (1977: 332).

adopting a mixed methods longitudinal research design, Truss was able to explain how Hewlett-Packard's people management philosophy, known as 'The HP Way', was translated into policies by the HR function.

The questionnaire data enabled comparison with other companies, showing, for example, that employees were significantly more positive regarding the effectiveness of recruitment at Hewlett Packard (HP). Overall, employees received more training and development than in the other high-performance companies, and appraisals were regularly conducted. However, once the researchers attempted to probe beneath the surface, it emerged that 'The HP Way' was open to quite different interpretations. For example, during the first wave of data collection it was found that, prior to the redundancies in the 1980s, employees had believed that 'The HP Way' meant they

would have 'jobs for life'. It was also found that the move towards flexible working was having an adverse effect on staff loyalty. In terms of recruitment and selection, the strength of corporate values expressed in 'The HP Way' had given rise to a rather narrow view of the HP employee, and individuals who did not fit this profile were unlikely to survive within the company. These findings suggest that changes in the company's environment, which was becoming increasingly competitive and hostile, were having a negative effect on HRM. In conclusion, the research provides only limited support for the view that effective HRM is the key to achieving sustained competitive advantage, instead suggesting that environmental events and conditions play a significant part. Finally, Truss concludes that these findings are the direct result of the qualitative aspect of the study:

Research in focus 27.5
Expanding on quantitative findings with qualitative research in a study of leadership

Currie et al. (2009) drew on institutional theory to illuminate the connections between leadership and organizational change. They note that increasingly school leaders in the UK operate within a system within which a particular kind of leadership (results-oriented leadership) is increasingly valued over traditional leadership patterns within the sector (professional value-based leadership). They wanted to examine whether the former leadership approach was more effective than the latter and to examine how far institutional forces (the values and norms about leadership) affects leadership as it is practised on the ground. In order to investigate the relationship between leadership and effectiveness, the researchers conducted a content analysis of 200 Ofsted Reports covering the period 2002–2004. These are reports produced by inspectors acting for the UK Office of Standards in Education when they inspect standards in a school. Inspections are carried out on a regular basis. Through the content analysis it was possible to identify the leadership pattern for 182 of the 200 reports. Of these, 49 were results-oriented and 133 were professional value-based. School performance was measured as the percentage of students at each school who achieved grade C or above in five or more General Certificate of Secondary Education subjects. Currie et al. found that whether the predominant leadership approach was results-oriented or professional value-based was unrelated to school performance. The researchers then conducted thirty semi-structured interviews with heads or deputy heads at 30 schools. Some of the questions asked were informed by the findings deriving from the content analysis. The findings from this phase of the research strongly suggest that professional value-based leadership is still prevalent and that the old institutional environment is fairly resistant to policy-driven values that emphasize results. As one of the researchers' interviewees put it:

> 'We educate children, not make widgets. Good lessons. Nothing else matters at all. All we need is high quality teachers that teach high quality lessons. My job is to provide a role model and give them a receptive context in which to do it. I don't care for anything else. Obviously this leads to better results.'
>
> (a School Principal quoted in Currie et al. 2009: 673)

The researchers show that heads and deputy heads sometimes grafted a results-based orientation onto a traditional professional value-based leadership as can be seen in this quotation. Principals who express a commitment to professional value-based leadership are in effect moderating their approach by instilling a focus on results as well. Straddling both leadership approaches allowed the heads and deputy heads to enhance the legitimacy of their leadership in the eyes of the two different constituencies—peers and colleagues and policy-makers and inspectors. Adopting a mixed methods approach allowed Currie et al. to establish the lack of a relationship between the predominant leadership approach and performance and to embellish that finding with qualitative findings that demonstrate the subtle interplay between the two leadership approaches and the institutional forces at play. As Stentz et al. (2012) observe, this is a good example of a sequential explanatory study in which the quantitative component has priority (i.e. QUAN→qual).

> Had we relied on questionnaire data obtained from a single informant (the HR director, as in other studies) and carried out a quantitative analysis linking performance with human resource processes, we would have concluded that this organization was an example of an organization employing 'High Performance Work Practices' to good effect. However, employing a contextualized, case-study method has enabled us to see below the surface and tap into the reality experienced by employees, which often contrasts sharply with the company rhetoric.
>
> (2001: 1145)

The quantitative research results could thus be seen as somewhat misleading, in that they reflect the organization's rhetorical position rather than the reality experienced by employees. Truss is suggesting that the latter would not have been exposed without the addition of qualitative methods of investigation. Another mixed methods study in which qualitative findings allowed the authors to arrive at a more rounded picture than the quantitative data alone revealed can be found in Research in focus 2.16. The questionnaire data collected by Holmberg et al. (2008) revealed the general pattern whereby leadership was found to influence the success or failure of the implementation of evidence-based treatment practices for drug abuse and criminal behaviour in Sweden, but the qualitative data brought out the specific significance of leaders being actively interested in the programme and being available for support.

Studying different aspects of a phenomenon

This category of mixed methods research incorporates two forms Bryman has referred to in earlier work as 'the relationship between "macro" and "micro" levels' and 'stages in the research process', but provides a more general formulation (Bryman 1988a: 147–51). The former draws attention to the tendency to think of quantitative research as most suited to the investigation of 'macro' phenomena (such as social mobility) and qualitative research as better suited to 'micro' ones (such as small-group interaction).

In the example shown in Research in focus 27.6, Chan and Li (2010) combined quantitative research and qualitative research in order to examine different facets of

consumer interactions in a virtual community. The combination produced greater understanding that might have been possible using only one research strategy.

In Table 17.1, the category 'stages in the research process' draws attention to the possibility that quantitative and qualitative research may be suited to different phases in a study. However, it now seems to us that these are simply aspects of a more general tendency for quantitative and qualitative researchers to examine different aspects of their area of interest.

A further illustration of the use of mixed methods research to explore different aspects of a phenomenon can be found in a study conducted by Perlow (1997, 1999) of how people use their time at work, previously encountered in Chapter 17 and Key concept 19.1. Although this study mainly comprised ethnographic methods, which included participant observation and semi-structured interviewing, Perlow also used a time-use diary (see Chapter 10), similar to the one used by R. Stewart (1967; see Research in focus 10.4), to record and measure quantitatively the time that

Research in focus 27.6
Combining netnography and an online survey in a study of a virtual community of consumers

Chan and Li (2010) were interested in virtual communities: in particular the reasons why participants help each other and how such help relates to participants' commitment to the communities, as well as their behavioural intentions in the form of online shopping. The researchers set up several hypotheses. In order to address these hypotheses, the researchers combined netnography (see Research in focus 28.4) and an online survey. However, the survey was used for testing all of the hypotheses and the netnography's role was to explore and provide 'a preliminary understanding of the practice, potential drivers, and impacts of reciprocity' (Chan and Li 2010: 1037) among participants in an online community. The netnography comprised an examination of postings on a popular Chinese women's Web site (***www.onlylady.com***, accessed 4 November 2014) and in particular on its cosmetic message board, which is a source of information and discussions concerning beauty products. The researchers read and interpreted postings covering the period September 2004 to January 2005. The researchers show through their netnography that the conveying of information and support through virtual interactions was itself a motivator of reciprocal help and support. In some cases, the discussion threads indicate that participants felt impelled to purchase products to get bigger discounts for others and for themselves in the future. For the survey, the researchers obtained permission to conduct a survey of participants. They initiated a thread and invited members of the online community to participate in the survey, resulting in a sample of 899. The resulting data allowed the researchers to test their hypotheses and as a result to find, for example, that stronger social ties among participants and greater enjoyment derived from interaction are associated with greater reciprocity. Reciprocity in turn was found to be associated with the propensity to co-shop.

This is an example of a study in which the combination of quantitative research and qualitative research allowed different facets of the phenomenon of interest—consumer interactions in a virtual community—to be examined. Greater understanding could be gleaned than from one research strategy alone. The research has the characteristics of an embedded mixed methods design with the quantitative research as the priority approach.

software engineers spent on various activities each day. She explains:

> On randomly chosen days, I asked three or four of the twelve software engineers to track their activities from when they woke up until they went to bed. I asked them to wear a digital watch that beeped on the hour and, at each beep, to write down everything that they had done during the previous hour. I encouraged them to write down interactions as they occurred and to use the beeps as an extra reminder to keep track of their activities.
>
> (Perlow 1999: 61)

The ethnographic methods were intended to capture the cultural norms and values held by the software engineers, while the time-use diary was specifically directed towards measurement of their time use. Using this combined approach, Perlow was able to build up a picture of *how* the engineers use their work time (using a quantitative strategy) and an understanding of *why* they use their work time in this way (using qualitative methods). In this study, mixed methods research was geared to addressing different kinds of research question. After each tracking log had been completed, Perlow conducted a debriefing interview with each engineer, who explained the patterns of interaction recorded on the log sheets. From this Perlow was able to calculate the total time the engineer spent at work and the proportion of that time spent on interactive versus individual activities. Perlow found that, although 60 per cent of the engineers' time was spent on individual activities, and just over 30 per cent was spent on interactive activities, the time spent alone did not occur in one consecutive block.

> Rather, examination of the sequences of individual and interactive activities revealed that a large proportion of the time spent uninterrupted on individual activities was spent in very short blocks of time, sandwiched between interactive activities. Seventy-five percent of the blocks of time spent uninterrupted on individual activities were one hour or less in length, and, of those blocks of time, 60 percent were half an hour or less in length.
>
> (Perlow 1999: 64)

This finding forms the basis for the theoretical conclusions that Perlow is able to draw in relation to the crisis mentality induced by the engineers, their work patterns, and the heroic acts that this culture encourages and rewards. In her analysis, she is able to illustrate these themes through presentation of the ethnographic research data. However, it is the *quantitative* analysis of time use that provides the initial impetus for the theoretical conclusions that Perlow is able to draw.

This form of mixed methods research entails making decisions about which kinds of research question are best answered using a quantitative research method and which by a qualitative research method, and about how best to interweave the different elements, especially since, as suggested in the context of the discussion about triangulation, the outcomes of mixtures of methods are not always predictable.

Solving a puzzle

The outcomes of research are, as suggested by the last sentence, not always easy to anticipate. Although people sometimes cynically suggest that social scientists find what they want to find or that social scientists just convey the obvious, the capacity of the obvious to provide us with puzzling surprises should never be underestimated. When this occurs, employing a research method associated with a research strategy not initially used can be helpful. One context in which this might occur is when qualitative research is used as a salvage operation, when an anticipated set of results from a quantitative investigation fails to materialize (Weinholtz, Kacer, and Rocklin 1995). Research in focus 27.7 provides an interesting illustration of this use of mixed methods research. Another situation arises when questionnaire response rates are too low to be used as the sole data source upon which to base findings. P. Stiles (2001; see Chapter 9), for example, generated only a 14 per cent response rate from the 900 questionnaires that were sent to members of the Institute of Company Secretaries and Administrators. Interview and case study data provided him with alternative data sources upon which to focus.

Like unplanned triangulation, this category of mixed methods research is more or less impossible to plan for. It essentially provides the quantitative researcher with an alternative either to reconstructing a hypothesis or to filing the results away (and probably never looking at them again) when findings are inconsistent with a hypothesis. It is probably not an option in all cases in which a hypothesis is not confirmed. There may also be instances in which a quantitative study could shed light on puzzling findings drawn from a qualitative investigation.

Research in focus 27.7
Using mixed methods research to solve a puzzle: the case of displayed emotions in convenience stores

An example of combining quantitative and qualitative research to solve a puzzle is Sutton and Rafaeli's (1988) study of the display of emotions in organizations. Following a traditional quantitative research strategy, based on their examination of such studies as Hochschild (1983), Sutton and Rafaeli formulated a hypothesis suggesting a positive relationship between the display of positive emotions to retail shoppers (smiling, friendly greeting, eye contact) and the level of retail sales. In other words, we would expect that, when retail staff are friendly and give time to shoppers, sales will be better than when they fail to do so. Sutton and Rafaeli had access to data that allowed this hypothesis to be tested. The data derived from a study of 576 convenience stores in a national retail chain in the USA.

Structured observation of retail workers provided the data on the display of positive emotions, and sales data provided information for the other variable. The hypothesis implied that there would be a positive relationship— that is, that stores in which there was a more pronounced display of positive emotions would report superior sales. When the data were analysed, a relationship was confirmed, but it was found to be negative; that is, stores in which retail workers were *less* inclined to smile, be friendly, and so on tended to have better sales than those in which such emotions were in evidence. This was the reverse of what the authors had anticipated they would uncover. Sutton and Rafaeli (1992: 124) considered restating their hypothesis to make it seem that they had found what they had expected, but fortunately resisted the temptation!

Instead, they conducted a qualitative investigation of four case study stores to help understand what was happening. This involved a number of methods: unstructured observation of interactions between staff and customers; semi-structured interviews with store managers; brief periods of participant observation; casual conversations with store managers, supervisors, executives, and others; and data gathered through posing as a customer in stores. The stores were chosen in terms of two criteria: high or low sales, and whether or not staff typically displayed positive emotions. The qualitative investigation suggested that the relationship between the display of positive emotions and sales *was* negative, but that sales were likely to be a cause rather than a consequence of the display of emotions. This pattern occurred because, in stores with high levels of sales, staff were under greater pressure and encountered longer queues at checkouts. Staff therefore had less time and inclination for the pleasantries associated with the display of positive emotions. The quantitative data were then re-analysed with this alternative interpretation in mind and it was supported.

Thus, instead of the causal sequence being

> display of positive emotions → retail sales

it was

> retail sales → display of positive emotions.

This exercise also highlights the main difficulty associated with inferring causal direction from a cross-sectional research design (see Key concept 3.12 and Figure 3.2).

Quality issues in mixed methods research

There can be little doubt that mixed methods research is becoming far more common than when one of us first started writing about it (Bryman 1988a). Two particularly significant factors in prompting this development are:

1. a growing preparedness to think of research methods as techniques of data collection or analysis that are not as encumbered by epistemological and ontological baggage as is sometimes supposed; and

2. a softening in the attitude towards quantitative research among feminist researchers, who had previously been highly resistant to its use (see Chapter 17 for a discussion of this point).

Other factors are doubtless relevant, but these two developments do seem especially significant. However, it is important to realize that mixed methods research is not intrinsically superior to mono-method or mono-strategy research. It is tempting to think that mixed methods research is more or less inevitably superior to research that relies on a single method on the grounds that more, and more varied, findings are inevitably 'a good thing'. Indeed, social scientists sometimes display such a view (Bryman 2007b).

However, several points must be borne in mind. These reflections are influenced by recent writings concerned with indicators of quality in mixed methods research (e.g. Bryman, Becker, and Sempik 2008; O'Cathain, Murphy, and Nicholl 2008). Rather than include all possible quality criteria that can or have been applied to mixed methods research (e.g. O'Cathain 2010), the approach taken here is to emphasize criteria that recur in discussions of quality in connection with mixed methods research (Bryman 2014).

1. Mixed methods research, like mono-method research, must be competently designed and conducted. Poorly conducted research will yield suspect findings, no matter how many methods are employed.

2. Just like mono-method or mono-strategy research, mixed methods research must be appropriate to the research questions or research area with which you are concerned. There is no point collecting more data simply on the basis that 'more is better'. Mixed methods research has to be dovetailed to research questions, just as all research methods must be. It is, after all, likely to consume considerably more time and financial resources than research relying on just one method.

3. It is best to be explicit about why you have conducted mixed methods research. Providing a rationale for its use gives the reader a better sense of the relationship between the research questions and the research methods and also what the use of two or more methods was meant to achieve in terms of the overall project.

4. Try not to think of mixed methods research as made up of separate components. It is best to consider how the quantitative and qualitative components are related to each other from the outset. There is a feeling among many writers with an interest in such research that many so-called mixed methods projects are not really mixed at all, because the researchers do not adequately integrate their quantitative and qualitative findings. This is particularly evident when researchers present and discuss their quantitative and qualitative findings separately rather than bringing the evidence together. We will return to this issue in Chapter 29.

5. Make sure that you provide a sufficiently detailed account of all of the methodological details of the research for both the quantitative and the qualitative components. Sometimes researchers provide more detail concerning one element or give only a surface treatment of both. So, make sure that information about sampling, design, and administration of research instruments, analysis of the data, and the like are provided for both components.

6. As awareness of the different types of mixed methods design has spread, there is a growing expectation that the researcher stipulates the kind of design he or she is using and the reasons for that choice. The designs outlined in the section above on 'Different types of mixed methods design' provides an outline of the fundamental types of design.

In other words, mixed methods research should not be considered as an approach that is universally applicable or as a panacea. It may provide a better understanding of a phenomenon than if just one method had been used. It may also frequently enhance our confidence in our own or others' findings—for example, when a triangulation exercise has been conducted. It may even improve our chances of access to settings to which we might otherwise be excluded; Milkman (1997: 192), for example, has suggested in the context of her research on a General Motors factory that the promise that she 'would produce "hard," quantitative data through survey research was what secured [her] access', even though she had no experience in this method. But the general point remains: that mixed methods research, while offering great potential in many instances, is subject to similar constraints and considerations as research relying on a single method or research strategy.

On the other hand, Molina-Azorín (2012) compared the mixed methods articles published between 1980 and 2006 in *Strategic Management Journal* with an equivalent set of mono-method articles from the same journal. He found that mixed methods articles were noticeably more likely to be cited in other publications than the mono-method articles. ('Citation', the citing of a particular article in other articles, is sometimes treated as an indicator of the impact of a piece of work within its field.) For example, eight years after publication the mean number of citations of a mixed methods article was around 6 but the equivalent number of citations of a mono-method article was around 3.5. Molina-Azorín's findings suggest that mixed methods articles typically make a greater impact than their mono-method counterparts.

Key points

- While there has been a growth in the amount of mixed methods research, not all writers support its use.

- Objections to mixed methods research tend to be the result of a view that there are epistemological and ontological impediments to the combination of quantitative and qualitative research.

- There are several ways of combining quantitative and qualitative research and of representing mixed methods research.

- The outcomes of combining quantitative and qualitative research can be planned or unplanned.

Questions for review

- What is mixed methods research?

The argument against mixed methods research

- What are the main elements of the embedded methods and paradigm arguments in terms of their implications for the possibility of mixed methods research?

Two versions of the debate about quantitative and qualitative research

- What are the main elements of the technical and epistemological versions of the debate about quantitative and qualitative research? What are the implications of these two versions of the debate for mixed methods research?

The rise of mixed methods research

- How does the field of business research compare with other areas of the social sciences in terms of the frequency with which it is employed?

Approaches to mixed methods research

- Why might it be helpful to distinguish between different mixed methods research designs in terms of the priority and the sequence of the quantitative and the qualitative components?

- What are the chief ways in which quantitative and qualitative research have been combined?

- What is the logic of triangulation?

- Traditionally, qualitative research has been depicted as having a preparatory role in relation to quantitative research. To what extent do the different forms of mixed methods research reflect this view?

Quality issues in mixed methods research

- Why is it important to integrate the quantitative and the qualitative strands in mixed methods research as far as possible?

- Is mixed methods research necessarily superior to single strategy research?

Online Resource Centre
www.oxfordtextbooks.co.uk/orc/brymanbrm4e/

Visit the Interactive Research Guide that accompanies this book to complete an exercise in Mixed Methods Research: Combining Quantitative and Qualitative Research.

28

E-research: Internet research methods

Chapter outline

This chapter is concerned with the ways in which the Internet can be used in research. Most readers will be familiar with using the Internet as a means of searching for material on companies or on topics for essays and various other uses. It can be very valuable for such purposes, but this kind of activity is not the focus of this chapter. Instead, we are concerned with the ways in which Internet websites can be used as objects of analysis in their own right and with the ways that the Internet can be used as a means of collecting data, much like the post and the telephone.

Introduction

There can be little doubting that the Internet and online communication have proliferated since the early 1990s and indeed since the publication of the first edition of this book in 2003. For the UK, it has been estimated that Internet usage between 2000 and 2009 increased by 203 per cent: *www.internetworldstats.com/stats4.htm#europe* (accessed 4 November 2014)

Meanwhile, the Office for National Statistics has estimated that in 2009, 70 per cent of households had access to the Internet: *www.statistics.gov.uk/cci/nugget.asp?ID=88* (accessed 4 November 2014)

It would be surprising if this boom did not have implications for the practice of business research, and, as we will show, researchers have been quick to take advantage of the many research possibilities offered by the Internet.

Given this background of Internet expansion, many students are drawn to the Internet as an environment within which to conduct business research. The Internet offers several opportunities in this regard and in this chapter we will focus on:

- the Internet as object of analysis;
- ethnographic study of the Internet;
- qualitative research using online focus groups;
- qualitative research using online personal interviews;
- online social surveys.

The ongoing and burgeoning nature of the Internet and online communication makes it difficult to characterize this field and its impact on business research and its conduct in any straightforward and simple way. In this chapter, we will be concerned with the following areas of e-research:

1. websites and web pages as objects of analysis;
2. using the Internet or online communications as a means of collecting data from individuals and organizations.

In addition, we will address some of the broader implications and ramifications of the Internet for conducting business research.

While the choice of these two areas of online research and their classification is rather arbitrary and they tend to shade into each other somewhat, they provide the basis for a reasonably comprehensive overview in the face of a highly fluid field. This chapter does not consider the use of the Internet as an information resource or as a means of finding references. Some suggestions about the latter can be found in Chapter 5. The Internet is a vast information resource and has too many possible forms to be covered in a single chapter. Moreover, we advise caution about the use of such materials; while the Internet is a cornucopia of data and advice, it also contains a great deal of misleading and downright incorrect information. Healthy scepticism should guide your searches.

The Internet as object of analysis

Websites and web pages are potential sources of data in their own right and can be regarded as potential fodder for both quantitative and qualitative content analysis of the kind discussed in Chapters 13 and 23. Indeed, in the latter chapter, there is a section on 'virtual documents' that draws attention to websites as a form of document amenable to analysis. Sillince and Brown (2009), for example, examined the websites of all English and Welsh police constabularies for October 2005–March 2006. The websites were analysed using a rhetorical approach of the kind covered in Chapter 22 to explore how the constabularies' organizational identities were constructed. Through an analysis of such documents, Sillince and Brown (2009) show that organizational identity was rhetorically constructed through core themes:

1. the constabulary as effective or ineffective;
2. the constabulary as part of the community or as apart from the community;
3. the constabulary as progressive or not progressive.

Within each of these three organizational identity constructions Sillince and Brown identified distinctive rhetorical manoeuvres. Thus the last of the three themes, the identification of the constabulary as progressive or not progressive, was often placed within a wider narrative of improvement, particularly from being not progressive to progressive. Of particular theoretical significance is the investigation's finding, on the basis of the analysis, that organizational identity is not unitary but is often conflicting and ambiguous and is designed to support claims to legitimacy for both internal and external audiences.

However, there are clearly difficulties with using websites as sources of data in this way. Four issues were mentioned in Chapter 23, as identified by Scott (1990): authenticity, credibility, representativeness, and meaning. In addition to the issues raised there, the following additional observations are worth considering:

- You will need to find websites that relate to your research questions. This is likely to mean trawling the Web using a search engine such as Google. However, any search engine provides access to only a portion of the Web. Dorsey, Steeves, and Porras (2004) used several search engines to find websites that promote ecologically sensitive tourism, and even then there is evidence that the combined use of several search engines will allow access to only just under a half of the total population of websites (Ho, Baber, and Khondker 2002). While this means that the use of several search engines is highly desirable when seeking out appropriate websites, it has to be recognized that not only will they allow access to just a portion of the available websites but also that they may be a biased sample.

- Related to this point, seeking out websites on a topic can only be as good as the keywords that are employed in the search process. The researcher has to be very patient to try as many relevant keywords as possible (and combinations of them—known as Boolean searches) and may be advised to ask other people (librarians, supervisors, etc.) if the most appropriate ones are being used.

- New websites are continually appearing and others disappearing. Researchers basing their investigations on websites need to recognize that their analyses may be based on websites that no longer exist and that new ones may have appeared since data collection was terminated.

- Websites are also continually changing, so that an analysis may be based upon at least some websites that have been quite considerably updated. Thus, while the constabularies in Sillince and Brown's (2009) investigation may still have websites, their content is likely to be significantly different from the content that was available at the time of the research.

- The analysis of websites and web pages is a new field that is very much in flux. New approaches are being developed at a rapid rate. Some draw on ways of interpreting documents that were covered in Chapters 22 and 23, such as discourse analysis and qualitative content analysis. Others have been developed specifically in relation to the Web, such as the examination of hyperlinks between websites and their significance (Schneider and Foot 2004).

Most researchers who use documents as the basis for their work have to confront the issue that it is difficult to determine the universe or population from which they are sampling. The problems identified here and in Chapter 23 are not unique to websites, but the rapid growth and speed of change in the Web accentuate these kinds of problems for business researchers, who are likely to feel that the experience is like trying to hit a target that not only continually moves but is in a constant state of metamorphosis. The crucial issue is to be sensitive to the limitations of the use of websites as material that can be analysed, as well as to the opportunities they offer, especially in marketing research (see Research in focus 28.2). Employing both printed and website materials, as Aldridge (1998) did, has the potential to bring out interesting contrasts in such sources and can also provide the basis for cross-validating sources.

In addition, it is important to bear in mind the four quality criteria recommended by John Scott (1990) in connection with documents (see Chapter 23). Scott's suggestions invite us to consider quite why a website is constructed. Why is it there at all? Is it there for commercial reasons? Does it have an axe to grind? In other words, we should be no less sceptical about websites than about any other kind of document.

Research in focus 28.1
Conducting an analysis of websites

Gevorgyan and Manucharova (2009) investigated whether Internet users' cultural backgrounds influence their expectations of the form that websites should take. Their focus was upon possible differences between American and Chinese users and they formulated some hypotheses to explore aspects of this issue. They focused upon two of the dimensions of cultural difference examined by Hofstede (1984; see Research in focus 2.12): individualism versus collectivism, and low versus high power distance. Hofstede's research had revealed big differences between American and Chinese managers in terms of these two cultural dimensions. Gevorgyan and Manucharova formulated the following hypotheses after a review of the relevant literature:

> H1a: Compared to American Internet users, Chinese users will report more positive attitudes toward *collectivism and high power distance-orientated* Web design features.
>
> H1b: Compared to Chinese Internet users, American users will report more positive attitudes toward *individualism and low power distance-orientated* Web design features.
>
> H2a: American Internet users' favourite Web sites will have stronger *individualistic* and *low power distance* orientation than will Chinese Internet users' favourite sites.
>
> H2b: Chinese Internet users' favourite Web sites will have stronger *collectivistic* and *high power distance* orientation than will American users' favourite sites.
>
> (Gevorgyan and Manucharova 2009: 397, all emphases are in the original)

A questionnaire survey was conducted with convenience samples of American and Chinese students following focus groups to refine the measures used. The questionnaires were administered in a conventional offline context in order to test hypotheses H1a and H1b. In the course of the questionnaires, respondents were asked to nominate their 10 favourite websites. A total of 700 websites were identified by the American respondents and 442 websites were identified by the Chinese respondents. In addition, 87 websites were common to both samples and were excluded from the investigation. The resulting 1055 websites were then content analysed to explore hypotheses H2a and H2b. Collectivism was operationalized through an emphasis on 'group membership and many-to-many forms of communication' (Gevorgyan and Manucharova 2009: 399) such as chatrooms, while individualism was operationalized through an emphasis on user privacy and an ability to tailor retrieval of information to one's own interests. High power distance was indicated by such features as vision statements and top-down forms of communication, whereas low power distance was indicated by user control over content and the ability to steer a path through the site. The researchers found that Chinese students' favourite websites did exhibit a greater collectivist orientation than those of the American students, but there were no differences between the two sets of favourite websites in terms of individualism and power distance.

Tips and skills
Referring to websites

There is a growing practice in academic work that, when referring to websites, you should include the date you consulted them. This convention is very much associated with the fact that websites often disappear and frequently change, so that, if subsequent researchers want to follow up your findings, or even to check on them, they may find that they are no longer there or that they have changed. Citing the date you consulted the website may help to relieve any anxieties about someone not finding a website you have referred to or finding it has changed. This does mean, however, that you will have to keep a running record of the dates you consulted the websites to which you refer.

Research in focus 28.2
Analysing company websites

Hinson et al. (2014) were interested in the 'dialogic quality' of insurance companies' websites in Ghana, i.e. the extent to which websites allow for an element of dialogue with their various stakeholders. To this end they examined websites in terms of five factors: whether the site has information likely to be valuable for stakeholders; the degree to which the website affords opportunities for stakeholders to question the company in question and for the company to respond (the researchers call this the 'dialogic loop'); the ease with which it is possible to navigate around the site; how far return visits are encouraged through such features as regularly updating information and having question and answer sessions; and whether the site contains features that encourage the user to keep looking at the site. The researchers found that only fourteen insurance companies had active websites and these formed the sample that was analysed. The analysis comprised noting whether the five factors and aspects of them were present or not. For example, most of the insurance companies in the sample fared well in terms of the dialogic loop. Only two had websites that were not engaging and interactive and all of them supplied an email or feedback form. They fared less well in terms of whether a return visit was encouraged. None included an invitation to return and only one prompted the individual to bookmark the site. The authors show that companies varied quite a lot in terms of their overall performance with regard to the five factors and that local firms did better in than international firms.

One further point to register is that, just like most documents, websites can be subjected to both qualitative and quantitative forms of analysis. The example in Research in focus 28.1 involves a qualitative approach to the analysis of content, but quantitative content analysis of the kind covered in Chapter 13 is also feasible.

There is yet another kind of material that can be found on the Web that could be construed as a form of document—the postings that are made to discussion forums, chatroom interactions, and other kinds of contribution to online environments. An example can be found in Research in focus 28.4. Such data might be gleaned in real time, in which case they are closer to a form of observation, or they may be archived interactions, in which case they are forms of document. Sometimes chatroom/discussion forum contexts may be ones in which the researcher simply reads and analyses the various postings without any participation (see Research in focus 28.4 for an example to which this approach largely applies). This can often lead to accusations of 'lurking', where the researcher simply reads without participation and without announcing his or her presence; this is often regarded as being dubious in ethical terms, an issue that will be explored in greater detail below. On other occasions, the researcher may be a participant, and in such circumstances the research is much closer to the notion of what is variously called virtual or online ethnography. These considerations demonstrate that, in e-research, the analysis of online documents and virtual/online ethnography easily shade into each other. Emails too may provide sources of data for researchers. Nikiforova and Gregory (2013) analysed the content of 500 Nigerian letter scam emails which had been delivered over nine years to an institutional email box. They were keen to examine the rhetorical construction of the emails and in particular how Western language devices were employed to create a sense of trust among potential victims. Of course, there is no way of knowing how representative the 500 emails are but their findings have significance for the understanding of trust and of its cultural elements.

Using websites to collect data from individuals

In this section we examine research methods that entail the use of either the Web or online communications, such as email, as a platform for collecting data from individuals. At the time of writing, the bulk of the discussion concerned with this issue has emphasized four main areas:

1. virtual ethnography or the ethnography of the Internet;

2. qualitative research using online focus groups;

3. qualitative research using online personal interviews;

4. online social surveys.

These types of Internet-based research method do not exhaust the full range of possibilities but they do represent recurring emphases in the emerging literature on this subject. All of them offer certain advantages over their traditional counterparts because:

- they are usually more economical in terms of time and money;

- they can reach large numbers of people very easily;

- distance is no problem, since the research participant need only be accessible by computer—it does not matter whether he or she is in the same building or across the world;

- data can be collected and collated very quickly.

The chief general disadvantages tend to revolve around the following issues:

- Access to the Internet is still nowhere near universal, so certain people are likely to be inaccessible. Remote regions are still sometimes excluded from broadband access and, even when access is available, bandwidth varies considerably, with consequent implications for download speeds.

- People still vary considerably in their facility with computers, which can have implications for preparedness to be involved in research and the ease with which people can be research participants.

- Invitations to take part in research may be viewed as just another nuisance email.

- There is loss of the personal touch, owing to lack of rapport between interviewer and interviewee, including the inability to pick up visual or auditory cues.

- There are concerns among research participants about confidentiality of replies at a time of widespread anxiety about fraud and hackers.

More specific balance sheets of advantages and disadvantages relating to some of the individual e-research methods will be covered below.

There are two crucial distinctions that should be borne in mind when examining Internet-based research methods.

1. There is a distinction between *web-based* and *communication-based* methods. The former is a research method whereby data are collected through the Web—for example, a questionnaire that forms a web page and that the respondent then completes. A communication-based research method is one where email or a similar communication medium is the platform from which the data collection instrument is launched.

2. There is a distinction between *synchronous* and *asynchronous* methods of data collection. The former occur in real time. An example would be an interview in which an online interviewer asks a question and the respondent, who is also online, replies immediately, as in a chatroom. An asynchronous method is not in real time so that there is no immediate response from the respondent, who is unlikely to be online at the same time as the interviewer (or, if the respondent is online, he or she is extremely unlikely to be in a position to reply immediately). An example would be an interview question posed by the interviewer in an email that is opened and answered by the respondent some time later, perhaps days or weeks later.

With these distinctions in mind we can now move on to examine the four main forms of online research methods previously identified. However, one final point to note before concluding this section is that the issues discussed above can also be used to collect data from organizations as well as from individuals (see Research in focus 28.3 for an example).

Research in focus 28.3
Collecting data about companies: a study of language use on multinational company websites

Tiessen (2004) was interested in the language choices that multinational firms make in designing their websites. Focusing on the websites of 362 non-Japanese companies listed on the 'Fortune Global 500', Tiessen sought to identify factors associated with the companies' decision to use Japanese on their websites. The decision to focus on the Japanese language was made because it is the third most used online language and because Japan was at the time the world's second-largest economy. Japanese language use is also interesting because it has been associated with the country's emergence as a wealthy economy. The study could therefore provide insight into how managers are dealing with the language issues associated with the Internet and globalization. The results showed that business-to-consumer firms were more likely to offer Japanese than those in business-to-business markets because the former were using the Web to target a broader population of consumers who were typically less proficient in English. Firms from Anglo countries were just as likely to offer Japanese as those from non-Anglo nations, suggesting that 'economic necessity tends to overcome ethnocentric approaches to foreign markets' (2004: 187).

Virtual ethnography

Ethnography may not seem to be an obvious method for collecting data on Internet use. The image of the ethnographer is that of someone who visits places or locations, and, particularly in the context of business research, organizations. The Internet seems to go against the grain of ethnography, in that it seems a decidedly placeless space. In fact, as V. Hine (2000) has observed, conceiving of the Internet as a place—a cyberspace—has been one strategy for an ethnographic study of the Internet, and from this it is just a short journey to the examination of communities in the form of online communities or virtual communities. In this way, our concepts of place and space that are constitutive of the way in which we operate in the real world are grafted onto the Internet and its use. A further issue is that, as noted in Chapter 19, ethnography entails participant observation, but in cyberspace what is the ethnographer observing and in what is he or she participating? In particular, a virtual ethnography requires getting away from the idea that an ethnography is of or in a place in any traditional sense. It is also an ethnography of a domain that infiltrates other spaces and times of its participants, so that the boundaries of the virtual in a virtual ethnography are problematic to participants and analysts alike.

Early ethnographic research in connection with the Internet often entailed the use of semi-structured interviews which were administered online (e.g. Markham 1998). As the use of the Internet has changed, there has been a burgeoning of online discussion groups and these have increasingly become a focus of attention for researchers wanting to conduct online ethnographic research. One of the most significant approaches to doing such research is *netnography* (see Research in focus 28.4) which has been developed by Kozinets (2010, 2012). For

Kozinets, netnography is a form of ethnography because it entails the researcher's immersion in the online worlds under investigation, because it is an essentially naturalistic method, and because it relies considerably on observation though often supported by forms of online interview. Netnography is tailored to the examination of communities that have an exclusively online existence, although it can play a role in relation to communities that have both an online and an offline existence. With cases where a community has both an online and an offline presence, the offline element needs to be examined through a conventional ethnographic approach.

The growing focus on online communities suggests a number of different formats through which they can be studied using various combinations of netnography, traditional ethnography, and some interviewing. Three types of study are suggested. The three types entail a considerable degree of immersion in the postings, but Type 1 is the least likely of the three to be viewed as a form of online ethnography, as the researcher largely occupies a position as external observer.

Type 1. Study of online interaction only with no participation

These are studies that typically entail solely the examination of blogs, discussion groups, listservs, etc., without any participation or intervention on the part of the researcher(s). It can take the form of 'lurking' and conducting an analysis without the authors of the materials being aware of the researcher's(s') presence. However, a more ethical approach that is consistent with netnography is for the researcher to announce his/her presence, as Kozinets (2002; see Research in focus 28.4) did in his study of an online group of coffee enthusiasts and Chan and Li (2010; see Research in focus 27.6) did in their mixed methods study of a virtual community of consumers. The goal of such research is to uncover themes that derive from the threads in the online discussions.

Type 2. Study of online interaction with some participation plus online or offline interviews

These are studies that typically entail the examination of blogs, discussion groups, listservs, etc., but with some participation or intervention on the part of researcher(s). The researcher is not passive and instead intervenes (overtly or covertly) in the ongoing Internet-mediated postings and discussions. In addition the researcher interviews some of the people involved in the online interaction. The interviews may be online or offline. Research in focus 28.5 illustrates this kind of study. So too does Kozinets's (2001) study of *Star Trek* fandom and the construction of consumption, in particular in relation to memorabilia and merchandise. Kozinets, himself a *Star Trek* fan, collected data from three websites devoted to *Star Trek* and which exhibited a substantial amount of interaction between fans. In addition, he was a participant observer at meetings and conventions for fans and conducted face-to-face and email interviews with fans. Kozinets also contributed to some of the online interactions between fans on the websites.

Type 3. Study of online interaction plus offline research methods (in addition to online or offline interviews)

Same as Type 3, but in addition there is active participation of the researcher(s) in the offline worlds of those being studied, such as attending gatherings, as well as interviews (which may be online or offline). An example is Chen's (2012) study of group buying on the Internet, whereby groups of consumers approach businesses concerning their intention to purchase goods and services with a view to negotiating better terms by virtue of their greater leverage as a result of being part of a group. Chen focused upon Ihergo.com, which is the largest Taiwanese online community dedicated to group buying. Chen's methods are described as follows: 'This study used Netnography to gather data, including online participant-observation (e.g., observing participants' online discussion and buying behavior in Ihergo), online interviews (e.g., e-mail exchanges and online immediate interviews), offline participant observation (e.g., joining private parties/meetings), and offline (face-to-face in-depth) interviews' (Chen 2012: 258). Through the resulting data, Chen was able to identify four motivations for online group purchasing.

A further example of the use of ethnography in relation to the study of online worlds can be found in Research in focus 28.4, which shows how the study of online discussion groups can be revealing about enthusiasms in our era of consumerism and brands.

Research in focus 28.4
Netnography

Kozinets (2002, 2010) has coined the term 'netnography' to refer to a marketing research method that investigates computer-mediated communications in connection with market-related topics. As the author points out: 'Online communities are contexts in which consumers often partake in discussions whose goals include attempts to inform and influence fellow consumers about products and brands' (2002: 61). Kozinets illustrates his approach with reference to a study of the meanings surrounding coffee and its consumption. As with most specialized online discussion forums, groups that engage in computer-mediated communications about a certain topic are likely to be knowledgeable enthusiasts. Therefore, they are well placed to provide interesting market-related information about trends and meanings in relation to a consumer topic such as coffee. Kozinets began with a search for newsgroups that contained the word 'coffee' and homed in on one—<alt.coffee>—that contained a large amount of traffic. He read hundreds of posted messages but narrowed these down to 179. He followed through particular threads (for example, those to do with Starbucks) in terms of their connection with his research questions. For example, the netnography suggests that, among many of these enthusiasts, Starbucks is seen as having commodified coffee, and, as a result, its 'baristas' lack passion in their craft. There is a sense that the discussion participants felt that this lack of passion was transmitted to the quality of the coffee. Kozinets suggests that his analysis shows that 'coffee marketers have barely begun to plumb the depths of taste, status, and snob appeal that are waiting to be explored by discriminating coffee consumers' (2002: 70).

Studies such as these are clearly inviting us to consider the nature of the Internet as a domain for investigation, but they also invite us to consider the nature and the adaptiveness of our research methods. In the examples discussed in this section, the question of what is and is not ethnography is given a layer of complexity that adds to the considerations about this issue that were referred to in Chapter 19. But these studies are also invariably cases of using Internet-based research methods to investigate Internet use. Future online ethnographic investigations of issues unrelated to the Internet will give a clearer indication of the possibilities that the method offers. At the same time, both C. Hine (2008) and Garcia et al. (2009) have observed that there is a growing tendency and need for online ethnographers to take into account offline worlds, because even the most committed Internet user has a life beyond the computer. This development means taking into account that the members of the online communities that tend to be the focus of ethnographic studies have lives offline and that the two will have implications for the other. There is a corollary to this observation that, as the Internet becomes increasingly embedded in people's lives, practitioners of what might be thought of as conventional ethnography (in the sense of the ethnographic study of non-virtual lives and communities) will increasingly have to take into account individuals' commitments to life on the Internet. Earlier online/virtual ethnographies tended to emphasize people's involvement and participation in online worlds, perhaps because the relative newness of the Internet and its lack of reach into everyday life during those days meant that the virtual could be treated as a relatively autonomous domain.

One area of debate in recent years regarding online ethnography has been over the status of 'lurking'. This practice is disliked by members of online communities and can result in censure from participants, who are often able to detect the practice. At the same time, online ethnographers sometimes lurk as a prelude to their fieldwork in order to gain an understanding of the setting prior to their participation. Even when websites are used in this way, ethical issues arise (see below), while it has been suggested that 'ethnographers will get a more authentic experience of an online setting if they jump straight into participation' (Garcia et al. 2009: 60).

Research in focus 28.5
Using blogs in a study of word-of-mouth marketing

Kozinets et al. (2010) carried out a netnographic (see Research in focus 28.4) study of word-of-mouth marketing (WOMM), a technique increasingly used by firms who intentionally influence individuals who they believe are likely to communicate positive impressions of a product to others. Word of mouth has been known to be an important factor in influencing whether new products or changes to existing ones will take root. As a marketing device, WOMM is used to influence a formerly spontaneous process. A North American specialist WOMM firm (Buzzablog) 'seeded' a new camera-equipped mobile telephone with 90 influential bloggers whom the firm had previously screened and who were known to write about relevant issues and also to receive 400 or more readers per day. The authors did not participate in the study in the sense of contributing to any of the discussion surrounding the blogs, though they did have some discussions with Buzzablog, some of whose managers were interviewed. They focused upon the 83 bloggers whose blogs were maintained for the duration of the study. Their data set comprised 220 postings by the 83 bloggers and around 700 comments from readers. These were divided into postings that were sent before, during, or after the WOMM campaign. Through a qualitative content analysis of the blogs and associated discussions, four communication strategies were identified and were taken to suggest that WOMM does not simply amplify marketing messages. The content and meaning of marketing messages were transformed at the same time that they were being implanted. The authors conclude: 'Word-of-mouth marketing operates through a complex process that transforms commercial information into cultural stories relevant to the members of particular communities' (Kozinets et al. 2010: 86).

Qualitative research using online focus groups

There is a crucial distinction between synchronous and asynchronous online focus groups. With the former, the focus group is in real time, so that contributions are made more or less immediately after previous contributions (whether from the moderator or from other participants) among a group of participants, all of whom are simultaneously online. Contributions can be responded to as soon as they are typed (and with some forms of software, the contributions can be seen as they are being typed). As Mann and Stewart (2000) observe, because several participants can type in a response to a contribution at the same time, the conventions of normal turn-taking in conversations are largely sidelined.

With asynchronous groups, focus group exchanges are not in real time. Email is one form of asynchronous communication that is sometimes used (see Research in focus 28.6 for an example). For example, the moderator might ask a question and then send the email containing it to focus group participants. The latter will be able to reply to the moderator and to other group members at some time in the future. Such groups get around the time zone problem and are probably easier than synchronous groups for participants who are not skilled at using the keyboard. However, the spectre of dropouts is greater.

Huang and Hsu (2009) were interested in the experiences among cruise passengers of interaction with fellow North American passengers. To this end, they undertook both personal interviews and virtual focus groups. The researchers were participants in online cruise forums and used these as a springboard for securing participation in the online focus groups. Two of the groups were able to proceed in spite of some dropouts and took 25 and 28 days to complete. Four out of an initial seven completed the first group and six out of an initial seven completed the second group. The third group began with five participants and ended up with one person so that it became in effect an online personal interview.

One of the advantages of both types of online focus groups stems from the possibility of using a 'captive population' of people who are already communicating with each other, unlike face-to-face focus groups that are brought together for the purpose of the focus group meeting. This means researchers are often able to take advantage of pre-existing social groups of people who are already communicating with one another online (Stewart and Williams 2005). Online focus groups also enable geographical distances to be overcome. International focus groups can enable cross-cultural discussions

Research in focus 28.6
An asynchronous focus group study

Adriaenssens and Cadman (1999) report their experiences of conducting a market research exercise to explore the launch of an online share-trading platform in the UK. Participants were in two groups: one group of active shareholders (twenty participants) and a second group of passive shareholders (ten participants). They were identified through the MORI (Market & Opinion Research International) Financial Services database as 'upmarket shareholders who were also Internet users' (1999: 418–19). The participants who were identified were very geographically spread, so online focus groups were ideal. Questions were emailed to participants in five phases, with a deadline for returning replies, which were then copied anonymously to the rest of the participants. The questions were sent in the body of the email, rather than as attachments, to solve problems of software incompatibility. After each phase, a summary document was produced and circulated to participants for comment, thus injecting a form of respondent validation into the project. The researchers found it difficult to ensure that participants kept to the deadlines, which in fact were rather tight, although it was felt that having a schedule of deadlines that was kept to as far as possible was helpful in preventing dropouts. The researchers felt that the group of active shareholders was too large to manage and suggest groups of no more than ten participants.

at a relatively low cost. However, setting up a time and place for synchronous online focus group discussions between international participants may be problematic because of time zone differences, making it hard to find a time that is convenient to everyone (Stewart and Williams 2005).

Conferencing software is used for synchronous groups and is often used for asynchronous groups as well. This may mean that focus group participants will require access to the software, which can be undesirable if the software needs to be loaded onto their computers. Participants may not feel confident about loading the software and there may be compatibility problems with particular machines and operating systems.

Selecting participants for online focus groups is potentially difficult, not least because they must normally have access to the necessary hardware and software. One possibility is to use questionnaires as a springboard for identifying possible participants, while another possibility is to contact them by email, this being a relatively quick and economical way of contacting a large number of possible participants. For their study of virtual communities concerned with consumption issues, Evans et al. (2001) used a combination of questionnaires (both paper and online) and focus groups made up of respondents to the questionnaires who had indicated a willingness to take further part in the research. The British focus groups were of the face-to-face kind, but, in addition, international respondents to the questionnaire who were prepared to be further involved in the research participated in an online focus group. Other sources of participants for online focus groups might involve postings on appropriate special interest websites or on such outlets as special interest bulletin boards or chatrooms.

The requisite number of participants is affected by the question of whether the online focus group is being conducted synchronously or asynchronously. Mann and Stewart (2000) advocate that, with the former type, the group should not be too large, because it can make it difficult for some people to participate, possibly because of limited keyboard skills, and they recommend groups of between six and eight participants. Also, moderating the session can be more difficult with a large number. In asynchronous mode, such problems do not exist, and very large groups can be accommodated—certainly much larger ones than could be envisaged in a face-to-face context, although Adriaenssens and Cadman (1999) suggest that large groups can present research management problems.

Before starting the focus group, moderators are advised to send out a welcome message introducing the research and laying out some of the ground rules for the ongoing discussion. There is evidence that participants respond more positively if the researchers reveal something about themselves (Curasi 2001). This can be done in the opening message or by creating links to personal websites.

One problem with the asynchronous focus group is that moderators cannot be available online twenty-four hours a day, although it is not inconceivable that moderators could have a shift system to deal with this limitation. This lack of continuous availability means that emails or postings may be sent and responded to without any ability of the moderator to intervene or participate. This feature may not be a problem, but could become so if offensive messages were being sent or if it meant that the discussion were going off at a complete tangent from which it would be difficult to redeem the situation. Further, because focus group sessions in asynchronous mode may go on for a long time, perhaps several days or even weeks, there is a greater likelihood of participants dropping out of the study. A further problem arises from response rates, which may be lower than for face-to-face focus groups (Stewart and Williams 2005). Even though it is relatively easy for the researcher to contact a large number of possible respondents using email, the response rates of those wishing to participate in an online focus group has been found to be quite low (between 5 and 20 per cent). Further reservations have been expressed about the lack of non-verbal data obtained from online focus groups, such as facial expression.

Online focus groups are unlikely to replace their face-to-face counterparts. Instead, they are likely to be employed in connection with certain kinds of research topic and/or sample. As regards the latter, dispersed or inaccessible people are especially relevant to online focus group research. As Sweet (2001) points out, relevant topics are likely to be ones involving sensitive issues and ones concerned with Internet use—for example, the study discussed in Research in focus 28.6 and studies such as O'Connor and Madge (2001).

The discussion in Tips and skills 'Advantages and disadvantages of online focus groups and personal interviews compared to face-to-face focus groups and interviews in qualitative research' combines focus groups with online personal interviews, which are the subject of the next section, since most of the elements in the balance sheet of advantages and disadvantages are the same.

Tips and skills
Advantages and disadvantages of online focus groups and personal interviews compared to face-to-face focus groups and interviews in qualitative research

Here is a summary of the main advantages and disadvantages of online focus groups and personal interviews compared to their face-to-face counterparts. The two methods are combined because the tally of advantages and disadvantages applies more or less equally well to both of them.

Advantages

- Online interviews and focus groups are extremely cheap to conduct compared to comparable face-to-face equivalents. They are likely to take longer, however, especially when conducted asynchronously.

- Interviewees or focus group participants who would otherwise normally be inaccessible (for example, because they are located in another country) or hard to involve in research (for example, very senior executives, people with almost no time for participation) can more easily be involved.

- Large numbers of possible online focus group participants can be contacted by email.

- Interviewees and focus group participants are able to reread what they (and, in the case of focus groups, others) have previously written in their replies.

- People participating in the research may be better able to fit the interviews into their own time.

- People participating in the research do not have to make additional allowances for the time spent travelling to a focus group session.

- The interviews do not have to be audio-recorded, thus eliminating interviewee apprehension about speaking and being recorded.

- There is no need for transcription. This represents an enormous advantage because of the time and cost involved in getting recorded interview sessions transcribed.

- As a result of the previous point, the interview transcripts can be more or less immediately entered into a computer-assisted qualitative data analysis software (CAQDAS) program of the kind introduced in Chapter 25.

- The transcripts of the interviews are more likely to be accurate, because the problems that may arise from mishearing or not hearing at all what is said do not arise. This is a particular advantage with focus group discussions, because when playing back an audio recording it can be difficult to establish who is speaking and impossible to distinguish what is said when participants speak at the same time.

- Focus group participants can employ pseudonyms so that their identity can be more easily concealed from others in the group. This can make it easier for participants to discuss potentially embarrassing issues or to divulge potentially unpopular views. The ability to discuss sensitive issues generally may be greater in electronic than face-to-face focus groups.

- In focus groups, shy or quiet participants may find it easier to come to the fore.

- Equally, in focus groups overbearing participants are less likely to predominate, but in synchronous groups variations in keyboard skills may militate slightly against equal participation.

- Participants are less likely to be influenced by characteristics such as the age, ethnicity, or appearance (and possibly even gender if pseudonyms are used) of other participants in a focus group.

- The greater remoteness of individuals in Internet interviews and focus groups may make it easier for them to answer sensitive questions than when in a face-to-face context and they may be more inclined to disclose difficult information about themselves, especially in asynchronous mode.

- Similarly, interviewees and focus group participants are much less likely to be affected by characteristics of interviewers or moderators respectively, so that interviewer bias is less likely.

- When interviewees and participants are online at home, they are essentially being provided with an 'anonymous, safe and non-threatening environment' (O' Connor and Madge 2001: 11.2), which may be especially helpful to vulnerable groups.

- Similarly, researchers are not confronted with the potentially discomfiting experience of having to invade other people's homes or workplaces, which can themselves sometimes be unsafe environments.

Disadvantages

- Only people with access to online facilities and/or who find them relatively straightforward are likely to be in a position to participate.

- It can be more difficult for the interviewer to establish rapport and to engage with interviewees. However, when the topic is of interest to participants, this may not be a great problem.

- It can be difficult in asynchronous interviews to retain over a longer term any rapport that has been built up.

- Probing is more difficult though not impossible. Curasi (2001) reports some success in eliciting further information from respondents, but it is easier for interviewees to ignore or forget about the requests for further information or for expansion on answers given.

- Asynchronous interviews may take a very long time to complete, depending on cooperativeness.

- With asynchronous interviews and focus groups, there may be a greater tendency for participants to discontinue their involvement than is likely to be the case with face-to-face contexts.

- There is less spontaneity of response, since interviewees can reflect on their answers to a much greater extent than is possible in a face-to-face situation. However, this can be construed as an advantage in some respects, since interviewees are likely to give more considered replies (Adriaenssens and Cadman 1999).

- There may be a tendency for refusal to participate to be higher in online personal interviews and from possible online focus group participants.

- The researcher cannot be certain that the people who are interviewed are who they say they are (though this issue may apply on occasion to face-to-face interviews as well).

- In synchronous focus groups, variations in keyboard skills may make equal levels of participation difficult.

- Online interviews and focus groups from home require considerable commitment from interviewees and participants if they have to install software onto their computers and remain online for extended periods of time.

- The interviewer/moderator may not be aware that the interviewee/participant is distracted by something and in such circumstances will continue to ask questions as if he or she had the person's full attention.

- Online connections may be lost, perhaps because of a server crashing or a respondent's broadband going down, so research participants need to know what to do in case of such an eventuality.

- Interviewers cannot capitalize on body language or other forms of non-verbal data that might suggest puzzlement, or in the case of focus groups a thwarted desire to contribute to the discussion.

Sources: Clapper and Massey (1996); Adriaenssens and Cadman (1999); Tse (1999); Mann and Stewart (2000); Curasi (2001); O'Connor and Madge (2001); Sweet (2001); Hewson and Laurent (2008).

Qualitative research using online personal interviews

The issues involved in conducting online personal interviews for qualitative research are essentially the same as those to do with conducting online focus groups. In particular, the researcher must decide whether the interviews should take place in **synchronous** or **asynchronous** mode. The factors involved in deciding which to use are largely the same as with focus groups, although issues to do with variable typing speed or computer-related knowledge among focus group participants will not apply. Hewson and Laurent (2008) point out that research on the synchronous versus asynchronous issue seems to imply that interviews in the latter mode tend to generate richer, more thorough, and more thoughtful data than synchronous ones, which often produce data they describe as 'playful' as well as less detailed. Such research would seem to imply that asynchronous interviews are likely to be the preferred mode of administration, especially in view of the greater sophistication on the part of both researchers and their participants that is required for the use of the software platforms that are necessary for synchronous interviews. Interestingly, O'Connor et al. (2008) maintain that the adoption of synchronous interviews and focus groups has been low, perhaps because of greater understanding of what can be gleaned from asynchronous interviews and because of the perceived difficulty of implementing the software platforms.

Although online interviews run the risk relative to face-to-face interviews that the respondent is somewhat more likely to drop out of the exchange (especially in asynchronous mode, since the interviews can sometimes be very protracted), Mann and Stewart (2000: 138–9) suggest that in fact a relationship of mutual trust can be built up. This kind of relationship can make it easier for a longer-term commitment to the interview to be maintained, but also makes it easier for the researcher to go back to his or her interviewees for further information or reflections, something that is difficult to do with the face-to-face personal interview. The authors also suggest that it is important for interviewers to keep sending messages to respondents to reassure them that their written utterances are helpful and significant, especially since interviewing through the Internet is still an unfamiliar experience for most people.

A further issue for the online personal interviewer to consider is whether to send all the questions at once or to interview on the basis of a question followed by a reply. The problem with the former tactic is that respondents may read all the questions and then reply only to those that they feel interested in or to which they feel they can make a genuine contribution, so that asking one question at a time is likely to be more reliable.

There is evidence that prospective interviewees are more likely to agree to participate if their agreement is solicited prior to sending them questions and if the researcher uses some form of self-disclosure, such as directing the person being contacted to the researcher's website, which contains personal information, particularly information that might be relevant to the research issue (Curasi 2001; O'Connor and Madge 2001). The argument for obtaining prior agreement from interviewees before sending them questions to be answered is that unsolicited emails, often referred to as 'spam', are regarded as a nuisance among online users and receiving what is thought to be spam can result in an immediate refusal to take the message seriously.

Curasi (2001) conducted a comparison in which twenty-four online interviews carried out through email correspondence (and therefore asynchronous) were contrasted with twenty-four parallel face-to-face interviews. The interviews were concerned with shopping on the Internet. She found the following:

- Face-to-face interviewers are better able than online interviewers to maintain rapport with respondents.

- Greater commitment and motivation are required for completing an online interview, but, because of this, replies are often more detailed and considered than with face-to-face interviews.

- Online interviewers are less able to have an impact on whether the interview is successful or not because they are more remote.

- Online interviewees' answers tend to be more considered and grammatically correct, because they have more time to ponder their answers and because they can tidy them up before sending them. Whether this is a positive feature is debatable: there is the obvious advantage of a 'clean' transcript, but there may be some loss of spontaneity, which Gibson (2010) found in connection with her research when she compared email and face-to-face interviews.

- Follow-up probes can be carried out in online interviews, as well as in face-to-face ones.

On the other hand, Curasi also found that the worst interviews in terms of the amount of detail forthcoming were from online interviews. It may be that this and the other differences are to do with the fact that, whereas a qualitative face-to-face interview is *spoken*, the parallel online interview is *typed*. The full significance of this difference in the nature of the respondent's mode of answering has not been fully appreciated.

It is very clear from many of the discussions about online interviews by email that a significant problem for many interviewers is that of keeping respondents involved in the interview when questions are being sent one or two at a time. Respondents tend to lose momentum or interest. However, Kivits (2005) has shown that recontacting interviewees on regular occasions and adopting an accessible and understanding style can not only help to maintain momentum for many interviewees but also bring some who have lost interest or forgotten to reply back into the research.

An interesting issue with asynchronous personal interviews in particular is whether it is appropriate to describe them as interviews at all and indeed whether they are experienced by research participants as interviews. Given that the process of answering questions in an **asynchronous online interview** entails writing, particularly if there is minimal interaction with the researcher, it may be experienced by the 'interviewee' as more akin to answering open questions in a self-administered questionnaire.

Using Skype

Thus far, most of the discussion of online personal interviewing assumes that the exchange is conducted entirely in a textual context. However, the webcam and Skype may offer further possibilities for synchronous online personal interviews. Skype is available for use on many smartphones and tablets, as well as conventional computers. It makes the online interview similar to a telephone interview; in fact, although it is mediated by Internet technology, it is also similar to an in-person interview, since those involved in the exchange are able to see each other. Some researchers have begun to report and reflect on their experiences of using Skype in this way and the early indications are broadly positive (Deakin and Wakefield 2014; Hanna 2012; Weinmann et al. 2012). These early impressions suggest that the obvious advantage of Skype (or similar software, such as FaceTime) over telephone interviewing, namely that it allows a visual element that is akin to a face-to-face interview, is borne out. In addition, researchers' early impressions suggest several other advantages:

- The Skype interview is more flexible than the face-to-face interview, in that last-minute adjustments to the scheduling of the interview can be easily accommodated.

- There are obvious time and cost savings in that the need to travel to the interview is removed, which is a particular advantage with geographically dispersed samples.

- The convenience of being interviewed by Skype may actually encourage some people to agree to be interviewed when they might otherwise have declined.

- There are fewer concerns about the safety of both parties to an interview, particularly when the interview is being conducted at night.

- There seems little evidence that the interviewer's capacity to secure rapport is significantly reduced in comparison with face-to-face interviews.

There are some limitations that warrant mention too:

- There are potential technological problems with the use of Skype and similar platforms. Not everyone has the necessary Wifi connection, and familiarity with Skype is by no means universal.

- Skype can be prone to fluctuations in the quality of the connection (and sometimes outages) which can make the flow of the interview less than smooth. Breaking up of speech can result in poor recordings of the interview, which makes transcription difficult if not impossible at times.

- One of the principal advantages of the online interview is lost, in that the respondent's answers need to be transcribed as in traditional qualitative interviewing.

- Although it is clearly advantageous for interviewers and interviewees to see each other so that visual cues can be picked up, responses may be affected by visible characteristics of the interviewer, such as gender, age, and ethnic group.

- There is some evidence that prospective Skype interviewees are more likely than face-to-face interviewees to fail to be present for an interview.

- A study of German youth conducted in 2011 found that it was harder to secure agreement to participate in Skype interviews than in telephone interviews (Weinmann et al. 2012).

Interviewing via Skype clearly has great potential and it may be that some of the difficulties reported above will gradually become less pronounced as familiarity with the software increases and Wifi connections improve.

Online social surveys

There has been a considerable growth in the number of **surveys** being administered **online**. It is questionable whether the research instruments should be regarded as structured interviews (see Chapter 9) or as self-completion questionnaires (see Chapter 10); in a sense they are both. So far as online social surveys are concerned, there is a crucial distinction between surveys administered by email (email surveys) and surveys administered via the Web (**Web surveys**). In the case of the former, the questionnaire is sent via email to a respondent, whereas, with a Web survey, the respondent is directed to a website in order to answer a questionnaire. Sheehan and Hoy (1999) suggest that there has been a tendency for email surveys to be employed in relation to 'smaller, more homogeneous on-line user groups', whereas Web surveys have been used to study 'large groups of on-line users'.

Email surveys

With email surveys it is important to distinguish between **embedded** and **attached email surveys**. In the case of the embedded questionnaire, the questions are to be found in the body of the email. There may be an introduction to the questionnaire followed by some marking that partitions the introduction from the questionnaire itself. Respondents have to indicate their replies using simple notations, such as an 'x', or they may be asked to delete alternatives that do not apply. If questions are open, they are asked to type in their answers. They then simply need to select the reply button to return their completed questionnaires to the researcher. With an attached questionnaire, the questionnaire arrives as an attachment to an email that introduces it. As with the embedded questionnaire, respondents must select and/or type their answers. To return the questionnaire, it must be attached to a reply email, although respondents may also be given the opportunity to fax or send the completed questionnaire by postal mail to the researcher (Sheehan and Hoy 1999).

The chief advantage of the embedded questionnaire is that it is easier for the respondent to return to the researcher and it requires less computer expertise. Knowing how to read and then return an attachment requires a certain facility with handling online communication that is still not universally applicable. Also, the recipients' operating systems or software may present problems with reading attachments, while many respondents may refuse to open the attachment because of concerns about a virus. On the other hand, the limited formatting that is possible with most email software, such as using bold, variations in font size, indenting, and other features, makes the appearance of embedded questionnaires rather dull and featureless, although this limitation is rapidly changing. Furthermore, it is slightly easier for the respondent to type material into an attachment that uses well-known software like Microsoft Word, since, if the questionnaire is embedded in an email, the alignment of questions and answers may be lost.

Dommeyer and Moriarty (2000) compared the two forms of email survey in connection with an attitude study. The questionnaire that was attached was given a much wider range of embellishments in terms of appearance than was possible with the embedded one. Before conducting the survey, undergraduate students were asked about the relative appearance of the two formats. The attached questionnaire was deemed to be better looking, easier to complete, clearer in appearance, and better organized. The two formats were then administered to two random samples of students, all of whom were active email users. The researchers found a much higher response rate with the embedded than with the attached questionnaire (37 per cent versus 8 per cent), but there was little difference in terms of speed of response or whether questions were more likely to be omitted with one format rather than the other. Although Dommeyer and Moriarty (2000: 48) conclude that 'the attached e-mail survey presents too many obstacles to the potential respondent', it is important to appreciate that this study was conducted during what were still early days in the life of online surveys. It may be that, as prospective respondents become more adept at using online communication methods and as viruses become less of a threat (for example, as virus-checking software improves in terms of accessibility and cost), the concerns that led to the lower response rate for the attached questionnaire will be less pronounced. Also, the researchers do not appear to have established a prior contact with the students before sending out the questionnaires; it may be that the reaction to such an approach, which is frowned upon in the online community, may have been more negative in the case of the attached questionnaire format.

Web surveys

Web surveys operate by inviting prospective respondents to visit a website at which the questionnaire can be found and completed online. The Web survey has an important advantage over the email survey in that it can use a much wider variety of embellishments in terms of appearance. Plate 28.1 presents part of the questionnaire from the gym survey from Chapter 15 in a Web survey format and answered in the same way as in Tips and skills 'A completed and processed questionnaire' (Chapter 15). There are also greater possibilities than with paper-based questionnaires in terms of the use of colour and variety in the format of closed questions. With open questions, the respondent is invited to type directly into a boxed area (for example, question 2 in Plate 28.1).

However, the advantages of the Web survey are not just to do with appearance. The questionnaire can be designed so that, when there is a filter question (for example, 'if yes go to question 12, if no go to question 14'), it skips automatically to the next appropriate question. The questionnaire can also be programmed so that only one question ever appears on the screen or so that the respondent can scroll down and look at all questions in advance. Finally, respondents' answers can be automatically programmed to download into a database, thus eliminating the daunting coding of a large number of questionnaires. One of the chief problems with the Web survey is that, in order to produce the attractive text and all the other features, the researcher will either have to be highly sophisticated in the use of HTML or will need to use one of a growing number of software packages that are designed to produce questionnaires with all the features that have been described.

Plate 28.1 was created using Survey Monkey: *www.surveymonkey.com/MySurveys.aspx* (accessed 4 November 2014)

With commercial websites such as these, you can design your questionnaire online and then create a Web address to which respondents can be directed in order to complete it. The questions in Plate 28.1] were created using the software's basic features, which are free of charge. There is a fee for using this software if more advanced features are required. The fee will be affected by the number of respondents who complete the questionnaire and the length of time that the questionnaire is active. Each respondent's replies are logged, and the entire dataset can be retrieved once you have decided that the data collection phase is complete. This means that there is no coding of replies (other than with open questions) and entering of data into your software. Not only does this save time; it also reduces the likelihood of errors in the processing of data.

Potential respondents need to be directed to the website containing the questionnaire. Research in focus 28.7 provides an example of the kind of approach that might be used. Where there are possible problems to do with restricting who may answer the questionnaire, it may be necessary to set up a password system to filter out people for whom the questionnaire is not appropriate.

The use of mobile telephones as a platform for self-completion questionnaires

Although still very much in its infancy, there is growing interest in the potential of mobile phones and in particular smartphones as a means of administering self-completion questionnaires. Until fairly recently, the self-completion questionnaire was considered a research instrument that

Plate 28.1

Gym survey in Web survey format

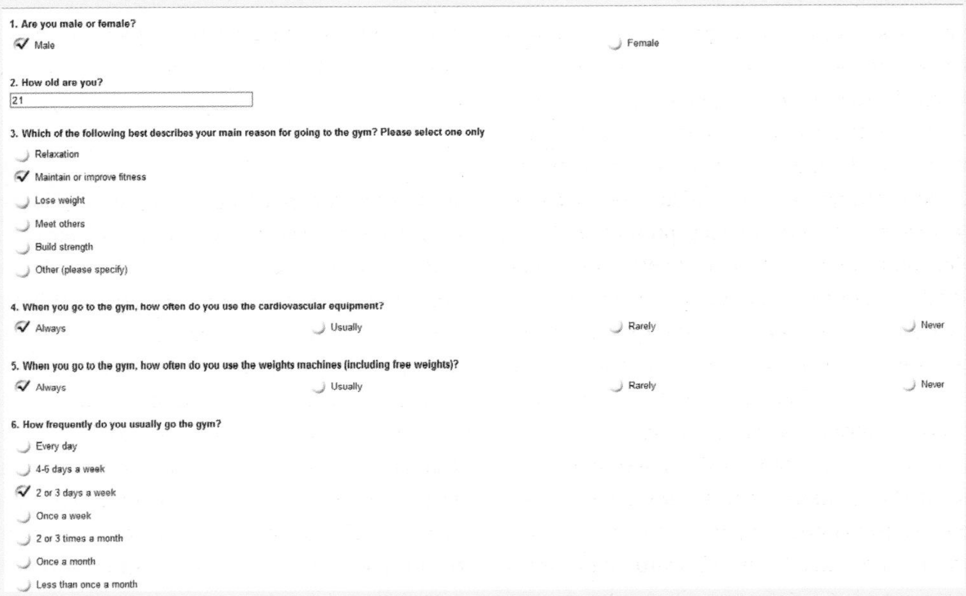
1. Are you male or female?
Male
Female

2. How old are you?
21

3. Which of the following best describes your main reason for going to the gym? Please select one only
Relaxation
Maintain or improve fitness
Lose weight
Meet others
Build strength
Other (please specify)

4. When you go to the gym, how often do you use the cardiovascular equipment?
Always
Usually
Rarely
Never

5. When you go to the gym, how often do you use the weights machines (including free weights)?
Always
Usually
Rarely
Never

6. How frequently do you usually go the gym?
Every day
4-6 days a week
2 or 3 days a week
Once a week
2 or 3 times a month
Once a month
Less than once a month

was primarily administered to people through the postal system. A format that is also sometimes encountered is when a sample is handed a questionnaire which is then returned to the researcher either immediately or left for later collection (Allred and Ross-Davis 2011). However, the growth in the ownership and use of smartphones in particular has begun to offer a new and potentially promising means of administration in addition to the Web survey answered via a computer, the subject of the previous section. It is too early in the development of this medium for a comprehensive assessment of mobile phone questionnaires to be presented but the following discussion aims to outline a small number of key points that can be derived from the emerging literature.

On the face of it, questionnaires administered on mobile devices share many features with web surveys whereby the respondent replies using a computer and keyboard. However, as Peytchev and Hill (2010) observe, smartphones and similar mobile devices differ from computers in three important ways: small screen size, navigation (mouse versus touchscreen or thumb wheel), and how information is inputted. Research by these authors suggests that Web surveys can be used with mobile phones but need to be adapted because features such as the small screen create difficulties for respondents, particularly when questions include a visual element. An early study in 2008 of a German sample's willingness to participate in a mobile phone survey found three factors were especially important: the perceived enjoyment of participating; attitudes towards participation (e.g. whether it is perceived to be exciting, absorbing, useful); and the perceived trustworthiness of the medium (e.g. anonymity, personal data not being misused) (Bosnjak et al. 2010). Such research provides pointers to factors that may be capable of being influenced in order to increase the likelihood of respondent participation.

An experiment conducted in Russia by Mavletova (2013) compared a survey administered by Web survey and answered using a computer with the same survey administered using a mobile phone in terms of data quality. The author found that the mobile format resulted in a lower level of completed questionnaires and fewer words being written in response to open questions. However, in respect of other aspects of data quality, there were no differences or only very minor ones. Thus, there was no difference in primary effects (whether answers to closed questions that are higher on a list of questions are more likely to be answered); in reporting levels in relation to sensitive questions; or in what the author calls 'non-substantive responses' (e.g. 'don't know', 'none of the above'). Findings from a similar study in the Netherlands suggests that there were no differences between mobile devices and computers in terms of the nature of the answers given but that when the questionnaire used for the experiment

was answered using a mobile device, it took longer to complete and had a lower response rate (de Bruijne and Wijnant 2013). These findings are quite promising, but it is too early to be confident about the use of mobile phones as a means of administering Web surveys. Also, the significance of tablet computers (such as the iPad and Android devices) raises the issue of whether these produce the same differences from computers as mobile phones.

Mixing modes of survey administration

The example in Research in focus 28.7 concerns a case in which a Web survey is combined with a conventional self-administered questionnaire. When this occurs, there are two different modes of administration of the research instrument in operation. Mixed modes of administering a survey raise the question of whether the mode of administration matters; in other words, do you get different results when you administer a questionnaire online from when you administer it offline (for example, by handing or mailing a questionnaire to respondents)? Obviously, it would not be desirable to aggregate data from two different modes of administration if part of the variation in respondents' replies could be attributed to the way they received and completed the questionnaire. Equally, researchers using solely a web-based questionnaire need to know how far their findings are different from conventional modes of administration.

Experiments with different modes of administration are quite reassuring on this point, because the differences may not always be large. In a study of American students' attitudes to various aspects of college experience, respondents were found to reply more positively when answering questions online than when using paper questionnaires. However, with the exception of one of the scales, the differences were not large (Carini et al. 2003). Fleming and Bowden (2009) conducted a travel cost questionnaire survey by mail and the Web of visitors to Fraser Island, Australia. They found the results from the two modes of administration to be similar and that, in particular, the estimates of the 'consumer surplus' (the amount the tourist would be willing to spend on the visit less the amount actually spent) were similar between the two. In spite of the fact that there is some evidence of differences in response between modes of survey administration, mixing postal and online questionnaires is often recommended as a survey approach (Van Selm and Jankowski 2006). Trau et al. (2013) were interested in how far web-based questionnaires could be used as a means of achieving greater inclusion of stigmatized groups into organizational research. They compared questionnaires distributed through the Web and mail and found that although data quality (amount of missing data) was worse for the Web survey, the findings from various scales that were administered (e.g. an organizational commitment scale) were roughly equivalent. In other words, the mode of administration was unrelated to the responses derived. Further, Wolfe et al. (2008) conducted an experiment on teachers in Ohio and South Carolina comparing mail questionnaire and Web surveys in terms of non-response at the level of the individual item or question in order to determine whether one mode of administration results in a higher level of failure to answer individual questions than the other. The authors found any differences to be very small.

Given that the differences in findings resulting from different modes of administration in surveys that combine a web-based mode with a conventional mode (such as a paper-based self-completion questionnaire) do not appear to be great, there is often a good case to be made for offering respondents an online option. A covering letter might draw prospective respondents' attention to a web-based option along with the necessary instructions for accessing it, so that those who prefer to work online are not put off responding to the questionnaire. However, there are grounds for caution when the survey in question is a mail questionnaire survey that offers respondents the option of responding through a web-based questionnaire. Medway and Fulton (2012) conducted a meta-analysis of studies that examined the impact of offering a Web option and found a clear tendency for such surveys to produce *lower* response rates than those that do not provide such an option. The authors explain this possibly surprising finding in terms of such factors as the provision of a Web option: increasing the overall complexity in responding; introducing a break in the process of responding; and sometimes causing technical difficulties that result in respondents giving up.

Sampling issues

Anyone who has read Chapter 8 must be wondering how the sampling principles described there might apply to online surveys. A major issue and limitation is that not everyone in any nation is online and has the technical ability to handle questionnaires online in either email or Web formats. Certain other features of online communications make the issue more problematic.

- Many people have more than one email address.
- Email addresses tend to be much more fleeting than postal addresses.
- Many people use more than one Internet service provider (ISP).

- A household may have one computer but several users.
- Internet users are a biased sample of the population, in that they tend to be better educated, wealthier, younger, and not representative in ethnic terms (Couper 2000).
- Few sampling frames exist of the general online population and most of these are likely to be expensive to acquire, since they are controlled by ISPs or may be confidential.

Such issues make the possibilities of conducting online surveys using probability sampling principles difficult to envisage. This is not to say that online surveys should not be considered. Indeed, for researchers in the field of business and management, there may be more opportunities than for researchers in other areas. For example, in many organizations, most if not all non-manual workers are likely to be online and to be familiar with the details of using email and the Internet, so that a suitable sampling frame of email addressees is available or can relatively easily be compiled. In such circumstances, surveys can be conducted using essentially the same probability sampling procedures as those outlined in Chapter 8. For certain kinds of business research, such as investigations involving surveys of organizational members, email-based surveys may present sampling problems that differ little from offline modes of administration, other than the possibility of higher levels of non-response. Similarly, surveys of members of commercially relevant online groups can be conducted using probability sampling principles. C. B. Smith (1997) conducted a survey of Web presence providers (people or organizations that are involved in creating and maintaining Web content). She acquired her sample from a directory of providers, which acted as her sampling frame. A further example of the use of a directory to generate a probability sample can be found in Research in focus 28.7.

As Couper (2000) notes of surveys of populations using probability sampling procedures:

> Intra-organizational surveys and those directed at users of the Internet were among the first to adopt this new survey technology. These restricted populations typically have no coverage problems . . . or very high rates of coverage. Student surveys are a particular example of this approach that are growing in popularity.
>
> (2000: 485)

Hewson and Laurent (2008) suggest that when there is no sampling frame, which is normally the case with samples to be drawn from the general population, the

Research in focus 28.7
Sampling for an online survey

Cobanoglu, Ward, and Moreo (2001) report the results of a study in which three different modes of survey administration were used: post, fax, and online. The questionnaires were administered to 300 hospitality professors in the USA, who had been randomly sampled from the online directory of the Council on Hotel, Restaurant, and Institutional Education. The sampling was carried out only from those who had an email address. The 300 professors were randomly assigned to one of the three modes of survey administration. The authors write:

> For the web-based survey, an email message was sent to the professors along with a cover letter and the website address. The respondents were informed that they could request a paper copy of the survey should they have problems accessing the survey online. A unique website address was created for each respondent.
>
> (2001: 447)

Compared with the postal administration of the questionnaire, the online administration achieved a higher response rate (26 per cent versus 44 per cent) and a faster response speed, and was cheaper.

main approach taken to generating an appropriate sample is to post an invitation to answer a questionnaire on relevant newsgroup message boards, to suitable mailing lists, or on web pages. The result will be a sample of entirely unknown representativeness, and it is impossible to know what the response rate to the questionnaire is, since the size of the population is also unknown. On the other hand, given that we have so little knowledge and understanding of online behaviour and attitudes relating to online issues, it could reasonably be argued that some information about these areas is a lot better than none at all, provided that the limitations of the findings in terms of their generalizability are appreciated.

A further issue in relation to sampling and sampling-related error is the matter of *non-response* (see Key concept 8.5). There is growing evidence that online surveys typically generate lower response rates than postal questionnaire surveys (Tse 1998; Sheehan 2001). In the early years, in the late 1980s, response rates for email surveys were quite encouraging (Sheehan and Hoy 1999), but since the mid-1990s they have been declining and are at lower levels than those for most postal questionnaires (Sheehan 2001), though there are clear exceptions to this tendency (for example, see Research in focus 28.7). Two factors may account for this decline: the novelty of email surveys in the early years and a growing antipathy towards unsolicited emails among online communities. A meta-analysis that compared Web surveys with other modes of survey administration found that on average,

Web surveys produce a response rate that is 11 per cent lower (Lozar Manfreda et al. 2008). However, response rates can be boosted by following two simple strategies.

1. Contact prospective respondents before sending them a questionnaire. This is regarded as basic 'netiquette'. Bosnjak et al. (2008) found that response rates to a web-based panel survey could be enhanced by prenotifying prospective participants. They found that prenotifications sent by text (SMS) message were more effective than when sent by email but that a combination of both was more effective than text messages alone.

2. As with postal questionnaire surveys, follow up non-respondents at least once.

The case for the first of these two strategies in boosting response rates is not entirely clear (Sheehan 2001), but seems to be generally advisable. However, as previously noted, with many online surveys it is impossible to calculate a response rate, since, when participants are recruited through invitations and postings on discussion boards, etc., the size of the population of which they are a sample is almost impossible to determine.

Crawford, Couper, and Lamias (2001) report the results of a survey of students at the University of Michigan that experimented with a number of possible influences on the response rate. Students in the sample were initially sent an email inviting them to visit the website, which allowed access, via a password, to the questionnaire. Some of those emailed were led to expect that the questionnaire would take 8–10 minutes to complete (in fact, it would take considerably longer); others were led to expect that it would take 20 minutes. As might be expected, those led to believe it would take longer were less likely to accept the invitation, resulting in a lower response rate for this group. However, Crawford et al. also found that those respondents who were led to believe that the questionnaire would take only 8–10 minutes were *more* likely to give up on the questionnaire part of the way through, resulting in unusable partially completed questionnaires in most cases. Interestingly, they also found that respondents were most likely to abandon their questionnaires part of the way through when in the middle of completing a series of open questions. The implications of this finding echo the advice in Chapter 9 that it is probably best to ask as few open questions in self-completion questionnaires as possible.

Further evidence regarding this survey suggests that having a progress indicator with a Web survey can reduce the number of people who abandon the questionnaire part of the way through completion (Couper, Traugott, and Lamias 2001). A progress indicator is usually a diagrammatic representation of how far the respondent has progressed through the questionnaire at any particular point. Couper et al. also found that it took less time for respondents to complete related items (for example, a series of Likert items) when they appeared on a screen together than when they appeared singly. Respondents also seemed less inclined to omit related questions when they appeared together on a screen rather than singly.

However, it is important not be too sanguine about some of these findings. One difficulty with them is that the samples derive from populations whose members are not as different from one another as would almost certainly be found in samples deriving from general populations. Another is that it must not be forgotten that, as previously noted, access to the Internet is still not universal, and there is evidence that those with Web access differ from those without, both in terms of personal characteristics and attitudinally. Fricker et al. (2005) compared the administration of a questionnaire by Web survey and by telephone interview among a general US sample. They found that telephone interviewees were much more likely to complete the questionnaire (though it is possible if not probable that the same effect would have been noted if they had compared the Web mode with a self-completion mode). By contrast, telephone interviewees were more likely to omit questions by saying they had 'no opinion' than in the Web administration, probably because respondents were prompted to answer if they failed to answer a question. One difficulty noted by Fricker et al. is that Web respondents were more likely than telephone interviewees to give undifferentiated answers to series of questions such as Likert items. In other words, they were more prone to response sets. Some of the questions were open questions inviting respondents to display their knowledge on certain issues. The researchers found that Web respondents took longer to answer the questions and were more likely to provide valid answers than the telephone interviewees. Couper (2008) summarized the results of several studies that compared the use of open questions in both web-based and paper-based questionnaire surveys and found that the former were at least as good as the mail questionnaires in terms of both quantity and quality of answers. In fact, in terms of the quantity written, the Web questionnaires were usually superior. More recently, Smyth et al. (2009) report that the quality of answers to open questions in Web surveys can be enhanced by: increasing the size of the space available for answers; drawing attention to the flexibility of the box into which answers are typed; and providing instructions that both clarify what is expected and motivate the respondent (such as pointing out the importance of their replies). A comparison of replies with an earlier equivalent paper-based questionnaire revealed that the quality of web-based replies was superior in several different ways. Smyth et al. observe that the use of open questions in surveys has declined because of the high costs of administering them and the poor quality of replies, but that, with growing evidence of their potential through a web-based mode of administration, they may enjoy a renaissance, especially when it is borne in mind that there is no need to transcribe people's sometimes illegible handwriting.

These findings suggest that it is difficult and probably impossible, given their relative newness, to provide a definitive verdict on Web surveys compared to traditional forms of survey administration. For one thing, it is difficult to separate out the particular formats that researchers use when experimenting with modes of administration from the modes themselves. It may be that, if they had displayed Web questions in a different manner, their findings would have been different—with obvious implications for how the Web survey fares when compared with any of the traditional forms. Further, Web surveys seem to work better than traditional survey forms in some respects more than others.

Tips and skills 'Advantages and disadvantages of online surveys compared to postal questionnaire surveys' summarizes the main factors to take into account when comparing online surveys with postal questionnaire surveys, and Table 28.1 compares the different methods of administering a survey.

Table 28.1

The strengths of email and web-based surveys in relation to face-to-face interview, telephone interview, and postal questionnaire surveys

Issues to consider	Mode of survey administration				
	Face-to-face interview	Telephone interview	Postal questionnaire	Email	Web
Resource issues					
Is the cost of the mode of administration relatively low?	✓	✓✓	✓✓✓	✓✓✓	✓ (unless access to low-cost software)
Is the speed of the mode of administration relatively fast?	✓	✓✓✓	✓✓✓	✓✓✓	✓✓✓
Is the cost of handling a dispersed sample relatively low?	✓ (✓✓ if clustered)	✓✓✓	✓✓✓	✓✓✓	✓✓✓
Does the researcher require little technical expertise for designing a questionnaire?	✓✓✓	✓✓✓	✓✓✓	✓✓	✓
Sampling-related issues					
Does the mode of administration tend to produce a good response rate?	✓✓✓	✓✓	✓	✓	✓
Is the researcher able to control who responds (i.e. the person at whom it is targeted is the person who answers)?	✓✓✓	✓✓✓	✓✓	✓✓	✓✓
Is the mode of administration accessible to all sample members?	✓✓✓	✓✓	✓✓✓	✓ (because of need for respondents to be accessible online)	✓ (because of need for respondents to be accessible online)
Questionnaire issues					
Is the mode of administration suitable for long questionnaires?	✓✓✓	✓✓	✓✓	✓✓	✓✓
Is the mode of administration suitable for complex questions?	✓✓✓	✓	✓✓	✓✓	✓✓
Is the mode of administration suitable for open questions?	✓✓✓	✓✓	✓	✓✓	✓✓
Is the mode of administration suitable for filter questions?	✓✓✓ (especially if CAPI used)	✓✓✓ (especially if CATI used)	✓	✓	✓✓✓ (if allows jumping)
Does the mode of administration allow control over the order in which questions are answered?	✓✓✓	✓✓✓	✓	✓	✓✓
Is the mode of administration suitable for sensitive questions?	✓	✓✓	✓✓✓	✓✓✓	✓✓✓
Is the mode of administration less likely to result in non-response to some questions?	✓✓✓	✓✓✓	✓✓	✓✓	✓✓
Does the mode of administration allow the use of visual aids?	✓✓✓	✓	✓✓✓	✓✓	✓✓✓
Answering context issues					
Does the mode of administration give respondents the opportunity to consult others for information?	✓✓	✓	✓✓✓	✓✓✓	✓✓✓

Table 28.1

Continued					
Issues to consider	Mode of survey administration				
	Face-to-face interview	Telephone interview	Postal questionnaire	Email	Web
Does the mode of administration minimize the impact of interviewers' characteristics (gender, class, ethnicity)?	✓	✓✓	✓✓✓	✓✓✓	✓✓✓
Does the mode of administration minimize the impact of the social desirability effect?	✓	✓✓	✓✓✓	✓✓✓	✓✓✓
Does the mode of administration allow control over the intrusion of others in answering questions?	✓✓✓	✓✓	✓	✓	✓
Does the mode of administration minimize need for respondent to have certain skills to answer questions?	✓✓✓	✓✓✓	✓✓	✓(because of need to have online skills)	✓ (because of need to have online skills)
Does the mode of administration enable respondents to be probed?	✓✓✓	✓✓✓	✓	✓✓	✓
Does the mode of administration reduce the likelihood of data entry errors by the researcher?	✓	✓	✓✓	✓	✓✓✓

Notes: Number of ticks indicates the strength of the mode of administration of a questionnaire in relation to each issue. More ticks correspond to more advantages in relation to each issue. A single tick implies that the mode of administering a questionnaire does not fare well in terms of the issue in question. Three ticks imply that it does very well, and two ticks imply that it is acceptable.
CAPI is computer-assisted personal interviewing; CATI is computer-assisted telephone interviewing.

Sources: This table has been influenced by the authors' own experience and the following sources: Dillman (1978); Czaja and Blair (1996); *www.restore.ac.uk/orm/* (accessed 5 November 2014).

Tips and skills
Advantages and disadvantages of online surveys compared to postal questionnaire surveys

This box summarizes the main advantages and disadvantages of online surveys compared to postal questionnaire surveys. The tally of advantages and disadvantages in connection with online surveys relates to both email and Web surveys. It should also be made clear that, by and large, online surveys and postal questionnaires suffer from one disadvantage relative to personal and telephone interviews—namely, that the researcher can never be certain that the person answering questions is who the researcher believes him or her to be. However, it has also been suggested that the remoteness of the Internet means that the problem of social desirability effects is less likely to be pronounced than with surveys conducted by structured interview.

Advantages

1. *Low cost*. Even though postal questionnaire surveys are cheap to administer, there is evidence that email surveys in particular are cheaper. This is in part due to the cost of postage, paper, envelopes, and the time taken to stuff covering letters and questionnaires into envelopes with postal questionnaire surveys. However, with Web surveys there may be start-up costs associated with the software needed to produce the questionnaire.

(continued)

2. *Faster response*. Online surveys tend to be returned considerably more quickly than postal questionnaires.

3. *Attractive formats*. With Web surveys, there is the opportunity to use a wide variety of stylistic formats for presenting questionnaires and closed-question answers. Also, automatic skipping when using filter questions and the possibility of immediate downloading of questionnaire replies into a database make this kind of survey quite attractive for researchers.

4. *Mixed administration*. Online surveys can be combined with postal questionnaire surveys, so that respondents have the option of replying by post or online. Moreover, the mode of reply does not seem to make a significant difference to the kinds of replies generated (see Research in focus 28.7).

5. *Unrestricted compass*. There are no constraints in terms of geographical coverage with online surveys. The same might be said of postal questionnaire surveys, but the problems of sending respondents stamped addressed envelopes that can be used in their own countries is overcome.

6. *Fewer unanswered questions*. There is evidence that online questionnaires are completed with fewer unanswered questions than postal questionnaires, resulting in less missing data. However, there is also evidence of little difference between the two modes of administering surveys.

7. *Better response to open questions*. To the extent that open questions are used, they tend to be more likely to be answered online and to result in more detailed replies.

8. *Better data accuracy, especially in Web surveys*. Data entry is automated with online surveys, so that the researcher does not have to enter data into a spreadsheet, and therefore errors in data entry are largely avoided.

Disadvantages

1. *Low response rate*. Typically, response rates to online surveys are lower than those for comparable postal questionnaire surveys. However, the difficulty that is often encountered with Internet surveys of finding suitable sampling frames means that for many such surveys it is more or less impossible to calculate a response rate.

2. *Restricted to online populations*. Only people who are available online can reasonably be expected to participate in an online survey. This restriction may gradually ease over time, but, since the online population differs in significant ways from the non-online population, it is likely to remain a difficulty. On the other hand, if online populations are the focus of interest, this disadvantage is unlikely to prove an obstacle.

3. *Requires motivation*. Online survey respondents must be online to answer the questionnaire, so, if they are having to pay for the connection and perhaps are tying up their telephone lines, they may need a higher level of motivation than postal questionnaire respondents. This suggests that the solicitation to participate must be especially persuasive.

4. *Confidentiality and anonymity issues*. It is normal for survey researchers to indicate that respondents' replies will be confidential and that they will be anonymous. The same suggestions can and should be made with respect to online surveys. However, with email surveys, since the recipient must return the questionnaire either embedded within the message or as an attachment, respondents may find it difficult to believe that their replies really are confidential and will be treated anonymously. In this respect, Web surveys may have an advantage over email surveys.

5. *Multiple replies*. With Web surveys, there is a risk that some people may mischievously complete the questionnaire more than once. There is much less risk of this with email surveys.

Sources: Based on Schaeffer and Dillman (1998); Tse (1998); Kent and Lee (1999); Sheehan and Hoy (1999); Cobanoglu, Ward, and Moreo (2001); Fricker and Schonlau (2002); Denscombe (2006).

Overview

Online surveys are clearly in their infancy, but they have considerable potential. There is evidence that having a Web survey or even an email option can boost response rates to postal questionnaires (Yun and Trumbo 2000). Several problems have been identified with Web and email surveys, but it is too early to dismiss them because researchers are only beginning to get to grips with this approach to survey research and may gradually develop ways of overcoming the limitations that are being identified. Moreover, as we have pointed out, for certain kinds of populations and as more and more people and organizations go online,

some of the sampling-related problems will diminish. As Yun and Trumbo (2000) observe: 'the electronic-only survey is advisable when resources are limited and the target population suits an electronic survey'.

It is also worth making the obvious point that, when conducting an online survey, you should bear in mind the principles about sampling, interview design, and question construction that were posed in Chapters 8–11 in particular. While online surveys are distinctive in certain ways, they require the same rigorous considerations that go into the design of conventional surveys that are conducted by postal questionnaire or by personal or telephone interview.

Ethical considerations in e-research

Conducting research by using the Internet as a method of data collection raises specific ethical issues that are only now starting to be widely discussed and debated. Some of these are related to the vast array of venues or environments in which these new forms of communication and possibilities for research occur, including blogs, listservs, or discussion groups, email, chatrooms, instant messaging, and newsgroups. The behaviour of Internet users is governed by 'netiquette', the conventions of politeness or definitions of acceptable behaviour that are recognized by online communities, as well as by service providers' acceptable use policies and by data protection legislation, and anyone contemplating using the Internet as a method of data collection should start by familiarizing themselves with these and by considering the general ethical principles discussed in Chapter 6. However, this section is concerned with the specific ethical issues raised by Internet research. One of the problems faced by social researchers wanting to use the Internet for data collection is that we are clearly in the middle of a huge growth in the amount of research being conducted in this way (M. Williams 2007). Not only is this trend creating the problem of over-researched populations who suffer from respondent fatigue; many of those involved in doing research with this new technology are not adhering to ethical principles. As a result, fatigue and suspicion are beginning to set in among prospective research participants, creating a less than ideal environment for future Internet researchers.

The Association of Internet Researchers (AoIR) (2002) recommends that researchers start by considering the ethical expectations established by the venue. For

instance, is there a posted site policy that notifies users that the site is public and specifies the limits to privacy? Or are there mechanisms that users can employ to indicate that their exchanges are private? The more the venue is acknowledged to be public, the less obligation there is on the researcher to protect the confidentiality and anonymity of individuals using the venue, or to seek their informed consent. However, the distinction between public and private space on the Internet is blurred and contested. Hewson et al. (2003) suggest that data that have been deliberately and voluntarily made available in the public Internet domain, such as newsgroups, can be used by researchers without the need for informed consent, provided anonymity of individuals is protected. However, other researchers (Hudson and Bruckman 2004) found that, although certain Internet venues might be considered by some to be public spaces, entering chatrooms and recording the conversation for research purposes provoked an extremely hostile response from chatroom users (see Research in focus 28.8).

Barnes (2004) identifies five types of Internet message, each presenting slightly different ethical concerns for anonymity, confidentiality, and informed consent.

- *Messages exchanged in online public discussion lists*. A typical forum for these would be discussion groups or newsgroups. Although most group members see their messages as public, Barnes (2004) found that some

Research in focus 28.8
Chatroom users' responses to being studied

Hudson and Bruckman (2004) designed an experiment to understand how potential participants react to being invited to participate in an online study. This involved entering a number of online moderated chatrooms and informing the participants that they were recording them and then recording how they responded. They downloaded a list of available chatrooms on 'ICQ Chat' each evening at 9.50 p.m. Dividing the chatrooms by size from very small (2–4 participants) to large (30 or more participants), they then randomly selected sixteen chatrooms from each set, then subdivided these into groups of four. Each group of four chatrooms was sent a different message as follows:

- *no message*: the researchers entered the chatroom using the nickname 'chat study' and said nothing;
- *recording message*: the researchers entered the chatroom as 'chat study' and announced that they were recording the chatroom for a study;
- *opt-out message*: the researchers entered the chatroom in the same way as above but posted a message giving the participants the option not to be recorded;
- *opt-in message*: the researchers entered the chatroom in the same way as before but gave participants the option to volunteer to be recorded.

Based on a sample of 525 chatrooms studied over a two-week period, Hudson and Bruckman found that posting a message about the study resulted in significant hostility, greatly increasing the likelihood of researchers being kicked out of the chatroom by the moderator. Moreover, the likelihood of being kicked out of a chatroom decreased as the number of participants in the chatroom increased. The comments that accompanied the researchers being kicked out included referring to the study as 'spamming' (unwanted electronic communication often involving some form of commercial advertising), objection to being studied, general requests to leave, and insults. When given a chance to opt in, only 4 of the 766 potential respondents actually did so. Hence, even when the option of fully informed consent was given, chatroom participants still objected to being studied. The researchers conclude that 'these results suggest that obtaining consent for studying online chatrooms is impracticable' (Hudson and Bruckman 2004: 135). This example highlights the potential ethical difficulties in intruding on a pre-existing Internet communication venue for research purposes, even if it is considered to be a public space.

consider them as private, despite having been sent statements upon joining the group indicating the public nature of the space. Barnes (2004) recommends as a general principle that the ideas of individuals who share their ideas on public lists should be attributed to their authors in the same way as you would attribute something they had written in a printed text under traditional copyright law. However, it is a good idea to check the welcoming messages of public discussion lists for guidance on how to cite email messages. Some discussion groups state that researchers must notify the group in advance of any research being undertaken. Barnes advises that, when researching any Internet group, it is a good idea to contact it in advance and to ask for permission to observe the members.

- *Messages exchanged in private discussions between individuals and on private lists*. Barnes (2004) suggests that in this situation the names of the lists and participants should never be revealed. To protect individual identities

further, she recommends that messages are combined, all headers and signatures are removed, references to the exact type of forum being studied are not made, and behaviour is described in general terms in a composite personality type rather than by referring to specific messages that could be traced to particular individuals.

- *Personal messages sent to the researcher*. In Barnes's (2004) research, these were sent on to her by a contact who had already deleted the names and email addresses of the original sender, but in any case she suggests that headers and signatures are removed to protect the authors' anonymity.

- *Messages re-posted and passed around the Internet*. This includes messages that people forward on to other people and discussion lists because they think they are interesting. They can contain the name of the original author or can be distributed as anonymous email. If they are distributed anonymously, Barnes (2004) believes it is worth trying to find the original author, so he or she can be properly credited in the research publication. She advises emailing the author and asking for permission to use the message.

- *Messages generated by computer programs*. This refers to messages generated by natural language computer programs that form the basis for interaction with people.

There may also be specific ethical considerations associated with certain types of research, such as virtual ethnography (see Research in focus 28.9).

A further ethical issue relates to the principle of protecting research participants from harm (see Chapter 6) and the related issues of individual anonymity and confidentiality. Stewart and Williams (2005) suggest that complete protection of anonymity is almost impossible in Internet research, since, in computer-mediated communication, information about the origin of a computer-generated message, revealed for instance in the header, is very difficult to remove. It is also more difficult to guarantee confidentiality, because the data are often accessible to other participants. In a similar vein, DeLorme, Zinkhan, and French (2001) suggest that the Internet raises particular ethical concerns for qualitative researchers that arise from the difficulty of knowing who has access to information. For example, a message posted on an Internet discussion group can be accessed by anyone who has a computer and an Internet connection. In addition, some Internet environments enable 'lurkers', people who listen to what is going on without making themselves identifiable. This makes it difficult for researchers to protect the confidentiality of data that they collect. A further concern arises from the potential for individuals to present a 'fake' identity during online interaction. If a research participant does this, it has implications for the validity of the data (see Chapter 17), but there is also potential for the researcher to deceive participants in the expectation that this will encourage them to respond more openly—for example, by pretending to be a man when conducting a focus group with all-male participants. This is thus a form of covert research, which, as discussed in Chapter 6, raises particular ethical issues because of the lack of informed consent.

These concerns have led some researchers to suggest that there is a need for an ethics code for Internet research. DeLorme, Zinkhan, and French (2001) surveyed qualitative researchers to find out whether or not they felt there was a need for an ethics code for qualitative researchers using the Internet and, if so, what kinds of issues it should cover. A majority of respondents thought that there should be an ethics code for qualitative Internet research. When asked what their reasons were for believing this, researchers expressed a rationale based on principles, driven by a professional view of what constitutes good research, and a practical rationale, based on the belief that dishonest practices will discourage Internet users from taking part in future online studies and undermine the reputation of legitimate researchers who use the Internet. DeLorme, Zinkhan, and French (2001) suggest that ethics codes designed by professional associations such as those discussed in Chapter 6 need to be revised to include an addendum that deals with these issues. However, the debates about the ethics of Internet research and the development of guidelines for researchers are ongoing, and, even though traditional ethical guidelines may need to be revised to reflect the ethical issues raised by Internet research, researchers should continue to be guided by the ethical principles discussed in Chapter 6.

Research in focus 28.9
Ethical issues in a virtual ethnography of change in the NHS

There have also been some attempts to highlight the ethical considerations associated with particular kinds of Internet research such as virtual ethnography. Clegg Smith (2004) was interested in organizational change and the role played by professionals in the NHS. While she was in the process of doing her research, she came across a listserv that was being used by British general practitioners (GPs) as a forum to discuss their feelings about the proposed reforms to the British health care system and their likely effects. She explains, 'essentially, I had stumbled on a "setting" in which GPs were "talking" among themselves about the significance of the proposed health care reforms for them as individuals, for the wider profession and generally about the future of general practice in Britain' (2004: 225). The geographically dispersed nature of GPs' work meant that the list provided a unique opportunity for them to interact with each other. Clegg Smith argues that one of the advantages of such virtual

(continued)

methods is that they provide the opportunity to conduct research with virtually no observer effects (see Research in focus 3.8). Therefore, her strategy was covert because, she explains, 'I anticipated difficulties in informing participants about my research without intruding in the ongoing interaction to an unacceptable extent' (2004: 232), and she feared that this might also arouse hostility because she observed that 'spam' messages were received unfavourably. For fifteen months she 'participated' in the list by receiving and reading messages daily without explicitly stating or explaining her presence to the majority of the listserv's members. A further difficulty in seeking informed consent arose from the nature of the list as an unmoderated forum; therefore there was no gatekeeper to whom she could address her request. Added to this, the membership of the list of around 500 members was in constant flux, so any single request for consent would have been impossible. Hence 'the only appropriate way to gain informed consent would be to repeatedly post requests to the entire list. Through my previous exposure to the list, however, I knew that such behaviour was clearly out of line with accepted practice in this domain' (2004: 233).

However, as Clegg Smith explains, 'I am aware that in making the decision not to expound my presence on the list, I may face considerable ethical critique. My research appears analogous with the notion of "covert" research so demonized in the usual discussions of research ethics' (2004: 225). One of the ways in which she justifies this is through discussion of the features of her study that distinguish it from other studies of virtual interaction. She notes how her study examined interaction between participants who were not engaged in the kind of 'fantasy interaction' associated with sexual or social virtual interaction. Therefore, Clegg Smith argues, her participants were not taking the opportunity to 'engage in behaviour with which they would not be comfortable engaging as part of their "real" lives' (2004: 228). A further ethical justification of her research arises from the extent to which participants saw the list as a public rather than a private space. Hence, the warning posted to each member on subscription and at monthly intervals stated 'MEMBERS ARE ADVISED TO CONSIDER COMMENTS POSTED TO LISTX TO BE IN THE PUBLIC DOMAIN' (2004: 229; capitalization in original). In addition, list members received guidelines on the copyright implications of email messages, which stated that comments posted to public lists are comparable to sending letters to a newspaper editor. Clegg Smith suggests that this provided justification for her 'electronic eavesdropping', since the ethical guidelines she was working to suggested that it was 'not necessary to explicitly seek permission for recording and analyzing publicly posted messages' because this is 'akin to conducting research in a marketplace, library or other public area, where observers are not necessarily expected to obtain informed consent from all present' (2004: 230).

A final ethical issue arising from the study concerns the principle of anonymity. Initially, Clegg Smith assumed she should protect the identity of participants when reporting her research findings, but through her involvement in the list she became aware that 'participants might wish to be "credited" for their postings' (2004: 234) because of the reaction when journalists used list messages without crediting the authors. However, despite this, she felt that, because she had not sought informed consent from all list members, it would be wrong to do this.

Telling it like it is
Informed consent in a research project involving the Internet

The use of the Internet as a method of data collection raises ethical considerations in relation to the issue of informed consent. Tore's dissertation project made use of data that had been collected for the purpose of enabling students to socialize with each other. As part of the process of joining the website, students were required to sign an agreement. Even though Tore did not anticipate using the data for his research at the time of setting up the website, the contract signed by students did include a clause in which they gave their consent for the data to be used for this purpose. Tore himself conceded that it was unlikely that the students had read the ten pages of small print that constituted the terms and conditions of the website, so they were probably not giving their fully informed consent to the use of the data for this purpose. However, since Tore was concerned with patterns of interaction and the profiles of individuals within these social networks and not with the content of the messages that were exchanged, he was able to avoid disclosure of potentially more sensitive aspects of the data and to protect the anonymity of individuals involved. Tore's research project also has implications relating to data protection legislation, which was discussed in Chapter 6.

The state of e-research

It should be apparent from the discussion above that, at least from a methodological viewpoint, e-research is very much a work in progress. New approaches are being developed, new fields of study are being envisioned, and the platforms for conducting research via software and the Internet are changing. The ethical terrain is changing too, and it is likely that some of the practices that were in evidence in the early years of e-research would be less likely to be considered now. Arriving at definitive statements about the various components of e-research is difficult because it is in fact an assemblage of research methods and approaches, each of which is developing in significantly different ways. The growing awareness of the interpenetration of online and offline worlds compounds the complexity of the issues. However, as we hope is clear from the presentation in this chapter, e-research offers huge opportunities for researchers as both a focus for research and a springboard for doing research. At the same time, a prospective user of e-research has to be aware that, although many methodological conventions have been developed, it is also a fast-developing area of research methodology.

Key points

● The growth in the use of the Internet offers significant opportunities for business researchers in allowing them access to a large and growing body of people.

● Many research methods covered elsewhere in this book can be adapted to online investigations.

● There is a distinction between research that uses websites as objects of analysis and research that uses the Internet to collect data from others.

● Online surveys may be of two major types: Web surveys and email surveys.

● Most of the same considerations that go into designing research that is not online apply to e-research.

● Both quantitative and qualitative research can be adapted to e-research.

Questions for review

The Internet as object of analysis

● In what ways might the analysis of websites pose particular difficulties that are less likely to be encountered in the analysis of non-electronic documents?

Using websites to collect data from individuals

● What are the chief ways of collecting data from individuals using the Internet and online communications?

● What advantages do these approaches have over traditional research methods for collecting such data?

● What disadvantages do they have in comparison to traditional research methods for collecting such data?

● What is the difference between web-based and communication-based research methods?

Virtual ethnography

● How does ethnography need to be adapted in order to collect data on the use of the Internet?

● Does the study of the impact of the Internet necessarily mean that we end up as technological determinists?

● Are ethnographies of the Internet really ethnographic?

Qualitative research using online focus groups

- What is the significance of the distinction between synchronous and asynchronous focus groups?

- How different is the role of the moderator in online, as against face-to-face, focus groups?

Qualitative research using online personal interviews

- Can online personal interviews really be personal interviews?

- To what extent does the absence of direct contact mean that the online interview cannot be a true interview?

Online social surveys

- What is the significance of the distinction between email and Web surveys?

- Are there any special circumstances in which embedded email questionnaires will be more likely to be effective than attached questionnaires?

- Do sampling problems render online social surveys too problematic to warrant serious consideration?

- Are response rates in online surveys worse or better than in traditional surveys?

Ethical considerations in e-research

- What ethical issues are raised by using the Internet as a method of data collection?

....

Online Resource Centre

www.oxfordtextbooks.co.uk/orc/brymanbrm4e/

Visit the Interactive Research Guide that accompanies this book to complete an exercise in Internet Research Methods.

....

29

Writing up business research

Chapter outline

It is easy to forget that one of the main stages in any research project, regardless of its size, is that it has to be written up. Not only is this how you will convey your findings, but being aware of the significance of writing is crucial, because your audience must be persuaded about the credibility and importance of your research. This chapter presents some of the characteristics of the writing-up of business research, including writing up a student research project. The chapter explores:

* why writing, and especially good writing, is important to business research;

* how to write up your research for a dissertation project;

* how quantitative and qualitative research are composed, using examples.

Introduction

The aim of this chapter is to examine some of the strategies that are used in writing up business research. As well as providing students with some practical advice on writing up a student research project, we will explore the question of whether or not quantitative and qualitative research reveal divergent approaches. As we will see, the similarities are frequently more striking and apparent than the differences. However, the main point of this chapter is to extract some principles of good practice that can be developed and incorporated into your own writing. This is important, since many people find writing up research more difficult than carrying it out. On the other hand, many people treat the writing-up stage as relatively unproblematic. But no matter how well research is conducted, others (that is, your readers) have to be convinced about the credibility of the knowledge claims you are making. Good writing is, therefore, very much

to do with developing your style so that it is *persuasive* and *convincing*. Flat, lifeless, uncertain writing does not have the power to persuade and convince. This chapter will provide some basic ideas about structuring your own written work that will be extremely useful if you have to write a dissertation.

In exploring these issues, we will touch on rhetorical strategies in the writing of business research (see Key concept 29.1). Writers in the area of theory and research known as the social studies of science have been concerned with the limitations of accepted distinctions between rhetoric and logic and between the observer and the observed (e.g. Gilbert and Mulkay 1984). The problematizing of these distinctions, along with doubts about the possibility of a neutral language through which the natural and social worlds can be revealed, opened the door for an evaluation of scientific and social scientific writing.

Key concept 29.1
What is rhetoric?

The study of rhetoric is fundamentally concerned with the ways in which attempts to convince or persuade an audience are formulated. We often encounter the term in a negative context, such as 'mere rhetoric' or the opposition of 'rhetoric and reality'. However, rhetoric is an essential ingredient of writing, because when we write our aim is to convince others about the credibility of our knowledge claims. To suggest that rhetoric should somehow be suppressed makes little sense, since it is in fact a basic feature of writing. The examination of rhetorical strategies in written texts based on business research is concerned with the identification of the techniques in those texts that are designed to convince and persuade.

Telling it like it is
Constructing rhetoric from rhetorical interview data

Tom was conscious of the process whereby his interviewees were using rhetoric to make sense of their experience of working in a call centre. 'The interviewees may well have been telling me things that they thought I wanted to hear. They may well have been giving a constructed account of what was going on. I took a mid-way position, I believed the data I collected wasn't simply call handlers giving me an accurate account of what was going on, but on the other hand I wouldn't say it was completely constructed and had no bearing on the sort of reality of the situation. I suppose I'd say that people were giving an account of what was going on, but there were inconsistencies in what they said. So, for example, some call handlers were quite keen to emphasize that when they left the building at 5 o'clock they didn't take any work issues home; they left them behind; but at other times in the interview they might say that at home they would be worrying about a stressful call or an angry call that had happened the previous day or something, so there were kind of inconsistencies in their accounts, which led me to think that they were kind of constructing a story to some extent which they'd like perhaps to believe themselves about their work as well as liking me to believe it.'

Tom's reflections on his interview data are interesting because they make explicit the process of interpretation. Tom is operating from a constructionist rather than an objectivist position (see Chapter 2). Once he had collected his data, he was in the position of having to interpret the rhetoric used by interviewees, looking for inconsistencies and contradictions and using this to inform his own rhetoric in his dissertation. His reflections on this process help to challenge the *interpretative omnipotence* that can be associated with certain types of ethnographic writing (see Chapter 19).

Writing up your research

It is easy to neglect the writing stage of your work because of the difficulties that you often encounter in getting your research underway. But—obvious though this point is—your dissertation has to be written. Your findings must be conveyed to an audience, something that all of us who carry out research have to face. The first bit of advice is . . .

Start early

It is easy to take the view that the writing-up of your research findings is something that you can think about after you have collected and analysed your data. There is, of course, a grain of truth in this view, in that you could hardly write up your findings until you know what they are, which is something that you can know only once you have gathered and analysed your data. However, there are good reasons for beginning writing early on, since you might want to start thinking about such issues as how best to present and justify the research questions that are driving your research or how to structure the theoretical and research literature that will have been used to frame your research questions. Students often tend to underestimate the time that it will take to write up their research, so it is a good idea to allow plenty of time for this, especially if you are expecting your supervisor to read and comment on an early draft, since you will also need to allow him or her a reasonable amount of time for this. A further reason why it is advisable to begin writing earlier rather than later is an entirely practical one: many people find it difficult to get started and employ (probably unwittingly) procrastination strategies to put off the inevitable. This tendency can result in the writing being left until the last minute and consequently being rushed. Writing under this kind of pressure is not ideal. How you represent your findings and conclusions is a crucial stage in the research process. If you do not provide a convincing account of your research, you will not do justice to it.

Telling it like it is
The benefits of writing up early . . . versus leaving it until later

Tom and Karen both found that there were advantages to having completed writing up their dissertations early so they were able to come back to them after a break before the deadline and make further changes. Tom said: 'The deadline was to hand it in by the end of August, but I had a holiday at the beginning of August and I was going to move house, so I knew I had to finish by the end of July because otherwise it was going to be a nightmare. And that was quite good, because it meant I finished, went off on holiday, then I just let it sort of settle for a couple of weeks and when I came back I was able to look at it with a fresh eye and give it a final kind of tidy up and tweak.'

Karen found that starting her research project early was an advantage in helping her to see her argument more clearly. 'I wanted to give it a lot of time to think about all the different issues. I did one draft and then just left it for four months and then came back to it, which I think was a definite benefit. because then I came back to it with fresh eyes and I'd had a couple of thoughts about different things; it was one of those things that was just constantly at the back of my mind. And I think that's definitely the best way to do it, because I had so many friends who sort of rushed it in the last two weeks, and I think then you lose all of the conceptual thinking and the ability to think more broadly about the topic and you just get a bit bogged down in all the detail.'

Tore was relatively late in starting to write up his research project, as he explained: 'I was maybe the last one to start writing up, I think, among all the students doing a research project. I think it is very important to know what you're writing about before you start writing, because otherwise you just start writing something and then you have to backtrack and change it and in a sense you're anchoring yourself to a certain text if you start writing. So I was actually very late at writing it up, but then it took less than a week to write it all up because I basically knew what I wanted to write. I had my headings and I knew where I was going on each heading. I had the data, I had the formulas, and then I sent it to all my friends to spell check and they questioned what it was all about. So I waited until I knew what I wanted to say and I had all the conclusions in order before I started writing up my results. I know it's kind of wrong to do it that way, but in a sense it made the writing very clear.'

Although Tore's experience might initially seem to contradict what we have said about the importance of starting early, he did have a clear sense of what he was intending to write about and how he was intending to structure his writing well before he started to write this final version. This understanding was derived in part from reading articles in his subject area and realizing that they have a consistent structure. As he explained: 'They go through certain things. They have a results section and then they have a conclusion section, so in a sense the layout is fixed. I just used what others had used before me.' Tore was thus able to replicate elements of the structure of these published articles in his own writing.

However, Lucie was more ambivalent about having left the writing-up of her dissertation towards the end of the time available, feeling that she had not had enough time to really do justice to her complex dataset, which included documentary, interview, participant observational, and statistical data. 'I think I let myself down a little bit at the end. I carried out all this research and it had the potential to be really good and then I kind of ran out of time before having to hand in the dissertation. You know, I didn't write it as well as I could have and didn't include as much as I could have, I don't think, so I was a bit disappointed with my final draft.' This is a particular consideration in mixed methods research that combines different kinds of qualitative data like Lucie's, because the process of analysing such varied data is likely to be complex and more time-consuming than in research designs that use one data collection method.

Telling it like it is
The rewards of being a supervisor

The experience of supporting a student research project can be a rewarding experience for supervisors. Some of the rewards that supervisors mentioned included:

- reading a well-written dissertation;
- finding out interesting things they did not already know;
- discussing interesting topics with students;
- obtaining additional references for their own research and writing;
- helping students to discover they have become an expert in their sub-field;
- hearing of someone doing well in his or her career after leaving university.

Be persuasive

This point is crucial. Writing up your research is not simply a matter of reporting your findings and drawing some conclusions. Writing up your research will contain many other features, such as referring to the literature on which you drew, explaining how you did your research, and outlining how you conducted your analysis. But, above all, you must be *persuasive*. This means that you must convince your readers of the credibility of your conclusions. Simply saying 'This is what I found; isn't it interesting?' is not enough. You must persuade your readers that your findings and conclusions are significant and that they are plausible.

Get feedback

Try to get as much feedback on your writing as possible and respond positively to the points anyone makes about what they read. Your supervisor is likely to be the main source of feedback, but institutions vary in what supervisors are allowed to comment on. Provide your supervisor with drafts of your work to the fullest extent that regulations will allow. Give him or her plenty of time to provide feedback. There will be others like you who will want your supervisor to comment on their work, and, if he or she feels rushed, the comments may be less helpful. Also, you could ask others on the same degree programme to read your drafts and comment on them. They may ask you to do the same. Their comments may be very useful, but, by and large, your supervisor's comments are the main ones you should seek out.

Tips and skills
The importance of an argument

One of the things that students can find difficult about writing up their research is the formulation of an argument. The writing-up of research should be organized around an argument that links all aspects of the research process from problem formulation, through literature review and the presentation of research methods, to the discussion and conclusion. Too often, students make a series of points without asking what the contribution of those points is to the overall argument that they are trying to present. Consider what your claim to knowledge is and try to organize your writing to support and enhance it. That will be your argument. Sometimes it is useful to think in terms of telling a story about your research and your findings. Try to avoid tangents and irrelevant material that may mean your readers will lose the thread of your argument. If you are not able to supply a clear argument, you are vulnerable to the 'so what?' question. Ask yourself: 'What is the key point or message that I want my readers to take away with them when they have finished reading my work?' If you cannot answer that question satisfactorily (and it may be worth trying it out on others), almost certainly you do not have an argument. The argument is a thread that runs through your dissertation (see Figure 29.1 for some examples of key phrases that can be used to construct and maintain an argument throughout the dissertation).

Figure 29.1

Typical ways of constructing an argument

Dissertation chapter		Commonly used phrases to make an argument
Introduction	**A**	In this dissertation I will argue that ... This dissertation argues that ... It is often argued that ... It is argued here that ... It could be argued that ...
Literature review	**R** **G** **U**	In the introduction I argued that ... This argument is illustrated by exploring the concept of ... The argument in this dissertation draws on ... My arguments build on the work of Mintzberg (1973) ... Some would argue that ... Others have argued ... As Bryman (1998) argued .../he suggests ... Bell (1999) argues that .../she claims that ... In this chapter I willl situate my argument in the literature on ...
Research methods	**M**	Following the arguments put forward by Willmott (1990) ...
Results/findings/cases	**E** **N**	This shows ... This demonstrates that ... This implies that ... From this I suggest ...
Discussion/analysis	**T**	Based on these findings I would argue that ... In an earlier chapter I argued that ...
Conclusion		In this dissertation I have argued for ... I conclude that ... In this dissertation I have argured for a more ...

Tips and skills
Non-sexist writing

One of the biggest problems (but by no means the only one) when trying to write in a non-sexist way is avoiding complex his/her formulations. The easiest way of dealing with this is to write in the plural in such circumstances. For example: 'I wanted to give each respondent the opportunity to complete the questionnaire in his or her own time and in a location that was convenient for him or her.' This is a rather tortuous sentence and, although grammatically correct, it could be phrased more helpfully as: 'I wanted to give respondents the opportunity to complete their questionnaires in their own time and in a location that was convenient for them.'

Avoid sexist, racist, and disablist language

Remember that your writing should be free of sexist, racist, and disablist language. The British Sociological Association provides very good general and specific guidelines on this issue, which can be found at: *www.britsoc.co.uk/NR/rdonlyres/4E70B7F7-58A1-43AB-A414-77F929A954D2/533/Equalityand-Diversity_LanguageandtheBSA_SexandGende.doc* (accessed 5 November 2014)

Structure your writing

It may be that you have to write a dissertation of around 10,000 to 15,000 words for your degree. How might it be structured? The following is typical of the structure of a dissertation.

Title page

You should examine your institution's rules about what should be entered here.

Acknowledgements

You might want to acknowledge the help of various people, such as gatekeepers who gave you access to an organization, people who have read your drafts and provided you with feedback, or your supervisor for his or her advice.

List of contents

Your institution may have recommendations or prescriptions about the form this should take.

Abstract

A brief summary of your dissertation. Not all institutions require this component, so check on whether it is required. Journal articles usually have abstracts, so you can draw on these for guidance on how to approach this task.

Introduction

- You should explain what you are writing about and why it is important. Saying simply that it interests you because of a long-standing personal interest is not enough.

- You might indicate in general terms the theoretical approach or perspective you will be using and why.

- You should also at this point outline your research questions. In the case of dissertations based on qualitative research, it is likely that your research questions will be rather more open-ended than is the case with quantitative research. But do try to identify some research questions. A totally open-ended research focus is risky and can lead to the collection of too much data, and, when it comes to writing up, it can result in a lack of focus.

- The opening sentence or sentences are often the most difficult of all. Becker (1986) advises strongly against opening sentences that he describes as 'vacuous' and 'evasive'. He gives the example of 'This study deals with the problem of careers', and adds that this kind of sentence employs 'a typically evasive manœuvre, pointing to something without saying anything, or anything much, about it. *What* about careers?' (Becker 1986: 51). He suggests that such evasiveness often occurs because of concerns about giving away the plot. In fact, he argues, it is much better to give readers a quick and clear indication of what is going to be meted out to them and where it is going.

Literature review

More detailed advice on how to go about writing this chapter of your dissertation is given in Chapter 5.

Research methods

The term 'research methods' is meant here as a kind of catch-all for several issues that need to be outlined: your research design; your sampling approach; how access was achieved, if relevant; the procedures you used (e.g. if you sent out a postal questionnaire, if you followed up non-respondents); the nature of your questionnaire, interview schedule, participant observation role, observation schedule, coding frame, or whatever (these will usually appear in an appendix, but you should comment on such things as your style of questioning or observation and why you asked the things you did); problems of non-response; note-taking; issues of ongoing access and co-operation; coding matters; and how you proceeded with your analysis. When discussing each of these issues, you should describe and defend the choices that you made, such as why you used a postal questionnaire rather than a structured interview approach, or why you focused upon a particular population for sampling purposes.

Results

In this chapter you present the bulk of your findings. If you intend to have a separate Discussion chapter, it is likely that the results will be presented with little commentary in terms of the literature or the implications of your findings. If there will be no Discussion chapter, you will need to provide some reflections on the significance of your findings for your research questions and for the literature. Bear these points in mind.

- Whichever approach you take, remember not to include *all* your results. You should present and discuss only those findings that relate to your research questions. This requirement may mean a rather painful process of leaving out many findings, but it is necessary so that the thread of your argument is not lost.

- Your writing should point to particularly salient aspects of the tables, graphs, or other forms of analysis you present. Do not just summarize what a table shows; you should direct the reader to the component or components of it that are especially striking from the point of view of your research questions. Try to ask yourself what story you want the table to convey and try to relay that story to your readers.

- Another sin to be avoided is simply presenting a graph or table or a section of the transcript of a semi-structured interview or focus group session without any comment whatsoever, because the reader is left wondering why you think the finding is important.

- When reporting quantitative findings, it is quite a good idea to vary wherever possible the method of presenting results—for example, provide a mixture of diagrams and tables. However, you must remember the lessons of Chapter 15 concerning the methods of analysis that are appropriate to different types of variable.

- A particular problem that can arise with qualitative research is that students find it difficult to leave out large parts of their data. As one experienced qualitative researcher has put it: 'The major problem we face in qualitative inquiry is not to get data, but to get rid of it!' (Wolcott 1990: 18). He goes on to say that the 'critical task in qualitative research is not to accumulate all the data you can, but to "can" (i.e., get rid of) most of the data you accumulate' (Wolcott 1990: 35). You simply have to recognize that much of the rich data you accumulate will have to be jettisoned. If you do not do this, any sense of an argument in your work is likely to be lost. There is also the risk that your account of your findings will appear too descriptive and lack an analytical edge. This is why it is important to use research questions as a focus and to orient the presentation of your findings to them. It is also important to keep in mind the theoretical ideas and the literature that have framed your work. The theory and literature that have influenced your thinking will also have shaped your research questions.

- If you are writing a thesis, for example for an M.Phil. or Ph.D. degree, it is likely that you will have more than one and possibly several chapters in which you present your results. Cryer (1996) recommends showing at the beginning of each chapter the particular issues that are being examined in the chapter. You should indicate which research question or questions are being addressed in the chapter and provide some signposts about what will be included in the chapter. In the conclusion of the chapter, you should make clear what your results have shown and draw out any links that might be made with the next results chapter.

Discussion

In the Discussion, you reflect on the implications of your findings for the research questions that have driven your research. In other words, how do your results illuminate your research questions? If you have specified hypotheses, the discussion will revolve around whether the hypotheses have been confirmed or not, and, if not, you might speculate about some possible reasons for and the implications of their refutation.

Conclusion

The main points here are as follows:

- A Conclusion is not the same as a summary. However, it is frequently useful to bring out in the opening paragraph of the Conclusion your argument thus far. This will mean relating your findings and your discussion of them to your research questions. Thus, your brief summary should be a means of hammering home to your readers the significance of what you have done. However, the Conclusion should do more than merely summarize.

- You should make clear the implications of your findings for your research questions.

- You might suggest some ways in which your findings have implications for theories relating to your area of interest.

- You might also suggest some ways in which your findings have implications for practice in the field of business and management.

- You might draw attention to any limitations of your research with the benefit of hindsight, but it is probably best not to overdo this element and provide examiners with too much ammunition that might be used against you!

- It is often valuable to propose areas of further research that are suggested by your findings.

- Two things to avoid are engaging in speculations that take you too far away from your data, or that cannot be substantiated by the data, and introducing issues or ideas that have not previously been brought up.

Telling it like it is
The challenges and constraints of length

For many students, the prospect of writing up a single piece of work of between 7000 and 15,000 words in length may at first seem a daunting prospect. However, the experiences of students interviewed for this book suggest that when it comes down to it the challenge is more often about how to keep within these limits. Chris's comments are typical: 'I'd never done a piece of work like this. You know, 3000 or 4000 words was probably as much as I'd written before and, although it was only meant to be 7000 words, it turned out to be 13,000.' Some students found the need to keep to a word limit a real struggle, particularly when presenting qualitative data. Angharad felt that her problems with the word limit were related to the nature of her data. 'I can't represent interview data in a table like other people might be able to do with their research. So the way that I had to write up the research meant that it was going to be over the word count.' Karen also found that her work exceeded the length guidelines provided by her institution, so she tried to cut it down by putting graphs and tables into the appendices, but this had drawbacks because the reader had constantly to keep checking the appendices, and some supervisors may suspect that the student has done this just to get around the word limit. It is therefore important to plan your work carefully and to edit your work if necessary during the revision process. Editing to meet a word limit can also help you to focus on what you really want to say. For example, Tom realized that his first draft was quite descriptive and therefore he could cut out some of this detail, and this left him more space for the analysis.

Note that institutions vary in the extent that they rigorously enforce a word limit, so check with your supervisor to find out if you have an element of discretion about this. But remember, while word limits may be viewed as a nuisance, especially when you feel that you have a lot to say or some really interesting data, they help ensure a level playing field for students, so that everyone has roughly the same amount of space in which to present their ideas and arguments. It is also worth noting that constraints of length apply to all academics, since the norm of writing in scholarly journals requires you to produce papers that are between 6000 and 8000 words in length. So you are being required to conform to similar norms as other business and management researchers.

Appendices

In your appendices you might want to include such things as your questionnaire, coding frame, or observation schedule, letters sent to sample members, and letters sent to and received from gatekeepers where the cooperation of an organization was required.

References

Include here all references cited in the text. For the format of the References section you should follow whichever approach is prescribed by your department.

Nowadays, the format is usually a variation of the Harvard method, such as the one employed for this book.

Finally

Remember to fulfil any obligations you entered into, such as supplying a copy of your dissertation if, for example, your access to an organization was predicated on providing one, and maintaining the confidentiality of information supplied and the anonymity of your informants and other research participants.

Tips and skills
Proofreading your dissertation

Before submitting your dissertation, make sure that it is spellchecked and check it for grammatical and punctuation errors. There are many useful guides and handbooks that can be used for this purpose. It may also be useful to ask someone else, such as a friend or family member, to proofread your work in case there are errors that you have missed. As well as being an important presentational issue, this will affect the ease with which your written work can be read and understood. It therefore has the potential significantly to affect the quality of your dissertation.

Writing up quantitative, qualitative, and mixed methods research

In the next three sections, research-based articles that have been published in journals are examined to detect some helpful features. One is based on quantitative research, one on qualitative research, and another on mixed methods research. The presentation of the quantitative and the qualitative research articles raises the question of whether or not practitioners of the two research strategies employ different writing approaches. It is sometimes suggested that they do, though, when Bryman compared two articles based on research in the sociology of work, he found that the differences were less pronounced than he had anticipated on the basis of reading the literature on the topic (Bryman 1998). One difference that we have noticed is that, in journals, quantitative researchers often give more detailed accounts of their research design, research methods, and approaches to analysis than qualitative researchers. This is surprising, because, in books reporting their research, qualitative researchers provide detailed accounts of these areas. Indeed, the chapters in Part Three of this book rely heavily on these accounts. Wolcott (1990: 27) has also noticed this tendency: 'Our [qualitative researchers'] failure to render full and complete disclosure about our data-gathering procedures give our methodologically orientated colleagues fits.

And rightly so, especially for those among them willing to accept our contributions if we would only provide more careful data about our data.' Being informed that a study was based on a year's participant observation or a number of semi-structured interviews is not enough to gain an acceptance of the claims to credibility that a writer might be wishing to convey.

However, this point aside, although one article based on quantitative research and one based on qualitative research will be examined in the discussion that follows, we should not be too surprised if they turn out to be more similar than might have been expected. In other words, although we might have expected clear differences between the two in terms of their approaches to writing, the similarities are more noticeable than the differences.

In addition to looking at examples of writing in quantitative and qualitative research, we will examine how mixed methods research can be written up and explore some guidelines that are being proffered by practitioners. The approach to dealing with the mixed methods research article is slightly different from the other two in that we will begin with some general suggestions for writing up mixed methods research, as this is an area that has not been given much attention.

An example of quantitative research

To illustrate some of the characteristics of the way quantitative research is written up for academic journals, we will take an article by Coyle-Shapiro and Kessler (2000). We are not suggesting that this article is somehow exemplary or representative, but rather that it exhibits some features that are often regarded as desirable qualities in terms of presentation and structure. The article is a secondary analysis of data from two surveys conducted in a large local-authority government organization, and it was accepted for publication in the *Journal of Management Studies*. The article has the following components, aside from the abstract:

1. introduction;
2. theory and hypotheses;
3. methods;
4. results;
5. discussion.

Introduction

Right at the beginning of the introduction, the opening sentences attempt to grab our attention, to give a clear indication of where the article's focus lies, and to provide an indication of the significance and importance of the subject of study for practitioners, policy-makers, and academics. This is what the authors write:

> The implications of globalization, organizational restructuring and downsizing on employment relations have renewed interest in the concept of the psychological contract. It has captured the attention of policy-makers in their efforts to 'change the deal' in response to increasing pressures to adapt to changing circumstances. For academics, the psychological contract presents another opportunity to re-examine the fundamental aspect of organizational life, the employee–employer relationship.
>
> (2000: 903)

This is an impressive start, because, in just over sixty words, the authors set out what the article is about and persuade us of its significance. Let us look at what each sentence achieves.

- The first sentence locates the article's focus as addressing an important aspect of business and management research that is currently the focus of renewed interest.
- The second sentence notes that the concept of the psychological contract has been used by policy-makers in response to pressure to adapt to changing circumstances.
- The third sentence goes on to suggest that this subject has also been of long-standing interest to academics. This sentence also widens the focus of the article by suggesting that the psychological contract is just one way of looking at the employee–employer relationship.

The rest of the paragraph then hints towards current challenges faced in managing the employment relationship, citing two further sources on this subject and hinting that the psychological contract has been proposed as a potential framework for understanding changes in the employee–employer exchange relationship. So, by the end of this paragraph, the contribution that the article is claiming to make to our understanding of the psychological contract has been outlined and situated within an established literature on the topic. This is quite a powerful start to the article, because the reader knows what the article is about and the particular case the authors are making for their contribution to the literature on the subject.

The authors go on to draw attention to the specific organizational context of their study, highlighting changes in the public sector that have led to increased financial and managerial accountability. Then they set out in much more precise terms exactly what this article will achieve, providing a summary of exactly where the researchers claim their contribution to this subject lies:

> In this study, we set out to examine the content and state of the psychological contract from the employer and employee perspective. The inclusion of the employer's perspective goes some way towards counteracting the exclusive emphasis on the employee perspective adopted in the majority of empirical studies undertaken to date.
>
> (2000: 904)

Notice how the second sentence aims to persuade us that this really is an important contribution to our understanding of this research area. The authors draw attention to a deficiency in existing knowledge (the tendency towards an 'exclusive emphasis on the employee perspective') and tell us that they are going to correct this situation.

This aim is then broken down into three distinct stages:

1. First, 'we explore employees' and managers' perceptions of employer obligations and how well the employer has fulfilled its obligations to its employees (i.e. contract behaviour)';
2. 'Subsequently, we investigate the consequences of perceived employer contract behaviour on employees' perceived organizational support, organizational commitment and organizational citizenship behaviour [OCB]';
3. This then enables examination of 'whether the psychological contract contributes to our understanding of the employee–employer exchange relationship . . .' (2000: 904).

Two important concepts—'contract behaviour' and 'organizational citizenship behaviour [OCB]'—are thereby introduced; the latter is defined as a 'readiness to contribute beyond literal contractual obligations' (Organ 1988: 22, cited in Coyle-Shapiro and Kessler 2000: 910). The authors then go on to review the literature on the psychological contract, from early contributions to recent developments.

Theory and hypotheses

Although this is not presented as a separate section of the paper—in fact it forms an extension of the introduction—it is where existing ideas and research on the topic of the psychological contract are presented; it is thus where the theory that the study builds on is introduced. The authors point to a tendency within the literature to downplay the mutuality in the exchange relationship and the 'near exclusive emphasis on the employee perspective' (2000: 905). They treat managers as agents of the organization and suggest 'their interpretation of the psychological contract may provide one way of capturing the employer's perspective' (2000: 907). The authors suggest that capturing the employer's perspective may add to understanding of employer violation or breach of the psychological contract and go on to cite empirical studies that suggest employer violations of the psychological contract are increasing in frequency. Importantly, they point out that none of the empirical studies has 'examined the relationship between employer contract behaviour and perceived organizational support' (2000: 909). Coyle-Shapiro and Kessler's ruminations on this issue lead them to propose the first of three hypotheses.

- *Hypothesis 1.* 'Fulfilment of the psychological contract by the employer will have a positive effect on employees' perceived organizational support' (2000: 909).

This hypothesis stipulates that fulfilment of the psychological contract by the employer has an impact on employee perception concerning the extent to which the organization values their contributions and cares for their well-being. This leads the researchers to suggest two further related hypotheses.

- *Hypothesis 2a.* 'Fulfilment of the psychological contract by the employer will have a positive effect on employees' commitment to the organization' (2000: 910).

- *Hypothesis 2b.* 'An employee's perception of who their employer is will moderate the relationship between psychological contract fulfilment and organizational commitment' (2000: 910).

Finally, the authors suggest a third hypothesis:

- *Hypothesis 3.* 'Fulfilment of the psychological contract by the employer will have a positive effect on employees' OCB behaviour' (2000: 911).

These three hypotheses suggest a relationship between fulfilment of the psychological contract by the employer—the dependent variable—and employees' perceived organizational support, commitment to the organization, and OCB behaviour, which constitute the independent variables in this study. We thus end up with very clear research questions, which have been arrived at by reflecting on existing ideas and research in this area.

Methods

In this section, the authors outline the methods that were used in conducting the research and provide details about the data that they draw on. They begin by describing the case study organization in which the data for the study were collected. The section then gives a general outline of the datasets and provides details of the sample sizes and response rates for the two questionnaire surveys that were conducted, one of managers and the other of employees. Information about the sample is given, including mean organizational and job tenure, mean age, gender proportions, and average earnings. The section also outlines the different ways in which the relationships between the variables might be conceptualized and discusses the control variables included in the study. The control variables are additional variables that may have an influence on the nature of the relationships between the main variables in the study. The authors then go on to explain how the main variables in their research were measured using a series of psychological scales.

Results

In this section, the authors provide a general description of their findings, which are based on factor analysis (see Chapter 7), and then consider whether or not their hypotheses are supported. In fact, it turns out that hypotheses 1 and 2 are supported, but hypothesis 3, which predicted that contract fulfilment would have a positive effect on OCB, is not supported. In fact, the effect of transactional fulfilment on OCB is found to be negative. The authors then offer a potential explanation that may account for this contrary finding related to the difficulties in conceptualizing OCB, arguing that what is measured in the study as citizenship behaviour and thus discretionary 'may actually be considered in-role behaviours from the employees' viewpoint' (2000: 920). They thus highlight differences in interpretation that OCB is prone to.

Discussion

In this final section, Coyle-Shapiro and Kessler return to the issues that have been driving their investigation. These are the issues they presented in the introduction and theory sections. They begin this section with a strong statement of their findings:

> Our findings suggest that the majority of employees are experiencing contract breach. Furthermore, managers responding as representatives of the employer broadly support this. The extent of perceived employer contract fulfilment has a significant effect on employees' perceived organizational support, organizational commitment and organizational citizenship behaviour.
>
> (2000: 922)

The authors go on to claim that their results are consistent with other empirical studies that suggest violation of the psychological contract, adding that 'our inclusion of the employer's perspective adds significant weight to the findings' (2000: 922).

In the last few paragraphs of the paper, Coyle-Shapiro and Kessler reflect on the implications of their findings for our understanding of the consequences of employer contract behaviour and the nature of the psychological contract, concluding that, 'overall, this study highlights the importance of employer's contract behaviour regarding the fulfilment of specific obligations in affecting employees' attitudes and behaviour' (2000: 923). After drawing attention to some of the limitations of the study, the authors then outline possibilities for further research. Finally, they outline some practical implications of the study, suggesting that 'employers need to take steps to understand employees' perceptions of the content of the psychological contract and from this alter the terms of the contract where circumstances permit' (2000: 925).

Many articles have a section called 'conclusion' in which the kinds of discussion that appear in these last few paragraphs are presented. Regardless of whether there is a separate conclusion or not, a presentation of the main conclusions will invariably be provided.

Lessons

What lessons can be learned from Coyle-Shapiro and Kessler's article? To some extent, these have been alluded to in the course of the above exposition, but they are worth spelling out.

- There is a clear attempt to grab the reader's attention with strong opening statements, which also act as signposts to what the article is about.
- The authors spell out clearly the rationale of their research. This entails pointing to the significance of the psychological contract as a framework for analysis of the employment relationship, highlighting reasons

for renewed interest in this concept, along with the neglect of the employer's perspective in most research.

- The research questions are spelled out in a very specific way. In fact, the authors present hypotheses that are a highly specific form of research question. As noted in Chapter 7, by no means all quantitative research is driven by hypotheses, even though outlines of the nature of quantitative research often imply that it is. Nonetheless, Coyle-Shapiro and Kessler chose to frame their research questions in this form.
- The research methods employed, the nature of the data, the measurement of concepts, the sampling, and the approaches to the analysis of the data are clearly and explicitly summarized.
- The presentation of the findings is orientated very specifically to the questions that drive the research.
- The discussion returns to the research questions and spells out the implications of the findings for them and for the theories examined earlier on in the paper. This is an important element. It is easy to forget that you should think of the research process as closing a circle in which you must return unambiguously to your research questions. There is no point inserting extraneous findings if they do not illuminate your research questions. Digressions of this kind can be confusing to readers, who might be inclined to wonder about the significance of the extraneous findings. In this section there is an attempt to consider the limitations of the study, in addition to its strengths, and to identify possibilities for further research. In addition, because business and management are an applied field of research, it is also common at this stage to draw attention to practical implications that arise from the study.

We also see that there is a clear sequential process moving from the formulation of the research questions through the exposition of the nature of the data and the presentation of the findings to the conclusions. Each stage is linked to and follows on from its predecessor (but see Thinking deeply 29.2). The structure used by Coyle-Shapiro and Kessler is based on a common one employed in the writing-up of quantitative research for academic journals in business and management. Sometimes, there is a separate Theory section that appears between the Introduction and the Data sections. Another variation is that issues of measurement and analysis may appear in separate sections from the one dealing with research methods. Finally, the structure employed by Coyle-Shapiro and Kessler involved just one final section entitled Discussion, in which the authors drew their conclusions, but in other articles these may be treated as separate sections.

Thinking deeply 29.2
An empiricist repertoire?

At this point, it is worth recalling the Chapter 26 discussion of Gilbert and Mulkay's (1984) research on scientists. The authors drew a distinction between an *empiricist repertoire and a contingent repertoire*. The former derived from 'the observation that the texts of experimental papers display certain recurrent stylistic, grammatical and lexical features which appear to be coherently related' (1984: 55–6). We should bear in mind that the same is true of papers written for social science journals. These too display certain features that suggest a degree of inevitability to the outcome of the research. In other words, the reader is given a sense that, in following the rigorous procedures outlined in the article, the researchers logically arrived at their conclusions. The contingent repertoire, with its recognition of the role of the researcher in the production of findings, is far less apparent in scientists' published work. Thus, we have to recognize the possibility that the impression of a series of linked stages leading to an inescapable culmination is to a large extent a reconstruction of events designed to persuade referees (who, of course, use the same tactics themselves) of the credibility and importance of one's findings. This means that the conventions about writing up a quantitative research project, some of which are outlined in this chapter, are in many ways an invitation to reconstruct an investigation in a particular way. The whole issue of the ways in which the writing-up of research represents a means of persuading others of the credibility of one's knowledge claims has been a particular preoccupation among qualitative researchers and has been greatly influenced by the surge of interest in postmodernism (Key concept 17.2). In Key concept 29.3, some of the rhetorical strategies involved in writing up quantitative research are outlined. Three points are worth making about these strategies in the present context. First, they are characteristic of the empiricist repertoire. Secondly, while the writing of qualitative research has been a particular focus since the 1980s (see below), some attention has also been paid to quantitative research. Thirdly, when Bryman (1998) compared the writing of quantitative and qualitative research articles, he found they were not as dissimilar in terms of rhetorical strategies as is sometimes proposed. However, he did find greater evidence of a management metaphor (see Key concept 29.3).

Key concept 29.3
What is a rhetorical strategy in quantitative research?

The rhetorical strategies used by quantitative researchers include the following:

- There is a tendency to remove the researcher from the text as an active ingredient of the research process in order to convey an impression of the objective nature of the findings—that is, as part of an external reality that is independent of the researcher (Gusfield 1976). Woolgar (1988*a*) refers to this as an externalizing device.

- The researcher surfaces in the text only to demonstrate his or her ingenuity in overcoming obstacles (Bazerman 1987; Bryman 1998).

- Key figures in the field are routinely cited to bestow credibility on the research (McCloskey 1985).

- The research process is presented as a linear one to convey an air of inevitability about the findings that are reached (Gusfield 1976).

- Relatively strict rules are followed about what should be reported in published research and how it should be reported (Bazerman 1987).

- The use of a *management* metaphor is common in the presentation of findings in which the researcher is depicted as ingeniously '"designing" research, "controlling" variables, "managing" data, and "generating" tables' (Bryman 1998: 146). See Shapiro (1985–6) and Richardson (1990) on this point.

Note that the first two points are somewhat inconsistent. There is some evidence that disciplines within the social sciences differ in respect of their use of an impersonal style of writing. But it may well also be that it sometimes depends on what the writer is trying to do; for example, sometimes getting across a sense of one's cunning in overcoming practical difficulties can be just as useful as giving a sense of the external nature of the findings. Therefore, sometimes the style of presentation may vary somewhat.

An example of qualitative research

Now we will look at an example of a journal article based on qualitative research. Again, we are not suggesting that the article is exemplary or representative, but that it exhibits some features that are often regarded as desirable qualities in terms of presentation and structure. The article is one that has been referred to in Chapter 19: a study of time use at work by Perlow (1999). The study is based predominantly on ethnographic methods and was published in *Administrative Science Quarterly*, a leading American journal.

The structure runs as follows:

1. introduction;
2. review of the literature;
3. methods;
4. presentation of main themes;
5. discussion;
6. implications.

What is immediately striking about the structure is that it is not dissimilar to that of Coyle-Shapiro and Kessler's (2000) article. Nor should this be all that surprising. After all, a structure that runs

Introduction → Literature review → Research design/ methods → Results → Discussion → Conclusions

is not obviously associated with one research strategy rather than the other. One difference from quantitative research articles is that the presentation of the results and the discussion of them are frequently rather more interwoven in qualitative research articles. We will see this in the case of Perlow's article. As with Coyle-Shapiro and Kessler's article, we will examine the writing in terms of the article's structure.

Introduction

The first two paragraphs give us an immediate sense of what the article is about and where its focus lies. Like Coyle-Shapiro and Kessler, Perlow uses the introduction to locate the article in relation to a subject of wide interest to business and management researchers, referring to the tendency for many workers routinely to work extremely long hours and to suffer as a result. She explains: 'The purpose of this paper is to explore what I refer to as their time famine—their feeling of having too much to do and not enough time to do it—and to question whether this famine must exist' (Perlow 1999: 57).

In the second paragraph, Perlow begins simply by stating what type of workers she intends to focus on: 'I chose to study a group of software engineers in a high-tech corporation' (1999: 57).

She then goes on to outline precisely the position that will be taken in the article:

> Several recent books have described with awe the fast-paced, high-pressure, crisis-filled environment in which software engineers work (Kidder 1981; Moody 1990; Zachary 1994). These authors portray the engineers as heroes for their willingness to work extremely long hours and celebrate the engineers' intensity and total devotion to work. I, in contrast, explore the engineers' actual use of time at work and the impact their use of time has on other individuals and the groups to which individuals belong, which reveals the problematic nature of the current way of using time. Ultimately, I therefore challenge the assumption that the current way of using time, which is so destructive to individuals' lives outside of work, is in the corporation's best interests (Perlow 1995, 1997).
>
> (1999: 57)

Like Coyle-Shapiro and Kessler's, this is a strong introduction. Although it must be noted that for the purpose of this analysis we have been selective in our direct quotation from these two paragraphs, it is useful to look again at what each of these sentences achieves.

- The first sentence introduces a primary theme, the idea of 'time famine', which is the main subject of this article.

- The second sentence provides a specific research focus—the study of software engineers.

- In the four sentences of the final block of text, however, our attention is jolted by the assertions that the author makes in relation to the existing literature. Like Coyle-Shapiro and Kessler, Perlow begins by pointing to a line of research interest in this subject, but interestingly, unlike them, she cites the work of these authors critically, using it to draw the reader's attention to what she is *not* going to do in *this* article. In addition, by highlighting the limitations of the existing literature, Perlow is preparing the reader for delivery of her alternative viewpoint.

- In the penultimate sentence, Perlow claims that, unlike previous studies, this article explores 'engineers' actual use of time', thereby implying her preference for qualitative, ethnographic research.

- The final sentence allows Perlow to elaborate on the argument that she is making, in which she directly contradicts some of the claims made by other writers.

Thus, after around 100 words, the reader has a clear idea of the focus of the research and has been led to anticipate that some of the findings presented within the article are likely to be unsupportive or indeed indirectly critical of existing studies of how people use their time at work. Unlike Coyle-Shapiro and Kessler, Perlow is more forthright in presenting an argument that is sometimes almost polemical in its criticism of other writers for their tendency to glamourize high-pressure work.

Review of the literature

This short section reviews existing theory and research on time use at work. Perlow proposes that the theory and research 'on time use contributes to a partial understanding of both how and why individuals do and should spend their time at work' (1999: 57). This point is important because it enables Perlow to acknowledge, yet also to distance her study from, existing literature in order to be able to develop an alternative theoretical position throughout the remainder of the article. Interestingly, even though this section is relatively short, approximately 600 words, it contains 28 references. Many of these are string references—this means that they are grouped together to

indicate a theoretical association. In contrast, there are only two references in the whole of the two subsequent sections.

Methods

This section covers a number of important issues relating to the methods and the analytical processes used within the study. The author outlines:

- what the organization that the software engineers worked for is like and why it was chosen as the research site for the study;

- how respondents were selected and access negotiated;

- the data sources used, which included participant observation, semi-structured interviews, shadowing, and tracking logs (see Key concept 19.1 and Chapter 27), and how the data were collected;

- the approach to analysing the data; this involved an iterative process of generating inferences that were related to emerging themes.

Presentation of main themes

The chief findings are outlined under separate headings: interdependent work patterns, enactment of work patterns, and effectiveness of work patterns. The presentation of the results is carried out so that there is some discussion of their meaning or significance in such a way as to lead onto the next section, which provides more detailed discussion of them. For example, in the first paragraph of the second main theme, which deals with enactment of work patterns, Perlow writes:

> Two components of the social context help explain why engineers perpetuated this disruptive pattern of interacting. I found that engineers experience both constant pressure to respond to crises and a reward system based on individual heroics. These two components, together, resulted in engineers doing whatever it took to solve the crisis of the moment. When individuals attempted to solve crises at the expense of all else, they frequently interrupted each other, thereby further perpetuating crises and the perceived need for individuals to do whatever it took to solve crises. I refer to this dynamic as the vicious work–time cycle.
>
> (1999: 65)

For all three themes, direct or verbatim quotations from the interview transcripts are used to reinforce or illustrate the analysis, in addition to extracts from time logs and field note observations. As with this direct quote from a project team leader:

'My team's work is less critical to the project, and therefore we get much less attention. This is good because it enables us to work along at our own pace, but we lack that extra push. We can never get the resources we need. It makes it all the harder to succeed.... Management will pay attention if we succeed in the end. But that makes it nearly impossible

to shine. It is all or nothing. We have no visibility along the way. And we lack the support to make sure that we'll make it in the end.'

(Perlow 1999: 67).

This is a common technique in presenting qualitative data but, as illustrated in Thinking deeply 29.4, the presentation of verbatim quotes can take other formats. Through the presentation of themes illustrated by verbatim quotes, the presentation of the results points forward to some themes that are taken up in the following sections and this demonstrates the significance of findings in relation to the previously discussed literature.

Thinking deeply 29.4
Using verbatim quotations from interviews

In presenting their findings, Perlow (1999) uses verbatim interview quotations to illustrate the themes identified in the data. This is a common approach. However, many articles published in North American journals tend to take a slightly different approach. Here, the tone and mode of presenting the findings is very formal and conforms to traditional, mainstream expectations of what a research article should comprise. In particular, there is a 'definite harkening to a more positivistic style' in the presentation of findings, which is associated with a 'generic and impersonal' use of quotations (Adler and Adler 2008: 13, 14). One way in which this is revealed is through presentation of verbatim quotations in a formal manner in tables rather than *en passant*. An example can be found in Table 29.1, which is taken from Maitlis and Lawrence's (2007) multiple case study ethnography of three British orchestras. The article was published in a highly regarded journal and adopts what Adler and Adler (2008) refer to as the 'mainstream ethnography' frame. This can be discerned in the more formalistic tone than is usually encountered in the other writing frames. The article is about how 'sensegiving' takes place in organizations—that is, how leaders and others frame perceptions for others. One of the key themes identified was the competence of the leader, and this theme had three components (referred to as 'first-order concepts', see Key concept 17.10). Maitlis and Lawrence provided 'representative quotations' for each of the three components in a table (see Table 29.1). This style of presenting quotations has become noticeably popular in some leading journals. It is likely that there are several reasons for this: the provision of a table provides a sense of something equivalent to the more commonly encountered table summarizing the results of a statistical procedure; it provides a more formal style in keeping with the prevalent tone of such journals; and possibly it gives less of a sense that the quotations are anecdotal or 'cherry-picked'.

Corden and Sainsbury (2006) conducted research into qualitative researchers' use of such quotations. They found that researchers employ verbatim quotations for interview transcripts for a variety of reasons, such as to illustrate a point; to give voice to participants; to provide evidence; or to deepen readers' understanding. When Corden and Sainsbury examined a wide range of publications in the social policy field, they found a wide variety of approaches to the use of quotations. There was a great deal of variety in how those quoted are referred to and in editing conventions, such as the removal of 'er' and 'erm' and of false starts, as well as whether pauses or laughter are indicated. Thus, there is a wide variety of practice in the use of verbatim quotations. Corden and Sainsbury recommend that researchers should decide which approach they want to use and why and be able to justify the choice made if necessary.

Table 29.1

The use of verbatim interview quotations in a table

Data Supporting the Theme 'Perceptions of a Lack of Leader Competence'

Associated First-Order Concepts	Representative Quotations
Poor organizational decision process	2.1 '[The associate leader] expressed concern over the lack of information from the office and wondered whether enough was being done to seek out potential leaders to work with the orchestra.' (minutes, BSO orchestra committee meeting) (BSO5)
	2.2 Commenting on the appointment decision process for an orchestra leader: 'It's one incredible grey area. Nobody seems to know what's happening with that and no one seems to know whose responsibility it is . . . . Eventually, the principals just made it so clear that basically they weren't happy [that the appointment was not made] . . . . But we have a theory that he may have promised the guy the job first, and got himself into a pickle.' (interview, BSO orchestra committee member) (BSO5)
	2.3 Commenting on a decision not to terminate a player, a LSO player board member commented: 'There was a decision over this player. The vote was taken and it went against the wishes of the chairman, and he said, "Well okay, we'll call a council of principals meeting" . . . . Most of the principals are more than happy to sit on the fence. They've got a hard enough job. They don't want to put their oar in and stir things up, so of course the vote went the other way. Now I think that's a misuse of power, if you like. You're widening the goal posts and moving them at the same time. I was more than a little pissed off about that because it didn't seem to be fair. What was the point of having a [board]?' (interview, LSO player board member) (LSO5)
Poor outcomes of leader decision making	2.4 'Programming is [the senior producer]—you couldn't ask for better repertoire. [The senior producer] is very successful. He has organized some very good programmes and concerts.' (interview, BSO player) (BSO1)
	2.5 'Looking back on all this. I would say that those judgments [of the chief executive] were fatally flawed for our organization on two counts: [the principal conductor's] availability and commitment, and his financial cost.' (interview, PSO player director) (PSO2)
	2.6 'It was like lambs to the slaughter. The contract [the principal conductor] was offered should never have been accepted.' (interview, PSO deputy CEO) (PSO2)
	2.7 'If you look at the main [home city] concerts, something has happened there, and we've lost our thread, because we had three distinct series . . . . So I think the [PSO], represented by the board and the senior management, has a duty to make sure that the repertoire actually fulfils the artistic strategy.' (interview, PSO player chairman-elect) (PSO1)
Lack of leader expertise	2.8 '[We need] someone who knows what they're doing, who has sufficient commercial grasp to know the effect of what they're doing, and appreciates the need to create a programme for [the PSO home city] that will also apply in [other regional towns]. It's that thorough vision that is lacking at the moment, causing all sorts of orchestral problems.' (interview, PSO finance director) (PSO1)
	2.9 'You have someone here [the chief executive] who has no understanding of orchestras at all.' (observation, musicians' union representative, PSO players meeting with musicians' union) (PSO6)

Source: Maitlis and Lawrence (2007: 67); reproduced with permission.

Discussion

This section discusses the findings in the light of the study's research questions about how people use time at work. The results are also related to many of the ideas introduced in the previous sections of the article, in particular to the notions of the 'vicious work–time cycle', which the author suggests is reinforced by 'individual heroics'. However, in this section the author takes these ideas in a more ambitious direction, suggesting that the emerging 'framework' lays the 'foundation' for development of 'a sociology of work time' that 'integrates components from several existing streams of research' (1999: 77). To support this claim she draws on the work of a number of highly regarded sociologists of work time (including D. Roy 1958 and Zerubavel 1981) and calls for a structuration approach (Giddens 1979) to writing work ethnographies (see Research in focus 2.1 for a summary of structuration theory). 'Researchers would consider simultaneously the role that these interdependent patterns play in the work process and both the social and temporal contexts that perpetuate and are perpetuated by these patterns' (Perlow 1999: 77–8).

Implications

In this section, the author spells out the implications of the research, which are claimed to be practical as well as theoretical in nature. To this end, Perlow suggests that the 'vicious circle' may be changed into a 'virtuous circle' through the actions of managers. She states: 'instead of interruptions perpetuating crises, reactive behaviour, and long work hours, synchronizing individual and interactive activities may minimize crises, perpetuate proactive behaviour, and even reduce the demand for such long work hours' (1999: 79). Thus, similarly to Coyle-Shapiro and Kessler, Perlow rounds off the article by drawing attention to the relevance of the findings for those who manage. The final sentence returns to the primary theme of 'time famine' and reiterates the main findings of the study in order to drive home this point: to mitigate the time famine experienced by employees whose

> work involves both individual and interactive activities a new type of collective time management is needed—one that takes into account individuals' interdependent work patterns, the macro context in which they work, and the interconnections between this context and their work patterns.
>
> (1999: 80)

Lessons

As with Coyle-Shapiro and Kessler's article, it is useful to review some of the lessons learned from this examination of Perlow's article.

- As in the illustration of quantitative research writing, there are strong opening sentences, which attract our

attention and give a clear indication of the nature and content of the article.

- The rationale of the research is clearly identified. To a large extent, this revolves around noting the limitations of existing literature that celebrates heroic attitudes towards time use at work and challenging the assumption that this is in either the individual's or the organization's interests.

- Research questions are specified, but they are somewhat more open-ended than in Coyle-Shapiro and Kessler's article, which is in keeping with the general orientation of qualitative researchers. The research questions revolve around the engineers' use of time at work and the impact that this has on other individuals and groups to which the engineers belong.

- The research methods are outlined, and an indication is given of the approach to analysis. The section in which these issues are discussed demonstrates greater transparency than is sometimes the case with articles reporting qualitative research.

- The presentation of main themes is geared to the broad research questions that motivated the researcher's interest in time use at work. However, this section also represents a major opportunity for the idea of the vicious work–time cycle and its dimensions to be articulated. The inductive nature of qualitative research means that the concepts and theories that are generated from an investigation must be clearly identified and discussed, as in this case.

- The discussion section allows concepts and theories to be developed into a more general framework, which is used to characterize the present study in the context of other qualitative studies of work time.

- The implications elucidate in a more specific way the significance of these results for managers, thereby addressing a requirement that is specifically made of business researchers to highlight the practical relevance of research findings.

 # An example of mixed methods research

Partly because interest in and the practice of mixed methods research has gained momentum only since the turn of the century, it has few if any writing conventions. More particularly, it is difficult to say what an

exemplary or model mixed methods research journal article might look like. To a certain extent, it is bound to borrow some of the conventions associated with writing up quantitative and qualitative research in terms of needing to start out with a research focus in the sense of a research problem and/or some research questions. Creswell and Tashakkori (2007: 108), the editors of the *Journal of Mixed Methods Research*, have suggested that 'good original/empirical mixed methods articles' should be:

- 'well-developed in both quantitative and qualitative components' (2007: 108); and
- 'more than reporting two distinct "strands" of quantitative and qualitative research; these studies must also integrate, link, or connect these "strands" in some way' (2007: 108).

They actually add a third feature of good mixed methods articles—namely, that they contribute to the literature on mixed methods research in some way. This seems a rather tall order for many writers and researchers, so that we would tend to emphasize the other two features.

The first implies that the quantitative and the qualitative components of a mixed methods article should be at the very least competently executed. This means that, in terms of the fundamental criteria for conducting good quantitative and good qualitative research, mixed methods research should conform to both quantitative and qualitative research criteria. In terms of writing, it means that, for each of the components, it should be clear what the research questions were, how the sampling was done, what the data collection technique(s) was or were, and how the data were analysed.

The second feature implies that a good mixed methods article will be more than the sum of its parts. This issue relates to a tendency that has been identified by some writers (e.g. Bryman 2007c; O'Cathain, Murphy, and Nicholl 2007) for some mixed methods researchers not to make the best use of their quantitative and qualitative data, in that they often do not link the two sets of findings so that they extract the maximum yield from their study. As Creswell and Tashakkori (2007) put it:

> The expectation is that, by the end of the manuscript, conclusions gleaned from the two strands are integrated to provide a fuller understanding of the phenomenon under study. Integration might be in the form of comparing, contrasting, building on, or embedding one type of conclusion with the other.
>
> (2007: 108)

To some extent, when writing up the results from a mixed methods study, researchers might make it easier for themselves to get across the extra yield associated with their investigations if they make clear their rationales for including both quantitative and qualitative components in their overall research strategy. The issue of rationales for conducting mixed methods research is one that was addressed in Chapter 27.

Further advice on writing up mixed methods research can be found in suggestions in Creswell and Plano Clark's (2007: 161) delineation of a structure for a mixed methods journal article. They suggest that the structure should be along the following lines:

- *Introduction*. This would include such features as: a statement of the research problem or issue; an examination of the literature on the problem/issue; an examination of the problems with the prior literature, which might include indicating why a mixed methods approach would be beneficial, perhaps because much of the previous research is based mainly on just quantitative or qualitative research; and the specific research questions.
- *Methods*. This would include such features as: indicating the rationale for the mixed methods approach; the type of mixed methods design (see, for example, Morgan's classification of approaches to mixed methods research in Chapter 27); data collection and data analysis methods; and indications of how the quality of the data can be judged.
- *Results*. The quantitative and the qualitative findings might be presented either in tandem or sequentially, but, if the latter, they would need to be merged in the Discussion.
- *Discussion*. Summarize and explain results, emphasizing the significance of the mixed methods nature of the research and what is gained from the presence of both quantitative and qualitative findings; draw attention to any limitations of the investigation; and possibly suggest avenues for future research.

In terms of the overall structure, Creswell and Plano Clark's (2007) suggestions are more or less the same as for an article based on quantitative research or an article based on qualitative research (see above). It is in the need to outline the mixed methods nature of the research and to bring the two sets of findings together that the distinctiveness of a mixed methods journal article can be discerned.

Many of these features can be seen in the study of organizational culture in Russia and the USA by Fey and Denison (2003). This article has previously been encountered in Research in focus 10.1. The following examination of the writing of this article is organized in terms of its structure.

Tips and skills
Do not separate your quantitative from your qualitative findings

We have noticed that some students who conduct mixed methods investigations treat their quantitative and qualitative findings as separate domains, so that they present one set and then the other. In Ph.D. theses and Master's dissertations, this can take the form of separate chapters labelled something like 'survey findings' and 'qualitative interview findings'. This may not be a problem if the two (or more) sets of findings are then integrated in the Discussion sections or chapters. However, treating findings in this way does tend to encourage a view of the quantitative and the qualitative findings as separate spheres and may therefore militate against integration, which, as writers like Creswell and Tashakkori (2007) imply, is increasingly an expectation in mixed methods studies. Instead, try to think of the quantitative and the qualitative findings thematically across the two sets of results, so that the findings are presented in terms of substantive issues rather than in terms of different methods.

Introduction

The article begins with a very strong and clear statement of the focus of the article:

> Many organizational researchers have examined corporate culture as a source of competitive advantage (Barney 1986, Ott 1989, Pfeffer 1994, Wilkins and Ouchi 1983), but explicit theories are few and empirical evidence is limited (Denison and Mishra 1995). The theories that do exist (Denison 1990, Kotter and Heskett 1992, O'Reilly 1989) have been developed and applied only in the United States. Scholars focusing on the applicability of American management theories abroad (Adler 1991; Boyacigiller and Adler 1991; Hofstede 1980a, 1993; Lammers and Hickson 1979) have asked, 'Is organization science, as it is currently conceived, applicable across countries?' and 'To what extent must organizational theorizing be modified due to national differences?' (Boyacigiller et al. 2003, p. 17). This paper contributes to the ongoing debate by presenting a study of organizational culture and effectiveness that focuses on a set of foreign-owned firms operating in Russia. The study also compares the Russian results to results previously obtained in the United States. Russia merits study for several reasons.
>
> (Fey and Denison 2003: 686)

This opening passage accomplishes the following:

- It explains more or less immediately what the article is about.

- It makes clear what the contribution of the article will be to our understanding of organizational culture.

- It locates the authors' work within an established literature on its subject matter, including a reference to Hofstede, whose work has been mentioned on several occasions in this book.

- It makes clear why it is important to compare US studies with those of other nations.

- It justifies the use of Russian companies as the point of comparison in the second paragraph.

In the third paragraph, the authors provide an account of the structure of the article that provides a route map for the reader.

The Russian context

In this section, the authors critically appraise and summarize some of the principal studies that relate to Russia, especially those findings that are particularly relevant to the article's focus on organizational culture.

Organizational culture and effectiveness

Here, the authors examine some of the literature on the relationship between organizational culture and effectiveness, which entails spelling out a model of organizational culture in which the four 'cultural traits' that they focus on—adaptability, mission, consistency, and involvement—are introduced. They also outline the mixed methods nature of the study, explaining that a quantitative study will be conducted to test the model and a qualitative, inductive study will be carried out to 'ground the concepts' (Fey and Denison 2003: 689). They then provide a clear rationale for their use of a mixed methods approach:

> Using two approaches simultaneously allowed us to go back and forth between them to gain a better understanding of what was 'behind the numbers' and to develop a better picture of areas where the concepts had a different meaning in Russia than in the United States.
>
> (2003: 689)

In this way, the reader has a clear sense of why both quantitative and qualitative research are employed in this research and what its contribution might be to understanding the organizational culture-effectiveness relationship.

Research questions

In this section the authors specify their research questions and how they relate to their use of a mixed methods approach. The research questions are:

> Research Question 1. To what extent are involvement, consistency, adaptability, and mission associated with the effectiveness of firms in Russia? . . . Research Question 2. What is the specific pattern between the four traits and various criteria of effectiveness in Russia? How does the pattern in Russia differ from the pattern in the United States? Do the traits of adaptability and involvement have a stronger impact in Russia than they do in the United States? . . . Research Question 3. What are the patterns of behavior that illustrate the concepts in the model in Russia? Which patterns of behavior are similar to those that might be observed in the United States? Which patterns of behavior are different from those that might be observed in the United States? What are some of the underlying forces that drive these different patterns of behavior?
>
> (2003: 689)

The authors explain that the first two research questions are to be examined through a quantitative study of 179 firms, while the third will be examined through 4 case studies.

Testing the model: a comparative study

This section comprises two distinct subsections: one dealing with the study's research methods for the survey element and the other with the ensuing results.

Methodology

The authors explain that the population for their survey study was all foreign-owned firms in Russia in October 1997. They explain how the firms were sampled and how questionnaires to the firms were administered. They also observe that the findings are based on 179 usable questionnaires, a response rate of 37 per cent. They tell us about their various measures, in particular that the measures of organizational culture are based on the Denison Organizational Culture Survey. It is precisely because this had been used in studies of US companies that the comparison with Russian findings can be forged.

Results

The authors analyse the Russian findings and compare these to the US findings. In fact, they find clear differences between the two. In Russia, adaptability and involvement were the cultural dimensions most closely correlated with effectiveness, whereas, among the US firms, it was mission. Involvement was also related to effectiveness in the USA, but this was less pronounced than among the Russian firms.

Taking a closer look: four case studies

The authors point out that, while the survey data suggest that the cultural traits developed in the US context appear to be broadly relevant, 'it could be a mistake to assume that the concepts have the same *meaning* in the Russian context as they do in the US environment. For example, empowerment [a dimension of involvement] may be important in both contexts, but empowerment may entail very different behaviors in the two contexts' (2003: 695; emphasis in original).

Case study methods

The authors outline their strategy for selecting the four case study firms. For example, they explain that, in order to control for national culture, they selected the four firms from the thirteen Swedish-owned companies among the sample of 179 firms. They also inform us that ten interviews were conducted in each firm and they describe the thinking behind the development of the interview guide they employed.

Four case studies: general background

The authors describe the four firms in terms of their activities and history.

Grounding the model in the Russian context

The authors begin by presenting the quantitative survey findings for each of the four companies and also some additional survey information collected specifically for the multiple-case study element of the research. Here the authors outline how the four cultural traits were perceived by their Russian interviewees. They note that the qualitative findings mirror the quantitative ones, because their interviewees gave a lot more examples of the significance of adaptability and involvement for their firms' effectiveness than of the other two traits.

Understanding organizational culture in the Russian context

In this section, the authors note that some qualitative findings had a good fit with the Western-based model they had previously developed for the US context and some had a weaker fit; they then go on to examine what they call the 'cultural dynamics' behind these contrasting results. At the end of this section they make a particularly interesting observation:

> The case studies highlight an interesting distinction between the behaviors that illustrate the concepts in the model and are similar to what one might observe in firms in the West and those behaviors that illustrate the concepts, but are very different from what one might observe in a firm in the West. This distinction is very helpful because it illustrates that the concepts may travel fairly well, helping to account for the quantitative support for the model, but that the specific patterns of behavior that exemplify the concepts may vary quite a bit across cultures.
>
> (2003: 701)

In other words, they suggest that the quantitative data tell only part of the story. The meaning of some of the cultural concepts are different for the interviewees in Russia, although the quantitative data suggest that, on the face of it, those same concepts are broadly applicable and relevant. There is a cautionary tale where cross-cultural studies are concerned about assuming 'sameness' when an underlying 'differentness' may be the reality.

Discussion

The authors begin this final section with a concise summary of their main findings. They gradually move on to discuss some of the broader implications of their findings, drawing attention at one point to the contribution and significance of using both quantitative and qualitative research:

> The novel combination of qualitative and quantitative methods used in this study will also be of interest to organizational researchers. The study began by using an existing model of organizational culture and effectiveness as a starting point for the research. The first part of the study presented a quantitative test of the model and showed that the model was useful in understanding effectiveness, but that the results were somewhat different from the results for a sample of US firms. The quantitative results were used as probes to inform our research questions rather than tools to refute falsifiable hypotheses. The second part of the study selected four firms for in-depth qualitative analysis. These case studies generated a number of examples that served to ground the theoretical concepts in the realities of the Russian context. The case studies offered examples that fit well with the model, but also highlighted themes that were invaluable in understanding the realities of the Russian context but were not fully anticipated by the model.
>
> (2003: 701)

In this way, Fey and Denison articulate the contribution made by a mixed methods approach (though they do not use the term) in arriving at a more complete and more nuanced understanding of the relationship between organizational culture and effectiveness in the Russian context. In the last sentence of the article they go further when they write: 'Combining these insights enabled us to both validate the model and to provide a more complete understanding of the dynamics of organizational cultures in the Russian context' (Fey and Denison 2003: 702). Thus, in their Discussion section, the authors make clear what the contribution of their research is to understanding the relationship between organizational culture; in particular there is an implicit warning that one should be wary of presuming the cultural generalizability of Western models of organizations. The final sentence provides a clear and striking message for the reader to take away. The message is partly substantive—to do with not assuming the applicability of Western models—and partly methodological—to do with the need to employ quantitative and qualitative findings to provide more comprehensive portrayals of complex organizational issues.

Lessons

One feature of this article that is striking is that in terms of structure and overall approach it is quite similar to the quantitative and the qualitative research articles previously examined. Indeed, we have noted that the qualitative research article was not dissimilar to the quantitative one. In large part, these similarities can be attributed to the fact that there are general conventions about how findings should be written up for academic audiences, and these conventions act as a template for, and to some extent restrict, much academic writing. What is striking about the article by Fey and Denison is their inclination to make as much of the mixed methods status and context of their research as possible, as recommended in the guidelines suggested by Creswell and Plano Clark (2007). On the face of it, this article seems to go against the advice in Tips and Skill 'Do not separate your quantitative from your qualitative findings', in that the two sets of results appear to be presented in different sections. However, Fey and Denison do align their qualitative findings to some of their survey data at the beginning of the section in which they present their case study results. Also, they constantly cross-refer between the two sets of results in both the

discussion of the case studies and in the Discussion. In fact, the main message of the article is that it would have been misleading if just the survey findings had been at their disposal, since the qualitative case studies strongly suggest that the understanding of the diffusion of the Western model of organizational culture needs to take into account local understandings of cultural traits, and these are best explored through in-depth probing through qualitative research.

While attention to the writing-up of mixed methods research is an area that is in its infancy, the suggestions of writers mentioned above such as Creswell and Tashakkori (2007) and Creswell and Plano Clark (2007), along with strong exemplars such as the article by Fey and Denison, provide helpful pointers to the ways in which this task should be approached. Fey and Denison meet the emerging expectations of good mixed methods research and writing, as outlined above and in Chapter 27, in that they

- are explicit about how the different components of the research were executed;

- are clear about why a mixed methods study was conducted;

- explain the nature of their research questions and the connection between these and a mixed methods approach;

- show what was gained by doing a mixed methods study;

- integrate the different elements of their research.

 # Reflexivity

It is an increasing expectation (especially, but by no means exclusively, among qualitative researchers) that researchers display a degree of reflexivity in their research writing. Reflexivity has several meanings in the social sciences. The term is employed by ethnomethodologists to refer to the way in which speech and action are constitutive of the social world in which they are located; in other words, they do more than merely act as indicators of deeper phenomena (see Chapter 22). The other meaning of the term carries the connotation that business researchers should reflect on the implications of their methods, values, biases, and decisions for the knowledge of the social world they generate and should try to be aware of how personal idiosyncrasies and implicit

assumptions affect their approach to study. Reflexivity also entails sensitivity to the researcher's cultural, political, and social context. As such, knowledge from a reflective position is always based on the researcher's location in time and social space. Also, unlike reflection, which takes place after the interaction or activity has passed, reflexivity is exercised in the moment as well as afterwards. However, most importantly, according to Riach (2009: 359), reflexivity 'requires a fundamental requestioning of what is knowable in a given context'. This notion is especially explicit in Pink's (2001) formulation of a reflexive approach to analysing visual images (see Chapter 19) and in Plummer's (2001) definition of a reflexive approach to life histories (see Chapter 20).

Reflexivity is related to the concept of postmodernism (Key concept 17.2), which in one sense can be seen as a form of sensitivity—a way of seeing and understanding that results in a questioning of the taken-for-granted. Postmodernism questions the very notion of the dispassionate social scientist seeking to uncover a pre-given external reality. As a result, 'knowledge' of the social world is relative; any account is just one of many possible ways of rendering social reality.

There has been growing evidence of reflexivity in organizational research in the form of an industry of books that collect together inside stories of the research process, detailing the nuts and bolts of research as distinct from the often sanitized portrayal in research articles. Reflexivity encourages greater awareness and acknowledgement of the role of the researcher as part of the construction of knowledge. In other words, the reflexive attitude is highly critical of the notion that the researcher extracts knowledge from observations and conversations with others and then transmits knowledge to an audience. Instead, the researcher is viewed as implicated in the construction of knowledge through the stance that he or she assumes in relation to the observed and through the ways in which an account is transmitted in the form of a text. This entails an acknowledgement of the implications and significance of the researcher's choices as both observer and writer. An explanation of different forms of reflexivity in business and management research is offered by Johnson and Duberley (2003), who differentiate between three forms. The form assumed depends upon the epistemological and ontological assumptions that guide the researcher.

- *Methodological reflexivity* stems from an objectivist view of ontology (see Key concept 2.11, which holds that social phenomena exist independently of social actors. Objectivism seeks to find a way of recording social phenomena in a way that is neutral, by ensuring that the social phenomena remain unaffected by the research. It is also related to a positivist epistemology (see Key concept 2.7) and also to empiricism (see Key concept 2.3), which both share a commitment to generating knowledge based on an observable reality. Methodological reflexivity therefore involves monitoring the behavioural impact of the researcher's actions on the social setting under investigation and detailing the nature of these effects in research writing.

- *Deconstructive reflexivity* arises from a constructionist ontological view (see Key concept 2.12), which presupposes that social phenomena are produced through social interactions involving social actors. This is often associated with an interpretative epistemology (see Key concept 2.9), which holds that the study of social phenomena involves trying to understand how social actors understand their behaviour. It also relates to the role of postmodernism, discussed in this chapter, in challenging existing conventions about how language is used to represent reality and invites the deconstruction of texts in order to reveal their narrative logic. The implications for reflexivity are significant, suggesting that the author must decentre him- or herself as a privileged voice within the narrative, instead allowing multiple voices to appear and disrupt each other. Deconstructive reflexivity therefore entails the researcher questioning his or her own taken-for-granted beliefs and accepting that there will always be multiple valid accounts of a research project.

- *Epistemic reflexivity* also relates to constructionism and interpretivism, but it goes further than deconstructive reflexivity in seeking out new modes of engagement with research subjects that are more amenable to the co-creation of knowledge through the adoption of more participatory approaches (Chapter 17, 'Researcher–subject relationships'). However, unlike deconstructive reflexivity, epistemic reflexivity retains the hope that some notion of truth can be attained through consensus based on engagement with research subjects. It is, therefore, more closely aligned with critical realism (see Key concept 2.8).

Writing academically

To conclude, as the preceding examples have hopefully made clear, in writing up business research it is important to write in a way that follows the conventions of logic, argumentation, and style that are associated with academic writing. Thinking deeply 29.5 provides some additional advice on how to write academically. One thing that can be noticed about Daft's (1995) list of reasons for rejecting academic manuscripts is that he makes little distinction between papers based on quantitative or qualitative methods, suggesting that they are evaluated according to similar conventions. These conventions, according to Czarniawska (1999), form part of the logico-scientific genre, which, as the dominant system of action in business and management research, has become institutionalized and made recognizable through repetition. They can be recognized as scientific because of the devices they use to indicate logical reasoning based on logical propositions. Genre boundaries define how texts should be constructed and impose constraints on the writing style that is adopted. The three examples of quantitative (Coyle-Shapiro and Kessler 2000), qualitative (Perlow 1999), and mixed methods (Fey and Denison 2003) research which we have analysed in this chapter are illustrative of the logico-scientific genre to which Czarniawska refers.

However, logico-scientific writing also uses aspects of storytelling, using literary devices, such as metaphor as well as rhetoric (which was mentioned at the start of this chapter), to engage the reader and convince them of the importance of the research subject and the rightness of the argument. Czarniawska (1990) likens this to a detective story, which, like academic writing, is written in the form of a problem or puzzle that needs to be solved. The central characters, the detective and the researcher, are often invisible narrators of the story who are called upon to investigate a situation and find a solution. As with any form of storytelling, it is vital to write in a way which is engaging and interesting in order to grab the reader's attention, but at the same time to retain the specificity and precision that is the hallmark of good academic writing. This task is made easier if you are researching something which interests you. The vast range of business-related research topics that can be studied, and the importance of business and management related topics in our lives today, means you should have much to choose from.

Thinking deeply 29.5
How to write academically

In an attempt to make the tacit rules of journal publishing more explicit, Daft (1995) draws upon his own experiences of writing papers and submitting them to journals. He lists 11 common manuscript problems based on analysis of 111 of his own reviews of manuscripts submitted to North American journals that took a traditional theory-based, hypothesis-testing approach. The common types of problems identified were:

- *No theory*: this involves a lack of explanation of the relationships among variables—'without a theory, there is nothing to pull the study together, nothing to justify why the variables should be studied' (1995: 167).

- *Concepts and operationalization not in alignment*: this problem occurs when the research design does not reflect the variables under study, sometimes because of differences in level of analysis. An example of this might involve using fluctuations in the number of employees in an organization as a measure of organizational change.

- *Insufficient definition—theory*: this occurs when authors do not explain what their concepts mean, since enacting a definition is often a part of theory development.

- *Insufficient rationale—design*: this problem arises when manuscripts fail to explain the procedures or methods used in the study, such as sample size or response rates, in sufficient detail.

- *Macrostructure—organization and flow*: this refers to whether or not the various parts of the paper, such as theory section, methods, and conclusions, fit together into a coherent whole. Problems arise when manuscripts contain measures in the results section that are not referred to in the theory section or when conclusions are reached that are not related to the paper's research questions.

- *Amateur style and tone*: indications of amateurism, according to Daft (1995: 170), include 'frequent use of underlining or exclamation marks'; exaggerating the importance of the research topic in order to make the case for publication; or tearing down the work of others to justify the author's own study rather than showing how it builds on previous work.

- *Inadequate research design*: this involves the inappropriate use of methods that cannot address the research question posed by the study, such as the use of an undergraduate student sample to analyse the selection of business strategies by corporate executives, as undergraduate students have little or no experience of strategy selection. These often constitute a fatal problem which cannot be put right after the study has been conducted.

- *Overengineering*: sometimes authors concentrate so much on the methodology that it becomes an end in itself, at the expense of making a theoretical contribution.

- *Conclusions not in alignment*: this problem involves manuscripts where conclusions are too short or lack sufficient interpretation of the findings, as well as manuscripts which generalize far beyond the data; 'the important thing is to use the conclusion section to fully develop the theoretical contribution and to point out the new understanding from the study' (1995: 173).

Daft suggests that papers based on qualitative research studies are prone to similar shortcomings as quantitative papers, especially in relation to lack of theory and misalignment of concepts and operationalization. Qualitative papers were often rejected 'not because referees did not like qualitative research, but because the investigators had not used the manuscript to build theory' (1995: 174).

He then goes on to suggest ways of overcoming these common problems, or what you can do to lessen the likelihood of having your manuscript rejected. His suggestions include:

- *Tell a story*. Think of each **variable** in the research as a character and explain how the characters interact with each other. This will give meaning to the observed relationships between variables.

- *Discuss fully your procedures and thought processes*. Be open about weaknesses and limitations, because it gives reviewers confidence that you are not hiding anything.

- *Concentrate on the macrostructure*. Make sure that all sections of the paper are coordinated and flow logically from one to another.

- *Find the operational base of your research and stick to it*. Think of the research design as the core of an empirical paper, to which the theory, results, and discussion correspond.

- *Don't exaggerate*. It is better to be cautious in your argument than to overstate your claims. Avoid statements like 'these findings prove' and instead say 'these findings suggest'.

While these comments and suggestions relate to writing papers for academic journals, much of this advice is relevant to anyone writing for an academic audience, including students.

Telling it like it is
Using direct quotations to enhance confidence and demonstrate reflexivity

When students reach the stage of writing up qualitative research, they can find the previous work that they have done in recording the comments of research participants in their own words extremely valuable when presenting their findings. Karen found that, when she was writing up her research project, the ability to include direct quotations based on the detailed notes she had taken during interviews was invaluable and that this enhanced her dissertation. Similarly, Angharad described how 'quite often there was a good quote or just a word that summed it up really well that I could use from the data'. A direct quotation from a research participant can help to convey the views of people being studied in a way that is engaging and interesting. Direct quotations can also enhance the perceived trustworthiness of the research project by enabling the researcher to provide an example from the data that illustrates the theoretical point that he or she is trying to make. They can also help convince the reader that a methodical and thorough approach to data collection and analysis has been adopted. Direct quotations can also help the researcher to demonstrate reflexivity and awareness of researcher–subject relationships, by showing that he or she has been aware of the power relations between the researcher and the people being studied, and has sought to deal with this by 'giving voice' to participants in a way that is not mediated by his or her own interpretations. Of course, the process of selecting a direct quotation and any subsequent process of analysis does involve the researcher in imposing meaning, but this does not mean that the use of direct quotations has no value.

Checklist

Issues to consider for writing up a piece of research

○ Have you clearly specified your research questions?

○ Have you clearly indicated how the literature you have read relates to your research questions?

○ Is your discussion of the literature critical and organized so that it is not just a summary of what you have read?

○ Have you clearly outlined your research design and your research methods? This includes:

  ○ why you chose a particular research design;

  ○ why you chose a particular research method;

  ○ how you selected your research participants;

  ○ if there were any issues to do with cooperation (e.g. response rates);

  ○ why you implemented your research in a particular way (e.g. how the interview questions relate to your research questions, why you observed participants in particular situations, why your focus group guide asked the questions in a particular way and order);

  ○ if your research required access to an organization, how and on what basis was agreement for access forthcoming;

  ○ steps you took to ensure that your research was ethically responsible;

  ○ how you analysed your data;

  ○ any difficulties you encountered in the implementation of your research approach.

○ Have you presented your data in a manner that relates to your research questions?

○ Does your discussion of your findings show how they relate to your research questions?

○ Does your discussion of your findings show how they shed light on the literature that you presented?

○ Are the interpretations of your data that you offer fully supported with tables, figures, or segments from transcripts?

○ If you have presented tables and/or figures, are they properly labelled with a title and number?

○ If you have presented tables and/or figures, are they commented upon in your discussion?

○ Do your conclusions clearly allow the reader to establish what your research contributes to the literature?

○ Have you explained the limitations of your study?

    ○ Do your conclusions consist solely of a summary of your findings? If they do, rewrite them!

    ○ Do your conclusions make clear the answers to your research questions?

    ○ Does your presentation of the findings and the discussion allow a clear argument and narrative to be presented to the reader?

    ○ Have you broken up the text in each chapter with appropriate subheadings?

    ○ Does your writing avoid sexist, racist, and disablist language?

    ○ Have you included all appendices that you might need to provide (e.g. interview schedule, letters requesting access, communications with research participants)?

    ○ Have you checked that your list of references includes *all* the items referred to in your text?

    ○ Have you checked that your list of references follows precisely the style that your institution requires?

    ○ Have you followed your supervisor's suggestions when he or she has commented on your draft chapters?

    ○ Have you got people other than your supervisor to read your draft chapters for you?

    ○ Have you checked to ensure that there is not excessive use of jargon?

    ○ Do you provide clear signposts in the course of writing, so that readers are clear about what to expect next and why it is there?

    ○ Have you ensured that your institution's requirements for submitting projects are fully met in terms of such issues as word count (so that it is neither too long nor too short) and whether or not an abstract and table of contents are required?

    ○ Have you ensured that you do not quote excessively when presenting the literature?

    ○ Have you fully acknowledged the work of others so that you cannot be accused of plagiarism?

    ○ Is there a good correspondence between the title of your project and its contents?

    ○ Have you acknowledged the help of others where this is appropriate (e.g. your supervisor, people who may have helped with interviews, people who read your drafts)?

Key points

- Good writing is probably just as important as good research practice. Indeed, it is probably better thought of as a part of good research practice.

- Clear structure and statement of your research questions are important components of writing up research.

- Be sensitive to the ways in which writers seek to persuade us of their points of view.

- The study of rhetoric and writing strategies generally teaches us that the writings of scientists and social scientists do more than simply report findings. They are designed to convince and to persuade.

- The emphasis on rhetoric is not meant to imply that there is no external social reality; it merely suggests that our understanding of that reality is profoundly influenced by the ways it is represented by writers.

- The basic structure of and the rhetorical strategies employed in most quantitative and qualitative research articles are broadly similar.

- We need to get away from the idea that rhetoric and the desire to persuade others of the validity of our work are somehow bad things. They are not. We all want to get our points across and to persuade our readers that we have got things right. The questions to ask are, do we do it well and do we make the best possible case? We all have to persuade others that we have got the right angle on things; the trick is to do it well. So when you write an essay or dissertation, do bear in mind the significance of your writing strategy.

Questions for review

- Why is it important to consider the ways in which business research is written?

Writing up quantitative research: an example

- Read an article based on quantitative research in an American business and management journal (e.g. *Academy of Management Journal* or *Administrative Science Quarterly*). How far does it exhibit the same characteristics as Coyle-Shapiro and Kessler's (2000) article?

- What is meant by rhetorical strategy? Why might rhetorical strategies be important in relation to the writing-up of business research?

- Do Coyle-Shapiro and Kessler employ an empiricist repertoire?

Writing up qualitative research: an example

- Read an article based on quantitative research in a European business and management journal (e.g. *Organization Studies*, *Journal of Management Studies*, or *Organization*). How far does it exhibit the same characteristics as Perlow's (1999) article?

- How far is the structure of Perlow's article different from Coyle-Shapiro and Kessler's?

Writing up mixed methods research: an example

- Read an article based on mixed methods research in a British management journal. How far does it exhibit the same characteristics as the one by Fey and Denison (2003)?

- Do Fey and Denison employ an empiricist repertoire?

Reflexivity and its implications for writing

- How has postmodernism called into question established ways of writing business research?

- What is reflexivity?

Online Resource Centre

www.oxfordtextbooks.co.uk/orc/brymanbrm4e/

Visit the Interactive Research Guide that accompanies this book to complete an exercise in Writing up Business Research.

Glossary

Terms defined elsewhere in the Glossary are in colour.

Abductive A type of reasoning with strong ties to *inductive* reasoning that grounds social scientific accounts of social worlds in the perspectives and meanings of participants in those social worlds.

Action research An approach in which the action researcher and a client collaborate in the diagnosis of a problem and in the development of a solution based on the diagnosis.

Ad libitum **sampling** A sampling approach in structured observation whereby whatever is happening at the moment that observation is due to occur is recorded.

Adjacency pair The tendency for certain kinds of activity in talk to be characterized by linked phases.

Analytic induction An approach to the analysis of qualitative data in which the researcher seeks universal explanations of phenomena by pursuing the collection of data until no cases that are inconsistent with a hypothetical explanation (deviant or negative cases) of a phenomenon are found.

Arithmetic mean Also known simply as the mean, this is the everyday average—namely, the total of a distribution of values divided by the number of values.

Asynchronous online interview or focus group Online interviews may be asynchronous or *synchronous*. In the case of the former, the transactions between participants are not in real time, so that there may be long spaces of time between interviewers' questions and participants' replies, and in the case of focus groups, between participants' contributions to the discussion.

Attached email survey A survey in which respondents are sent a questionnaire, which is received as an email attachment. Compare with *embedded email survey*.

Behaviour sampling A sampling approach in *structured observation* whereby an entire group is watched and the observer records who was involved in a particular kind of behaviour.

Biographical method See *life history method*.

Bivariate analysis The examination of the *relationship* between two *variables*, as in *contingency tables* or correlation.

CAQDAS An acronym of computer-assisted (or -aided) qualitative data analysis software.

Case study A *research design* that entails the detailed and intensive analysis of a single case. The term is sometimes extended to include the study of just two or three cases for comparative purposes.

Categorical variable See *nominal variable*.

Causality A concern with establishing causal connections between *variables*, rather than mere *relationships* between them.

Cell The point in a table, such as a *contingency table*, where the rows and columns intersect.

Census The enumeration of an entire *population*. Unlike a *sample*, which comprises a count of *some* units in a population, a census relates to *all* units in a population. Thus, if a *postal questionnaire* is mailed to every person in a town or to all members of a profession, the research should be characterized as a census.

Chi-square test Chi-square (χ^2) is a test of *statistical significance*, which is typically employed to establish how confident we can be that the findings displayed in a *contingency table* can be generalized from a *probability sample* to a *population*.

Closed question A question employed in an *interview schedule* or *self-completion questionnaire* that presents the respondent with a set of possible answers to choose from. Also called fixed-choice question and *pre-coded question*.

Cluster sample A sampling procedure in which at an initial stage the researcher samples areas (i.e. clusters) and then samples units from these clusters, usually using a *probability sampling* method.

Code, coding In *quantitative research*, codes are numbers that are assigned to data about people or other units of analysis when the data are not inherently numerical. In *questionnaire*-based research, the answer to a question (e.g. 'strongly agree') is assigned a number (e.g. 5) so that the information can be statistically processed. Thus, each person who answers 'strongly agree' will receive the same number (in this case 5). When answers are textual, respondents' answers must be grouped into categories and those categories are then coded. In *qualitative research*, coding is the process whereby data are broken down into component parts, which are given names.

Coding frame A listing of the codes used in relation to the analysis of data. In relation to answers to a *structured interview* schedule or *questionnaire*, the coding frame will delineate the categories used in connection with each question. It is particularly crucial in relation to the coding of *open questions*. With *closed questions*, the coding frame is essentially incorporated into the pre-given answers, hence the frequent use of the term *pre-coded question* to describe such questions.

Coding manual In *content analysis*, this is the statement of instructions to coders that outlines all the possible categories for each dimension being coded.

Coding schedule In *content analysis*, this is the form onto which all the data relating to an item being coded will be entered.

Cognitive mapping A method used to map the thought processes and decision-making sequences used by an individual or a group to solve a problem.

Collaborative enquiry A tradition founded on the assumption that the people who are the focus of study should be fully involved in the research process at all stages, from the identification of aims to the writing-up of findings. The tradition stems from a desire to challenge the conventional methods whereby knowledge is constructed in the social sciences and to dismantle the assumed authority of the researcher, and for this reason it is sometimes referred to as 'new paradigm' research or cooperative enquiry.

Comparative design A *research design* that entails the comparison of two or more cases in order to illuminate existing theory or generate theoretical insights as a result of contrasting findings uncovered through the comparison.

Concept A name given to a category that organizes observations and ideas by virtue of their possessing common features.

Concurrent validity One of the main approaches to establishing *measurement validity*. It entails relating a measure to a criterion on which cases (e.g. people) are known to differ and that is relevant to the *concept* in question.

Confounding variable A *variable* that is related to each of two variables the result of which is to produce the appearance of a *relationship* between the two variables. Such a relationship is a spurious relationship.

Connotation A term used in *semiotics* to refer to the principal and most manifest meaning of a *sign*. This may be contrasted with 'denotation', which refers to the meanings of a sign associated with the social context within which it operates that are supplementary to and less immediately apparent than its connotation.

Constant An attribute in terms of which cases do not differ. Compare with *variable*.

Constant comparison A central tool of *grounded theory* that entails constantly comparing new data with existing data, concepts, and categories. It also entails comparing categories with each other and categories with concepts.

Construct The same as a *concept*, but in much *quantitative research* 'construct' is the preferred term.

Construct validity An assessment of the *measurement validity* of a measure that tests hypotheses deduced from a theory that is relevant to the underlying concept. If the findings are consistent with the theory, confidence in the validity of the measure is enhanced.

Constructionism, constructionist An *ontological* position (often also referred to as 'constructivism') that asserts that social phenomena and their meanings are continually being accomplished by social actors. It is antithetical to *objectivism*.

Constructivism See *constructionism*.

Content analysis An approach to the analysis of documents and texts that seeks to quantify content in terms of predetermined categories and in a systematic and replicable manner. The term is sometimes used in connection with qualitative research as well—see *qualitative content analysis*.

Contingency table A table, comprising rows and columns, that shows the *relationship* between two *variables*. Usually, at least one of the variables is a *nominal variable*. Each cell in the table shows the frequency of occurrence of that intersection of categories of each of the two variables and usually a percentage.

Continuous recording A procedure in *structured observation* whereby observation occurs for extended periods, so that the frequency and duration of certain types of behaviour can be carefully recorded.

Convenience sample A sample that is selected because of its availability to the researcher. It is a form of *non-probability sample*.

Convergent validity An assessment of the *measurement validity* of a measure that compares it to another measure of the same concept that has been generated from a different method.

Conversation analysis The fine-grained analysis of talk as it occurs in interaction in naturally occurring situations. The talk is recorded and *transcribed* so that the detailed analyses can be carried out. The analysis is concerned with uncovering the underlying structures of talk in interaction and as such with the achievement of order through interaction. Conversation analysis is grounded in *ethnomethodology*.

Correlation An approach to the analysis of *relationships* between *interval/ratio variables* and/or *ordinal variables* that seeks to assess the strength and direction of the relationship between the variables concerned. *Pearson's r* and *Spearman's rho* are both methods for assessing the level of correlation between variables.

Covert research A term frequently used in connection with *ethnographic* research in which the researcher does not reveal his or her true identity. Such research violates the ethical principle of *informed consent*.

Cramér's V A method for assessing the strength of the *relationship* between two *variables*, at least one of which must have more than two categories.

Critical incident method A technique that usually relies on *structured interviewing* to elicit from respondents an account of key events or specific kinds of behaviour (critical incidents) and their consequences. Analysis involves interpretation of critical incidents so as to identify common patterns of behaviour.

Critical realism A *realist* epistemology that asserts that the study of the social world should be concerned with the identification of the structures that generate that world. Critical realism is critical because its practitioners aim to identify structures in order to change them, so that inequalities and injustices may be counteracted. Unlike a *positivist* epistemology, critical realism accepts that the structures that are identified may not be perceptible by the senses. Thus, whereas *positivism* is *empiricist*, critical realism is not.

Cross-sectional design A *research design* that entails the collection of data on more than one case (usually quite a lot more than one) and at a single point in time in order to collect a body of quantitative or quantifiable data in connection with two or more *variables* (usually many more than two), which are then examined to detect patterns of association. The cross-sectional design is also often called 'social survey design'.

Deductive An approach to the relationship between theory and research in which the latter is conducted with reference to hypotheses and ideas inferred from the former. Compare with *inductive*.

Dependent variable A *variable* that is causally influenced by another variable (i.e. an *independent variable*).

Diary In the context of social research methods, a term that can mean different things. Three types of diary can be distinguished: diaries written or completed at the behest of a researcher; personal diaries that can be analysed as a *personal document*, but that were produced spontaneously; and diaries written by social researchers as a log of their activities and reflections.

Dichotomous variable A *variable* with just two categories.

Dimension Refers to an aspect of a *concept*.

Discourse analysis An approach to the analysis of talk and other forms of discourse that emphasizes the ways in which versions of reality are accomplished through language.

Distribution of values A term used to refer to the entire data relating to a *variable*. Thus, the ages of members of a *sample* represent the distribution of values for that variable for that sample.

Ecological fallacy The error of assuming that inferences about individuals can be made from findings relating to aggregate data.

Ecological validity A concern with the question of whether or not social scientific findings are relevant and applicable to people's everyday, natural social settings.

Embedded email survey A social survey in which respondents are sent an email that contains a *questionnaire*. Compare with *attached email survey*.

Empiricism An approach to the study of reality that suggests that only knowledge gained through experience and the senses is acceptable.

Epistemology, epistemological A theory of knowledge. It is particularly employed in this book to refer to a stance on what should pass as acceptable knowledge. See *positivism*, *realism*, and *interpretivism*.

Eta (η) A test of the strength of the *relationship* between two *variables*. The *independent variable* must be a *nominal variable* and the *dependent variable* must be an *interval variable* or *ratio variable*. The resulting level of correlation will always be positive.

Ethnographic content analysis See *qualitative content analysis*.

Ethnography, ethnographer Like *participant observation*, a research method in which the researcher immerses him- or herself in a social setting for an extended period of time, observing behaviour, listening to what is said in conversations both between others and with the fieldworker, and asking questions. However, the term has a more inclusive sense than participant observation, which seems to emphasize the observational component. Also, the term 'an ethnography' is frequently used to refer to the written output of ethnographic research.

Ethnomethodology A sociological perspective concerned with the way in which social order is accomplished through talk and interaction. It provides the intellectual foundations of *conversation analysis*.

Evaluation research Research that is concerned with the evaluation of real-life interventions in the social world.

Experience sampling Also called 'event sampling', experience sampling refers to various methods that seek to capture affective states and/or behaviour at certain points in time. These 'points in time' are determined by the researcher and when they occur, research participants have to record such things as what they are doing or how they are feeling.

Experiment A *research design* that rules out alternative explanations of findings deriving from it (i.e. possesses *internal validity*) by having at least (*a*) an experimental group, which is exposed to a treatment, and a control group, which is not; and (*b*) *random assignment* to the two groups.

External validity A concern with the question of whether or not the results of a study can be generalized beyond the specific research context in which it was conducted.

Face validity A concern with whether or not an *indicator* appears to reflect the content of the *concept* in question.

Facilitator See *moderator*.

Factor analysis A statistical technique used for large numbers of *variables* to establish whether there is a tendency for groups of them to be inter-related. It is often used with *multiple-indicator measures* to see if the *indicators* tend to bunch to form one or more groups of indicators. These groups of indicators are called factors and must then be given a name.

Field notes A detailed chronicle by an *ethnographer* of events, conversations, and behaviour, and the researcher's initial reflections on them.

Field stimulation A study in which the researcher directly intervenes in and/or manipulates a natural setting in order to observe what happens as a consequence of that intervention.

Fixed-choice question See *closed question*.

Focal sampling A sampling approach in *structured observation* whereby a sampled individual is observed for a set period of time. The observer records all examples of whatever forms of behaviour are of interest.

Focus group A form of group interview in which: there are several participants (in addition to the *moderator* or facilitator); there is an emphasis in the questioning on a particular fairly tightly defined topic; and the emphasis is upon interaction within the group and the joint construction of meaning.

Frequency table A table that displays the number and/or percentage of units (e.g. people) in different categories of a *variable*.

Generalization, generalizability A concern with the *external validity* of research findings.

Grounded theory An approach to the analysis of qualitative data that aims to generate theory out of research data by achieving a close fit between the two.

Hawthorne effect See *reactivity*.

Hermeneutics A term drawn from theology that, when imported into the social sciences, is concerned with the theory and method of the interpretation of human action. It emphasizes the need to understand from the perspective of the social actor.

Hypothesis An informed speculation, which is set up to be tested, about the possible *relationship* between two or more *variables*.

Independent variable A *variable* that has a causal impact on another variable (i.e. a *dependent variable*).

Index See *scale*.

Indicator A measure that is employed to refer to a *concept* when no direct measure is available.

Inductive An approach to the relationship between theory and research in which the former is generated out of the latter. Compare with *deductive*.

Informed consent A key principle in social research ethics. It implies that prospective research participants should be given as much information as might be needed to make an informed decision about whether or not they wish to participate in a study.

Inter-coder reliability See *inter-rater reliability*.

Internal reliability The degree to which the indicators that make up a *scale* are consistent.

Internal validity A concern with the question of whether or not a finding that incorporates a causal *relationship* between two or more *variables* is sound.

Interpretative repertoire A collection of linguistic resources that are drawn upon in order to characterize and assess actions and events.

Interpretivism An *epistemological* position that requires the social scientist to grasp the subjective meaning of social action.

Inter-rater reliability The degree to which two or more individuals agree about the *coding* of an item. Inter-rater reliability is likely to be an issue in *content analysis*, *structured observation*, and when *coding* answers to *open questions* in research based on *questionnaires* or *structured interviews*.

Interval variable A *variable* where the distances between the categories are identical across its range of categories.

Intervening variable A *variable* that is affected by another variable and that in turn has a causal impact on another variable. Taking an intervening variable into account often facilitates the understanding of the *relationship* between two variables.

Interview guide A rather vague term that is used to refer to the brief list of memory prompts of areas to be covered that is often employed in *unstructured interviewing* or to the somewhat more structured list of issues to be addressed or questions to be asked in *semi-structured interviewing*.

Interview schedule A collection of questions designed to be asked by an interviewer. An interview schedule is always used in a *structured interview*.

Intra-coder reliability See *intra-rater reliability*.

Intra-rater reliability The degree to which an individual differs over time in the *coding* of an item. Intra-rater reliability is likely to be an issue in *content analysis*, *structured* *observation*, and when *coding* answers to *open questions* in research based on *questionnaires* or *structured interviews*.

Key informant Someone who offers the researcher, usually in the context of conducting an *ethnography*, perceptive information about the social setting, important events, and individuals.

Life history interview Similar to the *oral history interview*, but the aim of this type of unstructured interview is to glean information on the entire biography of each respondent.

Life history method Also often referred to as the 'biographical method', this method emphasizes the inner experience of individuals and its connections with changing events and phases throughout the life course. The method usually entails *life history interviews* and the use of *personal documents* as data.

Likert scale A widely used format developed by Rensis Likert for asking attitude questions. Respondents are typically asked their degree of agreement with a series of statements that together form a *multiple-indicator* (also called multiple-item) *measure*. The scale is deemed then to measure the intensity with which respondents feel about an issue.

Longitudinal research A *research design* in which data are collected on a *sample* (of people, documents, etc.) on at least two occasions.

Mail questionnaire Traditionally, this term has been synonymous with the *postal questionnaire*, but, with the arrival of email-based questionnaires (see *embedded email survey* and *attached email survey*), many writers prefer to refer to 'postal' rather than 'mail' questionnaires.

Mean See *arithmetic mean*.

Measure of central tendency A statistic, such as the *arithmetic mean*, *median*, or *mode*, that summarizes a *distribution of values*.

Measure of dispersion A statistic, such as the *range* or *standard deviation*, that summarizes the amount of variation in a *distribution of values*.

Measurement validity The degree to which a measure of a concept truly reflects that concept. See also *face validity* and *concurrent validity*.

Median The mid-point in a *distribution of values*.

Member validation See *respondent validation*.

Meta-analysis A form of *systematic review* that involves summarizing the results of a large number of quantitative studies and conducting various analytical tests to show whether or not a particular *variable* has an effect across the studies.

Meta-ethnography A form of *systematic review* that is used to achieve interpretative synthesis of *qualitative research* and other secondary sources, thus providing a counterpart to *meta-analysis* in *quantitative research*. It can

be used to synthesize and analyse information about a phenomenon that has been extensively studied.

Missing data Data relating to a case that are not available, for example, when a respondent in *survey research* does not answer a question. These are referred to as 'missing values' in *SPSS*.

Mixed methods research A term that is increasingly employed to describe research that combines the use of both *quantitative research* and *qualitative research*. The term can also be employed to describe research that combines just quantitative research methods or that combines just qualitative research methods. However, in recent times, it has taken on this more specific meaning of combining quantitative and qualitative research methods.

Mode The value that occurs most frequently in a *distribution of values*.

Moderated relationship A *relationship* between two *variables* is said to be moderated when it holds for one category of a third variable but not for another category or other categories.

Moderator The person who guides the questioning of a *focus group*. Also called a 'facilitator'.

Multiple-indicator measure A measure that employs more than one *indicator* to measure a *concept*.

Multi-strategy research A term used to describe research that combines *quantitative* and *qualitative research*; see also *mixed methods research*.

Multivariate analysis The examination of *relationships* between three or more *variables*.

Narrative analysis An approach to the elicitation and analysis of data that is sensitive to the sense of temporal sequence that people, as tellers of stories about their lives or events around them, detect in their lives and surrounding episodes and inject into their accounts. However, the approach is not exclusive to a focus on life histories.

Narrative review An approach to reviewing the literature that is often contrasted nowadays with a *systematic review*. It tends to be less focused than a systematic review and seeks to arrive at a critical interpretation of the literature that it covers.

Naturalism A confusing term that has at least three distinct meanings: a commitment to adopting the principles of natural scientific method; being true to the nature of the phenomenon being investigated; and a style of research that seeks to minimize the intrusion of artificial methods of data collection.

Negative relationship A *relationship* between two *variables* whereby as one increases the other decreases.

Nominal variable Also known as a 'categorical variable', this is a *variable* that comprises categories that cannot be rank ordered.

Non-manipulable variable A *variable* that cannot readily be manipulated either for practical or for ethical reasons and that therefore cannot be employed in an *experiment*.

Non-probability sample A sample that has not been selected using a *random sampling* method. Essentially, this implies that some units in the population are more likely to be selected than others.

Non-response A source of *non-sampling error* that occurs whenever some members of a sample refuse to cooperate, cannot be contacted, or for some reason cannot supply the required data.

Non-sampling error Differences between the *population* and the *sample* that arise either from deficiencies in the sampling approach, such as an inadequate *sampling frame* or *non-response*, or from such problems as poor question wording, poor interviewing, or flawed processing of data.

Null hypothesis A *hypothesis* of no *relationship* between two *variables*.

NVivo A *CAQDAS* package that derives from but goes beyond NUD*IST (Non-numerical Unstructured Data Indexing Searching and Theorizing).

Objectivism An *ontological* position that asserts that social phenomena and their meanings have an existence that is independent of social actors. Compare with *constructionism*.

Observation schedule A device used in *structured observation* that specifies the categories of behaviour that are to be observed and how behaviour should be allocated to those categories.

Official statistics Statistics compiled by or on behalf of state agencies in the course of conducting their business.

Online survey A very general term used to include any survey conducted online. As such, it includes the *Web survey*, the *attached email survey*, and the *embedded email survey*.

Ontology, ontological A theory of the nature of social entities. See *objectivism* and *inductivism*.

Open question A question employed in an *interview schedule* or *self-completion questionnaire* that does not present the respondent with a set of possible answers to choose from. Compare with *closed question*.

Operational definition The definition of a *concept* in terms of the operations to be carried out when measuring it.

Operationism, operationalism A doctrine, mainly associated with a version of physics, that emphasizes the search for *operational definitions* of *concepts*.

Oral history interview A largely *unstructured interview* in which the respondent is asked to recall events from his or her past and to reflect on them.

Ordinal variable A *variable* whose categories can be rank ordered (as in the case of *interval* and *ratio variables*), but

the distances between the categories are not equal across the range.

Outlier An extreme value in a distribution of values. If a *variable* has an extreme value—either very high or very low—the *arithmetic mean* or the *range* will be distorted by it.

Paradigm A term deriving from the history of science, where it was used to describe a cluster of beliefs and dictates that for scientists in a particular discipline influence what should be studied, how research should be done, and how results should be interpreted.

Participant observation Research in which the researcher immerses him- or herself in a social setting for an extended period of time, observing behaviour, listening to what is said in conversations both between others and with the fieldworker, and asking questions. Participant observation usually includes interviewing key informants and studying documents, and as such is difficult to distinguish from *ethnography*. In this book, 'participant observation' is employed to refer to the specifically observational aspect of ethnography.

Pearson's *r* A measure of the strength and direction of the *relationship* between two *interval* or *ratio variables*.

Personal documents Documents such as *diaries*, letters, and autobiographies that are not written for an official purpose. They provide first-person accounts of the writer's life and events within it.

Phenomenology A philosophy that is concerned with the question of how individuals make sense of the world around them and how in particular the philosopher should bracket out preconceptions concerning his or her grasp of that world.

Photo-elicitation Typically, photo-elicitation is a visual research method that entails getting interviewees to discuss one or more photographs in the course of an interview. The photograph(s) may be extant or may have been taken by the interviewee for the purpose of the research.

Phi (φ) A method for assessing the strength and direction of the *relationship* between two *dichotomous variables*.

Population The universe of units from which a *sample* is to be selected.

Positive relationship A *relationship* between two *variables*, whereby as one increases the other increases as well.

Positivism An *epistemological* position that advocates the application of the methods of the natural sciences to the study of social reality and beyond.

Postal questionnaire A form of *self-completion questionnaire* that is sent to respondents, and usually returned by them, by non-electronic mail.

Postmodernism A position that displays a distaste for master-narratives and for a *realist* orientation. In the context of research methodology, postmodernists display a preference for qualitative methods and a concern with the modes of representation of research findings.

Pre-coded question Another name for a *closed question*. The term is often preferred, because it describes an approach that removes the need for the application of a *coding frame* to the question after it has been answered. This is because the range of answers has been predetermined and a numerical *code* will have been pre-assigned to each possible answer. The term is particularly appropriate when the codes appear on the *questionnaire* or *interview schedule*.

Predictive validity An assessment of the *measurement validity* of a measure of a concept that uses a future benchmark as a criterion.

Probability sample A sample that has been selected using *random sampling* and in which each unit in the population has a known probability of being selected.

Projective techniques A method involving the presentation of ambiguous stimuli to individuals, which are interpreted by the researcher to reveal the underlying characteristics of the individual.

Purposive sampling, sample A form of *non-probability sample* in which the researcher aims to sample cases/participants in a strategic way, so that those sampled are relevant to the research questions that are being posed.

Qualitative content analysis An approach to documents that emphasizes the role of the investigator in the construction of the meaning of and in texts. There is an emphasis on allowing categories to emerge out of data and on recognizing the significance for understanding the meaning of the context in which an item being analysed (and the categories derived from it) appeared.

Qualitative research Qualitative research usually emphasizes words rather than quantification in the collection and analysis of data. As a *research strategy* it is *inductivist*, *constructionist*, and *interpretivist*, but qualitative researchers do not always subscribe to all three of these features. Compare with *quantitative research*.

Quantitative research Quantitative research usually emphasizes quantification in the collection and analysis of data. As a *research strategy* it is *deductivist* and *objectivist* and incorporates a natural science model of the research process (in particular, one influenced by *positivism*), but quantitative researchers do not always subscribe to all three of these features. Compare with *qualitative research*.

Quasi-experiment A *research design* that is close to being an experiment but that does not meet the requirements fully and therefore does not exhibit complete *internal validity*.

Questionnaire A collection of questions administered to respondents. When used on its own, the term usually denotes a *self-completion questionnaire*.

Quota sample A *sample* that non-randomly samples a *population* in terms of the relative proportions of people in different categories. It is a type of *non-probability sample*.

Random assignment A term used in connection with *experiments* to refer to the random allocation of research participants to the experimental group and the control group.

Random sampling Sampling whereby the inclusion of a unit of a *population* occurs entirely by chance.

Range The difference between the maximum and the minimum value in a *distribution of values* associated with an *interval* or *ratio variable*.

Rapid review A literature review that conforms to the main principles of a *systematic review* but is deliberately limited in scope so that the review can be completed in a relatively short time.

Ratio variable An *interval variable* with a true zero point.

Reactivity, reactive effect A term used to describe the response of research participants to the fact that they know they are being studied, also sometimes referred to as the Hawthorne effect. Reactivity is deemed to result in untypical behaviour.

Realism An epistemological position that acknowledges a reality independent of the senses that is accessible to the researcher's tools and theoretical speculations. It implies that the categories created by scientists refer to real objects in the natural or social worlds. See also *critical realism*.

Reflexivity A term used in research methodology to refer to a reflectiveness among social researchers about the implications for the knowledge of the social world they generate of their methods, values, biases, decisions, and mere presence in the very situations they investigate.

Relationship An association between two *variables* whereby the variation in one variable coincides with variation in another variable.

Reliability The degree to which a measure of a concept is stable.

Repertory grid technique A method for mapping the relationship between constructs used by an individual or a group of individuals to construct meaning. The method results in the production of a diagrammatic matrix representing the various constructs and elements involved in analysing this relationship, i.e. the repertory grid.

Replication, replicability The degree to which the results of a study can be reproduced. See also *internal reliability*.

Representative sample A *sample* that reflects the population accurately, so that it is a microcosm of the *population*.

Research design This term is employed in this book to refer to a framework or structure within which the collection and analysis of data takes place. A choice of research design reflects decisions about the priority being given to a range of dimensions of the research process (such as *causality* and *generalization*) and is influenced by the kind of *research question* that is posed.

Research question An explicit statement in the form of a question of what it is that a researcher intends to find out about. A research question influences not only the scope of an investigation but also how the research will be conducted.

Research strategy A term used in this book to refer to a general orientation to the conduct of social research (see *quantitative research* and *qualitative research*).

Respondent validation Sometimes called 'member validation', this is a process whereby a researcher provides the people on whom he or she has conducted research with an account of his or her findings and requests feedback on that account.

Response set The tendency among some respondents to *multiple-indicator measures* to reply in the same way to each constituent item.

Rhetoric A concern with the ways in which appeals to convince or persuade are devised.

Sample The segment of the population that is selected for research. It is a subset of the *population*. The method of selection may be based on *probability sampling* or *non-probability sampling*.

Sampling error Differences between a *random sample* and the *population* from which it is selected.

Sampling frame The listing of all units in the *population* from which a *sample* is selected.

Scale A term that is usually used interchangeably with 'index' to refer to a *multiple-indicator measure* in which the score a person gives for each component *indicator* is used to provide a composite score for that person.

Scan sampling A sampling approach in *structured observation* whereby an entire group of individuals is scanned at regular intervals and the behaviour of all of them is recorded at each occasion.

Secondary analysis The analysis of data by researchers who will probably not have been involved in the collection of those data for purposes that may not have been envisaged by those responsible for the data collection. Secondary analysis may entail the analysis of either quantitative data or qualitative data.

Self-administered questionnaire See *self-completion questionnaire*.

Self-completion questionnaire A *questionnaire* that the respondent answers without the aid of an interviewer. Sometimes called a 'self-administered questionnaire'.

Semiotics The study/science of *signs*; an approach to the analysis of documents and other phenomena that empha-

sizes the importance of seeking out the deeper meaning of those phenomena. A semiotic approach is concerned to uncover the processes of meaning production and how signs are designed to have an effect upon actual and prospective consumers of those signs.

Semi-structured interview A term that covers a wide range of types. It typically refers to a context in which the interviewer has a series of questions that are in the general form of an *interview guide* but is able to vary the sequence of questions. The questions are frequently somewhat more general in their frame of reference from that typically found in a *structured interview* schedule. Also, the interviewer usually has some latitude to ask further questions in response to what are seen as significant replies.

Sensitizing concept A term devised by Blumer to refer to a preference for treating a *concept* as a guide in an investigation, so that it points in a general way to what is relevant or important. This position contrasts with the idea of an *operational definition*, in which the meaning of a concept is fixed in advance of carrying out an investigation.

Sign A term employed in *semiotics*. A sign is made up of a signifier (the manifestation of a sign) and the signified (that idea or deeper meaning to which the signifier refers).

Simple observation The passive and unobtrusive observation of behaviour.

Simple random sample A *sample* in which each unit has been selected entirely by chance. Each unit of the *population* has a known and equal probability of inclusion in the sample.

Snowball sampling A *non-probability sample* technique in which the researcher makes initial contact with a small group of people who are relevant to the research topic and then uses these to establish contacts with others.

Social desirability bias A distortion of data that is caused by respondents' attempts to construct an account that conforms to a socially acceptable model of belief or behaviour.

Social survey See *cross-sectional design*.

Spearman's rho (ρ) A measure of the strength and direction of the *relationship* between two *ordinal variables*.

SPSS Originally short for Statistical Package for the Social Sciences, SPSS is a widely used computer program that allows quantitative data to be managed and analysed.

Spurious relationship A *relationship* between two *variables* is said to be spurious if it is being produced by the impact of a third variable on each of the two variables that form the spurious relationship. When the third variable is controlled, the relationship disappears.

Standard deviation A measure of dispersion around the mean.

Standard error of the mean An estimate of the amount that a *sample* mean is likely to differ from the *population* mean.

Statistical inference See *statistical significance (test of)*.

Statistical significance (test of) Allows the analyst to estimate how confident he or she can be that the results deriving from a study based on a randomly selected *sample* are generalizable to the *population* from which the sample was drawn. Such a test does not allow the researcher to infer that the findings are of substantive importance. The *chi-square test* is an example of this kind of test. The process of using a test of statistical significance to generalize from a sample to a population is known as 'statistical inference'.

Stratified random sample A *sample* in which units are *randomly sampled* from a *population* that has been divided into categories (strata).

Structured interview A research interview in which all respondents are asked exactly the same questions in the same order with the aid of a formal *interview schedule*.

Structured observation Often also called 'systematic observation', structured observation is a technique in which the researcher employs explicitly formulated rules for the observation and recording of behaviour. The rules inform observers about what they should look for and how they should record behaviour.

Survey research A *cross-sectional design* in relation to which data are collected predominantly by *self-completion questionnaire* or by *structured interview* on more than one case (usually quite a lot more than one) and at a single point in time in order to collect a body of quantitative or quantifiable data in connection with two or more *variables* (usually many more than two) which are then examined to detect patterns of *relationship*.

Symbolic interactionism A theoretical perspective in sociology and social psychology that views social interaction as taking place in terms of the meanings actors attach to action and things.

Synchronous online interview or focus group Online interviews may be *asynchronous* or synchronous. In the case of the latter, the transactions between participants are in real time, so that there will be only brief time lapses between interviewers' questions and participants' replies, and, in the case of focus groups, between participants' contributions to the discussion.

Systematic observation See *structured observation*.

Systematic review An approach to reviewing the literature that uses explicit procedures and exhaustive searches; the aim is to conduct a comprehensive and unbiased literature review and to leave a transparent record of the process used.

Systematic sample A *probability sampling* method in which units are selected from a *sampling frame* according to fixed intervals, such as every fifth unit.

Text A term that is used either in the conventional sense of a written work or in more recent years to refer to a wide range of phenomena. For example, in arriving at a *thick description*, Geertz refers to treating culture as a text.

Thematic analysis A term used in connection with the analysis of qualitative data to refer to the extraction of key themes in one's data. It is a rather diffuse approach and there are few generally agreed principles for defining core themes in data.

Theoretical sampling A term used mainly in relation to *grounded theory* to refer to sampling carried out so that emerging theoretical considerations guide the selection of cases and/or research participants. Theoretical sampling is supposed to continue until a point of *theoretical saturation* is reached.

Theoretical saturation In *grounded theory*, the point when emerging concepts have been fully explored and no new theoretical insights are being generated. See also *theoretical sampling*.

Thick description A term devised by Geertz to refer to detailed accounts of a social setting that can form the basis for the creation of general statements about a culture and its significance in people's social lives.

Time sampling A sampling method in *structured observation* that entails using a criterion for deciding when observation will occur.

Transcription, transcript, transcribe The written translation of an audio-recorded interview or *focus group* session; transcribing is the act of making such a transcript.

Triangulation The use of more than one method or source of data in the study of a social phenomenon so that findings may be cross-checked.

Trustworthiness A set of criteria advocated by some writers for assessing the quality of *qualitative research*.

Turn-takin The notion from *conversation analysis* that order in everyday conversation is achieved through orderly taking of turns in conversations.

Univariate analysis The analysis of a single *variable* at a time.

Unobtrusive methods Methods that do not entail the awareness among research participants that they are being studied and that are therefore not subject to *reactivity*.

Unstructured interview An interview in which the interviewer typically only has a list of topics or issues, often called an *interview guide*, that are typically covered. The style of questioning is usually very informal. The phrasing and sequencing of questions will vary from interview to interview.

Validity A concern with the integrity of the conclusions that are generated from a piece of research. There are different aspects of validity. See, in particular, *measurement validity*, *internal validity*, *external validity*, and *ecological validity*. When used on its own, *validity* is usually taken to refer to *measurement validity*.

Variable An attribute in terms of which cases vary. See also *dependent variable* and *independent variable*. Compare with *constant*.

Verbal protocol approach A method that involves asking respondents to think aloud while they are performing a task in order to capture their thought processes while they are making a decision or judgement or solving a problem.

Web survey A *social survey* conducted so that respondents complete a *questionnaire* via a website.

References

Abendroth, A. K., and Den Dulk, L. (2011). 'Support for the Work-life Balance in Europe: The Impact of State, Workplace and Family Support on Work-life Balance Satisfaction', *Work, Employment and Society*, 25(2): 234–56.

Abrahamson, E. (1996). 'Management Fashion', *Academy of Management Review*, 21(1): 254–85.

Addison, J. T., and Belfield, C. R. (2000). 'The Impact of Financial Participation and Employee Involvement on Financial Performance: A Reiteration Using the 1998 WERS', *Scottish Journal of Political Economy*, 47(5): 571–83.

Adler, N. (1983). 'A Typology of Management Studies Involving Culture', *Journal of International Business Studies*, 14(2): 29–47.

Adler, P. A., and Adler, P. (2008). 'Of Rhetoric and Representation: The Four Faces of Ethnography', *Sociological Quarterly*, 49: 1–30.

Adriaenssens, C., and Cadman, L. (1999). 'An Adaptation of Moderated E-mail Focus Groups to Assess the Potential of a New Online (Internet) Financial Services Offer in the UK', *Journal of the Market Research Society*, 41: 417–24.

Ainsworth, S., and Hardy, C. (2009). 'Mind over Body: Physical and Psychotherapeutic Discourses and the Regulation of the Older Worker', *Human Relations*, 62(8): 1199–229.

Alderson, P. (1998). 'Confidentiality and Consent in Qualitative Research', *Network: Newsletter of the British Sociological Association*, 69: 6–7.

Aldrich, H. E. (1972). 'Technology and Organizational Structure: A Re-Examination of the Findings of the Aston Group', *Administrative Science Quarterly*, 17(1): 26–43.

Aldridge, A. (1998). 'Reproducing the Value of Professional Expertise in Post-Traditional Culture: Financial Advice and the Creation of the Client', *Cultural Values*, 2: 445–62.

Alise, M. A., and Teddlie, C. (2010). 'A Continuation of the Paradigm Wars? Prevalence Rates of Methodological Approaches across the Social/Behavioral Sciences', *Journal of Mixed Methods Research*, 4(2): 103–26.

Allison, T. H., McKenny, A. F., and Short, J. C. (2013). 'The Effect of Entrepreneurial Rhetoric on Microlending Investment: An Investigation of the Warm-Glow Effect', *Journal of Business Venturing*, 28(6): 690–707.

Allred, S. B., and Ross-Davis, A. (2011). 'The Drop-off and Pick-Up Method: An Approach to Reduce Nonresponse Bias in Natural Resource Surveys', *Small-scale Forestry*, 10(3): 305–18.

Altheide, D. L. (1980). 'Leaving the Newsroom', in W. Shaffir, R. A. Stebbins, and A. Turowetz (eds), *Fieldwork Experience: Qualitative Approaches to Social Research*. New York: St Martin's Press.

Altheide, D. L. (1996). *Qualitative Media Analysis*. Thousand Oaks, CA: Sage.

Altschuld, J. W., and Lower, M. A. (1984). 'Improving Mailed Questionnaires: Analysis of a 96 Percent Return Rate', in D. C. Lockhart (ed.), *Making Effective Use of Mailed Questionnaires*. San Francisco, CA: Jossey-Bass.

Alvesson, M. (2002). *Postmodernism and Social Research*. Buckingham: Open University Press.

Alvesson, M. (2003). 'Methodology for Close Up Studies: Struggling with Closeness and Closure', *Higher Education*, 46: 167–93.

Alvesson, M. (2013). 'Do We Have Something to Say? From Re-search to Roi-search and Back Again', *Organization*, 20(1): 79–90.

Alvesson, M., and Kärreman, D. (2000). 'Varieties of Discourse: On the Study of Organization through Discourse Analysis', *Human Relations*, 53(9): 1125–49.

Alvesson, M., and Kärreman, D. (2007). 'Constructing Mystery: Empirical Matters in Theory Development', *Academy of Management Review*, 32: 1265–81.

Alvesson, M., and Kärreman, D. (2011). 'Decolonializing Discourse: Critical Reflections on Organizational Discourse Analysis', *Human Relations*, 64(9): 1121–46.

Alvesson, M., and Sandberg, J. (2011). 'Generating Research Questions through Problematization', *Academy of Management Review*, 36(2): 247–71.

Andersen, M. (1981). 'Corporate Wives: Longing for Liberation or Satisfied with the Status Quo?', *Urban Life*, 10: 311–27.

Andersen, M. F., Nielsen, K. M., and Brinkmann, S. (2012). 'Meta-Synthesis of Qualitative Research on Return to Work among Employees with Common Mental Disorders', *Scandinavian Journal of Work and Environmental Health*, 38(2): 93–104.

Anderson, N. (1990). 'Repertory Grid Technique in Employee Selection', *Personnel Review*, 19(3): 9–15.

Archer, M. (1995). *Realist Social Theory: The Morphogenetic Approach*. Cambridge: Cambridge University Press.

Argyris, C., Putnam, R., and Smith, M. (1985). *Action Science: Concepts, Methods and Skills for Research and Intervention*. San Francisco, CA: Jossey-Bass.

Armstrong, G. (1993). 'Like that Desmond Morris?', in D. Hobbs and T. May (eds), *Interpreting the Field: Accounts of Ethnography*. Oxford: Clarendon Press.

Armstrong, K. (2006). *Life after MG Rover: A Report Prepared for BBC Radio 4*. London: The Work Foundation.

Aronson, E., and Carlsmith, J. M. (1968). 'Experimentation in Social Psychology', in G. Lindzey and E. Aronson (eds), *The Handbook of Social Psychology*. Reading, MA: Addison-Wesley.

Arthur, J. (1994). 'Effects of Human Resource Systems on Manufacturing, Performance and Turnover', *Academy of Management Journal*, 37(3): 670–87.

Asch, S. E. (1951). 'Effect of Group Pressure upon the Modification and Distortion of Judgments', in H. Guetzkow (ed.), *Groups, Leadership and Men*. Pittsburgh: Carnegie Press.

Ashforth, B. E., Kreiner, G. E., Clark, M. A., and Fugate, M. (2007). 'Normalizing Dirty Work: Tactics for Countering Occupational Taint', *Academy of Management Journal*, 50: 149–74.

Association of Internet Researchers (AoIR) (2002). 'Ethical Decision Making and Internet Research: Recommendations from the AoIR Ethics Working Committee', aoir.org/reports/ethics.pdf (accessed 18 January 2014).

Atkinson, P. (1981). *The Clinical Experience*. Farnborough: Gower.

Atkinson, P. (1990). *The Ethnographic Imagination: Textual Constructions of Society*. London: Routledge.

Atkinson, P., and Coffey, A. (2004). 'Analysing Documentary Realities', in D. Silverman (ed.), *Qualitative Research: Theory, Method and Practice*, 2nd edn. London: Sage.

Atkinson, P., and Silverman, D. (1997). 'Kundera's Immortality: The Interview Society and the Invention of Self', *Qualitative Inquiry*, 3(3): 324–45.

Atkinson, P., Coffey, A., and Delamont, S. (2003). *Key Themes in Qualitative Research: Continuities and Changes*. Oxford: AltaMira Press.

Avolio, B. J., Reichard, R. J., Hannah, S. T., Walumbwa, F. O., and Chan, A. (2009). 'A Meta-Analytic Review of Leadership Impact Research: Experimental and Quasi-Experimental Studies', *Leadership Quarterly*, 20: 764–84.

Bacon, N., and Blyton, P. (2001). 'Management Practices and Employee Attitudes: A Longitudinal Study Spanning Fifty Years', *Sociological Review*, 49(2): 254–74.

Banks, M. (2001). *Visual Methods in Social Research*. London: Sage.

Bansal, P., and Roth, K. (2000). 'Why Companies Go Green: A Model of Ecological Responsiveness', *Academy of Management Journal*, 43(4): 717–36.

Barley, S. (1983). 'Semiotics and the Study of Occupational and Organizational Cultures', *Administrative Science Quarterly*, 28: 393–413.

Barley, S. (2006). 'When I Write My Masterpiece: Thoughts on What Makes a Paper Interesting', *Academy of Management Journal*, 49(1): 16–20.

Barley, S., Meyer, G., and Gash, D. (1988). 'Cultures of Culture: Academics, Practitioners and the Pragmatics of Normative Control', *Administrative Science Quarterly*, 33: 24–60.

Barnes, S. (2004). 'Issues of Attribution and Identification in Online Social Research', in M. D. Johns, S.-L. S. Chen, and G. J. Hall (eds), *Online Social Research*. New York: Peter Lang.

Barnett, R. (1994). 'Editorial', *Studies in Higher Education*, 19(2): 123–4.

Barthes, R. (1972). *Mythologies*. London: Jonathan Cape.

Bartunek, J. M., Bobko, P., and Venkatraman, N. (1993). 'Toward Innovation and Diversity in Management Research Methods', *Academy of Management Journal*, 36(6): 1362–73.

Bartunek, J. M., Rynes, S. L., and Ireland, R. D. (2006). 'What Makes Management Research Interesting and Why Does it Matter?', *Academy of Management Journal*, 49(1): 9–15.

Basbøll, T. (2010). 'Softly Constrained Imagination: Plagiarism and Misprision in the Theory of Organizational Sensemaking', *Culture and Organization*, 16(2): 163–78.

Bauman, Z. (1978). *Hermeneutics and Social Science: Approaches to Understanding*. London: Hutchison.

Baumgartner, R. M., and Heberlein, T. A. (1984). 'Applying Attitude Theories to the Return of Mailed Questionnaires', in D. C. Lockhart (ed.), *Making Effective Use of Mailed Questionnaires*. San Francisco: Jossey-Bass.

Bazerman, C. (1987). 'Codifying the Social Scientific Style: The APA *Publication Manual* as a Behaviorist Rhetoric', in J. S. Nelson, A. Megill, and D. N. McClosky (eds), *The Rhetoric of the Human Sciences*. Madison: University of Wisconsin Press.

Beardsworth, A. (1980). 'Analysing Press Content: Some Technical and Methodological Issues', in H. Christian (ed.), *Sociology of Journalism and the Press*. Keele: Keele University Press.

Bechhofer, F., Elliott, B., and McCrone, D. (1984). 'Safety in Numbers: On the Use of Multiple Interviewers', *Sociology*, 18: 97–100.

Becker, H. S. (1982). 'Culture: A Sociological View', *Yale Review*, 71: 513–27.

Becker, H. S. (1986). *Writing for Social Scientists: How to Start and Finish your Thesis, Book, or Article*. Chicago: University of Chicago Press.

Becker, H. S., and Geer, B. (1957a). 'Participant Observation and Interviewing: A Comparison', *Human Organization*, 16: 28–32.

Becker, H. S., and Geer, B. (1957b). ' "Participant Observation and Interviewing": A Rejoinder', *Human Organization*, 16: 39–40.

Becker, S., Bryman, A., and Sempik, J. (2006). *Defining 'Quality' in Social Policy Research*. Lavenham: Social Policy Association, www.social-policy.org.uk/downloads/defining%20quality%20in%20social%20policy%20research.pdf (accessed 18 January 2015).

Beech, N. (2000). 'Narrative Styles of Managers and Workers: A Tale of Star-Crossed Lovers', *Journal of Applied Behavioral Science*, 36(2): 210–28.

Belk, R. W., Ger, G., and Askegaard, S. (1997). 'Consumer Desire in Three Cultures: Results from Projective Research', *Advances in Consumer Research*, 24: 24–8.

Bell, C. (1969). 'A Note on Participant Observation', *Sociology*, 3: 417–18.

Bell, C., and Newby, H. (1977). *Doing Sociological Research*. London: George Allen & Unwin.

Bell, E. (1999). 'The Negotiation of a Working Role in Organizational Ethnography', *International Journal of Social Research Methodology*, 2(1): 17–37.

Bell, E. (2001). 'The Social Time of Organizational Payment Systems', *Time & Society*, 10(1): 45–62.

Bell, E. (2012). 'Ways of Seeing Death: A Critical Semiotic Analysis of Organizational Memorialization', *Visual Studies*, 27(1): 4–17.

Bell, E., and Bryman, A. (2007). 'The Ethics of Management Research: An Exploratory Context Analysis', *British Journal of Management*, 18(1): 63–77.

Bell, E., and Davison, J. (2013). 'Visual Management Studies: Empirical and Theoretical Approaches', *International Journal of Management Reviews*, 15(2): 167–84.

Bell, E., and Thorpe, R. (2013). *A Very Short, Fairly Interesting and Reasonably Cheap Book about Management Research*. London: Sage.

Bell, E., and Wade Clarke, D. (2013). 'Beasts, Burrowers and Birds: The Enactment of Researcher Identities in UK Business Schools', *Management Learning*, doi: 10.1177/1350507613478890.

Bell, E., and Wray Bliss, E. (2009). 'Research Ethics: Regulations and Responsibilities', in D. Buchanan and A. Bryman (eds), *The Sage Handbook of Organizational Research Methods*. London: Sage, 78–92.

Bell, E., Taylor, S., and Thorpe, R. (2001). 'Investors in People and the Standardization of Professional Knowledge in Personnel Management', *Management Learning*, 32(2): 201–19.

Bell, E., Taylor, S., and Thorpe, R. (2002). 'Organizational Differentiation through Badging: Investors in People and the Value of the Sign', *Journal of Management Studies*, 39(8): 1071–85.

Berelson, B. (1952). *Content Analysis in Communication Research*. New York: Free Press.

Berg, P., and Frost, A. C. (2005). 'Dignity at Work for Low Wage, Low Skill Service Workers', *Industrial Relations*, 60(4): 657–82.

Bettis, R. (1991). 'Strategic Management and the Straightjacket: An Editorial Essay', *Organization Science*, 2(3): 315–19.

Bettman, J., and Weitz, B. (1983). 'Attributions in the Board Room: Causal Reasoning in Corporate Annual Reports', *Administrative Science Quarterly*, 28: 165–83.

Beynon, H. (1975). *Working for Ford*, 2nd edn. Harmondsworth: Penguin.

Beynon, H. (1988). 'Regulating Research: Politics and Decision Making in Industrial Organizations', in A. Bryman (ed.), *Doing Research in Organizations*. London: Routledge.

Bhaskar, R. (1975). *A Realist Theory of Science*. Leeds: Leeds Books.

Bhaskar, R. (1989). *Reclaiming Reality: A Critical Introduction to Contemporary Philosophy*. London: Verso.

Bhojraj, S., Lee, C. M. C., and Oler, D. K. (2003). 'What's My Line? A Comparison of Industry Classification Schemes for Capital Market Research', *Journal of Accounting Research*, 41(5): 745–74.

Billig, M. (1991). *Ideology and Opinions: Studies in Rhetorical Psychology*. Cambridge: Cambridge University Press.

Billig, M. (1992). *Talking of the Royal Family*. London: Routledge.

Blackburn, R., and Stokes, D. (2000). 'Breaking down the Barriers: Using Focus Groups to Research Small and Medium-Sized Enterprises', *International Small Business Journal*, 19(1): 44–67.

Blauner, R. (1964). *Alienation and Freedom*. Chicago: University of Chicago Press.

Bloland, H. G. (2005). 'Whatever Happened to Postmodernism in Higher Education?', *Journal of Higher Education*, 76: 121–50.

Bloor, M. (2002). 'No Longer Dying for a Living: Collective Responses to Injury Risks in South Wales Mining Communities, 1900–47', *Sociology*, 36(1): 89–105.

Bluhm, D. J., Harman, W., Lee, T. W., and Mitchell, T. R. (2011). 'Qualitative Research in Management: A Decade of Progress', *Journal of Management Studies*, 48(8): 1866–91.

Blumer, H. (1954). 'What is Wrong with Social Theory?', *American Sociological Review*, 19: 3–10.

Blumer, H. (1956). 'Sociological Analysis and the "Variable"', *American Sociological Review*, 21: 683–90.

Blumer, H. (1962). 'Society as Symbolic Interaction', in A. M. Rose (ed.), *Human Behavior and Social Processes*. London: Routledge & Kegan Paul.

Blyton, P., Bacon, N., and Morris, J. (1996). 'Working in Steel: Steelworkers' Attitudes to Change Forty Years On', *Industrial Relations Journal*, 27(2): 155–65.

Boddy, C. (2005). 'A Rose by Any Other Name may Smell as Sweet but "Group Discussion" is Not Another Name for a "Focus Group" nor Should it Be', *Qualitative Market Research*, 8(3): 248–55.

Boden, D. (1994). *The Business of Talk: Organizations in Action*. Cambridge: Polity Press.

Bogdan, R., and Taylor, S. J. (1975). *Introduction to Qualitative Research Methods: A Phenomenological Approach to the Social Sciences*. New York: Wiley.

Boje, D. (1991). 'The Storytelling Organization: A Study of Performance in an Office Supply Firm', *Administrative Science Quarterly*, 36: 106–26.

Boje, D. (2001). *Narrative Methods for Organizational and Communication Research*. London: Sage.

Bolton, A., Pole, C., and Mizen, P. (2001). 'Picture This: Researching Child Workers', *Sociology*, 35(2): 501–18.

Bond, M., and Pyle, J. (1998). 'The Ecology of Diversity in Organizational Settings: Lessons from a Case Study', *Human Relations*, 51(5): 589–623.

Booth, C., and Rowlinson, M. (2006). 'Management and Organizational History: Prospects', *Management & Organizational History*, 1(1): 5–30.

Born, G. (2004). *Uncertain Vision: Birt, Dyke and the Reinvention of the BBC*. London: Secker & Warburg.

Bosley, S. L. C., Arnold, J., and Cohen, L. (2009). 'How Other People Shape our Careers: A Typology Drawn from Career Narratives', *Human Relations*, 62: 1487–520.

Bosnjak, M., Metzger, G., and Gräf, L. (2010). 'Understanding the Willingness to Participate in Mobile Surveys: Exploring the Role of Utilitarian, Affective, Hedonic, Social, Self-Expressive, and Trust-Related Factors', *Social Science Computer Review*, 25: 350–70.

Bosnjak, M., Neubarth, W., Couper, M. P., Bandilla, W., and Kaczmirek, L. (2008). 'Prenotification in Web-Based Access Panel Surveys: The Influence of Mobile Text Messaging Versus E-mail on Response Rates and Sample Composition', *Social Science Computer Review*, 26: 213–23.

Bottomore, T. B., and Rubel, M. (1963). *Karl Marx: Selected Writings in Sociology and Social Philosophy*. Harmondsworth: Penguin.

Bourdieu, P. (1984). *Distinction: A Social Critique of the Judgement of Taste*. Cambridge, MA: Harvard University Press.

Bowen, D. D., and Hisrich, R. D. (1986). 'The Female Entrepreneur: A Career Development Perspective', *Academy of Management Review*, 11: 393–407.

Bowen, G. A. (2008). 'Naturalistic Inquiry and the Saturation Concept: A Research Note', *Qualitative Research*, 8: 137–52.

Bowey, A., and Thorpe, R. (1986). *Payment Systems and Productivity*. Basingstoke: Macmillan.

Boyce, G., and Lepper, L. (2002). 'Assessing Information Quality Theories: The USSCo. Joint Venture with William Holyman and Sons and Huddart Parker Ltd, 1904–35', *Business History*, 44(4): 85–120.

Boyd, B. K., Haynes, K. T., Hitt, M. A., Bergh, D. D., and Ketchen, D. J. (2012). 'Contingency Hypotheses in Strategic Management: Use, Disuse, or Misuse', *Journal of Management*, 38(1): 278–313.

Bradburn, N. A., and Sudman, S. (1979). *Improving Interview Method and Questionnaire Design*. San Francisco: Jossey-Bass.

Brannick, T., and Coghlan, D. (2007). 'In Defense of Being "Native": The Case for Insider Academic Research', *Organizational Research Methods*, 10(1): 59–74.

Braun, V., and Clarke, V. (2006). 'Using Thematic Analysis in Psychology', *Qualitative Research in Psychology*, 3: 77–101.

Braverman, H. (1974). *Labor and Monopoly Capital: The Degradation of Work in the Twentieth Century*. London: Monthly Review Press.

Brayfield, A. and Rothe, H. (1951). 'An Index of Job Satisfaction', *Journal of Applied Psychology*, 35: 307–11.

Brengman, M., Geuens, M., Weijters, B., Smith, S. M., and Swinyard, W. (2005). 'Segmenting Internet Shoppers Based on their Web-usage Related Lifestyle: A Cross-cultural Validation', *Journal of Business Research*, 58: 79–88.

Bresnen, M., Goussevskaia, A., and Swan, J. (2004). 'Embedding New Management Knowledge in Project-based Organizations', *Organization Studies*, 25(9): 1535–55.

Brewis, J. (2005). 'Signing My Life Away? Researching Sex and Organization', *Organization*, 12(4): 439–510.

Bridgman, P. W. (1927). *The Logic of Modern Physics*. New York: Macmillan.

Briggs, C. L. (1986). *Learning How to Ask: A Sociolinguistic Appraisal of the Role of the Interview in Social Science Research*. Cambridge: Cambridge University Press.

Briner, R. B., Denyer, D., and Rousseau, D. (2009). 'Evidence-Based Management: Concept Cleanup Time?', *Academy of Management Perspectives*, 23(4): 5–18.

Broussine, M., and Vince, R. (1996). 'Working with Metaphor towards Organizational Change', in C. Oswick and D. Grant (eds), *Organization Development: Metaphorical Explanations*. London: Pitman Publishing.

Brown, A. D. (1998). 'Narrative, Politics and Legitimacy in an IT Implementation', *Journal of Management Studies*, 35: 35–58.

Bruce, C. S. (1994). 'Research Students' Early Experiences of the Dissertation Literature Review', *Studies in Higher Education*, 19(2): 217–29.

Bryman, A. (1974). 'Sociology of Religion and Sociology of Elites', *Archives de Sciences Sociales des Religions*, 38: 109–21.

Bryman, A. (1988a). *Quantity and Quality in Social Research*. London: Routledge.

Bryman, A. (1988b). *Doing Research in Organizations*. London: Routledge.

Bryman, A. (1989a). *Research Methods and Organization Studies*. London: Routledge.

Bryman, A. (1989b). 'The Value of Re-studies in Sociology: The Case of Clergy and Ministers, 1971 to 1985', *Sociology*, 23: 31–54.

Bryman, A. (1992). 'Quantitative and Qualitative Research: Further Reflections on their Integration', in J. Brannen (ed.), *Mixing Methods: Qualitative and Quantitative Research*. Aldershot: Avebury.

Bryman, A. (1994). 'The Mead/Freeman Controversy: Some Implications for Qualitative Researchers', in R. G. Burgess (ed.), *Studies in Qualitative Methodology*, vol. 4. Greenwich, CT: JAI Press.

Bryman, A. (1995). *Disney and his Worlds*. London: Routledge.

Bryman, A. (1998). 'Quantitative and Qualitative Research Strategies in Knowing the Social World', in T. May and M. Williams (eds), *Knowing the Social World*. Buckingham: Open University Press.

Bryman, A. (1999). 'Global Disney', in P. Taylor and D. Slater (eds), *The American Century*. Oxford: Blackwell.

Bryman, A. (2003). 'McDonald's as a Disneyized Institution: Global Implications', *American Behavioral Scientist*, 47: 154–67.

Bryman, A. (2004a). *Social Research Methods*, rev. edn. Oxford: Oxford University Press.

Bryman, A. (2004b). *The Disneyization of Society*. London: Sage.

Bryman, A. (2006a). 'Integrating Quantitative and Qualitative Research', *Qualitative Research*, 6: 97–113.

Bryman, A. (2006b). 'Paradigm Peace and the Implications for Quality', *International Journal of Social Research Methodology*, 9: 111–26.

Bryman, A. (2007a). 'Effective Leadership in Higher Education', *Studies in Higher Education*, 32: 693–710.

Bryman, A. (2007b). 'The Research Question in Social Research: What is its Role?', *International Journal of Social Research Methodology*, 9: 5–20.

Bryman, A. (2007c). 'Barriers to Integrating Quantitative and Qualitative Research', *Journal of Mixed Methods Research*, 1: 8–22.

Bryman, A. (2009). 'Mixed Methods in Organizational Research', in D. A. Buchanan and A. Bryman (eds), *The Sage*

Handbook of Organizational Research Methods. London: Sage.

Bryman, A. (2014). 'June 1989 and Beyond: Julia Brannen's Contribution to Mixed Methods Research', *International Journal of Social Research Methodology*, 17: 121–31.

Bryman, A., and Burgess, R. G. (1994*a*). 'Developments in Qualitative Data Analysis: An Introduction', in A. Bryman and R. G. Burgess (eds), *Analyzing Qualitative Data*. London: Routledge.

Bryman, A., and Burgess, R. G. (1994*b*). 'Reflections on Qualitative Data Analysis', in A. Bryman and R. G. Burgess (eds), *Analyzing Qualitative Data*. London: Routledge.

Bryman, A., and Burgess, R. G. (1999). 'Introduction: Qualitative Research Methodology: A Review', in A. Bryman and R. G. Burgess (eds), *Qualitative Research*. London: Sage.

Bryman, A., and Cramer, D. (2008). *Quantitative Data Analysis with SPSS 14, 15 and 16: A Guide for Social Scientists*. London: Routledge.

Bryman, A., and Cramer, D. (2011). *Quantitative Data Analysis with IBM SPSS 17, 18 and 19: A Guide for Social Scientists*. London: Routledge.

Bryman, A., Becker, S., and Sempik, J. (2008). 'Quality Criteria for Quantitative, Qualitative and Mixed Methods Research: The View from Social Policy', *International Journal of Social Research Methodology*, 11: 261–76.

Bryman, A., Gillingwater, D., and McGuinness, I. (1996). 'Industry Culture and Strategic Response: The Case of the British Bus Industry', *Studies in Cultures, Organizations and Societies*, 2: 191–208.

Bryman, A., Haslam, C., and Webb, A. (1994). 'Performance Appraisal in UK Universities: A Case of Procedural Compliance?', *Assessment and Evaluation in Higher Education*, 19: 175–88.

Bryman, A., Stephens, M., and A Campo, C. (1996). 'The Importance of Context: Qualitative Research and the Study of Leadership', *Leadership Quarterly*, 7: 353–70.

Buchanan, D. A. (1998). 'Representing Process: The Contribution of a Re-engineering Frame', *International Journal of Operations and Production Management*, 18(12): 1163–88.

Buchanan, D. A. (2001). 'The Role of Photography in Organization Research: A Reengineering Case Illustration', *Journal of Management Inquiry*, 10: 151–64.

Buchanan, D. A. (2012). 'Case Studies in Organizational Research', in G. Symon and C. Cassell (eds), *Qualitative Organizational Research: Core Methods and Current Challenges*. Los Angeles: Sage.

Buchanan, D., and Bryman, A. (2007). 'Contextualizing Methods Choice in Organizational Research', *Organizational Research Methods*, 10(3): 483–501.

Buchanan, D. A., Boddy, D., and McCalman, J. (1988). 'Getting In, Getting Out and Getting Back', in A. Bryman (ed.), *Doing Research in Organizations*. London: Routledge.

Bulmer, M. (1979). 'Concepts in the Analysis of Qualitative Data', *Sociological Review*, 27: 651–77.

Bulmer, M. (1980). 'Why Don't Sociologists Make More Use of Official Statistics?', *Sociology*, 14: 505–23.

Bulmer, M. (1982). 'The Merits and Demerits of Covert Participant Observation', in M. Bulmer (ed.), *Social Research Ethics*. London: Macmillan.

Bulmer, M. (1984). 'Facts, Concepts, Theories and Problems', in M. Bulmer (ed.), *Social Research Methods*. London: Macmillan.

Burawoy, M. (1979). *Manufacturing Consent*. Chicago: University of Chicago Press.

Burawoy, M. (2003). 'Revisits: An Outline of a Theory of Reflexive Ethnography', *American Sociological Review*, 68: 645–79.

Burawoy, M., Blum, J. A., George, S., Gille, Z., Gowan, T., Haney, L., Klawiter, M., Lopez, S. H., Riain, S. O., and Thayer, M. (2000). *Global Ethnography: Forces, Connections and Imaginations in a Postmodern World*. Berkeley and Los Angeles: University of California Press.

Burger, J. M. (2009). 'Replicating Milgram: Would People Still Obey Today?', *American Psychologist*, 64(1): 1–11.

Burgess, R. G. (1984). *In the Field*. London: Allen & Unwin.

Burman, E. (1994). 'Interviewing', in P. Banister, E. Burman, I. Parker, M. Taylor, and C. Tindall (eds), *Qualitative Methods in Psychology: A Research Guide*. Buckingham: Open University Press: 49–71.

Burrell, G. (1997). *Pandemonium: Towards a Retro-Organization Theory*. London: Sage.

Burrell, G., and Morgan, G. (1979). *Sociological Paradigms and Organisational Analysis*. Aldershot: Gower.

Business Week (1973). 'The Public Clams up on Survey Takers', 15 September, 216–20.

Buston, K. (1997). 'NUD*IST in Action: Its Use and its Usefulness in a Study of Chronic Illness in Young People', *Sociological Research Online*, 2, www.socresonline.org.uk/socresonline/2/3/6.html.

Butcher, B. (1994). 'Sampling Methods: An Overview and Review', *Survey Methods Centre Newsletter*, 15: 4–8.

Buttner, E. H. (2001). 'Examining Female Entrepreneurs' Management Style: An Application of a Relational Frame', *Journal of Business Ethics*, 29: 253–69.

Cable, D., and Graham, M. (2000). 'The Determinants of Job Seekers' Reputation Perceptions', *Journal of Organizational Behavior*, 21: 929–47.

Calder, B. J. (1977). 'Focus Groups and the Nature of Qualitative Marketing Research', *Journal of Marketing Research*, 14: 353–64.

Campbell, D. T. (1957). 'Factors Relevant to the Validity of Experiments in Social Settings', *Psychological Bulletin*, 54: 297–312.

Campbell, M. L. (1998). 'Institutional Ethnography and Experience as Data', *Qualitative Sociology*, 21(1): 55–73.

Caplan, R., Cobb, S., French, J., Harrison, R., and Pinneau, S. (1975). *Job Demands and Worker Health*. Washington: US Department of Health, Education and Welfare.

Carini, R. M., Hayek, J. C., Kuh, G. D., Kennedy, J. M., and Ouimet, J. D. (2003). 'College Student Responses to Web and Paper Surveys: Does Mode Matter?' *Research in Higher Education*, 44(1): 1–19.

Casey, C. (1995). *Work, Self and Society: After Industrialism*. London: Routledge.

Cassell, J. (1982). 'Harms, Benefits, Wrongs and Rights in Fieldwork', in J. E. Sieber (ed.), *The Ethics of Social Research: Surveys and Experiments*. New York: Springer, 7–31.

Catterall, M., and Maclaran, P. (1997). 'Focus Group Data and Qualitative Analysis Programs: Coding the Moving Picture as well as Snapshots', *Sociological Research Online*, 2, www.socresonline.org.uk/socresonline/2/1/6.html.

Cavendish, R. (1982). *Women on the Line*. London: Routledge & Kegan Paul.

Chamberlayne, P., Bornat, J., and Wengraf, T. (2000). 'Introduction: The Biographical Turn', in P. Chamberlayne, J. Bornat, and T. Wengraf (eds), *The Turn to Biographical Methods in Social Science: Comparative Issues and Examples*. London: Routledge.

Chan, I. Y. S., Leung, M.-Y., and Yu, S. S. W. (2012). 'Managing the Stress of Hong Kong Expatriate Professionals in Mainland China: Focus Group Study Exploring Individual Coping Strategies and Organizational Support', *Journal of Construction Engineering and Management*, 138(10): 1150–60.

Chan, K. W., and Li, S. Y. (2010). 'Understanding Consumer-to-Consumer Interactions in Virtual Communities: The Salience of Reciprocity', *Journal of Business Research*, 63: 1033–40.

Charmaz, K. (1983). 'The Grounded Theory Method: An Explication and Interpretation', in R. M. Emerson (ed.), *Contemporary Field Research: A Collection of Readings*. Boston: Little, Brown.

Charmaz, K. (2000). 'Grounded Theory: Objectivist and Constructivist Methods', in N. K. Denzin and Y. S. Lincoln (eds), *Handbook of Qualitative Research*, 2nd edn. Thousand Oaks, CA: Sage.

Charmaz, K. (2006). *Constructing Grounded Theory: A Practical Guide through Qualitative Analysis*. London: Sage.

Chatterjee, A., and Hambrick, D. C. (2007). 'It's All About Me: Narcissistic Chief Executive Officers and their Effects on Company Strategy and Performance', *Administrative Science Quarterly*, 52: 351–86.

Chen, C. C., and Meindl, J. R. (1991). 'The Construction of Leadership Images in the Popular Press: The Case of Donald Burr and People Express', *Administrative Science Quarterly*, 36: 521–51.

Chen, C.-P. (2012). 'Online Group Buying Behavior in CC2B e-Commerce: Understanding Consumer Motivations', *Journal of Internet Commerce*, 11: 254–70.

Cicourel, A. V. (1964). *Method and Measurement in Sociology*. New York: Free Press.

Cicourel, A. V. (1968). *The Social Organization of Juvenile Justice*. New York: Wiley.

Cicourel, A. V. (1982). 'Interviews, Surveys, and the Problem of Ecological Validity', *American Sociologist*, 17: 11–20.

Clapper, D. L., and Massey, A. P. (1996). 'Electronic Focus Groups: A Framework for Exploration', *Information and Management*, 30: 43–50.

Clarke, C., and Knights, D. (2014). 'It's a Bittersweet Symphony, This Life: Fragile Academic Selves and Insecure Identities at Work', *Organization Studies*, 35(3): 335–7.

Clarke, C., Knights, D., and Jarvis, C. (2012). 'A Labour of Love? Academics in Business Schools', *Scandinavian Journal of Management*, 28: 5–15.

Clegg, S. (2002). ' "Lives in the Balance": A Comment on Hinings and Greenwood's "Disconnects and Consequences in Organization Theory?" ', *Administrative Science Quarterly*, 47: 428–41.

Clegg Smith, K. (2004). ' "Electronic Eavesdropping": The Ethical Issues Involved in Conducting a Virtual Ethnography', in M. D. Johns, S.-L. S. Chen, and G. J. Hall (eds), *Online Social Research*. New York: Peter Lang.

Clifford, J. (1983). 'On Ethnographic Authority', *Representations*, 1: 118–46.

Cobanoglu, C., Ward, B., and Moreo, P. J. (2001). 'A Comparison of Mail, Fax and Web-Based Survey Methods', *International Journal of Market Research*, 43: 441–52.

Cockburn, C., and Ormrod, S. (1993). *Gender and Technology in the Making*. London: Sage.

Coffey, A. (1999). *The Ethnographic Self: Fieldwork and the Representation of Reality*. London: Sage.

Coffey, A., and Atkinson, P. (1996). *Making Sense of Qualitative Data: Complementary Research Strategies*. Thousand Oaks, CA: Sage.

Coffey, A., Holbrook, B., and Atkinson, P. (1996). 'Qualitative Data Analysis: Technologies and Representations', *Sociological Research Online*, 2, www.socresonline.org.uk/socresonline/1/1/4.html.

Coghlan, D. (2001). 'Insider Action Research Projects: Implications for Practising Managers', *Management Learning*, 32(1): 49–60.

Coleman, C., and Moynihan, J. (1996). *Understanding Crime Data: Haunted by the Dark*. Buckingham: Open University Press.

Coleman, J. S. (1958). 'Relational Analysis: The Study of Social Organization with Survey Methods', *Human Organization*, 16: 28–36.

Collins, G., and Wickham, J. (2004). 'Inclusion or Exploitation: Irish Women Enter the Labour Force', *Gender, Work and Organization*, 11(1): 26–46.

Collins, M. (1997). 'Interviewer Variability: A Review of the Problem', *Journal of the Market Research Society*, 39: 67–84.

Collins, R. (1994). *Four Sociological Traditions*, rev. edn. New York: Oxford University Press.

Collinson, D. L. (1988). 'Engineering Humour: Masculinity, Joking and Conflict in Shop Floor Relations', *Organisation Studies*, 9(2): 181–99.

Collinson, D. L. (1992a). *Managing the Shopfloor: Subjectivity, Masculinity and Workplace Culture*. Berlin: DeGruyter.

Collinson, D. L. (1992b). 'Researching Recruitment: Qualitative Methods and Sex Discrimination', in R. Burgess (ed.), *Studies in Qualitative Methodology*, vol. 3. London: JAI Press.

Colquitt, J. (2012). 'From the Editors: Plagiarism Policies and Screening at *AMJ*', *Academy of Management Journal*, 55(4): 749–51.

Colville, I., Pye, A., and Carter, M. (2013). 'Organizing to Counter Terrorism: Sensemaking amidst Dynamic Complexity', *Human Relations*, 66(9): 1201–23.

Combe, I. A., and Crowther, D. E. (2000). 'The Semiology of an Advertising Campaign: Brand Repositioning', University of North London, Social Marketing Working Paper Series, 1–32.

Conger, J. A., and Kanungo, R. N. (1998). *Charismatic Leadership in Organizations*. Thousand Oaks, CA: Sage.

Connell, R. (2007). *Southern Theory*. Cambridge: Polity.

Converse, J. M., and Presser, S. (1986). *Survey Questions: Handcrafting the Standardized Questionnaire*. Beverly Hills, CA: Sage.

Conway, N., and Briner, R. (2002). 'A Daily Diary Study of Affective Responses to Psychological Contract Breach and Exceeded Promises', *Journal of Organizational Behaviour*, 23: 287–302.

Cook, T. D., and Campbell, D. T. (1979). *Quasi-Experimentation: Design and Analysis for Field Settings*. Boston, MA: Houghton Mifflin.

Cooke, B. (2003). 'The Denial of Slavery in Management Studies', *Journal of Management Studies*, 40(8): 1895–918.

Cooke, B. (2006). 'The Cold War Origin of Action Research as Managerialist Cooptation', *Human Relations* 59(5): 665–93.

Corden, A., and Sainsbury, R. (2006). *Using Verbatim Quotations in Reporting Qualitative Social Research: Researchers' Views*. Social Policy Research Unit Report, www.york.ac.uk/inst/spru/pubs/pdf/verbquotresearch.pdf (accessed 18 October 2014).

Corley, K. G., and Gioia, D. A. (2004). 'Identity Ambiguity and Change in the Wake of a Corporate Spin-Off', *Administrative Science Quarterly*, 49: 173–208.

Cornelissen, J. P., Mantere, S., and Vaara, E. (2014). 'The Contradiction of Meaning: The Combined Effect of Communication, Emotions, and Materiality on Sensemaking in the Stockwell Shooting', *Journal of Management Studies*, doi: 10.1111/joms.12073.

Corti, L. (1993). 'Using Diaries in Social Research', *Social Research Update*, no. 2.

Corti, L., Foster, J., and Thompson, P. (1995). 'Archiving Qualitative Research Data', *Social Research Update*, no. 10.

Cotterill, P. (1992). 'Interviewing Women: Issues of Friendship, Vulnerability, and Power', *Women's Studies International Forum*, 15(5–6): 593–606.

Couper, M. P. (2000). 'Web Surveys: A Review of Issues and Approaches', *Public Opinion Quarterly*, 64: 464–94.

Couper, M. P. (2004). 'Internet Surveys', in M. S. Lewis-Beck, A. Bryman, and T. F. Liao (eds), *The Sage Encyclopedia of Social Science Research Methods*. Thousand Oaks, CA: Sage.

Couper, M. P. (2008). *Designing Effective Web Surveys*. Cambridge: Cambridge University Press.

Couper, M. P., and Hansen, S. E. (2002). 'Computer-Assisted Interviewing', in J. F. Gubrium and J. A. Holstein (eds), *Handbook of Interview Research: Context and Method*. Thousand Oaks, CA: Sage.

Couper, M. P., Traugott, M. W., and Lamias, M. J. (2001). 'Web Survey Design and Administration', *Public Opinion Quarterly*, 65: 230–53.

Coupland, C. (2005). 'Corporate Social Responsibility on the Web', *Journal of Business Ethics*, 62: 355–66.

Coutrot, T. (1998). 'How Do Institutional Frameworks Affect Industrial Relations Outcomes? A Micro-Statistical Comparison of France and Britain', *European Journal of Industrial Relations*, 4(2): 177–205.

Cowley, J. C. P. (2000). 'Strategic Qualitative Focus Group Research: Define and Articulate our Skills or We Will be Replaced by Others', *International Journal of Market Research*, 42(1): 17–38.

Coyle-Shapiro, J., and Kessler, I. (2000). 'Consequences of the Psychological Contract for the Employment Relationship: A Large Scale Survey', *Journal of Management Studies*, 37(7): 903–30.

Cramer, D. (1998). *Fundamental Statistics for Social Research*. London: Routledge.

Crang, P. (1994). 'It's Showtime: On the Workplace Geographies of Display in a Restaurant in South East England', *Environment and Planning D: Society and Space*, 12: 675–704.

Crawford, S. D., Couper, M. P., and Lamias, M. J. (2001). 'Web Surveys: Perception of Burden', *Social Science Computer Review*, 19: 146–62.

Creswell, J., and Plano Clark, V. L. (2007). *Designing and Conducting Mixed Methods Research*. Thousand Oaks, CA: Sage.

Creswell, J., and Plano Clark, V. L. (2011). *Designing and Conducting Mixed Methods Research*, 2nd edn. Los Angeles: Sage.

Creswell, J., and Tashakkori, A. (2007). 'Editorial: Developing Publishable Mixed Methods Manuscripts', *Journal of Mixed Methods Research*, 1(2): 107–11.

Croll, P. (1986). *Systematic Classroom Observation*. London: Falmer Press.

Cryer, P. (1996). *The Research Student's Guide to Success*. Buckingham: Open University Press.

Cullen, D. (1997). 'Maslow, Monkeys and Motivation Theory', *Organization*, 4(3): 355–73.

Cully, M., Woodland, S., O'Reilly, A., and Dix, G. (1999). *Britain at Work: As Depicted by the 1998 Workplace Employee Relations Survey*. London: Routledge.

Cunha, R. C., and Cooper, C. L. (2002). 'Does Privatization Affect Corporate Culture and Employee Wellbeing?', *Journal of Managerial Psychology*, 17(1): 21–49.

Curasi, C. F. (2001). 'A Critical Exploration of Face-to-Face Interviewing vs Computer-Mediated Interviewing', *International Journal of Market Research*, 43: 361–75.

Curran, J., and Blackburn, R. (1994). *Small Firms and Local Economic Networks: The Death of the Local Economy?* London: Paul Chapman.

Currie, G., Lockett, A., and Suhomlinova, O. (2009). 'Leadership and Institutional Change in the Public Sector: The Case of Secondary Schools in England', *Leadership Quarterly*, 20: 664–79.

Czaja, R., and Blair, J. (1996). *Designing Surveys: A Guide to Decisions and Procedures*. Thousand Oaks, CA: Sage.

Czarniawska, B. (1998). *A Narrative Approach to Organization Studies*. Thousand Oaks, CA: Sage.

Czarniawska, B. (1999). *Writing Management: Organization Theory as a Literary Genre*. Oxford: Oxford University Press.

Czarniawaska, B. (2007). *Shadowing and other Techniques for Doing Fieldwork in Modern Societies*. Malmö: Liber.

Czarniawaska, B. (2014). 'Why I Think Shadowing is the Best Field Technique in Management and Organization Studies', *Qualitative Research in Organizations and Management*, 9(1): 90–93.

Daft, R. L. (1995). 'Why I Recommended that your Manuscript be Rejected and What You can Do About It', in L. L. Cummings and P. J. Frost (eds), *Publishing in the Organizational Sciences.* London: Sage.

Daigneault, P.-M., Jacob, S., and Ouimet, M. (2012). 'Using Systematic Review Methods within a Ph.D. Dissertation in Political Science: Challenges and Lessons Learned from Practice', *International Journal of Social Research Methodology*, doi: 10.1080/13645579.2012.730704.

Dale, A., Arber, S., and Proctor, M. (1988). *Doing Secondary Analysis*. London: Unwin Hyman.

Dalton, M. (1959). *Men who Manage: Fusion of Feeling and Theory in Administration*. New York: Wiley.

Dalton, M. (1964). 'Perceptions and Methods in Men who Manage', in P. Hammond (ed.), *Sociologists at Work*. New York: Basic Books.

Davies, B., Browne, J., Gannon, S., Honan, E., and Somerville, M. (2005). 'Embodied Women at Work in Neoliberal Times and Places', *Gender, Work and Organization*, 12(4): 343–62.

Davies, C. A. (1999). *Reflexive Ethnography: A Guide to Researching Selves and Others*. London: Routledge.

Davies, J. (2001). 'International Comparisons of Labour Disputes in 1999', *Labour Market Trends*, April: 195–201.

Davies, R., Jones, M., and Lloyd-Williams, H. (2014). 'Age and Work-related Health: Insights from the UK Labour Force Survey', *British Journal of Industrial Relations*, doi: 10.1111/bjir.12059.

Davis, J. A. (1964). 'Great Books and Small Groups: An Informal History of a National Survey', in P. Hammond (ed.), *Sociologists at Work*. New York: Basic Books.

Davison, J. (2009). 'Icon, Iconography, Iconology: Visual Branding, Banking and the Case of the Bowler Hat', *Accounting, Auditing and Accountability Journal*, 22(6): 883–906.

de Bruijne, M., and Wijnant, A. (2013). 'Comparing Survey Results Obtained via Mobile Devices and Computers: An Experiment with a Mobile Web Survey on a Heterogeneous Group of Mobile Devices Versus and Computer-Assisted Web Survey', *Social Science Computer Review*, 31(4): 484–504.

Deacon, D., Bryman, A., and Fenton, N. (1998). 'Collision or Collusion? A Discussion of the Unplanned Triangulation of Quantitative and Qualitative Research Methods', *International Journal of Social Research Methodology*, 1: 47–63.

Deakin, H., and Wakefield, K. (2014). 'Skype Interviewing: Reflections of Two PhD researchers', *Qualitative Research*, doi: 10.1177/1468794113488126.

Deery, S., Iverson, R., and Walsch, J. (2002). 'Work Relationships in Telephone Call Centres: Understanding Emotional Exhaustion and Employee Withdrawal', *Journal of Management Studies*, 39(4): 471–96.

Delamont, S., and Hamilton, D. (1984). 'Revisiting Classroom Research: A Continuing Cautionary Tale', in S. Delamont (ed.), *Readings on Interaction in the Classroom*. London: Methuen.

Delbridge, R. (1998). *Life on the Line: The Workplace Experience of Lean Production and the 'Japanese' Model*. Oxford: Oxford University Press.

DeLorme, D. E., Zinkhan, G. M., and French, W. (2001). 'Ethics and the Internet: Issues Associated with Qualitative Research', *Journal of Business Ethics*, 33: 271–86.

Denscombe, M. (2006). 'Web-Based Questionnaires and the Mode Effect: An Evaluation Based on Completion Rates and Data Contents of Near-Identical Questionnaires Delivered in Different Modes', *Social Science Computer Review*, 24: 246–54.

Denscombe, M. (2010). *Ground Rules for Good Research: Guidelines for Good Practice*, 2nd edn. Maidenhead: Open University Press.

Denyer, D., and Tranfield, D. (2009). 'Producing a Systematic Review', in D. Buchanan and A. Bryman (eds), *The Sage Handbook of Organizational Research Methods*. London: Sage.

Denzin, N. K. (1968). 'On the Ethics of Disguised Observation', *Social Problems*, 15: 502–4.

Denzin, N. K. (1970). *The Research Act in Sociology*. Chicago: Aldine.

Denzin, N. K. (1994). 'Evaluating Qualitative Research in the Poststructural Moment: The Lessons James Joyce Teaches us', *International Journal of Qualitative Studies in Education*, 7: 295–308.

Denzin, N. K., and Lincoln, Y. S. (2000). *Handbook of Qualitative Research*, 2nd edn. Thousand Oaks, CA: Sage.

Denzin, N. K., and Lincoln, Y. S. (2005). 'Introduction: The Discipline and Practice of Qualitative Research', in N. K. Denzin and Y. S. Lincoln (eds), *Handbook of Qualitative Research*, 3rd edn. Thousand Oaks, CA: Sage.

Dhanesh, G. S. (2014). 'CSR as Organization-Employee Relationship Management Strategy: A Case Study of Socially Responsible Information Technology Companies in India', *Management Communication Quarterly*, 28(1): 130–49.

Diener, E., and Crandall, R. (1978). *Ethics in Social and Behavioral Research*. Chicago: University of Chicago Press.

Dillman, D. A. (1978). *Mail and Telephone Surveys: The Total Design Method*. New York: Wiley.

Dillman, D. A. (1983). 'Mail and Other Self-Administered Questionnaires', in P. H. Rossi, J. D. Wright, and A. B. Anderson (eds), *Handbook of Survey Research*. Orlando, FL: Academic Press.

Dingwall, R. (1980). 'Ethics and Ethnography', *Sociological Review*, 28: 871–91.

Ditton, J. (1977). *Part-Time Crime: An Ethnography of Fiddling and Pilferage*. London: Macmillan.

Doloriert, C., and Sambrook, S. (2009). 'Ethical Confessions of the "I" of Autoethnography: The Student's Dilemma', *Qualitative Research in Organizations and Management*, 4(1): 27–45.

Dommeyer, C. J., and Moriarty, E. (2000). 'Comparison of Two Forms of an E-mail Survey: Embedded vs Attached', *International Journal of Market Research*, 42: 39–50.

Dorsey, E. R., Steeves, H. L., and Porras, L. E. (2004). 'Advertising Ecotourism on the Internet: Commodifying Environment and Culture', *New Media and Society*, 6: 753–79.

Dougherty, D., and Kunda, G. (1990). 'Photograph Analysis: A Method to Capture Organizational Belief Systems', in P. Gagliardi (ed.), *Symbols and Artefacts: Views of the Corporate Landscape*. Berlin: DeGruyter.

Douglas, J. D. (1976). *Investigative Social Research: Individual and Team Field Research*. Beverly Hills, CA: Sage.

Duriau, V. J., Reger, R. K., and Pfarrer, M. D. (2007). 'A Content Analysis of the Content Analysis Literature in Organization Studies: Research Themes, Data Sources, and Methodological Refinements', *Organizational Research Methods*, 10(5): 5–34.

Durkheim, E. (1938). *The Rules of Sociological Method*, trans. S. A. Solavay and J. H. Mueller. New York: Free Press.

Dyer, W. G., and Wilkins, A. L. (1991). 'Better Stories, not Better Constructs, to Generate Better Theory: A Rejoinder to Eisenhardt', *Academy of Management Review*, 16: 613–19.

Easterby-Smith, M., Golden-Biddle, K., and Locke, K. (2008). 'Working with Pluralism: Determining Quality in Qualitative Research', *Organizational Research Methods*, 11(3): 419–29.

Easton, G. (2002). 'Marketing: A Critical Realist Approach', *Journal of Business Research*, 55(2): 103–9.

Eden, C. (1988). 'Cognitive Mapping: A Review', *European Journal of Operational Research*, 36: 1–13.

Eden, C., and Huxham, C. (1996). 'Action Research for Management Research', *British Journal of Management*, 7(1): 75–86.

Edwards, P. (1995). 'Human Resource Management, Union Voice and the Use of Discipline: An Analysis of WIRS 3', *Industrial Relations Journal*, 26(3): 204–20.

Edwards, P., Collinson, M., and Rees, C. (1998). 'The Determinants of Employee Responses to Total Quality Management: Six Case Studies', *Organization Studies*, 19(3): 449–75.

Edwards, R. (1979). *Contested Terrain*. New York: Basic Books.

Eisenhardt, K. M. (1989). 'Building Theories from Case Study Research', *Academy of Management Review*, 14: 532–50.

Eisenhardt, K. M., and Graebner, M. E. (2007). 'Theory Building from Cases: Opportunities and Challenges', *Academy of Management Journal*, 50(1): 25–32.

Elliott, H. (1997). 'The Use of Diaries in Sociological Research on Health Experience', *Sociological Research Online*, 2, www.socresonline.org.uk/socresonline/2/2/7.html.

Ellis, C. (2004). *The Ethnographic I: A Methodological Novel about Teaching and Doing Autoethnography*. Walnut Creek, CA: AltaMira.

Elsesser, K. M., and Lever, J. (2011). 'Does Gender Bias Against Female Leaders Persist? Quantitative and Qualitative Data from a Large-scale Survey', *Human Relations*, 64(12): 1555–78.

Erikson, K. T. (1967). 'A Comment on Disguised Observation in Sociology', *Social Problems*, 14: 366–73.

Evans, M., Wedande, G., Ralston, L., and van't Hul, S. (2001). 'Consumer Interaction in the Virtual Era: Some Qualitative Insights', *Qualitative Market Research*, 4: 150–9.

Fairclough, N. (1992). *Discourse and Social Change*. Cambridge: Polity Press.

Fairclough, N. (1995). *Critical Discourse Analysis: The Critical Study of Language*. London: Longman.

Fairclough, N. (2003). *Analysing Discourse: Textual Analysis for Social Research*. London: Routledge.

Fairclough, N. (2005). 'Discourse Analysis in Organization Studies: The Case for Critical Realism', *Organization Studies*, 26(6): 915–39.

Faraday, A., and Plummer, K. (1979). 'Doing Life Histories', *Sociological Review*, 27: 773–98.

Faulkner, X., and Culwin, F. (2005). 'When Fingers Do the Talking: A Study of Text Messaging', *Interacting with Computers*, 17: 167–85.

Fenton, N., Bryman, A., and Deacon, D. (1998). *Mediating Social Science*. London: Sage.

Fern, E. F. (2001). *Advanced Focus Group Research*. Thousand Oaks, CA: Sage.

Fernández, R., Taylor, S., and Bell, E. (2005). *How Long until We Get There? A Survival Analysis of the Investors in People Initiative 1991–2001*. Oxford and Warwick: SKOPE Working Paper, 56.

Fey, C. F., and Denison, D. R. (2003). 'Organizational Culture and Effectiveness: Can American Theory Be Applied in Russia?', *Organization Science*, 14(6): 686–706.

Fiedler, F. E. (1967). *A Theory of Leadership Effectiveness*. New York: McGraw Hill.

Fielding, N., and Lee, R. M. (1998). *Computer Analysis and Qualitative Research*. London: Sage.

Filmer, P., Phillipson, M., Silverman, D., and Walsh, D. (1972). *New Directions in Sociological Theory*. London: Collier-Macmillan.

Finch, J. (1984). ' "It's Great to have Someone to Talk to": The Ethics and Politics of Interviewing Women', in C. Bell and H. Roberts (eds), *Social Researching: Politics, Problems, Practice*. London: Routledge & Kegan Paul.

Finch, J. (1987). 'The Vignette Technique in Survey Research', *Sociology*, 21: 105–14.

Fine, G. A. (1996). 'Justifying Work: Occupational Rhetorics as Resources in Kitchen Restaurants', *Administrative Science Quarterly*, 41: 90–115.

Fioretti, G. (2012). 'Agent-based Simulation Models in Organization Science', *Organizational Research Methods*, 16(2): 227–42.

Flanagan, J. C. (1954). 'The Critical Incident Technique', *Psychological Bulletin*, 1: 327–58.

Fleetwood, S. (2005). 'Ontology in Organization and Management Studies: A Critical Realist Perspective', *Organization*, 12(2): 197–222.

Fleming, C., and Bowden, M. (2009). 'Web-Based Surveys as an Alternative to Traditional Mail Methods', *Journal of Environmental Management*, 90: 284–92.

Fletcher, D. (2002). ' "In the Company of Men": A Reflexive Tale of Cultural Organizing in a Small Organization', *Gender, Work and Organization*, 9(4): 398–419.

Fletcher, J. (1966). *Situation Ethics*. London: SCM Press.

Flint, A., Clegg, S., and Macdonald, R. (2006). 'Exploring Staff Perceptions of Student Plagiarism', *Journal of Further and Higher Education*, 30: 145–56.

Foddy, W. (1993). *Constructing Questions for Interviews and Questionnaires: Theory and Practice in Social Research*. Cambridge: Cambridge University Press.

Forster, N. (1994). 'The Analysis of Company Documentation', in C. Cassell and G. Symon (eds), *Qualitative Methods in Organizational Research*. London: Sage.

Foucault, M. (1974). *The Order of Things: An Archaeology of the Human Sciences*. New York: Vintage.

Foucault, M. (1979). *Discipline and Punish: The Birth of the Prison*. New York: Random House.

Foucault, M. (1980). *The History of Sexuality, i. An Introduction*. New York: Random House.

Fowler, F. J. (1993). *Survey Research Methods*, 2nd edn. Newbury Park, CA: Sage.

Fowler, F. J., and Mangione, T. W. (1990). *Standardized Survey Interviewing: Minimizing Interviewer-Related Error*. Beverly Hills, CA: Sage.

Franzosi, R. (1995). 'Computer-Assisted Content-Analysis of Newspapers: Can We Make an Expensive Research Tool More Efficient?', *Quantity and Quality*, 29(2): 157–72.

Frayne, C. A., and Geringer, J. M. (2000). 'Self-Management Training for Improving Job Performance: A Field Experiment Involving Salespeople', *Journal of Applied Psychology*, 85(3): 361–72.

Freeman, C. (2000). *High Tech and High Heels in the Global Economy: Women, Work and Pink-Collar Identities in the Caribbean*. Durham, NC: Duke University Press.

Frege, C. M. (2005). 'Varieties of Industrial Relations Research: Take-over, Convergence or Divergence?', *British Journal of Industrial Relations*, 43(2): 179–207.

Frey, J. H. (2004). 'Telephone Surveys', in M. S. Lewis-Beck, A. Bryman, and T. F. Liao (eds), *The Sage Encyclopedia of Social Science Research Methods*. Thousand Oaks, CA: Sage.

Frey, J. H., and Oishi, S. M. (1995). *How to Conduct Interviews by Telephone and in Person*. Thousand Oaks, CA: Sage.

Fricker, S., and Schonlau, M. (2002). 'Advantages and Disadvantages of Internet Research Surveys: Evidence from the Literature', *Field Methods*, 14: 347–67.

Fricker, S., Galesic, M., Tourangeau, R., and Yan, T. (2005). 'An Experimental Comparison of Web and Telephone Surveys', *Public Opinion Quarterly*, 69: 370–92.

Gabriel, Y. (1998). 'The Use of Stories', in G. Symon and C. Cassell (eds), *Qualitative Methods and Analysis in Organizational Research*. London: Sage.

Gallup, G. (1947). 'The Quintamensional Plan of Question Design', *Public Opinion Quarterly*, 11: 385–93.

Gallupe, R. B., Dennis, A. R., Cooper, W. H., Valacich, J. S., Bastianutti, L. M., and Nunamaker, J. F. (1992). 'Electronic Brainstorming and Group Size', *Academy of Management Journal*, 35: 350–69.

Galton, M., Simon, B., and Croll, P. (1980). *Inside the Primary Classroom*. London: Routledge & Kegan Paul.

Ganann, R., Ciliska, D., and Thomas, H. (2010). 'Expediting Systematic Reviews: Methods and Implications of Rapid Reviews', *Implementation Science*, 5, www.implementationscience.com/content/5/1/56.

Gans, H. J. (1962). *The Urban Villagers*. New York: Free Press.

Gans, H. J. (1968). 'The Participant-Observer as Human Being: Observations on the Personal Aspects of Field Work', in H. S. Becker (ed.), *Institutions and the Person: Papers Presented to Everett C. Hughes*. Chicago: Aldine.

Garcia, A. C., Standlee, A. I., Bechkoff, J., and Cui, Y. (2009). 'Ethnographic Approaches to the Internet and Computer-Mediated Communication', *Journal of Contemporary Ethnography*, 38(1): 52–84.

Gardner, W. L., Lowe, K. B., Moss, T. W., Mahoney, K. T., and Cogliser, C. C. (2010). 'Scholarly Leadership of the Study of Leadership: A Review of *The Leadership Quarterly*'s Second Decade, 2000–2009', *Leadership Quarterly* 21: 922–58.

Garfinkel, H. (1967). *Studies in Ethnomethodology*. Englewood Cliffs, NJ: Prentice-Hall.

Geertz, C. (1973). 'Thick Description: Toward an Interpretive Theory of Culture', in C. Geertz, *The Interpretation of Cultures*. New York: Basic Books.

Gephart, R. P. (1988). *Ethnostatistics: Qualitative Foundations for Quantitative Research*. Newbury Park, CA: Sage.

Gephart, R. P. (1993). 'The Textual Approach: Risk and Blame in Disaster Sensemaking', *Academy of Management Journal*, 36(6): 1465–514.

Gersick, C. J. G. (1994). 'Pacing Strategic Change: The Case of a New Venture', *Academy of Management Journal*, 37(1): 9–45.

Gerson, K., and Horowitz, R. (2002). 'Observation and Interviewing: Options and Choices', in T. May (ed.), *Qualitative Research in Action*. London: Sage.

Gevorgyan, G., and Manucharova, N. (2009). 'Does Culturally Adapted Online Communication Work? A Study of American and Chinese Internet Users' Attitudes and Preferences toward Culturally Customized Web Elements', *Journal of Computer-Mediated Communication*, 14: 393–413.

Gherardi, S., and Turner, B. (1987). 'Real Men Don't Collect Soft Data', pamphlet 13, Department of Social Policy, University of Trento.

Ghobadian, A., and Gallear, D. (1997). 'TQM and Organization Size', *International Journal of Operations and Production Management*, 17(2): 121–63.

Gibbons, M., Limoges, C., Nowotny, H., Schwartzman, S., Scott, P., and Trow, M. (1994). *The New Production of Knowledge*. London: Sage.

Gibson, D. R. (2005). 'Taking Turns and Talking Ties: Networks and Conversational Interaction', *American Journal of Sociology*, 110(6): 1561–97.

Gibson, L. (2010). 'Realities Toolkit #09: Using Email Interviews', *Realities* series, Morgan Centre for the Study of Relationships and Personal Life, University of Manchester.

Giddens, A. (1979). *Central Problems in Social Theory*. Berkeley, CA: University of California Press.

Giddens, A. (1984). *The Constitution of Society*. Cambridge: Polity.

Gilbert, G. N. (1977). 'Referencing as Persuasion', *Social Studies of Science*, 7: 113–22.

Gilbert, G. N., and Mulkay, M. (1984). *Opening Pandora's Box: A Sociological Analysis of Scientists' Discourse*. Cambridge: Cambridge University Press.

Gill, R. (1996). 'Discourse Analysis: Practical Implementation', in J. T. E. Richardson (ed.), *Handbook of Qualitative Research Methods for Psychology and the Social Sciences*. Leicester: BPS Books.

Gill, R. (2000). 'Discourse Analysis', in M. W. Bauer and G. Gaskell (eds), *Qualitative Researching with Text, Image and Sound*. London: Sage.

Gill, R., Barbour, J., and Dean, M. (2014). 'Shadowing in/as Work: Ten Recommendations for Shadowing Fieldwork Practice', *Qualitative Research in Organizations and Management*, 9(1): 69–89.

Gioia, D., Thomas, J., Clark, S., and Chittipeddi, K. (1994). 'Symbolism and Strategic Change in Academia: The Dynamics of Sensemaking and Influence', *Organization Science*, 5(3): 363–83.

Gioia, D. A., Corley, K. G., and Hamilton, A. L. (2012). 'Seeking Qualitative Rigor in Inductive Research: Notes on the Gioia Methodology', *Organizational Research Methods*, 16(1): 15–31.

Glaser, B. G. (1992). *Basics of Grounded Theory Analysis*. Mill Valley, CA: Sociology Press.

Glaser, B. G., and Strauss, A. L. (1967). *The Discovery of Grounded Theory: Strategies for Qualitative Research*. Chicago: Aldine.

Glock, C. Y. (1988). 'Reflections on Doing Survey Research', in H. J. O'Gorman (ed.), *Surveying Social Life*. Middletown, CT: Wesleyan University Press.

Glucksmann, M. (1994). 'The Work of Knowledge and the Knowledge of Women's Work', in M. Maynard and J. Purvis (eds), *Researching Women's Lives from a Feminist Perspective*. London: Taylor & Francis.

Godard, J. (1994). 'Beyond Empiricism: Towards a Reconstruction of IR Theory and Research', *Advances in Industrial and Labour Relations*, 6: 1–35.

Goffman, E. (1959). *The Presentation of Self in Everyday Life*. New York: Anchor Books.

Gold, R. L. (1958). 'Roles in Sociological Fieldwork', *Social Forces*, 36: 217–23.

Golden-Biddle, K., and Locke, K. D. (1993). 'Appealing Work: An Investigation of how Ethnographic Texts Convince', *Organization Science*, 4: 595–616.

Golden-Biddle, K., and Locke, K. D. (1997). *Composing Qualitative Research*. Thousand Oaks, CA: Sage.

Goldthorpe, J. H., Lockwood, D., Bechhofer, F., and Platt, J. (1968). *The Affluent Worker: Industrial Attitudes and Behaviour*. Cambridge: Cambridge University Press.

Goodall, H. L., Jr (1994). *Casing a Promised Land: The Autobiography of an Organizational Detective as Cultural Ethnographer*. Carbondale, IL: Southern Illinois University Press.

Goode, E. (1996). 'The Ethics of Deception in Social Research: A Case Study', *Qualitative Sociology*, 19: 11–33.

Gorard, S. (2002). 'Ethics and Equity: Pursuing the Perspective of Non-Participants', *Social Research Update*, no. 39.

Gottdiener, M. (1982). 'Disneyland: A Utopian Urban Space', *Urban Life*, 11: 139–62.

Gottdiener, M. (1997). *The Theming of America: Dreams, Visions and Commercial Spaces*. Boulder, CO: Westview Press.

Grant, A. M., and Wall, T. D. (2009). 'The Neglected Science and Art of Quasi-Experimentation: Why-to, When-to, and How-to Advice for Organizational Researchers', *Organizational Research Methods*, 12(4): 653–86.

Grant, D., Hardy, C., Oswick, C., and Putnam, L. L. (eds) (2004). *The Sage Handbook of Organizational Discourse*. London: Sage.

Grant, D., Keenoy, T., and Oswick, C. (1998). *Discourse and Organization*. London: Sage.

Greatbatch, D., and Clark, T. (2003). 'Displaying Group Cohesiveness: Humour and Laughter in the Public Lectures of Management Gurus', *Human Relations*, 56(12): 1515–44.

Greene, J. C. (1994). 'Qualitative Program Evaluation: Practice and Promise', in N. K. Denzin and Y. S. Lincoln (eds), *Handbook of Qualitative Research*. Thousand Oaks, CA: Sage.

Greene, J. C. (2000). 'Understanding Social Programs through Evaluation', in N. K. Denzin and Y. S. Lincoln (eds), *Handbook of Qualitative Research*, 2nd edn. Thousand Oaks, CA: Sage.

Greenland, P., and Fontanarosa, P. B. (2012). 'Ending Honorary Authorship', *Science Magazine*, 337: 1019.

Greenwood, D., Whyte, W., and Harkavy, I. (1993). 'Participatory Action Research as a Process and as a Goal', *Human Relations*, 46(2): 175–91.

Grele, R. J. (1998). 'Movement without Aim: Methodological and Theoretical Problems in Oral History', in R. Perks and A. Thomson (eds), *The History Reader*. London: Routledge.

Grey, C. (2010). 'Organizing Studies: Publications, Politics and Polemic', *Organization Studies*, 31(6): 677–94.

Grint, K. (2000). *The Arts of Leadership*. Oxford: Oxford University Press.

Grint, K., and Woolgar, S. (1997). *The Machine at Work: Technology, Work and Organization*. Cambridge: Polity Press.

Grinyer, A. (2002). 'The Anonymity of Research Participants: Assumptions, Ethics and Practicalities', *Social Research Update*, 36, sru.soc.surrey.ac.uk/SRU36.html.

Grinyer, P., and Yasai-Ardekani, M. (1980). 'Dimensions of Organizational Structure: A Critical Replication', *Academy of Management Journal*, 23: 405–21.

Gronn, P. (2011). 'Hybrid Configurations of Leadership', in A. Bryman, D. Collinson, K. Grint, B. Jackson, and M. Uhl-Bien (eds), SAGE Handbook of Leadership. London: Sage.

Guba, E. G. (1985). 'The Context of Emergent Paradigm Research', in Y. S. Lincoln (ed.), *Organization Theory and Inquiry: The Paradigm Revolution*. Beverly Hills, CA: Sage.

Guba, E. G., and Lincoln, Y. S. (1994). 'Competing Paradigms in Qualitative Research', in N. K. Denzin and Y. S. Lincoln (eds), *Handbook of Qualitative Research*. Thousand Oaks, CA: Sage.

Gubrium, J. F., and Holstein, J. A. (1997). *The New Language of Qualitative Method*. New York: Oxford University Press.

Guest, D. E., and Dewe, P. (1991). 'Company or Trade Union? Which Wins Worker's Allegiance? A Study of Commitment in the UK Electronics Industry', *British Journal of Industrial Relations*, 29(1): 73–96.

Guest, G., Bunce, A., and Johnson, L. (2006). 'How Many Interviews are Enough? An Experiment with Data Saturation and Variability', *Field Methods*, 18: 59–82.

Gummesson, E. (2000). *Qualitative Methods in Management Research*, 2nd edn. London: Sage.

Gusfield, J. (1976). 'The Literary Rhetoric of Science: Comedy and Pathos in Drinking Driving Research', *American Sociological Review*, 41: 16–34.

Haber, S., and Reichel, A. (2005). 'Identifying Performance Measures of Small Ventures: The Case of the Tourism Industry', *Journal of Small Business Management*, 43(3): 257–86.

Hackley, C. (2003). ' "We Are All Customers Now": Rhetorical Strategy and Ideological Control in Marketing Management Texts', *Journal of Management Studies*, 40: 1325–52.

Hackman, J., and Oldham, G. (1976). 'Motivation through the Design of Work: Test of a Theory', *Organizational Behavior and Human Performance*, 16(2): 250–79.

Hackman, J., and Oldham, G. (1980). *Work Redesign*. Reading, MA: Addison-Wesley.

Halfpenny, P. (1979). 'The Analysis of Qualitative Data', *Sociological Review*, 27: 799–825.

Hall, E. (1993). 'Smiling, Deferring and Flirting: Doing Gender by Giving "Good Service" ', *Work and Occupations*, 20(4): 452–71.

Hall, R., Workman, J., and Marchioro, C. (1998). 'Sex, Task, and Behavioral Flexibility Effects on Leadership Perceptions', *Organizational Behavior and Human Decision Processes*, 74(1): 1–32.

Hammersley, M. (1989). *The Dilemma of Qualitative Method: Herbert Blumer and the Chicago Tradition*. London: Routledge.

Hammersley, M. (1992a). 'By what Criteria should Ethnographic Research be Judged?', in M. Hammersley, *What's Wrong with Ethnography*? London: Routledge.

Hammersley, M. (1992b). 'Deconstructing the Qualitative–Quantitative Divide', in M. Hammersley, *What's Wrong with Ethnography*? London: Routledge.

Hammersley, M. (1997). 'Qualitative Data Archiving: Some Reflections on its Prospects and Problems', *Sociology*, 31: 131–42.

Hammersley, M., and Atkinson, P. (1995). *Ethnography: Principles in Practice*, 2nd edn. London: Routledge.

Hammersley, M., and Gomm, R. (2000). 'Bias in Social Research', in M. Hammersley (ed.), *Taking Sides in Social Research: Essays in Partisanship and Bias*. London: Routledge.

Hammond, P. (1964). *Sociologists at Work*. New York: Basic Books.

Haney, C., Banks, C., and Zimbardo, P. (1973). 'Interpersonal Dynamics in a Simulated Prison', *International Journal of Criminology and Penology*, 1: 69–97.

Hanna, P. (2012). 'Using Internet Technologies (such as Skype) as a Research Medium: A Research Note', *Qualitative Research*, 12(2): 239–42.

Hanson, D., and Grimmer, M. (2005). 'The Mix of Qualitative and Quantitative Research in Major Marketing Journals', *European Journal of Marketing*, 41(1/2): 58–70.

Hantrais, L. (1996). 'Comparative Research Methods', *Social Research Update*, no. 13.

Hardy, C. (2001). 'Researching Organizational Discourse', *International Studies of Management and Organization*, 31(3): 25–47.

Hardy, M., and Bryman, A. (2004). 'Introduction: Common Threads among Techniques of Data Analysis', in M. Hardy and A. Bryman (eds), *Handbook of Data Analysis*. London: Sage.

Harfield, T., and Hamilton, R. (1997). 'Journeys in a Declining Industry: Stories of Footwear Manufacturing', *Journal of Organizational Change Management*, 10(1): 61–70.

Harker, J., and Kleijnen, J. (2012). 'What is Rapid Review?: A Methodological Exploration of Rapid Reviews in Health Technology Assessments', *International Journal of Evidence-Based Medicine*, 10: 397–410.

Harlow, G., Bouldmetis, J., Clark, P. G., and Willis, G. H. (2003). 'Computer-Assisted Life Stories', *Computers in Human Behaviour*, 19: 391–406.

Harper, D. (1986). 'Meaning and Work: A Study in Photo Elicitation', *Current Sociology*, 34(3): 24–68.

Harré, R. (1972). *The Philosophies of Science*. Oxford: Oxford University Press.

Harris, H. (2001). 'Content Analysis of Secondary Data: A Study of Courage in Managerial Decision Making', *Journal of Business Ethics*, 34(3–4): 191–208.

Harrison, R. L., and Reilly, T. M. (2011). 'Mixed Methods Designs in Marketing Research', *Qualitative Market Research: An International Journal*, 14(1): 7–26.

Haslam, C., and Bryman, A. (1994). 'The Research Dissemination Minefield', in C. Haslam and A. Bryman (eds), *Social Scientists Meet the Media*. London: Routledge.

Hassard, J. (1991). 'Multiple Paradigms and Organizational Analysis: A Case Study', *Organization Studies*, 12(2): 275–99.

Hatch, M. J. (1996). 'The Role of the Researcher: An Analysis of Narrative Position in Organization Theory', *Journal of Management Inquiry*, 5(4): 359–74.

Hawkes, N. (2003). 'Close Shaves Beat Death by a Whisker', *The Times*, 6 February, 1.

Healey, M. J., and Rawlinson, M. B. (1993). 'Interviewing Business Owners and Managers: A Review of Methods and Techniques', *Geoforum*, 24(3): 339–55.

Heap, J. L., and Roth, P. A. (1973). 'On Phenomenological Sociology', *American Sociological Review*, 38: 354–67.

Heath, C. (1997). 'The Analysis of Activities in Face to Face Interaction Using Video', in D. Silverman (ed.), *Qualitative Research: Theory, Method and Practice*. London: Sage.

Heisley, D. D., and Levy, S. J. (1991). 'Autodriving: A Photoelicitation Technique', *Journal of Consumer Research*, 18(4): 257–72.

Heracleous, L., and Klaering, L. A. (2014). 'Charismatic and Rhetorical Competence: An Analysis of Steve Job's Rhetoric', *Group & Organization Management*, 39(2): 131–61.

Heritage, J. (1984). *Garfinkel and Ethnomethodology*. Cambridge: Polity Press.

Heritage, J. (1987). 'Ethnomethodology', in A. Giddens and J. H. Turner (eds), *Social Theory Today*. Cambridge: Polity Press.

Heron, J., and Reason, P. (2000). 'The Practice of Co-operative Inquiry', in P. Reason and H. Bradbury (eds), *Handbook of Action Research*. London: Sage.

Herzberg, F., Mausner, B., and Snyderman, B. B. (1959). *The Motivation to Work*, 2nd edn. New York: Wiley.

Hesse-Biber, S. (1995). 'Unleashing Frankenstein's Monster? The Use of Computers in Qualitative Research', *Studies in Qualitative Methodology*, 5: 25–41.

Hewson, C., and Laurent, D. (2008). 'Research Design and Tools for Internet Research', in N. Fielding, R. M. Lee, and G. Blank (eds), *The Sage Handbook of Online Research Methods*. London: Sage.

Hewson, C., Yule, P., Laurent, D., and Vogel, C. (2003). *Internet Research Methods: A Practical Guide for the Social and Behavioural Sciences*. London: Sage.

Heyes, J. (1997). 'Annualised Hours and the Knock: The Organisation of Working Time in a Chemicals Plant', *Work, Employment and Society*, 11(1): 65–81.

Hilton, G. (1972). 'Causal Inference Analysis: A Seductive Process', *Administrative Science Quarterly*, 17(1): 44–54.

Hine, C. (2000). *Virtual Ethnography*. London: Sage.

Hine, C. (2008). 'Virtual Ethnography: Models, Varieties, Affordances', in N. Fielding, R. M. Lee and G. Blank (eds), *The Sage Handbook of Online Research Methods*. London: Sage.

Hinings, C. R., and Greenwood, R. (2002). 'ASQ Forum: Disconnects and Consequences in Organization Theory?', *Administrative Science Quarterly*, 47: 411–21.

Hinings, C. R., Ranson, S., and Bryman, A. (1976). 'Churches as Organizations', in D. S. Pugh and C. R. Hinings (eds), *Organizational Structure: Extensions and Replications, The Aston Programme II*. Farnborough: Saxon House.

Hinson, R. E., van Zyl, H., and Agbleze, S. (2014). 'An Interrogation of the Dialogic Potential of Insurance Firm Websites in Ghana', *Information Develoment*, 30(1): 59–69.

Ho, K. C., Baber, Z., and Khondker, H. (2002). ' "Sites of Resistance": Alternative Websites and State-Society Relations', *British Journal of Sociology*, 53: 127–48.

Hochschild, A. R. (1983). *The Managed Heart*. Berkeley and Los Angeles: University of California Press.

Hochschild, A. R. (1989). *The Second Shift: Working Parents and the Revolution at Home*. New York: Viking.

Hodson, R. (1996). 'Dignity in the Workplace under Participative Management', *American Sociological Review*, 61: 719–38.

Hodson, R. (1999). *Analyzing Documentary Accounts*. Thousand Oaks, CA: Sage.

Hofmans, J., Gelens, J., and Theuns, P. (2013). 'Enjoyment as a Mediator in the Relationship Between Task Characteristics and Work Effort: An Experience Sampling Study', *European Journal of Work and Organizational Psychology*, 23(5): 693–705.

Hofstede, G. (1984). *Culture's Consequences: International Differences in Work Related Values*. Beverly Hills, CA: Sage.

Holbrook, A., Bourke, S., Fairburn, H., and Lovat, T. (2007). 'Examiner Comment on the Literature Review in Ph.D. Theses', *Studies in Higher Education*, 32: 337–56.

Holbrook, A., Green, M. C., and Krosnick, J. A. (2003). 'Telephone versus Face-to-Face Interviewing of National Probability Samples with Long Questionnaires: Comparisons of Respondent Satisficing and Social Desirability Response Bias', *Public Opinion Quarterly*, 67: 79–125.

Holdaway, E. A., Newberry, J. F., Hickson, D. J., and Heron, R. P. (1975). 'Dimensions of Structure in Complex Societies: The Educational Sector', *Administrative Science Quarterly*, 20: 37–58.

Holliday, R. (1995). *Investigating Small Firms: Nice Work?* London: Routledge.

Holliday, R. (2001). 'We've Been Framed: Visualising Methodology', *Sociological Review*, 48(4): 503–21.

Holman Jones, S. (2005). 'Autoethnography: Making the Personal Political', in N. K. Denzin and Y. S. Lincoln (eds), *Handbook of Qualitative Research*, 3rd edn. London: Sage.

Holmberg, R., Fridell, M., Arnesson, P., and Bäckvall, M. (2008). 'Leadership and Implementation of Evidence-Based Practices', *Leadership in Health Services*, 21(3): 168–84.

Holsti, O. R. (1969). *Content Analysis for the Social Sciences and Humanities*. Reading, MA: Addison-Wesley.

Homan, R. (1991). *The Ethics of Social Research*. London: Longman.

Honig, B., and Bedi, A. (2012). 'The Fox in the Hen House: A Critical Examination of Plagiarism among Members of the Academy of Management', *Academy of Management Learning and Education*, 11(1): 101–23.

Hood, J. C. (2007). 'Orthodoxy vs. Power: The Defining Traits of Grounded Theory', in A. Bryant and K. Charmaz (eds), *The SAGE Handbook of Grounded Theory*. Los Angeles: Sage.

Hooghe, M., Stolle, D., Mahéo, V., and Vissers, S. (2010). 'Why Can't a Student be more Like an Average Person? Sampling and Attrition Effects in Social Science Field and Laboratory Experiments', *Annals of the American Academy of Political and Social Science*, 628: 85–96.

Hoque, K. (2003). 'All in All, It's Just Another Plaque on the Wall: The Incidence and Impact of the Investors in People Standard', *Journal of Management Studies*, 40(2): 543–71.

Hough, J. R., and White, M. A. (2003). 'Environmental Dynamism and Strategy Decision-Making Rationality: An Examination at the Decision Level', *Strategic Management Journal*, 24: 481–9.

House, J. (1981). *Work Stress and Social Support*. Reading, MA: Addison-Wesley.

Howell, J. M., and Frost, P. J. (1989). 'A Laboratory Study of Charismatic Leadership', *Organizational Behavior and Human Decision Processes*, 43: 243–69, http://onlinelibrary.wiley.com.ezproxy3.lib.le.ac.uk/doi/10.1111/j.1083-6101.2008.01430.x/pdf.

Huang, J., and Hsu, C. H. C. (2009). 'Interaction Among Fellow Cruise Passengers: Diverse Experiences and Impacts', *Journal of Travel and Tourism Marketing*, 26: 547–67.

Huberman, A. M., and Miles, M. B. (1994). 'Data Management and Analysis Methods', in N. K. Denzin and Y. S. Lincoln (eds), *Handbook of Qualitative Research*. Thousand Oaks, CA: Sage.

Hudson, J. M., and Bruckman, A. S. (2004). ' "Go Away": Participant Objections to Being Studied and the Ethics of Chatroom Research', *Information Society*, 20: 127–39.

Hudson, S., Snaith, T., Miller, G., and Hudson, P. (2001). 'Distribution Channels in the Travel Industry: Using Mystery Shoppers to Understand the Influence of Travel Agency Recommendations', *Journal of Travel Research*, 40: 148–54.

Hughes, E. C. (1958). *Men and their Work*. Glencoe, IL: Free Press.

Hughes, J. A. (1990). *The Philosophy of Social Research*, 2nd edn. Harlow: Longman.

Hummerinta-Peltomäki, L., and Nummela, N. (2006). 'Mixed Methods in International Business Research', *Management International Review*, 46(4): 439–59.

Humphreys, M., and Watson, T. (2009). 'Ethnographic Practices: From "Writing-up Ethnographic Research" to "Writing Ethnography" ', in S. Ybema, D. Yanow, H. Wels, and F. Kamsteeg (eds), *Organizational Ethnography: Studying the Complexities of Everyday Life*. London: Sage.

Hunter, W. C. (2008). 'A Typology of Photographic Representations for Tourism: Depictions of Groomed Spaces', *Tourism Management*, 29: 354–65.

Hurworth, R. (2003). 'Photo-Interviewing for Research', *Social Research Update*, 40, sru.soc.surrey.ac.uk/SRU40.html.

Huselid, M. (1995). 'The Impact of Human Resource Management Practices on Turnover, Productivity and Corporate Financial Performance', *Academy of Management Journal*, 38(3): 635–72.

Hutt, R. W. (1979). 'The Focus Group Interview: A Technique for Counseling Small Business Clients', *Journal of Small Business Management*, 17(1): 15–20.

Huxley, P., Evans, S., Gately, C., Webber, M., Mears, A., Pajak, S., Kendall, T., Medina, J., and Catona, C. (2005). 'Stress and Pressures in Mental Health Social Work: The Worker Speaks', *British Journal of Social Work*, 35: 1063–79.

Hycner, R. H. (1985). 'Some Guidelines for the Phenomenological Analysis of Interview Data', *Human Studies*, 8: 279–303.

Hyde, P., McBride, A., Young, R., and Walshe, K. (2006). 'Role Redesign: New Ways of Working in the NHS', *Personnel Review*, 34(6): 697–712.

Insch, G., Moore, J., and Murphy, L. (1997). 'Content Analysis in Leadership Research: Examples, Procedures and Suggestions for Future Use', *Leadership Quarterly*, 8(1): 1–25.

Jack, G., and Westwood, R. (2006). 'Postcolonialism and the Politics of Qualitative Research in International Business', *Management International Review*, 46(4): 481–500.

Jack, L., and Kholief, A. (2007). 'Introducing Strong Structuration Theory for Informing Qualitative Case Studies in Organization, Management and Accounting Research', *Qualitative Research in Organizations and Management: An International Journal*, 2(3): 208–25.

Jackall, R. (1988). *Moral Mazes: The World of the Corporate Manager*. Oxford: Oxford University Press.

Jackson, B. (2001). *Management Gurus and Management Fashions*. London: Routledge.

Jackson, N., and Carter, P. (1991). 'In Defence of Paradigm Incommensurability', *Organization Studies*, 12(1): 109–27.

Jackson, N., and Carter, P. (1998). 'Management Gurus: What are we to Make of Them?', in J. Hassard and R. Holliday (eds), *Organization-Representation: Work and Organization in Popular Culture*. London: Sage.

Jackson, T. (2001). 'Cultural Values and Management Ethics: A Ten Nation Study', *Human Relations*, 54(10): 1267–302.

Jacobs, J., and O'Neill, C. (2003). 'On the Reliability (or Otherwise) of SIC Codes', *European Business Review*, 15(3): 164–9.

Jacques, R. S. (2010). 'Discourse Analysis', in A. J. Mills, G. Durepos, and E. Wiebe (eds), *Sage Encyclopedia of Case Study Research*. Thousand Oaks, CA: Sage, i: 304–8.

Janis, I. L. (1982). *Groupthink: Psychological Studies of Policy Decisions and Fiascos*, 2nd edn. Boston: Houghton-Mifflin.

Jayaratne, T. E., and Stewart, A. J. (1991). 'Quantitative and Qualitative Methods in the Social Sciences: Current Feminist Issues and Practical Strategies', in M. M. Fonow and J. A. Cook (eds), *Beyond Methodology: Feminist Scholarship as Lived Research*. Bloomington, IN: Indiana University Press.

Jenkins, G. D., Nader, D. A., Lawler, E. E., and Cammann, C. (1975). 'Standardized Observations: An Approach to Measuring the Nature of Jobs', *Journal of Applied Psychology*, 60: 171–81.

John, I. D. (1992). 'Statistics as Rhetoric in Psychology', *Australian Psychologist*, 27: 144–9.

Johns, G., Xie, J., and Fang, Y. (1992). 'Mediating and Moderating Effects in Job Design', *Journal of Management*, 18(4): 657–76.

Johnson, P., and Duberley, J. (2000). *Understanding Management Research*. London: Sage.

Johnson, P., and Duberley, J. (2003). 'Reflexivity in Management Research', *Journal of Management Studies*, 40(5): 1279–303.

Jones, G. (1983). 'Life History Methodology', in G. Morgan (ed.), *Beyond Method: Strategies for Social Research*. London: Sage.

Jones, M. L. (2004). 'Application of Systematic Review Methods to Qualitative Research: Practical Issues', *Journal of Advanced Nursing*, 48(3): 271–8.

Kabanoff, B., Waldersee, R., and Cohen, M. (1995). 'Espoused Values and Organizational Change Themes', *Academy of Management Journal*, 38(4): 1075–104.

Kandola, B. (2012). 'Focus Groups', in G. Symon and C. Cassell (eds), *Qualitative Organizational Research: Core Methods and Current Challenges*. Los Angeles: Sage.

Kanter, R. M. (1977). *Men and Women of the Corporation*. New York: Basic Books.

Keat, R., and Urry, J. (1975). *Social Theory as Science*. London: Routledge & Kegan Paul.

Keenoy, T., Oswick, C., and Grant, D. (1997). 'Organizational Discourses: Text and Context', *Organization*, 2: 147–58.

Kelan, E. K., and Mah, A. (2014). 'Gendered Identification: Between Idealization and Admiration', *British Journal of Management*, 25: 91–101.

Kelly, G. A. (1955). *The Psychology of Personal Constructs*. New York: Norton.

Kelly, L., Burton, S., and Regan, L. (1994). 'Researching Women's Lives or Studying Women's Oppression? Reflections on what Constitutes Feminist Research', in M. Maynard and J. Purvis (eds), *Researching Women's Lives from a Feminist Perspective*. London: Taylor & Francis.

Kent, J., Williamson, E., Goodenough, T., and Ashcroft, R. (2002). 'Social Science Gets the Ethics Treatment: Research Governance and Ethical Review', *Sociological Research Online*, 7(4), www.socresonline.org.uk/7/4/williamson.html.

Kent, R., and Lee, M. (1999). 'Using the Internet for Market Research: A Study of Private Trading on the Internet', *Journal of the Market Research Society*, 41: 377–85.

Ketchen, D. J., Ireland, R. D., and Baker, L. T. (2012). 'The Use of Archival Proxies in Strategic Management Studies', *Organizational Research Methods*, 16(1): 32–42.

Kiely, T. (1998). 'Wired Focus Groups', *Harvard Business Review*, 76(1): 12–16.

Kieser, A. (1994). 'Crossroads: Why Organization Theory Needs Historical Analyses—and How This Should Be Performed', *Organization Science*, 5(4): 608–20.

Kieser, A. (1997). 'Rhetoric and Myth in Management Fashion', *Organization*, 4: 49–74.

Kirk, J., and Miller, M. L. (1986). *Reliability and Validity in Qualitative Research*. Newbury Park, CA: Sage.

Kitzinger, J. (1994). 'The Methodology of Focus Groups: The Importance of Interaction between Research Participants', *Sociology of Health and Illness*, 16: 103–21.

Kivits, J. (2005). 'Online Interviewing and the Research Relationship', in C. Hine (ed.), *Virtual Methods: Issues in Social Research on the Internet*. Oxford: Berg.

Knight, K., and Latreille, P. (2000). 'Discipline, Dismissals and Complaints to Employment Tribunals', *British Journal of Industrial Relations*, 38(4): 533–55.

Knights, D., and McCabe, D. (1997). ' "How Would You Measure Something Like That?": Quality in a Retail Bank', *Journal of Management Studies*, 34(3): 371–88.

Kondo, D. K. (1990). *Crafting Selves: Power, Gender and Discourses of Identity in a Japanese Workplace*. Chicago: University of Chicago Press.

Kostova, T. (1999). 'Transnational Transfer of Strategic Organizational Practices: A Contextual Perspective', *Academy of Management Review*, 24(2): 308–24.

Kowalczyk, R. (2004). 'Tracing the Effects of a Hospital Merger', in S. Fleetwood and S. Ackroyd (eds), *Critical Realist Applications in Organisation and Management Studies*. London: Routledge.

Kozinets, R. V. (2001). 'Utopian Enterprise: Articulating the Meanings of *Star Trek*'s Culture of Consumption', *Journal of Consumer Research*, 28(1): 67–88.

Kozinets, R. V. (2002). 'The Field behind the Screen: Using Netnography for Marketing Research in Online Communities', *Journal of Marketing Research*, 39: 61–72.

Kozinets, R. V. (2010). *Netnography: Doing Ethnographic Research Online*. London: Sage.

Kozinets, R.V. (2012). 'Marketing Netnography: Prom/ ot(ulgat)ing a New Research Method', *Methodological Innovations Online*, 7(1): 37–45. www. methodologicalinnovations.org.uk/previous-issues/ (accessed 18 October 2014).

Kozinets, R. V., de Valck, K., Wojnicki, A. C., and Wilner, S. J. S. (2010). 'Networked Narratives: Understanding Word-of-Mouth Marketing in Online Communities', *Journal of Marketing*, 74: 71–89.

Kramer, A. D. I., Guillory, J. E., and Hancock, J. T. (2014). 'Experimental Evidence of Massive-Scale Emotional Contagion Through Social Networks', *Proceedings of the National Academy of Sciences*, 111(24): 8788–90, www. pnas.org/content/111/24/8788.

Krause, R., Whitler, K., and Semadeni, M. (2014). 'Power to the Principals! An Experimental Look at Shareholder Say-on-Pay Voting', *Academy of Management Journal*, 57: 94–115.

Kring, A. M., Smith, D., and Neale, J. (1994). 'Individual Differences in Dispositional Expressiveness: Development and Validation of the Emotional Expressivity Scale', *Journal of Personality and Social Psychology*, 66: 934–49.

Krishnan, J., and Press, E. (2003). 'The North American Industry Classification System and Its Implications for Accounting Research', *Contemporary Accounting Research*, 20(4): 685–717.

Kristof-Brown, A. (2000). 'Perceived Applicant Fit: Distinguishing between Recruiters' Perceptions of Person–Job and Person–Organization Fit', *Personnel Psychology*, 53: 643–71.

Krosnick, J. A., Holbrook, A. L., Berent, M. K., Carson, R. T., Hanemann, W. M., Kopp, R. J., Mitchell, R. C., Presser, S., Ruud, P. A., Smith, V. K., Moody, W. R., Green, M. C., and Conaway, M. (2002). 'The Impact of "No Opinion" Response Options on Data Quality: Non-Attitude Reduction or an Invitation to Satisfice?', *Public Opinion Quarterly*, 66: 371–403.

Krueger, R. A. (1988). *Focus Groups: A Practical Guide for Applied Research*. Newbury Park, CA: Sage.

Krueger, R. A. (1998). *Moderating Focus Groups*. Thousand Oaks, CA: Sage.

Kuhn, T. S. (1970). *The Structure of Scientific Revolutions*, 2nd edn. Chicago: University of Chicago Press.

Kunda, G. (1992). *Engineering Culture: Control and Commitment in a High-Tech Corporation*. Philadelphia: Temple University Press.

Kvale, S. (1996). *InterViews: An Introduction to Qualitative Research Interviewing*. Thousand Oaks, CA: Sage.

Ladge, J. J., Clair, J. A., and Greenberg, D. (2012). 'Cross-domain Identity Transition During Liminal Periods: Constructing Multiple Selves as Professional and Mother During Pregnancy', *Academy of Management Journal*, 55(6): 1449–71.

Langley, A. (2009). 'Studying Processes in and Around Organizations', in D. Buchanan and A. Bryman (eds), *The Sage Handbook of Organizational Research Methods*. London: Sage.

LaPiere, R. T. (1934). 'Attitudes vs Actions', *Social Forces*, 13: 230–37.

Lavin, D., and Maynard, D. W. (2001). 'Standardisation vs Rapport: Respondent Laughter and Interviewer Reaction during Telephone Surveys', *American Sociological Review*, 66(3): 453–79.

Lawlor, M. A., and Prothero, A. (2007). 'Exploring Children's Understanding of Television Advertising: Beyond the Advertiser's Perspective', *European Journal of Marketing*, 42(11/12): 1203–23.

Lawrence, P. R., and Lorsch, J. W. (1967). *Organization and Environment*. Boston: Addison Wesley.

Layder, D. (1993). *New Strategies in Social Research*. Cambridge: Polity Press.

Lazarsfeld, P. (1958). 'Evidence and Inference in Social Research', *Daedalus*, 87: 99–130.

Learmonth, M. (2008). 'Speaking Out: Evidence-Based Management: A Backlash against Pluralism in Organization Studies', *Organization*, 15(2): 283–91.

Learmonth, M. (2009). 'Rhetoric and Evidence: The Case of Evidence-Based Management', in D. Buchanan and A. Bryman (eds), *The Sage Handbook of Organizational Research Methods*. London: Sage.

Leavitt, H. J. (1989). 'Educating our MBAs: On Teaching what We Haven't Taught', *California Management Review*, 31(3): 38–50.

LeCompte, M. D., and Goetz, J. P. (1982). 'Problems of Reliability and Validity in Ethnographic Research', *Review of Educational Research*, 52: 31–60.

Lee, B., Collier, P. M., and Cullen, J. (2007). 'Reflections on the Use of Case Studies in the Accounting, Management and Organizational Disciplines', *Qualitative Research in Organizations and Management: An International Journal*, 2(3): 169–78.

Lee, C. K. (1998). *Gender and the South China Miracle: Two Worlds of Factory Women*. Berkeley and Los Angeles: University of California Press.

Lee, R. M. (2000). *Unobtrusive Methods in Social Research*. Buckingham: Open University Press.

Lee, R. M. (2004). 'Danger in Research', in M. S. Lewis-Beck, A. Bryman, and T. F. Liao (eds), *The Sage Encyclopedia of Social Science Research Methods*. Thousand Oaks, CA: Sage.

Lee, R. M., and Fielding, N. G. (1991). 'Computing for Qualitative Research: Options, Problems and Potential', in N. G. Fielding and R. M. Lee (eds), *Using Computers in Qualitative Research*. London: Sage.

Lee, T. W. (1999). *Using Qualitative Methods in Organizational Research*. London: Sage.

Legge, K. (1995). *Human Resource Management: Rhetorics and Realities*. Basingstoke: Macmillan.

Leidner, R. (1993). *Fast Food, Fast Talk: Service Work and the Routinization of Everyday Life*. Berkeley and Los Angeles: University of California Press.

Leitch, C.M., Hill, F.M., and Harrison, R.T. (2010). 'The Philosophy and Practice of Interpretivist Research in Entrepreneurship: Quality, Validation, and Trust', *Organizational Research Methods*, 13: 67–84.

Lilley, S., Harvie, D., Lightfoot, G., and Weir, K. (2012). 'What are We to Do with Feral Publishers?', *Organization*, 19(6): 905–14.

Lincoln, Y. S., and Denzin, N. K. (1994). 'The Fifth Moment', in N. K. Denzin and Y. S. Lincoln (eds), *Handbook of Qualitative Research*. Thousand Oaks, CA: Sage.

Lincoln, Y. S., and Guba, E. (1985). *Naturalistic Inquiry*. Beverly Hills, CA: Sage.

Linstead, S. (1985). 'Jokers Wild: The Importance of Humour and the Maintenance of Organizational Culture', *Sociological Review*, 33(4): 741–67.

Linstead, S. (1993). 'From Postmodern Anthropology to Deconstructive Ethnography', *Human Relations*, 46(1): 97–120.

Lippe, T. van der, Dulk, L. den, Doorne-Huiskes, A. van, Schippers, J., Lane, L., and Bäck-Wiklund, M. (2009). *Final Report: Quality of Life in a Changing Europe* [report of the European Commission's 'Quality' research project]. Utrecht: Utrecht University.

Little, L. M., Kluenper, D., Nelson, D. L., and Gooty, J. (2012). 'Development and Validation of the Interpersonal Emotion Management Scale', *Journal of Occupational and Organizational Psychology*, 85(2): 407–20.

Livingstone, S., and Lunt, P. (1994). *Talk on Television: Audience Participation and Public Debate*. London: Routledge.

Locke, K. (1996). 'Rewriting The Discovery of Grounded Theory after 25 Years?', *Journal of Management Inquiry*, 5: 239–45.

Locke, K. (2001). *Grounded Theory in Management Research*. London: Sage.

Locke, R. (1996). *The Collapse of the American Management Mystique*. Oxford: Oxford University Press.

Lofland, J. (1971). *Analyzing Social Settings: A Guide to Qualitative Observation and Analysis*. Belmont, CA: Wadsworth.

Lofland, J., and Lofland, L. (1995). *Analyzing Social Settings: A Guide to Qualitative Observation and Analysis*, 3rd edn. Belmont, CA: Wadsworth.

Lok, J., and de Rond, M. (2013). 'On the Plasticity of Institutions: Containing and Restoring Practice Breakdowns at the Cambridge University Boat Club', *Academy of Management Journal*, 56(1): 185–207.

Longenecker, J., Moore, C. W., Petty, J. W., Palich, L. E., and McKinney, J. A. (2006). 'Ethical Attitudes in Small Business and Large Corporations: Theory and Empirical Findings from a Tracking Study Spanning Three Decades', *Journal of Small Business Management*, 44(2): 167–83.

Lonkila, M. (1995). 'Grounded Theory as an Emergent Paradigm for Computer-Assisted Qualitative Data Analysis', in U. Kelle (ed.), *Computer-Aided Qualitative Data Analysis*. London: Sage.

Louhiala-Salminen, L. (2002). 'The Fly's Perspective: Discourse in the Daily Routine of a Business Manager', *English for Specific Purposes*, 21: 211–31.

Lowe, K. B., and Gardner, W. L. (2000). 'Ten Years of *The Leadership Quarterly*: Contributions and Challenges for the Future', *Leadership Quarterly*, 11(4): 459–514.

Lozar Manfreda, K., Bosnjak, M., Berzelak, J., Haas, I., and Vehovar, V. (2008). 'Web Surveys versus Other Survey Modes', *International Journal of Market Research*, 50(1): 79–104.

Lucas, R. (1997). 'Youth, Gender and Part-Time Work: Students in the Labour Process', *Work, Employment and Society*, 11: 595–614.

Lupton, T. (1963). *On the Shopfloor*. Oxford: Pergamon Press.

Macdonald, S., and Kam, J. (2007). 'Ring a Ring o' Roses: Quality Journals and Gamesmanship in Management Studies', *Journal of Management Studies*, 44(4): 640–55.

Madriz, M. (2000). 'Focus Groups in Feminist Research', in N. K. Denzin and Y. S. Lincoln (eds), *Handbook of Qualitative Research*, 2nd edn. Thousand Oaks, CA: Sage.

Maitlis, S., and Lawrence, T. B. (2007). 'Triggers and Enablers of Sensegiving in Organizations', *Academy of Management Journal*, 50: 57–84.

Malinowski, B. (1967). *A Diary in the Strict Sense of the Term*. London: Routledge & Kegan Paul.

Mangabeira, W. (1995). 'Qualitative Analysis and Microcomputer Software: Some Reflections on a New Trend in Sociological Research', *Studies in Qualitative Methodology*, 5: 43–61.

Mangham, I. (1986). *Power and Performance in Organizations: An Exploration of Executive Process*. Oxford: Blackwell.

Mangione, T. W. (1995). *Mail Surveys: Improving the Quality*. Thousand Oaks, CA: Sage.

Mann, C., and Stewart, F. (2000). *Internet Communication and Qualitative Research: A Handbook for Researching Online*. London: Sage.

Mantere, S., and Ketokivi, M. (2013). 'Reasoning in Organizational Science', *Academy of Management Review*, 38(1): 70–89.

Marcus, C. (1999). *Ethnography Through Thick and Thin*. Princeton, NJ: Princeton University Press.

Marginson, P. (1998). 'The Survey Tradition in British Industrial Relations Research: An Assessment of the Contribution of Large-Scale Workplace and Enterprise Surveys', *British Journal of Industrial Relations*, 36(3): 361–88.

Markham, A. (1998). *Life Online: Researching the Real Experience in Virtual Space*. London and Walnut Creek, CA: AltaMira Press.

Marsden, R. (1982). 'Industrial Relations: A Critique of Empiricism', *Sociology*, 16(2): 232–50.

Marsh, C. (1982). *The Survey Method: The Contribution of Surveys to Sociological Explanation*. London: Allen & Unwin.

Marsh, C., and Scarbrough, E. (1990). 'Testing Nine Hypotheses about Quota Sampling', *Journal of the Market Research Society*, 32: 485–506.

Marshall, J. (1981). 'Making Sense as a Personal Process', in P. Reason and J. Rowan (eds), *Human Inquiry*. Chichester: John Wiley.

Marshall, J. (1984). *Women Managers: Travellers in a Male World*. Chichester: Wiley.

Marshall, J. (1995). *Women Managers Moving On: Exploring Career and Life Choices*. London: Routledge.

Martin, J. (1992). *Cultures in Organizations: Three Perspectives*. Oxford: Oxford University Press.

Martin, J., and Siehl, C. (1983). 'Organizational Culture and Counterculture: An Uneasy Symbiosis', *Organizational Dynamics*, 12(2): 52–64.

Martin, P., and Bateson, P. (1986). *Measuring Behaviour: An Introductory Guide*. Cambridge: Cambridge University Press.

Martin, P. Y., and Turner, B. A. (1986). 'Grounded Theory and Organizational Research', *Journal of Applied Behavioral Science*, 22(2): 141–57.

Martinko, M. J., and Gardner, W. L. (1990). 'Structured Observation of Managerial Work: A Replication and Synthesis', *Journal of Management Studies*, 27(3): 329–57.

Marx, G. T. (1997). 'Of Methods and Manners for Aspiring Sociologists: 37 Moral Imperatives', *American Sociologist*, 28(1): 102–25.

Marzano, G., and Scott, N. (2009). 'Power in Destination Branding', *Annals of Tourism Research*, 36: 247–67.

Maslach, C., and Jackson, S. (1981). 'The Measurement of Experienced Burnout', *Journal of Occupational Behavior*, 2: 99–113.

Maslow, A. (1943). 'A Theory of Human Motivation', *Psychological Review*, 50: 370–96.

Mason, J. (1996). *Qualitative Researching*. London: Sage.

Mason, M. (2010). 'Sample Size and Saturation in PhD Studies Using Qualitative Interviews' [63 paragraphs], *Forum Qualitative Sozialforschung/Forum: Qualitative Social Research*, 11/3, art. 8, www.qualitative-research.net/index.php/fqs/article/view/1428 (accessed 14 October 2014).

Masterman, M. (1970). 'The Nature of a Paradigm', in I. Lakatos and A. Musgrave (eds), *Criticism and the Growth of Knowledge*. Cambridge: Cambridge University Press.

Matthewman, S., and Hoey, D. (2006). 'What Happened to Postmodernism?', *Sociology*, 40: 529–47.

Matza, D. (1969). *Becoming Deviant*. Englewood Cliffs, NJ: Prentice-Hall.

Mauthner, N. S., Parry, O., and Backett-Milburn, K. (1998). 'The Data are Out There, or Are They? Implications for Archiving and Revisiting Qualitative Data', *Sociology*, 32: 733–45.

Mavletova, A. (2013). 'Data Quality in PC and Mobile Web Surveys', *Social Science Computer Review*, doi:10.1177/0894439313485201.

Maynard, M. (1994). 'Methods, Practice and Epistemology: The Debate about Feminism and Research', in M. Maynard and J. Purvis (eds), *Researching Women's Lives from a Feminist Perspective*. London: Taylor & Francis.

Maynard, M. (1998). 'Feminists' Knowledge and the Knowledge of Feminisms: Epistemology, Theory, Methodology and Method', in T. May and M. Williams (eds), *Knowing the Social World*. Buckingham: Open University Press.

Mays, N., Pope, C., and Popay, J. (2005). 'Sytematically Reviewing Qualitative and Quantitative Evidence to Inform Management and Policy-Making in the Health Field', *Journal of Health Services Research and Policy*, 10(Supplement 1): S6–S20.

McCall, M. J. (1984). 'Structured Field Observation', *Annual Review of Sociology*, 10: 263–82.

McCall, M. J., and Lombardo, M. (1982). 'Using Simulation for Leadership and Management Research: Through the Looking Glass', *Management Science*, 28(5): 533–49.

McCartney, J. L. (1970). 'On Being Scientific: Changing Styles of Presentation of Sociological Research', *American Sociologist*, 5: 30–5.

McClelland, D. C. (1961). *The Achieving Society.* Princeton: Van Nostrand.

McCloskey, D. N. (1985). *The Rhetoric of Economics.* Brighton: Wheatsheaf.

McDonald, G. (2000). 'Cross-Cultural Methodological Issues in Ethical Research', *Journal of Business Ethics*, 27: 89–104.

McDonald, S. (2005). 'Studying Actions in Context: A Qualitative Shadowing Method for Organizational Research', *Qualitative Research*, 5(4): 455–73.

McKeever, L. (2006). 'Online Plagiarism Detection Services: Saviour or Scourge?', *Assessment and Evaluation in Higher Education*, 31: 155–65.

McPhail, C., and Rexroat, C. (1979). 'Mead vs Blumer: The Divergent Methodological Perspectives of Social Behaviorism and Symbolic Interactionism', *American Sociological Review*, 44: 449–67.

Medway, R. L., and Fulton, J. (2012). 'When More Gets You Less: A Meta-analysis of the Effect of Concurrent Web Options on Mail Survey Response Rates', *Public Opinion Quarterly*, 76(4): 733–46.

Meltzer, B. N., Petras, J. W., and Reynolds, L. T. (1975). *Symbolic Interactionism: Genesis, Varieties and Criticism.* London: Routledge & Kegan Paul.

Merton, R. K. (1967). *On Theoretical Sociology.* New York: Free Press.

Merton, R. K., Fiske, M., and Kendall, P. L. (1956). *The Focused Interview: A Manual of Problems and Procedures.* New York: Free Press.

Meyer, A. D. (1991). 'Visual Data in Organizational Research', *Organization Science*, 2(2): 218–36.

Meyer, R. E., Höllerer, M. A., Jancsary, D., and Van Leeuwen, T. V. (2013). 'The Visual Dimension in Organizing, Organization and Organization Research', *The Academy of Management Annals*, 7(1): 487–553.

Michel, A. (2011). 'Transcending Socialization: A Nine-year Ethnography of the Body's Role in Organizational Control and Knowledge Workers' Transformation', *Administrative Science Quarterly*, 56(3): 325–68.

Mies, M. (1993). 'Towards a Methodology for Feminist Research', in M. Hammersley (ed.), *Social Research: Philosophy, Politics and Practice.* London: Sage.

Miles, M. B. (1979). 'Qualitative Data as an Attractive Nuisance', *Administrative Science Quarterly*, 24: 590–601.

Miles, M. B., and Huberman, A. M. (1984). *Qualitative Data Analysis: A Sourcebook of New Methods.* London: Sage.

Miles, M. B., and Huberman, A. M. (1994). *Qualitative Data Analysis: An Expanded Sourcebook.* London: Sage.

Milgram, S. (1963). 'A Behavioral Study of Obedience', *Journal of Abnormal and Social Psychology*, 67: 371–8.

Milgram, S., and Shotland, L. (1973). *Television and Antisocial Behavior: Field Experiments.* New York: Academic Press.

Milkman, R. (1997). *Farewell to the Factory: Auto Workers in the Late Twentieth Century.* Berkeley and Los Angeles: University of California Press.

Millen, D. (1997). 'Some Methodological and Epistemological Issues Raised by Doing Feminist Research on Non-Feminist Women', *Sociological Research Online*, 2, www.socresonline.org.uk/socresonline/2/3/3.html.

Miller, A. G. (2009). 'Reflections on "Replicating Milgram" (Burger, 2009)', *American Psychologist*, 64(1): 20–7.

Miller, K. D., and Tsang, E. W. K. (2011). 'Testing Management Theories: Critical Realist Methods: Critical Realist Philosophy and Research Methods', *Strategic Management Journal*, 32: 139–58.

Miller, N., and Morgan, D. (1993). 'Called to Account: The CV as an Autobiographical Practice', *Sociology*, 27: 133–43.

Miller, R. L. (2000). *Researching Life Stories and Family Histories.* London: Sage.

Miner-Rubino, K., Jayaratne, T. E., and Konik, J. (2007). 'Using Survey Research as a Quantitative Method for Feminist Social Change', in S. N. Hesse-Biber (ed.), *Handbook of Feminist Research: Theory and Praxis.* Thousand Oaks, CA: Sage.

Mintzberg, H. (1973). *The Nature of Managerial Work.* New York: Harper & Row.

Mintzberg, H., and Rose, J. (2003). 'Strategic Management Upside Down: A Study of McGill University from 1829 to 1980', *Canadian Journal of Administrative Sciences*, 20(4): 270–90.

Mintzberg, H., Brunet, J. P., and Waters, J. A. (1986). 'Does Planning Impede Strategic Thinking? Tracking the Strategies of Air Canada from 1937 to 1976', in R. Lamb and P. Shrivastava (ed.), *Advances in Strategic Management.* Greenwich, CT: JAI Press, iv: 3–41.

Mirchandani, K. (1999). 'Feminist Insight on Gendered Work: New Directions in Research on Women and Entrepreneurship', *Gender, Work and Organization*, 6(4): 224–35.

Mishler, E. G. (1986). *Research Interviewing: Context and Narrative.* Cambridge, MA: Harvard University Press.

Mitchell, J. C. (1983). 'Case and Situation Analysis', *Sociological Review*, 31: 186–211.

Mitchell, T. (1985). 'An Evaluation of the Validity of Correlational Research Conducted in Organizations', *Academy of Management Review*, 10(2): 192–205.

Mohr, L. B. (1982). *Explaining Organizational Behavior: The Limits and Possibilities of Theory and Research.* San Francisco: Jossey-Bass.

Molina-Azorín, J. F. (2009). 'Understanding how Mixed Methods Research is Undertaken within a Specific Research Community', *International Journal of Multiple Research Approaches*, 3: 47–57.

Molina-Azorín, J. F. (2012). 'Mixed Methods in Strategic Management: Impact and Applications', *Organizational Research Methods*, 15(1): 33–56.

Molina Azorín, J. F., and Cameron, R. (2010). 'The Application of Mixed Methods in Organisational Research: A Literature Review', *The Electronic Journal of Business Research Methods*, 8(2): 95–105, www.ejbrm.com/volume8/issue2/p95.

Morgan, D. L. (1998*a*). *Planning Focus Groups.* Thousand Oaks, CA: Sage.

Morgan, D. L. (1998*b*). 'Practical Strategies for Combining Qualitative and Quantitative Methods: Applications for Health Research', *Qualitative Health Research*, 8: 362–76.

Morgan, D. L. (2014). *Integrating Qualitative and Quantitative Methods: A Pragmatic Approach.* Los Angeles: Sage.

Morgan, G. (1997). *Images of Organization*. Thousand Oaks: CA: Sage.

Morgan, G., and Smircich, L. (1980). 'The Case for Qualitative Research', *Academy of Management Review*, 5: 491–500.

Morrison, D. E. (1998). *The Search for a Method: Focus Groups and the Development of Mass Communication Research*. Luton: University of Luton Press.

Morse, J. M. (2004a). 'Purposive Sampling', in M. S. Lewis-Beck, A. Bryman, and T. F. Liao (eds), *The Sage Encyclopedia of Social Science Research Methods*. 3 vols. Thousand Oaks, CA: Sage.

Morse, J. M. (2004b). 'Sampling in Qualitative Research', in M. S. Lewis-Beck, A. Bryman, and T. F. Liao (eds), *The Sage Encyclopedia of Social Science Research Methods*. 3 vols. Thousand Oaks, CA: Sage.

Moser, C. A., and Kalton, G. (1971). *Survey Methods in Social Investigation*. London: Heinemann.

Mumby, D., and Clair, R. (1997). 'Organizational Discourse', in T. A. Van Dijk (ed.), *Discourse as Social Interaction, vol. 2 of Discourse Studies: A Multidisciplinary Introduction*. Newbury Park, CA: Sage.

Musson, G. (1998). 'Life Histories', in G. Symon and C. Cassell (eds), *Qualitative Methods and Analysis in Organizational Research*. London: Sage.

Myers, K. K., and Oetzel, J. G. (2003). 'Exploring the Dimensions of Organizational Assimilation: Creating and Validating a Measure', *Communication Quarterly*, 51: 438–57.

Newell, A., and Simon, H. A. (1972). *Human Problem Solving*. Englewood Cliffs, NJ: Prentice Hall.

Ng Kwet Shing, M., and Spence, L. (2002). 'Investigating the Limits of Competitive Intelligence Gathering: Is Mystery Shopping Ethical?', *Business Ethics: A European Review*, 11(4): 343–53.

Nichols, T., and Beynon, H. (1977). *Living with Capitalism: Class Relations and the Modern Factory*. London: Routledge.

Nielsen, K., Randall, R., and Christensen, K. B. (2010). 'Does Training Managers Enhance the Effects of Implementing Team-Working? A Longitudinal Mixed Methods Field Study', *Human Relations*, 63: 1719–41.

Nikiforova, B., and Gregory, D. W. (2013). 'Globalization of Trust and Internet Confidence Emails'. *Journal of Financial Crime*, 20(4): 393–405.

Noblit, G. W., and Hare, R. D. (1988). *Meta-ethnography: Synthesizing Qualitative Studies*. Newbury Park, CA: Sage.

Noy, C. (2008). 'Sampling Knowledge: The Hermeneutics of Snowball Sampling in Qualitative Research', *International Journal of Social Research Methodology*, 11: 327–44.

O'Cathain, A. (2010). 'Assessing the Quality of Mixed Methods Research: Toward a Comprehensive Framework', in A. Tashakkori and C. Teddlie (eds), *The Sage Handbook of Mixed Methods in Social and Behavioral Research*, 2nd edn. Los Angeles: Sage, 531–55.

O'Cathain, A., Murphy, E., and Nicholl, J. (2007). 'Integration and Publication as Indicators of "Yield" from Mixed Methods Studies', *Journal of Mixed Methods Research*, 1: 147–63.

O'Cathain, A., Murphy, E., and Nicholl, J. (2008). 'The Quality of Mixed Methods Studies in Health Services Research', *Journal of Health Services Research and Policy*, 13: 92–8.

O'Connor, H., and Madge, C. (2001). 'Cyber-mothers: Online Synchronous Interviewing using Conferencing Software', *Sociological Research Online*, 5, www.socresonline.org.uk/5/4/oconnor.html.

O'Connor, H., Madge, C., Shaw, R., and Wellens, J. (2008). 'Internet-Based Interviewing', in N. Fielding, R. M. Lee, and G. Blank (eds), *The Sage Handbook of Online Research Methods*. London: Sage.

O'Gorman, C., Bourke, S., and Murray, J. A. (2005). 'The Nature of Managerial Work in Small Growth-Oriented Businesses', *Small Business Economics*, 25: 1–16.

O'Reilly, K., Paper, D., and Marx, S. (2012). 'Demystifying Grounded Theory for Business Research', *Organizational Research Methods*, 15(2): 247–62.

O'Reilly, M., and Parker, N. (2013). ' "Unsatisfactory Saturation": A Critical Exploration of the Notion of Saturated Sample Sizes in Qualitative Research', *Qualitative Research*, 13(2): 190–97.

Oakley, A. (1981). 'Interviewing Women: A Contradiction in Terms', in H. Roberts (ed.), *Doing Feminist Research*. London: Routledge & Kegan Paul.

Oakley, A. (1998). 'Gender, Methodology and People's Ways of Knowing: Some Problems with Feminism and the Paradigm Debate in Social Science', *Sociology*, 32: 707–31.

Ojala, M. (2005). 'SIC Those NAICS on Me: Industry Classification Codes for Business Research', *Online*, 29(1): 42–4.

Okely, J. (1994). 'Thinking Through Fieldwork', in A. Bryman and R. G. Burgess (eds), *Analyzing Qualitative Data*. London: Routledge.

Omar, N. A., Aziz, N. A., and Nazri, M. A. (2011). 'Understanding the Relationship of Program Satisfaction, Program Loyalty and Store Loyalty among Cardholders of Loyalty Programs', *Asian Academy of Management Journal*, 16(1): 21–41.

Onwuegbuzie, A. J., and Collins, K. M. T. (2007). 'A Typology of Mixed Methods Sampling Designs in Social Sciences Research', *The Qualitative Report*, 12: 281–316, www.nova.edu/ssss/QR/QR12-2/onwuegbuzie2.pdf (accessed 18 October 2014).

Onwuegbuzie, A. J., and Leech, N. L. (2010). 'Generalization Practices in Qualitative Research: A Mixed Methods Case Study', *Quality and Quantity*, 44: 881–92.

Oppenheim, A. N. (1966). *Questionnaire Design and Attitude Measurement*. London: Heinemann.

Oppenheim, A. N. (1992). *Questionnaire Design, Interviewing and Attitude Measurement*. London: Pinter.

Organ, D. W. (1988). *Organizational Citizenship Behaviour: The Good Soldier Syndrome*. Lexington, MA: Lexington Books.

Orlitzky, M. (2011). 'Institutional Logics in the Study of Organizations: The Social Construction of the Relationship between Corporate Social and Financial Performance', *Business Ethics Quarterly*, 12(3): 409–44.

Orton, J. D. (1997). 'From Inductive to Iterative Grounded Theory: Zipping the Gap between Process Theory and Process Data', *Scandinavian Journal of Management*, 13(4): 419–38.

Oswick, C., Putnam, L., and Keenoy, T. (2004). 'Tropes, Discourse and Organizing', in D. Grant, C. Hardy,

C. Oswick, and L. Putnam (eds), *Handbook of Organizational Discourse*. London: Sage.

Palys, T. (2008). 'Purposive Sampling', in L. M. Given (ed.), *The Sage Encyclopedia of Qualitative Research Methods*, Thousand Oaks, CA: Sage, vol. 2.

Parboteeah, K. P., Hoegl, M., and Cullen, J. (2009). 'Religious Dimensions and Work Obligation: A Country Institutional Profile Model', *Human Relations*, 62(1): 119–48.

Park, C. (2003). 'In Other (People's) Words: Plagiarism by University Students: Literature and Lessons', *Assessment and Evaluation in Higher Education*, 28: 471–88.

Park, P. (1999). 'People, Knowledge, and Change in Participatory Research', *Management Learning*, 30(2): 141–57.

Park, S. H. (1996). 'Relationships between Involvement and Attitudinal Loyalty Constructs in Adult Fitness Programmes', *Journal of Leisure Research*, 28(4): 233–50.

Parker, I. (1992). *Discourse Dynamics*. London: Routledge.

Parker, M. (2000). *Organizational Culture and Identity*. London: Sage.

Partington, D. (2000). 'Building Grounded Theories of Management Action', *British Journal of Management*, 11: 91–102.

Patterson, M. G., West, M. A., Shackleton, V. J., Dawson, J. F., Lawthom, R., Maitlis, S., Robinson, D. L., and Wallace, A. M. (2005). 'Validating the Organizational Climate Measure: Links to Managerial Practices, Productivity and Innovation', *Journal of Organizational Behavior*, 26: 379–408.

Patton, M. (1990). *Qualitative Evaluation and Research Methods*, Beverly Hills, CA: Sage.

Patwardhan, A., Noble, S. M., and Nishihara, C. M. (2009). 'The Use of Strategic Deception in Relationships', *Journal of Services Marketing*, 23(5): 318–25.

Paulus, T. M., Lester, J. N., and Britt, V. G. (2013). 'Constructing Hopes and Fears Around Technology: A Discourse Analysis of Introductory Research Methods Texts', *Qualitative Inquiry*, 19(3): 639–51.

Pawson, R., and Tilley, N. (1997). *Realistic Evaluation*. London: Sage.

Peñaloza, L. (1999). 'Just Doing It: A Visual Ethnographic Study of Spectacular Consumption Behavior at Nike Town', *Consumption, Markets and Culture*, 2: 337–400.

Peñaloza, L. (2000). 'The Commodification of the American West: Marketers' Production of Cultural Meanings at the Trade Show', *Journal of Marketing*, 64: 82–109.

Peräkylä, A. (1997). 'Reliability and Validity in Research Based on Transcripts', in D. Silverman (ed.), *Qualitative Research: Theory, Method and Practice*. London: Sage.

Perlow, L. A. (1995). *The Time Famine: The Unintended Consequences of the Way Time is Used at Work*, unpublished Ph.D. thesis, Massachusetts Institute of Technology.

Perlow, L. A. (1997). *Finding Time: How Corporations, Individuals and Families can Benefit from New Work Practices*. Ithaca, NY: ILR Press.

Perlow, L. A. (1999). 'Time Famine: Toward a Sociology of Work Time', *Administrative Science Quarterly*, 44: 57–81.

Petticrew, M., and Roberts, H. (2006). *Systematic Reviews in the Social Sciences: A Practical Guide*. Oxford: Blackwell.

Pettigrew, A. (1985). *The Awakening Giant: Continuity and Change in Imperial Chemical Industries*. Oxford: Blackwell.

Pettigrew, A. (1990). 'Longitudinal Field Research on Change: Theory and Practice', *Organization Science*, 1(3): 267–92.

Pettigrew, A. (1997). 'What is a Processual Analysis?', *Scandinavian Journal of Management*, 13: 337–48.

Peytchev, A., and Hill, C. A. (2010). 'Experiments in Mobile Web Survey Design: Similarities to Other Modes and Unique Considerations', *Social Science Computer Review*, 28(3): 319–35.

Pfeffer, J. (1997). 'Pitfalls on the Road to Measurement: The Dangerous Liaison of Human Resource Management with the Ideas of Accounting and Finance', *Human Resource Management*, 36(3): 357–65.

Pfeffer, J., and Fong, C. T. (2002). 'The End of Business Schools? Less Success than Meets the Eye', *Academy of Management Learning and Education*, 1(1): 78–95.

Phillips, D. L. (1973). *Abandoning Method*. San Francisco: Jossey-Bass.

Phillips, N., and Brown, J. L. (1993). 'Analyzing Communications in and around Organizations: A Critical Hermeneutic Approach', *Academy of Management Journal*, 36: 1547–76.

Phillips, N., and Hardy, C. (2002). *Discourse Analysis: Investigating Processes of Social Construction*. London: Sage.

Phillips, N., Sewell, G., and Jaynes, D. (2008). 'Applying Critical Discourse Analysis in Strategic Management Research', *Organizational Research Methods*, 11(4): 770–89.

Piekkari, R., Welsh, C., and Paavilainen, E. (2009). 'Case Study as Disciplinary Convention: Evidence from International Business Journals', *Organizational Research Methods*, 12(3): 567–89.

Piercy, N. F., Harris, L. C., and Lane, N. (2002). 'Market Orientation and Retail Operatives' Expectations', *Journal of Business Research*, 55: 261–73.

Pink, S. (2001). *Doing Visual Ethnography*. London: Sage.

Pink, S. (2004). 'Visual Methods', in C. Seale, G. Gobo, J. F. Gubrium, and D. Silverman (eds), *Qualitative Research Practice*. London: Sage.

Pittaway, L., Robertson, M., Munir, K., Denyer, D., and Neely, A. (2004). 'Networking and Innovation: A Systematic Review of the Evidence', *International Journal of Management Reviews*, 5/6(3–4): 137–68.

Platt, J. (1981). 'The Social Construction of "Positivism" and its Significance in British Sociology, 1950–80', in P. Abrams, R. Deem, J. Finch, and P. Rock (eds), *Practice and Progress: British Sociology 1950–1980*. London: George Allen & Unwin.

Plummer, K. (2001). 'The Call of Life Stories in Ethnographic Research', in P. Atkinson, A. Coffey, S. Delamont, J. Lofland, and L. Lofland (eds), *Handbook of Ethnography*. London: Sage.

Podsakoff, P. M., and Dalton, D. R. (1987). 'Research Methodology in Organizational Studies', *Journal of Management*, 13: 419–44.

Poland, B. D. (1995). 'Transcription Quality as an Aspect of Rigor in Qualitative Research', *Qualitative Inquiry*, 1: 290–310.

Pollert, A. (1981). *Girls, Wives, Factory Lives*. London: Macmillan.

Porter, S. (1993). 'Critical Realist Ethnography: The Case of Racism and Professionalism in a Medical Setting', *Sociology*, 27: 591–609.

Potter, J. (1996). *Representing Reality: Discourse, Rhetoric and Social Construction*. London: Sage.

Potter, J. (1997). 'Discourse Analysis as a Way of Analysing Naturally Occurring Talk', in D. Silverman (ed.), *Qualitative Research: Theory, Method and Practice*. London: Sage.

Potter, J. (2004). 'Discourse Analysis', in M. Hardy and A. Bryman (eds), *Handbook of Data Analysis*. London: Sage.

Potter, J., and Wetherell, M. (1987). *Discourse and Social Psychology: Beyond Attitudes and Behaviour*. London: Sage.

Potter, J., and Wetherell, M. (1994). 'Analyzing Discourse', in A. Bryman and R. G. Burgess (eds), *Analyzing Qualitative Data*. London: Routledge.

Poutanen, S., and Kovalainen, A. (2010). 'Critical Theory', in A. J. Mills, G. Durepos, and E. Wiebe (eds), *Sage Encyclopedia of Case Study Research*. Thousand Oaks, CA: Sage, i: 260–64.

Powell, T. C. (1995). 'Total Quality Management as Competitive Advantage: A Review and Empirical Study', *Strategic Management Journal*, 16: 15–37.

Prasad, A., Prasad, P., and Mir, R. (2011). 'One Mirror in Another: Managing Diversity and the Discourse of Fashion', *Human Relations*, 64(5): 703–24.

Prasad, P. (1993). 'Symbolic Processes in the Implementation of Technological Change: A Symbolic Interactionist Study of Work Computerization', *Academy of Management Journal*, 36(6): 1400–29.

Prasad, P. (2003). 'The Return of the Native: Organizational Discourses and the Legacy of the Ethnographic Imagination', in A. Prasad (ed.), *Postcolonial Theory and Organizational Analysis: A Critical Engagement*. New York: Palgrave, 149–70.

Prasad, P., and Prasad, A. (2009). 'Endless Crossroads: Debates, Deliberations and Disagreements on Studying Organizational Culture', in B. Buchanan and A. Bryman (eds.), *The Sage Handbook of Organizational Research Methods*. London: Sage.

Pratt, M. G. (2008). 'Fitting Oval Pegs into Round Holes: Tensions in Evaluating and Publishing Qualitative Research in Top-Tier North American Journals', *Organizational Research Methods*, 11: 481–509.

Prichard, A. (2001). 'Tourism and Representation: A Scale for Measuring Gendered Portrayals', *Leisure Studies*, 20(2): 79–94.

Pringle, R. (1988). *Secretaries Talk: Sexuality, Power and Work* (London: Verso).

Prior, L. (2008). 'Repositioning Documents in Social Research', *Sociology*, 42: 821–36.

Psathas, G. (1995). *Conversation Analysis: The Study of Talk-in-Interaction*. Thousand Oaks, CA: Sage.

Pugh, D. S. (1983). 'Studying Organizational Structure and Process', in G. Morgan (ed.), *Beyond Method*. Newbury Park, CA: Sage.

Pugh, D. S. (1998). 'Introduction', in D. S. Pugh (ed.), *The Aston Study and its Developments, The Aston Programme I*. Dartmouth: Ashgate.

Pugh, D. S., Hickson, D. J., Hinings, C. R., and Turner, C. (1968). 'Dimensions of Organization Structure', *Administrative Science Quarterly*, 13: 65–105.

Punch, M. (1994). 'Politics and Ethics in Qualitative Research', in N. K. Denzin and Y. S. Lincoln (eds), *Handbook of Qualitative Research*. Thousand Oaks, CA: Sage.

Purkayastha, S., Manolova, T. S., and Edelman, L. F. (2012). 'Diversification and Performance in Developed and Emerging Market Contexts: A Review of the Literature', *International Journal of Management Reviews*, 13: 18–38.

Rafaeli, A., Dutton, J., Harquail, C. V., and Mackie-Lewis, S. (1997). 'Navigating by Attire: The Use of Dress by Female Administrative Employees', *Academy of Management Journal*, 40: 9–45.

Ragin, C. C., and Becker, H. S. (1989). 'How the Microcomputer is Changing our Analytic Habits', in G. Blank, J. L. McCartney, and E. Brent (eds), *New Technology in Sociology: Practical Applications in Research and Work*. New Brunswick, NJ: Transaction Publishers.

Ram, M. (1994). *Managing to Survive: Working Lives in Small Firms*. Oxford: Blackwell.

Ramirez, I., and Bartunek, J. (1989). 'The Multiple Realities and Experiences of Internal Organization Development in Healthcare', *Journal of Organizational Change Management*, 2(1): 40–57.

Ranson, S., Hinings, B., and Greenwood, R. (1980). 'The Structuring of Organizational Structures', *Administrative Science Quarterly*, 25: 1–17.

Raz, A. E. (1999). *Riding the Black Ship: Japan and Tokyo Disneyland*. Cambridge, MA: Harvard University Press.

Reason, P. (1999). 'Integrating Action and Reflection through Cooperative Inquiry', *Management Learning*, 30(2): 207–26.

Reason, P., and Marshall, J. (1987). 'Research as Personal Process', in D. Boud and V. Griffin (eds), *Appreciating Adult Learning*. London: Kogan Page.

Reason, P., and Rowan, J. (eds) (1981). *Human Inquiry*. Chichester: John Wiley.

Reay, T., Berta, W., and Kohn, M. K. (2009). 'What is the Evidence on Evidence-Based Management?', *Academy of Management Perspectives*, 23(4): 19–32.

Reed, M. I. (1985). *Redirections in Organizational Analysis*. London: Tavistock.

Reed, M. I. (1997). 'In Praise of Duality and Dualism: Rethinking Agency and Structure in Organizational Analysis', *Organization Studies*, 18(1): 21–42.

Reed, M. I. (2000). 'The Limits of Discourse Analysis in Organizational Analysis', *Organization*, 7: 524–30.

Reichl, C., Leiter, M. P., and Spinath, F. M. (2014). 'Work-nonwork Conflict and Burnout: A Meta-analysis', *Human Relations*, doi: 10.1177/0018726713509857.

Reid, D. J., and Reid, F. J. M. (2005). 'Online Focus Groups: An In-depth Comparison of Computer-Mediated and Conventional Focus Group Discussions', *International Journal of Market Research*, 47(2): 131–62.

Reinharz, S. (1992). *Feminist Methods in Social Research*. New York: Oxford University Press.

Reuber, A. R. (2010). 'Strengthening your Literature Review', *Family Business Review*, 23: 105–8.

Rhodes, C., and Brown, A. D. (2005). 'Narrative, Organizations and Research', *International Journal of Management*, 7(3): 167–88.

Riach, K. (2009). 'Exploring Participant-Centred Reflexivity in the Research Interview', *Sociology*, 43(2): 356–70.

Richards, L., and Richards, T. (1994). 'From Filing Cabinet to Computer', in A. Bryman and R. G. Burgess (eds), *Analyzing Qualitative Data*. London: Routledge.

Richardson, L. (1990). 'Narrative and Sociology', *Journal of Contemporary Ethnography*, 19: 116–35.

Richardson, L. (1994). 'Writing: A Method of Inquiry', in N. K. Denzin and Y. S. Lincoln (eds), *Handbook of Qualitative Research*. Thousand Oaks, CA: Sage.

Riessman, C. K. (1993). *Narrative Analysis*. Newbury Park, CA: Sage.

Rigby, M., and O'Brien-Smith, F. (2010). 'Trade Union Interventions in Work-Life Balance', *Work, Employment and Society*, 24: 203–20.

Ritchie, J., Spencer, L., and O'Connor, W. (2003). 'Carrying out Qualitative Analysis', in J. Ritchie and J. Lewis (eds), *Qualitative Research Practice: A Guide for Social Science Students and Researchers*. London: Sage.

Ritzer, G. (1975). 'Sociology: A Multiple Paradigm Science', *American Sociologist*, 10: 156–67.

Roethlisberger, F. J., and Dickson, W. J. (1939). *Management and the Worker: An Account of a Research Programme Conducted by the Western Electric Company, Hawthorne Works, Chicago*. Cambridge, MA: Harvard University Press.

Rorty, R. (1979). *Philosophy and the Mirror of Nature*. Princeton: Princeton University Press.

Rose, G. (2001). *Visual Methodologies*. London: Sage.

Rosen, M. (1991). 'Coming to Terms with the Field: Understanding and Doing Organizational Ethnography', *Journal of Management Studies*, 28(1): 1–24.

Rosén, M. E. (2014). 'From Ad-man to Digital Manager: Professionalization through Swedish Job Advertisements 1960–2010', *Journal of Communications Management*, 18(1): 16–39.

Rosenau, P. M. (1992). *Post-Modernism and the Social Sciences: Insights, Inroads, and Intrusions*. Princeton: Princeton University Press.

Rosnow, R. L., and Rosenthal, R. (1997). *People Studying People: Artifacts and Ethics in Behavioral Research*. New York: W. H. Freeman.

Roulston, K., DeMarrais, K., and Lewis, J. (2003). 'Learning to Interview in the Social Sciences', *Qualitative Inquiry*, 9: 643–68.

Rousseau, D. (1985). 'Issues of Level in Organizational Research: Multi-level and Cross-level Perspectives', in L. Cummings and B. Staw (eds), *Research in Organizational Behavior*, vol. 7. London: JAI Press.

Rousseau, D. M. (2006). 'Is There Such a Thing as Evidence-Based Management?' *Academy of Management Review*, 31(2): 256–69.

Rowlinson, M. (2004a). 'Historical Perspectives in Organization Studies: Factual, Narrative, and Archeo-Genealogical', in D. E. Hodgson and C. Carter (eds), *Management Knowledge and the New Employee*. Burlington, VT: Ashgate, 8–20.

Rowlinson, M. (2004b). 'Historical Analysis of Company Documents', in C. Cassell and G. Symon (eds), *Essential Guide to Qualitative Methods in Organizational Research*. London: Sage, 301–10.

Roy, A., Walters, P., and Luk, S. (2001). 'Chinese Puzzles and Paradoxes: Conducting Business Research in China', *Journal of Business Research*, 52: 203–10.

Roy, D. (1958). 'Banana Time: Job Satisfaction and Informal Interaction', *Human Organisation*, 18: 156–68.

Rubin, H. J., and Rubin, I. S. (1995). *Qualitative Interviewing: The Art of Hearing Data*. Thousand Oaks, CA: Sage.

Ryan, G. W., and Bernard, H. R. (2003). 'Techniques to Identify Themes', *Field Methods*, 15: 85–109.

Rynes, S. L., Hillman, A., Ireland, R. D., Kirkman, B., Law, K., Miller, C. C., Rajagopalan, N., and Shapiro, D. (2005). 'Everything you've Always Wanted to Know about *AMJ* (but May have been Afraid to Ask)', *Academy of Management Journal*, 48(5): 732–7.

Sacks, H., Schegloff, E. A., and Jefferson, G. (1974). 'A Simplest Systematics for the Organization of Turn-Taking in Conversation', *Language*, 50: 696–735.

Salancik, G. R. (1979). 'Field Stimulations for Organizational Behavior Research', *Administrative Science Quarterly*, 24: 638–49.

Saldaña, J. (2009). 'Popular Film as an Instructional Strategy in Qualitative Research Methods Courses', *Qualitative Inquiry*, 15(1): 247–61.

Samuel, R. (1976). 'Oral History and Local History', *History Workshop Journal*, 1: 191–208.

Sandberg, J., and Alvesson, M. (2011). 'Ways of Constructing Research Questions: Gap-Spotting or Problematization?', *Organization*, 18: 23–44.

Sanjek, R. (1990). 'A Vocabulary for Fieldnotes', in R. Sanjek (ed.), *Fieldnotes: The Making of Anthropology*. Ithaca, NY: Cornell University Press.

Sarsby, J. (1984). 'The Fieldwork Experience', in R. F. Ellen (ed.), *Ethnographic Research: A Guide to General Conduct*. London: Academic Press.

Savage, M. (2005). 'Working-Class Identities in the 1960s: Revisiting the Affluent Worker Study', *Sociology*, 39(5): 929–46.

Scandura, T. A., and Williams, E. A. (2000). 'Research Methodology in Management: Current Practices, Trends and Implications for Future Research', *Academy of Management Journal*, 43(6): 1248–64.

Scase, R., and Goffee, R. (1989). *Reluctant Managers: Their Work and Lifestyles*. London: Routledge.

Schaeffer, D. R., and Dillman, D. A. (1998). 'Development of a Standard E-mail Methodology', *Public Opinion Quarterly*, 62: 378–97.

Schegloff, E. A. (1997). 'Whose Text? Whose Context?', *Discourse and Society*, 8: 165–87.

Scherbaum, C. A., and Meade, A. W. (2013). 'New Directions for Measurement in Management Research', *International Journal of Management Reviews*, 15: 132–48.

Schlesinger, P., Dobash, R. E., Dobash, R. P., and Weaver, C. K. (1992). *Women Viewing Violence*. London: British Film Institute.

Schminke, M. (2009). 'Editor's Comments: The Better Angels of our Nature—Ethics and Integrity in Publishing Process', *Academy of Management Review*, 34(4): 586–91.

Schminke, M. (2014). 'Retraction Statement for "Ethics and Integrity of the Publishing Process: Myths, Facts, and a Roadmap" by Marshall Schminke and Maureen L. Ambrose', *Management and Organization Review*, 10: 157–62, http://onlinelibrary.wiley.com/doi/10.1111/more.12046/full (accessed 23 April 2014).

Schminke, M., and Ambrose, M. L. (2011). 'Ethics and Integrity in the Publishing Process: Myths, Facts, and a Roadmap', *Management and Organization Review*, 7(3): 397–406 [retracted].

Schneider, S. M., and Foot, K. A. (2004). 'The Web as an Object of Study', *New Media and Society*, 6: 114–22.

Schoneboom, A. (2007). 'Diary of a Working Boy: Creative Resistance among Anonymous Workbloggers', *Ethnography*, 8(4): 403–23.

Schoneboom, A. (2011). 'Workblogging in a Facebook Age', *Work, Employment and Society*, 25(1): 132–40.

Schoonhoven, C. B. (1981). 'Problems with Contingency Theory: Testing Assumptions Hidden within the Language of Contingency Theory', *Administrative Science Quarterly*, 26: 349–77.

Schuman, H., and Converse, J. (1971). 'The Effects of Black and White Interviewers on Black Responses in 1968', *Public Opinion Quarterly*, 35: 44–68.

Schuman, H., and Presser, S. (1981). *Questions and Answers in Attitude Surveys: Experiments on Question Form, Wording, and Context*. San Diego, CA: Academic Press.

Schutte, N., Toppinnen, S., Kalimo, R., and Schaufeli, W. (2000). 'The Factorial Validity of the Maslach Burnout Inventory—General Survey (MBI—GS) across Occupational Groups and Nations', *Journal of Occupational and Organizational Psychology*, 73(1): 53–67.

Schutz, A. (1962). *Collected Papers, i: The Problem of Social Reality*. The Hague: Martinus Nijhof.

Schwartzman, H. B. (1993). *Ethnography in Organizations*, Qualitative Research Methods Series 27. Newbury Park, CA: Sage.

Schwartz-Shea, P., and Yanow, D. (2012). *Interpretive Research Design*. London: Routledge.

Scott, A. (1994). *Willing Slaves? British Workers under HRM*. Cambridge: Cambridge University Press.

Scott, J. (1990). *A Matter of Record*. Cambridge: Polity Press.

Scott, W., Banks, J., Halsey, A., and Lupton, T. (1956). *Technical Change and Industrial Relations*. Liverpool: Liverpool University Press.

Seale, C. (1999). *The Quality of Qualitative Research*. London: Sage.

Sebba, J. (2004). 'Developing Evidence-Informed Policy and Practice in Education', in G. Thomas and R. Pring (eds), *Evidence-Based Practice in Education*. Maidenhead: Open University Press.

Shapiro, M. (1985–6). 'Metaphor in the Philosophy of the Social Sciences', *Cultural Critique*, 2: 191–214.

Sharpe, D. (1997). 'Managerial Control Strategies and Subcultural Processces', in S. Sackmann (ed.), *Cultural Complexity in Organizations*. London: Sage.

Sheehan, K. (2001). 'E-Mail Survey Response Rates: A Review', *Journal of Computer-Mediated Communication*, 6(2), www.ascusc.org/jcmc/vol6/issue2/sheehan.html.

Sheehan, K., and Hoy, M. G. (1999). 'Using E-mail to Survey Internet Users in the United States: Methodology and Assessment', *Journal of Computer-Mediated Communication*, 4(3), www.ascusc.org/jcmc/vol4/issue3/sheehan.html.

Shenoy, S. (1981). 'Organization Structure and Context: A Replication of the Aston Study in India', in D. J. Hickson and J. McMillan (eds), *Organization and Nation, The Aston Programme IV*. Aldershot: Gower.

Shepherd, C., and Challenger, R. (2013). 'Revisiting Paradigm(s) in Management Research: A Rhetorical Analysis of the Paradigm Wars', *International Journal of Management Reviews*, 15(2): 225–44.

Shrivasta, P., Mitroff, I. I., Miller, D., and Miglani, A. (1988). 'Understanding Industrial Crises', *Journal of Management Studies*, 25: 283–304.

Shuy, R. W. (2002). 'In-person versus Telephone Interviewing', in J. F. Gubrium and J. A. Holstein (eds), *Handbook of Interview Research: Context and Method*. Thousand Oaks, CA: Sage.

Sillince, J. A. A., and Brown, A. D. (2009). 'Multiple Organizational Identities and Legitimacy: The Rhetoric of Police Websites', *Human Relations*, 62(12): 1829–56.

Silverman, D. (1984). 'Going Private: Ceremonial Forms in a Private Oncology Clinic', *Sociology*, 18: 191–204.

Silverman, D. (1985). *Qualitative Methodology and Sociology: Describing the Social World*. Aldershot: Gower.

Silverman, D. (1993). *Interpreting Qualitative Data: Methods for Analysing Qualitative Data*. London: Sage.

Silverman, D. (2000). *Doing Qualitative Research: A Practical Handbook*. London: Sage.

Sin, C. H. (2005). 'Seeking Informed Consent: Reflections on Research Practice', *Sociology*, 39(2): 277–94.

Singh, G., Haddad, K. M., and Chow, C. W. (2007). 'Are Articles in Top Management Journals Necessarily of Higher Quality?', *Journal of Management Inquiry*, 16(4): 319–31.

Skinner, B. F. (1953). *Science and Human Behaviour*. New York: Macmillan.

Smith, C. B. (1997). 'Casting the Net: Surveying an Internet Population', *Journal of Computer-Mediated Communication*, 3(1), www.ascusc.org/jcmc/vol3/issue1/yun.html.

Smith, J. K. (1983). 'Quantitative versus Qualitative Research: An Attempt to Clarify the Issue', *Educational Researcher*, 12: 6–13.

Smith, J. K., and Heshusius, L. (1986). 'Closing down the Conversation: The End of the Quantitative–Qualitative Debate among Educational Enquirers', *Educational Researcher*, 15: 4–12.

Smith, T. W. (1995). 'Trends in Non-Response Rates', *International Journal of Public Opinion Research*, 7: 157–71.

Smyth, J. D., Dillman, D. A., Christian, L. M., and McBride, N. (2009). 'Open-Ended Questions in Web Surveys: Can Increasing the Size of Answer Spaces and Providing Extra Verbal Instructions Improve Response Quality?', *Public Opinion Quarterly* 73(2): 325–37.

Snyder, N., and Glueck, W. F. (1980). 'How Managers Plan: The Analysis of Managers' Activities', *Long Range Planning*, 13: 70–6.

Sonenshein, S., DeCelles, K. A., and Dutton, J. E. (2014). 'It's Not Easy Being Green: The Role of Self-evaluations in

Explaining Support of Environmental Issues', *Academy of Management Journal*, 57(1): 7–37.

Sørensen, J. B. (2004). 'The Organizational Demography of Racial Employment Segregation', *American Journal of Sociology*, 110(3): 626–71.

Spender, J. (1989). *Industry Recipes: An Enquiry into the Nature and Sources of Managerial Judgement*. Oxford: Blackwell.

Spradley, J. P. (1979). *The Ethnographic Interview*. New York: Holt, Rinehart & Winston.

Spradley, J. P., and McCurdy, D. (1972). *The Cultural Experience*. Chicago: Science Research Associates.

Sprokkereef, A., Larkin, E., Pole, C. J., and Burgess, R. G. (1995). 'The Data, the Team, and the Ethnograph', *Studies in Qualitative Methodology*, 5: 81–103.

Sprouse, M. (ed.) (1992). *Sabotage in the American Workplace*. San Francisco: Pressure Drop Press.

Sreedhari, D. D., Chugh, D., and Brief, A. P. (2014). 'The Implications of Marriage Structure for Men's Workplace Attitudes, Beliefs, and Behaviours Towards Women', *Administrative Science Quarterly*, 59(2): 330–65.

Stacey, J. (1988). 'Can there be a Feminist Ethnography?', *Women's International Studies Forum*, 11: 21–7.

Stake, R. E. (1995). *The Art of Case Study Research*. Thousand Oaks, CA: Sage.

Stake, R. E. (2005). 'Qualitative Case Studies', in N. K. Denzin and Y. S. Lincoln (eds), *The Sage Handbook of Qualitative Research*, 3rd edn. Thousand Oaks, CA: Sage.

Stanley, L., and Temple, B. (1995). 'Doing the Business? Evaluating Software Packages to Aid the Analysis of Qualitative Data Sets', *Studies in Qualitative Methodology*, 5: 169–97.

Starbuck, W. H. (1981). 'A Trip to View the Elephants and Rattlesnakes in the Garden of Aston', in A. H. van de Ven and W. F. Joyce (eds), *Perspectives on Organization Design and Behaviour*. New York: Wiley.

Starkey, K., Hatchuel, A., and Tempest, S. (2004). 'Rethinking the Business School', *Journal of Management Studies*, 41(8): 1521–31.

Steenkamp, J.-B. E. M., de Jong, M. G., and Baumgartner, H. (2010). 'Socially Desirable Response Tendencies in Survey Research', *Journal of Marketing Research*, 48: 199–214.

Stefani, L., and Carroll, J. (2001). 'A Briefing Note on Plagiarism', Assessment Series 10, www.sussex.ac.uk/tldu/documents/plag_ass0101.doc.

Stentz, J. E., Plano Clark, V. L., and Matkin, G. S. (2012). 'Applying Mixed Methods to Leadership Research: A Review of Current Practices', *Leadership Quarterly*, 23: 1173–83.

Stewart, K., and Williams, M. (2005). 'Researching Online Populations: The Use of Online Focus Groups for Social Research', *Qualitative Research*, 5(4): 395–416.

Stewart, R. (1967). *Managers and their Jobs*. London: Macmillan.

Stiles, D. R. (2004). 'Pictorial Representation', in C. Cassell and G. Symon (eds), *Essential Guide to Qualitative Methods in Organizational Research*. London: Sage.

Stiles, P. (2001). 'The Impact of the Board on Strategy: An Empirical Examination', *Journal of Management Studies*, 38(5): 627–50.

Stockdale, A. (2002). 'Tools for Digital Audio Recording in Qualitative Research', *Social Research Update*, 38.

Storey, J., Quintas, P., Taylor, P., and Fowle, W. (2002). 'Flexible Employment Contracts and their Implications for Product and Process Innovation', *International Journal of Human Resource Management*, 13(1): 1–18.

Strathern, M. (1987). 'The Limits of Auto-Anthropology', in A. Jackson (ed.), *Anthropology at Home*. London: Tavistock.

Strauss, A. (1987). *Qualitative Analysis for Social Scientists*. New York: Cambridge University Press.

Strauss, A., and Corbin, J. M. (1990). *Basics of Qualitative Research: Grounded Theory Procedures and Techniques*. Newbury Park, CA: Sage.

Strauss, A., and Corbin, J. M. (1998). *Basics of Qualitative Research: Techniques and Procedures for Developing Grounded Theory*. Thousand Oaks, CA: Sage.

Strauss, A., Schatzman, L., Ehrich, D., Bucher, R., and Sabshin, M. (1973). 'The Hospital and its Negotiated Order', in G. Salaman and K. Thompson (eds), *People and Organizations*. London: Longman.

Streiner, D. L., and Sidani, S. (2010). *When Research Goes Off the Rails: Why it Happens and What You Can Do About It*. New York: Guilford.

Sudman, S., and Blair, E. (1999). 'Sampling in the Twenty-First Century', *Journal of the Academy of Marketing Science*, 27(2): 269–77.

Sudman, S., and Bradburn, N. M. (1982). *Asking Questions: A Practical Guide to Questionnaire Design*. San Francisco: Jossey-Bass.

Sutton, R. I., and Rafaeli, A. (1988). 'Untangling the Relationship between Displayed Emotions and Organizational Sales: The Case of Convenience Stores', *Academy of Management Journal*, 31: 461–87.

Sutton, R. I., and Rafaeli, A. (1992). 'How we Untangled the Relationship between Displayed Emotion and Organizational Sales: A Tale of Bickering and Optimism', in P. J. Frost and R. Stablein (eds), *Doing Exemplary Research*. Newbury Park, CA: Sage.

Swales, J. M., and Rogers, P. S. (1995). 'Discourse and the Projection of Corporate Culture: The Mission-statement', *Discourse and Society*, 6(2): 223–42.

Sweet, C. (2001). 'Designing and Conducting Virtual Focus Groups', *Qualitative Market Research*, 4: 130–5.

Symon, G., Buehring, A., Johnson, P., and Cassell, C. (2008). 'Positioning Qualitative Research as Resistance to the Institutionalization of the Academic Labour Process', *Organization Studies*, 29(10): 1315–36.

Tashakkori, A., and Teddlie, C. (2003). *Handbook of Mixed Methods in Social and Behavioral Research*. Thousand Oaks, CA: Sage.

Tashakkori, A., and Teddlie, C. (2010). *Handbook of Mixed Methods in Social and Behavioral Research*, rev. edn. Thousand Oaks, CA: Sage.

Taylor, H. (1997). 'The Very Different Methods Used to Conduct Telephone Surveys of the Public', *Journal of the Market Research Society*, 39(3): 421–32.

Taylor, P., D'Cruz, P., Noronha, E., and Scholarios, D. (2013). 'The Experience of Work in India's Domestic Call Centre Industry', *International Journal of Human Resource Management*, 24(2): 436–52.

Taylor, S., Bell, E., and Cooke, B. (2009). 'Business History and the Historiographical Operation', *Management & Organizational History*, 4(2): 151–66.

Teddlie, C., and Yu, F. (2007). 'Mixed Methods Sampling: A Typology with Examples', *Journal of Mixed Methods Research*, 1: 77–100.

Thomas, R., and Linstead, A. (2002). 'Losing the Plot? Middle Managers and Identity', *Organization*, 9(1): 71–93.

Thompson, E. P. (1968). *The Making of the English Working Class*. London: Pelican.

Thompson, P. (1989). *The Nature of Work*, 2nd edn. London: Macmillan.

Tiessen, J. H. (2004). 'Multinational Multilingualism on the Internet: The Use of Japanese on Corporate Web Sites', *Canadian Journal of Administrative Sciences*, 21(2): 180–89.

Tight, M. (2010). 'The Curious Case of Case Study: A Viewpoint', *International Journal of Social Research Methodology*, 13(4): 329–39.

Tinker, T. (2004). ' "The End of Business Schools?" More Than Meets the Eye', *Social Text*, 22(2): 67–80.

Todd, P. A., McKeen, J. D., and Gallupe, R. B. (1995). 'The Evolution of IS Job Skills: A Content Analysis of IS Job Advertisements from 1970 to 1990', *Management Information Systems Quarterly*, 19(1): 1–27.

Tourangeau, R., and Smith, T. W. (1996). 'Asking Sensitive Questions: The Impact of Data Collection Mode, Question Format, and Question Context', *Public Opinion Quarterly*, 60: 275–304.

Townsend, K., and Burgess, J. (eds) (2009a). *Method in the Madness: Research Stories you Won't Read in Textbooks*. Oxford: Chandos.

Townsend, K., and Burgess, J. (2009b). 'Serendipity and Flexibility in Social Science Research: Meeting the Unexpected', in K. Townsend and J. Burgess (eds), *Method in the Madness: Research Stories you Won't Read in Textbooks*. Oxford: Chandos.

Tracy, S. J., Lutgen-Sandvik, P., and Alberts, J. K. (2006). 'Nightmares, Demons and Slaves: Exploring the Painful Metaphors of Workplace Bullying', *Management Communication Quarterly*, 20(2): 148–85.

Tranfield, D., and Starkey, K. (1998). 'The Nature, Social Organisation and Promotion of Management Research: Towards Policy', *British Journal of Management*, 9: 341–53.

Tranfield, D., Denyer, D., and Smart, P. (2003). 'Towards a Methodology for Developing Evidence-Informed Management Knowledge by Means of Systematic Review', *British Journal of Management*, 14: 207–22.

Trau, R. N. C., Härtel, C. E. J., and Härtel, G. F. (2013). 'Reaching and Hearing the Invisible: Organizational Research on Invisible Stigmatized Groups via Web Surveys', *British Journal of Management*, 24: 532–41.

Trethewey, A. (1999). 'Disciplined Bodies: Women's Embodied Identities at Work', *Organization Studies*, 20(3): 423–50.

Treviño, L. K., den Nieuwenboer, N. A., Kreiner, G. E., and Bishop, D. G. (2014). 'Legitimating the Legitimate: A Grounded Theory Study of Legitimacy Work among Ethics and Compliance Officers', *Organizational Behavior and Human Decision Processes*, 123: 186–205.

Tripp, T. M., Bies, R. J., and Aquino, K. (2002). 'Poetic Justice or Petty Jealousy? The Aesthetics of Revenge', *Organizational Behavior and Human Decision Processes*, 89: 966–84.

Trow, M. (1957). 'Comment on "Participant Observation and Interviewing: A Comparison" ', *Human Organization*, 16: 33–5.

Truss, C. (2001). 'Complexities and Controversies in Linking HRM with Organizational Outcomes', *Journal of Management Studies*, 38(8): 1121–49.

Tsang, E., and Kwan, K.-M. (1999). 'Replication and Theory Development in Organizational Science: A Critical Realist Perspective', *Academy of Management Review*, 24(4): 759–80.

Tse, A. C. B. (1998). 'Comparing the Response Rate, Response Speed and Response Quality of Two Methods of Sending Questionnaires: E-mail vs. Mail', *Journal of the Market Research Society*, 40: 353–61.

Tse, A. C. B. (1999). 'Conducting Electronic Focus Group Discussions among Chinese Respondents', *Journal of the Market Research Society*, 41: 407–15.

Tuhiwai Smith, L. (1999). *Decolonizing Methodologies: Research and Indigenous Peoples*. London: Zed Books.

Turner, B. A. (1983). 'The Use of Grounded Theory for the Qualitative Analysis of Organizational Behaviour', *Journal of Management Studies*, 20(3): 321–48.

Turner, B. A. (1994). 'Patterns of Crisis Behaviour: A Qualitative Inquiry', in A. Bryman and R. G. Burgess (eds), *Analyzing Qualitative Data*. London: Routledge.

Turner, S. (1980). *Sociological Explanation as Translation*. New York: Cambridge University Press.

Tüselmann, H. J., McDonald, F., and Heise, A. (2002). 'Globalisation, Nationality of Ownership and Employee Relations: German Multinationals in the UK', *Personnel Review*, 31(1): 27–43.

Tyler, M., and Cohen, L. (2010). 'Spaces that Matter: Gender Performativity and Organizational Space', *Organization Studies*, 31(2): 175–98.

UK Data Archive (2009). *Managing and Sharing Data: A Best Practice Guide for Researchers*. Colchester, Essex: UK Data Archive.

Urban, A-M., and Quinlan, E. (2014). 'Not for the Faint of Heart: Insider and Outsider Shadowing Experiences within Canadian Health Care Organizations', *Qualitative Research in Organizations and Management*, 9(1): 47–65.

Urch Druskat, V., and Wheeler, J. V. (2003). 'Managing from the Boundary: The Effective Leadership of Self-managing Work Teams', *Academy of Management Journal*, 46(4): 435–57.

Usunier, J. C. (1998). *International and Cross-Cultural Management Research*. London: Sage.

Uy, M. A., Foo, M., and Aguinis, H. (2010). 'Using Experience Sampling Methodology to Advance Entrepreneurship Theory and Research', *Organizational Research Methods*, 13(1): 31–54.

Van Dijk, T. A. (1997). 'Discourse as Interaction in Society', in T. A. Van Dijk (ed.), *Discourse as Social Interaction, vol. 2 of*

Discourse Studies: A Multidisciplinary Introduction. Newbury Park, CA: Sage.

Van Maanen, J. (1978). 'On Watching the Watchers', in P. Manning and J. Van Maanen (eds), *Policing: The View from the Street*. Santa Monica, CA: Goodyear.

Van Maanen, J. (1988). *Tales of the Field: On Writing Ethnography*. Chicago: University of Chicago Press.

Van Maanen, J. (1991*a*). 'Playing Back the Tape: Early Days in the Field', in W. B. Shaffir and R. A. Stebbins (eds), *Experiencing Fieldwork: An Inside View of Qualitative Research*. Newbury Park, CA: Sage.

Van Maanen, J. (1991*b*). 'The Smile Factory: Work at Disneyland', in P. J. Frost, L. F. Moore, M. R. Louis, C. C. Lundberg, and J. Martin (eds), *Reframing Organizational Culture*. Newbury Park, CA: Sage.

Van Maanen, J. (1996). 'On the Matter of Voice', *Journal of Management Inquiry*, 5(4): 375–81.

Van Maanen, J., and Kolb, D. (1985). 'The Professional Apprentice: Observations on Fieldwork Roles in Two Organizational Settings', *Research in the Sociology of Organizations*, 4: 1–33.

Van Selm, M., and Jankowski, N. W. (2006). 'Conducting Online Surveys', *Quality and Quantity*, 40(3): 435–56.

van Wanrooy, B., Bewley, H., Bryson, A., Forth, J., Freeth, S. Stokes, L., and Wood, S. (2013). *Employment Relations in the Shadow of Recession: Findings from the 2011 Workplace Industrial Relations Study*. Basingstoke: Palgrave Macmillan.

Vaughan, D. (1990). 'Autonomy, Independence and Social Control: NASA and the Space Shuttle *Challenger*', *Administrative Science Quarterly*, 35: 225–57.

Vaughan, D. (2006). 'The Social Shaping of Commission Reports', *Sociological Forum*, 21: 291–306.

Venter, E., Boshoff, C., and Maas, G. (2005). 'The Influence of Successor Related Factors on the Succession Process in Small and Medium-Sized Family Businesses', *Family Business Review*, 18(4): 283–303.

Vroom, V. H. (1964). *Work and Motivation*. New York: Wiley.

Waddington, D. (1994). 'Participant Observation', in C. Cassell and G. Symon (eds), *Qualitative Methods in Organizational Research*. London: Sage.

Waddington, K. (2005). 'Using Diaries to Explore the Characteristics of Work-Related Gossip: Methodological Considerations from Exploratory Multimethod Research', *Journal of Occupational and Organizational Psychology*, 78: 221–36.

Wagner, D. T., Barnes, C. M., and Scott, B. A. (2013). 'Driving it Home: How Workplace Emotional Labor Harms Employee Home Life', *Personnel Psychology*, doi: 10.1111/peps.12044.

Walker, J. (2010). 'Measuring Plagiarism: Researching What Students Do, Not What They Say', *Studies in Higher Education*, 35(1): 41–59.

Walsh, D. (1972). 'Sociology and the Social World', in P. Filmer, M. Phillipson, D. Silverman, and D. Walsh (eds), *New Directions in Sociological Theory*. London: Collier-Macmillan.

Warner, L. S., and Grint, K. (2006). 'American Indian Ways of Leading and Knowing', *Leadership*, 2(2): 225–44.

Warren, C. (1988). *Gender Issues in Field Research*. London: Sage.

Warren, C. A. B. (2002). 'Qualitative Interviewing', in J. F. Gubrium and J. A. Holstein (eds), *Handbook of Interview Research: Context and Method*. Thousand Oaks, CA: Sage.

Warren, S. (2002). 'Show Me How it Feels to Work Here: Using Photography to Research Organizational Aesthetics', *Ephemera*, 2(3): 224–45.

Warren, S. (2005). 'Photography and Voice in Critical, Qualitative, Management Research', *Accounting, Auditing and Accountability Journal*, 18(6): 861–82.

Warren, S. (2009). 'Visual Methods in Organizational Research', in D. Buchanan and A. Bryman (eds), *The Sage Handbook of Organizational Research Methods*. London: Sage.

Wasko, J., Phillips, M., and Meehan, E. R. (eds) (2001). *Dazzled by Disney: The Global Disney Audiences Project*. London: Leicester University Press.

Watson, T. (1994*a*). *In Search of Management: Culture, Chaos and Control in Managerial Work*. London: Routledge.

Watson, T. (1994*b*). 'Managing, Crafting and Researching: Words, Skill and Imagination in Shaping Management Research', *British Journal of Management*, 5S: S77–87.

Watson, T. (2000). 'Ethnographic Fiction Science: Making Sense of Managerial Work and Organizational Research Processes with Caroline and Terry', *Organization*, 7(3): 489–510.

Wax, M. L. (1982). 'Research Reciprocity Rather than Informed Consent in Fieldwork', in J. E. Sieber (ed.), *The Ethics of Social Research: Fieldwork, Regulation and Publication*. New York: Springer-Verlag.

Weaver, A., and Atkinson, P. (1994). *Microcomputing and Qualitative Data Analysis*. Aldershot: Avebury.

Webb, E. J., Campbell, D. T., Schwartz, R. D., and Sechrest, L. (1966). *Unobtrusive Measures: Nonreactive Measures in the Social Sciences*. Chicago: Rand McNally.

Weber, M. (1930). *The Protestant Ethic and the Spirit of Capitalism*. London: George Allen & Unwin.

Weber, M. (1947). *The Theory of Social and Economic Organization*, translated by A. M. Henderson and T. Parsons. New York: Free Press.

Weber, R. (1990). *Basis Content Analysis*, 2nd edn. Thousand Oaks, CA: Sage Publications.

Weick, K. E. (1990). 'The Vulnerable System: An Analysis of the Tenerife Air Disaster', *Journal of Management*, 16: 571–93.

Weick, K. E. (1995). *Sensemaking in Organizations*. Thousand Oaks, CA: Sage.

Weinholtz, D., Kacer, B., and Rocklin, T. (1995). 'Salvaging Quantitative Research with Qualitative Data', *Qualitative Health Research*, 5: 388–97.

Weinmann, T., Thomas, S., Brilmayer, S., Heinrich, S., and Radon, K. (2012). 'Testing Skype as an Interview Method in Epidemiologic Research: Response and Feasibility', *International Journal of Public Health*, 57: 959–61.

Weitzman, E. A., and Miles, M. B. (1995). *Computer Programs for Qualitative Data Analysis*. Thousand Oaks, CA: Sage.

Westwood, S. (1984). *All Day Every Day: Factory, Family, Women's Lives*. London: Pluto Press.

Wetherell, M. (1998). 'Positioning and Interpretative Repertoires: Conversation Analysis and Post-Structuralism in Dialogue', *Discourse and Society*, 9: 387–412.

Wharton, A. (1993). 'The Affective Consequences of Service Work', *Work and Occupations*, 20: 205–32.

White, H. (1987). *The Content of the Form: Narrative Discourse and Historical Representation*. London: Johns Hopkins University Press.

White, P. (2009). *Developing Research Questions: A Guide for Social Scientists*. Basingstoke: Palgrave Macmillan.

Whittington, R. (1989). *Corporate Strategies in Recession and Recovery*. London: Unwin Hyman.

Whyte, W. F. (1953). 'Interviewing for Organizational Research', *Human Organization*, 12(2): 15–22.

Whyte, W. F. (1955). *Street Corner Society*, 2nd edn. Chicago: University of Chicago Press.

Widdicombe, S. (1993). 'Autobiography and Change: Rhetoric and Authenticity of "Gothic" Style', in E. Burman and I. Parker (eds), *Discourse Analytic Research: Readings and Repertoires of Text*. London: Routledge.

Wilhite, A. W., and Fong, E. A. (2012). 'Coercive Citation in Academic Publishing', *Science Magazine*, 335: 542–3.

Wilkinson, S. (1998). 'Focus Groups in Feminist Research: Power, Interaction, and the Co-production of Meaning', *Women's Studies International Forum*, 21: 111–25.

Wilkinson, S. (1999a). 'Focus Group Methodology: A Review', *International Journal of Social Research Methodology*, 1: 181–203.

Wilkinson, S. (1999b). 'Focus Groups: A Feminist Method', *Psychology of Women Quarterly*, 23: 221–44.

Williams, M. (2000). 'Interpretivism and Generalization', *Sociology*, 34: 209–24.

Williams, M. (2007). 'Cybercrime and Online Methodologies', in R. King and E. Wincup (eds), *Doing Research on Crime and Justice*. Oxford: Oxford University Press.

Williams, R. (1976). 'Symbolic Interactionism: Fusion of Theory and Research', in D. C. Thorns (ed.), *New Directions in Sociology*. London: David & Charles.

Willman, P., Renton-O'Creevy, M., Nicholson, N., and Soane, E. (2002). 'Traders, Managers and Loss Aversion in Investment Banking: A Field Study', *Accounting, Organizations and Society*, 27: 85–98.

Willmott, H. (1990). 'Beyond Paradigmatic Closure in Organisational Enquiry', in J. Hassard and D. Pym (eds), *The Theory and Philosophy of Organizations*. London: Routledge.

Willmott, H. (1993). 'Breaking the Paradigm Mentality', *Organization Studies*, 14(5): 681–719.

Wilson, F. (1995). *Organizational Behaviour and Gender*. London: McGraw Hill.

Winch, P. (1958). *The Idea of a Social Science and its Relation to Philosophy*. London: Routledge & Kegan Paul.

Wolcott, H. F. (1990). *Writing up Qualitative Research*. Newbury Park, CA: Sage.

Wolcott, H. F. (1995). 'Making a Study More Ethnographic', in J. Van Maanen (ed.), *Representation in Ethnography*. London: Sage.

Wolfe, E. W., Converse, P. D., and Oswald, F. L. (2008). 'Item-level Nonresponse Rates in an Attitudinal Survey of Teachers Delivered by Mail and Web', *Journal of Computer-mediated Consumption*, 14: 35–66.

Wolfram Cox, J., and Hassard, J. (2007). 'Ties to the Past in Organization Research: A Comparative Analysis of Retrospective Methods', *Organization*, 14(4): 475–97.

Woodward, J. (1965). *Industrial Organization: Theory and Practice*. Oxford: Oxford University Press.

Woolgar, S. (1988a). *Science: The Very Idea*. Chichester: Ellis Horwood.

Woolgar, S. (1988b). *Knowledge and Reflexivity: New Frontiers in the Sociology of Knowledge*. London: Sage.

Wright, G. H. von (1971). *Explanation and Understanding*. London: Routledge, www.socialsciences.manchester.ac.uk/morgancentre/realities/toolkits/email-interviews/index.html.

Xian, H. (2008). 'Lost in Translation? Language Culture and the Roles of Translator in Cross-Cultural Management Research', *Qualitative Research in Organizations and Management*, 3(3): 231–45.

Yardley, L. (2000). 'Dilemmas in Qualitative Health Research', *Psychology and Health*, 15: 215–28.

Yauch, C. A., and Steudel, H. J. (2003). 'Complementary Use of Qualitative and Quantitative Cultural Assessment Methods', *Organizational Research Methods*, 6: 465–81.

Yin, R. K. (1984). *Case Study Research: Design and Methods*. Beverly Hills, CA: Sage.

Yin, R. K. (2003). *Case Study Research: Design and Methods*, 3rd edn. Thousand Oaks, CA: Sage Publications.

Yin, R. K. (2009). *Case Study Research: Design and Methods*, 4th edn. Los Angeles: Sage.

Yun, G. W., and Trumbo, C. W. (2000). 'Comparative Response to a Survey Executed by Post, E-Mail, and Web Form', *Journal of Computer-Mediated Communication*, 6(1), www.ascusc.org/jcmc/vol6/issue1/yun.html.

Zamanou, S., and Glaser, S. R. (1994). 'Moving toward Participation and Involvement', *Group and Organization Management*, 19(4): 475–502.

Zerubavel, E. (1981). *Hidden Rhythms: Schedules and Calendars in Social Life*. Chicago: University of Chicago Press.

Zhang, Z., and Spicer, A. (2014). 'Leader, You First: The Everyday Production of Hierarchical Space in a Chinese Bureaucracy', *Human Relations*, 67(6): 739–62.

Zimmerman, D. H., and Wieder, D. L. (1977). 'The Diary: Diary-Interview Method', *Urban Life*, 5: 479–98.

Zuber-Skerritt, O. (1996). *New Directions in Action Research*. London: Falmer.

Index of names

Subject index